Handbook of Research on the Education of School Leaders

D0217776

Sponsored by the University Council of Educational Administration, this comprehensive handbook will be the definitive work on leadership education in the United States. An in-depth portrait of what constitutes research on leadership development, this handbook provides a plan for strengthening the research-based education of school leaders in order to impact leadership's influence on student engagement and learning. Although research-oriented, the content is written in a style that makes it appropriate for any of the following audiences: university professors and researchers, professional development providers, practicing administrators, and policy makers who work in the accreditation and licensure arenas.

Michelle D. Young is the Executive Director of the University Council for Educational Administration (UCEA) and an Associate Professor in Educational Leadership and Policy at the University of Texas - Austin.

Gary M. Crow is Professor in the Department of Educational Leadership and Policy Studies at Indiana University.

Joseph Murphy is Frank W. Mayborn Chair and Associate Dean for Special Projects at the Peabody College of Education, Vanderbilt University.

Rodney T. Ogawa is Professor of Education in the Education Department at the University of California - Santa Cruz.

Handbook of Research on the Education of School Leaders

Editors:

Michelle D. Young
UCEA, University of Texas-Austin

Gary M. Crow
Indiana University

Joseph Murphy
Vanderbilt University

Rodney T. Ogawa
University of California-Santa Cruz

Routledge
Taylor & Francis Group

NEW YORK AND LONDON

First published 2009
by Routledge
270 Madison Ave, New York, NY 10016

Simultaneously published in the UK
by Routledge
2 Park Square, Milton Park, Abingdon, Oxon OX14 4RN

Routledge is an imprint of the Taylor & Francis Group, an informa business

© 2009 Routledge, Taylor and Francis

Typeset in Minion by EvS Communication Networx, Inc.
Printed and bound in the United States of America on acid-free paper by Sheridan Books, Inc.

Library of Congress Cataloging in Publication Data
Handbook of research on the education of school leaders / editors, Michelle D. Young ... [et al.].
p. cm.
Includes bibliographical references and index.
1. School administrators—Training of—United States—Handbooks, manuals, etc. 2. Educational leadership—
United States—Handbooks, manuals, etc. I. Young, Michelle D.
LB2831.82.H36 2009
371.20071'1—dc22
2008047987

ISBN 10: 0-8058-6157-2 (hbk)
ISBN 10: 0-8058-6158-0 (pbk)
ISBN 10: 0-203-87886-8 (ebk)

ISBN 13: 978-0-8058-6157 -0 (hbk)
ISBN 13: 978-0-8058-6158-7 (pbk)
ISBN 13: 978-0-203-87886-6 (ebk)

Contents

List of Tables

List of Figures

Preface

There is a pressing need for a research handbook on leadership education. The education of school and school system leaders is the subject of considerable research and theorizing because effective leadership is believed to be critical to improving educational outcomes and student performance. Until recently, however, there has been little research to demonstrate the effectiveness of program models and features or even agreement on outcome measures on which to assess effectiveness.

This handbook was developed as part of an effort to stimulate more, better quality research in the field of leadership preparation; to document the existing knowledge base in educational leadership preparation; and to identify gaps and new directions for research on leadership preparation. Thus, the handbook provides a rich resource for educational researchers, professional developers, practitioners, and policy makers, enabling them to access research on leadership education as well as on the political and contextual issues that impact leadership education.

The handbook is sponsored by the University Council for Educational Administration (UCEA), a consortium of research institutions with master's and doctoral programs in educational leadership, which is an organization dedicated to supporting research in educational leadership and using that research to improve educational leadership preparation, policy and, most importantly, practice. UCEA is structured around 10 major domains of research concerning the preparation and development of educational leaders: (a) Leadership Education as a Field of Study; (b) the Context of Leadership Education; (c) Models and Theories of Leadership Education; (d) Recruitment, Selection, and Development of Leadership Candidates; (d) Providers of Leadership Education; (e) Curriculum and Pedagogy in Leadership Education; (f) the Delivery of Leadership Preparation; (g) Student Assessment and Program Evaluation; (h) Professional Learning; and (i) Leadership Education Around the Globe.

This handbook is meant to make widely available the conceptual and research base on leadership education. Handbook authors cite research findings, primarily from the last decade; identify gaps in the leadership preparation knowledge base; and discuss the implications of what is known and changing contexts for the future of educational leadership preparation and research. The field now has a resource for basing research and practice on what is currently known about leadership education, allowing the implementation of a reform agenda that is informed, consistent, and forward thinking.

Michelle D. Young, Gary M. Crow, Joseph Murphy, and Rodney T. Ogawa

Acknowledgements

There is no question that a project of this size depends on the help and support of a good many people. We wish to acknowledge the part that many individuals have played in brining this handbook to fruition. First, we wish to acknowledge and thank Lane Akers of Routledge, an enthusiastic supporter of the handbook and a responsive and patient link to the publisher. Our thanks also go out to the authors who took on the enormous task of searching out, investigating, and reviewing large bodies of research in their efforts to produce chapters for the handbook. We realize that they had many other projects competing for their attention, and we appreciate that they chose to contribute to the handbook. Several of the authors also assisted in early editorial work, as Section Editors, for the handbook, including Robert Kottkamp, Fran Kochan, Diana Pounder, Martha McCarthy, Nelda Cambron-McCabe, Margaret Grogan, M. Terry Orr, Kent Petersen, and Miles Bryant. We deeply appreciate their efforts to assist authors and general editors in shaping the original chapters of the handbook.

Many individuals also contributed their expertise by serving as consulting editors and reviewing chapters for the handbook, including Professor Nan Restine, Texas Woman's University; Professor Stephen Jacobson, University of Buffalo; Professor Catherine Lugg, Rutgers University; Professor Bruce Cooper, Fordham University; Professor Mary Driscoll, New York University; Dr. James Cibulka, President of the National Council for the Accreditation of Teacher Education; Professor Tom Greenfield, Portland State University; Professor Robert Slater, Texas A& M University; Professor Brad Portin, University of Washington; Professor Karen Seashore, University of Minnesota; Professor Lenoard Burrelo, Southern Florida University; Professor Phillip Young, University of California-Davis; Professor Michael Dantley, Miami University of Ohio; Proessor John Tarter, St. Johns University; Professor Bruce Baker, Rutgers University; Professor Charol Shakeshaft, Virginia Commonwealth; Professor Robert Donmoyer, University of San Diego; Professor Kathleen Brown, University of North Carlina-Chapel Hill; Professor John Deresh, University of Texas-El Paso; Professor Jane Lindle, Clemson University; Professor Carolyn Riehl, Teachers College-Columbia; Professor Betty Malen, University of Maryland; Professor William Firestone, Rutgers University; Professor Ellen Goldring, Vanderbilt University; Professor Rick Reitzug, University of North Carolina-Greensboro; and Professor Tina Reyes, University of Houston.

Jennifer E. Cook provided invaluable service in the development of the handbook, carefully and closely copy editing each chapter and assisting in final phases of manuscript submission. Katherine Mansfield spearheaded the effort to acquire author agreements and up-to-date biographies. Christopher Ruggeri reliably provided high-quality assistance whenever it was needed. We greatly appreciate the expertise and assistance Jennifer, Christopher, and Katherine contributed to this project. Finally, we acknowledge each other as general editors, for working hard over the last few years to make this handbook substantive contribution to the field.

Michelle D. Young, Gary M. Crow, Joseph Murphy, and Rodney T. Ogawa

Introduction

Exploring the Broad Terrain of Leadership Preparation in Education

JOSEPH MURPHY, MICHELLE D. YOUNG,
GARY M. CROW, AND RODNEY T. OGAWA

Over the last half of the 20th century, a good deal of attention was devoted to the topic of preparing leaders for schools. In the last quarter century, in particular, the volume of that work has increased substantially. Yet, somewhat surprisingly, only a small proportion of the scholarship on school leader preparation has been empirical in nature, limiting the field's ability to use research to inform understanding and subsequent improvement initiatives in preparation. Recently, recognition of this research gap and the need to jumpstart empirical studies of leadership development has been spotlighted more boldly. As we will see throughout this volume, a number of forces are responsible for this change.

To be sure, the larger context in which education in general and school leadership in particular is nested deserves some of the credit. Specifically, we live in an environment in which action requires empirical support. Appeals to theory, critique, the wisdom of practice, and other foundations for change have less saliency in education today. The ascendancy of outcome-based accountability in education also has promoted the movement to examine empirical linkages in the chain of causality.

At the same time, forces internal to school leadership have been in play. On the one hand, the quite-limited empirical base informing understanding and action around the education of school leaders has been documented. On the other, professional associations, especially the University Council for Educational Administration (UCEA), have assumed a strong leadership position in an effort to address the research gap.

So, as we move into the 21st century, the problem has been laid bare; energy to act is being mustered; and, as we will see, some important initial steps at strengthening the research base are underway. Thus, it seems a propitious moment to offer macro-level frameworks for research on the education of school leaders. This handbook is one effort to furnish such scaffolding. Specifically, the handbook is designed to accomplish a number of goals. In its design, it establishes the broad contours as well as the integrative architecture for leadership preparation in education. For the first time in the history of school leadership, an in-depth cohesive portrait of what defines leadership preparation is provided. As we discuss more fully in the concluding chapter, this is essential in helping readers see the full landscape of preparation as well as in providing a cohesive empirical game plan for strengthening the education of school leaders.

At the micro level the handbook provides, in many cases, the first comprehensive reviews of empirical evidence on the various dimensions of leadership preparation (e.g., program evaluation). In other cases, it expands and deepens our knowledge about components of preparation programs (e.g., program pedagogy). Most of the chapters are designed to address similar aims: to inform readers about what is known concerning each element of leadership preparation (e.g., student selection); to highlight in detail the empirical portion of that narrative; and, finally, to establish a platform and an agenda for strengthening research on preparation over the next quarter century. Given the incipient stage of the journey to create more research-anchored preparation designs and the quite-limited body of available empirical work, the agenda-setting work in these chapters is of particular significance. As the reader will see, the authors enjoy a very unique position to mold research on the education of school leaders. In a very real sense, how effectively they accomplish this task will help determine how productively resources are devoted to the work of improving leadership preparation as well as to the speed and smoothness of the efforts.

The balance of this introductory chapter about the broad terrain of leadership preparation unfolds as follows. We begin with an overview of major critiques of educational leadership preparation programs in the United States. We include this review to historically contextualize the growing recognition in the field that a robust agenda of research was needed on the preparation and development of school leaders. In the second section, we outline action on the reform of leadership preparation over the last quarter century, which we view as fueling many significant developments in the field. We begin by pulling together the major "markers" on the path to reform. These include major reform initiatives, activities, reports, and other publications that have shaped and continue to influence the overhaul of leadership preparation. In this part of the chapter, we also introduce important trends in the recent evolution of leadership preparation. The third section provides a review of what was known about research on preparation programs at the outset of the handbook project. The storylines of each of these three sections are deepened in the subsequent chapters of the handbook. We close with a brief section describing the remaining chapters.

Major Critiques of Leadership Preparation: Driving a Research Agenda

As we reported above, the authors in this volume provide the first comprehensive reviews of research, however limited the raw material with which they have to work, on the various aspects of preparation programs. In this section, we foreshadow these contributions. Specifically, we review critiques of preparation programs, scaffolded on the functions and dimensions that influenced this volume. As the reader will observe, over the last quarter century in particular, reviewers have provided an often "dismal evaluation" (Shakeshaft, 1999, p. 237) of the preparation of future school leaders. Taken together, critiques built an image of a system of preparing school leaders that was seriously flawed and that was found wanting in nearly every aspect, including (a) the ways students were recruited and selected into training programs, (b) the education they received once there—including the content emphasized and the pedagogical strategies employed, (c) the methods used to assess academic fitness, and (d) the procedures developed to certify and select principals and superintendents (Griffiths, Stout, & Forsyth, 1988; Murphy 1992). Moreover, critics have gone as far as characterizing these shortcomings as contributors to and, in some cases, "as a major cause of dysfunction in American public schools" (Baker, Wolf-Wendel, & Twombly, 2007, p. 190). We discuss some of the more impactful critiques in the following subsections.

Increases in Program Numbers and Degree Production

Looking at the profession as a whole, it is clear that there is an expanding number of preparation programs in educational leadership and that these programs are granting escalating numbers of graduate degrees (Baker, Orr, & Young, 2007). At the time of the National Commission on Excellence in Educational Administration (1987) report, 505 institutions were offering coursework in educational leadership, with "less than 200 hav[ing] the resources and commitment to provide the excellence called for by the Commission" (p. 20). Today the number is just under 500, and many have opened in the last 10 years. In fact, from 1993 to 2003, master's degree programs increased by 16% and the number of master's degrees granted increased by 90%. According to Baker et al. (2007), degree production also shifted by institutional type, with research universities playing a much smaller role and Comprehensive Colleges and Universities showing over a four-fold increase in the share. Given that many of the newer programs are opening in smaller and less well-resourced institutions, Baker and colleagues argued that they likely lack the institutional capacity to provide high-quality preparation experiences. As a result, the critiques of the late 1980s, in which entrepreneurial and underresourced programs were characterized as "cash cows" that "offer graduate study in name only ... stint inquiry and survive by offering easy credentials and by working hard at legislative politics" may be relevant in today's context as well (Willower, 1983, p. 194).

Recruitment and Selection

Commentary and reviews of recruitment and selection processes employed by institutions in the administrator training business over the last quarter century consistently have characterized them as lacking in rigor (Levine, 2005). The general perception has been that procedures are often informal, haphazard, and casual and that because few programs have formal recruitment plans, prospective candidates are often self-selected (Young, Peterson, & Short, 2002). According to Creighton (2002), fewer than 10% of the students surveyed reported that they were influenced by the recruitment activities of the training institutions. Despite well-documented, if commonsense, reminders that training outcomes depend on the mix of program experiences and the quality of entering students (Creighton, 2002), research on the recruitment of school administrators remains quite thin (American Association of Colleges for Teacher Education, 1988; Browne-Ferrigno & Shoho, 2004; Miklos, 1988). As noted above, close to 500 educational-leadership preparation programs are located in universities and a growing number of nonuniversity programs (Baker et al., 2007). It is unclear what procedures or decision rules drive their selection processes today. While a growing body of evidence indicates that an increasing number of programs are using more rigorous and research-based strategies, many others likely continue to have "open admissions, with a baccalaureate degree the only prerequisite" (Griffiths et al., 1988, p. 290). As Jacobson (1990) put it, "For too many administrator preparation programs, any body is better than no body" (p. 35).

The UCEA-sponsored study in the mid-1970s (Silver, 1978a) discovered that the rejection rates to preparation programs were quite low—about 12% for master's students, 14% for 6th-year students, and 25% for doctoral students. In 1984, Gerritz, Koppich, and Guthrie found that only about 1 in 30 applicants was denied admission to certification programs they studied in California. It is not surprising, therefore, that the quality of applicants to leadership programs, when compared to other professional fields, has been rather low. In 1988, for instance, Griffiths (1988b) revealed, "Of the 94 intended majors listed in [the] Guide to the Use of the Graduate Record Examination Program 1985–86 ... educational administration is fourth from the bottom" (p. 12). The lack of rigorous recruitment and selection procedures and criteria reportedly had several negative effects:

> First, it lowers the level of training and experience possible, since courses are often geared to the background and intelligence of the students. Second, "eased entry downgrades the status of the students in the eyes of the populace." Third, the candidates themselves realize that anyone can get in and that nearly everyone will get the license if he or she just keeps paying for credits. In part, this lack of rigor at entry reflects a lack of clear criteria for training or clear

vision of what candidates and graduates will look like, and the realization that the graduate school experience itself is not very demanding. (Cooper & Boyd, 1987, p. 14)

The huge expansion in the number of programs over the last 10 years (Baker et al., 2007), paired with such a lack of rigor in selection, without a doubt contributes to the oversupply of credentialed administrators in the United States who are not fit for practice.

Over the last decade, two new lines of critical analysis in the area of recruitment and selection have surfaced. First, researchers are beginning to explore how well programs investigate the intentionality of preparation-program applicants to enter school administration (Darling-Hammond, LaPointe, Meyerson, & Orr, 2007; Murphy, Moorman, & McCarthy, 20008; Orr, 2008). This work has explored the fact that many students in leadership preparation programs have little or no interest in school leadership as a profession, a storyline spotlighted at least as early as 1975 by Dale Mann. The critique here is that by failing to address the issue of applicant intentionality in the recruitment and selection process, preparation programs (a) perpetuate a system of education that fails to target resources on those colleagues most likely to actually join the profession, (b) pull teachers away from coursework that actually can enhance instructional quality, and (c) distort instruction inside leadership preparation programs to meet the needs of the many educators with no intention of being school administrators (Darling-Hammond et al., 2007; Murphy et al., 2008).

Second, researchers have explored the relationship as well as the disconnect between recruitment and selection procedures and the espoused values and missions of preparation programs. Specifically, Murphy et al. (2008) studied programs across six states and reported almost no correlation between what programs claim to value (e.g., social justice, community, instructional leadership, standards-based leadership) and the recruitment processes and selection tools employed. That is, Murphy et al. found that almost all of the universities in these states—given a reform blueprint and an extended period to redesign their programs—continued to rely almost exclusively on selection procedures, tools, and scripts that have defined the profession for the last 50 years (e.g., grades, norm-referenced test scores, and letters of recommendations). The problem, Murphy et al. (2008) argued, is that there is no known relationship between these measures and important institutional values. Moreover, available research has not demonstrated a link between these measures and effective leadership practice (see Browne-Ferrigno & Muth, chapter 5 of this handbook).

Program Content

Turning to the content of preparation programs, critiques have focused on the following problems: the indiscriminate adoption of practices untested and uninformed by educational values and purposes; serious fragmentation; the separation of the practice and academic arms of the profession; relatively nonrobust strategies for generating new knowledge; the neglect of ethics, social justice, and other issues considered key to effective leadership preparation; and the concomitant failure to address outcomes. Critics aver that in many preparation programs "course content is frequently banal" (Clark, 1988, p. 5) and that they lack internal consistency. Students often confront a "confusing melange of courses, without clear meaning, focus, or purpose" (Cooper & Boyd, 1987, p. 14; see also Achilles, 1984), or what Levine (2005) labeled "an irrelevant curriculum" (p. 27). There is often an absence of a "continuum of knowledge and skills that become more sophisticated as one progresses" (Peterson & Finn, 1985, pp. 51–52). In practical terms, Erickson (1979) concluded, "The field consists of whatever scholars associated with university programs in 'educational administration' consider relevant. It is, to say the least, amorphous" (p. 9). What all this means is "that most administrators receive fragmented, overlapping, and often useless courses that add up to very little" (Cooper & Boyd, 1987, p. 13).

Until quite recently there has been little common agreement about the appropriate foundation for administrator preparation (Murphy, 1999a), especially for the "holistic, focused, and integrative design" (Pounder, Reitzug, & Young, 2002, p. 285) that some scholars and practitioners believe is needed. In the early 1980s, Goldhammer (1983) reported that although there were "general areas of concern that might dictate to preparatory institutions the names of courses that should be taught ... there [was] less agreement on what the content of such courses should actually be" (p. 269).

One of the most serious critiques of leader preparation content focuses on the belief that it does not reflect the realities of the workplace (Hess & Kelly, 2005; Lakomski, 1998; Murphy, 2006b; Young et al., 2002). Such content is therefore, at best, "irrelevant to the jobs trainees assume" (Mulkeen & Cooper, 1989, p. 1) and, at worst, "dysfunctional in the actual world of practice" (Sergiovanni, 1989, p. 18).

We know from historical reviews that as professors in school leadership attempted to develop a science of administration, they exacerbated the natural tension between the practice and academic arms of the profession (Campbell, 1981; Campbell, Fleming, Newell, & Bennion, 1987). The nurturance and development of the social sciences became ends in themselves (Erickson, 1977; Björk & Ginsbeg, 1995). As a result, the theory and research borrowed from the behavioral sciences "never evolved into a unique knowledge base informing the practice of school administration" (Griffiths, 1988b, p. 19). Mann (1975), Hills (1975), Bridges (1977), Carver (1988), Muth (1989), Sergiovanni (1989), Murphy (2007), and others all have written influential essays in which they question whether the processes and procedures stressed in university programs support or contrast conditions that characterize the workplace milieu of schools. Other thoughtful reviewers have concluded that administrators-in-training are often "given a potpourri of theory, concepts, and ideas—unrelated to one another and rarely useful in either understanding schools or managing them" (Mulkeen & Cooper, 1989, p. 12).

The pervasive antirecipe, antiskill philosophy that characterized many programs of educational leadership, it is argued, has resulted in significant gaps in the prevailing knowledge base: an almost complete absence of performance-based program components, a lack of attention to practical problem-solving skills, "a neglect of practical intelligence" (Sergiovanni, 1989, p. 17), and a truncated conception of expertise (Murphy, 2007). Administrators consistently report that the best way to improve training in preparation programs would be to improve the instruction on job-related skills (Erlandson & Witters-Churchill, 1988). Despite an entrenched belief that supervised practice "could be the most critical phase of the administrator's preparation" (Griffiths, 1988b, p. 17) and a long history of efforts to make field-based learning an integral part of preparation programs, little progress appears to have been made in this area (Cambron-McCabe, 2002). Clinical work remains impoverished in many of our preparation programs (Levine, 2005).

The field-based component has been "relegated to a secondary role" (Pounder et al., 2002, p. 282) in preparation programs. This component continues to be infected with weaknesses that have been revisited on a regular basis since the inception of the National Council of Professors of Educational Administration (NCPEA) and UCEA: (a) unclear objectives; (b) inadequate number of clinical experiences; (c) activities arranged on the basis of convenience; (d) overemphasis on role-centered as opposed to problem-centered experiences; (e) lack of individualization; (f) poor planning, supervision, and follow-up; (g) absence of "connecting linkages between on-campus experiences and field-based experiences" (Milstein, 1990, p. 121); and (h) overemphasis on low-level (orientation and passive-observation type) activities (McKerrow, 1998; Milstein, 1996; Murphy et al., 2008).

Woven deeply into the idea of "administration as an applied science" and, thus, the preparation of future administrators was the belief that there was a single best approach to educating prospective school leaders (Cooper & Boyd, 1987), including a dominant worldview of school leadership and administration as an area of study (content) and method of acting (procedure). Thoughtful analysts have maintained that this perspective has resulted in significant gaps in the knowledge base employed in training programs (English, 2007; Pounder et al., 2002; Young & Laible, 2000). Missing is consideration of the diversity of perspectives that inform scholarship and practice (English, 2007). For example, in her review of the literature on women administrators, Shakeshaft (1988) discovered "differences between the ways men and women approach the tasks of administration" (p. 403). She concluded that, although "these differences have implications for administrative training programs ... the female world of administrators has not been incorporated into the body of work in the field ... [n]or are women's experiences carried into the literature on practice" (Shakeshaft, 1988, pp. 403–406; see also Shakeshaft, 1999). Similar conclusions have been reached about the experiences of racial minorities (Young & Laible, 2000).

Moreover, most programs have shown "little interest in exploring the historical roots and social context of schooling" (Anderson, 1990, p. 53) and have done "a very bad job of teaching ... a wider vision of schools in society" (Mulkeen & Cooper, 1989, p. 12). Furthermore, critics have made a case that the content in training programs has been heavily influenced by the "pervasive managerial-administrative ethic" (Evans, 1998, p. 30) that undergirds the profession (Callahan, 1962; Murphy, 1992; Newlon, 1934). Further, preparation programs largely have ignored matters of teaching and learning, pedagogy, and curriculum (Murphy, 1990a, 1990b; Murphy et al., in press). Most of the interest and scholarly activity during the last half of the 20th century heavily reinforced the "separation of problems in administration from problems in education" (Greenfield, 1988, p. 144) and the emphasis on noneducational issues in training programs (Hallinger & Murphy, 1991). As Evans (1991) astutely chronicled, the focus has been on discourse and training primarily on "the administration of education" (p. 3), or administration qua administration—a major shift from the profession's formative years when the emphasis "was upon the adjective *educational* rather than upon the noun *administration*" (Guba, 1960, p. 115). The separation of educational administration "from the phenomenon known as instruction" (Erickson, 1979, p. 10) means that the typical graduate of a school administration training program can act only as "a mere spectator in relation to the instructional program" (Hills, 1975, p. 4; Murphy et al., 2008).

Program Standards

Thoughtful critiques of preparation programs have suggested that the lack of rigorous standards has been a serious problem touching almost every aspect of educational leadership (Murphy & Vriesenga, 2006). Previously, we noted the historical absence of standards in the recruitment and selection of candidates into preparation programs. According to critics, once students enter preparation programs, the lack of standards continued. Programs were often focused around organizational management issues and professors' areas of research interest, resulting in a good deal of content variety and quality unevenness across programs. The delivery system most commonly employed—part-time study in the evening or on weekends—exacerbated the problems resulting from program unevenness, as students came to their "studies worn-out, distracted, and harried" (Mann, 1975, p. 143). Exit requirements, in turn, were characterized as "slack and unrelated to the work of the profession" (Peterson & Finn, 1985, p. 54; also see Murphy et al., 2008). Many critics also argued that compounding the lack of standards at almost every phase of preparation programs were university faculty who were unable or unwilling to improve the situation (Hawley, 1988; Levine, 2005; McCarthy et al., 1988). Thus, not surprisingly, reviewers argued that the time had come to markedly elevate standards in school leadership (Young & Peterson, 2002).

Program Evaluation

In 1946, Grace identified an important gap in the preparation architecture: a lack of work devoted to the examination of the effectiveness of educational programs in school leadership. He held that institutions of higher education needed to be more diligent in assessing program quality and impact. The call for greater attention to program assessment was picked up in the 1950s by Wynn (1957); in the 1960s by Gregg (1960, 1969); in the 1970s by Farquhar (1977) and Silver (1978a, 1978b); and at the turn of the century by Glasman, Cibulka, and Ashby (2002) and by Orr and Kottkamp (2003).

Over the last quarter century, other scholars periodically have spotlighted the need for action on this line of work. Erickson (1977) reported that studies in the field "between 1954 and 1974 provided no adequate basis for outcome-oriented organizational strategy in education" (p. 128). Two years later, Erickson (1979) expanded on the ideas of his earlier essay, highlighting "the tendency to neglect the careful tracing of connections between organizational variables and student outcomes" (p. 12) and suggesting, "The current major emphasis in studies of organizational consequences, should be on postulated causal networks in which student outcomes are the bottom line" (p. 12). Glasman et al. (2002) summed up the situation somewhat charitably for the National Commission on the Advancement of Educational Leadership Preparation as follows: "Educational leadership programs have not had a strong tradition of engagement in self evaluation of their programs" (p. 258).

Until this area of research was supported by UCEA and the Teaching in Educational Administration special interest group in the early 2000s, this particular patch of the research landscape in the school leadership lay fallow. And, as we will see in later chapters, important work is finally getting underway in this area (Orr & Pounder, 2006), providing sorely needed evidence to guide program improvement.

Mapping the Change of Preparation Programs

Markers on the Path to Reform

In this section, we review key markers on this road to more productive preparation programs, and we tease out reform trends. Although it is impossible to prejudge what future historians of educational leadership will designate as the specific major events that helped shape the education of school leaders for the 21st century, certain events appear likely to receive considerable attention. An overview of significant events, initiatives, and publications follows.

National Commission on Excellence in Educational Administration (NCEEA) and the National Policy Board for Educational Administration (NPBEA)

One marker that surely will be singled out is the set of activities comprising the work of the NCEEA. Growing out of the deliberations of the Executive Council of the UCEA, the commission was formed in 1985 under the direction of Daniel E. Griffiths. The NCEEA produced three influential documents that promoted considerable discussion both within and outside educational leadership: the 1987 report, *Leaders for America's Schools*; Griffiths's highly influential address to the 1988 annual meeting of the American Educational Research Association (AERA), subsequently published as a UCEA paper (Griffiths, 1988b); and a UCEA-sponsored, edited volume containing background papers commissioned by the NCEEA (Griffiths et al., 1988). These three documents helped to crystallize the sense of what was wrong with the profession in general and with the preparatory function specifically. They also helped to extend discussion about possible solutions and, to a lesser extent, to provide signposts for those engaged in redefining school leadership and rebuilding preparation programs (see Forsyth, 1999).

Following up on these activities, then UCEA Executive Director Patrick Forsyth set about mustering support for one of the key NCEEA recommendations, the creation of the NPBEA. After considerable work on the part of UCEA, the NPBEA was created in 1988. The NPBEA has undertaken a series of activities designed to provide direction for the reconstruction of the profession, especially its training function. NPBEA released its first report, titled *Improving the Preparation of School Administrators: The Reform Agenda*, in May 1989. The report outlines an extensive overhaul and strengthening of preparation programs. Its recommendations were later adopted in slightly modified form by the universities comprising the UCEA. Following the release of *The Reform Agenda*, the NPBEA published a series of occasional papers that were designed to inform the reform debate on preparing the next generation of school leaders. NPBEA also sponsored, in conjunction with the Danforth Foundation, national conferences to help professors discover alternatives to deeply ingrained practices in training programs. The 1992 conference on problem-based learning drew nearly 150 participants from universities throughout the United States and Canada.

Reform Books and Reports on Preparation

In addition to the reform efforts described above, program change has been shaped by a series of volumes devoted to the analysis and improvement of the academic arm of the profession and its preparation programs. Each of these books has helped focus attention on the problems of the field and has provided alternative visions as well as solution paths to guide the voyage. Some of the most important of these preparation-focused volumes include the two volumes on the professoriate authored by Martha M. McCarthy and colleagues: *Under Scrutiny: The Educational Administration Professoriate* (McCarthy, Kuh, Newell, & Iacona, 1988) and a follow-up volume, *Continuity and Change: The Educational Leadership Professoriate* (McCarthy & Kuh, 19979). Other books devoted primarily to the reform of preparation programs include those edited by Murphy (1993), *Preparing Tomorrow's School Leaders: Alternative Designs*; Mulkeen, Cambron-McCabe, and Anderson (1994), *Democratic Leadership: The Changing Context of Administrative Preparation*; and Murphy and Forsyth (1999), *Educational Administration: A Decade of Reform*. They also include those authored by Beck and Murphy (1994), *Ethics in Educational Leadership Preparation Programs: An Expanding Role*; by Beck, Murphy, and Associates (1997), *Ethics in Educational Leadership Programs: Emerging Models*; by Milstein and Associates (1993), *Changing the Way We Prepare Educational Leaders: The Danforth Experience*; and by Murphy (1992, 2006a), *The Landscape of Leadership Preparation: Reframing the Education of School Administrators* and *Preparing School Leaders: Defining a Research and Action Agenda*.

A particularly influential marker coming at the dawn of the 21st century was Murphy's (1999a) invited AERA address (later published as a UCEA monograph) on the state of the profession of school administration: *The Quest for a Center: Notes on the State of the Profession of Educational Leadership*. Based on a comprehensive review of work underway throughout the field, the *Quest* document directs the profession to rebuild itself in general and its preparation programs specifically not on updated revisions of traditional blueprints but rather on the valued ends of schooling—school improvement, social justice, and democratic community (Murphy, 2002).

It is always a little difficult to decide what might count as a "reform report." The assignment is only complicated when we add the criterion of "potentially influential" to the identification equation. To be sure, the field has been defined by an almost never-ending cascade of critical analyses of preparation programs in school leadership over the last 20 years. We explored some of that work in the previous section. However, it is not the center of attention here. Rather, we target commission documents on the future of leadership preparation, not the analyses of single scholars or small teams of researchers. Using these criteria, five documents merit attention, two of which we already have highlighted: The NCEEA (1987) report, *Leaders for America's Schools,* and the NPBEA (1989) report, *Improving the Preparation of School Administrators: The Reform Agenda.* Later we reference a fourth potentially historically important document compiled under the banner of the National Commission on the Advancement of Educational Leadership Preparation in 2001.

In 1990, the National Commission for the Principalship, under the leadership of Scott D. Thomson, published a report titled *Principals for Our Changing Schools: Preparation and Certification.* The document represents an attempt to unpack the functional knowledge base required by principals. Working from this document, Thomson, under the aegis of the NPBEA—of which he was at the time executive secretary—assigned teams to flesh out each of the 21 knowledge domains identified in the report. The resulting document (National Commission for the Principalship, 1993) provides a comprehensive outline of the core knowledge and skills needed by principals to lead today's schools (Thomson, 1999). The final report was written by Arthur Levine and his colleagues at Teachers College, Columbia University. Generally referred to as the "Levine report," this 2005 analysis involved a critical examination of the preparation landscape in school leadership at the dawn of the 21st century and, like all its predecessors, lacked an understanding of the aggressive and complex changes underway in leadership preparation programs (Young, Crow, Orr, Ogawa, & Creighton, 2005). As a result, the report offers frequently cited and in many ways wrong-headed action steps to be taken to strengthen the education of future school leaders, including the development of a new professional master's degree and the elimination of the doctor of education degree (see also Finn, Broad, Meyer, & Feistritzer, 2003).

Interstate School Leaders Licensure Consortium (ISLLC)

Standards-defining activities are also likely to be heavily referenced in future reports of events shaping the evolution, and perhaps the transformation, of preparation programs in school leadership. The central line of activity here revolves around the work of the ISLLC. Created in the mid-1990s by the NPBEA and chaired by Joseph Murphy of Vanderbilt University, a group of 24 states and major professional associations developed the first set of standards for school leaders. Approved by the NPBEA late in 1996, the ISLLC standards have been adopted or adapted for use in over 40 states as the basis for operating preparation programs. The newly revised standards, renamed Educational Leadership Policy Standards: ISLLC 2008: As Adopted by the NPBEA (Flanary & Simpson, 2008), is an updated version of the 1996 ISLLC standards. To ensure that the revised standards were "based on current research concerning effective educational leadership, a nationally recognized research panel worked for two years to tie each of the functions of the revised standards to research-based pedagogical practice as well as empirical knowledge" (Young, 2008a, p. 9).

Over the last decade, many of the states that adopted the ISSLC standards have worked with their universities to rebuild preparation programs, including Ohio and Georgia (Murphy, 2005b). Some, such as New Jersey, North Carolina, and Delaware, have adopted whole-state review processes to energize the scholarly process (see Murphy et al., 2008). In addition, 13 states currently use the School Leaders Licensure Assessment, developed by the Educational Testing Service and based on ISLLC standards to license graduates of preparation programs, a particularly powerful leverage point for reshaping preparation programs. Equally important, on the professional front, the ISLCC standards have been adapted by the National Council for Accreditation of Teacher Education (NCATE) specialty-area review in educational leadership, conducted by the Educational Leadership Licensure Consortium (ELCC). The ELCC, which is an official program initiative of the NPBEA, has been using an adapted version of the ISLLC standards since 2001 to review program quality and grant those of high quality national recognition. The use of ISLLC by NCATE's ELCC resulted in focusing the content of hundreds of programs around these national standards, thus significantly enhancing ISLLC's influence on the preparation of school leaders (Murphy, 2005b; Murphy & Shipman, 1999; Murphy, Yff, & Shipman, 2000; Young, 2008b).

Foundation Initiatives

Histories of the field of school leadership reveal two conclusions about foundational support (Campbell et al., 1987; Murphy, 1992, 2006a). On the one hand, there has not been much of it. On the other hand, the resources that have been forthcoming have exerted an important influence on the academic arm of school leadership in general and on preparation programs in particular. This was true in the 1950s when the Kellogg Foundation supported the highly influential Cooperative Project in Educational Administration (Campbell et al., 1987) and the development of the UCEA (Culbertson, 1995). It held again in the 1980s and 1990s when Danforth Foundation support helped nudge preparation programs from a foundation of complacency and reset them on much stronger pillars (McCarthy, 1999; Milstein & Associates, 1993). In addition to its sponsorship of the NCEEA and its core support for the NPBEA during its inception, Danforth underwrote four significant efforts designed to assist self-analyses and preparation-program improvement efforts in educational leadership, all of which capture multiple elements from the various reform volumes and documents cited above: (a) a Principals' Program to improve preparation programs for prospective leaders; (b) a Professors' Program to enhance the capability of departments to respond to needed reforms; (c) research and development efforts, such as the Problem-Based Learning Project, that designed alternative approaches to understanding the profession and to educating tomorrow's leaders; and (d) a series of conferences and workshops created to help the professoriate grapple with important reform ideas in the area of preparing leaders for tomorrow's schools.

Our reading of the existing clues leads us to conclude that a current "third wave" of foundational support also will be identified in future reports as a key marker in the history of leadership preparation. Here, in particular, we reference three preparation-focused initiatives of the Wallace Foundation: (a) the creation of the State Action for Education Leadership Project (SAELP, later known as Cohesive Leadership System Initiative) through which some states (e.g., Missouri and New Mexico) are employing state policy in the service of strengthening preparation programs, either by creating new training avenues or by upgrading existing pathways; (b) the funding of the Stanford study that unpacked the elements of high-quality preparation programs (see Darling-Hammond et al., 2007); and (c) the funding of the Southern Regional Education Board to develop new curriculum and to work with universities to use this curriculum and related materials to redesign preparation programs.

In a similar vein, the Broad Foundation is supporting the creation of alternative models of preparation such as New Leaders for New Schools. A central dynamic of much of the Broad Foundation work is that, unlike earlier funding that employed professionally based reform strategies, market or political change engines are featured.

Recent Professional Initiatives

It is almost a certainty that recent actions by the leading professional associations—AERA, NCPEA, and UCEA—will stand the test of time when the history of administrator preparation is written. The NCPEA, an organization that has served as a network for professors of educational leadership since the 1940s, is likely to make its mark through two major initiatives introduced during the last decade. First, this group has worked to strengthen university faculty networks by creating state affiliates in many regions. Although the activities of these regional groups are variable, a number of them (e.g., in Missouri and California) have used their state networks to focus on program improvement. A second significant contribution of NCPEA is likely to be the online open-access publishing site they have developed in collaboration with researchers at Rice University. On this site, faculty can share research in progress as well as course materials.

We already have noted some of the hallmark contributions of the UCEA toward the strengthening of leadership preparation over the last quarter century, including the NCEEA. Three more recent initiatives also likely will be remembered for substantively shaping preparation programs for school leaders. The first major initiative it is important to discuss from UCEA was the creation under the leadership of Executive Director Michelle Young of the National Commission on the Advancement of Educational Leadership Preparation (NCAELP) in 2001. NCAELP included representatives from all the major stakeholder groups in the U.S. educational leadership field. Working in cooperation with the NPBEA, NCAELP engaged in systemic work (a) to develop a complex understanding of contemporary contextual factors impacting educational leadership and leadership preparation, (b) to examine exceptional and innovative educational leadership preparation and professional development programs, (c) to determine clearly and precisely what must take place both within and outside the university to ensure effective educational leadership preparation and professional development, and (d) to create a comprehensive and collaborative set of action plans for the future. Commission members working under the guidance of Professor Young engaged in a series of preparation program reform efforts (see special issue of *Educational Administration Quarterly*, 2002, *38*[2], especially Young & Peterson, 2002, and Grogan & Andrews, 2002).

A major theme within the work of NCAELP was the understanding that the field of educational leadership did not have enough research on educational leadership preparation to make strong statements about what preparation patterns and characteristics programs should employ. As a result, UCEA, under the leadership of Executive Director Michelle Young, developed a series of initiatives to address what it viewed as a serious impediment to progress. Initiatives included the development of the Joint Research Taskforce on Educational Leadership Preparation; the establishment of the *Journal of Research on Leadership Education*; the development of two major handbooks on the preparation of educational leaders (this volume and an international version published in cooperation with the British Educational Leadership and Management Association and the Commonwealth Council for Educational Administration and Management); and increased support to the evaluation research taskforce, jointly supported by UCEA and the Teaching in Educational Administration special interest group. Several of these initiatives are discussed below.

Of particular importance was the founding of *The Journal of Research on Leadership Education (JRLE)* by UCEA in 2005. This was a significant action because, unlike other professions, prior to the launch of the *JRLE,* there were no journals in the field concentrating on the preparation aspect of school leadership (Murphy & Vriesenga, 2004; Young et al., 2005).

Also as a follow-up to the work of NCAELP, UCEA in conjunction with AERA, again under the direction of Professor Young, launched a massive reform initiative at the dawn of the 21st century to examine all elements of leadership preparation and to provide the knowledge base and tools needed to engage reform efforts on a broad front (Young, 2004). Known as the Joint Research Taskforce on Educational Leadership Preparation, its primary impetus was to stimulate more and better research in our field focused on the preparation of leaders. Following up on the NCAELP concern that not enough was known about leadership reparation, the taskforce was intended to provide a foundation about existing research and theory in the field of leadership preparation.

The taskforce's inquiry was organized around 10 domains: (a) Leadership Education as a Field of Study; (b) the Context of Leadership Education; (c) Models and Theories of Leadership Education; (d) Recruitment, Selection, and Development of Leadership Candidates; (e) Providers of Leadership Education; (f) Curriculum and Pedagogy in Leadership Education; (g) the Delivery of Leadership Preparation; (h) Student Assessment and Program Evaluation; (i) Professional Learning; and (j) Leadership Education Around the Globe. Many of these same themes are reflected in the organization of this handbook, and many of the handbook authors participated in the taskforce work.

The taskforce was also intended to identify gaps and new directions for research on leadership preparation; to stimulate more, better quality research in the field of leadership preparation; to encourage new and experienced researchers to undertake research in the field; and to provide a community of scholars for ongoing conceptual and methodological work (Young, 2004). Along with the development of the new *JRLE* and the U.S. and international handbooks of research on leadership development, this taskforce has helped shift the focus of leadership program faculty to conducting and using high-quality research on and in their programs.

Also of particular significance is the program evaluation work that has been supported by UCEA and the Learning and Teaching in Educational Leadership (LTEL) special interest group, under the leadership of Terry Orr, Robert Kottkamp, and more recently Diana Pounder. These two organizations have established a joint UCEA/LTEL Evaluation Taskforce, which has worked with a national network of programs to (a) develop a valid and reliable survey instrument for graduates and alumni to assess their program preparation experiences, leadership learning, leadership practices, career advancement, and school improvement work and outcomes; (b) establish baseline results for comparing programs on these measures; (c) develop evaluation training and data analysis protocols; (d) harness Internet resources to facilitate data collection and analysis through online survey mechanisms; (e) establish strategies for obtaining and integrating state data systems to track graduate outcomes from institutions through their school leadership careers; and (f) establish protocols for obtaining institutional and individual consent for collecting and reporting evaluation information. As will be shown in a later chapter, a growing body of research on preparation demonstrates that selected program designs and features are more effective for leadership preparation and development and are more likely to yield better graduate outcomes (Davis et al., 2005; Jackson & Kelly, 2002; U.S. Department of Education, 2005). More efficacious, high-quality leadership preparation programs (Darling-Hammond et al., 2007; Orr, 2008) have the following characteristics: (a) rigorous selection, giving priority to underserved groups, particularly racial/ ethnic minorities; (b) clear focus and clarified values about leadership and coherently organized; (c) standards-based content and internships; (d) active, student-centered instruction; (e) supportive organizational structures to facilitate retention and engagement; (f) coherent, challenging, and reflective content and experiences; and (g) appropriately qualified faculty. Programs with such features yield better graduate outcomes—in what they learn and their career advancement, and, in turn, how they practice leadership and foster school improvement. By applying such research to evaluation, programs can improve their impact.

AERA, in turn, has exercised significant influence on preparation programs with the creation of the UCEA/LTEL special interest group. This group, along with Division A under the leadership of Rodney Ogawa, cosponsored the Joint Research Task Force on Educational Leadership Preparation with UCEA. In addition, the fingerprints of its members are visible on nearly every effort to improve leadership preparation in school leadership underway at the dawn of the 21st century.

State-Directed Initiatives

The report of the NCEEA in 1987 called for states to exercise increased influence in determining the shape and texture of leadership preparation programs in education. And consistent with their dramatically enhanced role in directing preK–12 education beginning in the 1980s (see Murphy, 1990d)—and often in conjunction with support from the Wallace Foundation—states have responded to that request. As we have noted above, in the late 1990s over 40 states adopted or adapted the ISLLC standards as the framework to guide leadership preparation in universities and school districts. Equally noteworthy, the states assumed the leadership role, under the direction of the NPBEA, to develop the standards in the first place. Over the last decade, state leaders increasingly have nudged their way into "professional" conversations about leadership preparation. For example, it was a small coalition of states (North Carolina, Mississippi, Illinois, Missouri, and Washington, DC) that banded together to fund the development of the ETS-developed School Leader Licensure Assessment, which we argued above has had an important influence on preparation programs across the country. Increasingly, states are pulling policy levers to exercise new forms of control over preparation programs, such as the use of whole-state program reviews with heretofore unused sanctions (New Jersey, Iowa, and Georgia) and the funding of full-time internship programs (Mississippi and North Carolina; see Murphy, 2006a; Murphy et al., in press).

Reform Trends

Our analysis of the changing face of leadership preparation—our first cut at reform trends—sets the stage for the chapters that follow. In effect, the perspectives that we describe below are hypotheses that will be explored by the authors in this volume. Collectively, they define our best sense of where preparation for school leaders was moving at the time the handbook was first conceptualized (Forsyth & Murphy, 1999; Murphy, in press; Murphy & Forsyth, 1999), refined by NCAELP and the work of the Joint Research Taskforce, and finally made a reality through the efforts of UCEA's Executive Director Michelle Young in 2005. We return to our hypotheses in the concluding chapter.

New Energy for Reform Work

One central conclusion of our collective work is that considerable energy is flowing into the reformation of preparation programs in school leadership. A second finding is that this energy is positively impacting school leadership and administrator preparation programs (Murphy & Forsyth, 1999; Young, 2008a; Young et al., 2002).

Earlier reports on the readiness of the field for change in its preparation programs were disheartening. Studies by McCarthy and her colleagues (McCarthy et al., 1988; McCarthy & Kuh, 1997) and by Murphy (1991) found a general level of complacency about preparation programs among professors of educational leadership. The assumption of the profession of a more active stance (Young et al., 2002) is therefore worthy of note. We expect that time is one variable in play in this shift in expectations. That is, unlike in the earlier studies, many of the critical reviews and reform reports in the area of leadership have had a chance to spread across the profession. There also has been sufficient time for programs to engage in change initiatives and for some of those efforts to take root.

It may also be the case that, as authors in the early chapters of the handbook show, the buffering these programs historically have enjoyed—buffering employed to fend off external influences—may be thinning considerably. That is, the option not to act may be becoming reduced. For example, the resurgence of more vigorous state control over preparation programs in a growing number of states may be propelling reform efforts (Murphy, 2005b). This certainly has been the case in states such as North Carolina, Mississippi, Kentucky, Delaware, and New Jersey. Concomitantly, the introduction of market dynamics into the licensure system may be influencing departments to strengthen training programs (Hess & Kelly, 2005; Murphy & Hawley, 2003). At least two such forces have surfaced over the past decade: the creation of alternative avenues for licensure and the growth of alternative providers of programs leading to licensure. Currently, it is unclear whether the introduction of such alternative providers will result in program improvement or if it will drive a race to the bottom. Only time will tell.

Professional forces also may lie behind recent reform work. There is a sense that the earlier widespread complacency about preparation programs among professors of educational leadership is being challenged as older members of the professoriate retire and new faculty begin to assume the reins of the profession. If, indeed, we are witnessing a lifting of the veil of complacency, it may be attributable to the influx of more women professors and of more faculty members who are joining the professoriate from practice (McCarthy, 1999) than was the case in earlier decades.

The growth of professional groups dedicated to program reform, such as the new AERA special interest groups on problem-based learning and LTEL, are noteworthy markers in the professional area. So, too, has been the development of professional networks of reformers over the last few decades: those nurtured through the Danforth initiatives of the late 1980s and early 1990s, the community of work led by Terry Orr and Robert Kottkamp on program evaluation, the integrative efforts of social justice scholars promoted by Catherine Marshall and a host of other colleagues, and work on technology in leadership preparation led by Scott McCloud. In short, it may be that the rather inhospitable landscape of the profession is being remolded to be more receptive to the seeds of change. It is worth noting that many more colleagues than was the case 15 years ago have staked at least part of their professional reputations on work related to preparation program development and reform.

Finally, it is possible that shifting norms in universities in general and in colleges of education in particular may be responsible for some of the increased attention to program reform. Specifically, at least three forces operating in education schools may be directing, or at least facilitating, program improvement: (a) the increased emphasis "on enhancing the quality of instruction [in] most colleges and universities" (McCarthy & Kuh, 1997, p. 245), (b) outcome focus of national accreditation, and (c) the demand by many colleges of education that meaningful connections to practice be established and nurtured. Although historically offset by other forces (e.g., the press for research respectability; Levine, 2005), these dynamics may be helping to energize efforts to strengthen preparation programs in the area of educational leadership.

Reforging the Technical Core

On the instructional front, a renewed interest in teaching is embedded in the preparation reform narrative. There is evidence of an increase in the use of technology in instruction—in redefining the classroom (e.g., field-based instruction), in classroom activities (e.g., teaching simulations), and in building working relationships with students outside the class (e.g., Blackboard and e-mail communications). There appears to be greater stress on applied approaches and relevant materials in general and on the additional use of problem- and case-based materials specifically (Black, Bathon, & Poindexter, 2007). The emergent cognitive perspectives that are helping to redefine learning seem to be working their way into instructional designs in leadership-preparation programs (Hart & Pounder, 1999; Pounder et al., 2002).

A number of issues in the area of curriculum stand out. To begin with, there is greater interest concerning matters of teaching and learning, including connections between principals' actions and the core technology. Ethics and values are more heavily featured in newly designed preparation programs, with coursework related to the normative dimensions of educational leadership. Closely connected to the growing interest in values is an expanded concern for the social and cultural influences shaping schooling. A subtheme that cuts across both of these areas—values and social context—has heightened attention to issues of diversity, race, and gender. Closely related to this last focus, programs for preparing school leaders are devoting more attention to topics related to underserved children and their families, especially to the equity agenda. Data use and data-based decision making are evident in increasing numbers of programs, as are field-based research strategies (e.g., collaborative inquiry and action research). Finally, approaches to inculcating habits of reflection and critical analysis are finding life in preparation programs as we push into the 21st century (Murphy, 1999b, 1999c).

Reunification of the Profession

A central component of recent efforts to reweave the somewhat tattered fabric that represents the profession of school leadership is collaboration. Although the practice and academic spheres of the profession have been estranged for nearly 50 years, preparation programs are being redesigned to repair that gash (Young et al., 2002). These endeavors are of two types: stronger field-based elements in preparation programs and more robust linkages between university faculty and district- and school-based administrators. On the first topic, preparation programs feature the use of practice-anchored materials to a greater extent than had been the norm in earlier times. There has been a revitalization of the internship. We also see more attention to related clinical activities—shadowing, interviewing administrators, community studies, and working with practitioners on projects. In general, reforging content has surfaced an underlying dynamic toward aligning preparation with the essential practice aspects of school leadership.

On the second topic, university–field connections, a number of trends are visible. The most evident is an enhanced emphasis on forging partnerships in preparation programs between university-based and school-based educators, including the legitimization of practitioner-based advisory groups to help inform preparation program design and content. Another piece of the university–field matrix underscores the rejuvenation of adjunct and clinical faculty roles (Murphy & Forsyth, 1999).

Alternative Preparation Models

During its short history, formal preparation for the role of school leader has been the purview of universities, with the imprimatur of state government agencies. Under the onslaught of critical analysis and the renewed interest in the power of markets described earlier, the monopolistic position of universities has come under attack (Finn et al., 2003; Hess & Kelly, 2005; Murphy & Hawley, 2003; Murphy, Hawley, & Young, 2005). It is increasingly being asserted that preparation might occur more productively in venues other than universities and might be provided more effectively by other agents than faculty members in departments of educational leadership.

In response to these forces, alternative pathways to the role of formal school leader are emerging, again with the warrant of the state. New pathways feature providers not historically associated with the preparation of school administrators. Six alternative models of preparation, roughly in degree of aggressiveness in opening up the preparation function, are outlined below.

Under *alternative university models*, the preparation function remains in institutions of higher education, but it is no longer restricted to colleges of education, or, if it is so restricted, departments other than school leadership are brought into the picture. For example, focusing on the former scenario, New Jersey allows anyone with a degree in administration (e.g., business administration, public administration) to become a school leader. Under the latter scenario, one could become a school administrator with a degree in psychology or curriculum and instruction for example.

Professional models transfer responsibility for preparation from universities to professional associations. For example, professional groups in California, Massachusetts, and New Jersey are all in the business of preparing newly minted school leaders. The New Jersey Principals and Supervisors Association's Expedited Certification for Education Leadership (EXCEL) programs employ practice-based educators to prepare teachers to become certified to be school administrators.

District models, in turn, make the employer the prime actor in the preparation drama. This is the case in Houston and other districts throughout the country, especially large-city school systems.

Entrepreneurial models combine the insights of creative individuals outside the university and the resources of committed reformers, almost always philanthropic foundations. The best known examples here are Dennis Litkey and his Big Picture Company with its school-based, mentoring model of preparation and Jon Schnur and the New Leaders for New Schools program to prepare nontraditional actors as school administrators for urban school systems.

The efforts of for-profit firms fall into the category of *private models*. The most extensive and visible example here is the Leadership for Learning master's program developed by Canter and Associates in partnership with the American Association of School Administrators.

Experiential models permit potential administrators to substitute work experience for coursework. Although to date almost all initiatives in this area have been ad hoc (e.g., a waiver to certification regulations), the profession likely will see more systematic initiatives to allow work experience to substitute for formal preparation in the future.

Findings About Research on Preparation Programs

In the introduction, we reported that only a very small proportion of the scholarship on school leader preparation is empirical in nature; that is, the research base informing understanding and subsequent change efforts is remarkably thin. This is a theme that will be reinforced continually in subsequent chapters. Here, we present a broad picture of what was known about research on the preparation function as this handbook took shape—the starting point, if you will. Our findings come from a study by Murphy and Vriesenga (2004) of empirical work on leadership preparation in four leading journals in school leadership (*Educational Administration Quarterly, Journal of Educational Administration, Journal of School Leadership*, and *Planning and Changing*) from 1975 to 2002.

1. *There is not an overabundance of scholarship in the area of administrator preparation.*
    At least when we focus on the leading journals in school leadership, it is clear that descriptions and analyses of preparation programs do not occupy much space in these outlets. Only 8% of the 2,000-plus articles in these journals from 1975 to 2002 dealt with preservice training programs. Given the applied nature of the profession and the centrality of preparatory activities to departments of educational leadership, the fact that serious academic work on preservice training remains a minor element in the school administration scholarship mosaic is as surprising as it is disappointing.
2. *Work in entire domains of administrator preparation is conspicuous by its absence.*
    Although in no area of administrator preparation is there a surfeit of work, at least on some topics an initial body of literature is developing. On the other hand, as we see in subsequent chapters, very little study has been directed toward entire sections of the preparatory landscape. Specifically, we know very little about issues ranging from how we recruit and select students, instruct them in our programs, and monitor and assess their progress. Organizational life inside programs is hardly touched upon in the research literature. We also learn remarkably little form the journals about the faculty members who develop and operate these programs. In particular, there is almost no empirical evidence on the education of those who educate prospective school leaders.

3. *The contours of school leadership are only weakly shaped by empirical evidence on preparation programs.*

Slightly less than 3% (56) of the 2,000-plus articles published between 1975 and 2002 in the leading journals in our field are empirically anchored investigations on administrator preparation. While we seem to know about this topic, as evidenced in the abundance of writing and professing in the area, very little of our understanding has been forged on the empirical anvil. While it is appropriate for the field to incorporate multiple ways of knowing about the preparation experience, the very limited attention devoted to empirical studies remains a serious problem.

4. *The amount of scholarship devoted to administrator preparation is expanding.*

Between 1975 and 1990, approximately 3% of the articles in the leading journals addressed administrator preservice training. Since that time, over 11% of the articles have attended to training issues. During the earlier time period, less than 1% of journal space was devoted to empirical work on preparation programs. Since 1990, nearly 4% of the articles in the four leading journals in our field have been given over to empirical studies of administrator preservice training. Concomitantly, individual faculty have become scholars of specific areas within preparation programs, conducting critical and empirical investigations on the topic at hand (see, for example, the extended work of Barnett, Basom, Yerkes, & Norris, 2000, in the area of student cohorts; that of Kochan & Twale, 1998, and Daresh, 1987, on clinical work; and that of McCarthy et al., 1988, and McCarthy & Kuh, 1997, on faculty issues).

5. *The methodological scaffolding supporting empirical studies has been expanded, yet it is not clear that quality has been greatly enhanced.*

When one steps back and examines the full landscape of empirical work on preparation programs, it is obvious that the terrain is populated not only more densely, but also by a greater variety of studies than has been the case in the field of school leadership in general in the past. In particular, incipient efforts into blended methods and the mushrooming use of naturalistic designs have significantly expanded the assortment of studies in the preparation area. Concomitantly, the importation of an entire new set of analytic strategies has enriched the architectural design undergirding preparation programs.

Although in many ways the expansion of the methods portfolio has strengthened the study of the preparatory function (e.g., it has helped us see issues from multiple angles and sometimes more deeply as well), it has not made a large dent in overcoming many of the deficiencies that characterize research in school administration in general. In particular, the expanded portfolio has not helped produce much traction on the following issues: the ad hoc nature of the work, an overreliance on cross-sectional investigations, the use of limited samples, inadequately developed (or at least described) analytic frames, and a lack of depth or a heavy focus on the surface issues of topics under investigation.

6. *Dissertation work comprises a small but not insignificant proportion of published research.*

Reviewers of research in school administration in general long have noted the prominent place that doctoral students occupy in building the knowledge base in the profession. However, when the lens is directed on published articles focusing on administrator preparation in refereed journals, that conclusion is muted. Of the 56 empirical studies published in the leading journals over the last quarter century, only 3 can be traced directly to a dissertation. When the names of the authors of these 56 pieces were matched with dissertations, 7 additional articles that could be coupled to dissertation research were located—for a total of 18%. In addition, 4 dissertations that were loosely linked to the content of an article published in one of the leading journals in school administration were found.

7. *There is almost no evidence of external support for empirical research on preparation programs.*

   For the 56 empirical studies, only 3 have either direct or indirect reference to external funding, and 2 of these represent very limited support. It appears that professors who engage in research on preparation programs continue to do so out of their back pockets, relying on (a) the good will of current and recent graduates to complete surveys or sit for interviews and (b) residual documents associated with preparation programs (e.g., admissions records). It is difficult to see how the profession can gain much leverage on developing systematic and programmatic work on preparation without additional support.

An Overview of the Handbook

Earlier, we outlined both the need for this handbook as well as its intended purpose. We also foreshadowed much of the material that will be examined in detail in later chapters. We close this introductory chapter with an overview of the chapters that follow. As was the case with this chapter, the authors in the first section of the handbook (chapters 1–4) focus on the general terrain of leadership preparation. In chapter 1, Kottkamp and Rusch describe the broad landscape of scholarship and narrower empirical research about leadership education for the preparation of future school leaders. In chapter 2, McCarthy and Forsyth examine the primary building blocks of professional preparation, review influences on the education of school leaders, and identify gaps related to effective preparation of school administrators. In chapter 3, LaMagdeleine and his colleagues zero in on the forces internal and external to universities that are shaping leadership preparation today. Finally, in chapter 4, Lumby and her coauthors explore why culture is a critical consideration in the design and delivery of programs, analyze the differing approaches to leader development (initial preparation and ongoing education) in a variety of countries, and suggest the major lessons emerging for U.S. leader preparation.

The second section of the handbook moves from the context in which leadership preparation takes place to the people involved in preparation and the experiences provided therein. In chapter 5 Browne-Ferrigno and Muth focus on the participants in educational administration and leadership programs, whereas Hackmann and his colleagues in chapter 6 discuss the faculty members of educational leadership preparation programs. In chapter 7, Osterman and Hafner review research on the curriculum used within leadership preparation programs, and in chapter 8 Taylor and her colleagues review research on pedagogy. In chapter 9, Barnett, Copland, and Shoho focus on the use of internships in the preparation of educational leaders, whereas in chapter 10 Grogan and her colleagues review research on the design and delivery of leadership preparation programs. The final chapter in this section, by Kochan and Locke, focuses on student assessment and evaluation.

The third and final section of the handbook is made up of three chapters that in turn focus on program evaluation, leadership development, and leadership mentoring. In the handbook's conclusion, we reflect on the contributions made by each of the handbook chapters and revisit our hypotheses concerning the state of research and research activity in the field around leadership preparation. As noted previously, the need for a knowledge base on educational leadership preparation has been made clear; energy to act has been mustered; and, as we will see throughout this handbook, some important initial steps at strengthening the research base are underway.

References

Achilles, C. M. (1984). Forecast: Stormy weather ahead in educational administration. *Issues in Education, 2*(2), 127–135.

American Association of Colleges for Teacher Education. (1988). *School leadership preparation: A preface for action.* Washington, DC: Author.

Anderson, G. L. (1990). Toward a critical constructionist approach to school administration: Invisibility, legitimization, and the study of non-events. *Educational Administration Quarterly, 26*(1), 38–59.

Baker, B. D., Orr, M. T., & Young, M. D. (2007). Academic drift, institutional production and professional distribution of graduate degrees in educational administration. *Educational Administration Quarterly, 43*(3), 279–318.

Baker, B. D., Wolf-Wendel, & Twombly, S. (2007). Exploring the faculty pipeline in educational administration: Evidence from the survey of earned doctorates, 1999 to 2000. *Educational Administration Quarterly, 43*(2), 189–220.

Barnett, B., Basom, M., Yerkes, D., & Norris, C. (2000). Cohorts in educational leadership programs: Benefits, difficulties and the potential for developing school leaders. *Educational Administration Quarterly 36*(2), 255–282.

Beck, L. G., & Murphy, J. (1994). *Ethics in educational leadership preparation programs: An expanding role.* Newbury Park, CA: Corwin Press.

Beck, L. G., Murphy, J., & Associates. (1997). *Ethics in educational leadership preparation programs: Emerging models.* Newbury Park, CA: Corwin Press.

Björk, L. G., & Ginsberg, R. (1995). Principles of reform and reforming principal training: A theoretical perspective. *Educational Administration Quarterly, 31*(1), 11–37.

Black, W. R., Bathon, J., & Poindexter, B. (2007, August). *Looking in the mirror to improve practice: A study of administrative licensure and master's degree programs in the State of Indiana.* Bloomington: Indiana University.

Bridges, E. M. (1977). The nature of leadership. In L. L. Cunningham, W. G. Hack, & R. O. Nystrand (Eds.), *Educational administration: The developing decades* (pp. 202–230). Berkeley, CA: McCutchan.

Browne-Ferrigno, T., & Shoho, A. (2004). Careful selection of aspiring principals: An exploratory analysis of leadership preparation program admission practices. In C. S. Carr & C. L. Fulmer (Eds.), *Educational leadership: Knowing the way, showing the way, going the way* (pp. 172–189). Lanham, MD: Scarecrow Education.

Callahan, R. E. (1962). *Education and the cult of efficiency.* Chicago: University of Chicago Press.

Cambron-McCabe, N. (2002). National Commission for the Advancement of Educational Leadership: Opportunity for transformation. *Educational Administration Quarterly, 38*(2), 289–299.

Campbell, R. F. (1981). The professorship in educational administration: A personal view. *Educational Administration Quarterly, 17*(1), 1–24.

Campbell, R. F., Fleming, T., Newell, L. J., & Bennion, J. W. (1987). *A history of thought and practice in educational administration.* New York: Teachers College Press.

Campbell, R. F., & Newell, L. J. (1973). *A study of professors of educational administration: Problems and prospects of an applied academic field.* Columbus, OH: University Council for Educational Administration.

Carver, F. D. (1988, June). *The evaluation of the study of educational administration.* Paper presented at the EAAA Allerton House Conference, University of Illinois, Urbana-Champaign.

Clark, D. L. (1988, June). *Charge to the study group of the National Policy Board for Educational Administration.* Unpublished manuscript.

Cooper, B. S., & Boyd, W. L. (1987). The evolution of training for school administrators. In J. Murphy & P. Hallinger (Eds.), *Approaches to administrative training* (pp. 3–27). Albany, NY: SUNY Press.

Creighton, T. (2002). Standards for educational administration preparation programs: Okay, but don't we have the cart before the horse? *Journal of School Leadership, 12*(5), 526–551.

Culbertson, J. A. (1995). *Building bridges: UCEA first 2 decades.* Washington, DC: UCEA.

Daresh, J. C. (1987). *The practicum in preparing educational administrators: A status report.* Paper presented at the annual meeting of the Eastern Educational Research Association, Boston.

Darling-Hammond, L., LaPointe, M., Meyerson, D., & Orr, M. (2007, April). *Preparing school leaders for a changing world: Lessons from exemplary leadership develop programs. Final report.* Palo Alto, CA: Stanford Educational Leadership Institute.

English, F. W. (2007, November). *An anatomy of professional practice: Reflections on practices, standards, and promising research perspectives on educational leadership.* Paper presented at the annual meeting of the University Council for Educational Administration, Arlington, VA.

Erickson, D. A. (1977). An overdue paradigm shift in educational administration, or how can we get that idiot off the freeway. In L. L. Cunningham, W. G. Hack, & R. O. Nystrand (Eds.), *Educational administration: The developing decades* (pp. 114–143). Berkeley, CA: McCutchan.

Erickson, D. A. (1979). Research on educational administration: The state-of-the art. *Educational Researcher, 8,* 9–14.

Erlandson, D. A., & Witters-Churchill, L. (1988, March). *Design of the Texas NASSP study.* Paper presented at the annual meeting of the National Association of Secondary School Principals.

Evans, R. (1991, April). *Ministrative insight: Educational administration as pedagogic practice.* Paper presented at the annual meeting of the American Educational Research Association, Chicago.

Evans, R. (1998). Do intentions matter? Questioning the text of a high school principal. *Journal of Educational Administration and Foundations, 13*(1), 30–51.

Farquhar, R. H. (1977). Preparatory program in educational administration. In L. L. Cunningham, W. G. Hack, & R. O. Nystrand (Eds.), *Educational administration: The developing decades* (pp. 329–357). Berkeley, CA: McCutchan.

Finn, C. E., Broad, E., Meyer, L., & Feistritzer, E. (2003). *Better leaders for America's schools: A manifesto.* New York: Thomas

20 • Joseph Murphy, Michelle D. Young, Gary M. Crow, and Rodney T. Ogawa

B. Fordham Institute.

Flanary, R. A., & Simpson, J. (2008, January 12). *Major projects*. Available from the National Policy Board for Educational Administration Web site: http://www.npbea.org/projects.php

Forsyth, P. (1999). A brief history of scholarship on educational administration. In J. Murphy & P. Forsyth (Eds.), *Educational administration: A decade of reform* (pp. 71–92). Newbury Park, CA: Corwin Press.

Forsyth, P., & Murphy, J. (1999). A decade of reform: Emerging themes. In J. Murphy & P. Forsyth (Eds.), *Educational administration: A decade of reform*. Newbury Park, CA: Corwin.

Gerritz, W., Koppich, J., & Guthrie, J. (1984, November). *Preparing California school leaders: An analysis of supply, demand, and training*. Berkeley: University of California, Policy Analysis for California Education.

Glasman, N., Cibulka, J., & Ashby, D. (2002). Program self-evaluation for continuous improvement. *Educational Administration Quarterly, 38*(2), 257–288.

Goldhammer, K. (1983). Evolution in the profession. *Educational Administration Quarterly, 19*(3), 249–272.

Grace, A. G. (1946). The professional preparation of school personnel. In N. B. Henry (Ed.), *Changing conceptions in educational administration* (45th NSSE yearbook, Part II, pp. 176–182). Chicago: University of Chicago Press.

Greenfield, T. B. (1988). The decline and fall of science in educational administration. In D. E. Griffiths, R. T. Stout, & P. B. Forsyth (Eds.), *Leaders for America's schools* (pp. 131–159). Berkeley, CA: McCutchan.

Gregg, R. T. (1960). Administration. In C. W. Harris (Ed.), *Encyclopedia of educational research* (3rd ed., pp. 19–24). New York: MacMillan.

Gregg, R. T. (1969). Preparation of administrators. In R. L. Ebel (Ed.), *Encyclopedia of educational research* (4th ed., pp. 993–1004). London: MacMillan.

Griffiths, D. E. (1988a). Administrative theory. In N. J. Boyan (Ed.), *Handbook of research on educational administration* (pp. 27–51). New York: Longman.

Griffiths, D. E. (1988b). *Educational administration: Reform PDQ or RIP* (Occasional paper, no. 8312). Tempe, AZ: University Council for Educational Administration.

Griffiths, D. E., Stout, R. T., & Forsyth, P. B. (Eds.). (1988). *Leadership for America's schools: The report and papers on the National Commission on Excellence in Educational Administration*. Berkeley, CA: McCutchan.

Grogan, M., & Andrews, R. (2002). Defining preparation and professional development for the future. *Educational Administration Quarterly, 38*(2), 233–256.

Guba, E. G. (1960). Research in internal administration—What do we know? In R. F. Campbell & J. M. Lipham (Eds.), *Administrative theory as a guide to action* (pp. 113–141). Chicago: University of Chicago, Midwest Administrative Center.

Hallinger, P., & Murphy, J. (1991). Developing leaders for tomorrow's schools. *Phi Delta Kappan, 72*(7), 524–520.

Hart, A. W., & Pounder, P. G. (1999). Reinventing preparation programs: A decade of activity. In J. Murphy & P. B. Forsyth (Eds.), *Educational administration: A decade of reform* (pp. 115–151). Thousand Oaks, CA: Corwin Press.

Hawley, W. D. (1988). Universities and the improvement of school management. In D. E. Griffiths, R. T. Stout, & P. B. Forsyth (Eds.), *Leaders for America's schools: The report and papers of the National Commission on Excellence in Educational Administration* (pp. 82–88). Berkeley, CA: McCutchan.

Hess, F. M., & Kelly, A. (2005). An innovative look, a recalcitrant reality: The politics of principal preparation reform. *Educational Policy, 19*(1), 155–180.

Hills, J. (1975). The preparation of administrators: Some observations from the "firing line." *Educational Administration Quarterly, 11*(3), 1–20.

IJacobson, S. L. (1990). Reflections on the third wave of reform: Rethinking administrator preparation. In S. L. Jacobson & J. A. Conway (Eds.), *Educational leadership in an age of reform* (pp. 30–44). New York: Longman.

Kochan, F., & Twale, K. (1998). Advisory groups in educational leadership: Seeking a bridge between town and gown. *Journal of School Leadership, 29*(4), 237–250.

Lakomski, G. (1998, Fall). Training administrators in the wild: A naturalistic perspective. *UCEA Review, 34*(3), 1, 5, 10–11.

Levine, A. (2005). *Educating school leaders*. Washington, DC: The Education Schools Project.

Mann, D. (1975). What peculiarities in educational administration make it difficult to profess: An essay. *Journal of Educational Administration, 13*(1), 139–147.

McCarthy, M. M. (1999). The evolution of educational leadership preparation programs. In J. Murphy & K. Seashore Louis (Eds.), *Handbook of research on educational administration* (2nd ed., pp. 119–139). San Francisco: Jossey-Bass.

McCarthy, M. M., & Kuh, G. D. (1997). *Continuity and change: The educational leadership professoriate*. Columbia, MO: University Council for Educational Administration.

McCarthy, M. M., Kuh, G. D., Newell, L. J., & Iacona, C. M. (1988). *Under scrutiny: The educational administration professoriate*. Tempe, AZ: University Council for Educational Administration.

McKerrow, K. (1998). Administrative internships: Quality or quantity? *Journal of School Leadership, 8*(2), 171–186.

Miklos, E. (1988). Administrator selection, career patterns, succession, and socialization. In N. J. Boyan (Ed.), *Handbook of research on educational administration* (pp. 53–76). New York: Longman.

Milstein, M. (1990). Rethinking the clinical aspects of preparation programs: From theory to practice. In S. L. Jacobson & J. A. Conway (Eds.), *Educational leadership in an age of reform* (pp. 119–130). New York: Longman.

Milstein, M. (1996, October). *Clinical aspects of educational administration preparation programs.* Paper prepared for a workshop of the Mississippi professors of educational administration, Jackson, MS.

Milstein, M., & Associates (1993). *Changing the way we prepare educational leaders: The Danforth experience.* Newbury Park, CA: Corwin.

Mulkeen, T. A., Cambron-McCabe, N. H., & Anderson, B. J. (Eds.). (1994). *Democratic leadership: The changing context of administrative preparation.* Norwood, NJ: Ablex.

Mulkeen, T. A., & Cooper, B. S. (1989, March). *Implications of preparing school administrators for knowledge-work organizations.* Paper presented at the annual meeting of the American Educational Research Association, San Francisco.

Murphy, J. (1990c). Preparing school administrators for the twenty-first century: The reform agenda. In B. Mitchell & L. L. Cunningham (Eds.), *Educational leadership and changing contexts of families, communities and schools* (1990 NSSE yearbook). Chicago: University of Chicago Press.

Murphy, J. (1990d). The educational reform movement of the 1980s: A comprehensive analysis. In J. Murphy (Ed.), *The reform of American public education in the 1980s: Perspectives and cases.* Berkeley, CA: McCutchan.

Murphy, J. (1990e). School administration responds to pressures for change. In J. Murphy (Ed.), *The reform of American public education in the 1980s: Perspectives and cases.* Berkeley, CA: McCutchan.

Murphy, J. (1991). The effects of the educational reform movement on departments of educational leadership. *Educational Evaluation and Policy Analysis, 13*(1), 49–65.

Murphy, J. (1992). *The landscape of leadership preparation: Reframing the education of school administrators.* Newbury Park, CA: Corwin Press.

Murphy, J. (1993). *Preparing tomorrow's school leaders: Alternative designs.* University Park, PA: University Council for Educational Administration.

Murphy, J. (1998). Preparation for the school principalship: The United States story. *School Leadership and Management, 18*(3) 359–372.

Murphy, J. (1999a). *The quest for a center: Notes on the state of the profession of educational leadership.* Columbia, MO: University Council for Educational Leadership.

Murphy, J. (1999b). The reform of the profession: A self portrait. In J. Murphy & P. Forsyth (Eds.), *Educational administration: A decade of reform* (pp. 39–68). Newbury Park, CA: Corwin.

Murphy, J. (1999c). Changes in preparation programs: Perceptions of department chairs. In J. Murphy & P. Forsyth (Eds.), *Educational administration: A decade of reform* (pp. 170–191). Newbury Park, CA: Corwin Press.

Murphy, J. (1999d). Reconnecting teaching and school administration: A call for a unified profession. *UCEA Review, 40*(2), 1–3, 6–7.

Murphy, J. (2002). Reculturing the profession of educational leadership: New blueprints. *Educational Administration Quarterly, 38*(3), 176–191.

Murphy, J. (2005a, February). Uncovering the foundations of the ISLLC standards and addressing concerns in the academic community. *Educational Administration Quarterly, 41*(1), 154–191.

Murphy, J. (2005b, September). Using the ISLLC Standards for School Leaders at the state level to strengthen school administration. *The State Education Standard,* 15–18.

Murphy, J. (2006a). *Preparing school leaders: An agenda for research and action.* Lanham, MD: Rowman & Littlefield.

Murphy, J. (2006b, Spring). Some thoughts on rethinking the pre service education of school leaders. [Electronic version]. *Journal of Research on Leadership Education, 1*(1).

Murphy, J. (2007, April). Questioning the core of university-based programs for preparing school leaders. *Phi Delta Kappan, 88*(8), 582–585.

Murphy, J. (in press). University-based preparation in the U.S.: A brief history and emerging trends. In M. Brundrett (Ed.), *Developing school leaders: An international perspective.* London: Routledge/Taylor and Francis.

Murphy, J., & Forsyth, P. (1999). A decade of change: An overview. In J. Murphy & P. Forsyth (Eds.), *Educational administration: A decade of reform* (pp. 3–38). Newbury Park, CA: Corwin Press.

Murphy, J., & Hawley, W. (2003). The AASA "Leadership for Learning" masters program. *Teaching in Educational Administration, 10*(2), 1–6.

Murphy, J., Hawley, W. D., & Young, M. F. (2005). Redefining the education of school leaders: Scaffolding a learning-anchored program on the ISLLC standards. *Educational Leadership Review, 6*(2), 48–57.

Murphy, J., Moorman, H., & McCarthy, M. M. (2008). A comprehensive framework for rebuilding initial certification and preparation programs in school administration: Lessons from whole-state reform initiatives. *Teachers College Record, 110*(10), 2172–2203.

Murphy, J., & Shipman, N. J. (1999, October). The Interstate School Leaders Licensure Consortium: A standards based approach to strengthening educational leadership. *Journal of Personnel Evaluation in Education, 13*(3), 205–224.

Murphy, J., & Vriesenga, M. (2004). *Research on preparation programs in educational administration: An analysis.* Columbia, MO: University Council for Educational Administration.

Murphy, J., & Vriesenga, M. (2005). Developing professionally anchored dissertations: Lessons from innovative programs. *School Leadership Review, 1*(1), 33–57.

Murphy, J., & Vriesenga, M. (2006). Research on school leadership preparation in the United States: An analysis. *School Leadership and Management, 26*(2), 183–195.

Murphy, J., Yff, I., & Shipman, N. J. (2000). Implementation of the Interstate School Leaders Licensure Consortium standards. *International Journal of Leadership in Education, 3*(1), 17–39.

Muth, R. (1989, October). *Reconceptualizing training for educational administrators and leaders: Focus on inquiry* (Notes on Reform, no. 2). Charlottesville, VA: National Policy Board for Educational Administration.

National Commission on Excellence in Educational Administration. (1987). *Leaders for America's schools.* Tempe, AZ: University Council for Educational Administration.

Newlon, J. H. (1934). *Educational administration as social policy.* New York: Scribner.

Orr, M. T. (2008, March). *How preparation influences school leaders and their school improvement: Comparing exemplary and conventionally prepared principals.* Paper presented at the annual meeting of the American Educational Research Association, New York.

Orr, M. T., & Kottkamp, R. (2003, April). *Evaluating the causal pathway from leadership preparation to school improvement.* Paper presented at the annual meeting of the American Educational Research Association, Chicago.

Orr, M. T., & Pounder, D. (2006). *UCEA/TEA-SIG Taskforce on evaluating leadership preparation programs. Report: Six years later.* New York: Bank Street College.

Peterson, K. D., & Finn, C. E. (1985, Spring). Principals, superintendents and the administrator's art. *The Public Interest, 79,* 42–62.

Pounder, D., Reitzug, U., & Young, M. D. (2002). Preparing school leaders for school improvement, social justice, and community. In J. Murphy (Ed.), *The educational leadership challenge: Redefining leadership for the 21st century* (pp. 261–288). Chicago: University of Chicago Press.

Sergiovanni, T. J. (1989). Mystics, neats, and scruffies: Informing professional practice in educational administration. *The Journal of Educational Administration, 27*(2), 7–21.

Shakeshaft, C. (1988). Women in educational administration: Implications for training. In D. E. Griffiths, R. T. Stout, & P. R. Forsyth (Eds.), *Leaders for tomorrow's schools* (pp. 403–416). Berkeley, CA: McCutchan.

Shakeshaft, C. (1999). The struggle to create a more gender-inclusive profession. In J. Murphy & K. Seashore Louis (Eds.), *Handbook of research on educational administration* (2nd ed., pp. 99–118). San Francisco: Jossey-Bass.

Silver, P. F. (1978a). Some areas of concern in administrator preparation. In P. F. Silver & D. W. Spuck (Eds.), *Preparatory programs for educational administrators in the United States* (pp. 202–215). Columbus, OH: University Council for Educational Administration.

Silver, P. F. (1978b). Trends in program development. In P. F. Silver & D. W. Spuck (Eds.), *Preparatory programs for educational administrators in the United States* (pp. 178–201). Columbus, OH: University Council for Educational Administration.

Thomson, S. D. (1999). Causing change: The National Policy Board for Educational Administration. In J. Murphy & P. B. Forsyth (Eds.), *Educational administration: A decade of reform* (pp. 93–114). Thousand Oaks, CA: Corwin.

Willower, D. J. (1983). Evolutions in the professorship: Past philosophy, future. *Educational Administration Quarterly, 19*(3), 179–200.

Wynn, R. (1957). Organization and administration of the professional program. In R. F. Campbell & R. T. Gregg (Eds.), *Administrative behavior in education* (pp. 464–509). New York: Harper.

Young, M. D. (2004). Next steps for NCAELP, UCEA and the field: A joint research taskforce on educational leadership preparation. *UCEA Review, 46*(3), 11–12.

Young, M. D. (2008a). Programs are making important progress in providing research-based preparation that supports student learning. *UCEA Review, 50*(2), 9–10.

Young, M. D. (2008b). Newly revised ISLLC standards released—Why is that important? *UCEA Review, 50*(1), 6–7.

Young, M. D., Crow, G., Orr, T., Ogawa, R., Creighton, T. (2005). An educative look to educating school leaders. *UCEA Review, 47*(2), 1–5.

Young, M. D., & Laible, J. (2000). White racism, anti-racism, and school leadership preparation. *Journal of School Leadership, 10*(5), 374–415.

Young, M. D., & Peterson, G. J. (2002). The National Commission for the Advancement of Educational Leadership Preparation: An introduction. *Educational Administration Quarterly, 38*(2), 130–136.

Young, M. D., Peterson, G. J., & Short, P. M. (2002). The complexity of substantive reform: A call for interdependence among key stakeholders. *Educational Administration Quarterly, 38*(2), 137–175.

1

The Landscape of Scholarship on the Education of School Leaders, 1985–2006

ROBERT B. KOTTKAMP AND EDITH A. RUSCH

In this chapter, we examine the broad landscape of scholarship related to the preparation of future school leaders and continuing professional development for current school leaders. Our primary focus is on scholarship that examines university-based, formal degree, and licensure programs. This chapter differs from others in this handbook because it consists primarily of original document based research.

Scholarship is broadly defined here as any form of systematic inquiry leaving an accessible record. Scholarship enfolds the narrower category of empirical research; it also includes many forms not considered to be empirical, including essays, construction of untested theoretical propositions, and position pieces arguing for particular perspectives. Including nonempirical work in our broad baseline allows us to capture and examine a larger portion of the scholarly interest in leadership preparation over this time period than would have been evident had we restricted our inquiry to empirically grounded research alone.

Specifically, we examine two sources of scholarship concerning education to become school leaders. The first source is the annual meeting programs of three educational research associations whose memberships are largely composed of university professors, the teachers in university leadership preparation programs. The second source is dissertations of doctoral students enrolled in formal leadership programs. These two sources receive limited attention in the other handbook chapters, whose sources are chiefly published scholarship.

Our rationale for choosing these two sources of scholarship is to capture the broadest possible array of work produced by scholars who have directly addressed preparation of school leaders. *Research on Preparation Programs in Educational Administration: An Analysis* (Murphy & Vriesenga, 2004) was an immediate precursor of our work and a major impetus for the handbook. In that monograph, the authors concentrated their analyses exclusively on published sources. Under their broad discussion of research on leadership preparation, Murphy and Vriesenga noted the "significant extent to which research in educational administration is a product of doctoral dissertations" (p. 10). To support this argument they cited two noted scholars: "'most of the research on educational administration is done by graduate students' (Immegart, 1977, p. 303) and 'the dissertation in educational administration [is] the primary method of creating knowledge in the field' (Miskel, 1988, p. 23)" (Murphy & Vriesenga, 2004, p. 10).

Under the heading of caveats, Murphy and Vriesenga (2004) stated that their exclusive attention to published sources "casts a shadow over non-published papers" and that "good information can be found in these sources" (p. 14). Murphy and Vriesenga further opined, "Research on preparation programs in educational administration is probably too thin at this point in history to dismiss out-of-hand unpublished papers presented at national conferences" (p. 14). With their encouragement, we take the broadest view possible on the scholarship of leadership preparation.

Professors who produced scholarship for national research meetings were reporting studies of their work related to leadership preparation. Proposals for presentations at these meetings undergo a blind review process, but the stringency of the process is less than that for journal articles. However, while some bias, known or unknown, enters the review process for meetings, existing filters probably screen out fewer scholars and topics than those at work in the processes among peer-referred journals. Thus, the total content of presentations at national research meetings likely captures the larger part of the systematic thinking about and study of the leadership preparation aspect of professorial work.

In terms of dissertation research, Immegart (1977) claimed that dissertation topics shifted as professional research shifted, and that both shifted based on emerging social issues or problems in the field. Furthermore, while dissertations encompass the interests of their authors, a considerable proportion of the topics researched is also influenced by the ongoing research and professional interests of students' major professors. Additionally, dissertations are typically one source from which doctoral graduates moving into the academy formulate research agendas. Following the suppositions that dissertations, although sometimes overlooked, are key to the development of knowledge in the profession and that they to a degree reflect the deep interests of their sponsoring professors and sometimes new professors, we take a closer look at the patterns of study found in them, topically, thematically, methodologically, and historically for the past 20 years. We believe that examining dissertations along with the scholarly contents of professional meetings yields a solid base for understanding the broad landscape of scholarship on the preparation of school leaders.

Purposes

Three specific purposes frame this chapter and serve as a broad introduction to the content of the entire handbook:

1. Provide the broad story of scholarly activity related to the preparation of school leaders over the past 20 years and nested within this story to explore the topical areas in which scholars have conducted research.
2. Provide a discussion of the methodological and theoretical approaches scholars have used to research leadership preparation.
3. Examine the context in which scholars conducted what research exists on the preparation of school leaders, including issues of resource availability and the perceived legitimacy of undertaking this research focus.

Method

We use content analysis as the basic method for our work with both meeting programs and dissertations. Yet, while our general orientation toward and procedures used with both data sources are generally parallel, there are differences specific to each source.

Samples and Universe

We chose to track scholarship on leadership preparation through examination of the annual meeting programs of three professional associations beginning with 1985 and doctoral dissertations listed in *Dissertations Abstracts International,* 1986–2006. Although our chosen professional meetings are only a sample of all potential professional group meetings, the data collected from the three organizations we chose constitute the universe of their contents during those years. The dissertation database constitutes the universe of applicable reported dissertations completed in those years.

Document Sources

Professional Organization Meetings

The three professional meetings we chose were (a) Division A of the American Educational Research Association (AERA) annual meeting (AERA-A), (b) the annual convention of the University Council for Educational Administration (UCEA), and (c) the annual program of the AERA Learning and Teaching in Educational Leadership Special Interest Group, which was formerly Teaching in Educational Administration Special Interest Group, which we reference hereafter as simply SIG. The rationale for selecting these organizations is that they cover well a wide swath of professional representation and activity in the larger profession.

The data we needed on individual presentations were located in the meeting programs of these three organizations, many of which we possessed. Lacking a number of the necessary programs, we put out a general call for help on the UCEA electronic mailing list and e-mailed many colleagues individually in an attempt to fill the holes in our collection. The program search was not easy. It required a trip to the AERA archive at their headquarters in Washington, DC, to retrieve information on meetings in the 1980s. Michelle Young, Diana Pounder, Gail Furman, and Charlie Russo were most helpful in locating and lending us various programs. But in the end, we still have not been able to locate the programs for the initial two UCEA convention meetings in Charlottesville and Cincinnati. If a scholar reading this chapter has access to these missing programs, we would love to be able to complete our analysis back to the UCEA convention origin.

We began with AERA-A in 1985 to provide a 2-year lead on the inception of the UCEA convention in 1987. We hoped to see whether the presentation profile of the AERA-A meetings began to change with the advent of the UCEA convention as part of its environment. We gathered all UCEA convention programs from 1989 through 2006 and all SIG programs (contained with the large AERA meeting programs) from its first program in 1994 (1993 was simply an organizing meeting with no presentations) through 2006.

Doctoral Dissertations

We used the *Dissertation Abstracts International* search engine to build a year-by-year database of dissertation abstracts using the search terms *educational administration* and *educational leadership.* We concluded that these two phrases would capture studies that connected in any way to leadership preparation and would exclude studies that focused on more general education topics. These terms functioned in a similar way to searching only the meeting programs of organizations specifically focused on the same two descriptors. We also hypothesized that during the past two decades the term *leadership* gradually displaced or overshadowed *administration* as a descriptive term.

Sample Limitation

There is an important limitation on the selection of professional meetings. In the best case, we would have included the National Council of Professors of Educational Administration (NCPEA), dating to 1947 and featuring a summer annual conference. We secured several recent NCPEA meeting programs with the intent of inclusion, but in the search learned that the organization has neither a permanent home nor a program archive. Without a nearly complete set of programs, we could not do justice to NCPEA given the universe of data we had for the other three organizations. We lacked the resources to find all NCPEA data.

Procedures for Meeting Program Analysis

Our primary means of making sense of the program data was content analysis. Each program listed the title of each presentation as well as its session context, the format of presentation (paper, symposium, round table or paper discussion, poster, conversation, charla, innovative session, etc.), the authors, and their institutional affiliations. Our first content analytic decision for each presentation was whether it primarily or substantively concerned leadership preparation along a number of more specific potential subcategories, or whether it was not related to preparation of leaders but to some other interest in the field. Once a presentation was coded as within the domain of leadership preparation, we then coded it into a subcategory, explained in detail below. When the coding was completed, we constructed longitudinal records for each of the three organizations across various large categories and smaller subcategories.

Content Analysis

Units of Analysis

The major concern with defining units of analysis adhered to the meeting program analyses. In pursuing content analysis of programs, we needed to establish units of analysis. Professional meetings were broken into time-block units in which typically a number of events were scheduled simultaneously in different rooms, though sometimes there was a single event, such as a meeting opening, keynote address, or banquet. These various events in time blocks were called sessions, each of which consisted primarily of various kinds of presentations but also included meetings of special interest groups, editorial boards, commissions, research work groups, workshops, or presessions and whole community meetings, such as major addresses, receptions, and banquets. Events within sessions were sometimes broken down into smaller subunits such as individual papers, round tables, paper discussions, or poster presentations.

For the content analytic process, we coded at the smallest, most specific unit of analysis possible. For consistency, we called these smallest units *presentations*. While most presentations were literally presentations, not all were; some were meetings. Our data were limited to titles given for either sessions or presentations. Symposia typically had a number of presenters and respondents but were given only a single title rather than naming a specific focus of each individual participant's presentation or response. The lowest unit we could code in these cases was the session, and so the *session* became synonymous with a single *presentation*. In other cases such as paper or round table sessions, as few as 2 and as many as 15 separate titled presentations were identified.

The upshot of coding at the most disaggregated level for which a title was provided is that the weights of the units we coded were not equal. A symposium with 5 participants taking individual perspectives received the same weight as a single paper or poster presentation in a cluster of such presentations within a session. Given only titles in programs, there was no way we could break some sessions into smaller presentations. Readers simply need to know that weighting of the entities coded was not inherently equal.

The unit of analysis for dissertation abstracts was straightforwardly the individual abstract. All of these had the same weighting and thus avoided the problem described above resulting from use of titles in meeting programs.

Content Categories

We needed to establish content categories into which to code the presentations found in the meeting programs and the dissertation abstracts. The single most useful attempt to describe the empirical research and broader scholarship on leadership education in preparation programs that we had available to us was *Research on Preparation Programs in Educational Administration: An Analysis*, a UCEA monograph by Murphy and Vriesenga (2004). We began with the 12 content categories they constructed to code the published articles they content analyzed. Their categories were based on categories put forth by earlier scholarly work in the field. Our second step was to examine the titles of the various chapters that the general editors had established for the *Handbook of Research on the Education of School Leaders* at the formative time in this volume's development.

We then compared the two category systems as indicated in Table 1.1. As may be seen, the fit between the two sets is reasonable, though not identical. There were no handbook chapter contents for two categories Murphy and Vriesenga (2004) had used (department goals and organizational climate), and similarly three chapters in the handbook did not match Murphy and Vriesenga's categories (professional development; mentoring, coaching, and induction; and context). Two categories related to students used by Murphy and Vriesenga (recruitment and selection) collapsed into a single chapter in the handbook, whereas two separate handbook chapters (design, delivery, and models and theories and program design) cut across two of Murphy and Vriesenga's categories (program structure and cooperative relations with other organizations).

From the several influences already discussed, we distilled 12 categories and then used them for content analytic coding of meeting programs and dissertation abstracts.[1] The categories and their content descriptions are the following:

1. *Program design, delivery, and models* includes elements of design, integration of design and delivery, coherence, historical roots and trends, dominant and emerging patterns, models, and effectiveness.

Table 1.1 Comparison of Content Areas for Empirical Articles From Murphy and Vriesenga (2004) and Chapters of the *Handbook of Research on the Education of School Leaders*

Murphy & Vriesenga (2004)	This handbook
Student selection	Student candidates
Monitoring progress of students	Student assessment
Clinical components	Clinical experiences
Curriculum	Curriculum
Instruction	Pedagogy
Program structure	Design and delivery (models and theories, program design)
Cooperative relations with other organizations	Design and delivery (models and theories, program design)
Faculty	Faculty preparation and development
Department goals	
Organizational climate	
Program evaluation	Program evaluation
	Professional development
	Mentoring, coaching, and induction
	Context

2. *Pedagogy* includes instructional approaches used primarily in the classroom, how faculty members teach, enumerating and describing specific strategies for instruction, and effectiveness of strategies employed.

3. *Curriculum* includes content areas taught, scope and sequence, forces a affecting curricular content, changes over time, rigor, and opportunities to learn provided by content.

4. *Program evaluation* includes levels of program review, evaluation, and accreditation; purposes, methods, and frequency of types; and uses and effects on programs.

5. *Faculty* includes pipeline for entry, personal and professional characteristics, work life and evaluation, role and role change, preparation and professional development, and conceptual grounding of preparation and professional development.

6. *Context* includes higher education environments and effects, kindergarten through Grade 12 contexts and effects, and larger environmental influences (political, economic, value, regulatory, and professional).

7. *Theory design* includes explicit theories or values underpinning programs or advocated as a basis for design, integration, and intended outcomes.

8. *Clinical experience* includes design and implementation, partnerships with schools, relationship to other program components, integration of theory and practice, and instructional approaches used in field experiences.

9. *Students* as a category includes candidates seeking initial and advanced leadership certification or degrees and their recruitment, selection, personal and professional characteristics, goals, and program choices.

10. *Professional development* includes continuous professional learning, ad hoc or focused and coherent, evaluations and their uses, and effects on the field.

11. *Student assessment and evaluation* as a category includes assessments or evaluations of students rendered on the basis of coursework, internships, and examinations; graduation and licensure recommendations; and design.

12. *Mentoring, coaching, and induction* as a category includes initial and ongoing relationships, nature and strategies employed, evaluation and effectiveness, and trends.

Content Analysis: Meeting Program Data

To this point, it has made sense to discuss together the two data sources, professional meetings and dissertations. However, whereas the broad strokes are reasonably parallel, the details of the data are different in many specifics. Consequently, beginning here we separate the remaining details of the methods and the resulting findings into distinct sections. The meeting program data are analyzed and reported first, followed by the dissertation data. In a later section where the research questions are answered, we also do some comparing and contrasting of findings from the two data sources.

Assembling and coding the data Creating the data set for content analysis required assemblage of hard copies of 53 meeting programs. Of these programs, the smallest (SIG for 1994) contained 3 sessions with a total of 7 presentations to be coded. The largest program, UCEA, 2006, contained 216 sessions totaling 399 presentations to be coded. Across all the meetings, 9,185 presentations required coding. None of the material was open to sorting via computer. Thus, coding meant reading through each presentation title and then coding it into either not related to education for leadership/preparation program or related to education for leadership/preparation program. Each related presentation (1,709) was then secondarily categorized into one of the 12 content categories defined above.

Coding limitations It is critical to understand that for the meeting analyses we were working with titles, with the exception of the last few UCEA conventions, for which the programs had very brief abstracts of several sentences. Because titles provide so little information about complex presentations, our content analytic process was fraught with difficulties, resulting in serious limitations.

First, more often than we wanted, there was no touchstone of certainty that we had allocated a specific leadership preparation related title to the best fit category among the 12. There were cases in which elements of both pedagogy and curriculum were either stated or easily imagined, and in some titles program design was indicated as a third element. Our approach was to attempt to identify the dominant element; if that was not possible, we coded the presentation into what seemed the most inclusive category. For example, when confronted with a title in which curriculum, pedagogy, and program design were all elements and in which we could not be assured of the dominant element, we coded the title under program design because, taken broadly, design included both of the other elements.

We sometimes had coding uncertainties with clinical experiences and one or two other category elements indicated in the title. The category of program design, delivery, and models was sometimes not perfectly distinguishable from that of theory and design. In the case of presentations about department chairs and their work and dilemmas, we consistently coded these presentations under the faculty category, for chairs retain their faculty status and often return to that primary status at the end of a term.

Second, it was almost impossible to discern whether the presentation described in the title was empirical or nonempirical. The exceptions to this were titles with words that clearly stated some element of research methodology indicating an empirical nature, such as *empirical, ethnography, survey, interview, action research*, and *evaluation*. On the other side, there were words that indicated the absence of an empirical undertaking: *proposal, advocacy, dialogue, conversation*, and so on. Most of the titles we analyzed lacked words, phrases, or other specific indicators we could put much trust in for differentiating between empirical and nonempirical content. After a frustrating attempt, we were unable to code leadership-related presentations into empirical and nonempirical categories. Titles alone simply lacked sufficient information for such coding with any assurance of validity. Furthermore, the content categories overlap; they are not mutually exclusive. Thus, even if we had the full text of the presentations, coding would not have been a clear-cut process. The upshot for our completed sorting into the 12 content areas is for the reader to understand that the materials were not adequate to accomplish ideal classification.

Analytical computations: meeting program data In order to answer our research questions, we needed to perform some calculations once we had allocated the data from meeting program titles into the large categories of not-leadership-preparation related versus leadership-preparation related and then subclassified the latter major category into the 12 content categories just described. We then made the following calculations:

1. The total number of presentations in each meeting for each year is simply the sum of all presentations.
2. The total number of presentations across all meetings for each year is the sum of the total number of presentations for each of the applicable meetings in a given year. For the years 1985–1988, this total included AERA-A only; from 1989 to 1993, the total included both AERA-A and UCEA; from 1994 forward it included totals for all three meetings.
3. The number of leadership preparation related presentations for each meeting for each year was the sum of all leadership preparation presentations for each meeting.
4. The total number of leadership preparation related presentations across all meetings for each year was the sum of the number leadership preparation presentations across all the applicable meetings for a given year as indicated above.
5. The number of leadership preparation related presentations for each meeting in each of the

12 content categories by year was the sum of the presentations in each content category for each program for each year.

6. We also calculated a number of proportions in terms of percentages. These included (a) the percentage all leadership preparation related presentations constituted of the grand total of all presentations for a given year by meeting and across meetings for each year and (b) the percentage of the total of all leadership preparation presentations for each of the 12 content categories by meeting by year.

Findings: Professional Meetings

Size

One means of depicting the landscape of the endeavor to research leadership preparation is to view the size of the undertaking. Such a view may be presented as an absolute total quantity of work, or alternatively as comparisons across the organizations that sponsor professional meetings, and as proportions of the total scholarship presented within meetings.

To provide context, we begin with a line graph (Figure 1.1) displaying four different lines. The top line is the total number of presentations across all meetings for each year. It is the universe of presentations—that is, both leadership preparation and non-leadership preparation related

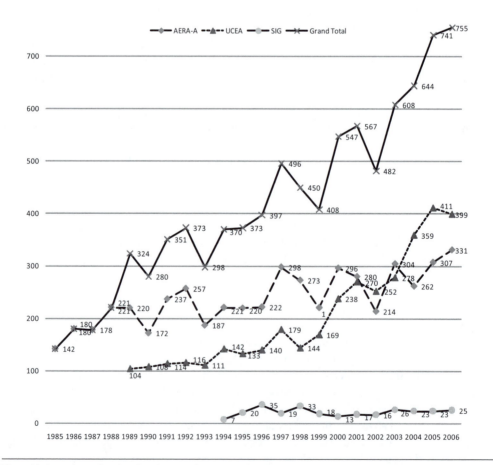

Figure 1.1 Comparisons of total number of presentations at meetings of AERA-A, UCEA, SIG, and the grand total of presentations across all three meetings by year.

presentations—at all of the meetings for which we have data, arrayed by meeting year. The second line is the total number of presentations at AERA-A; the third line is the total for UCEA; the fourth line is the total for SIG, all by year. Said differently, line 1 is the sum of the other three lines for each year.

Look first at the top line in Figure 1.1, the grand total for all meeting presentations by year. Beginning with a total of 142 presentations in 1985 and running to 1988, this line consists of AERA-A presentation data only. Although the UCEA convention began in 1987, we do not have data for either that year or 1988. The first peak in the top line occurs in 1989, the 1st year for which we have UCEA data; the total presentations jump to 324. In that 1st year of data for two meetings, AERA-A accounts for 220 of the presentations and UCEA for 105; thus, AREA-A is over twice the size in terms of presentations. Now note that line 2, AERA-A, though not smooth, generally slopes upward over time such that if a regression line were drawn the straight line would indicate a growth in sessions of about 100 from 1989 to 2006. Line 3, UCEA, begins more than 100 presentations lower than AERA-A, but its slope is considerably steeper, and by 2006 it increases by over 300 additional presentations, overtaking AERA-A in the period 2001–2003. The fourth line, SIG, in contrast to the other two meetings, shows the straightest and flattest line over its shorter history with its much smaller number of presentations compared to the other two organizations. In 2006, there were 755 total presentations of which UCEA accounted for 399, AERA-A for 331, and SIG for 25. This glimpse at the size of the organizational meetings provides a context of the venues in which presentations concerning leadership preparation had to compete for acceptance with all other submissions for inclusion.

It is noteworthy that both AERA-A and SIG sizes are regulated by their umbrella AERA organization on proportional basis of division and SIG membership size compared to total AERA membership. AERA-A was one of the first divisions, but over our time span new divisions and SIGs were created. To control total size of the annual meeting, AERA periodically recalibrates the total sessions for each division and SIG in proportion to the ever-growing total membership. Dips seen in the AERA-A line likely came with these recalibrations as AERA-A lost in its proportional membership to the whole.

We move now from considerations of total size to the size of the portion of presentations focused directly on some aspect of leadership preparation. These relationships are graphed in Figure 1.2. Note that there are five lines in the graph. The top line does not depict leadership preparation presentations alone, but is in fact the same grand total of all presentations across the three meetings line taken from Figure 1.1. It is reproduced in Figure 1.2 to provide a continuing context for the other four lines. The second line is the total of all leadership preparation oriented presentations from across all three meetings—put differently, the sum of the three lines below it. The third line represents the total number of leadership preparation presentations for UCEA, the fourth line represents the same for AERA-A, and the fifth line represents the total of leadership preparation presentations for SIG. When comparing Figures 1.1 and 1.2, the most striking difference in the latter is the close clustering of four lines and their increasing greater distance from line 1. Clearly, presentations concerned with leadership preparation do not constitute the bulk of all presentations at these meetings. In fact, their slopes of incline over time are much less that those in Figure 1.1, and they appear to be a relatively small portion of the grand total.

Note that during 1985–1988, line 2 and the line for AERA-A are synonymous, since only AERA-A data were available through 1988. In 1989, the third or UCEA line begins in a position elevated considerably above the fourth or AERA-A line. In that 1st year of our data, we coded fully 73% of all presentations (76 of 104) at UCEA as being related to leadership preparation.[2] The advent of the new meeting and its large proportion of leadership preparation related presentations drive line 2, the total of all preparation related presentations, up a steep incline to its first peak in 1989.

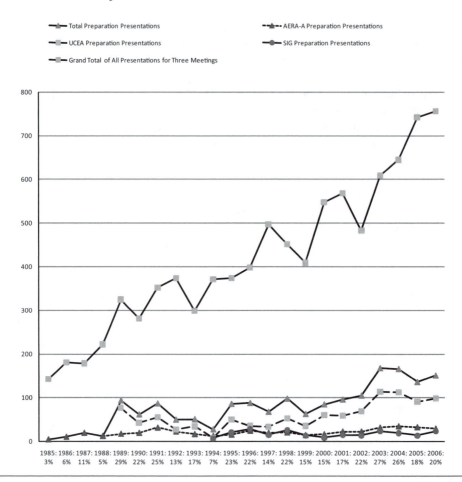

Total Preparation Presentations
AERA-A Preparation Presentations
UCEA Preparation Presentations
SIG Preparation Presentations
Grand Total of All Presentations for Three Meetings

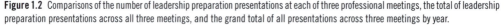

Figure 1.2 Comparisons of the number of leadership preparation presentations at each of three professional meetings, the total of leadership preparation presentations across all three meetings, and the grand total of all presentations across three meetings by year.

The fourth line represents AERA-A leadership preparation presentations and is the only meeting that runs continuously from 1985 through 2006. Notice that with the exception of 1994, the UCEA line always runs above that of AERA-A. The UCEA line begins higher than the AERA line and then declines toward it until the 1994 exception year; then, the UCEA line over the remaining time generally distances itself further from the AERA-A line. Since these lines represent actual numbers, the relationship of the two lines indicates that in its early years, UCEA, the smaller of the two meetings in terms of presentations, provided space for the proportionately larger number of leadership preparation presentations. Past 1999, the UCEA line inclined more steeply and distanced itself further from the AERA-A line. It is clear from these two lines alone that UCEA historically has been the organization more receptive to presentations related to leadership preparation. With the exception of the very first years, AERA-A's line is stable, almost level, over most of the time span; as the AERA-A meeting size grows, the number of preparation related presentations exhibits only a very slight incline over time

The fifth line, representing SIG, begins in 1994. In the years from 1994 through 1999, the AERA-A and the SIG lines are almost identical. Following 1999, the SIG line runs slightly under the AERA-A line. SIG is tiny in comparison to AERA-A.

For another means of comparison, the average grand total number of all presentations a year or line 1 is 416. For the total of all leadership preparation presentations for line 2 the average is

78; for line 3, UCEA, the average is 58; for line 4, AERA-A, it is 20; and for line 5, SIG the average is 17.

Some of the above discussion of organizational size and differential proportions of preparation related presentations at each of the three meetings is explained by differences in the professional organizations themselves. AERA-A maintains an explicit focus on *research*; presentation formats historically were for the most part paper sessions, symposia, paper discussions, and poster sessions; other formats such as interactive discussions and performances are of recent origin. UCEA opens its presentations to a *broader range of scholarship* than AERA and has from its inception; presentation formats from the UCEA convention's origin included those of AERA plus presessions, job-alike sessions, and a wider array of discussions sessions to accommodate broader forms of scholarship. Thus, AERA-A is a better measure of strict research interest in preparation; UCEA is a better measure of broad scholarly interest in preparation. SIG, in addition to its explicit preparation content focus, has an orientation for accepting work closer to that of UCEA than AERA.

Ira Bogotch (2002), who served as SIG's first program chair and found himself surrounded by debates about the legitimacy of introducing research on teaching and learning in the realm of AERA, reported the following:

> In 1995, blind written reviews of TEA-SIG proposals included statements like the topic and quality are not up to AERA, Division A [Administration] research standards. More than a few early reviewers opposed the writing style of self-reflexivity of the research proposals as well as the delimited classroom and/or program/institutional focus of the research designs themselves. The gist of their comments was that the topic of teaching and learning might be appropriate for extended conversations, but it did not qualify as research. (p. 95)

Bogotch's specifics make concrete the abstract discussion above about differentiating research and broader scholarship orientations among the professional organizations.

Proportions: Percentage of Presentations Concerned With Leadership Preparation

Before leaving Figure 1.2, note a percentage at the bottom associated with each year. These figures represent a proportion, expressed in percentage, that the total of all leadership preparation related presentations (line 2) constitutes of the grand total of all presentations across all meetings for that year (line 1). In the years of AERA only, the percentages are in the single digits except for one. In 1989, the 1st recorded year of UCEA, the percentage of total leadership preparation presentations to all presentations jumps to 29%, the highest percentage of total presentations of any year on the graph. In that year, 73% of UCEA presentations are leadership preparation related; that fact explains the huge jump in line 2 and the highest total percentage of total leadership preparation presentations in the whole 22-year run of investigation. However, the original burst of numbers of preparation related presentations at UCEA declines rapidly and with it the percentage of all presentations related specifically to preparation of leaders. Not until 2003 and 2004 do the percentages (27% and 26%) of all presentations across meetings related specifically to leadership preparation come close to the percentage height in 1989. The average proportion of the grand total of presentations related to leadership preparation across all the years is 18.6%. Yet, also note that UCEA in all but a few years makes the highest number of contributions to line 2, the yearly totals of all preparation related presentations. These figures provide broad strokes to begin examining the interest in and perhaps perceived legitimacy of presentations related to leadership preparation in these three professional venues.

We get a better understanding of the contributions of individual organizations by looking at Figure 1.3, the data of which are all in percentages of each organization's meeting program devoted

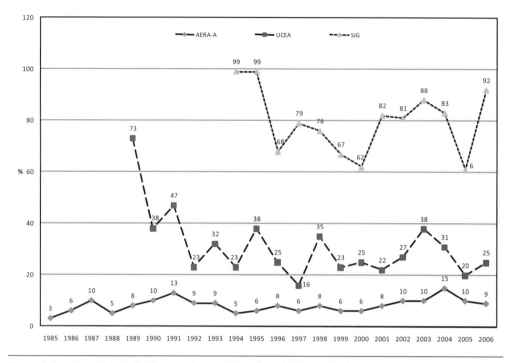

Figure 1.3 Percentage of total leadership preparation presentations for each of three professional meetings by year.

to leadership preparation presentations. In Figure 1.3 the lines representing the three meetings are starkly different, separated, and do not cross; each occupies a separate space relative to the percentage levels of the graph. Note that percentages put each of the three professional associations shown in a common metric, which is completely separate from the actual size of the meetings in total presentations. Thus, we see the tiny organization by size, SIG, having the highest percentages of presentations directly related to leadership preparation. This organization is ostensibly about leadership preparation. For the 13 years of its meetings, the average percentage of presentations related to leader preparation is 80%. The second line, UCEA, whose meeting began as half the size of AERA-A in presentations and grew to larger than AERA-A, shows a consistent second place in terms of the percentage of its presentations focused on leadership preparation; the high is 73%, the low is 16%, and average across 18 years is 31%. For AERA-A the highest was 15%, the lowest 3%, and the average 8%.

The pecking order of meetings in terms of privileging leadership preparation oriented presentations is clear; we assume that organizationally shared perceptions of importance and validity concerning presenting scholarship about preparation issues are evidenced by the consistent differences in acceptance rates. On the other hand, acceptance rates of presentations result from orientations of the organizations on a continuum of strictly research to varied forms of scholarship. AERA-A is the most research focused, resulting in fewer preparation presentations. UCEA and SIG accept a wider array of scholarship, resulting in acceptance of a larger number of preparation-oriented presentations.

Finer Focus: Comparative Analysis by Content Areas Within Leadership Preparation

The remaining analyses of professional meeting programs focus on the 12 specific content areas defined earlier and are related to specific chapters in this handbook. These are much finer grained

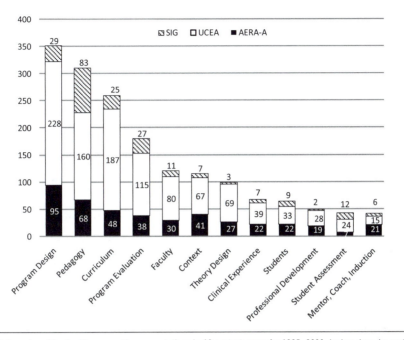

Figure 1.4 Total number of leadership preparation presentations in 12 content areas for 1985–2006, broken down by contribution of AERA-A, UCEA, and SIG to each.

than the prior analyses. We begin with an overview comparing the total number of presentations within each of the 12 content areas across all three professional organizations for the 22 years of 1985–2006. We then move to examining each content area, beginning with the largest and moving to the smallest. For each category, we examine first the total number of presentations across all three meetings by year.

Figure 1.4 shows the total number of presentations by content area across all three organizations for all years. Figure 1.4 also breaks down each content area into the number of presentations each organization—AERA-A, UCEA, and SIG—contributed to the total. Three content areas have totals greater than 200 presentations: (a) program design, delivery, and models with 352; (b) pedagogy with 311; and (c) curriculum with 260. Recall that the first three categories were also the hardest to separate definitively working from titles alone and that where more than one category was indicated we coded a presentation for the most inclusive category. Thus, coding decisions may have been the deciding matter in program design running in first place, since design likely included information about both pedagogy and curriculum at some level.

The fourth- through seventh-place content areas contain greater than 100 presentations: The fourth largest content area is program evaluation with 180 presentations. Fifth is faculty with 121, sixth is context with 115, and seventh is theory design with 101. The remaining content areas have less than 99 presentations each. There are clear differences in size among the content areas, with the largest being 8.4 times the size of the smallest.

Having compared the content areas by size, we now turn attention to each area separately. In these sets of analyses, we examine the total number of presentations across programs by year.

Program Design, Delivery, and Models

Program design, delivery, and models, the largest content area, contains 352 total presentations across the years. Figure 1.5 shows the general slope of the line is from a low in the single digits to

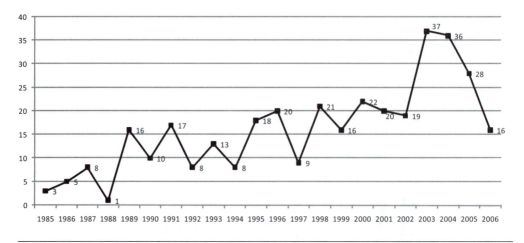

Figure 1.5 Total number of presentations related to program design for three professional meetings by year.

a high in the upper 30s and then some decline. The line neither is completely smooth nor does it bounce around a great deal. There are two large upward jumps: 1998 and 2003. The first jump, 1988–1989, is also our first capture of UCEA data; the jump is from one presentation to 16. In the previous year AERA-A had a single presentation coming out of the Danforth Program for the Preparation of Principals. In the 1989, AERA-A had two presentations concerning what works in administrator preparation and a program for minority administrators. In that year, UCEA put forward 14 presentations. One was a survey of Danforth principal preparation programs. Seven, or half, were descriptions of individual preparation programs, each working on reform and redesign: (a) Brigham Young, (b) State University of New York, Buffalo, (c) Colorado at Denver, (d) Fordham, (e) Hofstra, (f) Kansas, and (g) Northern Colorado. UCEA clearly had opened a gate for a new, less strictly research kind of presentation telling the story of individual program development.

The jump in 2003 takes this category to its height of 37 presentations, which is followed by 36 the next year. All three organizations contributed presentations in those years. AERA-A produced 7 in 2003 and 12 in 2004; UCEA contributed 27 and 20; SIG put forth 3 and 4. We treat all three organizations together and lump the 2 years together to get a sense of the specifics. The largest cluster of 15 focused on preparation programs as partnerships between universities and school systems, though for several the larger community was considered the partner. Designing programs to promote leadership for learning was the second cluster with 11. The next batch focused on number of specific designs for program graduates: 4 for equity and social justice, 3 for leaders of technology, 2 for urban contexts, 1 for rural contexts, and 1 for independent schools. Three addressed cohorts as a central element of design, and 4 addressed some version of online design. In contrast to 1989, when half of the presentations provided descriptions of single programs, 9 of 73 presentations did so in 2003–2004, a major drop in proportion. We note that the two presentations specifically comparing a number of programs were presented at AERA-A. The remaining 18 presentations were singletons not codable into a cluster. Clearly, the focus of the content with program design, delivery, and models presentations had shifted considerably between the two peaks situated near the ends of the continuum of years.

Pedagogy

The second largest content category for preparation presentations is pedagogy with 331 total presentations across our time span. As indicated in Figure 1.6, the configuration of the line that

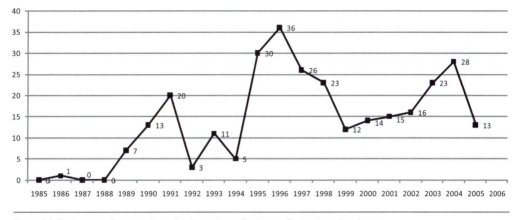

Figure 1.6 Total number of presentations related to pedagogy for three professional meetings by year.

shows the total number of pedagogy presentations by year differs from the gradually increasing line of program design. Pedagogy starts with only one presentation in the 4 years of AERA-A's time alone. When UCEA program statistics are added to the mix, the line begins to rise, but does not jump like the 1st year of UCEA as in program design. What we see are three sets of peaks followed by valleys. The first peak comes in 1991 (20 presentations), the second in 1996 (36 presentations), and the third in 2004 (28 presentations). We have no attributions for why these peaks appear at the times they do.

Looking into actual presentations given at the three high points, we found the following: In 1991, there were 20 presentations split in half by two organizations. AERA-A had 4 presentations on case methods and 1 on computer simulation. Presentations describing pedagogical strategies appeared for teaching values and ethics, platform writing, and fiction as a means of critical reflection and introduction of emotions into consideration of administrative work, something almost completely avoided in structural-functionalist approaches to administration. In the UCEA meeting, we found 6 job-alike presentations for specific content areas (e.g., teaching school law, organizational theory, etc.); 2 presentations mixing action research, cases, and simulation; and 1 presentation each for case writing and strategies of interactive exercises to developing multicultural awareness. Overall in 1991, case-study-based pedagogies predominated.

For 1996, of the 36 presentations, AERA contributed 6, UCEA 13, and SIG 17. It should be noted that SIG produced its highest ever number of sessions in this year by developing joint sessions with divisions and other SIGs. Looking across all organizations, we found 4 sessions each on problem-based learning, case methods, and feminist pedagogies. There were 3 sessions on teaching with technology, 2 on technological simulation use, and 2 on other simulations. A wide array of single presentations appeared for pedagogies related to cohorts, problem solving, portfolio construction, adult learning, story and narrative construction, shared decision-making groups, interviews, and action research.

In 2004, there were 28 presentations, of which AERA-A contributed 2, UCEA 20, and SIG 6. Across the organizations, there were 2 presentations on case studies; 5 on social justice pedagogies; 3 on technology and online teaching; 4 focused on pedagogies for the related areas of forming spirit, growing learning communities, developing sense of community, and collaborative inquiry; and 2 presentations on writing. As in the prior peak year, there were a number of diverse singleton presentations on pedagogical strategies for teaching with film, transformative learning, critical conversations, raising social consciousness, teaching literature reviews and law, and consideration of a signature pedagogy.

Clearly, across the years these presentations were very personal descriptions of "what I do in my classes" and at the widest "what we do in our program." A glance back at Figure 1.4 indicates that UCEA and SIG were venues particularly receptive to presentations on pedagogy. There were few apparent efforts to look at anything greater than an *N* of 1 in a single institution. Methods, where "research" might have been claimed, were invariably descriptive.

In a broad swath, our look at professional meeting presentations produced conclusions paralleling the more broad and intensive examination of pedagogy authored by Dianne Taylor, Paula Cordiero, and Janet Chrispeels in chapter 8 of this handbook, "Pedagogy." In their chapter is the particularly useful Figure 8.1, which graphically summarizes a great many of their total set of findings in the context of a multidimensional conceptual framework. They include knowledge outcomes on four dimensions: (a) declarative, (b) procedural, (c) contextual, and (d) somatic. They array from left to right a continuum ranging from classroom-learning locus to workplace-learning locus that runs through stages of knowledge and skills out of context, hypothetical problems, real-life problems, field applications, to knowledge and skills in workplace context. They present research data indicating that the normative pedagogies historically were lecture and discussion, at the extreme left of Figure 8.1 in the sector of classroom-based knowledge and skills out of context. It is likely that most presentations at the meetings we coded were attempts to describe and advocate pedagogical strategies to the right of the old and probably residual lecture and discussion pole.

In chapter 8, Taylor, Cordiero, and Chrispeels situate role play, case methods, simulated problem-based learning, narratives, film and video, and classroom-based reflective practice as pedagogies in the center of their continuum. We note that a large majority of the pedagogy presentations at these meetings fall into this middle zone. To the right side of Figure 8.1, Taylor et al. located pedagogies including site visits, simulations, action research, authentic problem-based learning, field-based projects, and reflective practice drawing on field-based experience and data. We found a few pedagogical presentations situated in this zone. At the extreme right of the continuum, the authors place cognitive apprenticeships, internships, and on-the-job learning. None of the presentations we coded were located in the zone of workplace-grounded learning. One category in the workplace-located zone not found in our pedagogical coding is internships. We separated this category and examine it later.

Curriculum

The third most populated content category is curriculum with 260 presentations. Figure 1.7 shows these presentations spread over an irregular pattern. In the 4 earliest years with only AERA-A contributing, there are but 2 presentations. When UCEA data come on line in 1989, the graph shoots up to a peak of 25 presentations and then falls and hits minor peaks in 1991 and 1995. There is then a little dip and a slower rise to a peak of 28 presentations in 2003 and then a final slow decline. We now examine the contents of the 4 peak years.

The theme of the 1989 UCEA convention was "The Knowledge Base of Educational Administration: Moving Beyond the Theory–Practice Dilemma." That program contributed 24 of the 25 curriculum presentations for that year, whereas AERA-A contributed but 1 concerning research on administrative behavior and its implications for preparation. It appears that there was a pent-up need or desire to address curricular issues that the UCEA convention and perhaps especially its theme for that year addressed. Seven of the 24 UCEA presentations actually contained the phrase *knowledge base*. However, the objects of the knowledge differed considerably: instructional leadership, improved school learning, group leadership skills, organizational and administrative theory, special education, educational administration (in general), and school board–superintendent relationships. Five presentations focused on curricula for reflective practice or reflection of various

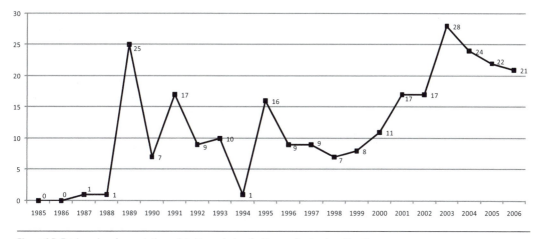

Figure 1.7 Total number of presentations related to curriculum for three professional meetings by year.

sorts, and 2 were directed at educational law. More than half of the presentations, then, could be classified into three topical clusters. There were quite a number of singleton foci: supervision of instruction; training needs of executive officers; need for emphasis on race, ethnicity, culture and values; fiction; and metaphorical policy analysis.

Two years later, AERA-A contributed 7 of 17 presentations and UCEA contributed 10. The phrase *knowledge base* still figured in 5 of the total, but the objects were varied: insights for restructuring, notes from the field, postpositivist reflections, focus on beginning leaders, and global and multicultural orientation. Five presentations had gender themes related to supervision, career paths, feminist thought, stories women are told, and integrating women's perspectives across the curriculum. Thus, more than half of the presentations clustered under two themes. The remainder included various singletons: social construction of administration through practice, administration as a caring profession, knowledge for restructuring schools, humanities perspectives, and curricular reform.

In 1995, with a peak consisting of 16 presentations, it was basically a UCEA show. AERA-A contributed none; SIG contributed 1 concerning ethics. The largest theme was 3 author forums featuring books for topics of school–community relations, professionalism and reforming urban education, and educating teachers for leadership and change. There were 2 presentations on case methods. Single topics were arrayed widely: moral education, communitarianism and leadership, exaggerated influence of positivism on social functionalism, metaphors and chaos theory, and non-traditional texts for educational administration. Other presentations had designated implications for leadership preparation: school reform, alternative perspectives, and multicultural competencies.

The largest number of curricular presentations occurred in 2003. Of the 28 we coded, AERA-A presented 5, UCEA presented 20, and SIG presented 3. The largest cluster (6) across organizations was social justice. One simply referenced social justice; the others referenced specific aspects as they related to leadership preparation: antioppression, ethics, equity and caring, activism for civil rights, sexual identity, diversity, and citizenship. Three presentations referenced literacies for preparation: research, assessment, and technology; the technology study was grounded in a national study. Two presentations focused on dilemmas of schooling and leadership: responding to dilemmas of leaders and Dewey's philosophy related to dilemmas. A number of singleton presentations advocated particular approaches: constructivism, building a knowledge base for professional practice, instructional leadership for diverse learners, multicultural leadership, rural superintendent preparation, and instructional leadership for assistant principals. There was a report of asynchronous, Web-based learning related to cohorts.

Across the total of 86 curricular presentations in the 4 peak years, UCEA was numerically the primary venue and probably most receptive to acceptance, with 68 or 79%. The often bimodal foci of curricular topics of these peak periods varied from knowledge base (7) and reflective practice (5) in 1998 to knowledge base (5) and gender (5) in 1991, to author forums (3) and case methods (2) in 1995, and to social justice (6) and specific literacies (3) in 2003. The only sustained pattern was concentration on the knowledge base in the first two peaks, but even there the specific foci of the individual presentations were often quite varied. The big picture looks more like scatter-shot than research agendas systematically pursued over time. The vast majority of presentations appear from the titles alone to have been grounded in individual courses or programs at one location or simply personal advocacy. A notable exception was a national study of technologic literacy and perhaps some of the knowledge base presentations, which may have had some larger descriptive, survey-based foundation.

We find some comparisons between our findings and chapter 7 of this handbook, "Curriculum in Leadership Preparation: Understanding Where We Have Been in Order to Know Where We Might Go," authored by Karen Osterman and Madeline Hafner. Although these authors reference a few presentations from the three professional meetings, the huge majority of their sources are from published articles, national reports, and book chapters. So, the comparisons seem to be across basically different sources.

Osterman and Hafner carefully define curriculum and then adopt and adapt a seven-component framework of curricular conceptions from Glatthorn (2000) as the structure for their chapter: (a) recommended—what scholars and practitioners believe should be included; (b) written—planned, intended, or formal written statements and expectations for teachers to deliver to students; (c) taught—enacted or experiential, what teachers actually deliver; (d) supported—material recourses supporting curriculum; (e) assessed—what is tested or otherwise assessed; (f) learned—what students actually learn; and (g) hidden—what is not taught in school. The two components of assessed and learned are merged for chapter 7.

Osterman and Hafner find the most saturated component of the framework to be recommended curriculum; our findings, working from titles alone, suggest that a very large portion of the presentations fit into this same component. The National Policy Board for Educational Administration (NPBEA, 1989) report, "Improving the Preparation of School Administrators: An Agenda for Reform," is a major document in the recommended curriculum component and is what sparked the knowledge base controversy that followed. We note this is the same year as the first peak in our data and that the knowledge base is the modal cluster of presentations. UCEA responded to the NPBEA's call with its knowledge base project and in 1994 published *Educational Administration: The UCEA Document Base,* also known as PRIMIS. However, we found only one presentation directly referencing the knowledge base discussion in 1995, though it had been one of the bimodal clusters again in 1991. The desire to address the knowledge base in professional meetings seems to have run its course pretty much by the time the actual outcomes of the UCEA project were published. There has been little direct attention to the knowledge base in these meetings since 1995. Other kinds of recommendations for all sorts of particular curricular orientations and thrusts may be seen in the clusters and scatter-shot, singleton presentations noted topically above. What seems to be absent is a track record of consistently pursued curricular scholarly or research agendas, even in the relatively nonempirically grounded, recommended curriculum.

We find some titles whose contents might indicate elements of a written or taught curriculum, but we cannot be sure. Of those that we think may fall into these curricular components, the majority emanates from participant perceptions of single program reform efforts, and we found no attempt to synthesize these. What are probably wholly absent are presentations on the taught and learned curriculum components that are grounded in any kind of data gathered from students.

These are two components that Osterman and Hafner (chapter 7) strongly advocate as in need of major, sophisticated research investment; they are components we simply do not know about. We note that Osterman and Hafner's advocacy here is related to SIG's name change (see Silverberg & Kottkamp, 2006, for rationale) from Teaching in Educational Administration to Learning and Teaching in Educational Leadership and that both authors are active members of SIG. In sum, we find the conceptual frame for chapter 7 useful in examining our findings and see a number of parallels to what the authors report there.

Program Evaluation

The trajectory of the line seen in Figure 1.8 representing leadership preparation related presentations focused on program evaluation differs from previous graphs. It begins slowly with several fallow years and does not reach a total of 10 presentations in a single year until 2000.

There is no major jump with the advent of UCEA data in 1989 as with program design, pedagogy, and curriculum. The line shows a long, slow climb until the late 1990s and then an upward turn at a steeper incline, a picture of slow, then accelerating growth in its representation of 180 presentations. We look quickly at the first 13 years, 1985–1997, which evidence 29 presentations or 16% of the total.

The very first presentation, AERA-A 1986, was an evaluation of preparation developments in Nigeria, and this occurred in the midst of a fallow year preceding it and 3 years following it at AERA-A—a slow start. There was no self-evident, simple way to code these presentations, so a few were double coded because they might have occupied both a content and process category. The largest cluster (8) contained evaluations of some kind of learning or behavioral outcome. Included were learning the basics of administration or a change in supervisory practices, adult cognitive development, collaboration, leadership aspirations for females, or principal–teacher linkages. Five presentations focused on "innovative" programs. Four clustered because programs or aspects of them were evaluated through perceptions of program participants or stakeholders. Two concerned evaluations of the Danforth Program for the Preparation of School Principals, 2 were formative evaluations, 2 were evaluations of the dissertation process by those who wrote them, and 2 more evaluated programs from the perspective of 1st-year principals. In only 3 was it evident that the sample was greater than an *N* of 1 program: the Danforth studies and a California study of principals, which also appeared to have a longitudinal element. Only 1 presentation explicitly addressed methodology: Could micropolitical conceptions be used to evaluate clinical experiences? In sum,

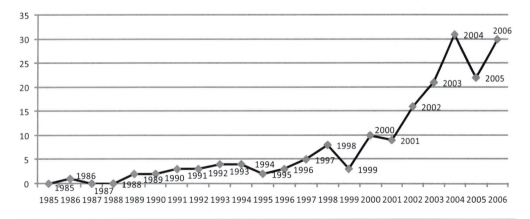

Figure 1.8 Total number of presentations related to program evaluation for three professional meetings by year.

there were few studies but lots of variation among those presented and no continuing research agenda, save perhaps evaluation of Danforth program experiences. AERA-A and UCEA provided roughly equal numbers, and SIG produced only 1 presentation in its 4 years in this time span.

We now consider the 9 years, 1998–2006, the period in which the line shifts to a steeper incline and that contains 151 presentations. As context, the line's upswing corresponds with period in which the federal government launched the No Child Left Behind Act of 2001 (NCLB), the National Council for Accreditation of Teacher Education (NCATE) incorporated Educational Leadership Constituency Council (ELCC) standards into preparation-program accreditation reviews, and university-based leadership preparation received targeted scrutiny through reports supported by conservative foundations and institutes (Broad Foundation & Thomas B. Fordham Institute, 2003; Hess & Kelly, 2005; Levine, 2005).

Again, there is wide variation in the content of these presentations. We were able to classify 72% of them in some meaningful category; the others were idiosyncratic singletons. We developed categories of specific content and specific relationships; other categories are specifically method-ological.

Four of our designated content categories have 6 presentation each: (a) principal or superintendent perceptions of leadership preparation program outcomes, generally or a specific outcome; (b) current students or graduates' evaluations of their own programs, either in general or in named specifics; (c) the outcomes or efficacy of cohort program designs, with or without comparisons to "traditional" programs; and (d) assessments of online learning settings, with or without comparison to face-to-face settings. We categorized 3 presentations as international evaluations, 1 of which had a comparison to the United States. Two presentations were evaluations of preparing students to be technology facilitators.

The categories we named relational contained more presentations than the content categories. The largest of these had a count of 24. Included were studies, typically of revised or redesigned programs or program components, that provided no sense or only a vague sense of the criteria of evaluation. Recall that we were working from titles, which often did not provide all the information one might like for coding. The second category contained 17 presentations parallel to the previous category, except their titles contained outcome measures for evaluation that we imagined could be operationalized. Outcomes included principal retention, teacher retention, career aspirations, transformative learning, problem framing, school improvement, employment, wages, career paths, collaboration, student achievement, school community, democratic processes, reflection, and equity.

The third class of categories captured various methodological issues. Five presentations clustered under longitudinal studies. We clustered 13 presentations that stated inclusion of multiple settings or *N* greater than 1 program or institution. Among these were comparing outcomes across various innovative program designs and structures, doctoral attrition across numerous institutions, Texas principal test scores across institutions, several statewide preparation program studies, technology use across programs, and Information Environment for School Leader Preparation (major computer simulation) assessment across programs. Another category with 7 presentations was use of specific methodologies. Examples here included developing causal pathways from leadership programs to school improvement or various student indicators, extrapolating leadership and learning theories that underpin preparation programs, backward mapping from exemplary principals to roots of their effectiveness, content analyzing NCATE/ELCC reports, and creating statewide program consortia for comparative program analysis. The final category in this group was presentations concerning development of specific criteria for use in evaluation studies. Among the 6 presentations so coded were standards for assessing reflective practice, criteria for comparing programs on Interstate School Leaders Licensure Consortium (ISLLC) standards, best-practice models, and criteria for outcomes of case-based programs.

We coded one final category of presentations, those resulting from the UCEA LTEL-SIG Taskforce on Evaluating Leadership Preparation Programs.[3] For transparency, both authors are group members, one a founder. During the time span we coded, the taskforce logged a total of 26 presentations: 8 presession or work sessions, 7 seminars and innovative sessions, and 11 paper presentations. The presession or work sessions at UCEA totaled 33 hours. Since presessions were not possible at AERA meetings, the group started with breakfasts and informal meetings; since 2005, it has logged 6 hours of work meetings using meeting space provided by AERA but not listed on the AERA program. The taskforce designed and launched a four-point strategy for evaluation studies: (a) mapping program designs and prevalence, (b) comparative longitudinal evaluations of programs and through their principal graduates and program outcomes on schools and students, (c) backward mapping on identified leadership effectiveness, and (d) studies of student experience in programs. The presentations we coded included work on and research results from all four designs. All designs are comparative; they move beyond N of 1, the solidly modal case in the total array of program evaluation presentations.

Calculated differently, the UCEA LTEL-SIG Taskforce on Evaluating Leadership Preparation Programs was responsible for 14% of all program evaluation presentations since 1985 and 20% of presentations from 2001–2006. Also, of the methodological categories discussed just above, 7 of the 13 multiple settings presentations, 6 of the 7 specific methodologies presentations, and 4 of the 6 criteria development presentations are attributable to the taskforce.

Faculty

The content area of faculty accounted for 121 presentations and ranked fifth. As can be imagined by examining Figure 1.9, a regression or general trend line would run on an incline, showing increase from the left to the right, but not a steep one, and such a line would eliminate the ups and downs that characterize the actual line. There are three visible peaks: 1991–1992, 2002–2004, and 2006. Upon content examination by year, we found that 2006 was similar to 2002–2004, so we lumped them together, though we cannot explain the dip in 2004–2005.

The 1991–1992 peak came at the time the Danforth initiatives for principal preparation and leadership faculty were ending. Reform was a major element in faculty related presentations: role of professors in, costs of, and politics of institutional reform; university social responsibility; constructive departmental debates; chair's role in reform; and the possibility of change. One third of presentations concerned supporting the roles of junior tenure-line and clinical faculty members;

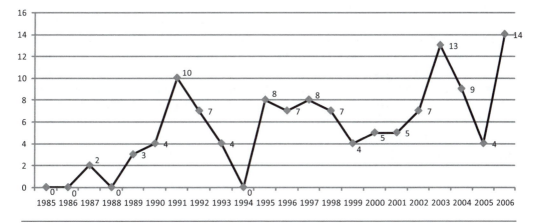

Figure 1.9 Total number of presentations concerning faculty for three professional meetings by year.

some of these were professional development events. AERA-A and UCEA sponsored presentations in a ratio of 9:8. The peak of 2002–2004 and 2006 was seated predominantly in the UCEA meetings, 31 of the total 42 presentations. Two thirds of these presentations focused on the following clusters: underrepresented faculty, race, and gender, 9; chair and program coordinator roles and change, 7; junior faculty, transition from grad student to professor, job search, and publishing, 5; differentiated staffing and clinical and adjunct professors, 4; and internal conversation as a vehicle of departmental change, 3. Thus, over the 16 years between peaks we see considerable continuity in emphasis on change and reform, junior and clinical professors, chairs, and faculty conversation; the new element in the later period was emphasis on underrepresented faculty members, totaling one fifth of the presentations.

Examining all 121 presentations together, we started with the major content divisions used in chapter 6 of this handbook, "Characteristics, Preparation, and Professional Development of Educational Leadership Faculty," based on published sources and authored by Donald Hackmann, Scott Bauer, Nelda Cambron-McCabe, and David Quinn. Their major chapter sections are faculty characteristics, work activities, attitudes and values, changing role expectations, academic preparation, and professional development. We found 9 presentations for faculty characteristics, 15 for work activities, 4 for values and attitudes, and 2 for academic preparation. The research on these sections in chapter 6 is generally survey based, atheoretical, or employs descriptive statistical analyses. From the titles alone, presentations at professional meetings for these sections seemed similar. Example content included presentations on characteristics and attitudes of female, minority, clinical, and adjunct professors; orientations toward teaching; attitudes of new hires; views about comprehensive exams, advisement, and publishing; and balancing research and publication with teaching and service in career building. Hackmann and colleagues find the first three of these sections to be the most researched, albeit not heavily; however, we found them the least populated with presentations.

Presentations in the meetings were more numerous in the chapter section categories of changes in role expectations and professional development, 21 and 17 presentations, respectively. Changes in role expectations came from three sources: (a) professors' internal drives for reform of leadership preparation such as shaping reform and resulting role redefinition, experiencing effects of working cohort programs, joint program development requiring greater trust among colleagues and across rank and race, and learning to work alongside students rather than over them; (b) external pressures from various sources such as distance learning and completion of market forces and demands for higher quality graduates; and (c) pressures from within the academy such as higher publication requirements (especially in research universities), unchanging reward systems, and overall increased complexity of the role.

The authors of chapter 6 report not finding much research on professional development. The presenters at meetings both described various professional development options and actually provided development opportunities for colleagues at the meetings. Nonparticipatory development presentations included topics of learning to model one's philosophy, becoming critically reflective of one's practice or developing a self-assessment system, and learning strategies to attract new tenure-line and clinical professors. Participative actives included an action lab on time management, developing a network of scholars of color (3 meetings), and presessions of the Educational Consortium (aka the Heretics Group), initiated by Laurence Marcus of Rowan University, which engaged participants in lively discussion of reform proposals and other "ahead of the mainstream" ideas.

Our final two categories do not coincide with the sections in chapter 6, though they might have been what we would consider forced into the existing structure. The first cluster of 23 presentations has two subsets, which we call junior professors and the path to the professorship. The presentations and interactive sessions provided strategies for aspirant use to propel themselves toward the academy and on the other hand provided sessions that were essentially magnets and mentoring opportunities to entice and support movement toward the professorship. In the junior professor set, some presentations (6) taught senior potential colleagues about the difficulties that women and professors of color confront and that universities and departments need to rectify if they expect to recruit and retain a faculty that is diverse. Closely related to these is another set (2) that presented phenomenological studies of actually experiences of new participants of color at professional meetings. Some other presentations concerned helping junior professors develop research agendas, and yet others were interactive discussions that likely included attempts at coaching and short-term mentoring of junior colleagues. The path to the professorship subset included 9 presentations and interactive sessions similar to those above, except that they were clearly developed for graduate students attending the professional meetings. Topics included the job search, writing and publishing, and information about the transition from one role to the other. These had inviting titles using words like *chats*.

While not targeted in chapter 6, we were encouraged to find that there has been a noteworthy stream of work around chairpersons and program coordinators dating all the way back to the beginning of our UCEA data. Some might argue that the chairpersons are not correctly considered under the category of faculty. We counter that chairs typically are faculty members on assignment for a period of time, generally maintaining significant duties as professors as well. Certainly, chairs figure importantly in the major deliberations and work of developing and executing preparation programs. Simply to leave them out seems unwise. We found 29 presentations covering role ambiguity, conflict, dilemmas, stress, and personal–professional tradeoffs; democratic departmental leadership and leadership for social justice; building community and programs through faculty dialogue, program promotion, and conflict resolution; and faculty evaluation, mentoring, and career paths. A good number of presentations were actually interactive action labs, job-alike discussions, and presessions with various topical foci. Almost all of these, in fact, the bulk of chair presentations occurred at the UCEA conventions.

Unusual in the whole array of preparation scholarship content areas are programmatic research agendas. However, study of faculty is one area with several long-term scholarly efforts. Walter Gmelch was director of the UCEA Center for the Study of Department Chair in Educational Administration. He has taken a very active role over the years. We coded him and his several colleagues 9 times in various action labs, presessions, and research presentations focused on the position of chair. Also, Martha McCarthy and her colleague George Kuh have been pursuing an agenda of studying the professorate in educational administration for decades and have presented findings of several national surveys at professional meetings.[4]

Context

The sixth most populated content area, context, with 115 total presentations, is graphed in Figure 1.10. The year-by-year line starts with 4 years of fallow AERA-A only meetings. The large jump in 1989 results from 1 AERA-A and 14 UCEA presentations in the 1st year of coding for the latter. In that year, the creation of the NPBEA was a big event in the context of leadership preparation. UCEA participants that year demonstrated considerable interest in context issues, but recall that in the 1st year of data for the UCEA convention, 73% of all presentations were leadership preparation related. The line then dips into some very lean years until about 1997 before rising to a small peak and then two peaks of 16 presentations, with valleys between the peaks. The years after the first spike were relatively quiet in the external environment; they did include the creation of SIG and the publication of the *Educational Administration: UCEA Document Base* or PRIMIS. Just before

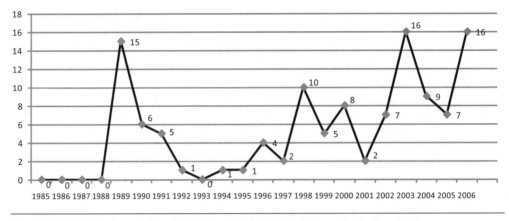

Figure 1.10 Total number of presentations related to the context of preparation for three professional meetings by year.

the last two peaks, the revised NCATE accreditation process with incorporated ELCC standards went into effect, and then in the next several years major reports questioning university-based principal licensure came out.

Following the large analytical structure of chapter 3 in this handbook, "The Context of University-Based Educational Leadership Preparation," authored by Donald LaMagdeleine, Brendan Maxcy, Diana Pounder, and Cynthia Reed, we began our content analysis with two large categories: internal and external influences. Beginning with quite general categories under external influences, we coded 3 for reform movements in general, 2 for the changing world of practice, 2 for framing new policy contexts, 2 for professional association interactions, 3 for a globalizing economy, 2 for cohorts in a changing context, 2 for general competency-based licensure, 2 for computers and information technology, 2 for comparing educational administration with professional preparation in other fields, and 4 for preparation programs in other national contexts—in short, a considerable number of small but varied groupings.

We coded 5 external context presentations in a grouping of various conservative policy components: market discipline, competition, and school choice. Accountability appeared 3 times. Eight presentations focused on agencies of state-level reform and specific state reform initiatives. We coded other presentations with specifically named organizations or initiative-taking commissions and councils: 2 for NPBEA, 1 for the National Commission for the Advancement of Education Leadership Preparation, 6 for NCATE and its new accreditation standards, 1 for NCLB, 13 for ISLLC standards, and 2 for licensure tests. Presentations on these specifics usually appeared within a few years of an action by one of the organizations.

Another group, 16 in number, consisted of specifics that generally cluster under a rubric of liberal policy concerns related to equity and social justice. The list of specifics includes equity and social justice; sociocultural effects; cultural pluralism and diversity; class, race, gender, and ethnicity; democratic leadership; ethics; and linguistic diversity. There were not many indications in presentation titles that external context-oriented offerings were empirical studies. Given titles, most appeared to be some combination of position statements, analyses, and simple descriptions of things. Very little work was deeper than description.

In comparison to the 88 presentations we classified into many categories as influences external to the university, there was a dearth of presentations focused on the internal university context, of which faculty and programs of leadership preparation are themselves but a small part. We found only 5 internal context presentations, each essentially a singleton: intransience of programs, leadership preparation as cash cows, school or college of education factors affecting reform implementation, connecting university faculty to the outside, and reform confronting university traditions. The last presentation may point best to internal contextual elements referenced in chapter 3: changing expectations of faculty role, reward and incentive systems, faculty recruitment and retention, and academic standards. It appears that internal context issues hold little interest for or are of little concern to faculty members in leadership preparation programs. However, the internal context contains the ideas, structures, and forces most likely to constrain some of our current conceptions of how we ought to alter programs. At the same time, these forces are likely to continue to create internal tension even if we are successful in altering what we currently do. It appears to us that if we were wise, this is one area in which investment and engagement in research would pay dividends.

Theory Design

The seventh content category is theory design, with 101 presentations. We coded presentations for this category if they named or advocated for specific theories or values as the major design element integrating preparation or indicating its intended outcomes. Presentations we coded as theory design might also be seen as responsive to leadership program platforms (Cambron-McCabe, Mulkeen &Wright, 1991) that emerged toward the end of the Danforth Professors Program. Figure 1.11 displays the total number of theory design presentations across all three meetings by year. The basic shape of the line looks the most like that for program evaluation (Figure 1.8) of the total presentations graphs seen so far. It has a steep slope upward in the most current time period and is relatively low and flat until that time except for the moderate spike in 1989, the year UCEA data begin, which did not occur in program evaluation.

There were only 4 presentations in the 1985–1988 AERA-A solo period. The spike in 1989 results from 5 contributions each from AERA-A and UCEA. Of the 10, 3 referenced knowledge-based or knowledge-work organizations, and 2 organized around preparation for ethnic minorities. Other design orientations included democratic authority and reflective practice. The years between 1990 and 2003 have relatively low totals, ranging from 1 fallow year to 2 years of 6 presentations each. The steep upward climb begins in 2004.

We coded as many of the 101 presentations as we could into clusters by theories or values that served as the organizing design factors. By far the largest category was organized by advocacy of value positions. We first coded presentations into a number of value-laden categories, but with more thought we came to view these groupings as subcategories of a more inclusive value position

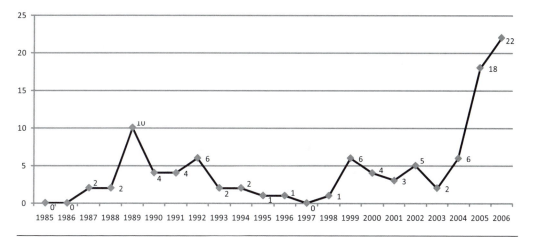

Figure 1.11 Total number of presentations related to program theory for three professional meetings by year.

we called social justice. The original subcategories were race and class, 1; racial ethnic minorities, 3; diversity, 4; diversity, critical theory, and democratic authority, 1; socially responsible leaders, 1; social reconstruction, 1; ethical leaders, 5; democratic authority and leadership, 3; democratic and ethical education leaders, 3; democracy and democratic or social justice, 6; equity and social justice, 3; critical theory and social justice, 1; instructional leadership and social justice, 1; and social justice, 9. The total count is 42 presentations or 42% of all theory design presentations. We first found the phrase *social justice* in a paper by Michelle Young presented at UCEA in 1999. By the time of line ascendency, the phrase seems to have become ubiquitous; it also appeared in the theme of the 2006 UCEA convention. A number of the recent presentations, up through 2007, seem to indicate that social justice as a concept is still evolving and that considerable attention is still focused on conceptual and operational definitions.

We identified other clusters of presentations that named alternative bases for overall design of preparation programs: combining or linking professional preparation of teachers and school leaders (sometimes also connected with democracy and social justice), 6; research and theory and practice, 3; community–school and district–university partnerships, 2; constructivist leadership, 2; and alternative dissertation designs that would alter doctoral program design, 2. The remaining presentations were singletons suggesting a wide variety of potential design foci.

Clinical Experiences

Figure 1.12 shows the number of presentations what we coded as clinical experiences within presentations concerned with leadership preparation. Note that the calibration changes in this graph. Prior figures have line increments in amounts of 10 and 5; here the increment changes to 1. Clinical experiences is the eighth content area in size, totaling only 64 presentations. There are two spikes at 1989 (8) and 2003 (9). The first may be explained by the entry of UCEA data, which account for 7 presentations; the second pike also has a predominance of 7 attributed to UCEA. In neither year is there a clear dominant theme that explains the spike.

We use the term *clinical experiences* for this category because we thought it more inclusive than *internships*, but note that chapter 9 uses the term *internships*. Out of curiosity, we coded the terms used in the presentations. The titles and number for each are internship program or internship, 26; field based or field experience, 9; clinically based or clinical experience, 8; apprenticeship, 2; residency (doctoral), 2; and practicum, 1. We did not choose the most typical title.

Our coding resulted in content oriented clusters except for one methodological designation,

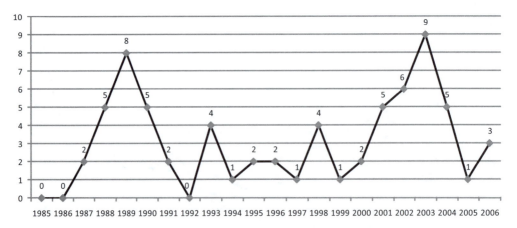

Figure 1.12 Total number of presentations related to clinical experiences for three professional meetings by year.

comparative studies (units greater than 1), of which there were 2 presentations. Our largest category (13 presentations) was one indicating a change from the status quo; a number of words indicated the change: *redesigned, restructured, revised, re-visioned,* and *innovative.* The second cluster of 12 presentations contained focused purposes that went beyond the general purposes described in chapter 9. The specific purposes included bridging theory and practice (4, with 1 for all others), diagnostic professional development, transformative leadership, learning about poverty, school improvement through action research, urban principal recruitment through research experiences in that context, transformative learning, and connecting university faculty to community and others outside the university. Of five categories of empirical studies described in chapter 9, we found only acculturation and socialization (5) and mentor role (1). We coded 6 presentations as simply descriptions; 5 presented perceptions of one or more role (administrator, intern); 4 concerned national reform, NCATE standards, and state governmental actions; 3 focused on the "triad," the interaction of the professor, mentor, and intern roles typically found in the internship structure; 3 addressed assessments of internship outcomes; and 1 focused on the analytical seminars typically prescribed as one component of an internship experience. There were a number of singletons; the 2 we deem important are questioning practices and assumptions, and comparisons with clinical experiences in other professions.

We observed several things in analyzing these data. First, there do not appear to be research agendas operative here. Even those presentations we clustered together contained wide differences, not an orderly progression that more likely would follow from a central question. Most of the presentations appeared simply to follow interests of their authors. Second, the great majority, from titles alone, appeared not to be empirical. Rather, they most likely were opinion, advocacy, and simple description pieces. Only from the 2 presentations containing *comparative* could we find any methodological indications. What struck us most, however, was the paucity of clinical experience presentations, especially in relationship to the categories of program design (which in fairness may have included internship descriptions within their content), pedagogy, and curriculum. The number of clinical experience presentations amounted to only 19%, 22%, and 25%, respectively, of the key areas of program design, pedagogy, and curriculum. Our conclusion of paucity squares with the findings of Bruce Barnett, Michael Copland, and Alan Shoho, authors of chapter 9 of this handbook, "The Use of Internships in Preparing School Leaders."

How could it be, we began to think, that in a field where internships and field experiences generally are touted as the grounding for preparing future leaders, there is so little research or even interest to anchor this assumption? Chapter 6, "Characteristics, Preparation, and Professional Development of Educational Leadership Faculty," authored by Donald Hackmann, Scott Bauer, Nelda Cambron-McCabe, and David Quinn, makes several points useful in searching for an answer to our question: Major surveys of educational leadership faculty characteristics historically tap only tenure-track professors; non-tenure-line faculty are virtually ignored. And the National Commission on Excellence in Educational Administration (1987) through *Leaders for America's Schools* advocated full-time, non-tenure-line professors having the role of monitoring program clinical experiences, including internship supervision (Griffiths, Stout, & Forsyth, 1988).

We began thinking about the backgrounds of colleagues who do supervision of the internship components in preparation programs. In our experience with research-oriented universities, the typical person associated with internship administration, supervision, and analytical seminars is often a non-tenure-track professor or adjunct viewed as practice oriented, a clinical professor, or a special professor on a limited contract. So the question: Why should we expect much scholarship on internships if many faculty members directly associated with this field component at research-productive universities are precisely those from whom the research and scholarly writing expectations have been lifted? In our experience at research universities, individuals doing the internship functions do not attend the meetings we are analyzing, much less do systematic scholarship and develop it for presentation at such meetings or for scholarly journals. The presentations on program design, pedagogy, and curriculum that show up in high proportions at these meetings are written by tenure-track professors directly responsible for these program structures and processes. These active scholars and researchers may not in large numbers identify personally with internship functions.

Our interest and line of thought about the paucity of research on internships raised by chapter 6 receive support from a central organizing proposition in chapter 2, "Historical Review of Research and Development Activities Pertaining to the Preparation of School Leaders," authored by Martha McCarthy and Patrick Forsyth. They argue that a central epistemological tension runs through the history of leadership preparation, tension between those who believe that core professional knowledge is technical-rational in origin and those who believe it is "artistry" derived from practice. Each epistemological position is embedded in a different culture: technical-rational knowledge in the university culture's tenure-line professors and knowledge of artistry in non-tenure-line clinical professors from the culture of school practice. If the internship component of preparation is staffed by those grounded in the epistemology of artistry, whereas the classroom component is staffed by those grounded in technical-rational epistemology, the tension is then held between separate program components. Formal scholarship and research is part of the university culture, not the culture of practice, so again we find a similar rationale for the lack of scholarship and research on clinical experiences. This line of thought brings us to the same hypothesis derived from chapter 6: Those who staff classrooms tend to research and write; those who staff internship work tend not to research and write. This hypothesis needs careful study.

We are aware of an empirical study that tracked a cohort of 9 interns through three semesters of internships and analytical seminars (Fishbein, 2000). Findings concerned direct and indirect socialization attempts from the conflicting assumptive worlds of teachers and administrators, each grounded on assumptions and practices antithetical to the collegial and collaborative thrust of the university preparation program: Focus on your own needs, don't trust, maintain distance, *quid pro quo*, and don't ask and don't tell. Fishbein's study consistently has been met with disbelief by academic audiences, despite being a well-crafted empirical study. Without programmatic clinical practice research open enough to produce findings potentially negative as well as positive, the field will continue to advocate field-based learning grounded on what, from a scholarly perspective, is essentially a position of ignorance and mystery.

Students

Preparation programs are developed and operated to educate candidates for leadership positions in schools. However, the importance of students among the 12 content categories ranked 9th with only 62 presentations. This finding of presumably low interest as a unit of study related to preparation is consistent with chapter 5 in this handbook, "Candidates in Educational Leadership Graduate Programs," authored by Tricia Browne-Ferrigno and Rodney Muth. The authors quote McCarthy's (1999, p. 134) statement that students in preparation programs "have been routinely overlooked" and Murphy's (2006a) statement that there is a "limited body of empirical knowledge" (p. 73) concerning candidates for preparation.

Figure 1.13 displays the total number of presentations about students across the three applicable professional meetings by year. First, note that the lines are in increments of 1. Relatively similar to Figure 1.9 for faculty, a regression line drawn on the graph would slope gently upward from left to right, and it would eliminate the considerable up-and-down fluctuation over the progression of years. Although there are some peaks, the numbers are so small that we simply deal with all presentations together.

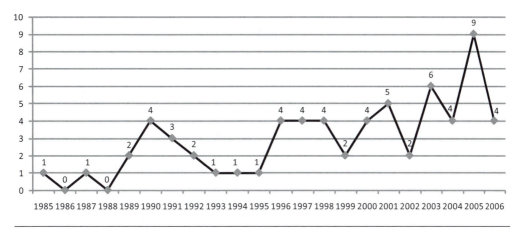

Figure 1.13 Total number of presentations related to students for three professional meetings by year.

In coding the 62 presentations, we came up with categories both the same and different from those in chapter 5. We had no presentations that fit into the category of student characteristics, which typically contains results of surveys eliciting demographic and biosocial descriptive data. Our largest category, experiences of and proposals to support students currently in preparation, contained 11 presentations. Eight of those either described the experiences of individuals of color or women and advocated for improvement or proposed specific changes. One presentation addressed the negative effects of ambiguity on aspirants for leadership positions; another gave information on aspirant attitudes toward the gay community. Two categories contained 8 presentations and are really integrally related, yet for some reason applied distinct language: recruitment and retention, and applicant selection. Three of the presentations under recruitment and retention focused on race and gender, whereas others named Generation X teachers and high-quality aspirants. A number of presentations simply addressed the processes without indicating specific target populations. In terms of selection, several presentations addressed general themes of improved process and better outcomes. Others described specific means of arriving at the desired results: portfolios; assessment processes and tools beyond standard academic credentials; and field-based, partnership-based, or cohort-based cooperation in arriving at admission decisions.

Professional Development

We coded 49 presentations for the content area of professional development. Figure 1.14 displays the total presentations distributed across the three professional meetings by year. The line shows the low number of presentations in this category. It begins at a low level, sinks in the middle to years of 1 presentation a year mixed with fallow years, and then rises to its top years of production beginning in 1998 and peaking in 2005. We have no explanation for the peak year.

We performed content analysis with the whole set of presentations together. The largest subset clustered around means or processes for providing professional development. Reflective practice and reflection was the largest group (4), followed by school district–university collaboration (2) and telecommunications and technology (2). The remaining presentations in this category were singletons: summer institute model, career portfolios, scaffolding, action research, and conflict resolution. Another cluster of 6 presentations emphasized the intended outcomes for professional development: social justice (2), equitable student outcomes, improved instructional leadership and supervision of instruction, learner-centered leadership, and growth of assistant principals. The final cluster contained 9 presentations focused on the larger view: 3 indicated longitudinal elements,

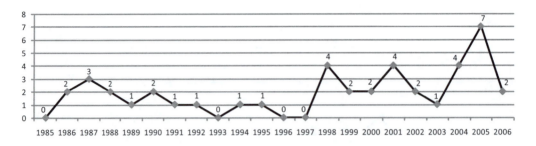

Figure 1.14 Total number of presentations related to professional development for three professional meetings by year.

including database development and long-term effects of professional development. Others indicated theory building or synthesis, developing and testing processes, assessing alternative models, and designing models of professional development. The remaining presentations were scatter-shot. Though there were clusters, we could discern no developing research threads across time.

Chapter 13, "Comprehensive Leadership Development: A Portrait of Programs," authored by Carolyn Kelley and James Shaw, provides a perspective quite different from the professional development presentations we examined from professional meetings. Kelley and Shaw focus exclusively on "comprehensive and embedded leadership development for principals." They present a focused chapter built on the embedded and comprehensive points grounded in both theory and empirical research. They also present five examples of such programs. None of these utilize anything like typical university courses or workshops. Thus, the presentations at national meetings seem mostly to represent a universe quite different from that found in chapter 13 in this handbook.

Student Assessment

The 11th content category is student assessment, accounting for 45 presentations among the three professional organizations. This content area contains 19 fewer presentations than the content area on students, the 9th in size. Figure 1.15 displays the presentations by year over the time span of interest. Two general movements are visible. The first is the saw-tooth, up-and-down motion that, with the exception of the middle section, is a general pattern; the second is a slow rise in the number of presentations over time, or from left to right. Five completely fallow years end at the midpoint. The patterns indicate moderate, intermittent activity and cast doubt on programmatic research in this area.

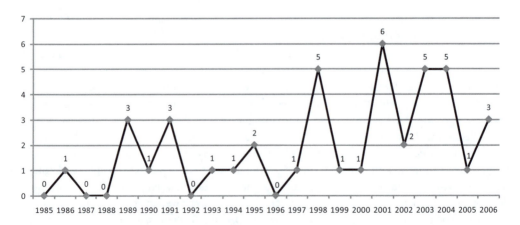

Figure 1.15 Total number of presentations related to student assessment for three professional meetings by year.

We coded the presentations into four clusters that in general are focused on quite specific and often operational methods of student assessment:

1. The first cluster of 11 presentations, portfolios, began to appear in 1990 and ran throughout the time span. A number of presentations seemed quite general, describing portfolios as alternative and self-assessments. Others considered the possibilities and potholes associated with using them. The UCEA Center for Study of Preparation Programs considered specific uses of student-prepared portfolios. One presentation addressed them as authentic assessments, whereas another argued that using them involved changing one's models and assumptions; yet another coupled platform writing with portfolio use. Others perceived them as straightforward ways of assessing management behaviors.

2   A second cluster had 12 presentations that were similar in that they appeared to encompass attempts to operationalize assessment instruments, which on the other hand were quite varied as to method, process, and purpose. Some examples included ADMIN-SIM, a computer-based assessment; an online evaluation tool to assess leadership experiences and outcomes; a low-inference observation tool for assessing school improvement and program evaluation; and an assessment center model. Others included assessing dispositions and student engagement in graduate programs. One presentation asked the question: How generic are the skills to be assessed? Others concerned using standards of reflective practice to assess development of reflection; demonstrating a Web-based, performance-assessment system for certification; and considering the context of reform in creating assessments. The array of tools and processes was quite wide.

3. A third cluster of 4 presentations was focused on performance appraisals: assessments based on national reports, expertise linking context with performance, development and implementation of performance appraisals, and performance data for assessing leadership effects.

4. Presentations in the final cluster were all related to ISLLC standards and fist appeared in 1998. One concerned developing a platform to support ISLLC standards, another addressed developing portfolios grounded in ISLLC for documenting growth, and a third linked platforms and portfolios to assess students and preparation programs. Two presentations described and tested the new School Leaders Licensure Assessment from the Education Testing Service, grounded in ISLLC standards.

The contents of these presentations stand in contrast to contents of chapter 11 in this handbook, "Student Assessment in Educational Leadership Preparation Programs: Looking at our Past, Examining out Present, and Framing our Future," authored by Frances Kochan and Demetriss Locke. Unlike more instrumental presentations, chapter 11 delineates the history of assessment in higher education generally and in schools of education and preparation programs in educational administration. It provides considerable information about the context of higher education and the forces hindering and supporting the implementation of student assessment. We found no presentations dealing with these broad historical and contextual issues in our meeting data. We also found no evidence in the presentations at professional meetings of attempts to synthesize various individual studies about, for example, portfolios, into a some kind of unified understanding or to generate a research agenda to create a substantial larger picture of even a piece of the assessment universe. Rather, at least working from titles alone, we perceived mostly isolated, single context-based, typically descriptive studies whose authors were not in some kind of larger conversation with others studying the same or similar phenomena to imagine a more whole picture or a more integrated understanding that extends beyond individual small samples and specific experiences.

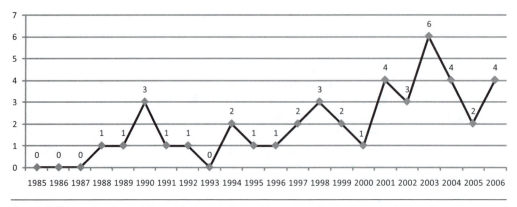

Figure 1.16 Total number of presentations related to mentoring, coaching, and induction for three professional meetings by year.

Mentoring, Coaching, and Induction

The 12th and final content category, mentoring, coaching, and induction, is a trio of preparation activities for guidance during actual workplace experience. The category yielded 42 presentations. These are activities that may occur during clinical experiences or as the student actually enters first employment as a school administrator or leader. Yet, they are activities that can be separated out from the content of clinical experiences broadly viewed. They are activities initiated by the experienced person or person in a role of organization power. A look at Figure 1.16 indicates a general increase in presentations in this area up to 2003, but it is an up-and-down process of increase. Note, too, that the calibrations between graph lines are diminished from 5 units in more saturated content categories to units of only 1 in Figure 1.16.

Coding the presentations into the three activities inciated in the content-area title was simple and revealing. Attending simply the words themselves, the three categories yielded *mentoring*, 37 titles; *coaching*, 1 title; and *inducting*, 4 titles. *Coaching* and *inducting* were more recent terms: *Inducting* first appeared in 1999, and half of these presentations related to a state preparation reform initiative in Kentucky; *coaching* entered in 2005 in a presentation about designing coaching positions across five school districts. The dominant activity, mentoring, was spread through the whole time span

Titles with *mentoring* were not easily put in tight categories. Many were quite general and many contained specific desriptors but were singletons in that specificity. The overall impression was of a content area still formulating its dimensions and common processes. We found some small and codable groupings of mentoring related to women and femanism, 3; urban contexts, 3; formal and informal dimensions, 3; and superintendents, 2 (most others were assumed to be principal preparation or so stated).

A Larger View: Size and Emphasis Among Professional Meetings

Here we combine size and proportion data to examine the relative importance of the 12 content areas within each of the three professional organizations and to compare emphasis across organizations. In Table 1.2, the numbers to the left are the absolute numbers of presentations in the given content area within the particular organization across all years. The percentage to the right is the proportional result when the number to its left is divided by the sum of the numbers in that professional meeting's column; it is the percentage that the given content category contributes to the grand total of all presentations across all years for that organization. Creating these percentages is a way of putting meetings of different size and term of years in the same metric to compare

Table 1.2 Total Number of Presentations by Organizational Meeting by Content Area and Percentage of Grand Total of Presentations Within Organizational Meeting by Content Area

Content area	AERA-A		UCEA		SIG	
	n	%	n	%	n	%
Program design	95	**24%**	228	**24%**	29	14%
Pedagogy	68	16%	160	17%	83	**36%**
Curriculum	48	10%	187	**15%**	25	13%
Program evaluation	38	8%	115	9%	27	**11%**
Faculty	30	6%	80	**9%**	11	4%
Context	41	**9%**	67	5%	7	3%
Theory design	27	**8%**	69	6%	3	2%
Clinical experiences	22	**6%**	39	**6%**	7	3%
Students	22	**6%**	33	3%	9	4%
Professional development	19	**4%**	28	2%	2	1%
Student assessment	7	2%	24	3%	12	**6%**
Mentoring, coaching, induction	21	**5%**	15	1%	6	4%

relative levels of importance of content areas within an organization and then in comparison with the other organizations.

We begin with size. Looking at the absolute numbers across the content rows, we find that UCEA hosted a larger number of presentations in every category except mentoring, coaching, and induction in its 18 years than either AERA-A in its 22 years or SIG in its 13-year run. In 10 of 12 categories, it is true that AERA-A hosted a larger number of presentations than did SIG. However, for pedagogy and student assessment, SIG hosed more presentations than AEREA-A.

Looking up and down the column within each organization at the percentages gives us a view of the relative importance of each of the 12 content areas within that organization. So for example, we find that program design receives the highest rank at the rate of 24% in both AERA-A and UCEA. The lowest rank of importance, however, is different across the organizations: student assessment for AERA-A; mentoring, coaching, and induction for UCEA; and professional development for SIG.

Looking across content rows at the percentages provides the relative importance given to that area by each organization. The highest percentage in the row is bolded to indicate its greatest comparative importance in that organization. Thus, AERA-A placed greater comparative importance than other organizations on program design (actually tied with UCEA); context; theory design; clinical experiences (tied with UCEA); students; professional development; and mentoring, coaching, and induction. UCEA gave highest importance to program design, curriculum, faculty, and clinical experiences. SIG gave greatest comparative emphasis to pedagogy, program evaluation, and student assessment. Why particular content areas find more or less support in one organization versus another is not readily evident, save for one situation. For SIG's greatest weight in program evaluation, the explanation is that it houses the UCEA LTEL-SIG Taskforce on Evaluating Leadership Preparation Programs. However, for the scholar looking to present work of a particular content, the differential importance weights are suggestive of probabilities of acceptance.

Dissertations: Assembling and Coding the Data Set

Here we continue with the parallel study of dissertations. Recall that shared elements of conception and method are presented early in the chapter for both the professional meeting and dissertation data. At this point, we describe those elements of data and analysis unique to the dissertation study.

Using the search engine, *Dissertation Abstracts*, we built a year-by-year database using the search terms *educational administration* and *educational leadership*. We concluded that these two phrases would capture studies that connected in any way to leadership preparation and exclude studies that focused on more general education topics. We also hypothesized that during the past two decades the term *leadership* gradually displaced or overshadowed *administration* as a descriptive term.

The first level of the search turned up 1,429 dissertation titles that were entered into *Dissertation Abstracts* between 1986 and 2006. The Search Results column of Table 1.3 displays the number of dissertations by year. Then, using the 12 content categories that guided this inquiry, we selected dissertations that appeared to connect in any way to leader preparation. Eliminated titles included studies completed at non-U.S.-based institutions, studies of higher education institutions, studies related to teachers and classrooms, and studies about leadership in professions outside of education. The Dissertations Selected column of Table 1.3 shows the number of titles we chose, by year, from this stage of the review, a total of 562 dissertations. Next, we reviewed the abstracts of the selected titles, looking specifically for any reference to leadership preparation. In some cases the dissertation was about preparation (e.g., a program review), in some cases preparation was a key finding, and in others preparation was part of the implications or recommendations. Dissertations that had no reference to preparation were eliminated at this point, leaving us with a group of 305 that we termed *Useful Dissertations* in the database.

Using information in the abstract, we created an Excel spreadsheet that included the author, year of completion, institution, title, content category of study, methodology, up to four findings, and up to four recommendations. We read and assigned each dissertation abstract to 1–4 of the 12 content categories. We coded the primary category to reflect the main focus of the study. Recognizing that research often addresses multiple or overlapping themes, we assigned additional content codes when appropriate. For example, when a study that examined the problems of beginning

Table 1.3 Search Results for Dissertations Related to Leadership Preparation

Year	Search results (N = 1,429)	Dissertations selected (n = 562)	Useful dissertations (n = 305)
1986	61	17	13
1987	68	18	16
1988	57	17	13
1989	67	16	11
1990	68	35	19
1991	74	37	17
1992	67	30	15
1993	75	29	15
1994	63	27	14
1995	46	13	8
1996	60	19	15
1997	72	25	14
1998	65	47	16
1999	61	29	22
2000	78	42	22
2001	68	20	17
2002	74	21	11
2003	105	33	21
2004	107	50	18
2005	68	24	7
2006	25	13	4

principals was designed as a program evaluation, it was coded for both categories. In many cases, content coding was limited to the most obvious category because the author provided minimal or very general information about the study. Coding dilemmas were less of an issue for the dissertation data if the abstract included rich descriptions of a study's purpose and design. Our final database for analysis contained 305 entries, representing 1986–2006.

Dissertations: Coding Limitations

The limitations to this data set are obvious, and thus our observations and inferences are open to question. First, our choice of search terms may have eliminated some studies with important recommendations for leadership preparation. Our decision was based on limited time and resources and an assumption that almost all dissertations prepared within educational leadership or educational administration programs are catalogued under those major search terms. Second, by only previewing titles for our first cut, we surely missed some dissertations that fit our coding categories. In order to mediate this issue, we overselected titles for each year, giving more weight to the later abstract reading. The abstracts themselves proved to be the most challenging limitation. Time precluded a full reading of the dissertations, and we suspect that some eliminated dissertations may contain important insights for leadership preparation. Frequently, titles or study designs suggested possible connections to our inquiry. However, the abstract itself was constructed in such a way that it provided almost no substantive information about the findings, conclusions, implications, or recommendations. In these cases, we had no choice but to eliminate the study.

Dissertation Data

We used Excel's data-sorting features to construct charts that displayed content categories by year that, in turn, allowed us to examine patterns of topics within a content category and patterns of methodological approaches. Finally, we transferred the data from the Excel spreadsheet to SPSS v.13 in order to enhance our descriptive analysis. We ran cross-tabs to identify primary and secondary categories, categories by particular historical eras, patterns of content development by years, an analysis of major recommendations by historical eras, and an analysis of the institutions most frequently sponsoring dissertations related to leadership preparation. Our analysis consisted of using a qualitative lens to examine the numerical data that, in turn, led us back to the content data in order to locate patterns that provoked important questions for the profession.

Findings: Dissertations

Leadership Content Categories Addressed 1986–2006

The categories, either primary or ancillary, addressed in dissertations (Figure 1.17) focused primarily on the categories of curriculum, program evaluation, and students. This section provides details about the dissertation questions that were most commonly studied during the chosen time frame. We also probed the data for the most used methodologies for the two most prominent categories.

Inquires Related to Curriculum

Dissertations about various aspects of leadership curriculum were prominent in 1989, 1992, 2000, 2003, and 2004. We surmised that attention to National Policy Board standards in the late 1980s and the emergence of the ISLLC standards in the early 1990s led to inquiries related to curriculum issues. This particular data sort allowed us to examine the specific content more closely, and Figure

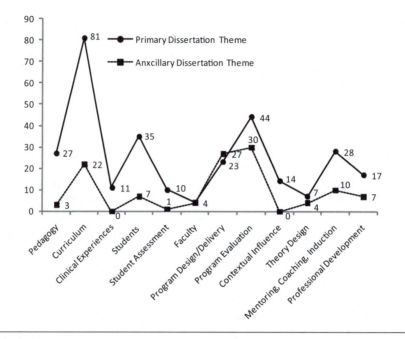

Figure 1.17 Leadership preparation content categories addressed in dissertations.

1.18 shows the primary foci of the dissertations coded as curriculum topics. Those coded as specific leader skills focused on leadership actions like decision making, communication, or instructional leadership. Examples of abstracts we coded as specific leader roles were studies of middle school principals, special education leaders, or technical school leaders. The topics we labeled as perception of quality were 16 descriptive studies that documented student perceptions of curricular relevance. The studies of women and leadership specifically looked at how curriculum supported women's ways of leading. The general topics included studies of Maslow's theory or the influence of prominent academics like Dan Griffiths. The least addressed topic in this category was professional standards, studies that examined the application of state, NPBEA, or ISLLC standards.

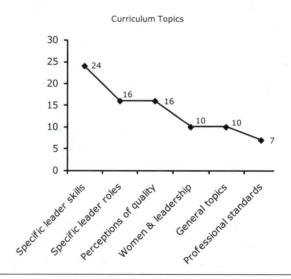

Figure 1.18 Analyses of dissertations on curricular topics.

Table 1.4 Percentage of Types of Methodologies for Curriculum Topics by Selected Time Frames

Years	Quantitative	Qualitative	Mixed
1986–1992	50	32	18
1993–1999	64	29	13
2000–2006	29	50	21

The methodological choices in this group of studies reflected change in research paradigms, with a visible movement from quantitative inquiry methods to an increased use of qualitative approaches. Yet, the overall statistics of the 20-year time frame show an interesting balance of research methods, with 42% of the studies conducted with quantitative approaches, 40% conducted with qualitative approaches, and 18% conducted with mixed methods. To gain a more nuanced look, we sorted the data by three general time frames that closely match educational reform eras (discussed later). Table 1.4 clearly shows how the research paradigm shift influenced dissertation studies in educational leadership.

The challenging, and perhaps disappointing, element of this data set is that the vast majority of the studies examined were based on descriptive survey data, open-ended questionnaires, interviews, or single case studies. Few study designs described in the abstracts suggested comprehensive or sophisticated methods of study.

Inquires Related to Program Evaluation

The next most frequently addressed topic was program evaluation. A total of 74 dissertations (Figure 1.19) had either a primary or secondary focus on evaluating leadership programs. However, only 3 of 74 addressed the topic from a national perspective. All the other dissertations were specific to one institution or one specific program within a department. Some studies focused on a recent innovation or alternative preparation models, but most were merely a review of in-place programs. Most often, the studies used surveys or questionnaires to gather data and, if described, the findings were labeled as "descriptive." We frequently were curious to know if these dissertations coincided with upcoming NCATE/ELCC accreditation processes.

We also examined the methods employed by dissertation students whose studies focused on program evaluation. More studies (43%) were designed using quantitative methods, but again, they

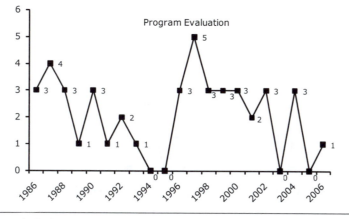

Figure 1.19 Program evaluation by year.

Table 1.5 Percentages of Types of Methodologies for Program Evaluation Studies by Selected Time Frames

Years	Quantitative	Qualitative	Mixed
1986–1992	53	34	13
1993–1999	36	45	18
2000–2006	29	35	35

were primarily surveys with findings presented as descriptive statistics. Based on methodological descriptions in the abstracts, we found only one fourth of these studies used more complex analytical tools to report findings. Thirty-five percent of the studies used qualitative approaches, but again, less than one fifth of those studies used multiple means to gather or triangulate data. Studies that we perceived as more methodologically complex reported data gathered and compared from multiple groups, such as surveys of faculty, students, and alumni. Typically, the study design was reported as using mailed questionnaire or personal interviews. Mixed methods were used for 18% of this group of dissertations. In most cases, these data-gathering procedures described more nuanced sources, such as student entry records, interviews, student achievement, or job placement data.

When the data were reconfigured by the same three reform eras, quantitative studies were clearly far less prevalent in the recent past (Table 1.5). However, the data show a steady increase in the use of mixed methods and challenge the notion that qualitative procedures are now dominating studies in the field.

Inquiries Related to Students

Figure 1.20 shows the patterns of dissertations that address student issues over the 20 years. Eleven of those studies focused on some aspect of student retention and persistence or variables that influenced attrition. Between 1986 and 1998, eight of those studies focused on comparison studies of men and women or the experiences of racial and ethic minorities. The remainder of the studies collected data on student perceptions of specific programs using mostly surveys or questionnaires. In most cases, these studies appeared to be evaluation studies, not unlike those described in the program evaluation section above.

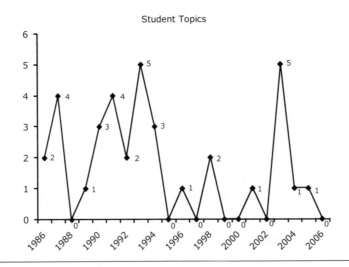

Figure 1.20 Dissertations related to student issues by year.

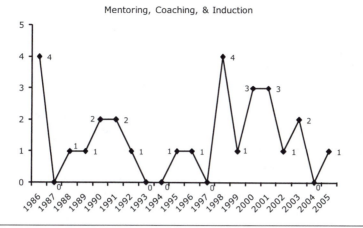

Figure 1.21 Dissertations related to mentoring, coaching, or induction.

Inquiries Related to Mentoring, Coaching, and Induction

One might predict that the topics related to mentoring, coaching, and induction would be of interest to both faculty and doctoral students, particularly as they relate to educational leadership program outcomes. To our surprise, this turned out to be a rather understudied topic, with a total of 28 dissertations over the 20-year period (Figure 1.21). After 2002, we identified only 1 study with mentoring as a primary or ancillary goal. We found surges of studies in 1986 and 1999, but interestingly, the studies focused specifically on the induction or mentoring of women and under-represented minorities, accounting for 32% of all the studies in the category.

Inquires Related to Pedagogy

Studies of pedagogical issues (Figure 1.22) in leadership programs were the only other topic with some prominence over the two decades. Six of the 27 inquires were conducted at Columbia Teachers College and dealt specifically with some type of simulation process. Three other dissertations focused on problem-based learning, and 2 investigated the process and practice of reflection.

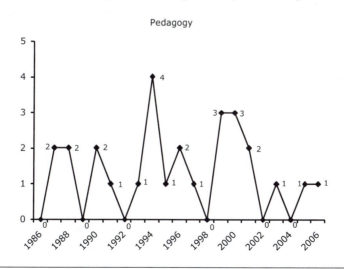

Figure 1.22 Dissertations related to pedagogy.

Inquiries Related to Clinical Experience or Internships

The data in Figure 1.17 that most interested us documented the inquiries related to clinical experiences or internships. The minimal attention to investigations of this issue suggested to us that dissertation research does not necessarily respond to the issues of the moment (Immegart, 1977). The lack of studies was extraordinary in light of the enormous emphasis on increasing and improving the internship or field-based experience in the past decade and the emphasis on documenting the internship by NCATE/ELCC since 1992. As a result, many programs increased required hours of clinical experiences, and some states modified licensure standards to require increased hours of field-related work. Yet, when we combine the two data sets reviewed for this chapter, there was an astounding lack of attention to research on clinical experiences. In fact, between 1988 and 1994, only 6 dissertations focused on practice or clinical experience. Then we found a 5-year gap until 1999 (1 study) followed by 3 studies in 2001, and 1 other in 2005. One might speculate that clinical or field-based practice is of no interest to the profession. Not only do we have an undeveloped knowledge base related to clinical practice, we also have limited evidence related to the effectiveness of the practice. Four of the 11 studies documented student perceptions of internships or clinical experiences, and 2 inquired into the qualifications of mentors and supervisors.

Neglected Themes

The other neglected themes were highly visible in recommendations for program change or future study. Although there was a slight surge in studies of mentoring between 1999 and 2001, we identified no studies with mentoring even as a secondary goal after 2003. Despite innovations in program design and delivery, increased emphasis on assessing student outcomes, and a plethora of activities related to professional development and socialization, the actual studies devoted to identifying factors related to effectiveness of these important issues were not in evidence.

As we compiled these data, we became increasingly troubled by the lack of work in each of the above areas. First of all, student dissertation research is often driven by, or related to, faculty interests. Admittedly, the complex on-site issues in schools often seem more pressing and probably garner more attention from both students and faculty members as dissertation topics are chosen. That said, we also contend that the fundamental knowledge base for developing quality school leaders is so understudied that all the other seemingly critical focuses may have little chance for improvement until we have a better understanding about preparing effective leaders. Second, during the two examined decades, policy makers, commissions, professional associations, and foundations invested heavily in questions about preparation. We began to wonder whether those evolving conversations had any effect on academic interests in research questions that would enlighten those of us who prepare school leaders.

Influence of Ferment in the Field

We borrowed Murphy's (1992) notion of "eras of ferment" and began to look at the dominant educational messages and issues that might have influenced choices of dissertation topics during these two decades. We wondered if particular themes warranted research because of particular "presses in the field" (Immegart, as cited in Boyan, 1981). We developed a chronology of the most prominent reform issues that fostered ferment for educators and potentially had implication for the preparation of school leaders. Because reform movements do not have defined beginnings and ends, we defined three eras, using overlapping years:

1. The Excellence Era, 1986–1992, had as primary influences the *A Nation at Risk* report (National Commission on Excellence in Education, 1983), Goodlad's (1984) *A Place Called*

School, federally sponsored state leadership academies, Danforth Foundation projects, the National Commission on Excellence in Educational Administration (1987) report, and the NPBEA Study Group. The primary focus was restructuring organizations.

2. The Proficiency Era, 1989–1998, had as primary influences the Effective Schools movement, *What Work Requires of Schools: A SCANS Report for America 2000* (Secretary's Commission on Achieving Necessary Skills, 1991), Goals 2000: Educate America Act (1994), Sizer's (1984) *Horace's Compromise*, reform models (e.g., Coalition for Essential Schools; Comer Schools, etc.), ISLLC standards, Danforth Model Programs, and NCATE/ELCC accreditation standards. The primary focus was school, program, and learner outcomes.

3. The Access and Equity Era, 1996–2006, had as primary influences NCLB, state adoption of ISLLC standards, Levine (2005), Wallace Foundation State Action for Education Leadership Project, Marzano and Water's research, and the Broad Foundation fellows preparation program. The primary focus was learners.

Figures 1.23 and 1.24 display the dissertation topics differentiated by these three educational eras. Readers are cautioned to look only at the prominent patterns of primary and secondary dissertation topics, remembering that some dissertations are counted in two different eras because of the overlapping years.

The Excellence Era 1986–1992

This time period generally matches the patterns of research topics described earlier over the 20 years of this inquiry. The most common study questions focused on perceptions of particular curricular topics (e.g., preparation for special education, ethical issues, technology competence), on evaluations of specific programs at single institutions, or on the profiles and characteristics of students. Three studies reflected the emerging influence of the NPBEA, with research questions about the knowledge domains. This era included negligible interest in program designs or delivery models, suggesting the Danforth work had not widely influenced preparation practices at this point.

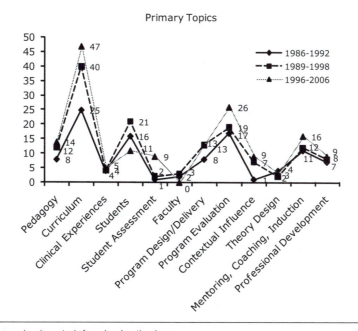

Figure 1.23 Differences in primary topic focus by educational eras.

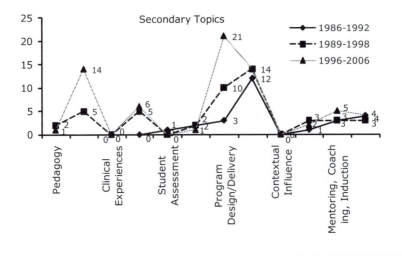

Figure 1.24 Differences in secondary topics by educational eras.

The Proficiency Era 1989–1998

Curricular topics were more prominent in this era, and many titles included the term *effective* (e.g., instructional leader, problem solver, or novice principals). Contents of the abstracts suggested that studies were beginning to reflect a shift from technical and managerial preparation to leadership preparation. While studies related to program evaluation and student experiences continued to be popular research topics, this era saw the first surge in studies on program design, particularly as an ancillary research question. The increased attention in dissertation research was similar to the reports on scholarly activity at AERA and UCEA meeting during that time frame. This is also the time period during which the results of the Danforth projects were more visible in both published accounts and professional conversations.

The Access and Equity Era 1996–2006

We noted the prominence of dissertation topics (both primary and secondary) related to curriculum during the 1996–2006 time frame and speculated that the implementation of ISLLC standards led to increasing interest in curricular questions. However, the theme of this era was reflected in the number of dissertations that focused on studies of women, women's ways of leading, and the experiences of particular racial and ethnic women in administration. Another topic that received attention during this time frame was program designs, suggesting that program changes fostered by the Danforth project were leading to more inquiries on preparation models. Titles included terms like *off-campus, alternative, restructured,* and *cohort.* This era also showed a marked spike in dissertations focused on student assessment, with questions related specifically to ISLLC standards. Delivery models emerged as a strong ancillary topic with titles and questions focused on cohorts and distance learning. Finally, this data display also revealed a visible drop in topics related to students. We wondered if increased attention to student selection processes and the adaptation of most preparation programs to the part-time student had diminished the concerns that we found in abstracts of the earlier eras.

Primary Recommendations in Dissertations for Leadership Preparation

Educational leadership programs produced hundreds of dissertations each year. Faculty advisors encourage students to present conference papers and submit versions of the studies to peer-

Table 1.6 Primary and Ancillary Recommendations in 1986–2006 Dissertation Abstracts

Year	Primary recommendations	Ancillary recommendations
1986	Social justice: Women	

1987	Curriculum:
	   Communication
	   Bilingual
	   Curriculum development	

1988	Curriculum:
	   Practical
	   Organizational development
	   Participatory management
		Clinical experience
		Pedagogy:
		   Simulation

1989	Social justice: Women Reflection	Pedagogy:

1990	Curriculum:
	   Communication
	   Participatory management
	   Special education
	   Interpersonal relationships
		Students:
		   Predicting success

1991	Social justice: Women	
1992	No primary topic	

1993	Curriculum:
	   Communication
		Social justice
		Pedagogy:
		   Simulation
		   Variety of instruction
		Clinical experience

1994	Curriculum:
	   Teaching-learning
	   Practical
	   Organizational theory	

1995	Curriculum:
	   Practical
	   Middle schools	

1996	Pedagogy:
	   Adult learning theory
		Faculty
		Curriculum:
		   School improvement
		   Transformational leadership

1997	Curriculum:
	   Practical
	   Effective Schools
	   Supervision	

1998	Curriculum:
	   Transformative leadership
	   Politics
		Mentoring

1999	Program design	Curriculum Social justice: Minorities

2000	Curriculum:
	   Total quality management
	   Technology
	   Special education
		Pedagogy:
		   Coaching
		Faculty:
		   More student contact, feedback
		   Hire practitioners

2001	Curriculum: Communication	Clinical experience Social justice: Women

(*continued*)

Table 1.6 Continued

Year	Primary recommendations	Ancillary recommendations

2002	Curriculum:
	  Special education
		Social justice: Women
		Pedagogy:
		  Practical application

2003	Curriculum:
	  Instructional leadership
	  Standards
	  Communication
		Assessment
		Delivery:
		  Cohorts
		  Partnerships

2004	Students:
	  Persistence
	  Character
	  Credo-values
		Curriculum:
		  Practical
		  Communication
		  Standards
		Delivery

2005	No primary topic	

2006	Curriculum:
	  Transformative leadership
	  Special education	

reviewed journals. Yet, we wondered to what degree the profession pays attention to dissertation findings that relate to leadership preparation. Again, following the Immegart (1977) and Miskel (1988) premise, we examined the categories of recommendations found in dissertation abstracts between 1986 and 2006 in an effort to understand how dissertation research had informed leadership preparation (adding to the knowledge base) or how it had followed emergent educational issues and social concerns. Using the Excel database, we documented and categorized all the recommendations relevant to leadership preparation and identified the most frequently repeated category for each year using our 12 themes. After analyzing the data, we found that in years where recommendations focused on women in administration, the recommendations typically included multiple categories (e.g., curriculum, recruitment, mentoring, and gender and racial biases). The term *social justice* was a more appropriate term for capturing the nature of the recommendations. Table 1.6 documents the results of that analysis and additionally identifies the specific recommendation cited for that category.

We trust that recommendations scaffold from study findings, yet frequently researchers (students and faculty) proffered recommendations that appeared to represent personal or political positions. For that reason alone, this category offered interesting insights into students' observations of leadership preparation. After looking at some of the consistent messages in the data, we began to wonder to what degree the profession was paying attention to student recommendations. For example, starting in 1987, a reoccurring recommendation was related to the importance of and need for the development of oral communication skills. Although it was not the primary recommendation every year, the suggestion reoccurred frequently enough that we began to wonder how many programs currently require either specific classes or demonstrated proficiency in communication skills. Another prominent theme was related to pedagogy, one of the most understudied topics among doctoral students. Recommendations typically focused on principles of adult learning, engaged learning, or applied learning. Mentoring and clinical experiences were two other understudied topics that were conspicuous recommendations throughout the 20 years.

One more time, we used the three reform eras described earlier to look for additional insights. Figure 1.25 provides a graphic picture of the "missing bricks in the wall" (Kempner, personal communication, 1987), the term one dissertation chair used to describe how one selected a dissertation

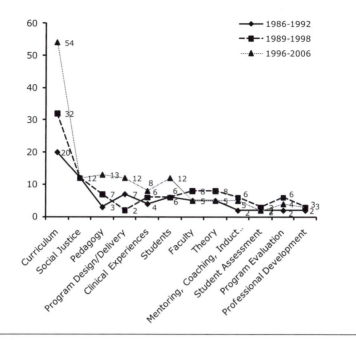

Figure 1.25 Categories of recommendations for leadership preparation by reform eras.

topic. Several things are interesting about this data display. First of all, curriculum topics continue to be the most prominent areas identified for further research and obviously have become more prominent in the last decade. Second, the next most recommended areas are related to social justice, pedagogy, program design and delivery models, and clinical experiences. Despite a decline in studies related to students, there has been an increase in recommendations related to students. We also noticed a set of recommendations related to faculty that had a very consistent message (e.g., experience in the field, hire more clinical faculty), yet found that research related to these questions was, for the most part, nonexistent.

Institutional Contributions to Research on Leadership Preparation

Our data set also provided a detailed look at the institutions that have supported and encouraged research on leadership preparation (Tables 1.7 and 1.8). Based on the observations noted above, the numbers may be influenced by individual faculty interests or departmental program evaluation needs. Only one institution (Columbia Teachers College) had more than 10 identified dissertations during the two decades, and a fair number of those were specific to a single pedagogical approach. It is also noteworthy that three of the other schools in the top five are Texas institutions. Although all the other institutional numbers are small, it was also interesting that almost all the institutions contributing to this data set hold Carnegie research classifications.

Comparison and Contrast of Scholarship by Professors and Doctoral Students

In this section, we compare and contrast the content of professor scholarship (the vast bulk of presentations at meetings) and doctoral student dissertations. To put the two sources of scholarship in a common metric, we use proportions. Separately for meetings and for dissertations, we divided the number of presentations or dissertations in each of the 12 content areas by the total presentations or dissertations. This procedure yielded percentages for each of the content areas

Table 1.7 Dissertations Completed at UCEA-Affiliated Institutions 1986–2006

UCEA-affiliated institution	Leadership preparation dissertations
Texas A & M	10
UT Austin	7
University of Houston	7
Fordham University	6
University of Oregon	6
Indiana University	5
University of Cincinnati	5
Illinois State University	5
University of Georgia	5
University of Alabama	4
University of Arizona	4
University of Denver	4
University of Missouri-Columbia	4
Auburn University	3
University of Nebraska	3
Ohio State University	3
SUNY Buffalo	3
Temple University	3

within each of the two scholarship classes. Thus, since percentages are a common metric, we were able to compare the two sources on a common basis. The results of the percentage calculations are shown in Figure 1.26.

Previous analyses showed the most studied categories by rank. For meetings (largely professor), the top four ranks in descending order are (a) program design, (b) pedagogy, (c) curriculum, and (d) program evaluation. (Content areas in Figure 1.26 are arranged by rank order at meetings.) For dissertations, the corresponding ranks are (a) curriculum; (b) program evaluation; (c) students; and (d) mentoring, coaching, and induction. Only curriculum and program evaluation share top interest and production across professors and students; however, the rank orders differ within the shared interest.

The high ranks for professors tell us that there is primary interest in the "whole" preparation enterprise—*program* design and *program* evaluation—and in the teaching role professors perform through pedagogy and curriculum. Middle ranks for professors include studying themselves and their roles, faculty; contextual effects on their work, context; and a conceptual and integrative approach to program, theory design.

The high ranks for doctoral students include what can be seen as focus on individual interests: What content my colleagues and I receive or should receive—a large 27%—curriculum; about my group and colleagues—students; and about supports for bridging my two real worlds of academy and school or district—mentoring, coaching, and induction. The high rank for program evaluation suggests a combination of two interests: (a) How good is what I receive, and (b) the need for program legitimacy, which contains both a personal property interest (the worth of my degree in the market) and collective interests of both professors and students in the same regard. Our meeting data show that program evaluation is a growing interest for professors but not a constant-across-time interest for students. The dissertation abstracts coded as program evaluation, we sug-

Table 1.8 Dissertations Completed at Non-UCEA-Affiliated Institutions 1986–2006

Non-UCEA-affiliated institution	Leadership preparation dissertations
Columbia Teachers College	14
East Tennessee State	4
St Louis University	4
University of Central Florida	4
University of West Virginia	4
University of South Carolina	3
University of North Carolina-Greensboro	3
Virginia Polytechnic	3
Western Michigan University	3
University of California-Los Angeles	3
Baylor	3
George Washington University	3

gest, easily could be seen as projects completed for the instrumental purpose of accreditation (i.e., NCATE), in which both professors and recent graduates have a stake. Middle ranks for doctoral students include the following: How I receive content from professors—pedagogy, how the whole that I experience is designed and intended—program design, and how my colleagues and I will stay current once we leave the academy—professional development. It appears that the pursuit of high- and middle-ranked content areas for both professors and doctoral students may spring from the same source, personal and self-interest, those areas that the individual perceives to affect him or her most directly—a hypothesis that needs testing.

Yet, what of the content areas that seem to evoke little interest, the neglected areas? Two methods of ascertaining the most neglected content areas produce the same result: student assessment and clinical experiences. Neither group includes these two areas in its high or middle ranks. If we add the percentage for professors to that for students from Figure 1.26, these areas also receive the lowest two combined percentages (as if out of 200%): student assessment, 5.9%, and clinical experiences,

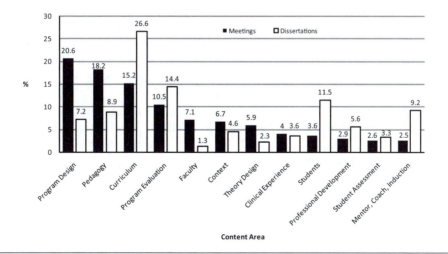

Figure 1.26 Comparison percentages of total professional meeting presentations and dissertations in each of 12 content areas.

7.6%. We already have suggested important meaning for the extreme neglect of clinical experiences in the sections on meetings and on dissertations. These lowest two areas are primary ways that the external world currently judges university-based preparation programs and finds us collectively wanting. Clinical experience is a point of perceived primary importance held by individual practitioners of educational leadership and their professional associations, American Association of School Administrators, National Association of Secondary School Principals, National Assessment of Educational Process, the corporate and business world, legislators, and foundations with research-funding potential. In collectively moving our programs in this direction, we are acting on personal belief, external pressure, and faith, because the empirical literature on what occurs in clinical contexts and what affect it has is miniscule. In the area of student assessments, after decades of compounding waves of excellence, proficiency, accountability, and mixed incarnations of them in NCLB, the entire national culture seems to assess the value of all things educational primarily in the limited assessment subcategory of tests. When we reach into our cupboards for evidence of worth in response to external pressures, we find almost nothing with empirical bases to address how our students are doing in the process of learning to become leaders.

Perhaps we have not perceived critical, public, programmatic, and empirical study of clinical experiences and student assessment to be in our self-interest. If so, it may be because these are, in a sense, collectively held elements of preparation omnipresent in university-based programs today, which may allow us to avoid concerted collegial inquiry. At the same time, they are areas in which we are found wanting collectively by a scrutinizing larger culture. Whatever the reasons are, professional commitment to solid research in those two areas, among others, seems a wise investment.

Two other missing dimensions in the scholarship and research we examined do not derive from the matrix of content areas but are important to mark for future work. First, we professors have emphasized teaching tremendously more in our work than learning (in all schooling, really). While it is possible to perceive pedagogy, curriculum, internships, program designs, and so on from the *learning element* of the interacting teaching and learning processes, our own enculturation process in behaviorist-grounded schooling probably has resulted in tacit, causal assumptions or theories-in-use that lead us to perceive primarily through the *teaching element* of the dual teaching and learning processes. Consequently, most of us attend much more to what we do in teaching than to what our students (or we) do in learning. This reasoning suggests that we spend more time and thought on curriculum, pedagogy, and structural elements like internships under that assumption that they are our primarily tools for teaching than under the assumption that they are the primary enabling tools for students to use in creating their individual meanings—learning. This assumption about a heavy imbalance weighted on the side of teaching is one thing that led Silverberg and Kottkamp (2006) to propose that SIG change its name from Teaching in Educational Administration to Learning and Teaching in Educational Leadership. Placing learning first was deliberate to cause a twinge of cognitive dissonance and reflectivity.

Smylie and Bennett (2005), in the context of proposing a new educational leadership research agenda for developing school leaders (Firestone & Riehl, 2005), implicitly took the learning orientation in responding to the question, What should we know about leadership development? Their answer, in part, was the following:

> We should know about the social, psychological, and cognitive processes by which capacity for leadership develops. Knowledge of these processes—*how* school leaders learn and *how* they develop skills and dispositions—…provides the conceptual and theoretical foundation for assessing the efficacy of known development strategies and for choosing among them. It provides a basis for developing new, potentially more effective strategies. (Smylie & Bennett, p. 140)

In saying this, they advocated looking through the learning end of the telescope or microscope. How much research do we design from this perspective? Not much.

The second, related issue was raised for the first author by Ira Bogotch (personal communication, January 2, 2006): student voice in research on leadership preparation. One reason for posing the question of student voice in research is that we professors need our students as dialogic partners to understand their learning (and ours!) in order to improve program outcomes. In years of wrestling with preservice and doctoral program revision, we authors have worked to create cohesion, integration, and consistency among curriculum, pedagogy, and delivery structures (i.e., courses), all resting on a public platform for leadership preparation (Cambron-McCabe et al., 1991). In this attempt to create "program curriculum and pedagogy" that inheres in the whole, not in separate courses, we were constantly buffeted by the headwind of what Murphy (2006b) later called "privileging of existing curriculum," for which he proposed the antidote of "zero-based curriculum development" (p. 2): Take all curriculum off the table; reintroduce only that which logically derives from the platform or "destination-defining goal-anchored" (p. 2) foundation.

Bogotch (personal communication, January 2, 2006) argued,

> Perceptions of pedagogy and curriculum [as program-wide vs. courses] have to be co-constructed. Voices of faculty describing their pedagogy and curriculum lack the constructivist validity that students' voices bring to the research project. While this seems so obvious, we still privilege faculty author voices in the research.

Examples of significant student voice—not professor-preordained survey question—in preparation-related research may be found, but they are precious few and quite recent (Brown-Ferrigno, 2007; Calabrese et al., 2007; Fishbein, 2000; Kottkamp & Silverberg, 2000).

Summary of Methodological and Theoretical Approaches to Leadership: Preparation Scholarship in Professional Meeting Programs and Dissertations

We already have described the difficult and flawed process of attempting to assess methodological and theoretical approaches to scholarship based on dissertation abstracts and titles of presentations. Such assessment attempt is at least partially a guessing game. Nonetheless, from what we are able to glean from the available evidence, a few salient phrases from Bridges's (1982) summary of his analysis of the published research in the *Educational Administration Quarterly* (*EAQ*) 1967–1980 are still applicable to the situation we found two and a half decades after his report:

> [Researchers] continue their excessive reliance on survey research designs, questionnaires of dubious reliability and validity, and relatively simplistic types of statistical analyses.... persist in treating research problems as in an ad hoc rather than a programmatic fashion ... most [research] proved to be atheoretical. (pp. 24–25)

In the time span of our investigation, there are increasing proportions of naturalistic and qualitative as well as mixed-methods research. Yet, new methods, while bringing different epistemological perspectives, do not affect the overwhelmingly modal character of reported research—descriptive, atheoretical, cross-sectional, based on convenience samples of one analytical unit (course, program, university)—regardless of the type of data collected. And while empirical research is the rule in dissertations in our field, it may be that half or more of the presentations we coded from meetings would not qualify as empirical.

Even the few exceptions to this norm may have embedded problems. For example, there are a limited number of fairly large sample empirical pieces in several of the content areas. However, the modal study in this small group drew its sample from UCEA institutions, we assume largely because it is easy to contact subjects for survey and other forms of research because the UCEA Web site provides accessible lists of names, addresses, e-mail addresses, and even the purchase of address labels for chairs and Plenary Sessions Representatives. Yet Baker, Orr, and Young (2007) recently informed us that UCEA institutions are anything but representative of the almost 500 colleges and universities granting master's degrees preparing teachers for educational administration and leadership. Baker et al. reported that regional Comprehensive I universities are now the primary producers (56%) of leadership preparation degrees, whereas the more selective Research I through Doctoral II universities that characterize UCEA institutions now produce only 36% of leadership preparation master's degrees nationally. So, samples drawn from UCEA institutions are not representative of the likely variation in experiences encountered by students earning degrees and certification across the nation. We need to invest in nationally representative samples.

We concur strongly with Murphy and Vriesenga (2004), who argued that the way forward is not a continuation of the past or much of the present: "The pathway to improvement passes through the doorway of programmatic research, research that is grounded in comprehensive and longitudinal analyses.… Discrete research pieces generally do not add up to much" (p. 31). Our future research will be more powerful if it also includes strong conceptual frameworks, multiple methods, and multiple strands integrated within a programmatic agenda.

The Context of Research on the Preparation of School Leaders: Perceived Legitimacy and Resource Availability

In this section we draw upon data we gathered from presentations at professional meetings and from dissertations. We extend beyond our documentary work to other sources useful in building understanding of the forces that attracted and repelled scholarship and research in leadership preparation.

Perceived Legitimacy

The norm for determining quality and legitimacy of individual pieces of scholarship in most scholarly fields is blind peer review. It is never a perfect process. It is a valuing process with supposed consensus on criteria, but there are also individual differences, which is why we trust that the process will triangulate among multiple referees. Kuhn (1970) also taught us that science (and a professional field by extrapolation) rests on socially constructed sets of assumptions or paradigms, none of which is empirically verifiable. As one outcome of such constructions, professional organizations and journals set parameters of content and method in soliciting proposals and manuscripts. This social construction process has operated historically in accepting or rejecting categories of method and content as well as individual proposals and research pieces in the organizations we studied. It also operates generally in determining the quality and legitimacy of doctoral dissertations. In that respect, there is the grand tradition of a whole field, generally followed, and the individual local cultures of specific departments in operation. The result is local variation in social constructions of meaning and standards of legitimacy concerning dissertation topics and methods.

Given its context, how could we locate the perceived legitimacy of scholarly work at the professorial and doctoral levels as regard study of leadership education as a legitimate undertaking? We return to figures above to probe perceived legitimacy among three professional organizations. Looking first at Figure 1.3, the percentage of the total presentations that concern leadership education, the order is clear: This scholarly area is perceived with the highest legitimacy by SIG, second by UCEA, and least by AERA-A. The lines on this graph never cross; the average preparation focused percentage of total presentations across all years for each meeting is 80% for SIG, 31% for

UCEA, and 8% for AERA-A. Each organization possesses a completely distinct realm of perceived legitimacy. Going backward to Figure 1.2, we see how these levels of legitimacy worked out in the actual volume of presentations, given also the size differentials. We see, for example, even before UCEA became larger in total presentations that AERA-A, that with one exception it always had more preparation presentations than AERA-A. In the same figure, we also see that between its inception in 1994 and 1999, though tiny by comparison, SIG had roughly the same number of preparation-related presentations as AERA-A.

Another indicator of AERA-A's comparatively low level of perceived legitimacy extended toward preparation scholarship may be seen by looking at the total leadership preparation content area graphs, Figures 1.5–1.16. Only 4 of 12 content categories exceed 2 presentations in the 4 years between 1985 and 1988, the AERA-A only years.

The consistent pattern of perceived legitimacy among the three different organizations is related directly to our previous discussion of the differing organizational criteria for accepting presentations: AERA holds the strongest research orientation, UCEA accepts a broader array of scholarship, and SIG is explicitly oriented to preparation and a broad definition of scholarship.

However, perceived legitimacy is not static. By 2002 AERA-A had divided its meeting program into five sections, each with its own program cochair. Section 5 is titled Leadership Development. Thus, AERA-A by early in the new millennium was running direct competition with SIG by seeking presentations in an area that included leadership preparation. There is evidence in some of AERA-A's newsletters of cooperation with SIG to create joint sessions at the AERA annual meeting. Another indicator of fluidity in perceptions of legitimacy comes from Bogotch's (2002) study of the first 8 years of SIG history: "During the last eight years [1994–2002] vocal objections to conducting research on teaching and learning in educational administration have been erased inside of the American Educational Research Association" (p. 96).

Looking across the period of 1985–2006, it is clear that the perceived legitimacy of preparation scholarship increased over time and took major steps upward with the introduction of each of the "new" meetings. In its 3rd year (1989) when we first have data, the UCEA convention proposal readers selected leadership preparation proposals at the level of 73% of its meeting's presentations. When SIG came on line in 1994, its first program gave 100% of its meeting to preparation-related presentations.

Another way to examine the context of perceived legitimacy in which scholars produced the research pieces we used as data was to examine the two editions of the *Handbook of Research on Educational Administration* (Boyan, 1988; Murphy & Seashore Lewis, 1999). Both were sponsored by AERA; the work was done largely by members of AERA-A. These volumes contain critical reviews of specific content and proposed agendas for areas of exploration along with new methods for conducting explorations. The handbooks yield a glimpse at the *weltanschauung* and dominant narratives embraced by members of the sponsoring organization that defined what was legitimate and, explicitly or by omission, what was not legitimate to pursue in the professional field at the times of their publications. UCEA launched its hotly contested Knowledge Base Project halfway between the publications of these two handbooks, a time of competing paradigms. Much of the heat was likely related to the issue of the power of project and handbook authors and editors to define the importance and legitimacy of particular content, interpretations, and proposed agendas.

For the first *Handbook of Research on Educational Administration* (Boyan, 1988), the research and writing was likely started when only AERA-A had a record of professional meetings and the UCEA convention was just beginning. Of the 44 authors, 59% were full professors, only 1 a woman. The other authors were associate professors, 18%; assistant professors, 7%; and "other," 16%, social scientists mostly in senior positions at centers or governmental offices (Boyan, 1988). Most senior authors played roles in the theory movement; the junior faculty members were probably educated under that paradigm.

Our method for exploring the context of legitimacy was to examine the tables of contents for references to the same leader or administrator preparation content with which we coded meeting presentations and doctoral dissertations. In the first handbook (Boyan, 1988), we found five entries that met our criterion. Three were secondary entries under the primary entry of Administrators: (a) Academic Qualifications of, (b) Preservice Training of, and (c) Assessment Centers for Adminstrators. The academic qualification entry consisted of a single paragraph. Preservice training included three paragraphs in one chapter. The paragraphs for Evaluation as an Administrative Function simply noted five universities where good program evaluation courses could be taken. The assessment centers entry consisted of a six-paragraph discussion of exactly that for in-service principals with no mention of applying the technology to preparation. The entry, Superintendence—University Training for, referred to a one-sentence quotation in a chapter on administrative theory. Leadership Training led to a critique on the point that many theoretical leadership-training models possessed insufficient empirical testing to validate their claims, a foreshadowing of the conclusion drawn from the present investigation. The entry, Training Program for Special Programs Staff and Leadership Personnel, led to a particular federal, college-level program not related to prekindergarten through Grade 12 preparation. Each entry referred to a single place in a single chapter. No entry we found led a reader to a discussion of anything like a university program for leadership preparation beyond merely naming a particular university. As an indicator of resource availability, the Danforth Foundation had no entry. We conclude that the authors and sponsoring organization took the implicit position that the perceived legitimacy of scholarship on preparation of administrators was nil within the content of "research on educational administration."

The second *Handbook of Research on Educational Administration* (Murphy & Seashore Louis, 1999) was published 11 years after the first, 5 years after the SIG's first program, and in a post–theory movement period evidencing multiple perspectives. It, too, was sponsored by AERA-A. Of the 43 authors, 81% were full professors, 6 of them women; associates and assistants each accounted for 3%; others constituted 5%. Six individuals or 14% authored in both volumes. The second handbook differed from the first in a number of ways, but in the particulars we looked for, the big difference was an entire chapter on our focal area, The Evolution of Educational Leadership Preparation Programs, authored by Martha McCarthy (1999).

Our content analysis of the table of contents was identical to that for the first edition. We noted the page range of McCarthy's dedicated chapter on preparation and scored each entry either for that chapter or for another chapter. For 5 entries, page numbers for both McCarthy's chapter and another were cited; we double scored those entries, a score in each of the two categories. There were 49 separate entries related to preparation content. We scored 39 for McCarthy's chapter and 15 entries for other chapters. The entries for 6 chapters beyond the dedicated one indicated that leadership preparation was perceived as a legitimate subject of scholarship beyond a direct focus. The content of the other chapters with page references included History of Scholarship in Educational Administration, Internationalization of Educational Administration, Changing Fabric of American Society and Education, Social Constructivist Learning, New Professionalism, and Resources for School Improvement (Murphy & Seashore Louis, 1999). This is a fairly broad array; we conclude that in the 11 years between the two handbook volumes there was considerable growth in the perceived legitimacy of studying preparation-related topics.

A third way of gauging the perceived legitimacy of scholarship on leader preparation in the broad context and the time frame of our study is to look into likely journal targets for scholars wishing to publish preparation related studies. Murphy and Vriesenga's (2004) UCEA-sponsored monograph, a direct precursor to this volume, contained a carefully documented study of preparation-related articles published in general and specialized journals over the period 1975–2002, a 10-year longer history on the front end than ours.

Murphy and Vriesenga (2004) first analyzed the contents of 61 general journals and magazines retrieved from the ERIC database. In these sources, they found a total of 134 articles in their 27-year period. That averages to 5 articles a year across 61 outlets. The modal number of preparation articles in these journals and magazines across 27 years was 1. Publications with the highest number of articles were *NASSP Bulletin* (17), *Peabody Journal of Education* (13), *Phi Delta Kappan* (8), *Education* (7), and *School Administrator* (6). All other publications had fewer than 5 preparation articles (Murphy & Vriesenga, 2004, pp. 15–16).

For specialized publication opportunities, Murphy and Vriesenga (2004) chose four "leading school administration journals": (a) *Journal of Educational Administration*, (b) *EAQ*, (c) *Journal of School Leadership*, and (d) *Planning and Changing*. For the 27-year period (*Journal of School Leadership* and *Planning and Changing* had shorter publications histories), these four peer-reviewed journals published a total of 162 preservice preparation articles. Broken down by individual journals the totals were *Journal of Educational Administration*, 20; *EAQ*, 26; *Journal of School Leadership*, 85; and *Planning and Changing*, 31. For context, the total article output of the four journals for these years was 2,038, of which the preparation articles constituted 7.9% (Murphy & Vriesenga, 2004, pp. 16–19, 77). The authors then broke the 162 articles down into empirical and nonempirical and did a fine-grained analysis of methods.

The summed figures above for general and specialized publication sources total 296 articles over the 27-year span, an average of 7 articles a year. About quantity of preparation articles, Murphy and Vriesenga (2004) concluded, "There is not an over abundance" (p. 28). In our conceptual frame, this level of production does not indicate a high level of perceived legitimacy. As we concluded from analysis of meeting data and both editions of the *Handbook of Research on Educational Administration* (Boyan, 1988; Murphy & Seashore Louis, 1999), perceived legitimacy has been dynamic, having shown growth over our period of study. Murphy and Vriesenga found parallel growth in publication of preparation articles in the period since 1990, which we take as an indicator of growing legitimacy.

We now explore the growth of perceived legitimacy for scholarship on preparation by examining the editorial policy of *EAQ*. Of Murphy and Vriesenga's (2004) three U.S.-based "leading journals," *EAQ* ran for the full 27 years but published the smallest number of preparation articles. Following is a catalogue of changes in *EAQ*'s editorial policy or statements to contributors. Under editor Roald Campbell, *EAQ*'s first issue, January 1965, made no mention of administrative preparation:

> Conceptual and theoretical pieces, analyses of empirical findings, projections of purposes and policies for schools and colleges, and critiques of important writing in the field will be sought. (p. iii)

In January 1973, in an "Invitation From the Editor" soliciting more articles and a wider array, Donald Carver made an oblique reference to preparation related scholarship:

> Professors of educational administration, especially, face the additional challenge of developing and operating training programs.… There are thus, more than enough knowledge bases to be expanded and explored and problems and issues to be studied. (pp. 1–2)

In 1975, *EAQ* published the first two preparation-related articles in its history (Boardman, 1975; Hills, 1975). January 1976 brought specific mention of preparation from *EAQ* editor, Daniel Griffiths:

Within the purview of the *Quarterly* are: articles that focus on significant issues in administration *or in the preparation of administrators* [emphasis added] and that explicate sound conceptual frameworks, research methodologies, and empirical findings; speculative or evocative … and historical or philosophical analyses. (p. ii)

In February 1987, under the editorship of Cecil Miskel, specific mention of preparation disappeared from the information for authors and was replaced by the phrase "knowledge about educational administration, broadly defined" (p. 2). By November 1990 under the editorship of Ann Weaver Hart, specific mention of preparation was back in the information for authors:

Papers on educational reform, governance and reform in colleges of education and the professional preparation of educational administrators—topics advancing the purposes and goals of the University Council for Educational Administration—are welcome. (p. 314)

In 1998, editor Gail Schneider added the phrase "the teaching of educational administration" (p. 4) to the 1990 statement to authors.
In "Letter From the Editor," Diana Pounder (2005) put forth a markedly different and longer contributor's message, from which we quote only the directly relevant portions:

As an editorial team, we embrace traditional and emergent research paradigms, methods, and issues. We particularly promote the publication of rigorous and relevant scholarly work that enhances the linkages between and utility for educational policy, practice, and research arenas, including work that examines … improved leadership preparation and development structures and processes and that assesses the relationship between leadership preparation and development and valued organizational outcomes. (p. 4)

Thus, *EAQ* editorial statements to contributors over a period of 40 years show a trend running from no mention of accepting preparation-related manuscripts in 1965 to an explicit and elaborated statement soliciting them in 2005.
EAQ published one special issue specifically on leadership preparation (Lindle, 2002). It contained six commissioned papers and a number of short responses, characterized as "thinking pieces," for the National Commission for the Advancement of Educational Leadership Preparation. None of these were strictly empirical, though several contained limited descriptions of specific preparation programs. The *EAQ* has scheduled a second special issue for 2009 featuring studies resulting from the work of the UCEA LTEL-SIG Task Force to Evaluate Leadership Preparation Effectiveness. The contents include five empirical studies and two essays. The forthcoming empirical articles alone exceed the total number of empirical preparation studies Murphy and Vriesenga (2004) found published in *EAQ* between 1965 and 2002! Thus, we glimpse the change in perceived legitimacy of leadership preparation related scholarship as evidenced in UCEA's flagship journal. Legitimacy grew very gradually—with one back step between 1987 and 1990—and then grew with increasing rapidity to the present.
Two more UCEA actions give credence to the assent of perceived legitimacy of scholarship on preparation, especially in the last 10 years. The *Journal of Cases in Educational Leadership* (*JCEL*) reached its 10th anniversary in 2008. Founded and supported by UCEA, *JCEL*

publishes, in electronic format, peer-reviewed cases appropriate for use in programs that prepare educational leaders. Building on a long tradition, the University Council for Education Administration sponsors this journal in an ongoing effort to improve administrative preparation. (Sage, n.d., Description section)

This journal publishes only materials for use with case analysis pedagogy in preparation programs; case content is also curricular material. From 1998 through 2006, *JCEL* averaged three issues a year with 3–6 cases per issue; the total for these years is105 cases.

The second UCEA-sponsored journal launched in the past decade is the *Journal of Research on Leadership Education,*

> an electronic peer-reviewed journal, sponsored by UCEA, [that] provides an international venue for scholarship and discourse on the teaching and learning of leadership across the many disciplines that inform the field of educational leadership. (Young, n.d., Aims and Scope section)

The name of this journal summarizes its purpose well. In addition to being international, it also welcomes submissions from scholars in various disciplines. The *Journal of Research on Leadership Education* inaugural issue appeared in April 2006. It included a commitment from the editor to "provide a seed bed for traditional and heretical discourse, while attending to the highest standards for scholarship" (Rusch, 2006, p. 2). Taken together, *JCEL* and the *Journal of Research on Leadership Education* are UCEA's statement that the issue of perceived legitimacy of scholarship on leadership education broadly construed is no longer in question.

Resource Availability

While we argue that perceived legitimacy of preparation research and scholarship has been and is on the rise, the same is not true of resource availability. As we perceive it, both funding availability and probability of receiving funding from limited sources probably has declined from an earlier point in our time period.

Only 4 years ago, Murphy and Vriesenga (2004) provided data that speak directly to resource availability. Of the 56 preservice-preparation, empirical research articles they gleaned from four leading journals in the 27 years ending in 2002, "there is either direct or indirect reference to external funding in only three, and two of these represent very limited funding" (p. 30). Murphy and Vriesenga concluded,

> It appears that professors who engage in research on preparation programs continue to do it out of their back pockets, relying on (1) the good will of current and recent graduates to complete surveys or sit for interviews and (2) residual documents associated with preparation programs. (p. 30)

Another study by Cooner, Dickmann, and Dugan (2006) aimed specifically to answer a research funding question: "Based on a rigorous review of descriptive, evaluative and research articles, how has outside funding helped to build the knowledge base for educational leadership preparation?" (p. 6). Three distinct literature searches broader then refereed journals alone together yielded 421 articles. Only 30 of these met the criteria of U.S.-based studies that received outside funding and whose participants were future educational leaders. Of the 30, 66% were supported by the Danforth Foundation, 1 by the Wallace Foundation, and the remainder by other sources. The array of funded articles by decade was 1980s, 6 or 20%; 1990s, 16 studies or 53% (Danforth era); and since 2000, 8 or 27%.

Another important—but not specifically mentioned—finding of the Cooner et al. (2006) study was the absence of federal support for any of the 30 funded studies they located. Funding came only from foundations, corporations, and professional organizations. There has been considerable controversy about the report of the National Research Council's Committee on Scientific Principles for Education Research, *Scientific Research in Education* (Shavelson & Towne, 2002), which laid the foundation for stringent research upon which the George W. Bush administration (Bush II) then overlaid their ideological orientation. Riehl and Firestone (2005) extrapolated from specific Bush II education policy initiatives an underlying vision of efficiency and effectiveness that

> rests on assumptions that educational problems are straightforward, solutions can be identi-
> fied, and educators will simply accept and implement "proven" practices.... The government
> has prioritized "scientifically based research," preferably experimental or quasi-experimental
> designs with random assignment. (pp. 160–161)

It is apparent that our existing research, largely at the descriptive level, added to the kinds of problems scholars and researchers of leadership preparation are tracking, did and does not easily fit within this federal vision. The upshot is the absence of federal funding for our research.

Locating external funded research from titles of presentations is impossible. However, from background generally known to professors about the Danforth Principal Preparation Program and Professor Programs (1987–1993) and affirmed by Cooner et al. (2006), the Danforth Foundation was the largest and perhaps single consistent funder of programs to improve and research univer-sity-based leadership preparation for schools in the time span we covered. Presentations resulting from Danforth funding were clearly in evidence during our coding process. Now gone is this once important source of funding. Exploration of Web sites identified with the Danforth Founda-tion revealed complete withdrawal from funding of national education projects. "As of 1997, the Danforth Foundation exclusively makes grants in metropolitan St. Louis" (Danforth Foundation, 1999). "The St. Louis-based Danforth Foundation has announced that it will shift its grantmak-ing focus to plant and life sciences and will cut its staff of eight employees to just two" ("Danforth Foundation Shifts Focus,"2003, ¶ 1).

Other foundations such as Wallace and Broad are funding development of and research on al-ternatives to university-based leadership preparation programs in a number of large urban school districts. The Broad Foundation also supports a program to bring private-sector and military leaders into school and district leadership. Smaller grants have supported some of the reports most critical of university-based leadership preparation. These foundations are unlikely to fund the kinds of research agendas generated in this handbook.

We now turn to the efforts of those of us within the "family" who profess educational leader-ship to secure resources to fund research. We note first that whereas institutions like UCEA and boards and commissions such as NPBEA and the National Commission on the Advancement of Educational Leadership Preparation have advocated for research agendas and for their funding, little material support has been realized from their efforts. We know of the multiyear efforts of the UCEA LTEL-SIG Taskforce on Evaluating Leadership Preparation Programs to secure funding for several research projects. With UCEA support in the form of serving as the receiving institution for proposed grants, the taskforce applied for three grants from the Fund for the Improvement of Postsecondary Education and five U.S. Department of Education grants for various strands of the research agenda. To date the taskforce has received no funding. Strangely, several taskforce-spawned, within-state groups are pursuing state-wide studies of preparation as part of the larger organization's research agenda and have received small amounts of support as pass-through funds from Wallace Foundation grants given to their state departments of education.

In brief summary, the resource availability for expanding research on leadership preparation appears to be next to nil. Major change in this situation does not appear likely. That finding led us to develop the next section.

UCEA LTEL-SIG Taskforce on Evaluating Leadership Preparation Programs: A Model

Given the need for longitudinal, programmatic research to move leadership education knowledge forward in an economy of extreme funding scarcity, the UCEA LTEL-SIG Taskforce on Evaluating Leadership Preparation Programs provides an adaptable and replicable model for any research focus. The taskforce is clearly a bootstrap operation, but one apparently achieving success in its 8th year at this writing. Several other chapters in this handbook refer to the taskforce; most address the specifics of program evaluation and its four-point programmatic research agenda. Here we describe the taskforce to encourage replication of its structure, processes, logistics, communication, affiliations, and kind of core research group it has developed. Later, we recommend to the major professional associations how they could restructure their meetings to support collective research efforts similar to this model.

Early History and Structure

The Taskforce on Evaluating Leadership Preparation Programs was created at the 2001 UCEA convention on a basis of experience with presessions on Reflective Practice and Sharing Best Practices—plus faith and a good deal of serendipity. Robert Kottkamp, a UCEA Plenary Session Representative and incoming chair of SIG, was fed up with cyclical discussion of our lack of data to indicate what our major collective expenditure of time and effort—preparing of school leaders—was yielding. Be they good, bad, or indifferent, we simply did not know what our outcomes were. Considering the potential of yoking UCEA and SIG efforts, he requested permission that new UCEA Executive Director Michelle Young allow a presession. Margaret Terry Orr responded to the call first. Thus, two strangers took up shared leadership for the first 5 years. Significantly, they had different but complementary strengths and leadership styles yet shared core beliefs and aspirations.

The first meetings (note the plural) were scheduled from noon to 5:00 p.m. and from 6:00 to 8:00 p.m. Thursday, preceding the convention opening. There was no fixed agenda. Scholars came in good number (25–30); some came and stayed; some came and went; some, like Kottkamp, were Plenary Session Representatives operating in time conflict with the Plenum. They broke for dinner but continued the conversation and reconvened for 2 more hours. Some engaged for the full 7 hours. Interest was clear; time allowed sufficient conversation for developing commitment, and participants designed follow-up. Inaugural members of the taskforce agreed to meet at the AERA annual meeting and to use the SIG as the logistical anchor point. Facilitating this arrangement was the fact that the two leaders were incoming SIG chair and program committee chair. At AERA, the work group met for breakfast, used the SIG business meeting to announce the taskforce and its objectives, and continued with dinner as a group following the meeting. Time was harder to garner at AERA meetings without presessions, but the taskforce found ways to secure it. Thus, the structure of meeting at UCEA in the fall and AERA in the spring was established. The taskforce became located in twice-yearly meetings, not on one or two university campuses, as with UCEA Program Centers. The decision to meet in this way made the taskforce's work sessions available to a wide array of individuals and institutions.

Supporting Processes, Structures, and Organizations

Being a bootstrap operation, the taskforce anchored its work in the SIG, which provided some of its time and room allocations to support taskforce work. Reaching out through Michelle Young, the leadership received UCEA Executive Committee's symbolic support and agreement to serve as a "brokering house" to sponsor attempts at grant funding—though none have been successful to date, validating our observations about the paltry resources available to the profession to support much-needed inquires. The driving force came mostly from the strong commitment of the members, who attended work sessions and developed a four-faceted programmatic research agenda. Provision of unbroken time blocks of 3 hours or more at UCEA and travel support by participants' institutions provided necessary resources.[5] So, by piggybacking taskforce work sessions onto national meetings, members acquired the resources necessary to create conditions for accomplishing real work: engaging in deep conversation about ideas, planning agendas and presentations, reflecting upon and critiquing past work, developing means of communication, solidifying purpose, and developing a professional learning community. The group maintained dedication and energy via accomplishment and becoming a magnet attracting new researchers. These processes and structures resulted in a diverse, committed assemblage of scholars from UCEA-affiliated and nonaffiliated, large and small, public and private colleges and universities. It is noteworthy that some members of the taskforce have reached out to local colleagues and created state-level communities of practice patterned on the operation of the parent taskforce to pursue state-wide studies of leadership preparation.

Conclusion

We began work on this chapter under the title, the Landscape of Research. To mix metaphors, we missed the boat. After binary coding of 9,185 meeting presentations and content coding 1,709 of them and reducing 1,429 dissertation titles to 305 abstracts and content coding them, we have an experiential understanding of unpublished scholarship in our field, especially that portion related to leadership preparation. A more appropriate title for what we found might shift the metaphor to the Seascape of Research.

What we as a field of researchers produce is a lot of islands sprinkled across a vast sea. A few islands are large because they consist of clusters of research done with different methods but focused on the same questions or problems, built upon one another to form substantial knowledge masses. A larger number of islands are small, arranged as archipelagoes, composed of loosely related research pieces generally about similar phenomena but spread out, not building solid knowledge masses. More numerous yet are tiny atolls sprinkled widely apart, with no possibility of building knowledge masses of substance. To move forward we need to construct large islands, even continents of knowledge. Ten or 15 more years of "researching" as we have done to date will take us nowhere beyond the present. The vast sea will continue to swallow our efforts. We will not grow knowledge substantial enough to support our work of preparing school leaders.

Having examined closely what exists in meeting programs and dissertations, we feel affective kinship with those who came before us in examining "what is" and prescribing that we give up our ad hoc, discrete, convenience-based, isolated, small-sample, atheoretical ways and get on the wagon of developing *research communities* with *shared agendas* for programmatic, longitudinal, conceptually underpinned research of a comprehensive and useful nature (e.g., Bridges, 1982; Erickson, 1979; Immegart, 1977; McCarthy, Kuh, Newell, & Iacona, 1988; Murphy & Vriesenga, 2004; Silver & Spuck, 1978).

Murphy and Vriesenga (2004) opined, "Absent funding, our exhortations for change from ad hoc to programmatic work will be no more successful than the dozen or so calls already sprinkled throughout the literature" (p. 31). Murphy and Vriesenga went on to argue that our professional associations ought to lead in "leveraging potential revenues" (p. 31). Authors of several other chapters in this handbook come to similar conclusions. While we think their prescription is solid and do not oppose it, we do not foresee strong financial support in current circumstances. Rather, we set forth a different question: In ways *other than* or *in addition to* funding, how might our professional associations leverage a better future for our research efforts? One potential response is for them to take the lead in altering the culture in which we conduct research, an issue not addressed in the litany of prior calls for different research processes and outcomes. Simply to assist in acquiring funding, for what is likely to be a small number of senior researchers in prestigious institutions, will do little to alter the culture in which most of us do research, a culture that lies within the internal context of universities, which LaMagdeleine, Maxcy, Pounder, and Reed in chapter 3 find we mostly ignore and certainly don't research deeply.

What resources do professional organizations possess to lead reculturing of our research processes? Their most important resource is time, for professional meetings are the places we most frequently interact directly with colleagues beyond our own institutions, places that have potential to serve as developmental meeting grounds for small, cross-institution research communities. That belief is our reason for including the structure and process description of the UCEA LTEL-SIG Taskforce on Evaluating Leadership Preparation Programs.

Professional meeting time is currently used primarily for presenting results of research developed in the now half-century modal pattern we simultaneously bemoan. The structuring of time at professional meeting dates to when positivist methods held hegemonic sway and a researcher in 12–15 minutes adequately could set out a brief statement of conceptual grounding, problem, method, findings, and conclusions. Even recent attempts at "innovative" sessions that feature conversation rather than telling by a few are confined to the same maximum of 1 hour and 20 minutes. This normative time allocation supports questionable tacit assumptions such as (a) a conversation of that length is sufficient to start and maintain something larger; (b) listening to others (one-way communication) is more important than engaging in creating, developing, and planning interactively (two-way communication); and (c) excitement about new ideas can be maintained in later isolation.

The UCEA LTEL-SIG Taskforce on Evaluating Leadership Preparation Programs, though imperfect, provides an example of different use of time and of the potential to grow cross-institution research communities. We advocate that our professional associations give deep consideration to providing "time spaces" of a minimum of 3 hours along with suitable meeting rooms for creation and nurture of ongoing, small, research communities pursuing programmatic research agendas. To enact such a proposal will be disruptive to a degree and is certainly not guaranteed to succeed. We are not suggesting that such time and space allocations be for everyone—we are not advocating a universal "respite for research" block schedule. We advocate simply making it possible for groups to request such time.

What other resources do professional associations have to support development of a different research culture? They possess the prestige to break tradition. They possess the institutional rectitude and recognition to serve as brokering houses to hold grants secured by small research communities with members from multiple universities, at least partly answering equity questions concerning who gets the best deal when a grant goes to one university but not the others represented in the endeavor. Technology is another resource possessed by professional organizations. It can be used for communication in the interim times between meetings once interpersonal bonds are formed, and motivation to continue communication makes sense using digital means. There are no doubt other resources to be discovered useful for nurturing small research communities focused on a new culture for doing research work. We believe our proposal worthy of pilot testing.

Acknowledgment

Robert Kottkamp acknowledges the support of Hofstra University through an academic leave during which he began early work on the empirical portion of this chapter.

Notes

1. As it turned out, the original working plan for chapter contents was altered after we had completed our content analyses in correspondence with it. To create new one-to-one correspondence between the slightly altered array of chapters and our content analyses would have meant starting over, which we lacked motivation and time to do.
2. Joseph Murphy (personal communication, April 25, 2008) noted that the high early proportion (73%) of UCEA presentations about preparation followed by a rapid decline was the same phenomenon that Murphy and Vriesenga (2004) observed at the origin of the *Journal of School Leadership*: The first issues were heavily concerned with preparation issues, but as research rigor grew, preparation articles declined.
3. The UCEA/LTEL-SIG Taskforce on Evaluating Leadership Preparation Programs has gone through a number of name iterations in the literature. For example, it was originally the Ad Hoc Committee on Evaluating the Effectiveness of Educational Leadership Preparation (all within the SIG), then with the formal UCEA/TEA-SIG joint sponsorship it took on that prefix and finally morphed into the current name.
4. Several other individuals and groups have pursued programmatic research in leadership preparation related areas: internships and mentoring, John Daresh; cohort delivery models, Bruce Barnett, Margaret Basom, Diane Yerkes, and Cynthia Norris; student learning during preparation (in clinical experiences, cohorts, technology/online), Rodney Muth with various colleagues; women in educational administration, Charol Shakeshaft; and evaluation of preparation programs, Margaret Terry Orr, the leading creator of programmatic research with the context of the UCEA/LTEL-SIG Taskforce on Evaluation of Leadership Preparation Programs.
5. In terms of necessary resources, citing the 2002 Committee on Scientific Principles for Education Research report, Riehl and Firestone (2005) indicated that the three necessary "enabling conditions" are "time, fiscal resources, and public support for sustained scientific study" (p. 169). In fact, Firestone and Riehl's (2005) whole edited book presented ideas on research agendas and focal research methods to accomplish them that stand as a supportive companion to this volume.

References

Baker, B., Orr, M. T., & Young, M. D. (2007). Academic drift, institutional production and professional distribution of graduate degrees in educational administration. *Educational Administration Quarterly, 43*(3), 279–318.
Bogotch, I. E. (2002). Emerging trends in teaching and learning educational leadership. *Educational Leadership and Administration: Teaching and Program Development, 14,* 93–111.
Boyan, N. (1981). Follow the leader: Commentary on research in educational administration. *Educational Researcher, 10*(2), 6–13.
Boyan, N. J. (Ed.). (1988). *Handbook of research on educational administration.* New York: Longman.
Bridges, E. M. (1982). Research on school administrators: The state of the art, 1967–1980. *Educational Administration Quarterly, 18*(3), 112–33.
Boardman, G. (1975). A computer-based simulation model for feedback and analysis of the administrative in-basket exercise. *Educational Administration Quarterly, 11*(1), 55–71.
Broad Foundation & Thomas B. Fordham Institute. (2003). *Better leaders for America's schools: A manifesto.* Retrieved April 2, 2008, from http://www.edexcellence.net/doc/Manifesto.pdf
Browne-Ferrigno, T. (2007). Developing school leaders: Practitioner growth during an advanced leadership development program for principals and administrator-trained teachers. *Journal of Research on Leadership Education, 2*(3), 1–30.
Calabrese, R. L., Zepeda, S. J., Peters, A. L., Hummel, C., Kruskamp, W. H., San Martin, T. S., et al. (2007). An appreciative inquiry into educational administration doctoral programs: Stories from doctoral students at three universities. *Journal of Research on Leadership Education, 2*(3), 1–29.
Cambron-McCabe, N., Mulkeen, T. A., & Wright, G. K. (1991). *A new platform for professors of school administration.* St. Louis, MO: Danforth Foundation.
Campbell, R. F. (1965). The editor's desk. *Educational Administration Quarterly, 1*(1), iii.
Carver, F. D. (1973). An invitation from the editor. *Educational Administration Quarterly, 9*(1), 1–2.
Committee on Scientific Principals for Education Research. (2002). *Scientific research in education* (R. J. Shavelson & L. Towne, Eds.). Washington, DC: National Research Council & National Academy Press.
Cooner, D., Dickmann, E., & Dugan, J. (2006, April). *The impact of funding on leadership preparation: a research synthesis.* Paper presented at the annual meeting of the American Educational Research Association, San Francisco.
Danforth Foundation. (1999). *About the Danforth Foundation.* Retrieved April 12, 2008, from http://www.orgs.muohio.edu/forumscp/Danfrth.html
Danforth Foundation shifts focus, cuts staff. (2003, January 31). *Philanthropy News Digest.* Retrieved April 12, 2008, from http://foundationcenter.org/pnd/archives/
Erickson, D. A. (1979). Research on educational administration: The state-of-the-art. *Educational Researcher, 8*(3), 9–14.
Firestone, W. A., & Riehl, C. (Eds.). (2005). *A new agenda for research in educational administration.* New York: Teachers College Press.

Fishbein, S. J. (2000). *Crossing over: The roles and rules of the teacher-administrator relationship.* Unpublished doctoral dissertation, Hofstra University, Hempstead, NY.

Glatthorn, A. A. (2000). The principal as curriculum leader: Shaping what is taught and tested (2nd ed.). Thousand Oaks, CA: Corwin Press.

Goals 2000: Educate America Act, Pub. L. 103-227 (1994).

Goodlad, J. I. (1984). *A place called school: Prospects for the future.* New York: McGraw-Hill.

Griffiths, D. E. (1976). [Editorial policy statement]. *Educational Administration Quarterly, 12*(1), ii.

Griffiths, D. E., Stout, R. T., & Forsyth, P. B. (Eds.). (1988). *Leaders for America's schools: The report and papers of the National Commission on Excellence in Educational Administration.* Berkeley, CA: McCutchan.

Hart, A. W. (1990). [Editorial policy statement]. *Educational Administration Quarterly, 26*(4), 314.

Hess, F. M., & Kelly, A. P. (2005). *Learning to lead? What gets taught in principal preparation programs.* Cambridge, MA: Harvard University. (ERIC Document Reproduction Services No. ED485999)

Hills, J. (1975). The preparation of administrators: Some observations from the "firing line." *Educational Administration Quarterly, 11*(3), 1–20.

Immegart, G. L. (1977). The study of educational administration, 1954–1974. In L. L. Cunningham, W. G. Hack, & R. O. Nystrand (Eds.), *Educational administration: The developing decades* (pp. 298–328). Berkeley, CA: McCutchan.

Kottkamp, R. B., & Silverberg, R. P. (2000). Learning formal theory through constructivism and reflective practice: Professor and student perspectives. *Educational Administration and Leadership: Teaching and Program Development, 11,* 47–59.

Kuhn, T. S. (1970). *The structure of scientific revolutions.* Chicago: University of Chicago Press.

Levine, A. (2005). *Educating school leaders.* Washington, DC: The Education Schools Project.

Lindle, J. C. (2002). Editor's note: Ensuring the capacity of university-based educational leadership preparation: The collected works of the National Commission for the Advancement of Educational Leadership Preparation. *Educational Administration Quarterly, 38*(2), 129.

McCarthy, M. M. (1999). The evolution of educational leadership preparation programs. In J. Murphy & K. Seashore Louis (Eds.), *Handbook of research on educational administration* (2nd ed., pp. 119–139). San Francisco: Jossey-Bass.

McCarthy, M. M., Kuh, G. D., Newell, L. J., & Iacona, C. M. (1997). *Under scrutiny: The educational administration professoriate.* Tempe, AZ: University Council for Educational Administration.

Miskel, C. G. (1987). [Editorial policy statement]. *Educational Administration Quarterly, 23*(1), 2.

Miskel, C. (1988, October). *Research and the preparation of educational administrators.* Paper presented at the annual meeting of the University Council for Educational Administration, Cincinnati, OH.

Murphy, J. (1992). *The landscape of leadership preparation: Reframing the education of school administrators.* Newbury Park, CA: Corwin.

Murphy, J. (2006a). *Preparing school leaders: Defining a research and action agenda.* Lanham, MD: Rowman & Littlefield Education.

Murphy, J. (2006b). Some thoughts on rethinking the pre-service education of school leaders. *Journal of Research on Leadership Education, 1*(1), 1–4.

Murphy, J., & Seashore Louis, K. (1999). *Handbook of research on educational administration* (2nd ed.). San Francisco: Jossey-Bass.

Murphy, J., & Vriesenga, M. (2004). *Research on preparation programs in educational administration: An analysis.* Columbia, MO: University Council for Educational Administration.

National Commission on Excellence in Education. (1983, April). *A nation at risk: The imperative for educational reform.* Washington, DC: U.S. Department of Education.

National Commission on Excellence in Educational Administration. (1987). *Leaders for American schools: The report of the National Commission on Excellence in Educational Administration.* Tempe, AZ: University Council for Educational Administration.

National Policy Board for Educational Administration. (1989). *Improving the preparation of school administrators: An agenda for reform.* Charlottesville, VA: Author. (ERIC Document Reproduction Service No. ED310495)

Pounder, D. G. (2005). Letter from the editor. *Educational Administration Quarterly, 41*(1), 3–6.

Riehl, C., & Firestone, W. A. (2005). What research methods should be used to study educational leadership? In W. A. Firestone & C. Riehl (Eds.), *A new agenda for research in educational leadership* (pp. 156–170). New York: Teachers College Press.

Rusch, E. A. (Ed.). (2006). [Special issue]. *Journal of Research on Leadership Education, 1*(1).

Sage. (n.d.). *Journal of Cases in Educational Leadership.* Retrieved January 8, 2009, from http://www.sagepub.com/journalsProdDesc.nav?prodId=Journal201765

Schneider, G. T. (1998). [Editorial policy statement]. *Educational Administration Quarterly, 34*(1), 4.

Secretary's Commission on Achieving Necessary Skills. (1991, June). *What work requires of schools: A SCANS report for America 2000.* Washington, DC: U.S. Department of Labor.

Shavelson, R. J., & Towne, L. (Eds.). (2002). *Scientific research in education.* Washington, DC: National Academy Press.

Silver, P. F., & Spuck, D. W. (Eds.). (1978). *Preparation programs for educational administration in the United States.* Columbus, OH: University Council for Educational Administration.

Silverberg, R. P., & Kottkamp, R. B. (2006). Language matters. *Journal of Research on Leadership Education, 1*(1). Retrieved April 1, 2008, from http://www.ucea.org/JRLE/issue_vo1.php

Sizer, T. R. (1984). *Horace's compromise.* Boston: Houghton Mifflin.

Smylie, M. A., & Bennett, A. (with Konkol, P., & Fendt, C. R.). (2005). What do we know about developing school leaders? A look at existing research and next steps for new study. In W. A. Firestone & C. Riehl (Eds.), *A new agenda for research in educational leadership* (pp. 138–155). New York: Teachers College Press.

Young, M. D. (n.d.). *Journal of Research on Leadership Education: Aims and scope.* Retrieved January 8, 2009, from the University Council for Educational Administration Web site: http://www.ucea.org/JRLE/index.cgi

2

An Historical Review of Research and Development Activities Pertaining to the Preparation of School Leaders

MARTHA M. MCCARTHY AND PATRICK B. FORSYTH

Believe the past as well as doubt it.
—Weick, 1996, p. 302

Different Kinds of Knowledge

How are we to understand and interpret the history of changes in the preparation of school leaders? Why does leadership preparation have a certain content and process at a particular moment in time? No small part of the answer can be found in how educators function as part of a larger society and workforce. There are a number of ways workers in postagricultural societies are defined, exercise power, and influence their monetary compensation. Historically, various skilled and unskilled workers have organized and used the threat of strike to negotiate a living wage, benefits, and humane working conditions. In contrast, professional workers have used their claims to possession of expert knowledge, along with market forces, to procure autonomy in the workplace as well as personal, material benefit. Larson (1977) described professionalization as "an attempt to translate one order of scarce resources—special knowledge and skills—into another—social and economic rewards" (p. xvii). Larson, Johnson (1972), and other Marxist scholars have embraced a critical explanation of profession, one that we believe is at best incomplete.

In addition to the admittedly powerful drives toward survival and self-aggrandizement, there are other forces, altruism among them, that function as subthemes in the social process of professionalization. We think altruism, in itself a complex motive and construct, provides a productive way to examine the history of school leader preparation. The ability of occupations to sustain claims to professionalization is based on the extent to which their work is perceived as essential, exclusive, and complex (Elmore, 2006; Forsyth & Danisiewicz, 1985). The motives for launching such a claim can be self-interest, communitarianism, or commonly a complex synthesis. That is, both an altruistic motive, such as the commitment to provide engaging and useful learning opportunities for all children, and self-interest play a part in shaping how society, the education establishment, and education workers enact school leader preparation.

If we concede that the story of school leader preparation involves more than an elitist plot by individuals and the aggregate profession to acquire power and wealth, much of the historic debate about leadership preparation can be situated in the tension between those who believe that technical-rational knowledge is the bedrock for the profession and those who believe professional knowledge is based on what Schön (1987) has called "artistry." This dichotomy is fundamental to understanding the history, politics, and research on school leader preparation as well as other service occupations.

Oakeshott (1962) defined technical knowledge as an organized system of theoretical explanation and systematic evidence related to a set of phenomena comprising the focus of a professional practice, or in other words, codified, specialized knowledge. In the literature of educational leadership, Leithwood and Steinbach (1995), for example, referred to this knowledge as expertise dependent on propositional knowledge produced through scientific research. This knowledge and understanding can be acquired through individual study and traditional academic learning environments.

Schön's (1987) concept of artistry is consistent with Simon's (1973) notion of expertise growing out of experience: the learned capacity to discern quickly what is critical and germane from what is routine or pedestrian in professional work (Chase & Simon, 1973). Pattern recognition is part of this kind of expertise. Harris (1993) called the artistry domain "practice knowledge" and defined it as "know-how, artistry, insight, judgment, and connoisseurship . . . expressed only in practice and learned only through experience with practice" (p. 22). Generally, practice knowledge can be learned, but it is extremely difficult to teach. Cognitive psychologists disagree on exactly how this kind of expertise is acquired; however, there is general agreement that it requires a more active, constructivist, learning-by-doing set of experiences than conventional classrooms offer. Occupational preparation has long recognized the importance of practice knowledge, as for example, in the apprentice system of medieval Europe, the modern internship and residency requirements for many professions, and the technical education movement in this country.

There is an important third constituent of professions running parallel to the dichotomy described above and having to do with individual and collective valuation. Valuation has been conceptualized in a variety of ways and embraced by the professions from their earliest days and recently for educational leaders in the work of Willower and Licata (1997), among others. The Hippocratic oath held early physicians to high standards of care and dedication to patient well-being beyond all else. Modern-era trait and process sociologists who study professions have discussed valuation using the constructs *altruism* and *codes of ethics* (Ozga & Lawn, 1981). T. B. Greenfield (1988) has attacked "positivist" science as a basis for school leadership and would have valuation enter the professional model through a "new science of administration [that] must be free to talk about the values that power serves" (p. 134). He further has asserted, "We must seek a new definition of science in administration—one that can accommodate the view that values pervade the entire realm of administration and, indeed, constitute the proper focus of study" (T. B. Greenfield, p. 135).

The earliest professions incorporated socialization to benevolence and altruism into the preparation of their practitioners. The reform of professional preparation following Flexner (1910) gave way to the university's bias toward technical-rational knowledge production, in most cases ignoring or minimizing issues of valuation. In the near century since Flexner's work, the valuation feature of profession has been marginalized by the focus on science and has been problematized by the proliferation of occupations claiming to be professions and the lack of societal agreement on value questions. Still, the conceptualization of true professions clearly has retained a mandate for benevolent service in the interests of clients, and it is this enduring social belief in the protection of the vulnerable that prohibits equating profession with mere expertise, whether it be technical-rational or practice expertise. Occupations that claim professional status but are transparently motivated primarily by commercial interests are under public suspicion as professions.

In the theoretical model we introduce here, valuation enters the process in conjunction with influences, although a strong argument can be made that valuation should be part of both technical-rational knowledge (as argued by T. B. Greenfield, 1988) and practice knowledge, as fledglings are socialized by senior practitioners. It seems likely that valuation will remain problematic in our society and in the preparation of school leaders. Nonetheless, an understanding of the history; sources; process; and critical, contemporary, moral dilemmas inherent in valuation are certainly essential to the formation of school leaders (Starratt, 1991).

The fight for dominance between the two polar opposite sources of expertise described above has fueled reactive changes in professional preparation for more than a century in the United States. Within a constantly changing social context, the building blocks of professional preparation (induction practices, curriculum, program structure, pedagogical approach, and field components) wax and wane through the interventions of various social agents, advocates of technical-rationality, artistry, or valuation. In the field of educational leadership, as in other professional fields, the long-term debate has been between those who believe preparation of school leaders should be controlled by universities and those who believe it should be controlled by practitioners. Ostensibly, universities are disposed to emphasize technical-rationality, whereas practitioner-initiated preparation and professional development are disposed to emphasize artistry.

The argument should not be overstated, however. Even after the Carnegie Foundation enlisted Flexner to study the professions and the consequent closing of the proprietary medical schools after 1910, new university preparation of physicians included attention to the development of practice knowledge through internship and residency. However, to varying degrees, professional preparation hosted by universities tends to emphasize the esoteric and to underemphasize practice. Brubacher (1962) cited a most extreme example in which Oxford and Cambridge continued exclusively to teach Roman jurisprudence long after it ceased being the law of the land. Those wishing to practice law in the courts of Britain were prepared outside of its two most prestigious universities.

We should point out that the dichotomy discussed here has much to do with how knowledge, experience, and skill are derived, rather than content. This is not to deny that there are content debates within each of these sources of expertise, among them whether emphasis should be placed on managerial or instructional expertise in the preparation of educational leaders. The state of educational leadership preparation is never what academics think it should be, and it never perfectly meets the perceived needs of practitioners and the public.

In the next section, we examine the primary building blocks (variables) of professional preparation, the history of their use in this field, and any evidence about the relative importance and utility of these building blocks for producing competent practitioners (see Figure 2.1). Next, we turn our attention to the primary influences on the preparation of school leaders. These are of two types: contextual factors and agency factors, the latter usually consisting of organized forces having specific intentions to stabilize or change how school leaders are prepared. Our argument is that fluctuations in the degree to which school leadership preparation emphasizes technical knowledge or practice knowledge are the consequence of a complex array of contextual and agency factors. The tepid and intermittent efforts to value both of these sources of professional expertise simultaneously have been chronicled by many (Clark, 1988; Daresh, 1987; Forsyth & Murphy, 1999; Milstein, 1990). In the last section, we identify troubling knowledge gaps related to the effective preparation of school leaders. These gaps may function as a suggested research agenda aimed at the systemic and incremental improvement of the field. It is our hope and intention to interpret and explain the history of leadership preparation in such a way as to provide a basis for incremental, long-term reform and improvement of leadership preparation and the schools leaders serve.

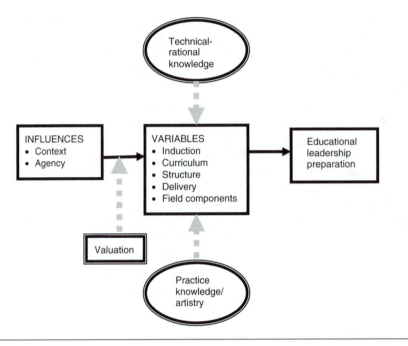

Figure 2.1 Model of educational leadership preparation formation.

The Primary Building Blocks of Professional Preparation: Variables and Evidence

Historically, the approaches and features of professional preparation have been limited in number. We believe five variables can be used to describe what practitioner preparation looks like in any given profession at any given time. Standardizing and categorizing the components of preparation allows for comparisons across time and promotes a theoretical understanding of how the various influences specifically affect professional preparation. Moreover, identifying specific variables permits us to accumulate empirical evidence related to their efficaciousness. The five variables are (a) induction, (b) curriculum, (c) structure, (d) delivery, and (e) field components.

Induction: Recruitment and Selection to Leadership Preparation

Recruitment and selection are concepts we use to examine how individuals are inducted into the field of educational leadership, or how they are prevented from induction. The state, the public, and the organized profession all have an interest in the competence of individuals who will practice vital professions. Competing political and economic interests beyond the question of practitioner competence also come into play.

Scholars who study profession and expertise as it relates to professional practice long have claimed that to prepare individuals for competent practice, the preparation programs must develop the candidates' requisite knowledge, skills, and dispositions; must recruit and admit those who already possess the requisite qualifications; or must use some combination of selection and preparation. The most critical questions to be answered, then, are what knowledge, skills, and dispositions are required for minimal competent practice, and what selection and preparatory activities most certainly will produce individuals with the requisite attributes?

If the answer to the first question were uncontested, the answer to the second question at least would be discernable through a systematic research program. However, the answer to the first question is not so obvious; moreover, recent critics have argued that the essential work of school leaders has changed rather dramatically in the last decade (Bottoms & O'Neill, 2001; Levine, 2005; Murphy, 1999c), contributing to the absence of consensus about the essential work of school leaders and the difficulty of selecting appropriate candidates.

We have not found comprehensive, systematic research examining the recruitment and admission of school leaders to preparation programs, but occasional observations and data can be found in the literature. Achilles (1988) noted, "Future leaders tend to self-select into preparation programs; there is little attempt to recruit selectively or to screen vigorously for the programs" (p. 44). Murphy (1992, 1999c, 2006) has concurred that the absence of sound recruitment practices remains a very serious problem. If recruitment has become more evident in recent years, it may be partly because of increased competition to fill seats in the expanding numbers of regional college and entrepreneurial preparation programs, along with efforts to achieve diversity, rather than a commitment to select recruits more carefully. Instead, recruitment practices may well be contributing to what Levine (2005) has called "a race to the bottom" (p. 24).

Although there has been some movement toward cooperative recruitment efforts between universities and school districts, the Institute for Educational Leadership found in 2000 that "only 27 percent of school districts reported having a program to recruit or prepare aspiring principals" (p. 9). Thus, with the caution that systematic analysis of recruitment appears absent, it seems that universities, states, and school districts do little to recruit individuals to school leadership careers (Björk & Murphy, 2005).

There is only slightly more information on the quality of recruits. In 1966, McIntyre charged, "The average student of educational administration is so far below the average student in most other fields, in mental ability and general academic performance, that the situation is little short of being a national scandal" (p. 17). Silver's 1978 study found that school leader preparation rejection rates were very low, approximately 12% for master's students, 14% for 6th-year students, and 25% for doctoral students. Ten years later, Achilles (1988) concurred: "Seldom are persons denied admission to or 'successful' exit from leader preparation programs" (p. 44).

Griffiths, Stout, and Forsyth (1988) reported comparative Graduate Record Examination (GRE) data on those who specified educational administration as their intended career, as did Levine (2005). Comparing educational leadership candidates with others who took the GRE, during 1981–1984 educational leadership candidates scored 37 points below average on the verbal section and 71 points below average on the quantitative section. Levine cited data showing that in 2004 educational leadership candidates scored 46 points below average on verbal and 81 points below average on the quantitative section, both measures reflecting approximately a 10-point decline for educational leadership candidates compared to all others taking the GRE during the past 20 years. The performance of candidates could be overstated by these data, since some educational leadership applicants, especially those wishing to avoid having their quantitative skills tested, may take the Miller Analogies as a substitute for the GRE.

Keedy and Grandy (2001), claiming that excellent problem-solving and analytic abilities distinguish outstanding school administrators from their mediocre peers, argued that the GRE measures analytic abilities. Thus, they urged use of higher GRE scores in educational leadership admissions, noting that the scores of applicants to school administration programs continue to be lower than those of most other fields.

Tests like the GRE, of course, measure preparedness to do graduate academic work, which may not equate with potential in school leadership. Some have argued that the most successful leaders of human enterprises are not necessarily the most academically oriented (Bennis & Biederman, 1997). On the other hand, we have not seen arguments or data suggesting that school leaders should be selected from the pool of the academically inept. Universities admit individuals to graduate study, not the profession, and thus their interests are in assessing the likelihood of applicant success in graduate school, not school leadership. The assumption that success in educational leadership graduate study produces successful school leaders is at least as precarious as the parallel assumption about medical school graduation.

Duke (1992) has argued that admissions standards may have remained flexible because of the difficulty in recruiting more able candidates and concerns about recruiting minority candidates. For these and other reasons, some educational leadership programs are moving away from GRE scores in admission decisions. In a 2006 study of educational leadership preparation programs in Indiana, only 6 of 17 programs required designated GRE scores in their principal preparation programs (Black & Bathon, 2006).

Despite questions about the relevance of GRE-like tests, most concur that admission standards in educational leadership programs need more rigor. Cooper and Boyd (1987) have outlined what they believe are the consequences of low admission standards.

> First, it lowers the level of training and experience possible since courses are often geared to the background and intelligence of students. Second, "eased entry downgrades the status of the students in the eyes of the populace." Third, the candidates themselves realize that anyone can get in and that nearly everyone will get the license if he or she just keeps paying for credits. In part, this lack of rigor at entry reflects a lack of clear criteria for training or clear vision of what candidates and graduates will look like, and the realization that the graduate school experience itself is not very demanding. (p. 14)

This brings us back to the earlier stated problem of agreement on what knowledge, skills, and dispositions individuals should have before being admitted to preparation programs and prior to receiving administrative licenses. In sum, there is little systematic or comprehensive research on either recruitment or selection to school leadership preparation programs. All that is known is that school leader applicants appear to be less prepared to do successful, traditional graduate study than most graduate school applicants, and this preparedness appears to have declined in the past 20 years. As Cooper and Boyd (1987) have suggested, this fact does not appear to have negative consequences for graduation rates, since school leadership programs seem to have kept the bar low to meet the challenge.

Murphy (1999a) reported data on school leadership department chairs' perceptions of changes in recruitment and selection of candidates between 1989 and 1996. Although department chairs perceived more changes in the ways they recruited and selected candidates during this period, the changes were both small and quite variable across universities. In 2005, Björk and Murphy were less sanguine as they reported to the Centre for Education Management Research, "In general, [U.S.] candidates self-select into educational administration programs" (p. 13).

A study by Creighton and Jones (2001) examined the admission practices of 450 school leadership programs in the United States. They concluded that common admission practices focus on GRE scores, previous college grade point averages, and letters of recommendation. How these data were used varied considerably among programs. In a companion study by Creighton and Shipman (2002), professors of educational leadership were asked to express their beliefs about school leadership applicants that might predict successful and lifelong learning. Ironically, it was found that professors do not think letters of recommendation, undergraduate grades, or performance on the GRE, which are the most often-used criteria, are important indicators. Instead, professors pointed to cognitive skills and behaviors related to practice as the most important criteria predicting lifelong learning.

Some positive trends, in addition to the espoused need to use multiple admission criteria, seem to be gaining interest and acceptance (Hess & Kelly, 2005). It should be noted, however, that these trends are emerging without consensus on what school leaders should know and be able to do (see Murphy, 2003). First, there is greater interest in collaborating with school districts in the recruitment and selection process (Browne-Ferrigno & Shoho, 2002; Keedy & Achilles, 2001; Southern Regional Education Board [SREB], 2002). Crow and Glascock (1995) have reported an especially detailed demonstration project of such collaboration. In addition to collaborative efforts, some school districts have assessed their future needs and developed succession plans, under which they identify leadership candidates and provide experiences to prepare them for leadership roles. For example, with some foundation support, Boston runs a field-based leadership institute, and the district has an arrangement with the state to license institute graduates who do not already hold administrative licenses. Instead of school leaders self-selecting into university preparation programs, candidates in such grow-your-own programs are identified and prepared (at least in part) by their school districts. However, we found no research on the comparative quality or sustainability of these programs.

Despite little evidence of widespread and sustained implementation across university-based school leadership preparation, the chorus calling for greater selectivity in choosing candidates has been growing for some time. Starting with McIntyre (1966), continuing with various commentators and the NCEEA 22 years later (Cooper & Boyd, 1987; Griffiths et al., 1988), and becoming more strident recently (Levine, 2005; Murphy & Forsyth, 1999; Muth & Barnett, 2001; Pounder & Young, 1996), the press for selectivity nags the profession. These discussions are laced with the reasoning that selecting candidates on the basis of their preparedness to do graduate work alone is wrong minded. Less academic notions have been entertained, such as the possession of high energy, enthusiasm, and the capacity to persuade and communicate. Last, there is emerging interest in a much more diverse palate of selection assessments (Browne-Ferrigno & Shoho, 2002; McCarthy, 1999; Murphy, 1999c) that could measure capacity and skills more directly related to the identified successful practice of school leadership (Creighton, 2001; Crow & Glascock, 1995).

In summary, induction is a variable that has not varied all that much over the history of school leader preparation. Recruitment to the initial stages of leader preparation has been left to universities, which have shown little interest in their recruitment practices. Selection criteria, despite periodic calls for increased selectivity by blue-ribbon panels, foundations, and political reformers, seem to have been responsive to market factors rather than reform rhetoric.

Curriculum Content

Like student selection practices, the courses offered by most educational leadership units have been relatively stable since the 1970s and perhaps even earlier. There are reports, however, that some units are incorporating content grounded in new perspectives on leadership, teaching, and learning. Whether these changes eventually will influence the curriculum of preparation programs nationally remains an open question.

Historical Overview

Educational leadership analysts have documented various stages in the orientation of university coursework for prospective school leaders (McCarthy, 1999; Murphy, 1993a). In the 1950s, when separate school administration units were starting to be established independent of curriculum and instruction or secondary education, professors usually were recruited from the ranks of practice. These professors often taught primarily by anecdote and were faulted for having little interest in research or theory building (Hills, 1965; Marland, 1960). As a response, those interested in reforming leadership preparation shifted their attention from practice to expanding the educational leadership knowledge base, drawing primarily on the social sciences (Getzels, 1977; Griffiths, 1964).

This movement to infuse the social sciences into the curriculum and to develop a science of school administration stimulated a decade (1947–1957) of ferment in the field (Culbertson, 1965; Murphy, 1993b). Most activity was concentrated at a few universities and involved a small group of researchers, but the movement's focus on the social sciences eventually affected the curriculum and faculty hiring practices of many leadership preparation programs (Farquhar, 1977; W. D. Greenfield, 1975; McCarthy, 1999). The social sciences emphasis in educational leadership course-work and the desire to hire faculty who were discipline-based scholars rather than practitioners or generalists reached a high point in the early 1980s (Miklos, 1983; Nagle & Nagle, 1978; Newell & Morgan, 1980).

During the past quarter century, however, there has been a decline in the proportion of faculty who identify themselves as social scientists, and belief in the utility of the social sciences frameworks also has declined (McCarthy, 1999). Murphy (1990) observed that a major force contributing to calls for reform in educational leadership units has been increasing disillusionment with the useful-ness of the theory movement grounded in the social sciences, particularly an "overemphasis on the hypothetico-deductive approach and the concomitant failure to stress inductive approaches and to use qualitative lenses to examine organizational phenomena" (p. 284). An alternatiave explanation might include the observation that the ranks of educational leadership scholars were never graced by more than a handful of trained social scientists. Thus, inferior social science may have shaped a shaky platform for practice, one that eventually tumbled.

Criticisms of the educational leadership curriculum have been directed beyond the social sci-ences orientation and unsuccessful efforts to model arts and sciences degrees. Preparation programs have been faulted for giving insufficient attention to curriculum, instruction, and learning and to linkages between preparation and what administrators actually do on the job (Griffiths, 1988; Murphy, 2006). Courses have been referred to as banal and outdated, lacking clear focus or purpose, fragmented and overlapping, without a continuum of knowledge and skills, containing weak clini-cal components, lacking rigor, and unrelated to administrative roles (Achilles, 1984; Clark, 1988; Cooper & Boyd, 1987; Levine, 2005; Mulkeen & Cooper, 1989; National Governors Association, 1990; K. D. Peterson & Finn, 1985; Van Berkum, Richardson, & Lane, 1994).

At a number of universities, educational leadership course titles, and in many instances the topical areas addressed within courses, have remained essentially the same for four decades or more. Griffiths (1966) reported that doctoral programs in the mid-1960s followed the traditional core of basic courses in educational organization and administration, curriculum, supervision, finance, school law, research, educational psychology, history and philosophy of education, school plant, and personnel. This description still applied to many programs throughout the 1990s and into the 21st century (Levine, 2005; McCarthy & Kuh, 1997; Murphy, Moorman, & McCarthy, 2008; Pohland & Carlson, 1993).

The National Policy Board for Educational Administration (NPBEA, 1989) recommended that the curriculum of educational leadership preparation programs focus on societal and cultural in-fluences on schooling, teaching, and learning processes and school improvement; organizational theory; methodologies of organizational studies and policy analysis; leadership and management processes and functions; policy studies and politics of education; and the moral and ethical dimen-sions of schooling. Yet, of these content areas, only two—leadership and organizational theory—were among the seven most frequently reported content specializations of faculty members in 1994 (McCarthy & Kuh, 1997). Similar to findings in the 1960s, faculty in the mid-1990s most often listed leadership, law, organizational theory, the principalship, economics and finance, and supervision of instruction as their primary areas of specialization.

More recently, Murphy et al. (2008) reported that across 54 educational leadership preparation programs reviewed from 1993 to 2005, almost all entered a curriculum reform process by advan-taging the existing curriculum; there was little evidence of changes in course offerings. Also, this privileged curriculum in most instances did not match the respective program's asserted foundation, if there was one. For example, some universities stated that teaching and learning constituted the core of their educational leadership programs but rarely offered a course on student learning or exemplary instructional practices (Murphy et al., 2008). The researchers also found few preparation programs to be cohesive and grounded in principles of cognition or leadership.

However, Levine (2005) painted a slightly different picture of educational leadership course offerings. Based on a survey of principals, he reported that more than 80% of the respondents said they took the same nine courses in their principal preparation programs: (a) instructional leadership (92%), (b) school law (91%), (c) educational psychology (91%), (d) curriculum development (90%), (e) research methods (89%), (f) historical and philosophical foundations of education (88%), (g) teaching and learning (87%), (h) child and adolescent development (85%), and (i) the school principalship (84%). Most of these courses are similar to those cited in earlier studies, but the fact that the vast majority of respondents indicated that they had taken a course in teaching and learning conflicts with the recent findings of Murphy et al. (2008).

Levine (2005) further asserted that few of the 600 educational leadership preparation programs nationally provided a coherent and rigorous curriculum designed to provide principals and superintendents with the preparation they need. Contending that the curriculum usually consists of survey courses, he concluded that the intent is for students to meet minimum state licensure requirements rather than to lead schools effectively. Hess and Kelly (2007) recently reviewed courses taught in 31 programs and reported considerable consistency across types of institutions in course offerings. They found that less than 5% of the instruction focused on school accountability and improvement through data management, technology, or empirical research, which made them question whether leadership preparation is attuned to current needs in an era of accountability.

Notwithstanding the discrepancy regarding a few topical areas, studies over time for the most part have reported similar educational leadership course titles, subjects emphasized, and areas of faculty expertise. Moreover, there is some evidence that state licensure requirements encourage keeping courses the same and do not nurture cohesive programs centered on learning. Adams and Copland (2005) recently reported, "No state has crafted licensing policies that reflect a coherent learning-focused school leadership agenda" (p. 1). Also, Elmore (2006) has asserted that licensure is designed primarily to retain the existing actors in the preparation of school administrators.

Yet, course title stability does not necessarily mean that the content of individual educational leadership courses has remained the same. Similarities in course titles may obscure substantive changes in content. Some units may circumvent the time-consuming course approval process by offering new content under old course names and numbers (McCarthy, 1999).

Efforts to Redesign the Curriculum

Although most educational leadership programs appear to have remained relatively unchanged, some substantially have redesigned the content of their preparation programs based on a concept of leadership that shifts the focus from plant manager to educational leader. Since the early 1990s, some of the most active curriculum reformers in educational leadership units have focused on the centrality of student learning (Cambron-McCabe, 1993; Murphy, 2006; Wilson, 1993).

Doolittle and Jacobson (2003) reported that the promotion of transformational leadership requires the preparation curriculum to focus on altering the culture instead of making only superficial changes in instructional orientation. Analysts often mention that essential elements in redesigning the curriculum are a common vision of what constitutes desirable leadership preparation and a sense of community among faculty and students, who embrace a core set of values and are striving toward common objectives (Bennis & Nanus, 1985; Daresh & Barnett, 1993; Geltner

& Ditzhazy, 1994; Milstein, 1993; Murphy et al., 2008; Reitzug, 1989). For example, Jackson and Kelley (2002) studied six leadership preparation programs that were "identified by experts in the field as exceptional or innovative" and reported that these units were distinguished by having a clear vision that drives programmatic decisions (p. 197).

A few units have shifted the focus of the curriculum from an empiricist approach (see Atkinson & Hammersley, 1994) to a constructivist paradigm, emphasizing multiple perspectives to address complex school issues that include some nontraditional perspectives, such as the feminist perspective (Achilles, 1994; Cambron-McCabe & Foster, 1994; Marshall & Oliva, 2006; Milstein, 1993; Rusch, 2005). Advocates of changing to a constructivist paradigm have asserted that it empowers the learner by changing the focus from teaching to learning and from consuming knowledge to creating it (Schmuck, 1992; Wilson, 1993).

An emphasis on ethics is evident across programs reporting major curricular redesigns during the past 15 years; most of the revised programs include seminars or courses on ethics. In contrast to Farquhar's (1981) findings that little attention was being given to ethical issues in University Council for Educational Administration (UCEA) leadership preparation programs in the late 1970s, by the 1990s most UCEA programs were addressing ethics to some extent (Beck & Murphy, 1994; Murphy, 1993c). Increased emphasis on ethics received widespread support among educational leadership faculty surveyed in 1994, and unit heads concurred that the expansion of ethics instruction was a major curricular change in their programs within the preceding decade (McCarthy & Kuh, 1997).

Several of the redesigned programs give greater emphasis to the foundations of education in their core experiences than do traditional programs, and they give far less attention to technical topics such as management of school facilities (Cambron-McCabe, 1993; McCarthy & Kuh, 1997; Shakeshaft, 1993). Cambron-McCabe (1993) observed that some leadership preparation programs have moved "the social and cultural context of schools to center stage" (p. 161). Yet, despite these assertions, there is little, if any, research linking such foundational changes in the preparation program curriculum to more effective school leaders. Moreover, these content shifts may enhance practitioner claims that university-based preparation is far removed from everyday practice.

Related to the emphasis on cultural foundations is the trend for reconstructed programs to give more attention to cultural diversity and social activism (Maniloff & Clark, 1993; Murphy, 1993a). Some educational leadership professors are introducing students to the concepts of privilege, power, the ethic of care, spirituality, and related topics (see hooks, 2000; Marshall & Oliva, 2006; Noddings, 1984; Starratt, 1991) and are including authors from a range of ethnicities and backgrounds in their course readings (see Marshall & Gerstl-Pepin, 2005). This movement is being nurtured by the Leadership for Social Justice network of faculty members across educational leadership units nationally, which is committed to infusing social justice in leadership preparation programs and in prekindergarten through Grade 12 (preK–12) schools (see Marshall, 2004; Marshall & Oliva, 2006).

Another noticeable trend since the early 1980s has been for some faculty to encourage students to pursue qualitative approaches in conducting research (Denzin & Lincoln, 1994). Given that few educational leadership faculty are trained in sophisticated quantitative research design and statistical analysis, qualitative studies have been given more prominence throughout the curriculum in educational leadership programs (McCarthy & Kuh, 1997). However, the federal government's current emphasis in funding research is on quantitative studies (Delandshere, 2004; U.S. Department of Education, 2005). Debate continues about the merits of polarizing research into qualitative and quantitative approaches instead of allowing research questions to guide methods (Ercikan & Roth, 2006).

Since the late 1990s, a major curricular change has been the focus on standards-based preparation programs. In an increasing number of states, professional standards boards are requiring the curriculum of educational leadership preparation programs to reflect administrative standards that are tied to licensure. Indeed, by 2005, 46 states had adopted leadership standards for administrator licensure and preparation program approval (Sanders & Simpson, 2005). Universities usually are being asked to scaffold their initial licensure programs on the Interstate School Leaders Licensure Consortium (ISLLC, 2006) Standards for School Leaders, and 41 states specifically have adopted or slightly modified the ISLLC standards (ISLLC, 2006). About half of the states also are requiring administrative licensure candidates to pass examinations (Adams & Copland, 2005). The most commonly used test is the School Leaders Licensure Assessment (SLLA) developed by the Educational Testing Service (ETS) and based on the ISLLC standards; 16 states currently use SLLA (ETS, 2006). In addition, states are beginning to apply stringent outcome accountability measures to preparation programs, whereas program accountability traditionally has been weak across most states (Murphy, 2006).

Although many educational leadership programs are purported to have become standards based and even document which standards each course addresses, it is debatable whether the actual substance of most courses has changed substantially. The standards movement definitely has altered the conversation, but whether the rhetoric has been translated into substantive curricular changes remains to be documented. Murphy et al. (2008) reported that the 54 programs they reviewed for the most part continue to emphasize the curriculum in place before the standards were adopted. Thus, instead of taking all existing courses off the table and actually building a standards-based program that focuses on increasing student learning, many educational leadership units have simply plugged the standards into existing courses. The critical need for research in this arena is revisited in the concluding section of this chapter.

Structure of Preparation Programs

As in other professions, the structural template for the preparation of school leaders has become synonymous with graduate degree programs offered by colleges and universities. Several degree configurations have been tried in this field over time, all in an effort to match preparation to the leadership and management needs of America's schools. The master's degree, EdD, and PhD continue to be strong; the Education Specialist (EdS) degree grew in popularity between the 1960s and 1980s and then waned (McCarthy, 1999). The master's and doctoral degrees are more universally recognized and seem to have gained more acceptance in the context of school leadership roles. The university as host for the preparation of school leadership practitioners has had immense and enduring effects on the structure of leadership preparation as it exists today.

Educational leadership did not emerge as a separate specialty until the 20th century and was even slower to have specific training or academic preparation attached to it. When the field did emerge, it was in the context of the modern research university, taking on the familiar forms of graduate study, including master's degrees, theses, doctoral degrees, and dissertations. However, unlike many other professions, no particular degree was designated as the required gateway for practicing specific school leadership roles, such as the principalship or superintendency (Murphy, 1992; Shulman, Golde, Bueschel, & Garabedian, 2006). In 1924, only two thirds of the nation's principals held any college degree, 1 in 5 had a master's degree, and 1 in 100 held a doctorate (Eikenberry, 1925). Even today, neither the master's degree nor the doctorate in educational leadership is universally required for school leadership roles from high school department chair to state commissioner of education, nor are advanced degrees universally attached to licensing practices across states. These degrees never attained the *sine qua non* stature of professional degrees in other fields.

One consequence of the lack of attachment of specific degrees to specific positions is that the curricula of the various degrees often lack focus and relevance for particular leadership positions.

Unlike many professions with a preparation tradition and degree specifically related to practice (e.g., the MD, JD, and DDS), universities offered advanced graduate programs in education that appeared to prepare candidates for research careers rather than the practice of school leadership. The primary requirement for obtaining the advanced degrees tended to be related to the production of original research. This misalignment might have been solved by the widespread adoption of the EdD degree developed at Harvard in 1920. However, as embraced across the nation, this degree became indistinguishable from the PhD (Osguthorpe & Wong, 1993; Shulman et al., 2006).

In a detailed study comparing research competencies required by the EdD and PhD degrees, out of nine competencies, only advanced inferential statistics (required by 89% of PhD and 71% of EdD programs) differed significantly between the two degrees (Osguthorpe & Wong, 1993). Unlike other professional degrees, education degrees continue to require dissertations and the coursework that leads up to this culminating research activity. As research–practice hybrids, education master's and doctoral degrees never gained universal traction as necessary qualification for practice or even state licensure, a condition unthinkable in most other professions. Calls to transform these degrees into high-quality, dedicated practitioner degrees have been largely ignored by academe.

A number of alternative degree configurations have been suggested. Goodlad (1990) recommended the establishment of a Doctor of Pedagogy (D Paed) as the only terminal degree in education, eliminating both the PhD and EdD. Arguing for the establishment of a new dedicated practitioner degree in education, the Professional Practice Doctorate (PPD), Shulman et al. (2006) estimated that only about one quarter to one third of doctoral graduates enters the professoriate (probably fewer for school leadership, where the doctorate increasingly is sought in candidates for the superintendency). The Carnegie Initiative on the Doctorate (CID), a cross-disciplinary project aimed at engaging higher education institutions in the reform of doctoral education, reported,

> The education departments that participated in the CID are now on a path of reflection and change. USC [University of Southern California] took the most dramatic path, distinguishing explicitly between the Ph.D. and the Ed.D. On the Ph.D. side, several departments have engaged in clear movement toward enrolling students full time, creating full-immersion and unequivocally research-focused programs. (as cited in Shulman et al., 2006, p. 27)

It is yet unclear how extensive the effects of the CID may be. In 1989, 163 institutions still offered the EdD, and 142 offered the PhD in education (Shulman et al., 2006). Osguthorpe and Wong (1993) pointed to several significant trends in the 1980s. First, nearly half of the doctoral-granting universities offered both the EdD and PhD. Second, research universities appeared to be moving away from the EdD as the only terminal education degree, preferring to offer both. Finally, the data revealed a significant increase in comprehensive universities offering the EdD as their only degree and a parallel decrease in research universities offering only the EdD. In 1994, across degree-granting educational leadership units, 92% offered master's degrees, and 54% offered either the EdD (44%) or PhD (28%) (McCarthy & Kuh, 1997). Further, 21% of the research institutions offered the master's, EdD, and PhD, whereas none of the comprehensive universities offered all three degrees.

One important question is whether the exclusive PhD in education now offered by many research universities is a full-fledged academic research degree as envisioned by some of the CID institutions or simply the continuation of the research–practice hybrid that has been the norm in many schools or colleges of education. Another important question is whether the EdD degree increasingly offered by comprehensive universities is an authentic practice degree or also a hybrid.

Levine (2005) recently has called for the elimination of the doctorate altogether in the preparation of school leaders. Instead, Levine recommended the creation of the Master's of Educational Administration (MEA), a new degree "rigorously combining the necessary education subject matter and business/leadership education" (p. 66). We seem no closer to consensus regarding which degrees should be offered for school leaders than was true several decades ago.

In summary, the paucity of evidence on the extant structures suggests that university-based school leadership preparation continues to be structured as graduate work at the master's and doctoral levels in a variety of institutions, ranging from research universities to regional state universities offering master's degrees as their most advanced degrees. Generally, none of the degrees awarded in educational leadership (MA, MS, MEd, EdS, PhD, and EdD) has been necessarily linked to distinctive career paths in practice (assistant principal, principal, central district office, superintendency, or state department service) or research (professor, school district research, and government or other institutional research). For the most part, these degrees are characterized by vestigial or full-fledged structural features (Griffiths, 1988) borrowed from traditional arts and sciences academic degrees (comprehensive examinations, theses or dissertations, and research methods courses) rather than structural features characteristic of professional preparation (full-time internships, rotations, residency, and mentoring). The academically focused approach to the preparation of school leaders may explain findings like those of Haller and Brent (1997), who compared principals having completed degrees in school leadership from master's to doctorates and found that "taken collectively, graduate programs in educational administration seem to have little or no influence on the attributes that characterize effective schools" (p. 225). This topic is addressed in more detail in the final section of this chapter.

It is quite peculiar that schools of education prepare school leaders and other graduate students in the manner of academic scholars, rather than as professional practitioners. It has been argued that, at the time education graduate study in universities developed, there was no credible technical-rational knowledge base in education, and the spirit of the age was turning against practice knowledge (Forsyth & Murphy, 1999). Seeking credibility, education programs borrowed from other university fields of study. Sociology, history, and philosophy had education branches that were incorporated into "educational foundations" programs. School leadership borrowed from finance, economics, management, and human relations. These borrowings did provide some credible content to the fledgling specialty, but in the process might have incorporated the ill-fitting structures attached to the study of arts and sciences.

Instructional Delivery Systems

As with curriculum and program structure, pedagogy or instruction in educational leadership preparation is as traditional as instruction in other university departments. In recent decades, however, the pedagogy of the field has been energized somewhat by innovations such as problem-based learning (PBL), cohort delivery, and experiments with design studios and collaborative research. Hallinger, Leithwood, and Murphy (1993), examining the problems of cognition inherent in the preparation of school leaders, identified specific conditions associated with successful instructional experiences. Such experiences (a) provide models of expert problem solving, (b) provide practice opportunities across a wide variety of problem types, (c) sequence increasingly complex task demands, (d) provide performance feedback on individual problem solving, (e) ensure participation in sophisticated group problem-solving processes, (f) encourage individual reflection on one's own as well as group problem solving, and (g) provide performance feedback on the contribution of the individual to group problem-solving processes. Many of the instructional delivery approaches being experimented with or revived during recent decades take these conditions into consideration.

Having graduate students matriculate through their programs as a cohort has become a commonplace structural feature of many, if not most, school leadership preparation programs. Cohort delivery usually involves clusters of students moving through a multiyear leadership preparation program together. Cohort students take many (if not most) courses together, collaborate on research and practice projects, and often enjoy enhanced social contact with fellow students and faculty. The cohort approach, because it is situated in an enduring learning group, facilitates many of the conditions associated with the cognitive development and skill acquisition cited above, especially the sequencing of complex task demands and the group aspects of problem solving.

Several commentators have cited a variety of social theories that together suggest cohort-style learning may be especially effective for school leadership students (Herbert & Reynolds, 1992; Leithwood, Jantzi, Coffin, & Wilson, 1996; Milstein & Krueger, 1993; Murphy, 1993c; Zander, 1982). Specifically, Barnett, Basom, Yerkes, and Norris (2000) as well as Teitel (1997) have noted that using cohorts results in a variety of benefits to students, including increased academic motivation, more social support, and greater likelihood of program completion.

Additional benefits for students participating in cohort structures may include enduring post-program contact and support as well as perceptions of colleagues that graduates of cohort programs are more successful leaders (Leithwood & Steinbach, 1995). In a study of faculty members who use and do not use student cohorts, Barnett et al. (2000) reported that faculties adopting the cohort model justify the approach based on "organizational efficiency and benefits to students' learning and development" (p. 274). In a study of faculty members who use and do not use student cohorts, Barnett et al. reported that faculties adopting the cohort model justify the approach based on "organizational efficiency and benefits to students' learning and development" (p. 274). Both cohort and noncohort program faculty tend to focus on how students are affected during their graduate studies rather than on how the cohort structure or its absence can affect students' later success in the workplace. What we do know for certain is that cohorts have been around for more than two decades, and no one is claiming that this structural feature is a panacea to address the defects in school leader preparation.

PBL gained attention in the 1990s as law and medical schools experimented with the approach (Evensen & Hmelo, 2000). PBL requires students to work in small groups solving significant and often complex problems. Unlike the case method, PBL is student centered. Proponents of PBL have argued that in addition to gaining mastery of problem finding, "students learn teamwork, administrative and project development skills, and problem solving" (Hart & Pounder, 1999, p. 12). Examining the cognitive underpinnings of PBL, Bridges and Hallinger (1997) noted that, as a process, it activates prior knowledge, creates realistic context, and encourages the elaboration of newly acquired knowledge.

If PBL is implemented as designed, it represents a significant departure from conventional instructional delivery. The roles of instructors and students are very different from those we see in typical university courses, generating some discomfort for faculty and possibly accounting for its low level of implementation among educational leadership programs. Despite some evidence of the method's effectiveness in medicine, for instance (Vernon & Blake, 1993), its widespread use in the preparation of educational leaders probably will depend on making professors familiar and comfortable with this strategy and the planning time it requires. How widespread its use is in educational leadership pedagogy remains unknown, but PBL seems to be garnering less attention at professional meetings in the field than was evident in the 1990s.

Another example of an instructional delivery system is one designed by the SREB (2002), entailing a 14-module curriculum that "engages school teams in applying research-based knowledge and processes to real problems that are creating barriers to comprehensive school improvement" (p. 15). The modules are sequenced and flexible enough to be used by school districts in a professional development series; in otherwise conventional preparation courses; and in workshops offered to school professionals through, for example, their state associations.

SREB requires facilitators to be trained in the use of the modules, thus reducing some of the stress associated with new delivery systems. A four-step delivery approach has been designed to include (a) a brief introduction to key concepts, (b) 6–8 weeks of application and reflection, (c) a few days of analysis, and (d) extended school-based application and portfolio development. One of the unique features of this approach is that school-site colleagues learn together and jointly apply new knowledge to their real-life educational problems. These features are highly consistent with the conditions associated with successful instructional experiences and cognitive theory discussed earlier.

Despite these and other glimmers on the horizon of instructional delivery innovation, Hess and Kelly (2005), in reviewing the evolving school leader preparatory structures, found little that is new in delivery systems among conventional university providers, district-based programs, and nontraditional providers. They claimed that universities and districts in general merely have tweaked traditional preparation, and for-profit providers are prevented from innovation in part by government policies related to licensure and competition from conventional providers.

There is a great deal of advice, but very little is known about the optimum instructional delivery system, including the appropriate sequencing of courses and the effectiveness of Web-based instruction versus conventional or PBL approaches. Certainly, more attention to what we know about the cognitive processes of learners and a commitment to connect preparation and practice (Glasman & Glasman, 1997) can steer us toward more effective instructional delivery.

Field Components

The graduated transition to independent practice is a major problem for many professions and historically has been seriously flawed in school leadership preparation (Milstein, 1993). Done adequately, this transition requires significant resources and time commitments in an arena that has been often viewed as an add-on to university-based school leader preparation. Few policy makers, professors, school districts, or leadership candidates themselves have been persuaded of the cost-benefit of intensive field preparation and mentored transition into practice.

In the past half century, various approaches to field learning have emerged and been tried. Most approaches can be sorted into two distinct types, face-to-face field learning and document-centered field learning. The first type, as suggested by its name, involves the field learner interacting intensely with expert practitioner leaders and researchers while learning to practice. This dynamic has the experts and field learners probing, questioning, exhorting, and critiquing the thought processes and proposed interpretations and interventions of the field learner as work progresses. It exposes the cognitive processes of both expert and field learners mutually and simultaneously. Examples of face-to-face approaches include full-time internships during school hours (Williams, Matthews, & Baugh, 2004), professional rounds (Elmore, 2006; Forsyth & Murphy, 1999), and engaged mentoring approaches (Browne-Ferrigno, 2004; Williams et al., 2004).

Document-centered field learning, as its name suggests, is field learning reviewed and critiqued after it is completed and reported. It often produces valuable practice experiences for field learners but suffers from the absence of dynamic exchange during the work process and provides only limited access to the situated cognitive processes of experts. Examples of document-centered approaches include portfolios (Barnett, 1995); project work; part-time internships during off hours; simulated field experiences; and practitioner mentoring translated as open-door, on-demand consultation. Most of these approaches focus on products as evidence of experience and learning.

Despite little credible research on field learning and the preparation of school leaders, Leithwood and Steinbach (1995) have provided a treatise on the acquisition of expertise from a cognitive perspective. They have included a summary of theory and research evidence on instructional conditions fostering the formation of expertise. These sets of instructional conditions are concerned with developing and refining (a) procedural schema to guide problem solving, (b) the role of social interaction in learning, (c) learning conditions approximating practice conditions, (d) increasingly automatic responses to routine problems, (e) flexible and mindful responses and knowledge use in the face of ill-structured problems, and (f) skills in reflection and metacognition.

As a consequence of their research, Leithwood and Steinbach (1995) were able to make two tentative claims relevant to field learning. First, they cited support

> for the special value of using authentic problems, small group, collaborative work on such problems, modeling effective processes, feedback to students, and a framework of components and subskills to cue the use of processes and to serve as a scaffold for problem solving. (p. 307)

Second, Leithwood and Steinbach claimed that simply stepping into an administrative role and learning from "on-the-job experience is a slow and unreliable way to improve one's problem solving expertise" when compared to a set of problem experiences carefully designed to develop practice skills and knowledge (p. 307). In the absence of other persuasive research, the above six criteria and findings can serve as a starting place to begin the analysis and study of field-learning approaches for school leaders. The categories of our simple taxonomy, face-to-face and document-centered learning approaches, differ significantly on these criteria.

Face-to-face approaches are more likely to generate a dynamic, cognitive environment characterized by intensity, immediacy of feedback and clarification, and broad and deep analyses of problems and intervention alternatives, coupled with the formation of decision scaffolding and patterns. These positive features also are fostered by the social structures in which they are embedded.

Document-centered field-learning approaches, focusing on products, are usually less intense, immediate, and interactive than face-to-face approaches. Thus, they are less likely to stimulate the same level of cognitive development. Unfortunately, their focus on products and artifacts rather than process makes them the favorites of licensing and accrediting groups like the National Council for Accreditation of Teacher Education (NCATE) and states whose program approvals are affiliated with NCATE.

Some would argue that PBL approaches utilized in otherwise conventional university courses or structured simulations bridge the gap between face-to-face and document-based field-learning approaches (Creighton, 2001). Yet, such compromises have been faulted; Williamson and Hudson (2001) have described how quickly anything less that a full-fledged internship disintegrates to maintaining minimal appearances of engaged field learning.

As with other building blocks of professional preparation, little credible evidence indicates which field-learning experiences foster the practice knowledge and skills related to expert school leadership. From existing scholarship, we are drawn to approaches based on the specific cognitive processes that are involved in school leadership, such as those reported by Leithwood, Seashore, Anderson, and Wahlstrom (2004). There is no dearth of advice, much of it contradictory, emanating from commissions, foundations, and business-sponsored reports about how field learning in school leadership preparation should be organized and conducted. However, we actually know very little.

Influences on Preparation

The five variable features of school leadership preparation described above have been influenced or affected by a number of social and economic contextual trends as well as by a set of agency factors, that is, institutions and sometimes informal groups with an interest and intention in changing or stabilizing school leadership preparation. The former set of external influences we cluster under the heading of *contextual factors,* as they are societal developments or forces to which school leaders must respond. The latter set we label *agency factors* because of their specific and conscious intent to shape or reshape professional preparation of school leaders. Educational leadership may be particularly vulnerable to contextual and agency forces because it encompasses large, eclectic, loosely defined knowledge sets from law to child psychology (Campbell, Fleming, Newell, & Bennion, 1987; Clark & Astuto, 1988; Forsyth, 1992; McCarthy, 1999; Murphy, 1999c).

Contextual Factors

Systematic investigation of the context of leadership preparation in general has been lacking, which is especially troubling when external conditions are rapidly changing and are having an increasingly significant impact on educational institutions (see McCarthy, 2002; Murphy, 2006). Indeed, Murphy (1999b) argued, "Institutional shifts in education are primarily a response to changes in the larger environment in which schools reside in the economy, the society, and the polity" (p. 405). Among significant contextual factors are economic and societal globalization, technological advances that have revolutionized communication and where education takes place, the shift from government control toward market control of education, and the changing demographics in the United States. These factors are highlighted below.

Globalization and Technological Advances

Few would dispute that schools are currently functioning in an increasingly global society and economy. Cheng (2003) has defined globalization as "the transfer, adaptation, and development of values, knowledge, technology, and behavioral norms across countries and societies in different parts of the world" (p. 9). Apple (2000) has noted that the politically conservative educational trend in the United States, embodied by higher standards and additional student testing and other accountability measures, is directly related to fear of international competition and the loss of jobs to other nations. Given the widespread use of outsourcing from the United States to other countries (Friedman, 2005), an understanding of global interdependence is essential.

It is imperative for schools to expose students to multiple perspectives and experiences globally, as children's lives will be linked to those around the world. Most analysts agree that knowledge is the central resource in a global society and economy (Davies, 2002). Barber (2004) observed,

> Education not only speaks to the public,… it is how individuals are transformed into responsible participants in the communities of the classroom, the neighborhood, the town, the nation, and (in schools that recognize the new interdependence of our times) the world to which they belong. (p. 10)

School leaders and other educators need to have a global perspective and international communication skills so they can provide appropriate guidance to teachers and students. Those students in school today will not have lifelong jobs with one company in a single locale, so they must learn to be creative, critical thinkers who can adapt to new environments. A study distributed by the Association of Supervision and Curriculum Development (1990) reported that effective school principals were more aware of the global complexities of education than were their less effective counterparts. Flanary and Terehoff (2000) have argued that school leaders in the United States must have opportunities not only to learn about schools and the roles of school leaders in other countries, but also to develop connections globally. Commentators have recognized the lack of research pertaining to the specific skills successful school leaders need to facilitate student learning in a global economy and have called for research to assess how well principals are prepared to play an ecological role in borderless environments and to engage in international networking so they can better understand the world in which they must function (Bottery, 2006; Cheng, 2003).

Connected to globalization are the incredible technological advances that have revolutionized how we communicate, conduct research, and receive information. These developments allow diverse parts of the world to be connected through distance education and are even changing the concept of *school*. Davies (2002) asserted, "The application of information and communications technology (ICT) has been the most powerful change agent in the educational world over the last 20 years" (p. 200).

During the past decade, almost all public schools (99%) have established Internet connections, with an average of one computer for every five students (DeSchryver, 2005). Furthermore, a number of virtual schools are currently operational, and a few states are experimenting with virtual school districts (see Boss, 2002; Hassel & Terrell, 2004). Even in some traditional school districts, policy makers are opting to connect families to schools electronically rather than to add space to school buildings. A recent survey sponsored by the Sloan Consortium documented that 700,000 K–12 students took online or blended courses during the 2005–2006 school year; online learning was predicted to expand substantially in the near future (Picciano & Seaman, 2007). Socialization is substantially different in the information age when students can interact with others at a distance more easily than they can with classmates at school.

The advances in technology, which provide unlimited and exciting opportunities, also may have some undesirable long-term effects. Whether the advances will unite or divide our society remains an open question (see Davies, 2002). Although educators are not usually driving the technological developments, they have an important role to play in shaping responses to new technologies at all levels of education. Thus, school leaders and those preparing them need to devote serious attention to this topic and its implications for leadership preparation and for education in general (Tirozzi, 2001).

The rapidly changing technological landscape has important repercussions not only for how we prepare future school leaders, such as the incorporation of distance education, Web-enhanced courses, and online programs, but also for the skills school administrators need to acquire to lead schools effectively in the current environment, such as using available instructional technologies, managing information systems to facilitate data-driven decisions, and communicating with students and parents electronically. Technological advances also mean that school leaders must take on new roles in setting standards for distributed education, student use of the Internet, and electronic confidentiality. In addition, they must be knowledgeable regarding Internet censorship concerns, cyber bullying, and numerous related issues. The extent that leadership preparation programs are being redesigned to address these issues is not known.

Shift From Government Control to Market Control of Education

Policy makers are giving considerable attention to marketplace models of schooling and their focus on competition to reform education. The school privatization movement has significant implications for school leaders and those who prepare them. Marketplace models of schooling range from state-funded private initiatives, such as voucher systems to enable children to attend private schools or to be educated at home, to public–private partnerships, such as private management of public schools and districts. The focus on the consumer and competition across schools represents a dramatic departure from the "near monopoly that government-run schools have enjoyed for more than a century in our nation" (McCarthy, 2002, p. 92).

Little research is available on the merits of various efforts to privatize education (Etscheidt, 2005), but much has been written supporting ideological positions. Advocates of marketplace models of schooling contend that poor parents deserve to have choices that the wealthy always have enjoyed and argue that in a competitive environment schools must improve or they will go out of business (see Chubb & Moe, 1990; B. Fuller, 2000; Whittle, 2005). Critics counter that opening education to the marketplace will doom the American common school, exacerbate economic and racial segregation, unconstitutionally entangle church and state, and turn the public schools into pauper schools that serve primarily disadvantaged and special-needs students (see Berliner, Farrell, Huerta, & Mickelson, 2000; F. C. Fowler, 1991; Goodlad, 1997; McCarthy, 2002; Molnar, 2001).

A political shift toward the right in the United States has increased acceptance of school privatization. Marketplace models of schooling, which might not have been considered by policy makers a quarter century ago, are now being adopted in state and federal laws. This political change is reflected in the federal No Child Left Behind Act of 2001 (NCLB, 2002) that encourages opening education to the marketplace and providing options for students who have been attending public schools that are not making sufficient progress in specified areas over time. In fact, a federally supported national voucher program has been proposed for the reauthorization of NCLB; this provision would allow low-income children in persistently underperforming public schools to attend private, including religious, schools at public expense (Paley, 2007; Schemo, 2006).

Although the U.S. Supreme Court has ruled that publicly funded voucher plans, under which state aid flows to religious schools, do not violate the Establishment Clause of the First Amendment (*Zelman v. Simmons-Harris*, 2002), voucher plans recently have not fared well in state courts. Several plans have been struck down as abridging state constitutional provisions prohibiting the use of public funds for private purposes or placing an obligation on the legislature to provide for a uniform system of free education (see *Anderson v. Town*, 2006; *Bush v. Holmes*, 2006; *Colorado Congress of Parents v. Owen*, 2004). Nonetheless, states continue to consider voucher plans. In 2007, Utah voters rejected the most comprehensive legislative plan to date, which would have provided vouchers, varying by family income, for all Utah students to attend private schools (Warchol, 2007). As additional plans are adopted and challenged in their respective state courts, we seem destined to have 50 standards regarding the legality of school vouchers instead of a national policy in this regard.

In contrast to the few statewide voucher plans that have been adopted, charter schools have been much more politically palatable because they remain public schools with some state requirements waived. In 1993 only 2 states had enacted charter school legislation; by 2005, the District of Columbia, 40 states, and Puerto Rico had such laws (Lake & Hill, 2005). Charter schools are accountable to their sponsors, which usually are the local or state boards of education or universities. Advocates view charter schools as drawing on the strengths of public and private schools, representing a good compromise (Buechler, 1996). Yet, some commentators view charter schools as a backdoor approach to vouchers and assert that they skim off the most involved families from public schools and do not provide appropriate programs for children with disabilities (Cobb, Glass, & Crockett, 2000).

The private management of public schools, including some charter schools, is increasing each year (Molnar, Morales, & Wyst, 2000). Education is a huge market, so it is not surprising that private firms increasingly are interested in reaping some of the benefits from education spending. The most influential school management initiative, the Edison Project, was conceptualized by entrepreneur Chris Whittle to provide radically different experiences from traditional schools by using multiage grouping, differentiated staffing, extensive use of technology, and a longer school day and year ("Edison Schools," 2004). Companies providing targeted instructional services, such as Sylvan, Voyager, Berlitz, Laureate, and others, increasingly are signing contracts with public schools to address student performance in targeted areas. These companies seem to face fewer hurdles and to be more acceptable to teachers' organizations than companies seeking contracts to manage entire schools.

Results of the few studies on the merits of voucher plans, charter schools, and private management of schools and districts are mixed. To date, no conclusive data have established that these alternative models are superior to regular public schools. In fact, a study released in 2006 by the U.S. Department of Education confirmed the results from an earlier study that charter school students performed slightly lower in reading and math on average than did their school district peers (Braun, Jenkins, & Grigg, 2006). Also, there have been mixed reports on the few operational voucher programs and on the benefits of private management of public schools (Etscheidt, 2005; H. Fuller & Caire, 2001; Gill, Timpane, Ross, & Brewer, 2001; Metcalf, 2004; Molnar et al., 2000; Witte, 1998). The only consistent finding across studies is that parents are more satisfied when allowed to select the school their children will attend (Metcalf, 2004; P. Peterson, Howell, & Greene, 1999).

Under marketplace models, individual schools will become more homogeneous, because families will select schools where students and staff share their characteristics and values. Some view this as healthy, asserting that such homogeneity will reduce conflicts about mission and goals within schools; each school will appeal to a limited segment of the population (Chubb & Moe, 1990). However, others are concerned that this development could threaten the U.S. national commitment to instill in youth respect for diversity in backgrounds, perspectives, and ideas (Apple, 2000; Goodlad, 1997). Privatization models emphasize competition and individual advancement rather than values traditionally attributed to public schools that are intended to advance the common good. Barber (1996) observed that whereas "consumers speak the elementary rhetoric of 'me,' citizens invent the common language of 'we'" (p. 243).

Despite a plethora of ideological assertions, we lack sufficient research on the impact and implications of the various strategies to privatize education that can guide policy makers in their deliberations on this critically important topic. If school privatization becomes dominant, the change in the nature and structure of education in our nation could be as momentous as the common school movement in the 1800s and could have substantial ramifications on the preparation of school leaders (McCarthy, 2005).

In a consumer-driven environment, school leaders must be prepared for different roles, which may necessitate a new set of skills. For example, school administrators will have to acquire more political and business acumen. School leaders also will face new pressures as traditional public schools compete for students with an expanded set of private schools and charter schools. Educational leadership preparation programs will be affected by the mounting school privatization movement because they will be expected to produce leaders who have the ability to market the salient aspects of their schools, engage in fund-raising activities, exhibit sensitivity toward preferences of parents, and demonstrate competence in other activities associated with a competitive environment. Yet, there have been few efforts to assess whether preparation programs have been altered to address the significant implications of the political shift from government control toward market control of education.

Demographic Changes

The shifting U.S. demographics also are affecting where school leaders will be needed and the types of skills they should possess. Sixty percent of the nation's public school students currently live in the South and West, and enrollments are expected to rise continually in these regions while they decline in the Midwest and Northeast (National Center for Education Statistics, 2006). More than two fifths of the students attend school in suburban areas (urban fringe), whereas 31% attend urban schools, and 29% attend school in towns or rural areas (Center on Education Policy [CEP], 2006). However, the racial percentages differ significantly by locale, with half of African American and Latino students, compared to 19% of White students, attending urban schools.

About 13 million children (1 in 6) live in poverty, according to the Children's Defense Fund (2004). More than one third of all students qualify for free or reduced-price school lunches, with

African American and Latino students far more likely than White students to attend schools where more than three fourths of the students are eligible for free or reduced-price lunches. Also, more than half of African American and Latino students nationally are enrolled in public schools where at least three fourths of the students are children of color (CEP, 2006).

The racial composition of public schools nationally, and especially in certain states, is changing rapidly. More than 4 out of 10 students nationally are children of color, which is predicted to climb to half of the students by 2020. The biggest change is in Latino students, who comprised 19% of students nationally in 2004 and are expected to comprise about one fourth of the students nationally by 2020. Students of color currently are in the majority in Hawaii, Texas, California, Mississippi, New Mexico, and Louisiana and in numerous large urban school districts across states. Indeed, children of color constitute a majority of students in two thirds of the nation's 50 largest school districts (CEP, 2006). In some districts, including Chicago; Houston; Los Angeles; Washington, DC; and Detroit, the student population is more than 90% children of color (Sable & Hoffman, 2005).

Despite significant attention being given to the changing demographics in schools, there is little research on how leadership preparation is being altered as a result. Riehl (2000) has argued that school leaders must be prepared to foster "new meanings about diversity," promote "inclusive school cultures and instructional programs," and build "relationships between schools and communities" (p. 55). Support for the previously dominant strategy of assimilation to address diversity in public education is waning as more attention is focused on cultural pluralism and valuing cultural differences (Baptiste, 1999). Yet, school leaders generally have been prepared to accept the existing social order, including its hierarchies, so that leaders who encourage social change may experience conflict (Parker & Shapiro, 1993). Some argue that to prepare school leaders to serve diverse populations, changes are needed in each domain of leadership preparation from finance to curriculum to assessment, and coursework needs to address conditions that pose barriers to administrators being innovative and socially transformative (Riehl, 2000). Those who study the increasing racial diversity in schools contend that school leaders must acquire skills in facilitating democratic discourse if all groups—professionals, parents, students, and the public—are to become invested in promoting teaching and learning that is culturally responsive for diverse students (Riehl, 2000; Rusch, 1998). In addition to personalizing instruction, teachers need support from administrators in examining their classroom practices for possible bias (Parker & Shapiro, 1993). To date, there are no systematic investigations of whether school leaders have acquired these skills to enable them to better serve racially and ethnically diverse learners and their families.

Also, little research has been conducted on how school leaders are facilitating the education of children with disabilities and how universities are preparing school leaders to address the special needs of these children. The number of children with disabilities has not increased dramatically in recent years, remaining about 14% of all students (CEP, 2006). Yet, the responsibilities placed on public schools to identify and serve these children have increased steadily (Wagner, Newman, Cameto, & Levine, 2005). School leaders face particular challenges in ensuring that these students are provided appropriate instructional programs and procedural protections in placement and disciplinary decisions.

Challenges also are posed by the fact that English language learners (ELLS) are increasing in public schools. In fact, there was a 65% increase in ELLs between 1993–1994 and 2003–2004 (National Clearinghouse for English Language Acquisition, 2006). In 2004, 10% of all public school students were ELLs. Also, about one fifth of school-age children have parents who are immigrants, either legal or undocumented (Capps et al., 2005). Almost three fourths of these children were born in the United States. Yet, widespread changes are not evident in school leadership programs to prepare administrators to work with ELLs.

Another demographic trend, the aging of American society, has different implications for public education. The percentage of the population over 65 is projected to rise from less than 13% in 2003 to 20% by 2030, with an accompanying decline in the growth of the working population (*Aging Global Population,* 2003). Unlike the impact of the shifting student characteristics, the graying of American society may reduce support for education as the significant and costly needs of senior citizens become more prominent. The increasing proportion of the citizenry over 65 has implications not only for Social Security benefits, but also for decisions on how to use the limited tax resources available. Some funds for education may be redirected to programs targeting the elderly.

The increasing transiency of the American population also presents significant challenges in efforts to sustain educational continuity (Tirozzi, 2001). In some schools a majority of the students enrolled in May started the school year elsewhere. All of these demographic changes and related developments have significant implications for who should become schools leaders, how they are prepared, and how they function in their roles. Yet, research pertaining to the preparation and support of school leaders to deal with these significant demographic shifts is scarce.

Agency Factors

Agency factors pertain primarily to organizations or institutions that intend to change or stabilize school leader preparation. Each has a history and a set of values with respect to preparation. Each also has a variety of tools it uses to exert influence on the constitutive variables discussed above.

The University and College or School of Education as Host Institutions

Historically, the university has hosted school leadership preparation and has exerted important direct influence by defining the work of professors and the plan of study for professional degrees. In the past the university decided what kind of knowledge was worthwhile and what kind of professorial scholarship and teaching should be rewarded. As organized structurally and culturally, the university leaned toward an emphasis on technical-rational knowledge. However, in the last decade the power to shape the reform agenda for school leadership preparation has shifted from universities, individually and collectively, to a coalition of foundations, government, and to a lesser extent the business establishment. This is in stark contrast to the late 1980s and early 1990s when the UCEA, the Holmes Group, and the NPBEA—at the time, all university-friendly and influential organizations—controlled that reform agenda.

Three watershed events, beginning with the publication of *Leaders for America's Schools* (Griffiths et al., 1988), chronicle the marked transfer of some power over school leadership preparation from universities to other agents. Griffiths et al.'s *Leaders for America's Schools* was a report by the National Commission on Excellence in Educational Administration (NCEEA), a blue-ribbon panel of political leaders, educational practitioners, and university leaders. This report can be described as a university-sponsored effort to heal itself. Hosted by UCEA, the NCEEA held hearings across the country, heard from every interested sector, and subjected its draft recommendations to multiple reviews. Griffiths, NCEEA chair, managed a democratic process that produced a practical reform agenda and touched on every aspect of preparation from purpose to curriculum and licensure.

During the NCEEA process, there was recognition that university-based school leader preparation could not effectively change without corresponding changes in the profession itself—its practice and its licensure. Thus, Griffiths et al. (1988) included among their most far-reaching recommendations the call for the establishment of the NPBEA that would especially concern itself with issues of licensure and certification. The first meeting of the NPBEA in 1988 brought together the executive directors of 10 national associations having critical interest in the preparation of school leaders. Of the 10, 3 were higher education associations (American Association of Colleges of Teacher

Education, National Council of Professors of Educational Administration [NCPEA], and UCEA), 6 were associations of practitioners (Association for the Study of Curriculum Development, Association of School Business Officers, National School Boards Association, American Association of School Administrators [AASA], National Association of Elementary School Principals, National Association of Secondary School Principals [NASSP]), and 1 was an association of state governments, the Council of Chief State School Officers. David Clark, then professor at the University of Virginia, was selected as the NPBEA's original executive secretary. Clark shepherded an aggressive effort to reform preparation, which included the publication of *Improving the Preparation of School Administrators: An Agenda for Reform* (NPBEA, 1989).

The agenda was developed by an NPBEA-appointed study group consisting entirely of professors and included several radical departures from then-current practice. Some recommendations were ill advised, such as making the EdD the sole route to legitimate practice of school leadership. The agenda was not well received, and the NPBEA reversed its approval following a contentious "Convocation of 100 Education Leaders" held in Charlottesville to consider the reform proposals. Shortly after the convocation, Clark resigned as executive secretary, and the leadership of the NPBEA aligned itself with the practitioner associations as Scott Thomson, recently retired executive director of NASSP, was named NPBEA executive secretary.

A third blow to university control over the reform agenda came after the NPBEA had written a proposal to the Pew Charitable Trusts to fund a project developing common and higher standards for state licensure. One of the NPBEA's member associations, the Council of Chief State School Officers, persuaded the foundation instead to award it the grant to do this work, rather than the NPBEA, effectively placing control and management of the project in the hands of representatives of state governments (Thomson, 1999) under the title of the Interstate School Leaders Licensure Consortium (ISLLC). A new era emerged with publication of the ISLLC standards and the ultimate adoption of these standards by NCATE. Reform of school leader preparation was now prescriptively delivered to university providers in the form of standards, licensure and accreditation requirements, and evaluation methods. Bureaucratic reporting of measured outcomes to states and accrediting bodies became the accepted evidence of reform, although no persuasive evidence that these accountability approaches have produced more effective school leadership has been produced thus far (Hess & Kelly, 2005).

The most recent examination of leadership preparation by Levine (2005) has reaffirmed the possible demise of university-based preparation of school leaders first sounded by Griffiths in 1988. Levine simultaneously found that preparation is not scholarly enough, too academic, too eclectic, not practical or useful enough, lacking faculty with school experience, and using too many former practitioners who do not value scholarship. It is difficult to establish a reform agenda when critics embrace contradictory goals. Levine does endorse a few preparation programs, like those of the United Kingdom's National College for School Leadership, which appear to be as eclectic as those in the United States, albeit incorporating more coherent processes for the preparation of school leaders. In a candid summary of its failures, Levine argued that educational administration preparation is

> a field rooted neither in practice nor research, offering programs that fail to prepare school leaders for jobs, while producing research that is ignored by policy makers and practitioners and looked down on by academics both inside and outside of education schools. As a field, despite some strong programs around the country, educational administration is weak in its standards, curriculum, staffing, the caliber of its student body, and scholarship. Its degrees are low in quality and inappropriate to the needs of school leaders. (p. 61)

For at least two reasons, the Levine report failed to advance the reform of school leader preparation. First, Levine repeated the criticisms of the past without providing a coherent explanation of the current state of affairs or directions as to where we should go. Second, like its many predecessors, the report exhorted, largely without evidence or persuasive argument.

It is interesting that Levine's (2005) analysis suggests that, faced with the dichotomy we introduced at the outset of this chapter, our field chose to embrace neither technical nor practice knowledge as its foundation. At this point in time, although universities continue to prepare the vast majority of school leaders (88%), universities collectively may not be able to retain control over school leadership preparation or to protect the field from evisceration in the name of reform inspired by political and commercial interests.

Consumers (School Districts and Educational Leadership Students)

The users of school leader preparation, prospective administrators and school districts, have not historically had a significant, organized effect on that preparation. Virtually all school leader preparation is graduate work done part time while students are holding full-time jobs as teachers or administrators. In some states, half of the graduates of these programs are not employed as school administrators in the 10 years after they receive their degrees and administrative licenses, suggesting that the school leadership master's degree is often used by teachers to advance on the district's salary schedule (Forsyth & Smith, 2002, 2004). Professors and blue-ribbon panels long have claimed that such students choose preparation programs based on low cost, convenience, and lack of challenge, thus exerting a kind of negative pressure and competition for nonrigorous, low-quality programs (Griffiths et al., 1988; Levine, 2005). Although not a formally organized influence, the nature of the students attracted to these programs has had a collective negative effect on sustainable improvement. There is much to suggest that many, perhaps most, consumers of this preparation do not really seek its improvement.

School districts, on the other hand, have become increasingly interested in the improvement of school leader preparation, particularly as state and federal accountability audits make school-by-school academic performance public and penalize schools for not reaching legislated levels of annual progress. Growing dissatisfaction with the quality of applicants to administrative positions has caused some districts to look elsewhere, that is, to seek out alternatively prepared or licensed candidates. As noted previously, other districts have mounted their own preparation programs, sometimes collaborating with universities or other institutions. It seems clear that school districts have a daunting task, that of meeting the school improvement expectations of parents, lay boards, and both state and federal governments. However, as institutions, they are not designed to provide preservice preparation of school professionals, and sporadic efforts to do this work generally have not been sustainable. A number of authors have pointed to some of the problems, especially in university-district collaborations: lack of continuity and stability, communication, power balance, and funding (Bullough & Kauchak, 1997; SREB, 2002).

Federal and State Governments

Even though education is not mentioned in the U.S. Constitution, the federal government has influenced educational priorities through its powers to tax and spend funds for the general welfare and its authority to enact legislation to implement federal constitutional provisions (U.S. Constitution, Art. 1). In fact, federal assistance started with the Northwest Ordinances that provided for the proceeds from some federal lands to be used for the maintenance of schools.

Yet, the major federal influence on public education started in the 1960s; federal legislation coupled with judicial rulings placed responsibilities on public schools to reduce discriminatory practices and provide compensatory services for students with special needs. When Congress enacted the Elementary and Secondary Education Act (ESEA) of 1965, federal aid to education tripled, and Title I of ESEA focused national attention on improving educational opportunities for economically and educationally disadvantaged children. The infusion of federal aid into public schools also affected higher education, and leadership preparation programs benefited from faculty hired using federal funds (Bowen & Shuster, 1986; Ladd & Lipset, 1975). Subsequent federal civil rights laws protected individuals against discrimination based on race, ethnicity, gender, religion, age, and disabilities and made some federal aid available to prepare school leaders to become change agents and to address injustices against vulnerable minority groups (McCarthy & Kuh, 1997).

In contrast to the indirect federal involvement in public education, all state constitutions place a duty on the state legislature to provide for a system of free public schools. States have an obvious societal, moral, and economic interest in providing citizens with the best possible education and protecting citizens and children from incompetent school leaders. Traditionally, state education agencies were fairly weak, and fewer than half the states required school administrators to be licensed until the mid 1900s. The AASA reported in 1939 that 33 states issued administrative licenses, but only 19 states required school leaders to be licensed by the state. By the mid-1950s, more than four fifths of the states required the completion of some graduate coursework for administrative licensure, and more than half of the states required completion of a master's degree (McCarthy, 1999). States slowly began using a variety of other tools to influence the preparation of school leaders, including test requirements, professional development policies, and various program accountability measures.

The National Commission on Excellence in Education's (1983) report, *A Nation at Risk*, asserted that the quality of education in the United States had declined significantly since the early 1960s and that this decline weakened the nation's economy. This report focused national attention on school reform and further emphasized that state governments, rather than the federal government, must lead school improvement efforts. During the 1980s, education became prominent on state political agendas; state education departments were strengthened; and many states enacted comprehensive educational reform packages mandating statewide testing at designated grade levels, performance-based school accreditation, longer school years, and other initiatives designed to enhance student learning (Bull, 1998).

At the same time, federal aid for public education was reduced; federal education assistance declined from its high of 9.8% of total education funds in 1979–1980 to 6.1% of the total in 1989–1990. Yet, some initiatives focusing on school leadership received federal assistance during this time. The Leadership Development Act established technical support centers in every state to provide inservice activities for practitioners and to disseminate promising school leadership practices (Moorman, 1989). Federal aid has started to increase again and by 2005 had climbed back to more than 8% of total education funds (NCES, 2006b).

As part of states' more elaborate educational accountability initiatives, many states have adopted professional standards for teachers and school leaders and established professional standards boards to handle licensure of educational professionals. Several states also have created leadership academies to provide professional development for school administrators. In addition, a few states have undertaken statewide assessments of leadership preparation programs. These assessments usually entail comprehensive self-studies, which are reviewed by external panels. Some state evaluations are low stakes, such as critical friends reviews providing programs feedback that they can use as they wish, whereas other assessments are high stakes in that they can result in some programs being closed or facing a moratorium on admissions until reforms are implemented (Murphy et al., 2008).

Despite the strengthened state role, the federal government still is influential in setting the education reform agenda. The ESEA has been reauthorized several times with slightly different emphases. The reauthorization in NCLB (2002) entails the most significant changes since ESEA was first enacted. NCLB represents a conceptual shift in school accountability from assessing school inputs to measuring school outcomes, primarily student performance on statewide tests in specified areas. The federal law requires states to strengthen accountability processes, using annual student testing based on academic standards. In short, it holds states, school districts, and schools accountable for the basic skills achievement of all students. NCLB requires states to report student achievement data by poverty, race, ethnicity, disability, and English proficiency to ensure that no group of students is left behind. Schools that do not meet their annual yearly progress toward the goal of 100% student proficiency in basic skills may face reorganization, with parents provided other educational options for their children.

Elmore (2006) has asserted that the NCLB was not adopted based on research and that credible documentation of its impact on student learning is not available. Other critics have faulted the NCLB, asserting that it narrows the curriculum, relies heavily on student testing, and contains unfunded mandates. They also lament the impossibility of most schools' meeting annual yearly progress for every student group (Linn, Baker, & Betebenner, 2002; Popham, 2003). Nonetheless, the federal government's emphasis on standards-based accountability with its reliance on proficiency testing is influencing state policies governing every level of education, including the preparation of school leaders.

Professional and Philanthropic Organizations

Many professional organizations are associated with education job categories and institutions, which individually, together in consortia, or in cooperation with foundations have exerted influence and pressure on what we have called the building blocks of professional preparation. These professional and philanthropic organizations have attempted to influence school leader preparation most often by (a) defining and clarifying the body of professional knowledge logically attached to school leadership; (b) establishing learning outcomes to guide school leadership preparation and standardize administrative licensure across states; (c) evaluating, critiquing, and promoting effective leadership preparation; and (d) providing opportunities for those who prepare school leaders to develop their knowledge and skills. Because some efforts to stimulate or mandate change have consisted of value and political advocacy unsupported by credible research, implementation has often been controversial and resisted or subverted.

Defining and clarifying the body of professional knowledge First, with respect to defining and clarifying professional knowledge, a few projects have had a broad impact on the field nationally (McCarthy, 1999). For example, the Kellogg Foundation in 1950 supported the Cooperative Program in Educational Administration at five universities recognized as national leaders and added three additional Cooperative Program in Educational Administration centers in 1951 to improve leadership preparation through multidisciplinary approaches (Gregg, 1969; McCarthy, 1999; Murphy, 1993b). Reports sponsored by the Cooperative Program in Educational Administration in the 1950s brought new substance to the field, replacing descriptive analyses with deductive theory and the behavioral sciences, and these ideas dominated preparation programs for more than 30 years (McCarthy, 1999). In this instance, the Kellogg Foundation subsidized a limited number of elite universities, which, acting with little coordination, advanced a social science curriculum for school leader preparation (Moore, 1964). Kellogg funded the university-based project instead of supporting a national commission proposed by the AASA that the association would have controlled.

UCEA, with Danforth Foundation support, began a knowledge development project in 1989 specifically aimed at defining necessary knowledge and skills for urban principals (Forsyth & Tallerico, 1993). Uniquely, the project developed nine problems of practice conceptualized around the primary work of principals identified by exceptional urban practitioners, for example "motivating urban children to learn," and integrated these problem foci with existing technical knowledge (Forsyth, 1999). Although this work had little immediate effect, probably because universities were unwilling to build scholarly specialties around practice rather than what have become traditional disciplines like organizational theory, some later reform approaches imitated this approach because of its obvious relevance to practice. UCEA's urban initiative was novel in its simultaneous emphasis on technical knowledge and practice knowledge.

In the 1990s, there was considerable debate about the core knowledge on which the curriculum is built, and professional associations were active in efforts to articulate the educational leadership knowledge base. Again, with the support of major philanthropies, two projects sponsored by the NPBEA and UCEA attempted to delineate the knowledge and skill base for school leaders (see Hoy, 1994; Thomson, 1993). In the preface of the NPBEA compendium, *Principals for Our Changing Schools,* Thomson asserted, "The knowledge and skill base of a profession should provide a platform for practice" and "must address core professional responsibilities so that persons qualifying for practice can fulfill the essential tasks of the profession in various contexts" (p. ix). This comprehensive publication was a collaboration of practicing school administrators and university professors. Supported by the Lilly Endowment and the Danforth and Geraldine Rockefeller Dodge Foundations, *Principals for our Changing Schools* (Thomson, 1993) was widely distributed and arrived on the scene as states were starting to develop standards for school leaders. Although subsequent projects reduced and combined the knowledge and skill domains from the original 21 domains, this document was influential in establishing the basic content.

The UCEA project identified leading scholars who developed taxonomies, overviews, case studies, and other materials depicting the nature and scope of knowledge in each of the following seven domains: (a) societal and cultural influences on schooling; (b) teaching and learning processes; (c) organizational studies; (d) leadership and management processes; (e) policy and political studies; (f) legal, moral, and ethical dimensions of schooling; and (g) economic and financial dimensions of schooling. McGraw-Hill became interested in this project, mainly because of its potential products and their fit with the publisher's experiment with electronic texts. For each domain, a taxonomy, overview of the domain, annotated bibliography, selected illustrative scholarship, and a salient case were published in the *Primis* system under the title, *Educational Administration: The UCEA Documents Base* (Hoy, Astuto, & Forsyth, 1996).

Scholars have debated the orientation of these projects. For example, some have claimed they gave insufficient attention to diverse perspectives, and a few even have questioned the wisdom of attempting to explicate the knowledge base at all (Bartell, 1994; Donmoyer, 1995; Gosetti & Rusch, 1994; Scheurich & Laible, 1995). Wilson (1993) took the extreme position that since learners must construct knowledge for themselves and be actively engaged in the process, efforts to articulate a knowledge base are misguided. Others, continuing in a neo-scientific paradigm, believe these periodic, stock-taking exercises contribute to important syntheses in understanding the knowledge base that leads to course corrections in preparation programs.

Establishing learning outcomes A second approach to influencing school leader preparation is through the mechanism of establishing learning outcomes to guide preparation and standardizing state licensure requirements. In 1987, professional associations joined forces with several foundations and a consortium of state education departments to advance this agenda. As described earlier, the ISLLC standards, developed under a grant from the Pew Charitable Trusts to the NPBEA and managed by the Council of Chief State School Officers, can be characterized as a key part of the most comprehensive nationwide effort to reform school leader preparation in the United States. Unlike previous and subsequent reform projects, ISLLC built a set of standards carefully and thoroughly tied to relevant research (Murphy, 2005).

Despite little evidence that the adoption of standards has driven meaningful change in the curriculum of preparation programs, the standards have influenced accreditation criteria. The Educational Leadership Constituent Council, with representation from practitioner organizations, was created to review educational leadership preparation programs for NCATE and to assess the conversion to standards-based programs. The ISLLC standards were incorporated in NCATE's 2002 revision of its standards for educational leadership programs. As with most professional program reviews, the Educational Leadership Constituent Council relies heavily on self-reporting by university programs, which can lead to little more than formal compliance with standards (e.g., a matrix displaying where the standards are addressed in traditional courses). Nonetheless, the standards movement has given states the leverage they need to require university-based school leadership programs to implement changes based on licensure requirements and program accreditation by associations such as NCATE. Some states, such as New Jersey and Delaware, have engaged in rigorous reviews of leadership preparation programs as part of their school improvement and accountability efforts. It is too early in this movement to predict whether this approach will have transformative effects.

Evaluating, critiquing, and promoting effective leadership preparation With respect to promoting effective school leadership preparation, several foundations and professional organizations have played prominent roles. The Danforth Foundation became dominant in supporting reforms in the preparation of school leaders across universities in the 1980s and 1990s (Cambron-McCabe, 1993). The Danforth principalship preparation program was offered by 22 universities from 1987 until 1991. This field-based program focused in part on recruiting talented people, and one of its goals was to increase minority and female representation among school leaders (Playko & Daresh, 1992). Candidates for the principal preparation program were classroom teachers identified by their school districts as having the potential to be outstanding school leaders. Many of the participating universities adopted common features in their principal preparation programs, such as student cohort groups, an emphasis on clinical experiences and field mentors, substantial collaboration with school districts, and a coordinated curriculum (Milstein, 1993).

The Danforth program for professors affected educational leadership programs at 21 universities 1987–1993 and was designed to create opportunities for faculty to share ideas with colleagues from other universities and to engage in comprehensive program development with the assistance of outside consultants (McCarthy, 1999). Many, if not most, of the educational leadership units that have been involved in substantial preparation program reforms since the 1990s participated in one of these two Danforth initiatives. As noted, Danforth support of the NPBEA also was critical in facilitating collaboration across professional organizations with an interest in the work and preparation of school leaders.

In 2001, UCEA established the National Commission on the Advancement of Educational Leadership Preparation to examine exceptional preparation and professional development programs and to create action plans for the improvement of leadership preparation nationally. This commission produced a series of papers as well as a special issue of the *Educational Administration Quarterly* (Lindle, 2002). In 2005, UCEA also launched the *Journal of Leadership Education* to broaden the opportunities to publish articles focusing on improvements in preparation programs.

The creation of the American Educational Research Association (AERA) special interest group, Learning and Teaching in Educational Leadership (LTEL, formerly Teaching in Educational Administration), in 1993 was significant in focusing attention on the reform of leadership preparation programs and encouraging research in this arena. Since 2000, LTEL has been sponsoring an ad hoc task force focusing on the evaluation of leadership preparation programs across states (Orr &

Pounder, 2006). Also, in 2004 LTEL, UCEA, the NCPEA, and Division A of AERA jointly created a task force to identify research on leadership preparation in seven domains.

In addition to support for leadership preparation reform initiatives managed by professional organizations and other institutions, some foundations have attempted to change the conversation regarding educational leadership preparation more directly. For example, the Danforth Foundation in 1991 issued a platform for preparing school administrators, declaring that leadership is an intellectual, moral, and craft practice and emphasizing hands-on experiences and clinical inquiry regarding practical problems (Cambron-McCabe, Mulkeen, & Wright, 1991). More recently, the Broad Foundation and Fordham Institute (2003) jointly sponsored a report, *Better Leaders for America's Schools: A Manifesto,* calling for more rigorous candidate selection and deregulation of licensure to give prospective school leaders more preparation choices. *Better Leaders* has called into question the assumption that there is requisite, general knowledge for school leadership or even effective ways to prepare school leaders, relying instead on ascribed characteristics like energy and determination, ad hoc skill building based on needs identified locally by school boards and school leaders, and military metaphors likening superintendents to field marshals (Broad Foundation, 2003). Thus, foundation influence on leadership preparation has extended beyond funding improvement projects to endorsing position statements, some, like *Better Leaders,* aimed at dismantling university-based preparation.

The Wallace Foundation is the primary funding catalyst in the current wave of reform efforts in educational leadership preparation, having supported research projects as well as policy initiatives in selected states and school districts. Wallace has funded a series of comprehensive studies to explore the types of leadership that promote student success and to investigate the elements of high-quality preparation programs for school principals (see Davis, Darling-Hammond, LaPointe, & Meyerson, 2005; Knapp et al., 2003; Leithwood, Louis, Anderson, & Wahlstrom, 2004). Wallace also created the State Action for Education Leadership Project through which some states are employing state policy to inform and strengthen leadership preparation, and recently Wallace funded two universities to provide a 5-year executive leadership program for key state-level and other top education leaders.

The Annenberg, Ford, Kauffman, and Wallace foundations also sponsored the recent Education Schools Project and its examination of school leader preparation in *Educating School Leaders,* known as the Levine Report (Levine, 2005), which has been discussed previously in some detail. Written and researched by academics, this report leaves room for universities in the future preparation of school leaders but also calls for greater involvement by school districts and practitioners; Levine warned that little time remains for conventional school leadership preparation to heal itself.

Providing opportunities for those who prepare school leaders to develop their knowledge and skills With respect to providing opportunities for professional development, several organizations have made it their mission to enhance the knowledge and skills of professors of educational leadership, perhaps most notably NCPEA and UCEA, and to a lesser extent AERA and AASA. NCPEA, which has no permanent staff, was formed in 1947 as a loose organization of educational leadership faculty members. Each year since, NCPEA has held a summer conference, which traditionally involved professors and their families meeting on university campuses but has evolved into an annual meeting resembling other job-alike conferences. These meetings and other NCPEA activities afford opportunities for professors to present ideas about leadership preparation and to engage in professional development activities.

UCEA historically was a consortium of elite universities promoting quality scholarship, program experimentation, and faculty development through its democratic governance, the Plenum, and project work to enhance the field. In recent years, UCEA has broadened its membership, welcoming some regional universities as members. UCEA has played a central role in efforts to reform university preparation of school leaders, and since 1989 has served the field through its annual conference that provides a forum for dialogue and research on preparation programs and other issues pertinent to school leadership. For decades, UCEA has demonstrated a commitment to equity concerns and more recently has assumed an advocacy role in connection with social justice issues.

Division A of AERA has been the professional home for scholars who study schools; how they work; and the significance of school leadership, management, and administration for their success. AERA historically has not taken an interest in preparation programs, but rather in advancing scientific knowledge that might serve as the technical knowledge practitioners could use. Like UCEA, Division A of AERA recently has shifted more of its attention to advocacy, social justice concerns, and equity. As noted, creation of the LTEL Special Interest Group has provided an AERA niche for those researchers interested in preparation program reform.

Some practitioner organizations, most notably AASA, have had leadership preparation and faculty development as a focus over time. For more than a decade AASA has included a *conference within a conference* for professors as part of its national convention for superintendents, board members, and other central office school leaders. This conference within a conference is coordinated by NCPEA and starting in 2007 began rotating among annual meetings of other practitioner organizations. It was held in conjunction with the NASSP convention in 2007. The NASSP also offers assessment tools that universities can use in identifying needs of individuals matriculating through their preparation programs and that school districts can use to design professional development activities (Tirozzi, 2001).

In summary, the agency forces we have discussed clearly have been designed to influence school leader preparation, but their motives are complex and not entirely self-serving. Universities have been accused of emphasizing theory and research only marginally relevant to the practice of school administration. Foundations, states, and practitioner associations have been accused of catering to a narrow set of business and military interests in their recent recommendations that seek an antidote to the claimed failure of the American educational system. The best vision for school leader preparation probably lies somewhere in the middle of these opposing forces. We next try to identify gaps in our knowledge that are especially troublesome in that they prevent us from persuading the multiple arms of the profession (practitioners, professional associations, states, and preparation programs) to act in concert and enthusiastically.

Gaps in our Knowledge About the Preparation of School Leaders

A review of research on the preparation of school leaders reveals more gaps than it does answers to questions regarding what constitutes best practices. A recent Wallace Foundation study focusing on preparing successful principals recognized the essential role that principals play in guiding successful schools but also acknowledged the knowledge void regarding the optimal ways to prepare and develop school leaders (Davis et al., 2005). For decades, leadership preparation has been criticized, and there have been numerous calls for more research on the effectiveness of university programs (Achilles, 1994; Griffiths, 1988; Murphy, 1992). Criticisms have become increasingly strident in the absence of data to combat assertions that preparation programs are inadequate or misdirected (see Levin, 2006; Levine, 2005).

Despite recent attention devoted to preparation program reform, significant changes have been modest at best. Murphy et al. (2008) concluded that many institutions have committed themselves to rebuilding their programs and are pumping considerable reform energy into program development. However, Murphy et al. concluded that across 54 educational leadership programs only a few are building exemplary preparation programs:

A second cluster is putting up a good fight, but often with, at best, very mixed results. The third and by far the largest number of institutions, even given the infusion of support and sanction, has been unable to gain traction on anything that could be thought of as real improvement. The great bulk of the programs appears unable to move beyond existing values (often implicit), processes, norms, structures, and systems. These conditions relegate improvement efforts to changes on the margin. (p. 19)

A few of the gaps in research on leadership preparation, which need serious attention to move the reform efforts forward, are discussed in this section.

Research on Educational Leadership Students and Faculty Members

Empirical research on educational leadership students across programs is noticeably lacking. A national database on the personal and professional characteristics of educational leadership master's and doctoral students would be enlightening (McCarthy, 1999). What are their educational backgrounds and work experiences, visions of schooling, and attitudes toward leadership and educational reform? Do these characteristics vary by type of institution where students are enrolled? Given some evidence that female graduate students are more research oriented than their male counterparts (Bean & Kuh, 1988; McCarthy & Kuh, 1997), has the increase in female educational leadership students altered the nature and caliber of dissertation research? Do male and female students differ as to professional backgrounds and goals, and has the change in gender composition altered the student culture of educational leadership units in significant ways? Has the racial composition of students changed over time, and does the composition vary by type of institution and by state? Are racial differences evident in professional experiences and attitudes toward education? Do graduates who plan to become faculty members rate their programs more favorably than do aspiring practitioners? To date, trend data on student characteristics and attitudes across programs are not available, even though calls for such data are not new (see McCarthy, 1999; Murphy, 1992).

Particular attention should focus on strategies to recruit intelligent and capable individuals to pursue graduate degrees in educational leadership. As noted previously, recruitment standards and practices have not been studied systematically, and such research across programs is sorely needed. Griffiths et al. (1988) urged educational leadership units to place greater emphasis on selective recruitment, noting, "There are no recorded examples of good dumb principals or successful stupid superintendents" (p. 290). Jacobson (1990) observed, "For too many administrator preparation programs, *any body* is better than *no body*" (p. 35). Murphy (2006) concluded that student recruitment and selection consistently lack rigor, with prospective candidates often self-selected. Yet, data on recruitment practices across institutions have not been collected systematically. Particularly useful would be data on strategies that programs have found successful in recruiting higher caliber students.

There has been more research on educational leadership faculty than on students, but additional studies on educational leadership faculty also would be instructive. Data for the last comprehensive study of educational leadership faculty were collected in 1994 (McCarthy & Kuh, 1997), although an investigation of the characteristics, activities, and attitudes of faculty members in the field currently is underway (Hackmann, personal communication, December 15, 2007). Studies are needed to track the research productivity of faculty members and to examine the types of projects they are pursuing and the relative influence of these projects on preparation programs, leadership practices, and the improvement of learning in U.S. schools (McCarthy, 1999). Are recently hired faculty more or less likely than their veteran colleagues to have administrative experience? Also, are the changing characteristics of faculty, such as the increase in women, affecting the structure and content of preparation programs and the nature of research conducted in the field? These and related questions about the composition and characteristics of educational leadership faculty need serious attention.

Research Across Institutions on the Structure and Content of Preparation Programs

Little has been done across educational leadership preparation programs to assess what is taught in specific educational leadership courses and how courses are aligned in graduate programs. Are new perspectives on leadership and the nature of knowledge and learning guiding revisions in preparation programs? What effects are schools of thought, such as postmodernism, poststructuralism, feminist theory, and critical race theory, having on curriculum development and pedagogy in educational leadership units? Are the notions of instructional leadership, school improvement, and democratic education guiding revisions in preparation programs? Is the movement to prepare leaders to advance social justice having an impact on the orientation of leadership preparation, and what are the ramifications of NCATE dropping social justice language from its accreditation standards? Also, are advocacy and identity politics squeezing out new contributions of normal science and methodologically decapacitating junior scholars (Levin, 2006)? Murphy (2006) has urged researchers to conduct comprehensive studies of the status of leadership preparation at regular intervals, similar to those published on the professoriate, noting that the last comprehensive study of the structure and content of preparation programs was more than a quarter century ago. The field needs credible research and a paradigm of practice so we do not continue to tinker with ineffective components of the curriculum.

Research on the Impact of Standards-Based Accountability

Similar to the lack of scholarship pertaining to the content and structure of preparation programs, there is a dearth of research on the impact of standards for school leaders. As noted, the standards movement, with its reliance on high-stakes testing, is the dominant school improvement strategy at all levels of education and is driving the curriculum in K–12 schools as well as teacher and administrator preparation programs (McCarthy, 2005). Passage of high-stakes tests is required for grade promotion, high school graduation, and teacher and administrator licensure across most states, and test scores are used to evaluate schools and university preparation programs.

The ISLLC (2006) standards for school leaders have garnered surprising support among policy makers and national and regional accrediting agencies. These standards have been praised for adding more rigor to leadership preparation and for shifting the focus from school management to the central responsibility of school leaders, which "is to improve teaching and learning" (NPBEA, 2002, p. 8). Critics, however, are concerned that the standards overlook important leadership characteristics such as cultural competence, provide few incentives to collaborate with school districts, and will reduce preparation to a single "approved" method, which perpetuates the status quo (English, 2001).

Many leadership preparation programs are purported to be standards based, and state leaders increasingly are demanding that programs move in this direction, but there is little evidence that many educational leadership units have actually recreated their programs based on the standards (Murphy et al., 2008). More commonly, it appears that units have attempted to incorporate the standards in existing courses without altering programmatic features in any meaningful ways.

And, even if some leadership preparation programs are truly standards based, data are not available to confirm or disprove that standards-based programs produce better school leaders. As discussed, many states have adopted passage of an exam as a condition of administrative licensure, and the most popular instrument is ETS's SLLA. Does aligning university admissions and curriculum with SLLA have a positive impact on the quality of preservice programs and the school leaders they prepare? Or, will use of a licensure test narrow the focus of preparation and downplay creativity and imagination, ethical dimensions of leadership, and important social justice perspectives (English, 2001)? Although there is some evidence that licensure tests disproportionately eliminate minority candidates (Flippo & Canniff, 2000; Gitomer, Latham, & Ziomek, 1999), critics' other contentions have not been substantiated or disproven. Standards-based accountability has far-reaching implications for the preparation of school leaders and deserves to be carefully investigated as to its impact on the caliber of programs, their graduates, and the schools their graduates lead.

Research Linking Preparation Programs to Success as School Leaders

In addition to evaluating the effects of standards-based accountability, the efficacy of leadership preparation programs in general needs to be assessed. Few people are championing the status quo, but considerable debate surrounds *how* and *what* to change in preparation programs (McCarthy, 2005). Which criteria are most important in judging preparation effectiveness, and what strategies should be used? Should we use backward mapping to identify elements of preparation that influence leader behaviors with the greatest positive effect on student learning as measured by performance tests? Should we focus on how leadership is distributed and teachers are empowered within the school? Should the emphasis be on social justice concerns, such as how leaders' actions nurture democratic schools and affect various groups of children and their families? Are there ways to assess leadership preparation that would incorporate all of the above and draw on various strategies and perspectives? Considering the complexities involved in conducting such studies, it is not surprising that limited assessments of preparation programs have been conducted to date. Murphy (personal communication, December 21, 2006) observed, "Until quite recently, the field has appeared to be genetically incapable of gaining traction on this matter."

There appears to be universal agreement that empirical documentation of the merits of leadership preparation is lacking and that much written about this topic cannot be considered research (Achilles, 1994; Griffiths, 1988; Levine, 2005; Murphy, 2006). In short, we do not have credible evidence to counter the allegations that the current preparation of school leaders is wrongheaded or that the significant costs associated with graduate education for school leaders (Haller, Brent, McNamara, & Rufus, 1994) could be better spent elsewhere. Most of the reports of leadership preparation program success have entailed self-reports from students or faculty, and a few studies have assessed coworkers' perceptions of school leaders. Educational leadership graduates traditionally have been less positive about their preparation programs than faculty have been (Heller, Conway, & Jacobson, 1988; House, Sommerville, & Zimmer, 1990). However, in the 1990s some case studies of redesigned programs included favorable faculty and student assessments of certain program features, such as student cohort groups, field mentors, PBL, field-based research, and policy-oriented alternatives to traditional dissertations (Clark, 1997; McCarthy, 1999; Milstein et al., 1993; Murphy, 1993c; Sirotnik & Mueller, 1993). These perception studies are useful in determining the level of satisfaction among those directly involved in preparation programs, but they are not sufficient to conclude that particular preparation program features will produce better school leaders (McCarthy, 1999).

Several studies using national data from the School and Staffing Survey developed measures of leader effectiveness and have related these effectiveness scores to the amount and type of graduate preparation. Disturbingly, these studies have not found a relationship between the amount of graduate education or major and perceived effectiveness of principals as instructional leaders (W.

J. Fowler, 1991; Haller et al., 1994; Zheng, 1996). A few other studies across states also have failed to find positive correlations between amount of graduate education and administrators' perceived effectiveness (Bauck, 1987; Gross & Herriott, 1965). Each of these studies has its own set of problems, and none has addressed the effect of specific elements of the preparation received.

Researchers only recently have begun to isolate particular components of preparation programs in perception studies. Leithwood et al. (1996) gathered data from principals who graduated from nine institutions involved in the Danforth Foundation principalship preparation program and from teacher colleagues of these graduates. Graduates highly valued their participation in group learning activities, internships, and mentoring experiences. Colleagues agreed that the graduates used effective leadership practices, rating highest the graduates' success in fostering staff development and setting school directions. Leithwood et al. (1996) concluded that the innovative program features in the Danforth principals' program were valued by graduates and enhanced how colleagues viewed graduates. More recently, Orr and Orphanos (2007) found a small but positive relationship between teachers' perceptions of leaders prepared in innovative leadership programs (e.g., those with rigorous selection, program focus on leadership for learning, standards-based content, etc.) and teacher engagement measures contrasted with data gathered on teachers in schools led by traditionally prepared principals.

One problem in trying to link leader preparation to school or student performance is the lack of agreement on which school and student outcomes to use in determining success. Slavin (1988) observed, "One major factor inhibiting systematic progress in education is the lack of agreement about what constitutes progress and what constitutes adequate evidence to support action" (p. 753). There is considerable dissatisfaction with using student test scores as the sole measure (Amrein & Berliner, 2002; Linn et al., 2002; Pringle & Martin, 2005), but nonetheless test results are the primary criterion currently employed in state accountability systems and in NCLB (2002).

Although consensus has not been reached regarding what constitutes administrative effectiveness, there is general agreement that a school leader's influence on student learning is an important consideration. Studies have documented that school leaders account for up to one quarter of the school's influence on student learning, with about 20% of the total variance attributed to school variables and the remaining 80% accounted for by student and family characteristics (Firestone & Riehl, 2005; Leithwood & Jantzi, 1999; Leithwood et al., 2004; Ross & Gray, 2006). Given the recent narrative syntheses and quantitative meta-analyses documenting the impact of school leaders on student learning (Cotton, 2003; Leithwood et al., 2004; Marzano, Waters, & McNulty, 2005), the sparse research linking leadership preparation to how program graduates perform their jobs is disappointing. Research is needed to evaluate more precisely the elements of redesigned preparation programs in relation to student performance in schools where the program's graduates are employed. In essence, data are needed to link empirically leadership practices that enhance student learning with specific elements of leadership preparation.

There are some promising signs regarding the evaluation of leadership preparation in recent initiatives supported by various professional associations, accrediting agencies, and task forces. For example, as noted, some states have engaged in critical friends reviews of their educational leadership preparation programs. Yet, there are only a few of these efforts, and they are not coordinated across states. Also, in some instances responses by educational leadership units to the critical friends' reviews are purely voluntary (Murphy et al., 2008).

Some states also recently have engaged in statewide audits or other reviews of leadership preparation programs, involving an analysis of documents and on-site visits that usually are overseen by a formal committee or task force. The advantage of this strategy is that state leaders can take a broader look at the licensure, preparation, and professional development of school leaders in light of state needs and current practices. Again, only a handful of states have engaged in such systematic evaluation efforts, but more states are considering statewide assessments as a vehicle to reform the preparation of school leaders.

Also, the task force launched by the LTEL Special Interest Group of AERA focuses on evaluating leadership preparation programs and linking preparation to leaders' performance in schools. One of its proposed projects is to conduct field studies of six schools in three different states to study the relationship between preparation, leadership practice, and school improvement outcomes (Pounder, Orr, & Black, 2006). More research along these lines is critically needed in the field.

Evaluation of Administrative Licensure Requirements and Various Alternative Approaches to Prepare School Leaders

State licensure as a warrant for minimum competence in a field never has been touted as ensuring success in a specific role. Indeed, the asserted purpose of licensure is to prevent entry of incompetent individuals into the profession and not to ensure that licensees will excel. However, research on the effectiveness of administrative licensure requirements in achieving this purpose is practically nonexistent. Organizations such as the Education Commission of the States have documented what is required for licensure across states, but little is known about how these requirements relate to job performance. The few studies that have been conducted have not shown a relationship between criteria for administrative licensure and competence as a school leader. For example, 46 states require teaching experience for an individual to become licensed as a principal (Adams & Copland, 2005), and intuitively such experience seems appropriate. Yet, data are not available to confirm that a designated amount of teaching experience influences the practices of school principals.

Licensure serves as the gatekeeper to professional practice as a school leader, but no studies have substantiated that current licensure requirements across states are linked to improvements in the caliber of school leaders. Indeed, some analysts have contended that the opposite may be true in that licensure requirements favor the status quo and deter some bright, innovate individuals from becoming school administrators (Adams & Copland, 2005; Elmore, 2006). The future of licensure practices in educational leadership should rest on evidence rather than on polemical claims and counterclaims.

A number of states are considering or adopting provisions that eliminate licensure requirements for school leaders, and a few states, such as Michigan and South Dakota, already have done so. Other states, including California and Iowa, are allowing alternative routes to leadership preparation in lieu of traditional university programs, although some of the alternatives are linked in various ways to universities. These alternative preparation routes, some totally online, are lucrative for entrepreneurs willing to develop consumer-friendly options. Levine (2005) declared, "The signs that the states have pulled back from their historic alliance with university-based educational administration programs are unmistakable" (p. 49). Considerable attention has focused on several major cities, including Chicago, Los Angeles, Miami, and New York City, which have hired noneducators to lead their public school systems. Also, the Knowledge Is Power Program trains principals to work in charter schools for at-risk students, New Leaders for New Schools was created in 2000 to recruit and train talented people to lead schools, and the Broad Foundation has established the Urban Superintendents Academy. In addition, there are numerous avenues for individuals to receive administrative licenses and graduate degrees in educational leadership through online programs, such as the University of Phoenix, and through a combination of online instruction and applied work in their school settings, such as the American College of Education.

With the technological ease of providing entire programs online, alternatives to traditional university preparation of school leaders are destined to increase. Those contemplating enrollment in university degree programs already are regularly receiving advertisements for virtual programs in which they can obtain the same degree from home in a very short period of time. Although some of these online programs offer high-quality instruction, personal interactions with faculty and classmates are often nonexistent. Levine (2005), Murphy (2006), and others have observed that we know very little empirically about the myriad of alternative leadership preparation strategies offered by school districts, professional associations, foundations, and private entrepreneurs, and we have no documentation as to whether they are more or less successful than traditional programs. Given our earlier analysis of the changing context of leadership preparation, we know that these alternatives to university leadership preparation and licensure are not a passing fad and must be addressed in a thoughtful manner.

Conclusion

Wallace Foundation President DeVita (2005) recently noted that although better training for school leaders "isn't the whole answer, it is surely a big part of it" (p. i). Few would disagree that effective school leadership influences student learning. Leithwood et al. (2004) noted, "There's nothing new or especially controversial about that idea" (p. 1). Yet, they also recognized that what remains elusive after decades of reform efforts "is just how leadership matters, how important those effects are in promoting the learning of all children, and what the essential ingredients of successful leadership are," causing those trying to increase the investment in school leadership to "rely more on faith than fact" (Leithwood et al., 2004, p. 1).

Never has it been more important to have leaders who understand teaching and learning, engage in critical analysis of current conditions, and are willing to question structures and deeply rooted cultural norms in the service of children and their families. It is not productive to become entrenched in polar opposite positions about what is needed; we must fashion opportunities for real collaboration among all interested parties. Creative tension is healthy, and we certainly are not advocating that those preparing school leaders all should embrace a single perspective. Yet currently, those adopting specific positions are not recognizing the legitimacy of other points of view; a review of reference lists of journal articles in our field verifies that those espousing particular perspectives cite like-minded colleagues (McCarthy, 2005). Debate is healthy, but we do need to reduce the fragmentation in our field so resources and energies can be directed toward conducting meaningful research that can help us respond to the many challenges and pressures school leaders face (Willower & Forsyth, 1999).

We can learn a great deal from the past but should not be bound by it. We can benefit from new approaches and ideas, but simply because they are new does not always suggest that they are better. Indeed, transformative leadership does not mean that we throw out all that has been done in the past or that we blindly embrace a new orthodoxy. Rather, it means that we critically assess the impact of everything we do and question our own assumptions and activities, drawing on multiple perspectives to expand our thinking. Our field is at a crossroads, and current decisions will affect generations to come. We need credible research on leadership preparation to guide those decisions.

We began this chapter by constructing a theoretical model to examine influences and variables that constitute and affect the preparation of school leaders in the United States. We also identified key intellectual forces and conflicting perspectives that problematize this field. Historically, the main forces buffeting the field have been the dichotomy between technical-rational knowledge and practice knowledge and artistry. Also, during the past 20 years, the need for readdressing valuation in the contemporary social context has gained momentum, although the approaches to and content of valuation remain controversial in their implications for school leadership preparation and practice. Levin (2006) has recently reminded us, "There is disagreement on which educational goals leaders should strive for and use as criteria for judging their effectiveness" (p. 40). Absent some consensus on these essential matters, the task of studying and designing effective school leadership preparation continues to be daunting.

References

Achilles, C. M. (1984). Forecast: Stormy weather ahead in educational administration. *Issues in Education, 2*(2), 127–135.

Achilles, C. M. (1988). Unlocking some mysteries of administration and administrator preparation: A reflective prospect. In D. E. Griffiths, R. T. Stout, & P. B. Forsyth (Eds.), *Leaders for America's schools: The report and papers of the National Commission on Excellence in Educational Administration* (pp. 284–304). Berkeley, CA: McCutchan.

Achilles, C. M. (1994). Searching for the golden fleece: The epic struggle continues. *Educational Administration Quarterly, 30,* 6–26.

Adams, J. E., & Copland, M. A. (2005). *When learning counts: Rethinking licenses for school leaders.* Seattle: University of Washington, Center on Reinventing Public Education.

Aging global population: Hearings before the Special Committee on Aging, United States Senate (2003, February 27) (testimony of Alan Greenspan).

American Association of School Administrators. (1939). *Standards for superintendents of schools: Preliminary report of the Committee on Certification of Superintendents of Schools.* Washington, DC: Author.

Amrein, A., & Berliner, D. (2002). High-stakes testing, uncertainty, and student learning. *Education Policy Analysis Archives, 10*(18). Retrieved October 10, 2006, from http://epaa.asu.edu/epaa/v10n18/

Anderson v. Town of Durham, 895 A.2d 944 (Me. 2006), *cert. denied,* 127 S. Ct. 661 (2006).

Apple, M. (2000). *Are vouchers really democratic?* (Education Policy Project No. 00-08). Milwaukee: University of Wisconsin, Center for Education Research, Analysis, and Innovation.

Association of Supervision and Curriculum Development. (1990). *Global education from thought to action: The 1991 ASCD yearbook.* Alexandria, VA: Author.

Atkinson, P., & Hammersley, M. (1994). Ethnography and participant observation. In N. K. Denzin & Y. S. Lincoln (Eds.), *Handbook of qualitative research* (pp. 248–261). Thousand Oaks, CA: Sage.

Baptiste, H. P., Jr. (1999). The multicultural environment of schools: Implications for leaders. In L. W. Hughes (Ed.), *The principal as leader* (2nd ed., pp. 105–127). Upper Saddle River, NJ: Merrill.

Barber, B. (1996). *Jihad vs. McWorld.* New York: Ballantine Books.

Barber, B. R. (2004, May). Taking the public out of education. *School Administrator.* Retrieved October 10, 2006, from http://www.aasa.org/publications

Barnett, B. G. (1995). Portfolio use in educational leadership preparation programs: From theory to practice. *Innovative Higher Education, 19*(3), 197–206.

Barnett, B. G., Basom, M. R., Yerkes, D. M., & Norris, C. J. (2000). Cohorts in educational leadership programs: Benefits, difficulties, and the potential for developing school leaders. *Educational Administration Quarterly, 36,* 255–282.

Bartell, C. A. (1994, April). *Preparing future administrators: Stakeholder perceptions.* Paper presented at the annual meeting of the American Educational Research Association, New Orleans, LA.

Bauck, J. M. (1987). Characteristics of the effective middle school principal. *NASSP Bulletin, 71*(500), 90–92.

Bean, J., & Kuh, G. D. (1988). The relationship between author gender and the methods and topics used in the study of college students. *Research in Higher Education, 28,* 130–144.

Beck, L., & Murphy, J. (1994). *Ethics in educational leadership programs: An expanding role.* Newbury Park, CA: Corwin.

Bennis, W. G., & Biederman, P. W. (1997). *Organizing genius: The secret of creative collaboration.* New York: Persius Books.

Bennis, W. G., & Nanus, B. (1985*). Leaders: The strategies for taking charge.* New York: Harper & Row.

Berliner, D., Farrell, W., Huerta, L., & Mickelson, R. (2000). *Will vouchers work for low-income students?* Milwaukee: University of Wisconsin, Center for Education Research, Analysis, and Innovation.

Björk, L. G., & Murphy, J. (2005). *School management training, country report: The United States of America.* Oslo, Norway: Norwegian School of Management.

Black, W., & Bathon, J. (2006). *Looking in the mirror to improve practice: A study of administrative licensure and master's degree programs in the state of Indiana.* Indianapolis: Indiana Department of Education.

Boss, S. J. (2002, January 8). Virtual charters: Public schooling at home. *Christian Science Monitor, 94*(31), 14–15.

Bottery, M. (2006). Educational leaders in a globalizing world: A new set of priorities? *School Leadership and Management, 26*(1), 5–22.

Bottoms, G., & O'Neill, K. (2001). *Preparing a new breed of school principals: It's time for action.* Atlanta, GA: Southern Regional Education Board.

Bowen, H., & Shuster, J. (1986). *American professors: A national resource imperiled.* New York: Oxford University Press.

Braun, H., Jenkins, F., & Grigg, W. (2006, August). *A closer look at charter schools using hierarchical linear modeling.* Washington, DC: National Center for Education Statistics.

Bridges, E. M., & Hallinger, P. (1997). Using problem-based learning to prepare educational leaders. *Peabody Journal of Education, 72*(2), 131–146.

Broad Foundation & Fordham Institute. (2003). *Better leaders for America's schools: A manifesto.* Washington, DC: Author.

Browne-Ferrigno, P. (2004). Principals Excellence Program: Developing effective school leaders through unique university-district partnership. *Education Leadership Review, 5*(2), 24–36.

Browne-Ferrigno, P., & Shoho, A. (2002, November). *An exploratory analysis of leadership preparation selection criteria.* Paper presented at the annual meeting of the University Council for Educational Administration, Pittsburgh, PA.

Brubacher, J. S. (1962). The evolution of professional education. In N. B. Henry (Ed.), *Education for the professions: The sixty-first yearbook of the National Society for the Study of Education* (pp. 47–67). Chicago: National Society for the Study of Education.

Buechler, M. (1996). Out on their own. *Technos, 5*(3), 30–32.

Bull, B. (1998). School reform in Indiana since 1980s. In B. Reese (Ed.), *Hoosier schools: Past and present* (pp. 194–217). Bloomington: Indiana University Press.

Bullough, R., & Kauchak, D., Jr. (1997). Partnerships between higher education and secondary schools: Some problems. *Journal of Education for Teachers, 23*(3), 215–233.

Bush v. Holmes, 919 So. 2d 392 (Fla. 2006).

Cambron-McCabe, N. (1993). Leadership for democratic authority. In J. Murphy (Ed.), *Preparing tomorrow's school leaders: Alternative designs* (pp. 157–176). University Park, PA: University Council for Educational Administration.

Cambron-McCabe, N., & Foster, W. (1994). A paradigm shift: Implications for the preparation of school leaders. In T. Mulkeen, N. Cambron-McCabe, & B. Anderson (Eds.), *Democratic leadership: The changing context of administrative preparation* (pp. 49–60). Norwood, NJ: Ablex.

Cambron-McCabe, N., Mulkeen, T., & Wright, G. (1991). *A new platform for preparing school administrators.* St. Louis, MO: The Danforth Foundation.

Campbell, R. F., Fleming, T., Newell, L. J., & Bennion, J. W. (1987). *A history of thought and practice in educational administration.* New York: Teachers College Press.

Capps, R., Fix, M., Murray, J., Ost, J., Passel, J. S., & Herwantoro, S. (2005). *The new demography of America's schools: Immigration and the No Child Left Behind Act.* Washington, DC: The Urban Institute.

Center on Education Policy. (2006). *A public education primer.* Washington, DC: Author.

Chase, W. G., & Simon, H. A. (1973). Perception in chess. *Cognitive Psychology, 5,* 55–81.

Cheng, Y. C. (2003, April). *New principalship for globalization, localization and individualization: Paradigm shift.* Paper presented at the International Conference on Principalship and School Management Practice in the Era of Globalization: Issues and Challenges, University of Malaya City Camus, Kuala Lumpur.

Children's Defense Fund. (2004). *Poverty.* Retrieved December 4, 2006, from http://www.childrensdefense.org/site/PageServer?pagename=Programs_Cradle_Poverty.

Chubb, J. E., & Moe, T. M. (1990). *Politics, markets, and America's schools.* Washington, DC: Brookings Institute.

Clark, D. L. (1988, June). *Charge to the study group of the National Policy Board for Educational Administration* (unpublished manuscript).

Clark, D. L. (1997, March). *The search for authentic educational leadership: In the universities and in the schools.* Division A invited address presented at the annual meeting of the American Educational Research Association, Chicago.

Clark D. L., & Astuto, T. A. (1988). Paradoxical choice options in organizations. In D. E. Griffiths, R. T. Stout, & P. B. Forsyth (Eds.), *Leaders for America's schools: The report and papers of the National Commission on Excellence in Educational Administration* (pp. 41–67). Berkeley, CA: McCutchan.

Cobb, C. D., Glass, G. V., & Crockett, C. (2000, April). *The U.S. charter school movement and ethnic segregation.* Paper presented at the annual meeting of the American Educational Research Association, New Orleans, LA. (ERIC Document Reproduction Service No. ED445414)

Colorado Congress of Parents, Teachers, and Students v. Owens. 92 P.3d 933 (Colo. 2004).

Cooper, B. S., & Boyd, W. L. (1987). The evolution of training for school administrators. In J. Murphy & P. Hallinger (Eds.), *Approaches to administrative training* (pp. 3–27). Albany, NY: SUNY Press.

Cotton, K. (2003). *Principals and student achievement: What the research says.* Alexandria, VA: Association for Supervision and Curriculum Development.

Creighton, T. (2001). Lessons from the performing arts: Can auditioning help improve the selection process in university administration preparation programs in the 21st century? In T. J. Kowalski & G. Perreault (Eds.), *21st century challenge for school administration* (pp. 101–112). Lanham, MD: Scarecrow Press.

Creighton, T., & Jones, G. (2001, August). *Selection or self-selection? How rigorous are selection criteria in education administration programs?* Paper presented at the annual meeting of the National Council of Professors of Educational Administration, Houston, TX.

Creighton, T. B., & Shipman, N. J. (2002). Putting the H.O.T.S. into school leadership preparation. *Education Leadership Review, 3*(3), 26–31.

Crow, G. M., & Glascock, C. (1995). Socialization to a new conception of the principalship. *Journal of Educational Administration, 33*(1), 22–43.

Culbertson, J. A. (1965). Trends and issues in the development of a science of administration. In W. W. Charters, Jr. (Ed.), *Perspectives on educational administration and the behavioral sciences* (pp. 3–22). Eugene: University of Oregon, Center for the Advanced Study of Educational Administration.

Daresh, J. C. (1987, February). *The practicum in preparing educational administrators: A status report.* Paper presented at the annual meeting of the Eastern Educational Research Association, Boston.

Daresh, J. C., & Barnett, B. G. (1993). Restructuring leadership development in Colorado. In J. Murphy (Ed.), *Preparing tomorrow's school leaders: Alternative designs* (pp. 129–156). University Park, PA: University Council for Educational Administration.

Davies, B. (2002). Rethinking schools and school leadership for the twenty-first century: Changes and challenges. *International Journal of Educational Management, 16,* 196–206.

Davis, S., Darling-Hammond, L., LaPointe, M., & Meyerson, D. (2005). *School leadership study: Developing successful principals.* Stanford, CA: Stanford Educational Leadership Institute.

Delandshere, G. (2004). The moral, social and political responsibility of educational researchers: Resisting the current quest for certainty. *International Journal of Educational Research, 41,* 237–256.

Denzin, N. K., & Lincoln, Y. (1994). *Handbook of qualitative research.* Thousand Oaks, CA: Sage.

DeSchryver, D. (2005, September 28). The digital pivot No. 1: Copyright. *The Doyle Report, 5.40.* Retrieved from http://www.thedoylereport.com/archives.aspx?page_id=spotlight

DeVita, M. C. (2005). Getting the facts on school leadership preparation. In S. Davis, L. Darling-Hammond, M. LaPointe, & D. Meyerson (Eds.), *School leadership study: Developing successful principals* (p. 5). Stanford, CA: Stanford University, Stanford Educational Leadership Institute.

Donmoyer, R. R. (1995, April). *The very idea of a knowledge base.* Paper presented at the annual meeting of the American Educational Research Association, San Francisco.

Doolittle, V., & Jacobson, S. (2003, April). *Tracking leadership preparation to practice and back.* Paper presented at the annual meeting of the American Educational Research Association, Chicago.

Duke, D. L. (1992). The rhetoric and the reality of reform in educational administration. *Phi Delta Kappan, 73,* 764–770.

Edison schools to serve more than 250,000 students in 2004–2005. (2004). Retrieved December 6, 2006, from http://www.edisonschools.com/news/news.cfm?ID=174

Educational Testing Service. (2006). *State requirements.* Retrieved November 12, 2006, from http://www.ets.org

Eikenberry, D. H. (1925). *Status of the high school principal* (Bulletin No. 24). Washington, DC: U.S. Government Printing Office.

Elmore, R. (2006, November). *Leadership and professional practice in education.* Mistifer Lecture at the annual meeting of the University Council for Educational Administration, San Antonio, TX.

English, F. W. (2001, April). *The epistemological foundations of professional practice: Do they matter? The case for the ISLLC standards and the national exam for administrative licensure.* Paper presented at the annual meeting of the American Educational Research Association, Seattle, WA.

Ercikan, K., & Roth, W. M. (2006). What good is polarizing research into qualitative and quantitative? *Educational Researcher, 35*(5), 14–24.

Etscheidt, S. (2005). Vouchers and students with disabilities. *Journal of Disability Policy Studies, 16,* 156–162.

Evensen, D. H., & Hmelo, C. E. (2000). *Problem-based learning: A research perspective on learning interactions.* Mawah, NJ: Erlbaum.

Farquhar, R. (1977). Preparatory programs in educational administration, 1954–1974. In L. Cunningham, W. Hack, & R. Nystrand (Eds.), *Educational administration: The developing decades* (pp. 329–357). Berkeley, CA: McCutchan.

Farquhar, R. (1981). Preparing educational administrators for ethical practice. *Alberta Journal of Educational Research, 27,* 192–204.

Firestone, W. A., & Riehl, C. (Eds.). (2005). *A new agenda for research in educational leadership.* New York: Teachers College Press.

Flanary, R. A., & Terehoff, I. I. (2000). The power of leadership in a global environment. *NASSP Bulletin, 84*(617), 44–50.

Flexner, A. (1910). *Medical education in the United States and Canada* (Bulletin No. 4). New York: Carnegie Foundation for the Advancement of Teaching.

Flippo, R., & Canniff, J. (2000). Teacher competency whitewash: How one high-stakes test eliminates diversity from the teaching force. *Connection: New England's Journal of Higher Education & Economic Development, 15*(2), 28–31.

Forsyth, P.B. (1992). Fury, flutter, and promising directions: Notes on the reform of educational administrator preparation. In E. Miklos & E. Ratsoy (Eds.), *Educational leadership: Challenge and change* (pp. 319–337). Edmonton, Alberta, Canada: University of Alberta.

Forsyth, P. B. (1999). The work of UCEA. In J. Murphy & P. B. Forsyth (Eds.), *Educational administration: A decade of reform* (pp. 253–272). Thousand Oaks, CA: Corwin.

Forsyth, P. B., & Danisiewicz, T. J. (1985). Toward a theory of professionalization. *Work and Occupations, 12,* 59–76.

Forsyth, P. B., & Murphy, J. (1999). A decade of changes: Analysis and comment. In J. Murphy & P. B. Forsyth (Eds.), *Educational administration: A decade of reform* (pp. 253–272). Thousand Oaks, CA: Corwin.

Forsyth, P. B., & Smith, T.O. (2002, April). *Patterns of principal retention: What the Missouri case tells us.* Paper presented at the annual meeting of the American Educational Research Association, New Orleans, LA.

Forsyth, P. B., & Smith, T. O. (2004, April). *Licensure and the practice of superintendency.* Paper presented at the annual meeting of the American Educational Research Association, San Diego, CA.

Forsyth, P. B., & Tallerico, M. T. (1993). *City schools: Leading the way.* Newbury Park, CA: Corwin.

Fowler, F. C. (1991). The shocking ideological integrity of Chubb and Moe. *Journal of Education, 173,* 119–132.

Fowler, W. J. (1991, April). *What are the characteristics of principals identified as effective teachers?* Paper presented at the annual meeting of the American Educational Research Association, Chicago.

Friedman, T. L. (2005). *The world is flat: A brief history of the twenty-first century.* New York: Farrar, Straus, & Giroux.

Fuller, B. (2000). *Inside charter schools: The paradox of radical decentralization.* Cambridge, MA: Harvard University Press.

Fuller, H., & Caire, K. (2001). *Lies and distortions: The campaign against school vouchers.* Milwaukee, WI: Marquette University, Institute for the Transformation of Learning.

Geltner, B. B., & Ditzhazy, H. E. (1994, October). *Shaping departmental community: Engaging individualism and collegiality in pursuit of shared purpose.* Paper presented at the annual meeting of the American Educational Research Association, Philadelphia.

Getzels, J. W. (1977). Educational administration twenty years later, 1954–1974. In L. L. Cunningham, W. G. Hack, & R. O. Nystrand (Eds.), *Educational administration: The developing decades* (pp. 3–24). Berkeley, CA: McCutchan.

Gill, B., Timpane, M., Ross, K. E., & Brewer, D. J. (2001). *Rhetoric versus reality: What we know and what we need to know about vouchers and charter schools.* Santa Monica, CA: Rand Foundation.

Gitomer, D. H., Latham, A. S., & Ziomek, R. (1999). The academic quality of prospective teachers: The impact of admissions and licensure testing. Princeton, NJ: Educational Testing Service.

Glasman, N. S., & Glasman, L. D. (1997). Connecting the preparation of school leaders to the practice of school leadership. *Peabody Journal of Education, 72*(2), 3–20.

Goodlad, J. L. (1990). Teachers for our nation's schools. San Francisco: Jossey-Bass.

Goodlad, J. L. (1997, July 9). Making democracy safe for education. *Education Week, 40,* 56.

Gosetti, P. P., & Rusch, E. A. (1994, April). *Diversity and equity in educational administration: Missing in theory and in action.* Paper presented at the annual meeting of the American Educational Research Association, New Orleans, LA.

Greenfield, T. B. (1988). The decline and fall of science in educational administration. In D. E. Griffiths, R. T. Stout, & P.B. Forsyth (Eds.), *Leaders for America's schools: The report and papers of the National Commission on Excellence in Educational Administration* (pp. 131–159). Berkeley, CA: McCutchan.

Greenfield, W. D. (1975, April). *Organizational socialization and the preparation of educational administrators.* Paper presented at the annual meeting of the American Educational Research Association, Washington, DC.

Gregg, R. T. (1969). Preparation of administrators. In R. L. Ebel (Ed.), *Encyclopedia of educational research* (4th ed., pp. 993–1004). London: Macmillan.

Griffiths, D. E. (Ed.) (1964). *Behavioral science and educational administration.* Chicago: University of Chicago Press.

Griffiths, D. E. (1966). *The school superintendent.* New York: Center for Applied Research in Education.

Griffiths, D. E. (1988). *Educational administration: Reform PDQ or RIP* (UCEA Occasional Paper No. 8312). Tempe, AZ: University Council for Educational Administration.

Griffiths, D. E., Stout, R. T., & Forsyth, P. B. (Eds.). (1988). *Leaders for America's schools: The report and papers of the National Commission on Excellence in Educational Administration.* Berkeley, CA: McCutchan.

Gross, N. C., & Herriott, R. E. (1965). *Staff leadership in public schools: A sociological inquiry.* New York: Wiley.

Haller, E. J., & Brent, B. O. (1997). Does graduate training in educational administration improve America's schools? *Phi Delta Kappan, 79*(3), 222–228.

Haller, E. J., Brent, B. O., McNamara, J. F., & Rufus, C. (1994, April). *Does graduate training in educational administration improve America's schools? Another look at some national data.* Paper presented at the annual meeting of the American Educational Research Association, New Orleans, LA.

Hallinger, P., Leithwood, K., & Murphy, J. (Eds.). (1993). *Cognitive perspectives on educational leadership.* New York: Teachers College Press.

Harris, I. B. (1993). New expectations for professional competence. In L. Curry & J. F. Wergin (Eds.), *Educating professionals: Responding to new expectations for competence and accountability* (pp. 17–52). San Francisco: Jossey-Bass.

Hart, A. W., & Pounder, D. G. (1999). Reinventing preparation programs: A decade of activity. In J. Murphy & P. B. Forsyth (Eds.), *Educational administration: A decade of reform* (pp. 115–151). Thousand Oaks, CA: Corwin.

Hassel, B. C., & Terrell, M. G. (2004). *How can virtual schools be a vibrant part of meeting the choice provisions of the No Child Left Behind Act?* (White paper). Washington, DC: U.S. Department of Education.

Heller, R., Conway, J., & Jacobson, S. (1988). Here's your blunt critique of administrator preparation. *The Executive Educator, 10*(9), 18–22.

Herbert, F. T., & Reynolds, K. C. (1992). *Cohort groups and intensive schedules: Does familiarity breed learning?* Unpublished manuscript.

Hess, F. M., & Kelly, A. P. (2005). An innovative look, a recalcitrant reality: The politics of principal preparation reform. *Educational Policy, 19*(1), 155–180.

Hess, F. M., & Kelly, A. P. (2007). Learning to lead: What gets taught in principal-preparation programs, *Teachers College Record, 109,* 244–274.

Hills, J. (1965). Educational administration: A field in transition. *Educational Administration Quarterly, 1*, 58–66.

hooks, b. (2000). *Feminism is for everybody: Passionate politics*. Cambridge, MA: South End Press.

House, J. E., Sommerville, J. C., & Zimmer, J. W. (1990, October). *Make haste slowly: The linkage between tradition, preparation, and practice*. Paper presented at the annual meeting of the University Council for Educational Administration, Pittsburgh, PA.

Hoy, W. K. (1994). Foundation of educational administration: Traditional and emerging perspectives. *Educational Administration Quarterly, 30*, 178–198.

Hoy, W. K., Astuto, T. A., & Forsyth, P. B. (Eds.). (1996). *Educational administration: The UCEA document base*. New York: McGraw-Hill.

Institute for Educational Leadership. (2000). *Leadership for student learning: Reinventing the principalship*. Washington, DC: Author.

Interstate Consortium on School Leadership. (2006, June). *ISLLC standards*. Retrieved November 12, 2006, from http://www.ccsso.org/projects/interstate_consortium_on_school_leadership/ISLLC_Standards/

Jackson, B. L., & Kelley, C. (2002). Educational and innovative programs in educational leadership. *Educational Administration Quarterly, 38*, 192–212.

Jacobson, S. L. (1990). Reflections on the third wave of reform: Rethinking administrator preparation. In S. L. Jacobson & J. A. Conway (Eds.), *Educational leadership in an age of reform* (pp. 30–44). New York: Longman.

Johnson, T. J. (1972). *Professions and power*. New York: Macmillan.

Knapp, M. S., Copland, M. A., Ford, B., Markholt, A., McLaughlin, M. W., Milliken, J., et al. (2003). *Leading for learning sourcebook: Concepts and examples*. Seattle: University of Washington, Center for the Study of Teaching and Policy.

Keedy, J. L., & Achilles, C. M. (2001). The intellectual firepower needed for educational administration's new era of enlightenment. In T. J. Kowalski & G. Perreault (Eds.), *21st century challenges for school administrators* (pp. 89–100). Lanham, MD: Scarecrow Press.

Keedy, J., & Grandy, J. (2001). Trends in GRE scores for principal candidates in the United States: A call for international debate on the intellectual quality of principal candidates. *International Journal of Educational Reform, 10*, 306–325.

Ladd, E., & Lipset, S. (1975). *The divided academy: Professors and politics*. New York: McGraw Hill.

Lake, R. J., & Hill, P. T. (2005). *Hopes, fears, & reality: A balanced look at American charter schools in 2005*. Seattle: University of Washington, National Charter School Research Project.

Larson, M. S. (1977). *The rise of professionalism: A sociological analysis*. Berkeley: University of California Press.

Leithwood, K., & Jantzi, D. (1999). The relative effects of principal and teachers sources of leadership on student engagement with school. *Educational Administration Quarterly, 35*, 679–706.

Leithwood, K., Jantzi, D., Coffin, G., & Wilson, P. (1996). Preparing school leaders: What works? *Journal of School Leadership, 6*, 316–342.

Leithwood, K., Seashore Louis, K., Anderson, S., & Wahlstrom, K. (2004). *How leadership influences student learning*. Minneapolis: University of Minnesota.

Leithwood, K., & Steinbach, R. (1995). *Expert problem solving: Evidence from school and district leaders*. Albany, NY: SUNY Press.

Levin, H. M. (2006). Can research improve educational leadership? *Educational Researcher, 35*(8), 38–43.

Levine, A. (2005). *Educating school leaders*. Washington, DC: Education Schools Project.

Lindle, J. C. (Ed.). (2002). *Educational Administration Quarterly, 38*(2).

Linn, R. L., Baker, E. L., & Betebenner, D. W. (2002). Accountability systems: Implications of requirements of the No Child Left Behind Act of 2001. *Educational Researcher, 31*(6), 3–6.

Maniloff, H., & Clark, D. (1993). Preparing effective leaders for schools and school systems: Graduate study at the University of North Carolina-Chapel Hill. In J. Murphy (Ed.), *Preparing tomorrow's school leaders: Alternative designs* (pp. 177–203). University Park, PA: University Council for Educational Administration.

Marland, S. P. (1960). Superintendents' concerns about research applications in educational administration. In R. F. Campbell & J. M. Lipham (Eds.), *Administrative theory as a guide to action* (pp. 21–36). Chicago: University of Chicago Midwest Administration Center.

Marshall, C. (2004). Social justice challenges to educational administration. *Educational Administration Quarterly, 40*, 5–15.

Marshall, C., & Gerstl-Pepin, C. (2005). *Re-framing and re-visioning education politics*. Boston: Allyn & Bacon.

Marshall, C., & Oliva, M. (Eds.). (2006). *Leadership for social justice*. Boston: Allyn & Bacon.

Marzano, R. J., Waters, T., & McNulty, B. A. (2005). *School leadership that works*. Alexandria, VA: Association for Supervision and Curriculum Development.

McCarthy, M. (1999). The evolution of educational leadership preparation programs. In J. Murphy & K. S. Louis (Eds.), *Handbook of research on educational administration* (pp. 119–139). San Francisco: Jossey-Bass.

McCarthy, M. (2002). The changing environment for school leaders: Market forces. In G. Perreault & F. Lunenburg (Eds.), *The changing world of school administration* (pp. 91–108). Lanham, MD: Scarecrow Press.

McCarthy, M. (2005). Prologue. In T. Creighton, S. Harris, & J. C. Coleman, *Crediting the past, challenging the present, creating the future* (pp. 1–4). Houston, TX: Sam Houston State University, National Council of Professors of Educational Administration.

McCarthy, M., & Kuh, G. (1997). *Continuity and change: The educational leadership professoriate.* Columbia, MO: University Council for Educational Administration.

McIntyre, K. E. (1966). *Selection of educational administrators.* Columbus, OH: University Council for Educational Administration.

Metcalf, K. (2004). *Evaluation of the Cleveland scholarship and tutoring grant program, 1998–2003.* Bloomington, IN: Indiana Center for Evaluation.

Miklos, E. (1983). Evolution in administrator preparation programs. *Educational Administration Quarterly, 19,* 153–177.

Milstein, M. (1990). Rethinking the clinical aspects in administrative preparation: From theory to practice. In S. L. Jocobson & J. Conway (Eds.), *Educational leadership in an age of reform.* New York: Longman.

Milstein, M. (Ed.). (1993). *Changing the way we prepare educational leaders: The Danforth experience.* Newbury Park, CA: Corwin.

Milstein, M., & Krueger, J. A. (1993). Innovative approaches to clinical internships: The University of New Mexico experience. In J. Murphy (Ed.), *Preparing tomorrow's school leaders: Alternative designs* (pp. 19–38). University Park, PA: University Council for Educational Administration.

Molnar, A. (2001, May 6). *School vouchers: The law, the research, and public policy implications.* Paper presented at the Hechinger Institute on Education and the Media, Columbia University, New York.

Molnar, A., Morales, J., & Wyst, A. van der. (2000). *Profiles of for-profit education management companies, 2000–2001.* Milwaukee: University of Wisconsin, Center for Education Research, Analysis, and Innovation.

Moore, H. A. (1964). The ferment in school administration. In D. E. Griffiths (Ed.), *Behavioral science and educational administration: The sixty-third yearbook of the National Society for the Study of Education* (pp. 11–32). Chicago: National Society for the Study of Education.

Moorman, H. (1989). The LEAD program at Age 2: Accomplishments and future directions. *Educational Considerations, 16*(2), 70–72.

Mulkeen, T. A., & Cooper, B. S. (1989, March). *Implications of preparing school administrators for knowledge-work organizations.* Paper presented at the annual meeting of the American Educational Research Association, San Francisco.

Murphy, J. (1990). The reform of school administration: Pressures and calls for change. In J. Murphy (Ed.), *The reform of American public education in the 1980s: Perspectives and cases* (pp. 277–303). Berkeley, CA: McCutchan.

Murphy, J. (1992). *The landscape of leadership preparation: Reframing the education of school administrators.* Newbury Park, CA: Corwin.

Murphy, J. (1993a). Alternative designs: New directions. In J. Murphy (Ed.), *Preparing tomorrow's school leaders; Alternative designs* (pp. 225–253). University Park, PA: University Council for Educational Administration.

Murphy, J. (1993b). Ferment in school administration: Rounds 1–3. In J. Murphy (Ed.), *Preparing tomorrow's school leaders: Alternative designs* (pp. 1–38). University Park, PA: University Council for Educational Administration.

Murphy, J. (Ed.). (1993c). *Preparing tomorrow's school leaders: Alternative designs.* University Park, PA: University Council for Educational Administration.

Murphy, J. (1999a). Changes in preparation programs: Perceptions of department chairs. In J. Murphy & P. B. Forsyth (Eds.), *Educational administration: A decade of reform* (pp. 170–191). Thousand Oaks, CA: Corwin.

Murphy, J. (1999b). New consumerism: Evolving market dynamics of the institutional dimension of schooling. In J. Murphy & K. S. Louis (Eds.), *Handbook of research on educational administration* (pp. 405–419). San Francisco: Jossey-Bass.

Murphy, J. (1999c). *The quest for a center: Notes on the state of the profession of educational leadership.* Columbia, MO: University Council for Educational Administration.

Murphy, J. (2003, September). *Reculturing educational leadership: The ISLLC Standards ten years out.* Arlington, VA: National Policy Board for Educational Administration.

Murphy, J. (2005). Unpacking the foundations of ISLLC standards and addressing concerns in the academic community. *Educational Administration Quarterly, 41,* 154–191.

Murphy, J. (2006). *Preparing school leaders: Defining a research and action agenda.* Lanham, MD: Rowman & Littlefield Education.

Murphy, J., & Forsyth, P. B. (Eds.). (1999). *Educational administration: A decade of reform.* Thousand Oaks, CA: Corwin.

Murphy, J., Moorman, H. N., & McCarthy, M. (2008). A framework for rebuilding initial certification and preparation programs in educational leadership: Lessons from whole-state reform initiatives. *Teachers College Record, 110,* 2172–2203.

Muth, R., & Barnett, B. (2001). Making the case for professional preparation: Using research for program improvement and political support. *Educational Leadership and Administration: Teaching and Program Development, 13,* 109–120.

Nagle, J., & Nagle. E. (1978). Doctoral programs in educational administration. In P. Silver & D. Spuck (Eds.), *Preparatory programs for educational administrators in the United States* (pp. 114–149). Columbus, OH: University Council for Educational Administration.

National Center for Education Statistics. (2006). *Digest of education statistics, 2006.* Washington, DC: Author.

National Clearinghouse for English Language Acquisition and Language Instruction Educational Programs. (2006). Home page. Retrieved August 1, 2006, from http://www.ncela.gwu.edu/

National Commission on Excellence in Education. (1983). *A nation at risk: The imperative for educational reform.* Washington, DC: U.S. Department of Education.

National Governors Association. (1990). *Educating America: State strategies for achieving the national education goals.* Washington, DC: Author.

National Policy Board for Educational Administration. (1989). *Improving the preparation of school administrators: An agenda for reform.* Charlottesville, VA: Author.

Newell, L. J., & Morgan, D. A. (1980). [Study of professors of higher education and educational administration]. Unpublished raw data.

No Child Left Behind Act of 2001, Pub. L. No. 107-110 (2002).

Noddings, N. (1984). *Caring: A feminine approach to ethics and moral education.* Berkeley: University of California.

Oakeshott, M. (1962). *Rationalism in politics and other essays.* New York: Basic Books.

Orr, T., & Orphanos, S. (2007, April). *Learning leadership matters: Teachers' experiences of innovatively and conventionally prepared principals.* Paper presented at the annual meeting of the American Educational Research Association, Chicago.

Orr, T., & Pounder, D. (2006, November). *UCEA/TEA-SIG taskforce on evaluating leadership preparation programs.* Report distributed at the annual meeting of the University Council for Educational Administration, San Antonio, TX.

Osguthorpe, R. T., & Wong, M. J. (1993). The Ph.D. versus the Ed.D.: Time for a decision. *Innovative Higher Education, 18*(1), 47–63.

Ozga, J. T., & Lawn, M. A. (1981). *Teachers, professionalism and class: A study of organized teachers.* London: Taylor & Francis.

Paley, A. R. (2007, January 25). Bush proposes adding private school vouchers to "No Child" law. *Washington Post,* p. A16.

Parker, L., & Shapiro, J. P. (1993). The context of educational administration and social class. In C. A. Capper (Ed.), *Educational administration in a pluralistic society* (pp. 36–65). Albany, NY: SUNY Press.

Peterson, K. D., & Finn, C. E. (1985, Spring). Principals, superintendents and the administrator's art. *The Public Interest, 79,* 42–62.

Peterson, P., Howell, W., & Greene, J. (1999). *An evaluation of the Cleveland voucher programs after two years.* Cambridge, MA: Harvard University Program on Education Policy and Governance.

Picciano, A. G., & Seaman, J. (2007). *K–12 online learning: A survey of U.S. school district administrators.* Needham, MA: Sloan Consortium.

Playko, M. A., & Daresh, J. C. (1992). *Field-based preparation programs: Reform of administrator training or leadership development?* Paper presented at the annual meeting of the University Council for Educational Administration, Minneapolis, MI.

Pohland, P., & Carlson, L. (1993). Program reform in educational administration, *UCEA Review, 34*(3), 4–9.

Popham, W. J. (2003). *Crafting curricular aims for instructionally supportive assessment.* Retrieved December 5, 2006, from http://www.education.umn.edu/NCEO/Presentations/CraftingCurricula.pdf

Pounder, D. G., Orr, T., & Black, W. (2006). *From preparation to practice and school improvement: Comparing leadership preparation program approaches and outcomes across three states.* Proposal submitted to the U.S. Department of Education, Institute of Education Sciences.

Pounder, D. G., & Young, I. P. (1996). Recruitment and selection of educational administrators: Priorities for today's schools. In K. Leithwood, J. Chapmen, D. Corson, P. Hallinger, & A. Hart (Eds.), *International handbook of educational leadership* (pp. 279–308). Boston: Kluwer.

Pringle, R. M., & Martin, S. C. (2005). The potential impacts of upcoming high-stakes testing on the teaching of science in elementary classrooms. *Research in Science Education, 35,* 347–361.

Reitzug, U. C. (1989, October). *Utilizing multiple frameworks to integrate knowledge and experience in educational administration preparation programs.* Paper presented at the annual meeting of the University Council for Educational Administration, Scottsdale, AZ.

Riehl, C. J. (2000). The principal's role in creating inclusive schools for diverse students: A review of normative, empirical, and critical literature on the practice of educational administration. *Review of Educational Research, 70,* 55–81.

Ross, J. A., & Gray, P. (2006). School leadership and student achievement: The mediating effects of teacher beliefs. *Canadian Journal of Education, 29,* 798–822.

Rusch, E. A. (1998). Leadership in evolving democratic school communities. *Journal of School Leadership, 8,* 214–250.

Rusch, E. A. (2005). Gender and race in leadership preparation. *Educational Administration Quarterly, 40,* 14–46.

Sable, J., & Hoffman, L. (2005). *Characteristics of the 100 largest public elementary and secondary school districts in the United States.* Washington, DC: National Center for Education Statistics.

Sanders, N. M., & Simpson, J. (2005). State policy framework to develop highly qualified administrators. Washington, DC: Council of Chief State School Officers. Retrieved December 8, 2006, from http://www.ccsso.org/projects/Interstate_Consortium_on_School_Leadership/.

Schemo, D. J. (2006, July 19). *Republicans propose national school voucher program.* The New York Times, p. A17.

Scheurich, J., & Laible, J. (1995). The buck stops here in our preparation programs: Educational leadership for all children (no exceptions allowed). *Educational Administration Quarterly, 31,* 313–322.

Schmuck, P. (1992). Educating the new generation of superintendents. *Educational Leadership, 49*(5), 66–71.

Schön, D. A. (1987). *Educating the reflective practitioner*. San Francisco: Jossey-Bass.

Shakeshaft, C. (1993). Preparing tomorrow's school leaders: The Hofstra University experience. In J. Murphy (Ed.), *Preparing tomorrow's school leaders: Alternative designs* (pp. 205–223). University Park, PA: University Council for Educational Administration.

Shulman, L. S., Golde, C. M., Bueschel, A. C., & Garabedian, K. J. (2006). Reclaiming education's doctorates: A critique and a proposal. *Educational Researcher, 35*(3), 25–32.

Silver, P. F. (1978). Some areas of concern in administrator preparation. In P. F. Silver & D. W. Spuck (Eds.), *Preparatory programs for educational administrators in the United States* (pp. 202–215). Columbus, OH: University Council for Educational Administration.

Simon, H. A. (1973). The structure of ill-structured problems. *Artificial Intelligence, 4,* 181–201.

Sirotnik, K. A., & Mueller, K. (1993). Challenging the wisdom of conventional principal preparation programs and getting away with it (so far). In J. Murphy (Ed.), *Preparing tomorrow's school leaders: Alternative designs* (pp. 57–83). University Park, PA: University Council for Educational Administration.

Slavin, R. (1988). Contributions of educational research to policy and practice: Constructing, challenging, changing cognition. *Educational Researcher, 17*(7), 4–11.

Southern Regional Education Board. (2002). *"Uneasy collaborators" must learn to redesign leadership preparation together.* Atlanta, GA: Author.

Starratt, R. J. (1991). Building an ethical school: A theory for practice in educational leadership. *Educational Administration Quarterly, 27*(2), 185–202.

Teitel, L. (1997). Understanding and harnessing the power of the cohort model in preparing educational leaders. *Peabody Journal of Education, 72*(2), 66–85.

Thomson, S. D. (Ed.). (1993). *Principals for our changing schools: The knowledge and skill base*. Fairfax, VA: National Policy Board for Educational Administration.

Thomson, S. D. (1999). Causing change: The National Policy Board for Educational Administration. In J. Murphy & P. B. Forsyth (Eds.), *Educational administration: A decade of reform* (pp. 93–114). Thousand Oaks, CA: Corwin.

Tirozzi, G. N. (2001). The artistry of leadership: The evolving role of the secondary school principal. *Phi Delta Kappan, 82,* 434–439.

U.S. Department of Education. (2005, December). *Fiscal Year 2006 performance plan.* Washington, DC: Author.

Van Berkum, D. W., Richardson, M. D., & Lane, K. E. (1994, August). *Professional development in educational administration programs: Where does it exist?* Paper presented at the annual meeting of the National Council of Professors of Educational Administration, Indian Wells, CA.

Vernon, D. T. A., & Blake, R. L. (1993). Does problem-based learning work? A meta-analysis of evaluative research. *Academic Medicine, 68,* 559–563.

Wagner, M., Newman, I., Cameto, R., & Levine, P. (2005). *Changes over time in the early postschool outcomes of youth with disabilities (a report of findings from the National Longitudinal Transition Study and the National Longitudinal Transition Study 2).* Menlo Park, CA: SRI International.

Warchol, G. (2007, November 7). Vouchers go down in crushing defeat. *The Salt Lake Tribune.* Retrieved December 20, 2007, from http://www.districtadministration.com/newssummary.aspx?news=yes=48679

Weick, K. E. (1996, June). Drop your tools: An allegory for organizational studies. *Administrative Science Quarterly, 41,* 301–313.

Whittle, C. (2005). *Crash course: Imagining a better future for public education.* New York: Riverhead Books.

Williams, E. J., Matthews, J., & Baugh, S. (2004). Developing a mentoring internship model for school leadership: Using legitimate peripheral participation. *Mentoring and Tutoring, 12*(1), 53–70.

Williamson, R., & Hudson, M. (2001, August). *The good, the bad, the ugly: Internships in principal preparation.* Paper presented at the annual meeting of the National Council of Professors of Educational Administration, Houston, TX. (ERIC Document Reproduction Service No. ED461931)

Willower, D. J., & Forsyth, P. B. (1999). A brief history of scholarship on educational administration. In J. Murphy & K. Seashore Louis (Eds.), *Handbook of research on educational administration* (pp. 1–23). San Francisco: Jossey-Bass.

Willower, D. J., & Licata, J. W. (1997). *Values and valuation in the practice of educational administration.* Thousand Oaks, CA: Corwin.

Wilson, P. (1993). Pushing the edge. In M. Milstein (Ed.), *Changing the way we prepare educational leaders* (pp. 219–235). Newbury Park, CA: Corwin.

Witte, J. (1998). The Milwaukee voucher experiment. *Educational Evaluation and Policy Analysis, 20,* 229–251.

Zander, A. F. (1982). *Making groups effective.* San Francisco: Jossey-Bass.

Zelman v. Simmons-Harris, 536 U.S. 639 (2002).

Zheng, H. (1996, April). *School contexts, principal characteristics, and instructional leadership effectiveness: A statistical analysis.* Paper presented at the annual meeting of the American Educational Research Association, New York.

3

The Context of University-Based Educational Leadership Preparation

DONALD LAMAGDELEINE, BRENDAN D. MAXCY, DIANA G. POUNDER, AND CYNTHIA J. REED

The purpose of this chapter is to address forces internal and external to universities that influence educational leadership preparation today. Admittedly, leader preparation programs have extended beyond the walls of universities. However, it is still true that the clear majority of school leader candidates obtain their administrative degrees and licenses through university preparation programs. Thus, we have focused on forces internal and external to universities in our discussion of the context of educational leadership preparation.

However, before addressing these contextual influences, we begin by describing the current state of the educational leadership field—particularly as it pertains to university-based leadership preparation. Empirical study of leadership education is in very early stages (Hoyle, 2003a, 2003b; Murphy, 2006; Murphy & Vriesenga, 2004; Papalewis, 2005), creating uncertainty in leader preparation strategies. This condition, coupled with ideological contention in the field, contributes to the vulnerability and the malleability of preparation programs to influences from within and outside of the university.

The Educational Leadership Preparation Field

The field of educational leadership (or educational administration) is an applied field preparing school leadership professionals. The educational leadership knowledge base draws heavily from social and behavioral science disciplines and from corporate business management, as well as from education literature. University graduate students may be introduced to multiple dimensions of the foundational educational administration literature, such as historical, philosophical, political, economic, cultural, psychological, legal, managerial, technological, and organizational components of the field of study. However, unlike some of these foundational disciplines, educational leadership has responsibilities to link traditional scholarly priorities such as formal knowledge production with improvement of professional practice, often rooted in experiential learning (Pounder, 2006). University preservice programs teach both the structure of the discipline and the applied field components of educational administration (Pounder, Young, & Reitzug, 2002). This bridging role can create a degree of internal tension within preparation programs in university settings—particularly research university settings, where knowledge production is heavily stressed. Cambron-McCabe (2002) described this as a "tension [occurring] between traditional academic disciplines and practice-based knowledge" and claimed it occurs "while challenging our cultural and philosophical bases that are grounded in scientific knowledge" (p. 289).

As a field, we experience dissonance about best ways to prepare educational leaders and, to date, have relatively little empirical evidence to inform best practices in administrator preparation. Consequently, this debate fuels the criticisms of both insiders and outsiders to the leadership preparation enterprise. The lack of a clear understanding about what educational leadership preparation programs should be and what content, instructional methods, and structures should frame them is at the heart of this tension. There is even debate about what to call these preparation programs, with names and terms ranging from *educational leadership* to *administration and supervision*, or *instructional leadership* (Southern Regional Education Board [SREB], 2006).

Some believe educational leadership is an applied science (Lunenburg, 2003), requiring refinement, revision, and extension of knowledge development (Lunenburg & Ornstein, 2004). Others believe that leadership education is a developing science anchored in sound theory, research, and patterns of behavior (Hoy & Miskel, 2005). Educational leadership also has been referred to as a skilled craft (Cicchelli, Marcus, & Weiner, 2002), suggesting that to become effective, one must learn at the side of a "master leader," promoting an apprentice model of leader preparation. Still others argue the need to emphasize specific theories of leadership and organizational development, providing a rationale for how leaders can transform themselves and their institutions.

Within these various world views are a variety of theories and preferences for preparing educational leaders. Although not an exhaustive list, these include Griffiths's (1995, 1997) theoretical pluralism, which is linked to problems of practice; Willower's (1998) philosophical naturalism and pragmatism, which relies on logic and evidence; Hoy's (1996) support of the heuristic value of social science research and theory and its usefulness as frames of reference for practitioners; and others differing from these (as cited in Lunenburg, 2003). Murphy's (1992, 2002) dialectic strategy offers, according to Lunenburg (p. 3), some "unifying concepts—a synthesizing paradigm," relying on a modernistic mindset that is open to postmodern perspectives, especially the concept of social justice. For example, Dantley (2003) purported purpose-driven educational leadership as an approach that helps schools leaders balance multidimensional administrative challenges with the inner personal strength needed to resist system inequities and oppression. Other researchers have stated that preparation should focus on reflective practice (Kottkamp & Silverberg, 2003), democratic practice (Gale & Densmore, 2003), social justice (Brown, 2006; Marshall, 2004; Rusch, 2004; Scheurich, Skrla, & Johnson, 2000), the spiritual side of leadership (Capper, Hafner, & Keyes, 2002; Dantley, 2003; Hafner & Capper, 2005; Hoyle, 2002a, 2002b; Thompson, 2004), or theory-in-action (Cordeiro, 1998). Other scholars have stressed the interpersonal side of preparing school administrators and professors to lead with morality, soul, and love (Bolman & Deal, 1993; Fullan, 2003; Hoyle, 2002a, 2002b; Marshall, Patterson, Rogers, & Steele, 1996; Sergiovanni, 1992).

Although few argue about the need for effective educational leaders, debates about appropriate preparation and assessment of leaders abound among those within and outside of university-based educational leadership programs. Efforts to shape the preparation of educational leaders can be traced back to the early 1950s, when collaboration between the National Council for the Accreditation of Teacher Education (NCATE) and the American Association of School Administrators (AASA) resulted in general standards for administrator preparation and development. In the early 1980s, standards were revived and refined by the National Council of Professors of Educational Administration (NCPEA) with consultation and advisement by several national professional associations, including the AASA, the National Association of Secondary School Principals, the National Association of Elementary School Principals, and the Association of Supervision and Curriculum

Development. The standards movement was pushed further with the development of Interstate School Leader Licensure Consortium (ISLLC, 1996) standards, including modest modification by the National Policy Board for Educational Administration (NPBEA) and subsequent adoption by the Educational Leadership Constituent Council (ELCC), resulting in NCATE's educational administration standards for program accreditation. (See further elaboration in subsequent sections of this chapter.)

More recently, external forces and some professors within the ranks have begun calling for another "systemic overhaul" in leadership preparation programs (Barnet, 2004, p. 121). These critics argue for the formation of stronger ties between K–12 public education and university faculty, for authentic and regularly occurring school-based learning experiences to better develop the skills needed for today's school leaders (Grogan & Andrews, 2002; Hoyle, Björk, Collier, & Glass, 2005; Jackson & Kelley, 2002; Murphy, 2002; Young, Petersen, & Short, 2002).

However, debates abound about whether there should be imposed professional standards for preparation (G. L. Anderson, 2001a; English, 2003, 2006; Hoyle, 1985, 1987; Murphy, 2002, 2005). Additionally, proposals about who should select candidates (SREB, 2006), about limits on the numbers of candidates prepared, and about the merits of emerging preparation models similar to those offered through alternative licensure programs (Teitel, 2006) or in clinical positions at hospitals (Browne-Ferrigno & Muth, 2004) add to the debates about best practices in leadership preparation. Levine (2005) reminded us that programs must be more than a random collection of courses. Teitel (2006) emphasized that the two major criticisms of leadership preparation are the lack of coherence and lack of relevance or utility.

From the early 1960s through the mid-1980s, professors' teaching and learning activities often were designed around the business management and social science research literature, with varying and sometimes loose connections to pressing demands and problems of pre-K–12 school settings (Murphy, 1992, 2002, 2006). By the 1990s, there was a heightened emphasis on the need to keep preparation programs focused on instructional leadership (SREB, 2006) or standards such as ISLLC, ELCC, and NCATE (Achilles & Price, 2001; Hoyle et al., 2005; Murphy, 2002, 2005). Murphy (2002), in particular, called for a recentering of the profession to have a focus on education, specifically, on what he referred to as the valued outcomes of schooling: school improvement (or effectiveness), equity (or social justice), and democratic community. However, most recently, critics have argued that these approaches emphasize a deficit model of leader preparation and pre-K–12 student learning (Achilles & Price, 2001; G. L. Anderson, 2001a, 2001b; English, 2003, 2006). These researchers emphasize the need to embrace the ways schools *should* be run. For example, these critics argue that priority should be given to developing a transformative curriculum that addresses issues of diversity and privilege (Allen & Estler, 2005). Other models suggest engaging teachers in professional learning communities (Cambron-McCabe, 2003) or partnering with local school districts and practitioners to focus on problem-based learning so aspiring principals "gain the ability to analyze complex systems even as they act within them" (Stein, 2006, p. 523).

Equally controversial are views on how best to assess the competency and craft of current and future educational leaders (Brundrett, 2000; Orr, 2006). Some call for preparation programs to assess administrative candidates using completion of tasks today's school leaders will face (Barnet, 2004), whereas others demand passing scores on standardized tests (Murphy, Yff, & Shipman, 2000). Marshall (2004) further reminded us of the tension occurring as schools are experiencing narrowed curriculum and increased accountability, while educational leadership reforms are calling for schools and universities to engage in novel ways of thinking and doing.

This complexity of world views, multiplicity of leader preparation goals and purposes, and uncertainty regarding appropriate program content and effective preparation methods is the backdrop against which forces internal and external to universities are influencing today's educational leadership preparation programs. Although the field recently has embraced empirical investigation of leader preparation program issues and effectiveness, our knowledge base about our own leader preparation practices is not well developed—and thus easily influenced by forces within and outside university settings.

Internal Influences on Educational Leadership Preparation

Internal influences within university settings can limit or enhance educational leader preparation reform. This part of the chapter begins by considering changes in the nature and mission of universities—to become more engaged with local communities; to promote democratic purposes; and to provide socially relevant research, teaching, and service to constituents. The following sections address conditions within university settings that hold implications for leader preparation programs, including changing expectations for faculty roles and responsibilities, faculty reward and incentive systems, faculty recruitment and retention challenges, and academic or professional standards. This portion of the chapter ends with a summary of these major internal contextual influences on educational leadership programs in higher education settings.

Engaged Universities and Changing Expectations for Faculty Roles and Responsibilities

For years, many have viewed universities as "Ivory Towers," places where professors work and reside in protected castles isolated from the rest of the world. New trends in higher education are pushing the importance of active engagement with the communities surrounding universities (Peters, Jordan, Adametk, & Alter, 2005), altering the traditional role of professor, and instead providing an avenue for faculty members to be social activists rather than passive observers or impartial documenters of social phenomena. Peters et al. noted "heightened concern" about the "apparent erosion of the overall quality and vitality of American civic life and even of democracy itself" (p. 4). Increased scrutiny on the value-added aspects of universities in communities has fueled university attention on the types of research conducted and with whom it is conducted, how teaching and other services are delivered, and the other types of responsibilities faculty and administrators have within communities.

Scholars are being called upon to engage in civic work alongside their fellow citizens (Boyer, 1990). Engaged universities, according to Peters et al. (2005), offer promise for contributing to the larger task of renewing democracy as the academy revisits its civic mission by engaging with campus and community. Peters et al. stated the democratic practices, purposes, and contributions of faculty in higher education can serve as a "guiding theme in faculty and organizational development efforts" (p. 4) at universities. For example, Imagining America (n.d.) is a national consortium whose mission is to strengthen the public role and democratic purposes of the arts, humanities, and design while both studying and enacting positive social change. Other groups are promoting similar causes. Campus Compact (2007) was formed in 1985 to support civic engagement, community building, and campus engagement in higher education. Currently, 542 Campus Compact member presidents have signed the Presidents' Declaration on the Civic Responsibility of Higher Education, 300,000 students were mobilized during Campus Compact's multiyear Raise Your Voice service and civic action campaign, 886,536 hours of community work were clocked in 2004–2005 by volunteers recruited through Campus Compact state offices, and $24 million in funding has been raised by Campus Compact since 1992 to support service initiatives connecting higher education with its surrounding communities. Based on findings from the Campus Compact Annual Member Survey in 2004, the annual dollar value of service contributed to the community by students at Campus Compact member schools was $4.45 billion (Campus Compact, 2007). Proponents of this approach to teaching and learning claim higher education students learn more about themselves, their career goals, and the complexity of the world through their engagement in service learning work focused on civic responsibility (Peters et al., 2005).

This emphasis on active engagement of faculty and students in democratic action, particularly to promote education reform and social justice, is becoming evident in educational leadership preparation programs. For example, at the University of Utah, Assistant Professor Madeline Hafner initiated service learning as a pedagogy in her instructional leadership courses because it required students to become actively involved in understanding and developing culturally relevant curriculum and instructional practices with local Latino students and community members. Also, Assistant Professors Enrique Aleman and Andrea Rorrer actively involved educational leadership doctoral students in research and advocacy activities to address the state's achievement gap for K–12 students of color. Additionally, the collective educational leadership faculty implemented a field-based project requirement as the capstone experience to the EdD degree in an effort to place heightened value on actively and directly influencing educational organizations, policies, and leadership practices. These initiatives are illustrative of an action-oriented, advocacy approach implemented in the context of leadership preparation programs to encourage democratic action, educational reform, and social justice for historically marginalized student populations.

Corresponding to this shift in institutional mission is a similar shift in expectations for faculty roles and responsibilities. Characterized as naïve and idealistic, university professors often have been viewed as disconnected from the problems facing the real world. "Surrounding each university is a world—actually, many worlds—as divisive, insular, bounded, and contested as one can imagine" (Cantor, 2003, p. 5). Greenwood and Levin suggested that when university faculty set research agendas, research "nearly always focuses on questions that are not relevant to disenfranchised populations" (as cited in Peters et al., 2005, p. 345).

Typically, professors are expected to teach, conduct research, and provide service to the university, scholarly communities, professionals, or others, although the relative emphasis on each of these responsibility areas varies substantially depending on the type of institution and institutional setting. Land-grant universities, for example, are explicit about the importance of service and outreach as one of the three parts to the mission of these schools. "The land-grant mission signifies a responsibility to share the research knowledge of the university with the people and community of their respective states" (Peters, 2005, p. 399). Teaching or regional universities place greater emphasis on teaching, whereas research universities typically place more emphasis on research and scholarly publication yet also expect quality teaching. The institutional weight given to research, teaching, and service or outreach may be reflected in the formal reward system policies as well as in the faculty norms regarding promotion, tenure, and merit pay. The more that is expected in one performance domain (e.g., research and publication), the less time that faculty may have available for other performance domains (e.g., service and outreach; Jaeger & Thornton, 2006).

More recently, however, comprehensive public universities are experiencing greater expectations for civic engagement with and contributions to their local communities, especially in high-need urban centers. These (typically public) universities are building university–community partnerships and developing community-based, integrated service systems—not unlike the original land-grant university model of research-teaching-service extension (Corrigan, 1997). For example, the University of Utah, under the leadership of its former President Bernie Machen, developed University Neighborhood Partners (n.d.), a partnership between the University and Salt Lake City's West Side, a community of largely lower income persons of color and linguistically diverse residents. University Neighborhood Partners has sponsored research and outreach initiatives, including Adelante, a project developed by Education Department faculty, Enrique Aleman, Dolores Delgado-Bernal, and Octavio Villalpando, to create conditions for elementary-aged Latino/a students to be educationally successful and aspire to a college education. Similarly, the University of Wisconsin–Madison, through the leadership of Professor Gloria Ladson-Billings and nationally prominent school district superintendents (and now directed by Dr. Madeline Hafner), formed the Minority Student Achievement Network (2008) designed to bring school district leaders and education researchers together to address the problem of racial disparity in K–12 student educational achievement.

Increased expectations for university engagement have resulted in additional or different expectations for university faculty. Professors are expected to be active service and outreach providers in their local communities, in addition to being excellent teachers and readily available advisors (K. A. Adams, 2002); exemplary researchers able to conduct and fund their own research through solicitation of contracts and grants (Katz, 1992); and strong mentors to students, junior faculty, and adjunct faculty (Kochan & Sabo, 1995). For educational leadership faculty, this outreach can include regular engagement with practitioners in pre-K–12 settings (Achilles, 2005; Darling-Hammond, 2006; McCarthy, 2005; SREB, 2006; Young & Peterson, 2002a, 2002b), providing educator professional development; collaboration with stakeholders (Pounder, 1998; SREB, 2006; Young et al., 2002); and interaction with all stakeholders in a manner demonstrating trust, commitment, and openness (Cambron-McCabe, 2003). In addition, faculty are expected to maintain an active teaching and research and publication agenda (Carroll, 2003).

Although the public historically has placed trust in colleges and universities, allowing faculty members the freedom to "pursue their individual work, needs, and interests" (Lindholm, 2004, p. 604), communities are now more vocal about the social responsibilities faculty members must have to their institutions and larger communities. Professors traditionally have been able to engage in research they found intellectually stimulating and rewarding, with little emphasis on the direct relationship that research had on society. Now, there is more demand for research with immediate and high utility to educational policy makers and education practitioners (Pounder, 2000). Education faculty members are also now expected to be highly visible in pre-K–12 schools and within the education community (SREB, 2006; Young et al., 2002). This is consistent with changing trends regarding the responsibilities of faculty and staff in engaged universities (Peters et al., 2005) and with the examples of activist or advocacy approaches to leadership preparation offered above.

These changing expectations have both favorable and challenging implications for leadership preparation programs. On the one hand, if professors are expected to invest in more active and direct outreach to schools and the education community, there is greater potential to build partnerships between university leader preparation programs and local schools and districts. These partnerships have greater capacity for addressing both the academic knowledge-base elements of leader preparation as well as the applied or field-based experiential knowledge associated with professional learning. University faculty typically have greater capacity for instructing administrative candidates about the formal knowledge base and research findings in educational leadership literature because their jobs are often focused around reading and writing for publication in this arena. By contrast, school district personnel may have greater capacity for providing high-quality field-based experiences due to their access to day-to-day administrative problems, practices, and dilemmas. As university faculty become more engaged with school personnel, leadership preparation programs may benefit from the dual and complementary contributions of both scholars and practitioners.

Educational leadership programs have increased use of advisory councils and K–12 partnerships (SREB, 2006). Similar to the work of professional development schools (Darling-Hammond, 2006), these approaches generally take more time to work through, require faculty members to work collaboratively with others, and blur the boundaries between higher education and public school settings. As programmatic efforts become more collaborative with public education and other agencies, it has become more typical to utilize tools such as Memoranda of Agreement to ensure each partner is clear about goals, expectations, and requirements. Use of these agreements helps to make explicit the work of programs and facilitates deeper understanding of the needs, resources, and abilities of each participating organization (Reed, 2006).

Similarly, as engaged universities promote more faculty activism and investment in local school and community issues, these issues may be reflected in the content of university-based leader preparation programs. For example, if university faculty are working with school and community citizens to enhance the educational opportunities and outcomes for historically marginalized student populations (e.g., low-income students, English language learners, or students of color), this focus is also more likely to be reflected in the leader preparation program curriculum and field-based activities. Also, pedagogies such as service learning may become more prominent in leader preparation programs.

However, changing faculty role expectations may challenge some of the traditional norms and working conditions of university faculty, such as faculty autonomy. Professors tend to be intelligent, with a strong need for achievement and autonomy (Lindholm, 2004). Intellectual challenge and freedom tend to be two of the main reasons why people pursue a teaching and research career in the academy (Astin, Korn, & Dey, 1990; Lindholm, Astin, Sax, & Korn, 2002). In traditional higher education organizational cultures, faculty members have become used to having autonomy (Cambron-McCabe, 2003), although this situation is changing with increased emphasis on faculty members' becoming involved in civic life (Boyer, 1990). Increased engagement with outreach efforts may place more constituent demands on faculty, thus limiting much of their work autonomy. Of course, other influences, such as licensure or accreditation requirements, also may decrease the autonomy of professors' work by prescribing curricular content, candidate assessment procedures, or other preparation program elements (see also the chapter section on external influences). Thus, although constituent groups and professional standards may enhance some aspects of leader preparation, professors' autonomy in teaching, research, and program development may be inhibited.

Some private, for-profit institutions have recognized the limitations of these multiple demands on professors' time and have promoted more efficient and financially profitable models of instructional delivery by "unbundling" teaching functions from the research, service, and outreach dimensions of more comprehensive institutions (e.g., University of Phoenix). These for-profit institutions focus exclusively on teaching and instructional delivery, offering no promise of research (i.e., academic knowledge development) or service and outreach to the broader community. These institutions may gain even more efficiency by hiring few, if any, full-time professional faculty to develop course and program curriculum, while hiring a very large cadre of (low-paid) adjunct faculty to deliver the prescribed curriculum uniformly across multiple institutional locations. This approach to curriculum development and instructional delivery allows greater cost-effectiveness for more limited services, relative to that of comprehensive public universities.

Faculty Reward and Incentive Systems

Reward and incentive systems, like faculty role expectations, may vary somewhat by type of institution. Although most university tenure and promotion systems are based on teaching, research, and service performance indicators, the type and amount of teaching, research, and service that are rewarded may vary considerably by institutional type and setting. For example, most graduate faculty members, such as those educational leadership programs, especially in research institutions (versus teaching institutions), are rewarded to a large degree on research productivity. Research productivity is often measured by the number and scholarly quality of publications and the amount of external funding (e.g., grants, contracts, and foundation money) brought into the university by a faculty member (K. A. Adams, 2002).

Teaching is a primary responsibility for most professors, and with most educational leadership preparation programs offered in teaching institutions (Murphy, 1992), teaching functions may take priority over other responsibilities for many educational leadership faculty. By contrast, some critics, like Edgerton (1993), have argued,

> Teaching loads in research universities and elite liberal arts colleges have declined to such an embarrassing point that faculty are pressured into doing research that is of no particular value to society, and that there are fewer and fewer faculty to count on to perform tasks of university citizenship. (p. 14)

These critics, like those promoting engaged universities, are calling upon universities to recapture and redirect faculty energy toward agendas of higher social value. Faculty members also are expected to advise students and work on teaching-related initiatives and preparation program revisions, often engaging in partnership building and advocacy work with local school personnel. Additionally, some institutions are putting increasing emphasis on university faculty coteaching with practitioners and clinical or contract faculty, although these auxiliary personnel are typically involved in direct instruction only and are rarely expected to participate in student advising, programmatic reform, or other teaching-related academic work (O'Meara, 2006).

Service to the university and outreach in schools is expected from nearly all faculty members, yet it often does not count much on performance reviews and tenure decisions (K. A. Adams, 2002). Some claim there are large differences between real and espoused expectations for promotion and tenure. For example, although professors often serve as experts for policy makers, most policy initiative and advocacy work gets little or no credit in tenure and promotion reviews (Marshall, 2004). Social justice advocacy work may be seen as "working out personal problems and detracting from the 'main work' directed toward preparing principals for current practice and publishing on topics related to current practice" (Marshall, 2004, p. 5). Most universities expect faculty members to engage in service activities within the college and university; yet, as described above, more recently there are also increasing external demands for outreach to school systems and other community organizations.

Changes in faculty roles and responsibilities can create dilemmas for faculty members as performance expectations change, but reward and incentive policies and practices on campus do not respond to these changing demands. Cantor and Lavine (2006) challenged universities to take public scholarship and engagement seriously, rewarding faculty for these efforts when they are being considered for promotion and tenure. They claimed that although public and creative scholarship is flourishing at campuses around the country, the faculty members and graduate students engaging in this work are not. These faculty and students are instead pressured to postpone their work with community-based research and civic collaboration until they have earned tenure. Cantor and Lavine further challenged university leaders to take public scholarship seriously and to consider broader and more flexible definitions as well as more inclusive processes for reviewing faculty work. However, it is yet unclear whether universities will adapt their reward and incentive systems to correspond to these newer expectations for civic engagement. Unless universities make corresponding adjustments in other performance expectations (e.g., research and publication productivity), university faculty members may fail to engage in these partnerships or may become overwhelmed by the many types of demands placed upon them (K. A. Adams, 2002; LaRocco & Bruns, 2006).

Calls to revise traditional university reward systems to more adequately reflect the full range of faculty work responsibilities have particular relevance for applied disciplines such as educational leadership (Boyer, 1990). For example, Boyer argued that scholarship takes many forms and is reflected in faculty members' teaching, service, and outreach activities as well as their research. Boyer argued for promotion and tenure policies based on the "scholarship of discovery," the "scholarship of integration," the "scholarship of application," and the "scholarship of teaching" (pp. 15–25). These standards include attention to traditional knowledge development as well as knowledge application, knowledge transmission, knowledge dissemination, knowledge utilization, and related scholarly activities.

Although universities expect faculty members to be effective teachers, competent researchers, active participants in academic life (K. A. Adams, 2002; Boyer, 1990), and more recently engaged activists in community outreach, few institutions have modified their reward and incentive policies to more adequately reflect the balance or potential synergy among these various performance domains. Fewer yet have established norms that reflect the realities of time limitations for faculty to invest in an increasing array of performance activities. As workloads continue to increase for full-time faculty members, there is greater need for creating a culture that values differences yet keeps an improvement-focused ethos (Kuh, Kinzie, Schuh, & Whitt, 2005).

For reward systems to keep pace with changing role expectations, promotion and tenure policies and norms may need to shift from current thinking that considers each performance domain as separate and distinct and often differentially weighted. Instead, we need to begin thinking about how a faculty member makes contributions across multiple domains (e.g., research, teaching, service, and outreach) in ways that are mutually reinforcing and that promote the broader mission of our applied discipline. For example, rather than focusing on how many top-tier, refereed publications an individual has, we may need to consider how one's empirical research that is published in top-tier journals is related to and made possible by one's engagement with schools and how the research addresses important and timely educational leadership challenges or issues. Further, how is the knowledge gained by this empirical work communicated to school practitioners (rather than only to fellow academicians) and to students in leader preparation programs? In other words, how do one's empirical and conceptual research and publications, practitioner publications, outreach engagement with schools, and leadership preparation teaching form a synergistic whole? How can we assess and reward the overall impact of this collective educational leadership professorial work? How can we promote and reward balance and integration of faculty activity across these multiple domains? These are important faculty reward and incentive considerations if our leader preparation programs and education schools are going to retain their viability and prominence in an environment of increasing accountability and critique (see also the chapter section on external influences).

Tenure is supposed to provide a reasonable assurance to faculty members that they have academic freedom and cannot lose their jobs because they pursue a particular line of research or teaching emphasis that may be out of favor with university administrators or constituents. There has been criticism of tenure, with claims that tenure decreases productivity and shelters unproductive faculty (Benjamin, 1998). Edgerton (as cited in Benjamin, 1998) claimed tenured faculty may substitute their own priorities for those of the institution. Some believe that academics must have freedom of expression, but only when it is in appropriate contexts or situations (Brecher, 2006), whereas others feel that without tenure, faculty members would be unable to engage in controversial research or to challenge the practices of university administration (Benjamin, 1998). There are increased calls for faculty to be public scholars, working with specific publics and engaging in social criticism (Peters et al., 2005). If faculty are expected to become public scholars or activists and advocates in their communities, then they are more likely to engage in controversial activities, necessitating stronger tenure policies to enable professors greater security for fulfilling these professional responsibilities. Currently, educational leadership faculty who publicly advocate for educational changes to better serve historically marginalized student populations (e.g., students of color; English language learners; special education students; or gay, lesbian, or transgendered students) may be vulnerable without the protection of tenure policies.

Opportunities for professional renewal and recognition are important for faculty members, but the opportunities vary by university and college. Those professors who are successful at writing grants, publishing, and conducting research tend to be afforded more opportunities for graduate students to support their work efforts, funding to purchase needed equipment and supplies, and travel to professional conferences where they can network with other successful scholars. Junior faculty members and those with less prominent academic careers are often not afforded as many of these benefits. Similarly, sabbaticals of one or more semesters are sometimes available for faculty members who are actively engaged in research and have been serving at the university for a lengthy time. Selection procedures and criteria for sabbaticals may be difficult for many faculty members to negotiate; there are usually a limited number of these available on a campus each year.

In response to these typical faculty incentive systems, Stein (2006) suggested three types of incentives that should be developed to support effective reform of educational leadership programs: (a) Release time, space, and resources to create opportunities to work together with practitioners; (b) pay for faculty to learn how to use pedagogies and develop curricular materials to use in simulations and case studies (or other teaching methods requiring application of knowledge to typical administrative challenges); and (c) use promotion and tenure decisions to reward faculty for innovative teaching practices that prepare educational leaders for real work. Stein suggested these three approaches would send a clear message and provide adequate incentive to facilitate a shift in thinking and practice among faculty members. These and other revisions to tenure and promotion policies and norms (described above) warrant serious consideration to better align current university faculty reward and incentive systems with the changing mission of universities, the demands of applied fields such as educational leadership, and the expanding roles and responsibilities of university faculty. Careful alignment of reward systems with the goals and mission of improved leader preparation may encourage faculty to invest in the multiple activities and efforts required to build and sustain high-quality leader preparation programs.

Faculty Recruitment and Retention Challenges

Because of the applied nature of the field of educational leadership, not only are faculty members with traditional research and teaching skills needed, but it is also highly desirable that these same faculty members have strong backgrounds as educational practitioners (e.g., school teachers, administrators, or other education professionals) so that they have professional understandings of schools and other educational organizations and can work collaboratively with school communities. There is particularly pressure to hire professors of educational leadership who have administrative experience (SREB, 2006). Some retired administrators make the transition from administrator to professor, seeking a position that allows them to utilize their expertise and experience while preparing new educational leaders—although relatively few may actively engage in research and publication activity. Critics claim some of these professors make the transition expecting an easy lifestyle and opportunities for consulting work they can enjoy until their next retirement (Benjamin, 1998). Livingston, Davis, Green, and DeSpain (2001) cautioned about those transitioned professors who "just recount war stories" and do not effectively teach students about research knowledge in the field or engage in knowledge development through research (p. 135). Since 1994, there has been an increasing trend to hire those with recent administrative experience, although many of these new faculty members may have served as adjunct professors while working as administrators prior to joining the faculty full time (Livingston et al., 2001).

There is also a need for more diversity, particularly racial and gender diversity, among educational leadership faculty (Lindholm, 2004). University leaders want to attract educational leadership faculty who can promote effective leadership preparation for diverse school settings, which means having expertise about how to change schools to better serve historically marginalized student populations, increasing their educational opportunities and outcomes. Because the fields of education and educational leadership in particular tend to be conservative in views and practices (Ridenour & Twale, 2005), many professors are not prepared to deal with issues of poverty, language minority, special needs, gender, race, and sexuality (Marshall, 2004). There is often a mismatch between the culture and background of professors and those they may serve in institutions of higher education (Lindholm, 2004; Marshall, 2004).

Given this complexity of job requirements and qualifications, strong competition for educational leadership faculty is not surprising. Few faculty members hold all of these qualifications: research, teaching, and service or outreach skills, coupled with a practitioner background and experience in nurturing and strengthening the educational experiences of diverse school communities. Those who do are in particularly high demand.

There is also a mismatch between graduate training and the many responsibilities facing new faculty members (Austin, 2002). Alexander (2006) suggested scholars face a cultural adjustment after graduate school, shifting from a viewpoint that education is an adventure to one where, for college professors, education is more about customer satisfaction. For example, university students typically evaluate faculty members' teaching and advisement performance, and these evaluations are generally included as one part of a faculty member's merit consideration or promotion and tenure review. As a result, some students try to hold faculty members hostage, expecting a good grade in return for a positive evaluation (Addison, Best, & Warrington, 2006; Heckert, Latier, & Ringwald-Burton, 2006). Often students in graduate programs expect to earn a grade of A or possibly B but not lower. When this is the case, there may be pressure on professors either to demonstrate the difficulty of their expectations and course material or to accommodate student expectations for good grades (Landrum, 1999).

Additionally, although educational leadership faculty often teach about the importance of mentoring, it is not unusual for new faculty members in educational preparation programs to be expected to learn about norms, culture, and expectations in their department without the support of a mentor or advocate. Instead, new faculty members are often left to fend for themselves as they prepare for and teach classes, advise students and serve on committees, begin or continue to develop a research agenda, find avenues for service within their department or college, and begin to establish collegial working relationships with the other professors in their program and department. Each university, and often each department within the university, has different normative nuances and practices within the established governance structure and regulations of the campus. These norms and informal practices may be unclear or invisible to new faculty, potentially putting the new professor in a perilous position with respect to more established and powerful colleagues, students, and supervisors.

Coupled with this cultural adjustment is a troubling trend in faculty compensation. According to the American Association of University Professors (2006), in 2005–2006 the average faculty salaries increased by less then the inflation rate for the 2nd consecutive year, adding to the reasons why faculty positions may be less appealing for new scholars. Further, with educational leadership entry-level faculty salaries typically much lower than those of school practitioners, relatively few doctoral graduates move to the ranks of educational leadership faculty versus returning to administrative practice (Pounder, Crow, & Bergerson, 2004).

Given these combined conditions, universities are facing considerable challenges in attracting and retaining high-quality faculty among their ranks. The academic labor market has been changing for over a decade. The increase in the number of faculty members has not kept pace with the increase in the number of students (Benjamin, 1998). Increasing numbers of adjunct or contract faculty members are being hired instead of tenure-track faculty as a cost-saving measure (Elman,

2002). Many educational leadership programs utilize practicing school administrators as adjunct faculty members in their departments. There are concerns this situation can create disjointed programs, tiered classes of faculty, and lessened access to faculty members for students (Schneider, 2003). Although auxiliary faculty may be competent teachers, they are often disengaged from other academic responsibilities such as student advisement, active reading and investment in academic scholarship, program development work, or collaboration with peers (Elman, 2002). Further, the predictability and quality control of educational leadership programs may be vulnerable to the ups and downs of frequently varying auxiliary faculty involved in teaching assignments. These adjunct faculty, however, may become an important pool from which to attract and develop full-time faculty by encouraging them to transition to full-time faculty roles (Livingston et al., 2001). Creative solutions are needed to meet both the fiscal and staffing needs facing departments and programs, providing assistance to program and student development while remaining in line with budgetary concerns challenging many universities.

Gappa, Austin, and Trice (2005) claimed faculty and their work are at the heart of colleges and universities, having a lasting impact on the lives they touch. Gappa et al. cited four changes affecting faculty work life since tenure was first widely recognized in 1940: (a) higher education institutions experiencing numerous external pressures and needing faculty members who can respond to con-strained financial environments, calls for accountability, new technologies, expanding knowledge, shifting disciplinary boundaries, and increasingly diverse student bodies; (b) a proliferation of new types of faculty appointments whereby the majority of faculty members are no longer in full-time tenured or tenure-track positions; (c) diverse faculty populations largely with increased numbers of women and people of color; and (d) new faculty members with different expectations about the workplace, including their need to balance work with other life responsibilities. These changes can have a profound impact on current faculty and institutional needs and necessitate a review and possible reframing of academic structures, policies, and purposes.

K. A. Adams (2002) further suggested five areas needing attention when preparing new faculty members for a successful career: (a) teaching, (b) research, (c) academic life, (d) job search skills, and (e) understanding academic options. Rarely are all of these areas addressed in academic preparation programs. Without opportunities for ongoing professional development, mentoring, and profes-sional renewal as well as a valuing of professors as professionals, high-quality faculty members are unlikely to enter or remain in the field. One needs only to review the numerous advertisements for professors of educational leadership to realize the difficulty of hiring and retaining quality faculty members able to negotiate the numerous and often conflicting demands of professorial roles. Given the labor-intensive nature of educational enterprises generally, the strength of leader preparation programs is, in large measure, dependent on the quantity and quality of faculty attracted to and retained in the professorate.

Academic Standards

There are numerous points of view about how to assess the quality of an academic program. Since 1983, the *U.S. News and World Report*, a popular lay-person magazine, has ranked universities, colleges, graduate schools, and departments according to indicators of "excellence." Since beginning this process, critics have expressed concern about the weighting of the indicators and the accuracy of the overall scores (Clarke, 2004), yet colleges and universities, as well as the public at large, pay attention to these rankings. High-ranking colleges and graduate schools often advertise their rank-ing in promotional materials. Ehrenberg (2003) warned that an institutional obsession with these rankings exacerbates their competitiveness and influences them to alter their behavior in ways that do not benefit students or higher education as a whole. Although efforts are often made to recruit underrepresented groups and provide access to the university, many colleges and programs pride themselves, and are rated, on the difficulty or exclusivity of their admissions criteria (e.g., Graduate Record Exam scores) rather than on the diversity of their student population.

Programs are also assessed through internal peer reviews and accreditation processes, with particular attention to student outcomes such as retention rates; job placement rates; and a variety of learning and performance outcomes of students, including on-the-job performance after graduation (Pounder, 1995; SREB, 2006). Educational leadership programs are also expected to be accountable to area school systems, national professional standards, and external agencies such as state education offices and accrediting boards. Programs and individual professors are encouraged to undergo self-evaluation and reflection in order to facilitate continuous improvement. Although these measures suggest a process of continuous improvement is in place, many universities and their programs are viewed by the public as resistant to change (SREB, 2006).

The leadership education standards movement began in 1954, with NCATE collaborating with AASA to create a set of general standards to guide administrator preparation and professional development. However, the new standards were not widely adopted in preparation programs (Moore, 1964). When these general guidelines were revised in 1982 by a committee composed of professors, practicing school administrators, and leaders of professional administrator associations, the standards movement and related accountability issues gained some national attention with university-based leadership preparation programs. These standards were reflected in NCPEA's *Leadership Guidelines* in 1984 and subsequently revised in 1995 (as cited in Peterson & Finn, 1985). Peterson and Finn said it was surprising that "no such work existed previously that gave those responsible for administrator preparation clear notions about what essential knowledge constitutes higher achievement among their own students" (p. 43). Peterson and Finn summed up the use of the new standards this way: "Under these headings, the AASA suggests administrators need a mix of empirical and theoretical knowledge and they need a feel for how to put their knowledge and skills into operation within the school organization so as to increase its effectiveness" (p. 53). Thus, these eight standards established the original model for standards developed by AASA (superintendents), the National Association of Secondary School Principals, the National Association of Elementary School Principals, and the Association for Supervision and Curriculum Development.

Some feel the increased emphasis on accountability for educational leadership professors came to a head with the implementation of the ISLLC Standards (English, 2006), prompting the restructuring of numerous training programs so graduates would be well versed on the topics covered by these standards. Certainly no previous standards had such an impact on university-based leadership preparation programs, largely through state-mandated program-accreditation and administrator-licensure exams. Some claim the adoption of these standards implied university faculty would not change their practices without being forced to do so, and faculty were not in touch with what educational leaders needed to know in order to be effective leaders and change agents (G. L. Anderson, 2001a; English, 2003, 2006).

A warning foreshadowed forced standards on leadership preparation with the creation of the *AASA Guidelines for the Preparation of School Administrators* (Hoyle, 1983) and the AASA *Professional Standards for the Superintendency* (Hoyle, 1993). Hoyle, English, and Steffy (1985) warned about the negative impact of rigid application of standards on leadership preparation programs:

> AASA recognizes the danger inherent in developing guidelines/standards that may vary substantially from the programs provided by some institutions. Professionals depend on creativity and the capacity of individuals and institutions to capitalize on these unique strengths. Since the uniform patterns rigidly applied may impair the flexibility of that program's need to meet local and regional needs, AASA desires that these guidelines/standards not be used to limit program development or expertise of a given faculty. (p. 2)

These various bodies and processes designed to promote and uphold high academic standards may be used to encourage leadership preparation program development and improvement. In fact, it is quite common for educational leadership faculty members to participate frequently in revisions of curricula and programs in response to changing standards and accreditation requirements. A variety of considerations may be embraced in program reform initiatives. These include the following three: (a) program content priorities such as emphasis on learning-focused leadership (Young & Peterson, 2002a), contextual understandings of schools, administrative management skills, and culture-building strategies, including promoting socially just school cultures; (b) instructional strategies and delivery systems that address the needs of adult professional learners, including case study methods, problem-based learning, or service learning; and (c) programming considerations such as the use of distance-learning strategies, cohort groups, and scheduling and location of classes to better serve program enrollees. As part of the self-evaluative process, deliberation also should occur among faculty members and others about embedding the practices of leadership development in authentic practices and school reform efforts as part of the programmatic culture (Young et al., 2002).

An additional practical consideration in program revision is the degree to which the university system requires extensive review and approval of program and curriculum changes at multiple levels of the institution (e.g., department, college, graduate school, academic senate, board of trustees, or university system level). In many institutions, even after department faculty have reached consensus about specific educational leadership program reforms, this curriculum review and approval process can take a year or more to complete. Although universities are advantaged by having strong professional expertise to develop, review, and approve educational programs, universities are also often constrained from responding quickly to internally or externally motivated programmatic change. Although the text above does not capture all of the internal contextual influences on university-based leader preparation, certainly the changing roles and responsibilities of faculty in engaged universities, alignment of faculty rewards and incentives, challenges of attracting and retaining faculty, and academic standards are strong influences to be considered in the context of educational leader preparation scholarship and practice.

External Influences on Educational Leadership Preparation: Recent Trends and Challenges

We now turn our attention to external contextual influences on educational leadership preparation. We begin by describing an historical shift in education policy paradigms. Specifically, through the 1970s, a supply-side focus premised on the establishment of a coherent, scientifically grounded approach to educating school leaders held sway in the United States and most other places (Culbertson, 1988; Donmoyer, 1999). Over the past two decades, however, a market-oriented approach stressing the merits of a demand-side orientation has emerged (Gronn, 2003). The change has featured what Gronn described as "an intimate relationship between standards and standardisers" as well as an inherent bias toward "standard-setting" itself (p. 9). As we discuss in this section, the shift created pressures on preparation programs to supply leaders for a field of education changing dramatically since the 1980s. Increasingly, administrative preparation programs struggle to satisfy a conflicting set of demands that pits their longstanding reliance on internal norms and mission-driven curricula against highly prescriptive guidelines policed by external onlookers (e.g., vigilant accreditation and licensure agencies) skeptical of higher education in general. Below we briefly discuss the external influences behind the rise of the demand-side orientation, the subsequent new modalities of regulation and control coenacted by the states and accreditation bodies, and the challenges these pose for the programs that prepare educational leaders.

Critique of Public Education in the 1980s

Critiques from various sources mounted in the 1980s. From the left, Anyon (1980), Apple (1981), Bowles and Gintis (1976), Oakes (1985), and others offered incisive critiques challenging the "achievement ideology" (Habermas, 1975, p. 81) foundational to the public's faith in the American public school system (Tyack & Cuban, 1995). These critiques increasingly informed the discourse of educational administration (G. L. Anderson, 1990; Blase & Anderson, 1995; Foster, 1986; Marshall, 1993; Maxcy, 1994). From within, teacher organizations in concert with powerful policy actors (notably the Carnegie Forum on Education and the Economy and the National Governors Association) pressed for greater professional influence on school decision making (Ogawa, 1994). The result was widespread governance restructuring (see Leithwood & Menzies, 1998; Murphy & Beck, 1995) that promoted site- or school-based management and stressed the administrative skills required to manage teachers effectively.

Meanwhile, during the Reagan administration (1980–88), U.S. public education came under fire from the right. Perhaps most iconically in *A Nation at Risk* (National Commission on Excellence in Education, 1983), the business-oriented blue ribbon commission members who authored the report argued that schools must be dramatically retooled if the United States was to compete in the new, high-technology, knowledge-based economy being shaped by postindustrialism. *A Nation at Risk* also echoed the claims of cultural conservatives arguing that schools were overburdened with accommodating special interests rather than instilling traditional knowledge and values vital for the preservation of American society (Bennett, 1988; Hirsch, Kett, & Trefil, 1988).

The tone of this discourse, consistent with the statements and policy of the Reagan administration in general, was markedly different from that of the 1950s and 1960s. Then, public schools had been charged with the vitally important task of catapulting the Cold War (and later, post-Sputnik) United States back into the position of world educational leader, fueled by all the financial and policy aid that could be directed their way. Next, following the need to accommodate the *Brown v. Board of Education* decision, in the 1960s and 1970s federal officials took an even stronger stance vis-à-vis state and local officials in assisting public schools' efforts to desegregate students (Schofield, 1991). Though technically a state function, the federal concern with public education at the time represented a significant increase in government investment in public education.

Ronald Reagan cast the strong federal role in public education very differently in his first inaugural address in 1981, arguing, "Government isn't the solution to our problem, it *is* the problem." His administration's Department of Education aligned itself with both the neo-conservative educational critique and a growing group of neo-liberals (e.g., Chubb & Moe, 1988; Friedman & Friedman, 1980) advocating for the privatization of educational delivery.

Thus, a "perfect storm" of criticism from left, right, and within yielded a systematically critical discourse among federal policy makers decrying the educational establishment as ineffective, muddled, and largely incapable of reforming itself (Cibulka, 1997; Cuban, 1990; Timar & Kirp, 1987), a charge that those preparing teachers and school administrators found difficult to ignore. Public schools since have faced increasing demands to enhance performance accountability by documenting their activities and student learning (J. E. Adams & Kirst, 1999; Elmore, Abelman, & Fuhrman, 1996). Meanwhile, in order to further "tighten the grip" (Malen, 2003, p. 195) on the training of educational professionals, national accreditation bodies and state licensure guidelines underwent major changes. The increasing emphasis on standardized documentation alongside the creation of alternative routes toward licensure significantly restructured the field of leadership preparation (Fusarelli, 2002; Meyer, 2002). By the mid-1990s these performance accountability systems had become the order of the day (Cibulka & Derlin, 1998).

The new operating environment featured explicitly articulated curricula and iterative assessments, new systems of performance monitoring, and public comparisons of results (Elmore et al., 1996; Fuhrman, 1999). The performance comparisons purportedly foster improved student achievement by facilitating consumer choice among education providers. While this may be so, it is still too early to accurately assess the results objectively. It is definitely the case that within this regime of heightened expectations, teachers and administrators operate under greater scrutiny. In addition, the new environment has served as a brake on educators' professional autonomy in the interest of a consumer-driven restructuring of public schools. As noted, the animus for these developments has been neo-liberal theories of public choice and organizational dynamics (Terry, 1998). As a result of this shift, administrative preparation programs struggle with the mandate to provide school leaders for public schools.

The Rise of New Public Management

Within the larger context of public institutions, the above developments parallel those that occurred in the public service sector over roughly the same period. Termed *New Public Management* (NPM) by Hood (1991), the movement was reflective of, and in part inspired by, Reagan's claim that government is problematic. NPM emerged across many fields and in many countries during the 1980s as part of Reagan's general push for deregulation (Kaboolian, 1998). Its rise was mirrored in the UK during the Thatcher administration, and in both countries NPM became the favored paradigm for bringing the purported efficiencies of the private sector to public administration. Its main premise is that introducing market discipline to government agencies by contracting services and adopting a customer-driven orientation improves civil service training and protocols (Barzelay, 1992; Osborne & Gabler, 1992). Based loosely on a combination of business and corporate management literature, NPM became the *leit motif* of governmental discourse in the United States and Britain (Kaboolian, 1998; Pollitt, 1990, 2003; Reich, 1990). NPM also figured prominently in the Blair and Clinton administrations, which further hastened its global application (via Organization for Economic Development and other international coalitions) to prisons, hospitals, the military, and social service agencies as well as school systems (Ball, 1998; Fusarelli & Johnson, 2004; Pollitt, 2003; Whitty & Power, 2003).[1]

NPM proponents characterize the former government reliance on civil service cultural norms for public administration as ineffective, inefficient, unresponsive to clients, and prone to mission expansion rather than service improvement (Osborne & McLaughlin, 2002). Proponents offer NPM principles to cure or mitigate these "bureau-pathologies" (Kaboolian, 1998, p. 190) by reconfiguring the operating environment. Five of these principles are (a) decentralizing authority over operational decisions, (b) reconfiguring accountability relationships, (c) promoting private-sector management techniques, (d) specifying and clarifying incentives for attaining performance targets, and (e) invoking competition among providers through market-like pressures (Hood, 1991; Pollitt, 2003). Although not often directly linked with it, NPM is highly congruent with neo-classical conceptions of global capitalism (Robison & Hewison, 2005; Whitty & Power, 2003). Thus, proponents eschew the premise of autonomous professions and professional schools, which previously had been trusted to educate competent civil servants who were also members of well-defined professions, as impediments to the market (Friedman & Friedman, 1980; Larabee, 1997).

Whereas NPM is depicted by proponents as a pragmatic solution to problems that are of a different nature than those that emerged during earlier epochs (e.g., the agrarian or early industrial eras), its critics charge that it strategically blurs the line between prescription and description (Bottery, 2003). Hood (1991), for instance, has expressed concern that NPM may overplay efficiency and effectiveness in organizations at the expense of other valued outcomes like fairness, honesty, or resilience. Pollitt (2003) similarly has described NPM as a "paradoxical" set of principles that has facilitated a modest level of improvement in institutional practices yet "has achieved a level of rhetorical dominance that far outruns its impact on practice" (p. 26). Finally, Fusarelli and Johnson (2004) argued that NPM appropriation of neo-corporatism overplays the real and significant differences between public- and private-sector management.

An Altered Operating Environment for Leader Preparation

The preceding brief discussion of the rise of NPM directly impinges upon the practices and loci of educational leadership preparation. Paralleling the ends of the "new accountability" (Fuhrman, 1999, p. 1), NPM premises appear to have held sway in the new state and federal educational regulatory changes affecting public education, as epitomized by the No Child Left Behind Act of 2001 (NCLB, 2002). In view of the post-Reagan appetite for deregulation, NCLB appears (paradoxically) to constitute a new order of K–12 regulation with important implications for the preparation of school leaders. The law mandates high-stakes testing only for public schools, in effect creating a K–12 "market" that includes only schools that already have been cast as doing a bad job.

As with the NPM-steeped discourse against public schools as an inefficient monopoly, the institution of standards for administrative preparation was accompanied by the invocation of competition among service providers. Meanwhile, the delegitimatization of the former order (public institution as civil service) was counterbalanced by legitimation of market-like mechanisms. The latter were cast as antidotes to the perceived bureau-pathologies of the public sector. The result is a quasi-market (Gordon & Whitty, 1997) lacking the attributes through which (idealized) markets yield economic and social efficiency. It is not really a market environment so much as a neo-Tayloristic form of management training designed to accompany school accountability (Terry, 1998).

The next few paragraphs further analyze how these processes have occurred, particularly as they affect administrative preparation. In brief, the larger influence of NPM induced many states' policy makers to subject traditional leader preparation programs to high-stakes regulation even as they created new avenues for licensure certification. For example, the NPBEA member organizations[2] and state agencies cooperated to create and promulgate the ISLLC (1996) standards and associated state examinations and accreditation requirements. This process occurred just as many states, with the encouragement of NPBEA and numerous foundations intent on restructuring public education, created fast-track alternative licensure routes that bypassed university programs, while facing less scrutiny than such programs do. Thus, a new leadership preparation market with little regulation was created to stand alongside traditional providers.

As has been noted by NPBEA, one important benefit of the ISLLC codification has been the thoughtful review and assessment of the entire history of school leadership preparation. Another, less fortunate by-product is the possibility of schools and districts hiring celebrity candidates who may know very little about schools but quickly can satisfy the new licensure requirements (Hess, 2003). Meanwhile, the operating assumptions of traditional preparation programs have been cast into serious doubt.

As one might expect, the emergence of the ISLLC standards has been highly contentious. For example, one leader in the administrative standards movement has described it as "a concerted effort to rebuild the foundations of school administration, both within the practice and academic domains of the profession … [enabling the field] to grow out of its adolescence" (Murphy, 2003, p. 1). By contrast, others have argued that by inappropriately codifying educational administration as static and atomistic, the standards privilege convenient and affordable licensure programs over ones that convey a more nuanced appreciation of the role of school leader. The result is an environment that undermines the legitimacy of basic research on the field because its content appears cut and dried (English, 2006). Others recognize the value of standards and the importance of program accreditation but argue that merely passing students through standards-based programs designed for ELLC/NCATE approval will not necessarily inspire the spiritual side of students (Hoyle, 2003a, 2003b). Similarly, some argue that the heightened emphasis on school accountability reflected in ISLLC ought to be balanced with other valued ends of schooling, such as the promotion of social justice and democratic community (Starratt, 2003).

It is precisely at this point that the NPM-like aspects of the standards movement come into focus. Broadly, the ISLLC standards' emphasis on the role of the principal in promoting school improvement privileges some perspectives on school leadership over others. Specifically, the Effective Schools (ES) literature's approach to school leadership includes six focal points for preparing school leaders: (a) vision, (b) school culture, (c) organizational management, (d) parent and community relations, (e) ethics, and (f) operational context (Marzano, Waters, & McNulty, 2005). While these standards underscore the ES emphasis—as an aspect of ethics—on the equitable delivery of education in a democratic society, they also stress the role of data-driven oversight of all school activities in a very prescriptive manner. Within the current high-stakes environment in which schools operate, such an approach can lead to inappropriately narrow definitions of *effectiveness* as well as a leadership discourse more dictatorial than democratic (G. L. Anderson, 2001a).

The first level of leadership attention as indicated by ES literature is incremental and amounts to ongoing data collection and systemic modifications where indicated (Marzano et al., 2005). Here the literature is mainstream, in line with both John Dewey's (1916/1944) approach to schools (pp. 139–206; also see Tannen, 1997) and Edward Deming's (1966) quality assurance model. However, at the second, "sudden reversal" level, abrupt change is mandated in terms that parallel NCLB's prescribed reconstitution of failing schools. The school leader is encouraged to apply dramatic methods to achieve the desired learning outcomes (Marzano et al., 2005), a premise that puts the leader above the school's community and organizational structure in a way uncharacteristic of both Dewey and Deming. Thus, while the ISLLC standards echo the ES literature's emphasis on the school leader who promotes the success of all students, they also harbor its affinity for unilateral leadership measures that could be based on a seriously skewed picture of overall learning because they are premised on only the easily quantified data.

For example, and notwithstanding the ES concern for equitable education, some have criticized its emphasis on quantitative performance over other potential measures of school effectiveness, such as equity for otherwise marginalized students (Starratt, 2003). Gronn (2003) also has noted the administrative standards movement's embrace of transformational leadership and other variations of heroic individualism that have been largely discredited due to an inability to withstand empirical test.

Challenges and Choices: Operating in and Responding to Current Conditions

The ISLLC standards attained nearly complete dominance in their initial decade. A review by Sanders and Simpson (2005) for the Council of Chief State School Officers found 46 states using some version of the ISLLC standards. Eight states adopted the ISLLC standards outright, 23 others added to or modified the standards for leadership frameworks, and 10 states use separately developed leadership standards found to align with the standards. Sanders and Simpson noted that states not using the ISLLC standards nonetheless use others with marked similarities to them. According to a report from NPBEA (2005), 29 states have adopted or adapted the ISLLC-based ELCC program standards associated with the NCATE review of administrator preparation programs. More than 150 university programs met the ELCC/NCATE Program Standards in 2005. According to the Educational Testing Service (2008), the ISLLC-based School Leader Licensure Assessment is currently a requirement in 17 states and the District of Columbia. Thus, the standards compel preparation programs' compliance as a condition of state agency approval and professional accreditation by independent authorities such as NCATE and through candidate testing. With widespread adoption of the standards, ISLLC holds sway over preparation programs and couples them to problems of field-based practice in powerful new ways (Murphy, 2003).

Put in broader theoretical terms, the administrative standards movement has placed schools, school leaders, and their preparation programs in the midst of a formidable "legitimation crisis" (Habermas, 1975, p. 46). Certainly, public and governmental discourse concerning schools now routinely calls into question their competence. Bottery (2003) has argued that NPM-style protocols simultaneously anticipate, and contribute to, a culture of minimal trust within schools. They do so by eschewing the premise that altruism plays much of a role as a motivator in the work of public servants like public school educators. Instead, NPM protocols rely upon extrinsic reward systems more akin to traditional piecework than professional job roles; in historical terms, reminiscent of the business-oriented administrative progressives (R. E. Anderson, 1990; Ball, 1998; Callahan, 1962). Such assumptions bear significant implications for leadership preparation and practice. In contemporary public schools, administrators now find themselves in the ambiguous position of ensuring the public's trust by monitoring teachers whose motivations and methods are assumed to be suspect. Meanwhile, they are themselves assumed to be cravenly self-interested (Terry, 1998) and only marginally competent (cf., Levine, 2005).

Moreover, Gronn (2003) has argued that the resulting reconstruction of the principalship is founded on faulty assumptions. It also has resulted in aspiring school leaders' sense that they are now obliged to anticipate a career of intense public scrutiny in a lonely—if purportedly heroic— role that demands virtually unlimited time demands (see also Pounder & Merrill, 2001). Moreover, Gronn has suggested that recruitment may be further undermined as intergroup relations among teachers and between teachers and administrators erode to the point of creating habitually tense work environments. These trends may help account for the apparent administrator shortage occurring in some states (Baker, Orr, & Young, 2006; Hoyle, 2002c; Pounder, Galvin, & Shepard, 2003) and related calls to expand the candidate pool to include noneducators (cf., Finn, 2003; Hess, 2003; Levine, 2005).

With regard to the NPM-style reforms of the 1980s and 1990, Rhodes (1994) argued the UK public sector was effectively "hollowed out" through efforts to increase economy and effectiveness in service delivery, in part by opening competition to private-sector providers and in part by reducing the scope of professional discretion. O'Sullivan (2005, p. 17) noted an associated "sea-change" in leadership preparation following these reforms, which fostered a marketized education sector and scaled back and streamlined public spending on administrator preparation. In this context, university-based programs—the traditional home of preparation—faced a "double whammy" of reduced public support for research and teaching amid increasing competition from low-cost providers offering skill-based management training. Such a scenario does not bode well for ongoing involvement of those preparing new leaders in the development of the field's base of knowledge.

While one might argue the UK context differs substantially, Baker, Orr, and Young (2006) found a substantial shift in degree production patterns between 1993 and 2003 away from more research-oriented and selective universities to less selective comprehensive U.S. institutions. Admittedly, not all research or comprehensive institutions are alike. Still, the data available suggest that leadership preparation is increasingly occurring in settings with lower levels of financial support and institutional security. Baker et al. also noted wide variations in degree production, even substantial overproduction, in a number of states relative to projected needs. These findings suggest the need for redirecting public policy analysis and resources to preparation programs that produce knowledgeable school leaders who understand the breadth of organizational and human complexity within any school's array of students, teachers, and community resources.

As of this writing, one potential counterbalance to the proliferation of programs and expansion of degrees granted among leadership preparation programs is state-level efforts to better inform state legislatures about the patterns and dynamics of administrative preparation. Such efforts are underway in Florida, Indiana, Missouri, New Jersey, and Utah, among others. For instance, state affiliates of the University Council for Educational Administration (UCEA) have spearheaded efforts to document program content and evaluate delivery of administrator preparation, working more closely with state policy makers to establish meaningful levers to control degree production and ensure quality in program delivery. Other efforts underway to improve the quality of preservice preparation include efforts to research and document the scope and specifics of trends discussed here.

Also, working collectively under the joint UCEA/TEA-SIG Taskforce on Evaluating Leadership Preparation headed by Terry Orr and Diana Pounder, researchers from Indiana, Missouri, and Utah were pursuing federal monies for a multistate study of preparation program effectiveness and impact. The taskforce also had undertaken a study of licensure preparation patterns among 14 programs across the country, with results anticipated in 2007. Finally, the taskforce, which sponsored the Baker et al. (2006) study on institutional trends in educational leadership degrees and licensure production discussed above, was seeking further funding from the U.S. Department of Education for a multistate study of leader preparation and administrative career outcomes. These activities are indicative of recent efforts within the field to move from a defensive to a responsive posture in addressing the changes in the operating environment and the erosion (or dismantling) of the institutional position once taken for granted.

Implications for Leader Preparation

Given the array of internal and external influences on university-based leader preparation described above, it is difficult to argue that these forces create a cohesive whole or push leader preparation in any single direction. Let us first consider the potential implications of internal influences.

Internal influences described above include changing trends in university missions to be more engaged with local communities, corresponding expanding faculty roles and responsibilities, potentially misaligned reward and incentive systems, faculty recruitment and retention challenges, and academic standards. Although these collective internal influences present challenges to universities and to leader preparation programs and their faculty, these influences also offer renewed possibilities for colleges of education and their various professional preparation programs.

Due to the applied nature of educational leadership preparation, reform of long-held practices and assumptions within universities may benefit those professional fields that have been constrained by more narrowly defined academic norms and standards. Specifically, trends of engaged universities may help define faculty roles and responsibilities in ways that benefit applied professional disciplines such as educational leadership. Standards of engaged universities push university faculty to be more service and outreach oriented—to bring their expertise to local community issues and challenges and to teach their students using hands-on pedagogies such as service learning. This influence may actually help colleges of education and educational leadership programs to be more authentically who they are; that is, education and education leadership may benefit from being truer to their applied disciplinary roots. Similarly, the research generated from outreach and real-world issues may contribute to the knowledge base in ways that not only serve academia, but also connect more strongly to educational leadership practice and better inform leader preparation.

However, for these internal influences to have any substantial impact, colleges of education and educational leadership programs must exercise the courage to embrace their applied roots to design and shape reward and incentive systems to more strongly support faculty outreach work and field-based research. Faculty are not likely to be successful sustaining activities of both engaged universities as well as those of more strictly defined traditional scholarly roles without becoming overwhelmed. If colleges of education will embrace these activist-oriented changes and align faculty reward and incentive systems accordingly, these same colleges may gain increased stature within the university by more authentically representing their discipline and its mission. Additionally, they may gain more respect and appreciation from local communities and the practitioner arm of the educational leadership profession.

We also posit that educational leadership programs that honor the integration of outreach and advocacy work, research, and teaching to promote social and educational improvement are likely to attract highly committed faculty with experiential backgrounds that reflect priorities of both schools and universities. By redefining faculty roles and responsibilities to be more closely engaged with the broader education profession, schools, and communities, the professoriate may be able to attract candidates who find this modified role appealing. That is, for those who have started their professional careers as practitioners, professorial roles that embrace and support the applied roots of educational leadership may be more attractive than roles defined in terms of strict arts and sciences academic disciplines. Further, faculty strongly committed to and engaged in the education profession broadly and the improvement of conditions for children will continue to redefine and refine academic and professional standards in the educational leadership field to reflect these priorities. These combined internal influences may be utilized to promote improved, responsive, and relevant educational leadership preparation in university settings.

Let us turn our attention now to the implications of external contextual influences on university-based leader preparation. Following the logic of the section above, there are at least two broad sets of implications concerning the immediate future and prospects for university-based school leader preparation programs. The first is a response to the most historically, philosophically, and research-substantiated aspects of the standards movement. In line with the stated ISLLC standards (as well as the first level of the prescribed principal focus of attention according to ES), preparation programs must better instruct aspiring administrators to be able to identify, research, assess, and remediate gaps in curricular content and student mastery of such content. For now, this process certainly must include the standardized tests mandated by the federal government, but they also should place these scores within the larger context of student learning.

Doubtless core aspects of NCLB (2002)—indeed, any well-constructed mandated test—not only are important measures of learning, but also incorporate the tacit need for students to negotiate the realities of life in a complex capitalist economy in which first impressions—be they visual or data based—carry weight. However, aspiring school leaders need the time and the expertise to consider other, less benign, aspects of high-stakes testing. Thus, preparation programs need to instruct their students in the more problematic aspects of the standards movement, whether applied to student outcomes or administrative licensure. Indeed, it is only by including this aspect of the new curriculum of ISLLC that school leaders may be expected to recognize the potential for inequitable, unintended consequences that may emerge from it. We have identified a few such consequences that apply to preparation programs (e.g., deskilling, demoralization of potential applicants, reduced resources, and priority for research institutions). However, the parallel implications for public schools and public education are at least as important.

The second set of implications directly concerns the future of research and theory on school leadership, which has been the traditional forte specific to research universities that prepared future administrators. Certainly, the prevailing conditions are against such institutions producing research outside the quantitative, NPM-friendly paradigm that produced the recent administrative standards movement. In the United States, the reasons for this situation go far beyond any set of administrator preparation standards. Indeed, the Institute for Education Sciences, which was created by the

George W. Bush administration to make education a more scientifically grounded field of research and scholarship, consistently has stated that only quantitative data that approximate experimental research deserve research funding (What Works Clearinghouse, 2007). To some extent, this same premise informs the ISLLC standards, particularly as manifested in the Educational Testing Service School Leader Licensure Assessment test format that has been criticized by ISLLC detractors. It also may be reflected in the current, outcome-based, educational leadership program accreditation trends, such as those of NCATE and ELCC. The net effect of this combination of licensure standards, program accreditation standards, and federal-funding policy construction is to create a paradigm of school leadership that is more hard science oriented than one with which many educational leadership faculty are comfortable. Put another way, some feel that school leadership is being pushed toward an earlier behaviorist paradigm merged with a prior era of Taylorism and other manifestations of the cult of efficiency (Callahan, 1962).

Thus, the collective internal and external contextual influences on university-based leader preparation are complex and in some instances contradictory, with perhaps leadership preparation standards central among these influences. At the very time that colleges of education and educational leadership preparation programs have an opportunity to embrace their authentic and applied disciplinary roots, they are being asked to stretch to fit a hard-science or business-bottom-line paradigm of accountability. The challenge for educational leadership preparation is not to cast these dilemmas and conflicting tensions into either–or propositions, devolving into paradigm wars that distract from the work at hand. That is, the education profession broadly and leadership preparation specifically need to consistently ask what norms, standards, procedures, and accountability are authentic and appropriate to an applied discipline. How can we support and enact educational leadership standards and preparation procedures that collectively will benefit schools and their students? In other words, how can the field of educational leader preparation sustain an internal locus of control in the face of its many and complex contextual influences?

Acknowledgment

We wish to thank Professor John Hoyle of Texas A&M University for his contributions on the early history of the educational leadership preparation standards movement.
Note: All authors contributed equally in the development of this chapter; authors' names are alphabetically ordered.

Notes

1. In the latter administration, Al Gore's push to "reinvent government," was informed by NPM principles though with greater emphasis on worker empowerment (Terry, 1998).
2. NPBEA includes representatives from the following: AASA, American Association of Colleges for Teacher Education (AACTE), Association for Supervision and Curriculum Development, the Council of Chief State School Officers, National Association of Elementary School Principals, National Association of Secondary School Principals, NCATE, National Council of Professors of Educational Administration (NCPEA), National School Boards Association (NSBA), and the UCEA.

References

Achilles, C. M. (2005). *Drama in educational administration: A farce or a morality play? Crediting the past, challenging the present, creating the past.* Paper presented at the National Council of Professors of Educational Administration Summit on the Preparation of School Leaders, Flagstaff, AZ.
Achilles, C. M., & Price, W. J. (2001). What is missing in the current debate about educational administration standards? *AASA Professor, 24*(2), 8–14.
Adams, J. E., Jr., & Kirst, M. W. (1999). New demands and concepts for educational accountability: Striving for results in

an era of excellence. In J. Murphy & K. S. Louis (Eds.), *Handbook of research on educational administration: A project of the American Educational Research Association* (2nd ed., pp. 463–489). San Francisco: Jossey-Bass.

Adams, K. A. (2002). *What colleges and universities want in new faculty. Preparing future faculty occasional paper series.* Washington, DC: Association of American Colleges and Universities and Council of Graduate Schools.

Addison, W. E., Best, J., & Warrington, J. D. (2006). Student perceptions of course difficulty and their ratings of the instructor. *College Student Journal, 40*(2), 409–416.

Alexander, M. S. (2006, September 1). Taking all the fun out of education. *The Chronicle of Higher Education,* p. B20.

Allen, E., & Estler, S. (2005). Diversity, privilege, and us: Collaborative curriculum transformation among educational leadership faculty. *Innovative Higher Education, 29*(3), 209–232.

American Association of University Professors. (2006). The devaluing of higher education: The annual report on the economic status of the profession 2005–2006. *Academe, 92*(2), 24–50.

Anderson, G. L. (1990). Toward a critical constructivist approach to school administration: Invisibility, legitimization and the study of non-events. *Education Administration Quarterly, 26*(1), 38–59.

Anderson, G. L. (2001a). Disciplining leaders: A critical discourse analysis of the ISLLC national examination and performance standards in educational administration. *International Journal of Leadership in Education, 4*(3), 199–216.

Anderson, G. L. (2001b). Promoting educational equity in a period of growing social inequity: The silent contradictions of Texas reform discourse. *Education and Urban Society, 33*(3), 320–332.

Anderson, R. E. (1990). The advantages and risks of entrepreneurship. *Academe, 76*(5), 9–14.

Anyon, J. (1980). Social class and the hidden curriculum of work. *Journal of Education, 161*(1), 67–93.

Apple, M. W. (1981). Social structure, ideology and curriculum. In L. Barton & M. Lawn (Eds.), *Rethinking curriculum studies: A radical approach* (pp. 133–159). New York: Wiley.

Astin, A. W., Korn, W. S., & Dey, E. (1990). *The American college teacher: National norms for 1989–90.* Los Angeles: UCLA Higher Education Research Institute.

Austin, A. U. (2002). Preparing the next generation: Graduate school as socialization to the academic career. *The Journal of Higher Education, 73*(94), 94–122.

Baker, B., Orr, T., & Young, M. (2006). Academic drift, institutional production and professional distribution of graduate degrees in educational administration. *Educational Administration Quarterly, 43*(3), 279–318.

Ball, S. J. (1998). Big policies/small world: An introduction to international perspectives in education policy. *Comparative Education, 34*(2), 119–130.

Barnet, D. (2004). School leadership preparation programs: Are they preparing tomorrow's leaders? *Education, 125*(1), 121–129.

Barzelay, M. (1992). *Breaking through bureaucracy: A new vision for managing in government.* Berkeley: University of California Press.

Benjamin, E. (1998). Declining faculty availability to students is the problem—But tenure is not the explanation. *American Behavioral Scientist, 41*(5), 716–736.

Bennett, W. J. (1988). *Our children and our country: Improving America's schools and affirming the common culture.* New York: Simon and Schuster.

Blase, J., & Anderson, G. (1995). *The micropolitics of educational leadership: From control to empowerment.* New York: Teachers College Press.

Bolman, L., & Deal, T. (1993). *Leading with soul: An uncommon journey of spirit.* San Francisco: Jossey-Bass.

Bottery, M. (2003). The leadership of learning communities in a culture of unhappiness. *School Leadership and Management, 23*(2), 187–207.

Bowles, S., & Gintis, H. (1976). *Schooling in capitalist America: Educational reform and the contradictions of economic life.* New York: Basic Books.

Boyer, E. L. (1990). *Scholarship reconsidered: Priorities of the professoriate.* Lawrenceville, NJ: Princeton University Press.

Brecher, B. (2006, August 25). A time and place to shout out "fire." *The Times Higher Education Supplement, 1757,* 42.

Brown, K. M. (2006). Leadership for social justice and equity: Evaluating a transformative framework for andragogy. *Educational Administration Quarterly, 42*(5), 700–745.

Browne-Ferrigno, T., & Muth, R. (2004). Leadership mentoring in clinical practice: Role socialization, professional development, and capacity building. *Educational Administration Quarterly, 40*(4), 468–494.

Brundrett, M. (2000). The question of competence: The origins, strengths, and inadequacies of a leadership training program. *School Leadership and Management, 20*(3), 353–369.

Callahan, R. E. (1962). *Education and the cult of efficiency: A study of the social forces that have shaped the administration of the public schools.* Chicago: University of Chicago Press.

Cambron-McCabe, N. H. (2002). Commentary: National Commission for the Advancement of Educational Leadership: Opportunity for transformation. *Educational Administration Quarterly, 38*(2), 289–299.

Cambron-McCabe, N. H. (2003). Rethinking leadership preparation: Focus on faculty learning communities. *Leadership and Policy in Schools, 2*(4), 285–298.

Campus Compact. (2007). Home page. Available from http://www.compact.org

Cantor, N. (2003). *Transforming America: The university as public good. Forseeable futures No. 3.* Position paper presented at the Imagining America Conference, Urbana, IL.

Cantor, N., & Lavine, S. D. (2006, June 9). Taking public scholarship seriously. *The Chronicle of Higher Education, 52*, p. B40. Retrieved June 19, 2006, from http://chronicle.com/cgi-bin/printable.cgi?article=http://chronicle.com

Capper, C. A., Hafner, M.., & Keyes, M. W. (2002). The role of community in spiritually centered leadership for justice. In G. Furman-Brown (Ed.), *School as community: From promise to practice* (pp. 77–94). Albany: State University of New York Press.

Carroll, V. S. (2003). The teacher, the scholar, the self: Fitting thinking and writing into a four-four load. *College Teaching, 51*(1), 22–26.

Chubb, J. E., & Moe, T. M. (1988). Politics, markets, and the organization of schools. *The American Political Science Review, 82*(4), 1065–1087.

Cibulka, J. (1997). Two eras of urban schooling: The decline of the old order and the emergence of new organizational forms. *Education and Urban Society, 29*(3), 317–341.

Cibulka, J., & Derlin, R. (1998). Accountability policy adoption to policy sustainability: Reforms and systemic initiatives in Colorado and Maryland. *Education and Urban Society, 30*(4), 502–515.

Cicchelli, T., Marcus, S., & Weiner, M. (2002). Superintendents' dialogue in a professional development model. *Education and Urban Society, 34*(4), 415–421.

Clarke, M. (2004). Weighing things up: A closer look at "U.S. News & World Report" ranking formulas. *College and University, 79*(3), 3–9.

Cordeiro, P. A. (1998). Problem-based learning in educational administration: Enhancing learning transfer. *Journal of School Leadership, 8*, 280–302.

Corrigan, D. C. (1997). The role of the university in community building. *The Educational Forum, 62*(1), 14–24.

Cuban, L. (1990). Reforming again, again, and again. *Educational Researcher, 19*(1), 3–13.

Culbertson, J. A. (1988). A century's quest for a knowledge base. In N. J. Boyan (Ed.), *Handbook of research on educational administration: A project of the American Educational Research Association* (pp. 3–26). New York: Longman.

Dantley, M. E. (2003). Purpose-driven leadership: The spiritual imperative to guiding schools beyond high-stakes testing and minimum proficiency. *Education and Urban Society, 35*(3), 273–291.

Darling-Hammond, L. (2006). Constructing 21st-century teacher education. *Journal of Teacher Education, 57*(3), 300–314.

Deming, W. E. (1966). *Out of the crisis*. Cambridge, MA: MIT Press.

Dewey, J. (1944). *Democracy and education*. New York: Macmillan. (Original work published 1916)

Donmoyer, R. (1999). The continuing quest for a knowledge base: 1976–1998. In J. Murphy & K. S. Louis (Eds.), *Handbook of research on educational administration: A project of the American Educational Research Association* (2nd ed., pp. 25–44). San Francisco: Jossey-Bass.

Edgerton, R. (1993). The re-examination of faculty priorities. *Change, 25*(4), 10–24.

Educational Testing Service. (2008). Home page. Retrieved May 11, 2008, from http://www.ets.org

Ehrenberg, R. G. (2003). Reaching for the brass ring: The "U.S. News and World Report" rankings and competition. *Review of Higher Education, 26*(2), 145–162.

Elman, S. E. (2002). Part-time faculty and student learning: A regional accreditation perspective. *Peer Review, 5*(1), 15–18.

Elmore, R. F., Abelman, C., & Fuhrman, S. (1996). The new accountability in state education reform: From process to performance. In H. Ladd (Ed.), *Holding schools accountable: Performance-based reform in education* (pp. 65–98). Washington, DC: Brookings Institute.

English, F. W. (2003). Cookie-cutter leaders for cookie-cutter schools: The teleology of standardization and the de-legitimization of the university in educational leadership preparation. *Leadership and Policy in Schools, 2*(1), 27–46.

English, F. W. (2006). The unintended consequences of a standardized knowledge base in advancing educational leadership programs. *Educational Administration Quarterly, 42*(3), 461–472.

Finn, C. (2003). *Better leaders for America's schools: A manifesto*. Washington, DC: Thomas Fordham Institute.

Foster, W. P. (1986). *Paradigms and promises: New approaches to educational administration*. Buffalo, NY: Prometheus Books.

Friedman, M., & Friedman, R. D. (1980). *Free to choose: A personal statement*. New York: Harcourt Brace Jovanovich.

Fuhrman, S. H. (1999). *The new accountability (CPRE policy brief)*. Philadelphia: University of Pennsylvania, Consortium for Policy Research in Education.

Fullan, M. (2003). *The moral imperative of school leadership*. Thousand Oaks. CA: Corwin Press.

Fusarelli, L. D. (2002). Tightly coupled policy in loosely coupled systems: Institutional capacity and organizational change. *Journal of Educational Administration, 40*(6), 561–575.

Fusarelli, L. D., & Johnson, B. (2004). Educational governance and the new public management. *Public Administration and Management: An Interactive Journal, 9*(2), 118–127.

Gale, T, & Densmore, K. (2003). Democratic educational leadership in contemporary times. *International Journal of Leadership in Education, 6*(2), 119–136.

Gappa, J. M., Austin, A. E., & Trice, A. G. (2005). Rethinking academic work and workplaces. *Change: The Magazine of Higher Learning, 37*(6), 32–40.

Gordon, L., & Whitty, G. (1997). Giving the hidden hand a helping hand? The rhetoric and reality of neoliberal education reform in England and New Zealand. *Comparative Education, 33*(3), 453–467.

Griffiths, D. (1995). Theoretical pluralism in educational administration. In R. Donmoyer, M. Imber, & J. J. Scheurich (Eds.), *The knowledge base in educational administration: Multiple perspectives* (pp. 300–309). Albany: State University of New York Press.

Griffiths, D. E. (1997). The case for theoretical pluralism. *Educational Management and Administration, 25,* 371–380.

Grogan, M., & Andrews, R. (2002). Defining preparation and professional development for the future. *Educational Administration Quarterly, 38*(2), 233–256.

Gronn, P. (2003). *The new work of educational leaders: Changing leadership practice in an era of school reform.* London: Sage.

Habermas, J. (1975). *Legitimation crisis.* Boston: Beacon Press.

Hafner, M. M., & Capper, C. (2005). Defining spirituality: Critical implications for the practice and research of educational leadership. *Journal of School Leadership, 15,* 624–638.

Heckert, T. M., Latier, A. & Ringwald-Burton, A. (2006). Relations among student effort, perceived class difficulty appropriateness, and student evaluations of teaching: Is it possible to "buy" better evaluations through lenient grading? *College Student Journal, 40*(3), 588–596.

Hess, F. (2003). *License to lead? A new leadership agenda for America's schools.* Washington, DC: Progressive Policy Institute.

Hirsch, E. D., Kett, J. F., & Trefil, J. S. (1988). *The dictionary of cultural literacy.* Boston: Houghton Mifflin.

Hood, C. (1991). A public management for all seasons? *Public Administration, 69,* 3–19.

Hoy, W. K. (1996). Science and theory in the practice of educational administration: A pragmatic perspective. *Educational Administration Quarterly, 32,* 366–378.

Hoy, W., & Miskel, C. (2005). *Educational administration: Theory and practice* (7th ed.). Boston: McGraw-Hill.

Hoyle, J. (1983). *Guidelines for the preparation of school administrators.* Arlington, VA: The American Association of School Administrators.

Hoyle, J. (1985). Programs in educational administration and the AASA preparation guidelines. *Educational Administration Quarterly, 21*(1), 91–95.

Hoyle, J. (1987). The AASA model for preparing school leaders. In J. Murphy & P. Hallinger (Eds.), *Approaches to administrative training in education* (pp. 83–98). Albany: State University of New York Press.

Hoyle, J. (1993). *Professional standards for the superintendency.* Arlington, VA: The American Association of School Administrators.

Hoyle, J. R. (2002a). The highest form of leadership. *School Administrator, 59*(8), 18–21.

Hoyle, J. R. (2002b). *Leadership and the force of love: Six keys to motivating with love.* Thousand Oaks, CA: Corwin Press.

Hoyle, J. (2002c) *Superintendents for Texas school districts: Solving the crisis in executive leadership.* Fort Worth, TX: Sid Richardson Foundation.

Hoyle, J. (2003a). Educational administration: Atlantis or phoenix. NCPEA Distinguished Lecture. In F. Lunenburg & C. Carr (Eds.), *Shaping the future: Policy, partnerships, and emerging perspectives* (pp. 5–15). Lanham, MA: Scarecrow Education.

Hoyle, J. (2003b). Educational administration: Atlantis or phoenix? *UCEA Review, 45*(1), 11–14.

Hoyle, J., Björk, L., Collier, V., & Glass, T. (2005). *The superintendent as CEO: Standards based performance.* Thousand Oaks, CA. Corwin Press.

Hoyle, J., English, F., & Steffy, B. (1985). *Skills for successful school leaders.* Arlington, VA: American Association of School Administrators.

Imagining America. (n.d.). Home page. Retrieved May 11, 2008, from http://www.imaginingamerica.org/

Interstate School Leaders Licensure Consortium. (1996). *Standards for school leaders.* Washington, DC: Council of Chief State School Officers.

Jackson, B. L., & Kelley, C. (2002). Exceptional and innovative programs in educational leadership. *Educational Administration Quarterly, 38*(2), 192–212.

Jaeger, A. J., & Thornton, C. H. (2006). Neither honor nor compensation: Faculty and public service. *Educational Policy, 20*(2), 345–366.

Kaboolian, L. (1998). The new public management: Challenging the boundaries of the management vs. administration debate. *Public Administration Review, 58*(3), 189–193.

Katz, J. A. (1992). *Endowed positions and the infrastructure of entrepreneurship.* Saint Louis, MO: Jefferson Smurfit Center for Entrepreneurial Studies. (ERIC Document Reproduction Services No. ED409928)

Kochan, F. K., & Sabo, D. J. (1995). Transforming educational leadership programs through collaboration: Practicing what we preach. *Planning and Changing, 26,* 168–178.

Kottkamp, R. B., & Silverberg, R. P. (2003). Leadership preparation reform in first person: Making assumptions public. *Leadership and Policy in Schools, 2*(4), 299–326.

Kuh, G. D., Kinzie, J., Schuh, J. H., & Whitt, E. J. (2005). Never let it rest. *Change, 37*(4), 44–51.

Landrum, R. E. (1999). Student expectations of grade inflation. *Journal of Research and Development in Education, 32*(2), 124–128.

Larabee, D. F. (1997). Public goods, private goods: The American struggle over educational goals. *American Educational Research Journal, 34*(1), 39–81.

LaRocco, D. J., & Bruns, D. A. (2006). Practitioner to professor: An examination of second career academics' entry into academia. *Education, 126*(4), 626–639.

Leithwood, K., & Menzies, T. (1998). A review of research concerning the implementation of site-based management. *School Effectiveness and School Improvement, 9*(3), 233–285.

Levine, A. (2005). *Educating school leaders.* Washington, DC: The Education Schools Project.

Lindholm, J. A. (2004). Pathways to the professoriate: The role of self, others, and environment in shaping academic career aspirations. *Journal of Higher Education, 75*(6), 603–635.

Lindholm, J. A., Astin, A. W., Sax, L. J., & Korn, W. S. (2002). *The American college teacher: National norms for the 2001–2002 HERI Faculty Survey.* Los Angeles: UCLA Higher Education Research Institute.

Livingston, M., Davis, L., Green, R. L., & DeSpain, B. C. (2001). Strengthening the professorial role through collaboration: A guide to school administrators. *Education, 122*(1), 135–140.

Lunenburg, F. C. (2003, April). Paradigm shifts in educational administration: A view from the editor's desk of *Educational Leadership Review* and *NCPEA Yearbook.* Paper presented at the annual meeting of the American Educational Research Association, Chicago.

Lunenburg, F. C., & Ornstein, A. O. (2004). *Educational administration: Concepts and practices.* Belmont, CA: Wadsworth/Thomson Learning.

Malen, B. (2003). Tightening the grip? The impact of state activism on local school systems. *Education Policy, 17*(2), 195–216.

Marshall, C. (Ed.). (1993). *The new politics of race and gender.* London: Falmer.

Marshall, C. (2004). Social justice challenges to educational administration: Introduction to a special issue. *Educational Administration Quarterly, 40*(1), 3–13.

Marshall, C., Patterson, J., Rogers, D., & Steele, J. (1996). Caring as a career: An alternative perspective on educational administration. *Educational Administration Quarterly, 32*(2), 271–294.

Marzano, R., Waters, T., & McNulty, B. (2005). *School leadership that works: from research to results.* Washington, DC: Association for Supervision and Curriculum Development.

Maxcy, S. J. (1994). *Postmodern school leadership: Meeting the crisis in educational administration.* Westport, CT: Praeger.

McCarthy, M. (2005). Prologue. In T.Creighton, S. Harris, & J. C. Coleman (Eds.), *Crediting the past, challenging the present, creating the future* (pp. 1–4). Flagstaff, AZ: The National Council of Professors of Educational Administration.

Meyer, H.-D. (2002). From "loose coupling" to "tight management"? Making sense of the changing landscape in management and organization theory. *Journal of Educational Administration, 40*(6), 515–521.

Minority Student Achievement Network. (2008). Home page. Retrieved May 11, 2008, from http://msan.wceruw.org/

Moore, H. (1964). The ferment in school administration. In E. E. Griffiths (Ed.), *Behavioral science and educational administration* (pp. 11–32). Chicago: National Society for the Study of Education.

Murphy, J. (1992). *The landscape of leadership preparation: Reframing the education of school administrators.* Newbury Park, CA: Corwin Press.

Murphy, J. (2002). Reculturing the profession of educational leadership: New blueprints. *Educational Administration Quarterly, 38*(2), 176–191.

Murphy, J. (2003). *Reculturing educational leadership: The ISLLC standards ten years out.* Washington, DC: National Policy Board for Educational Administration.

Murphy, J. (2005). Unpacking the foundations of the ISLLC standards and addressing concerns in the academic community. *Educational Administration Quarterly, 41*(1), 154–191.

Murphy, J. (2006). *Preparing school leaders: Defining a research and action agenda.* Lanham, MD: Rowman & Littlefield Education.

Murphy, J., & Beck, L. G. (1995). *School-based management as school reform: Taking stock.* Thousand Oaks, CA: Corwin Press.

Murphy, J., & Vriesenga, M. (2004). *Research on preparation programs in educational administration: An analysis* (UCEA monograph series). Columbia, MO: University Council for Educational Administration.

Murphy, J., Yff, J., & Shipman, N. (2000). Implementation of the Interstate School Leaders Licensure Consortium standards. *International Journal of Leadership in Education, 3*(1), 17–39.

National Commission on Excellence in Education. (1983). *A nation at risk: The imperative for educational reform. A report to the nation and the Secretary of Education, United States Department of Education.* Washington, DC: U.S. Government Printing Office.

National Policy Board for Educational Administration. (2005). *A listing of nationally recognized educational leadership preparation programs at NCATE accredited colleges and universities.* Washington, DC: Author.

No Child Left Behind Act of 2001, Pub. L. No. 107-110 (2002).

Oakes, J. (1985). *Keeping track: How schools structure inequality.* New Haven, CT: Yale University Press.

Ogawa, R. T. (1994). The institutional sources of educational reform: The case of school-based management. *American Educational Research Journal, 31*(3), 519–548.

O'Meara, K.A. (2006). Encouraging multiple forms of scholarship in faculty reward systems: Influence on faculty work life. *Planning for Higher Education, 34*(2), 43–53.

Orr, M. T. (2006). Mapping innovation in leadership preparation in our nation's schools of education. *Phi Delta Kappan, 87*(7), 492–499.

Osborne, S. P., & Gabler, T. (1992). *Reinventing government: How the entrepreneurial spirit is transforming the public sector.* Reading, MA: Addison-Wesley.

Osborne, S. P., & McLaughlin, K. (2002). The new public management in context. In K. McLaughlin, S. P. Osborne, & E. Ferlie (Eds.), *New public management: Current trends and future prospects* (pp. 7–14). New York: Routledge.

O'Sullivan, F. (2005). Education leadership prepartion: A view from the UK. *UCEA Review, 45*(1), 17–20.

Papalewis, R. (2005). The discipline of educational administration: Crediting the past. In T. Creighton, S. Harris, & J. C. Coleman (Eds.), *Crediting the past, challenging the present, creating the future* (pp. 5–22). Flagstaff, AZ: National Council of Professors of Educational Administration.

Peters, S. (2005). Chapter eleven: Findings. In S. J. Peters, N. R. Jordan, M. Adamek, & T. R. Alter (Eds.), *Engaging campus and community: The practice of public scholarship in the state and land-grant university system* (pp. 393–459). Dayton, OH: Kettering Foundation Press.

Peters, S. J., Jordan, N. R., Adamek, M, & Alter, T. R. (Eds.) (2005). *Engaging campus and community: The practice of public scholarship in the state and land-grant university system.* Dayton, OH: Kettering Foundation Press.

Peterson, K. D., & Finn, C. E. (1985). Principals, superintendents and administrator's art. *Public Interest, 79,* 42–62.

Pollitt, C. (1990). *Managerialism and the public services: The Anglo-American experience.* Cambridge, England: Basil Blackwell.

Pollitt, C. (2003). *The essential public manager.* Philadelphia: Open University Press.

Pounder, D. G. (1995). Theory to practice in administrator preparation: An evaluation study. *Journal of School Leadership, 5*(2), 151–162.

Pounder, D. G. (Ed.). (1998). *Restructuring schools for collaboration: Promises and pitfalls.* Albany: State University of New York Press.

Pounder, D. G. (2000). Research and inquiry in educational administration: A call for quality and utility, *Educational Administration Quarterly, 36*(3), 336–340, 465–473.

Pounder, D. G., Young, M., & Reitzug, U. (2002). Restructuring the preparation of school leaders. In J. Murphy (Ed.), *The educational leadership challenge: Redefining leadership for the 21st century* (pp. 261–288). Chicago: National Society for the Study of Education/University of Chicago Press.

Pounder, D. G. (2006). Leader preparation research and reform agendas: A response to charting the changing landscape. In J. Murphy (Ed.), *Preparing school leaders: Defining a research and action agenda* (pp. 87–92). Lanham, MD: Rowman & Littlefield Education.

Pounder, D. G., Crow, G., & Bergerson, A. (2004). Job desirability of the university professorate in the field of educational leadership. *Journal of School Leadership, 14*(5), 497–529.

Pounder, D. G., Galvin, P., & Shepard, P. (2003). An analysis of the United States educational administrator shortage. *Australian Journal of Education, 47*(2), 133–145.

Pounder, D. G., & Merrill, R. (2001). Job desirability of the high school principalship: A job choice theory perspective. *Educational Administration Quarterly, 37*(1), 27–57.

Reed, C. J. (2006, November). *Creating powerful partnerships.* Paper presented at the annual meeting of the Southern Regional Council of Educational Administration, Atlantic Beach, FL.

Reich, R. (1990). *Public management in a democratic society.* Englewood Cliffs, NJ: Prentice Hall.

Rhodes, R. A. W. (1994). The hollowing out of the state: The changing nature of the public service in Britain. *The Political Quarterly, 65*(2), 138–151.

Ridenour, C. S., & Twale, D. J. (2005). Academic generations exploring intellectual risk taking in an educational leadership program. *Education, 126*(1), 158–164.

Robison, R., & Hewison, K. (2005). Introduction: East Asia and the trials of neo-liberalism. *Journal of Development Studies, 41*(2), 183–196.

Rusch, E. A. (2004). Gender and race in leadership preparation: A constrained discourse. *Educational Administration Quarterly, 40*(1), 14–46.

Sanders, N. M., & Simpson, J. (2005). *State policy framework to develop highly qualified administrators.* Washington, DC: Council of Chief State School Officers.

Scheurich, J. J., Skrla, L., & Johnson, J. E. (2000). Thinking carefully about equity and accountability. *Phi Delta Kappan, 82*(4), 293–299.

Schneider, J. (2003). *The unholy alliance between departments of educational administration and their "invisible faculty"* (Occasional paper). Arlington, VA: American Association of School Administrators.

Schofield, J. W. (1991). School desegregation and intergroup relations: A review of the literature. *Review of Research in Education, 17,* 335–409.

Sergiovanni, T. (1992). *Moral leadership: Getting to the heart of school improvement*. San Francisco: Jossey-Bass.

Southern Regional Education Board. (2006). *Schools can't wait: Accelerating the redesign of university preparation programs*. Atlanta, GA: Author. Retrieved September 15, 2006, from http://www.sreb.org/programs/hstw/publications/special/SchoolsCantWait.asp_

Starratt, R. J. (2003). *Centering educational administration: Cultivating meaning, community, responsibility*. Mahwah, NJ: Erlbaum.

Stein, S. J. (2006). Transforming leadership programs: Design, pedagogy, and incentives. *Phi Delta Kappan, 87*(7), 522–524.

Tannen, D. (1997). *Dewey's laboratory school*. New York: Teachers College Press.

Teitel, L. (2006). Mapping the terrain of "alternative" leadership education: Lessons for universities. *Phi Delta Kappan, 87*(7), 500–507.

Terry, L. D. (1998). Administrative leadership, neo-managerialism, and the public management movement. *Public Administration Review, 58*(3), 194–200.

Thompson, S. (2004). Learning from the eye of the storm. *Educational Leadership, 61*(7), 60–63.

Timar, T. B., & Kirp, D. L. (1987). Educational reform and institutional competence. *Harvard Educational Review, 57*(3), 309–330.

Tyack, D. B., & Cuban, L. (1995). *Tinkering toward utopia: A century of public school reform*. Cambridge, MA: Harvard University Press.

University Neighborhood Partners. (n.d.). Home page. Retrieved May 11, 2008, from http://www.partners.utah.edu/

What Works Clearinghouse. (2007). *Review process*. Retrieved May 11, 2008, from http://ies.ed.gov/ncee/wwc/overview/review.asp

Whitty, G., & Power, S. (2003). Making sense of education reform: Global and national influences. In C. A. Torres & A. Antikainen (Eds.), *The international handbook on the sociology of education: An international assessment of new research and theory* (pp. 305–324). Lanham, MD: Rowman & Littlefield.

Willower, D. J. (1998). Fighting the fog: A criticism of postmodernism. *Journal of School Leadership*, 8, 448–463.

Young, M. D., & Petersen, G. J. (2002a). Enabling substantive reform in the preparation of school leaders. *Educational Leadership Review, 3*(1), 1–15.

Young, M. D. & Petersen, G. J. (2002b). The National Commission for the Advancement of Educational Leadership Preparation: An introduction. *Educational Administration Quarterly, 38*(2), 130–136.

Young, M. D., Petersen, G. J., & Short, P. M. (2002). The complexity of substantive reform: A call for interdependence among key stakeholders. *Educational Administration Quarterly, 38*(2), 137–175.

4

Research on Leadership Preparation in a Global Context

JACKY LUMBY, ALLAN WALKER, MILES BRYANT,
TONY BUSH, AND LARS G. BJÖRK

EDITED BY JACKY LUMBY AND MILES BRYANT

Challenging Narcissism

In this chapter we view U.S. leadership preparation from a global stage. We bring together voices from various parts of the world to consider why stepping outside a U.S. perspective may help develop U.S. programs. We explore why culture is a critical consideration in the design and delivery of programs, analyze the differing approaches to leader development (initial preparation and ongoing education) in a variety of countries, and suggest the major lessons emerging for U.S. leader preparation. Our premise is that engaging with the plurality of systems with their rich spectrum of values, cultural underpinning, and variation in practice is a means of both enriching U.S. programs and contributing to the worldwide development of education leaders. We argue for recognition, valuing, and utilization of difference. Consequently, we adopt an approach that is consistent with this value base, allowing the writers' different voices to be discernible. While we construct a coherent sequence of arguments and explorations, we make no attempt to homogenize the chapter into a composite, single voice. Rather, the chapter requires the orientation being suggested to those involved with preparation programs, that readers engage with different perspectives and views to reflect on their own assumptions and practice. The writer is consequently identified for each of the four sections of the chapter.

The focus is the preparation and continuing development of leadership. However, leadership is a highly contested concept. As a starting point we take House, Hanges, Javidan, Dorfman, and Gupta's (2004) definition: "the ability of an individual to influence, motivate, and enable others to contribute toward the effectiveness and success of the organizations of which they are members" (p. 15). This definition was conceived as part of an international study in relation to generic organizations. Our view in relation to school leadership views the field of influence as wider, not just contributing to the effectiveness of the organization, but also directly interacting with and contributing to the community. The chapter therefore is concerned with how preparation programs relate to the global context and thereby contribute to leaders' efforts to support the success of both school and community.

The first section of the chapter, written by Jacky Lumby, begins by justifying and exploring further the key question: Is an international perspective vital for the future health of U.S. leader preparation? Lumby approaches this question by considering the forces of globalization and their relation to an international perspective. This section examines the impact of global pressures, which are suggested to impel both homogeneity and diversity. Political, professional, and personal rationales for educational leaders to respond to such a paradoxical context are explored.

In the second section of the chapter, Allan Walker considers the relationship of culture to leadership development programs (LDPs). He argues that the efficacy of leader development is dependant on cultural fit, and that sensitivity to cultural context is as relevant to the design of U.S. programs as it is to considering the transmission of practice from one national context to another. He provides examples of fit or lack of fit for what he distinguishes as content-based and community-based programs.

Miles Bryant and Tony Bush detail and analyze systems in developing and developed economies throughout the world. They argue that the distinctions made between systems illuminate different choices of the optimum means of developing leaders but also suggest that what is perceived as different can sometimes be less so than appears. Their typology of approaches offers stimulation for considering the nature and underpinning of practice globally and in the United States. Finally, Lars Björk, Miles Bryant, and Jacky Lumby conclude the chapter by relating an international perspective to five key challenges facing leadership preparation in the United States (Björk, Kowalski, & Young, 2005).

The Importance of an International Perspective on Leadership Preparation

The current orientation of U.S. leaders and those who prepare them is widely believed to be circumscribed. For well over two decades, various commentators have noted what W. G. Walker (1984) termed the narcissism of those researching and preparing leaders. Most research, even when considering future trends, adopts a firmly national perspective (Crisci & Tutela, 1987; Hills, 1983; Hoy, 1986). Critiques of ethnocentric and isolationist perspectives have highlighted the propensity of U.S. faculty to turn inward, evolving leadership preparation programs with little cognizance of developments outside North America (Foskett & Lumby 2003; Griffiths, Stout, & Forsyth, 1988; Hallinger, 1995; Hallinger & Leithwood, 1998; A. Walker & Dimmock, 2004). Reviews of the development of educational leadership preparation programs and prognostications or prescriptions of future trends have little to say about an international perspective (A. Levine, 2005). A North American perspective is taken for granted, its cultural implications unexplored (Burlingame & Harris, 1998). A lack of awareness of one's own culture may be evident globally. However, the worldwide lack of self-awareness of acculturation may be exacerbated by numerous factors in the United States. Why this is the case is worthy of a chapter in its own right but briefly may include relative geographical isolation from the rest of the world and the size of the population, which may lend a seeming self-dependence.

Since W. G. Walker's criticism in 1984, the context has changed radically. Depictions of political, economic, and cultural globalization and its influence on education, though contested, are nevertheless ubiquitous and pressing (Bottery, 1999; Crossley & Watson, 2003; Foskett & Lumby, 2003, Ohmae, 2000; Scholte, 2000). In this chapter we argue that such is the force of global change, narcissism, if ever it was an appropriate stance, is no longer tenable. We consider leadership preparation in a globalized context and challenge educational leaders and those who prepare them to think anew about the relevance of an international perspective. Definitions of the term are multiple and contested, and, in part, the purpose of this chapter is to clarify our understanding of the nature and purpose of such a perspective. The chapter does not adopt a cross-cultural stance, that is, the comparison of two or more cultures with the aim of distinguishing past and present differences, a mosaic pattern of divergence. Such a stance would risk being ethnocentric, aiming to underpin effective performance in alien cultures. Rather the international stance adopted is more akin to a systems approach, searching not just for differences, but critically "for patterns of interconnectedness" (Paige & Mestenhauser, 1999, p. 502) that subsume and color patterns of difference. As Paige and Mestenhauser stressed, it is a process of knowledge construction that attempts to transcend the ethnocentric; an international stance renders one's own position merely one tale in a meta story.

The empirical base to support such an enterprise is weak. There is a dearth of research investigating the nature and degree of international perspective in leadership preparation programs in North America or the attitudes of those delivering or participating in programs towards the necessity for or benefits of such a perspective. In the absence of an empirical base, this chapter initially constructs a case for adopting an international perspective. This serves as a foundation from which we explore the impact of culture on preparation programs, the varying approaches to preparation adopted in different parts of the globe, and the possibilities for a research agenda that is global in reach. The underlying premise is that preparation programs need to develop the capacity of leaders to connect to and understand the community. What is in question is whether the school community and the community of practice of educators are to be understood merely as local or also as regional, national, and international.

The Context of Global Change

Globalization is a term that appears ubiquitously in texts relating to the social, political, and economic sciences (Giddens, 1999; Rosenberg, 2000). Nevertheless, its definition is problematic, given the contested understanding of global forces and the infinitely variable interrelationship of the latter to individual, organizational, and national psyches (Brown &Lauder, 1997; Parsons, 1995; Rhoten, 2000). Levin (2001) unpacked the multiple meanings in the term:

> Globalization is a multi-dimensional term. It suggests a condition: the world as a single place. It is viewed as a process: the linking of localities, separated by great distances and intensifying relations between these localities. Globalization is also implicitly connected to international economies, as in the concept of a world economy; and to international relations or politics, as in the concept of global politics; and to culture, as in the concept of global culture. Furthermore, the term *global* is used as an adjective for both singular and plural nouns, suggesting that there are multiple economies, political systems, and cultures globally as well as a single integrative economy, political system, and culture. (p. 8)

Paradox is implicit in the definition, reflecting tension between effects that delete the unique but also bolster determination to retain what is distinctive. Globalization theories therefore present a potentially infinite variation in interpretation of the existence, degree, interplay, and impact of political, economic, and cultural change (Waters, 1995). The implications for educational leaders and systems to prepare them are multiple and profound. Scholte (2000) argued that globalization has affected ontology and epistemology. First, conceptions of space have changed, as distance no longer separates nations and peoples or schools, curricula, and educators, all of which are linked by readily available, efficient means of travel and virtual means of connection. Schools increasingly function and create knowledge in virtual space, where an ocean of knowledge pours through screens in classrooms, and ties to a school thousands of miles away may be stronger than those with the school down the road. Leaders function in a context that is partly the physical location of their school and partly cyberspace. Second, Scholte argued that our notions of time have shifted as time has become decoupled from distance, accelerating the creation and transmission not only of goods and services, but also of knowledge across regional and national boundaries. The impact on education of such global volition is not only the seemingly simultaneous adoption of common solutions, but also a degree of homogenization of problems. School-based management, outcomes-based curricula, and target-driven assessment are examples of practices that assume a place on a global stage irrespective of cultural, political, and economic differences in context.

Lakomski (2001) argued that culture is embedded neurologically. Relatedly, neuroepistemological approaches to studying educational leadership strengthen the conviction that there is a connection between ontology, epistemology, and neurology (Allix & Gronn, 2005). As globalization creates epistemological and axiological tides of change, the connection between educators in all parts of the world is a function of often unconscious shared patterns of thinking and not just of conscious links through communication technology.

As global forces sweep migrants and their culture across local, regional, and national perimeters, the incursion of the distant is matched by pressure from divergent ideas close at hand, evident in the increasingly heterogeneous local context. Scholte (2000) asserted that long-standing state-nations have been overlain by ethnonations and the diasporas of global tribes (Kotkin, 1992), transworld communities tied by religion or nation of origin. Globalization, therefore, is not experienced as the wholesale adoption of a particular ontology, epistemology, and axiology in all parts of the world, but rather as a common context where pressures towards both homogeneity and heterogeneity are simultaneously experienced. The result is a thrust for change that alters the texture of the world (Bottery, 1999; Brown & Lauder, 1997; Ohmae, 2000; Parsons, 1995; Waters, 1995).

As a result, education and educators stand at the heart of the boundaryless world and the rapidly evolving maelstrom of engagement with the problems of society and the proposed solutions. Whether the globalized, boundaryless world is seen as utopian or dystopian, at the fulcrum stand educators, the "key linking agents" (Hallinger, 1995, p. 1). If, as Hallinger (1995, p. 4) suggested over a decade ago, "school leadership development has become a global enterprise," there are compelling reasons why narcissism among those who prepare educational leaders is unsustainable.

How to counter narcissism is the challenge. Rhetorical commitment to inclusion of different world views requires a practical strategy if it is to become more than rhetoric. An international perspective is one such strategy aiming at a global reach appreciation of the culture and practice of others in order to increase consciousness of one's own parameters, strengths, and limitations. It entails viewing values and practice in locations across the world, including one's own, with sufficient openness to reach insights about similarities, differences, and their scale and translating such insights into renewed commitment to and ideas for developing one's own practice. It is qualitatively different from the "travellers' tales" (Crossley & Watson, 2003, p. 12) that observe alternative practice outside the nation state with curiosity, often assumed superiority, and engage at most, magpie like, by borrowing seemingly useful practice from the great elsewhere.

Global Utopia and Dystopia

The concept of globalization therefore provides a powerful argument for the need for those who prepare and develop educational leaders to look across the world. Two positions are discernible in response. First, the positive is discovered in possibilities, as Burbules and Torres (2000) put it, for "an international educational organisation and agenda that could create a new hegemony in curriculum, instruction, and pedagogical practices, in general, as well as in policies concerning school financing, research, and evaluation" (p. 4). Globalization is interpreted as a positive integrative force, with a goal of harmonization. As a result, future learners may have more similar and therefore more equitable opportunities, to their benefit. Such a vision is rejected by many, and globalization is frequently interpreted by educators negatively, as resulting in worldwide trends that are inimical to the professional values of educators. The "McDonaldization" of education (Levin, 2001, p. 9) neatly sums up the pejorative view of the effects of globalization in the view of some. There is no space here to explore in depth the arguments propounded to welcome or resist the global sweep of educational reform. However, implications for the preparation and continuous development of leaders are evident. If the effects of globalization are to create worldwide pressures and trends, such as outlined by Levin, then the response of educators to welcome, accommodate, or repel the overt or covert incursion of new values, priorities, and practice must be based on an understanding that transcends analysis based on the immediate location (Foster, 2004).

What then are the professional, political, and personal rationales for responding to the scenario depicted and supporting leaders to achieve a global reach in their engagement with and understanding of educational issues and practice? Each of these perspectives may offer an impetus for engagement, and they are explored in turn.

Professional Rationale

K. M. Cheng (1998) suggested that few classrooms in the United States are not multiethnic, touched by the global tribes and diasporas referred to earlier. In response, the necessity for cultural competence to be an effective educator and leader, though not accepted by all (Lopez, 2003), is widely adopted at least rhetorically by those who prepare leaders (Rusch, 2004). The resulting challenge is how to provide for intercultural competence in leaders, and how it can best be supported through programs that focus on the diversity of North America or that attempt to incorporate an international perspective on worldwide diversity. Such a perspective would include different conceptualizations of education, leadership, schooling and learning, and the resulting practice, looking beyond the North American cultural and ethnic mix.

An international perspective is sometimes taken to mean the "travellers' tales" (Crossley & Watson, 2003, p. 12) referred to earlier: knowledge and understanding of education in different parts of the world. For some, and for many in North America, the stance may assume that "elsewhere" is viewed rather as a specimen, novel and interesting but of limited relevance. This version of an international perspective may be interpreted as the very opposite, a perspective that is essentially bound by one culture. As such, it is likely to reinforce limitations of reflection on practice rather than the contrary.

Those preparing leaders are culture bound; blinkered by narcissism, their engagement with alternative approaches, theoretical frames, and practices is constrained. As a result, theoretical frames and resulting practice come to seem unquestioned. Adler (1997) suggested that capacity to learn is impeded by the dominance of patterns of seeing and knowing, which are accrued by a lifetime's acculturation. It is not that we do not wish to see what challenges our experience, but that we cannot. Gudykunst (1995) depicted our relations with others as "strangers" (p. 10) who provoke a powerful psychological response to defend our mental and physical well-being, our status, and our self-image. Communication processes are designed to filter out difference or to render it unthreatening by reducing the stranger to a recognizable formula: Such a threat is easier to defuse than the complex uniqueness of those deemed "other." Such deletion of difference is played out in classrooms throughout North America (Benson, 2002). Dramatic and novel contrasts may be necessary to shift embedded thinking and ways of relating (Allix & Gronn, 2005).

An international perspective may provide such a shift. It challenges leaders to rethink what they know and to apply what they have learned to their own practice. It demands that preconceptions are set aside to view familiar and accepted practice from new perspectives, to reach new insights. As such, an international perspective is not about knowing of education overseas, a scientific typology of the alien, but about leaders reaching a deeper understanding of their own acculturation and resulting practice. It challenges complacency in knowing and unsettles assumptions. As such, it is essential not only directly to develop leaders and managers, but also to model for learners openness to a wider range of ways of knowing, reflecting, and acting.

Acculturation creates mental barriers, automatic emotional and cognitive processes that simplify difference through creating stereotypes, filtering experience through preconceived frameworks. Breaking free of a lifetime's practice of proscribed views presents huge challenges and is not easily achieved. It is as if the short sighted are asked to remove their spectacles and achieve a sharp focus. An international perspective attempts a parallel psychological shift, acting as a support for leaders to become more mindful—that is, consciously to start to construct a more accurate, less culturally preconceived picture of individuals and communities both within the United States and more widely (Gudykunst, 1995). As such, it is not a worthy but peripheral broadening of knowledge, but a powerful strategy to prepare leaders to be mindful in responding to diversity in their own school and their local community.

A second professional justification for an international perspective is that it provides perspective on the scale of issues with which leaders must contend. Complaints about underresourcing of U.S. schools come into sharp focus when contrasted with the difficulties facing many teachers, for example, in Africa. The scale of challenge in terms of behavioral problems in U.S. schools is thrown into relief by viewing the order of many Asian or African classrooms. Such a perspective may reprioritize issues or, kaleidoscope like, give fresh views of previously accepted and seemingly immutable perspectives.

Third, the role of "confrere" (A. Walker & Dimmock, 2004, p. 275), that is, a relationship of mutual professional interest where one colleague learns from another, is opened through an international perspective. Numerous commentators have argued that the world has learned much, sometimes appropriately and sometimes inappropriately, from the United States (Dimmock, 2000; Hallinger & Kantamara, 2000; Heck, 1996). It is possible for U.S. leaders to learn both about the preparation of leaders and about the practice of leadership through adopting a confrere orientation to an international perspective. This orientation to the international is perhaps the most superficial of the three, though ironically the one most commonly adopted. Nevertheless, it potentially has benefits to offer if linked to the mindfulness, which attempts to step outside cultural boundaries and view practice elsewhere as potentially legitimate in its own right rather than as "travellers' tales" (Crossley & Watson, 2003, p. 12).

Political Rationale

There are also political reasons why an international perspective is important in preparation programs. Many globalizing values and practices are perceived to emanate from the United States (Giddens, 1999). The resulting American ascendancy in political and economic arenas places them in a particular relation to much of the rest of the world (Foskett & Lumby, 2003). It also lends its citizens power along all three dimensions defined by Lukes (1975): (a) power to influence the behavior of others, (b) power to define the agenda, and (c) power to define values and beliefs. Henze, Katz, Norte, Sather, and Walker (2001) suggested, "Inherent in being in the dominant position is that we are blind, to greater or lesser degrees, to the negative consequences of our power over others" (p. 4). Preparation programs may exhibit such blindness. Ethnocentrism is an alternative expression of narcissism, and though the intention may be unconscious, the resulting programs are complicit with the inappropriate global ascendancy of Western theory and practice. The latter has been the subject of more comment than the lack of an international perspective in U.S. preparation programs (Gronn, 2001; Hallinger & Leithwood, 1998; Leithwood & Duke, 1998).

Leaders therefore are subject to a double negative. Their ethnocentric preparation renders them complicit in sustaining the hegemony of Western values and practice. Simultaneously, the global sweep of change potentially means "educational managers will continue to find themselves pressurised into marching line by line" (Bottery, 1999, p. 309). North American leaders therefore will be subject to similar demands to those experienced elsewhere and may wish to resist. At the same time, they are engaged in the creation of the pressures. Educational leaders will require a perspective that is sufficiently broad to allow them to understand, assess, and devise their response to pressures, ideas, and policies that, though locally implemented, find their force in their adoption by multiple nations. For example, notions of raising attainment, of testing, and of quality follow the contours of global trends. To adequately shape understanding and response, resistance or acceptance, knowledge of origin, implementation, and effect is needed.

Personal Rationale

There are also personal reasons for preparation and continuing development programs to attempt to connect educators with those in similar roles elsewhere in the world. Isolation is a reality for many in education. Contact is often primarily with children, and time to work with other adults is severely limited. A sense of community may sustain individuals through isolation. Community can be variously conceived (Bamberg 2003; Rose, 2003). Bamberg contrasted definitions that imply a range of individuals, groups, and organizations in some way linked to a school, even when geographically distant, to the alternative: community seen as a location, the people in relation to the structures, the history, and the economy of the area surrounding a school. Bamberg queried whether the latter is feasible, given that not all the individuals and groups in any location will have a link to or interest in the local school, particularly if some families send children to an alternative school in another area. She suggested that community can be understood in multiple ways, of which physical proximity is only one. Given that the shared interest sets within a school may include ethnic and religious groups whose networks extend outside national boundaries and sometimes worldwide (Rose, 2003), *community* can be conceived as international as well as local. Linking to the international community of education leaders can reduce the sense of both isolation and of coping with unique problems in leading a school. For example, one of the shared experiences may be the necessity to support children who live in poverty. An international perspective may open wider understanding of the global forces that create and impact on poverty as well as the theoretical frame and implementation of strategies that are called on in response throughout the world. There is comfort in the solidarity of difficulties and sometimes dangers as a shared experience. The two quotations below are the words of a principal, first in a rural primary school in KwaZulu-Natal in South Africa and second in an U.S. high school. Lumby (2003) quoted the South African principal as follows:

> There is a lack of funds … to repair the old buildings of the school … therefore during rainy days my teachers and pupils suffer very much as the corrugated iron has big holes and rust. I have written many letters to the inspectors but the funds are helping better schools near big main roads. As I have worked here at school for 22 years as principal, riots and faction fights in the area have depressed me, as the whole of the good work that I did in my first year has gone. Hooligans, thieves, robbers have stolen doors, tables, chairs, desks and burnt valuable schoolbooks. They have killed a female teacher near the school. (pp. 181–182)

Parkray and Hall (1992) quoted an American school principal:

> I wondered if I could do it … if a woman could do it … if I had the guts to do it. Knowing I would be the one to walk into a volatile situation and maybe in some cases put my life on

the line as opposed to somebody else's. Those things you have to think about before you become a principal, because when you become a principal, you don't have time to think about it then. (p. 1)

The principals from the United States and from South Africa confront an entirely different context, but the moral challenges and physical dangers they face resonate. The potential sense of shared professional and moral challenges is qualitatively different from the kind of more superficial link frequently adopted by, for example, video links between schools.

While most leaders might support the creation of an international focus in the abstract or in others such as their students, they do not always adopt such a focus in their own practice. In common with all learners and learning programs, an international perspective can considerably enhance learning and a sense of agency in educational leadership preparation programs (Robertson & Webber, 2000).

Looking Forward

Adopting an international perspective in developing leader preparation programs is not a peripheral luxury, distant from the more important element related to instruction. Rather, it is an integral part of reshaping programs to reflect a commitment to democratic and socially just processes. An international perspective has the potential to provide the psychological leverage and substantive content to challenge the acculturation of the leader's socioeconomic class, ethnicity, gender, and citizenship (Crowther & Limerick, 1998; Wilkins, 2002). Neuroepistemological analyses of educational leaders' incapacity to modify the acculturated perceptions provide theoretical underpinnings. Yet, there is little evidence of any examination of the implications this theoretical perspective has for adjusting preparation programs (Allix & Gronn, 2005; Lakomski, 2001; Waite, 2002). This may be in part because those researching and designing the programs share the limitations of acculturation and remain largely unaware of the boundaries that enclose. As a consequence, they do not experience any pressure to change. On the contrary, remaining within the dominant cultural parameters provides psychological security (Lumby, 2007). Also, strategies to shift neurological habits are not part of the training of faculty. Adopting an international perspective may be a partial response. It also would allow leaders a greater sense of agency in responding to the integrative and homogenizing, divisive and diversifying pressure of a globalized world.

The next section takes up the thread of arguing that awareness of culture, both of the cultural context within which other nations work and of the cultural boundedness of one's own approach, is a critical feature of self-reflection. The discussion reflects the two levels of diversity identified in the opening of the chapter; nation-states may have a discernible and dominant culture that provides the context for developing leaders. Simultaneously, each nation-state or subunit within it may have multiple cultures relating to the intensifying heterogeneity of societies and the multiple identities of each individual. Cultural fit is therefore an issue within as much as across nations.

The Influence of Culture

This section of the chapter asserts that leaders make a difference in schools, that the context within which they lead makes a difference to *how* they lead, and that culture forms an important part of this context. While acknowledging the multifaceted hypercomplexity that typifies all school leaders' lives regardless (Moos, 2005), we suggest that cultural value sets have a potent influence on leaders in different societies. Furthermore, we propose that if people accept the influence of culture on why and how school leadership is exercised, then it is axiomatic that it must impact how they conceptualize, structure, and run leader development programs (LDPs). The inseparable link between improving leader development (defined as preparation and continuous development) and understanding leadership itself is also made.

A number of examples are provided to illustrate the influence of culture on leader development. These are grouped under content-based and more currently in-vogue community-based approaches. Five general propositions that may inform those interested in school leader development across societies are outlined. Among the propositions is a reminder that although the focus of the paper is on societal culture, this does not imply that other external and personal factors do not influence what leaders do; rather, the influence of culture on leader development is important but is generally underestimated. While decrying the absence of research on the influence of societal culture, K. M. Cheng (1995) stated, "The (societal) cultural element is not only necessary, but essential in the study of educational administration" (p. 99). K. M. Cheng, along with others (Dimmock &Walker, 1998; Hallinger & Leithwood, 1996), lamented the fact that much research was conducted on school culture without reference to the larger macrosociety culture or on school culture without reference to educational administration.

It is important that we understand the influence of culture on leader development for at least four interrelated reasons, which relate to the themes of the opening discussion and have important implications for equity, opportunity and social justice at both local and global levels. We have introduced in this chapter the idea of cultural boundedness, by which we mean the limitations we almost unavoidably carry with us as a result of own cultural upbringing. These include how we see the world, perceive human relationships, and categorize certain actions or opinions. To be able to see others' cultures and values, we need to learn to look beyond these limitations. We restate these four themes of cultural awareness and cultural boundedness more explicitly:

1. First, if programs are to make a difference to what leaders do in specific contexts and cultures, the design—and, indeed, content—must hold legitimacy and currency within that context. For example, there is little point of transmitting notions of democratic learning communities constructed within culturally restricted understandings to leaders in vertically aligned culture systems where democracy may hold very different meanings (Begley, 2000).
2. If school leaders themselves are to grow, regardless of where they operate, they need to be aware of how their cultural values underpin the ways they see the world, interact with others, view learning, and construct community. In other words, they need to develop an awareness of how their own cultural values filter and in some cases restrict their views and actions.
3. In an increasingly intercultural world, leaders often operate as cultural outsiders, separated by values, understandings, and aspirations from their students, communities, and even their teachers. This applies as much within as it does between national, societal, or geographic boarders. Although this section does not delve into leader development in intercultural schools, it may well hold messages for leaders in such circumstances (A. Walker & Chen, 2007).
4. Awareness of different cultures and cultural influence will support agency in responding to the simultaneously homogenizing and diversifying pressures of globalization and will help to balance the often one-sided argument that globalization inevitably will lead to values convergence and so dissolution of difference. As Dorfman, Hanges, and Brodbeck (2004) stated,

> While we acknowledge that global communication, technical innovation and industri-
> alization can create a milieu for cultural change, a convergence among cultural values is
> by no means assured. In fact, cultural differences among societies may be exacerbated

as they adapt to modernization while simultaneously striving to preserve their cultural heritage. (p. 709)

Understanding and interpreting the influence of culture on leader development, or anything else, however, is a difficult task, mainly because of cultural boundedness; it is so difficult to find or see where others are coming from. Hoppe (2004) explained that developing cultural self-awareness is a difficult business, adding, "Awareness of their subjective culture is particularly difficult for Americans, since they often interpret cultural factors as characteristics of individual personality" (p. 334).

Guiding Assumptions

Any discussion of the effect of culture on leader development rests on at least five interrelated assumptions:

1. The first is that leadership makes a difference in schools, even as we remain unsure of exactly how this works. This assumption is founded on international literature that confirms the centrality of school leadership to school improvement and quality schooling and that it most effectively influences school outcomes indirectly through multiple variables (Y. C. Cheng, 2001; Hallinger, 2003; Hallinger & Heck, 1999; Huber, 2004; Southworth, 2005). It is also now widely accepted that *how* leaders make a difference is contingent upon the context within which they lead. In other words, what leaders do is mediated and moderated by both their personal internal states as well as the organizational and external milieu of the school. This context then is not only extremely complex, but also constantly shifting and evolving in response to factors such as personality, ethnicity, gender, politics, history, economics, and culture.
2. The interplay between these value sets plays out in an assortment of forms in schools as leaders attempt to make sense of what is needed. The second assumption, therefore, is that multiple contexts influence how school leaders lead.
3. Given that leadership is centrally concerned with the interpretation and enactment of values, it is reasonable to assume that one of the most influential contextual factors on how leadership is conceptualized and exercised is the cultural values, norms, and beliefs that help to define the society within which leaders live and work. For our purpose here, *culture* can be defined very broadly as patterns of shared values, beliefs, and norms held by a particular group and or society that combine in various ways to influence behavior and action. Recent work has asserted the influence of societal culture on school leadership and organization (Dimmock & Walker, 2005; Hallinger, Walker, & Bajunid, 2005; Tippeconnic, 2006). An acceptance that culture matters, however, as with leader effects, still leaves us unsure just how much it matters—this probably will never be definitively resolved. However, the bottom line appears to be that even though cultural values exist within a complex and vibrant broader context, they continue to exert a strong influence on people's lives. As such, they form a key element of the environment within which leaders lead and on how they lead.
4. Building on the previous hypothesis, the fourth assumption holds that the study of leader development cannot be separated from the study of leaders themselves or from what constitutes effective leadership in different societies. An example of this link can be inferred from the recently completed Global Leadership and Organizational Behaviour Effectiveness (GLOBE) study, which investigated specifically the influence of cultural values on leadership across 61 societies (House et al., 2004). The GLOBE researchers aimed to develop an empirically based theory to describe, understand, and predict the influence of cultural variables on leadership

and organizational processes. They attempted to show that both individuals and groups of individuals in certain societies possess an implicit leadership theory. In other words, the GLOBE researchers "wanted to show that societal and organizational culture influences the kind of leadership found to be acceptable and effective by people within that culture" (Grove, 2005, p. 4). Whereas it is not possible to discuss sufficiently the outcomes of this major study, it identified ways in which people worldwide distinguish between leaders who are effective and ineffective, and, perhaps more importantly, the extent to which the differences in leader styles and effectiveness across societal clusters can be explained in terms of the values that prevailed in those clusters.

5. The final assumption is that leader development actually makes a difference, be it in different ways, to what leaders do in schools. Beyond largely anecdotal evidence, this can be difficult to verify (Jones, 2006). However, there appears now some general agreement that certain approaches to leader development have at least the potential to be an important factor in improving leader practice. For example, recent wide-ranging reviews by Huber (2004), Hallinger (2003), Hallinger and Snidvongs (2005), Earley and Weindling (2004), and Wales and Welle-Strand (2005) have identified elements that are increasingly prominent in leader development programs. These include program linkage to leadership reality and school life, opportunities for reflection, involvement of experienced practitioners as mentors or coaches, formal and informal grouping, and networking and intentional design. These developments provide better understandings of useful generic development approaches. Yet, in terms of how they travel, or the shape they may take in different societies, questions remain. Such questions may include those below (Hoppe, 2004):

- Are the models and practices of leader development being used by context-specific organizations and development programs applicable across cultural contexts?
- What adjustments need to be made in methods, practices, assessment and philosophies so that they will work in or across cultures?
- What can be done to successfully transfer western (or other) leadership development models and practice?
- And, indeed, should western (or other) leader development models and practices be transferred? And if so, how? (p. 331)

The Influence of Culture on Leader Development

Jones (2006, p. 483) interpreted LDPs as sites of "ritual process" wherein the larger cultural, historical, and national conflicts that confront human societies are confronted and redressed as they manifest themselves in the particular organizations and individual lives of program participants. In very simple terms, current education LDPs most often include both content and process components. Some are more heavily loaded one way than the other. For example, content comprising many programs in East Asia rests mainly on theory, knowledge, and skills built on Anglo-American understandings and values. Such content is often imparted using variations of a transmission model, whereby experts pass down theory and knowledge through assorted media to others, moderated to varying degrees by localized familiarity. Import can take any number of forms; two of these serve as examples. The first can be referred to as *theory-wrapped knowledge*, normally flown in as part of university-based programs, overseas experts, local scholars, and trainers returning from overseas study, textbooks, journals, simulations, case studies, Web sites, and so on. The second takes the form of values-driven, neatly *prepackaged programs* built around lists of preset competencies.

Increasingly fashionable process components of LDPs are also often developed in foreign settings but, at least at first glance, appear more suited to working with indigenous values and knowledge.

Processes models are normally built around particular notions of community, or more specifically communities of (leader) learners. Such models as currently in vogue in the United Kingdom, parts of the United States and Australia, Singapore, and Hong Kong incorporate elements such as workplace learning, mentoring and coaching, internship, and action learning. The worth of these elements depends largely on relational processes such as discussion, debate, and feedback self-analysis and open contextual analysis, all built on some type of structural scaffolding.

Content-Based Elements

While acknowledging the positive aspects of cross-fertilization, the weaknesses of directly importing decontexualized content are fairly widely recognized (A. Walker, 2006). The basic argument is that content is too often transmitted with insufficient sensitivity to or understanding of how leadership is constructed or how schools operate in different cultural contexts—indigenization is largely left to serendipity. As Jones (2006) noted when discussing content used by the Center for Creative Leadership in cross-national LDPs,

> Simulations are, in effect, prefigured with "rational" decisions made by "rational" actors with whom participants must interact. Such normative assumptions are not culturally neutral; rather, they are distinctly western in their assumptions about human behavior and the psychological backdrop of decision making. (p. 485)

This criticism, of course, holds equally well within as between societies, particularly when addressing leadership within indigenous or intercultural communities.

Two brief examples serve to illustrate this point. The first relates to the current popularity in the some societies of the concept of distributed leadership. At least as often conceptualized, this makes little sense to leaders in high-power distance societies where hierarchical inequities are accepted and leadership is closely tied to position and ordered responsibilities. This is true throughout the Middle East, Southeast and East Asia, and also in many African societies (Jansen, 2006). The second example is that of democratic school communities. Democratizing reforms call for teachers to openly assert their views, even if they dissent with community values. Such notions may be flawed in cultures where the open expression of diverse views is believed to unnecessarily complicate decision situations and challenge smooth relationships. This does not mean that people do not hold or communicate diverse views; rather it is a matter of how, when, and why they do it. It is here that cultural nuance emerges and challenges the relevance of theory and associated knowledge included in many LDPs.

Perhaps one of the most worrying trends in terms of content–culture misfit is apparent in LDPs assembled around generalized lists of competencies, or what is sometimes called indicators of *best practice*. Given the rise of the standards movement, it is unsurprising that some educators are even trying to develop a list of international school leadership best practice. Defining best practice implies an attempt to regulate or "bottle a prescriptive formula" (A. Walker & Stott, 2000, p. 65), which may disregard that social expressions, and so effective leadership and leader development, differ across cultures in respect to power, communication, change, and action. Criticisms of competency lists are common within relatively homogenous systems (Glatter & Kydd, 2003; Loudon & Wildy, 1999; A. Walker & Quong, 2005b), but when used to underpin LDPs in very different societal cultures, even more serious questions about their legitimacy surface. Leader values and behaviors broken down into competency indicators and considered effective in places like East Asia and the Middle East, which emphasize respect for authority and position, tradition, and religion or indirectness in communication, are less likely to be part of Western LDPs, and vice versa. For example, a study of leaders across cultures asked participants to list the top five functions of leadership (Hoppe,

2004). In the U.S. sample, one of the top five was "get results—manage strategy to action" (Hoppe, 2004, p. 338). However, this was not rated in the top five choices by leaders in France, Germany, Japan, Korea, and Spain.

In sum, imported content components, regardless of their directional flow, which focuses predominantly on transferring knowledge, risk separating leadership performance from the cultures within which content is constructed. Knowledge and skills, according to Brooks (2005), touch only the most superficial components of human capital and ignore other more complex forms, such as cultural, social, moral, cognitive, and aspirational capital, which are manifested somewhat differently in different cultures' contexts. When programs are, for example, based on competency approaches that primarily reflect Anglo-American values and models of human behavior, important issues of cultural bias and generalizability come to the fore. This suggests that we look more closely at the learning processes involved in leader development. It may be that these transfer more easily and effectively than knowledge or competencies, but it is important to note that cultural considerations remain.

Community-Based Elements

An increasingly popular approach to leader development is the building of communities of practice. This acknowledges the power of learning together and places informal learning in its social setting of work relationships and group dynamics. Communities of practice can be based within an organization or be constructed outside organizations based on shared need. They often involve the purposeful building of cohorts or groups specifically to share learning. Development programs fitting this mold assume leader learning is most effective when it explicitly taps leaders' tacit knowledge, becomes integral to their job, is based firmly within the purpose and context of the school (and, more specifically, student learning), involves multiple opportunities for social interaction, and encourages group and individual reflection. All of these aim to embed a sense of community among leader learners where mutual support, shared wisdom, and meaningful dialogue drive learning. If collections of leaders are to transform into learning communities, a number of conditions are necessary; these include open self-analysis and group analysis (for example, through 360-degree feedback), trust, meaningful feedback, challenge, partnership, debate, and openness (for example, see Lambert, 2005; Sackney & Walker, 2006). Specifically, 360-degree feedback involves leaders in collecting feedback on their performance from different groups relevant to their work as a means of providing them with a broader perspective on their effectiveness. For principals, for example, this may involve gathering feedback from students, teachers, inspectors, or parents.

In general, community-based elements may be more readily transferable across cultures in that they are designed around existing professional knowledge (although this does not exclude the infusion of more formal knowledge) and driven by relational processes. However, it is here that the nuances of cultural influence become important to program efficacy: Once again, the devil is in the details. Attention to cultural nuance is perhaps even more important when learning becomes more dependent on social and professional relationships. This does not imply that they are out of place in particular cultures—people in all cultures share wisdom in some way—but that implementation processes, relational norms, and formalized designs are sensitively considered. This holds whether they are being passed from east to west, north to south, or any other direction. Three interrelated examples built around some of the relation dynamics or processes of leader learning communities help illustrate the point: (a) support, (b) feedback, and (c) challenge.

Support Support components in LDPs are those that aim partly to maintain self-esteem and to reduce professional isolation by letting leaders know that their strengths are important and valued.

They aim to engage leaders in new experiences and change processes by providing a comfortable, trusting environment. Support is usually expressed through interpersonal encouragement or resources and norms that value personal growth. Sounds good, but even here culture can complicate things. Using GLOBE terminology, a comparison between Anglo and Confucian contexts exemplifies the possible influence of culture on building support into LDPs. Hoppe (2004) claimed U.S. leaders can have difficulty seeking support because of the deep tradition of individualism and independence as well as cultural admiration for the self-made woman or man, where the high achiever succeeds through individual talent, ability, and effort. As such, an overdependence on another can be seen as a sign of weakness. Success, then, is seen as something to be achieved in competition with others.

In contrast, Europeans construct leadership in "a more social-cultural (vs. individual-psychological) assessment of accomplishment and responsibility that prevails as a cultural value" (Jones, 2006, p. 486). Hence, accepting support through LDPs may be a somewhat smoother process. In some ways, programs designed to establish supportive relationships between leaders for learning can cause fewer problems in more collective societies, like Indonesia, where group needs take precedence. However, closer examination exposes differently shaped problems and ways of enactment. First, support from outside a relationally defined in-group can be discouraged, as leaders appear more comfortable receiving support from people they are close to and seem reluctant because of "face" issues to open up to people outside their in-group. Second, in cultures where collectivism is combined with high power distance, it can be difficult to give or receive support. Within some cultures, accepted power inequity is accompanied by care and support, but, in return, loyalty and subordination are expected. In other words, sources of personal support are limited by status and position. As a result, available supportive learning relationships can be somewhat proscribed (Hoppe, 2004).

Given relational intricacies across cultures, sensitivity is needed when selecting individuals to be paired or grouped for mentoring or coaching. For example, depending on the dominant values, it can be hazardous to match people of different ethnic or national backgrounds, across genders or across levels of schooling; all may make people feel uncomfortable. In Hong Kong mentoring and coaching for local Chinese principals is best done in small groups rather than one on one; these are called Learning Squares (A. Walker & Quong, 2005a). Grouping also must take careful account of hierarchy and seniority and cannot cross school-level bounds such as elementary and high schools.

Feedback Communities of practice require feedback of one form or another. In its various forms, feedback basically aims to provide leaders with knowledge of their strengths and weaknesses, successes and failures, and insights into their blind spots. Feedback can come from different groups, such as leader peers grouped for specific long- or short-term programs; ongoing leadership learning clusters; or within the school community where the leader works, perhaps through a development-oriented, 360-degree feedback process. Feedback can take verbal, written, or other visual forms.

Leslie, Gryskiewicz, and Dalton (1998) identified assumptive differences between cultures about 360-degree feedback and the interpretation of results. They found that feedback data in the United States were assumed to be "owned" by the individual, whereas in more collectivist China, even if collected for developmental purposes, data were seen as the property of the group. There were also differences in ratings according to whether anonymity was guaranteed. In such circumstances, peers in France tended to rate their colleagues down in order to gain an advantage, the Chinese tended to inflate the ratings to please their superiors, and individual leaders in the United States boosted ratings out of career concerns (Hoppe, 2004). In terms of self-ratings, U.S. leaders tended to rate themselves higher than their supervisors or peers, whereas in Taiwan they were more likely to rate themselves lower. According to Hoppe, this "is due in part to the cultures' different emphasis on competition versus collaboration" (p. 352). Hoppe also claimed that Chinese leaders avoid extreme ratings because of the cultural importance of maintaining harmonious relations and preserving status. If such differences hold, LDPs need to account not only for the methods and processes of the mechanisms included, but also (and perhaps even more importantly) for relational understandings and values.

A second illustration relates to how feedback is interpreted by leaders holding different cultural values. Different interpretations of direct, face-to-face feedback (or lack thereof) are illustrative because of their growing place within programs based on mentoring or coaching, both of which hold cultural messages. Dorfman et al. (1997) compared leaders in the United States, Japan, Mexico, South Korea, and Taiwan across a number of areas. Out of this sample, only U.S. leaders said that they responded positively to negative feedback. On the other hand, positive feedback had a positive impact in all five countries. In other words, feedback that is direct, honest, specific, and measurable tends to be welcome in U.S. workplaces, whether it points out strengths or shortcomings, but this is not necessarily so elsewhere. Dorfman et al.'s finding was confirmed by Javidan (2004), who found that leaders in achievement cultures (where status is based on accomplishments) welcome and value feedback as an indication of how they are doing, whereas those in ascribing cultures (where status is based upon who the person is) avoid direct feedback because they see it as commenting on the person, rather than on what they do in their jobs.

The acceptance of feedback also relates to the form and path of feedback. For example, in Chinese societies like Hong Kong, negative feedback between those of unequal status (whether up or down the hierarchy), especially but not exclusively within the same organization, tends to be unacceptable if given directly; however, such feedback is more accepted if provided through intermediaries and if delivered in a somewhat impersonalized, polite format (Wearley, 2006). Feedback within like-status groups is acceptable but still only if done gently and in a roundabout way.

Communities of practice involve moving from solely content-driven, university or training provider classrooms to the workplace and hence to the real world of leaders. This takes various paths, but increasingly common forms include action and experiential learning, or learning-by-doing. Experiential learning is a process whereby individuals learn through their experience at work. Action learning involves working on an action-centered project in the school. Within themselves, these are certainly worthwhile structures for leadership learning, but cultural nuances endure.

Challenge Hoppe (2004) suggests that a common thread across learning-by-doing learning is that of challenge. In other words, assignments such as action-learning projects, whether internally or externally prescribed, are designed to challenge the leaders in order to help them learn. In very basic terms, challenge uses mechanisms designed to extend people beyond their existing levels of thought, skills, and expertise through exposing them to new, difficult, or ill-defined situations. It aims to induce cognitive conflict through exposing a gap between what people know and what else is possible. On the surface, challenge is a powerful learning strategy, but in terms of either work-based or non-work-based LDPs how it is done and what it involves are important. Some questions we might ask include the following (Hoppe, 2004):

- How do members of different cultures respond to uncertainties and ambiguities which accompany challenge?
- What does challenge look like in collectivist cultures where the group rather than the individual is the focus?
- How will leader development react to this? (p. 353)

Some cultures value challenge and subsequent feedback and reflection as a learning strategy. For example, cross-cultural literature has suggested that mainstream U.S. culture is open to experiences of change, personal growth, and lifelong mobility. Hoppe (2004) noted that *hero leaders* are those who have failed many times before succeeding. In such cultures, where people are more comfortable with change, they tend to value learning by doing, which implies the learners cannot know what will happen next. Leaders in the United States, Great Britain, and Sweden seem to follow cultural norms that suit an active approach to learning. In contrast, leaders in France, Germany, and Turkey seem more concerned with stability, continuity, and certainty. In other words, they may be less comfortable in novel situations or potential conflicts that push them too far beyond their comfort zone. Leaders in these societies seem to find comfort in rules, structure, standard procedures, functional expertise, intellectual models, and predictability (Hoppe, 2004).

Cultural dynamics around challenge are also relevant in collectivist cultures such as Japan, where group loyalty is very important. In these cultures the learning needs and aspirations of the individual are subordinated to those of the group. As such, challenging activities as part of LDPs may need to be more staggered and designed to avoid failure, embarrassment, and discomfort. An emphasis on loyalty and group belonging may result in different approaches to development in that the group instead of the individual is the target. The individual then becomes the agent of the group, and the individual's performance is embedded within collective effort. This may call for different approaches in LDPs.

Culturally Aware Leader Development

The ideas explored may be informative to those interested in school leader development and its potential for improving schools regardless of their place within, across, or outside their cultures of origin. These ideas may be relevant to considering cultural fit within as much as across nations. Below are five propositions related to building culturally aware LDPs.

1. The transportation of leader development approaches across cultures needs to move beyond surface concepts and their too-neatly attached content and to focus more on the processes that place these in context and thereby respect deeply embedded cultural norms. For example, emerging understandings that leader development is most successfully instituted through diverse, work-related, and practitioner-supported developmental experiences are likely to travel well across boundaries—but only as long as they are done in context and are sensitive to cultural norms. Certainly, generalizability may be burred by globalization, technology, and industrialization as the global economy takes root, and similar leader qualities across cultures and organizations may well emerge. However, the way in which knowledge and processes are enacted and interpreted will continue to differ according to cultural values and norms, even as they hybridize.

2. In any leader development activity, cross-fertilization across sites, countries, cultures, and schools is desirable, but what is happening now in many parts of the world is not cross-fertilization; rather, it is largely a one-way flow that sometimes holds insufficient respect for local traditions. Unfortunately, this phenomenon is often mirrored within multiethnic and multicultural societies themselves and is played out in leader development activities that gloss over the value orientations of cultural groups. For LDPs this suggests the importance of an emphasis on values, particularly in terms of their formulation and intentionality, regardless of their cultural base. The unthinking import of knowledge or ideas applies equally regardless of the direction it flows.

3. When programs travel across cultural boundaries, their associated beliefs and knowledge must not be (or seem) a hegemonic device or a desire to impose one best way. In terms of leader development, the purpose of sharing ideas and thoughts between societies is to increase

understanding and tolerance and to question existing conceptions in order to make schools better places for students. In short, such ideas should provoke our curiosity and not be about domination. Whereas it is fine to challenge cultural norms and ways of working—this is good for leader learning—it is very different from culturally restricted or biased approaches, which too often slip across borders.

4   As highlighted in the assumptive base of this section of the chapter, we cannot study leader development without studying leaders; the two agendas must be amalgamated. This has at least two faces. First, we cannot work out how to support leaders' learning across cultures unless we know more about the cultures themselves and how these influence what leaders do. Second, amalgamating understanding of leadership and leader learning may be a fruitful avenue for improving our programs, even if cultural variation is minimal. The exercise of working out how to cater for difference, whether it is obvious or subtle, only can help us produce more connected, meaningful learning opportunities for leaders.

5.   Given that leaders learn in different ways both within and between cultures, and that learning should be a continuous, lifelong affair, it is important that multiple, varied opportunities for learning are available. This calls not just for differentiated content, but also for multiple delivery modes (for example, story-based learning) that allow for differing learning purposes and styles. What is involved here should remain in a fluid state so that programs cover not only the necessary basics, but also the variable situations where culturally aware learning takes place. Such models may be usefully based around curiosity and may promote flexibility within structure in response to dominant cultural values.

Culture Matters

Leadership makes a difference, culture matters, and culture influences how leaders think and what they do. If we accept this, it is axiomatic that culture will influence leader development. However, a final warning: When discussing anything to do with difference, we must avoid the raw dichotomization of cultures and societies and should not overlook the powerful effect of personality and other contextual variables. While respecting these, however, they should not become shields that block recognition of the powerful role that different cultural values play in shaping what leaders do and how schools operate. We must recognize that key values and beliefs position leaders in a "cultural space" and that leader development agendas must address the substance and exercise of what leaders do within this space. In other words, we should try to be aware of what we "don't know we don't know" and accept that this will always be confusing (Shweder, 2000, p. 167).

Having set the context of a global stage and considered the relationship of culture to leader development, the next section of the chapter reviews the variation in content and process in systems in varying nation states. The purpose is not only to offer "confrere" opportunities (A. Walker & Dimmock, 2004, p. 275), that is, possibilities of learning from the professional practice of others, but also to shake the kaleidoscope, to destabilize acculturated reflection. The differences between national systems may be predicated on differences in culture and interpretation of preferred means ends, but the differences also may be less distinct than is sometimes imagined. The deficiency model, often applied particularly to systems in developing economies, is challenged, with the aim of encouraging reconsideration of U.S. and other practice.

International Patterns in the Selection and Development of School Administrators

Overview of Selection and Development

Selection, certification, and development practices for school administrators vary by national and regional context. Those wanting to be school administrators can select themselves as aspirants (United States, Australia, and France); they can be nominated for a leadership position by a hierarchical authority or local authority (Azerbaijan, Belarus, and China). In many countries, individuals can start nongovernmental, private schools and serve as head teachers. In Bangladesh thousands of village schools are private and run by entrepreneurial locals. Those wanting to be school administrators can develop their skills and talents through preservice education (United States, England, and France) or, depending on how development is targeted, through in-service education or on-the-job learning (Sweden, Denmark, Germany, and Hong Kong). There are two contrasting approaches to helping educators acquire administrative knowledge and skills. One approach provides or requires that individuals study school administration prior to obtaining a post or position. A contrasting approach places the individual in a position with the proviso that the new administrator participate in development activities. Each approach is predicated on different assumptions about how best to develop leaders, and each approach requires a very different infrastructure of support.

Those wanting to be school leaders can earn their positions through demonstrated merit (England, France, and the United States) or by taking advantage of family, clan, or political connections (Nigeria, Botswana, and Azerbaijan). Some places have few requirements for those who wish to be administrators (Cyprus and Nigeria). In other places, a substantial set of requirements has been established for those who wish to be school leaders (England, United States, and Australia). There are many routes to administrative positions in the school systems of the world. Not all hold promise for improving the life chances of children, but some approaches hold great promise. This section identifies basic patterns in how school administrators are selected, appointed, and developed outside of the United States. First, we wish to add our own justification for the importance of attending to leadership preparation in any system of education.

The Case for Expanding Leadership Preparation

Because many places in the world lack the purposeful selection and development of school administrators, we first present the argument for an educational system that does require careful selection and development of school leaders. March (1978) famously observed, "Any effort to improve American education by changing its organization or administration must begin with scepticism. Changing education by changing educational administration is like changing the course of the Mississippi by spitting into the Allegheny" (p. 219). March was speaking of American education, but his observation easily could apply to any national system of education.

However, many current practitioners of educational administration preparation have rejected March's (1978) scepticism. To the contrary, contemporary scholars find that good educational administrators do change education and they do so at the building level. Huber (2004) wrote,

> The pivotal role of the school leader as a factor in effective schools has been corroborated by findings of school effectiveness research for the last decades. Extensive empirical efforts of the quantitatively oriented school effectiveness research—mostly in North America, Great Britain, Australia, and New Zealand, but also in the Netherlands and in the Scandinavian countries—have shown that the leadership is a central factor for the quality of a school. (p. 1)

Huber cited many scholars in support of this claim: Reynolds (1976); Rutter, Maughan, Mortimore, and Ouston (1979); Mortimore, Sammons, Stoll, Lewis, and Ecob (1988); Sammons, Hillman, and Mortimore (1995); Brookover, Beady, Flood, Schweitzer, and Wisenbaker (1979); Edmunds (1979); D. U. Levine and Lezotte (1990); Teddlie and Stringfield (1993); Creemers (1994); and Scheerens and Bosker (1997). Grady, Wayson, and Zirkel (1979) published a review of research on effective schools for UCEA's monograph series, adding to the chorus of those supporting the relationship of effective leadership with effective schools. More recently, the National College for School Leadership (2001) and Bush (2003) have argued for the relationship of successful leadership and effective schools. The weight of this scholarship is convincing. As a consequence, the role of educational administration preparation in the efficacy of national systems of education assumes paramount importance. This discussion is important, for one of the distinguishing characteristics of systems that do seek to develop school-based leadership is a process for familiarizing educators with accumulated knowledge about education. If those interested in advancing into leadership positions are to be schooled in the knowledge of preferred educational practice, there must be in place a means of producing and disseminating that knowledge. It needs to be noted that as preferred educational or best practice is transmitted across national and cultural boundaries, it must be tempered by the local context in which it is delivered.

To achieve the promise of contributing to an effective school, a person must be selected for a position, appointed to it, and provided with some means of developing leadership skills and wisdom. Selection, appointment, and development practices constitute the basic elements of placing educators in leadership-role positions in schools.

The Absence of Governmental Selection and Development Practices

In some places in the world, education and educational administration lack resources. Schools have scant equipment, teachers may not be trained, and administrators lack knowledge of effective educational practices. In some areas, selection practices are political in nature, based on connections and favoritism; development activities for the appointed individual are few (Aghammadova, 2006; Dutta, 2006). Knowledge of existing educational research may be vague or nonexistent. Scholars examining such systems implicitly or explicitly compare existing practices with those of developed countries. For example, writing of Kenya, Kitavi and Westhuizen (1997) noted,

> The means by which most principals in developing countries are trained, selected, inducted and in-serviced are ill-suited to the development of effective and efficient school managers … neither the old nor the new educational system [in Kenya] gives attention to either formal training or induction of beginning school principals. (p. 251)

John (2002), in a study of administrator preparation in Pondicherry, India; Sommerbakk (1994), in a study of Norwegian training programs; Ogunu (1999), in a study of preparation in Nigeria; and Rakhashani (1980), in examining principal education in Iran, all argued that their national systems for preparing educational leaders were inadequate and did so to varying degrees by contrasting their systems with those in Western countries. In a way, criticisms of leadership preparation in developing nations spring from a deficiency model in which a Western standard is implicitly applied; in other words, the system failed to live up to a Westernized approach. This deficiency model, of course, feeds the forces of globalization that seek to integrate, harmonize, and homogenize leadership preparation.

As has been argued earlier in this chapter, there is no doubt that the development of leaders in such educational systems, indeed educational systems everywhere, is needed. Yet, one needs to be cautious in adopting a deficiency approach, for so doing may create barriers to perceiving how local culture and values inevitably impact and shape the education of children.

Comparative Studies of Educational Leadership Preparation

There have been systematic efforts to compare leadership preparation programs across national and state systems of education. Huber (2004) studied programs in Europe, Asia, Australia and New Zealand, and North America. He categorized systems of preparation, giving labels to the core distinctiveness of the different national approaches (see Table 4.1).

Table 4.1 Huber's Models for Administrator Preparation

Country	Model
Sweden	Split responsibility between state and cities
Denmark	No need for regulation and standards
England	Moving toward a coherent national provision
Netherlands	Diversity and choice
France	Recruitment and extensive training is state responsibility
Germany	Courses at state-run teacher training institutions
Switzerland	Canton-specific qualifications
Austria	Mandatory training according to state guidelines
South Tyrol	Qualifying at a government selected private provider
Singapore	Full-time preparation
Hong Kong	A task-oriented short course
Australia	Development of a learning community
New Zealand	Variety and competition
Ontario, Canada	Qualifying school leaders according to standards
United States	Extensive qualification programs and long history of school leader preparation

Huber's (2004) distinctions suggest variety in terms of centralization versus decentralization and in terms of those tapped as providers of preparation and training. Selection and development are left entirely to local discretion in some places (Denmark) and in others controlled by a centralized system, like that of Austria, where training is mandatory and provided by the state.

Watson (2003) edited a volume of case studies on leadership selection and development in 23 European countries. Watson suggested that the head teacher position now carries with it far more responsibility for curricular and regulatory oversight. The case studies in this edited volume reveal significant variety in selection and development. Cisneros-Cohernouri, Adler, Young, and Muth (2004) conducted a comparative study of administrator preparation across national boundaries. The abstract of their study reported that little is known about leadership preparation practices across national boundaries.

Studies of leadership preparation in developing countries are challenging in part because there are often significant regional and local differences that make broad generalizations difficult. For example, the growth and development opportunities for educators in a large South American city will contrast significantly with the opportunities available to those in nearby rural regions. However, efforts to capture the landscape of leader preparation in the developing regions of the world do exist. Bush and Oduro (2006) examined leadership preparation in Africa and concluded that preparation for school principals was inadequate throughout the continent. Ratliff (2006) reported that preparation of teachers and administrators in Latin American countries generally fell far short of what was needed in order to improve the quality of schooling. Bottoms and O'Neill (2001) argued that across the Latin American region, principals are needed who "understand school and classroom practices that contribute to student achievement" (p. 8). Borden (2002) added,

> On the one hand, it is clear that principals have an important role to play in assuring school effectiveness and success. Yet at the same time, most principals do not assume the leadership and management functions that are required to contribute to the improvements in learning and teaching that lead to the school's success. (p. 23)

From what one can learn about leadership preparation in Latin American countries, there are initiatives to improve the levels of knowledge that principals possess relative to teaching and learning.

Borden cited a number of these in her commissioned study of administrative training in Latin American countries. She concluded that large systemic changes would be needed before principals really could attend to instructional and curriculum improvement.

Some parts of the world are relatively unexamined in terms of studies of management and leadership programs. Haiplik (2003) and Sperandio (2006) examined rural schools in Bangladesh and discovered a vast system of paraprofessionals at work with very little training, operating over 35,000 village schools. There are few comparative studies that "probe the administrative framework within which Arab school systems operate" (Mazawi, 1999, p. 341). Cisneros-Cohernouri et al. (2004) suggested that little is known about leadership preparation in many countries. What we discuss below, therefore, are selection and development practices that take place in more developed areas of the world and geographical locations with either an existing or emerging body of literature examining leadership preparation.

The Systemic Elements of Locating Leaders in Schools

Two facets are associated with placing a leader in a school: selection practices and development practices. There is substantial variety in each of these two aspects of locating the principal or head teacher, *rector,* or *directeur* in a school. Selection can be based on a competency that may be demonstrated in various ways: a test (France and Germany), performance on the job (Sweden and China), a formal preparation program (England and Austria), or personal considerations (Africa). Appointments can be made in an orderly and merit-based manner done by a central authority (France), by a municipal or regional authority (Sweden and China), or by a local authority (Norway and Denmark). Appointments may be predicated on the certification of participation in a program (Hong Kong and Germany) or the certification of mastery (New Zealand, France, and Ontario). Induction or development may occur prior to the assumption of a position (preservice), afterwards (in-service or on the job), or both (United States and England). We discuss each of these elements of leadership preparation—selection, appointment, and development—in turn and provide examples of how different countries achieve these elements.

Selection Practices

Two basic patterns exist in the selection process. First, school leaders are selected based on criteria that have little to do with the position (kinship, partisanship, or favoritism). Second, school leaders are selected based on objective criteria that emanate from some merit-based assessment (prior performance, satisfaction of pre-established criteria, completion of a preservice or in-service program, or participation in a carefully constructed mentor program). Variation in the selection process can be understood in terminology developed by Perrow (1979): particularism versus universalism.

Particularism When the selection of an employee is based on elements of ascribed status—family background, religion, political affiliation, or social status—scholars may refer to this as *particularism*. Perrow (1979) held, "Particularism means that irrelevant criteria (e.g., only relatives have a chance at a top position) are employed in choosing employees" (p. 8). Yet, one may argue that particularism in selection does not necessarily mean that irrelevant criteria are used. The criteria may be extremely relevant for the cultural context of the national system of education. The social structure and stability of a country or region may be quite dependent upon social forces that arise from particularism in selecting individuals for positions.

Still, particularism means that individuals are hired based on factors that may have little to do with personal competence or promise as educational leaders. While almost any system will select educational leaders based in part on an individual's connections and sponsorship from well-placed authorities, a system that emphasizes particularism will use key non-job-related factors in making appointments. Johnson (1995) noted one example, South Africa: "Over the years there has been increasing evidence that political considerations influenced the selection process" (p. 224). Or, when a teacher in Azerbaijan, for example, is able to pay a fee for a position that exceeds what other individuals are willing to pay, that is often sufficient for an appointment (Aghammadova, 2006; Bryant, Aghammadova, Krupenikava, Dutta, & Hu, 2006). When an individual in Nigeria is selected because of kinship in an important and powerful clan, particularism is at work. Bush and Oduro (2006) noted that personal characteristics, including gender, are often used in the selection process in Africa. The great majority (93%) of primary school principals in Kenya are male, and they also dominate in South Africa and Ghana (Bush & Oduro, 2006).

Particularism as a selection practice may be masked, leading to the theoretical construct developed by Gouldner (1954), the *mock bureaucracy*. The official public practices in such systems appear to be based on transparent processes and criteria related to performance. In fact, they are not. Thus, some former Soviet bloc nations describe their selection process in universalistic terms (see below) but may practice particularism (Bryant et al., 2006; Krupenikava, 2006). To a degree, parallel selection processes are at work. An aspirant must look officially qualified and also have the personal resources to secure the favor of hiring authorities. To some observers, this is a form of cronyism and is reputed to be common in educational systems controlled more by political than educational goals.

Universalism The opposite of particularism is what Perrow (1979) referred to as *universalism*. Under universalism, selection is made by attempting to match the talents and capabilities of the individual with the requirements of the position. This approach is the more dominant approach in developed nations and is common to those systems in which some formal educational requirements are mandated as a condition of selection. A universalistic system first establishes educational criteria and expectations for those who wish to become school leaders or who will be nominated for leadership positions. These criteria are then applied in making selection decisions. Those criteria normally include experience as a teacher and either the completion of some program of learning prior to appointment or participation in a program while newly on the job. Most developed and many developing nations subscribe to a selection process that is universalistic in nature. Educators must complete a preservice program of instruction in an approved program of study, must be enrolled in an induction or in-service program as a condition of their selection, or must pass a test or assessment certifying their competence to be appointed to a position of leadership in a school.

For example, South Africa is one of several African countries moving towards a universal process. Aspiring principals will need to acquire an Advanced Certificate of Education (Management) before appointment (Bush & Oduro, 2006). We cover the details of these educational development programs below in our discussion of how universalistic systems set out to develop their educational leaders. The critical factor is that under the conditions of universalism, the selection process is objective. Individuals are selected after they have responded successfully to a set of demands grounded in what the system proponents claims are indicators of competence. In some countries these indicators are captured in standardized assessments, such as the School Leaders Licensure Assessment (Bryant, 2002) currently being developed in the United States or the National Professional Qualification for Headship process in England.

Particularism and universalism are constructs, which, rather than being viewed as absolutes evident in selection practice, are better seen as a spectrum, or perhaps two processes viewed in parallel. Consideration of systems throughout the world initially may invite conclusions in relation to a dichotomy and frequently a sense of superiority in apparently universalist systems. This is a prime example of the ability of an international perspective to destabilize assumptions. Even a cursory glance at employment statistics in developed countries would reveal the extent to which irrelevant factors such as gender and ethnicity are at play in selection of leaders. The binary of universalist and particularist systems and the comfortable sense of superior practice cannot be sustained in the face of the similarities as well as the differences in how selection is undertaken.

Development and Induction Practices

What are the core characteristics any system may exhibit in developing individuals for administrative roles in schools? It is important to note that systematic programs for developing school administrators through formal educational efforts are relatively recent phenomena. Whereas all systems have some way of selecting school heads, not all have formal foci for developing or training those individuals. Additionally, certainly the comprehensiveness of training varies significantly across countries.

It is also important to note that scholars have recorded a shift in the landscape of administrator preparation. Grace (2000) distinguished between the preparation of principals that is utilitarian and practical in nature and the preparation that includes a critical scholarship examining the "large culture, organization, and ethos of schooling" (p. 232). The examination of the philosophical foundations that underlie the preparation programs for educational leaders is a complex field. We acknowledge that historically formal preparation programs have gone through cycles. In some eras, what Grace referred to as "management studies" are emphasized, periods when the field seeks to enhance the pursuit of instrumental and utilitarian knowledge of school practices. At other times, programs approach development through a more reflective and inquiry-based approach, in which some professors of educational administration even advocated the use of literature as content in development programs (Brieschke, 1990; Bryant, 1989; Popper, 1990; Sergiovanni, 1991). Our analysis focuses more on the structural processes of providing development and induction activities than on the actual content of that preparation. We identify the following six factors as elements of development and induction approaches:

1. Authorities: Who sets the requirements for development?
2. Providers: Who is authorized to provide the training and developing?
3. Processes are passive activities, formal mentoring or coaching, and action learning.
4. Timing: When and to what extent are development opportunities provided or demanded?
5. Content: What do new administrators or aspirants learn?
6. Knowledge base is the extent of and process for the dissemination of knowledge about school leadership.

Authorities In many developing and developed countries, education is viewed as a responsibility of the national or regional government. Given that most modern nation-states seek to develop human capital through education, it follows that national, regional, or state governments may sustain some means of developing school leaders. As indicated above, how those authorities exercise control over the development of educational leaders varies.

Three common conditions characterize authority over principal preparation and development. First, national governments establish standards and criteria and promulgate these to their citizenry and educational system. An example is in Belarus, where national guidelines call for aspiring school leaders to be under the age of 40 (Krupenikava, 2006). Under centralized authority, relatively proscriptive programs may be established.

A second condition is that in which the national government delegates authority to state, regional, provincial, or urban jurisdictions. Such systems are much more decentralized. This is not unusual in many places. China, for example, has relaxed central authority over all of its educational system in favor of delegating more responsibility to provincial and municipal authorities.

A third condition is where the national authority is permissive, allowing private networks and owners of schools (nongovernmental schools) to develop their own training and development programs. In many instances, religious school systems function in this way, largely free from governmental oversight. Other private schools function in a similar manner. Typically, nongovernmental schools achieve some legitimacy through accreditation agencies. The large mix of private schools described by Sperandio (2006) in Bangladesh illustrates this national approach to authority over education.

Providers Educational policy makers exercise several choices when it comes to determining the entities that will provide development activities to aspirants or new administrators. The most common practices are for the government (a) to provide training and development through government-run institutions or technical schools; (b) to turn to universities and colleges to provide an approved training and development program; or (c) to leave preparation and training programs in the hands of local education agencies, school districts, or sometimes municipal districts. Examples of this third approach to leader preparation can be found in countries where no governmental authority regulates or requires particular types of preparation or certification. The second approach, delegating responsibility for preparation to colleges and universities, is increasingly common. This is the practice commonly followed in the United States and is the model planned for South Africa. In China, both government organizations and private providers work to improve educational leadership qualities of new principals.

It is not all that uncommon for school district entities to provide their own development activities for principals. For example, in Norway, there was a proposal some years ago to require school leaders (called *rektors* in that country) to undertake training at the university level, but this was defeated. Today, in some countries state colleges do run induction programs for rectors, but these decisions are made at the local level (Lein, 2003).

Timing For the educator who is to be appointed as a new administrator, training for that position may occur at two distinct periods, each with significant implications. The common approach in the United States, England, France, and South Africa is to provide preservice training. Educators go through a program of learning and induction prior to obtaining a position. In Norway, Sweden, New Zealand, and much of Africa the timing of the development activities occur after an individual has been appointed as the leader (in-service).

There are advocates of both positions. Educational leadership preparation has been criticized in the United States for being too removed from practice and for insisting that aspirants learn material of little relevance to practice. Supporters of preservice preparation point to a record of school leadership that consistently has elevated the quality of schooling. There is no doubt that this approach has a role in the enormous amount of research literature that has accumulated at an ever-increasing pace over the past century. Preservice education requires established curricular content that focuses the learning of aspirants on such topics as educational leadership and management, educational law, and instructional leadership.

The advocates of in-service training claim that only when the new leader is in a position does she or he begin to understand the type of new knowledge needed. Grounded more in theories of adult learning and the importance of practical relevancy, in-service training can be adapted to the needs of the individual learner and more easily can be provided independent of a third-party institution like a university or government institution. Certainly in countries that lack a well-developed tertiary system that can provide preservice training, the approach that develops administrators through in-service training may offer benefits. In-service approaches also allow the development processes to be grounded in the specific cultural context in which leadership is to be enacted.

Content The content of training and development activities varies widely as well. Bush and Jackson (2002) claimed that the main components of leadership preparation programs appear across national boundaries. Drawing on a study of 11 leadership centers in seven countries (Australia, Canada, Hong Kong, New Zealand, Singapore, Sweden, and the United States), Bush and Jackson noted,

> The content of educational leadership and development programmes has considerable simi-
> larities in different countries, leading to a hypothesis that there is an international curriculum
> for school leadership preparation. Most courses focus on leadership, including vision, mission,
> and transformational leadership, give prominence to issues of learning and teaching, often
> described as instructional leadership, and incorporate consideration of the main task areas
> of administration or management, such as human resources and professional development,
> finance, curriculum and external relations. (p. 421)

Huber (2004) also examined the content of development programs and found similarities across national contexts. However, in instances where countries rely far more on local resources, the provision of standardized curricula from international resources is less pronounced.

In some countries, such as England and South Africa, there is increasing interest in preparation processes and the development of leadership skills. Mentoring is a feature of preparation programs in both countries as well as in Singapore, Australia, and the United States. Coaching is utilized in several programs offered by the English National Conference of State Legislatures, and action learning is increasingly advocated. The rationale for this emphasis is that learning about leadership theories and research provides incomplete preparation for the practice of leadership. Such approaches are usually seen as more appropriate for in-service than preservice programs (Bush & Glover, 2005).

Knowledge and dissemination An important part of the training and development of new administrators has to do with providing these educators with linkages to the growing research-based knowledge pertaining to student learning, development, and educational attainment. In most developed countries, a rich network of research-based associations, practitioner organizations, scholarly and professional journals, conferences, and meetings of educators at all levels serves as a necessary resource of knowledge that informs school leadership. In developing countries, however, leaders have limited access to such resources, and those that are available tend to be Anglo-American rather than being grounded in the specific cultural context where development activities are being forged.

Future Trends in Preparation

Based on the examples of leadership selection and development that we have covered, we suggest the following four trends for the short term:

1. First, we believe that many systems of education will seek to establish a more transparent system of selection that will reduce the influence of political or noneducational forces on selection. The increasing use of formal training programs will tend to lead to selection based more on demonstrated performance. Still, in many places, cultural conditions will continue to influence the reasons why some are selected for principal or head positions. In such con-

texts, developing communities of practice as described earlier in this chapter hold promise for improving school leadership.

2. Different systems appear to be moving in different directions relative to devolution. Not all systems will decentralize authority over selection and development. Two significant examples of the centralization and standardization of selecting and training are the National Professional Qualification for Headship managed and controlled by the National College for School Leadership in England and, in South Africa, the Advanced Certificate in Education program, which serves as another example of a more centralized process.

3. We believe that the use of tertiary institutions as providers of training and development will increase and will spread to national systems that are currently struggling to provide developmental opportunities. Again, there are examples where this is not the case, notably that of England. Yet, we think these same tertiary institutions will not control the selection of leaders, as has been true in many places. Local participation within a local context seems to be expanding in many places.

4. We believe that a global network of scholars researching educational leadership and educational issues will become an important resource for national systems of education everywhere. Earlier we have used the metaphor of a boundaryless world as a way to capture the context in which educators will practice. The very inclusion of this chapter makes more elastic the body of knowledge about ways to prepare and develop educational leaders, stretching the knowledge base across national contexts.

In this section we have attempted to illustrate the message with which we began the chapter. There are many reasons to believe that what comes to us from elsewhere can help us see our own practices with greater clarity. By looking at the variation and diversity in just the concrete and basic practices that select and develop educational leaders, we hope this broad examination of different approaches helps U.S. preparation programs examine their own practices.

Lessons for the United States

Thus far the chapter has presented an argument for an international perspective both in terms of expanding awareness of how leadership preparation is carried out in other places and, perhaps more importantly, suggesting that those in the field of educational administration need to reflect on structural and cultural variation in leadership preparation and what these differences might mean for preparation in the United States. That is, we have argued that it is important for learners to be open to a wider range of ways of knowing, reflecting, and acting and that looking outward sharpens discernment and deepens understanding when looking inward. We have discussed both the opportunity and the challenge presented by globalization, and we have provided comparative examples of different approaches to leadership preparation. This final section seeks to distil from what is known about leadership preparation about the globe those trends and practices that appear to be of significance for leadership preparation in the United States.

Historically, the nature of leadership preparation in the United States has progressed through four major evolutionary phases between 1820 and today (Murphy, 2005). The preparation of school administrators during the Ideological Era (1820–1900) was not differentiated from the training received by teachers. Rather, it emphasized teaching, ideology, character, and philosophy. During the Prescriptive Era (1900–1946), university-based administration programs emphasized providing aspiring school administrators with the managerial skills they would need to successfully administer schools (Campbell, Fleming, Newell, & Bennion, 1987). Faculty members consisted largely of former district superintendents who carried heavy teaching loads and who "preferred descriptive statistics" (Griffiths, 1959, p. 9) and "personal success stories and lively anecdotes" (Marland, 1960, p. 25) to engaging in research or theoretical discussions of a school administrator's work. During the Scientific Era (1947–1985) educational administration programs sought to enhance their status in the academic community (Björk & Ginsberg, 1995), embraced the disciplines and empirical research methods (McCarthy, 1999), and hired professors with backgrounds in the social sciences (Campbell et al., 1987). The quest for a science of school administration (Björk, 1996) not only altered the structure, nature, and content of preparation programs, but also separated the academic and practitioner sides of the profession (Crowson & McPherson, 1987).

The contemporary era, the Dialectic Era (1986–2008), has been characterized by Björk (2001) as possessing "the most intense, comprehensive, and sustained effort to improve education in America's history" (p. 19). This era of educational reform has focused on the need to increase accountability, enhance student learning, improve curriculum, and strengthen teaching (Björk, Kowalski, & Young, 2005). Commission reports have underscored the importance of reconfiguring LDPs that were accused of being decoupled from the reality of practice. Analysts (Björk, Kowalski, & Young, 2005) identified five key recommendations relating to how the next generation of aspiring principals and superintendents should be identified, recruited, and prepared:

1. Strengthen connections to the field.
2. Revise course content.
3. Modify instructional strategies.
4. Achieve social and organizational justice.
5. Evaluate program effectiveness.

Under these five broad recommendations one may locate most of the significant challenges facing leadership development in the United States. Knowledge of how leaders are identified and prepared in other national contexts may stimulate new thinking about how those in the United States may best serve the recommendations made for the field during this Dialectic Era. Indeed, the point of the earlier sections of this chapter is that, were leadership preparation providers in the United States more informed about practices elsewhere, the scholars and practitioners of educational leadership might find unique and efficacious ways to address their challenges.

Strengthening Connections to the Field

A consistent theme that has emerged from the educational reform reports during the past two decades has been the admonition that all forms of university-based professional programs should strengthen connections with the field of practice. We have argued that the field might be seen as a global practice community and not just as local and national. An international perspective can result in a sense of connection to a wider field of practice and to solidarity with educational leaders facing similar and dissimilar challenges throughout the world and also can result in recommendations related to how leadership preparation is conducted in other countries in which one finds many different approaches to strengthening connections to the field.

A number of key commission reports (Björk, 1996, 2001; Björk, Kowalski, & Browne-Ferrigno, 2005; Björk, Kowalski, & Young, 2005) recommended adopting work-embedded learning, the creation of partnership sites with school districts, field residencies, principal apprenticeship programs, and action research. For example, several national commission reports recommended that LDPs collaborate with school districts to recruit individuals that have demonstrated commitment and talent to lead schools. Because a number of countries have processes that do identify and develop targeted individuals for leadership positions (in contrast to the largely self-nominated aspirants that flood the aspirant pool in the United States), those working to create the next generation of administrators may find cause to be more intentional about who is selected to receive leadership preparation.

It is instructive as well that in some national systems of education the role of the higher education institution has been altered. Some national systems even go so far as to provide for development experiences so embedded in practice (through mentoring or coaching, for example) that the descriptive phrase *educational administration program* is no longer operable. In such settings the higher education sector provides specific instruction but does not design and deliver a total program of instruction. Yet, the field in the United States tends to consign to the educational administration program the dominant role in reconfiguring the selection and development of educational leaders.

New patterns of connecting the development with the field are evident in many places; these are grounded in literature on adult learning theory and findings from studies on work-embedded learning (Björk, Kowalski, & Browne-Ferrigno, 2005). Two possible lessons emerging for the United States are questioning the current parameters of what constitutes *the field* and calling into question the traditional definition and understanding of the *educational administration program*.

Revising Course Content

Recommendations for leadership preparation in the United States include significant changes to revisions in course content (National Commission on Excellence in Educational Administration, 1987; National Policy Board for Educational Administration, 1989; Young, 2002). The Danforth Foundation (1987) recommended a move away from school management to an emphasis on school leadership, a leadership compatible with the decentralized school focused on student learning. Scholarship from a number of countries re-enforces the centrality of the principal as leader as we discussed earlier. In 1994 the Council of Chief State School Officers convened representatives from the National Policy Board for Educational Administration, who acknowledged that principals are vital to improving student learning and formed The Interstate School Leadership Licensure Consortium (ISLLC). The ISLLC (1996) standards provided a research-based template for improving the content, instruction, and clinical experiences of principal preparation programs that aligned with the new realities of practice. These national licensure standards intended to shift preparation and practice away from management towards leadership and to recenter the field to focus on improving student learning. In 2007 a draft of revised ISSLC standards was circulated to members of the National Policy Board for Educational Administration members for comment. Although significant progress has been made to improve professional preparation, the need to end curricular disarray (A. Levine, 2005) and to develop a coherent and rigorous curriculum focused on enhancing the capacity of new principals to improve student learning remains a prominent challenge.

In 2000, the American Educational Research Association, in collaboration with UCEA and the Laboratory for Student Success at Temple University, formed a task force, Developing Research in Educational Leadership. This taskforce released its report, *What We Know About Successful School Leadership* (Leithwood & Riehl, 2003). The report linked positive outcomes for student learning with the following: (a) distributing leadership; enacting moral, instructional, and transformational leadership roles; and establishing high student expectations; (b) setting directions and building the capacity of school staff; (c) viewing accountability as an opportunity to improve practice; (d) examining prevailing practices in light of the needs of diverse student groups; and (e) building trust and improving communication, providing parents with knowledge and resources (Leithwood & Riehl, 2003).

The report (Leithwood & Riehl, 2003) has a hegemonic U.S. culture as taken for granted. As argued earlier, an implicitly assumed culture has potential disadvantages. The assumption of cultural homogeneity among those preparing leaders and program participants cannot be assumed; a supposed common culture may ensure a poor cultural fit for some within richly diverse U.S. communities. Additionally, assumptions of shared culture may encourage cultural blindness and reinforce a lack of reflection on differing ways of doing things. Finally, culturally grounded ideas may be exported elsewhere, whatever the fit, so that the cultural underpinning of the five factors related to positive outcomes for students may be taken not as related to the U.S. context, but as in some sense universal.

The latter appears born out by analyses of program content. As we have discussed previously, there are similarities in curriculum content across national boundaries. Bush and Jackson (2002) have suggested that these similarities present a "hypothesis that there is an international curriculum for school leadership preparation" (p. 421). There is relatively little research on how we might understand the *international* label and how far the dominance and diffusion of values and ideas from U.S. research, reports, and programs results in positives or negatives for student learning in the United States and elsewhere. A lesson emerging is the necessity for researchers and program leaders or tutors to be more self-aware, more explicit, and more reflective on the cultural assumptions that underpin their work.

Modifying Instructional Strategies

The importance of modifying instructional strategies in preparing educational leaders has been urged in a number of reform reports issued by the American Association of Colleges of Teacher Education (1988), National Association of Secondary School Principals (1985), National Commission on Excellence in Educational Administration (1987), and National Commission for the Advancement of Education Leadership Preparation (2002); licensure standards (ISLLC, 1996); and recent reports by A. Levine (2005) and LaPointe and Davis (2006). Convincing theoretical and empirical evidence supports the use of active learning, including simulations, case studies, and practice-based and problem-based learning; collaborative action research (Milstein, 1993); integration of formal and experiential knowledge (Björk, 1999); and more student-oriented rather than professor-centered instructional strategies. These initiatives called for professional preparation programs to be research based, standards aligned, work embedded, and performance assessed. Situating aspiring leaders in actual work contexts and enlisting them in real-world problem-finding and problem-solving activities is similar to what Bush (2003) referred to as process-oriented leadership development models that are presently in vogue in the United Kingdom, Australia, Singapore, and Hong Kong. The adoption of work-embedded learning in preservice programs captures the need for practical relevancy that is central to postappointment in-service training preferred in Norway, Sweden, and New Zealand.

Opinions vary as to whether practice should be a sheltered experience or an opportunity to participate in actual high-risk work (Björk, 2001). Schön (1992) posited that the purpose of engaging in field-based learning experiences is to "represent essential features of a practice to be learned while enabling students to experience at low risk, vary the pace and focus of the work, and go back to do things over when it seems useful to do so" (p. 179). Hoberman and Mailick (1994), however, asserted that the absence of risk may diminish rich opportunities for work-embedded learning. They argued that work-embedded learning should reflect a full range of complex social, economic, and political circumstances that enable and constrain administrator action. In their view, work-embedded learning should involve actual, rather than sheltered, activities that have real consequences for the learner. We have argued that confronting a full range of complex social, economic, and political circumstances requires a global perspective; without such a perspective, leaders are ill equipped to assess their position and their response to the pressures and changes that buffet them as part of a global tide. Some programs have addressed such a necessity by ensuring a program component that demands engagement with the unfamiliar context through a variety of strategies (McClellan & Dominguez, 2006).

We have observed that notions of experiential learning and action learning should be designed to challenge learners and to extend present levels of knowledge, skills, and expertise. Creating the circumstances to induce cognitive conflict that exposes the gap between what people presently know and what they may need to know to adapt to change is crucial. Cultural norms in the United States, Great Britain, and Sweden value challenge and consequentially are more open to change and comfortable with personal growth and career mobility. In general, people in these cultures tend to be more tolerant of ambiguity and value learning by doing. On the other hand, education leaders in France, Germany, and Turkey, whose cultures place a high value on stability, continuity, and certainty, may be less comfortable with ambiguity and intentionally induced conflict and prefer more conventional learning environments. In addition, collectivist cultures like Japan, in which aspirations of leaders are subordinated to the well-being of the group, pose additional circumstances that may call for different LDP learning models. Although these cultural characteristics are distinct, they also may fit individuals and groups within a given nation. Given the variability of individuals participating in LDPs and the range of school contexts, it may be advisable to be circumspect as to how to promote growth among leaders who exhibit different characteristics across and within cultural settings.

Leadership preparation and performance cannot be separated from cultures within which they are constructed. Thus, assuming that practices are generic and transferable across cultures may be less useful than acknowledging that they differ in respect to power, patterns of communication, and approaches to change and action. In addition, providers of LDPs may want to consider how supportive relationships may be enacted within cultures and select communication patterns that align with accepted conditions of power and status configurations. These issues are particularly important when using mentoring and coaching and providing feedback. The emerging lesson is a universal requirement for acute sensitivity to the multiple cultures and value bases within any community, including those of the United States, and that engagement with practice globally may prove the most effective means to achieve such sensitivity in local practice.

Achieving Social Justice

Leadership preparation in the United States has adopted as part of its agenda a commitment to the achievement of social justice. This commitment has fuelled any number of initiatives to increase full membership, opportunity, and participation by all races and classes of individuals. Generally, in the United States this commitment has been a response to demographic changes that have occurred over past two decades, changes that have altered the landscape of education and heightened awareness of the lack of correspondence between the gender and race of those who teach and lead public schools. National commission and task force reports have recognized that increasing access and equity for marginalized groups is in the national interest (Ryan, 1993) and have recommended rectifying this imbalance (Cross, Bazron, Dennis, & Isaacs, 1989; Commission on Policy for Racial Justice of the Joint Center for Political Studies, 1989; Commission on Minority Participation in American Life, 1988; Commission on Minority Participation in American Life, 1988; Davis, 1997; Isaacs & Benjamin, 1991; Leithwood & Riehl, 2003; Quality Education for Minorities Project, 1990; Young, 2002; Young et al., 2002). Thus, notions of social and organizational justice are becoming important dimensions of efforts to reconfigure how the next generation of school and district leaders are identified, prepared, and hired.

However, from an international perspective, the changing demographics of the United States are anything but unique. Most countries are experiencing demographic shifts as populations move from place to place and as global economic activity opens local cultures to sometimes wrenching change. Educational systems offer one way to mitigate the damaging effects of demographic and economic change in promoting equity for individuals. Enhancing cultural knowledge through education is perhaps the most important task facing all of the educational systems of the world, if social justice is to be promoted.

Above we noted that culture is viewed as an integrated pattern of human behavior that encompasses the values, beliefs, and attitudes of a group of individuals, made known through their customs, and individual actions involving racial, ethnic, religious, or social groups. The notion of competence implies that institutions and individuals have the capacity to function within multicultural and multiethnic settings. Thus, those who are regarded as being culturally competent are sensitive to cultural differences at all levels of schooling (i.e., policy, governance, administration, and instruction) and model professional attitudes and behaviors that enable schools and districts to work effectively in cross-cultural situations. Cultural competence is the integration of knowledge about individuals and groups of people into policies and practices that increase the quality of education for all children to enhance learning. Being competent in cross-cultural and cross-national settings requires learning new patterns of behavior and effectively applying them in a wide range of cultural contexts. Being sensitive to and capable of working in diverse cultural settings is important to leader success and should be an integral dimension of LDPs rather than being left to serendipity. Such an attribute not only is central to whether educational leaders are able to successfully enact their leadership roles, but also governs agency to achieve social and organizational justice at the local and global levels.

Evaluating Program Effectiveness

Efforts to align leadership preparation programs with student academic performance as well as other school and community-related outcomes are facilitated by adoption of national leadership standards by state licensing agencies and program self-evaluation. As noted previously, in 1994, the Council of Chief State School Officers formed the ISLLC to develop a set of national licensure standards intended to shift preparation and practice away from management towards leadership and to recenter the field to focus on improving student learning. The ISLLC (1996) standards are intended as a template for improving the content, instruction, and clinical experiences of principal preparation programs. The six ISLLC standards are (a) building a shared vision; (b) creating a culture of learning; (c) ensuring safe and productive learning environments; (d) working together with parents and community citizens; (e) working in a fair and ethical manner; and (f) understanding broad socioeconomic, legal, political, and cultural contexts in which schools are embedded. The notion of performance-based licensure is a significant departure from previous models based solely on completion of a state-approved program of study and level the playing field in the United States as the range of potential leadership development providers expands. At this juncture, expectations for all LDPs are that they will be research based, standards compliant, work embedded, and performance assessed. Although these standards allow for a wide range of learning formats, all providers are expected to guarantee that graduates have the demonstrated capacity to lead schools and are capable of improving student learning, developing the capacity for change, and engaging parents and community citizens. During the last several years, heightened interest ascertaining the efficacy of school leaders and a wide range of LDPs has called for designing assessment systems that align school leaders and their preparation programs with student academic test scores. Although most scholars concur that principals are central to improving student learning, their effect is indirect, presenting them with an unprecedented challenge in research and public policy arenas.

Bush (2003) and Bryant (2002) noted that developing school leaders is often viewed as the responsibility of national, regional, or state governments that may exercise varying degrees of control. In these instances, governments that establish standards and criteria, such as Belarus and the United States, through state adoption of national standards like ISLLC (1996), influence establishment of proscriptive LDPs that fail to recognize the need for contextual and cultural relevance.

Concluding Comments

There are many lessons those in the United States can glean from learning about leadership in other countries and about how others are preparing leaders. We know that the United States is exporting its programs and its knowledge base. We have suggested that special responsibilities and accountability accompany this trend. We also have suggested that given the diversity of practices to be found elsewhere, the rather restrictive model of U.S. preparation and development may be missing many opportunities. Also, we have suggested that educating leaders as global citizens needs to be an important part of leader preparation in the United States.

Globalization is heightening awareness of the importance of building human capital through education that has provided grist for an international conversation about the nature of leadership and leadership preparation. Although evidence suggests that there is a shared belief that the work of the principal is related to the quality of schooling, how they make a difference and how they are prepared are highly dependent on contexts and cultures. These insights are particularly relevant for nations that are anticipating or are presently engaged in school reform and reconfiguring leadership development. These insights are also edifying for those seeking involvement in other countries as advisors, experts, consultants, or collaborative partners. The notion that there is one best way of preparing school leaders is the hallmark of the uninformed. Those who recognize that effective leadership and leadership development cannot be separated from the context and culture in which they are constructed may draw upon rich international perspectives to gain insights into their own values and practice and into how leadership development and practice may be improved. The discernable pattern of lessening control of institutions of higher education on leadership preparation and locating it in the field rather than in the classroom provides an extraordinary opportunity for bridging academic and practice arms of the profession and increasing the rigor and relevance of leadership development. Regardless of whether work-embedded leadership development occurs at the pre- or in-service point in time, it is evident that mentoring and coaching are being viewed as central to their success. Although it is promising that schools and universities in the United States recognize the need to recenter the profession to focus on student learning and situate leadership development in work settings, progress has been slow.

Adopting an international perspective on leader preparation and continuing development programs is not a peripheral luxury, the equivalent of the 19th-century European Grand Tour to view the quaint and the uplifting and thereby achieve a rounded person who is thereby fitted to do very little on return home. Rather, we have argued strongly that an international perspective can do the following:

1. Increase leaders' reflection on practice through making strange the familiar.
2. Act as a primary strategy to support the development of cultural competence.
3. Contribute to social justice through offering a wider understanding of the extent and provenance of issues such as child poverty and their impact on education and school leaders.
4. Promote greater sensitivity to the need for preparation program evaluation models to be contextually and culturally relevant.
5. Offer an extensive pool of practical knowledge and wisdom based on different approaches and experience globally.

6.   Inhibit the unthinking export of U.S. ideas to other contexts.

Such aims imply that U.S. preparation programs, rather than importing some international element as a token gesture, could benefit from embedding an international perspective in every aspect of development to equip leaders for this, our diverse and global world.

References

Adler, N. (1997). *Organizational behaviour* (3rd ed.). Cincinnati, OH: South Western.

Aghammadova, F. (2006). *The selection of school administrators in Azerbaijan: A case study.* Lincoln: University of Nebraska.

Allix, N., & Gronn, P. (2005). "Leadership" as a manifestation of knowledge. J. Lumby, N. Foskett, & B. Fidler (Eds.) Researching leadership [Special issue]. *Educational Management, Administration and Leadership, 33*(2), 181–196.

American Association of Colleges of Teacher Education. (1988). *School leadership preparation: A preface to action.* Washington, DC: Author.

Bamberg, I. (2003) L'ecole comme centre de la vie communitaire. *Cahiers d'Etudes Africaines, 43*(1-2), 121–142.

Begley, P. (2000) Cultural isomorphs of educational administration: Reflections on western-centric approaches to values and leadership. *Asia Pacific Journal of Education, 20*(2), 23–33.

Benson, C. (Ed.). (2002). *America's children: Key national indicators of well-being, 2002.* Washington, DC: Federal Interagency Forum on Child and Family Statistics.

Björk, L. (1996). The revisionists' critique of the education reform reports. *Journal of School Leadership, 6,* 290–315.

Björk, L. (1999, April). *Integrating formal and experiential knowledge: A superintendent preparation model.* Paper presented at the annual meeting of the American Educational Research Association, Montreal, Quebec, Canada.

Björk, L. (2001). Preparing the next generation of superintendents: Integrating formal and experiential knowledge. In C. C. Brunner & L. Björk (Eds.), *The new superintendency: Advances in research and theories of school management and educational policy* (pp. 19–54). Greenwich, CT: JAI Press.

Björk, L. G., & Ginsberg, R. (1995). Principles of reform and reforming principal training: A theoretical perspective. *Educational Administration Quarterly, 31*(1), 11–37.

Björk, L., Kowalski, T., & Browne-Ferrigno, T. (2005). Learning theory and research: A framework for changing superintendent preparation and development. In L. Björk & T. Kowalski (Eds.), *The contemporary superintendent: Preparation, practice and development* (pp. 71–106). Thousand Oaks, CA: Corwin Press.

Björk, L., Kowalski, T., & Young, M. (2005). National education reform reports: Implications for professional preparation and development. In L. Björk & T. Kowalski (Eds.), *The contemporary superintendent: Preparation, practice and development* (pp. 45–70). Thousand Oaks, CA: Corwin Press.

Borden, A. (2002, April). *School principals in Latin America and the Caribbean: Leaders for change or subjects of change?* Paper presented at the meeting of the Education and Human Resources Training Network. Available from the Inter-American Development Bank Web site: http://wwwt.iadb.org/int/DRP/esp/Red4/Documentos/BordenAbril4-5-2002eng.pdf

Bottery, M. (1999). Global forces, national mediations and the management of educational institutions. *Educational Management and Administration, 27*(3) 299–312.

Bottoms, G., & O'Neill, K. (2001). *Preparing a new breed of school principals: It's time for action.* Atlanta, GA: Southern Regional Education Board.

Brieschke, P. A. (1990). The administrator in fiction: Using the novel to teach educational administration. *Educational Administration Quarterly, 26*(4), 376–393.

Brookover, W., Beady, C., Flood, P., Schweitzer, J., & Wisenbaker, J. (1979). *School social systems and student achievement: Schools can make a difference.* New York: Praeger.

Brooks, D. (2005, November 13). Psst! "Human capital." *New York Times,* p. A12.

Brown, P., & Lauder, H. (1997). Education, globalization and economic development. In A. H. Halsey, H. Lauder, P. Brown, & A. S. Wells (Eds.), *Education, economy and society* (pp. 172–192). Oxford, England: Oxford University Press.

Bryant, M. (1989). An inquiry-based orientation for programs in educational administration. *National Forum of Applied Educational Research Journal, 2*(1), 3–39.

Bryant, M. T. (2002). Face to face with ISLLC: Understanding the new School Leaders Licensure Assessment. *Planning and Changing, 33*(3-4), 171–185.

Bryant, M., Aghammadova, F., Krupenikava, A., Dutta, S., & Hu, X. (2006, November). *Patterns in administrative preparation: Four case studies.* Paper presented at the annual meeting of the University Council of Educational Administration, San Antonio, TX.

Burbules, N., & Torres, C. (2000). *Globalization and education: Critical perspectives.* London: Routledge.

Burlingame, M., & Harris, E. L. (1998). Changes in the field of educational administration in the United States from 1967 to 1996 as a revitalization movement. *Educational Management and Administration, 26*(1), 21–34.

Bush, T. (2003). *Theories of educational leadership and management* (3rd ed.). London: Sage.

Bush, T., & Glover, D. (2005). Leadership development for early headship: The New Visions experience. *School Leadership and Management, 25*(3), 217–239.

Bush, T., & Jackson, D. (2002). Preparation for school leadership: International perspectives. *Educational Management and Administration, 30*(4), 417–429.

Bush, T., & Oduro, G. (2006). New principals in Africa: Preparation, induction and practice. *Journal of Educational Administration, 44*(4), 359–375.

Campbell, R. F., Fleming, T., Newell, L. J., & Bennion, J. W. (1987). *A history of thought and practice in educational administration.* New York: Teachers College Press.

Cheng, K. M. (1998). Can education values be borrowed? Looking into cultural differences. *Peabody Journal of Education, 73*(2), 11–30.·

Cheng, K. M. (1995). The neglected dimension: Cultural comparison in educational administration. In K. C. Wong & K. M. Cheng (Eds.), *Educational leadership and change: An international perspective* (pp. 87–104). Hong Kong: Hong Kong University Press.

Cheng, Y. C. (2001). Multi-models of education quality and principal leadership. In K. H. Mok & D. Chan (Eds.), *The quest for quality education in Hong Kong: Theory and practice* (pp. 69–88). Hong Kong: Hong Kong University Press.

Cisneros-Cohernouri, E., Adler, A., Young, M., & Muth, R. (2004, April). *Cultural, sociopolitical and economic issues in the preparation of school principals: An international perspective.* Paper presented at the annual meeting of the American Educational Research Association, Chicago.

Commission on Minority Participation in American Life. (1988). *One third of a nation.* Washington, DC: American Council on Education and Education Commission of the States.

Commission on Policy for Racial Justice of the Joint Center for Political Studies. (1989). *Visions for a better way: A Black appraisal of public schooling.* Washington, DC: Joint Policy Center for Political Studies.

Creemers, P. M. (1994). *The effective classroom.* New York: Cassell.

Crisci, P. E., & Tutela, A. D. (1987, August). *Program development trends and issues: The Cleveland Leadership Academy.* Paper presented at the National Conference for Professors of Educational Administration, Chadron, NE.

Cross T., Bazron, B., Dennis, K., & Isaacs, M. (1989) *Towards a culturally competent system of care, Vol. I.* Washington, DC: Georgetown University Child Development Center, CASSP Technical Assistance Center.

Crossley, M., & Watson, K. (2003). *Comparative and international research in education.* London: Routledge Falmer.

Crowson, R. L., & McPherson, R. B. (1987). The legacy of the theory movement: Learning from the new tradition. In J. Murphy & P. Hallinger (Eds.), *Approaches to administrative training in education* (pp. 45–64). Albany: State University of New York Press.

Crowther, F., & Limerick, B. (1998). Leaders as learners: Implications for postmodern leader development. *International Studies in Education Administration, 26*(2), 21–29.

Danforth Foundation. (1987). *Program for the preparation of school principals (DPPSP).* St. Louis, MO: Author.

Davis, K. (1997). *Exploring the intersection between cultural competency and managed behavioral health care policy: Implications for state and county mental health agencies.* Alexandria, VA: National Technical Assistance Center for State Mental Health Planning.

Dimmock, C. (2000). *Designing the learning-centred school: A cross-cultural perspective.* London: Falmer.

Dimmock, C., & Walker, A. (1998). Comparative educational administration: Developing a cross-cultural comparative framework. *Educational Administration Quarterly, 34*(4), 558–595.

Dimmock, C., & Walker, A. (2005). *Educational leadership: Culture and diversity.* London: Sage.

Dorfman, P. W., Hanges, P. J., & Brodbeck, F. C. (2004). Leadership and cultural variation: The identification of culturally endorsed leadership profiles. In R. J. House, P. J. Hanges, M. Javidan, P. W. Dorfman, & V. Gupta (Eds.), *Culture, leadership and organizations: The GLOBE study of 32 societies* (pp. 670–713). Thousand Oaks, CA: Sage.

Dorfman, P. W., Howell, J. P., Hibino, S., Lee, J. K., Tate, U., & Bautista, A. (1997). Leadership in western and eastern countries: Commonalities and differences in effective leadership process across cultures. *Leadership Quarterly, 8*(3), 233–274.

Dutta, S. (2006). *Selection and preparation of administrators in West Bengal.* Lincoln: University of Nebraska.

Earley, P., & Weindling, D. (2004). *Understanding school leadership.* London: Paul Chapman.

Edmunds, R. (1979). Some schools work and more can. *Social Policy, 9*(2), 28–32.

Foskett, N., & Lumby, J. (2003). *Leading and managing education: International dimensions.* London: Paul Chapman.

Foster, W. P. (2004). The decline of the local: A challenge to educational leadership. *Educational Administration Quarterly, 40*(2), 176–191.

Giddens, A. (1999). *Runaway world.* London: Profile Books.

Glatter, R., & Kydd, L. (2003). "Best practice" in educational leadership and management: Can we identify it and learn from it? *Educational Management & Administration, 31*(3), 231–243.

Gouldner, A. W. (1954). *Patterns of industrial democracy.* Glencoe, IL: Free Press.

Grace, G. (2000). Research and the challenges of contemporary school leadership: The contribution of critical scholarship. *British Journal of Educational Studies, 48*(3), 231–247.

Grady, M., Wayson, W., & Zirkel, P. (1979). *A review of effective schools research as it relates to effective principals.* Austin, TX: University Council for Educational Administration.

Griffiths, D. E. (1959). *Administrative theory*. New York: Appleton-Century-Crofts.

Griffiths, D. E., Stout, R. T., & Forsyth, P. B. (1988). *National Commission on Excellence in Educational Administration (U.S.) Leaders for America's schools: The report and papers of the National Commission on Excellence in Educational Administration*. Berkeley, CA: McCutchan.

Gronn, P. (2001). Commentary. Crossing the Great Divides: problems of cultural diffusion for leadership in education. *International Journal for Leadership in Education, 4*(4), 401–414.

Grove, C. N. (2005). *Introduction to the GLOBE research project on leadership worldwide*. Retrieved September 16, 2008, from the Grovewell Web site: http://www.grovewell.com/pub-GLOBE-leadership.html#HowTeamProceeded

Gudykunst, W. (1995). Anxiety/uncertainty management (AUM) theory. In R. Wiseman (Ed.), *International communication theory* (Vol. 19, pp. 8–65). London: Sage.

Haiplik, B. (2003, March). *BRAC's non-formal primary education (NFPE) teacher training program*. Paper presented at the annual meeting of the Comparative and International Education Society, New Orleans, LA.

Hallinger, P. (1995). Culture and leadership: Developing an international perspective in educational demonstration. *UCEA Review, 406*(2), 1–13.

Hallinger, P. (Ed.). (2003). *Reshaping the landscape of school leadership development: A global perspective*. Lisse, The Netherlands: Swets and Zeitlinger.

Hallinger, P., & Heck, R. (1999). Can school leadership enhance school effectiveness? In T. Bush, L. Bell, R. Bolam, R. Glatter, & P. Ribbons (Eds.), *Educational management: Redefining theory, policy and practice* (pp. 179–190). London: Paul Chapman.

Hallinger, P., & Kantamara, P. (2000) Educational change in Thailand: Opening a window onto leadership as a cultural process. *School Leadership and Management, 20*(2), 189–205.

Hallinger, P., & Leithwood, K. (1996). Culture and educational administration: A case of finding out what you don't know you don't know. *Journal of Educational Administration, 34*(5), 98–116.

Hallinger, P., & Leithwood, K. (1998). Leading schools in a global era. *Peabody Journal of Education, 73*(2), 1–10.

Hallinger, P., & Snidvongs, K. (2005). *Adding value to school leadership and management: A review of trends in the development of managers in the education and business sectors*. Nottingham, England: National College for School Leadership.

Hallinger, P., Walker, A., & Bajunid, I. A. (2005). Educational leadership in East Asia: Implications for education in global society. *UCEA Review, 45*(1), 1–5

Heck, R. (1996). Leadership and culture: Conceptual and methodological issues in comparing models across cultural settings. *Journal of Educational Administration, 34*(5), 74–97.

Henze, R., Katz, A., Norte, E., Sather, S., & Walker, E. (2001). *Leading for diversity: How school leaders promote positive interethnic relations*. Berkeley: University of California, Center for Research on Education. Diversity and Excellence. Retrieved December 9, 2005, from http://repositories.cdlib.org/crede/edupractrpts/epr07

Hills, J. (1983). *The preparation of educational leaders: What's needed and what's next?* (RUF89025). Columbus, OH: University Council for Educational Administration.

Hoberman, S., & Mailick, S. (Eds.). (1994). *Professional education in the United States: Experiential learning, issues and prospects*. Westport, CT: Praeger.

Hoppe, M. H. (2004) Cross-cultural issues in development of leaders. In C. D. McCauley & E. V. Velsor (Eds.), *Handbook of leadership development* (pp. 331–360). San Francisco: Jossey-Bass.

House, R. J., Hanges, P. J., Javidan, M., Dorfman, P. W., & Gupta, V. (Eds.). (2004). *Culture, leadership and organizations: The GLOBE study of 32 societies*. Thousand Oaks, CA: Sage.

Hoy, W. (Ed.). (1986). *Educational administration: The UCEA document base* (Vols. 1–3). London: McGraw-Hill.

Huber, S. G. (2004). *Preparing school leaders for the 21st century*. New York: Routledge Falmer.

Interstate School Leaders Licensure Consortium. (1996). *Standards for school leaders*. Washington, DC: Council of Chief State School Officers.

Isaacs, M. R., & Benjamin, M. P. (1991). *Towards a culturally competent system of care. Vol. 2: Programs which utilize culturally competent principles*. Washington, DC: Georgetown University Child Development Center, Center for Child Health and Mental Health Policy, CASSP Technical Assistance Center.

Jansen, J. (2006). Leading against the grain: The politics and emotions of leading for social justice in South African. *Leadership and Policy in Schools, 5*, 37–51.

Javidan, M. (2004). Performance orientation. In R. J. House, P. J. Hanges, M. Javidan, P. W. Dorfman, & V. Gupta (Eds.), *Culture, leadership and organizations: The GLOBE study of 62 societies* (pp. 239–281). Thousand Oaks, CA: Sage.

John, P. (2002). *The training needs of principals of private schools in the Union Territory of Pondicherry, India*. Unpublished doctoral dissertation, Fordham University, New York.

Johnson, D. (1995). Developing an approach to developing educational management in South Africa. *Comparative Education Review, 31*(2), 223–241.

Jones, A. (2006). Developing what? An anthropological look at the leadership development process across cultures. *Leadership, 2*(4), 481–498.

Kitavi, M., & Westhuizen, P. van der. (1997). Problems facing beginning principals in developing countries: A study of beginning principals in Kenya. *International Journal of Educational Development, 17*(3), 251–263.

Kotkin, J. (1992). *How race, religion, and identity determine success in the new global economy.* New York: Random House.

Krupenikava, A. (2006, November). *Educational administrator selection in Belarus: A case study.* Paper presented at the annual meeting of the University Council for Educational Administration, San Antonio, TX.

Lakomski, G. (2001). Organizational change, leadership and learning: Culture as cognitive process. *The International Journal of Educational Management, 15*(2), 68–77.

Lambert, L. (2005). Constructivist leadership. In B. Davies (Ed.), *The essentials of school leadership* (pp. 93–109). London: Paul Chapman and Corwin Press.

LaPointe, M., & Davis, S. (2006). *School leadership study: Developing successful principals.* Stanford, CA: Stanford University.

Lein, E. (2003). The selection and development of head teachers in Norway. In L. Watson (Ed.), *Selecting and developing heads of schools: Twenty-three European perspectives.* Sheffield, England: Sheffield Hallam University.

Leithwood, K., & Duke, D. L. (1998). Mapping the conceptual terrain of leadership: A critical point for departure for cross-cultural studies. *Peabody Journal of Education, 73*(2), 31–50.

Leithwood, K., & Riehl, C. (2003). *What we know about successful school leadership.* Philadelphia: Temple University, Laboratory for Student Success.

Leslie, J. B., Gryskiewicz, B. D., & Dalton, M. A. (1998). Understanding cultural influences on the 360-degree feedback process. In W. W. Tornow & M. London (Eds.), *Maximizing the value of 360-degree feedback: A process for successful individual and organizational development* (pp. 196–216). San Francisco: Jossey-Bass.

Levin, J. (2001). *Globalizing the community college.* New York: Palgrave.

Levine, A. (2005). *Educating school leaders.* New York: Columbia University, The Education Schools Project.

Levine, D. U., & Lezotte, L. W. (1990). *Unusually effective schools: A review and analysis of research and practice.* Madison, WI: National Center for Effective Schools Research and Development. (ERIC Document Reproduction Service No. ED330032).

Lopez, G. R. (2003). The (racially neutral) politics of education: A critical race theory perspective. *Educational Administration Quarterly, 39*(1), 68–94.

Loudon, W., & Wildy, H. (1999). Short shrift to long lists: An alternative approach to the development of performance standards for school principals. *Journal of Educational Administration, 37*(2), 99–121.

Lukes, S. (1975). *Power, a radical view.* London: Palgrave Macmillan.

Lumby, J. (2003). Transforming schools: Managing the change process. In T. Bush, M. Thurlow, & M. Coleman (Eds.), *Leadership and strategic management in South African schools* (pp. 101–116). London: Commonwealth Secretariat.

Lumby, J. (with Coleman, M.). (2007). *Leadership and diversity.* London: Sage.

March, J. (1978). American public school administration: A short analysis. *School Review, 86*(2), 217–250.

Marland, S. P. (1960). Superintendents' concerns about research applications in educational administration. In R. F. Campbell & J. M. Lipham (Eds.), *Administrative theory as a guide to action* (pp. 21–36). Chicago: University of Chicago, Midwest Administration Center.

Mazawi, A. E. (1999). The contested terrains of education in Arab states: An appraisal of major research trends. *Comparative Education Review, 43*(3) 341–352.

McCarthy, M. M. (1999). The evolution of educational leadership preparation programs. In J. Murphy & K. Seashore Louis (Eds.), *Handbook of research on educational administration* (2nd ed., pp. 119–139). San Francisco: Jossey-Bass.

McClellan, R., & Dominguez, R. (2006). The uneven march toward social justice: Diversity, conflict, and complexity in educational administration programs. *Journal of Educational Administration, 44*(3), 225–238.

Milstein, M. (Ed.). (1993). *Changing the way we prepare educational leaders: The Danforth experience.* Newbury Park, CA: Corwin.

Moos, L. (2005). How do schools bridge the gap between external demands for accountability and the need for internal trust? *Journal of Educational Change, 6,* 307–328.

Mortimore, P., Sammons, P., Stoll, L., Lewis, D., & Ecob, R. (1988). *School matters.* Wells, England: Open Books.

Murphy, J. (2005). *Charting the changing landscape of the preparation of school leaders: An agenda for research and action.* Unpublished manuscript, Vanderbilt University, Stanford Grant on Innovative Principal Training Programs, Nashville, TN.

National Association of Secondary School Principals. (1985). *Performance-based preparation of principals: A framework for improvement.* Reston, VA: Author.

National College for School Leadership. (2001). *First corporate plan: Launch Year 2001-2002.* Nottingham, England: Author.

National Commission on Excellence in Educational Administration. (1987). *Leaders for America's schools.* Tempe, AZ: University Council for Educational Administration.

National Policy Board for Educational Administration. (1989). *Improving the preparation of school administrators: An agenda for reform.* Charlottesville, VA: Author.

Ogunu, M. A. (1999). *The development of a model training program in educational planning and management for the preparation of school administrators in Nigeria.* Unpublished doctoral dissertation, Michigan State University, East Lansing.

Ohmae, K. (2000). *The invisible continent: Four strategic imperatives of the new economy.* London: Nicholas Brealey.

Paige, R. M. & Mestenhauser, J. A. (1999). Internationalizing educational administration. *Educational Administration Quarterly, 345*(4), 500–517.

Parkray, F., & Hall, G. (Eds.). (1992). *Becoming a principal: The challenges of beginning leadership.* Boston: Allyn and Bacon.

Parsons, W. (1995). *Public policy.* Cheltenham, England: Edward Elgar.

Perrow, C. (1979). *Complex organizations: A critical essay.* Glenville, IL: Scott, Foresman and Company.

Popper, S. (1990). *Pathways to the humanities in school administration.* Tempe, AZ: University Council for Educational Administration.

Quality Education for Minorities Project. (1990). *Education that works: An action plan for the education of minorities.* Cambridge: Massachusetts Institute of Technology.

Rakhashani, A. A. (1980). *A developmental model for the preparation and continuing education of secondary school principals in Iran.* Unpublished doctoral dissertation, University of Wyoming, Laramie.

Ratliff, W. (2006). *Doing it wrong and doing it right: Education in Latin America and Asia.* Stanford, CA: Stanford University, Hoover Institution.

Reynolds, D. (1976). The delinquent school. In M. Hammersley & P. Woods (Eds.), *The process of schooling: A sociological reader* (pp. 217–229). London: Routledge & Kegan.

Rhoten, D. (2000). Education decentralization in Argentina: A "global-local conditions of possibility" approach to state, market and society change. *Journal of Education Policy, 15*(6), 593–620.

Robertson, J. M., & Webber, C. F. (2000). Cross-cultural leadership development. *International Journal of Leadership in Education, 3*(4), 315–330.

Rose, P. (2003). Community participation in school policy and practice in Malawi: Balancing local knowledge, national policies and international agency priorities. *Compare, 33*(1), 47–64.

Rosenberg J. (2000). *The follies of globalisation theory.* London: Verso.

Rusch, E. A. (2004). Gender and race in leadership Preparations: A Constrained Discourse, *Educational Administration Quarterly, 40*(1), 14–16.

Rutter, M., Maughan, B., Mortimore, P., & Ouston, J. (1979). *Fifteen thousand hours.* London: Open Books.

Ryan, B. (1993). "And your corporate manager will set you free …": Devolution in South Australian education. In J. Smyth (Ed.), *A socially critical view of the self-managing school* (pp. 191–212). London: Falmer Press.

Sackney, L., & Walker, K. (2006). Canadian perspectives on beginning principals: Their role in building capacity for learning communities. *Journal of Educational Administration, 44*(4), 341–358.

Sammons, P., Hillman, J., & Mortimore, P. (1995). *Key characteristics of effective schools: A review of school effectiveness research.* London: OFSTED.

Scheerens, R. J., & Bosker, J. (1997). *The foundations of educational effectiveness.* Oxford, England: Pergamon.

Scholte, J. A. (2000). *Globalisation: A critical introduction.* Basingstoke, England: Palgrave.

Schön, D. (1992). The crisis of professional knowledge and pursuit of an epistemology of practice. *Journal of Interprofessional Care, 6*(1), 8–19.

Sergiovanni, T. (1991). *The principalship: A reflective practice perspective.* Boston: Allyn and Bacon.

Shweder, T. (2000). Moral maps, "first world" conceits and the new evangelists. In L. Harrison & S. Huntington (Eds.), *Culture matters: How values shape human progress* (pp. 158–177). New York: Basic Books.

Sommerbakk, V. (1994). *A study of beginning principals in Norway.* Unpublished doctoral dissertation, University of Oregon, Eugene.

Southworth, G. (2005). Learning-centred leadership. In B. Davies (Ed.), *The essentials of school leadership* (pp. 75–92). London: Paul Chapman.

Sperandio, J. (2006, October). *Women leading and owning schools in Bangladesh: Opportunities in public, informal, and private education.* Paper presented at the annual meeting of the Women in Educational Leadership Conference, Lincoln, NE.

Teddlie, C., & Stringfield, S. (1993). *Schools make a difference: Lessons learned from a 10-year study of school effects.* New York: Teachers College Press.

Tippeconnic, J. W. III. (2006). Identity-based and reputational leadership: An American Indian approach to leadership. *Journal of Research on Leadership Education, 1*(1), 1–5.

Waite, D. (2002). The "paradigm wars" in educational administration: An attempt at transcendence. *International Studies in Education Administration, 30*(1), 66–81.

Wales, C., & Welle-Strand, A. (2005). *School management training country report: Norway, studies in education management research* (No. 16). Oslo, Norway: CEM Centre for Education Management Research, Norwegian School of Management, & University of Oslo Institute of Educational Research.

Walker, A. (2006). Leader development across cultures. *Journal of Research on Leadership Education. 1*(1), 1–4.

Walker, A., & Chen. S. (2007). Leader authenticity in intercultural school contexts. *Educational Management, Administration and Leadership, 35*(2), 185–204.

Walker, A., & Dimmock, C. (2004). International role of the NCSL. *Educational Management and Administration, 32*(3), 269–287.

Walker, A., & Quong, T. (2005a). *Blue skies: A professional learning programme for beginning principals—An overview booklet.* Hong Kong: Hong Kong Centre for the Development of Educational Leadership.

Walker, A., & Quong, T. (2005b). Gateways to international leadership learning: Beyond best practice. *Educational Research and Perspectives, 32*(2), 97–121.

Walker, A., & Stott, K. (2000). Performance improvement in schools: A case of overdose? *Educational Management and Administration, 28*(1), 63–76.

Walker, W. G. (1984). Administrative narcissism and the Tyranny of Isolation. *Educational Administration Quarterly* 20 (4), 6–32.

Waters, M. (1995). *Globalization.* London: Routledge.

Watson, L. (2003). *Selecting and developing heads of schools: Twenty-three European perspectives.* Sheffield, England: Sheffield Hallam University.

Wearley, L. (2006). *Coaching with Confucian values: Reflections on coaching Asian-Americans.* Retrieved September 16, 2008, from the Grovewell Web site: http://www.grovewell.com/pub-coach-Confucian.html

Wilkins, R. (2002). Transatlantic perceptions of secondary education. *International Studies in Education Administration, 30*(1), 13–35.

Young, M. (2002). *National Commission for the Advancement of Educational Leadership Preparation: Ensuring the university's capacity to ensure learning focused leadership.* Columbia, MO: University Council for Educational Administration.

Young, M., Petersen, G., & Short, P. (2002). The complexity of substantive reform: A call for interdependence among key stakeholders. *Educational Administration Quarterly, 38*(2), 137–175.

5

Candidates in Educational Leadership Graduate Programs

TRICIA BROWNE-FERRIGNO AND RODNEY MUTH

This chapter about participants in educational administration and leadership programs is framed by two propositions. The first is that the intent of leadership preparation is "to produce leaders" (Milstein, 1992, p. 10) able and willing to assume responsibilities as educational administrators of prekindergarten through Grade 12 (preK–12) schools and districts. The second is that leadership preparation is a developmental process that prepares individuals for new responsibilities and career opportunities (Browne-Ferrigno & Muth, 2004; Lashway, 2006; Matthews & Crow, 2003; Ortiz, 1982; Young & McLeod, 2001). Viewed from these two perspectives, information about the characteristics and experiences of individuals actively engaged in formal leadership development activities—prospective candidates for school administrator and leader positions—is critically important for assessing the effectiveness of leadership preparation.

Yet, the field's research on program participants as the unit of study has been sparse; instead, they "have been routinely overlooked" (McCarthy, 1999, p. 134) in research on preparation programs. Indeed, a "limited body of empirical knowledge" (Murphy, 2006, p. 73) about prospective candidates is evident in the results of an analysis of articles published in key journals between 1975 and 2002 (Murphy & Vriesenga, 2004, 2006). Additionally, we have reviewed numerous studies by professors and doctoral students published between 2001 and 2007 and likewise found few examinations of candidates in educational administration and leadership program. In contrast, studies about career paths of program graduates are more common.

The first section of this chapter is a presentation of personal and professional characteristics of prospective candidates in initial preparation programs, gleaned from research published in articles, book chapters, and dissertations. National statistics about preK–12 school principals and research findings about career paths of program completers are presented in the second section, followed by our recommendations for research about candidates in educational administration and leadership. Because universities no longer hold a monopoly on leadership preparation, the third section describes some of the program choices available for aspiring and practicing educational leaders gleaned from the Internet. Because university-based preparation programs generally regulate entrance into the field of educational administration, we present an overview of program admission practices described thus far in various research studies and then present our perspectives about selective admission to university-based programs. Our chapter closes with implications for our continuing failure to address the long-existing gap in research on program participants and recommendations for future studies.

Personal and Professional Characteristics

In the second edition of the *Handbook of Research on Educational Administration* (Murphy & Seashore Louis, 1999), McCarthy cited the need for "a national database on the personal and professional characteristics of educational leadership graduates" (p. 134). Data collected nationally and maintained at a single location would allow the field to conduct trend analyses about candidates' attitudes and characteristics, their assessments of changes in program design and delivery, and their career paths following program completion. A national database likewise would "build the reputation of the educational leadership profession" by having data readily available to "publicize the performance of program completers" (Browne-Ferrigno, Barnett, & Muth, 2003, p. 283).

The University Council for Educational Administration (UCEA) Learning and Teaching in Educational Leadership Special Interest Group (LTEL-SIG) Taskforce on Evaluating Leadership Preparation Programs has begun to collect such data through a survey of program graduates (Orr & Pounder, 2006). Results of statewide studies in Indiana, Missouri, and Utah (W. R. Black, Bathon, & Poindexter, 2007; Pounder & Hafner, 2006; Waddle & Watson, 2005) and a study of exemplary leadership development programs using the same survey (Darling-Hammond, LaPointe, Meyerson, Orr, & Cohen, 2007) have been released recently. Additional studies at both the state and program levels are in progress. Collection of such comparative data is a promising first step toward developing a national database, making feasible large-scale longitudinal studies about "who we are and what we are doing in the area of leadership preparation" (Murphy & Vriesenga, 2006, p. 192). Further, such data can provide foundations for needed longitudinal studies of program impact through effects on school outcomes (Barnett & Muth, 2003).

Describing participants in educational administration and leadership programs is complicated further by the fact that not much research is available about candidates who are actively engaged in leadership development activities (Murphy, 2006). When they are mentioned in the few publications reporting empirical studies, the information typically is simply the number of participants in the sample. Only rarely do the researchers report demographic information about candidates (Murphy & Vriesenga, 2004). Within the limited body of research on leadership preparation, participants indeed are "routinely overlooked" (McCarthy, 1999, p. 134). Further, because recruitment and admission practices among programs vary considerably across the United States, the individuals enrolled may or may not "mirror the existing demographic composition of the local district and community" (Carr, Chenoweth, & Ruhl, 2003, p. 207). Thus, the location of a program does not necessarily predict characteristics of participants in it, an issue in a time when calls for diverse leadership, particularly in urban schools, are so prominent.

Research on program graduates typically has targeted those serving as administrators, whose contact information is supplied by state certification or licensure offices. Data about program graduates choosing to remain in teaching or pursue other career paths rarely have been collected. The discussion about candidates in educational administration and leadership that follows is gleaned from information provided by research published between 1975 and 2007. The terms used to describe personal characteristics throughout this chapter have been standardized for consistency (e.g., Caucasian rather than White or non-Hispanic White).

Student Characteristics: 1975–2002 Article Analysis

Among the 2,038 articles published between 1975 and 2002 in the four leading journals in the field (Murphy & Vriesenga, 2004)—*Educational Administration Quarterly, Journal of Educational*

Administration, Journal of School Leadership, and *Planning and Changing*—only 162 (8%) were about preservice preparation of school leaders. Among them, 56 (35%) reported findings from empirical studies; only 7 (4%) reported demographic information about the program participants. For example, Parker and Shapiro (1992) used purposeful sampling to explore the extent to which diversity was integrated into three preparation programs across the United States: A total of 28 candidates (22 female, 6 male; 6 African American, 22 Caucasian) participated in semistructured interviews. To assess the effectiveness of a pilot program, Norris and Lebsack (1992) asked all 18 participants (14 female, 4 male) to complete a survey.

Further, Cordeiro and Sloan (1996) used purposeful sampling to select 18 interns (14 female, 4 male) among the first four cohorts of a new program to investigate impact of the internship on participants' learning. Examining the quality of internship experiences at two other university-based programs, McKerrow (1998) analyzed internship logs prepared by 45 candidates (30 female, 15 male; 6 African American, 39 Caucasian). Two other empirical articles were qualitative (Rapp, Silent X., & Silent Y., 2001; Shapiro, Briggs-Kenney, Robinson, & DeJarnette, 1997). One traced the rites of passage experienced by 4 women (3 African American, 1 Caucasian) during 2 years of doctoral studies, and the other examined the extent to which patriarchy silenced the voices of 4 female candidates, each from a different program.

Six of the seven articles cited by Murphy and Vriesenga (2004) presented findings from data gathered or documents created while candidates were actively enrolled in programs. Assuming that each participated in only one study, the total number of subjects was 117. Purposeful sampling used by some researchers may account for the skewed gender distribution: 88 of the 117 (75%) participants were female; more likely is that a significant gender shift has taken place in programs nationally, but this is undocumented. Only three articles mention race, indicating that 15 of the 77 (19%) candidates were African American. The seventh article (Veir, 1993) presented results from content analysis of program application files; not reported was the time period spanned or the admission status of applicants. Among 143 applications, 94 (66%) were submitted by women and 49 (34%) by minorities (17 African American, 32 Hispanics).

Student Characteristics: 2001–2007 Review

During the closing years of the 20th century and beginning of the 21st, forces external to higher education generated new interest in leadership preparation. First, the Interstate School Leader Licensure Consortium (1996) introduced national standards for administrative practice (also see Murphy, 2005), which forced universities and colleges to revise their preparation programs to meet changed accreditation standards (National Policy Board for Educational Administration, 1989, 2002a, 2002b) but did not force them to align admission requirements with the preparation program expectations for learning outcomes (Muth, 2002; Muth et al., 2001) inherent in the new standards. Second, the federal government initiated accountability requirements for all preK–12 schools receiving Title I funds (No Child Left Behind Act, 2002), which forced states to examine closely the learning performance of all students. Third, the principalship became a popular topic for criticism and scrutiny (Bottoms, O'Neill, Fry, & Hill, 2003; Educational Research Service [ERS], National Association of Elementary School Principals, & National Association of Secondary School Principals, 2000; Gates, Ringel, Santibanez, Ross, & Chung, 2003; Institute for Educational Leadership, 2000).

Projection of a nationwide principal shortage (ERS, 1998; National Association of Secondary School Principals, 2003), when proven to be unsubstantiated, transformed into criticism about the quality of principals (Hess, 2003; Levine, 2005). Calls for reforms in leadership preparation have been voiced by groups outside the academy (Fry, O'Neill, & Bottoms, 2006; Hale & Moorman, 2003) and by professors (Darling-Hammond et al., 2007; Knapp, Copland, Plecki, & Portin, 2006;

Portin, Schneider, DeArmond, & Gundlach, 2003). Despite these external forces, the field continues to eschew research on leadership preparation (Murphy & Vriesenga, 2006).

Only a few studies about educational administrator and leadership preparation, published between 2001 and 2007, contain demographic information about program participants. Among the sources cited in Table 5.1, only one article, based on a dissertation, was published in a leading journal identified by Murphy and Vriesenga (2004). Interestingly, this article has been among the top 50 most read articles in that journal since its publication in 2003. The only other empirically based article in the table was published in a journal on the periphery of educational administration. The remaining sources are book chapters—all but one published in yearbooks of the National Council of Professors of Educational Administration—or dissertations by doctoral candidates in educational administration and leadership. The Kentucky statistics (Rinehart, Winter, Björk, & Keedy, 2002; Rinehart, Winter, Keedy, & Björk, 2002) came from a study by professors of educational administration and leadership, requested by the state department of education and supported by the Wallace Foundation.

The only observations about data displayed in Table 5.1 are that (a) women outnumbered men and (b) the range of ages among program participants is quite wide. Table 5.1 also shows that data reported are not standardized, which makes comparisons across studies difficult. If a national database of information about candidates and graduates in educational administration and leadership is created, then standardized data types will need to be established to support comparative, longitudinal analyses.

Table 5.1 Students in Educational Leadership: 2000–2007

State	Gender		Race				Age range (avg.)	Years as an educator	Source
	F	M	A	C	H	O			
AZ	35	16	10	23	18	0	—	—	Danzig, Blankson, & Kiltz (2007)
CO	11	7	1	16	1	0	24–60	2–27	Browne-Ferrigno (2001, 2003)
CO	38	22	—	52	—	8	24–60	3–33	Browne-Ferrigno & Muth (2006)
IL	64	24	—	—	—	—	22–59	—	Israel & Maddocks (2007)
IL	40	16	—	—	—	—	—	1–13	Sims, Sukowski, & Trybus (2007)
KY	303	207	27	476	5	2	23–59	—	Rinehart, Winter, Keedy, & Björk (2002)
NY	10	5	—	2	—	13	—	—	Durden (2006)
NY	12	9	9	6	5	1	—	4–27	Effinger (2005)
NY	76	24	—	—	—	—	30–50+	3–20+	Hung (2001)
NY	3	3	3	1	2	0	—	—	Rockwood (2006)
OH	25	18	7	35	0	1	25–57	1–24	Brooks (2002)
OH	30	40	2	67	1	0	23–59	—	Zimmerman, Bowman, Salazar-Valentine, & Barnes (2004)
TX	93	61	9	125	19	1	23–52+	—	Border (2004)
TX	88	71	26	118	13	2	25–51	2–20	Franklin (2006)
TX	30	27	—	—	—	—	22–45+	3–20	Harris, Crocker, & Hopson (2002)
TX	—	—	5	12	5	0	—	—	Hines (2006)
TX	2	2	0	1	3	0	—	5–7	Ruiz (2005)
U.S.	524	336	68	524	62	42	—	—	Bass (2004)

Note. F = Female, M = Male, A = African American, C = Caucasian, H = Hispanic, O = other minorities (Native American, Pacific Rim)

Candidate Characteristics: Summary

Among the minority of professors of educational administration and leadership who conduct disciplined inquiry and publish findings in leading journals of the field (Murphy & Vriesenga, 2006), few have selected candidates in educational leadership as the unit of study. When professors collect data from those participating in preparation programs, their intent typically is to assess effectiveness of program design formats or learning activities. Only one published study was found that intentionally sought to capture participants' perspectives on their learning—at multiple intervals throughout their active engagement in preservice preparation—to assess professional growth attributed to program experiences (Browne-Ferrigno, 2003). Thus, it is troubling that "practically no empirical investigations of students inside preparation programs" (Murphy, 2006, p. 73) are found in published research. Without evidence-based information collected regularly from candidates at multiple intervals from their entry to their exit of formal preparation, the field is without a foundation for understanding program influences on candidates' leadership development and their eventual career choices.

Professional Goals and Career Choices

School administration is a career aspiration for many educational practitioners who seek greater responsibility and organizational mobility. Gaining an administrative position requires the successful merger of an aspirant's "attributes or capabilities and the organization's efforts" (Ortiz, 1982, p. 146). Placement is also influenced by the supply of candidates and demand for principals (Doyle, 1984). During the past two decades, the proliferation of preparation programs increased enrollments of students in educational administration and leadership (Hess, 2003; McCarthy, 1999), which in turn increased supply of potential candidates by approximately "2 to 3 times the number of job vacancies" (Grogan & Andrews, 2002, p. 237). Determining demand for principals, however, is much more complicated (Baker, Orr, & Young, 2007).

When districts began to report difficulty filling positions vacated by retiring principals in the late 1990s, concerns of an impending shortage were voiced (ERS, 1998; McAdams, 1998). Research on principal supply and demand, however, found "little evidence of a nationwide crisis in the market for certified school administrators" (RAND, 2003, p. 1). Replacing retiring principals of high-need schools—characterized by students living in poverty, low accountability test scores, limited resources, and high staff turnover—is nonetheless problematic for many districts (Gates et al., 2003; Knapp, Copland, & Talbert, 2003; Roza, 2003), and the issue of the availability of quality candidates matched to employers' needs is idiosyncratic. Further, according to Roza and Swartz (2003), those located in isolated, economically distressed areas with "high concentrations of poor and minority students, low per-pupil expenditures, and low principal salaries" appear to face the greatest challenge (p. 2). Moreover, although 1 of every 6 school-age children attends a rural school (Arnold, 2004), little national attention has been directed toward rural education issues (Arnold, Newman, Gaddy, & Dean, 2005; Browne-Ferrigno & Allen, 2006; Howley & Pendarvis, 2002).

Our discussion of professional goals of candidates in educational administration and leadership and their career paths as program completers begins with an overview of principal characteristics gleaned from national and statewide research conducted by governmental agencies, research foundations, and universities. A presentation of career decisions of students and graduates found in research conducted by professors and doctoral students follows. The section closes with an examination of why becoming a principal might not be a good idea for many who now populate our programs, too many of whom never do become school administrators and leaders.

Recent National Studies on the Principalship

Results from the National Center for Education Statistics 2003–2004 schools and staffing survey (Strizek, Pittsonberger, Riordan, Lyter, & Orlofsky, 2006) provide useful information about the principalship. First, public school principals identified themselves predominately as Caucasian (82%). Among the 18% reported in minority groups were African American (11%) and Hispanic (5%); the remaining 2% represented American Indian or Alaska Native, Asian, and Native Hawaiian or other Pacific Islander groups. Second, principals of public schools (i.e., inclusive of both traditional and charter schools serving at least one of Grades 1–12) have on average 7.8 years of experience as a school leader, remaining an average of 4.3 years at the same school as its head administrator. Those rates are relatively the same across all school classifications.

Third, the "average number of principals who were newly hired for grades K–12" across all public school districts is 0.7 (Strizek et al., 2006, p. 88). The number is higher for districts with 20 or more schools (2.8) and more than 10,000 students (2.5), whereas the rate is lower for districts with 5 or fewer schools and student enrollments less than 5,000 (0.6). The number of newly hired principals in rural communities and small towns is near the national average (0.5). However, due to limited resources, 38.0% of rural and small-town principals teach classes in addition to handling administrative duties.

Finally, principals reported serving in various leadership positions before assuming administrative responsibility for a school (Strizek et al., 2006). Their roles include assistant principal or program director (68.0%), club sponsor (52.7%), athletic coach or director (33.9%), department head (35.6%), curriculum specialist or coordinator (23.4%), guidance counselor (7.5%), or library-media specialist (1.3%).

A national study conducted by the RAND Corporation (Gates et al., 2003) at the same time the National Center for Education Statistics survey was administered provides another snapshot of the principalship. In this study, the average age of public school principals increased from 47.8 years in 1988 to 49.3 years in 2000. Moreover, public schools "are now less likely to hire people under 40 into a principalship than they were a decade age" (Gates et al., 2003, p. xiv). Gates et al. (2003) also found

> no evidence that administrators left [the field of education] to take jobs in other sectors of the economy … that the more-experienced principals were choosing not to work in urban schools serving larger populations of disadvantaged students, [or] … that there is a nationwide crisis in the ability of schools to attract and retain school administrators. (pp. xv–xvii)

Between 1983 and 1999, exit rates (ranging from 15–33% per year) and entry rates (ranging from 19–29% per year) remained relatively stable (Gates et al., 2003). Although the number of certified individuals available to fill vacancies was adequate nationwide, some regions and districts reported shortages. For instance, population growth in the West increased demand for public school principals by 18% and private schools by nearly 14%. The turnover rate of principals in New York City has exceeded 25%. Recently, Los Angeles had to recall retired principals to fill vacancies until replacements could be found, a common occurrence nationally but generally not on such scale.

Recent Statewide Studies on the Principalship

The Wallace Foundation has invested over $43 million since 2001 on educational administration and leadership initiatives. Twenty-one states have been selected to participate in the State Action for Education Leadership Project, each receiving 1- to 3-year grants to improve student achievement through improved school and district leadership. Assisting with this initiative are the Council of Chief State School Officers, the Education Commission of the States, the National Association of State Boards of Education, the National Conference of State Legislatures, and the National Governors Association. Although most of the studies described below were supported by grants from the Wallace Foundation, the research methodologies differed, making direct comparisons precarious.

The research teams that conducted the Illinois, North Carolina, New York, and Texas investigations used available datasets from the respective state governments. The Kentucky study findings were produced from surveys designed specifically for that investigation, whereas the research teams in Indiana and Utah used a survey developed by UCEA/LTEL-SIG Taskforce on Evaluating Leadership Preparation Programs. Because research foci were dissimilar among the studies, discussions of findings are presented separately and chronologically.

Kentucky

Researcher-developed surveys were sent to all 999 principals of public schools during 2001–2002 (Rinehart, Winter, Björk, et al., 2002). Analysis of the 587 surveys returned at that time revealed that 48.6% of the principals were female and their average age was 46.8 (range of 24–68 years). Racial distribution among the respondent group was 94.4% Caucasian, 3.5% African American, and 2.1% other minorities (e.g., Asian, Hispanic, Native American), which aligned with statewide population demographics at that time. The modal year that the principals obtained their administrator certification principal was 1998 (range of 1968–2001). The principals reported interviewing for school leadership positions an average of 2.61 times (range of 0–20) and received an average of 1.6 job offers (range of 0–8) before assuming their first principalship. Gender bias was apparent because male principals were invited for interviews and received job offers more often than did female principals.

A nearly identical survey was sent to all 1,285 educators in the state database who had completed requirements for administrator certification but had never held a position as principal (Winter, Rinehart, Keedy, & Björk, 2002). The demographics of this respondent group ($N = 548$) were quite similar to those of the practicing principal sample: 48.0% were female, and average age was 44.3 (range 24–68 years). Racial distribution was 94.0% Caucasian, 3.6% African American, and 2.4% other minorities (e.g., Hispanic, Asian, Native American). The modal year for obtaining administrator certification was 1999 (range of 1960–2001). The administrator-certified respondents reported interviewing for a principalship an average of 1.6 times (range of 0–13) and received an average of 0.68 job offers (range of 0–10).

New York

A study of the attributes and career paths of principals (Papa, Lankford, & Wyckoff, 2002) revealed that in 2000 the state educational system employed approximately 4,380 principals (average age 51.3 years) and 16,280 educators holding administrator certification but not working in leadership positions (average age 48.7 years). Among the 2000 cohort of first-time principals, 61.5% were females, who disproportionately were serving as principals of high-need schools, and 66.0% were at least 50 years old. When compared with the 1990 group of first-time principals, the 2000 cohort had less experience as educators (16.8 years vs. 18.6 years) but more prior experience as building or district administrators.

Career paths to the principalship varied by school type, location of school, and student enrollment size (Papa et al., 2002). Only 16% of all first-time principals moved directly from teaching to administration, and they typically were found in elementary schools and small schools outside metropolitan areas. They were younger than their peers, "much less likely to have graduated from a less competitive college," and "more likely to work in schools with more highly qualified teachers and better performing students" (Papa et al., p. 11). Their average tenure as a principal was 7 years. Within 6 years of assuming their first position, approximately 66% of all principals in this study left the school where they began their administrative careers, most often locating to other schools within the same district. According to Papa et al., trend analysis of administrator salaries indicated that compensation for New York City principals was lowest among all districts, which may account for "the reportedly small and weak applicant pools for leadership positions" (p. 16). When urban principals change jobs, they are more likely to stay in the same district or leave the state education system rather than transfer to suburban districts.

Illinois

From 1990 to 2000, the average age of first-time principals in Illinois increased from 42.5 to 44.1 years, while female representation among all principals grew from 26% to 47% (Ringel, Gates, Chung, Brown, & Ghosh-Dastidar, 2004). Among all first-time principals in 2000, nearly 24% were over the age of 50, and approximately 61% were female. Racial distribution was 78% Caucasian, 18% African American, and 3% Hispanic. The most common career path in Illinois is from teacher to principal (51%), followed by moving from teacher to assistant principal to principal (35%).

A surprising discovery in the Illinois data was that "relative to women in elementary schools, women in middle and high schools are actually more likely to become principals or assistant principals" (Ringel et al., 2004, p. xv). For all years examined, Ringel et al. reported that men were nearly "2.5 times more likely to becoming principals directly," but among the group of principals who first served as assistant principals, "women were nearly 20 percent more likely to become principals" (p. xv). Finally, the Illinois principalship appeared quite stable: Only 3% of 1st-year principals returned to teaching after 6 years. Others leaving the principalship either assumed other administrative positions in the state or left public education.

North Carolina

The North Carolina investigation used data from the 10-year period 1990–2000, showed an average age increase from 41.5 to 45.1 years and increased overall representation of female principals from 25.5% to 47.8% (Gates et al., 2004). Among the first-time principal cohort in 2000, 26% were over the age of 50, and females were a majority (59.6%). Racial distribution was 74% Caucasian and 25% African American, with less than 1% from other minority groups. The career path to the North Carolina principalship is predominately from teacher to assistant principal to principal (72%). Among the 13% who moved directly from teacher to administrator, gender-based discrimination was apparent, according to Gates et al.: "Men were four times more likely than women to become principals directly, and over three times more likely than women to become assistant principals" (p. 62).

Analysis of the career paths of principals 6 years after assuming their first position revealed that only 48% were still practicing principals (Gates et al., 2004). Sixteen percent had returned to teaching in North Carolina, 14% moved to other administration positions, and 14% left the public school system. Analysis of state data indicates that African Americans are twice as likely as Caucasians to become principal. The pool of minority candidates for open principalships, however, is diminishing because African Americans teachers leave the system more often than Caucasian teachers do.

Utah

Representatives of five university-based programs, the three state-level professional organizations for administrators, and the state office of education formed a consortium in 2004 for the purpose of conducting a statewide study of leadership preparation in Utah (Pounder & Hafner, 2006). During the spring and summer of 2006, the research team collected data from program completers. The UCEA/LTEL-SIG Taskforce survey was sent to 172 graduates. The response group ($N = 88$) was evenly balanced with regard to gender but not race (7% persons of color). Thirty-three (37.5%) graduates were serving as principals, assistant principals, or central office administrators at or shortly after program completion. The study is in its initial phase of implementation, and thus the report of early findings did not include information about all practicing principals in the state.

Indiana

The Indiana study was a trend analysis based on data collected during the 5-year period 2001–2005 (W. R. Black et al., 2007). Interestingly, the number of approved preparation programs increased from 10 to 17 during that period, and half of all initially licensed principals graduated from only 3 programs: Indiana Wesleyan, Ball State, and Indiana State. Women earned 51% of all building-level administrative licenses issued during the 5 years, yet they comprised only 39% of all practicing principals. Racial distribution among current principals was 91.3% Caucasian, 7.8% African American, and 1.0% other minority.

Among all program completers receiving initial building-level licenses, 53% had found administrative positions by October 31, 2005 (W. R. Black et al., 2007). Among the 833 new building-level administrators, 45% were serving as principals and 55% as assistant principals. Most new administrators worked near the university where they completed their leadership preparation. Gender distribution among new administrators was not balanced in relation to the gender distribution among program completers (51% female): Whereas 64% of the male graduates had obtained positions, only 51% of female graduates were serving as building-level administrators. Although the number of men and women holding principal positions was nearly equal, 60% of assistant principals were male.

Texas

Characteristics and attributes of teachers earning principal certification were the foci of a longitudinal study of career paths in Texas (Fuller, Young, & Orr, 2007). Using multiple datasets of public school educator personnel statistics from the state department of education, Fuller et al. identified a subset of who obtained principal certification ($n = 15,081$) among all teachers ($N = 238,094$) employed in Texas public schools during the 1994–1995 academic year. The subset became the unit of study for multiple analyses. The cohort was racially diverse, with 66.9% Caucasian, 13.3% African American, 19.0% Hispanic, and less than 1.0% other minorities (i.e., Asian, Native American). Although more females (66.4%) than males obtained certification in 1994–1995, the percentage of males earning certification among all male teachers that year (9.7%) was disproportionately higher than the percentage of females (5.4%) among their gender peers. Approximately 48% of the cohort had 5 or fewer years experience as educators and were aged 21–35. Further, a disproportionate percentage of physical- and health-education teachers were in the cohort.

During the 1993–1994 and 1994–1995 academic years, 4,105 teachers obtained principal certification; of those, 1,732 (42.2%) served as public school principals in Texas during the next decade (Fuller et al., 2007). Although 55.4% of the principals were female, a disproportionate percentage of men were employed as principals (49.6%) among the certificate holders because the female principals represented only 37.6% of their gender group. Also, Hispanics were more likely as a group to be employed as school leaders. Attrition rates among principals in this group were high: Within 5 years of becoming principals, only 52.2% continued as principals, and 34.8% were no longer employed in the Texas public education system. By the 10th anniversary of assuming a first principalship, only 23.4% of the original cohort was still employed as a principal—and 61.6% were no longer employed in the Texas system.

Program Studies About the Principalship

In contrast to the previous discussion about national and statewide research on principals and career paths of program graduates, this section presents findings from small-scale studies. Although many articles and dissertations have been published about preparation programs, only a few have included demographic information about what students in educational administration and leadership do following graduation.

Florida

In Florida, graduates of preparation programs serving as 1st-year principals during the 1996–1997 academic year shared perceptions about their preservice preparation through interviews and questionnaires (Cox, 1998). At the time that data were collected, the 19 study participants (14 female, 5 male) were working as principals in three different districts purposefully selected to provide diversity of context (i.e., location in state, size of student population). The group included 14 Caucasians, 4 African Americans, and 1 Hispanic. The modal age range for assuming a principalship was 41–50 years; 2 principals were in their 30s, and 2 others were in their 50s. The median year that principals received their administrator certificate was 1985 (range of 4–19 years since certification), indicating a significant time lapse between program completion and assumption of a principalship. During the intervening years, the principals served as curriculum coordinators and resource teachers, deans, assistant principals, and district coordinators. The most common step to the principalship in Florida at that time was the assistant principalship: Fourteen principals served in that capacity from 1 year to over 10 years.

Professors at the University of South Florida recently redesigned and implemented an executive model preparation program in partnership with local school districts (Bruner, Greenlee, & Hill, 2007). To assess success of the project, faculty surveyed department chairs and program coordinators at 25 randomly selected preparation programs located in 18 states to build a base for comparison. Among the student group described by respondents, an estimated 65% were female, and 80% worked within 50 miles of the college or university campus. Among program graduates, an estimated 81% intended to pursue a building-level administrative position and 48% would achieve their goal within a year of program completion. Department chairs and program coordinators estimated that 62% of their graduates would assume administrative positions within 50 miles of campus, suggesting that relocation for career reasons was not common across the 25 programs.

Georgia

Because Valdosta State University prepares administrators living in a region encompassing 41 rural districts in southern Georgia, faculty determined a principal profile was needed to inform their recruitment efforts. Grubbs, Leech, Gibbs, and Green (2002) developed a career path survey, which was validated by an expert panel composed of active and retired administrators and then mailed to all 241 principals in the service area. The returned surveys ($N = 106$) were from elementary (53%), middle (23%), and high (24%) school principals, of whom 44.4% were female and 16.7% minorities. Grubbs et al.'s composite study findings suggested that the typical principal in south Georgia at that time was "a Caucasian male with an average age of 48, possessing an average of 11.67 years teaching experience combined with 13.23 years of administrative experience" (p. 6). According to Grubbs et al., this profile was nearly identical to the profile of a typical principal 10 years earlier (Doud, 1989; North Carolina State Department of Public Instruction, 1992).

North Carolina

The North Carolina Principal Fellows Program provides loans for selected candidates to participate as full-time students in approved preparation programs in the state (Laing, 2006). Serving as a principal in the state for 4 years immediately after completing the program forgives the loan. Fellows fulfilling their loan-forgiveness obligation were recruited to participate in a study about cohort networking. The sample of 45 novice administrators was predominately female (73%) and included principals (18%), assistant principals (73%), and central office support personnel (9%). The modal age range among participants was 25–35 years ($n = 28$), followed by 36–45 years ($n = 14$) and 46 years or older ($n = 3$). These recent program completers often relied on former cohort peers for professional advice and personal support. One male expressed disappointment about a lack of career advisement during his preparation.

Reasons for not Becoming Principals

Successful placement as a principal requires an alignment between aspirant characteristics and school needs (Ortiz, 1982). In fact, two candidates "with identical training may be very different in their ability to 'fit' a particular vacancy in a school district" due to "idiosyncratic leadership preferences" (Painter, 2005, p. 9). Placement success is likewise influenced by the supply of candidates and demand for principals (Baker et al., 2007; Doyle, 1984).

Recall that National Center for Education Statistics survey results indicated that the average number of newly hired principals was only 0.7 for all public school districts in 2003–2004 (Strizek at al., 2006). Because the number is lower for schools located in small towns or rural communities (0.5), where principal characteristics often are defined narrowly, many aspirants have few opportunities to become a principal (Browne-Ferrigno, Allen, & Maynard, 2003; Grady, 1989). Because research investigating reasons why program candidates and graduates do not seek placement as principals is not disseminated widely, criticisms about preparation program ineffectiveness are unavoidable.

Job Inhibitors

A sample of 860 candidates in educational administration courses at 52 UCEA-member institutions participated in a survey study about their career plans (Bass, 2004). The candidates cited these top five inhibitors to their becoming principals: (a) perceived job-related stress, (b) time and work requirements, (c) accountability testing, (d) family responsibilities, and (e) excessive paperwork. Among this respondent group, gender and race also appeared to influence career-path decisions: Females more often than males cited concerns for personal safety, fear of failure, lack of job security, and political pressure as inhibitors. Caucasians more often than African Americans or Hispanics identified isolation from students and alienation from teachers as reasons for not becoming principals, according to Bass. Candidates in other studies cited potential litigation, discouragement by family and friends, and politics of administration as additional inhibitors (Hancock, Black, & Bird, 2006: Hung, 2001).

Socialization Inhibitors

The decision not to seek placement as a principalship also is influenced by candidates' self-perception of their readiness for the role. Some report that their youth, limited teaching experience, or lack of experience as a leader prevent or delay their becoming principals (Browne-Ferrigno, 2001, 2003; Schmidt, 2002). Others cite socialization difficulties (e.g., inability to make self-identity transformation from teacher to administrator, limited opportunities to work closely with administrators) as inhibitors (Begley & Campbell-Evans, 1992; Browne-Ferrigno & Muth, 2004, 2006; Crow & Glascock, 1995; Gronn & Lacey, 2005; Matthews & Crow, 2003). Stereotypical role conception of the principalship, gender-based discrimination, and few role models or mentors of same gender or ethnicity of aspirant can further hinder placement success (Grogan & Andrews, 2002; Larson & Murtadha, 2002; Ortiz, 1982; Young & McLeod, 2001). Socialization and job-demand issues likewise influence principals' decisions to leave school administration (Hertling, 2001; Williamson & Hudson, 2003).

Many program graduates and teachers also cite similar disincentives to becoming a principal (Flanary, 1998; Portin, 2000; Winter, Rinehart, & Munoz, 2002; Young & Creighton, 2002). Even before new expectations for school leadership transformed the principalship, 80% of teachers holding administrator certification in Louisiana reported disinterest in the position because it was becoming too complex and demanding (Jordan, McCauley, & Comeaux, 1994). Studies conducted in California (Adams, 1999) and Indiana (Malone, Sharp, & Walter, 2001) revealed similar findings. Practitioners in New York cited discriminatory hiring practices as reasons they did not seek principalships (Hammond, Muffs, & Sciascia, 2001). Teachers, both those holding administrator credentials and those not, perceive the principalship "as an unpleasant task undertaken by individuals substantially different from themselves" (Howley, Andrianaivo, & Perry, 2005, p. 773). It may be that many program graduates simply cannot make the transformation from teacher to administrator because it requires relinquishing an important self-identity and assuming another, less attractive one.

Graduate Career Paths: Summary

As the number of preparation programs increased nationally, educational administration departments began "to open their doors to and actively recruit individuals" (Daresh, 1984, p. 42) to increase enrollments. Although that action generates tuition dollars, many program participants seek graduate degrees for salary—not career—advancement. Not only are they "unwilling to devote adequate time and efforts" (Murphy & Forsyth, 1999, p. 22) toward leadership preparation because they never intend to become principals, but also their failure to become principals provides considerable foundation for current criticisms of university-based preparation, which appear to some critics mostly interested in increasing enrollments and tuition rather than focusing on leadership outcomes.

Reports of fewer applicants for vacant urban principalships and projected retirements among veteran principals ignited concerns of an impending principal shortage and focused public attention on the preparation of prospective candidates (ERS, 1998; McAdams, 1998; Young, Petersen, & Short, 2002). When research indicated that most regions of the United States have more than sufficient numbers of qualified candidates to fill immediate and future vacancies (Gates et al., 2003; Grogan & Andrews, 2002; Roza, 2003), preservice preparation became the target. Because universities controlled entry into the profession for decades (McCarthy, 1999), critics claim university-based programs are ineffective, evidenced by the abundance of graduates unwilling to be principals (Fry et al., 2006; Hale & Moorman, 2003; Hess, 2003; Lauder, 2000; Levine 2005).

While claiming that universities do not produce quality candidates, critics fail to mention job-related issues (e.g., low salary for time and work requirements, limited decision-making power, increased job-related stress) or placement challenges (e.g., gender and racial biases about who can serve as principals, few opportunities to serve due to low principal turnover or limited candidate mobility). Special-interest groups likewise suggest deregulation of the school principal profession as a solution to assuring sufficient quantities of quality applicants (Finn, 2003; Gutherie & Sanders, 2001; Herrington & Wills, 2005; Kanstroom & Finn, 1999). Unfortunately, the field has not responded quickly or intentionally to these criticisms through research-based arguments about career decisions of graduates, perhaps because only limited research is available and because the field lacks means of dissemination of such research.

Recommendations for Research

In the late 1990s, a task force appointed by a past vice president of American Educational Research Association Division A began exploring ways to "improve research and knowledge production in educational administration and leadership" (Pounder, 2000a, p. 336). After working 2 years on this project, the Task Force on Research and Inquiry recommended that research in our field "should be communicated effectively to its primary audience" and "subject to public evaluation" (Pounder, 2000b, p. 472). It is thus perplexing why research on candidates in educational administration and leadership continues to be nearly nonexistent in refereed publications (Murphy & Vriesenga, 2004, 2006). The review of research for this chapter clearly surfaces a significant gap in this critically important area of our work.

Likewise, very few documents on all aspects of preparation programs appear in the Educational Resources Information Center (ERIC) database. For example, using the key word *principal preparation* as the search descriptor produced 149 items. Narrowing the search to *principal preparation* and *students* yielded 42, whereas *principal preparation* and *candidates* produces only 19 items. Limiting either search to full-text, peer-reviewed sources produced nothing. Conversely, using *community college* and *students* as keywords in ERIC produced a list of 20,152 entries with no restrictions and 215 when the search was restricted to full-text, peer reviewed sources. Moreover, the Academic Search Premier database yielded 34 items about *preparation program,* whereas the same search in the Professional Development Collection database produced only 21; many of the same citations appear in these two databases.

Every year, professors and candidates of educational administration and leadership present dozens of research-based papers at conferences sponsored by the American Educational Research Association, National Council of Professors of Educational Administration, and UCEA. Building a knowledge base about participants in our programs requires access to these studies. Hence, to expand our database of studies about program participants, those who present research about preparation programs—particularly in the leadership development strand of American Educational Research Association Division A and the LTEL-SIG program—need to submit their conference papers to ERIC. With open access to copies of refereed conference papers and other publications, such research would be more widely available for public scrutiny and evaluation and perhaps usable to address concerns about preparation and practice cited herein. Further, the identity of scholars in our field whose research agenda is leadership development would become public, perhaps generating a community of scholars whose purpose is to close the gap in research about candidates in educational administration and leadership.

According to Murphy and Vriesenga (2006), dissertations contribute significantly to the knowledge base about leadership preparation in our field. Without dissertations, important information about candidates in educational administration and leadership simply would not exist. For instance, a search for articles written by the authors of those dissertations yielded only one, published in *Educational Administration Quarterly* in 2003. How can dissertations contribute significantly to the knowledge base, if dissertation reports are not published in refereed or practitioner journals? Unless a search for research is intentional, like those required for doctoral students and by us for this chapter, the findings generated from dissertations rarely are cited in educational administration and leadership literature, perhaps because such studies may be deemed less rigorous than those produced following the dissertation experience. Unfortunately, this constitutes a tremendous waste of resources, because more than 80% of the research concluded in the United States is buried in dissertations (Murphy & Vriesenga; for discipline-wide commentary, cf. Lovitts, 2007; Tronsgard, 1963; Walker, Golde, Jones, Bueschel, & Hutchings, 2008).

Thus, dissertations need to be converted into papers presented at professional meetings and then submitted to ERIC, published as articles in refereed journals, and shared more broadly in appropriate popular journals. But evidence here suggests that the task historically has not been completed by novice scholars working alone. Accordingly, senior faculty need to step up and assist doctoral graduates with the important, and sometimes arduous, task of converting hundreds of pages in a dissertation into a manuscript of presentable or publishable length. Some faculty do this, securing secondary authorship for their work.

Likewise, journal editors or new journals particularized to the task need to be willing to publish articles about leadership development. This two-pronged effort may be the only way that dissertations can contribute systematically to our knowledge base. Regardless how the task is accomplished, more research is needed about candidates in educational administration and leadership across the board but particularly their experiences while participating in administration- and leadership-preparation programs. For example, one of us currently is studying knowledge acquisition, use, and transfer among students in upper level graduate courses in school leadership. The fundamental purpose is to discern whether students (a) learn what is intended; (b) actually use what is learned; and (c) can transfer that learning to other situations, particularly their practice settings. Data from threaded discussions and student work collected in an online course are being analyzed now; later, two surveys will examine use and transfer over time to see whether concepts and skills carry over to relevant situations and settings.

Because research on candidates in educational administration and leadership is woefully underdeveloped, we have unique opportunities to develop and standardize methodologies that support cross-study comparisons. Two examples are the methodologies used by Fuller et al. (2007) to examine career paths of Texas teachers across a 10-year period and by Papa et al. (2002) to examine certification in New York. Both studies used existing personnel databases, and assuming that most states allow professors access to such for research purposes, these two studies could be replicated in other states.

Another important consideration is standardization in data collection and a national database. As evidenced by the entries in Table 5.1, data about candidates in educational administration and leadership are not gathered or reported in any standard way. The UCEA/LTEL-SIG taskforce has developed and field tested surveys that collect data intended for future use in national studies about the effectiveness of preparation programs (e.g., W. R. Black et al., 2007; Pounder & Hafner, 2006; Waddle & Watson, 2005). Professors and researchers in several states now are conducting studies using these instruments. A national database on students in educational administration and leadership is becoming a reality. Decisions about ownership, location, and maintenance of data as well as data accessibility and use need to be determined before the database becomes operational. Perhaps most importantly, professors need to disseminate research about candidates and graduates through practitioner-oriented publications.

Program Choices

Prospective candidates select leadership preparation programs for diverse reasons, such as a program's purpose and admission requirements, convenience for students (e.g., proximity to home or work location, time requirements), tuition costs and financial incentives, and external support (DeMoss, Wood, & Howell, 2007; Zimmerman, Bowman, Salazar-Valentine, & Barnes, 2004). From an historical perspective, it appears that program choices began to emerge when the Danforth Foundation supported university-program redesign beginning in 1987, followed soon after with the introduction of information technology and the World Wide Web that made online program delivery possible.

When urban school districts began reporting difficulty attracting and retaining principals for their high-need schools, several foundations became partners in program design and delivery. Through its School Leadership Development Program authorized through enactment of the No Child Left Behind Act (2002), the U. S. Department of Education also became a funding partner. With the launch of its Learner-Centered Leadership Program, the Southern Regional Education Board began lobbying the 16 state governments in its southeastern region to redesign leadership preparation toward a school-improvement orientation (Bottoms & O'Neill, 2001).

To present "a fuller picture of the terrain" (Murphy & Vriesenga, 2004, p. 13) of program options beyond those offered at universities and colleges, it was necessary to review information posted on the Web as well as publications and documents available through traditional venues. A member of the UCEA/LTEL-SIG Taskforce on Evaluating Leadership Preparation Programs recently conducted a comprehensive review of the Internet and identified non-university-based preparation programs as "for-profits (private companies online and face-to-face), state-based alternative preparation programs, foundations, and partnerships" (Barbour, 2005, p. 2). We use those descriptors in this section to present program choices available to candidates in educational leadership and administration.

Online For-Profit Programs

Some for-profit programs appear to be delivered strictly online and have no apparent affiliation with a recognized institution of higher education (e.g., Capella University, Strayer University), whereas other programs are combined online and face-to-face models sponsored by recognized institutions (e.g., Jones International University, University of Phoenix, Walden University). Online nonuniversity programs appear to be accredited through the Higher Leadership Commission of the North Central Association of Colleges and Schools, which accredits educational institutions in the 19 states in its region. Although providing convenience of "study anytime, anywhere, 24/7" (Barbour, 2005, p. 5), the programs appear to be somewhat costly ($400–600 per credit hour) and require participants to make their own arrangements for observations and internships.

State-Based Programs

The Maryland Merrimack Leadership Academy, New Jersey Expedited Certification for Educational Leadership, and California School Leadership Program are examples of state-sanctioned alternative preparation programs. Admission requirements, training experiences, and credentials earned vary significantly. Another type of state-based program is the Tennessee State Educational Leadership Preparation Redesign Initiative sponsored by the Southern Regional Education Board and funded through a U.S. Department of Education grant. Its purpose is to assist local school districts and universities, with support from state policy makers and agencies, in developing leadership programs that produce school leaders able to improve student achievement through successful school improvement efforts. Specific details about the initiative were not available on the Southern Regional Education Board Web site.

Partnership Programs

The Danforth Foundation pioneered the concept of university–district partnerships through its Danforth Programs for the Preparation of School Principals initiative begun in the late 1980s. Partnering with the National Policy Board for Educational Administration and National Commission on Excellence in Educational Administration, the foundation supported efforts by 22 university educational leadership departments and local school districts in the redesign of programs. Recruitment of high-quality principal candidates, integration of field experiences throughout preparation, and development of curricula more relevant to the principalship were among the innovative redesign strategies (Milstein, 1993; Miracle, 2006; Murphy, 1998).

Although not participants in the Danforth program, professors at the University of Colorado Denver were early adopters of university–district partnerships because faculty there had participated in the Danforth program at other universities. Following the state adoption of professional standards in 1994, the faculty transformed its leadership preparation program from a series of on-campus courses into off-campus cohorts developed through school district partnerships (Martin, Ford, Murphy, & Muth, 1998). This design format, with curriculum delivered as domains facilitated by professors and practitioners, supports active learning experiences aligned with authentic problems of practice confronted by principals (Muth, 2000).

Other examples of partnership programs identified through our Internet search are Project ISAIL: Improving Student Achievement through Instructional Leadership (Charlotte-Mecklenburg School System and University of North Carolina in Charlotte), Southwest Michigan Educational Leadership Consortium (Kalamazoo Regional Educational Service Center and Western Michigan University), and Potential Administrator Development Program (Halifax County Schools in North Carolina, East Carolina University, and National Association of Secondary School Principals). The New York City Board of Education and St. John's University partnership selects participants from low-performing schools, which become research sites for the doctoral candidates while they are engaged in training as future educational leaders.

The Laboratory for Student Success and the Institute for Educational Leadership maintain on the e-Lead (n.d.) Web site a database of professional development programs, both preservice and inservice, situated across the United States. Most programs in the database are delivered through strong partnerships between districts and universities and tailored to specific needs. The threshold criterion for inclusion in the database is that the program curriculum is driven by standards that articulate what principals need to know and be able to do. The intent of e-Lead is to provide examples of program designs that include environmental contexts and leadership challenges to assist others in developing their own unique initiatives. Several programs included in the e-Lead list are supported by external funding sources.

Foundation and Funded Programs

Many leadership preparation programs described on the Internet are sponsored by major foundations. For example, New Leaders for New Schools (2008) is a nonprofit organization whose goal is to produce "exceptional leaders with the skills to dramatically improve school performance and drive educational excellence on a national scale." The organization has programs in nine metropolitan areas (e.g., Baltimore, Chicago, Memphis, Milwaukee, New Orleans, and New York City). Among the 21 supporters of New Leaders for New Schools are the Bill and Melinda Gates Foundation, Broad Foundation, Walton Family Foundation, and the U.S. Department of Education.

Other examples of foundation-sponsored leadership preparation programs are the Boston Principal Fellowship Program (partnership between the Boston Public Schools and University of Massachusetts–Boston), and the Highly Qualified Leaders Project (partnership between Providence Public School District and University of Rhode Island). Both initiatives are supported by the Wallace Foundation, perhaps one of the most influential organizations in redesigning school leadership preparation. A complete listing of all grantees and project types is available on the Wallace Foundation (n.d.) Web site.

Although not a foundation, the federal government became involved in principal making when Congress authorized the U.S. Department of Education School Leadership Development Program (No Child Left Behind Act, 2002) and allocated grant funds to support design and implementation of partnership-based initiatives. Although some rural-based projects have been supported through this federal grant program, most projects are urban based and occasionally linked to projects also supported by foundations. Descriptions of the projects funded in 2002, 2003, and 2005 are available on the U.S. Department of Education (n.d.) Web site.

Nationally Recognized Programs

During the spring of 2004, WestEd convened an external advisory panel that included Dick Flanary (National Association of Secondary School Administrators), Libia Gil (New American Schools), Betty Hale (Institute for Educational Leadership), Frederick Hess (American Enterprise Institute), Lynn Liao (Broad Foundation), Kent Peterson (University of Wisconsin at Madison), Terry Ryan (Fordham Institute), and John Schnur (New Leaders for New Schools). With assistance from the advisory panel, WestEd researchers conducted an extensive review of nearly 60 leadership initiatives nationally to identify programs that offered innovative strategies in school leadership development. The six programs selected as finalists were (a) the Boston Principal Fellowship Program, (b) First Ring Leadership Academy (Cleveland State University and 13 local districts), (c) Leadership Academy and Urban Network for Chicago, (d) New Jersey Expedited Certification for Educational Leadership, (e) New Leaders for New Schools, and (f) Principals Excellence Program (University of Kentucky and Pike County Public Schools). The first five initiatives offer initial preparation for school leaders in urban areas. The Principals Excellence Program, funded through a 3-year grant from the U.S. Department of Education, provided intensive, field-based professional development for practicing principals and administrator-certified teachers in a high-need, rural district.

WestEd researchers visited each site and conducted multiple interviews with project designers and program participants. Among the 10 features common to all six programs were "candidate selection criteria and screening process that reflects the vision and capability of the program" and "structured program monitoring and assessment through feedback, participants' performance in the program, and participants' success on the job after the program" (U.S. Department of Education, 2005, p. 29). Both the Boston Principal Fellowship and Leadership Academy and Urban Network for Chicago reported 100% placement of program completers; 95% of New Leaders for New Schools graduates were serving as principals (60%) or assistant principals (35%). Among the teacher participants in the Principal Excellence Program, 73% now work as administrators.

Program Choices: Summary

When Milstein (1992) examined impact of the Danforth Program for the Preparation of School Principal 6 years after implementation, he found that placement rates among graduates a year after program completion varied considerably, from a high in California (67%) to a low in Florida (11%). Findings from case studies of these sponsored programs prompted Milstein (1992) to suggest that principal making requires three critically important steps: (a) careful selection of candidates into preparation programs to control entrance into the profession, (b) participation in effective preservice leadership preparation, and (c) purposeful involvement in job placement after the program.

The partnership and funded programs described above use selective admissions for their participants because the primary intent of those programs is to produce school leaders—who use their training as quickly as possible. Some foundation- and state-sponsored programs (e.g., Boston Principal Fellowship Program, North Carolina Principal Fellows) require graduates to repay the cost of that training if they fail to seek positions as school administrators or leave the partnership system before a specific time period. Because this type of leadership preparation involves high-stakes accountability for all concerned, prospective candidates are carefully screened and selected based on specific criteria stated in application materials.

In the closing sections of this chapter, we present an overview of program admission practices used by university-based programs. Based on these practices, we offer our recommendations and justifications for changing them.

Program Admission Practices

Amid the myriad calls for reform of preparation programs from a wide array of voices (Achilles, 1987; Barnett & Caffarella, 1992; Coleman, Copeland, & Adams, 2001; Griffiths, Stout, & Forsyth, 1988; Hill & Lynch, 1994; Milstein, 1992; Murphy, 1992, 1993), we also have heard arguments against and for standardizing program criteria (English, 2006; Van Meter & Murphy, 1997) as well as recommendations for developing better, stronger, and more relevant admission criteria connected to standards or preferred outcomes (American Association of School Administrators, 1960; Creighton, 2001, 2002; Creighton & Jones, 2001; Creighton & Shipman, 2002; Stout, 1973). Despite these calls, arguments, and recommendations for selective admission, we still have a field suffused with inertia, traditionalism, exploitation, and laissez-faire attitudes.

This means that the field of educational administration and leadership continues to use nonselective approaches to determining admissions to educational administration and leadership program programs nationwide (see Table 5.2, which lists typical criteria and explanations with several citations). That is, programs generally admit students as long as they meet minimum academic criteria for grade point average (GPA, both undergraduate and graduate), Graduate Record Examination (GRE) scores, letters of recommendation, and sometimes writing samples or interviews (Browne-Ferrigno & Shoho, 2003, 2004; Creighton, 2002; Lad, Browne-Ferrigno, Shoho, & Gulek, 2007). Such indicators can tell us about—but not predict fully—student performance in academics but are virtually useless in projecting performance in administrative practice. As Bridges (1977) intoned years ago and we seem to have ignored or forgotten, academic expectations—individual work, written analyses and explanations, a contemplative pace—conspire to work against the very skills—collaboration, oral engagement, and quick action—necessary to be a successful field practitioner.

Further, internships still are the typical fare, providing limited exposure to administrative activities under the part-time guidance of a field mentor, with only occasional visits—if any—by professors; such training experiences simply are inadequate (Heller, Conway, & Jacobson, 1988) for the level and complexity of engagement necessary for effective administrative practice. Given (a) the shortcomings of such experiences; (b) the idiosyncratic exposure of candidates to a range of roles and models in such internships; and (c) the limited capacity of the field, including school districts, to support full-time preparation, candidates' academic experiences probably do not compensate, leaving those who do enter the profession to wait for on-the-job experiences to learn the ropes of effective practice.

Table 5.2 Analysis of Criteria for Admission of Students to Educational Leadership-Preparation Programs

Traditional criterion	Arguments for the criterion	Arguments against the criterion
Graduate Record Exam (GRE)	Provides national norms	Nonpredictive of commitment to profession
	Supplies comparative data	Nonpredictive of on-the-job performance
Undergraduate GPA	Indicator of successful academic preparation, required by some states[abc]	Not related to or an assessment of potential for leadership[a]
Graduate GPA	Indicator of successful academic preparation[abc]	Not related to or an assessment of potential for leadership[a]
Letters of recommendation	Cited by many programs as important[a]	Such letters may tap potential but often are written by those not able to judge[c]
Open enrollment	We "need numbers to survive"	Taking all comers is inimical to program excellence[e]
	We need "students to fill courses"[d]	Professionalism comes from selectivity[f]

[a]Browne-Ferrigno & Shoho, 2004. [b]Creighton & Jones, 2001. [c]Lad, Browne-Ferrigno, Shoho & Gulek, 2007. [d]Browne-Ferrigno & Shoho, 2003, p. 16. [e]Murphy, 1992. [f]American Association of School Administrators, 1960; Stout, 1973.

Professors generally are inadequate role models for practitioners because success in academe cannot be equated with success in the field, and mastery of university expectations does not translate well into skills required for practice (Bridges, 1977). Too often, the skills "that make practitioners effective [are invalidated by the university], making clear ... the irrelevance of university-based education for seasoned administrators" (Barnett & Muth, 2008, p. 12; see also J. A. Black & English, 1986; Haller, Brent & McNamara, 1997).

Our successive, almost generational failures to shift focus can be explained by many factors, including the field's obeisance to liberal arts and sciences approaches to graduate education in denial of those of the more practice-oriented professions such as architecture, engineering, law, and medicine. Moving away from these traps requires a simple but radical change in perspective: Determine what those in preparation need to know and to be able to do to be successful as practicing principals and focus on preparing these preprofessionals to accomplish those ends. Further, those in the field have opined for years about such standards and even created ones that lead us in the this direction (e.g., Interstate School Leadership Licensure Consortium, 1996; Murphy, 2005; Van Meter & Murphy, 1997), even though we remain uncertain about the empirical bases for such directions (see English, 2006; Murphy & Vriesenga, 2004, 2006).

Nevertheless, we seem unable so far to wean ourselves from the admissions and teaching-learning mess that we have created that uses our standards for neither identifying recruits nor establishing selection criteria that focus on what successful principals do and how they do it. Further, we then compound this by imposing teaching strategies that turn a virtual deaf ear to what we know about adult learning and professional practice (Barnett & Muth, 2008; Browne-Ferrigno, Choi, & Muth, 2000; Browne-Ferrigno & Muth, 2008; Muth et al., 2001). Even with the guidance provided in a standards-based, knowledge-and-skill-oriented curriculum, our programs still fall prey to Bridges's (1977) admonitions.

Recruitment and Selection of Certification and Licensure Students

We now take a look at the criteria for admissions generally used historically, according to the research on admissions practices over the last 45 or so years. While many states require 2 or more years of teaching experience, completion of state-approved preparation programs, or state-issued credentials for administrator practice, only a few require all three conditions; 11 states do not require verification of teaching experience as part of their certification procedures (Browne-Ferrigno & Shoho, 2003, 2004). At the time of this analysis, 31 states did require completion of an approved preparation program, and some of these adhered to some type of state or national preparation standards, including those developed by the Interstate School Leadership Licensure Consortium (Murphy, 2005). Nevertheless, what Murphy posited in 1992, that "little progress has been made in resolving the deeply ingrained weaknesses that have plagued training systems for so long" (p. 79), remains so today, and this is most apparent in how people are selected for these programs. That is, recruitment, if it occurs at all, and selection continue to be "informal, haphazard, and casual" (Murphy, 1992, p. 80).

The same position was taken almost 50 years ago, when the American Association of School Administrators (1960) found that preparation programs used "*admission* rather than *selection* procedures" (p. 83), thereby limiting the potential for professionalism and impact. For a long time, entrance into principal preparation programs seems to have required only a "B.A. and the cash to pay the tuition" (Tyack & Cummings, 1977, p. 60). Despite some careful and proactive efforts (Crow & Glascock, 1995; Murphy, 1999; Pounder & Young, 1996), most admission processes in educational administration remain as they were in the 1960s (Creighton & Jones, 2001): Of 450 programs surveyed, only 40% required teaching credentials or K–12 teaching experience, and 60% permitted program completion while candidates were simultaneously "satisfying the minimum years of teaching experience required for state certification" (Browne-Ferrigno & Shoho, 2004, p. 178). Clearly, many preparation programs do not consider "first-hand knowledge and understanding of the school setting, students, teachers, administrators, and instruction" (Creighton & Jones, p. 24) relevant to success in school administration or necessary to understanding program expectations. According to Creighton and Jones, such actions constitute a "disservice to the candidates themselves … [and] a disservice to the teachers, students, and community members in the schools these aspiring principals will someday attempt to lead" (p. 24). Thus, we cannot assume that those who enter principalship programs are able and willing to assume responsibilities as educational administrators of preK–12 schools and districts, as we might want to believe, not when 50% or more of those who achieve certification or licensure as school administrators never use their credentials.

What We Need to Think About

Based on recent studies, it appears that admission to an educational administration and leadership preparation program, aside from traditional, university-based criteria (e.g., GPA, test scores, letters of recommendation), often devolves simply to warm bodies, showing up to fill classes in programs totally dependent on full-time equivalents. Thus, anyone who meets the minimum standards, regardless of career aspirations, abilities, or experience, is accepted. One outcome of this haphazard, almost random process is that at least 50% of program graduates never use the certificates or licenses that they earn, costing states, districts, and universities significant resources that could be used otherwise (Muth & Browne-Ferrigno, 2004). Besides this waste of resources, this laissez-faire approach suggests an agenda that forswears excellence, professionalism, commitment, and rigor.

Following a long-standing tradition in public education, born perhaps of the unionization of teaching (and in some places administration as well) and longevity-based salary scales, teachers often are viewed as interchangeable, none better than the other, with awards and commendations for excellence or outstanding achievement frowned upon because they exalt one teacher at the expense of others (Labaree, 2006). It may be that those admitting teachers to administrator preparation programs assume that these applicants do not differ from one another in ability, so that anyone who steps forward is equally likely to succeed. Although this is somewhat facetious, it does reflect an underlying problem in public education in which rewards and expectations are leveled both to protect teachers and to "regularize" how rewards and incentives are apportioned. To expect a system—teacher unions and their members, districts and schools, universities, and state departments and other regulators—to behave differently without significant intervention is naïve: Too many interests, vested in the status quo, find success in what they currently do. Reform from within is extremely difficult, yet not impossible (Labaree, 2006).

Even so, such "equality" of expectations at the level of school leadership is dysfunctional, if any credence is given to any of the critics cited earlier: Those who enter educational administration and leadership programs must distinguish themselves by what they know, can do, and can get done through others to ensure that all children learn (Bellamy, Fulmer, Murphy, & Muth, 2007). Instead of taking everyone and anyone and running them through academically oriented programs, we should seek out those with special abilities and experiences who might not consider a career in educational administration and leadership or even those who might not otherwise "pursue careers in educational organizations" (Daresh, 1984, p. 43). Such highly promising and select individuals then could be provided intense and broad exposure to what constitutes effective administrative and leadership practice in effective schools where all students learn.

Recommendations for Practice

In Table 5.2 we summarize current methods of admitting students to educational administration and leadership programs and suggest in our commentary that an open-admissions approach is not conducive to developing a strong profession. To change our practices, we offer a different set of criteria in Table 5.3, conveying that educational administration and leadership program leaders need to discuss such criteria in order to change their admissions practices to recruitment and selection practices. While many of the criteria in Table 5.2 will need to be minimum entry criteria—as long as programs are affiliated primarily in universities—Table 5.3 provides criteria

Table 5.3 Alternative Criteria for Selection of Students Into Educational Leadership-Preparation Programs

Nontraditional criterion	Arguments for inclusion of criterion	Arguments against inclusion of criterion
Advanced degree	Increase functional credibility Increase leadership legitimacy Supply broad-based skills Facilitate more specific and intense focus in principal preparation programs	Elitist Unnecessary as current programs can address such background adequately Would limit available students Would keep some very good people out of leadership positions
Teaching experience	Greater understanding of teaching, learning, and school functioning Possible wider range of experiences Greater maturity and insight More likely committed to administrative or leadership career	Loss of potential "stars" Ideas and insights not stunted by experience Greater creativity "New blood"
Leadership experience	Insights about how to lead schools Experience in leadership Know what getting into Experience working with and through adults	Principal preparation programs support and develop such experiences Teacher-leader experience not the same as preparing for or being a principal
Commitment to school administration and working with adults	Demonstrated commitment to school administration and leadership as a career Prior successful work with adults in educational settings	Principal preparation programs inculcate such commitments All teachers work with adults in various settings and ways

that might lead the field "to identify, attract, recruit, and screen candidates for leadership prepara-tion" (Young, 2004, p. 49).

An Advanced Degree

Too many teachers now take school administration courses and complete licensing and master's programs in educational administration and leadership simply to move up the salary scale, bring-ing to their studies of school administration and leadership little or no desire to make a difference. Rather, they sit through classes, take tests, submit papers, and perform pseudo-administrative tasks to get credits (Labaree, 1999). While all of us might imagine that their experiences enrich their work lives, benefiting what children and youth learn, we have no data on this. In fact, it has been estimated that as many as 250,000—at least 5,000 per state—educators credentialed as school administrators never have used their credentials to get an administrative position (Muth & Browne-Ferrigno, 2004). Besides being costly to all involved and all of the possible ancillary benefits, such overcredentialing is no way to build a profession.

On the other hand, should all applicants to educational administration and leadership programs be required to have a master's degree in a core field in education (e.g., curriculum, English as a second language, reading, mathematics, science, or another curriculum-related area), our program graduates not only might have greater credibility and legitimacy among those whom they seek to lead, but also might bring with them stronger and broader based skills necessary to improv-ing student learning. Thus, leadership preparation programs could build upon such background instead of having to address such areas cursorily, perhaps limiting other, more valuable (at this level) learning experiences.

Although some might say that requiring a graduate degree prior to admissions to formal leadership preparation is elitist, unnecessary, or limits access, why would we not want our school administrators and leaders to be more fully and better prepared to lead than others might be? Should we not demand more knowledge, better skills, and greater experience of those who are to lead the education of our children? Should we not demand more commitment?

More Teaching Experience

Too many of the teachers who enter educational administration and leadership programs are young, are inexperienced, and do not commit to an administrative career after they finish one of our educational administration and leadership programs (Browne-Ferrigno, 2001, 2003; Browne-Ferrigno & Muth, 2004, 2006). If we demand that recruits to our programs have at least 5–7 years of experience in classrooms and other educational pursuits, we might find more of them actually do take administrative positions directly following program completion. Additionally, greater experience might bring greater maturity and insight into effective leadership practices.

Some might argue instead that potential "stars" would be selected out by this criterion, and all of us have ready examples of this student or that whose maturity and ability clearly outstripped their experience. Yet, for the loss of a very few such stars, why should we continue to allow wholesale entry to anyone, no matter how inexperienced or committed, just because they approach our door? Should we not recognize that more experienced educational professionals are more likely to pursue administrative and leadership jobs and stay the course once in them?

Leadership Experience

To further this move toward greater experience, maturity, and commitment, teachers and others in schools who have had leadership experiences, and thus have been validated by their schools and districts, also might be better equipped and more likely to move directly into administrative positions subsequent to program completion—and to move into them successfully (Browne-Ferrigno & Muth, 2004, 2006). Requiring leadership experience as a selection criterion also means that recruits would have experience working with adults, which is, after all, a prime responsibility of school leaders and a stumbling block for many who continue to prefer to work in classrooms even after completing a principal preparation program.

On the other hand, it could be said that teaching leadership is just what principal preparation programs are designed to do, and that the amount and quality of leadership in a school is not necessarily a good indicator for success in a preparation program. On the contrary, what better indicator could we use of the ability to transition from leading student learning in the classroom to leading learning for all students? Demonstrating an ability to work with adults toward learning goals, working with and through them to improve curriculum and student outcomes, gives such students excellent awareness of the core technology of administration and leadership, is preclusive to what lies ahead in formal preparation, and can make such preparation more focused and intense than when dealing with inexperienced teachers who have so much to learn.

Commitment to Administration and Working With Adults

Do we even ask our potential students whether they want to work as administrators with adults? Do we make this a condition of entry to our programs? In our studies (Browne-Ferrigno, 2003; Browne-Ferrigno & Muth, 2004, 2006), we have found that many students in educational administration and leadership programs are more committed to continuing to work with their classroom students at the end of their programs than to assuming administrative positions. This commitment seems to be correlated with age and experience—and perhaps maturity and the comfort with working with adults that comes from working beyond the classroom.

Some might suggest that this criterion, too, would limit those who might apply, from whom an occasional star might arise. We would suggest that we enhance our ability to groom people for leadership and administrative positions in schools who will seek such positions on program completion the more that we select those who are readier than others.

Summary

These four areas, artfully orchestrated, can lead to improved programmatic outcomes, because starting with candidates more experienced, both as teachers or as other certified personnel and as leaders of adults, and more knowledgeable about education generally and specifically, will strengthen where we start our programs. If we can work closely with districts to ensure that only the very best and experienced professionals are identified, recruited, nominated, and selected for formal preparation as educational administrators and leaders, our program graduates can only be more effective when they enter administrative and leadership positions in schools.

Closing Thoughts

Conducting the literature review to write this chapter affirmed our concerns that professors of educational administration and leadership need to be actively—even aggressively—engaged in research about candidates in their programs and then need to disseminate those findings widely. Because our literature search within traditional venues yielded little information about candidates, we were forced to look elsewhere for information. In the process, we reviewed publications and Web sites sponsored by special interest groups actively engaged in leadership preparation, discovering that in many cases institutions of higher education—particularly research universities—appear to be excluded. Whereas departments of educational administration once held a monopoly on the preparation of school administrators (Baker et al., 2007; McCarthy, 1999), it is no longer so.

Our literature review also revealed that special interest groups claim our preparation programs are ineffective and fail to produce quality graduates, as evidenced by the excessive numbers who never assume principalships (Fry et al., 2006; Hale & Moorman, 2003; Hess, 2003; Lauder, 2000; Levine, 2005). Although we found evidence that job-related and placement issues influence the career paths chosen by our graduates, that information does not appear to have been disseminated via peer-reviewed publications read by professors, professional publications read by practitioners, or documents read by policy makers or lobbyists. Moreover, results of recent state studies about administrator-certified personnel support the assertion that the supply of potential candidates is approximately "2 to 3 times the number of job vacancies" (Grogan & Andrews, 2002, p. 237).

Additionally, among the six programs identified as "innovative pathways to school leadership" (U.S. Department of Education, 2005), only one—the First Ring Leadership Academy—provides initial leadership preparation through a partnership involving a university. Four others are administered by foundations in partnership with urban school districts or with professional organizations. Among the seven resources listed in Appendix B of the same U.S. Department of Education publication are the Broad Foundation and the Thomas B. Fordham Foundation. The two are cosponsors of *Better Leaders for American's Schools: A Manifesto* (Finn, 2003), which "contends that American public education faces a 'crisis in leadership' that cannot be alleviated from traditional sources of school principals and superintendents" or "fixed by conventional strategies for preparing, certifying, and employing education leaders" (U.S. Department of Education, 2005, p. 59).

We believe that we can avert the continuing charge that university-based administrator- and leadership-preparation programs are irrelevant—but only if we face the fact that we are becoming so—and that the current political agenda does not intend to help us change. It is thus entirely up to us to recognize the problems that we have and aggressively collaborate to attack them to ensure that our graduates produce fundamental change in learning for public school students. Anything less presages our deepening irrelevance and eventual demise.

References

Achilles, C. M. (1987, November). *Toward a model for preparation programs for education's leaders.* Paper presented at the annual meeting of the Southern Regional Council for Educational Administration, Gatlinburg, TN.

Adams, J. P. (1999). Good principals, good schools. *Thrust for Educational Leadership, 29*(1), 8–11.

American Association of School Administrators. (1960). *Professional administrators for America's schools: Thirty-eighth AASA yearbook.* Washington, DC: National Educational Administration.

Arnold, M. (2004). *Guiding rural schools and districts: A research agenda.* Aurora, CO: Mid-continent Research for Education and Learning.

Arnold, M. L., Newman, J. H., Gaddy, B. B., & Dean, C. B. (2005). A look at the condition of rural education research: Setting a difference for future research. *Journal of Research in Rural Education, 20*(6). Retrieved April 30, 2005, from http://www.umain.edu/jrre/20-6.pdf

Baker, B. D., Orr, M. T., & Young, M. D. (2007). Academic drift, institutional production, and professional distribution of graduate degrees in education leadership. *Educational Administration Quarterly, 43,* 279–318.

Barbour, J. D. (2005, November). *Non-university-based principal preparation programs: Analysis and discussion of findings.* Paper presented at the annual meeting of the University Council for Educational Administration, Nashville, TN.

Barnett, B. G., & Caffarella, R. S. (1992, October). *The use of cohorts: A powerful way for addressing issues of diversity in preparation programs.* Paper presented at the annual meeting of the University Council for Educational Administration, Minneapolis, MN.

Barnett, B. G., & Muth, R. (2003). Assessment of cohort-based educational leadership preparation programs. *Educational Leadership and Administration: Teaching and Program Development, 15,* 97–112.

Barnett, B., & Muth, R. (2008). Using action research strategies and cohort structures to ensure research competence for practitioner-scholar leaders. *Journal of Research on Leadership Education, 3*(1). Retrieved July 6, 2008, from http://www.ucea.org/JRLE/vol3–issue1_2008/Barnettfinal.pdf

Bass, T. S. (2004). Principalship inhibitors and motivators: Factors influencing educators' decisions to enter principal positions. *Dissertation Abstracts International, 65*(12), 4406. (UMI No. 3159484)

Begley, P. T., & Campbell-Evans, G. (1992). Socializing experiences of aspiring principals. *Alberta Journal of Educational Research, 38*(4), 285–299.

Bellamy, G. T., Fulmer, C. L., Murphy, M. J., & Muth, R. (2007). *Principal accomplishments: How school leaders succeed.* New York: Teachers College Press.

Black, J. A., & English, F. W. (1986). *What they don't tell you in schools of education about school administration.* Lancaster, PA: Technomic.

Black, W. R., Bathon, J., & Poindexter, B. (2007, August). *Looking in the mirror to improve practice: A study of administrative licensure and master's degree programs in the state of Indiana* [Report prepared under state grant from the Wallace Foundation]. Indianapolis: University of Indiana, Center for Urban and Multicultural Education.

Border, K. (2004). University-based principal preparation programs in Texas: Perceptions of program completers and supervisors in the Texas Lighthouse Project. *Dissertation Abstracts International, 65*(11), 4052. (UMI No. 3151936)

Bottoms, G., & O'Neill, K. (2001). *Preparing a new breed of school principals: It's time for action.* Atlanta, GA: Southern Regional Education Board.

Bottoms, G., O'Neill, K., Fry, B., & Hill, D. (2003). *Good principals are the key to successful schools: Six strategies to prepare more good principals.* Atlanta, GA: Southern Regional Education Board.

Bridges, E. M. (1977). The nature of leadership. In L. L. Cunningham, W. G. Hack, & R. O. Nystrand (Eds.), *Educational administration: The developing decades* (pp. 202–230). Berkeley, CA: McCutchan.

Brooks, G. E. (2002). Visual ethnography of emerging leadership in an educational leadership training program. *Dissertation Abstracts International, 63*(07), 2420. (UMI No. 3060321)

Browne-Ferrigno, P. A. (2001). Preparing school leaders: A case study of practitioner growth during a principal licensure cohort program. *Dissertation Abstracts International, 62*(03), 851. (UMI No. 3007743)

Browne-Ferrigno, T. (2003). Becoming a principal: Role conception, initial socialization, role-identity transformation, purposeful engagement. *Educational Administration Quarterly, 39*(4), 468–503.

Browne-Ferrigno, T., & Allen, L. W. (2006). Preparing principals for high-need rural schools: A central office perspective about collaborative efforts to transform school leadership. *Journal of Research in Rural Education, 21*(1). Retrieved February 12, 2006, from http://www.umaine.edu/jrre/21-1.htm

Browne-Ferrigno, T., Allen, L. W., & Maynard, B. (2003, November). *Developing school leaders for Kentucky high-need rural schools: Principals Excellence Program.* Paper presented at the annual meeting of the University Council for Educational Administration, Portland, OR.

Browne-Ferrigno, T., Barnett, B., & Muth, R. (2003). Cohort program effectiveness: A call for a national research agenda. In F. C. Lunenburg & C. S. Carr (Eds.), *Shaping the future: Policy, partnerships, and emerging perspectives* (pp. 274–290). Lanham, MD: Scarecrow Press.

Browne-Ferrigno, T., Choi, C., & Muth, R. (2000, November). *Comparing student learning in onsite and distance programs.* Paper presented at the annual meeting of the University Council for Educational Administration, Albuquerque, NM.

Browne-Ferrigno, T., & Muth, R. (2004). Leadership mentoring in clinical practice: Role socialization, professional development, and capacity building. *Educational Administration Quarterly, 40*(4), 468–494.

Browne-Ferrigno, T., & Muth, R. (2006). Leadership mentoring and situated learning: Catalysts in principalship readiness and lifelong mentoring. *Mentoring & Tutoring: Partnership in Learning, 14*(3), 275–295.

Browne-Ferrigno, T., & Muth, R. (2008). Generative learning communities: Preparing leaders for authentic practice. In R. Papa, C. Achilles, & B. Alford (Eds.), *Leadership on the frontlines: Changes in preparation and practice. Sixteenth annual yearbook of the National Council of Professors of Educational Administration* (pp. 73–86). Lancaster, PA: Pro Active.

Browne-Ferrigno, T., & Shoho, A. (2003, April). *Do admission processes in administrator preparation programs assure students with potential to become effective principals?* Paper presented at the annual meeting of the American Educational Research Association, Chicago.

Browne-Ferrigno, T., & Shoho, A. (2004). Careful selection of aspiring principals: An exploratory analysis of leadership preparation program admission practices. In C. S. Carr & C. L. Fulmer (Eds.), *Educational leadership: Knowing the way, showing the way, going the way* (pp. 172–189). Lanham, MD: ScarecrowEducation.

Bruner, D. Y, Greenlee, B. J., & Hill, M. S. (2007). The reality of leadership preparation in a rapidly changing context: Best practice vs. reality. *Journal of Research in Leadership Education, 2*(2). Retrieved October 10, 2007, from http://www.ucea.org/JRLE/pdf/vol2_issue1_2007/Bruneretal.pdf

Carr, C. S., Chenoweth, T., & Ruhl, T. (2003). Best practice in educational leadership preparation programs. In F. C. Lunenburg & C. S. Carr (Eds.), *Shaping the future: Policy, partnerships, and emerging perspectives* (pp. 204–223). Lanham, MD: ScarecrowEducation.

Coleman, D., Copeland, D, & Adams, R. C. (2001). University education administration program development: Administrative skills vs. achievement standards as predictors of administrative success. In T. J. Kowalski & G. Perreault (Eds.), *21st century challenges for school administrators* (pp. 53–61). Lanham, MD: Scarecrow Press.

Cordeiro, P. A., & Sloan, E. S. (1996). Administrative interns as legitimate participants in the community of practice. *Journal of School Leadership, 6*(1), 4–29.

Cox, H. S. (1998). Effectiveness of principal preparation in Florida as perceived by selected superintendents, first-year principals and other key informants. *Dissertation Abstracts International, 59*(06), 1945. (UMI No. 9838576)

Creighton, T. (2001). Lessons from the performing arts: Can auditioning help improve the selection process in university administration preparation programs in the 21st century? In T. J. Kowalski & G. Perreault (Eds.), *21st century challenges for school administration* (pp. 101–112). Lanham, MD: Scarecrow Press.

Creighton, T. (2002). Standards for education administration preparation programs: Okay, but don't we have the cart before the horse? *Journal of School Leadership, 12,* 526–551.

Creighton, T., & Jones, G. (2001, August). *Selection or self-selection? How rigorous are selection criteria in education administration programs?* Paper presented at the annual meeting of the National Council of Professors of Educational Administration, Houston, TX.

Creighton, T. B., & Shipman, N. J. (2002). Putting the H.O.T.S. into school leadership preparation. *Education Leadership Review, 3*(3), 26–31.

Crow, G. M., & Glascock, C. (1995). Socialization to a new conception of the principalship. *Journal of Educational Administration, 33*(1), 22–43.

Danzig, A. B., Blankson, G., & Kiltz, G. (2007). A learner-centered approach to leadership preparation and professional development. In A. Danzig, K. Borman, B. Jones, & W. Wright (Eds.), *Learner-centered leadership: Policy, research, and practice* (pp. 51–71). Mahwah, NJ: Erlbaum.

Daresh, J. C. (1984). The making of a principal: Mixed messages from the university. In J. J. Lane (Ed.), *The making of a principal* (pp. 31–46). Springfield, IL: Charles C. Thomas.

Darling-Hammond, L., LaPointe, M., Meyerson, D., Orr, M. T., & Cohen, C. (2007). *Preparing school leaders for a changing world: Lessons from exemplary leadership development program* [Study commissioned by the Wallace Foundation]. Stanford, CA: Stanford University, Stanford Educational Leadership Institute.

DeMoss, K., Wood, C. J., & Howell, R. (2007). Eliminating isolation to foster learner-centered leadership: Lessons from rural schools and research universities. In A. Danzig, K. Borman, B. Jones, & W. Wright (Eds.), *Learner-centered leadership: Policy, research, and practice* (pp. 149–170). Mahwah, NJ: Erlbaum.

Doud, J. L. (1989). The K–8 principal in 1998. *Principal, 68*(3), 6–12.

Doyle, C. R. (1984). Obtaining an administrative position. In J. J. Lane (Ed.), *The making of a principal* (pp. 129–152). Springfield, IL: Charles C. Thomas.

Durden, P. (2006). Creating connectivity: An urban collaboratory for preparation and practice in educational leadership. In F. L. Dembowski & L. K. Lemasters (Eds.), *Unbridled spirit: Best practices in educational administration* (pp. 117–126). Lancaster, PA: ProActive.

Educational Research Service. (1998). *Is there a shortage of qualified candidates for openings in the principalship? An exploratory study* [Report prepared for the National Association of Elementary School Principals and National Association of Secondary Principals]. Arlington, VA: Author.

Educational Research Service, National Association of Elementary School Principals, & National Association of Secondary School Principals. (2000). *The principal, keystone of a high-achieving school: Attracting and keeping the leadership we need.* Arlington, VA: Educational Research Service.

Effinger, R. L. (2005). Reform in the preparation of educational leaders: A partnership between a university and a school district. *Dissertation Abstracts International, 66*(03), 840. (UMI No. 316656)

e-Lead. (n.d.). *Professional development programs.* Retrieved July 26, 2008, from http://www.e-lead.org/programs

English, F. W. (2006). The unintended consequences of a standardized knowledge base in advancing educational leadership preparation. *Educational Administration Quarterly, 42,* 461–472.

Finn, C. (2003). *Better leaders for America's schools: A manifesto.* Retrieved May 13, 2006, from the Thomas B. Fordham Institute Web site: http://www.edexcellence.net/institute/publication/publication.cfm?id=1

Flanary, W. R. (1998). A qualitative study of individuals holding principalship endorsement in Tennessee yet not working as such in a public school letting. *Dissertation Abstracts International, 59*(03), 672. (UMI No. 9827631)

Franklin, S. F. (2006). Exploratory comparative case studies of two principal preparation programs. *Dissertation Abstracts International, 67*(07). (UMI No. 3225408).

Fry, B., O'Neill, K., & Bottoms, G. (2006). *Schools can't wait: Accelerating the redesign of university principal preparation programs.* Atlanta, GA: Southern Regional Education Board.

Fuller, E., Young, M. D., & Orr, M. T. (2007, April). *Career pathways of principals in Texas.* Paper presented at the annual meeting of the American Educational Research Association, Chicago.

Gates, S. M., Guarino, C., Santibanez, L., Brown, A., Ghosh-Dastidar, B., & Chung, C. H. (2004, May). *Career paths of schools administrators in North Carolina: Insights from an analysis of state data* [Study commissioned by the Wallace Foundation]. Santa Monica, CA: RAND Corporation. Retrieved September 15, 2007, from http://www.rand.org/pubs/technical_reports/TR129/

Gates, S. M., Ringel, J. S., Santibanez, L., Ross, K., & Chung, C. H. (2003). *Who is leading our schools? An overview of school administrators and their careers.* Retrieved June 9, 2003, from the RAND Corporation Web site: http://www.rand.org/pubs/monograph_reports/MR1679/

Grady, M. L. (1989, October). *Women with administrative certification: Iowa, Kansas, Nebraska, North Dakota, South Dakota.* Paper presented at the annual meeting of the National Rural Education Association, Reno, NV.

Griffiths, D. E., Stout, R. T., & Forsyth, P. B. (Eds.). (1988). *Leaders for America's schools: The report and papers of the National Commission on Excellence in Educational Administration.* Berkeley, CA: McCutchan.

Grogan, M., & Andrews, R. (2002). Defining preparation and professional development for the future. *Educational Administration Quarterly, 38,* 233–250.

Gronn, P., & Lacey, K. (2005). Positioning among aspirant school principals. *School Management and Leadership, 24*(4), 405–424.

Grubbs, S., Leech, D. W., Gibbs, A., & Green, R. (2002, November). *Who's leading our south Georgia schools? A profile of principals.* Paper presented at the annual meeting of the Georgia Educational Research Association, Savannah, GA.

Gutherie, J. W., & Sanders, T. (2001, January 7). Who will lead the public schools? *New York Times,* p. 4A.

Hale, E. L., & Moorman, H. N. (2003). *Preparing school leaders: A national perspective on policy and program innovations.* Washington, DC: Institute for Educational Leadership.

Haller, E. J., Brent, B. O., & McNamara, J. F. (1997). Does graduate training in educational administration improve America's schools? Another look at some national data. *Phi Delta Kappan, 79*(3), 222–227.

Hammond, J., Muffs, M., & Sciascia, S. (2001). The leadership crisis: Is it for real? *Principal, 81*(2), 28–29, 31.

Hancock, D. R., Black, T., & Bird, J. J. (2006). A study of factors that influence teachers to become school administrators. *Journal of Educational Research & Policy Studies, 6*(1), 91–103. Retrieved October 1, 2007, from http://normes.uark.edu/erps/V6N1_FINAL.pdf

Harris, S., Crocker, C., & Hopson, M. H. (2002). Issues that mentors share with protégés. In G. Perreault & F. C. Lunenburg (Eds.), *The changing world of school administration* (pp. 199–208). Lanham, MD: ScarecrowEducation.

Heller, R. W., Conway, J. A., & Jacobson, S. L. (1988). Here's your blunt critique of administrator preparation. *Executive Educator, 10*(9), 18–21, 30.

Herrington, C. D., & Wills, B. K. (2005). Decertifying the principalship: The politics of administrator preparation in Florida. *Educational Policy, 19*(1), 181–200.

Hertling, E. (2001, April). *Retaining principals.* Eugene: University of Oregon, Clearinghouse on Educational Policy and Management. Retrieved March 26, 2005, from http://eric.uoregon.edu/publications/digests/digest147.html

Hess, F. M. (2003). *A license to lead? A new leadership agenda for America's schools.* Washington, DC: Progressive Policy Institute, 21st Century Schools Project.

Hill, M. S., & Lynch, D. W. (1994). Future principals: Selecting educators for leadership. *NASSP Bulletin, 78*(565), 81–84.

Hines, M. T., III (2006). From practicing pedagogy to embracing andragogy: How to switch "gogys" to develop a "self-as-principal" voice in principal preparation classrooms. In F. L. Dembowski & L. K. Lemasters (Eds.), *Unbridled spirit: Best practices in educational administration* (pp. 190–197). Lancaster, PA: ProActive.

Howley, A., Andrianaivo, S., & Perry, J. (2005). The pain outweighs the gain: Why teachers don't want to become principals. *Teachers College Record, 107,* 757–782.

Howley, A., & Pendarvis, E. (2002, December). *Recruiting and retaining rural school administrators.* Charleston, WV: AEL ERIC Clearinghouse on Rural Education and Small Schools. (ERIC Document Reproduction Service No. ED470950)

Hung, S. S. Y. (2001). The nature of administrative internships on principal preparation. *Dissertation Abstracts International, 62*(05), 1654. (UMI No. 3014777).

Institute for Educational Leadership. (2000, October). *Leadership for student learning: Reinventing the principalship.* Washington, DC: Author.

Interstate School Leaders Licensure Consortium. (1996). *Standards for school leaders.* Washington, DC: Council of Chief State School Officers.

Israel, M. S., & Maddocks, A. M. (2007). Reclaiming the concepts of calling, professional, and professional obligations: A mindful pedagogy for teaching the ethics of school administration to future and practicing school leaders. In L. K. Lemasters & R. Papa (Eds.), *At the tipping point: Navigating the course for the preparation of educational administrators* (pp. 478–489). Lancaster, PA: ProActive.

Jordan, D. W., McCauley, H. S., & Comeaux, J. B. (1994). *The supply and demand trends of public school principals and administrators in Southwestern Louisiana: 1993–1997.* (ERIC Document Reproduction Service No. ED375525)

Kanstroom, M., & Finn, C. E., Jr. (Eds.). (1999). *Better teachers, better schools.* New York: Thomas B. Fordham Foundation.

Knapp, M. S., Copland, M. A., Plecki, M. L., & Portin, B. S. (2006, October). *Leading, learning, and leadership support.* Seattle: University of Washington, Center for the Study of Teaching and Policy.

Knapp, M. S., Copland, M. A., & Talbert, J. E. (2003, February). *Leading for learning: Reflective tools for school and district leaders.* Seattle: University of Washington, Center for the Study of Teaching and Policy.

Labaree, D. F. (1999). *How to succeed in school without really learning: The credentials race in American education.* New Haven, CT: Yale University Press.

Labaree, D. F. (2006). *The trouble with ed schools.* New Haven, CT: Yale University Press.

Lad, K., Browne-Ferrigno, T., Shoho, A., & Gulek, J. C. (2007). Admissions to university-based preparation programs: Faculty assessments of current practices and implications for navigating the future. In L. K. Lemasters & R. Papa (Eds.), *At the tipping point: Navigating the course for the preparation of educational administrators* (pp. 241–254). Lancaster, PA: ProActive.

Laing, P. (2006). Networking practices of cohort model graduates. *Dissertation Abstracts International, 67*(06). (UMI No. 3221579)

Larson, C. L., & Murtadha, K. (2002). Leadership for social justice. In J. Murphy (Ed.), *The educational leadership challenge: Redefining leadership for the 21st century* (pp. 134–161). Chicago: National Society of the Study of Education.

Lashway, L. (2006). Developing school leaders. In S. C. Smith & P. K. Piele (Eds.), *School leadership: Handbook for excellence in student learning* (pp. 104–128). Thousand Oaks, CA: Corwin Press.

Lauder, A. (2000). The new look in principal preparation programs. *NASSP Bulletin, 84,* 23–28.

Levine, A. (2005). *Educating school leaders.* New York: The Education School Project.

Lovitts, B. E. (2007). *Making the implicit explicit: Creating performance expectations for the dissertation.* Sterling, VA: Stylus.

Malone, B. G., Sharp, W. L., & Walter, J. K. (2001, April). *What's right about the principalship?* Paper presented at the annual meeting of the Midwestern Educational Research Association, Chicago. (ERIC Document Reproduction Services No. ED458710)

Martin, W. M., Ford, S. M., Murphy, M. J., & Muth, R. (1998). Partnerships: Possibilities, potentialities, and practicalities in preparing school leaders. In R. Muth & M. Martin (Eds.), *Toward the Year 2000: Leadership for quality schools* (pp. 238–247). Lancaster, PA: Technomic.

Matthews, L. J., & Crow, G. M. (2003). *Being and becoming a principal: Role conceptions for contemporary principals and assistant principals.* Boston: Allyn and Bacon.

McAdams, R. P. (1998). Who'll run the schools? The coming administrator shortage. *The American School Board Journal, 29*(8), 37–39.

McCarthy, M. M. (1999). The evolution of educational leadership preparation programs. In J. Murphy & K. Seashore Louis (Eds.), *Handbook of research on educational administration* (2nd ed., pp. 119–139). San Francisco: Jossey-Bass.

McKerrow, K. (1998) Administrative internships: Quality or quantity? *Journal of School Leadership, 8*(2), 171–186.

Milstein, M. M. (1992, October). *The Danforth Program for the Preparation of School Principals (DPPSP) six years later: What we have learned.* Paper presented at the annual meeting of the University Council for Educational Administration, Minneapolis, MN.

Milstein, M. (Ed.). (1993). *Changing the way we prepare educational leaders.* Newbury Park, CA: Corwin Press.

Miracle, T. L. (2006). An analysis of a district level aspiring principals training program. *Dissertation Abstracts International, 67*(08). (UMI No. 3228666)

Murphy, J. (1992). *The landscape of leadership preparation: Reframing the education of school administrators.* Newbury Park, CA: Corwin Press.

Murphy, J. (Ed.). (1993). *Preparing tomorrow's school leaders: Alternative designs.* University Park, PA: University Council for Educational Administration.

Murphy, J. (1998). Preparation for the school principalship: The United States' story. *School Leadership & Management, 18*(3), 359–372.

Murphy, J. (1999). Changes in preparation programs: Perceptions of department chairs. In J. Murphy & P. B. Forsyth (Eds.), *Educational administration: A decade of reform* (pp. 170–191). Thousand Oaks, CA: Corwin Press.

Murphy, J. (2005). Unpacking the foundations of ISLLC standards and addressing concerns in the academic community. *Educational Administration Quarterly, 41*(1), 154–191.

Murphy, J. (2006). *Preparing school leaders: Defining a research and action agenda.* Lanham, MD: Rowman & Littlefield Education.

Murphy, J., & Forsyth, P. B. (Eds.). (1999). *Educational administration: A decade of reform.* Thousand Oaks, CA: Corwin Press.

Murphy, J., & Seashore Louis, K. (Eds.). (1999). *Handbook of research on educational administration: A project of the American Educational Research Association.* San Francisco: Jossey-Bass.

Murphy, J., & Vriesenga, M. (2004). *Research on preparation programs in educational administration: An analysis* [UCEA monograph series]. Columbia, MO: University Council for Educational Administration.

Murphy, J., & Vriesenga, M. (2006). Research on leadership preparation in the United States: An analysis. *School Leadership and Management, 26*(2), 183–195.

Muth, R. (2000). Toward a learning-oriented instructional paradigm: Implications for practice. In P. Jenlink & T. Kowalski (Eds.), *Marching into a new millennium: Challenges to educational leadership. Eighth Annual Yearbook of the National Council of Professors of Educational Administration* (pp. 82–103). Lanham, MD: Scarecrow Press.

Muth, R. (2002). National standards and administrator preparation. *Educational Leadership and Administration: Teaching and Program Development, 14,* 73–92.

Muth, R., Banks, D., Bonelli, J., Gaddis, B., Napierkowski, H., White, C., et al. (2001). Toward an instructional paradigm: Recasting how faculty work and students learn. In T. J. Kowalski & G. Perreault (Eds.), *Twenty-first century challenges for school administrators* (pp. 29–53). Lanham, MD: Scarecrow Press.

Muth, R., & Browne-Ferrigno, T. (2004). Why don't our graduates take administrative positions, and what's the cost? In C. S. Carr & C. L. Fulmer (Eds.), *Educational leadership: Knowing the way, showing the way, going the way* (pp. 294–306). Lanham, MD: Scarecrow Press.

National Association of Secondary School Principals. (2003). *Selecting and developing the 21st century principal.* Reston, VA: Author.

National Policy Board for Educational Administration. (1989, May). *Improving the preparation of school administrators: The reform agenda.* Charlottesville, VA: Author.

National Policy Board for Educational Administration. (2002a). *Instructions to implement standards for advanced programs in educational leadership for principals, superintendents, curriculum directors, and supervisors.* Retrieved November 24, 2003, from http://www.npbea.org/ELCC

National Policy Board for Educational Administration. (2002b). *Standards for advanced programs in educational leadership for principals, superintendents, curriculum directors, and supervisors.* Retrieved April 12, 2002, from http://www.npbea.org/ELCC

New Leaders for New Schools. (2008). *About us: Goals.* Retrieved May 7, 2008, from http://www.nlns.org/NLWeb/Goals.jsp

No Child Left Behind Act of 2001, Pub. L. No. 107-110, 115 Stat. 1425 (2002).

Norris, C. J., & Lebsack, J. (1992). A pathway to restructuring: Discussion of a university pilot for principal preparation. *Journal of School Leadership, 2*(1), 45–58.

North Carolina State Department of Public Instruction. (1992). *Personnel file: Characteristics of certified public school employees 1980–81 through 1990–91.* Raleigh, NC: Division of LEA Personnel Services. (ERIC Document Reproduction Service No. ED364563)

Orr, M. T., & Pounder, D. (2006, November). *Report of the UCEA/TEA-SIG Taskforce on Evaluating Leadership Preparation Programs: Six years later.* Paper presented at the annual meeting of the University Council for Educational Administration, San Antonio, TX.

Ortiz, F. I. (1982). *Career patterns in education: Women, men and minorities in public school administration.* New York: Praeger.

Painter, S. R. (2005). Considering institutional character and leadership domains in K–12 principal training, licensing, and selection. *Connection: Journal of Principal Preparation and Developments, 7,* 2–12.

Papa, F. C., Jr., Lankford, H., & Wyckoff, J. (2002). *The attributes and career paths of principals: Implications for improving policy.* Albany: State University of New York. Retrieved June 18, 2007, from http://www.teacherpolicyresearch.org

Parker, L., & Shapiro, J. P. (1992). Where is the discussion of diversity in educational administration programs? Graduate students' voices addressing an omission in their preparation. *Journal of School Leadership, 2*(1), 7–33

Portin, B. S. (2000, April). *Principal distinctives in the United States: The intersection of principal preparation and traditional roles between education reform and accountability.* Paper presented at the annual meeting of the American Educational Research Association, New Orleans, LA. (ERIC Document Reproduction Service No. ED447598)

Portin, B., Schneider, P., DeArmond, M., & Gundlach, L. (2003, September). *Making sense of leadership schools: A study of the school principalship* [Report prepared under a grant from the Wallace Foundation]. Seattle: University of Washington, Center on Reinventing Public Education.

Pounder, D. G. (2000a). A discussion of the task force's collective findings. *Educational Administration Quarterly, 36,* 465–473.

Pounder, D. G. (2000b). Introduction to special issue. *Educational Administration Quarterly, 36,* 336–339.

Pounder, D., & Hafner, M. (2006, November). *Utah leader preparation study: Early findings.* Paper presented at the annual meeting of the University Council for Educational Administration, San Antonio, TX.

Pounder, D. G., & Young, I. P. (1996). Recruitment and selection of educational administrators: Priorities for today's schools. In K. Leithwood, J. Chapment, D. Corson, P. Hallinger, & A. Hart (Eds.), *International handbook of educational leadership* (pp. 279–308). Boston: Kluwer.

RAND. (2003). *Are schools facing a shortage of qualified administrators?* Retrieved September 28, 2007, from http://www.rand.org/pubs/research_briefs/RB8021/RB8021.pdf

Rapp, D., Silent X., & Silent Y. (2001). The implications of raising one's voice in educational leadership doctoral programs: Women's stories of fear, retaliation, and silence. *Journal of School Leadership, 11*(4), 279–295.

Rinehart, J. S., Winter, P. A., Björk, L. G., & Keedy, J. (2002, August). *State Action for Educational Leadership Policy (SALEP) principal survey results* [Report prepared under state grant from the Wallace Foundation]. Lexington: University of Kentucky.

Rinehart, J. S., Winter, P. A., Keedy, J., & Björk, L. G. (2002, August). *State Action for Educational Leadership Policy (SALEP) aspiring principal preparation survey results* [Report prepared under state grant from the Wallace Foundation]. Lexington: University of Kentucky.

Ringel, J., Gates, S., Chung, C., Brown, A., & Ghosh-Dastidar, B. (2004, May). *Career paths of school administrators: Insights from an analysis of state data* [Study commissioned by the Wallace Foundation]. Santa Monica, CA: RAND Corporation. Retrieved September 15, 2007, from http://www.rand.org/pubs/technical_reports/TR129/

Rockwood, K. D. (2006). Parent and community outreach: Profiles of community internship experiences. In F. L. Dembowski & L. K. Lemasters (Eds.), *Unbridled spirit: Best practices in educational administration* (pp. 146–155). Lancaster, PA: ProActive.

Roza, M., with Cello, M. B., Harvey, J., & Wishon, S. (2003, January). *A matter of definition: Is there truly a shortage of school principals?* Seattle: University of Washington, Center for Reinventing Public Education.

Roza, M., & Swartz, C. (2003, April). *A shortage of school principals: Fact or fiction? Policy brief.* Seattle: University of Washington, Center for Reinventing Public Education.

Ruiz, R. D. (2005). Linguistically and culturally diverse school leaders: A qualitative study of principal pre-service preparation. *Dissertation Abstracts International, 66*(02), 439. (UMI No. 3165000)

Schmidt, M. (2002). Emotions in educational administration: An unorthodox examination of teachers' career decisions. In K. Leithwood & P. Hallinger (Eds.), *Second international handbook of educational leadership and administration* (pp. 1103–1131). Dordrecht, The Netherlands: Kluwer Academic.

Shapiro, J. G., Briggs-Kenney M., Robinson, R. W., & DeJarnette, P. M. (1997). Autobiographical stories of rites of passage of Caucasian and African-American doctoral students in educational administration. *Journal of School Leadership, 7*(2), 165–193.

Sims, P., Sukowski, M., & Trybus, M. (2007). Reaching the tipping point: The interconnectedness of a school leadership program. In L. K. Lemasters & R. Papa (Eds.), *At the tipping point: Navigating the course for the preparation of educational administrators* (pp. 409–415). Lancaster, PA: ProActive.

Stout, R. T. (1973). *New approaches to recruitment and selection of educational administrators.* Columbus, OH: University Council for Educational Administration.

Strizek, G. A., Pittsonberger, J. L., Riordan, K. E., Lyter, D. M, & Orlofsky, G. F. (2006). *Characteristics of schools, districts, teachers, principals, and school libraries in the United States: 2003–04 Schools and Staffing Survey* (NCES 2006-313 Revised). Washington, DC: National Center for Education Statistics.

Tronsgard, D. T. (1963). A common sense approach to the dissertation: Should the graduate schools take a fresh look at this traditional requirement. *The Journal of Higher Education, 34*(9), 491–495.

Tyack, D. B., & Cummings, R. (1977). Leadership in American public schools before 1954: Historical configurations and conjectures. In L. L. Cunningham, W. G. Hack, & R. O. Nystrand (Eds.), *Educational administration: The developing decades* (pp. 46–66). Berkeley, CA: McCutchan.

U.S. Department of Education. (n.d.). Home page. Retrieved July 26, 2008, from http://www.ed.gov

U.S. Department of Education. (2005). *Innovative pathways to school leadership.* Washington, DC: Office of Innovation and Improvement. Retrieved March 1, 2005, from http://www.ed.gov/admins/recruit/prep/alternative/index.html

Van Meter, E., & Murphy, J. (1997). *Using ISLLC standards to strengthen preparation programs in school administration.* Washington, DC: Council of Chief State School Officers.

Veir, C. (1993). Gender and race differentiation among applicants in educational leadership programmes: Multivariant strategies for equity. *Journal of Educational Administration, 31*(4), 67–79.

Waddle, J. L., & Watson, R. (2005, November). *Working collaboratively to compare and improve school leadership preparation programs in Missouri.* Paper presented at the annual meeting of the University Council of Education Administration, Nashville, TN.

Walker, G. E., Golde, C. M., Jones, L., Bueschel, A. C., & Hutchings, P. (2008). *The formation of scholars: Rethinking doctoral education for the twenty-first century.* San Francisco: Jossey-Bass.

Wallace Foundation. (n.d.). *Contracts and grants.* Retrieved July 26, 2008, from http://www.wallacefoundation.org/GrantsPrograms

Williamson, R., & Hudson, M. (2003, April). *Walking away: New women school leaders leaving the career track.* Paper presented at the annual meeting of the American Educational Research Association, Chicago.

Winter, P. A., Rinehart, J. S., Keedy, J., & Björk, L. G. (2002, August). *State Action for Educational Leadership Policy (SALEP) principal certified personal survey results* [Report prepared under state grant from the Wallace Foundation]. Lexington: University of Kentucky.

Winter, P. A., Rinehart, J. S., & Munoz, M. A. (2002). Principal recruitment: An empirical evaluation of a school district's internal pool of principal certified personnel. *Journal of Personnel Evaluation in Education, 16*(2), 129–141.

Young, M. (2004). Preparing school and school system leaders: A call for collaboration. In C. S. Carr & C. L. Fulmer (Eds.), *Educational leadership: Knowing the way, showing the way, going the way* (pp. 46–58). Lanham, MD: Scarecrow Press.

Young, M., & Creighton, T. B. (2002, August). *Who is framing the nation's understanding of educational leadership preparation and practice?* Paper presented at the annual meeting of the National Council of Professors of Educational Administration, Burlington, VT.

Young, M. D., & McLeod, S. (2001). Flukes, opportunities, and planned interventions: Factors affecting women's decisions to become school administrators. *Educational Administration Quarterly, 37*(4), 462–502.

Young, M. D., Petersen, G. J., & Short, P. M. (2002). The complexity of substantive reform: A call for interdependence among key stakeholders. *Educational Administration Quarterly, 38,* 137–175.

Zimmerman, J. A., Bowman, J. S., Salazar-Valentine, M., & Barnes, R. L. (2004). The Principal Cohort Leadership Academy: A partnership that connects theory and practice. In C. S. Carr & C. L. Fulmer (Eds.), *Educational leadership: Knowing the way, showing the way, going the way* (pp. 224–239). Lanham, MD: Scarecrow Press.

6

Characteristics, Preparation, and Professional Development of Educational Leadership Faculty

DONALD G. HACKMANN, SCOTT C. BAUER,
NELDA H. CAMBRON-MCCABE, AND DAVID M. QUINN

It is axiomatic that high-quality leadership preparation programs must be staffed by a critical mass of faculty members who collectively have the foundational knowledge, skills, and commitments to educate the next generation of aspiring school leaders. In 1987 the National Commission on Excellence in Educational Administration (NCEEA), advocating for the improvement of educational leadership program quality, asserted that faculties "should have varied academic backgrounds and experience" and "should reflect balanced diversity" (p. 21), so that they would evidence the necessary academic preparation and administrative experience base to provide quality learning experiences for their students. Because educational leadership is a professional area of study, it is vitally important for faculty to maintain connections with the field and to provide opportunities for aspiring administrators to apply classroom theory to practice (Foster, 1988). Yet, sustaining these connections can be challenging when professors, particularly those working in research universities, are promoted and rewarded primarily based upon their research and scholarly activities (Griffiths, Stout, & Forsyth, 1988; McCarthy, 1999c). Consequently, educational leadership faculty members often are torn between addressing the needs of the field and fulfilling the performance expectations of their institutions (Young, Petersen, & Short, 2002).

This tension has become increasingly apparent over the past 50 years as educational leadership units have worked to address field relationships while simultaneously attending to academic responsibilities. Until the 1960s professors were more aligned with practitioners (McCarthy, 1999b), but by the 1980s the typical faculty member was more interested in scholarly pursuits than preparing aspiring school leaders (Murphy, 1993). Because of this increased focus on research, school administrative experience no longer was considered the gateway to the educational leadership professoriate (McCarthy, 1988). As a result, the profession has been challenged to respond to concerns that many programs are disconnected from the real world of practice because they are staffed by faculty members who lack administrative experience (Bredeson, 1996; Levine, 2005) or whose school leadership experience no longer is perceived as being current (McCarthy, 1999b). Additionally, educational leadership professors are being challenged to assist school leaders as they address the accountability demands for increased student achievement.

In this chapter we review the research literature related to faculty members in educational leadership preparation programs. The first section addresses the characteristics of faculty members, including tenure-line faculty members, clinical faculty members, and adjunct instructors. The second section presents the research related to the professional work activities of educational leadership faculty, regarding balancing responsibilities in the areas of teaching, scholarship, and service. The third section discusses trends related to attitudes and values of professors, as the educational leadership professoriate is becoming increasingly diverse. The fourth section highlights the changing role expectations of educational leadership faculty members, as they are called to be more responsive to problems in the field. Fifth, the academic preparation of educational leadership faculty is presented, related to their training to fulfill teaching and research responsibilities. The sixth section reviews the research about the types of professional development opportunities provided for faculty members and their effectiveness in improving practice. The seventh section notes tensions within the professoriate. The final section presents recommendations for future research activities related to educational leadership faculty.

Characteristics of Educational Leadership Faculty

Educational leadership graduate programs have a comparatively brief history (McCarthy, 1999b; Forsyth & Murphy, 1999). The first formal university-based programs were organized in the early years of the 20th century, and approximately 125 programs were in existence by the middle part of that century. Rapid expansion of the number of programs followed during the 1950s and 1960s, paralleling growth in public school enrollments due to the post-World War II baby boom and expansion of funding available to postsecondary institutions (McCarthy, 1999b). Over the past 30 years, estimates of the number of entities offering educational leadership programs have varied: McCarthy and Kuh (1997) noted that 375 degree programs existed in 1976, 372 in 1986, and 371 in 1994 with approximately 100 additional entities offering license-only programs. However, the NCEEA (1987) stated that 505 institutions offered school administration courses in 1987, although this group declared that fewer than 200 possessed the necessary institutional commitment and resources to offer quality programs. Despite the NCEEA (1987) assertion that "only institutions willing to support such excellence should continue to prepare school leaders" (p. 24), it appears that few institutions have heeded this recommendation. Levine (2005) estimated that approximately 500 institutions currently offer graduate programs for school administrators, with approximately 100 additional non-degree-granting programs, such as state-sanctioned programs being offered by professional associations and school districts.

With the expansion of programs over the past several decades, it is important to review trend data related to the types of individuals who are staffing these programs. This section reports the research that has been conducted related to tenure-line educational leadership faculty members and persons who serve in non-tenure-track appointments, including clinical and adjunct faculty members. Included in this overview are demographic data, including professors' gender, ethnicity, and administrative backgrounds.

Several national studies of the educational leadership professoriate have been conducted over the past four decades, with the research primarily focusing on identifying characteristics of faculty in tenure-line positions (Boyan, 1981; Campbell & Newell, 1973; Hills, 1965; McCarthy, 1988; McCarthy & Kuh, 1997; McCarthy, Kuh, Newell, & Iacona, 1988). These systematic examinations of leadership programs and their faculty tend to be promulgated from within the profession (McCarthy, 1999c). The studies, which have utilized survey research methods and have been conducted approximately each decade, have been highly informative in disclosing trends related to the composition of tenure-line educational leadership faculty, denoting a gradual shift from a relatively homogeneous group in the 1960s to a more diverse faculty in the 1990s.

During the decades of the 1960s and 1970s, educational leadership units overwhelmingly were staffed by professors who were White males, former school administrators, and generally unengaged in research. Subsequent studies, however, disclosed that some shifts in faculty characteristics were beginning to occur. In 1965, Hills reported that 90% of faculty were seasoned school administrators, and Campbell and Newell (1973) noted that a mere 2% were females and 3% were people of color. During the 1970s and early 1980s, leadership experience began to diminish in importance within the professoriate, as fewer new hires had served as school administrators (Boyan, 1981). By 1986, McCarthy (1988) reported that some diversification was happening, as 12% of faculty were female and 8% were minorities.

The last comprehensive examination of the educational leadership professoriate, sponsored by the University Council of Educational Administration (UCEA), was undertaken by McCarthy and Kuh in 1994, and the results were published 3 years later (McCarthy & Kuh, 1997). Based on an exhaustive exploration of the existing literature on the educational leadership professoriate, it is apparent that relatively little attention has been paid to this area in the past decade. Two major sources of data have relevance for understanding characteristics of the professoriate today: the Mc-Carthy and Kuh study, which offers a wealth of information on leadership programs, characteristics of faculty, and faculty perceptions relating to their employment, and data from the 2004 National Study of Postsecondary Faculty (NSOPF:04; Cataldi, Fahimi, Bradburn, & Zimbler, 2004). This analysis primarily draws from these two sources for information about faculty characteristics.

As noted, the McCarthy and Kuh (1997) study is the most recent in a series of studies of the educational leadership professoriate in the United States and Canada. It involved separate surveys of department chairs and faculty, which were designed to replicate earlier work and thus permit longitudinal comparisons. Department heads from the 371 educational leadership programs identified by the researchers were sent surveys dealing with program characteristics (unit size, composition, and structure); 254 surveys were returned for a 68% response rate for the department head survey. A random sample of 940 individual faculty members from the 371 identified university programs received surveys dealing with faculty demographics, activities, and attitudes toward various aspects of work. Usable surveys were collected from 486 respondents, reflecting a 55% response rate for the individual faculty surveys.

The NSOPF was sponsored by the U.S. Department of Education to address the need for data on faculty and instructors working in postsecondary institutions. This longitudinal survey initially was conducted in 1987–1988 and was repeated in 1992–1993, 1998–1999, and most recently in 2003–2004. The last survey included a sample of 1,080 public and private not-for-profit, degree-granting institutions from a universe of 3,381 institutions and a sample of approximately 35,000 faculty and staff. The weighted response rate for the faculty survey was 76%. Faculty surveys included questions about demographic characteristics of faculty, workloads, work responsibilities, salaries and benefits, and attitudes about various aspects of work (e.g., job satisfaction). The NSOPF:04 is the most recent source on educational leadership faculty; data were collected in the Fall 2003 semester and were released in May 2006. Although no published research was identified that uses the NSOPF:04 data, the Institute of Education Sciences makes basic descriptive statistical analyses from NSOPF:04 available through its online Data Analysis System (National Center for Education Statistics [NCES], n.d). Thus, for purposes of this chapter, the NSOPF:04 dataset was accessed to provide the most current information on educational leadership faculty.

One additional source of salary data was identified from the review of literature. Since the early 1980s, the College and University Personnel Association (CUPA) has conducted annual faculty salary studies by discipline. Two CUPA surveys are conducted: one for senior public colleges and universities and one for senior private institutions. Howe (2000) used data from the 1996–1997 surveys to establish baseline data and analyzed salary trends for faculty classified in the educational administration and supervision specialty area using the 1999–2000 CUPA surveys. Two hundred ninety-six institutions participated in both the 1997–1998 and 1999–2000 public institution surveys, and 390 institutions participated in both private institution surveys. Howe's analysis excluded faculty working less than 51% of full-time employment and included 9- or 10-month salary data only (excluding summer salary, fringe benefits, and other compensation).

It is important to address some limitations of these studies of educational leadership faculty. The McCarthy and Kuh (1997) study provided faculty comparisons with the Campbell and Newell (1973) and McCarthy et al. (1988) surveys. In presenting these data, however, they cautioned that comparisons across studies are somewhat problematic, because the earlier studies included faculty with concentrations in higher education administration (14% of respondents in 1986, 8% in the 1992), whereas the 1994 survey was sent only to professors whose focus was preparing school leaders. The NSOPF:04 data reported in this chapter are delimited to only full-time professors and to those who classify themselves in the education administration and supervision specialty, which may include faculty specializing in higher education administration.

Profile of Tenure-Track Faculty

From the 1970s to the mid-1990s, the face of the educational leadership professoriate reflected both stability and change (McCarthy, 1999a). One characteristic that seems to have changed very little is the size of the educational leadership program: Units offering leadership degrees averaged 6.5 full-time equivalent faculty in the mid-1970s, 5.0 full-time equivalents in the mid-1980s, and 5.6 full-time equivalents in 1994 (McCarthy, 1999b). Roughly 40% of educational leadership programs employed fewer than five full-time faculty members in 1994 (McCarthy & Kuh, 1997), the minimum recommended by the NCEEA (1987). McCarthy (1999a) attributed the slight increase in the number of faculty between the 1980s to 1990s to expansion of units housed in comprehensive universities, which represent over half of all educational leadership programs; in fact, the mean size of programs housed at research universities declined slightly from the 1980s to the 1990s.

The McCarthy et al. (1988) study predicted that at least half of the educational leadership professoriate would retire by the year 2000, implying that the field would see an influx of new faculty well into the new millennium. This prediction appears to have been realized, as many faculty hired during the expansion of programs in the 1960s indeed have retired (McCarthy, 1999b). Murphy's (1999c) survey of senior faculty members also provided a feeling that "a changing of the guard" (p. 47) has been underway in the faculty ranks. Approximately 40% of the respondents to the 1994 survey reported having been hired within the preceding decade, with 21% reporting that they were appointed within the previous 5 years (McCarthy, 1999a). From among respondents to the NSOPF:04 survey, 46.4% reported that they were employed for 5 or fewer years, and just under 70% had 10 or fewer years of service at their current institution. Of course, because experienced faculty move from one postsecondary institution to another, these percentages may overestimate the number of individuals new to the professoriate. Data from the McCarthy and Kuh (1997) survey indicate that 71% of respondents worked at universities in their most recent position prior to their current employment. A separate NSOPF:04 item reveals that about half of all full-time educational leadership faculty reported that their present job was their first position at a postsecondary institution, however, suggesting that there indeed has been an influx of new faculty in the past decade.

Despite a significant amount of faculty turnover, the educational leadership professoriate appears to be aging. McCarthy (1999a) reported that in 1972 the average professor was approximately 48 years old, and 1994 survey data reported a mean age of 54. McCarthy (1999c) observed, "Between 1972 and 1994, the percentage of faculty members under age 40 dropped from 22 percent to 2 percent, and the percentage over age fifty climbed from 40 percent in 1972 to 70 percent in 1994"

(p. 78). Further, professors were starting their teaching careers later in life, averaging around 9 years older when they entered the professoriate (with a mean age of 45). NSOPF:04 survey data discloses these trends continued through 2003: The mean age of full-time faculty in educational administration and supervision was 57.8 years, with faculty averaging 50 years of age when starting the professoriate. The age distribution in 2003, utilizing NSOPF:04 data, indicates that 4% were under 35 years of age, 9% were 35–44, 22% were 45–54, 35% were 55–64, 20% were 65–70, and 10% were over 70 years of age.

One explanation for the rise in the average age of leadership faculty was offered by McCarthy (1999a): Faculty are entering at an older age because an increasing number join the academy after serving as school administrators. Data from the 1994 survey of leadership faculty (McCarthy & Kuh, 1997) showed that one third of the professoriate had served as school administrators before joining the teaching ranks at a postsecondary institution, and new faculty were even more likely to have served as school administrators (45%). Professors with administrative experience were less likely to work at research-intensive universities: 57% were employed at comprehensive universities, 24% at doctoral universities, and 19% at research universities. Research by Pounder, Crow, and Bergerson (2004) indicated that hiring practices related to experienced administrators appear to be holding steady; approximately 35% of new professors responding to their survey possessed K–12 administrative experience.

The practice of hiring faculty with administrative experiences has gone through some changes over time. Although faculty in the early years of the profession came to the academy from administrative ranks, most typically from among retiring superintendents (Hills, 1965), during the theory movement in the mid-1950s and 1960s the emphasis shifted to hiring faculty with expertise in the traditional social sciences (Forsyth & Murphy, 1999). From the 1960s through the early 1980s, faculty ranks became increasingly specialized; new hires were less likely to have administrative experience, tended to identify with narrower subfields (e.g., law, finance, policy, politics), and were less concerned with administrative practice than with scholarship (McCarthy, 1986, 1999b). By 1994 the field experienced a "renewed commitment to field connections" (McCarthy, 1999c, p. 78) as concern grew about the perceived detachment of the professoriate from the real world of school administration. As S. L. Harris (2006) noted, the criticism that leadership preparation programs were not establishing theory-to-practice connections served as a catalyst for reexamining master's and doctoral programs, prompting "an emphasis on merging theory and practice rather than maintaining them as two separate entities" (p. 5). One result has been a renewed preference for hiring faculty with administrative experience and a renewed focus on problems associated with administrative practice in preparation programs (Jackson & Kelley, 2002; McCarthy, 1999c). Levine's (2005) research disputed these findings: He noted that only 6% of faculty have served as principals and 2% as superintendents. However, Levine's research methodology has been challenged by scholars in the field of educational leadership (Young, Crow, Orr, Ogawa, & Creighton, n.d.), and professors may have served in various school leadership posts besides the principalship and superintendency, including assistant principalships and assistant superintendencies, which certainly would be considered to be relevant and valid administrative experiences.

Although approximately half of faculty hired in the most recent 5-year period prior to the 1994 survey possessed administrative experience (McCarthy, 1999c), it is curious that the Doctor of Philosophy degree had overtaken the Doctor of Education as the prevalent terminal degree among full-time faculty (though the difference represented only a 51% to 45% split; McCarthy & Kuh, 1997). In addition, roughly two thirds of the 1994 survey respondents indicated their major field was educational administration, similar to responses in the 1972 and 1986 surveys. When compared with faculty at comprehensive universities, research university faculty were more likely to hold a PhD than an EdD. In contrast to the Campbell and Newell (1973) study, which showed that nearly half of all respondents had received their degrees from about 20 prestigious universities, more recent studies showed that professors were being trained at a diverse range of institutions. For the 1994 sample, 119 different institutions were listed; the most mentioned institution accounted for fewer than 4% of the responses, and "the top ten producers combined prepared less than one third of all faculty in both [1986 and 1994] studies" (McCarthy & Kuh, 1997, p. 90).

Faculty content-area specializations mirror, for the most part, traditional course offerings in leadership preparation programs, which in turn relate directly to state licensure requirements for school leaders. Leadership was the most frequently mentioned specialization (16%), with school law (13%) mentioned next. Organizational theory, which was the primary specialization in 1986 (16%), dropped to Number 3 in 1994 (9%), with principalship (8%), economics and finance (8%), and supervision of instruction (7%) following in the rankings (McCarthy & Kuh, 1997).

In terms of professorial rank, some changes have occurred over the past several decades. The percentage of full professors remained relatively stable for two decades: In 1972, fully half of survey respondents were classified as "professor" (Campbell & Newell, 1973), 59% held this rank in 1986 (McCarthy et al., 1988) and 54% in 1994 (McCarthy & Kuh, 1997). Almost three fourths of the educational leadership professoriate was tenured in 1994 (McCarthy & Kuh, 1997). NSOPF:04 data (Table 6.1) suggest that when compared with faculty in all fields, the educational leadership professoriate no longer appears quite as top heavy as was once the case. Only 31% of leadership faculty are full professors, and the distribution of leadership faculty among all ranks is quite similar to the distribution of faculty across all fields. In terms of tenure status, among NSOPF:04 respondents classified as full-time educational administration faculty, the 2003 survey noted that 32% of respondents were tenured, 35% were nontenured but in a tenure-track position, 23% were not in tenure-track positions, and 10% reported that they worked in an institution without a tenure system. Among all respondents to the 2003 survey, 48% were tenured, 21% were nontenured but in a tenure-track position, 24% were not on a tenure track, and 8% worked in institutions that did not offer tenure. These results seem logical given the amount of turnover and relative newness of the educational leadership professoriate, but nonetheless the shift is somewhat dramatic in just one decade.

Trend data indicate that impending retirements continue to be a significant concern. McCarthy (1999b) cautioned, "Given the mean age of faculty members and their anticipated retirement dates, continued faculty turnover can be expected into the twenty-first century. But an adequate supply of new faculty members to replenish professional ranks is not assured" (p. 130). Analysis of the NSOPF:04 data discloses that retirements of many full-time educational leadership faculty members are imminent: 30.4% intended to retire within the next 5 years, with an additional 24% retiring in 6–10 years. These retirements are problematic because there has been a decline in the number of programs placing an emphasis on preparing a new generation of faculty, and salary differentials between administrative jobs and faculty positions make it unlikely that a growing percentage of doctoral graduates will elect to join the professoriate (McCarthy & Kuh, 1997). Ad-

Table 6.1 Percentage Distribution of Faculty Ranks, 2003

Rank	Educational leadership	All fields
Professor	31	29
Associate Professor	24	23
Assistant Professor	26	24
Instructor/lecturer	5	16
Other (e.g., administrative faculty, Emeritus)	15	9

ditionally, Murphy's (1999c) surveys of senior faculty disclosed that many were concerned whether new professors were being adequately prepared in both core content and research methods, and whether they ultimately may be successful in attaining promotion and tenure.

Research conducted by Rayfield, Meaon, and Ughrin (2004) dealing with promotion and tenure policies affecting educational administration and higher education programs suggested that the vagaries of the tenure process represent an issue affecting faculty. Although certain aspects of the tenure process are predictable (e.g., most schools have a mandatory 3rd-year review for untenured faculty), the majority of faculty reported that there are not clear minimum standards associated with scholarship. Further, despite the increasing trend toward field-based activities within leadership programs, most faculty feel that "professional work cannot be substituted for refereed journal publications" (Rayfield et al., 2004, p. 4).

Women in the Professoriate

Perhaps the most significant change in the profile of the educational leadership professoriate has been the continued increase in the percentage of female faculty members (McCarthy & Kuh, 1997). Griffiths (1988) recalled that there was only one female educational leadership professor in the nation in 1961: Evelyn B. Martin of Florida A&M. Even by 1972 females comprised only 2% of faculty ranks (Campbell & Newell, 1973). Analyzing the 1983–1984 *Educational Administration Directory*, Ortiz and Marshall (1988) identified approximately 200 women professors in a listing of 2,553 professorships; they noted that women constituted 8% of all faculty members, but more than half were in temporary positions or were assistant professors. By 1988, women represented 12% of faculty (McCarthy, 1988). By 1994 women represented 20% of faculty, about 40% of all faculty hired from 1984 to 1994 were women, and more than half of all new hires at research universities were women (McCarthy & Kuh, 1997). McCarthy and Kuh predicted, "If these hiring trends continue, women may soon dominate educational leadership programs at research institutions and those affiliated with UCEA" (p. 197). These trends do appear to have continued into the 21st century, although not quite yet attaining that prediction: NSOPF:04 data reveal that by Fall 2003, women comprised 37% of all full-time faculty in educational leadership.

Although the trends appear encouraging, the percentage of females in the professoriate still do not parallel those percentages of females employed in elementary-secondary school systems. Marshall (2004) called this phenomenon a "mismatch of the demographics of profession and clientele" (p. 6). Although women comprise nearly 80% of the teaching force, data from the 1999–2000 school year indicated that they held only 46% of public and private school principalships (NCES, 2005). Marshall noted that 87% of superintendents are male. As women historically have struggled to move into the ranks of school administration (Blount, 1998; Grogan, 1999; Shakeshaft, 1999), they also have faced similar obstacles to attaining professorial status. Due to the relatively recent ascendancy of women into the educational leadership professoriate, it is not surprising that in 1994 fewer females were full professors and that they were less likely to be tenured (McCarthy & Kuh, 1997).

Relatively little research has been conducted on characteristics of female educational leadership professors. Iacona (1987) surveyed over 1,300 faculty members, of which approximately 200 were women and minorities. Females were more likely to report research skills as their primary strength, and they reported devoting more time to their research activities. Female faculty members were significantly less satisfied than males with their current positions, their salaries, and their departmental structures. In a qualitative study of 7 women faculty members who were full professors, Obeng-Darko (2003) found that these women not only had been highly productive scholars, but also had assumed various leadership roles, both in academic positions within their institutions and serving as officers of professional associations. Reporting on survey research of 114 educational administration faculty members in UCEA institutions, Rusch (2004) found a "troubling fault line" (p. 39) between male and female professors regarding issues related to gender and race. Women perceived that discussions related to these topics were held only half as frequently as men reported them to occur. Although men believed that these discussions were open and insightful, women characterized them as stilted and uncomfortable.

Minorities in the Professoriate

Trends related to minorities within educational leadership faculties are not as encouraging as the growth in numbers of female faculty. McCarthy and Kuh (1997) found a modest increase in the percentage of faculty who identified themselves as minorities from the early 1970s to the 1994 survey, from under 3% in 1972 to 11% in 1994. Minority composition was higher at comprehensive universities than at research universities or those affiliated with UCEA, and trends between 1986 and 1994 disclosed that people of color were more likely to list research as their primary strength (McCarthy, 1999a). Further, McCarthy (1999a) noted,

> The prospects for race equity do not seem as bright as the prospects for gender equity in educational leadership units. It was disappointing that in 1994, minority representation among those hired during the prior 5 years (10%) was smaller than among faculty hired during the prior 5 year period (15%). (p. 195)

Unfortunately, the pool of minority candidates does not appear to be growing appreciably; Pounder et al. (2004) found that only 12% of recent doctoral graduates were persons of color.

NSOPF:04 data suggest that the concern regarding minority representation is not unwarranted, as survey data from the educational administration faculty cohort in 2003 showed that 87% of respondents identified themselves as White non-Hispanic, 10% as Black, and 3% as other. Thus, data suggest that the aggregate percentage of racial minorities in the educational leadership professoriate has moderately inched up from 11% in 1994 to 13% in 2003. About half of the respondents to the 1994 McCarthy and Kuh (1997) survey felt that the small number of minorities in the profession was a serious problem. To echo McCarthy's (1999a) conclusion,

> This is worrisome because it is difficult to imagine that the educational leadership profession can respond effectively to the changing demographics of the American schools and prepare future leaders for those schools without a racially and ethnically diverse professoriate. (p. 195)

Although research has focused on minority faculty members in higher education (Björk & Thompson, 1989; Granger, 1993; Olsen, Maple, & Stage, 1995; Tack & Patitu, 1992), scholars generally have concluded that minority faculty members are significantly underrepresented in university settings. Unfortunately, the literature specific to educational leadership professors is very sparse. In some instances, scholars have attempted to address issues related to both gender and ethnicity, but the attention primarily is directed at gender with scant consideration to race issues (Grogan, 1999; Rusch, 2004). Quezada and Louque (2004) asserted that when educational leadership faculties include persons of color, they can be more effective in attracting students of color to their programs. Noting that retention of minority faculty can present even more challenges than recruiting and hiring persons of color, Quezada and Louque advocated for effective mentoring by senior faculty to include "developing and providing moral support, guidance, encouragement and feedback" (p. 218). In a survey of educational administration professors, Iacona (1987) found minimal differences between Caucasian and minority faculty members related to their job satisfaction and perceptions of their departmental structure.

Faculty Compensation

Faculty salaries can be an important consideration, particularly when the profession attempts to attract experienced school administrators—many who command high salaries—to the professoriate. McCarthy (1999b) noted that although mean academic year salaries of educational leadership faculty "compared favorably with those of faculty members in other academic units in the mid-1980s" (p. 131), this was no longer the case in 1994. The mean academic-year salary for education leadership faculty was $52,500 in 1994. However, the mean salary for the NSOPF:93 respondents who classified themselves as educational administration professors was $48,676, above the average salary for all education faculty but well below the $56,000 average salary for faculty across all disciplines (McCarthy & Kuh, 1997).

Prior research has identified a gender gap in compensation for educational leadership faculty (McCarthy et al., 1988; Pounder, 1989). The 1994 survey data also showed that average academic-year salaries of females were approximately $7,500 below their male counterparts, which further analysis attributed primarily to differences in experience (McCarthy & Kuh, 1997). Gender-based disparities documented in the 1980s had disappeared by 1994 when controlling for rank and length of service (McCarthy, 1999a). The difference in mean salary between faculty who were employed at research universities and those at doctoral or comprehensive universities persisted even when controlling for rank and experience; mean salaries at research universities were approximately $2,000 higher than at doctoral universities, and $4,500 higher than at comprehensive universities (McCarthy & Kuh, 1997). Using the McCarthy and Kuh dataset, Pounder (1989) conducted multiple regression techniques and concluded that gender discrimination in educational administrator professor salaries does exist; she determined that females earned over $3,000 less than their male counterpoints, after controlling for variables related to experience, rank, and administrative appointments.

The vast majority of educational leadership professors augment their academic-year salaries with other income. Although most of the additional compensation involves summer teaching responsibilities, the overall percentage of faculty earning summer salary consistently dropped, from a high of 92% of respondents in 1972 to 76% in 1986 and 73% in 1994 (McCarthy & Kuh, 1997). The mean summer income in 1994 was $6,900. Over 80% of faculty in the 1994 study reported additional types of external income, including royalties, lecture fees, and consulting contracts.

More recent information suggests that mean academic-year salaries of educational leadership faculty may be creeping up to the aggregate average for all faculty. Howe's (2000) analysis of CUPA salary survey data revealed that 100 of the 296 public institutions surveyed had educational administration units, and the average salary among 811 faculty was $51,512 in 1996–1997, 1% higher than the average salary for faculty in all major fields. For the 1999–2000 survey, educational administration units were reported in 110 of 226 public institutions; the average salary was $55,435, reflecting a 3-year increase of about 5.6%, which Howe noted was approximately 0.7% below the cost-of-living increase over this 3-year period. This average is approximately 3.5% lower than the average salary for faculty in all major fields.

Howe's (2000) analysis of CUPA survey results for respondents who work at private postsecondary institutions included data for only 33 of the 390 institutions surveyed (i.e., only 33 had school leadership preparation programs). These data reflected 141 individual respondents. Mean academic-year salaries for these respondents in 1996–1997 were $50,208, just 0.1% higher than the salary for respondents in all fields. By 1999–2000, for the 37 of 390 institutions that reported having educational leadership programs ($N = 159$ faculty), the mean salary had risen to $55,167, nearly 1% higher than the mean salary for respondents in all fields ($54,710). The increase in salary for faculty in private postsecondary units from 1996–1997 to 1999–2000 was 9.9%, some 3.3% above the cost-of-living change. It appears that over this time period, salaries for private college faculty in education leadership caught up to their public-sector counterparts.

Analysis of the NSOPF:04 data shows that the relative parity between educational leadership faculty and all other faculty revealed in the CUPA survey is likely a result of sampling bias. Whereas the McCarthy et al. (1988) surveys and the NSOPF involve broad, national samples of institutions, including those with educational leadership units, the CUPA survey includes only members of that organization. Examination of the more representative NSOPF:04 data disclosed that the average "basic salary from the institution" for faculty reporting themselves to be employed at 4-year institutions as specialists in educational administration was $63,660, which is about 10% above the average for all faculty in education ($57,996) but 11% *below* the average for faculty in all fields ($70,739). When examining the variable of total income from the institution, the difference between the average salaries for leadership faculty and all education faculty widens to about 13.5%, although the differential between leadership faculty and faculty in all disciplines narrows: Educational administration faculty have a mean total income of $71,253, compared with an average for all faculty of $75,801, about a 6.4% differential. These data suggest that leadership faculty may rely on summer salary and other sources of income from the institution to augment their earnings to a greater extent than other faculty in education or faculty in other fields. Of course, given that many educational leadership programs offer summer coursework to meet the needs of practicing teachers and administrators, this finding is not unexpected.

When comparing NSOPF:04 average salary data by institution type (i.e., doctoral versus non-doctoral-granting institutions), the average basic salary for educational leadership faculty at non-doctoral-granting institutions was slightly higher than at doctoral universities, but the total income from the institution was about 2% higher at doctoral-granting institutions, possibly suggesting that faculty at doctoral institutions rely on income from a greater variety of sources (including, for instance, income from grants and contracts).

Faculty in Non-Tenure-Track Appointments

Acknowledging the need to be more fully engaged with the practitioner realm, in 1987 the NCEEA recommended that educational leadership programs should have a balanced faculty that reflected diverse experiences and academic backgrounds. More recently, Levine (2005) expressed a similar desire for a high-quality faculty composition:

> The faculty includes academics and practitioners, ideally the same individuals, who are expert in school leadership, up to date in their field, intellectually productive, and firmly rooted in both the academy and the schools. (p. 13)

As one method of accomplishing this goal, NCEEA (1987) proposed the creation of clinical professor positions, staffed by practicing school administrators. The addition of these positions represented an opportunity for educational leadership faculties to diversify beyond the traditional tenure-track faculty model and the institutional research expectations for these positions. NCEEA did not advance a definition of the clinical position, but subsequent scholars have begun to articulate some responsibilities inherent in the clinical role, with sometimes differing expectations.

Griffiths et al. (1988) envisioned full-time faculty roles in non-tenure-track appointments that were "differentiated by both scholarly focus and responsibility for the many aspects of a professional preparation program" (p. 300). They advocated for *information specialists,* who were nonteaching professors whose responsibilities focused on student admission, student testing, and monitoring of student data systems, and *field specialists* who would monitor the clinical elements of the program, including internship supervision and field-based research. The full-time clinical faculty model also was endorsed by Peper (1988), who noted that programs must "balance their academic teaching faculty with a skilled clinical faculty if the paradigm of university-directed clinical education is to succeed" (p. 362). In contrast, Hawley (1988) described the clinical faculty role as a part-time position for active professionals, an approach similar to that employed in medical schools.

In the two decades since the clinical faculty model was proposed, numerous programs appear to have implemented this concept. A cursory review of educational leadership departmental Web sites revealed that a number of individuals have been hired in full-time, non-tenure-track appointments, with their titles described in various ways, such as clinical professor, clinician, professor of practice, temporary professor, lecturer, instructor, and clinical associate. These non-tenure-track lines also may include visiting professor positions, which typically are 1-year term appointments. In addition, the educational leadership programs may employ part-time adjunct instructors and other individuals who work in other positions on the university campus while enjoying part-time appointments or *courtesy* affiliation to the program area.

Characteristics of Non-Tenure-Track Faculty

Although the characteristics of educational leadership faculty have been documented adequately over the past several decades, the research is limited because it has focused only on those individuals who hold tenure-track positions. Virtually ignored has been an examination of characteristics and contributions of colleagues who work in faculty roles that are complementary to tenure-track lines, whether they serve in full-time, clinical positions or part-time, adjunct faculty appointments. It is important to include these individuals in descriptions of the overall faculty composition in order to obtain a more comprehensive picture of leadership preparation program faculty. Although a large number of universities employ clinical or adjunct faculty in educational administration programs (Schneider, 2003), there is a paucity of descriptive studies and virtually no comprehensive research on the topic. Data from the NSOPF:04 indicated that in Fall 2003, 36% of educational administration faculty were full time and 64% part time, as compared to 56% full time and 44% part time in all fields. A breakdown by rank revealed professors, associate professors, and assistant professors accounted for 81% of educational administration positions; 5% were instructors or lecturers, and 15% were coded as other, which included administrative, adjunct, emeritus, and other faculty. Unfortunately, a low sample size prevented further disaggregation of these positions by variables such as gender and ethnicity.

In a report profiling full-time, non-tenure-track professors, Benjamin, Hollinger, and Knight (2005) asserted, "By 2001, the number of full-time non-tenure-track professors in U.S. colleges and universities was just over 213,000, or 34 percent, of nearly 618,000 full-time faculty members" (p. 60). These data have elicited much concern from groups such as the American Association of University Professors (2003), who recommended that no more than 25% of the total instruction within any department should be provided by "contingent faculty," which includes both full- and part-time faculty who are not in tenure-line positions. The high percentage (64%) of part-time instructors utilized within the field of educational leadership far exceeds this 25% threshold advocated by the American Association of University Professors. Citing problems with instructional methods, academic background, and a lack of dedication to effective lesson preparation, critics assert that the profession's heavy reliance on adjunct faculty has eroded overall program quality (Levine, 2005; Schneider, 2003).

Attraction to the Job

Although these studies are informative, they have not addressed the central issues relevant to clinical and adjunct faculty in educational leadership programs. Hart and Naylor (1992) presented an American Educational Research Association (AERA) conference paper examining the university socialization process experienced by clinical professors who also were practicing administrators. Their findings illustrated the sense of ambiguity that many of these individuals faced as they adapted to their roles as clinical or adjunct faculty. Pounder (1994) ascertained that many practicing school administrators who applied for clinical faculty positions were motivated by their desire to prepare future leaders and for their own intellectual growth. This finding was confirmed by a later study in which superintendents indicated their primary motivation for working as adjunct professors was to improve the training of new school administrators (Schneider, 2003).

The topic of adjunct professors was a central theme in the November 2002 issue of *The School Administrator*, the publication of the American Association of School Administrators—the nation's professional organization for school superintendents ("Adjunct Professors," 2002). Although the articles included were neither empirical nor research based, the fact that a prominent practitioner journal would devote an entire issue to the subject does merit discussion and provides additional justification for further research.

Effectiveness of Non-Tenure-Track Faculty

The American Association of School Administrators conducted an informal self-report study that explored the nature of practicing administrators working as adjuncts or the *invisible faculty*, as Schneider (2003) referred to them. Because this study was not designed to be a rigorous research endeavor, there are limitations to the findings. Respondents were 295 superintendents who taught part time in educational administration graduate programs. Salient findings include the following four: (a) 62% teach in master's degree programs, 25% teach in post-master certificate programs, and 13% teach courses leading to the EdD or PhD; (b) only 18% of the adjuncts reported having a formal process for the evaluation of their teaching, and only 6% indicated they are reviewed by regular faculty; (c) 35% create their own syllabi without guidance; and (d) 53% responded that they only teach a course they know a lot about (Schneider, 2003, pp. 5–8).

Superintendents also were asked to state their levels of satisfaction with several aspects of adjunct relationships The percentage of individuals indicating they were strongly satisfied or satisfied with the aspects were the following: receiving regular communications from department or university (83%), receiving professional development opportunities (38%), receiving adequate orientation from department or university (64%), being provided an opportunity to network with other adjunct professors (49%), and networking with professors (54%; Schneider, 2003).

The latest research report addressing the issue of clinical or adjunct faculty does not shine a flattering light upon this practice. In 2005, Levine analyzed surveys, interviews, and observation data from 25 schools with educational leadership programs. Levine asserted, "The adjunct professoriate employed at the schools that were visited consisted largely of local superintendents and principals…. Their dominant mode of instruction, according to faculty and student reports, was telling war stories" (p. 36). His findings indicate that the number of clinical and adjunct faculty has grown substantially, due in large part to educational leadership program faculty members' decisions to increase their numbers of off-campus delivery sites. Former students of these programs asserted that many adjunct instructors did not integrate practice with theory and research, had narrow perspectives, were unprepared in the subject area they were teaching, and were ineffective instructors.

Professional Work Activities and Scholarly Productivity

Individuals who serve as university professors have the benefit of a great amount of professional autonomy in their work lives, yet they also must struggle continually to fulfill the numerous responsibilities inherent in their positions. Often, professors can experience anxiety and stress as they struggle to satisfy the expectations emanating from their jobs and to maintain balance between their professional and personal lives. In contrast to many other disciplines, the profession of educational leadership also creates additional challenges related to developing connections with practitioners, sustaining outreach activities, and solving problems of practice (Murphy, 1999c). This section reports the research related to the professional work activities of educational leadership professors, as they traditionally have been divided into the areas of scholarship and research, teaching, and service. This research is reported both for tenure-line professors and faculty who serve in non-tenure-track appointments.

Professional Activities of Tenure-Track Faculty

In terms of what McCarthy and Kuh (1997) called "primary role orientation" (p. 96), strikingly similar percentages of professors historically have identified teaching as their primary strength (71% in 1986, 70% in 1994), with research (15% and 16%, respectively) and service (15% and 14%) cited by virtually the same proportion of respondents. Differences between respondents at research and comprehensive universities diminished somewhat from 1986 to 1994, with 73% of the respondents at comprehensive universities identifying teaching as their primary strength, versus 66% at research universities.

Allocation of Time

Professors are engaged in complex work responsibilities within an academic culture that is increasingly demanding (Houston, Meyer, & Paewai, 2006). Universities are notoriously open systems, and recently there has been a growing insistence on compliance with a variety of accountability measures; innovation in teaching and research; and partnerships with a variety of local, state, and national entities. In their study relating work environment to job satisfaction, Houston et al. found that faculty are challenged to stretch their time to meet these expanding and often competing demands.

Faculty reports of time investments in position responsibilities clearly indicate that educational leadership professors have increased their levels of commitment to the profession, and their hourly workweeks now are consistent with professors in other disciplines. In 1994 professors reported spending an average of 39.0 hours weekly on professional activities, considerably below the mean of 54.0 hours reported across disciplines in the 1993 NSOPF (McCarthy & Kuh, 1997). The NSOPF:04 study disclosed that educational administration faculty have increased their workweeks to 52.2 hours, as compared with 53.3 hours for faculty in all disciplines. Two responsibilities stand out as different for leadership faculty: They reported serving more hours per week on administrative committees (8.1 hours) than faculty in all disciplines (4.9 hours), and they devoted more time to office hours (13.6) than faculty in all disciplines (7.4). Leadership faculty devoted about the same percentage of time on instruction (59.7%) as faculty in all disciplines (61.3%), but they spent 6.7% less time on research (28.6% for faculty in all disciplines, 21.9% for educational administration and supervision), due to the increased time dedicated to administrative tasks.

Scholarship and Research

The percentage of leadership faculty reporting research involvement has grown steadily over the past four decades. In 1965, about half of all respondents indicated some involvement in research (Hills, 1965), whereas by 1994, 85% of all respondents indicated involvement in research. The percentage of time dedicated to research also has increased. In 1994 professors spent an average of 14.4% of their time on research-related activity (McCarthy & Kuh, 1997). NSOPF:04 respondents in the educational administration and supervision specialization reported spending about 23% of their time on research. These trends point to a narrowing in the research gap between leadership faculty and faculty in all disciplines, which was 12% in 1994 (McCarthy & Kuh, 1997). These trends support that, through the decades, leadership professors have continued to shift their role orientation to the more scholarly aspects of the job (Pounder et al., 2004).

Scholarly productivity also has increased, as measured by tangible indicators such as books, articles, and other scholarly works. The mean number of books or monographs published by faculty over the course of their careers increased from around 5 in 1986 to 8.5 in 1994, the percentage of respondents who wrote or edited at least 1 book increased from 55% in 1972 to 85% in 1994, and the percentage reporting that they had produced 9 or more books rose from 5% in 1972 to 23% in 1994 (McCarthy & Kuh, 1997). Articles and book chapters produced in a 5-year period increased, from an average of 9.4 articles in the 5 years preceding the 1986 survey (McCarthy et al., 1988) to an average of 12.6 articles or chapters in 1994 (McCarthy & Kuh, 1997). In 1994, about one fifth of educational leadership professors (21%) reported receiving research time or external funding to support their research, as compared with 19% in 1986 and 23% in 1972 (McCarthy & Kuh, 1997). Women (26%) and professors of color (28%) were more likely to report having research support than men (20%) or Caucasians (20%). Respondents at doctoral universities were slightly more likely than faculty at research institutions to be receiving such support (26% as compared with 24%), with just 15% of faculty at comprehensive universities receiving release time or external funding. Faculty at research universities produced more scholarly products than those working at either doctoral or comprehensive universities.

The NSOPF:04 also included a variety of indicators of scholarly productivity, but the questions differed slightly from those used in prior studies, making comparisons problematic (Table 6.2). Educational leadership professors were asked about their scholarly productivity over their careers. For 2002 and 2003, the mean number of books produced over the duration of the respondents' careers was somewhat lower than the number reported a decade earlier in 1997 by McCarthy and Kuh (6.6 vs. 8.5).

In 1994, faculty reported spending 4.4% of their time attending professional conferences, and as intimated in the NSOPF:04 data (Table 6.2), leadership faculty are quite active in presenting papers at national conferences. The 1994 survey showed that 85% of all leadership faculty reported making at least one presentation within the preceding year, up from about two thirds in 1986, with the average number of presentations at 3.2 (McCarthy & Kuh, 1997). Not surprisingly, faculty from research and doctoral universities made more conference presentations than faculty at comprehensive universities. The number of presentations did not differ by gender, though faculty

Table 6.2 Scholarly Productivity for Education Administration and Supervision Faculty, 2003

Type of work	Career	Last 2 years
Articles, nonrefereed journals	13.0	2.9
Articles, refereed journals	11.6	3.3
Book reviews, chapters, creative works	4.0	—
Books, textbooks, reports	6.6	—
Conference presentations	38.8	6.4
Total publications/scholarly works	30.5	6.7

Note. Number could not be estimated due to low *n* for two table cells.

of color reported making more presentations than their Caucasian counterparts (3.9 vs. 3.2; McCarthy & Kuh, 1997). Interestingly, McCarthy and Kuh chose to classify professional conference presentations as a service activity, rather than as research; because papers at professional conferences typically are reported as scholarly activities, we include this information in the scholarship and research section.

Levine (2005) conducted surveys to gauge educational leadership faculty research productivity by Carnegie classification. Faculty identified as more or most productive had engaged in at least three of these four activities in the past 2 years: (a) book publication, (b) peer-reviewed article, (c) conference paper presentation, and (d) obtaining external funding. The percentages of faculty identified as more or most productive by Carnegie type were as follows: 55% in Doctoral Extensive, 32% in Doctoral Intensive, 26% in Masters I, and 12% in Master's II. It is not surprising that expectations for faculty productivity are greater for professors working in doctoral institutions.

Teaching

Data on teaching activities reveal that not only do the vast majority of faculty continue to cite teaching as their primary area of strength, but they also report spending a large proportion of their time teaching and advising students. However, the average percentage of faculty time dedicated to teaching declined from 41% in 1986 to 35% in 1994, with faculty at comprehensive institutions reporting spending a higher proportion or their time teaching than those at doctoral or research universities, whereas those at research and doctoral institutions spent a higher proportion of their time advising doctoral students (McCarthy & Kuh, 1997). Over successive iterations of the NSOPF, the proportion of faculty time spent on teaching has increased, from 35% in 1988 to 45% in 1993 (McCarthy & Kuh, 1997), and to 59.7% for the NSOPF:04 data.

The mean number of credits taught per semester has varied through the years, averaging 7.5 credits in 1986 and 6.3 in 1994 (McCarthy & Kuh, 1997). NSOPF:04 data showed that educational administration faculty averaged 8.3 credits in the Fall 2003 semester; respondents reported spending 9.7 hours per week teaching credit-earning classes, with class enrollments averaging 21.1 students. Each average was lower than the corresponding average for all faculty responding to the NSOPF:04 survey, although when delimiting the comparison to leadership and other faculty who teach graduate or first professional students, leadership faculty teach, on average, more credit hours per semester (8.0 compared with 5.9), and they spend more hours per week teaching credit classes (8.6 compared with 7.7). However, leadership faculty taught smaller classes (18.3 vs. 32.9 students) and had smaller total student loads (45.9 vs. 63.6) than all full-time faculty who teach graduate or first professional classes.

Advising is an important responsibility for the educational leadership faculty member, and studies have indicated it is becoming more time intensive for faculty. Whereas in 1986 faculty reported advising an average of 11.5 masters students, the mean number of advisees in 1994 had burgeoned to 31.9 (McCarthy & Kuh, 1997). The number of master's advisees was considerably greater at comprehensive universities in 1994. These increased advisee numbers may be attributed, in part, to what Levine (2005) described as a "proliferation of off-campus programs" (p. 35). The overall percentage of respondents who reported having chaired doctoral committees over the previous 3 years increased from about half in 1972 to 58% in 1994. In 1994 faculty reported having served on (but not chaired) an average of 9 doctoral committees (McCarthy & Kuh, 1997). According to NSOPF:04 data, educational administration faculty reported spending an average of 3.9 hours weekly on dissertation or thesis committee work, about 1.5 hours per week more than faculty in all disciplines. Administration faculty reported spending, on average, 5.0 hours per week with all advisees, whereas faculty in all disciplines averaged about 3.9 hours per week on advising.

Service

Educational leadership faculty devote themselves to a variety of service and outreach activities, including those that primarily benefit their departments and institutions, their communities, and the profession in general. In terms of institutional service, which might include governance activities, administrative tasks, and committee work, McCarthy and Kuh (1997) reported that faculty were less involved in service activities in 1994 and 1986 than in 1972. The 1994 and 1986 cohorts reported devoting only 7% of their time to university committee work and other governance activities, although about 7 in 10 noted that they spent at least some of their time on governance. The mean percentage of time devoted to university administrative responsibilities dropped from 17.6% in 1972 to 9.9% in 1994, with only about 1 in 3 professors reporting any involvement in administrative activity in 1994. Men were more likely than women to be totally uninvolved in governance, and women reported higher means in time allocated to university administrative duties, which McCarthy and Kuh suggested may be due to institutional goals for diverse committee representation.

NSOPF:04 survey data revealed that full-time educational administration faculty devoted an average of 8.3 hours weekly to administrative committee work, which exceeded the 4.9 hours per week spent by faculty in all disciplines. Although NSOPF data do not permit estimating the mean percentage of faculty time spent on governance alone, respondents were asked to estimate the percentage of time spent on "all other activities at this institution like administration, professional growth, service, and other activities not related to teaching or research." Data showed that full-time leadership faculty at 4-year institutions spent on average 34.2% of their time on such activities (McCarthy & Kuh, 1997).

Faculty in 1994 reported dedicating almost 8% of their time to field-based activities, with faculty with school administrative experience somewhat more likely to be involved in such activity than those without administrative experience (McCarthy & Kuh, 1997). Faculty at comprehensive universities spent a slightly higher proportion of their time on fieldwork. Due to increased support for field-based activities being advocated over the past few years (Murphy, 1999c; Young et al., 2002), it is likely that future studies would disclose increased faculty time spent on relationships with practitioners. In addition, nearly 60% of the 1994 respondents reported some involvement in outside consulting, with women and minorities somewhat less likely to engage in consulting activities. The mean amount of time devoted to consulting was fairly consistent across subgroups at 5.5% (McCarthy & Kuh, 1997).

Involvement with professional organizations for academics and practitioners is another important service activity. Quite possibly indicative of the dual focus on the scholarly and practitioner aspects within the educational leadership profession as well as the existence of associations dedicated to subspecializations within the field, there are no professional organizations in which the majority of educational leadership professors reported involvement. Furthermore, the associations ranked highly by professors include both practitioner and academic circles. In 1994 the most frequently cited organization was the AERA (noted by 22% of respondents), followed by the American Association of School Administrators, the Association for Supervision and Curriculum Development, the National Organization on Legal Problems in Education (now called the Education Law Association), the UCEA, and the National Association of Secondary School Principals (McCarthy & Kuh, 1997). Interestingly, women were also far more likely to list involvement in AERA.

This overview of professional responsibilities indicates that the average educational leadership professor's reported workweek has expanded over 13 hours in the past decade, to a current average of 52.2 hours weekly. Additionally, all areas of responsibility have evidenced an increase, including measures of research productivity, time dedicated to teaching and advising, service on committees, and time spent maintaining field connections. It appears highly likely that professors are experiencing difficulties maintaining an effective balance among these varied responsibilities as well as balancing their personal and professional obligations.

Professional Activities of Non-Tenure-Track Faculty

This section presents information on the professional activities of individuals who serve in non-tenure-track appointments. Non-tenure-track positions in educational leadership units consist of full-time clinical faculty positions and part-time adjunct appointments.

NCEEA (1987) suggested that clinical professor positions should be added to the ranks of leadership preparation programs. Although the clinical position initially was not fully defined, NCEEA (1987) noted that some individuals in these positions should be "professional, practicing administrators" (p. 21). In contrast to tenure-line positions, clinical faculty typically would be employed to focus on practice, rather than to engage in scholarly research pursuits (Hearn & Anderson, 2001). As experienced practitioners, clinical faculty members could teach practice-oriented courses, assist with student recruitment and evaluation, develop mentoring programs, and supervise internship activities. Griffiths et al. (1988) proposed a well-conceived differentiated staffing model for educational leadership departments, which was more fully aligned to the professional school model. Educational leadership programs would include both tenure-track and clinical faculty in full-time lines, with delineations in scholarly focus appropriate for a professional school. Clinical faculty primarily would direct the program's field-based elements, according to Griffiths et al.: "They would supervise interns, run the weekly intern seminars, and coordinate opportunities for colleagues and students to solve problems in the field.… These professors might also teach field-study methods, case analysis, and other clinical studies" (p. 300).

In a discussion of faculty staffing arrangements in three educational leadership departments, Bredeson (1996) explained that clinical professors who supervised students' internship experiences brought both administrative experience and credibility to their faculties. The job responsibilities for the clinical position within each department were context-bound, as each program "aggressively and creatively infused its teaching faculty with clinical professors" (Bredeson, 1996, p. 269). Similarly, a qualitative study of 8 clinical professors in educational leadership programs disclosed that clinical professors perceived they were hired to enhance their program's credibility; they focused on internship supervision and teaching responsibilities and generally were not expected to engage in research (Hackmann, 2007). It appears leadership preparation programs typically assign clinical faculty members the responsibilities of supervising students' field experiences and teaching courses, with additional responsibilities based upon each department's unique programmatic needs.

Although tenure-track faculty members' duties typically are divided into teaching, research, and service, these expectations do not appear to be the same for non-tenure-track faculty members. On university campuses, those faculty members who hold nontenurable faculty appointments principally engage in teaching activities (Benjamin et al., 2005). However, Griffiths et al. (1988) recommended that non-tenure-track faculty might conduct research that would "center on applied studies, the effects of administrator intervention, and case analysis.… Despite the nontraditional nature of these roles, all professors would be expected to produce new knowledge directly related to school administration" (p. 300). In practice, however, most clinical faculty members neither engage in research nor are typically required to be productive scholars. Service expectations for clinical faculty members tend to involve maintaining relationships with practitioners, through supervision of internships and involvement with state practitioner organizations as well as such activities as student recruitment and admissions oversight (Hackmann, 2007).

In addition to full-time, non-tenure-track faculty appointments, leadership preparation programs also utilize part-time, adjunct instructors, who typically are practicing administrators from local school districts. Adjuncts certainly can be important and effective contributors to the instructional core of the program, but excessive reliance on adjunct instructors potentially can result in substantially diminished program quality (Levine, 2005; Shakeshaft, 2002). Schneider (2003) noted that there often is very little interaction between tenure-track faculty and adjuncts. Merely utilizing adjuncts to teach courses, without ensuring that they are integrated and socialized into the departmental culture, does little to promote university–school connections and does not ensure that high standards for instructional quality and student performance will be maintained.

Attitudes and Values of Professors

The beliefs of educational leadership faculty members are an important consideration because they provide a more comprehensive understanding of those individuals who prepare aspiring leaders. Professors' value systems affect their decisions related to the inclusion—or exclusion—of curricular content and the learning activities to which they expose their students. These beliefs may be internalized by these aspiring leaders and subsequently will influence their practices when they assume administrative posts. Belief systems are akin to the dispositions identified within the Interstate School Leaders Licensure Consortium (ISLLC, 1996) standards for school leaders. Although the ISSLC task force expressed some concern over the inability to assess dispositions, it is nevertheless valuable to gain some insight into professors' values and attitudes.

Faculty Attitudes

Attitudes expressed by professors have held relatively constant across the decades, even as the demographic characteristics of the educational leadership professoriate have begun to change (Campbell & Newell, 1973; McCarthy & Kuh, 1997; McCarthy et al., 1988). Historically, professors have asserted that they are satisfied with their positions, their students, and the effectiveness of their preparation programs (McCarthy, 1999a), despite others' criticisms of both student quality and program quality (Levine, 2005; Schneider, 2003). However, relatively few recent studies have been conducted related to professors' perceptions and personal beliefs. Murphy and Vriesenga (2004) have noted that the research on administrator preparation programs is expanding, and program restructuring has occurred in many institutions. Therefore, given the combined effects of program reforms and projected turnover of leadership faculty in the past decade, it is likely that belief systems of the professoriate may have experienced a shift.

The reasons that individuals have elected to become professors have remained consistent through the decades (Campbell & Newell, 1973; McCarthy & Kuh, 1997; McCarthy et al., 1988). Highest-ranked items influencing individuals' selection of the educational leadership professoriate as a career are interest in ideas and the extension of knowledge and interest in students and teaching (McCarthy & Kuh, 1997). An additional category was added in the 1994 study, the desire to improve education, which also was cited favorably. Women were more likely to cite both interest in ideas and desire to improve education as reasons for entering the profession. The vast majority of respondents—between 84% and 90% across studies—stated that if they were able to reconsider their career choice, they still would become professors.

A variety of factors—both organizational and personal—can influence an individual's satisfaction with the position and ultimately prompt him or her to change institutional affiliations. When asked what factors might encourage respondents to move to another institution, educational leadership professors consistently have responded by citing the opportunity for a significant increase in salary (Campbell & Newell, 1973; McCarthy & Kuh, 1997; McCarthy et al., 1988); other factors typically cited were more stimulating colleagues and a more attractive geographic area. Faculty compensation can become increasingly important when average faculty salaries do not keep pace with the rate of inflation, as is currently the case (American Association of University Professors, 2006). Satisfaction with pay has been associated with overall job satisfaction, turnover, and motivation levels (Terpstra & Honoree, 2004). Although the prospect of lower professorial salaries, when compared with the larger salaries earned by school administrators, may discourage individuals from entering the professoriate (Pounder et al., 2004), faculty compensation may not be an issue once an individual has reached the decision to enter academe. In a study of 5,000 faculty across disciplines from over 100 universities, Terpstra and Honoree found that education professors were only slightly less satisfied with their salaries than professors in other disciplines, and these differences were not significant. As the professoriate becomes more diverse, reasons for job relocations also may become more varied. For example, males were more likely to cite salary considerations, females cited family considerations, and minority faculty were more likely to cite geographical location and family considerations (McCarthy & Kuh, 1997). These responses indicate that, although important, salary is not the only factor affecting faculty retention.

Faculty members have reported both gratifying and undesirable facets of their position responsibilities. The opportunity to teach graduate students consistently has been rated as the most enjoyable aspect, with research and publishing ranking a distant second (McCarthy & Kuh, 1997; McCarthy et al., 1988). Possibly reflecting the desires of former administrators to remain connected with practitioners, field-based responsibility also has been cited as a positive feature. In a study of factors related to job desirability of the professoriate, Pounder et al. (2004) found that, although publishing expectations discouraged some individuals from seeking academic positions, those individuals who became educational leadership professors positively associated publication responsibilities with their intention to remain in the professoriate. These surveys have disclosed differences related to gender and ethnicity. Males cited teaching and advising as the most enjoyable activities, whereas females cited research and writing. Minority professors were more likely than Caucasians to cite research and writing and field aspects as positive features. The least desirable aspects of the position, ranked in decreasing order of disfavor, included faculty governance and committee work, university administration, and research and writing (McCarthy & Kuh, 1997; McCarthy et al., 1988).

Over time, professors have noted differing needs and problems within the profession. The most critical need in the 1970s was building a more extensive knowledge base (Campbell & Newell, 1973). Curricular reforms were the primary issue in the 1980s (McCarthy et al., 1988), and addressing the theory-to-practice gap was the most significant need in the 1990s (McCarthy & Kuh, 1997). Generally, professors' perceptions of problems within the profession have not changed significantly over the past several decades. However, two items have been identified by a majority of professors as serious concerns: the small number of minority professors and the lack of graduate student financial support (McCarthy & Kuh, 1997).

Faculty Values

Surveys of faculty values related to the profession have disclosed only slight shifts in the past three decades (Campbell & Newell, 1973; McCarthy & Kuh, 1997; McCarthy et al., 1988). In the 1990s belief statements receiving support from over 80% of professors were that universities should reward service to school districts and state associations and that greater emphasis should be placed on ethics in leadership preparation. Other items with which a majority of professors voiced agreement were the following: Greater attention to field studies would strengthen practice (76%), faculty should participate extensively in professional meetings (72%), quality teaching and research are interdependent (71%), faculty should be centrally involved in university governance (69%), social sciences should be emphasized in leadership preparation (66%), I would like more contact with professors at other universities (64%), faculty preparing school leaders should have served as school administrators (59%), faculty should be more concerned about the well-being of their universities (58%), more emphasis at conferences should be placed on teaching and program reform (58%), there are not enough full-time students in preparation programs (57%), increased emphasis on qualitative research would strengthen inquiry (57%), curriculum should be organized around problems rather than disciplines (54%), and too many adjunct instructors are used in preparation programs (51%; McCarthy & Kuh, 1997, pp. 168–169).

Faculty diversity brings with it diverse perspectives. Women and minority faculty were significantly more likely than men to express a desire to develop contacts with faculty at other universities (McCarthy & Kuh, 1997). This finding may be attributed to the low percentages of female and minority faculty in leadership programs, because they may find it more difficult to find colleagues with which they identify and share interests within their institutions. Women believed that admissions standards should be increased, yet minority faculty members did not share this viewpoint. Finally, minority faculty members desired clear and explicit tenure and promotion criteria. Although more women have been hired into educational leadership professorial positions, these increased numbers, as of yet, have not produced significant shifts in faculty values. McCarthy (1999a) noted that, rather than changing overall faculty values, women's attitudes have come into closer alignment with their male colleagues. Given that 37% of faculty members now are female (NCES, n.d.), one can anticipate that future studies may show that women have influenced a shift in the overall attitudes and values within the profession.

The theory-to-practice continuum and scholar–practitioner debates are not settled. Although many faculty members believed the best professors are former practitioners (42%), a solid group believed that scholars with training in related disciplines are best (21%; McCarthy & Kuh, 1997). One's academic and experiential background, however, tends to drive these opinions: Former administrators believe that school leadership experience is important, and scholars trained in related disciplines believe their preparation is best. Of course, this issue may be better addressed from a perspective of faculty balance rather than an either–or approach.

Research has indicated that students enrolled in leadership preparation programs appreciate both theoretical and practical orientations in the classroom. Reporting the results of a survey of 74 specialist and doctoral degree-seeking students enrolled in one university, Styron, Maulding, and Hull (2006) found that students overwhelmingly preferred professors with administrative backgrounds who were strongly grounded in theory. Gender differences were present, however; female students preferred theory over administrative experience, and males stated a preference for professors with administrative experience.

Attitudes About Programs and Research

Faculty attitudes about program orientations have changed in the past few decades (Campbell & Newell, 1973; McCarthy & Kuh, 1997; McCarthy et al., 1988). In the 1970s, program faculties were nearly evenly split on whether their primary responsibilities were to prepare professors and researchers or to prepare practitioners (Campbell & Newell, 1973). However, more recent studies have determined that over 80% of programs are oriented to practitioner preparation (McCarthy & Kuh, 1997; McCarthy et al., 1988). This shift in mission most likely is due to the increase in the number of institutions that offer graduate programs in educational leadership—many of which are not at major research universities. In 1986 and 1994, 37% of professors believed that their programs should be equally balanced between preparing practitioners and preparing professors and researchers.

The emphasis on research varies greatly in educational leadership units. Approximately one fifth of programs do not emphasize research preparation in their leadership curricula (McCarthy & Kuh, 1997; McCarthy et al., 1988); one could assume that these programs offer only the master's-level principalship curriculum. More recently, Levine (2005) noted that 89% of principals had completed research courses in their principalship training; however, only 56% found this coursework to be valuable for their jobs. It is arguable, however, that including a course or two does not constitute adequate preparation for research. At this point, more programs may be requiring research courses to assist principals in becoming consumers of research, due to the increased emphasis on data-driven leadership skills and the No Child Left Behind (2002) accountability mandates.

Faculty members' research in the field of educational leadership has been challenged through the years by a number of scholars (Boyan, 1981; Bridges, 1982; Erickson, 1967, 1979; Immegart, 1977; Levin, 2006; Levine, 2005) with admonitions to improve its quality and relevance to practice. Levine has been especially critical, noting that the scholarship is "atheoretical and immature; it neglects to ask important questions; it is overwhelmingly engaged in non-empirical research; and it is disconnected from practice" (p. 44). Survey research has been identified as the dominant data collection method (Bridges, 1982; Miskel & Sandlin, 1981), although quantitative methods began to be utilized with greater frequency in the 1970s and 1980s (Riehl, Larson, Short, & Reitzug, 2000). Firestone and Riehl (2005) noted that research on educational leadership "has been weakened by a lack of overall focus and by the frequent failure to articulate how a given instance of research addresses linkages among leadership, learning, and equity" (p. 1). Due to the calls for accountability in the nation's schools, scholars have asserted that research efforts must be refocused on student achievement—what Murphy (1999b) called a "research agenda grounded in school improvement" (p. 58) and Firestone and Riehl described as "leadership for learning" (p. 2). Both quantitative and qualitative methods have gained acceptance, to the point that they are both now termed "conventional research" (Riehl et al., 2000, p. 396). Riehl and Firestone proposed that research efforts must be much more comprehensive, including more rigorous methodological approaches such as comprehensive case studies, design research, quasi-experimental methods, and experimental research. Future studies no longer may ask professors to classify their research orientations as either qualitative or quantitative but may inquire into additional research methodologies that are being employed.

Generally, educational leadership professors perceive that the quality of their programs is either good or excellent; over 80% specified this rating (McCarthy & Kuh, 1997; McCarthy et al., 1988). Nearly two thirds of professors asserted in 1994 that their programs had been improved within the previous 5 years (McCarthy & Kuh, 1997). Unfortunately, studies of professors have not been conducted since the development of the ISSLC standards, the subsequent adoption of these standards in over 40 states (Sanders & Simpson, 2006), and the use of the Educational Leadership Constituent Council standards for National Council for Accreditation of Teacher Education (NCATE) accreditation (National Policy Board for Educational Administration, 2002). Currently, 157 educational leadership programs have attained "national recognition" through the NCATE (n.d.) process, which implies faculty have been engaged in programmatic revisions over the past 5 years.

Faculty surveys have disclosed some developments within leadership programs, including increased emphasis on field connections, shifting away from management duties to an emphasis on leadership, enhanced focus on ethics, and increased used of distance learning (McCarthy & Kuh, 1997). Faculty in 1994 asserted that ethics; human relations or communications; problem solving; and issues related to diversity, leadership, and managing change deserved more attention within the curriculum (McCarthy & Kuh, 1997). Certainly, these elements have been addressed within a number of programs. In the past decade, faculty have advanced a number of additional issues in the professional literature, including social justice and equity (McKenzie, Skrla, & Scheurich, 2006); leadership for learning; more expansive understandings of diversity to include minority students, socioeconomic status, gay/lesbian/bisexual/transgender, and issues related to power and privilege; critical race theory, distributed leadership; and data-driven decision making. Although research is lacking to determine whether the new leadership discourse has had a widespread influence on leadership programs, the scholarship published in journals and books has indicated these concerns have gained significant attention and have affected many programs (Cambron-McCabe & McCarthy, 2005; Lopez, 2003; Marshall & Oliva, 2006; Marshall & Ward, 2004).

Job Satisfaction

Studies have demonstrated a relationship between university faculty job satisfaction and a variety of outcomes such as motivation, absenteeism, and turnover (Terpstra & Honoree, 2004). Theories postulate that a high level of faculty job satisfaction results in a greater investment in the organization, a higher likelihood of significant engagement in the job, and hence greater productivity (Hagedorn, 2000), although Oshagbemi (1997) suggested that there have been relatively few studies of the causes of faculty job satisfaction and dissatisfaction.

Educational leadership professors appear to be content with their current positions: Over 80% noted being either very satisfied or satisfied, and a majority reported that these levels of satisfaction extend to all aspects of their professional responsibilities (McCarthy & Kuh, 1997; McCarthy et al., 1988). Additionally, over 70% of faculty also expressed approval of the caliber of their students and overall program quality. On the opposite end of the spectrum, faculty dissatisfaction extended to three aspects of the job: (a) salary (29%), (b) the structure of their department (25%), and (c) the mission or focus of their unit (23%). Minor differences in satisfaction were present within subgroups: Men were slightly more satisfied than women, and people of color were somewhat more satisfied than Caucasians; however, these differences were not statistically significant.

In the NSOPF:04 survey, respondents also were asked questions regarding satisfaction with various aspects of their jobs. The 1999–2000 iteration of the NSOPF survey showed that overall most faculty were satisfied with their jobs, particularly with respect to the autonomy faculty enjoy to make decisions and conduct their work (Clery, 2002). A study conducted by Rosser (2005), however, suggested that faculty satisfaction and perceptions of their work lives had changed a great deal from the 1993 survey to the 1999 study, with faculty perceiving most dimensions of work and all aspects of job satisfaction more positively in 1999. Administrative support was the only dimension of work not rated higher by the 1999 cohort; this factor includes clerical support, library support, and the assignment of graduate assistants.

Table 6.3 displays the results for educational administration and supervision faculty in the most recent NSOPF survey. Patterns in the NSOPF:04 satisfaction data are quite similar to the McCarthy and Kuh (1997) study. Faculty overwhelmingly were satisfied with all aspects of their jobs, although more than one fourth were dissatisfied with salary and benefits. Although not included in the data here, these patterns are similar to responses for all university faculty. In general, leadership faculty reported being somewhat more satisfied than faculty in all other disciplines.

In the NSOPF:04 survey, faculty were asked a few additional opinion items. Specifically, they were asked whether they perceived that female and minority faculty were treated fairly at their institutions and whether they felt that teaching was rewarded. Again, the overwhelming majority of responses was positive: Over 90% either strongly agreed or agreed that women were treated fairly, and 89% strongly agreed or agreed that racial minorities were treated fairly. Faculty were slightly less likely to suggest that teaching is rewarded: 36% strongly agreed with this sentiment and 52% agreed.

In 1986, McCarthy wrote, "The current climate for inquiry in educational administration is promising and that the conditions are in place for significant progress to be made in generating

Table 6.3 Satisfaction of Educational Administration/Supervision Faculty, Percentage Responses, Fall 2003

Item	Very satisfied	Satisfied	Dissatisfied	Very dissatisfied
Salary	34.4	39.7	18.2	7.7
Benefits	34.3	40.2	16.7	8.9
The job overall	55.9	41.9	2.3	0.0
Workload	40.3	45.5	13.3	0.9
Decision-making authority	76.7	21.9	1.4	0.0
Institutional support for teaching	40.0	43.0	11.8	5.2

new knowledge" (p. 4). There was a growing diversity among scholars, a greater interest in research overall, and an increasing heterogeneity among researchers in terms of methods and interests. As Milstein (1999) observed, though, the basic conclusion from the research of McCarthy and Kuh (1997) was that more continuity emerged than change during the period 1986–1994. "Not only is continuity the reality," Milstein (1999) wrote, "but . . . there is a high level of self-satisfaction with that continuity on the part of faculty members" (p. 538).

Changing Roles for Educational Leadership Faculty

Leadership preparation has undergone a series of conceptual transformations during its relatively short history as a field of study, as scholars and reformers have worked to establish a knowledge base for educational leadership (Culbertson, 1988; Donmoyer, 1999). Prior to the 1950s, university-based educational leadership programs primarily were staffed by former school administrators who drew upon their experiences and taught through personal anecdotes (Marland, 1960; McCarthy, 1999b). Forsyth and Murphy (1999) noted the deficiencies of this approach: "The curriculum effectively conveyed neither technical nor practice knowledge about school administration—merely secondhand experiences as filtered through the recollections of retired school leaders" (p. 258). In the 1950s, a group of scholars promoted a science of administration that predominately drew upon the social sciences; this "theory movement" resulted in an increased emphasis on theoretical principles in coursework, the employment of discipline-based scholars as faculty members, and a decrease in practical experiences for students (Foster, 1988; Forsyth & Murphy, 1999; McCarthy, 1999b). The focus on administrative theory that reached a peak in the 1980s ultimately brought criticisms that the curriculum was not relevant to the real world of schools, that it provided insufficient attention to the development of technical skills, and that it lacked sufficient opportunities for aspiring administrators to apply theory to practice. Subsequently, McCarthy (1999b) noted "a sharp decline in faculty support for the utility of theory" (p. 125), and by the late 1990s the majority of institutions had integrated clinical experiences into their programs that addressed problems of practice.

Forsyth and Murphy (1999) identified two forms of knowledge that are involved in leadership preparation—technical and practice—and argued that professors have a legitimate interest in ensuring that both components are included within the curriculum. They asserted that historically a pendulum effect has occurred as programs have responded to concerns and criticisms, and noted, "Extreme imbalance has tended to promote correction" (Forsyth & Murphy, 1999, p. 257). The challenge is for leadership preparation programs to maintain an appropriate balance of both technical and practice knowledge. Asserting that programs should reflect "important responsibilities connected with professional life," Griffiths et al. (1988, p. 300) recommended that leadership preparation should include five strands: (a) theoretical study of educational administration, (b) the technical core of educational administration, (c) the solution of problems through the use of applied research and the development of administrative skills, (d) involvement in supervised practice, and (e) the demonstration of competence.

Recent trends indicate that the focus of leadership education is shifting away from management functions to an increased emphasis on school improvement, particularly as it relates to improving student achievement (Huber & West, 2002). This restructuring is due, in part, to the critical need to prepare educational leaders who can lead school systems that are responsive to the demands brought by changing student demographics (Reyes, Wagstaff, & Fusarelli, 1999). Trend data indicate an increasingly diverse student population: Whereas minority students comprised only 24% of public school enrollments in fall 1993, this percentage had increased to 42% by fall 2003 (NCES, 2005). The number of children living in poverty and who live in single-parent homes continues to increase, as well (Reyes et al., 1999). The accountability mandates of the No Child Left Behind (2002) legislation require educators to address the achievement gaps between White and minority students. Student achievement data from 2005 indicated that minimal progress has been made in eliminating these gaps (NCES, 2005).

Developments within the profession over the past decade have had implications for leadership preparation curricula and for faculty members' professional responsibilities. The ISLLC (1996) standards have created a framework guiding course restructuring for the majority of the nation's leadership preparation programs. These standards were developed to address three central changes that need to occur in educational institutions for quality schooling to exist for all students: (a) a redefinition of teaching and learning to challenge and engage all students in the educational process, (b) an increase in community-focused and caring conceptions of schools, and (c) increased involvement of stakeholders external to the schools (ISLLC, 1996). An advocate of reculturing the educational leadership profession, Murphy (2002) asserted that leaders must be moral stewards, educators, and community builders. Other areas that have received increased attention in leadership preparation curricula in recent years have included leadership for learning (Glickman, 2002); ethics (Murphy, 1999a); data-driven leadership and uses of technology (Murphy, 2005); and issues related to diversity, social justice, and equity (English, 2006; Marshall & Oliva, 2006; McKenzie et al., 2006). In addition to influencing curricular revisions, these developments can serve as a catalyst for changing role expectations for educational leadership faculty.

A significant change has occurred with respect to upgrading the quality of the field-based components of leadership preparation programs. As recently as the late 1980s, the clinical features of most programs could be described as "notoriously weak" (Murphy, 1999b, p. 22). Leading the efforts in reconceptualizing the clinical elements of leadership preparation, the 22 universities participating in the Danforth Program for the Preparation of School Principals were instrumental in including structured field experiences as a central feature of their program redesign efforts (Milstein, 1993). Surveys of these programs noted broad disparity in the total number of clock hours dedicated to internship experiences: The hours ranged from 120–1,703, with an average duration of 632 hours (Cordeiro, Krueger, Parks, Restine, & Wilson, 1993). Murphy's (1999a) survey research involving educational leadership department heads also disclosed an enhanced focus on improving the quality of field-based experiences. In addition, changing state administrative licensure mandates and national accreditation requirements are requiring educational leadership programs to include field-based elements and more extensive internship experiences (Young et al., 2002). McCarthy (1999b) noted that the field components of the 1990s differed significantly from leadership programs of the 1950s, "when theory and research were downplayed" (p. 128).

Current effective models encourage multiple perspectives in addressing problems of practice, including the integration of clinical experiences throughout coursework as well as formal internships. Despite the reported improvements in clinical experiences, Levine (2005) has remained highly critical of these activities, reporting that clinical instruction was inadequate and "well respected in name only" (p. 40). Of course, these enhanced field-based experiences necessitate that faculty must be integrally involved with the clinical components of the program in order to ensure that high-quality experiences are provided to students.

The improvement of field-based experiences is closely correlated with what Murphy (1999c) described as a "greater willingness to acknowledge the applied nature of the profession" (p. 50). As a result, and consistent with changing instructional practices in elementary and secondary classrooms, professors' instructional methods have begun to embrace constructivist strategies, through the use of authentic learning experiences, problem-based learning activities (Bridges, 1992), case studies, and reflective methods (Murphy, 1999b). Hart and Pounder (1999) have termed such improvement efforts as "practice-based reforms" (p. 130) to reflect a reliance on knowledge from experience.

Educational leadership programs also have experienced structural changes, beyond classroom instructional practices, that make them more responsive to the learning needs of adult learners. Many programs now utilize cohort groups, so students are exposed to sequenced courses and scaffolded learning experiences, develop a sense of community, and form professional networks (Barnett, Basom, Yerkes, & Norris, 2000; Scribner & Donaldson, 2001). Additionally, a growing number of programs are utilizing distance-learning mechanisms, including off-campus locations, online courses, two-way interactive video, and blended-delivery models. In a survey of 109 educational leadership programs that offered doctoral degrees, Hackmann and Berry (1999) found that 50 programs (45.9%) offered off-campus courses, 27 (24.8%) used interactive video, and 18 (16.5%) delivered online courses; over 30% of respondents intended to expand their distance-learning options. Distance learning has not gained universal acceptance, however, as many faculty members have expressed serious reservations related to maintaining course quality (Hackmann & Berry, 1999). Levine (2005) also expressed concerns about inferior courses, noting that many leadership programs offer "low cost, high volume, off-campus programs" (p. 24) that primarily are staffed by adjunct instructors; he noted that these programs tend to be "cash cows" for universities. English (2006) also has been critical of the for-profit entities that compete with traditional university-based programs, displaying heavy reliance in distance-learning models. Each of these structural changes has implications for faculty members' roles and responsibilities.

Involvement with distance learning creates additional demands on educational leadership professors, whether it involves learning and mastering the necessary technology to deliver online coursework, extensive time commitments when traveling to off-campus locations, sustaining one's research agenda, or ensuring that teaching and learning standards remain high when using approaches that do not involve face-to-face instruction. Hackmann (2003) reported his initial experiences with distance learning as an untenured assistant professor, which included teaching at off-campus locations and using interactive video. Although he found the experience challenging, he was able to identify and utilize a variety of creative approaches that ultimately permitted him to maintain and improve teaching quality and ensure that research activities remained on track. When educational leadership programs adopt distance-learning delivery mechanisms, it is important to acknowledge the personal and professional needs of faculty members and to provide appropriate support.

Expanding Field Connections

School leaders believe that educational leadership professors should be actively engaged with the field, through such initiatives as conducting applied research, supervising the clinical activities of aspiring administrators, working with professional associations, providing support to administrator academics and leadership centers, and assisting administrators in finding solutions to problems of practice. Although these connections traditionally have been prized by the educational leadership professoriate, they have not necessarily been perceived as important across the university campus. Consequently, these field connections have gone through periods of close relationships and benign neglect. Seventeen years ago, Murphy (1992) observed, "Faculty linkages to schools have actually atrophied over the last two generations" (p. 102). On a promising note, upon surveying 105 educational leadership professors in 1999, Murphy (1999c) noted that many faculty members perceived that field connections were being strengthened and rebuilt. Hart and Pounder (1999) identified several positive trends related to enhanced field connections that occurred in the 1990s, such as close partnerships that included universities, school districts, business and industry, state departments of education, and professional organizations; participation of practitioners as clinical or adjunct instructors; and courses and seminars grounded in local school settings.

Despite acknowledging some reconnections, Murphy (1999c) found that relationships with professional associations have not been restored to their levels before the theory movement took hold; for example, a continued separation was noted between the American Association of School Administrators and the UCEA. Young et al. (2002) asserted that a variety of groups have expressed a commitment to the improvement of preparation programs, including professional organizations, professors, higher education organizations, practitioners, and state and federal agencies. Revealing that few initiatives have been joint endeavors, Young et al. (2002) argued, "The success of any effort to positively and substantively improve the preparation of educational leaders will depend on commitment among key stakeholders to collaborate" (p. 142).

Although some increase in faculty participation within school settings was documented from 1989–1996, Murphy (1999a) characterized this involvement as moderate. Other than required supervision of students' clinical experiences, faculty members' linkages tended to be highly individualistic. Programs also provided fairly traditional services to school administrators, such as seminars, conferences, and professional development workshops (Murphy, 1999a). Levine (2005) noted that, although faculty members believe that involvement with schools is a worthwhile activity, they lack sufficient time to get involved.

The Professional School Model

Although extensive faculty involvement with practitioners and within schools is an important and valued activity, the university culture often discourages these practices. Although educational leadership is an applied field of study, in an effort to enhance their status on the university campus, colleges of education adopted an arts and sciences model rather than a professional school model of education. According to Griffiths et al. (1988), this action has resulted in "the single most destructive trend" (p. 299) affecting leadership preparation, causing the school of education to be an "ugly stepsister of arts and sciences instead of taking its place with the other professional schools housed in the university" (p. 299). Furthermore, Griffiths et al. continued, this approach has restricted and delimited faculty activities to a "single, narrowly construed research path to tenure" (p. 299) that focuses on theoretical and empirical models rather than applied research.

Within the arts and sciences model, field-based connections are classified merely as service activities that are given relatively little consideration when assessing faculty performance and productivity. As a consequence, because professors are promoted and rewarded primarily on the basis of scholarly activities that are disseminated through recognized academic channels, they are discouraged from establishing close working relationships with practitioners, from conducting applied research activities, and even from presenting and publishing their research in practitioner venues (Bredeson, 1996; Young et al., 2002). Untenured faculty often report that involvement with the field creates substantial conflicts and tensions for them, because this unrewarded work takes valuable time away from their scholarly pursuits (Levine, 2005; McCarthy & Kuh, 1997). Assistant professors who engage in field-based projects and supervise the clinical activities of aspiring administrators—despite the fact that they may be providing an invaluable service to current and aspiring practitioners—potentially can jeopardize their ability to advance in the professorial ranks and therefore can cause irreparable harm to their academic careers (Levine, 2005; McCarthy, 1999b).

A singular emphasis on research can have multiple negative consequences for educational leadership programs. Rather than working cohesively within a department, research-oriented professors can operate as an independent collection of individuals who are disinterested in curricular revisions, field connections, clinical experiences, and student advising (Griffiths et al., 1888). Relationships with school districts can disintegrate rapidly if professors do not continuously maintain these connections, so departments strive to preserve a balance between the interests of the university and the field. Peterson and Finn (1988) have noted that educational leadership professors are ambivalent whether their primary responsibilities are clinical or intellectual. This uncertainty has produced unsatisfactory results; as Murphy (1992) noted, "In attempting to address the need to develop intradepartmental balance between professor-scholars attuned to the disciplines and professor-practitioners oriented to the field, departments have generally produced the worst of both" (p. 101). In a qualitative study involving interviews of 16 productive senior scholars in educational administration, Tschannen-Moran and Nestor-Baker (2004) noted that these professors acknowledged the difficulties in coping with the competing demands of teaching, research, and service to the field. They acknowledged, "As an applied field education cannot afford to become disconnected from the practice of schools" (p. 1502). Some of these individuals published in practitioner journals to ensure that their work remained relevant to practitioners. Of course, senior scholars have more flexibility in determining their publication outlets; untenured assistant professors may not be permitted similar levels of freedom with their scholarly decisions.

The triad upon which university faculty historically have been evaluated, promoted, and rewarded is comprised of the domains of teaching, research, and service. Faculty responsibilities within these three areas typically are apportioned into 40% teaching, 40% research, and 20% service. Particularly within major research universities, primary emphasis is placed upon demonstrating one's research competency and performance, and the service aspects of the position receive minimal consideration (McCarthy & Kuh, 1997). However, nearly two decades ago, Boyer (1990) challenged the prevailing wisdom of this approach and advanced a new and enlarged perspective related to faculty scholarship. Boyer noted that faculty should be engaged in the scholarship of four interrelated components: (a) discovery, (b) integration, (c) application, and (d) teaching. The scholarship of application is of particular relevance to the educational leadership profession, as it involves the application of knowledge to solve significant societal issues. Functioning under Boyer's definition of scholarship would permit educational leadership faculty members to engage in applied research activities and field-based projects in school settings and also to take a lead role in helping practitioners solve problems of practice. This approach is also consistent with Wynn's (1957/1972) observation 50 years ago that the "ideal professor of educational administration ought to be a competent scholar, teacher, counselor, researcher, field worker, and professional leader" (p. 493).

In 1987 the NCEEA recommended the adoption of the professional school model for educational leadership programs, noting, "Administrator preparation programs should be like those in professional schools which emphasize theoretical and clinical knowledge, applied research, and supervised practice" (p. 20). This model also has been endorsed by several scholars (Griffiths et al., 1988; Murphy, 1992; Wilson, 1993). The professional school model would help to resolve two enduring problems faced by the profession: promoting the restructuring of faculty reward systems in universities and valuing enhanced connections between universities and schools (Murphy, 1992).

Faculty have a collective mission that reaches beyond scholarship into the "important responsibilities that [are] connected with professional life" (Griffiths et al., 1988, p. 300), and they should be rewarded appropriately for field-based work, including applied research and clinical activities involving students and practitioners.

Griffiths et al. (1988) proposed a well-conceived, differentiated staffing model for educational leadership departments, which is more fully aligned to the professional school model. Educational leadership programs would include both tenure-track and clinical faculty in full-time lines, with role delineations in scholarly focus and responsibilities appropriate for a professional school. Clinical and tenure-track lines would operate on complementary appointments, with clinical faculty conducting applied research activities and tenure-track faculty engaged with scholarly research and theory-building activities. Describing clinical faculty as *field specialists*, Griffiths et al. explained that they primarily would direct the program's field-based elements:

> They would supervise interns, run the weekly intern seminars, and coordinate opportunities for colleagues and students to solve problems in the field. Their research would center on applied studies, the effects of administrator intervention, and case analysis. These professors might also teach field-study methods, case analysis, and other clinical studies. Despite the nontraditional nature of these roles, all professors would be expected to produce new knowledge directly related to school administration. (p. 300)

Hiring full-time clinical faculty also was endorsed by Peper (1988), who noted that programs must "balance their academic teaching faculty with a skilled clinical faculty if the paradigm of university-directed clinical education is to succeed" (p. 362).

As programs move toward a field orientation, issues related to faculty reward structures and the significant time investments necessary to build field partnerships continue to arise (Cambron-McCabe, 1999; Young et al., 2002). Reporting on the experiences of universities participating in the Danforth Program for the Preparation of School Principals, Wilson (1993) explained that professors were required to embrace new roles as they participated in clinical experiences and collaborative school-based research projects. Wilson noted, "The time-consuming and complex nature of developing and managing field-based programs must be recognized, allotted adequate time and resources, and rewarded" (p. 229). Staffing educational leadership faculties with some full-time, clinical faculty lines may be helpful in resolving some issues related to tenure-track faculty reward structures because, as field specialists, these individuals would assume primary responsibility for maintaining these connections.

Fully implementing a professional school model similar to that utilized in medical and law schools may prove to be a challenging undertaking for educational leadership professors, as they design a program based upon authentic problems of practice that are approached from a clinical training perspective. Forsyth and Murphy (1999) explained, "Having separated the delivery of practice knowledge and technical knowledge for so long, and having effectively removed practice preparation from the university, professors are not well prepared to plan, organize, and provide this critical part of professional preparation" (p. 268).

Even though it has been 20 years since the NCEEA recommended the professional school approach for leadership preparation, it does not appear that this suggestion has been implemented in a large number of institutions. The literature does not contain any reports of changed models, and no empirical evidence appears to exist documenting educational leadership professors' restructured performance expectations. As recently as 2002, Young et al. highlighted the continuing dilemma of the profession: "We are measured, promoted, and expected to become prolific scholars" (p. 160). Therefore, although professors' roles appear to be changing to embrace connections to the field (McCarthy, 1999b), faculty members continue to be confronted with institutional norms that reinforce traditional conceptions of the professoriate.

Preparation of Faculty for University Educational Leadership Positions

There is very little research that specifically describes the preparation of faculty for educational leadership positions. Yet, there is an abundance of information analyzing the preparation and development programs available to general faculty at colleges and universities throughout the country. This section examines the essential elements within faculty preparation programs currently in place and the impact on university faculty.

One trend that emerged from the literature was the role of faculty mentoring and its influence on preparation of faculty members. Mentoring of beginning and newly hired faculty by experienced members of a department or college can have a positive influence on the trust, collaboration, and professional growth of faculty members (Perna, Lerner, & Yura, 1995; Savage, Karp, & Logue, 2004). In addition, mentoring can be helpful in socializing new faculty members into the norms of the profession and of the institution. Furthermore, the use of mentoring can enhance faculty collegiality (Heller & Sindelar, 1991), which is deemed to be the one of the most critical issues for college faculty (Ambrose, Huston, & Norman, 2005). Additional overarching outcomes that arise through the use of mentoring are empowering faculty by supporting their professional growth (Ambrose et al., 2005; Boice, 1992); improving the recruitment, retention, and promotion of new faculty (Kaye, 2000); and increasing productivity (Benson, Morahan, Sachdeva, & Richman, 2002).

The Department of Educational Leadership at Sam Houston State University exemplified the success that can be achieved when a successful mentoring program is implemented to support new and junior faculty. Edmonson et al. (2002) described how faculty collegiality helps each individual faculty member in all aspects of the professoriate, including teaching, scholarship, and service. The study illustrated how mentors assist new faculty in learning the culture of the institution. The end result is a continuous support system that ultimately will enhance and enrich the professional lives of the faculty.

Preparation for Research Development and Implementation

Preparation for research development has been emphasized as a key component for faculty growth. Although novice professors appear to perceive publishing responsibilities as a positive feature of the position (Pounder et al., 2004), the depth of research training provided within doctoral programs varies, and research requirements may be different for PhD and EdD degrees. Additionally, some individuals enter the professoriate several years after receiving their doctoral degrees and after they have concluded their K–12 educational careers (McCarthy & Kuh, 1997; Pounder et al., 2004). Therefore, individuals who do not transition into a professorial position immediately upon doctoral completion, as well as those who do not have extensive research training, may benefit from additional research training upon entering their faculty positions. One strategy found in the research was the use of an independent learning plan. This professional growth tool can be an effective mechanism for faculty members to plan, implement, assess, and evaluate their action research (Hubbell & Poole, 2004). Furthermore, the use of faculty presentations, cohort discussions, collaborative projects, and peer review all can have a dramatic influence on preparing faculty to conduct effective research (Hubbell & Poole, 2004).

Preparation for Teaching of Potential School Leaders: Pedagogical

The improvement of pedagogical skills of university faculty was determined to be another element of faculty preparation and development. Teaching and learning within the realm of higher education has been enhanced by recent advances in higher education pedagogical research and the willingness of institutions to use that research to assist faculty in improving their instructional approaches (Kilgore, 2001; Kolb & Boyatis, 2001). Effective strategies for enhancing faculty pedagogy include team teaching, collective faculty discussions regarding their teaching practices, and a shift in focus from mere curriculum content to a broader focus on teaching and student learning outcomes (Hubbell & Poole, 2003).

Preparation for Teaching of Potential School Leaders: Conceptual

Preparing aspiring professors for the teaching responsibilities may not be an arduous task, because many candidates already possess K–12 teaching and leadership experience. Furthermore, research consistently has disclosed that educational leadership professors perceive teaching duties in a favorable light and value this opportunity to influence the next generation of school leaders (McCarthy & Kuh, 1997; Pounder et al., 2004). Because of their previous K–12 teaching experiences, aspiring professors may not need training in instructional methods; however, they may need to develop a more comprehensive understanding of the teaching preferences and learning needs of adult learners.

One component of an effective faculty preparation program is increasing the ability of faculty members to use conceptual approaches when teaching. The conceptual approach to cooperative learning involves training professors to apply an overall system to build cooperative activities, lessons, and strategies (Johnson & Johnson, 1992). This approach is based on a theoretical framework that provides general principles regarding how to structure cooperative learning activities in a teacher's specific subject area, curriculum, students, and setting. Hubbell and Poole (2004) explained the influence on one's teaching through this approach: "I have developed a sound pedagogical knowledge, and acquired various conceptual frameworks for teaching and learning" (p. 21).

Numerous trends emerge when analyzing what the future may hold for faculty in leadership preparation programs. Balancing faculty roles increasingly will be important as faculty members take on teaching, research, service, advising, grant proposal writing responsibilities, and administrative roles (Austin, 2003). Additionally, the role of technology integration, a commitment to diversity, new instructional approaches, and assessment of teaching and student learning outcomes will alter the scope and sequence of current faculty preparation programs (Dezure, 1993). The goal of the institution is to adapt to these changes while ensuring that teaching excellence is sustained and—ideally—improved. It is this excellence in teaching that will lead to excellence in student learning (Austin, 2003).

The issue of balance is an important consideration, because novice professors need to maintain equilibrium between their personal lives and professional responsibilities. For example, Pounder et al. (2004) found that "married persons were less likely to pursue or accept an educational leadership professor position" (p. 517). This finding may be explained by a variety of factors, including one's inability to relocate absent employment for the trailing spouse, an unwillingness to accept a professor's salary, and the professional demands of the professoriate. Individuals with doctoral degrees have indicated that they are only somewhat likely to seek out an educational leadership professor position (Pounder et al., 2004), which should be cause for concern among those currently holding professorial positions.

Professional Development of Educational Leadership Faculty

This section reviews the research on the types of professional development activities that are designed primarily to enhance educational leadership faculty members' effectiveness in the areas of scholarship and teaching. Professional development can take two forms: providing professors with the skills to better prepare school leaders for their dramatically changing roles and assisting professors in remaining current with research methods. Unfortunately, very little published literature exists related to professional growth of educational leadership faculty.

A program of continuous professional growth is an important element to ensure that educational leadership faculty members maintain current with the practice elements of the profession and also improve their professional performance. The NCEEA (1987) acknowledged this fact, recommending that professors' annual performance reviews should include a professional development component:

> Changes in preparation programs, a maturing research capacity, and requirements for knowledge relevant to administrative practice, make professional development of professors of educational administration particularly crucial. The development plan should be formalized so that its importance is evident and so that planning can be done to fund aspects of the plan calling for external resources. (p. 21)

Hawley (1988) noted that institutional support for professional growth has been deficient: "There is virtually no investment in targeted and systematic professional upgrading of faculty" (p. 84). According to Griffiths et al. (1988), travel to professional conferences and institutional support for professors' research were the two primary mechanisms by which educational leadership faculty members improved their competence in the 1980s. A decade later, McCarthy's (1999b) research disclosed that professors' primary professional development venues were conference attendance and reading on their own. For those universities that have experienced decreasing state support for higher education, fewer funds are available to support the professional development needs of faculty, including travel to conferences (Murphy, 1999a; Young et al., 2002).

McCarthy and Kuh (1997) have taken a very narrow view of faculty professional development, viewing it only as "travel to professional meetings" (p. 283). A variety of additional approaches also can assist professors, including "services to improve instruction, sabbaticals, exchange programs, retooling opportunities, career development services, and fellowship programs" (Griffiths et al., 1988, p. 302). Other mechanisms include partnering with school districts and collaborating with other educational leadership programs to share experiences related to program improvements (Young et al., 2002). Although these mechanisms undoubtedly are utilized by educational leadership professors, no published research was uncovered documenting their efficacy in improving professors' practices. Therefore, the quality of these experiences and their effectiveness in promoting professors' growth or facilitating the improvement of their preparation programs currently is unknown (Young et al., 2002).

Analysis of the very limited research on educational leadership faculty professional development confirmed that these opportunities are exceedingly limited (Murphy, 1999a; Young et al., 2002). Reporting the results of a survey conducted with 44 chairs of UCEA-member educational leadership departments, Murphy (1999a) found that development opportunities for faculty members were minimal and "were almost uniformly ad hoc in nature" (p. 189). Nearly all identified opportunities were individualistic, consisting mainly of professors attending conferences to present papers or to learn from other research presentations. Relatively few activities were linked to organizational improvement, with the exception being workshops designed to upgrade faculty members' skills with technology. Interviewing educational leadership department chairs in five research universities, M. J. Harris (2005) concluded that effective chairs perceive that they do, indeed, provide resources and professional development opportunities for their faculty members. Wolverton and Ackerman (2006) reported on faculty professional development seminars at the University of Nevada–Las Vegas; these seminars, however, were provided only for professors who had been identified as prospective academic department chairs. This program was judged beneficial in providing networking opportunities for aspiring chairs, providing context-specific training, fostering leadership growth, and permitting faculty an opportunity to explore chair leadership to determine occupational fit. In a dissertation study of college of education faculty in one university, Albrecht (2003) determined that professors who worked together to prepare and deliver a teacher education course were engaged in a form of collaborative professional development. Through their activities, these individuals learned from one another and ultimately transformed their teaching practices.

Unlike such fields as law and medicine, where university faculty members remain current by continuing to practice their profession, educational leadership professors rarely are able to serve as school administrators. However, such arrangements as consulting with local districts and contracting services with state agencies do provide opportunities for professors to remain engaged in the profession. Sabbaticals or "faculty improvement leaves" also can permit professors to return to school administrative positions, upgrade their administrative skills, and experience the changing role expectations of school leaders. Whitaker (1999) reported being involved in a job exchange, in which she served a 1-year stint as elementary principal, after 10 years in the professoriate. She experienced a tremendous learning curve, finding that the work environment had changed significantly and had become more chaotic. She discovered that the principal's workload had greatly expanded and that principals must maintain access to a multitude of information. The principal's role also had changed dramatically, as principals were expected to be instructional leaders and to involve others in the decision-making process. Certainly, sabbatical opportunities such as the one experienced by Whitaker can assist professors in understanding the evolving challenges of leading today's schools and school systems and can enhance their teaching effectiveness when they return to their academic posts.

University faculty mentoring programs afford an opportunity to socialize novice assistant professors into the profession as well as to assist new professors in learning institutional policies and practices (Savage et al., 2004). Reporting on such a program at the University of Wisconsin–Madison, Ackerman, Ventimiglia, and Juchniewicz (2002) asserted that both senior faculty members who served as mentors and novice professors (the protégés) experienced professional growth from these collaborative relationships. Other reported benefits of formal mentoring programs included a more supportive faculty culture throughout the university campus, encouragement to participate in the university's governance system to effect change, and enhanced faculty relationships.

The Danforth Program for Professors of School Administration, funded by the Danforth Foundation, involved faculty teams from educational leadership programs in 22 universities over a 6-year period (1987–1993) and represented an opportunity for faculty members to explore their craft. The programs encouraged faculty teams to incorporate knowledge about current key issues into their course experiences, and many reported that their faculty improved their teaching effectiveness. All programs adopted the cohort format and implemented extensive field-based experiences, finding that these approaches were important to ensure program integrity. Additionally, a significant majority of programs reported extensive collaboration with school districts, professional organizations, and educational agencies (Cordeiro et al., 1993). Undoubtedly, these activities were important mechanisms to promote the professional growth of participating faculty members. Those involved in the Danforth program asserted that the procurement of "risk capital" was vitally important to ensure that faculty could engage in program planning, design, and implementation (Milstein, 1993, p. 207); again, the importance of appropriate funding levels is highlighted to ensure continuous faculty development.

The Danforth Foundation also funded a second program that focused on doctoral programs in the Danforth Program for Professors of Administration that involved four cycles and 21 universities (1987–1993). This program gave faculty an in-depth opportunity to come together in teams to engage in substantive reforms of their leadership preparation programs (Mulkeen, Cambron-McCabe, & Anderson, 1994). As the cycles progressed, some common understandings developed about the nature of leadership, leaders' roles in schools, and faculty roles in preparing leaders. Overarching ideas included leadership as an intellectual and moral practice, instructional approaches that provide opportunities for future leaders to become reflective about their actions, need for a wide array of laboratory settings collaboratively operated by universities and school districts, program structures that enable students to function as members of a learning community, and a research agenda focused on clinical inquiry in the problems of practice (Cambron-McCabe, Mulkeen, & Wright, 1991) The program provided an opportunity for faculty to identify their professional development needs relative to the new programs that were being created.

Despite the dearth of current research on professional development, Young et al. (2002) noted that several professional groups have emerged in recent years that are dedicated to changing instructional practices and revising curricular content in educational leadership preparation programs. These groups include the Learning and Teaching in Educational Leadership Special Interest Group of the AERA, networks that grew out of the Danforth Program for the Preparation of School Principals, and the Taskforce on Evaluating Leadership Preparation Programs sponsored jointly by the Learning and Teaching in Educational Leadership Special Interest Group and the UCEA. These initiatives hold the potential for creating quality of professional development opportunities for educational leadership faculty and for researching their effectiveness.

Tensions Within the Professoriate

As we reviewed the research about the professoriate, we noted several tensions that merit consideration. These areas have implications for how faculty members think about their teaching and scholarship as well as the design of their preparation programs.

Roles and Orientation of Faculty

As is evident in this chapter, faculty in educational leadership programs fill varied roles—from tenure-line faculty to clinical or field-based faculty to part-time adjunct faculty. Examining the research regarding these roles offers only a partial understanding of the faculty who specialize in this field or the mix of roles needed to achieve program goals. Further, these faculty roles vary significantly across different types of institutions (i.e., research, doctoral, comprehensive, master's), with each holding diverse expectations for its faculty members. Yet, the critiques of educational leadership faculty members and programs tend to conflate the role and institutional differences— differences that create tension within specific programs and among different types of institutions (Levine, 2005; NCEEA, 1987). Starratt (2006) argued that such tensions in faculty roles and orientations must be made explicit and considered by departments as they attempt to achieve program goals. Tensions exist regarding differences in faculty members' backgrounds, experiences, capacities, leadership views, and role expectations.

Recognizing the complexity of describing this landscape without oversimplifying the tensions, Starratt (2006) offered a three-dimensional matrix that examines faculty members' research-and-practice orientation, leadership orientation, and role and background. Under the research-and-practice dimension, three orientations are identified: (a) research, (b) reflective practice, and (c) practice. The research orientation is one most associated with research universities where faculty members conduct and publish research and prepare others to do research. The reflective-practice orientation includes faculty focused on integrating theory and practice in their scholarship and teaching as well as preparing leaders for reflective practice. Faculty members with a practice orientation work in schools to support leaders in change and improvement efforts. These three orientations can be seen in various combinations in educational leadership programs. The tension centers on how faculty connect to the program goals and how they are valued for that contribution within the program and broader institution.

Starratt's (2006) second dimension relates to faculty members' deeply held beliefs about the role of leaders. Under the leadership dimension, three orientations are described: (a) transactional leadership, (b) transformational leadership, and (c) radical leadership. Faculty members focusing on transactional leadership work to sustain traditional institutions and their core values; technical and political skills to management the schools are paramount. Faculty members adhering to transformational leadership prepare leaders to transform the school structures and processes to attain more equitable, quality programs for all students. Those who focus on radical leadership work to educate leaders to challenge existing structures and power relationships; their work is embedded in concerns for social justice and promoting democratic deliberation and civic engagement. Faculty members' leadership orientation drives not only their own teaching and research, but also program content.

The third dimension that Starratt (2006) identified is the role that individual faculty members fill in the department and their related background and experiences. This role and background dimension has three orientations: (a) tenure-track faculty with doctorates in educational leadership, administration, and policy; (b) tenure-track faculty with doctorates outside the education field; and (c) clinical faculty with doctorates in the field and careers in practice. Tenure-track faculty with educational administration backgrounds typically direct their scholarship toward the traditional educational leadership arenas, such as leadership, organizational change, school reform, and law. Tenure-track faculty with doctorates in other fields supplement instruction from wide-ranging fields, such as social theory, political science, anthropology, and psychology. Although some of these faculty members hold full-time appointments in educational leadership programs, most do not. The last role, one that has grown in prominence, is the clinical professor. These faculty members come to programs with extensive leadership experience and often work under 4- or 5-year contracts. Under the arts and sciences model that dictates faculty culture, this two- or three-tiered faculty system is fraught with tension as programs attempt to meet the needs and expectations of an applied field of study.

Starratt's (2006) orientations and roles matrix highlights tension-producing dimensions of the faculty role—dimensions that vary significantly across types of institutions. For the most part, research has examined the types of faculty roles more from a demographic perspective than an analysis of the specific roles, the relationships among the roles, expectations for the different roles, and value or desirability of diverse roles. As McCarthy and Kuh (1997) noted, leadership programs have made substantial movement toward field-based practice, collaboration, and broad-based stakeholder involvement. What is not clear is which faculty members bear the responsibility for this work.

Gap Between Perceptions of Faculty Members and School Leaders

Tension has existed over time between how faculty members and practicing school leaders see the nature of administrators' daily work and its connection to preparation programs. Regardless of where administrators received their preparation, most of them neither see higher education preparation as relevant to their work nor see faculty members involved in the work of schools (Cambron-McCabe & Cunningham, 2002; Nestor-Baker & Hoy, 2001; Portin, Schneider, DeArmound, & Gundlach, 2003). Even though McCarthy and Kuh (1997) documented an increase in faculty members' involvement in the field, only 8% or slightly more of their time was dedicated to field activities—a fact that reinforces administrators' perception of a gap in understanding between the field and the academy. Although this refrain sounds familiar, it is far more than the long-standing theory versus practice divide.

Specifically, since 2000 school administrators have noted the increasing complexity of leading schools and the failure of higher education faculty members to respond to the new demands on schools and their leaders (Portin et al., 2003). Administrators describe demanding school environments that require wide-ranging capabilities spanning in-depth data analysis, diagnosis of problems, improvement of student learning, quality instruction, cultural competence, shared leadership, professional learning communities, technology expertise, and management of human and other resources. According to Portin et al., principals report that most of these capabilities are being developed through on-the-job experiences rather than through academic training. Such findings point to an impending crisis for faculty members and their relevance to leadership preparation. Young et al. (2002) noted the imperative for all stakeholders in the preparation of school leaders to come together "to develop shared understandings and common goals with regard to the future of leadership preparation" (p. 156). The current gap between leadership preparation and practice points to the critical need to bring educational leadership faculty members and school leaders together to create substantive changes in preparation programs.

Recommendations for Future Research on Educational Leadership Faculty

Although we have provided an exhaustive review of the research related to profiles of the educational leadership professoriate, many limitations and gaps are apparent within the existing literature base. The extent to which we have relied on data from the McCarthy and Kuh (1997) study is an indicator that no current data are available related to the profession. Many of the questions raised by these researchers persist and, given that we have now marched well into the 21st century, it is high time to expand upon the previous studies of the professoriate. Therefore, the profession must set out to amass current, comprehensive, descriptive data on a variety of issues that we have addressed in this chapter. In reviewing this research, we often found ourselves presenting data information or extrapolating data based on comprehensive studies focused on related questions or more generalized populations. In this concluding section, we provide a brief analysis of the research and present our recommendations for future research activities in these topical areas.

Characteristics of Faculty

Historically, characteristics of educational leadership faculty have received the most intensive and sustained attention, as documented by studies that have occurred approximately each decade since the 1960s (Boyan, 1981; Campbell & Newell, 1973; Hills, 1965; McCarthy & Kuh, 1997; McCarthy et al., 1988). Certainly, this research has been effective in providing a basic demographic profile of those individuals who teach in leadership preparation units, so that trends can be analyzed with each subsequent decade. Yet, these studies have some limitations. To date, these studies have not been grounded within any conceptual frameworks, such as those related to faculty role expectations or faculty socialization. One exception is the Pounder et al. (2004) study, which utilized job choice theory. Future studies could explore the existing literature base related to university faculty, to examine theoretical frameworks that may be applicable to educational leadership professors.

Comparisons across studies have been problematic, because earlier studies included faculty with concentrations in higher education administration (Campbell & Newell, 1973; McCarthy et al., 1988), and the NSOPF:04 dataset does not differentiate between educational leadership and higher education program faculties. Furthermore, few attempts have been made to distinguish characteristics of faculty across a variety of dimensions, such as tenure-line versus non-tenure-track appointments, full-time versus part-time faculty, educational leadership faculty versus all university faculty, and institutional classifications. Finally, survey methods have been the research tool of choice, and data have been reported through descriptive statistics. Future studies could employ qualitative methods, and quantitative studies could employ inferential statistics to identify any significant differences across faculty.

Research questions that cannot be answered fully based on existing research include the following: What are the current demographic profiles of the educational leadership professoriate holding tenure-line positions, including such factors as sex, ethnicity, age, marital status, administrative experience, salary, academic preparation, and rank? What are the demographic profiles of faculty who are not in tenure-track positions, including full-time clinical faculty and individuals maintaining part-time adjunct appointments? What are the perceptions of educational leadership professors who are members of underrepresented groups, including faculty of color, women, and gay/lesbian/bisexual/transgender professors? How do professors perceive that they enrich and diversify the profession as well as raise issues that need to be addressed? What challenges affect these individuals' effectiveness as productive faculty members? In what innovative ways have programs reconfigured salary structures, in order to attract experienced administrators into the professoriate?

Professional Work Activities and Changing Expectations

Changes have occurred in leadership preparation programs over the past several decades. First, despite calls for the elimination of traditional administrator training, the number of institutions offering leadership preparation continues to grow, existing programs continue to expand their off-campus offerings (Levine, 2005), and programs increasingly are experimenting with distance-learning options (Hackmann & Berry, 1999). This prolonged expansion, obviously, has implications for student quality, as multiple programs compete for a limited candidate pool. Consequently, to ensure sufficient student enrollments, faculty may elect to lower admissions criteria or may decide to recruit more aggressively. Either option has workload implications, as faculty either must dedicate more of their time to student recruitment or must devote more attention to improving the skills of students who are admitted with academic deficiencies. Additionally, anecdotal evidence exists indicating that the number of institutions offering doctoral degrees in educational leadership has increased, and trend data indicate that expectations for faculty productivity have increased (Houston et al., 2006; McCarthy & Kuh, 1997). NSOPF:04 data indicate that the professors' workweek has expanded in the past decade. Also, leadership preparation programs are being encouraged to develop more expansive relationships with practitioners and professional organizations (Murphy, 1999c; Young et al., 2002), which bring additional and unique demands for professors.

Although some attempts have been made in prior studies to differentiate programs according to the institutional classifications developed by the Carnegie Foundation for the Advancement of Teaching, the different faculty performance expectations that exist within institutional classifications could be explored in a more comprehensive fashion. However, making comparisons across studies is hindered by the fact that these Carnegie classifications have undergone several transformations in the past decade. For example, the highest classification initially was termed Research I, then Doctoral/Research–Extensive, and now Research Universities–Very High Research Activity (RU/VH). Further complicating comparisons, criteria for each classification have been modified with each subsequent iteration.

Although scholars have argued for a professional school model, the research does not clarify whether institutions are embracing this model. Evidence suggests that programs are relying on part-time faculty to a greater extent, but it is unclear whether the roles and responsibilities of tenure-track faculty have adjusted as programs incorporate more part-time appointments. Because the extant research on educational leadership faculty in non-tenure-track appointments—including both full-time clinical and part-time adjunct faculty—is very limited, there is little information to document the extent of use of individuals in these positions and to disclose how their roles and responsibilities are differentiated from tenure-track faculty positions. Also, changing NCATE and state accreditation requirements have necessitated that professors devote additional time to curriculum revision and performance-based assessments. It is not clear whether these changes have caused professors to reallocate their time to encompass these new responsibilities.

Additional research also is needed in the following areas: How are the work expectations of tenure-track faculty changing among the traditional responsibilities of teaching, scholarship and research, teaching and advising, and service? In what ways have programs implemented Boyer's (1990) expanded definition of scholarship in defining faculty roles and responsibilities? How are full-time, non-tenure-line faculty and part-time faculty responsibilities defined, and how are these positions conceptualized to complement tenure-track lines? How are programs reconceptualizing field connections, and what implications does a shift in orientation to the field have on faculty work and, perhaps, the structure of programs themselves? How do faculty perceptions of the roles and responsibilities of school administration compare with school administrators' perceptions? What implications does the use of distance-learning delivery mechanisms have for faculty work and scholarly productivity? Are programs embracing expanded definitions of research, and in what ways are research and publishing expectations changing for tenure-track faculty? Has the emerging federal emphasis on the "gold standard" of randomized experimental designs had an influence on professors' research and grant-writing activities?

Values and Attitudes

Existing studies have explored numerous values and attitudes of professors, including their job satisfaction, attractions to the profession, willingness to relocate, desire to connect with practitioners, perceptions of problems within the profession, attitudes regarding the programs' mission to prepare academics or practitioners, belief systems regarding research, and perceptions of program quality. The literature has indicated that professors' values and attitudes have remained generally unchanged (Campbell & Newell, 1973; McCarthy & Kuh, 1997; McCarthy et al., 1988). These findings, however, must be tempered in light of the significant retirements that were forecast for the profession. Undoubtedly, an infusion of new professors—particularly those who increase the diversity within programs—would influence the institutional culture and prevailing faculty norms. Although McCarthy and Kuh noted that women have tended to adopt the values and attitudes of male professors, more recent research (Rusch, 2004) has indeed noted differences in perceptions between male and female professors. Minority professors also have expressed beliefs and values that differ from those of Caucasian faculty members (McCarthy & Kuh, 1997).

While future research should continue to explore the values and attitudes that traditionally have been surveyed, other topics could be explored. For example, research related to the extent of faculty members' commitment to social justice issues, equity, and diversity would be valuable. Faculty members' values and attitudes regarding the No Child Left Behind (2002) accountability mandates have not been investigated. Another topic that has remained unexplored is faculty members' levels of commitment to the training and placement of females and minorities in school leadership posts and professorial positions. Potential research questions include the following: What differences exist in values and attitudes of minority and majority faculty and of men and women? Have these values and attitudes changed over time? How do educational leadership professors' values and belief systems compare with other university faculty? What conflicts, if any, have ensued within leadership programs as the faculties become more diverse, and how have faculty members resolved these conflicts? How have faculty reconciled increasing institutional expectations for scholarly research with their commitments to the field?

Preparation of Faculty for University Educational Leadership Positions

Although an extensive amount of literature is related to preparation of aspiring faculty members, the research related to educational leadership professors is minimal. Within the literature, concerns have been expressed regarding the adequacy of preparation of future educational leadership faculty members, particularly as it relates to research training (Murphy, 1999c). Research has indicated that a number of individuals enter the professoriate after successful administrative careers (McCarthy & Kuh, 1997; Pounder et al., 2004), a phenomenon that may or may not be unique to the field of educational leadership on university campuses. However, relatively unexplored has been the role socialization of these individuals into their new professions. Hackmann's (2007) study of clinical faculty, all former school administrators, disclosed that these individuals experienced some difficulties in adjusting to the university norms and governance systems as well as in understanding issues related to faculty autonomy.

Because the topic of the preparation of aspiring educational leadership professors has not been examined adequately, this area is ripe for investigation. Questions that can be explored include the following: What formal programs exist, if any, to provide training for aspiring educational leadership professors, and how effective have these programs been in preparing individuals to assume these positions? What unique features should be included for underrepresented groups (i.e., women and minorities) to more fully prepare them for their roles? What programs exist, if any, to provide training for individuals currently in administrative roles who aspire to the professoriate? What unique training needs do these individuals have, to assure that they understand the university culture, norms, and role expectations?

Professional Development of Faculty

An analysis of the research related to professional development of educational leadership faculty disclosed that scholars traditionally have narrowly defined this activity—as travel to professional conferences (McCarthy & Kuh, 1997). The literature indicates that faculty primarily are left to their own devices, as they must seek out individual opportunities for professional growth (Murphy, 1999a). With the possible exception of activities emerging from the Danforth Program for the Preparation of School Principals (Milstein, 1993) and the Danforth Program for Professors of School Administration (Mulkeen et al., 1994), it does not appear that any formal professional development opportunities have been designed for those who serve in educational leadership faculty positions. Therefore, at this point in time, research efforts would be limited to ascertaining faculty members' involvement in those activities in which they have participated as individuals.

Research into this area, of necessity, must begin with an identification of professional development activities in which professors engage. Subsequent studies could investigate faculty members' perceptions of the quality of these experiences and their efficacy in promoting their professional growth. As programs continue to shift emphasis, it is important to know what options exist for current faculty for development in emerging programmatic emphases and pedagogies. Further, it would be interesting to learn whether professors of color and women seek out different professional growth opportunities. Also, it would be of interest to learn whether novice professors assert the need for different professional development experiences than veteran professors.

Conclusion

As noted from the extensive agenda identified for future research, this chapter may be more enlightening for what we did not discover than for the research that we have reported. The documented paucity of recent research about educational leadership faculty challenges both faculty and their graduate students to consider the identified research gaps as they develop their own research agendas. For too long, critiques of educational leadership faculty and programs have been based on partial knowledge and understandings, or on data that may no longer be current. Furthermore, a broad brush has been used to paint a composite profile of faculty across the nation, in the process blurring the differences between leadership preparation programs in different institutional types. The resultant profile of the profession, unfortunately, does not illuminate the complexity of the roles and the wide-ranging contexts that exist across programs and institutions. Expanding the research on who we are and what we value and believe can inform the profession as we grapple with the evolution of faculty roles and preparation programs and at the same time enlighten our critics. In learning more about ourselves as a profession, we can be better positioned to train future generations of school leaders.

References

Ackerman, R., Ventimiglia, L., & Juchniewicz, M. (2002). The meaning of mentoring: Notes on a context for learning. In K. Leithwood & P. Hallinger (Eds.), *Second international handbook of educational leadership and administration* (pp. 1133–1161). Dordrecht, the Netherlands: Kluwer.

Adjunct professors. (2002, November). [Special issue]. *School Administrator.*

Albrecht, N. M. R. (2003). University faculty collaboration and its impact on professional development (Doctoral dissertation, Kansas State University, 2003). *Dissertation Abstracts International, 64,* 1546.

Ambrose, S., Huston, T., & Norman, M. (2005). A qualitative method for assessing faculty satisfaction. *Research in Higher Education, 46*(7), 803–830.

American Association of University Professors. (2003, November). *Contingent appointments and the academic profession.* Retrieved January 31, 2007, from http://www.aaup.org/AAUP/pubsres/policydocs/conting-stmt.htm

American Association of University Professors. (2006). The devaluing of higher education: The annual report of the economic status of the profession 2005–06. *Academe, 92*(2), 24–50.

Austin, A. E. (2003). Creating a bridge to the future: Preparing new faculty to face changing expectations in a shifting context. *The Review of Higher Education, 26*(2), 119–144.

Barnett, B. G., Basom, M. R., Yerkes, D. M., & Norris, C. J. (2000). Cohorts in educational leadership programs: Benefits, difficulties, and the potential for developing school leaders. *Educational Administration Quarterly, 36,* 255–282.

Benjamin, E., Hollinger, D. A., & Knight, J. (2005). Professors of practice. *Academe, 91*(1), 60–61.

Benson, C. A., Morahan, P. S., Sachdeva, A. K., & Richman, R. C. (2002). Effective faculty preceptoring and mentoring during reorganization of an academic medical center. *Medical Teacher, 24,* 550–557.

Björk, L. G., & Thompson, T. E. (1989). The next generation of faculty minority issues. *Education and Urban Society, 21,* 341–351.

Blount, J. M. (1998). *Destined to rule the schools: Women and the superintendency, 1873–1995.* Albany: State University of New York Press.

Boice, R. (1992). *The new faculty member: Supporting and fostering professional development.* San Francisco: Jossey-Bass.

Boyan, N. (1981). Follow the leader: Commentary on research in educational administration. *Educational Researcher, 10*(2), 6–13.

Boyer, E. L. (1990). *Scholarship reconsidered: Priorities of the professoriate.* Lawrenceville, NJ: Princeton University Press.

Bredeson, P. V. (1996). New directions in the preparation of educational leaders. In K. Leithwood, J. Chapman, D. Corson, P. Hallinger, & A. Hart (Eds.), *International handbook of educational leadership and administration* (pp. 251–277). Dordrecht, The Netherlands: Kluwer.

Bridges, E. M. (1982). Research on the school administrator: The state of the art, 1967–1980. *Educational Administration Quarterly, 18,* 12–33.

Bridges, E. M. (1992). *Problem-based learning for administrators.* Eugene, OR: ERIC Clearinghouse on Educational Management.

Cambron-McCabe, N. H. (1999). Confronting fundamental transformation of leadership preparation. In J. Murphy & P. B. Forsyth (Eds.), *Educational administration: A decade of reform* (pp. 217–227). Thousand Oaks, CA: Corwin Press.

Cambron-McCabe, N., & Cunningham, L. (2002). National Commission for the Advancement of Educational Leadership: Opportunity for transformation. *Educational Administration Quarterly, 38,* 289–299.

Cambron-McCabe, N. H., & McCarthy, M. (2005). Educating school leaders for social justice. *Educational Policy, 19,* 201–222.

Cambron-McCabe, N., Mulkeen, T., & Wright, G. (1991, April). *A new platform for preparing school leaders: The Danforth Program for Professors of School Administration.* St. Louis, MO: Danforth Foundation.

Campbell, R. F., & Newell, L. J. (1973). *A study of professors of educational administration.* Columbus, OH: University Council for Educational Administration.

Cataldi, E. F., Fahimi, M., Bradburn, E. M., & Zimbler, L. (2004). *2004 national study of postsecondary faculty (NSOPF:04) report on faculty and instructional staff in Fall 2003*. Washington, DC: National Center for Education Statistics. Retrieved January 5, 2007, from http://nces.ed.gov/pubs2005/2005172.pdf

Clery, S. (2002). Faculty satisfaction. *NEA Higher Education Research Center Update, 8*(2). Retrieved December 20, 2006, from http://www2.nea.org/he/heupdate/images/vol8no2.pdf

Cordeiro, P. A., Krueger, J. A., Parks D., Restine, N., & Wilson, P. T. (1993). Taking stock: Learnings gleaned from universities participating in the Danforth program. In M. M. Milstein (Ed.), *Changing the way we prepare educational leaders: The Danforth experience* (pp. 17–38). Newbury Park, CA: Corwin Press.

Culbertson, J. A. (1988). A century's quest for a knowledge base. In N. J. Boyan (Ed.), *Handbook of research on educational administration* (pp. 3–26). White Plains, NY: Longman.

DeZure, D. (1993). Using cases about teaching in the disciplines. *Change, 25*(6), 40–43.

Donmoyer, R. (1999). The continuing quest for a knowledge base: 1976–1998. In J. Murphy & K. S. Louis, *The handbook of research on educational administration* (2nd ed., pp. 25–44). San Francisco: Jossey-Bass.

Edmonson, S., Fisher, A., Brown, G., Irby, B., Lunenburg, F., Creighton, T., et al. (2001, August). *Creating a collaborative culture*. Paper presented at the annual meeting of the National Council of Professors of Educational Administration, Houston, TX. (ERIC Document Reproduction Service No. ED470755)

English, F. W. (2006). The unintended consequences of a standardized knowledge base in advancing educational leadership preparation. *Educational Administration Quarterly, 42*, 461–472.

Erickson, E. A. (1967). The school administrator. *Review of Educational Research, 37*, 417–432.

Erickson, E. A. (1979). Research on educational administration: The state-of-the-art. *Educational Researcher, 8*(3), 9–14.

Firestone, W. A., & Riehl, C. (Eds.). (2005). *A new agenda for research in educational leadership*. New York: Teachers College Press.

Forsyth, P. B., & Murphy, J. (1999). A decade of changes: Analysis and comment. In J. Murphy & P. B. Forsyth (Eds.), *Educational administration: A decade of reform* (pp. 253–272). Thousand Oaks, CA: Corwin.

Foster, W. (1988). Educational administration: A critical appraisal. In D. E. Griffiths, R. T. Stout, & P. B. Forsyth (Eds.), *Leaders for America's schools: The report and papers of the National Commission on Excellence in Educational Administration* (pp. 68–81). Berkeley, CA: McCutchan.

Glickman, C. D. (2002). *Leadership for learning: How to help teachers succeed*. Alexandria, VA: Association for Supervision and Curriculum Development.

Granger, M. (1993). A review of the literature on the status of women and minorities in the professoriate in higher education. *Journal of School Leadership, 3*, 121–135.

Griffiths, D. E. (1988). The professorship revisited. In D. E. Griffiths, R. T. Stout, & P. B. Forsyth (Eds.), *Leaders for America's schools: The report and papers of the National Commission on Excellence in Educational Administration* (pp. 273–283). Berkeley, CA: McCutchan.

Griffiths, D. E., Stout, R. T., & Forsyth, P. B. (Eds.). (1988). *Leaders for America's schools: The report and papers of the National Commission on Excellence in Educational Administration*. Berkeley, CA: McCutchan.

Grogan, M. (1999). Equality/equality issues of gender, race, and class. *Educational Administration Quarterly, 35*, 518–536.

Hackmann, D. G. (2003). The promotion/tenure dilemma: Maintaining a research agenda while developing distance learning teaching excellence. *Journal of Technology and Teacher Education, 11*, 307–319.

Hackmann, D. G. (2007). Roles and responsibilities of clinical faculty in selected educational leadership programs. *Planning and Changing, 38*, 17–34.

Hackmann, D. G., & Berry, J. E. (1999). Distance learning in educational administration doctoral programs: The wave of the future? *Journal of School Leadership, 9*, 349–367.

Hagedorn, L. S. (2000). Conceptualizing faculty job satisfaction: Components, theories, and outcomes. In L. S. Hagedorn (Ed.), *New Directions for Institutional Research*: Vol. 105. *What contributes to job satisfaction among faculty and staff* (pp. 5–20). San Francisco: Jossey-Bass.

Harris, M. J. (2005). Effective leadership by department chairs in educational leadership/administration departments (Doctoral dissertation, University of Missouri-Columbia, 2004). *Dissertation Abstracts International, 66*, 426.

Harris, S. L. (2006). Changing leadership paradigms and practices of doctoral students. *AASA Journal of Scholarship and Practice, 2*(4), 5–11.

Hart, A. W., & Naylor, K. (1992, April). *The organizational socialization of clinical faculty*. Paper presented at the annual meeting of the American Educational Research Association, San Francisco. (ERIC Reproduction Service No. ED345612)

Hart, A. W., & Pounder, D. G. (1999). Reinventing preparation programs: A decade of activity. In J. Murphy & P. B. Forsyth (Eds.), *Educational administration: A decade of reform* (pp. 115–151). Thousand Oaks, CA: Corwin Press.

Hawley, W. D. (1988). Universities and the improvement of school management. In D. E. Griffiths, R. T. Stout, & P. B. Forsyth (Eds.), *Leaders for America's schools: The report and papers of the National Commission on Excellence in Educational Administration* (pp. 82–88). Berkeley, CA: McCutchan.

Hearn, J. C., & Anderson, M. S. (2001). Clinical faculty in schools of education: Using staff differentiation to address disparate goals. In W. G. Tierney (Ed.), *Faculty work in schools of education: Rethinking roles and rewards for the twenty-first century* (pp. 125–149). Albany: State University of New York Press.

Heller, M., & Sindelar, N. (1991). *Developing an effective teacher mentoring program: Fastback 319.* Bloomington, IN: Phi Delta Kappa Educational Foundation.

Hills, J. (1965). Educational administration: A field in transition. *Educational Administration Quarterly, 1*(1), 58–66.

Houston, D., Meyer, L. H., & Paewai, S. (2006). Academic staff workloads and job satisfaction: Expectations and values in academe. *Journal of Higher Education Policy and Management, 28*(1), 17–30.

Howe, R. D. (2000). *Salary-trend study of faculty in educational administration and supervision for the years 1996–97 and 1999–00.* Washington, DC: College and University Personnel Association. (ERIC Document Reproduction Service No. ED442381)

Hubbell, H., & Poole, G. (2003). A learning-centered faculty certificate programme on university teaching. *International Journal for Academic Development, 8*(1/2), 11–24.

Huber, S. G., & West, M. (2002). Developing school leaders: A critical review of current practices, approaches, and issues, and some directions for the future. In K. Leithwood & P. Hallinger (Eds.), *Second international handbook of educational leadership and administration* (pp. 1071–1101). Dordrecht, The Netherlands: Kluwer.

Iacona, C. M. (1987). A study of women and minority faculty of educational administration (Doctoral dissertation, Indiana University, 1987). *Dissertation Abstracts International, 48,* 2206.

Immegart, G. L. (1977). The study of educational administration, 1954–1974. In L. L. Cunningham, W. G. Hack, & R. O. Nystrand (Eds.), *Educational administration: The developing decades* (pp. 298–328). Berkeley, CA: McCutchan.

Interstate School Leaders Licensure Consortium. (1996). *Standards for school leaders.* Washington, DC: Council of Chief State School Officers.

Jackson, B. L., & Kelley, C. (2002). Exceptional and innovative programs in educational leadership. *Educational Administration Quarterly, 38,* 192–212.

Johnson, D. W., & Johnson, R. T. (1992). Positive interdependence: Key to effective cooperation. In R. Hertz-Lazarowitz & N. Miller (Eds.), *Interaction in cooperative groups: The theoretical anatomy of group learning* (pp. 174–199). New York: Cambridge University Press.

Kaye, H. J. (2000, April 21). One professor's dialectic of mentoring [Electronic version]. *Chronicle of Higher Education,* p. A68.

Kilgore, D. W. (2001). Critical and postmodern perspectives on adult learning. In S. Merriam (Ed.), *The new update on adult learning theory* (pp. 53–62). San Francisco: Jossey-Bass.

Kolb, D. A., & Boyatis, R. E. (2001). Experiential learning theory: Previous new directions. In R. J. Sternberg & L. Zhang (Eds.), *Perspectives on thinking, learning, and cognitive styles* (pp. 227–247). Mahwah, NJ: Erlbaum.

Levin, H. M. (2006). Can research improve educational leadership? *Educational Researcher, 35*(8), 38–43.

Levine, A. (2005). *Educating school leaders.* Washington, DC: The Education Schools Project. Retrieved December 20, 2006, from http://www.edschools.org/pdf/Final313.pdf

Lopez, G. (2003). The (racially neutral) politics of education: A critical race theory perspective. *Educational Administration Quarterly, 39,* 68–94.

Marland, S. P. (1960). Superintendents' concerns about research applications in educational administration. In R. F. Campbell & J. M. Lipham (Eds.), *Administrative theory as a guide to action* (pp. 21–36). Chicago: University of Chicago, Midwest Administration Center.

Marshall, C. (2004). Social justice challenges to educational administration: Introduction to a special issue. *Educational Administration Quarterly, 40,* 3–13.

Marshall, C., & Oliva, M. (2006). *Leadership for social justice: Making revolutions in education.* Thousand Oaks, CA: Corwin Press.

Marshall, C., & Ward, M. (2004). Strategic policy for social justice training for leadership. *Journal of School Leadership, 14,* 530–563.

McCarthy, M. M. (1986). Research in educational administration: Promising signs for the future. *Educational Administration Quarterly, 22,* 3–20.

McCarthy, M. M. (1988). The professoriate in educational administration: A status report. In D. E. Griffiths, R. T. Stout, & P. B. Forsyth (Eds.), *Leaders for America's schools: The report and papers of the National Commission on Excellence in Educational Administration* (pp. 317–331). Berkeley, CA: McCutchan.

McCarthy, M. M. (1999a). The "changing" face of the educational leadership professoriate. In J. Murphy & P. B. Forsyth (Eds.), *Educational administration: A decade of reform* (pp. 192–214). Thousand Oaks, CA: Corwin.

McCarthy, M. M. (1999b). The evolution of educational leadership preparation programs. In J. Murphy & K. S. Louis (Eds.), *The handbook of research on educational administration* (2nd ed., pp. 119–139). San Francisco: Jossey-Bass.

McCarthy, M. M. (1999c). How are school leaders prepared? Trends and future directions. *Educational Horizons, 77*(2), 74–81.

McCarthy, M. M., & Kuh, G. D. (1997). *Continuity and change: The educational leadership professoriate.* Columbia, MO: University Council for Educational Administration.

McCarthy, M. M., Kuh, G. D., Newell, L. J., & Iacona, C. M. (1988). *Under scrutiny: The educational administration professoriate.* Tempe, AZ: University Council for Educational Administration.

McKenzie, K., Skrla, L., & Scheurich, J. (2006). Preparing instructional leaders for social justice. *Journal of School Leadership, 16*, 158–170.

Milstein, M. M. (Ed.). (1993). *Changing the way we prepare educational leaders: The Danforth experience.* Newbury Park, CA: Corwin Press.

Milstein, M. (1999). Reflections on "The evolution of educational leadership programs." *Educational Administration Quarterly, 35*, 537–545.

Miskel, C., & Sandlin, T. (1981). Survey research in educational administration. *Educational Administration Quarterly, 17*(4), 1–20.

Mulkeen, T., Cambron-McCabe, N., & Anderson, B. (1994). *Democratic leadership: The changing context of administrative preparation.* Norwood, NJ: Ablex.

Murphy, J. (1992). *The landscape of leadership preparation: Reframing the education of school administrators.* Newbury Park, CA: Corwin Press.

Murphy, J. (1993). Ferment in school administration: Rounds 1–3. In J. Murphy (Ed.), *Preparing tomorrow's school leaders: Alternative designs* (pp. 1–38). University Park, PA: University Council for Educational Administration.

Murphy, J. (1999a). Changes in preparation programs: Perceptions of department chairs. In J. Murphy & P. B. Forsyth (Eds.), *Educational administration: A decade of reform* (pp. 170–191). Thousand Oaks, CA: Corwin Press.

Murphy, J. (1999b). *The quest for a center: Notes on the state of the profession of educational leadership.* Columbia, MO: University Council for Educational Administration.

Murphy, J. (1999c). The reform of the profession: A self-portrait. In J. Murphy & P. B. Forsyth (Eds.), *Educational administration: A decade of reform* (pp. 39–68). Thousand Oaks, CA: Corwin Press.

Murphy, J. (2002). Reculturing the profession of educational leadership: New blueprints. *Educational Administration Quarterly, 38*, 176–191.

Murphy, J. (2005). Unpacking the foundations of ISSLC standards and addressing concerns in the academic community. *Educational Administration Quarterly, 41*, 154–191.

Murphy, J., & Vriesenga, M. (2004). *Research on preparation programs in educational administration: An analysis* (UCEA monograph series). Columbia, MO: University Council for Educational Administration.

National Center for Education Statistics. (n.d.). *2004 National Study of Postsecondary Faculty—Institution Survey.* Retrieved December 1, 2006, from http://nces.ed.gov/dasol/tables/#ipeds

National Center for Education Statistics. (2005). *Digest of education statistics, 2005.* Washington, DC: Author.

National Commission on Excellence in Educational Administration. (1987). *Leaders for America's schools: The report of the National Commission on Excellence in Educational Administration.* Tempe, AZ: University Council for Educational Administration.

National Council for Accreditation of Teacher Education. (n.d.). *List of recognized programs per accredited institutions for educational leadership (ELCC).* Retrieved January 10, 2007, from http://www.ncate.org/public/recogPgmSPA.asp

National Policy Board for Educational Administration. (2002, January). *Standards for advanced programs in educational leadership for principals, superintendents, curriculum directors, and supervisors.* Retrieved January 10, 2007, from http://www.npbea.org/ELCC/ELCCStandards%20_5-02.pdf

Nestor-Baker, N. S., & Hoy, W. K. (2001). Tacit knowledge of school superintendents: Its nature, meaning, and content. *Educational Administration Quarterly, 37*, 59–86.

No Child Left Behind Act of 2001, Pub. L. No. 107-110, 115 Stat. 1425 (2002).

Obeng-Darko, E. (2003). Navigating the four-dimensional space of higher education: Storied narratives of women full professors as scholars and leaders in educational administration (Doctoral dissertation, University of Cincinnati, 2003). *Dissertation Abstracts International, 64*, 1929.

Olsen, D., Maple, S. A., & Stage, F. K. (1995). Women and minority faculty job satisfaction. *Journal of Higher Education, 66*, 267–291.

Ortiz, F. I., & Marshall, C. (1988). Women in educational administration. In N. J. Boyan (Ed.), *Handbook of research on educational administration* (pp. 123–141). White Plains, NY: Longman.

Oshagbemi, T. (1997). Job satisfaction and dissatisfaction in higher education. *Education & Training, 39*, 354–359.

Peper, J. B. (1988). Clinical education for school superintendents and principals: The missing link. In D. E. Griffiths, R. T. Stout, & P. B. Forsyth (Eds.), *Leaders for America's schools: The report and papers of the National Commission on Excellence in Educational Administration* (pp. 360–366). Berkeley, CA: McCutchan.

Perna, F. M., Lerner, B. M., & Yura, M. T. (1995). Mentoring and career development among university faculty. *Journal of Education, 17*(7), 31–45.

Peterson, K. D., & Finn, C. E., Jr. (1988). Principals, superintendents, and the administrator's art. In D. E. Griffiths, R. T. Stout, & P. B. Forsyth (Eds.), *Leaders for America's schools: The report and papers of the National Commission on Excellence in Educational Administration* (pp. 89–111). Berkeley, CA: McCutchan.

Portin, B., Schneider, P., DeArmound, M., & Gundlach, L. (2003). *Making sense of leading schools: A study of the school principalship.* Seattle, WA: Center on Reinventing Public Education.

Pounder, D. (1989). The gender gap in salaries of educational administration professors. *Educational Administration Quarterly, 25*, 181–201.

Pounder, D. (1994). Work incentives to attract clinical faculty. *People and Education, 2*(1), 14–36.

Pounder, D. G., Crow, G. M., & Bergerson, A. A. (2004). Job desirability of the university professoriate in the field of educational leadership. *Journal of School Leadership, 14,* 497–529.

Quezada, R. L., & Louque, A. (2004). The absence of diversity in the academy: Faculty of color in educational administration programs. *Education, 125,* 213–221.

Rayfield, R., Meahon, D., & Ughrin, T. (2004). Scholarly productivity: One element in the tenure process in educational administration and higher education programs. *AASA Journal of Scholarship and Practice, 1*(1), 3–6.

Reyes, P., Wagstaff, L. H., & Fusarelli, L. D. (1999). Delta forces: The changing fabric of American society and education. In J. Murphy & K. S. Louis (Eds.), *The handbook of research on educational administration* (2nd ed., pp. 183–201). San Francisco: Jossey-Bass.

Riehl, C., Larson, C. L., Short, P. M., & Reitzug, U. C. (2000). Reconceptualizing research and scholarship in educational administration: Learning to know, knowing to do, doing to learn. *Educational Administration Quarterly, 36,* 391–427.

Rosser, V. J. (2005). Measuring the change in faculty perceptions over time: An examination of their worklife and satisfaction. *Research in Higher Education, 46*(1), 81–108.

Rusch, E. A. (2004). Gender and race in leadership preparation: A constrained discourse. *Educational Administration Quarterly, 40,* 14–46.

Sanders, N. M., & Simpson, J. (2006, March). *Information and handouts for state education agencies updating the ISLLC Standards for School Leaders and the ELCC/NCATE program standards.* Washington, DC: Council of Chief State School Officers. Retrieved January 10, 2007, from http://www.ccsso.org/content/PDFs/ISLLC%20Update%20Talking%20Points%203%2D20%2D%2006.pdf

Savage, H. E., Karp, R. S., & Logue, R. (2004). Faculty mentorship at colleges and universities. *College Teaching, 52*(1), 21–24.

Schneider, J. (2003). *The unholy alliance between departments of educational administration and their "invisible faculty"* (Occasional paper). Arlington, VA: American Association of School Administrators. (ERIC Document Reproduction Service No. ED474643)

Scribner, J. P., & Donaldson, J. F. (2001). The dynamics of group learning in a cohort: From nonlearning to transformative learning. *Educational Administration Quarterly, 37,* 605–636.

Shakeshaft, C. (1999). The struggle to create a more gender-inclusive profession. In J. Murphy & K. S. Louis (Eds.), *The handbook of research on educational administration* (2nd ed., pp. 99–118). San Francisco: Jossey-Bass.

Shakeshaft, C. (2002). The shadowy downside of adjuncts. *The School Administrator, 59*(10), 29–30.

Starratt, R. J. (2006). *Preliminary considerations of conceptual debates and potential gaps in the research on "providers" of graduate educational leadership programs* (UCEA working paper on educational administration leadership programs). Austin, TX: University Council for Educational Administration.

Styron, R. A., Maulding, W., & Hull P. (2006). Practitioner vs. professor—Teacher preferences of educational leadership students. *College Student Journal, 40,* 293–303.

Tack, M. W., & Patitu, C. L. (1992). *Faculty job satisfaction: Women and minorities in peril.* Washington, DC: The George Washington University.

Terpstra, D. E., & Honoree, A. L. (2004). Job satisfaction and pay satisfaction levels of university faculty by discipline type and by geographic region. *Education, 124,* 528–539.

Tschannen-Moran, M., & Nestor-Baker, N. (2004). The tacit knowledge of productive scholars in education. *Teachers College Record, 106,* 1484–1511.

Whitaker, K. S. (1999). Going back to school as principal. *The School Administrator, 56*(8), 50–51.

Wilson, P. T. (1993). Pushing the edge. In M. M. Milstein (Ed.), *Changing the way we prepare educational leaders: The Danforth experience* (pp. 219–235). Newbury Park, CA: Corwin Press.

Wolverton, M., & Ackerman, R. (2006). Cultivating possibilities: Prospective department chair professional development and why it matters. *Planning for Higher Education, 34*(4), 14–23.

Wynn, R. (1972). *Unconventional methods and materials for preparing educational administrators* (ERIC/CEM state-of-the-knowledge series No. 15; UCEA monograph series No. 2). Danville, IL: Interstate. (Original work published 1957)

Young, M. D., Crow, G., Orr, M. T., Ogawa, R., & Creighton, T. (n.d.). *An educative look at "Educating school leaders."* Retrieved January 8, 2007, from www.ucea.org

Young, M. D., Petersen, G. J., & Short, P. M. (2002). The complexity of substantive reform: A call for interdependence among key stakeholders. *Educational Administration Quarterly, 38,* 137–175.

7

Curriculum in Leadership Preparation

*Understanding Where We Have Been in Order
to Know Where We Might Go*

KAREN F. OSTERMAN AND MADELINE M. HAFNER

Empirical study of leadership preparation programs in the last two decades has been neglected, with scholars and practitioners alike perceiving it as second-rate area of scholarly inquiry, less than rigorous (Levin, 2006), lacking legitimacy (Bogotch, 2001; M. D. Young, Peterson, & Short, 2002), and even "anemic" (Murphy, 2006, p. 60). Sustained investigation of curricular issues within leadership preparation has received even less attention. To address this gap, we offer an extensive review and discussion of research and scholarship pertaining to the curriculum in leadership preparation.

To provide a comprehensive understanding of curricular issues in leadership education as an area of study, we posed the following questions: What do we know empirically about the curriculum that shapes leadership preparation, and, conversely, what don't we know? How do we know, or what modes of inquiry have researchers used to develop this information? Finally, where might scholars focus future efforts regarding curricular issues in the field of leadership preparation? To respond to these and other questions, we (a) review research on the curriculum in the field of leadership preparation, (b) identify gaps in the research, and (c) offer suggestions to build a future research agenda that will enrich our understanding of the role that curriculum plays in the preparation of educational leaders. Before reviewing the literature, we provide a framework for thinking about this often-nebulous construct.

Defining Curriculum

Curriculum is an important topic within the field of educational leadership, particularly within the context of kindergarten through Grade 12 (K–12) schooling. The ideas of curriculum leadership, instructional leadership, and leadership for learning have evolved in our field as a stronger focus on student academic achievement has framed the broader educational conversation (J. F. Johnson & Uline, 2005; Mullen, Gordon, Greenlee, & Anderson, 2002; Pounder, Reitzug, & Young, 2002). Academics and administrators alike have engaged in debate on topics such as curriculum wars, culturally imbedded curriculum, multicultural curriculum, and the hidden curriculum (e.g., Eisner, 1996; Goodlad, 1994; P. Jackson, 1968, 1992; Pinar, 1999). While the focus of these scholars has been primarily on the curriculum enacted in K–12 schools rather than the curriculum offered in educator preparation programs, we draw our conceptualization of the term *curriculum* from this knowledge base in teacher education and curricular studies.

Derived from "the Latin *currere*, which means 'to run,' and its associated noun, translated as a *course*, or 'following a course of study'" (Neary, 2002, p. 33), curriculum is generally understood as what gets taught or what is learned in a given subject or content area, or a plan for learning (van den Akker, 2003). At the same time, in the absence of "orderly, technical terminology" (Toombs & Tierney, 1993, p. 177), the term is defined in different ways. Toombs and Tierney defined curriculum broadly as "an intentional design for learning negotiated by faculty in light of their special knowledge and in the context of social expectations and students' needs" (p. 183). Other scholars (Gwele, 2005; Kerr, as cited in Kelly, 2004; Toombs & Tierney, 1993; Walker, 2003) have referred to curriculum as the general plan for learning, the instructional system, the learning that actually occurs, or the substance that is being taught. For our purposes here, we define curriculum in a narrow way as the "what" of a given course or classroom interaction or the content of a particular educational endeavor.

Glatthorn (2000) delineated seven aspects of curricula: (a) the recommended curriculum, (b) the written curriculum, (c) the taught curriculum, (d) the supported curriculum, (e) the assessed curriculum, (f) the learned curriculum, and (g) the hidden curriculum. We describe each element of Glatthorn's framework next.

The *recommended curriculum* was described by Glatthorn (2000) as "that which is recommended by scholars and professional organizations" (p. 83). The recommended curriculum is what scholars in the field believe should be included.

The *written curriculum* is also referred to as the planned (Kelly, 2004), intended (Porter & Smithson, 2001), or formal (Goodlad, 1979) curriculum. The written curriculum involves "intentions as specified in curriculum documents and/or materials" (van den Akker, 2003, p. 3). In terms of K–12 schools, written curriculum is what "appears in state and locally produced documents, such as state standards, district scope and sequence charts, district curriculum guides, teachers' planning documents, and curriculum units" (Glatthorn, 2000, p. 83). It also includes "such policy tools as curriculum standards, frameworks, or guidelines that outline the curriculum teachers are expected to deliver" (Porter & Smithson, 2001, p. 2). In leadership education, then, the written curriculum includes professional standards as well as those statements of purpose, goals, and objectives typically reflected in program descriptions, course requirements, syllabi, and other program documents.

The *taught curriculum* is "that which teachers actually deliver day by day" (Glatthorn, 2000, p. 83). Also referred to as the enacted curriculum (Porter & Smithson, 2001, p. 3) or the experiential curriculum (Goodlad, 1979), the taught curriculum is the content that is designed and transmitted to students through the instructional process. According to Eisner (1985), the taught or operational curriculum "is the unique set of events that transpire within a classroom. It is what occurs between teachers and students and between students and students" (p. 47). Distinct from what students are actually learning in a given course of study, the taught curriculum includes descriptions of the learning experiences that take place within certain classes.

The *supported curriculum* is discussed less frequently in the literature on types of curriculum. The supported curriculum can be thought of as "those resources that support the curriculum—textbooks, software, and other media" (Glatthorn, 2000, p. 84) or, more generally, all of the informational resources that are part of the curriculum.

The *assessed curriculum,* according to Glatthorn (2000), is "that which appears in tests and performance measures" (p. 8). Porter and Smithson (2001) described it simply as "the knowledge that is assessed" (p. 3).

The *learned curriculum* or received curriculum (Kelley, 2004) is "the bottom-line curriculum—

the curriculum that students actually learn" (Glatthorn, 2000, p. 84). This dimension of curriculum is experiential, according to van den Akker (2003), and involves "learning experiences as perceived by learners" (p. 3) as well as outcomes of learning, including those measured by test scores (Porter & Smithson, 2001).

The *hidden curriculum,* also referred to as the null curriculum, includes what is not taught in schools. Curricular scholars have identified the presence of a hidden curriculum within any field of study (Glatthorn, 2000; Glatthorn, Boschee, & Whitehead, 2006; Kelly, 2004; Neary, 2002). Attributed to Philip Jackson in the late 1960s, the hidden curriculum consists of the unwritten purposes and goals of schooling, shaped by societal and organizational structures. According to Glatthorn, it is "the unintended curriculum. It defines what students learn from the physical environment, the policies, and the procedures of the school" (p. 84).

For the purposes of this chapter, we focus primarily on four of the seven dimensions of curriculum: (a) recommended, (b) written, (c) supported, and (d) taught. Although research regarding the remaining dimensions is addressed in other chapters in this book, we also review briefly research regarding learning that is linked directly to curriculum. Please see chapter 8 of this volume for a detailed discussion on learning and pedagogy, chapter 11 for specifics on assessing students, and chapter 12 for particulars on program evaluation.

Methods

Murphy and Vriesenga's (2004) review of empirical studies regarding leadership preparation was the starting place for the collection of articles that informed this chapter. Their review incorporated research articles published between 1975 and 2002 in four journals: (a) *Educational Administration Quarterly,* (b) the *Journal of School Leadership,* (c) the *Journal of Educational Administration,* and (d) *Planning and Changing.* We began with articles categorized as dealing with curriculum. We then reviewed the table of contents from issues of these same journals published from 2002–2006. After this initial search, we located abstracts for all pertinent articles then coded them as either empirical or nonempirical. Articles classified as empirical were those that included descriptive or analytic data. Nonempirical articles were retained only if they dealt with the "recommended" curriculum, that is, they maintained an advocacy stance regarding the leadership preparation curriculum. We then located the full text for all journal articles and categorized them, using Glatthorn's (2000) framework.

At this point, we expanded the search to identify other relevant articles through a series of ERIC database searches, focusing primarily on the period 1990–2006. In the first step, we focused exclusively on journal articles and then extended our search to include papers presented at professional conferences. We used a combination of search terms such as the following: *educational administration preparation, school leadership preparation, leadership* and *knowledge, administration preparation curriculum,* and *educational administration knowledge.* Other key words included *administrator education, leadership training/preparation, school administration, educational leadership literature,* and *knowledge base.* From these searches, we identified articles that included any reference to the curriculum in leadership preparation. In some cases, references in the articles led to other publications. In all, we reviewed over 400 articles, abstracting and analyzing for content themes.

The Recommended Curriculum

In this section, we review the literature in the field of leadership education that describes the recommended curriculum, that is, assertions regarding what "should" be included in the preparation of school administrators. Stated somewhat differently, this research studied perceptions regarding what school leaders should know and be able to do. Much of the literature regarding the leadership curriculum falls into this category.

It is important to note that the majority of recommendations regarding what should be included in the curriculum are theoretical arguments based on logic, with the rationale grounded in theory or research. Such arguments frequently are responses to perceived or documented problems or shortcomings in K–12 schools and school leadership or weaknesses and omissions in the curriculum of educational leadership preparation programs. However, a few primary research studies have concentrated specifically on the recommended curriculum. These studies typically examined student, graduate, and administrator perceptions of what should be included in the leadership preparation curriculum. The rationale for many of these studies reflected the view that the voices of these groups needed to be incorporated into ongoing efforts to reform leadership preparation. Before we review the major themes in the recommended literature, we first describe two major initiatives that attempted to define the knowledge base for leadership preparation.

The Knowledge Base for Educational Administration

In 1989, the National Policy Board spearheaded the formal debate over what should be included in a knowledge base in educational administration in a report entitled *Improving the Preparation of School Administrators: An Agenda for Reform* (as cited in Hoy, 1994b). In 1992, the University Council of Educational Administration (UCEA) responded to the National Policy Board's call and initiated a collaborative effort to identify "relevant knowledge for practice and inquiry in educational administration" (Hoy, 1994b, p. 178). Different phases of this scholarly endeavor resulted in two significant publications: *Educational Administration: The UCEA Document Base* (Hoy, 1994a) and *The Knowledge Base in Educational Administration: Multiple Perspectives* (Donmoyer, Imber, & Scheurich, 1995). According to Donmoyer et al., these two publications were the result of investigations by scholars asked to "catalog the knowledge that the practitioners of a particular field ought to possess and employ, and in the process, to legitimate the authority of those who possess, employ, or teach the designated knowledge base" (p. 1).

The authors of *The UCEA Document Base*, often referred to simply as PRIMIS, were charged with a daunting task: to "define the knowledge in the field, set curriculum goals, and foster systemic inquiry" (Hoy, 1994b, p. 179). Study teams organized the essential content and processes or essential knowledge in the field within the following seven domains of knowledge: (a) societal and cultural influences on schooling, (b) teaching and learning processes, (c) organizational studies, (d) leadership and management processes, (e) policy and political studies, (f) legal and ethical dimensions of schooling, and (g) economic and financial dimensions of schooling. Each study team of three to six scholars had the responsibility for the following:

1. Identify the essential content and processes of their domain.
2. Attend to both empirical and interpretive perspectives.
3. Include both the wisdom of practice and the knowledge of scholarship.
4. Incorporate multicultural, emergent, feminist, and traditional perspectives.
5. Recommend future directions for the development of the field.

The development of PRIMIS was an effort to circumscribe the most important elements of a comprehensive knowledge base, or "the relevant knowledge for practice and inquiry in educational administration" (Hoy, 1994b, p. 178), and to identify specific sources of that knowledge. At the same time, Hoy (1994b) provided a substantive caveat to the work, emphasizing "the overview of these domains [of knowledge] should be seen as a beginning, not an end" (p. 192). Given this opening, other scholars in the field continued the discussion of what constitutes the knowledge base in educational administration and followed with the second publication by Donmoyer et al. (1995).

Problematizing the very goal and process of defining a knowledge base within the field of educational administration, Donmoyer et al. (1995) asked readers to look "critically at the assumptions and beliefs that underlie efforts to create a knowledge base in educational administration and the possibility of developing and legitimating such a knowledge base" (p. 2). While the contributors to PRIMIS (Hoy, 1994a) were clear in admitting the unfinished nature of the knowledge-base project, they asked scholars and practitioners to look beyond the question "What are the multiple dimensions of the content of our knowledge base?" and consider instead, "How does knowledge develop and become legitimated in our particular field?"

Donmoyer et al. (1995) argued that understanding the knowledge base in educational leadership is an incomplete project without grappling with epistemological and ontological questions, such as how knowledge and the process of knowledge development reflect "values, interests, and biases" (p. 6). Donmoyer et al. also asserted that the knowledge legitimated within leadership education programs, located predominantly in higher education settings, was "largely irrelevant and out of touch with practical concerns" (p. 6). They also explored important omissions in leadership education, with respect to issues such as critical theory, feminism, race, gender, and ethnicity.

While PRIMIS (Hoy, 1994a) provided an overview of an identifiable and stable knowledge base and how the exploration and understanding of that knowledge base leads to improvements in educational leadership, Donmoyer et al. (1995) problematized these underlying assumptions. These efforts raised important questions that affect the dialogue and efforts to shape and assess the curriculum in the field today.

In addition to the knowledge-base project, other scholars' recommendations about what should be included as the curriculum in leadership preparation are grounded in distinct conceptualizations of the nature and purpose of educational leadership. One of the most widely discussed topics in the leadership preparation literature is the notion of leadership for social justice, reflecting the belief that a key responsibility of educational leaders is to address social inequities that influence the nature and outcomes of school leadership for social justice (e.g., K. M. Brown, 2003, 2004; Cambron-McCabe & McCarthy, 2005; Fierro & Rodriguez, 2006; Larson & Murtadha, 2002; McKenzie, Skrla, & Scheurich; 2006; Marshall, 2004, 2006; Parker & Shapiro, 1992; Shields, 2004; Rusch, 2004).

Scholars articulating the centrality of moral or ethical leadership, a theme that appeared frequently throughout the leadership preparation literature (Beck & Murphy, 1994; Bolman & Deal, 1994; K. M. Brown, 2004; Campbell, 1997; Carr, Chenoweth, & Ruhl, 2003; Hills, 1978; Murphy, 2002, 2005; Smith, 1993) provide another lens through which to understand the nature and purpose of leadership. Additionally, transformational leadership is an overarching conceptualization of leadership emphasizing organizational change and school improvement through the use of collaborative, democratic, or distributed leadership strategies and characterized by data-based and critical analysis of problems (Bredeson, 2004; Johansson, 2004; Murphy, 2001; Spillane, 2004; Starratt, 2004).

Although these different conceptualizations are not necessarily discrete—Murphy (2005), for example, claimed that leadership education should be framed by three "valued ends of schooling" that include "school improvement, community, and social justice" (p. 163)—they provide a useful framework for analyzing the literature with respect to ideas about what educational leaders should be prepared to do and the curriculum that is linked to those intended outcomes. The literature prescribing the recommended curriculum generally focuses on the development of knowledge and understanding as well as on the development of a range of skills that are both cognitive and technical. In the following sections, we highlight curricular recommendations associated with key themes. First, we focus on leadership for social justice and discuss curricular recommendations that focus on subsequent knowledge, dispositions, and competencies. Second, we concentrate primarily on skills associated with leaders' ability to enact educational improvement and change. In this section, too, we focus on cognitive skills, including self-awareness and critical thinking, interpersonal competencies, and managerial competencies.

Social Justice

The discourse in the literature regarding issues of educational equity and social justice has burgeoned in the past 15 years. Some scholars have based their advocacy for changes in the curriculum on their understanding of leadership for social justice as a moral imperative (Allan & Estler, 2005; Pounder et al., 2002; Riehl, 2000; Solomon, 2002).

Within this framework, school leaders engage in moral dialogue (Shields, 2004) and act as moral agents, or moral stewards (K. M. Brown, 2004). Place and Reitzug (1992) argued that the curriculum should be framed by Starratt's model for ethical school leadership that includes "promoting an ethic of critique, of caring, and of justice" (p. 407). Reiterating his beliefs about the centrality of enacting and teaching the principles of democratic leadership in education, Starratt (2004) specifically called upon leadership faculty to "modify their laissez-faire programs to promote … a pro-active, moral kind of leadership that will … more actively promote authentic democratic learning processes and learning outcomes" (p. 731). Citing the work of Grogan and Andrews (2002) and Murphy (2002), Carr et al. (2003) also placed values and ethics at the forefront of leadership preparation to ensure "school leaders are prepared to meet the needs of an increasingly diverse K–12 student body" (p. 211). Drawing on Beck and Murphy's (1994) study of ethics in administrator-preparation programs, Mullen et al. (2002) focused on "two ethical capacities needed by leaders: one, the ability to transcend individual preferences when investigating problems and making decisions; and two, the ability to be ethical in various situations and knowledgeable about one's self and beliefs" (p. 170).

Within this area of the recommended literature, scholars have provided a plethora of recommendations regarding the knowledge, skills, and dispositions needed so that school leaders will be able to ensure educational equity and work toward social justice. Some maintained that traditional preparation programs do not include the requisite knowledge or skill base that would enable administrators to recognize inequities and to work to change them (Marshall, 2004; Pounder et al., 2002; Riehl, 2000). Others, like Cambron-McCabe and McCarthy (2005), asserted that school leaders must possess "new analytical skills, knowledge and dispositions to promote social justice in schools" (p. 214). The recommendations in these areas highlight the relationship between educational inequity and larger societal issues such as demographic diversity, poverty, racism, ethnocentrism, language differences, homophobia, and sexism (e.g., K. M. Brown, 2004; Cambron-McCabe & McCarthy, 2005; Capper, 1993; Foster, 1986; Marshall, 2004; Parker & Shapiro, 1992; Pounder et al., 2002; Scheurich & Skrla, 2003; Scheurich & Young, 1997; M. D. Young & Laible, 2000).

Knowledge

Regarding the knowledge undergirding equity, scholars recommend developing new conceptions of leadership. These include an understanding of social, political, and economic issues.

New conceptions of leadership Cambron-McCabe and McCarthy (2005) provided a comprehensive analysis of the social justice discourse in educational administration and encouraged programs to redefine the core purposes of schooling and think differently about organizational structures and leadership roles. To achieve this goal, Cambron-McCabe and McCarthy recommended that the curriculum include "new" concepts of schooling aimed at social justice. To develop new conceptualizations of leadership rooted in a social justice framework, Murtadha and Watts (2005) advocated learning about and understanding the history of African American leaders who might "serve as models for school leadership, providing a source for understanding predominantly Black student populations and communities" (p. 592).

Other scholars recommended reframing educational leadership to focus on the core technologies of schooling—teaching and learning—and the instructional methods needed to ensure the academic success of diverse learners (Cambron-McCabe & McCarthy, 2005; J. F. Johnson & Uline, 2005; McKenzie et al., 2006; Pounder et al., 2002; Riehl, 2000; Solomon, 2002). J. F. Johnson and Uline, for example, provide detailed descriptions of the powerful role of leadership in ensuring access to strong instructional techniques and closing achievement gaps. They provided a comprehensive review of research delineating how knowledge of certain leadership practices can lead to improved academic outcomes. Additionally, McKenzie et al. outlined an equity-based approach to instructional leadership that emphasizes the leader's role in promoting "equity-oriented teaching strategies" (p. 160).

Social, political, and economic influence To respond to social justice concerns, leaders also should know how the social, political, and economic contexts of the larger society influence educational policies and practices (F. Brown, 2005; K. M. Brown, 2004; Cambron-McCabe & McCarthy, 2005; Larson & Murtadha, 2002; Lopez, 2003; Lyman & Villani, 2002; Marshall, 2004; Murtadha & Watts, 2005; Pounder et al., 2002). Based on their study of "whether and how school leadership preparation programs emphasize understanding poverty's substantial complexity" (p. 257), Lyman and Villani (2002) concluded that the leadership preparation curriculum should include "an in-depth understanding of poverty, its complex interrelated causes, typical American attitudes toward causes of poverty, and poverty's effects on families, children, and learning" (p. 246).

Advocates of an activist-oriented curriculum have claimed "leadership for social justice requires that leaders understand that schools are not neutral grounds but contested political sites" (Pounder et al., 2002, p. 272). Accordingly, the curriculum would include a thorough history of social inequities, such as racial discrimination, homophobia, or other examples of oppression experienced by individuals based on social-group identity markers, and the impact of social, political, and economic forces on education and student learning. Based on his empirical investigation of how principals utilize antiracist pedagogy in their schools, Solomon (2002) recommended providing "historically informed and politically shaped" (p. 189) conceptions of education to preservice leaders.

Recognizing the powerful influence of the broader social, economic, and political context, Thrupp and Willmot (2003) maintained that prospective leaders should be aware of significant contextual issues, including

> increasingly polarized schools and communities, a narrowed educational focus in schools and the loss of authenticity in the teaching and learning process, a reduction in the sociability of schools and communities, the commodification and marginalization of children, the distraction of existing teachers and school leaders from educational matters, the discouragement of potential teachers and school leaders, and the undermining of more progressive policies. (p. 150)

Based on a textual analysis, Thrupp and Willmot contended that current educational leadership texts, for the most part, fail to address these issues, lack criticality, and help to reproduce social inequality. In response, the authors called for antimanagerialist school leadership texts that explicitly acknowledge the inextricable link between education, politics, and sociology and address structural and political issues in order to stimulate social action toward equity.

In a more pragmatic vein, an interview study by Herrity and Glasman (1999) determined what administrators need to know to be effective in working with racially and ethnically diverse student populations. Twenty-seven principals in Southern California nominated by superintendents as highly effective in administering programs for linguistically and culturally diverse students recommended knowledge development in 15 areas. Topics recommended by two thirds or more included knowledge of the rationale and theory of bilingual education, second-language acquisition, bilingual instructional methodology, organizational models and scheduling for bilingual instruction, cultural norms and diversity issues, and pragmatics related to diversity.

Many of the recommendations that fall under a social justice or equity umbrella have been articulated by scholars who take an "openly ideological stance" (Lather, 1991) toward preparing school leaders. The authors who claimed an advocacy-oriented stance made no apologies for centering leadership preparation curriculum within a social justice or equity perspective because, as Marshall (2004) so passionately defended, "we see social justice efforts as more important than traditional research concerns" (p. 5).

The recommended curriculum emphasizing social justice or equity requires leaders to develop a deep knowing of "a social context that continues to be rife with inequity and school practices that are inequitable and lead to inequitable outcomes" (Pounder et al., 2002, p. 270). However, the curriculum also addresses skill sets and attitudinal positions needed by school leaders to address issues of demographic diversity, poverty, racism, ethnocentrism, language differences, homophobia, sexism, and their intersections within educational policies and practices.

Skills

A curriculum oriented toward social justice strongly emphasizes the notion of leaders as agents of change. Scholars argue that preparation programs should develop skills and dispositions that will enable school leaders to recognize, critique, and change inequitable structures, policies, and practices within our nation's schools, thereby closing achievement gaps and ensuring high academic achievement of all students in our schools.

To address educational inequities requires skills in working successfully with diverse students and families, knowing how to identify and transform teachers' beliefs and practices, and engaging in discussions about larger societal oppression and how it impacts school policies and practices. Lopez (2003), for example, recommended, "School leaders must be prepared to work with individuals who are culturally different and help create learning environments that foster respect, tolerance, and intercultural understanding" (p. 71). Based on findings from her study of faculty perceptions of race and gender in leadership preparation programs, courses, and departments, Rusch (2004) recommended preparation programs provide a venue where students have "an opportunity to practice difficult conversations about race and gender" (p. 16). McKenzie et al. (2006) recommended leaders create an instructional environment that promotes "equity-oriented teaching strategies" (p. 160).

Other examples of leadership skills include knowing how to "disrupt the normative discourse" (Marshall, 2004, p. 6) by supporting a language of critique. Further, leaders should know how to use data to "challenge assumptions and myths about student abilities..." (J. F. Johnson & Uline, 2005, p. 46). To stop harassment of lesbian, gay, or transgendered students, leaders must create "schools that are welcoming and affirming for all students and families, regardless of the school leaders' personal beliefs about sexual-minority individuals or regardless of the community's values and beliefs about homosexuality" (Capper et al., 2006, p. 145).

Dispositions

Often discussed as the belief systems or mental models that inform a leader's practice, dispositions are another important yet highly understudied (K. M. Brown, 2003, 2004; Hafner, 2006) aspect of the recommended social-justice curriculum. Drawing on Paulo Friere's notion of conscientization, Fierro and Rodriguez (2006) recommended that "learning to perceive social, political, and economic contradictions and to take action against the oppressive elements of reality" (p. 183) be embedded throughout the curriculum for leadership preparation.

In keeping with the development of an "equity consciousness," McKenzie et al. (2006) highlighted four key beliefs associated with this perspective:

- that all children—except only a very small percentage, that is, those with profound disabilities—are capable of high levels of academic success;
- that this academic success equitably includes all student groups, regardless of race, social class, gender, sexual orientation, learning differences, culture, language, religion, and so forth;
- that the adults in schools are primarily responsible for seeing that all children reach this success; and
- that traditional school practices result in inequity for individual students and groups of students and that these must be changed to ensure success for every child. (p. 160)

Other scholars who linked the belief that every student can achieve success in school with social justice leadership include J. F. Johnson and Uline (2005); McKenzie et al. (2006); Pounder et al. (2002); Riehl (2000); and M. D. Young and Laible (2000). As J. F. Johnson and Uline (2005) noted, leaders who adopt a social justice agenda believe that every student can achieve success and foster within the educational community "a sense of collective relentlessness about educating all students to high levels of achievements" (p. 46).

Additionally, Brunner (2002a) emphasized the importance of leadership preparation programs exploring and developing particular conceptions of power among leaders. Brunner (2002a) argued,

If educators wish to eliminate social injustice in schools, we cannot overlook the importance of re-creating a notion of leadership that is generated from a conception of power understood to be collective and caring—something that requires equal, authentic participation across race, class, gender, sexual preference, and other categories of difference. (p. 705)

Educational Improvement and Change

As the focus in leadership preparation shifted from management to leadership, scholars (Carr et al., 2003; Duke, 1992; Miskel, 1990; Murphy, 2001, 2005; Smith, 1993; Stevenson & Doolittle, 2003) urged that prospective leaders needed to know more about teaching and learning, or what Miskel (1990) described as "the core technologies of educational organizations" (p. 40). In one interview study, Lease (2002) indicated that practitioners shared this conception of leadership, with superintendents reporting that they desired visionary principals with expertise in teaching, learning, and instruction to lead a school toward improved learning.

This increased emphasis on student learning was accompanied by new approaches to leadership and transformational leadership in particular. Building on an expanding knowledge base that linked dimensions of leadership behavior with improved outcomes, scholars like Mullen et al. (2002) argued for a reconceptualization of leadership that is transformational in nature. The responsibility of a transformational leader, Mullen et al. offered, is to "maintain a collaborative culture, foster teacher development, and assist teachers to improve problem solving" (p. 180). Scholars urged not only collaboration, but also distribution of leadership authority (Marks & Printy, 2003; Spillane, 2004, 2006). Within this broad perspective of educational improvement and change, the recommended curriculum included attention primarily to the development of skills, but skills that are both cognitive and behavioral.

Personal Awareness and Critical-Thinking Skills

In research over the last 15 years, we find increasing emphasis on the importance of cognition and intentionality. This cognitive perspective suggests that what we believe, what we value, and what we think are reflected in action. Beginning with effective-schools research, we have seen a growing emphasis on developing and articulating a vision, as a motivating factor and as a means to assess progress toward stated goals. The importance of cognition and metacognition is also reflected in research on decision making, problem framing, and problem solving (Bolman & Deal, 1994; Davis, 2004; Davis & Davis, 2003; Reitzug & Cornett, 1990). This perspective is reflected in attention to the development of self-awareness and critical-thinking skills.

Self-Awareness

Arguing that mindscapes or personal theories of leaders should be the focus of the curriculum in leadership preparation programs, Sergiovanni (1991) asserted, "Theoretical models and technical practices have not worked [and] educational research and administrative theory constructed in the past decades have failed" (p. 39). More recently, as Elmore, Peterson, and McCarthy (1996) and others have established through empirical studies, structural reform without change in underlying beliefs is unlikely to generate meaningful changes (K. M. Brown, 2004; Murphy, 2005; Reitzug & Cornett, 1990). As a basis for organizational change, and grounded in the work of Argyris and Schön (1974), authors such as Keedy (2005), Osterman and Kottkamp (1993, 2004), Senge (1990), and Sergiovanni (1999) encouraged leaders to examine their theories-in-use, their mental models, or their assumptions, all elements of cognition that affect action. Osterman and Kottkamp (1993, 2004) presented systematic procedures for incorporating reflective practice into professional development programs.

This emphasis on personal awareness and development is and has been an important theme in the literature on leadership preparation. Bolman and Deal (1994) reported on a gathering of scholars and leaders from outside the field of education, convened "to discuss and distill their thoughts about leadership and to discover what education might learn from other sectors, such as business, the military, and public administration" (p. 78). Emphasizing the importance of personal values within the practice of leadership, participants argued that "developing leadership requires a shift in emphasis. We do more than enough about issues of control—planning, budgeting, performance, appraisal—but far too little on the human and spiritual dimensions" (Bolman & Deal, 1994, p. 93). To develop human and spiritual dimensions of leadership, participants in Bolman and Deal's study recommended school leaders work with "prospective teachers to know themselves, their strengths, limitations, and inner feelings" (p. 92) and to "connect learning with emotions or ethics" (p. 93).

In addition to developing a broad and critical understanding of one's beliefs and mental models, the recommended curriculum addresses the need to develop an understanding of emotions and one's emotional intelligence. Beatty and Brew (2004), building on the work of Hargreaves (2001), maintained, "There is a need to address the emotions of leadership as part of a comprehensive approach to preparing leaders for the challenges in today's schools" (p. 329). "Deep transformation in schools," Beatty and Brew asserted, "relies on the capacity of the individuals within them to value, integrate, and collaborate about this all-important 'motivating sphere of consciousness'" (p. 331). Accordingly, "school leadership programs need ways to broach the subject of their students' emotional preparedness to create trusting communities of respect and candour" (Beatty & Brew, 2004, p. 332).

McDowelle and Bell (1998) argued, "Research associated with the concept of emotional intelligence provides a vocabulary and empirical support for leadership preparation programs in their attempt to pinpoint and develop the intangibles of leadership" (p. 190). Basing their concepts on the work of Salovey and Mayer (1990), McDowelle and Bell characterized emotional intelligence as

> combining the intrapersonal and interpersonal intelligences described by Gardner (1993) and consisting of five skills domains. These include: (a) being self-aware, knowing yourself and recognizing your feelings; (b) managing emotions, regulating your feelings; (c) motivating yourself, persisting in the face of frustration and difficulties; (d) empathizing, perceiving life as others perceive it; and (e) handling relationships by managing emotions in others. (p. 191)

McDowelle and Bell argued that school leaders should

> be self-aware and cognizant of the effects that they have on the people that they lead,… empathize with a variety of stakeholders and constituencies,… work well as a member of a team or as a team leader, [and] be able to transmit the hope that regardless of current problems or issues, things will get better in the future. (p. 192)

Critical Thinking

In addition to an increased awareness of self, other authors encouraged the development of critical-thinking skills within leadership preparation. *Reflective inquiry*[1] is an area of study recommended by many scholars in the field (Carr et al., 2003; Davis, 2004; Murphy, 2001; Norris, 1990; Reitzug & Cornett, 1990; Rettig, 2004; Sergiovanni, 1988, 1991; Williamson & Hudson, 2000). Stevenson and Doolittle (2003) professed, "Educational leaders should employ critically reflective inquiry as an integral component of their practice such that individual and collective decisions and actions are informed by the outcomes of thoughtful inquiry and moral deliberation" (p. 670).

Emphasizing the importance of analytical skills, Mulkeen and Cooper (1992), for example, described a new Ed.D. program aimed to shift from management-in-training to "develop educational leaders who think of themselves as change agents, who think analytically about education as it exists, and who think critically about how education might be" (p. 20). Smith (1993), too, recommended that programs "provide frameworks to assist students in assessing moral and ethical implications" (p. 47) of policies and practices. Richardson and Lane (1994) suggested that the curriculum of principal preparation programs center on "developing students' critical analysis capability" (p. 14), based on their belief that "the issue of critical analysis and the ability to apply such skills to the school setting is the essence of improving administrative leadership and student academic performance" (p. 15). Richardson and Lane also emphasized the importance of leaders' "ability to apply inventiveness and ingenuity to the job, to create a learning environment and opportunities for learning, and the acquisition of the learning mentality" (p. 14) and proposed a curriculum that prepares administrators who can "unlearn and learn with equal ability" (p. 17). Miskel (1990) advocated, "The curriculum should place a strong emphasis on developing abilities to analyse situations and solve problems" (p. 39).

The recommendations for developing critical-thinking skills are diverse. Based on discussions with principals about decision making and an examination of educational administration course curricula, Davis and Davis (2003) concluded, "Principals relied very little on classical forms of decision analysis when resolving complex problems," yet "university administrative training programs continued to place a heavy emphasis on courses that taught classical/analytical decision-making" (p. 138). In response, they recommended an "alternative framework" for administrative decision making including both rational analytical decision-making skills and heuristic and intuitive thinking.

According to Dimmock and Walker (1998), inclusion of a comparative analytical approach to studying educational administration would assist leaders in seeing "the relationship between the organization and its social environment" (p. 563). Inclusion also would enhance problem-solving and program-design capabilities (Brundrett, 2001: Dimmock, 1998; Dimmock & Walker, 1998).

Miskel (1990) maintained that leaders should "conduct and use research as a basis of problem solving and program design" (p. 36). Accordingly, they need to develop basic research competencies, such as "gathering, analyzing, and interpreting data; understanding descriptive and inferential statistics, using evaluation and planning models and methods; and selecting, administering, and interpreting evaluation instruments" (Miskel, 1990, p. 36). Yet, having completed a comprehensive review of literature on preparation programs, Miskel reported he had found "not a single work that was devoted solely to the research aspect in preparation" (p. 34). Discussing the relationship between research and leadership, Ramsey (1975) proposed that the development of skills in participant observation would facilitate data gathering and problem solving. In another study (Lease, 2002), superintendents also viewed research skills as highly important to facilitate interpretation and use of data.

Other scholars focused attention on the paradigmatic perspectives or theoretical frameworks that influence the practice and theory of school leadership. Critiquing the traditional or positivistic paradigm that dominated research and inquiry, researchers made recommendations to include alternate paradigms in order to foster critical perspectives on research, organizational theory and practice, and social issues. To counteract the dominance of positivist thought, English (1997) advocated discussion of the role of postmodernity in educational administration and seeking out a "coherentism" centered program where no single truth or reality is sought or tested.

Some recommended inclusion of multiple or alternate perspectives, including critical theory, to develop critical capability (K. M. Brown, 2004; Capper, 1993; English, 1997; Place & Reitzug, 1992; Rettig, 2004; Scheurich & Laible, 1995; Williamson & Hudson, 2000; B. Young, 1994; M. D. Young & Laible, 2000). Scheurich and Laible claimed that including a critical perspective in the curriculum was necessary to develop leaders able to "recognize the erroneously destructive effects of race, gender, and class biases on our children" (p. 319). Noting the omission of the voices of African Americans from the traditional paradigms that frame understanding of leadership practice and research, F. Brown (2005) and Rettig also recommended the inclusion of critical race theory, queer legal theory, and chaos theory. Based on her feminist analysis of past and present scholarship in Canadian, English-language education administration, B. Young (1994), like others, urged leadership preparation programs to "make women and gender more visible in our conceptualizations of organizations" (p. 364). Rettig characterized preparation programs historically as positivistic in perspective, with a unidimensional view of educational organizations as closed bureaucratic systems, and suggested a curriculum that emphasizes critical theory can create substantial educational reform.

In contrast, Berrel and Macpherson (1995) contended that social critical and phenomenological theories as well as positivism are problematic because they "rely on arbitrary and unjustified claims to validate the partitions they employ" (p. 26). Berrel and Macpherson suggested that "a non-foundational, pragmatic and coherentist epistemology and a combination of empirical and extra-empirical criteria" (p. 28) would further knowledge in the field.

Interpersonal Competencies

Murphy (2001) proposed that, as a field of study, educational administration should "rethink the business of school leadership" (p. 1) and "reculture the field" to shift the focus from "educational administration as management to educational administration primarily concerned with teaching and learning" (p. 2). To achieve this goal, according to Murphy (2001), leaders need

> an understanding of caring and humanistic concerns as a key to effective leadership; knowledge of the transformational and change dynamics; … an appreciation of the collegial and collaborative foundations of school administration; and an emphasis on the ethical and reflective dimensions of leadership. (p. 2)

This humanistic perspective, with its emphasis on collegial and collaborative leadership, highlights the importance of interpersonal and group process skills, or what Murphy (2005) referred to as "working together skills" (p. 165). The development of human relation competencies is reflected in recommendations for attention to communication and group process, team building, collaborative inquiry, and conflict resolution (Beach & Lindahl, 2000; Brunner, 2002b; Duncan, 2003; Grove, 1992; Kowalski, 1998). According to Beach and Lindahl, strong communication skills are essential for leaders if they are to understand the culture, ethics, values, and beliefs of the organizations and environments where they serve. Towards that end, they recommended that leadership preparation programs teach skills that facilitate collaboration, consensus, negotiation, and conflict resolution. Duncan maintained that respectful and open listening is important among leaders. To develop that ability, she urged the use of democratic, inclusive, and humane principles in leadership preparation. If prospective leaders' experience supports an individual's voice rather than classroom lecture and discussion of textbooks, the assumption is that leaders then would incorporate these practices in their own leadership.

Brunner (2002b), too, recommended attention to listening skills. Based on findings from an analysis of "small samples of traditional discourse on communication found in superintendency texts and nontraditional narratives from women superintendents" (p. 402), her research advanced the idea of proactive listening as the cornerstone of transforming discourse surrounding the superintendency.

Practitioners concurred on the importance of interpersonal skills as a part of leadership preparation but reported that these areas are sorely neglected (Daresh, 1992; Lindauer, Petrie, Leonard, Gooden, & Bennett, 2003; Polite, 1990). Based on an internal review of their courses, the faculty in one program determined that "students were required to use interpersonal skills … in group interaction and project development" but did not receive instruction or critical feedback that would enable them to understand "how and why some exchanges were more successful than others" (Polite, 1990, p. 159). A survey of 15 students, practicing and aspiring administrators, confirmed their assessment. All participants in Polite's study indicated that such a course "should be included in their program of study" (p. 161), and 63% indicated that "in the context of the numerous skills needed for effective school administration, they would rate human interaction/human relations skills as more important than other skills" (p. 162). Rated most important was effective listening.

Examining the value of group process skills and the quality of preparation, Lindauer et al. (2003) analyzed survey responses from 262 elementary, middle, and high school principals. The majority of respondents felt that group process skills were essential for the job but reported there was little formal training and that the preparation provided was of poor quality. Noting the advent of site-based decision making, Lindauer et al. concluded that university preparation programs should do more. In a study by Herrity and Glasman (1999), expert leaders reported that working effectively in schools with diverse student populations required good listening skills, strong interpersonal skills, and being able to speak the language of the target population in order to work with parents in a collaborative manner.

Daresh, Myrna, Dunlap, and Hvizdak (2000) developed a two-phase study to gain "insights of rank-and-file principals" (p. 72) regarding characteristics of effective school principals and curricular components that should be included in an effective principal preparation program. In the first phase, they used the Delphi process to gather information from 30 peer-nominated principals. From these data, Daresh et al. identified 28 items viewed as necessary components of an effective preparation program. The researchers then surveyed 306 principals and assistant principals who ranked the items. The analysis identified six factors: (a) technical skills influenced by human relations, (b) technical skills influenced by legal mandates, (c) creating an inviting culture, (d) building community, (e) ethics in practice, and (f) understanding relationships. Most important were human relations competencies, which included conducting a meeting, managing an office, implementing site-based management, integrating student learning styles with appropriate pedagogical methods, forming and working with teams, planning strategically for future needs and growth, and identifying the special population.

Managerial Competencies

The traditional canon in administrator preparation ostensibly consisted of courses that separated theory and practice and focused either on the knowledge that educators needed (leadership theory, organizational theory, school law, politics of education) or on specific tasks or managerial functions (budgeting and finance, personnel management, supervision). Interestingly, there was little discussion of these traditional topics. There was some affirmation for the importance of traditional topics like school law in studies of practitioner perspectives (Daresh et al., 2000; Lease, 2002) as well as calls for a reconceptualization of certain areas of study and attention to other topics, not typically included in the curriculum, including professional development, educational technology, school improvement, and planning and change.

Based on their extensive review of contemporary research in leadership, Mullen et al. (2002) argued that the curriculum needed revision to reflect the changing understanding of the leader's role. They also focused on needed changes in the conceptualization of organizational theory, curriculum and instructional leadership, and school–community relations.

Mullen et al. (2002) suggested that students in leadership preparation programs need to view school organizations through "'multiple lenses (i.e. structural, political, symbolic, cultural, emotional, learning, critical, postmodern, feminist, systems, chaos, community, and moral)" (p. 181). This, Mullen et al. contended, "helps students to better understand complexity, to critically examine their own assumptions, and to identify and solve problems" (p. 181). Beach and Lindahl (2000) and B. L. Johnson and Fauske (2005) also recommended including concepts and skills that enable students to create a common school culture, develop shared meaning, and articulate a mission and vision.

Mullen et al. (2002) echoed calls for less hierarchical leadership strategies and proposed that the curriculum emphasize "a collegial rather than a hierarchical relationship between teachers and supervisors … and focus on teacher growth rather than compliance, teacher collaboration for instructional improvement, and facilitation of teachers' reflective inquiry" (p. 181). Concurring that a primary function of the school leader is to improve instruction, Shapiro, Benjamin, Hunt, and Shapiro (1996) contended that leaders need to be able to direct and develop a quality curriculum and proposed a theory of curriculum development in response to perceived problems in schools. Mullen et al. (2002) also framed an orientation to school–community relations that would challenge and enable students to "move beyond traditional public relations to collaboration with families and community members, responding to diverse community needs, mobilizing community resources, and developing formal partnerships with the private sector, community agencies, and postsecondary education" (p. 181).

Aside from Hess and Kelly's (2005a) assertion that certain managerial skills needed to be reintroduced into preparation programs, there has been little attention to this aspect of the leader's role, even among practitioners. In one study, for example, superintendents characterized skills in business management, budget, finance, and facilities management as less important for effective leadership than courses in human relations, planning, technology, diversity, and school law (Lease, 2002).

The Written Curriculum

Including the goals, standards, and plans that guide the delivery of curriculum, elements of the written curriculum appear in program descriptions and are reflected in course requirements and course documents, including syllabi. What does the literature tell us, then, about the curriculum that students encounter in educational leadership preparation programs? What are the learning goals, what courses do student take, and what is the nature of these courses?

The first source of information about the written curriculum consisted of descriptions or evaluations of programs considered distinctive. None of these studies was specifically designed to describe or assess the curriculum at the program level, but they provided some information about learning goals, the conceptual framework or beliefs shaping the curriculum, and the curriculum itself. With few exceptions, references to the curriculum lacked specificity or consistency. Some provided only general information about the stated purpose of the programs; others gave a more detailed statement of learning objectives. Some included a list of courses or modules, others only general areas of study. Although chapter 9 of this volume deals specifically with field components, it is important to mention here that this part of the preservice preparation appears to have a dual purpose in some programs, to convey knowledge as well as to develop experience or skill.

In addition to the literature on program design and evaluation, additional studies examined course offerings within and across institutions. Some were survey studies intended to gather information about courses and topics included in the curriculum; others consisted of systematic analyses of syllabi and texts.

Programs: Themes and Course Requirements

Program descriptions and evaluations of preservice preparation programs commonly defined their purpose as the development of leaders and leadership ability. Although management or administrative skills and competencies were not excluded, for the most part there was an intentional shift from a focus on management to one on leadership. At the same time, there were differing definitions of leadership; whereas programs were seldom unidimensional, there were distinctive differences in orientation and curriculum among programs. Some programs, for example, framed leadership as a cognitive process and emphasized the development of knowledge, cognitive skills, and self-understanding as a means of developing leader ability. Others focused more directly on the development of leadership competencies. Others emphasized desired outcomes such as school improvement, equity, or social justice and highlighted dimensions of leadership associated with these outcomes. Although programs differed in the statement of primary purposes, all addressed the development of knowledge and skills, theory, and practice. Some programs were designed intentionally to correspond to state or national performance standards.

Whereas the majority of programs seemed to retain a traditional course structure, others used alternative delivery formats, engaging students in intensive full-time programs and utilizing modules rather than the standard 3-credit course. From these descriptions, it is apparent that some titles digress from the traditional canon. In a few instances titles reflected the unique perspective outlined in the goals. At the same time, given possible discrepancies between titles and content, it is impossible to determine from course titles alone any alignment between curriculum and stated goals. Another important feature of curriculum design that is evident is a shift from a palette of discrete elective courses dealing with various administrative functions to a set of required and integrated courses. It is also clear that the conceptualization of the knowledge base differs very noticeably between programs and that the programs themselves are very different. At the same time, it is important to note that the information is based on reports from a relatively few institutions, a substantial number of which had received financial support through the Danforth Foundation or other grants to initiate reform efforts. Nonetheless, they do provide insight into the curricular landscape of preservice leadership preparation. In the following section, we review information about curricular goals and course content, based on a predominant orientation: the development of cognitive skills and abilities, the achievement of social justice or school improvement goals, and the development of management competencies.

Cognition and Self-Understanding

A number of preparation programs leading to initial certification or the doctorate emphasized the development of cognitive understanding and skill, with particular attention to self-awareness and inquiry skills (Bredeson, 2004; Milstein, 1993; Mulkeen & Cooper, 1992; Noonan, 1991; Wilmore & Thomas, 1998). Program reform efforts at the University of Wisconsin–Madison in 1991, for example, were intended to lead to a "complex view of school leadership as a shared, reflective, intellectual activity" (Noonan, 1991, p. 4). According to Noonan, the new curriculum was "based on three integrative spheres necessary to develop educational leaders" (p. 4): a contextual component, including "knowledge bases and skills relative to the historical, philosophical, social, legal, political, and community development perspectives" (p. 5); an administrative component; and a teaching and learning component. Illustrating the changing nature of the curriculum, Bredeson provided an updated perspective on program redesign and curriculum development efforts at the same institution approximately 10 years later. With a stated mission statement to "create, integrate, exchange, and apply knowledge about leadership, learning and organizational performance" (Bredeson, 2004, p. 715), the program seems to have retained its emphasis on cognition. At the same time, the mission statement now included the social justice goal to advance educational quality and opportunity, and the modified curriculum was now organized around three areas: (a) Professional Socialization (Intro to K–12 Administration, Professional Development, Student Services); (b) Instructional Leadership (Research Methods, School Principalship, Theory and Design of Curriculum); and (c) Integrative Leadership (Legal Aspects of Education, Instructional Leadership and School Improvement, Finance). Also included was a Capstone Field Experience.

Three programs at two institutions (The University of Texas at Arlington and Texas Christian University) ranged in design from an entirely field-based program to a more conventional approach. Wilmore and Thomas (1998) indicated redesign at Texas Christian University had shifted "from a traditional, managerially oriented educational administration program to one that better reflects the strands in Texas' new administrative certification standards" (p. 175). Designed to "convey a vision of administration that is congruent with the values shaping these standards" (p. 175), the program articulated the belief that self-awareness provides the basis for leadership, according to Wilmore and Thomas:

A critical measure of preparedness today is the development of a coherent, complex viewpoint on the nature and function of learning, teaching, and schooling. In other words, while students must acquire leadership skills, they must also begin to better understand what they believe, why they believe it, how to communicate and provide leadership based on their beliefs, and the importance of reflection/critical thought as a way to adjust beliefs when needed. (pp. 175–176)

Both programs Wilmore and Thomas studied mentioned their intent to link "theories of management with the realities of administrative practice" and indicated that reflective-critical thought is the "key to successful teaching, leading, and learning (p. 177)." Wilmore and Thomas noted, "In order to lead, you must first know who you are" (p. 176).

The Danforth Foundation initiated and supported the redesign of leadership preparation programs. At the completion of the project, participant institutions completed case studies to describe program reform. Given this broad perspective, the reports offer limited detail about the curriculum, but they did identify the general goals or orientation (Milstein, 1993). The University of Washington program, for example, emphasized reflection and community building, resting on an underlying belief that effective leadership requires an understanding of self, core beliefs, leadership styles, and decision making as well as an ability to work with others.

Several descriptions of reform at the doctoral level highlighted the development of inquiry skills. Mulkeen and Cooper (1992), as noted earlier, reported that the goal of the program at Fordham was to "help administrators become intellectual leaders" (p. 21). Mulkeen and Cooper described the curriculum only as a "planned sequence of core experiences related to school leadership, organizational design, educational policy, critical theory, the change process, and the history, philosophy, and sociology of education" (p. 21) and as based on an assumption that the "initial preparation programs" had provided a foundation of basic skills.

Two Ed.D. programs at Wichita State University and University of Utah both emphasized field-based inquiry. Furtwengler, Furtwengler, Hurst, Turk, and Holcomb (1996) described "an innovative doctoral program that prepares students to become expert leaders in educational administration" (p. 512). Furtwengler et al. described the program as a "hands on clinical process" (p. 517) that is "inquiry and data oriented" (p. 518) and focused on "situated cognition, organizational decision making and leadership" (p. 521). Replacing a set of standardized courses, the integrated curriculum combined theory and practice in field-based settings and thus required field-based studies representing complex problems, frequently developed in conjunction with partnering districts.

As part of a detailed assessment of program effectiveness, Pounder (1995) outlined the orientation and curriculum of the Ed.D. program at the University of Utah. The program was explicit that participation in the doctoral program should enhance administrative practice. Toward this goal, the central purpose of the curriculum was to link theory and research to the improvement of practice. In the 1st year, students completed core requirements in areas of leadership, organization, and ethics. In the 2nd and subsequent 2 years, students completed elective specializations drawing from courses in instructional management, legal issues, finance, politics and policy analysis, human resource administration, or higher education options. Pounder observed, "All content areas, including core requirements and specialization electives, include a theory/research seminar paired with a field-based application course. Students use their respective employment settings as a 'field laboratory' to do applied projects and problem-solving" (p.155). The projects were intended to "provide opportunities for students to address a problem of practice relevant to their own organizational or professional setting" (Pounder, 1995, p. 154). The research component of the program consisted of Principles of Inquiry, described as a conceptual approach to administrative decision making and problem solving and to methods and techniques of research. Like the program at Wichita State University, this program required a final project integrating theory and research to address a significant problem of practice.

School Change and School Improvement

Some programs framed their purpose in terms of change. Twale and Short (1989) described the reform efforts of the leadership program at Auburn University as beginning with a vision of the leader as one who is able to make a difference. Operating from a "broad, deep knowledge base," the leader would be proactive, reflective, and an inspirational change agent, "helping to develop a school culture conducive to collective purpose and committed to the larger community" (Twale & Short, 1989, p. 150). Whereas the existing research generally concludes that attention to women and technology is neglected in leader preparation, this is one example of a program that formally recognized these issues in the written curriculum, a set of nine modules (14 credit hours) including the following topics: (a) group dynamics and critical reflective thinking; (b) perspectives on education: historical, social, political, psychological, legal, and economic; (c) organizational theory and analysis in education; (d) management, administration, and policy making; (e) leadership in education; (f) women in educational leadership; (g) resources and technology in education; (h) research design, methodology, and analysis; and (i) education: tomorrow through the next century. Twale and Short claimed that the program "promoted the integration of educational theory with administrative practice" (p. 151), but, as in many other articles, their emphasis was on instructional methods rather than curricular content.

Also part of the Danforth Program, Southwest Texas State University modified its leadership preparation program in 1995 and began an assessment in 2000. According to Slater, McGhee, and Capt (2001), the reform drew on prior efforts, notably reports from the Danforth Program, and identified the central theme for the program as leadership and school improvement. Included was a sequence of core courses: (a) Understanding Self: Developing a Personal Vision for Leadership; (b) Shaping Organizations and Using Inquiry: Management and Leadership; (c) Understanding People: Professional Development; (d) Understanding Environments: Social, Political, Economic, Legal, and Technological; and (e) Understanding Curriculum and Instructional Leadership.

It is interesting to note that a similar, nontraditional course framework appeared in other program descriptions (Daresh, 1992; Osterman, 1994), suggesting the possible influence of the Danforth initiative in generating dialogue and reform. As Daresh and Playko (1994) explained, their newly developed program had shifted "from a collection of courses such as school law, supervision, finance, school-community relations and personnel to a set of integrated learning experiences which provide students with needed knowledge, skills, and attitudes through a coherent program" (p. 437). From the perspective of curriculum design and assessment, programs like this represent an important shift from those that consisted largely of elective options to a more cohesive approach.

Social Justice

Some programs focused on social problems dealing with equity, justice, and inclusion. B. L. Jackson and Kelley (2002) indicated that University of Washington and East Tennessee State emphasized the development of moral and ethical leadership. California State University at Fresno joined Danforth in an effort to better prepare leaders for area schools—specifically, to prepare school leaders to lead in a multicultural environment and to have a positive impact on educational performance of diverse student groups (Milstein, 1993). Wilmore and Thomas (1998), too, indicated that The University of Texas at Arlington placed a great deal of emphasis on the value of diversity and a multicultural environment. Stevenson and Doolittle (2003), in a programmatic self-study, identified moral leadership as a core belief guiding program development. "Educational leadership," Stevenson and Doolittle noted, "involves making moral commitments that should guide one's decision about practical actions (e.g., equity, social justice and care for others, effectiveness, and efficiency)" (p. 670).

Within this framework of social justice, Anderson (2006) completed a comprehensive study to describe and assess the California State University at Los Angeles Educational Administration faculty's "efforts to design and foster a program that prepares school administrators to be advocates for equity and social justice in their schools" (p. 2). Drawing on a detailed examination of program documents, course syllabi, and student work, Anderson's study (like Copland, 2001), was an in-depth exploration of a program curriculum offering detailed information about the conceptual framework, the knowledge base, course requirements, and effectiveness.

The program was shaped by the faculty's stated beliefs about the curriculum, its goals, and its content, according to Anderson (2006):

> Students should be taught the skills of critical pedagogy, develop an understanding of the power of personal awareness and reflection; be taught the skills and values of being a change agent; how to assess schools in the context of larger systems, using a variety of proven strategies and technological tools; be able to assess students' needs in light of the realities of the school and community systems in which they function, serving the needs of students in their community; and have the will to put her or his knowledge and passion into practice. (pp. 15–16)

Recommended components of knowledge base within the curriculum generally corresponded to the key areas identified in the *UCEA Document Base* (Hoy, 1994a). Anderson reported a typical course sequence included (a) Leadership for Organizational Transformation, (b) Fieldwork, (c) Leadership in Current Social and Political Issues, (d) Educational Research and Decision Making, (e) School Leadership and Technology, (f) Instructional Leadership, (g) Leadership in School Law, (h) Leadership in Human Resource Development, (i) Leadership in School Finance, (j) Problems and Practices in Special Education, and (k) Reflection and Portfolio Assessment.

In another comprehensive case study, Copland (2001) reported that a principal preparation master's program at Stanford (no longer offered) reflected faculty beliefs that the role of the principal was to lead people and to manage self, ideas, and things in order to achieve worthwhile results for a diverse student population. Copland (2001) noted,

> To confront the challenges of meeting the needs of a diverse student population, principals … need a thorough grounding in curriculum and instruction and exceptional skills in problem-solving, evaluating proposals that respond to the needs of these students, implementing change, and communicating with and relating to a diverse population. (p. 340)

Although the faculty maintained that "teaching is the most important activity that occurs within the public schools, and its importance should be reflected in all aspects of a training program for prospective principals," they also recognized that leaders "must have exceptional managerial and organizational skills," according to Copland (2001, p. 340). The emphasis on the development of managerial and organizational skills within the curriculum is important to note because, as program change has evolved, recent criticisms concern the neglect of these skills (Hess & Kelly, 2005a).

The design of the curriculum also reflected the faculty's beliefs about the failures of leadership preparation in general. The faculty, Copland (2001) noted, made "a conscious attempt to respond to criticisms of preparation," specifically that faculty are drawn almost exclusively from educational administration, with a curriculum consisting "largely of retired school and district administrators telling war stories" or "traditionally accepted frameworks, which for 40 years had shaped administrator preparation programs" (p. 336).

Overall, the program Copland (2001) studied consisted of three, consecutive, 8-week summer sessions of resident study, during which students completed nine core courses. A practicum, consisting of 13 problem-based learning projects, accounted for approximately 40% of the total curriculum. In addition to "developing students' capacity to examine school culture, supervise and evaluate teachers, lead change initiatives, organize time and schedules effectively, conduct a job search, and develop a professional portfolio," the faculty perceived that the problem-based learning projects would "foster an intimate examination of self and cause students to make serious inquiry into their personal readiness for future school leadership roles" (Copland, 2001, p. 345). The nine required courses—seven "designed specifically for the program and two adapted from existing courses to make them more relevant to future principals" (Copland, 2001, p. 358)—were as follows: (a) Instruction of Socially Heterogeneous Populations; (b) Education of Immigrants in Cities; (c) The Role of Personality and Emotions in Organizations; (d) The Analysis of Teaching; (e) The Role of Knowledge and Learning in Teaching; (f) Good Schools: Research, Policy, and Practice; (g) School-Based Decision Making; (h) Politics of Education; and (i) Curriculum: A Policy Focus. The nontraditional course titles illustrated a shift in design from a curriculum focused on discrete knowledge or functions to a more integrated, interdisciplinary approach. As Copland (2001) noted, information normally included in courses in school law, finance, or program assessment was "woven into the problem-based practicum projects" (p. 348). The course titles also corresponded to program goals.

Leadership Competencies

Whereas all preparation programs aim to develop competencies, for some the development of leadership or managerial competencies was explicit. Some focused on specific aspects of leadership, whereas others framed goals within the context of state or national standards or aimed more generally at the development of certain competencies. The courses associated with these programs were notably different.

Instructional and special education leadership Programs at California State University at Fresno (B. L. Jackson & Kelley, 2002), and the University of Alabama (Milstein, 1993), another Danforth program, reportedly organized their curricula around instructional leadership. Although special education was frequently identified as an area largely omitted from preservice preparation, an exception was Lehigh University's program to prepare preservice administrators to lead inclusionary schools (Collins & White, 2002). An assessment of the project that had been funded for 3 years (1998–2001) stated goals to produce administrator candidates who would be able to institute legally defensible and educationally sound special education programs, direct curriculum development, encourage the use of instructional strategies appropriate for the implementation of effective inclusionary models for special education, and create a seamless integration of the special education program into the general education program.

As part of the evaluation report, Collins and White (2002) provided an overview of the curriculum. Although the authors described the learning goals as "competencies," a number of the descriptors focused exclusively on knowledge: knowledge of the learning and behavioral characteristics of special education students, special education law, research and best practice on inclusive programs, and interventions for the integration of emotionally and behaviorally disturbed students. Students were expected to develop competencies in supervision of staff in inclusive classrooms; program design, implementation, and assessment of curriculum and instruction designed to meet the needs of special education students; and dissemination of legal information and best techniques to school administrators, teachers, parents, and community. A final goal was skill in financial analysis and management of special education programs. The program description, however, provided little information on the curriculum.

Standards-based In an article describing innovative programs in UCEA institutions, B. L. Jackson and Kelley (2002) reported that the University of Louisville "works with the student to develop a knowledge and experiential base related to the ISLLC [Interstate School Leaders Licensure Consortium] standards and instructional leadership" (p. 203). Further, The University of Texas at San Antonio apparently used both National Association of Secondary School Principals assessments and the ISLLC standards to shape the content of the program.

As part of an evaluation study, Kim (1997) noted that California State University designed an educational administration program to address the California Commission on Teaching Credentials' new standards for administrator preparation. The program consisted of "an induction course, and three required core courses, electives, practicum, and a candidate's assessment course," with the curriculum organized into "five thematic areas: organizational and cultural environment, dynamics of strategic-issues management, ethical and reflective leadership, analysis and development of public policy, and management of information systems and human and fiscal resources" (Kim, 1997, p. 3).

A master's program and Ph.D. leadership programs offered by the University of Colorado were also redesigned to respond to new state standards (Muth, Murphy, Martin, & Sanders, 1996). According to Muth et al., the curriculum was framed around four domains that "provide umbrellas for clinical analysis and intervention, theoretical content, skill-building field activities, and instructional collaboration" (p. 218): (a) administrative leadership in educational organizations, (b) supervising the curricular and instructional program, (c) administering the school improvement process, and (d) administering the environment of education.

General managerial competencies Glasman (1997) described the development of an experimental program designed to respond to criticisms dealing with lack of relevant coursework, separation of knowledge and skills, and weaknesses in the internship. The first revision (1993–1994) included seven leadership topics. In the subsequent year (1994–1995), reflecting critical assessment at the end of the pilot, the program was expanded to 12 learning modules, all focused on different dimensions of leadership: (a) dealing with leadership tasks; (b) vision in curriculum and instructional leadership; (c) teacher personnel administration; (d) budget administration; (d) exercising authority, power, and influence; (f) problem solving and decision making; (g) communication; (h) managing conflict; (i) school leadership style; (j) school change; (k) technology; and (l) enhancing student achievement.

Descriptions of two doctoral programs also focused on leadership competencies within an explicit conceptual framework. Holifield, Cox, Holman, Foldesy, and King (1994) described a doctoral program in Educational Leadership at Arkansas State University organized around the model for effective educational leadership and targeting the development of eight leadership skills and eight task areas. Leadership skills were (a) problem analysis, (b) judgment, (c) organizational ability, (d) decisiveness, (e) leadership, (f) sensitivity, (g) stress tolerance, and (h) oral and written communication. The task areas were (a) school climate, (b) school and community relations, (c) instructional management, (d) organization and allocating resources, (e) instructional focus, (f) monitoring and measuring school and student progress, (g) innovative programs, and (h) personnel evaluation and development.

In 1984, with grant support, East Texas State University developed an alternative program to respond to challenges in public education (student performance, teacher effectiveness, and leadership competency) and the perceived public dissatisfaction with the state education system (Vornberg & Davis, 1997). While the traditional program coursework focused on "structure, governance, law and policy matters" (p. 4), students in the alternative, 15-month, full-time, intensive program specialized in "communications and intergroup dynamics … listening, meaning, reflection, decision-making, group processes, and management of differences" (Vornberg & Davis, 1997, p. 4). Aside from course work, students also participated in staff development programs focused on topics including

> learning styles, teacher observation and conferencing, improving staff climate, improving classroom management and discipline, alternative assessment strategies, situation management, effective schools movement, curriculum development and alignment, facilitator practices for teamwork, school safety/security, strategic planning, site based management, teaming for effective instruction, school restructuring [and] exemplary school practices. (Vornberg & Davis, 1997, p. 5)

Courses

A small body of research examined course offerings within or across preparation programs. These studies utilized surveys to identify courses students were taking in preparation programs and conducted analyses to establish the content of these courses. Essentially, each concluded that the curriculum retained a traditional orientation and minimally represented emerging perspectives.

Pohland and Carlson (1993) initiated a national survey study to determine what courses students were taking in licensure and doctoral courses. Including responses from 40 UCEA institutions, the data set included 1,068 courses offered in fall 1992 and spring 1993. Based only on titles, these courses were grouped into 23 different categories and subcategories. According to Pohland and Carlson, the courses offered most frequently by institutions dealt with organization and administration, school law, politics and policy, leadership, personnel administration, organizational studies, research, supervision, economics and finance, and school business management. The percent of institutions offering these courses ranged from 100% (organization and administration) to 57.5% (school business management). Courses in school and community, curriculum and program evaluation, and technology and foundations were offered by 35–50% of the institutions. Courses offered by 30% or fewer dealt with planning, instructional processes, management and systems, facilities planning, ethics and values, cultural diversity and multiculturalism, students, and educational futures. Interestingly, of the three courses listed in the student category, none dealt with students in the preK–12 system. The report identified only a small number of courses "unlikely to be taught a decade or more ago." The majority of courses were 3-credit courses (83.0%). The next-largest category included 4-credit courses (4.4%).

Pohland and Carlson (1993) contrasted their findings with a study conducted approximately 15 years earlier by Silver and Spuck and concluded, "Content change in preparatory programs in educational administration is occurring but within the context of a stable framework" (p. 7). Although they did report a new emphasis on qualitative research, the researchers concurred with other critics that the social sciences paradigm continued to dominate preparatory programs. It is important to remember that their study focused exclusively on course titles that might or might not reflect content. As Pohland and Carlson noted, "Given full academic freedom and the loose constraint of faculty norms … faculty can redesign course syllabi at will" (p. 8). Additionally, the study preceded many of the reform initiatives described in the preceding section.

In 1992, Beck and Murphy surveyed department chairs from 50 UCEA institutions to determine the extent to which they were providing learning opportunities concerning ethics. On one forced-choice question, chairs rated the extent to which their department was offering learning opportunities. Responses from 42 institutions were not at all (1), very little (16), somewhat (21) and a great deal (4). The enactment of this concern about ethics in the curriculum elicited varying responses. Seven reported that they were doing "little (or nothing)" (Beck & Murphy, 1992, p. 38) and had no plans to change; 12 described a "concerted effort to integrate ethics into other courses within their curricula" (p. 42); and 17 stated that "they currently offer courses that specifically focus on administrative ethics" (p. 43).

Behar-Horenstein (1995) analyzed requirements for initial principal certification in Florida and Illinois because of what she viewed as a shift "away from core elements of schooling, such as teaching and learning" (p. 28). She reviewed course requirements for initial principal certification at eight Florida institutions and categorized them in four areas: (a) administration, (b) curriculum, (c) computers, or (d) research. Reflecting implicit and explicit assumptions about the curriculum, Behar-Horenstein reported that the bulk of requirements dealt with administration, whereas seven of the institutions offered one course in curriculum. Six programs included one computer course; two offered a research course. Only one required a course in foundations; two required a course in the principalship. Providing an interesting historical perspective, only one school required field-based experience. In Illinois, apparently requirements were standardized, and the curriculum included two required courses in administration (school administration and school supervision), one in curriculum and instruction, one in statistical methods, and one in educational psychology and philosophy of education. Students also had three elective options.

Hirth and Valesky (1990) surveyed a random sample ($N = 123$) of educational administration departments to determine the extent to which programs required knowledge of special education and special education law and how that information was offered. While 66 of the respondents (54%) included special education in their general school law course, over 74% of them devoted less than 10% of instructional time to the subject, and 57% of the universities had no state requirement for even a general knowledge of special education.

Course Content

Only a few studies have gathered information about course content, and few are in-depth. Based on analysis of syllabi or course descriptions, Beck and Murphy (1994) categorized courses dealing with ethics as those intended to develop a knowledge base, courses focusing on problems of practice, and those that combined theory and practice.

In reporting findings from a study of principal decision making, Davis and Davis (2003) referred to a prior study where they examined curricula from the top 20 schools of education in America, as ranked by *U.S. News and World Report*. They provided no detail on the study but concluded that, even though principals relied very little on classical forms of decision analysis when resolving complex problems, programs continued to place a heavy emphasis on courses that taught classical or analytical decision-making. "In fact," Davis and Davis noted, "we were unable to find even one course that focused on non-quantitative forms of decision making and problem solving" (p. 138). Nicolaides and Gaynor (1992) similarly reported that topics dealing with decision making as irrational processes were less frequent in syllabi dealing with organizational theory and administration.

Interested in the knowledge base of administrative and organizational theory that informs doctoral preparation programs, Nicolaides and Gaynor (1992) initiated a study to describe the "concepts, topics, themes, and theoretical frameworks reflected in current theory courses and specifically to identify the extent to which emergent perspectives available in the literature were represented" (p. 240). In response to an invitation to 50 UCEA institutions, 61 professors from 37 universities submitted 70 syllabi dealing with administrative and organizational theory. The 36 selected for in-depth analysis dealt with organization theory and education (29), organizational processes (4), advanced theory (2), and leadership in education (1). The researchers reviewed each section of the syllabi and recorded, coded, and then grouped concepts by topic. The 32 conceptual categories that emerged were combined into 10 theoretical frameworks: (a) historical-theoretical (human relations, bureaucracy, functionalism), (b) processual (decision making and planning; change, innovation, maintenance), (c) structural (state, federal, institutional; district, community, school; macro- and microstructures), (d) technical, (e) sociopolitical, (f) cultural, (g) symbolic, (h) ethical, (i) leadership (roles and actors, communication, motivation), and (j) new perspectives (loose and tight coupling, "garbage can" model).

Nicolaides and Gaynor (1992) provided a detailed description of findings in each of these areas but generally concluded that the syllabi "most frequently described positions located within general systems theory and geared toward functionalism" (p. 257). Underrepresented were alternative perspectives such as

> phenomenology, symbolic interactionism, ethnomethodology, and critical theory as well as areas recommended by the National Commission on Excellence in Administration: (a) the history and philosophy of education … (b) educational leadership as the embodiment of community, including minorities, and (c) issues related to women in educational leadership. (Nicolaides & Gaynor, 1992, p. 260)

Emphasizing the idiosyncratic development of curricula, all 11 female professors in the study, however, did include readings on women in leadership. Only a few syllabi cited authors writing from the critical or interpretive-phenomenological perspectives. Nicolaides and Gaynor's major conclusion, similar to that of Thrupp and Willmott (2003) and Pohland and Carlson (1993), was that "with a few notable exceptions, teaching in these courses is limited to topics and themes shaped by traditional perspectives" (p. 262).

Hess and Kelly (2005a) conducted an in-depth analysis of course syllabi to determine what gets taught in principal preparation programs. Hess and Kelly (2005a) proposed that preparation programs should include "significant attention to accountability, managing with data, and utilizing research; to hiring, recruiting, evaluating, and terminating personnel; to overseeing an effective instructional program; and to exposing candidates to diverse views regarding educational and organizational management" (p. 4). They analyzed 210 syllabi from core courses (or 2,424 course weeks) included in 31 preparation programs with attention to seven categories of management skills.

Procedurally, using the U.S. Department of Education's Integrated Postsecondary Education Data System listing of 496 administrator preparation programs, Hess and Kelly's (2005a) study drew a sample of elite, large, and more typical programs. Included were programs ranked as the top 20 by *U.S. News & World Report* in 2004, a group of 20 educational leadership preparation programs awarded the largest number of M.Ed. degrees in 2003, and another group of 20 programs randomly drawn from the remaining IPEDS institutions. After excluding institutions without principal preparation programs or courses with syllabi, 56 qualified for analysis: 19 elite, 17 large, and 20 typical. In the next phase of the study, Hess and Kelly (2005a) collected syllabi from the core courses and electives required of aspiring principals. Recognizing the limitations of using course syllabi, Hess and Kelly (2005a) stated,

> The study rests on the notion that syllabi are like blueprints; they reveal structure and design, even if they do not fully reflect what real life instruction looks like. Recognizing that blueprints necessarily lack context, we sought to avoid relying on simple word counts. Rather we gauged the emphasis of each lesson and coded each into one of seven areas of principal competency. Within each area, we then coded the various lessons based on their primary focus. (p. 5)

The findings represented the percentages of course weeks devoted to the each of the seven major coding categories and subcategories by type of institution and total. Since Hess and Kelly (2005a) found "little evidence of systematic variation among programs" (p. 17), their results primarily reflected averages by category, in rank order.

Technical Knowledge

Instruction pertaining to law, finance, facilities, data and research training, and technology—including issues like school funding, budgeting, due process, church and state, student and teacher freedoms, tort law, literature reviews, sampling, statistical analysis, and database management—accounted for 29.6% of the overall time (Hess & Kelly, 2005a). Interestingly, this is an area where the greatest differences between the elite institutions and others appeared, with the elite programs devoting far less attention to research, technology, and data training than their counterparts. Hess and Kelly (2005a) observed, "Elite programs devoted more than 85% of attention to law and finance but just 5% to data, research skills, and technology" (p. 25). In contrast, large and typical programs spent 27–32% on these three areas. While large and typical institutions spent 7.0% and 7.3 % of time on technology, respectively, the syllabi from the elite institutions did not include any examples.

Managing for Results

Of the total course weeks, 15.7% were devoted to school-level program implementation, evaluation, and organizational change efforts that require an active principal role, including topics like accountability, evaluation, assessments, data management, decision making, strategy, organizational structure, and change (Hess & Kelly, 2005a). Looking specifically at the emphasis on accountability and data and research, Hess and Kelly (2005a) found that about 13% "linked school management to standards-based accountability systems, state assessments, or the new demands of No Child Left Behind" (p. 18); only 11% "referenced statistics, data, or empirical research in some context" (p. 19).

Managing Personnel

The curriculum dealing with principal's relations with school employees, including issues like recruitment, selection, induction, teacher evaluation, clinical supervision, motivation, conflict management, professional development, termination, or dismissal accounted for 14.9% of course weeks (Hess & Kelly, 2005a). Of this, 11.4% of time focused on recruitment and hiring; 23.6% focused on evaluating teachers; and 3.3% and 2.5%, respectively, addressed teacher dismissal and compensation. Coding the treatment of teacher evaluation as tough minded (linking evaluation to student performance, using nonobservational data, rewarding excellence, or remediating or dismissing low-performing faculty) or supportive (observation, clinical supervision, coaching, or mentoring), Hess and Kelly (2005a) found the focus was predominantly supportive (74.1%). They concluded that preparation programs give little attention to teaching new principals to hire, evaluate, reward, or terminate employees.

Norms and Values

Exposure to different educational and pedagogical philosophies; purpose of schooling; and the racial, ethnic, and socioeconomic context of education—including issues like stratification, multicultural-ism, diversity, constructivism, inequality, equity, social justice, and gender—accounted for 12.1% of the curriculum (Hess & Kelly, 2005a). Within this category, Hess and Kelly (2005a) coded as "left-leaning" content that "advocated concepts like social justice and multiculturalism, focused on inequality or discrimination, emphasized notions of silenced voices and child-centered instruction, or were critical of testing and choice-based reform" (p. 28). Categorized as "right-leaning" were "weeks that critiqued notions of social justice and multiculturalism, critiqued a focus on inequality or discrimination as engaging in 'victimhood,' advocated phonics and back-to-basics instruction, or framed discussions of testing or choice-based reform in positive terms" (Hess & Kelly, 2005a, p. 28). Those weeks that did not "display clear normative direction or … included a variety of normative views were coded 'neutral'" (p. 28). Using this framework, Hess and Kelly (2005a, p. 28) found a "distinct left-leaning normative tilt," with 64.8% overall coded as normative left, only 0.3% as normative right (the single instance occurred in an elite program), and the balance (34.8%) as balanced or neutral. The authors also noted that the words *diversity, diverse, multiculturalism*, and *multicultural* appeared in only 3.0% of all course weeks.

Managing Classroom Instruction

Overall, 10.9% of course weeks addressed the leaders' role and influence on what goes on in the classroom (Hess & Kelly, 2005a). These weeks included issues like curriculum, learning theories, instructional leadership, pedagogy, classroom management, collaborative learning.

External Leadership

Only 8.0% of the curriculum dealt with principals' relationship with constituents, including issues like board relations, collective bargaining, public relations and marketing, parent and community relations, politics, and policy (Hess & Kelly, 2005a). Within that category, the most attention was focused on understanding politics and policy (30.4%) and community relations (22.7%). Small business skills and collective bargaining received significant attention in large programs (42.3%) but far less in elite (19.5%) or typical (18.6%) programs. Parental relations received scant attention in any program: 2.6% overall, ranging from 0.0% in large programs to 4.3% in elite programs.

Leadership and School Culture

Perhaps most surprising, only 6.0% of course weeks were devoted to leadership theory and school culture (Hess & Kelly, 2005a). These course weeks included issues like frames of leadership, symbolic leadership, leadership versus management, creating a school culture, leading with vision, and school climate.

The Supported Curriculum

The supported curriculum encompasses the information or ideas that support learning and is a tangible manifestation of the knowledge base. The most obvious source of information is published materials: the textbooks, texts, and articles that students encounter as required or recommended reading. As technology advances, faculty and students have wider access to materials in the form of films, tapes, or unpublished reports. Equally and perhaps more important, we argue, are the knowledge and perspectives that the faculty themselves bring into the classroom, shaping the curriculum through formal or informal lectures or simply by guiding discussion.

Although research on the supported curriculum is limited, there is sufficient information to conclude that the knowledge base that students encounter is extremely broad and diverse and differs from program to program, course to course, and even semester to semester. Despite evidence of a declining use of textbooks and reliance on multiple and frequently changing sources of information, systematic research is largely limited to the examination of textbooks.

Faculty Perspectives

After spending 10 months in Canada examining preparation programs in 12 prominent universities, Thomas (1975) concluded that course content more often reflected the interests and knowledge of faculty than the specific titles. Nearly 20 years later, even with comprehensive program plans to guide preparation, Mulkeen and Cooper (1992) also reported, "Topics for class were most often dictated by the academic interest of the faculty" (p. 26). Although individual faculty may play the most important role in shaping the curriculum, few studies have focused directly on faculty and the way that they influence the development and enactment of curriculum.

Several studies utilized national surveys to explore faculty perceptions about what should be included in preparation programs: computer skills (Garland, 1989), essential readings (Fero & Fero, 1991), general instructional topics (Cordeiro, Krueger, Parks, Restine, & Wilson, 1993), ethics (Beck & Murphy, 1994), and poverty (Lyman & Villani, 2002). Interestingly, even though a substantial portion of administrative preparation courses are taught by other than full-time faculty, these surveys were directed to department or program administrators and full-time faculty.

Fero and colleagues (1991) surveyed chairs of departments of educational administration in American Association of Colleges for Teacher Education institutions with graduate programs and asked them "to list up to ten books other than textbooks that they would consider to be required reading for students in educational administration/leadership" (p. 5). Of the 275 institutions contacted, 55 respondents listed 1–50 books. Excluding textbooks, a total of 308 books remained. With the exception of *A Place Called School* (Goodard, 1984) and *In Search of Excellence* (Peters & Waterman, 1983) each appearing on at least 20% of the lists, there was little agreement. Cordeiro et al. (1993) distributed a survey to 22 Danforth Program facilitators, asking them to rate the importance of 77 instructional topics in 17 content areas. Of the content areas, 90% of respondents rated leadership as most important, with 95% highlighting oral expression, human relations, interpersonal skills, and problem solving. Rated as highly important by more than 50% were 42 topics, including supervision, planning, governmental and legal issues, technology, and public relations. Five content areas not rated highly were business management and administration, labor management relations, politics, administration of special programs, and job skills.

In a survey of UCEA institutions, 42 department chairs rated the extent to which their department was offering learning opportunities concerning ethics (Beck & Murphy, 1994). From open-ended questions, Beck and Murphy noted a prevailing view among those reporting little or no activity that students would simply "absorb" an awareness of moral issues and ways to think about these issues in the course of their preparation (p. 41).

Lyman and Villani (2002) conducted an e-mail survey of 408 educational administration departments to determine "whether and how school leadership preparation programs emphasize understanding poverty's substantial complexity, including its systemic causes and effects" (p. 257). Of 279 (68.4%) who responded, 68.5% rated the issue as greatly or extremely important, but 94.0% did not have a course devoted to the topic, and only 19.9% felt that there was a strong or very strong emphasis on poverty. Interestingly, these perceptual studies correspond with other data suggesting a lack of attention to special education and the relative neglect of social justice issues, like poverty, within preparation programs.

Reading Requirements

Literature on preparation programs emphasizes the importance of the knowledge base and the need to integrate theory and practice. Whereas some articles include information about reading requirements, there is little information on the nature of the knowledge base included in the curriculum. Hart (1990), for example, described three ways of knowing: (a) theoretical, (b) empirical, and (c) experiential. The literature about preparation programs contains specific references to the personal and experiential knowledge that practicing administrators and students bring to programs and a recognition that this is an important part of the curriculum. In at least one instance (Parker & Shapiro, 1992), students directly attributed their learning, in this case about social justice, to interaction with other students. In contrast, there were few (if any) references to the expertise that full-time academic faculty contribute to programs, and very little information about the utilization and contribution of knowledge drawn from theoretical and empirical research.

Several studies included information on readings in courses dealing with social justice and ethics. Anderson (2006), in a case study of a single program with an intentional focus on social justice, identified "explicitly social justice-oriented texts" (p. 20) included in the syllabi. Lyman and Villani (2002) identified the specific readings in a course designed to sensitize students to the impact of poverty. From an interview study of 28 students or graduates in three colleges of education, Parker and Shapiro (1992) determined that about half had received "no exposure to the new scholarship on women, race, social class, and other areas of difference" (p. 13). According to Beck and Murphy (1994), ethics courses focused on problems of practice used *The Ethics of School Administration* or *The Ethics of Administration* (Strike, Haller, & Soltis; Strike & Soltis, both as cited in Beck & Murphy). Others reportedly drew from philosophy; sociology; literature; and works about professionalism, ethics, and professional issues.

Several other articles, describing curricular innovations, also included information on reading assignments. In a course on school culture, Barbour (1994) offered students a selection of novels and ethnographies, as did a leadership course intended to develop self-awareness (Whitaker, 1999). Henning and Robinson (2002), as they combined a traditional educational research course with one on change and transformation, shifted from a standard research text to texts on assessment and data analysis, written for practitioners. Although there were few references to the use of articles from peer-review journals, this course assigned additional readings from *Educational Evaluation and Policy Analysis* and the *Journal of Educational Administration*.

Ideas and Perspectives

Several studies relied on content analysis to determine the nature of the information and the messages that are being communicated. These studies revealed historical themes, textual apologism, and accountable management.

Historical Themes

A major historical analysis of textbooks from 1820–2000 clearly indicated that the perspectives on educational administration have changed over time, reflecting changing values; the impact of various influential groups or models; and the relative influence of theory, research, and practice (Glass, 2004). It is important to note that the "textbook" is a particular genre in the educational administration literature that is closely linked with a particular curriculum structure. Hess and Kelly (2005b), for example, focused on the general textbook because they assumed that the curriculum for preparation typically included an introductory course that provides an overview of administration. A second assumption was that the textbook is the primary source of information within a course.

Although 1955–1985 is "generally perceived to be an era of the ascendance and dominance of the social sciences in educational administration," Glass (2004) described texts from this period as "descriptive tomes of expert opinion and administrative practice" (p.140). From 1985–2000, the literature was dominated by school-reform efforts, with some texts slanted toward theory, others combining theory and practice. New on the scene were case-studies texts, specialized texts, and texts written to help meet new professional standards. The general textbook, in contrast, began to "fade out during this era" with only one completely new general text published; policy texts, including what Glass described as "near 'pulp quality' substitutions," (p. 111) began to replace general textbooks.

Several additional studies examined syllabi and course materials to identify themes that students encounter in preparation programs. While reflecting different philosophies about leadership, each reflected critical assumptions about what was needed or missing from the preparation programs. Sirotnik and Kimball (1994), for example, reviewed National Policy Board Reports (1993), *Educational Administration Quarterly* volumes from 1988–1992, and a 1993 report from the Council of Administrators of Special Education Preliminary regarding special education issues in administrative preparation programs. Sirotnik and Kimball found minimal attention to special education administration.

In her review of three introductory research texts, Ranis (2003) concluded that positivist perspectives predominate. From a feminist postmodern perspective, Brunner (2002a) analyzed "traditional discourse of the superintendency as reflected in 11 textbooks published from 1990–1999" (p. 406). Brunner's conclusion was that textbooks most often describe superintendents as "'talkers' or 'tellers'" (p. 408) and advise them (in explicit or implicit messages) "to be the communicators (the talkers) and distributors of carefully shaped information" (p. 408).

Textual Apologism

Thrupp and Willmott (2003) analyzed educational management texts reflecting textual apologism. Although offering a detailed description of their methods of selecting texts, they did not provide specific information on the numbers or names of the texts included in the analysis or coding procedures. In general, their conclusion was consistent with their original premise. Thrupp and Willmott were particularly critical of the literature in school leadership and school change, commenting that they were "linked to managerialism" and permeated by "bureaucratization and individualism" (p. 230).

Accountable Management

In contrast, Hess and Kelly (2005b) urged greater attention to management. In their analysis of syllabi, Hess and Kelly (2005b) also sought to determine whether the reading in preparation programs was preparing principals "for the rigors of accountable management" (p. 1). From the 210 core syllabi, they identified a total of 1851 readings, including books, articles, edited volume chapters, newspaper articles, and law cases. Of these, 43% were books or book sections. For the analysis, Hess and Kelly (2005b) selected "11 of the 13 educational administration texts most frequently assigned" (p. 1) and determined the degree to which texts emphasized performance, achievement, and accountability; covered important management skills "like the evaluation of personnel, the use of incentives, and removing ineffective educators"; and evinced a progressive or "politically correct" bias (p. 4).

Using a detailed coding system, Hess and Kelly (2005b) analyzed text on each page. Concepts appearing most frequently were performance or achievement (44.30/100 pages), evaluation (37.87), culture (28.77), data (16.82), values (15.91), resources (15.90), and compensation (15.70). Least frequent were efficiency (5.86), accountability (5.41) and termination or dismissal (3.09). Hess and Kelly (2005b) concluded, "The texts appear to reflect the current consensus regarding the importance of school performance and outcomes rather than the traditional emphasis on inputs and resources" (p. 13). The topics receiving the least amount of attention were those dealing with "thorny personnel management issues like compensation and termination or dismissal" (p. 14). Hess and Kelly (2005b) attributed the lack of attention to the "confines of traditional public school management," rather than to the fact that management was simply not a focus of many of the texts in the analysis (p. 14). Like Thrupp and Willmott (2003), Hess and Kelly (2005b) found infrequent references to the terms *diversity* (4.29) or *multicultural* (1.27) and concluded that "the themes conventionally imagined to signal an explicit progressive bias were largely absent" (p. 24), particularly so in the general and specialized texts.

Taught Curriculum

When students enter the classroom, what curriculum do they actually encounter? This section deals with articles that offered a closer look at what takes place in the classroom as faculty and students interact. The taught curriculum is essentially the enactment of different dimensions of the curriculum. Because this handbook includes a separate chapter on pedagogy, we limit our discussion here to ways that faculty conceptualize learning and how they utilize support materials to facilitate student learning. This section, then, reviews articles that portray faculty in their instructional roles as they design curriculum and explore the links among knowledge, pedagogy, and student learning. It is important to note that this is the smallest section, reflecting perhaps the lack of attention to the craft of teaching in leadership preparation.

Maintaining that effective problem-solving processes are essential for the development of expert administrators, Leithwood and Steinbach (1992) developed an experimental program to determine whether these skills can be taught. The 4-day program was evenly spaced over a period of 4 months, and instruction was organized around a specific model of administrative problem solving. Each component of the model and its subskills were explicitly taught. Each session focused on one or two components of the model, and typically participants would identify the problem-solving strategy used by others, analyze and evaluate the processes used by the problem solver, practice the strategies themselves using a new problem, and then reflect on their strategy use. Participants worked on a total of nine problems that varied in their degree of structure and complexity. Although this curriculum was designed for an in-service program, it illustrates the use of theory and research to shape instructional activities with intent to facilitate learning.

Several other articles also focused on the nature of instruction within preparation programs and illustrated how theory and practice are integrated in the classroom. Glasman and Glasman (1997) provided a detailed description of modules designed to develop students' understanding and use of strategies dealing with authority, power, and influence. Osterman (1994) described a curricular effort to develop communication skills. Whitaker (1999) outlined the self-strand, a required component of the preparation program at the University of Northern Colorado that was "designed to assist future leaders in gaining a greater awareness of their values and beliefs as they relate to leadership" (p. 168). Beatty and Brew (2004) explained a course designed to "address the emotions of leadership" (p. 329). In each instance, the instructors identified the informational materials that they introduced, described the instructional strategies they used to facilitate understanding and skill development, and provided some assessment data.

Providing the most direct and comprehensive look at the taught curriculum was a case study by Riehl, Larson, Short, and Reitzug (2000), an in-depth look at teaching and learning in the context of a doctoral course. In this study, we see doctoral faculty engaged in the work of curriculum development, assessing the effectiveness of their work relative to predefined goals as they interacted with students in the class and then used those data to modify the curriculum. It is particularly interesting because we see how decisions were made about the content as well as about pedagogical strategies. The purpose of Riehl et al.'s study was to "explore common and emerging conceptions of what constitutes knowledge in educational administration, how knowledge relates to practice, and how individuals in universities and schools can engage in a particular kind of knowledge work-research" (p. 391). The New York University faculty initially asked beginning doctoral students questions: "What does the term scholar mean to you? What do scholars do? What habits do scholars regularly practice?" (Riehl et al., 2000, p. 413). The ensuing discussion reflected the traditional notion of scholar as academic and the distinction between scholar and practitioner.

The faculty then prompted students to expand their narrow definition to conceive of scholarship as "a way of being, knowing, and doing" (Riehl et al., 2000, p. 413). Small-group conversations widened the definition to include a scholar as an inquirer, or "someone who always remains open to learning something new or who changes one's view in light of new evidence" (p. 413). According to Riehl et al., faculty subsequently "developed an introductory seminar that differed from traditional course work in that it brought the habits of scholarship necessary for scholarly practice to the fore" and involved a "two way examination of scholarship" (p. 414). The faculty acknowledged that doctoral students bring experience, respect, and knowledge from the field into the classroom and upon entering the program are relegated to a place of ignorance in the face of unfamiliar literature, theories and terminology. Hence, Riehl et al. noted that the faculty focused on "how students read and respond to research" (p. 415) in order to view literature through the students' eyes.

The faculty's observations of student learning shaped their approach to the curriculum (Riehl et al., 2000). They noted that initially students did not know how to read research. Some students read it as a novel, and when they did not understand it on the first read-through, they stopped reading and rejected the author. Others skipped sections deemed irrelevant or inaccessible (often methodology or theory). According to Riehl et al., in response, faculty assigned "fewer readings and slowed down the pace of instruction to examine our students' habits of scholarship more closely" and found as "students learned to read deep text, their confidence in themselves as scholars grew" (p. 418).

As they discovered that students had views of the way things are in education without any evidentiary support, the faculty felt it was important to uncover this and encourage students to "become more intentional about examining their own ways of knowing" (Riehl et al., 2000, p. 418). They also learned that students need practice writing and rewriting early and often. When they addressed this, "students became intentional about developing the habits of scholarship that ultimately helped them to read, use and apply research" (Riehl et al., 2000, p. 420). "By changing the way we think about and teach scholarship in educational administration," Riehl et al. concluded, "we can make our preparation programs more relevant to our students, regardless of the role they choose to play in education" (p. 420).

The Learned Curriculum

Perhaps the most important question confronting the field of leadership preparation deals with learning. Does the curriculum support learning, and, if so, how? Various studies have attempted to determine the effectiveness of leadership preparation programs on different dimensions of learning: Have students developed new knowledge and new ways of thinking, have they developed leadership competencies, and is preparation associated with more effective leadership? Since other chapters focus exclusively on assessment and program evaluation, here we provide only a brief overview of selected studies that directly examined the relationship between curriculum and learning.

Changes in Perspectives

Several evaluation studies were designed to explore cognitive changes associated with participation in a program or course. Two reported data about changes in leadership perspective and attempted to determine ways in which the program fostered learning. Responding to a survey, 20 students, all members of a cohort who had completed the program as an intact group, rated their preparation program favorably on meeting its objectives (Hermond, 1999). Respondents indicated that the program enabled them to explore leadership theories and develop a broad understanding of leadership, to refine their leadership philosophy, to think critically about solutions to current issues, to become more self-directed and better able to sense and respond to problems in creative manner, and to develop new insights into urban leadership (Hermond, 1999). In response to open-ended questions, students identified introductory and concluding leadership courses as important sources of learning about leadership theories. In contrast, Browne-Ferrigno (2001), while reporting changes in perspective, concluded that personal characteristics of the participants and their experience in the workplace might have had a stronger influence on learning than the program.

While assessment studies typically focused on predetermined outcomes or criteria, Slater et al. (2001) adopted an open-ended approach to develop an understanding of student learning. Twenty-two current students and recent graduates participated in five focus-group sessions regarding how they had changed during the program. Comments centered on personal transformation, according to Slater et al.: "Participants did not speak about learning specific job tasks such as preparing a budget, disciplining students, or conducting workshops. Rather, they focused on how they saw themselves differently, how they saw others differently, and how they had come to see school administration" (p. 9). They described becoming more aware of how they learn and more excited about learning. The curriculum emphasized research and data-based decision making; correspondingly, the graduates reported a new sense of confidence in their skills as problem solvers and thinkers.

In the area of social justice, several studies looked at changes relative to course or program objectives. In assessing a course on School Culture and the Principalship, Barbour (1994) concluded that the students were developing an understanding and appreciation of culture and were able to identify professional applications. Lyman and Villani (2002) assessed a course designed to increase students' understanding of poverty; in an analysis of class assignments, 87% of the students described "change in perception or attitude about poverty itself, or about persons who are economically poor" (p. 265). According to Lyman and Villani, responses on the Webb and Sherman Causes of Poverty questionnaire also showed that students who had taken the course were more likely than the control group to attribute poverty to structural problems ($p < .05$) and less likely to blame poverty on individual failures ($p < .01$).

Anderson (2006), however, who sought evidence of learning transfer by examining work samples, was less successful. As part of a case study to determine how a leadership preparation program implemented a social-justice oriented program, Anderson explored "the impact of this curriculum on students' self-reported attitudes toward social justice" (p. 2). Whereas Barbour (1994) and Lyman and Villani (2002) essentially explored students' espoused theories regarding poverty, Anderson probed deeper to determine if students were integrating social justice concepts by examining work not directly focused on social justice. Vision statements provided several examples where students appeared to apply learning from courses. At the same time, most students' descriptions of their fieldwork did not reflect the social justice and critical reflection curriculum. Like Browne-Ferrigno (2001), Anderson also concluded, "Discourses and practices promoted by students' school districts tended to be more powerful than those of the program" (p. 23).

Anderson (2006) clearly established that social justice was an integral part of this preparation program; yet, the findings suggest that, with few exceptions, students failed to integrate or apply social justice principles. Although these findings may be discouraging, it is also important to note that this is one of the few studies that used indirect methods to gather data. Further, the study established an important point—the development of new knowledge or a change in espoused theory does not necessarily lead to change in behavior (Osterman & Kottkamp, 1993, 2004).

Development of Competencies

A number of studies sought to determine if participation in preparation programs developed skills or competencies associated with leadership. In the self-report studies, graduates typically reported that the preparation programs were successful in developing their leadership capability; however, program differences were also clear. Other studies relied on authentic assessment and gathered performance data within the context of the preparation program, often focusing on specific competencies. They ranged from informal assessment of student learning in single courses to more comprehensive assessment of student learning in courses and programs. In each instance, the studies established a direct link between curriculum and the development of specific competencies.

Three comparative studies (Orr & Barber, 2006; Orr, LeTendre, & Silverberg, 2006; Orr & Pounder, 2007) enable us to determine that there are program differences in curriculum and that these differences are related to learning. Utilizing data generated by institutional members of the UCEA Teaching in Educational Leadership Special Interest Group (TEA-SIG) Task Force on Evaluating Leadership Preparation Effectiveness, these studies compared survey responses from graduates of 3, 5, and 17 programs, respectively. The second study (Orr et al., 2006) included as independent measures two aspects of curriculum content: leading learning and challenging and reflective. Although there were differences between schools, two curriculum features, challenging content and focus on leading learning, were the highest rated of the nine program features. Regression analysis indicated that these two curricular dimensions as well as three other program features predicted self-reported learning on two outcomes, leading learning and organizational learning. These studies are important not only for their findings, but also because the cross-institutional design represents an effective way to expand considerably our knowledge regarding the nature, quality, and effectiveness of preparation programs.

Another comparative study (Leithwood, Jantzi, Coffin, & Wilson, 1996) assessed the effectiveness of 11 university-based programs, using self-report data from program participants supplemented by responses from teachers working with the graduate administrators. All had been developed with Danforth Foundation support and were to have included common features, including specific curricular themes. On a 75-item survey, 136 program graduates rated nine structural features, including program content. The "overall rating of program features was 3.45" on the 4-point scale, suggesting that graduates "considered the programs to have been valuable to their development as school leaders" (Leithwood et al., 1996, p. 325). More important, teachers also perceived that administrators were demonstrating effective leadership in the schools.

A regression analysis determined that about 8% of the variation in perceptions of effective leadership was accounted for by the nine program features ($F = 4.688$, $df = 9,522$), but only three program features—instructional strategies, cohort membership, and program content—"made significant unique contributions of 2, 1, and 1 percent respectively" (Leithwood et al., 1996, p. 338). Their study is important because, as Leithwood et al. (1996) noted, it established that preparation programs make a difference in leadership effectiveness and that variations in leader effectiveness can be traced to even minor variations in program features. It also suggests that program content, as distinct from other program features, plays an important role in the development of leadership competencies.

Educational Improvement

To assess the effectiveness of theory–practice linkages in an Ed.D. program, Pounder (1995) evaluated the degree and ways in which Ed.D. student field-based projects and clinical research studies resulted in program or policy changes. Using a survey, researchers gathered information about student field-application projects that had been completed in their courses. Students also submitted copies of the projects for document analysis. Of 14 respondents, mostly middle-management educational administrators at midcareer, each had completed 4–6 field-application projects; 4 had completed the culminating clinical research study or dissertation. Of 83 completed projects, 54 lent themselves to adoption or implementation, and 69% of these (37) resulted in a program or policy change. Illustrating the practical value of the formal knowledge base, Pounder noted that the students felt that the level of support "was often influenced by the strength of their project's supporting theoretical and/or research rationale" (p. 160).

Problem Framing and Problem Solving

Frequently included in program goals, problem solving is one area where rigorous studies have utilized authentic assessment to establish competency and link the development of skills to the curriculum in the preparation program. The first of these was an experimental pre- and posttest conducted as part of an experimental in-service program to develop problem-solving expertise among principals and vice principals (Leithwood & Steinbach, 1992). Both groups took pre- and posttests in which they worked on varied problems. Expert raters assigned an overall score, reflecting thoroughness and quality, and scores for each of six components: (a) problem interpretation, (b) goals, (c) principles, (d) constraints, (e) solution processes, and (f) affect. Scores indicated that the experimental group improved more than the control group on both dimensions of the overall rating, but differences were not statistically significant.

In the detailed analysis, Leithwood and Steinbach (1992) reported,

> The experimental group showed significantly greater expertise in their thinking related to the interpretation of the problem, the goals set for solving the problem, and their understanding of the importance of anticipating and planning for the handling of possible constraints. (p. 338)

At the same time, with respect to the solution processes component, Leithwood and Steinbach noted, "Although the differences between groups were not statistically significant, the control group showed greater improvement than the experimental group" (p. 338). There was little change with respect to the values and affect component, and the researchers speculated that the lack of impact occurred "because these areas did not receive systematic instructional attention" (p. 339). Leithwood and Steinbach concluded that problem solving can be taught and seemed to have a positive impact on performance, with administrators seeming "better able to solve swampy administrative problems than they could before the program" (p. 340).

On the basis of two experimental studies, Copland (2000) also concluded that problem-framing ability "can be successfully taught and developed in students during the process of preparing for the principalship" (p. 603). The first study (Copland, 2000), a quasi-experimental, posttest-only design, involved 18 students enrolled in three cohorts in 3 successive years ($n = 6$ students per cohort). Over this 3-year period, the Stanford University Prospective Principals Program gradually increased students' exposure to problem-based learning. Whereas the first cohort had no program exposure to problem framing, the second cohort completed approximately seven problem-based learning projects, and the third completed approximately 12 problem-based learning projects. The purpose of Copland's (2000) study was to determine whether "greater exposure to problem based preparation experiences is associated with greater problem-framing ability among prospective principals" (p. 586).

Each of the 18 participants responded in writing to five administrative problem scenarios (Copland, 2000). Three raters, experienced as principals, scored responses. Highlighting the significance of individual differences, the analysis established that GRE scores, and particularly the quantitative and analytic subtests, had a significant positive correlation with problem-framing ability. At the same time, there were significant differences between the cohort groups on problem-framing ability: the more exposure to problem framing practice, the higher the mean score. Given the quasi-experimental nature of the design, Copland (2000) noted,

> Although the findings cannot imply a causal argument, … they do provide an indication that instructional practices that activate prior knowledge and situate learning in contexts similar to those encountered in practice are associated with the development of students' ability to understand and frame problems. (p. 604)

A second study addressed some of these limitations (Copland, 2003). This study focused on one cohort of 6 female students of diverse ethnicity enrolled in the Prospective Principals Program. As in the earlier study, for the pre- and posttest, students completed five problem scenarios that were then rated, using the same 10-item scoring instrument. Following the pretest, the treatment involved participation in a series of approximately 13 problem-based learning projects over three consecutive summers. A t test for dependent samples (9.259) established that the participants' mean scores on the posttest (2.057 on a 0–3 scale) were significantly higher than those on the pretest (1.006). Although pointing out the limitations of the study, Copland (2003) concluded again, "Greater exposure to PBL [problem-based learning] was associated with greater problem-framing ability" among these students (p. 541).

Leadership Effectiveness

One study specifically examined the effect of curriculum on leadership behavior and performance. As a follow-up study to the pre- and posttest analysis of the development of problem-framing ability, Copland (2003) conducted an interview study of 12 graduates from the Prospective Principals Program to determine whether the skills learned in problem-based preparation had transferred to their practice. The interviews began with open-ended questions about how the overall preparation program had influenced and supported their practice as school leaders. In the analysis, graduates identified clearly understanding problems as a key leadership characteristic, uniformly mentioned their ability to understand and frame problems as useful in their work as leaders, and attributed the development of these abilities to their specific experiences in problem-based learning.

What We Know and What We Don't Know

For this chapter, we defined curriculum in a comprehensive way. The recommended literature is an expression of vision and serves as standards to assess program efforts. The written curriculum identifies program goals and indicates how those goals are embodied in course requirements and course documents. The supported curriculum refers to the information and ideas that inform learning, the taught curriculum is the enactment of the course plans, and the learned curriculum is the learning that is linked to the instructional experience.

From the review of research regarding curriculum in leadership preparation programs, it is apparent that what we know about any single dimension of the curriculum is limited. With the exception of UCEA's attempts to develop a comprehensive knowledge base for the field, the recommended curriculum is an outgrowth of specific interests or perspectives of individual scholars. Information on the written curriculum is incorporated in program descriptions but is not addressed in any systematic or comparative fashion. In terms of the assessed or learned curriculum, although there is an obvious need to know more, a number of well-designed studies provide important data about the quality and effectiveness of leadership preparation programs and serve as models for future research. The areas least explored, however, deal with the curriculum that students encounter in preparation programs. Although there is substantive research on the supported curriculum, given its likely flux and breadth, it is particularly limited, given its almost exclusive attention to textbooks. We know little about the information and ideas that shape learning or how they are integrated into the learning experience.

In terms of research design, although several outstanding research studies inform our understanding of the curriculum and its relationship to learning, the majority of the information about the curriculum is drawn from articles or studies with other purposes. Few were designed specifically to examine curriculum in the field of leadership education, within or across programs. At the same time, the existing literature is informative and provocative and suggests areas for additional and more focused inquiry.

Does Curriculum Matter?

Perhaps one of the most interesting and important findings is that programs differ and the curriculum does matter. In general, criticisms of leadership preparation programs reflect assumptions about the uniformly poor quality of curriculum and its lack of relevance for leadership. This inquiry challenges these assumptions. Although there is insufficient information to develop a deep or comprehensive portrait of the curriculum, information from various sources indicates that, despite commonalities, programs differ in substantive ways.

At a very broad level, preservice programs have a shared purpose: to develop individuals' ability to function effectively as educational leaders. Yet, leadership is defined in multiple ways, and these conceptions of leadership are reflected in diverse program goals and curriculum design. They differ in stated goals and in their beliefs about the content and structure of the curriculum needed to realize these goals. Whereas some preparation programs emphasized the development of cognitive abilities and self-awareness, others focused on the development of leadership competencies. Others grounded their purpose in educational and social concerns. Despite the different emphases, programs were still multidimensional, but it is not clear how programs link their curriculum to the development of the full range of knowledge, skills, and dispositions associated with leadership.

Preparation programs generally have been criticized for lack of cohesiveness and loose requirements. Again, recognizing that the information about the curriculum draws upon a limited data base and may represent outliers rather than the average, these descriptive reports and studies presented a different picture. According to Levine (2005), preparation programs lack rigor and consist simply of one or two core requirements supplemented by elective options. An examination of program descriptions and analyses, however, identifies a number of universities that have developed cohesive programs, consisting of nontraditional courses that integrate theory and practice and are designed to develop a full range of cognitive and behavioral competencies incorporated in state and professional standards.

In contrast with criticisms that undermine the legitimacy of university preparation, individual and comparative evaluations affirm that graduates are generally complimentary about the quality of their experience in preparation programs and its relevance to their own leadership. From individual and comparative assessments, we learn that graduates were complimentary about the quality of the programs, attributed development of knowledge and competencies to the program, and perceived their learning as relevant to their work as educational leaders. An informal analysis of responses across programs, however, suggests that some programs are more successful than others in certain competency areas. Identifying program strengths and determining how the curriculum is organized to achieve those objectives would be helpful.

Although only a few studies have examined performance outcomes associated with leadership preparation, this research, too, suggests that student learning is related to the curriculum: Students learn what we teach. At the same time, the research also suggests that it is more difficult to achieve the deep cognitive change associated with high transfer. We also know that the content of the curriculum, in contrast with other design features, contributes importantly to student learning, but we still have limited knowledge of what is being taught or how elements of the curriculum contribute to learning.

To What Extent Are the Recommended, Written, and Enacted Curricula Aligned?

The recommended literature and statements in the written curriculum about program goals and objectives serve as standards. One assessment of program effectiveness, then, would be the alignment between stated goals and objectives and the curriculum design. From the recommended literature, we can identify aspects of the curriculum perceived as important, but when we examine information about the written and learned curriculum, it is not possible to determine how or to what extent those themes are embodied in the curriculum. While it is clear that these themes are central in selected programs, other studies suggest that areas prioritized in the literature are not widely addressed in the leadership curriculum.

Cognitive Awareness and Ability

One of the most prominent themes in the literature regarding the recommended and written curriculum focuses on the development of cognitive awareness and ability. To be effective leaders, the literature indicates, for example, that it is important for students to develop self-awareness, a critical perspective, sensitivity to issues of social justice and equity, knowledge of teaching and learning, and skills of inquiry associated with the analysis and resolution of problems.

Self-awareness and reflection Developing a deeper understanding of self through reflection is a pervasive theme, conceptually linked to leadership. Program descriptions associate effective leadership with awareness of one's emotions, beliefs, and values, and several studies describe or assess curricular efforts to develop self-awareness. At the same time, we know relatively little about how programs are defining or attempting to realize these goals. Some programs identify reflection as an integral component of the program. Some include stand-alone courses, while in others the development of awareness is a goal associated with the practicum. Reflective practice seems to play an important role in the design of programs, but again, there is little specific research and discussion of how reflective practice is defined or enacted in programs.

Inquiry skills Another common focus in programs is the development of inquiry skills. Knowledge of research and research strategies, in theory, develop a critical perspective and facilitate the development of problem-framing, problem-solving, and decision-making skills. This is one area where several studies provide an in-depth perspective on the taught, supported, and learned curricula. Riehl et al. (2000) offered perhaps the only in-depth reflective analysis on teaching research in a class of doctoral students and enabled us to see direct connections between the materials the faculty selected and the learning that occurred. Leithwood and Steinbach (1992) provided us with a detailed description of classroom-based instruction in problem solving. Later studies (Copland, 2000, 2003; Leithwood, Riedlinger, Bauer, & Jantzi, 2003; Pounder, 1995) evaluated the effectiveness of instruction in problem framing and problem solving and demonstrated that systematic instruction leads to the development of knowledge and competency. In light of this, the finding from Hess and Kelly (2005a) that leadership preparation programs at elite institutions devoted only 5% of the curriculum to data analysis, research skills, and technology is intriguing.

At the same time, in sharp contrast to the recommended literature, there is little evidence that the preparation curriculum adequately reflects what scholars consider emerging or critical perspectives. The findings are consistent that programs place more emphasis on positivistic frameworks and quantitative methodologies than on qualitative methodologies and pay little attention to newer perspectives (Brunner, 2002b; Davis & Davis, 2003; Nicolaides & Gaynor, 1992; Pohland & Carlson, 1993; Scheurich & Laible, 1995; Thrupp & Willmott, 2003).

Social justice Despite a strong emphasis on preparing leaders to address social justice concerns and issues of inequity in the recommended literature and within individual programs, analyses of course requirements, syllabi, and texts revealed relatively little attention to the topic. Pohland and Carlson (1993) found few courses dealing with topics of cultural diversity or multiculturalism. Hess and Kelly (2005b), concerned about a perceived overemphasis on social justice in the curriculum, were surprised to find a relatively small proportion (3%) devoted to left-leaning issues like diversity and multiculturalism. On the other end of the political spectrum, Thrupp and Willmott (2003) were dismayed at what they felt was an inattention to social inequality in texts.

Research utilizing survey data from graduates and faculty, as well as text analyses, also suggests that preparation programs provide scant attention to another area of social justice—special education leadership. Given trends toward inclusion as well as expanding administrative requirements associated with the No Child Left Behind Act and the Individuals With Disabilities Education Act, this omission may have important consequences for administrators and students.

Teaching and learning The recommended curriculum identified the need to provide prospective school leaders with a strong foundation in the core technologies of schooling—teaching and learning. Descriptions of some individual programs highlighted teaching and learning as key components and identified specific courses dealing with the topic. At the same time, other studies suggested that this area may be neglected. Pohland and Carlson (1993), for example, found that courses dealing with instructional processes were offered by less than 30.0% of the programs surveyed, and Hess and Kelly (2005a) found only 10.9% of course weeks devoted to managing classroom instruction. The knowledge base in the area of teaching and learning has expanded considerably (Hutchings & Shulman, 1999), and attention to this area should have important implications for instructional leadership. However, few studies have examined the ways that preparation programs address the topic or explore connections between dimensions of curriculum and practice.

Leadership Competencies

Despite a decided shift in emphasis from management to leadership in the recommended and the written curriculum, there is a surprising lack of clarity about how programs attempt to develop important leadership perspectives or specific competencies associated with effective leadership. The descriptive literature provides explicit references to leadership goals. Some program descriptions include courses with titles aimed at leadership in general or at specific dimensions of leadership. Some scholars are explicit in identifying a knowledge base that is essential for effective leadership. The emphasis on transformational leadership requires leaders to work effectively with others in the immediate and extended school community; accordingly, there is a focus on the development of interpersonal skills. In general, however, aside from the concentration of studies dealing with problem analysis, the literature is relatively silent on the development of other competencies. Despite an assumption that programs support the development of skills necessary for transformational leadership, instructional leadership, and the full range of managerial tasks associated with leadership roles, there is surprisingly little attention to programs' efforts to develop competencies in these different areas.

From analysis of course titles, Pohland and Carlson (1993) concluded that the curriculum retained a traditional management orientation. At the same time, it is evident that in some programs course titles digress from those viewed as "standard" components of the repertoire. Instead of courses aligned with specific administrative tasks or functions, for example, some report that they now integrate these topics into a set or sequence of required courses. Course titles, however, are not necessarily an accurate representation of content, and program descriptions are drawn from a very small number of institutions, many of which were members of UCEA or participants in the Danforth Program, both reform-minded groups. Hess and Kelly's (2005a) analysis of 210 syllabi in core courses is perhaps the most detailed and recent effort to examine the inclusion of managerial topics in leadership preparation programs. Among the seven areas they examined, technical knowledge, including law and finance, received the most attention. The category receiving least attention (6%) dealt with leadership and school culture, and there was even less attention to matters dealing with the community. The reality is that the scope of leadership preparation programs is broad, and our knowledge about the alignment of curriculum to goals is very limited.

What Is the Nature of the Enacted Curriculum?

Beyond course titles and even syllabi, how are courses organized, and what is the knowledge base that informs the leadership preparation curriculum? Regarding the taught curriculum, a handful of articles offered brief descriptions of courses or modules, and only a few provided any in-depth information regarding the enacted curriculum in programs or courses (Leithwood & Steinbach, 1992; Riehl et al., 2000). Even more elusive, despite several commendable research efforts, is the understanding regarding the nature of the knowledge base, the types of information that are selected to support learning, the reasons for these choices, and any evidence on how or if these choices actually enhance learning.

In a not-too-distant past, it was common to hear preparation courses described as theory *or* practice. In the current literature, this is no longer apparent. In terms of program design, there is an almost universal emphasis on the integration of theory and practice throughout the curriculum. In fact, one program describes the practicum itself as a strategy to facilitate application of knowledge gained from previous courses and also a way to develop new knowledge (Copland, 2001). At the same time, perhaps in response to criticisms about overemphasis on theory and inattention to practice, articles deal predominantly with reforms intended to increase relevance and to insure development of competencies. Consequently, while we learn a great deal about instructional strategies that facilitate the application of theory to practice, there is little information about the theory or research that students encounter, how that information is disseminated, or the efficacy of those materials in supporting learning.

Information does suggest, however, that the knowledge base is broad and constantly changing, with little consistency in use of materials across programs. Hess and Kelly (2005a), for example, noted that the 210 syllabi they examined included 1,851 readings, with over half from sources other than textbooks. Their analysis, while detailed, concentrated on specific themes represented in only a selected group of textbooks, giving us no insight into these other materials and texts. Reflecting the changing nature of the knowledge base, books and authors identified as prominent in one study do not appear in others, and while course titles may be inflexible, there is no indication that the supported curriculum is stable or tightly bounded.

Findings from a research study exploring the knowledge base in teacher education may be relevant to educational leader preparation. Christensen (1996) analyzed 42 National Council for Accreditation of Teacher Education institutional reports, focusing on two standards. These required the units to explicate the goals, philosophy, and objectives of the program; describe the knowledge base; and demonstrate that the knowledge base is reflected in the curriculum. According to Christensen, 31 of the 42 institutions identified "a theme statement that described its program design or conceptualization.... Yet, programs with similar theme statements had substantially different approaches" and "scholars cited in all of the reports numbered more than 1,000" (pp. 40–41). Christensen also referred to a 1994 study by Hall et al. where a review of 44 reports submitted by Teacher Education Council of State Colleges and Universities also determined that there was no single, generally accepted knowledge base. To the contrary, the programs incorporated a vast and differing array of sources.

The Christensen (1996) study is interesting not only for its findings on the nature of the knowledge base, but also for the methodology. Institutions who participate in accreditation review regularly complete extensive reports regarding multiple dimensions of the program, including the curriculum. These reports are readily accessible sources of data about the knowledge base and other dimensions of the curriculum. If we assume that the knowledge base is diverse and constantly changing, what information is being included, what are the sources for that information, and what perspectives do they represent?

Although much of the research regarding the knowledge base relies on analysis of texts and specifically administrative textbooks, the use of the textbook appears to be declining. Attention to the textbook seems to reflect assumptions about the curriculum that may no longer be relevant. Hess and Kelly (2005b), for example, viewed the lack of representativeness in general and foundational texts as problematic because they assumed that "overview classes are an inevitable component of any preparation program and will tend to employ general and foundational texts" (p. 27).

While at one time the general textbook might have played an important role in the curriculum, this no longer seems to be the case. Hess and Kelly's (2005b) data showed that the general textbook appeared infrequently in syllabi. As Glass (2004) noted, only one "entirely new general-type textbook in the field has been published since 1993" (p. vi). Based on his experience, Anderson (2006) speculated, "Fewer and fewer ... [programs] are using traditional texts in educational administration, organizational theory, finance, and supervision" (p. 25). Glass suggested that more professors are using trade books, many emerging from the private sector. If these assertions about the declining use of both general and specialized textbook use are true, what materials are replacing them and why?

Although the data are limited, program descriptions provide some evidence of a shift away from the reliance on general core courses supplemented by specialized courses—school law, supervision, the principalship—toward a more integrated set of courses that are not organized around specific tasks or functions. Such a change would contribute to the decline in the use of general or specialized textbooks; additionally, there has been a tremendous expansion of information that is available for use in preparation programs. As Thrupp and Willmott (2003) pointed out, "Since the late 1980s there has been a phenomenal increase in the publication of educational (especially *school)* management books" (p. 3), and "the education management offerings of just the 1990s potentially constitute thousands of books and journal articles" (p. 57). With technology, these books, articles, and other forms of information are more readily available. The sheer volume of potential resources suggests that efforts to identify a single or even predominant knowledge base would be relatively fruitless; however, that does not minimize the need to have a better understanding of the information that students encounter in preparation programs.

Some researchers expressed concerns about the absence of certain prominent thinkers and researchers from course syllabi. The fact that these scholars do not directly appear on the syllabi, however, does not necessarily mean that their perspectives are not represented in the course, either through their influence on the specific professors or on other authors in the field. However, the changing nature of the knowledge base does raise questions about what information is reaching students and the quality of the information. Whereas Hess and Kelly (2005a), for example, characterized Covey as an important management theorist, English (2002) was strongly critical of Covey's work, concluding that it had no empirical foundation yet has been incorporated widely into the educational administrative literature as if it did. Bomer, Dworin, May, and Semingson (2007) directed a similar critique toward Payne's *A Framework for Understanding Poverty*, a book widely used in professional development, but whose assertions regarding the social structure, daily life, language, and characteristics of individuals in poverty were "contradicted by anthropological, sociological, and other research on poverty" (p. 1).

English's (2002) concern was based on beliefs about the type of information that should be included in the knowledge base. He maintained, "No boundary could be more important to anchor a claim that the preparation of educational administrators rests on empiricism and its laws." (p. 20). English (2002) continued,

> Covey's penetration of educational administration texts means that professors have failed to understand the historic claims that were made in the creation of educational administration as a science in the first place—and in so doing undermine their own efficacy, validity, and professionalism. (p. 20)

This concern is relatively unexplored in the literature on the curriculum.

Levine (2005) asserted that the administrative preparation curriculum lacks rigor, which he attributed partly to a lack of rigorous scholarship. To support his case, he provided several comments from faculty in educational administration programs. There is "no substantial, meaningful body of theory and research to expose students to," one noted; another talked about "avoiding journals in educational administration in preference to *Harvard Business Review, Education Week,* and *Kappan*" (Levine, 2005, p. 44). While the broad generalizations from Levine's study rely on a very limited database, these comments raise questions about the role of research in the leadership education curriculum.

With the exception of a few studies (Anderson, 2006; Pounder, 1995; Riehl et al., 2000), we have little information about the logic underlying the development of the curriculum in leadership preparation programs or the selection of specific materials. Why do faculty members make the choices that they do? Why do they select one source over another? Are decisions based on relevance to specific learning objectives, level of student (initial certification or doctorate), or accessibility? With respect to theory and research, do faculty members believe, as English (2002) suggested, that empirical research matters? If so, do they introduce students to primary sources, or do they rely on secondary sources or lectures? Is there a preference for certain types of materials (e.g., audio-visual vs. print)? Do selections differ depending on the background, experience, education, and status of the faculty? Are there differences in choices, for example, between full-time and part-time faculty, corresponding to education and experience?

The choice of materials may reflect changes in and differences in pedagogical beliefs and strategies. During this current period of reform, approaches to pedagogy have changed noticeably, with a greater emphasis on the integration of theory and practice and the introduction of hands-on or problem-based learning, often reflecting constructivist beliefs (see chapter 8 of this volume). These beliefs about learning may very well influence instructors' choices of materials.

Directions for Future Research

Sources of information about the leadership preparation curriculum include scholarly recommendations and program and course descriptions as well as a variety of empirical studies. Although the majority of the research relies on surveys, there are also single and multiple case studies, usually mixed-methods; content analyses of texts and syllabi; historical analyses; and experimental stud-ies utilizing pre- and posttest or posttest-only designs. Survey data were drawn from full-time faculty or department chairs; from educational administrators without connection to any specific program or, more typically, from students and graduates; and occasionally from school personnel and students in schools employing program graduates. A number of studies also incorporated qualitative data drawn from interviews and focus groups; observations; and work samples, such as field projects and internship journal entries.

Despite diversity in approach and a number of well-designed and informative studies, the re-search is limited in a number of ways. Many of the studies are limited in scope and focus narrowly on one or more dimensions of the curriculum. Perhaps even more important, with very few studies designed directly to examine any dimension of the curriculum, pertinent information emerges almost as an afterthought. Although single studies have begun to address important connections, much of the existing research regarding the curriculum is segmented and deals with single aspects of the curriculum, rather than exploring links between different dimensions. For example, to what extent does the written curriculum correspond to scholarly recommendations? To what extent does the taught curriculum correspond to the written curriculum? And, perhaps most important, to what extent does the enacted curriculum (taught and supported) facilitate learning relative to specific goals and objectives in the written curriculum and lifelong leadership practice? Similarly, some areas of the curriculum have received more attention than others. Although still insufficient, information on the written curriculum, for example, is more available than information on the taught or supported curriculum.

Across several studies, a consistent finding was that students in preparation programs are more likely to encounter positivist approaches to research than approaches emanating from other re-search paradigms. Similarly, positivist and postpositivist research approaches are reflected in the majority of the empirical studies regarding the curriculum, and even studies that utilized mixed methods tended to underreport qualitative data. Although quantitative inquiry is important and appropriate as a means to explore certain questions, our knowledge of the curriculum is limited by the lack of qualitative inquiry. From comparative survey data, for example, there is evidence that some programs were more successful than others relative to certain goals, but we do not know how the curriculum relates to these differential outcomes. Interviews with some students identify important abstract learning outcomes that are intriguing. What, for example, is the nature of the transformation that students describe? What is the significance when students talk about develop-ing a deeper understanding of their own learning and becoming better teachers as a result of their preparation? More in-depth qualitative inquiry would enable us to develop a deeper understand-ing of student learning and to examine links between curriculum, understanding, and different levels of transfer.

Much of the literature, whether descriptive or analytic, represents innovative program devel-opment efforts and emanates from a limited number of institutions. UCEA institutions figure prominently as do institutions that had received financial support to encourage innovation, notably from the Danforth and DeWitt-Wallace foundations. UCEA's active support for the advancement of leadership preparation and ease of communication among its members facilitate research, but most individuals prepared as school administrators in the United States do not attend UCEA institutions (Baker, Orr, & Young, 2007).

Much of the research in this area seems to be reactive rather than proactive. It seems that many of the descriptive and analytic reports and studies were designed to respond to criticisms directed toward university preparation. Consequently, articles emphasized the role of practitioners and omitted any mention of the role or influence of full-time faculty. They emphasized the practicality of programs and highlighted field projects and internships but ignored the role of theory and research. They sought to determine relevance of preparation for practice but failed to examine the specific ways in which preparation fosters the development of the knowledge, skills, and dispositions associated with effective leadership. This is not to undermine the value of these studies or the importance of the questions but simply to say that there are other questions.

Despite evidence to suggest that initial preparation and doctoral programs differ in objectives and curriculum, this distinction is relatively unexplored. Additionally, several studies suggested that context, the educational settings where students are employed, influences learning, but we encountered no studies that explored this issue. In summary then, based on our review of the existing literature, we make the following five recommendations:

1. With evidence to suggest that curriculum does make a difference in the nature and quality of student learning, this is an important area of inquiry. We encourage attention to the curriculum as an important component of leadership preparation programs.

2. To expand the scope and depth of studies and develop a comparative cross-institutional perspective, we recommend the development of collaborative research efforts. Individual academicians in most institutions have limited resources that preclude in-depth and comparative studies. Kottkamp and Orr, organizers of the UCEA TEA-SIG Taskforce to Evaluate Educational Leadership Preparation Program Effectiveness, developed a collaborative model in which researchers from different institutions gather to design and implement research in their individual programs. The data, then, become part of a common pool. This alternate paradigm offers great potential to expand research in this area.

3. Although we have some information on the written curriculum, utilizing technology to facilitate data collection and analysis and drawing on existing databases would enrich our understanding of this dimension of the leadership curriculum and perhaps permit a wider exploration of preparation programs. Many preparation programs now include the programmatic information that constitutes at least some of the written curriculum (goals, program requirements, and syllabi) on the Internet. Additionally, as we noted earlier, a rich body of information is available from standardized accreditation reports that could enhance our understanding of the written curriculum.

4. Considering both the apparent diversity in the taught and supported curriculum and the lack of information regarding the learning experiences that students encounter as part of their preparation programs, we encourage inquiry—and particularly in-depth qualitative inquiry—that not only will describe the enacted curriculum, but also will generate a deeper understanding of the learning process and the way that the enacted curriculum facilitates learning. Since schools and school districts participate in and influence learning in all leadership preparation programs, we also encourage specific attention to the ways in which these partnerships may affect learning. Notably absent from the existing research, longitudinal studies and backward mapping would be valuable contributions.

5. Finally, we commend and encourage the continued efforts of researchers to utilize rigorous research designs, regardless of the method, to examine and assess the curriculum.

Acknowledgment

Dr. Osterman would like to thank graduate assistant Francine Newman for her assistance with this chapter.

Note

1. It is important to note here that *reflective inquiry* and *reflective practice* are not necessarily equivalent concepts. Reflective practice, according to Argyris and Schön (1974) and Osterman and Kottkamp (1993, 2004), involves systematic data-based assessment of personal practice; the term *reflective inquiry* is often used to refer generically to a retrospective thoughtful analysis of actions and outcomes.

References

Allan, E. J., & Estler, S. E. (2005). Diversity, privilege, and us: Collaborative curriculum transformation among educational leadership faculty. *Innovative Higher Education, 29*(3), 209–232.

Anderson, G. (2006). *Can we effectively build credential programs for educational administrators on principles of social justice? A case study.* Retrieved June 4, 2006, from http://www.leadershipforsocialjustice.org

Argyris, C., & Schön, D. A. (1974). *Theory in practice: Increasing professional effectiveness.* San Francisco: Jossey-Bass.

Baker, B. D., Orr, M. T., & Young, M. D. (2007). Academic drift, institutional production, and professional districution of graduate degrees in educational leadership. *Educational Administration Quarterly, 43*(3), 278–318.

Barbour, J. D. (1994). A novel idea: Changing the landscape of administrator preparation through literature and ethnographies. *Journal of School Leadership, 4*(4), 366–381.

Beach, R. H., & Lindahl, R.A. (2000). New standards for the preparation of school administrators: What conceptualization of educational planning do they portray? *Planning and Changing, 31*(1-2), 35–52.

Beatty, B. R., & Brew, C. R. (2004). Trusting relationships and emotional epistemologies: A foundational leadership issue. *School Leadership and Management, 24*(3), 329–356.

Beck, L. G., & Murphy, J. (1994). *Ethics in educational leadership programs.* Thousand Oaks, CA: Corwin Press.

Behar-Horenstein, L. S. (1995). Promoting effective school leadership: A change-oriented model for the preparation of principals. *Peabody Journal of Education, 70*(3), 18–40.

Berrel, M. M., & Macpherson, R. J. S. (1995). Educational sociology and educational administration: Problems with paradigms, epistemology, research and theory. *Journal of Educational Administration, 10*(1), 9–32.

Bogotch, I. E. (2001, April). *Emerging trends in teaching and learning educational leadership.* Paper presented at the annual meeting of the American Educational Research Association, Seattle, WA.

Bolman, L. G., & Deal, T. E. (1994). Looking for leadership: Another search party's report. *Educational Administration Quarterly, 30*(1), 77–96.

Bomer, R., Dworin, J. E., May, L., & Semingson, P. (2007). Miseducating teachers about the poor: A critical analysis of Ruby Payne's claims about poverty. *Teachers College Record, 110*(12), 19.

Bredeson, P. V. (2004). Creating spaces for the development of democratic school leaders. A case of program redesign in the United States. *Journal of Educational Administration, 42*(6), 708–723.

Brown, F. (2005). African Americans and school leadership: An introduction. *Educational Administration Quarterly, 41*(4), 585–590.

Brown, K. M. (2003, November). *Assessing preservice leaders' beliefs, attitudes and values regarding issues of diversity, social justice and equity: A review of existing measures.* Paper presented at the annual meeting of the University Council for Educational Administration, Portland, OR.

Brown, K. M. (2004). Leadership for social justice and equity: Weaving a transformative framework and pedagogy. *Educational Administration Quarterly, 40*(1), 79–110.

Browne-Ferrigno, T. (2001, November). *Preparing school leaders: Case study summary and implications.* Paper presented at the annual meeting of the University Council for Educational Administration, Cincinnati, OH.

Brundrett, M. (2001). The development of school leadership preparation programmes in England and the USA: A comparative analysis. *Educational Management & Administration, 29*(2), 229–245.

Brunner, C. C. (2002a). Professing educational leadership: Conceptions of power. *Journal of School Leadership, 12*(6), 693–720.

Brunner, C. C. (2002b). A proposition for the reconception of the superintendency: Reconsidering traditional and non-traditional discourse. *Educational Administration Quarterly, 38*(3), 402–431.

Cambron-McCabe, N., & McCarthy, M. M. (2005). Educating school leaders for social justice. *Educational Policy, 19*(1), 201–222.

Campbell, E. (1997). Ethical school leadership: Problems of an elusive role. *Journal of School Leadership, 7*(4), 287–300.

Capper, C. A. (Ed.). (1993). *Educational administration in a pluralistic society.* Albany: State University of New York Press.

Capper, C. A., Alston, J., Gause, C. P., Koschoreck, J. W., Lopez, G., Lugg, C. A., et al. (2006). Integrating lesbian/gay/bisexual/transgender topics and their intersections with other areas of difference into the leadership preparation curriculum: Practical ideas and strategies. *Journal of School Leadership, 16*(2), 142–157.

Carr, C. S., Chenoweth, T., & Ruhl, T. (2003). Best practice in educational leadership preparation programs. In F. C. Lunenburg & C. S. Carr (Eds.), *Shaping the future: Policy, partnerships, and emerging perspectives* (pp. 204–223). Lanham, MD: Scarecrow Education.

Christensen, D. (1996). The professional knowledge-research base for teacher education. In J. Sikula, T. Buttery, & E. Guyton (Eds.), *Handbook of research on teacher education* (2nd ed., pp. 38–52). New York: Macmillan.

Collins, L., & White, G.P. (2002). *Leading inclusive programs for all special education students: A pre-service training program for principals.* Bethlehem, PA: Lehigh University.

Copland, M. A. (2000). Problem-based learning and prospective principals' problem-framing ability. *Journal of School Leadership, 36*(4), 585–607.

Copland, M. A. (2001). The reform of administrator preparation at Stanford: An analytic description. *Journal of School Leadership, 11*(4), 335–366.

Copland, M. A. (2003). Developing prospective principals' problem-framing skills. *Journal of School Leadership, 13*(5), 529–548.

Cordeiro, P. A., Krueger, J. A., Parks, D., Restine, N., & Wilson, P. T. (1993). Taking stock: Learnings gleaned from universities participating in the Danforth Program. In M. Milstein (Ed.), *Changing the way we prepare educational leaders: The Danforth experience* (pp. 17–38). Newbury Park, CA: Corwin Press.

Daresh, J. C. (1992). In search of a knowledge base to guide program development in educational leadership. *Journal of School Leadership, 2,* 429–442.

Daresh, J. C., Myrna, M. W., Dunlap, K., & Hvizdak, M. (2000). Words from "the trenches": Principals' perspectives on effective school leadership characteristics. *Journal of School Leadership, 10*(1), 69–83.

Daresh, J. C., & Playko, M. A. (1994). Aspiring and practicing principals' perceptions of critical skills for beginning leaders. *Journal of Educational Administration, 32*(3), 35–45.

Davis, S.H. (2004). The myth of the rational decision maker: A framework for applying and enhancing heuristic and intuitive decision making by school leaders. *Journal of School Leadership, 14,* 621–654.

Davis, S. H., & Davis, P. B. (2003). *The intuitive dimensions of administrative decision making.* Lanham, MD: Scarecrow Press.

Dimmock, C. (1998). Towards comparative educational administration: Building the case for a cross-cultural school-based approach. *Journal of Educational Administration, 36*(4), 379–401.

Dimmock, C., & Walker, A. (1998). Comparative educational administration: Developing a cross-cultural conceptual framework. *Educational Administration Quarterly, 34*(4), 558–595.

Donmoyer, R., Imber, M., &Scheurich, J. J. (Eds.). (1995). *The knowledge base in educational administration.* Albany: State University of New York Press.

Duke, D. L. (1992). The rhetoric and the reality of reform in educational administration. *Phi Delta Kappan, 73*(10), 764–770.

Duncan, P. K. (2003). Professing educational leadership: The value of listening. *Journal of School Leadership, 13*(4), 464–491.

Eisner, E.W. (1985). *The educational imagination on the design and evaluation of school programs.* New York: Macmillan.

Eisner, E. W. (1996). *Cognition and curriculum reconsidered* (2nd ed.). London: Paul Chapman Educational.

Elmore, R., Peterson, P., & McCarthy, S. (1996). *Restructuring in the classroom: Teaching, learning, and school organization.* San Francisco: Jossey-Bass.

English, F. W. (1997). The cupboard is bare: The postmodern critique of educational administration. *Journal of School Leadership, 7,* 4–26.

English, F. W. (2002). The penetration of educational leadership texts by revelation and prophecy: The case of Stephen R. Covey. *Journal of School Leadership, 12*(1), 4–22.

Fero, M. A., & others. (1991, August). *Readings in educational administration: Coming to consensus on the top ten books recommended for educational administration students.* Paper presented at the annual meeting of the National Conference of Professors of Educational Administration, Fargo, ND.

Fierro, E., & Rodriguez, M. A. (2006). Leadership for bilingual education: Reflections on social justice. *Journal of School Leadership, 16,* 182–196.

Foster, W. P. (1986). *Paradigms and promises: New approaches to educational administration.* Amherst, NY: Prometheus Books.

Furtwengler, C. B., Furtwengler, W. J., Hurst, D., Turk, R. L., & Holcomb, E. (1996). Preparing expert leaders: A fresh clinical model. *Journal of School Leadership, 6*(5), 512–539.

Garland, V. E. (1989). Planning for the 1990's: Computer use in programs preparing school administrators. *Planning and Changing, 20*(4), 231–236.

Glasman, N. S. (1997). An experimental program in leadership preparation. *Peabody Journal of Education, 72*(2), 42–65.

Glasman, N. S., & Glasman, L. D. (1997). Connecting the preparation of school leaders to the practice of school leadership. *Peabody Journal of Education, 72*(2), 3–20.

Glass, T. (with Mason, R., Eaton, W., Parker, J. C., & Carver, F.). (2004). *The history of educational administration viewed through its textbooks.* Lanham, MD: Scarecrow Education.

Glatthorn, A. A. (2000). *The principal as curriculum leader: Shaping what is taught and tested* (2nd ed.). Thousand Oaks, CA: Corwin Press.

Glatthorn, A. A., Boschee, F., & Whitehead, B. M. (2006). *Curriculum leadership: Development and implementation.* Thousand Oaks, CA: Sage.

Goodlad, J. I., & Associates. (1979). *Curriculum inquiry: The study of curriculum practice.* New York: McGraw-Hill.

Goodlad, J. I. (1994). *Educational renewal: Better teachers, better schools.* San Francisco: Jossey-Bass.

Grogan, M., & Andrews, R. (2002). Defining preparation and professional development for the future. *Educational Administration Quarterly, 38*(2), 233–256.

Grove, R. W. (1992). Integrating the beliefs of Dewey, Lewin, and Rogers into a rationale for effective group leadership *Journal of School Leadership, 2,* 201–211.

Gwele, N. S. (2005). Education philosophy and the curriculum. In L. R. Uys & N. S. Gwele (Eds.), *Curriculum development in nursing: Process and innovation.* New York: Routledge.

Hafner, M. M. (2006). Teaching strategies for developing leaders for social justice. In C. Marshall & M. Oliva (Eds.), *Leadership for social justice: Making revolutions in education* (pp. 167–193). Boston: Allyn & Bacon.

Hargreaves, A. (2001) Emotional geographies of teaching, *Teachers College Record, 103*(6), 1056–1080.

Hart, A. W. (1990). Effective administration through reflective practice. *Education and Urban Society, 22*(2), 153–169.

Henning, J. E., & Robinson, V. (2002). Change and transformation in an educational leadership program. In G. Perreault & F. C. Lunenburg (Eds.), *The changing world of school administration* (pp. 209–221). Lanham, MD: Scarecrow Press.

Hermond, D. (1999). Evaluating a leadership preparation program: Participants' perspective. *Planning and Changing, 30*(3–4), 198–217.

Herrity, V. A., & Glasman, N. S. (1999). Training administrators for culturally and linguistically diverse school populations: Opinions of expert practitioners. *Journal of School Leadership, 9*(3), 235–253.

Hess, F. M., & Kelly, A.P. (2005a). *Learning to lead? What gets taught in principal preparation programs.* Cambridge, MA: Harvard University, Program on Educational Policy and Governance.

Hess, F. M., & Kelly, A. P. (2005b). *Textbook leadership? An analysis of leading books used in principal preparation.* Cambridge, MA: Harvard University, Program on Educational Policy and Governance.

Hills, J. (1978). Perspective: Problems in the production and utilization of knowledge in educational administration. *Educational Administration Quarterly, 14*(1), 1–12.

Hirth, M. A., & Valesky, T.C. (1990). Survey of universities: Special education knowledge requirements in school administrator preparation programs. *Planning and Changing, 21*(3), 165–172.

Holifield, M., Cox, D., Holman, D., Foldesy, G., & King, D. (1994). The development of a doctoral program in educational leadership at Arkansas State University. In J. Burdin (Ed.), *Leadership and diversity in education: The second yearbook of the National Council of Professors of Educational Administration* (pp. 234–237). Lancaster, PA: Technomic.

Hoy, W. K. (Ed.). (1994a). *Educational administration: The UCEA document base.* New York: McGraw-Hill.

Hoy, W. K. (1994b). Foundations of educational administration: Traditional and emerging perspectives. *Educational Administration Quarterly, 30*(2), 178–198.

Hutchings, P., & Shulman, L. S. (1999). The scholarship of teaching: New elaborations, new developments. *Change, 31*(5), 10–15.

Jackson, B. L., & Kelley, C. (2002). Exceptional and innovative programs in educational leadership. *Educational Administration Quarterly, 38*(2), 192–212.

Jackson, P. (1968). *Life in classrooms.* New York: Holt, Rinehart & Winston.

Jackson, P. W. (Ed.) (1992). *Handbook of research on curriculum: A project of the American educational research association.* New York: Macmillan Library Reference.

Johansson, O. (2004). Democracy and leadership—Or training for democratic leadership. *Journal of Educational Administration, 42*(6), 620–624.

Johnson, B. L., Jr., & Fauske, J. R. (2005). Organization theory, educational leadership and educational research. *Journal of Educational Administration, 43*(1), 5–8.

Johnson, J. F., Jr., & Uline, C. L. (2005). Preparing educational leaders to close achievement gaps. *Theory Into Practice, 44*(1), 45–52

Keedy, J. L. (2005). Reconciling the theory and practice schism in educational administration through practitioner-developed theories in practice. *Journal of Educational Administration, 43*(2), 134–153.

Kelley, A. V. (2004). *The curriculum: Theory and practice.* Thousand Oaks, CA: Sage.

Kim, L. (1997). *Ready, set, let's go: An evaluation study of an educational administration program for beginning administrators.* (ERIC Document Reproduction Service No. ED415582)

Kowalski, T. J. (1998). The role of communication in providing leadership for school restructuring. *Mid-Western Educational Researcher, 11*(1), 32–40.

Larson, C. L., & Murtadha, K. (2002). Leadership for social justice. In J. Murphy (Ed.), *The educational leadership challenge: Redefining leadership for the 21st century* (pp. 134–161). Chicago: The University of Chicago Press.

Lather, P. (1991). *Getting smart: Feminist research and pedagogy with/in the postmodern.* New York: Routledge.

Lease, A. J. (2002). New administrators need more than good grades. *School Administrator, 59*(6), 40–41.

Leithwood, K., Jantzi, D., Coffin, G., & Wilson, P. (1996). Preparing school leaders: What works? *Journal of School Leadership, 6*(3), 316–342.

Leithwood, K., Riedlinger, B., Bauer, S., & Jantzi, D. (2003). Leadership program effects on student learning: The case of greater New Orleans school leadership center. *Journal of School Leadership, 13*(6), 707–738.

Leithwood, K., & Steinbach, R. (1992). Improving the problem-solving expertise of school administrators. *Education and Urban Society, 24*(3), 317–345.

Levin, H.M. (2006). Can research improve educational leadership? *Educational Researcher, 35*(8), 38–43.

Levine, A. (2005). *Educating school leaders.* Washington, DC: The Education Schools Project.

Lindauer, P., Petrie, G., Leonard, J., Gooden, J., & Bennett, B. (2003). Preparing principals for leadership success. *ERS Spectrum, 21*(1), 23–28.

Lopez, G. R. (2003). The (racially neutral) politics of education: A critical race theory perspective. *Educational Administration Quarterly, 39*(1), 68–94.

Lyman, L. L., & Villani, C. J. (2002). The complexity of poverty: A missing component of educational leadership programs. *Journal of School Leadership, 12*(3), 246–280.

Marks, H. M., & Printy, S. M. (2003). Principal leadership and school performance: An integration of transformational and instructional leadership. *Educational Administration Quarterly, 39*(3), 370–397.

Marshall, C. (2004). Social justice challenges to educational administration: Introduction to a special issue. *Educational Administration Quarterly, 40*(1), 5–15.

Marshall, C. (2006). Tapping in to fury and passion. *Journal of Research on Leadership Education, 1*(1), 1–7.

McDowelle, J. O., & Bell, E. D. (1998). Emotional intelligence and educational leadership. In R. Muth & M. Martin (Eds.), *Toward the Year 2000: Leadership for quality schools. The sixth yearbook of the National Council of Professors of Educational Administration* (pp. 190–196). Lancaster, PA: Technomic.

McKenzie, K. B., Skrla, L., & Scheurich, J. J. (2006). Preparing instructional leaders for social justice. *Journal of School Leadership, 16,* 158–170.

Milstein, M. (Ed.). (1993). *Changing the way we prepare educational leaders.* Newbury Park, CA: Corwin Press.

Miskel, C. (1990). Research and the preparation of educational administrators. *Journal of Educational Administration, 28*(3), 33–47.

Mulkeen, T. A., & Cooper, B. S. (1992). Implications of preparing school administrators for knowledge work organizations: A case study. *Journal of Educational Administration, 30*(1), 17–28.

Mullen, C. A., Gordon, S. P., Greenlee, B. J., & Anderson, R. H. (2002). Capacities for school leadership: Emerging trends in literature. *International Journal of Educational Reform, 11*(2), 158–198.

Murphy, J. (2001). The changing face of leadership preparation. *School Administrator, 58*(10), 14–17.

Murphy, J. (Ed.). (2002). *The educational leadership challenge: Redefining leadership for the 21st century.* Chicago: The University of Chicago Press.

Murphy, J. (2005). Unpacking the foundations of ISLLC standards and addressing concerns in the academic community. *Educational Administration Quarterly, 41*(1), 154–191.

Murphy, J. (2006). *Preparing school leaders: Defining a research and action agenda.* Lanham, MD: Rowman & Littlefield Education.

Murphy, J., & Vriesenga, M. (2004). *Research on preparation programs in educational administration: An analysis* (UCEA Monograph Series). Columbia, MO: University Council for Educational Administration.

Murtadha, K., & Watts, D. M. (2005). Linking the struggle for education and social justice: Historical perspectives of African American leadership in schools. *Educational Administration Quarterly, 41*(4), 591–608.

Muth, R., Murphy, M. J., Martin, W. M., & Sanders, N. M. (1996). Assessing knowledge and skills through portfolios. In J. L. Burdin (Ed.), *Prioritizing instruction: The fourth yearbook of the National Council of Professors of Educational Administration* (pp. 216–231). Lancaster, PA: Technomic.

Neary, M. (2002). *Curriculum studies in post-compulsory and adult education: A teacher's and student teacher's study guide.* Cheltenham, England: Nelson Thormes.

Nicolaides, N., & Gaynor, A. K. (1992). The knowledge base informing the teaching of administrative and organizational theory in UCEA universities: A descriptive and interpretive survey. *Educational Administration Quarterly, 28*(2), 237–265.

Noonan, M. (1991, October). *Curriculum reform in educational administration: Fantasy or frustration.* Paper presented at the annual meeting of the University Council for Educational Administration, Baltimore.

Norris, C. (1990). Developing visionary leaders for tomorrow's schools. *NASSP Bulletin, 74*(526), 6–10.

Orr, M. T., & Barber, M. E. (2006). Collaborative leadership preparation: A comparative study of partnership and conventional programs and practices. *Journal of School Leadership, 16,* 709–739.

Orr, M. T., LeTendre, B., & Silverberg, R. (2006, April). *Comparing leadership development from pipeline to preparation to advancement: A study of multiple institutions' leadership preparation programs.* Paper presented at the annual meeting of the American Educational Research Association, San Francisco.

Orr, M. T., & Pounder, D. (2007, November). *Comparing leadership education from pipeline to preparation to advancement: A study of multiple institutions' leadership preparation programs.* Paper presented at the annual meeting of the University Council for Educational Administration, Alexandria, VA.

Osterman, K. F. (1994). Communication skills: A key to collaboration and change. *Journal of School Leadership, 4*(4), 382–398.

Osterman, K. F., & Kottkamp, R. B. (1993). *Reflective practice for educators: Improving schooling through professional development.* Newbury Park, CA: Corwin Press.

Osterman, K. F., & Kottkamp, R. B. (2004). *Reflective practice for educators.* Thousand Oaks, CA: Corwin Press.

Parker, L., & Shapiro, J. P. (1992). Where is the discussion of diversity in educational administration programs? Graduate students' voices addressing an omission in their preparation. *Journal of School Leadership, 2*(1), 7–33.

Pinar, W. F. (1999). *Contemporary curriculum discourses: Twenty years of JCT.* New York: Peter Lang.

Place, A. W., & Reitzug, U. C. (1992). Educational administration research, practice, and preparation: Lessons from woodworking and Indian philosophy. *Journal of School Leadership, 2,* 396–409.

Pohland, P. A., & Carlson, L. T. (1993). Program reform in educational administration. *UCEA Review, 34*(3), 4–9.

Polite, M. (1990). Human relations skills for administrators: A context for instructional leadership. *Planning and Changing, 21*(3), 158–164.

Porter, A. C., & Smithson, J. L (2001, December). *Defining, developing, and using curriculum indicators* (CPRE Research Report Series RR-048). Philadelphia: Consortium for Policy Research in Education.

Pounder, D. G. (1995). Theory to practice in administrator preparation: An evaluation study. *Journal of School Leadership, 5*(2), 151–162.

Pounder, D., Reitzug, U., & Young, M. D. (2002). Preparing school leaders for school improvement, social justice, and community. In J. Murphy (Ed.), *The educational leadership challenge: Refining leadership for the 21st century* (pp. 261–288). Chicago: The University of Chicago Press.

Ramsey, M. A. (1975). The administrator-observer as policy maker. *Educational Administration Quarterly, 11*(1), 1–10.

Ranis, S. H. (2003, April). *Needing to know: Education leadership preparation and research literacy.* Paper presented at the annual meeting of the American Educational Research Association, Chicago.

Reitzug, U. C., & Cornett, J. W. (1990). Teacher and administrator thought: Implications for administrator training. *Planning and Changing, 21*(3), 181–192.

Rettig, P. R. (2004). Beyond organizational tinkering: A new view of school reform. *Educational Horizons, 82*(4), 260–265.

Richardson, M., & Lane, K. (1994). Reforming principal preparation: From training to learning. *Catalyst for Change, 23*(2), 14–17.

Riehl, C. J. (2000). The principal's role in creating inclusive schools for diverse students: A review of normative, empirical, and critical literature on the practice of educational administration. *Journal of School Leadership, 70*(1), 55–81.

Riehl, C., Larson, C., Short, P., & Reitzug, U. C. (2000). Reconceptualizing research and scholarship in educational administration: Learning to know, knowing to do, doing to learn. *Educational Administration Quarterly, 36*(3), 391–427.

Rusch, E. A. (2004). Gender and race in leadership preparation: A constrained discourse. *Educational Administration Quarterly, 40*(1), 16–48.

Salovey, P., & Mayer, J. D. (1990). Emotional intelligence. *Imagination, Cognition, and Personality, 9,* 185–211.

Scheurich, J. J., & Laible, J. (1995). The buck stops here—In our preparation programs: Educative leadership for all children (no exceptions allowed). *Educational Administration Quarterly, 31*(2), 313–322.

Scheurich, J. J., & Skrla, L. (2003). *Leadership for equity and excellence: Creating high-achievement classrooms, schools, and districts.* Thousand Oaks, CA: Corwin Press.

Scheurich, J. J., & Young, M. D. (1997). Coloring epistemologies: Are our research epistemologies racially biased? *Educational Researcher, 26*(4) 4–16.

Senge, P. M. (1990). *The fifth discipline: The art and practice of the learning organization.* New York: Doubleday.

Sergiovanni, T. J. (1988). Mystics, neats and scruffies: Informing professional practice in educational administration *Journal of Educational Administration, 27*(2), 7–21.

Sergiovanni, T. (1991). Constructing and changing theories of practice: The key to preparing school administrators. *The Urban Review, 23*(1), 39–49.

Sergiovanni, T. J. (1999). *Educational governance and administration* (4th ed). Boston: Allyn & Bacon.

Shapiro, A. S., Benjamin, W. F., Hunt, J. J., & Shapiro, S. (1996). A theory of curriculum development. In J. L. Burdin (Ed.), *Prioritizing instruction: The fourth yearbook of the National Council of Professors of Educational Administration.* Lancaster, PA: Technomic.

Shields, C. M. (2004). Dialogic leadership for social justice: Overcoming pathologies of silence. *Educational Administration Quarterly, 40*(1), 111–134.

Sirotnik, K. A., & Kimball, K. (1994). The unspecial place of special education in programs that prepare school administrators. *Journal of School Leadership, 4*(4), 598–630.

Slater, C. L., McGhee, M. W., & Capt, R. L. (2001). Review and renewal of an educational administration program. *Planning and Changing, 32*(1-2), 2–23.

Smith, J. M. (1993). Preparing administrators for the world of practice: A proactive view of principalship preparation. *Journal of School Leadership, 3*(1), 45–58.

Solomon, R. P. (2002). School leaders and antiracism: Overcoming pedagogical and political obstacles. *Journal of School Leadership, 12*(2), 174–197.

Spillane, J. (2004). Educational leadership. *Educational Evaluation and Policy Analysis, 26*(2), 169–172,

Spillane, J. (2006). *Distributed leadership.* San Francisco: Jossey-Bass.

Starratt, R. J. (2004). Leadership of the contested terrain of education for democracy. *Journal of Educational Administration, 42*(6), 724–731.

Stevenson, R. B., & Doolittle, G. (2003). Developing democratic and transformational school leaders: Graduates' perceptions of the impact of their preparation program. *Journal of School Leadership, 13,* 666–687.

Thomas, A. R. (1975). The preparation of educational administrators in Canadian universities: Laying on of the hands. *Journal of Educational Administration, 13*(1), 35–60.

Thrupp, M., & Willmot, R. (2003). *Educational management in managerialist times: Beyond the textual apologists.* Berkshire, England: Open University Press.

Toombs, W. E., & Tierney, W. G. (1993). Curriculum definitions and reference points. *Journal of Curriculum and Supervision, 8*(3), 175–195.

Twale, D. J., & Short, P. M. (1989). Shaping school leaders for the future: Innovation in preparation. *Planning and Changing, 20*(3), 149–157.

van den Akker, J. (2003). Curriculum perspectives: An introduction. In J. van den Akker, W. Kuiper, & U. Hameyer (Eds.), *Curriculum landscapes and trends* (pp. 1–10). Norwell, MA: Kluwer Academic.

Vornberg, J. A., & Davis, J. (1997, August). *The Meadows Principal Improvement Program: A preservice field based model for the preparation of principals.* Paper presented at the annual meeting of the National Council of Professors of Educational Administration, Vail, CO.

Walker, D. F. (2003). *Fundamentals of curriculum: Passion and professionalism.* Mahwah, NJ: Erlbaum.

Whitaker, K. S. (1999). Principal role changes and implications for principalship candidates. *International Journal of Educational Reform, 8*(4), 352–362.

Williamson, R. D., & Hudson, M. B. (2000, April). *Democracy is hard work: The struggle to define one leadership preparation program.* Paper presented at the annual meeting of the American Educational Research Association, New Orleans, LA.

Wilmore, E., & Thomas, C. (1998). Linking theory to practice: Authentic administrative preparation. *International Journal of Educational Reform, 7*(2), 172–177.

Young, B. (1994). An other perspective on the knowledge base in Canadian educational administration. *Canadian Journal of Education, 19*(4), 351–367.

Young, M. D., & Laible, J. (2000). White racism, antiracism, and school leadership preparation. *Journal of School Leadership, 10*(5), 374–415.

Young, M. D., Peterson, G. J., & Short, P. M. (2002). The complexity of substantive reform: A call for interdependence among key stakeholders. *Educational Administration Quarterly, 38*(2), 137–175.

8
Pedagogy

DIANNE L. TAYLOR, PAULA A. CORDEIRO, AND JANET H. CHRISPEELS

As a field, educational administration and leadership has a history of approximately 130 years, beginning with the 1875 publication of the first book on the topic written by former teacher, principal, and superintendent William H. Payne of Michigan (Culbertson, 1988). Histories of scholarship in the field can be found in a number of sources (e.g., Callahan & Button, 1964; Campbell, Fleming, Newell, & Bennion, 1987; Culbertson, 1988; Willower & Forsyth, 1999). Much harder to find is a history of educational leadership as a field of practice, especially the principalship, as opposed to a field of scholarship. Cubberley, for example, in his 1916 textbook, *Public School Administration*, focused his discussion on administrators at the district level. Cubberley merely commented that "the school principal was evolved" (p. 56) and devoted a brief two and a half pages to a discussion of the job.

More problematic is the scant history available about the educational leadership of people of color and women. Tillman (2004) reminded us, "Many of the historical and contemporary contributions of African Americans have not been documented in the traditional literature on educational leadership and administration" (p. 101). Nor have the contributions of Native Americans, Hispanics, and women. For example, the contributions of women like Ella Flagg Young, whose innovations in education are often attributed to John Dewey (Seigfried, 1996), are seldom mentioned in the traditional literature.

Absent from the literature as well is a history of the pedagogy associated with preparing principals and other educational leaders. When compared to the wealth of books available on pedagogy relevant to teacher preparation, the miniscule amount of published empirical work on pedagogy in educational administration and leadership should be embarrassing to researchers in the field. This paucity persists despite the fact that educational leadership is an applied field making obligatory a strong focus on improving practice, and despite the assertion of Campbell et al. (1987) 20 years ago that any history of educational administration must address not only scholarship, but also practice and preparation.

Thus, as authors, we faced a daunting task when we accepted the invitation to write a chapter that reviews, describes, and evaluates research about pedagogy in educational leadership programs. Among other issues we confronted in writing is the virtual inseparability of curriculum, pedagogy, and learning theory. Because certain instructional strategies are more appropriate for some aspects of the curriculum than others, and because learning theory should influence pedagogy, the discussion below necessarily involves the three issues. Also, throughout the chapter, we seek to acknowledge the contributions of diverse groups to the field of educational leadership and to press the need to ensure that issues of social justice, ethics, and human relations are considered in the preparation of future leaders regardless of the pedagogical approaches used.

To address these several issues, the chapter is divided into five sections. The first section provides a brief history of the field of educational administration followed by a section in which we discuss learning theories. The third section highlights trends influencing pedagogy. Pedagogical practices themselves are addressed in the fourth section where we review and critique the empirical research on selected pedagogical approaches. Finally, the fifth section offers recommendations for future research on pedagogy appropriate for preparation programs.

History and Background

Educational administrators were rare until after the Civil War (Callahan & Button, 1964). Prior to the war, schools were small in size, making the "administration of schools … hardly differentiated from teaching" (Campbell et al., 1987, p. x). Administrative duties that needed attention in most schools serving White communities were carried out by teachers and the three or so trustees of the local school committee (Cubberley, 1916). During these post–Civil War years, Black communities actively pursued the establishment of schools for children and adults, most of whom had been legally prohibited from learning to read and write prior to the Civil War. Black leaders were instrumental in securing funds to establish both public and private schools. Principals of these schools were prominent role models in their respective communities and stressed the importance of educating Black children.

Black women such as Anna Julia Cooper and Septima Clark (Murtadha & Watts, 2005) overcame both racial and gender stereotypes to establish schools in the North and the South. Sarah Smith, appointed principal of the African School in Brooklyn, New York, in 1863, was "the first African American female principal in the New York public school system" (Tillman, 2004, p. 108). Fanny Jackson Coppin, renowned principal of the Institute for Colored Youth in Philadelphia, held that position for the last three decades of the 1800s. Under her leadership, the school developed into a premier secondary school where students studied the classics and graduates often went into one of the professions (Tillman, 2004). Unfortunately, we were not able to locate any information on the preparation programs of these outstanding leaders.

During the 1700s and throughout the 1800s, population growth among Whites and their concentration in large towns and cities forced a transition from the one-room school to "graded multi-room schools with several faculty members" (Campbell et al., 1987, p. 126). The need for coordination in these larger schools exceeded what could be provided by the lay trustees of the school committee; thus, head masters (Cubberley, 1916) and head teachers at the elementary level (Cayce, as cited in Messinger, 1939) were appointed to fulfill those tasks. Although these positions eventually evolved into the contemporary principalship, the close association between principals and teachers inhibited the development of educational administration as a field of study and professional preparation (Culbertson, 1988). Campbell et al. (1987) made this point clearly: "Educational administration was not generally recognized as a *specialized* [italics added] field of practice or thought" (p. x) until the 20th century.

Growth in the size of city school districts led to establishment of the superintendency for schools attended by White students in the mid-19th century. These superintendents were expected to fill a philosopher-scholar-statesman role rather than an administrative one (Callahan & Button, 1964; Culbertson, 1988) and typically served as clerk of the school board with few administrative duties (Callahan & Button, 1964). They traveled to district schools and, according to Cubberley (1916), were to inspire teachers and to be responsive to their needs. Schools serving Black students did not appear to have superintendents; however, the school principal enjoyed middle-class status and was viewed as a servant-leader in the community (Tillman, 2004).

Women also moved into the superintendency in the mid- to late 1800s. Important figures include Phebe Sudlow, the first female superintendent in the Unites States, who in 1847 was appointed to lead schools in Davenport, Iowa ("Phebe Sudlow," n.d.), and Ella Flagg Young, the first woman to superintend a large urban district, who in 1887 was appointed superintendent of Chicago Public Schools (Webb & McCarthy, 1998). Although histories of school administration omit the substantial contributions of both women, each served with distinction as superintendent, each presided over districts in which teacher discontent quickly gave way to teacher satisfaction, and both were appointed as university professors.

Notwithstanding the success of superintendents like Sudlow and Young, by the 1870s the need for some sort of formal preparation in educational leadership was recognized. Among the vanguard were other superintendents, especially Payne, mentioned above, and William T. Harris of St. Louis schools. The first college course on educational administration was taught in 1879 by Payne, then a professor at the University of Michigan (Callahan & Button, 1964). Two years later he inaugurated the "*first* course designed to train principals and superintendents" (Culbertson, 1988, p. 4).

The actual pedagogy used in the original courses was not reported; still, some insight into teaching practices was offered by Culbertson (1988). He explained that in 1897, the dean of Teachers College, Columbia, wanted a year-long course taught for principals. A superintendent of a nearby district was asked to teach it. Although this superintendent had written a book on school management, he replied that he could teach the requested course in 6 weeks. Determined that the course last a year, the dean "suggested ... that students in the course could investigate 'what the schools are doing' and 'how school systems are being managed'" (Russell, 1937, as cited in Culbertson, 1988, p. 8) to gain a realistic understanding of administration. The superintendent strongly objected to this proposal, and said "'all that the superintendent wants the public to know can be found in his reports.... Snooping around just can't be done; it isn't ethical'" (Russell, 1937, as cited in Culbertson, 1988, p. 8).

Such resistance to the study of educational administration combined with very rudimentary techniques for conducting social science research to prevent systematic knowledge about administration from accumulating until the mid-20th century. The administrative preparation that did exist was in the hands of practitioners who used their experience rather than scholarship as the basis for teaching. Formal preparation for Black educators, especially principals, often came through preparation for the ministry. Both Black and female educators only occasionally gained access to formal preparation through avenues available to White, male superintendents and principals. Still, leaders in the Black community well understood the value of education for economic and social status advancement and established a number of institutions of higher education, including Tougaloo University in Mississippi and Morris Brown College in Atlanta (Murtadha & Watts, 2005).

The 20th century brought a dramatic change of attitude toward the study of educational administration; the first university department of educational administration was established at Teachers College, Columbia, by 1910 (W. J. Davis, 1978). The forerunner to the American Educational Research Association was founded in 1915 (Culbertson, 1988). Several texts on educational administration were published between 1900 and 1920 (Callahan & Button, 1964). The departments for secondary and elementary school principal as units of the National Education Association were founded in 1920. In short, educational administration "emerged ... as a distinct professional field in this country" (Campbell et al., 1987, p. 3), though not in most other Western countries (J. Murphy, 1998). During these same decades, the African American principal continued to represent "the Black community; was regarded as the authority on educational, social, and economic issues; and was responsible for establishing the all-Black school as the cultural symbol of the Black community"

(Tillman, 2004, p. 102), important contributions that continue to be overlooked in contemporary histories of educational administration.

By midcentury, improvements in social science research methodology, which provided the foundation for a public sense that such research was important, contributed to a change in attitude toward educational administration in the dominant society. These developments led to a boom in both research and theory development in educational administration. The theoretical developments mirrored a White, male perspective and overlooked theories about the importance of nurturing students in their intellectual endeavors that more recent research has revealed is instrumental and that was historically practiced by Black (Lomotey, 1989) and female (Noddings, 1984) educational leaders. This omission is surprising given that Dewey sought to replicate "the best form of family life" in the University of Chicago Laboratory School (Dewey, 1915, as cited in Seigfried, 1996, p. 49). Here, Dewey drew on the work of teachers, almost exclusively women, at the school and noted,

> It has been popularly assumed that I am the author of these ready-made ideas and principles. … I take this opportunity to say that the educational conduct of the schools, as well as its administration, … [and] actual instruction of children have been almost entirely in the hands of the teachers of the schools. (as cited in Seigfried, 1996, p. 48)

Thus, Dewey acknowledged the momentous contributions of female teachers and administrators but stopped short of naming them. Likewise, the important administrative skill of nurturing those who were led did not receive serious consideration in preparation programs until near the end of the 20th century.

A number of major events and trends, both in this country and internationally, affected education and its leadership. These included industrialization, widespread enchantment with the business model (Callahan & Button, 1964), two world wars with the Great Depression sandwiched in between, continuing urbanization, tremendous population growth through immigration, and greater overall prosperity, all of which sent "vast numbers of new students" to school (Callahan & Button, 1964, p. 79; see also Campbell et al., 1987).

Milestones in the field of educational administration during these middle decades of the 1900s included the establishment of the National Conference of Professors of Educational Administration in 1947 (Campbell et al., 1987) and of the University Council for Educational Administration (UCEA) in 1957 (Culbertson, 1988), the publication of a number of important books such as *Administrative Behavior* by Herbert Simon, published in 1945 (as cited in Campbell et al., 1987) as well as the inauguration of journals devoted to the study of educational administration, such as *Educational Administration Quarterly*, begun in 1965 (Campbell et al., 1987). However, as is seen in the unfolding of the empirical research below, these associations and journals were slow to promote, support, encourage, or publish empirical studies of pedagogy used in administrative preparation programs.

At least three major forces account for the lack research attention to pedagogy. One force was the theory movement, which began in the 1950s. This movement gave shape and substance to administrative preparation programs and defined the pedagogy to be used. The successes of female leaders such as Ella Flagg Young and Fanny Jackson Coppin were ignored (as they are today), and education administration programs were largely comprised of White, male faculty who were former practitioners and often prepared in other social science disciplines, most notably, sociology, psychology, political science, economics, and history. The dominant form of instruction in these disciplines from 1950 to the present was lecture, driven by behaviorist concepts of learning theory, a second major force shaping pedagogy in preparation programs and an area of development discussed more fully below. Both of these factors combined to stymie research on pedagogy based on the belief that if knowledge were to be transmitted to relatively passive students, there was not much to study.

A third factor that inhibited the study of pedagogy in leader preparation programs was that scholarly associations and journals in the field would not have accepted manuscripts on administrative pedagogy, especially those that were small scale and primarily conducted as action research by professors studying their own programs. Editorial policies in major journals were heavily influenced by the theory movement, and positivist research methods with which action research methods were incompatible. Hence, any efforts by professors of education administration to more closely link instruction with practice in field settings and to experiment with alternate forms of instruction would not qualify for a hearing beyond the institution in which the professors worked.

One exception to prevailing disinterest in research on pedagogy is a nationwide study conducted in 1975 under the auspices of UCEA and reported by Silver and Spuck (1978). Using survey research methods that were popular in the social sciences in the 1970s, a questionnaire that included eight items related to instruction was distributed across the country. Based on these eight items, Alkire (1978) reported that at the master's level "only about 31% of students' instructional time" included lectures according to both students and professors, while "about 56% of the instructional time is spent in discussion" (p. 59). Based on data from other questionnaire items, Alkire inferred that respondents grouped teaching strategies such as simulations and case study with the strategy of discussion, thereby augmenting the time respondents indicated was spent in discussion. Similar teaching patterns were reported regarding educational specialist programs (Evans & Shapiro, 1978). At the doctoral level, however, lecture and discussion were the most prevalent teaching strategies, but case studies, simulations, and role play were also frequently used, according to Nagle and Nagle (1978). Although authors contributing to the Silver and Spuck (1978) report indicated that lecture and discussion were the pedagogies of choice for most professors of educational administration, they also suggested that faculty were experimenting, if on a small scale, with other instructional methods.

The theory movement and associated research failed to produce the hoped-for knowledge base in educational administration, and the field drifted during the 1970s and 1980s (Campbell et al., 1987). The efficacy of public education itself was questioned during this time, as demonstrated by the publication of *A Nation at Risk* (National Commission on Excellence in Education, 1983). Educational administration was not exempt from the critique. University programs were criticized for having low student-selection standards and for inadequately preparing the students for the demands of administration. These criticisms led to the development by the mid-1990s of standards for school leaders, by the Interstate School Leaders Licensure Consortium (ISLLC) and the Educational Leadership Constituent Council, which is now part of the National Council for the Accreditation of Teacher Education, developments that are discussed in more detail below.

Here we note only that most states either adopted the standards of one of these groups or patterned their own standards after them. State departments of education in turn required that university programs be redesigned in congruence with the standards or risk having state certification denied to their graduates. Thus, amid much flurry and trepidation, the standards led to substantial changes in the structure of many educational leadership programs, especially at the master's degree level. At the same time rival programs were established by organizations such as the National Association of Secondary School Principals (NASSP), the Southern Regional Education Board, and the Broad Foundation. Whether the structural changes in university program configuration resulted in changes in the actual pedagogy used is not certain. As Björk and Ginsberg (1995) pointed out, there is within the professoriate much resistance to change, a recurrent theme in the literature on attempts to advance pedagogy in preparation programs.

To provide a foundation for pedagogy used in and appropriate for educational leadership programs, an understanding of advances in research on learning and learning theory is important. These advances help to explain both why more attention is being given to pedagogy in administration preparation programs now than previously and why there is currently an increase in empirical study of the pedagogy used in these programs.

Learning and Learning Theory

We teach so that others may learn; the learning of others is the *raison d'être* of teaching. Teaching and learning have been pursued for millennia. Even in prehistoric times, children were taught the mores of their clan or tribe, skills necessary for survival, and whoever invented the wheel certainly at least modeled its use to other adults. The historical importance ascribed to learning notwithstanding, our capacity to study it scientifically is an artifact of the last century or so (Shuell, 1986).

Scientific study has not made learning as a construct easy to define, however. Many researchers agree that learning is a process (Iran-Nejad, McKeachie, & Berliner 1990; Resnick, 1989; Shuell, 1990) and that it involves change. Learning is also considered to occur through an interaction between the external environment and the internal characteristics of the learner (Iran-Nejad et al., 1990; Knowles, 1984). Learning can be formal (Marsick & Watkins, 2001) and intentional (Bereiter & Scardamalia, 1989; Knowles, 1984), pursued with purpose, strategy, and effort, such as when the learner prepares for a test or demonstration of what has been learned. But learning also can be incidental, requiring no planning and occurring unintentionally (Kerka, 2000) in ways that are tacit or unconscious (Marsick & Watkins, 2001), such as learning that occurs from unremarkable daily experiences and social interactions. In this section, we examine learning as a formal process linked to pedagogy in educational leadership preparation programs. In doing so, we review the tenets of behavioral and constructivist theories. We precede our review of these theories with a short discussion of pedagogy and andragogy.

Pedagogy and Andragogy

The *Oxford English Dictionary* (1989) defines *pedagogy* as the art or science of teaching, a definition with which there is wide agreement. The etymology of the word is Greek; it is derived from *paidagōgos*, an attendant, usually a male slave, who took young boys to and from school. There is some disagreement about whether pedagogues taught their charges or merely accompanied them to school; nevertheless, contemporary use of the term is virtually synonymous with teaching. Another term to denote teaching that is coming into increased use is *andragogy*. Andragogy is associated with the teaching of adults. Adult learning was the subject of much research activity in the last century in both the United States and Europe. Andragogy was used by these researchers to differentiate strategies used for teaching adults from those used for teaching children, or pedagogy.

Knowles is a prominent theorist in adult learning. In referring to Knowles's work, Brown (2006b) indicated that andragogy can be defined as "the art and science of helping others to learn," (p. 2). Instructive to note in this definition is the use of the word *others* rather than *adults*. Knowles's work in adult learning led him to conceptualize pedagogy and andragogy as complementary rather than as distinctly different. That is, both pedagogy and andragogy offer strategies that may be useful for both children and adults. The goal of learning and the learner's readiness to learn guide the teacher in selecting pedagogical or andragogical strategies, not the learner's age (Knowles, 1984). As Knowles (1984) pointed out, "youth might learn better, too, when their needs and interests, life situations, experience, self-concepts, and individual differences are taken into account" (p. 31). In this chapter, we use *pedagogy* as a generic term encompassing the art and science of teaching individuals, regardless of age.

Mezirow, another prominent scholar in the field of adult learning, introduced the concept of transformative learning, through which adult learners change their frame of reference as they become discriminating, self-reflective learners. Transformative learning is no easy task, as Mezirow (1997) explained:

We transform our frames of reference through *critical reflection on the assumptions* upon which our interpretations, beliefs, and habits of mind or points of view are based. We can become critically reflective of the assumptions we or others make when we learn to solve problems instrumentally or when we are involved in communicative learning. We may be critically reflective of assumptions when reading a book, hearing a point of view, engaging in task-oriented problem solving (objective reframing), or self-reflectively assessing our own ideas and beliefs (subjective reframing). Self-reflection can lead to significant personal transformations. (p. 7)

Frames of reference are resistant to change. They are assumptive understandings acquired through repeated experiences with normative behaviors and attitudes in the dominant society. Assumptive understandings in our society, for example, include that men, unless they are running for political office, do not cry in public; African Americans, in general, do not care about schooling; and women are not capable of captaining a Boeing 747 jet airliner.

Changing the frames of reference of adults in educational leadership preparation programs is one of the pedagogical tasks confronting those who teach in those programs. It would be rare to find a single class session, much less a full semester course, that successfully engages learners in experiences that challenge their frames of reference so that assumptions may be critiqued and changed, enabling new behaviors to emerge that alter students' world view. Mezirow (1997) urged, "Learners need practice in recognizing frames of reference and using their imaginations to redefine problems from a different perspective" (p. 10). Such practice implies ongoing experiences that challenge assumptions and build new ways of understanding the complex problems that confront educational leaders almost constantly. Brown (2004) reinforced this point when she wrote, "The overall purpose of adult development is to realize one's agency through increasingly expanding awareness and critical reflection" (p. 87). These issues of identifying one's frames of reference are fully discussed in the section on reflective practice below.

We touch on andragogy and adult learning theory here to highlight the need of adults to build on prior experiences; to connect learning to life, task, or problem-centered matters; and to attend to the internal motivators and independent learning goals that adults bring to formal learning settings, such as the university. In other words, those who teach adults mindfully should use strategies that more fully engage the learner in the process of constructing meaning. Such strategies are constructivist in nature and contrast with behavioral approaches that dominated most of the latter half of the 1900s.

Research related to andragogy and constructivism informs the development of pedagogical approaches that more authentically engage adult learners in the acquisition of knowledge and skills and the development of complex understandings about the effective use of knowledge and skills. Such authentic engagement is appropriate for the preparation of future education leaders and reflects advances in learning theory. Simon (1993), in his treatise urging that leader preparation programs incorporate advances in learning theory, asserted, "Professional schools have an opportunity for the deep contact with [the] real world" (p. 393), or authentic engagement with actual problems of practice. Authentic engagement requires pedagogical strategies that are primarily situated from the center to the right in Figure 8.1, a figure to which we refer throughout this chapter.

Figure 8.1, Learning and Teaching Continuum in Educational Leadership Programs, was developed by Cordeiro (2006) and modified for this chapter. The figure presents a conceptualization of pedagogies used in educational leadership programs. Contributions to learning theory from cognitive and developmental psychology and the neurosciences indicate that appropriate pedagogical practices in preparation programs should span the range of strategies and move away from the historical near-exclusive focus on the far left side of Figure 8.1. In other words, lecture and discussion, personal goal setting, reading and reflection, and independent study are useful teaching strategies; however, only by engaging fully in a workplace community of practice can adult

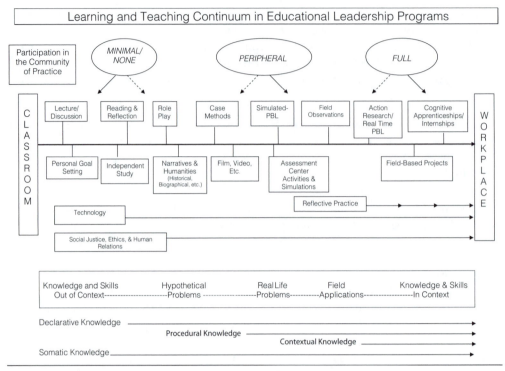

Figure 8.1 Learning and teaching continuum in educational leadership programs. Adapted from *Educating at the Border: Learning and Teaching on the Threshold*, by P. Cordeiro, 2006. Keynote address at the world assembly of the International Council for the Education of Teachers, Fortaleza, Brazil.

learners in our preparation programs garner fully the extent of knowledge and critical reflection they need as emerging educational leaders.

Among the important elements in Figure 8.1 are (a) the extent of participation in a community of practice, (b) the types of pedagogy used and their relationship to learner engagement (not all of which have been well researched), (c) the range of knowledge application from out-of-context to fully embedded in-context, and (d) the types of knowledge developed by the various pedagogical strategies. Important points to note are that the research is sometimes ahead of the pedagogy used in university preparation programs and that the extent to which actual changes in pedagogy have occurred to date is uneven within and across universities (Cambron-McCabe, 2003). A better understanding of pedagogical practices reflected in Figure 8.1 is dependent on a basic understanding of behavioral and constructivist learning theories.

Behaviorist Theory

According to Rowan (1995b), "Behaviorist models of learning and teaching … dominated educational thinking" (pp. 115–116) from the mid-1960s to the mid-1990s. The continued influence of behaviorist thinking is evident today in the attention given to learning objectives in many school districts (Rowan, 1995b). Although McInerney (2005) reminded us that Skinner, the father of behaviorism, "acknowledged that people … thought, deliberated, felt, and so on" (p. 587), behaviorists assert that learning has to be observable to provide "a path to a science of behaviour" (p. 587). Consequently, a change in behavior verifiable through observation is essential for behaviorists. Teaching from a behaviorist perspective involves the "direct transfer of knowledge" (Resnick, 1989, p. 2), commonly referred to as *direct instruction* (Rowan, 1995b). In leadership preparation programs, direct instruction is delivered through the lecture format.

Behavioral theory posits that knowledge is made accessible to the learner by decomposing complex concepts into discrete components that are taught sequentially (McInerney, 2005). Instruction is a linear process that builds from "lower to higher, easier to more difficult, basic to complex" (Prestine, 1995, p. 136). Iran-Nejad et al. (1990) applied the term "simplification by isolation" (p. 509) to behaviorist pedagogy. One key assumption of this paradigm is that the learner, with little difficulty, is able to link together the discrete, isolated bits of information that build toward a complex understanding. A second key assumption is that learning that takes place in one context, say, the university classroom, can be transferred successfully to a far different context, say, the actual practice of leadership in a school.

These assumptions are challenged by constructivist researchers, a contrast explored below. Suffice it to note at this point that behaviorist theory influenced pedagogy in educational leadership programs for decades. Consequently, those who taught in preparation programs assumed that future administrators would be able to pull together appropriate knowledge from discrete disciplines and disparate courses and apply that knowledge successfully in solving the complex, ill-structured problems faced by school leaders. Cognitive theorists also challenge the assumption that knowledge is easily transferable (Iran-Nejad et al., 1990; Resnick, 1989). Moreover, they criticize behaviorist-based pedagogy as "discourag[ing] the kinds of teaching behaviors associated with the achievement of higher order learning goals" (Rowan, 1995b, p. 119).

Constructivist Theory

Research over the past 20 years involved a convergence of developmental psychology, cognitive psychology, and the neurosciences, leading to a radical departure from behaviorist conceptions about learning and effective pedagogy. Insights into the workings of the brain and mind, as well as research about learning, are critical not only to prekindergarten through Grade 12 (preK–12) schooling, but also to the preparation of educational leaders. One important way cognitive psychologists differ from their behaviorist counterparts is in conceptualizing learning as a process that is not necessarily immediately observable and in which understanding is deemed an important aspect of learning though it is not behaviorally demonstrated.

According to cognitive theorists, learning has three aspects, which were explained by Resnick (1989):

> First, learning is a process of knowledge *construction*, not knowledge recording or absorption. Second, learning is *knowledge-dependent*; people use current knowledge to construct new knowledge. Third, learning is highly tuned to the *situation* in which it takes place. (p. 1)

In essence, cognitive theorists "emphasize that learning is an active, constructive, cumulative, and goal-oriented process that involves problem solving" (Shuell, 1990, p. 532) in a particular context. Iran-Nejad et al. (1990) explained further, "The starting point [of learning] is a complex problematic situation or an indeterminate zone of practice characterized by uncertainty, conflict, and uniqueness" (p. 512). The goal-oriented and problem-solving aspects of learning not only are consistent with research on adult learning (Knowles, 1984), but also are particularly salient for teaching and learning in educational leadership preparation and reflect the right side of the Figure 8.1 pedagogies.

Educational leaders are typically confronted with hundreds of ill-structured problems, many of them quite serious, as a typical aspect of their job (Leithwood, 1995). A pedagogy that engages students in identifying and resolving these ill-defined problems more meaningfully prepares them for the field of practice than a pedagogy that does not. Cognitive theories of learning suggest that dramatically different forms of pedagogy are needed if the learner is to be successful in not merely acquiring information but in constructing knowledge that can inform practice. One dilemma that has faced leadership preparation programs in the last several decades is that the many faculty teaching in these programs were educated as children and then groomed as undergraduate and graduate students in the behaviorist paradigm during the 1960s, 1970s, and 1980s. Developing modes of teaching that draw upon gains made in the cognitive sciences has not been easy (Kottkamp & Silverberg, 2000, 2003).

The focus of instruction is another point of contrast between behavioral and cognitive theories. Rather than teaching discrete parts that, when mastered, lead to understanding the whole, cognitive models begin with the whole and introduce the parts as relevance indicates. This important difference raises issues not only for pedagogical approaches, but also for the curricular structure of leader preparation programs in which disciplinary knowledge is usually divided into discrete courses, with little attempt to point out linkages between and among various sources of knowledge. Iran-Nejad et al. (1990) referred to learning as a multisource phenomenon with "diverse sources [of information] converging on a coherent organic whole" (p. 512). The emerging pedagogy of cognitive apprenticeship provides an example and is discussed more completely in chapter 9 of this handbook.

Cognitive apprenticeships are analogs to apprenticeships in the trades and reflect a pedagogy found at the right side of the Figure 8.1 pedagogies. The learner, or apprentice, is situated in the context in which learning is to be applied (Resnick, 1989). Rowan (1995b) explained, "In cognitive apprenticeship ... teachers begin the instructional process by modeling a whole task, and then teach component tasks by reference to this whole" (p. 123). What is learned is thus contextualized, not isolated, minimizing the difficulty of transferring knowledge from classroom to the field of practice. However, a caveat is in order. Because in educational leadership much of the work of the master, or expert, is mental, it is often not observable to the apprentice (Resnick, 1989). To address this issue, cognitive theorists emphasize the critical nature of knowledge construction as an interactive process between expert and novice, with the expert scaffolding the learning so that the novice is able to move from dependent to interdependent to independent, that is, from novice toward increasing expertise. This move is essential to the exercise of successful leadership in schools and deserves elaboration.

Moving From Novice to Expert in Five Difficult Steps

Learning, according to cognitive theorists, is a "process of organizing information into coherent representations of knowledge variously called schemata, scripts, frames, or cognitive structures" (Rowan, 1995b, p. 120). Schemata turn out to be very important in distinguishing experts from novices (Leithwood, 1995; Perkins & Salomon, 1989). It is worth noting here that knowledge the novice brings to a situation may be faulty (Bransford, Brown, & Cocking, 1999, p. xvi), in which case the novice's schemata are flawed and must be changed if expertise is to be gained. The novice-to-expert progression is relevant to all learning, including educational leadership preparation. Shuell (1990), citing work by Dreyfus and Dreyfus, described the steps of this progression. As novices continuously acquire knowledge and hone skills, they progress to advanced beginners, then to competent, next to proficient, and finally to expert (Shuell, 1990). Each step requires constant application and refinement of the knowledge and skills that have been acquired.

During this progression, knowledge is processed and organized differently, building toward complex schemata that hold large amounts of information that are accessed during problem solving (Leithwood, 1995; Perkins & Salomon, 1989; Rowan, 1995a, 1995b). Using highly elaborated schemata, the expert frees working memory from holding factual and procedural information. The expert is therefore able to attend to more nuanced but important aspects of the problem, thereby building a more complete and sophisticated understanding of the problem, which in turn leads more quickly to an effective solution. Attaining expertise is no easy task. Simon (1993) estimated that it takes a minimum of "10 years of intense application" (p. 407) to develop expertise in one's field.

Although expertise is domain specific (Yekovich, 1993), Perkins and Salomon (1989) gave us a "general profile of expertise" (p. 18). Perkins and Salomon noted,

> Expert performance entail[s] (a) a large knowledge base of domain-specific patterns…; (b) rapid recognition of situations where these patterns apply; and (c) reasoning that moves from such recognition directly toward a solution by working with the patterns, often called *forward reasoning.* (p. 18)

Novices, lacking well-developed schemata, have a more superficial understanding of the problem (Yekovich, 1993), may frame the problem incorrectly, and may use backward reasoning. That is, novices generate a hypothesis and then fit information about the situation to the hypothesis (Ohde & Murphy 1993) in a trial-and-error fashion. Therefore, novices reason more haphazardly, less efficiently, and less effectively. Shuell (1990) added, "A task that once constituted a problem for the new learner (and elicited various problem-solving strategies) becomes little more than a simple recall task for the more experienced and sophisticated learner" (p. 531), or expert.

As a learner moves from novice to expert, four types of knowledge are developed, as represented in Figure 8.1: (a) declarative, (b) procedural, (c) contextual, and (d) somatic. Declarative knowledge includes domain-related facts, principles, concepts, and generalizations (Ohde & Murphy, 1993). Procedural knowledge, as the name implies, involves understanding how to use the declarative knowledge to solve the problem at hand. Yekovich (1993) explained, "Procedural knowledge provides experts with specialized mental algorithms and heuristics for dealing with domain-related information" (p. 149). How one responds to the problem situation depends heavily on procedural knowledge, according to Yekovich.

Contextual knowledge, also referred to as conditional knowledge (Paris, Lipson, & Wixson, as cited in Garner, 1990), enables one to know when to use certain strategies. Somatic knowledge combines one's experience with sensory information in a mind–body interaction (Matthews, 1998), a source of knowledge largely ignored in Western cultures. According to Sellers-Young (1998), a somatic approach "implies an education that trusts individuals to learn from their ability to attend and to listen to the information they are receiving from interaction of self with the environment" (p. 176). Howard Gardner's (1983) concepts of the intrapersonal (knowledge of self) and interpersonal (skill in interacting with others) intelligences are closely connected to somatic knowledge. As is discussed below, it is contextual knowledge that enables declarative and procedural knowledge to be used to greatest effect, but contextual knowledge is seldom attended to in most curricula. Somatic knowledge, on the other hand, is ignored almost completely, though feminist and postmodernist discourses (J. A. Davis, 1997) as well as literature from the field of leadership studies (Getz, 2008; Monroe, 2000, 2003, 2004) have opened a window on the topic.

The difficulty of mastering these four types of knowledge and thereby attaining expertise in a field should not be underestimated. Expertise requires not only amassing an enormous amount of declarative knowledge, but also years of practice and experience in the field (Ohde & Murphy, 1993) to build reliable procedural, contextual, and somatic knowledge. Therefore, as with other professional fields, it is specious to think that students in school leader preparation programs, as they are currently configured, could emerge upon graduation as expert school leaders.

Despite the above caveat, the pedagogical benefit to be gained from knowing how experts in educational leadership solve problems is of some consequence. Leithwood (1995) reported that compared to novices, expert school leaders take more time to understand an ill-structured problem thoroughly before moving to solution, are more likely to contextualize both the problem and its solution in the multifaceted context of the school, develop "more precise, manageable goals" (p. 121) in the problem-solving process, are less invested personally in a particular solution and more interested in arriving at an optimal solution when working in a group, and are more adept at managing constraints on problem solving. Leithwood also noted that the field of educational leadership lacks empirical research about the nature of problematic situations confronting principals, hampering the study of school leader expertise and leaving a troubling gap in our knowledge about both the optimal content and pedagogy for preparation programs.

The research that does exist on novice–expert differences suggests that instructors in educational leadership programs might give thoughtful consideration to both curricula and pedagogy that consciously build students' schemata through authentic experiences and in a manner that fosters the progression from novice to competent during university study. Doing so would provide a foundation for school leaders to begin the move to proficient during the first several years of practice. Sans the development of schemata that contain not only declarative but also procedural, contextual, and somatic knowledge, the new school leader begins practice as an advanced beginner at best. In building such a foundation, instructors also consciously might teach metacognitive strategies that are helpful in both facilitating problem identification and solving (Leithwood, 1995) and acquiring new learning (Glaser, Raghavan, & Baxter, 1992; Rowan, 1995a, 1995b). Indeed, Leithwood urged educational researchers to use "the rich array of theoretical tools" (p. 122) offered by the cognitive sciences to understand more completely how expert educational leaders think about and respond to problems of practice. Such research could produce more valuable content and more appropriate pedagogy for preparation programs.

Given that contextual knowledge is important for expert problem solving in a domain, if learners in educational leadership preparation programs are to benefit from developments in the cognitive sciences, particular attention to the learning environment, or the workplace community of practice depicted at the right side of the Figure 8.1 pedagogies, is needed. Attention to the learning environment indicates a contextual shift from the classroom exclusively to field contexts as well as a pedagogical shift from teacher centered to learner centered. If the learning environment includes more content-rich workplace experiences, the learner's current declarative and procedural knowledge, which may be faulty, as noted, would be more successfully challenged. Declarative and procedural knowledge could be enhanced by including students' awareness of their somatic knowledge using a variety of pedagogies found in Figure 8.1. Teaching approaches such as the case-in-point method (Acker-Hocevar, Pisapia, Coukos-Semmel, 2002; Getz, 2008; Monroe, 2003) or simulations, such as those described by Brunner, Miller, and Hammel (2003), can result in particularly powerful personal learning experiences that could move the learner further along the novice-to-expert progression.

Support for the importance of context and a workplace-centered learning environment comes from the work of social constructivist theorists such as Vygotsky, whose work, along with that of his colleagues, has emerged as a dominant theory of learning in the new millennium. Social constructivists posit that knowledge construction is accelerated by the social context in which it occurs. Iran-Nejad et al. (1990) agreed; they noted, "The more meaningful, the more deeply or elaboratively processed, the more situated in context, and the more rooted in cultural, background, metacognitive, and personal knowledge an event is, the more readily it is understood, learned, and remembered" (p. 511).

One implication of the work of cognitive and social constructivist theorists is that the pedagogy in our preparation programs is in need of research that documents how cooperative learning groups assigned to address complex problems of practice contribute to the learning and problem-framing ability of prospective educational leaders. With this foundation, we turn our focus to the actual pedagogies that have been used in educational leadership preparation. From there we move to an examination of the research, limited though it is.

Influences in Educational Leader Preparation: 1970–2000

As we noted at the beginning of this chapter, our task was to review, describe, and evaluate research about pedagogy in educational leadership preparation programs. In this section, we summarize in broad strokes developments that shaped pedagogical approaches used in preparation programs for educational leaders during the decades 1970–2000. We selected this period in part because of space limitations and in part because of the upsurge in interest concerning pedagogy that characterizes those decades. We reiterate, however, that concern about the pedagogy appropriate for preparation programs was not new in the 1970s. Willower and Forsyth (1998) noted, for example, that the 1948 meeting of the National Council of Professors of Educational Administration quickly "turned to [issues of] recruitment and selection, courses and problems, surveys, internships, social science knowledge, and the principles that would *integrate* [italics added] such experiences in a program" of study (p. 16).

The case is made above that behavioral psychology and the theory movement drove pedagogy in the 1970s through the 1990s and led professors to rely heavily on lecture and discussion, approaches that only minimally engage the learner in a community of practice, as depicted in Figure 8.1. The 1970s saw increased interest in the preparation of managers and administrators across several fields, however. Deep (1971), for example, developed a program for business that was designed to enhance both personal growth and organizational development by engaging participants in case studies, role plays, sensitivity training,[1] and programmed instruction, all pedagogical practices with the more constructivist bent found near the middle of the Figure 8.1 pedagogies. Indeed, it can be argued that the development of a program such as Deep's was a harbinger of the impending decline of behaviorism.

At the same time, in education Lutz (1971) pointed out that insufficient funds were being spent on similar programs in educational leadership preparation, and researchers such as Markus and Huys (1973) and Silver (1979b) urged that preparation focus on problems of practice and student learning rather than on theory out of context. Pedagogies these researchers advocated were interactive instruction, especially role play, reflective practice, and field-based experiences. They argued that such strategies enhance a learner's ability to differentiate symptoms from problems and to identify problems with greater accuracy, first hypothetically in the classroom and then in context through the field experiences. In other words, these pedagogical strategies help preservice leaders develop a more complex schemata composed of declarative, procedural, and contextual knowledge and to begin the move from novice toward expert. Silver (1979b), in particular, worked to move the pedagogy in preparation programs toward the constructivist strategies located in the middle of Figure 8.1 and closer to engagement in the authentic activities of workplace located at the right end of the figure.

Two developments of the 1970s that affected educational administration were the reemergence of human relations training for in-service and preservice administrators and the availability of new technologies, especially the computer. Development of human relations skills was reported to be particularly successful in addressing leadership issues related to the desegregation of schools for both pre- and in-service leaders. The advent of available technologies, however, found the field of educational leadership typically slow to adapt. By the late 1980s, about one third of the leadership preparation programs provided students with neither experiences with computers nor instruction about uses to which computers could be put in schools (Spuck & Bozeman, 1988). To the extent that computers were incorporated into preparation programs, it was often as an additional course (House, 1989); thus, "relatively few practicing school administrators [made] effective use of personal computer technology" (p. 4).

By the end of the 1980s, increasing numbers of university professors in educational leadership programs recognized the need for on-the-job learning. Two often-cited dissertation studies, Jack

(1983) and Witters-Churchill (1988), offered two recommendations. First, administrative preparation programs should include a practicum as an integral part of the program; second, practitioners should be involved in instruction at the university. These preservice administrators were particularly interested in "practice-oriented faculty" who "keep … up-to-date with the field" and "have periodic experience in the field" (Witters-Churchill, 1988, p. 342). The suggestion that practicing administrators be involved in teaching prospective administrators should not be overlooked by professors in the academy. Prospective administrators are telling us that it is important not only to gain on-the-job experience, but also to learn from those doing the job of leading schools.

The Witters-Churchill (1988, 1991) study merits special focus. Sponsored by the University Consortium for the Performance-Based Preparation of Principals of the National Association of Secondary School Principals University Consortium, Witters-Churchill surveyed 400 Texas principals and assistant principals, garnering a response rate of 81%. These in-service leaders not only identified the internship as the most favored aspect of their leadership development, but also recommended longer internships accompanied by better supervision. Not surprisingly, lecture and discussion were the most frequently used pedagogical strategies in participants' preparation but were described by them as "only minimally to moderately effective" (Witters-Churchill, 1991, p. 341).

A number of studies, especially survey studies, conducted during the period from the 1970s through the 1990s (Hoachlander, Alt, & Beltranenam, 2001; Jack, 1983) confirmed Witters-Churchill's (1988) findings. These studies reinforce the conclusion that preparation programs have been "mindlessly dependant on lectures and classroom-based instruction rather than on experiential learning" (Witters-Churchill, 1988, p. 6) despite an ardent press from colleagues (e.g., Osterman & Kottkamp, 1993, 2004; Silver, 1979a) that more effective pedagogies be used and advances in learning theory that undergird those pedagogical strategies. Still, there is a glimmer of evidence that university instruction was inching toward the right side of the Figure 8.1 pedagogies. In addition to the internship, other pedagogies from which Witters-Churchill's (1988) respondents reported they benefitted were clinical study, computer-assisted instruction, instructional modules, group process training, and games and simulations, all pedagogies that include more field-based and problem-based experiences.

By the 1990s, discussion about preparing educational leaders was gaining strength and momentum. As noted earlier, educational leadership preparation was again under attack as irrelevant, admitting weak students and graduating students who were little more than callow novices (Cambron-McCabe, 2003). Concomitantly, the standards movement, mentioned above, had begun with the Council of Chief State School Officers giving impetus to the development of standards for educational leaders. The council sponsored a collaborative endeavor known as the ISLLC, which in 1996 promulgated standards for educational leaders.

Development of the ISLLC standards represents a significant milestone in redefining educational leadership preparation programs. The standards document (ISLLC, 1996) presents a daunting list of knowledge, skills, and dispositions that educational leaders need if they are to lead schools and school systems successfully. Concomitantly, standards were also developed by other groups. The wording in these various versions of standards differed only slightly and emphasized that school leaders must focus on instruction aimed at fostering high levels of learning by students in preK–12 schools. This emphasis included traditional management activities that further press educational leaders to think and act in the service of student learning.

The standards for educational leaders suggest a need for preparation programs to use pedagogical approaches that develop in future leaders the four types of knowledge posed in Figure 8.1, especially contextual and somatic knowledge. Doing so necessitates genuine involvement in a workplace community of practice. Applicable teaching approaches are supported by advances in learning theory, including adult learning theory, discussed above.

Research and the development of standards induced the professorate to begin to grasp the need for genuine change. As evidence of a sea change in the field, many university preparation programs dropped *administration* in favor of *leadership* as the departmental name and degree focus, UCEA began to welcome more presentations on pedagogical approaches, and the *Journal of Cases in Educational Leadership* was established. In addition, the *Journal of School Leadership* was founded and published research articles on pedagogies used in preparing school leaders and a special interest group of AERA, Teaching in Educational Administration was founded in 1993. In 2006, the name was changed to Learning and Teaching in Educational Leadership Special Interest Group to emphasize the salience of learning to the development of effective leadership practices. The context of the original name and the rationale for its change was laid out by Silverberg and Kottkamp (2006).

J. Murphy (1998) and others (e.g., Osterman & Kottkamp, 2004; Rusch, 2004) continue the press for more relevant teaching strategies, including problem-based learning (PBL), reflective practice, portfolio development, cognitive apprenticeships, case studies, multimedia communications, and so on. In arguing for authentic learning opportunities, these researchers envision faculty and students as co-learners (Kottkamp & Silverberg, 2000) who use collaborative learning models that are consonant with the Figure 8.1 pedagogies. Despite the number of scholars during this period who recognized the urgent need for attention to pedagogy, there were relatively few empirical studies about the merits or effectiveness of the approaches.

Review and Critique of Research About the Pedagogy Used in Educational Leadership Preparation Programs

The discussion above indicates that students enrolled in educational leadership preparation programs strongly feel they profit more from an authentic, field-based pedagogy, as opposed to the current overreliance on lecture and discussion. Their sensibilities comport with the research on constructivist pedagogy and adult learning theory. This section reviews research regarding authentic pedagogical strategies used in some educational leadership preparation programs and reflected in the Figure 8.1 pedagogies. Because many of the pedagogical strategies at the left side of the figure are discussed above or are self-explanatory (and there is little research on these approaches), we focus this review on pedagogies that begin to involve the learner more actively in the learning process, moving from left to right as we present what is known about these strategies as they have been incorporated into various preparation programs.

We preface the review with a brief discussion of the important concepts of social justice, ethics, and human relation strategies, which we believe must be considered throughout the preparation of future leaders and need to be addressed through a variety of pedagogical approaches. Similarly, as can be seen in Figure 8.1, technology is an underlying theme that can be drawn upon to support a variety of pedagogical approaches. For example, technological simulations have been used to help students explore social justice issues (Brunner, Hitchon, & Brown, 2002). While we discuss the different dimensions of technology separately, it needs to be seen as an underlying and integrative tool, which can be incorporated into a variety of pedagogical approaches.

Although we discuss cognitive apprenticeships above, we neither review the research on this strategy nor include internships or on-the-job learning. These pedagogical techniques are discussed in chapter 11 of this volume. As might be presumed by the reader, some of these strategies overlap or include other strategies as subcategories. For example, simulations can be conducted in the traditional classroom or can incorporate various technologies. Because most of these strategies are problem focused, they are congruent with adult and cognitive learning theories.

Social Justice, Ethics, and Human Relations

Social Justice and Ethics

Like many constructs, social justice is defined differently by different scholars. For example, Bogotch (2002) asserted that social justice is inseparable from action. It is the actions of a leader that make social justice a reality rather than the espousal of a belief system. Brown (2006a) and Mezirow (as cited in Brown, 2006a) echoed the importance of activism as part of adult learning and the transformative learning process that leads to social justice and ethical actions. In this vein, Theoharis (2007) studied principals specifically identified as social justice advocates. Theoharis defined "social justice leadership to mean that these principals make issues of race, class, gender, disability, sexual orientation, and other historically and currently marginalizing conditions in the United States central to their advocacy, leadership practice, and vision" (p. 223). In our analysis, we define social justice and ethical practices used by university instructors as those designed to raise the conscious awareness of aspiring educational leaders regarding the discrimination against or the marginalization of people based on race; gender; national origin; social class; and lesbian, gay, bisexual, and transgendered (LGBT) people and to translate that awareness into ethical practice.

The press for a pedagogy that centers on rather than minimizes social justice, ethics, and equity issues emerged in the educational leadership preparation literature during the late 1990s. Informed by the writings of teacher education researchers (e.g., Delpit, 2006; Ladson-Billings, 1994), critical theorists (e.g., Apple, 1993; Freire, 1970/1996; Freire & Macedo, 1995; Giroux, 1992), and adult-learning theorists (Knowles 1975; Mezirow 1991), several researchers began to conceptualize and describe programs and teaching methods that facilitated graduate students' learning about issues of social justice. Some writings in this vein include Capper (1993), Cunningham and Cordeiro (2006), Scheurich and Laible (1995), and Dantley (2005). Although most of these writings were not empirical, they synthesized the research from several fields, and most authors advocated a similar focus for school leadership preparation.

Principals included in studies by Theoharis (2007), Scheurich and Skrla (2003), and Tripses and Risen (2005) were specifically selected for their reputations as social justice advocates. In each study, principals pressed for transformations in teachers' belief structures from a deficit view of students of color to a belief structure that students of color could learn as well as White students. As might be expected, teacher resistance was encountered, but principal persistence led to new insights by teachers. Research using practicing principals as participants indicated that school leaders could be instrumental in replacing the deficit assumptions prevalent among many teachers with new beliefs about the abilities of students of color that were being discounted or ignored. Leithwood, Seashore Louis, Anderson, and Wahlstrom (2004) reinforced this finding, observing, "Leadership not only matters, it is second only to teaching among school-related factors in its impact on student learning" (p. 3). As a result, a number of empirical studies on preparing preservice leaders began to emerge. Research designs varied, and many studies were conducted by the professors themselves.

Simulations, located to the center on Figure 8.1, represent a pedagogical approach that is commonly used to challenge hegemonic race-related assumptions and explore related ethical issues. Chance and Chance (2000) used simulation to engage preservice leaders in a reconsideration of their beliefs and assumptions about people of a different culture. Though some students were initially uncomfortable, the experience led them to greater insight about nondominant cultures. Brunner et al. (2003) described simulations in a virtual school. Though empirical results were not reported, Brunner et al. described the technique as an "innovative approach to leadership preparation that resulted in a dramatic shift in thinking necessary for administrators and others to co-create democratic, socially just learning organizations" (p. 2). In an earlier publication, Brunner et al. (2002) offered descriptive information on the use of technologically delivered experiential simulations that modify a person's appearance. Through this process they provided administrative candidates with an immersion experience of other's perceptions of them in this new altered persona, which deepened their understanding of democratic principles and social justice issues.

Other studies examined social injustice evident in daily school routines and attitudes exhibited by adults in schools. One such study resulted in the development of the construct of equity traps, proposed by McKenzie and Scheurich (2004). Equity traps, according to McKenzie and Scheurich, "are ways of thinking or assumptions that prevent educators from believing that their students of color can be successful learners" (pp. 601–602). These researchers conducted a participatory action research study involving 8 experienced, White, elementary-level teachers from one school attended by mostly low-income Latina/o and African American students. Based on findings from their study, McKenzie and Scheurich developed "concepts and tools to assist educators in increasing equity in our nation's schools" (p. 607).

Jost, Whitfield, and Jost (2005) conducted research using as participants students enrolled in a required course on diversity. Although these researchers did not use the terminology of *equity traps*, the game strategy they employed provided a platform that encouraged students to think about equity traps. Using the game Monopoly™, students played by the rules with one modification: Pairs of students entered the game in stages and only after prior groups had the chance to play several rounds and buy and improve property. Even though late starters were allowed to negotiate the purchase of property or houses on property acquired by members privileged to have entered the game earlier, the privileged players were often reluctant to share the wealth. The first group to enter the game always won. Members of groups entering later were often content to sit in jail to preserve whatever wealth they might have accumulated and, according to Jost et al., were "discouraged by their inability to get a lead in the game" (p. 17). Jost et al. noted that this game experience had lasting effects on many students, giving "them a deeper insight into the role of history and the consequences of cumulative privilege" (p. 19).

Experiences such as the Monopoly™ game help provide an intellectual and experiential foundation for graduate students regarding the construct of equity traps. Skrla, Scheurich, Garcia, and Nolly (2004) conducted a follow-up study to the McKenzie and Scheurich (2004) study and found "substantial and persistent patterns of inequity internal to schools (i.e., embedded within the many assumptions, beliefs, practices, procedures, and policies of schools themselves)" (p. 143). They used their findings not only to raise the awareness of teachers and administrators at the participating school, but also to assist preservice leaders in recognizing their deficit-based approach to thinking about students of color. One outcome of the Skrla et al. research was the development of 12 indicators that they termed "equity audits" (p. 144). Equity audits and gaming strategies like the Monopoly™ technique could be used both in principal preparation and in principal professional development to raise consciousness about characteristics of society and its deleterious effects on certain children in school.

Reflective writing is another consciousness-raising pedagogical strategy. Research by Mendez-Morse (2004) and Tripses and Hatfield (2004) involved preservice educational leaders in writing end-of-course essays. In Tripses and Hatfield's this study, graduate students were to address an "issue related to poverty and … apply these understandings to their professional or personal life to make a positive difference in the lives of others" (pp. 8–9). Tripses and Hatfield also examined the reflections of two researchers who "had taught the course multiple times" (p. 9). One unexpected finding was the powerful effect that the reflective writing project had on the professors.

Regarding the students' work, Tripses and Hatfield (2004) found "support [for] the literature on change agentry for social justice" (p. 25). They also reported that students developed varying capacities for change agentry, including those who were purposeful change agents, those who were emerging change agents, and those who were compliance change agents and exhibited little change.

Brown (2006a), citing Mezirow, stated, "The overall purpose of adult development is to realize one's agency through increasingly expanding awareness and critical reflection" (p. 709). Such school leaders are likely to develop an increased understanding of the role of ethics in leadership.

Mendez-Morse (2004) reported that students changed differentially. Graduate students in her course interviewed elderly persons of color about their experiences with racism. Although some students saw the assignment as a learning opportunity, others regarded it as another "task that they needed to get done" (p. 13). Undaunted, Mendez-Morse argued that it is crucial for educational leadership preparation programs to design "course activities that can connect students to real, lived experiences of racism" (p. 22) and reported that the assignment was an effective way to prepare aspiring school leaders to work in schools with racially and ethnically diverse student bodies. Although assumptive beliefs may be slow to change for some aspiring leaders, Mendez-Morse engaged students actively in exploring social justice issues using a constructivist strategy. To find that some students were resistant when they encountered challenges to deeply held beliefs is not only to be expected, but also replicates the experiences of practicing principals regarding teachers.

Tripses and Risen (2005) built on the study by Tripses and Hatfield (2004) to compare "developing change agent graduate students against practicing school leaders with proven records as change agents in high poverty schools" (p. 1). The researchers reported that few of the graduate students achieved the extent of understanding regarding social justice that was exhibited by the principals participating in the study, but such a finding should not be surprising given the reputations of the practicing principals against whom the students were compared. Tripses and Risen concluded, "Using the works of recognized authors and experts on social justice has a clear impact on graduate students who aspire to become change agents" (p. 19).

A quasi-experimental study utilizing both quantitative and qualitative methods was conducted by Brown (2006a) to explore preservice leaders' attitudes toward multicultural education issues. Two cohorts, with a combined total of 40 full-time students enrolled in a school leadership program, participated in the following strategies: cultural autobiographies, life histories, prejudice reduction workshops, reflective analysis journals, cross-cultural interviews, diversity panels, and activist action plans. Participants completed a 63-item Likert-type scale questionnaire. Qualitative data were collected through reflective journals kept by students throughout their year-long, full-time internship. Brown (2006a) concluded,

> The results of the quantitative analysis suggest that under particular conditions, an important prerequisite of administrators' ability to lead for social justice and equity—an awareness of and openness to issues of diversity—might be successfully taught and developed in students during the process of preparing for the principalship. (p. 718)

Acker-Hocevar et al. (2002) conducted a cross-case analysis of nine action learning sets involving 30 doctoral students who were divided into teams that worked on projects for 12 weeks. Acker-Hocevar et al. were particularly interested in the "learning aspects" of action learning (p. 3). Using a variety of pedagogical approaches that more actively involve students, such as simulations, case studies, action research, and PBL, Acker-Hocevar et al. summarized "the contributions and limitations of each method" (p. 8) and identified "eight assertions regarding the value of action learning for leadership development" (p. 12). These findings led them to continue to use action learning to bridge the theory–practice gap, which would move students along the novice-to-expert progression.

Thus far, we have reported research addressing racial and cultural differences. Unmentioned is research that increases social justice awareness regarding LGBT people and how it can be meaningfully taught in preparation programs. Unfortunately, we found no research on pedagogy that specifically focused on consciousness raising among prospective principals regarding social justice and

LGBT individuals at the school. Indeed, an ERIC search using *gay, lesbian,* and *principals* returned seven sources, few of which were empirical and none of which addressed pedagogy. One matter that makes this deficit in the research particularly problematic is the very real physical danger and loss of employment LGBT people face by being open about their sexual preferences (Frankfurt, 2000; Gibson, as cited in Lugg, 1997). Even when administrators and teachers honestly confided their nonheterosexual preferences to those they considered close friends, they often soon found themselves perfunctorily dismissed from their jobs (Lugg, 1997).

Pace (2004), a principal at the time, related an anecdotal event in which a gay student planned to attend the senior prom with his boyfriend. The student had confided his sexual orientation to a few close friends who kept his confidence. The principal consulted colleagues at other schools about what to do, but they had no advice. Pace felt he could not deny the boy the right to attend the prom, especially when no one else was denied that right. To Pace's surprise, both students and teachers at the prom unobtrusively found ways to defuse situations that had potential to become problematic, and the prom proceeded without incident.

Things rarely go so smoothly for LGBT persons. Lugg (2003) recounted several incidents in which principals and teachers tolerated physical abuse of male students presumed to be gay. The prejudice was so deep that in one instance when an especially brutal attack caused a student to be hospitalized, the principal accused the student of provoking the attack because of his sexual preference. Clearly, overtly addressing LBGT issues is much needed in the pedagogy of educational leadership programs. Principals encounter LBGT adults, students, and parents during their careers, yet there is little research regarding strategies for dealing sensitively with LBGT individuals of all ages.

Human Relations

The field of human relations grew out of the Hawthorne studies of the 1920s and 1930s but fell out of favor in the 1950s. One reason for its decline was its inconsistency with the then-dominant behaviorist orientation, which required a teacher-centered pedagogy and observable evidence of learning. Behaviorist pedagogies, however, proved inadequate in preparing administrators to successfully address persistent and deep prejudice among teachers from one cultural background who teach students from another.

In the social turmoil of the 1960s and 1970s, human relations resurfaced as a strategy to overcome racial divides in schools. Unfortunately, in education, most references to human relations programs targeted teachers (e.g., Comstock, 1975; K. L. Davis & Gazda, 1975) and student teachers (e.g., Higgins, Moracco, & Danford, 1981; McEwen, Higgins, & Pipes, 1982); few references were found that focused on human relations programs that targeted principals or aspiring principals.

One study (L. W. Hughes, 1971) investigated a human relations program for principals in response to matters attending desegregation and poverty in Appalachia. The University of Tennessee redesigned their principal preparation program to promote change agency (L. W. Hughes, 1971). According to L. W. Hughes (1971), "Course work proceeded from developing adequate insights into contemporary social problems to integrating knowledge and skills in effective problem-solving" (p. 6). Techniques included sensitivity experiences in a human relations laboratory, work with field-based problems, and simulations. Both university students and faculty rated the human relations laboratory as among the best aspects of the program.

Using a similar professional development approach for in-service principals and assistant principals, Memphis State University partnered with the Memphis Principals Association to respond to leadership needs arising from desegregation efforts (Markus & Huys, 1973). A series of workshops focused on improving "understanding and implementation of policies and procedures which enhance desegregation practices" (p. 15). Strategies included film, role play, and small discussion groups. Markus and Huys cited both positive evaluative responses from the participants and the large number of school leaders who elected to participate in the workshop series, nearly 200, as evidence of success.

The enthusiasm pre- and in-service principals expressed for the Tennessee and Memphis programs was not unique. Rost (1980) cited a 1978 study by NASSP in which principals overwhelmingly indicated support for human relations courses, describing the courses as "essential" and "highly useful" (p. 84). Respondents in Rost's study indicated that techniques used in human relations development deviated from the pedagogical norm. Lecture was infrequent, whereas strategies such as role play, structured exercises, and simulations were common. Responding professors in the Rost study reported that participant evaluations confirmed the effectiveness of both human relations programs and the way content was taught. Nonetheless, professors who adhered to the behaviorist paradigm resisted such courses, with nearly two thirds in Rost's study indicating they did "not consider human relations training as … important" (p. 90).

As was illustrated in the previous two sections, a variety of pedagogies have been and continue to be used to develop future educational leaders' skills in addressing social justice, ethical, and human relations issues. We now turn our attention to examining research studies, which are quite limited in many instances, of pedagogies found in the center to the right in Figure 8.1.

Teaching Educational Leadership Through Narratives and the Humanities

One of the earliest references to using the humanities in preparing educational administrators can be found in an analysis of the literature by Piele (1970). His review examined then-current trends in the literature concerned with the preparation of school administrators. Piele found that university-based school administration programs were planning to make greater use of the humanities in preparing educational administrators; however, the literature subsequent to Piele's study showed little evidence of this happening during the 1970s.

In 1979, Calder published a multimedia resource guide for professors to use with prospective school leaders. The nonprint materials in the guide included films, videotapes, audiotapes, multimedia kits, filmstrips, and simulations. One can infer that, although there was no descriptive or empirical research on using these types of teaching materials, they were indeed used, given that a guide of this type was published.

It was not until the 1990s that publications by professors of educational leadership describing their use of narratives and arts and media-based teaching approaches began to appear. Professor of educational administration at Hofstra University, Brieschke (1993) maintained that involving imagination and aesthetic experience is key to narrative fiction, which can help prepare educational leaders. She advocated the use of novels to examine social issues such as class, gender, race, language, and politics.

In a paper exploring use of biographies and other life writings to teach educational leadership, English (1994) detailed criteria professors can use to select and critique biographies that offer insights needed by educational leaders. In addition to biographies, he maintained that related writings, such as autobiographies, portraits, profiles, case studies, memoirs, diaries, and journals, are powerful tools to expand the curriculum and pedagogy of preparation programs. English (1995) argued that these forms of life writing have been neglected in the preparation of educational administrators in favor of approaches such as case studies or PBL projects, which he regarded as grounded in the positivist paradigm. He propounded that if the field is to change ideas about organizational realities, then values, reflective practice, and the dichotomy between management and leadership should be examined. Biography and other forms of life writing are excellent vehicles to do so, in English's view.

English and Steffy (1995) examined the use of film to assist leadership students to attain a better understanding of the importance of culture and context for moral leadership. They maintained that film is a particularly effective vehicle for teaching and suggested criteria that professors can use to select relevant films. Among the many strengths of using film, two that they reported are providing a longitudinal view of a leader and her or his decisions and the ability to show the connection between values and action. Thus, film is an effective pedagogy for addressing issues of social justice and ethical leadership.

In line with the above studies, Meyer (2001) proposed using live performances or readings of original works based on true-life, dramatic scenarios as a useful developmental tool for both aspiring administrators and in-service professionals. Meyer referred to this as *theatre as representation* (TAR) and asserted, "TAR as a pedagogical device in administration preparation programmes can be very useful in helping participants to experience the complexity of the principal (in this case) beyond what is possible in using descriptive text alone" (p. 167). Meyer differentiated case methods from a TAR scenario, stating,

> A case study is an external documentation that requires a passive reading and linear analysis.... A TAR scenario takes the participants to a higher level of involvement from simply describing the case to exploding its language into an emotional reality. (p. 151)

Because a TAR scenario requires the learner to use the first person, Meyer asserted that TAR is similar to simulations. Both are reflection in action and "further ... students' understanding of leadership practice" (p. 152).

Emerging from the interdisciplinary field of leadership studies is the proposition that the traditional lecture approach is more appropriate for the study of leadership than it is for developing the practice of leadership (Pillai & Stites-Doe, 2003). The field of educational leadership is moving from studying school leadership to developing practitioners. The Figure 8.1 strategies offer techniques to facilitate that transition.

Film, Video, and Multimedia Technology

Figure 8.1 includes pedagogies that incorporate the use of film, video, and various forms of multimedia technologies. The literature on educational leadership in the United States contains no empirical research on these pedagogies. In addition, it is difficult to single out the use of multimedia as a unique pedagogy, since it could be a part of other pedagogical approaches such as narratives or simulations. Some authors have maintained that although film, video (English & Steffy, 1995), or in more recent years various forms of multimedia are readily available, they are rarely used. Given the exponential increase in technology applications in education and the widespread use of assessment exercises used in other field such as business, this is a fertile area for empirical research.

Case Methods

In 1870, the dean of Harvard's Law School, Christopher Langdell, developed and used the case method. Nearly 50 years elapsed before the Harvard Business School faculty created their first casebook. Interestingly, the Harvard Medical School did not use cases until the mid-1980s, and the Harvard Education School began using cases in the late 1980s. Today, many professional schools throughout the world, including law, business, medicine, and education, use case methods as a highly effective pedagogy. Overall, the empirical research on teaching using case methods focuses on single classes or experiences of faculty within one university program. The empirical findings tend to be descriptive and rely heavily on student perceptions of the value of the case method as an instructional strategy. Studies involving quasi-experimental, qualitative, or mixed-methods designs were not found. Nevertheless, from the descriptive work that does exist, it is clear that case methods are pedagogically more engaging for students.

The case study method is consistent with adult learning theory. The goal of using the method is to provide students with a real-life, problematic situation that challenges them to grapple with the multifaceted issues of the case. Students work in teams or individually to develop solutions to the dilemmas presented. Case studies and their variants, case records (Silver, 1986) and case stories (Ackerman & Maslin-Ostrowski, 1995, 1996), are a way to bring the world of practice into the controlled environment of the classroom, where students can try out and hone problem-solving strategies and receive feedback on their thinking before confronting similar problems in the actual work environment. When used in a small-group format, the case method moves students from passively receiving information through lecture to interactive engagement with both content and peers, a peripheral level of participation in a community of practice, as depicted in Figure 8.1.

Teacher education has used the case method longer than educational administration, and thus the body of empirical research is larger in that area than in the field of educational leadership preparation (e.g., Doyle, 1990; Levin, 2003; Merseth, 1991; Shulman, 1992; Sudzina, 1999; Sykes, 1989; Welty, 1989). The overall conclusion of these teacher education studies was that case methods can be a powerful teaching tool. The same findings emerged from the research in educational leadership, where researchers concluded that case studies can provide interesting and relevant opportunities for students to learn. Several books have described the case method and offered samples of case studies for the university classroom, including Kirschmann (1995), Kowalski (2007), Norton and Lester (1998), Piltch and Quinn (2006), and Weishaar and Borsa (2004).

The first reference to using the case method to teach educational administrators came in the form of a guide used in teaching by the Asia and Pacific Office of the United Nations Educational, Scientific and Cultural Organization. Pareek and Rao (1981), who created the guide, included simulations, games, in-basket activities, role plays, field activities, self-study, small-group work, instrument training, and the case method. This guide was intended to serve educational leadership programs in preparing others in a variety of settings.

The first paper describing the use of the case method in university programs for educational administrators also came from outside of the United States. Williams (1985), a West Indian professor, delivered a paper at the conference of the Professional Preparation and Development of Educational Administrators in Commonwealth Developing Areas held in Barbados, wherein she described in detail the history of the case method, features of cases, and her experience with the case method as an effective technique for teaching educational leadership.

During the 1990s, the use of the case method expanded exponentially in a variety of professional fields. In educational administration, UCEA created the Case Study Project with a goal of creating "a set of materials that will be widely available for use in the programs that prepare educational administrators" ("UCEA Cases Project," 1994, p. 5). Although it is unclear whether the cases created for this project were "widely" used by educational leadership professors, those who did touted the learning potential of the method, which prompted UCEA to found the electronically formatted, peer-reviewed *Journal of Cases in Educational Leadership* in 1998. UCEA noted that it "sponsors this journal in an ongoing effort to improve administrative preparation" (Sage, 2006). As a result, professors of educational leadership from throughout the world have access to case studies on a variety of topics as well as teaching notes that accompany each case, outlining how the material might be used in professional preparation programs.

Descriptions of the case method in preparation programs include Geltner's (1995) description of a university program that applied the case method department-wide and infused case teaching in all department courses. Diamantes (1996, 1997) described his use of cases as discussion starters, and he and a colleague (Diamantes & Williams, 1997) detailed a modified case method geared to the ISLLC standards that they used successfully in Kentucky.

Ackerman and Maslin-Ostrowski (1995) compared case study methods and storytelling as companion teaching tools. They found that "case study and case story are not mutually exclusive but complementary teaching techniques" (p. 11) and that both encouraged skill development and reflection on practice. Building upon this work, Ackerman and Maslin-Ostrowksi (1996) conducted a study that explored the case story teaching method with 60 graduate students in three educational administration programs. Data collection methods included "questionnaires, interview transcripts, portfolios of case stories and some audio-taped discussions ... in order to better understand how case stories influence the relationships between student and student, student and teacher and the culture of the classroom" (Ackerman & Maslin-Ostrowksi, 1996, p. 2). As with other case methods, Ackerman and Maslin-Ostrowksi (1996) found that "using case stories is a learning strategy that has the potential to enhance [students'] understanding and growth as educational administrators" (p. 4).

Borsa, Klotz, and Uzat (1998) collaborated on a case study problem using Internet technology to study the work of 20 graduate students in educational leadership programs at two universities. As often occurs when technology capabilities vary from location to location, these researchers concluded that reliable technological resources must be ensured for collaborative work to be effective. They recommended that evaluation criteria be clearly stated prior to beginning work on a case.

Dissertation studies also have contributed to the research base on case methods. Four doctoral candidates at Columbia University (DeFeo, 1997; Parra, 1996; Rodriguez 1995; Urgenson, 1994) examined the perceptions of students in leadership classes in which the case method was used. All four studies examined students' perceptions of the teaching method and found that the students believed the case method was an effective strategy for preparing school administrators.

Donmoyer, Garcia, and Robinett (2005) stressed the importance of "keeping principal preparation attached ... to the inquiry-oriented university setting" (p. 2) and suggested that a case study action-research project at a low-performing school could be a helpful tool in bridging the theory–practice gap. An innovative preparation program they described involved projects in which data were gathered in schools and used by the preservice leaders in the preparation program to generate case studies of the low-performing schools. Donmoyer et al.'s use of action research moved the pedagogy considerably further toward involvement in the workplace community of practice depicted in Figure 8.1.

English (1996) has been a critic of the case method, warning that these approaches "de-emphasize people and emphasize analytic skills" (p. 2) in the search for solutions. He asserted that the normative culture and value-laden environment of a school is neutralized substantially in cases. Therefore, he argued, a case is unlikely to be representative of the emotionally charged atmosphere in which many school problems are nested. In Figure 8.1, case methods are located toward the center, or peripheral level of involvement in a workplace community of practice, underscoring the decontextualized nature of many cases, consistent with the concern raised by English. Another limitation is that case studies may focus students primarily on problem solving rather than on problem framing, which the PBL pedagogy has worked to address (see discussion below).

The combination of case study generation and action research as described by Donmoyer et al. (2005) represents a potentially powerful way of more deeply engaging students in the learning and in problem finding, addressing the concerns raised by English (1996). So, too, in the teaching approach called PBL, a problematic situation is the central focus. In the next section, we outline how PBL developed in educational administration preparation and provide both descriptive and empirical studies of this teaching method.

Simulated Problem-Based Learning (PBL)

A key development in the research on teaching in educational leadership programs was the rise of PBL. Originally developed as a teaching method in medical education, PBL began appearing in the pedagogy of a variety of fields, and in the 1990s it became a key approach for those wanting to bridge the theory–practice gap.

In 1992, a national forum sponsored by the Danforth Foundation and the National Policy Board for Educational Administration focused on PBL in educational leadership programs. This 2-day seminar included a collection of papers that examined key issues in the emerging discussion about PBL (see Barbour, 1992; Jenlink, 1992; Norton, 1992). A year later, Bridges and Hallinger led a week-long National Training Institute in Problem-Based Learning at Stanford University for faculty in educational administration. Approximately 25 educational administration faculty (mostly in pairs of representatives from more than 11 universities across the nation) attended the institute. In 1995, Hallinger and Bridges led a follow-up, 2.5-day Advanced Training Institute in Problem-Based Learning.

From 1994 to 1999 dozens of papers, some descriptive and others empirical, appeared at national conferences (Achilles & Hoover, 1996; Badiali & Cambron-McCabe, 1996; Chenoweth, 1996; Chenoweth & Everhart, 1995; Chrispeels, Caston, Brandon, & Venter, 1996; Cordeiro, 1996; Cordeiro & Campbell, 1997; Cordeiro, Kraus, Hastings, & Binkowski, 1997; Estes, 1999; Grady, Macpherson, & Mulford, 1995; Hallinger, Chantarapana, & Sriboonma, 1995; Larson & Ovando, 1996; M. J. Murphy, Martin, Ford, & Muth, 1996; Ponmanee, 1995), as journal articles (Chrispeels & Martin 1998; Cordeiro, 1998; Martin, Chrispeels, & D'Emidio-Caston, 1998; Muth, Murphy, & Martin, 1994; Tanner, Keedy, & Galis, 1997), in newsletter articles (Hallinger & Bridges, 1991), as book chapters (Cordeiro, Krueger, Parks, Restine, & Wilson, 1993; Van Tassel-Baska, 1998), and as a book (Bridges & Hallinger, 1995). Many of these authors participated in the original Stanford training institute or the advanced training institute. The majority of this output described what PBL is, its theoretical underpinnings, and how it can be used in graduate programs preparing future educational leaders. Several of these works offered strong rationales for using PBL, whereas others critiqued the method. Below we report the empirical studies conducted on PBL as a teaching method.

Over the course of a year, Martin et al. (1998) collected data from 23 students enrolled in two problem-based seminars. Using a grounded theory approach, they analyzed student papers, video taped data, and conducted follow-up interviews with those students who had moved into administrative positions. The researchers examined (a) whether students developed the problem-solving skills needed by school leaders and (b) what group processing skills they had learned from their use of PBL in the seminars. Martin et al. found,

> Problem-based learning classes can contribute to students' abilities to define or frame problems, identify theories in use, and work collaboratively in groups. Students who found themselves embroiled in conflict in the first PBL class indicated they were "pleased to be able to make the group process work" in the second class. (p. 490).

In the reflection papers, students indicated to Martin et al. that they "were able to see patterns in their own growth and thus have ownership in their learning process" (p. 493), a key component of adult and constructivist learning theory. From their analysis, Martin et al. also identified recommendations that might assist faculty in designing and teaching PBL courses, such as being more explicit in teaching group-process skills, assisting students to work through conflict, and using more metacognitive reflective processes as the PBL simulation was unfolding.

Using the same initial data set, Chrispeels and Martin (1998) conducted a follow-up study that focused on 3 of the students who secured principalships immediately upon graduation. The purpose of the follow-up interviews was to learn how the students were able to link theory and practice and to explore the affect of the PBL classes on their work as principals. The students reported being able to link what they learned in their classes to their jobs as administrators. In addition, although the students had entered the preparation program with varying levels of problem-framing and problem-solving skills, all 3 perceived that PBL had enhanced these skills.

Using two PBL projects as the teaching method, Cordeiro, Kraus et al. (1997) examined learning transfer in a staff development program involving in-service leaders. Twenty-nine individuals from one school district participated in two 3-day sessions that took place in consecutive years. Using a questionnaire, participants were surveyed both immediately after each 3-day session and 1 year later. Consistent with research on staff development, participants had difficulty transferring what they learned in the first training session to the workplace, citing that they lacked adequate practice to make the transfer successfully. After the second session, participants felt more confident about their skills.

The effectiveness of PBL also has been reported in dissertations. Envig (1997) explored the perceptions of professors who had participated in the institute at Stanford University, mentioned above. She found that all participants had implemented PBL activities. Envig wrote, "The process which took place was not one of changing one way of teaching to another" (p. v). Rather, these professors saw many similarities between PBL and how they taught before. Shackleford (1998) examined "the use of problem-based learning in administrative preparation and assessed whether its application does address some of the criticism of administrator preparedness" (p. 16). He found that participants who experienced PBL felt it made learning more meaningful and realistic, whereas participants who were not taught with PBL methods reported that the transition into administration might have been less stressful if PBL had been used in their preparation programs.

Copland (1999, 2000), in his dissertation, used a mixed-methods design to examine two aspects of student learning using PBL, specifically students' development of self and their problem-framing abilities. The students in the study matriculated in three cohorts and experienced the use of PBL to varying extents. Using quasi-experimental techniques, Copland first developed a reliable measure of problem-framing ability. He then conducted an analysis of covariance and found that students' problem-framing abilities differed significantly and were associated with their extent of exposure to PBL. Copland (1999) found that "greater exposure to, and practice with, problem-based learning is associated with greater problem-framing ability among students" (p. 98), an ability critical for successful problem resolution.

Like case methods, little empirical research exists regarding the efficacy of PBL methods in educational leadership preparation. Copland's (1999, 2000) study provides an important quasi-experimental design and could be used as a model for future studies of PBL and other pedagogical approaches. Both PBL and case methods can be used to build aspiring leaders' sense of social justice and ethical decision making. We did not examine the empirical research in related professions but urge that such analysis be conducted.

Competency- and Performance-Based Preparation: Assessment Centers and Simulations

Faculty in preparation programs using primarily traditional instructional approaches such as lecture; discussion; and even narratives, role plays, and case methods struggle to determine how best to assess candidate competency and potential on-the-job performance. Two pedagogical strategies that offer the potential for job-like assessments without being on the job are assessment centers and simulations. Both of these approaches can be seen as moving pedagogy toward the right of the Figure 8.1 continuum. They engage the learner in situations that may be encountered on the job and require application and integration of knowledge and skills. In this section we describe how these approaches have evolved and been incorporated into preparation programs and discuss the limited evidence that exists regarding their outcomes and effectiveness.

Assessment Centers

Evidence from the literature in the last half of the 1900s illustrates the growing role of assessing candidates for school administration to identify those who demonstrated the requisite competencies for the job. Over this time period, university faculty and practitioners developed competency-based education, what some call performance-based education, which involves preservice students and in-service professionals in assessment center exercises and other forms of simulations.

The roots of assessment centers began in Germany during the 1920s and 1930s and later were established in England during the 1940s for the selection of military officers. These assessment centers used a standardized evaluation of behavior, which was based on multiple data sources. Multiple assessors (e.g., in the above instances, psychologists, officers, and physicians) and multiple measurement techniques were used by trained observers to make judgments about behaviors observed from specifically developed assessment simulations. Usually these judgments were pooled and feedback was provided to the candidate. Considerable research was conducted on the assessments, and assessment center methodology later spread to Australia and Canada (Waldron & Joines, 1994). These methods also became part of civil service exams in the United States.

In a longitudinal study of managers, Bray, Campbell, and Grant (1974) examined assessment center exercises as potential measures for business management and introduced the first industrial use of the technique at AT&T in 1956. Additional studies by Bray and others led a large number of organizations (IBM, Sears, GE, etc.) to use assessment center methods to identify potential employees for managerial positions. In 1973, the First International Congress on the Assessment Center Method was held, and by the end of the decade over 1,000 U.S. organizations had established assessment center programs (Waldron & Joines, 1994).

Competency- and performance-based approaches to educational leadership began to appear in the literature in the early 1970s. A special interest group on competency-based education for preservice administrators and supervisors was founded by the National Council of Professors of Education Administration in 1970. During these same years, NASSP collaborated with the Division of Industrial and Organizational Psychology of the American Psychological Association to establish an assessment center (Hersey, 1977) that focused on performance-based administrator preparation. Using generic skills identified by NASSP, a series of simulations and other activities were used to assess the performance of current and potential school principals.

In the mid-1970s, NASSP developed the Assessment Center Project, which consisted of in-basket exercises, analysis exercises, fact finding, and role playing. Practitioners and professors of educational administration began to use, describe, research, and promote the use of NASSP simulations and assessment center methodology during the 1980s and 1990s (Bradshaw, Bell, McDowelle, & Perreault, 1997; L. W. Hughes, 1986; Licata & Ellett, 1990; McCleary, 1986; Miller, 1987; Milstein, 1990; Prickett, 1990; Reynolds, 1994; Rohr, 1984; Veir, 1990; Wendel, Yusten, & Gappa, 1989; Westhuizen, 1988). NASSP created the Springfield Development Seminar as a follow-up activity to the Assessment Center experiences. This simulation provided experiences in a number of typical school district positions. However, because many of the simulation materials were inadequately developed, NASSP discontinued the seminar. NASSP remained committed to the use of simulations and in 1998 unveiled an updated version of the Assessment Center. It included two skills assessment programs, Selecting and Developing the 21st Century Principals, a face-to-face skills assessment model, and the Professional Skills Assessment Program, an online tool. The online tool provides authentic simulations of experiences a principal might encounter on the job.

Numerous small, empirical studies of NASSP Assessment Center methodology have been conducted and are briefly reviewed here. To determine the extent to which the assessment center was used in selecting principals, Baltzell and Dentler (1983) conducted a case study of 10 randomly chosen school districts and found that 5 of the districts used assessment centers. Wendel et al. (1989) mailed questionnaires to all 50 state chief certification officers and conducted follow-up interviews to explore whether states used assessment centers in certifying or hiring teachers and administrators. Although a variety of exams and observable behaviors were required across the country, Wendel et al. found that only one state reported planning to require assessment center participation for certification. Similarly, in a study of project sites that used the Leadership in Educational Administration Development (LEAD) program, Wildman (1988) found that 30% of the LEAD centers worked directly or in collaboration with administrator assessment centers.

Witters-Churchill and Erlandson (1990) reported on three research projects undertaken in collaboration with several universities and NASSP. One project occurred in Texas. Whereas Texas principals preferred performance-based pedagogies such as games, simulations, and computer-assisted instruction, the researchers found little evidence that these strategies were used in most preparation programs. In another report, Witters-Churchill (1991) cited other research (Ashe, Haubner, & Troisi, 1991; Voit, 1989) that supported the finding that performance-based strategies were seldom used. However, she also cited research by Gagne conducted in Texas and Utah in which performance-based pedagogies were important elements of principal preparation.

Schmuck (1992) reported outcomes of a 2-year, pilot leadership preparation program in Oregon that included NASSP's Assessment Center and noted that the center programs were most effective when used prior to beginning the internship. Using questionnaire methods, Wendel and Baack (1992) reported that participants in the Nebraska NASSP Assessment Center found the written report and oral feedback from the Assessment Center to be the greatest motivational force for pursuing further professional development. Least motivating were leaderless group and fact-finding exercises. Gender discrimination was also reported. Schneider and Wallich (1990), for example, examined gender differences in career development efforts of assessment center participants. Males received preferential treatment regardless of skill level.

Simulations

Assessment centers reflect one type of simulation. With advances in computer technology, other types of simulations have been incorporated into educational leader preparation programs. Importantly, as previously discussed, simulations have been used effectively to advance the social justice agenda (Brunner, Hitchon et al., 2002; Brunner, Miller et al., 2003; Chance & Chance, 2000).

Nelson (1993), a proponent of simulations, reviewed the historical literature on the development of systems simulations. Nelson proposed a theoretical rationale for creating computer-based simulations for educational leaders, noting, "Simulations have been a promising model available to educational leaders for over 35 years" (p. 3). Given the wide applicability, he urged that computer-based simulations be used to assist practicing administrators in school instructional and operational matters.

Bradshaw and Buckner (1998) offered a descriptive comparison of the two NASSP simulation programs, the Springfield Development Program, which was part of the NASSP Assessment Center activities, and its replacement, 21st Century School Administrator Skills Program. The Springfield Development Program was useful to school districts in identifying potential administrators. With the advent of the principal shortage, the Springfield Development Program was less useful. Therefore, it was redesigned, aligned with the ISLLC standards, and renamed. The 21st Century School Administrator Skills Program offers simulation experiences. Understandably, in-service administrators find the simulations threatening, according to Bradshaw and Buckner, but preservice administrators welcome the opportunity to practice through simulation. Skills developed through the simulations are judgment, sensitivity, oral communication, organizational ability, results orientation, setting leadership direction, teamwork and team leadership, and written communication. Bradshaw and Buckner offered no empirical findings regarding the simulations but reported that feedback from participants was positive.

Perreault and Bradshaw (1998) described an innovative principal preparation program that used the old NASSP Springfield Development Program simulations to develop skill areas similar to those named above. Through work with the Springfield simulations, students became more reflective, which would enable them to move toward socially just practices by identifying and dealing with previously unrecognized personal assumptions and beliefs that hinder effective leadership. Perrault and Bradshaw "found that Springfield provided a common language to use to discuss developmental opportunities" (p. 248) and that the materials associated with the Springfield Development Program were useful in assessing "the leadership skills of Principal Fellows upon entry to and graduation from the program" (p. 249).

UCEA was involved in developing one of the first simulations for use in the preparation of educational administrators, the Jefferson Township Simulation (Culbertson, 1967). This simulation used game theory instruments to provide feedback to administration students regarding their decision making. Subsequently, UCEA developed the Monroe City simulations, the first completed simulation involving an urban district (Blough, 1972). Blough collected data from participants in university-sponsored institutes and from workshop participants who evaluated various components of the Janus Junior High Principalship simulation from Monroe City project. His findings indicated that housing the institute at a university is an effective dissemination strategy. However, Blough did not report findings regarding the actual effectiveness of the simulation in helping to prepare educational leaders.

UCEA continued its work with simulations and in 1993, launched the Information Environment for School Leader Preparation (IESLP), a computer-based simulation project that contains Web-based exercises. These exercises integrate a rural school database with a variety of analytical and reporting templates that allow learners to identify and attempt to solve school problems, thereby incorporating PBL. In essence, IESLP is not a simulation; rather, it provides an authentic problem environment using real, not hypothetical, data.

In addition to the simulations created by NASSP and UCEA, various individual faculty in departments of educational leadership around the nation developed simulations. Poppenhagen and McArdle (1982) developed a simulation to increase students' comfort with using a quantitative management tool. Using a pre- and posttest design, the 35 participating students used a computer simulation and decision-making game. Students indicated that their ability to identify organizational variables and relate them to decision making was increased, as was their ability to see relationships among variables. Poppenhagen and McArdle also found that the simulation led to a significant positive attitude change regarding the use of the management tool.

Hallinger and a number of his colleagues have been involved in developing computer-based simulations. For example, In the Center of Things, developed in the 1980s by Vanderbilt researchers, was revised as a problem-based computer simulation (Hallinger & McCary, 1990). Based on many years of research on school change and improvement, this simulation is used to develop the instructional leadership capacities of school principals. More recently, Hallinger (2005b) adapted the board game Making Change Happen, developed by Carol Bershad and Susan Mundry (1999) for the Network, Inc., as a computer-based simulation. This simulation encompassed many of the concepts of PBL (Bridges & Hallinger, 1993; Hallinger & McCary, 1990), a pedagogical approach that has been reported to support students' problem-framing and problem-solving abilities (Copland, 1999, 2000). No empirical research has been published on the effectiveness of these simulations.

The Department of Educational Administration (now Educational Policy Studies) at the University of Alberta, Canada, has experimented with simulations for over a decade. Maynes, McIntosh, and Mappin (1996) collected data over this period from students' reactions and interactions with the simulation. Based on data collected as well as increasing versatility and refinements of the technology, Maynes et al. created a second-generation junior high school principalship simulation, which included "frighteningly real and very rich" (p. 588) events drawn directly from practicing junior high school principals. This simulation increased the interactivity between the simulation and the learner, including such events as phone interruptions, which thus enhanced the verisimilitude to the actual work experiences, time pressures, and emotional challenges faced by principals. Changes such as these require students to draw on all four types of knowledge presented in Figure 8.1.

The usefulness of simulations as a teaching strategy was discussed in papers presented by Jenlink, Lansing and Cropper, and Picus at the1992 PBL National Training Institutes. In his paper, Jenlink (1992) urged the use of the business management simulation, Looking Glass. Lansing and Cropper (1992) described a simulated community named Kaibab. Picus (1992) presented a computer simulation that can be found in his textbook on school finance. These papers are helpful for implementing simulations; however, they provided no evidence of the effectiveness of simulations as a teaching technique.

Chance and Chance (2000) described the results of two studies that explored the use of two simulations in the principal preparation program at the University of Nevada, Las Vegas. One is the IESLP Web-based simulation. Twenty-four master's students enrolled in a school leadership preparation program completed questionnaires before and after the IESLP simulation, in a pre- and posttest design. Results indicated that students reported substantial growth in several areas, including accessing information and using electronic spreadsheets and databases.

The second simulation studied by these authors was Bafa Bafa (Shirts, 1977). According to Chance and Chance (2000), Bafa Bafa focuses on diverse "cultures and allows students to become involved in a cross-cultural experience" (p. 133). The study involved 43 graduate students and used a pre- and posttest design. A questionnaire entitled Culture and Values was used to gather data. According to Chance and Chance, the questionnaire "consisted of fifteen statements geared to measure students' understanding of culture and intercultural relations" (p. 134). Chance and Chance reported, "Bafa Bafa encourages aspiring principals to reflect upon their personal values and their understanding of other cultures before they are faced with serious issues 'on the firing line' of the principalship" (p. 138).

As can be concluded from the above review of research, simulations have been used for many years in educational leadership for both preservice and in-service purposes. While the studies reported above and others (e.g., Tracy & Schutenberg, 1990) explored various aspects of assessment centers and simulation activities, none is comprehensive or in depth. Thus, a solid body of research on assessment center and simulation methods in educational administration does not now exist. This circumstance is particularly problematic given improvements in computer technology and the increase in available simulations. In the section that follows, we review research about the use of technology as a tool to teach program content and as a delivery mode of instruction.

Technology in Leader Preparation Programs: Competency, Instruction, and Program Delivery

As indicated in Figure 8.1, technology spans the leading and teaching continuum in educational leadership programs. Developing knowledge and skills about technology and its implications for both administrative and instructional practice is an important curricular area in which preservice and in-service administrators must be competent. We touch on this dimension, but this section primarily focuses on research about the use of technology as a component or tool to support many different types of pedagogy in preparation programs and on the use of technology to deliver preparation programs.

Substantive writings related to technology in preparation programs began to appear in the late 1980s. The descriptive as well as empirical literature had three lines of direction: (a) the need for students (and faculty) in preparation programs to demonstrate competency in the use of technology as an administrative tool, (b) the creation and implementation of instructional materials (simulation, cases, etc.) using various types of technology (computers, Web-based materials, etc.), and (c) the use of technology to deliver programs of educational leadership via distance learning.

Demonstrating Competency in Using Technology for Applications in Schools

Whereas earlier studies focused on practicing school administrators and described current conditions and applications with regard to microcomputer use in public schools, House (1989) and others (Comerford & Carlson, 1985; Heller, Chafee, & Davison, 1974; Spuck & Bozeman, 1988) maintained that all students in school administration preparation programs should acquire a basic competency in the use of computer software. A companion suggestion was the inclusion of a course to fill that need. In this regard, it should be noted that practitioners themselves voiced the need to be technology savvy and to look to preparation programs to meet that need (Dikkers, Hughes, & McLeod, 2005; Witters-Churchill, 1991).

J. E. Hughes, McLeod, Dikkers, and Whiteside (2005) noted "the critical nationwide shortage of administrators who can effectively facilitate the implementation of technology in schools and school districts" (p. 2). J. E. Hughes et al. created the School Technology Leadership Initiative (STLI), which "offers 15 one-credit school technology leadership" (p. 2) modules based on the National Educational Technology Standards for Administrators. To study the STLI effects, the authors conducted a qualitative study of 13 participants from the first STLI cohort. Data included course work products such as assignments, discussions, and course reflections. Findings indicated the need for "any technology leadership program to be comprehensive enough to meet the needs of all its participants while also being flexible enough to accommodate students' varied interests" (p. 18). J. E. Hughes et al. questioned the feasibility "of developing one course that can meet all of those needs" (p. 18).

Another study by McLeod, Hughes, Richardson, and Dikkers (2005) described 15 partner educational leadership programs that sought the assistance of STLI "to increase integration and coverage of technology leadership issues within their programs" (p. 1). Through their case study research design, several themes emerged, among them logistics, assessment of faculty training needs, current knowledge about using technology, financial considerations, choosing appropriate technology tools, and concerns about distance education.

Using Technology for University Classroom Instruction

One way for university instructors to teach technology uses to preservice administrators is to model it in our own teaching. The UCEA simulation project, IESLP, previously mentioned, was designed to address six elements; (a) information analysis, (b) a research access system, (c) IESLP navigating and reporting system, (d) problem-finding exercises, (e) problem-provided exercises, and (f) a training system The Web-based exercises integrated actual school data with a variety of analytical and reporting templates that allowed learners to identify and propose solutions to school problems. In 1997, UCEA added a new fictional school district, the Crawford Public Schools, that was again "based on [a] comprehensive data set from a real Midwestern district" ("IESLP Developers Sample St. Louis," 1997, p. 4). Although funding was sought from foundations for the project, apart from the initial funding, fiscal support did not materialize, and the only publication from the project was a paper by Howland, Musser, and Mayer (1999). Nevertheless, the simulation was used by some professors of educational administration (see syllabus by Repa, 1997).

As discussed in the section on simulations, in the past two decades computer technology has played an increasingly powerful part in simulation (Hallinger, 2005a, 2005b; Maynes et al., 1996) and interactive case study development (Valesky, 2006). For example, the University of Alberta uses a computer-based simulation as part of their university preparation program (Maynes et al., 1996) "to redress the balance between theory- and experience-based learning" (p. 579) of aspiring school leaders. The simulation depicts situations that confront the principals of Pembina Elementary School, a hypothetical school in a metropolitan area attended by an ethnically and economically diverse student body. Reasoning that internships often fall short of acquainting aspirants with the full range of demands and problems that are implicit in school leadership, the simulation seeks to develop skills of problem analysis, "the personal demands exacted by the professional role, and one's personal fit with the demands of the role" (Maynes et al., 1996, p. 581). Again, although Maynes et al. discussed the theory and general content of the simulation experiences, they did not report empirical findings regarding effects. Another simulation for electronic delivery was reported by Brunner, Miller et al. (2003). The simulation used a "Web site, chat room, threaded discussion, and video and audio clips" (p. 5), but Brunner, Miller et al. did not report empirical studies documenting the effectiveness of this simulation relative to other approaches.

Opsal, Brunner, and Virnig (2005) documented the affects of the online experiential simulations technology as a means of assisting aspiring leaders in recognizing bias toward traditional marginalized groups. Students' identities are masked from each other as they participate in chat rooms through the Internet and collaborate on projects before meeting in person, thereby allowing students to demonstrate their leadership online before gender, race, or disability is known. They found from this experience that the leadership skills of a previously marginalized deaf student were now recognized and utilized during the remainder of the course. As Sherman and Beaty (2007) pointed out,

> While there is a dearth of information available in regard to how technology has been used or is currently being used to prepare educational leaders ... those that do exist seem to highlight potential positive effects of the use of distance technology in the preparation of school and district leaders—at least in terms of how the technology can be useful for nontraditional administrative aspirants. (p. 611)

PBL also is increasingly incorporating technology as part of the design (Hallinger, 2005a). Hallinger (2005a) argued, "PBL and learning technology have the potential to enhance each other's strengths. The question is one of relationship and fit" (p. 1). He outlined several ways in which there may be a technology–PBL fit. For example, technology can be used to present the problem, even immersing the participants in the situation through video clips. In the problem-framing stage, technology can be used to access information about the problem. In the problem-solution phase, technology can have a role in analyzing information and options to facilitate decision making; finally, technology can be a resource to a PBL team in presenting or disseminating the product.

A noninteractive use of technology for preservice and in-service educators is portfolio development. Portfolios came into use in school leadership preparation programs in the late 1990s but have received wider use in teacher preparation. The rapid development of technologies has permitted video and audio as well as text entries to be included in a portfolio. Portfolio development is not hampered by the usual constraints of time and money investments from professors. Artifacts produced as part of the preparation program, such vision statements, educational philosophies, and presentations, can be included in an electronic portfolio and used for formative and other purposes.

Program Delivery

Despite a pervasive absence of technology use in educational leader preparation programs, the 1990s witnessed efforts to deliver such programs electronically (Sherman & Beaty, 2007). The literature describes online delivery of both courses and entire programs; the use of interactive video networks; and various types of Web enhancements for courses that are delivered on site, including electronic simulations, chat rooms, online multimedia, electronic meeting systems, pod and video casting, compressed video, and online learning modules. The majority of the published articles, paper presentations, and so on are descriptions of how a university program or class has integrated various types of technology into a course or delivered courses via technology. Due to the limitations of technology during the 1990s, few programs were delivered completely online, and most papers discuss technical and structural barriers to online delivery.

MacNeil and Garcia (1997) maintained that using electronic meeting systems in school leader preparation courses can serve "as a way to enhance decision making while incorporating creative problem solving skills and techniques" (p. 73). Muth (2000) described development of an online delivery project that led professors not only to reconceptualize the program and to rethink the teaching and learning processes, but also to adapt "program requirements and outcome expectations to this new medium" (p. 1).

As indicated, not all experiences with technology are smooth. Hackman and Berry (1999) surveyed 109 doctoral-granting university educational leadership programs and reported that approximately half used some form of distance learning (e.g., interactive video or online courses), whereas most others indicated an intention to do so. Obstacles inhibiting the change included faculty concern about program quality, workload, technical issues, the costs of technology, and the availability of resources to support technology delivery. North Dakota State University and its collaborators developed a plan to deliver programs statewide using an interactive video network (Stammen, 1993) but also encountered several obstacles. Using survey methods, Kaurala (1998) described the reaction of students and faculty to use of interactive television to deliver five graduate-level courses. From student survey results, his own reactions, and the finding of other studies, Kaurala reported the advantages and disadvantages of the delivery model and concluded, "Developing a relationship with students at a remote site and of students developing relationships with each other needs to be carefully considered" (p. 212). External pressures sometimes force preparation programs to adopt distance delivery methods. Ashby, Hecht, and Klass (1999) described feeling the threat of competition from programs at other universities as well as from external standards, which forced consideration of program delivery options through distance education.

In a recent review of 49 educational leadership programs in the United States, Sherman and Beaty (2007) reported that universities used a variety of program structures and types of distance technology. Most universities seem to be experimenting with hybrid program structures. Although a wide range of distance technologies is in use, Sherman and Beaty (p. 613) found that the most frequently used approaches are asynchronous Internet programs (75.5%), synchronous Internet programs (46.9%), and two-way interactive video and audio (34.7%). Their study is particularly useful in highlighting the variety of challenges faced by institutions in tapping distance technology for program delivery. Malfunctions of technology and student disengagement were the two most commonly cited problems. Quality control, especially over student work, was also a challenge. Sherman and Beaty argued that although their data provide important insights into the current delivery of educational leadership programs via distance technology, follow-up studies are needed to explore the "relationship between the use of distance technology and the transformative preparation of school leaders" (p. 605).

Various delivery strategies include technology and are useful in teaching educational leadership courses, according to Van Patten and Holt (2002). Among these strategies are hybrid courses that combine distance learning and compressed video with face-to-face methods. Van Patten and Holt stated that school administrators need to increase their knowledge of all operations of technology in their schools; therefore, preparation programs must incorporate the technology standards into programs and use distance education to teach educational leadership.

In an *UCEA Review* article, Enomoto (2003) described her reflections on "using electronic technologies in various ways to deliver instruction" in an educational leadership program (p. 1). The technologies included courses delivered through interactive television and Web-based courses. Enomoto concluded, "There is reason to be optimistic about the new distance learning courses, which promise greater convenience, ease of access, and learning on demand. Students may become more actively engaged in self-directed learning and individual problem solving" (p. 4).

In an empirical study of educational administration preparation students, Browne-Ferrigno, Choi, and Muth (2000) compared an on-site course with 30% of the instruction involving online delivery and a distance-delivered class with 100% of the instruction taught online. The study consisted of four types of data collection: (a) a series of questionnaires completed by the students, (b) personal interviews with 6 informants, (c) observations of the cohort sessions, and (d) a review of various artifacts. Browne-Ferrigno et al. found, "Online communication among learners can provide mutual support and stimulate sharing of ideas and information, risk-taking and reflecting on practice" (p. 29). Browne-Ferrigno et al. also found that "online exchanges are richer in context because of the time allowed for reflection prior to response," but they cautioned, "More research analysis is needed to determine ways to improve the efficacy of online learning activities" (p. 30). Van Patten and Holt (2002) advocated for distance education because it can be used not only to deliver instruction efficiently and eliminate entrance barriers to a field with a shortage of candidates, but also to increase knowledge of various applications of technology in schools.

Using technology in its myriad forms in educational leadership preparation programs can and will play a major role in preparation programs in the future. Much can be learned from the research literature coming from other fields about the effectiveness of Web-enhanced teaching as well as online delivery and the use of many forms of electronic technology. In addition, the field of educational leadership is in its infancy with regard to understanding the efficiency and effectiveness of electronic technologies and the possibilities for application.

As the field stands today, hesitancy to use technology and distance-delivery methods is more prominent in educational leadership preparation than in other fields, such as teacher preparation. This hesitancy deprives our students of the opportunity to gain proficiency with technologies they will be expected to be knowledgeable about on the job. Again, members of the academy should take notice. Our students understand the need for technology proficiency and have asked that it be included in preparation programs. Recurrent problems encountered in studying our pedagogy arise relative to the use of technology, specifically limited time for development, sample size issues, and funding support. Nevertheless, the data that do exist suggest that technology-based methods engage learners more actively and engage students in an off-site community of practice interacting with peers in their courses. These methods move learners toward the right end of the Figure 8.1 pedagogies. Technologies are part of life in this century and should be incorporated into leader preparation programs with subsequent, well-designed research studies conducted on the effects.

Action Research, Action Learning, and Real-Time PBL

Uses of technology not mentioned above involve action research, action learning, and real-time PBL. We differentiate real-time PBL from simulated PBL because real-time PBL occurs in the field, rather than in the classroom. Below we review research related to these pedagogical techniques, found near the far right of the Figure 8.1 continuum.

Action Research

Action research has a long history in teacher education (Corey, 1953; Stringer, 2004), where it is frequently used to assist preservice and master's-level candidates to research their own practice as a way to strengthen reflection, professional learning, and changes in practice (Elliott, 1991). As a pedagogical strategy, action research falls on the right side of Figure 8.1 because, through action research, the learner is fully involved in a real work setting and in the learning process. The level of engagement in one's own learning is intense as the student-practitioner systematically investigates a problem of practice in the hope of informing and potentially changing or validating practice.

In spite of its prevalence in teacher education, the use of action research as a pedagogical approach in leadership preparation programs is much less common, and consequently little research exists regarding its effects on student competencies and performance. As discussed earlier in this review, Donmoyer et al. (2005) creatively combined action research and case study methods with leadership students researching conditions and attributes of a low-performing school and using the information to prepare a case study. Through this project, students were engaged in data collection and analysis in a real school setting.

It is noteworthy that a number of school reform initiatives, such as Accelerated Schools (Hopfenberg, Levin, & Associates, 1993), School Renewal (Glickman, 1993), and the Bay Area School Reform Collaborative (Porter & Snipes, 2006), typically involve an action research inquiry cycle, which, to be implemented successfully, requires full support and guidance from the principal. In addition, a number of scholars have written books to assist educational leaders in conducting action research as an approach to whole-school reform (Anderson, Herr, & Nihlen, 1994; Calhoun, 1994, Sagor, 2000, 2005); yet, few educational leadership preparation programs require principals to learn about or conduct action research that would prepare them to lead their schools in such inquiry processes. Given the current use of action research in many teacher education master's programs and as a option in teacher evaluation systems, the lack of attention to preparing educational leaders to conduct action research suggests a significant missed opportunity for engaged learning as well as lost potential to effectively lead school reform. It is interesting to note, however, that many educational doctorate theses have an action research dimension, though these are not fully acknowledged, since many EdD students conduct research on their own practice or in their educational system. Herr and Anderson (2005) recently brought this reality to the foreground in their book, *The Action Research Dissertation*.

Action Learning and Real-Time PBL

Closely related to action research is action learning. Acker-Hocevar and Miller-Keating (2002) provided a useful comparison of these two approaches and illustrated how each approach might be used to address a district's problem of low performance in reading. Action research engages the student-practitioner in concrete cycles of inquiry that usually lead to the testing of new approaches to resolve an identified problem. In contrast, action learning involves the students as researchers for a client exploring and seeking to solve a real problem the client has identified, thus real-time PBL. The student researchers collect data, explore options, and present a report to the client who may or may not take action on the recommendations. Acker-Hocevar et al. (2002) studied the effects of action learning on nine sets of aspiring leaders in their preparation program who worked with districts to research and develop action plans to address identified problems. Acker-Hocevar et al. used a multiple case study design and collected data from multiple sources, such as e-mail correspondence between class members and clients, memoranda, agendas and minutes for set meetings, reflective journals, and final presentations and reports to district clients. They reported that students gained important practice in applying knowledge and skills to the workplace, developed insights into why educational change is so difficult, and built better relationships with local educational agencies. In addition, they found through action learning that students practiced and developed a full range of leadership skills, including managerial, transformational, political, and professional, as they applied their academic learning to real problems (Acker-Hocevar et al., 2002). The action learning work required students to draw on all four types of knowledge presented in Figure 8.1—declarative, procedural, contextual, and somatic—as they worked in groups, conducted investigations of current practices, visited schools, discussed and debated best practices, and had to prepare and present a final report for a real client. The field of leadership preparation would benefit considerably from replications of their study with perhaps the use of quasi-experimental designs. There is also a need for follow-up studies to explore how students who participated in action learning or action research projects perform as educational leaders compared to students who do not participate in such programs.

As was documented in a number of the studies discussed throughout this chapter, reflective journals often served as a data source to document the affect of certain pedagogical approaches on students in educational leadership preparation programs. It is fitting, therefore, to conclude our review of specific pedagogical practices with reflection. As shown in Figure 8.1, reflection can be incorporated to support and deepen the learning of other pedagogies.

Reflective Practice

Osterman and Kottkamp (2004) described reflective practice as "careful observation and data-based analysis of practice as well as experimentation with new ideas and new strategies" (p. xi). Brown (2006a) added,

> Within the context of preparation programs, the educational tasks of critical reflection involve helping future leaders become aware of oppressive structures and practices, developing tactical awareness of how they might change these, and building the confidence and ability to work for collective change. (p. 709)

Reflective practice is inexorably bound to social justice. Without reflecting on how one's biases and assumptions shape one's beliefs, and therefore one's actions, no change can occur.

A sustained push to include reflective practice as part of university preparation for educational leaders is due in no small part to the work of Kottkamp and Silverberg (1999a, 1999b, 2003), Osterman and Kottkamp (1993, 2004), and Silver (1984, 1986). Silver used reflective practice strategies successfully to improve the effectiveness of practicing principals. According to Osterman (1990), Silver urged "principals to keep case records, detailed accounts of problems which they encountered in their daily practice in the principalship" (p. 9), reasoning that the reflection involved in writing the case served as a vehicle of professional growth and development, a reasoning that emerges in some of the research we review below. Silver's thinking was highly consistent with adult learning theory and constructivist approaches discussed earlier in this chapter. As adult learners, these principals were asked to address problems of practice that had high relevance to them. Standard operating procedures did not suffice to solve the problems they confronted. By reflecting on these knotty problems, principals developed or constructed unique solutions, contextually bound to the schools in which they worked.

As a result of Silver's work with reflective practice, a joint venture between UCEA and Hofstra University led to the establishment of the Silver Center for Reflective Principals in 1988 and development of a database of case records (see the Case Methods section of this chapter for a discussion of case studies). In addition to case records, other materials used successfully in teaching reflective practice include literature from the humanities (Achilles, 1989) and having students interview practicing principals and construct stories regarding a salient situation (Danzig, 1997), film, and TAR (Meyer, (2001). Common to these materials is an ill-defined, ill-structured dilemma that becomes the subject of reflection.

Engaging in reflective practice requires the capacity to assume the dual roles of engaged performer and detached critic, according to Osterman and Kottkamp (1993, 2004). The engaged performer enacts certain behaviors anticipated to solve a problem of practice, while the detached critic contemplates the effectiveness of the behaviors. Novices are less likely to act as the detached critics of their behaviors while actually engaged in those behaviors, but as the novice moves toward expertise, reflection during practice becomes easier, more common, and eventually automatic. According to Osterman (1998) and others (Geltner, 1993; Silver, 1984), reflective practice can provide an effective bridge over the theory-to-practice chasm, enabling the school leader to amass a "repertoire of professional knowledge" (Lipton, 1993, p. 1) that can be retrieved to better resolve subsequent problematic situations.

This pedagogical technique extends from the middle to the right side of Figure 8.1 and aims at improving practice (Doolittle, 2003; Lipton, 1993; Osterman & Kottkamp, 1993, 2004; Schön, 1987). Here, as with other pedagogical techniques that move the learner toward meaningful involvement in the workplace, clarifying the precise nature of the problematic situation is essential for reflection to be effective.

Osterman and Kottkamp (1993, 2004) and others (Argyris & Schön, 1978; Keedy & Achilles, 1997; Osterman & Fishbein, 2001) explained that improving practice is dependent upon examining our espoused theories, that is, those theories which we claim to implement in our practice, for congruence with our theories-in-use, or the theories we actually practice. Espoused theories are easily described, are malleable, and may change as a result of new learning. In contrast, theories-in-use are rooted in tacit assumptions and beliefs gained through enculturation and are less amenable to change because they are subliminal in nature (Argyris & Schön, 1978; Doolittle, 2003; Kottkamp & Silverberg, 2003). For example, a university instructor might espouse a theory of establishing a learning community among herself and students in her course, but instead she employs a theory-in-use that relies primarily on lecture and discussion. There is a marked incongruence between the two theories. When a learning community is established, the instructor both facilitates students' active learning and is a learner herself. When the instructor lectures and leads discussion, she is the dispenser of knowledge to primarily passive students and has little role as a learner herself.

Scholars remind us that "how people act is based on how they think" (Kottkamp & Silverberg, 2003, p. 301) and the assumptions they hold (Keedy & Achilles, 1997). The "images, beliefs, and assumptions we have" (Cambron-McCabe, 2003, p. 288) both color and skew our biases; thus, reflective practice is needed to bring the beliefs and assumptions that undergird our actions to the surface for examination. Reflective practice, like school improvement, is a cyclical process that repeats itself on an ongoing basis. Osterman and Kottkamp (2004) described a four-step cycle for reflection on practice. The cycle begins with an indentified problematic concrete experience that is not amenable to standard operating procedures (Osterman & Kottkamp, 2004). The multidimensional, multifaceted context of education requires the skills of the detached critic to separate symptoms from the actual problem (Osterman & Kottkamp, 2004).

The next step in the cycle is to gather and analyze data relative to the experience. These data then become the subject of reflection and interpretation. This is the point in the cycle when the theory-in-use changes from being implicit, tacit, and theretofore unrecognized by the individual to being explicit, describable theory that is available for examination (Argyris & Schön, 1978). Sharing the revelations that emerge from this examination with trusted colleagues is an important part of the process (Cambron-McCabe, 2003; Doolittle, 2003; Lipton, 1993; Read & Hausman, 1998; Rusch, in press). The incongruence between the espoused theory and the theory-in-use becomes evident, enabling the individual to reconceptualize, experiment with, and transform the theory-in-use (Argyris & Schön, 1978; Osterman & Kottkamp, 2004).

Often, the reported research on reflective practice stems from action research conducted by professors and related to their own teaching. Lipton (1993) reported qualitative results of a study with 17 of 55 educators who had participated in a multiday experiential workshop designed to develop capacity in reflective practice and that included self-guided strategies to enhance implementation when the educators returned to the workplace. Respondents in the study, who were teachers and central office administrators, indicated that they were able to return to their workplaces and implement the knowledge and skills they had learned during the workshop. Among the techniques they implemented was changing emotionally tense reactions from the people with whom they worked to productive encounters in which listening skills, positive body language, flexibility, and adept questioning were important. Use of these strategies enabled the individuals presenting a problem to move from a sometimes hostile stance to being able to develop ideas for addressing the problem. Such positive outcomes were reported despite the workshop participants' explaining that they felt they were taking risks by foregoing their prior practice of imposing solutions. The respondents also noted that as a result of the workshop they developed a tolerance for uncertainty in the process of interacting with teachers and others.

Rusch (in press) conducted action research on her teaching using reflective practice. Aiming not only to change her own practice, but also to enable graduate students to become transformative leaders, she administered a learning pattern inventory, which she also completed, to 138 master's and doctoral students in courses she taught over a 4-year period. She used journaling to record her practices; collected student artifacts, such as student papers, e-mails, online conversations; and used course reflections. Rusch disclosed to her students her own learning patterns, which enabled some students to identify, examine, and disclose their own preferences. As she analyzed the data gathered over the years, Rusch shared the findings with students and modified her own pedagogy. Students with certain learning patterns resisted the reflection in which Rusch was asking them to engage. Through verbal exchanges with these students and support from groups formed in the courses, these students gradually began to see reflective practice as an asset. Rusch concluded that the reflective practices students learned "enhanced self-awareness in a recursive process … [and] also supported reflective inquiry about the values, knowledge, and actions that undergird transformative leadership behaviors" (p. 24), the very behaviors Rusch sought to foster.

Merging three pedagogical strategies, formative portfolio assessment, reflective practice, and cognitive coaching, Geltner (1993) provided evidence about 17 preservice school leaders in a cohort program. She reported that the students gained a deeper understanding and meaning of their practice, were able to use theory to understand practice, and enhanced their sense of efficacy as novice leaders.

Danzig (1997) used a procedure similar to the case stories described above. He had each of the 17 students in a leadership preparation course conduct several interviews with a principal of their selection. These interviews aimed to capture the principals' biographies, including their entry into the principalship, the recounting of a particular problem of practice, and a description of how their leadership skills were used to resolve the problem. According to Danzig, students "crafted these into 'stories of professional practice'" (p. 123) and then reflected on these stories, adding "what they had learned from the experience" (p. 123).

This experience helped students connect theory with practice, according to Danzig (1997), and provided a window into the kinds of thinking strategies principals used when confronting a dilemma of practice. Danzig noted, "Issues related to school culture, personal relations, values and beliefs, and rituals and myths, take on more meaning as they are presented in stories of practice" (p. 129). The thought that went into writing the stories, combined with students' reflection on the principal's problem-solving strategies, helped to make the practitioner's implicit knowledge and skills explicit to the student in a way similar to that of cognitive apprenticeships. Moreover, the stories contextualized the particular event related by the principals, leading to a holistic rather than fragmented understanding of the problem and its resolution. As important, the students' reflections on the stories they recounted often uncovered the student's own tacit beliefs and assumptions, bringing them to the surface for inspection and change.

One problem in teaching reflective practice is the tendency of some students to focus on surface-level issues. Doolittle (2003) reported case study action research that involved 7 students in a doctoral program, 6 of whom were practicing principals. All 7 struggled to move from surface analyses focused on the behavior of others to deeper understandings of their own leadership capacities and a focus on their own behaviors. Doolittle explained that the novelty of engaging in reflection was an obstacle that required much faculty assistance (and the faculty members' own reflection on the problem) to overcome. Faculty engagement in self-reflective practice was an important component of the doctoral program and is a recommendation that is also proffered by others (Pohland, 1990; Rusch, in press). Because most of the students in Doolittle's study were practicing principals, they were, by the end of their doctoral studies, able to describe changes in their theories-in-use that resulted from the reflection required in the program.

Pohland (1990) analyzed 34 case records developed by 11 administrative interns placed at school, district, and regional offices. Although the development of these case records was to be reflective work, Pohland found that most interns were unskilled at reflection, with only one third reflecting "upon their own actions" (p. 5). Most interns opted for means–ends solutions rather than serious analysis of alternative courses of action. This problem may indicate a lack of skill in problem specification, making genuine reflection more difficult. In the complex, untidy world of educational leadership (Leithwood, 1995), problems of practice are often difficult to specify for both in-service and preservice leaders (Achilles, 1989). Because accurate identification and specification of the problem is essential to effective reflection, Lipton (1993) recommended that techniques of problem specification be taught overtly.

Another pedagogical problem that may arise when incorporating reflective practice into preparation programs is initial student resistance. Resistance likely has many sources, not the least of which is the novelty of reflection for many adult learners. Read and Hausman (1998) required reflective journaling of 14 aspiring leaders during their 3 years in a preparation program and also used reflective practice themselves to analyze their own instructional practice in a course they co-taught. For the professors, reflection uncovered concerns about students who resisted participating in reflective journaling and the professors' feelings of being confronted and disrespected by these students. Students engaged in small-group, in-class discussions about the reflections they produced. Over time, this setting proved to be a safe environment to confront and challenge assumptions that otherwise might have gone unquestioned. Eventually, many students found that reflection built confidence, facilitated personal insight, and led to an "evolving and integrative understanding of school leadership" (Read & Hausman, 1998, p. 9).

In their analysis of student preparation, Kottkamp and Silverberg (1999a) reported that nearly two fifths of the students developed new approaches to problem situations, approaches that these students actively tested in the work environment. Similarly, over two thirds of the students indicated an intention to change behavior. In short, Kottkamp and Silverberg (1999a) found reflective practice to be "a powerful vehicle of self-initiated change of thought and action for educators in various roles and levels" (p. 2). Osterman (1990) provided additional insight, noting that students' "response has been positive with comments to the effect that the process leads to new perspectives, new insights and a greater understanding of the change process" (p. 9).

The studies reported in this section indicate that reflective practice as a constructivist approach can be used effectively to move students in educational leadership along the novice to expert continuum. Used as a pedagogical strategy, reflection occurs both individually and collaboratively through in-class group work. By critically examining dilemmas and tensions signaled by emotions that emerge when engaged in leadership behaviors, students in educational leadership programs began to develop a sharper awareness not only about the nature of problems, but also about their leadership behaviors in response to the problems (Osterman & Kottkamp, 1993, 2004; Silver, 1984).

Summary

In this section, we offered a review of the research on pedagogical strategies reflected in the middle to the right portion of Figure 8.1. In particular, we discussed humanities-based practices, case method, PBL, simulations and assessment center exercises, teaching with and through technology, action research and learning, and reflective practice. Again, we emphasize that social justice, ethics, and human relations sensibilities should undergird each of these pedagogies. Throughout, we noted the general lack of research on pedagogical techniques that engage prospective administrators peripherally and fully in a workplace community of practice, although techniques we reviewed appear to hold much promise for more adequately preparing aspiring school leaders. The conclusions below further summarize our findings and offer directions for moving research in the field ahead.

Conclusions and Recommendations

The charge for this chapter was to investigate research and studies of pedagogical practices used in preparing or supporting the development of educational leaders. We began with a review of the historical development of pedagogical practices, especially since the 1950s, and explored the literature that seems best to inform the field. We used the theoretical framework presented in Figure 8.1, adapted from the work of Cordeiro (2006), to guide our review. The framework captures both the major processes of teaching and learning and the position of instructor and learner within each process. The Figure 8.1 framework also places the primary pedagogies found in the literature along a continuum that move the learner from a passive recipient of transmitted information to an active participant and knowledge generator, which is most likely to occur when the student is engaged. The framework helps the reader take account of the increasing understandings about how adults learn and the kinds of pedagogical approaches needed to support that learning. Seven important conclusions can be drawn from this review.

1. First, we found limited empirical evidence on which to base decisions about how best to prepare future educational leaders. Some of the reasons for this include (a) dominance of the lecture-discussion format of instruction, which has been taken for granted as effective and appropriate; (b) difficulty of studying one's own practice; (c) lack of financial or professional support for the scholarly study of pedagogical practices in the preparation of educational leaders; (d) difficulty of conducting large-scale, rigorous, and comparative evaluations that

could provide more substantial evidence of effectiveness; and (e) lack of venues and respect for presenting findings from case study and action research regarding preparation programs. Fortunately, as this review shows, since the 1990s, assumptions and structures of the behavioral paradigm that worked against serious research on leader preparation have begun to shift. To advance the study of preparation, we conclude our chapter with several suggestions for further research that are detailed in the recommendations section below.

2. A second conclusion is that existing empirical evidence is drawn from small-scale studies conducted by individual professors or their doctoral students and tends to focus on one or two classes or one degree program. These studies are often weakly conceived and conceptualized, are rarely grounded in learning theory, and are often of short duration with research questions of limited utility and inadequate methodology. Fortunately, several dissertation studies have made important contributions to the field of pedagogical approaches, but they do not compensate for the absence of large-scale, rigorous research.

3. We point out that only rarely does research on pedagogical approaches represent a sustained research agenda. One important exception has been the work on reflective practice by Silver (1984), Osterman and Kottkamp (1993, 2004), and Kottkamp and Silverberg (1999a, 1999b, 2003). Use of technology may emerge as an area where a body of research will begin to build. Again, we posit as a critical factor the lack of federal grant monies (or foundation monies, with the past exception of the Danforth Foundation) available to support development of the pedagogy and research regarding the efficacy of promising teaching techniques. While professional associations such as UCEA and NASSP have supported important work in the development of some pedagogies, such as case studies and simulations, the capacity of these organizations is limited, making sustaining the research impossible. The effect of the limited capacity of professional associations is particularly problematic when, after the development phase, research is needed to demonstrate effects, but funds do not exist to support the studies. Thus, the research that exists has been small scale, of short duration, and conducted by faculty in their own settings, usually with their own resources.

4. Another conclusion concerns survey studies. The survey research we reviewed tends to report either the presence of some pedagogical practice or preferences for certain practices, as opposed to an analysis of outcomes accruing from the pedagogical approaches. A few larger scale efforts exist, for example, efforts to develop exemplary case studies that are peer reviewed and then posted for others to use (*Journal of Cases*), but no cross-university studies of the effectiveness of using these case studies as a pedagogical approach have been undertaken. Similarly, while the two national institutes that were conducted to assist faculty in implementing PBL were an important advance in attention to pedagogy, only a few individual professors subsequently documented their efforts and outcomes; no comparative research was conducted across multiple sites. Again, we suppose this is due to a lack of financial support. The several studies of PBL in the literature suggest it is an effective strategy in helping administrative candidates develop skills such as problem framing and developing group problem-solving skills, but the studies tend to stand independently, to be somewhat idiosyncratic and context based, and to represent only an emerging body of knowledge about effectiveness of PBL in leader preparation.

5. Researchers are not consistent in defining concepts, for example, the range of ways in which case methods are described (e.g., case study, case records, and case stories). This inconsistency in concepts is compounded by the use of different instruments and methods to describe and assess concepts. Particularly critical is the lack of information about instrument validity and reliability in quantitative studies and data trustworthiness in qualitative studies. These meth-

odological issues may be due in part to the need to construct, perhaps hastily, instruments for assessing the effectiveness of a particular approach. Also, since many evaluations of instructional methods take place at the conclusion of a course, studies rarely measured long-term effectiveness or actual candidate ability to apply concepts once in the work environment.

6. There is scant evidence that educational leadership scholars are linking the studies they conduct to research in related fields such as management, business, law, or medicine. For example, studies of PBL and case methods often cite the medical and legal fields as a stimulus for the development and use of these strategies in educational leader preparation, but rarely are results of such studies in these other professional fields compared with results of their use in educational leadership preparation. Linking the field of educational leader preparation more substantially to other fields may be one way to enhance the validity of findings, even those from small-scale studies.

7. Finally, it is important to recognize that scholars are currently conducting research on pedagogies reflected in the middle to the right side of Figure 8.1. This finding suggests that professors of educational leadership are increasingly interested in using approaches to learning that more closely reflect a constructivist and social constructivist orientation to learning. Given what is known about adult learning, this is a positive sign and suggests that if this trend continues, future administrators are being prepared in ways that more closely resemble what they will encounter on the job. It is imperative that as a discipline we continue with a more rigorous research trajectory.

Recommendations for Further Research

In light of the conclusions presented above, we see several implications and suggest five areas for further research.

1. Since most states have adopted standards for school leaders, a critical first agenda for future research might be joining states together to support research that explores which pedagogical approaches best support acquisition of standards among future administrators. An essential subquestion worthy of exploration is this: Once mastered, are the standards actually relevant to the skills, knowledge, and dispositions needed to lead a school or district to addresses the learning needs of all students successfully?

2. Professional associations might support more systematic research programs on pedagogical practices by maintaining an easily accessed database on recent and current pedagogical investigations open to professors and graduate students. This would enable scholars to link their work more substantially to that of others and could begin to build a more conceptually and methodologically sound research base.

3. There is a need for more longitudinal studies of how particular pedagogical approaches, such as PBL or various technologies, actually influence practice once administrators are in the workplace.

4. We need to understand how educational leader preparation programs and particular pedagogies support or are effective with diverse participants, including women, men, African Americans, Latina/os, urban, rural, and so on.

5. As a profession, we need to find better ways financially, conceptually, and methodologically to assist those who want to study their own practice to ensure that these studies reflect high-quality scholarship that can make a difference to the field. Then, we need to be sure the findings are disseminated widely to help inform the practice of others.

Note

1. We acknowledge instances when the term *training* is used instead of alternatives such as *teaching* or *learning* because terminology develops in a context that is inherently embedded with prevailing paradigms, which essentially dictate the use of one term, *training*, over another, *learning*.

References

Achilles, C. M. (1989, October). *Challenging Narcissus, or reflecting on reflecting*. Paper presented at the annual meeting of the University Council for Educational Administration, Scottsdale, AZ. (ERIC Document Reproduction Service No. ED312772)

Achilles, C. M., & Hoover, S. P. (1996, November). *Exploring problem based learning (PBL) in Grades 6-12*. Paper presented at the annual meeting of the Mid-South Educational Research Association, Tuscaloosa, AL. (ERIC Document Reproduction Service No. ED406406)

Acker-Hocevar, M., & Miller-Keating, C. (2002, April). *An integrative model of action learning and action research: The alchemy of learning organizations*. Paper presented at the annual meeting of the American Education Research Association, New Orleans. LA. Retrieved May 9, 2008, from the Florida Atlantic University Web site: http://www.leadership.fau.edu/facultyhomepages/AERA.pdf

Acker-Hocevar, M., Pisapia, J., & Coukos-Semmel, E. (2002, April). *Bridging the abyss: Adding value and validity to leadership development through action learning—Cases-in-point*. Paper presented at the annual meeting of the American Educational Research Association, New Orleans, LA.

Ackerman, R., & Maslin-Ostrowski, P. (1995, April). *Developing case stories: An analysis of the case method of instruction and storytelling in teaching educational administration*. Paper presented at the annual meeting of the American Educational Research Association, New York. (ERIC Document Reproduction Service No. ED390132)

Ackerman, R., & Maslin-Ostrowski, P. (1996, April). *Real talk: Toward further understanding of case story in teaching educational administration*. Paper presented at the annual meeting of the American Educational Research Association, New York. (ERIC Document Reproduction Service No. ED396644)

Alkire, G. (1978). Master's programs in educational administration. In P. F. Silver & D. W. Spuck (Eds.), *Preparatory programs for educational administrators in the United States* (pp. 52–82). Columbus, OH: University Council for Educational Administration.

Anderson, G. L., Herr, K., & Nihlen, A. S. (1994). *Studying your own school: An educator's guide to qualitative practitioner research*. Thousand Oaks, CA: Corwin.

Apple, M. (1993). The politics of official knowledge: Does a national curriculum make sense? *Teachers College Press, 95*(2), 222–241.

Argyris, C., & Schön, D. A. (1978). *Organizational learning: A theory of caution perspective*. Reading, MA: Addison-Wesley.

Ashby, D., Hecht, J. B., & Klass, P. H. (1999, April). *Implications of distance education for educational administration programs*. Paper presented at the annual meeting of the American Educational Research Association, Montreal, Quebec, Canada. (ERIC Document Reproduction Service No. ED430475)

Ashe, J., Haubner, J., & Troisi, N. (1991). University preparation of principals: The New York Study. *NASSP Bulletin, 75*(536), 145–150.

Badiali, B. J., & Cambron-McCabe, N. (1996, April). *Problem based learning in educational leadership: The Miami experience*. Paper presented at the annual meeting of the American Educational Research Association, New York.

Baltzell, D. C., & Dentler, R. A. (1983). *Selecting American school principals: A sourcebook for educators*. Washington, DC: National Institute of Education. (ERIC Document Reproduction Service No. ED238206)

Barbour, J. D. (1992, April). *Quilting with problem-based thread*. Paper presented at the San Francisco Forum on Problem Based Learning, Danforth Foundation and the National Policy Board for Educational Administration, San Francisco.

Bereiter, C., & Scardamalia, M. (1989). Intentional learning as a goal of instruction. In L. B. Resnick (Ed.), *Knowing, learning and instruction: Essays in honor of Robert Glaser* (pp. 361–392). Hillsdale, NJ: Erlbaum.

Bershad, C., & Mundry, S. (1999). *The change game*. Rowley, MA: The Network.

Björk, L. G., & Ginsberg, R. (1995). Principles of reform and reforming principal training: A theoretical perspective. *Educational Administration Quarterly, 31*(1), 11–37.

Blough, J. A. (1972, April). *Participant evaluation of UCEA urban simulation materials and workshops*. Paper presented at the annual meeting of the American Educational Research Association, Chicago.

Bogotch, I. E. (2002). Educational leadership and justice: Practice into theory [Electronic version]. *Journal of School Leadership, 12*(2), 138–156.

Borsa, J., Klotz, J., & Uzat, R. (1998, November). *Utilizing distance learning and the case study method to enhance instruction between two universities*. Paper presented at the annual meeting of the Mid-South Educational Research Association, New Orleans, LA. (ERIC Document Reproduction Service No. ED429470)

Bradshaw, L., Bell, E., McDowelle, J., & Perreault, G. (1997, November). *Building school district–university partnerships around leadership assessment and development: The time has come.* Paper presented at the meeting of the Southern Regional Council on Educational Administration, Charleston, SC.

Bradshaw, L., & Buckner, K. (1998). *From the "Springfield Development Program" to the "21st Century School Administrator Skills (SAS) Program."* Paper presented at the annual meeting of the National Association of Secondary School Principals assessment directors, Louisville, KY. (ERIC Document Reproduction Service No. EA029689)

Bransford, J. D., Brown, A. L., & Cocking, R. R. (Eds.). (1999). *How people learn: Brain, mind, experience, and school.* Washington, DC: National Academy Press.

Bray, D. W., Campbell, R. J., & Grant, D. L. (1974). *Formative years in business: A long-term AT&T study of managerial lives.* New York: Wiley.

Bridges, E., & Hallinger, P. (1993). Problem-based learning in medical and managerial education. In P. Hallinger, K. Leithwood, & J. Murphy (Eds.), *Cognitive perspectives on educational leadership* (pp. 253–267). New York: Teachers College Press.

Bridges E. M., & Hallinger P. (1995). *Implementing problem based learning in leadership development.* Eugene, OR: ERIC Clearinghouse on Educational Management.

Brieschke, P. A. (1993). Interpreting ourselves: Administrators in modern fiction. *Theory Into Practice, 32*(4), 228–235.

Brown, K. M. (2004). Leadership for social justice and equity: Weaving a transformative framework and pedagogy. *Educational Administration Quarterly, 40*(1), 77–108.

Brown, K. M. (2006a). Leadership for social justice and equity: Evaluating a transformative framework and andragogy. *Educational Administration Quarterly, 42*(5), 700–745.

Brown, K. M. (2006b). A transformative andragogy for principal preparation programs. *UCEA Review, 45*(2), 1–5.

Browne-Ferrigno, T., Choi, C., & Muth, R. (2000, November). *Comparing student learning in onsite and distance programs.* Paper presented at the annual meeting of the University Council for Educational Research, Albuquerque, NM.

Brunner, C. C., Hitchon, W. N. G., & Brown, R. (2002). Advancing social justice as a part of educational leadership development: The potential for imagining technologies. *On the Horizon, 10*(3), 12–15.

Brunner, C. C., Miller, M. D., & Hammel, K. (2003, November). *Leadership preparation and the opposite of control: A technologically-delivered Deweyan approach.* Paper presented at the annual meeting of the University Council for Educational Administration, Albuquerque, NM.

Calder, C. (1979) *Multimedia resources for educational administrators.* Toronto, Ontario, Canada: Ontario Institute for Studies in Education. (ERIC Document Reproduction Service No. ED181602)

Calhoun, E. (1994). *How to use action research in the self-renewing school.* Alexandria, VA: Association of Supervision and Curriculum Development.

Callahan, R. E., & Button, H. W. (1964). Historical change of the role of the man in the organization: 1865–1950. In D. E. Griffiths (Ed.), *Behavioral science and educational administration. The sixty-third yearbook of the National Society for the Study of Education, Part II* (pp. 73–92). Chicago: University of Chicago Press.

Cambron-McCabe, N. H. (2003). Rethinking leadership preparation: Focus on Faculty learning communities [Electronic version]. *Leadership and Policy in Schools, 2,* 285–298.

Campbell, R. F., Fleming, T., Newell, L. J., & Bennion, J. W. (1987). *A history of thought and practice in educational administration.* New York: Teachers College Press.

Capper, C. (1993). *Educational administration in a pluralistic society.* Albany: State University of New York Press.

Chance, E. W., & Chance, P. L. (2000). The use of simulations in principal preparation programs: A bridge between the classroom and field-based experiences. In R. Muth & M. Martin (Eds.), *Toward the Year 2000: Leadership for quality schools: Sixth annual yearbook of the National Council of Professors of Educational Administration* (pp. 132–139). Lancaster, PA: Technomic.

Chenoweth, T. G. (1996, April). *The efficacy of problem-based learning in Ed.D. research: Training school administrators to deal with diversity.* Paper presented at the annual meeting of the American Educational Research Association, New York.

Chenoweth, T. G., & Everhart, R. B. (1995, April). *Taking problem-based learning for school administrators on the road: An inservice application.* Paper presented at the annual meeting of the American Educational Research Association, San Francisco.

Chrispeels, J., Caston, M., Brandon, J. L., & Venter, K. (1996, April). *Action, reflection, action: The power of problem-based learning in developing future administrators.* Paper presented at the annual meeting of the American Educational Research Association, New York.

Chrispeels, J. H., & Martin, K. J. (1998). Becoming problem solvers: The case of three future administrators. *Journal of School Leadership, 8*(3), 303–331.

Comerford, J. P., & Carlson, M. (1985, March). *A methodology for training administrators to use microcomputers in educational administration.* Paper presented at the annual meeting of the American Educational Research Association, Chicago. (ERIC Document Reproduction Service No. EA017925)

Comstock, J. A. (1975). A study of in-service human relations training in Minnesota's public schools. *Pupil Personnel Services Journal, 4*(1), 6–12.

Copland, M. A. (1999). *Problem-based learning, problem-framing ability and the principal selves of prospective school principals*. Unpublished doctoral dissertation, Stanford University, Stanford, CA.

Copland, M. (2000). Problem-based learning and prospective principals' problem-finding ability. *Educational Administration Quarterly, 36*(4), 585–607.

Cordeiro, P. A. (1996, April). *Problem-based learning in educational administration: Enhancing learning transfer*. Paper presented at the annual meeting of the American Educational Research Association, New York.

Cordeiro, P. (1998). Problem-based learning in educational administration: Enhancing learning transfer. *Journal of School Leadership, 8*(3), 280–302.

Cordeiro, P. (2006, July). *Educating at the border: Learning and teaching on the threshold*. Keynote address at the world assembly of the International Council for the Education of Teachers, Fortaleza, Brazil.

Cordeiro, P. A., & Campbell, B. (1997, April). *Increasing the transfer of learning through problem-based learning in educational administration*. Paper presented at the annual meeting of the American Educational Research Association. Chicago.

Cordeiro, P. A., Kraus, C., Hastings, S., & Binkowski, K. (1997). *Simulated and authentic problem based learning*. Paper presented at the annual meeting of the American Educational Research Association, Chicago.

Cordeiro, P., Krueger, J., Parks, D., Restine, L. N., & Wilson, P. (1993). Taking stock: Lessons gleaned from universities participating in the Danforth program. In M. Milstein (Ed.), *Changing the way we prepare educational leaders* (pp. 17–38). Newbury Park, CA: Corwin Press.

Corey, S. M. (1953). *Action research to improve school practices*. New York: Teachers College.

Cubberley, E. P. (1916). *Public school administration*. Boston: Houghton Mifflin.

Culbertson, J. A. (1967). *Revising and updating the Jefferson Township simulation materials: Final report*. Columbus, OH: University Council for Educational Administration. (ERIC Document Reproduction Service No. ED018012)

Culbertson, J. A. (1988). A century's quest for a knowledge base. In N. J. Boyan (Ed.), *Handbook of research on educational administration: A project of the America Educational Research Association* (pp. 3–26). New York: Longman.

Cunningham, W. G., & Cordeiro, P. A. (2006). *An introduction to educational leadership: A problem-based approach*. Boston: Allyn & Bacon.

Danforth Foundation. (1992). *Taking stock: A survey of the Danforth Programs for the Preparation of Principals*. St. Louis, MO: Author.

Dantley, M. E. (2005). African American spirituality and Cornel West's notions of prophetic pragmatism: Restructuring educational leadership in American schools. *Educational Administration Quarterly, 41*(4), 651–674.

Danzig, A. B. (1997). Leadership stories: What novices learn by crafting the story of experienced school administrators. *Journal of Educational Administration, 35*(2), 122–137.

Davis, J. A. (1997). *Meadows Principal Improvement Program: A program assessment for preparing principals*. Unpublished doctoral dissertation, Texas A&M University, Commerce.

Davis, K. L., & Gazda, G. M. (1975). Results of the 1973 Association of Teacher Education Human Relations Training summer workshop. *Education, 96*(2), 184–189.

Davis, W. J. (1978). Departments of educational administration. In P. F. Silver & D. W. Spuck (Eds.), *Preparatory programs for educational administrators in the United States* (pp. 23–51). Columbus, OH: University Council for Educational Administration.

DeFeo, A. E. (1997). *Using multimedia as a tool in administrative decision-making: A teaching case designed to foster collaborative management strategies*. Unpublished doctoral dissertation Columbia University Teachers College, New York.

Delpit, L. (2006). *Other people's children*. New York: The New Press.

Deep, S. D. (1971, September). *Use of management training simulations in a university educational administration program: The program of exercises for management and organizational development*. Paper presented at the annual meeting of the American Association of School Administrators, Atlantic City, NJ.

Diamantes, T. (1996, August). *A case for cases: Using the case method in the preparation of administrators*. Paper presented at the annual meeting of the National Council of Professors of Educational Administration, Corpus Christi, TX. (ERIC Document Reproduction Service No. ED399624)

Diamantes, T. (1997). Discussion-starters: Using modified case methods in administrator preparation programs. In L. Wildman (Ed.), *School administration: The new knowledge base. The fifth annual yearbook of the National Council of Professors of Educational Administration* (pp. 65–68). New Carlisle, PA: Technomic.

Diamantes, T., & Williams, M. (1997, August). *The perceptive ear/eye game: An activity that encourages practice on best practices. Honing observation and problem solving skills of administrators*. Paper presented at the annual meeting of the National Association of Professors of Education Administration, Vail, CO. (ERIC Document Reproduction Service No. ED427403)

Dikkers, A. G., Hughes, J. E., & McLeod, S. (2005). A bridge to success: STLI—In that no man's land between school technology and effective leadership, the University of Minnesota's School of Technology Leadership Initiative is a welcoming bridge. *T.H.E. Journal, 32*(11). Retrieved January 16, 2007, from the EBSCOhost database.

Donmoyer, R., Garcia, J., & Robinett, D. (2005, April). *Grounding principal preparation in doing case studies of low performing schools*. Paper presented at the annual meeting of the American Educational Research Association, Montreal, Quebec, Canada.

Doolittle, G. (2003). Preparing leaders for reflective practice: New practices, methods, and models. In F. Lunenburg & C. Carr (Eds.), *Shaping the future. The eleventh annual yearbook of the National Council of Professors of Educational Administration* (pp. 244–261). Lanham, MD: Scarecrow.

Doyle, W. (1990). Case methods in the education of teachers. *Teacher Education Quarterly, 17*(1), 1–22.

Elliott, J. (1991). *Action research for educational change.* Bristol, PA: Open University Press.

English, F. W. (1994, April). *Biography as a focus for teaching leadership.* Paper presented at the annual meeting of the American Educational Research Association, New Orleans, LA. (ERIC Document Reproduction Service No. ED378634)

English, F. W. (1995). Toward a reconsideration of biography and other forms of life writing as a focus for teaching in educational administration. *Educational Administration Quarterly, 31*(2), 177–203.

English, F. W. (1996, April). *Promising directions in case-, problem-, and narrative-based teaching in educational administration.* Paper presented at the annual meeting of the American Educational Research Association, New York. (ERIC Document Reproduction Service No. ED396367)

English, F. W., & Steffy, B. E. (1995, April). *Using film to attain a cultural contextual understanding of moral leadership.* Paper presented at the annual meeting of the American Educational Research Association, San Francisco. (ERIC Document Reproduction Service No. ED385945)

Enomoto, E. K. (2003). Faculty reflections on teaching at a distance. *UCEA Review, 45*(2), 1–4.

Envig, M. B. (1997). *Professors' adoption and implementation of problem-based learning.* Unpublished doctoral dissertation, Stanford University, Stanford, CA.

Estes, D. M. (1999, August). *An attempt at problem-based learning.* Paper presented at the annual meeting of the National Council of Professors of Educational Administration, Jackson Hole, WY. (ERIC Document Reproduction Service No. ED450468)

Evans, S., & Shapiro, A. (1978). Certification and specialist degree programs. In P. F. Silver & D. W. Spuck (Eds.), *Preparatory programs for educational administrators in the United States* (pp. 83–113). Columbus, OH: University Council for Educational Administration.

Frankfurt, K. (2000). A place for everyone [Electronic version]. *Principal Leadership, 1*(2), 64–67.

Freire, P. (1996). *Pedagogy of the oppressed* (20th anniversary ed.). New York: Continuum. (Original work published 1970)

Freire, P., & Macedo, D. P. (1995). A dialogue: Culture, language and race. *Harvard Educational Review, 65*(3), 377–402.

Gardner, H. (1983). *Frames of mind: The theory of multiple intelligences.* New York: Basic Books.

Garner, R. (1990). When children and adults do not use learning strategies: Toward a theory of settings. *Review of Educational Research, 60*(4), 517–529.

Geltner, B. B. (1993, October). *Integrating formative portfolio assessment, reflective practice, and cognitive coaching into preservice preparation.* Paper presented at the annual meeting of the University Council for Educational Administration, Houston, TX. (ERIC Document Reproduction Service No. ED365702)

Geltner, B. (1995, June). *Shaping new leaders for new schools: Using the case method for innovative teaching and learning.* Paper presented at the annual meeting of the International Conference on Case Method Research and Application, Leysin, Switzerland. (ERIC Document Reproduction Service No. ED381507)

Getz, C. (2008, March). *Enhancing one's pedagogical approach to teaching leadership: Learning and teaching in real time.* Paper presented at the annual meeting of the American Educational Research Association, New York.

Giroux, H. A. (1992). *Educational leadership and the crisis of democratic culture* (UCEA monograph series). Austin, TX: University Council for Educational Administration.

Glaser, R., Raghavan, K., & Baxter, B. P. (1992). *Cognitive theory as the basis for design of innovative assessment: Design characteristics of science assessment* (CSE Technical Report No. 349). Los Angeles: National Center for Research on Evaluation, Standards, and Student Testing.

Glickman, C. D. (1993). *Renewing America's schools: A guide for school-based action.* San Francisco: Jossey-Bass.

Grady, N. B., Macpherson, R. J. S., & Mulford, B. R. (1995, April). *Problem-based learning in block delivery modes.* Paper presented at the annual meeting of the American Educational Research Association, San Francisco.

Hackman, D. G., & Berry, J. E. (1999). Distance learning in educational administration doctoral programs: The wave of the future? *Journal of School Leadership, 9*, 349–267.

Hallinger, P. (2005a, April). *Integrating learning technologies and problem-based learning: A framework and case study.* Paper presented at the annual meeting of the American Educational Research Association, Montreal, Quebec, Canada.

Hallinger, P. (2005b, August). *Making change happen: A problem-based computer simulation.* Paper presented at the Second International Conference on Learning for Knowledge-Based Society, Bangkok, Thailand.

Hallinger, P., & Bridges, E. M. (1991). Problem-based learning: A promising approach for preparing educational administrators. *UCEA Review, 32*(3), 3–5, 7.

Hallinger, P., Chantarapana, P., & Sriboonma, U. (1995, July). *Implementing problem-based leadership development in Thailand.* Paper presented at the International Conference in Teacher Education, Bangkok, Thailand.

Hallinger, P., & McCary, M. (1990). Developing the strategic thinking of instructional leaders. *Elementary School Journal, 9*(12), 90–108.

Heller, R., Chafee, L. M., & Davison, R. J. (1974). Two computer-based school scheduling programs analyzed. *NASSP Bulletin, 58*(380), 64–82.

Herr, K., & Anderson, G. L. (2005). *The action research dissertation: A guide for students and faculty*. Thousand Oaks, CA: Sage.

Hersey, P. W. (1977). NASSP's Assessment Center: From concept to practice. *NASSP Bulletin, 61,* 74–76.

Higgins, E., Moracco, J., & Danford, D. (1981). Effects of human relations training on education students [Electronic version]. *Journal of Educational Research, 75*(1), 22–25.

Hoachlander, G., Alt, M., & Beltranenam R. (2001, March). *Leading school improvement: What research says*. Atlanta, GA: Southern Regional Education Board.

Hopfenberg, W., Levin, M. H., & Associates, Inc, (1993). *The Accelerated Schools resource guide*. San Francisco: Jossey-Bass.

House, J. E. (1989, October). *The impact of personal computing technology on the educational administration knowledge base*. Paper presented at the annual meeting of the University Council for Educational Administration, Scottsdale, AZ. (ERIC Document Reproduction Service No. ED387895)

Howland, J., Musser, D., & Mayer, C. (1999). Information environment for school leader preparation: Web-based software for preparing reflective educational leaders. In *Proceedings of 1999* (pp. 1342–1343). Chesapeake, VA: Association for the Advancement of Computing in Education.

Hughes, L. W. (1971, March). *A program to prepare administrator/change agents for Southern Appalachia*. Paper presented at the annual meeting of the American Educational Research Association, New York.

Hughes, L. W. (1986). This administrator assessment center aims for excellence. *Executive Educator, 8*(3), 21–21, 33.

Hughes, J. E., McLeod, S., Dikkers, A. G., & Whiteside A. (2005, April). *Preparing technology leaders in the STLI program: Individual and institutional change*. Paper presented at the annual meeting of the American Educational Research Association, San Diego, CA.

IESLP developers sample St. Louis, present first exercises. (1997). *UCEA Review, 38*(3), 4–5.

Interstate School Leaders Licensure Consortium. (1996). *Standards for school leaders*. Washington, DC: Council of Chief State School Officers.

Iran-Nejad, A., McKeachie, W. J., & Berliner, D. C. (1990). The multisource nature of learning: An introduction. *Review of Educational Research, 60*(4), 509–515.

Jack, W. B. (1983). *An evaluation of the preparation of present secondary school principals*. Unpublished doctoral dissertation, Vanderbilt University, Nashville, TN.

Jenlink, P. M. (1992, April). *Problem-focused simulated experiences*. Paper presented at the San Francisco Forum on Problem Based Learning, Danforth Foundation and the National Policy Board for Educational Administration, San Francisco.

Jost, M., Whitfield, E. L., & Jost, M. (2005). When the rules are fair, but the game isn't [Electronic version]. *Multicultural Education, 31,* 14–21.

Kaurala, E. B. (1998). Interactive television: Reactions of students and faculty. In R. Muth & M. Martin (Eds.), *Toward the Year 2000: Leadership for quality schools. Sixth annual yearbook of the National Council of Professors of Educational Administration* (pp. 231–237). Lancaster, PA: Technomic.

Keedy, J. L., & Achilles, C. M. (1997). The need for school-constructed theories in practice in U.S. school restructuring [Electronic version]. *Journal of Educational Administration, 35,* 102–121.

Kerka, S. (2000). *Incidental learning. Trends and Issues Alert No. 18*. Columbus, OH: ERIC Clearinghouse on Adult, Career, and Vocational Education.

Kirschmann, R. E. (1995). *Educational administration: A collection of case studies*. Upper Saddle River, NJ: Prentice-Hall.

Knowles, M. (1975) Adult education: New dimensions. *Educational Leadership, 33*(2), 85–88.

Knowles, M. (1984). *The adult learner: A neglected species* (3rd ed.). Houston, TX: Gulf.

Kowalski, T. J. (2007). *Case studies on educational administration* (5th ed.). Boston: Allyn & Bacon.

Kottkamp, R. B., & Silverberg, R. P. (1999a, April). *Exploring the mental models of administrative aspirants: Assumptions about students, teaching, and learning*. Paper presented at the annual meeting of the American Educational Research Association, Montreal, Quebec, Canada.

Kottkamp, R. B., & Silverberg, R. P. (1999b). *Reconceptualizing the idea of "students at risk": Teachers' assumptions about "problematic students."* Paper presented at the Research Network: Children and Youth at Risk and Urban Education, European Education Research Association, Malta.

Kottkamp, R. B., & Silverberg, R. P. (2000). Learning formal theory through constructivism and reflective practice: Professor and student perspectives. *Educational Administration and Leadership: Teaching and Program Development, 11,* 47–59.

Kottkamp, R. B., & Silverberg, R. P. (2003). Leader preparation reform in first person: Making assumptions public [Electronic version]. *Leadership and Policy in Schools, 2*(4), 299–326.

Ladson-Billings, G. (1994). *Dreamkeepers: Successful teachers of African American children*. San Francisco: Jossey-Bass.

Lansing, P., & Cropper, A. P. (1992). *"Kaibob" simulation: A teaching strategy*. San Francisco: Danforth Foundation and National Policy Board for Educational Administration.

Larson, C., & Ovando, C. (1996, April). *Preparing administrators for multicultural leadership: An inquiry driven view of problem-based learning*. Paper presented at the annual meeting of the American Educational Research Association, New York.

Leithwood, K. (1995). Cognitive perspectives on school leadership. *Journal of School Leadership, 5*(2), 115–135.

Leithwood, K., Seashore Louis, K., Anderson, S., & Wahlstrom, K. (2004). *How leadership influences student learning.* New York: The Wallace Foundation.

Levin, B. B. (2003). *Case studies of teacher development: An in-depth look at how thinking about pedagogy develops over time.* Mahwah, NJ: Erlbaum.

Licata, J. W., & Ellett, C. D. (1990). LEAD program provides support development for new principals. *NASSP Bulletin, 74*(525), 5–10.

Lipton, L. (1993). *Transforming information into knowledge: Structured reflection in administrative practice.* (ERIC Document Reproduction Service No. ED361903)

Lomotey, K. (1989). *African-American principals: School leadership and success.* Westport, CT: Greenwood Press.

Lugg, C. A. (1997, November). *No trespassing: U.S. public schools and the border of institutional homophobia.* Paper presented at the annual meeting of the University Council for Educational Administration, Orlando, FL. (ERIC Document Reproduction Service No. ED429252)

Lugg, C. A. (2003). Sissies, faggots, lezzies, and dykes: Gender, sexual orientation, and a new politics of education? [Electronic version]. *Educational Administration Quarterly, 39*(1), 95–134.

Lutz, F. W. (1971). Funding and educational administration programs. *Educational Administration Quarterly, 7*(1), 1–7.

MacNeil, A., & Garcia, J. H. (1997). Technology, case studies, and creativity in the preparation of school leadership. In L. Wildman (Ed.), *School administration: The new knowledge base. The fifth annual yearbook of the National Council of Professors of Educational Administration* (pp. 69–74). New Carlisle, PA: Technomic.

Markus, F. W., & Huys, G. (1973, November). *Measuring effectiveness of a principals' desegregation workshop.* Paper presented at the annual meeting of the Mid-South Educational Research Association, Memphis, TN.

Marsick, V. J., & Watkins, K. E. (2001). Informal and incidental learning [Electronic version]. *New Directions for Adult and Continuing Education, 89,* 25–34.

Martin, K. J., Chrispeels, J. H., & D'Emidio-Caston, M. (1998). Exploring the use of problem-based learning for developing future administrators, *Journal of School Leadership, 8*(5) 470–500.

Matthews, J. C. (1998). Somatic knowing and education. *Educational Forum, 62,* 236–242.

Maynes, B., McIntosh, G., & Mappin, D. (1996). Computer-based simulations of the school principalship: Preparation for professional practice. *Educational Administration Quarterly, 32*(4), 579–594.

McCleary, L. (1986). Implications for universities: Bringing ancillary benefits to the university. *NASSP Bulletin, 70*(486), 51–53.

McLeod, S., Hughes, J. E., Richardson, J., & Dikkers, A. (2005, April). *Building capacity for technology leadership in educational administration preparation programs.* Paper presented at the annual meeting of the American Educational Research Association, Montreal, Quebec, Canada.

McEwen, M. K., Higgins, E. B., & Pipes, R. B. (1982). The impact of developmental issues on human relations training for preservice teachers. *The Personnel and Guidance Journal, 61,* 163–168

McInerney, D. M. (2005). Educational psychology—Theory, research, and teaching: A 25-year retrospective. *Educational Psychology, 25,* 585–599.

McKenzie, K. B., & Scheurich, J. J. (2004). Equity traps: A useful construct for preparing principals to lead schools that are successful with racially diverse students. *Educational Administration Quarterly, 40*(50), 601–632.

Mendez-Morse, S. (2004, November). *Emerging non-racist educational leaders: White aspirants constructing the "other."* Paper presented at the annual meeting of the University Council for Educational Administration, Kansas City, MO.

Merseth, K. K. (1991). *The case for cases in teacher education.* Washington, DC: American Association of Colleges for Teacher Education.

Messinger, M. G. (1939). *The non-teaching elementary school principal in the state of New Jersey.* Collegeville, PA: The Independent.

Meyer, M. J. (2001). Reflective leadership training in practice using theatre as representation. *International Journal of Leadership in Education, 4*(2), 149–169.

Mezirow, J. (1991). *Transformative dimensions of adult learning.* San Francisco: Jossey-Bass.

Mezirow, J. (1997). Transformative learning: Theory to practice. *New Directions for Adult and Continuing Education, 74,* 5–12.

Miller, E. (1987). *A new balance: Reshaping the principalship. A special report to the profession.* Eugene, OR: Clearinghouse of Educational Management. (ERIC Document Reproduction Service No. ED290200)

Milstein, M. (1990, October). *Preparing educational leaders for rural school districts: New Mexico's state-wide collaborative approach.* Paper presented at the annual meeting of the University Council for Educational Administration, Pittsburgh, PA.

Monroe, T. (2000, November). *Moving administrative preparation "out of the box": A data-based discussion of three experimental initiatives.* Paper presented at the annual meeting of the University Council for Educational Administration, Albuquerque, NM.

Monroe, T. (2003). *Key concepts that inform group relations work.* San Diego, CA: The Leadership Institute.

Monroe, T. (2004). Boundaries and authority. In G. R. Goethals, G. J. Sorenson, & J. MacGregor Burns (Eds.), *Encyclopedia of Leadership: Vol. 1* (pp. 112–117). Thousand Oaks, CA: Sage.

Murphy, J. (1998). Preparation of the school principalship: The United States' story [Electronic version]. *School Leadership and Management, 18*, 359–372.

Murphy, M. J., Martin, W. M., Ford, S. M., & Muth, R. (1996, October). *Problem-based learning: An idea whose time has come.* Paper presented at the annual meeting of the University Council for Educational Administration, Louisville, KY.

Murtadha, K., & Watts, D. M. (2005). Linking the struggle for education and social justice: Historical perspectives of African American leadership in schools. *Educational Administration Quarterly, 41*, 591–608.

Muth, R. (2000). Toward a learning-oriented instructional paradigm: Implications for practice. In P. M. Jenlink (Ed.), *Marching into the new millennium: Challenges to educational leadership* (pp. 82–103). Lanham, MD: Scarecrow.

Muth, R., Murphy, M., & Martin, W. M. (1994). Problem-based learning at the University of Colorado at Denver. *Journal of School Leadership, 4*(4), 432–450.

Nagle, J. M., & Nagle, E. E. (1978). Doctoral programs in educational administration. In P. F. Silver & D. W. Spuck (Eds.), *Preparatory programs for educational administrators in the United States* (pp. 114–149). Columbus, OH: University Council for Educational Administration.

National Commission on Excellence in Education. (1983). *A nation at risk: The imperative for educational reform.* Washington, DC: U.S. Department of Education.

Nelson, J. O. (1993, November). *School system simulation: An effective model for educational leaders.* Paper presented at the annual meeting of the Mid-South Educational Research Association, New Orleans, LA. (ERIC Document Reproduction Service No. ED371444)

Noddings, N. (1984). *Caring: A feminine approach to ethics and moral education.* Berkeley: University of California Press.

Norton, M. M. (1992, April). *Problem-based learning through case studies and simulations: Historical overview and current assessment.* Paper presented at the San Francisco Forum on Problem Based Learning, Danforth Foundation and the National Policy Board for Educational Administration.

Norton, M. M., & Lester, P. E. (1998). *K–12 case studies for school administrators.* London: Taylor & Francis.

Ohde, K. L., & Murphy, J. (1993). The development of expertise: Implications for school administrators. In P. Hallinger, K. Leithwood, & J. Murphy (Eds.), *Cognitive perspectives on educational leadership* (pp. 75–87). New York: Teachers College Press.

Opsal, C., Brunner, C. C., & Virnig, S. (2005, November). *Unprecedented liberation, unparalleled leadership: The case of a deaf school administrator's superintendency preparation experience.* Paper presented at the annual meeting of the University Council for Educational Administration, Nashville, TN.

Osterman, K. F. (1990). The Silver Center for reflective principals. *UCEA Review, 31*(2), 9–10.

Osterman, K. F. (1998, April). *Using constructivism and reflective practice to bridge the theory/practice gap.* Paper presented at the annual meeting of the American Educational Research Association, San Diego, CA. (ERIC Document Reproduction Service No. ED435518)

Osterman, K. F., & Fishbein, S. (2001, April). *Reshaping the administration internship through research and reflective practice.* Paper presented at the annual meeting of the American Educational Research Association, Seattle, WA. (ERIC Document Reproduction Service No. ED463275)

Osterman, K. F., & Kottkamp, R. B. (1993). *Reflective practice for educators: Improving schools through professional development.* Newbury Park, CA: Corwin.

Osterman, K. F., & Kottkamp, R. B. (2004). *Reflective practice for educators: Professional development to improve student learning* (2nd ed.). Thousand Oaks, CA: Corwin.

Oxford English dictionary (2nd ed.). (1989). Oxford, England: Clarendon Press.

Pace, N. J. (2004). You've got to talk him out of it [Electronic version]. *Principal Leadership, 4*(9), 24–39.

Pareek, U., & Rao, T. V. (1981). *Handbook for training in educational management—With special reference to countries in Asia and the Pacific.* Bangkok, Thailand: United Nations Educational, Scientific, and Cultural Organization. (ERIC Document Reproduction Service No. ED324746)

Parra, J. L. (1996). *Geographic information systems in school administration: Processes, products, and perceptions in the teaching case method.* Unpublished doctoral dissertation, Columbia University Teachers College, New York.

Perkins, D. N., & Salomon, G. (1989). Are cognitive skills context-bound? *Educational Researcher, 18*, 16–25.

Perreault, G., & Bradshaw, L. (1998). Integrating simulations, extended internships, and portfolios in a principal preparation program. In R. Muth & M. Martin (Eds.), *Toward the Year 2000: Leadership for quality schools. The sixth annual yearbook of the National Council of Professors of Educational Administration* (pp. 247–257). Lancaster, PA: Technomic.

Phebe Sudlow: Iowa's first lady of education. (n.d.). Retrieved January 2, 2007, from the Davenforth Public Library Web site: http://www.qcmemory.org

Picus, L. O. (1992, April). *Computer simulation for school finance.* San Francisco: Danforth Foundation and National Policy Board for Educational Administration Forum.

Piele, P. K. (1970). *New programs for training school administrators. Analysis of literature and selected bibliography. Analysis and bibliography series, No. 10.* Eugene, OR: ERIC Clearinghouse on Educational Management. (ERIC Document Reproduction Service No. ED043119)

Pillai, R., & Stites-Doe, S. (Eds.). (2003). *Teaching leadership: Innovative approaches for the 21st century. Leadership horizons series.* Greenwich, CT: Information Age. (ERIC Document Reproduction Service No. ED481538)

Piltch, B., & Quinn, T. (2006). *Real time problem solving in schools: Case studies for school leaders.* Blue Ridge Summit, PA: Rowman & Littlefield.

Pohland, P. A. (1990, October). *Reflective practice and the internship in educational administration.* Paper presented at the annual meeting of the University Council for Educational Administration, Pittsburgh, PA.

Ponmanee, S. (1995, April). *Using problem based learning (PBL) in preparing the graduate: Students' readiness for research work.* Paper presented at the Advanced Institute in Problem-Based Learning, San Francisco.

Poppenhagen, B. W., & McArdle, R. J. (1982, July). *Computer simulation and decision-making: The preparation of mid-level managers for higher education.* Paper presented at the International Conference on Improving University Teaching, Berlin. (ERIC Document Reproduction Service No. ED224463)

Porter, K. E., & Snipes, J. C. (2006). *The challenge of supporting change: Elementary student achievement and the Bay Area School Reform Collaborative's focal strategy.* Oakland, CA: MDRC.

Prestine, N. A. (1995). Crisscrossing the landscape: Another turn at cognition and educational administration. *Educational Administration Quarterly, 31,* 134–142.

Prickett, R. L. (1990, August). *Assessment for instructional leadership.* Paper presented at the annual meeting of the National Council of Professors of Educational Administration, Los Angeles. (ERIC Document Reproduction Service No. ED341157)

Read, A. M., & Hausman, C. S. (1998, April). *Developing critically reflective leaders (and teachers of leaders) through reflexive self-study.* Paper presented at the annual meeting of the American Educational Research Association, San Diego, CA.

Repa, J. T. (1997). *Syllabus for E65.3015 Seminar in (Management) Theories of (Educational) Administration.* Retrieved February 18, 2008, from the New York University Web site: https://pages.nyu.edu/~jtr1/3015/3015syl.html

Resnick, L. B. (Ed.). (1989). *Knowing, learning, and instruction: Essays in honor of Robert Glaser.* Hillsdale, NJ: Erlbaum.

Reynolds, J. C. (1994). *The application of the knowledge base in the preparation of school leaders.* Eugene, OR: Clearinghouse for Educational Management. (ERIC Document Reproduction Service No. ED377558)

Rodriguez, D. M. (1995). *Application of geographic information systems in school administration: A teaching case of school redistricting.* Unpublished doctoral dissertation, Columbia University Teachers College, New York.

Rohr, K. K. (1984). Training administrators. *Spectrum, 2*(4), 14–19.

Rost, J. C. (1980). Human relations training in educational administration programs: A study based on a national survey. *Group and Organization Studies, 5,* 80–95.

Rowan, B. (1995a). Learning, teaching, and educational administration: Toward a research agenda. *Educational Administration Quarterly, 31*(3), 344–354.

Rowan, B. (1995b). Research on learning and teaching in K–12 schools: Implications for the field of educational administration. *Educational Administration Quarterly, 31*(1), 115–133.

Rusch, E. A. (2004, November). *Transformative learning: The foundation for transformative leadership.* Paper presented at the annual meeting of the University Council for Educational Administration, Kansas City, MO.

Rusch, E. A. (in press). Self-knowledge that transforms: A study of learning reflective practice. *Journal of Teaching in Higher Education.*

Sage. (2006). *Journal of Cases in Educational Leadership.* Retrieved December 27, 2006, from http://www.sagepub.com/journalsProdDesc.nav?prodId=Journal201765

Sagor, R. (2000). *Guiding school improvement with action research.* Alexandria, VA: Association of Supervision and Curriculum Development.

Sagor, R. (2005). *The action research guidebook: A four-step process.* Thousand Oaks, CA: Corwin

Scheurich, J., & Laible, J. (1995). The buck stops here—In our preparation programs: Educational leadership for all children (no exceptions allowed). *Educational Administration Quarterly, 31*(2), 313–322.

Scheurich J. J., & Skrla, L. (2003). *Leadership for equity and excellence: Creating high-achievement classrooms, schools, and districts.* Thousand Oaks, CA: Corwin Press.

Schmuck, R. A. (1992). *Beyond academics in the preparation of educational leaders: Four years of action research.* Eugene, OR: Clearinghouse for Educational Management. (ERIC Document Reproduction Service No. ED354610)

Schneider, G. T., & Wallich, L. (1990). Assessment centers as avenues to administrative career advancement. *Planning and Changing, 21*(4), 225–238.

Schön, D. A. (1987). *Educating the reflective practitioner.* San Francisco: Jossey-Bass.

Seigfried, C. H. (1996). *Pragmatism and feminism: Reweaving the social fabric.* Chicago: University of Chicago Press.

Sellers-Young, B. (1998). *Somatic processes: Convergence of theory and practice.* Baltimore: John Hopkins University Press.

Shackleford, M. C. (1998). *Narrowing the gap: The use of problem-based learning in administrator preparation.* Unpublished doctoral dissertation, Vanderbilt University, Nashville, TN.

Sherman, W. H., & Beaty, D. M. (2007). The use of distance technology in educational leadership preparation programs. *Journal of Educational Administration, 44*(5), 605–620.

Shirts, M. (1977). *Bafa Bafa: A simulation training system.* Retrieved January 15, 2008, from http://www.SimulationTrainingSystems.com

Shuell T. J. (1986). Cognitive conceptions of learning [Electronic version]. *Review of Educational Research, 56*, 411–436.

Shuell, T. J. (1990). Phases of meaningful learning [Electronic version]. *Review of Education Research, 60*, 531–547.

Shulman, L. S. (1992). Toward a pedagogy of cases. In J. H. Shulman (Ed.), *Case methods in teacher education* (pp. 1–30). New York: Teachers College Press.

Silver, P. F. (1979a, April). *Changes in preparation programs: 1974–1978.* Paper presented at the annual meeting of the American Educational Research Association, San Francisco.

Silver, P. F. (1979b, April). *Some needed developments in research for building a "theory of administrative practice."* Paper presented at the annual meeting of the American Educational Research Association, San Francisco.

Silver, P. F. (1984). Reflectiveness in the professions. *Case Report, 1*(1), 1–4.

Silver, P. F. (1986). Case records: A reflective practice approach to administrator development. *Theory Into Practice, 25*(3), 161–167.

Silver P. F., & Spuck, D. W. (Eds.). (1978). *Preparatory programs for educational administrators in the United States.* Columbus, OH: University Council for Educational Administration.

Silverberg, R. P., & Kottkamp, R. B. (2006). Language matters. *Journal of Research on Leadership Education, 1*(1), 1–5.

Simon, H. (1993). Decision making: Rational, nonrational, and irrational. *Educational Administration Quarterly, 29*(3), 392–441.

Skrla, L., Scheurich, J., Garcia, J., & Nolly, G. (2004, April). *Equity audits: A practical tool for increasing equity in schooling.* Paper presented at the annual meeting of the American Educational Research Association, New Orleans, LA.

Spuck, D., & Bozeman, W. C. (1988). Training school administrators in computer use. *Journal of Research on Computing in Education, 21*, 229–239.

Stammen, R. (1993). An assessment: Teaching educational administration courses over a statewide interactive video network. *Educational Planning, 9*(2), 11–21.

Stringer, E. (2004). *Action research in education.* Upper Saddle River, NJ: Pearson Merrill Prentice Hall.

Sudzina, M. R. (Ed.). (1999). *Case study applications for teacher education: Cases of teaching and learning in the content areas.* Boston: Allyn and Bacon.

Sykes, G. (1989). Learning to teach with cases. *Colloquy, 2*, 7–13.

Tanner, C. K., Keedy, J. L., & Galis, S. A. (1997). Problem-based learning: Relating the "real world" to principalship preparation. *Clearinghouse, 68*(3), 154–157.

Theoharis, G. (2007). Social justice educational leaders and resistance: Toward a theory of social justice leadership. *Educational Administration Quarterly, 43*, 221–258. Retrieved January 2, 2008, from http://eaq.sagepub.com

Tillman, L. (2004). African American principals and the legacy of *Brown. Review of Research in Education, 28*, 101–146.

Tracy, S. J., & Schutenberg, E .M. (1990). Do assessment centers promote educational administrator development? An initial study. *Planning and Change, 21*(1), 13–25.

Tripses, J., & Hatfield, K. (2004, April). *Social change agents: Counselors, principals, and human service administrators' action for social justice.* Paper presented at the annual meeting of the American Educational Research Association, Montreal, Quebec, Canada.

Tripses, J. S., & Risen, M. (2005, April). *Social change agents: Counselors, principals, and human service administrators' action for social justice.* Paper presented at the annual meeting of the American Educational Research association, Montreal, Quebec, Canada.

UCEA Cases Project issues call. (1994). *UCEA Review, 35*(3), 5.

Urgenson, S. H. (1994). *Applications of geographic information systems in school administration: Development and evaluation of teaching cases.* Unpublished doctoral dissertation, Columbia University Teachers College, New York.

Valesky, T. (2006). *Interactive case study simulations in educational leadership.* Retrieved April 28, 2008, from http://cnx. org/content/m1400/latest/

Van Patten, J. J., & Holt, C. (2002, April). *Using distance education to teach educational leadership.* Paper presented at the annual meeting of the American Educational Research Association, New Orleans, LA. (ERIC Document Reproduction Service No. ED468529)

Van Tassel-Baska, J. (1998). A study of problem-based learning in teaching educational administration courses. In R. Muth & M. Martin (Eds.), *Toward the Year 2000: Leadership for quality schools. The sixth annual yearbook of the National Council of Professors of Educational Administration* (pp. 279–288). Lancaster, PA: Technomic.

Veir, C. A. (1990, October). *Perspectives on the future: Identifying potential leaders through pre-admittance assessment.* Paper presented at the annual meeting of the University Council for Educational Administration, Pittsburgh, PA. (ERIC Document Reproduction Service No. ED326962)

Voit, L. B. (1989). *Perceptions and evaluations of university principal preparation programs by Michigan public school principals.* Unpublished doctoral dissertation, Western Michigan University, Kalamazoo.

Waldron, B., & Joines, R. (1994, June). *Introduction to assessment centers.* Paper presented at the Conference on Public Personnel Assessment, Charleston, SC.

Webb, L. D., & McCarthy, M. M. (1998). Ella Flagg Young: Pioneer of democratic school administration. *Educational Administration Quarterly, 34*, 223–242.

Weishaar, M. K., & Borsa, J.C. (2004). *Inclusive educational administration: A case study approach.* Long Grove, IL: Waveland Press.

Welty, W. (1989). Discussion method teaching: How to make it work. *Change, 21,* 41–49.

Wendel, F. C., Yusten, C., & Gappa, L. (1989). *Measurement practices used in the certification of educators.* Reston, VA: National Association of Secondary School Principals. (ERIC Document Reproduction Service No. ED310547)

Wendel, F. C., & Baack, L. T. (1992). *The effect of assessment upon developmental activities.* Lincoln: University of Nebraska. (ERIC Document Reproduction Service No. ED352699)

Westhuizen, P. C. van der. (1988, April). *Implementing an assessment centre in educational management training at universities.* Paper presented at the annual meeting of the British Educational Management and Administration Society, Cardiff, Wales, UK. (ERIC Document Reproduction Service No. ED 371437)

Wildman, L. (1988). *Where will LEAD lead?* (ERIC Document Reproduction Service No. ED318078)

Williams, G. (1985, August). The case method: An approach to teaching and learning in educational administration. In *The Professional Preparation and Development of Educational Administrators in Commonwealth Developing Areas: A Symposium,* Barbados. (ERIC Document Reproduction Service No. EA018975)

Willower, D. J., & Forsyth, P. B. (1998). A brief history of scholarship on educational administration. In J. Murphy & K. S. Louis (Eds.), *Handbook of research on educational administration* (2nd ed., pp. 1–23). San Francisco: Jossey-Bass.

Witters-Churchill, L. J. (1988). *University preparation of the school administrator: Evaluation by Texas principals.* Unpublished doctoral dissertation, Texas A&M University, College Station.

Witters-Churchill, L. J. (1991). University preparation of school principals. *School Organization, 11,* 339–345.

Witters-Churchill, L. J., & Erlandson, D. A. (Eds.). (1990). *The principalship in the 1990s and beyond: Current research on performance-based preparation and professional development. UCEA monograph series.* Austin, TX: University Council for Educational Administration.

Yekovich, F. R. (1993). A theoretical view of the development of expertise in credit administration. In P. Hallinger, K. Leithwood, & J. Murphy (Eds.), *Cognitive perspectives on educational leadership* (pp. 146–169). New York: Teachers College Press.

9

The Use of Internships in Preparing School Leaders

BRUCE G. BARNETT, MICHAEL A. COPLAND, AND ALAN R. SHOHO

Internships, practica, and field experiences have been touted as important ingredients to preparing effective school leaders. Clinical experiences have been incorporated in educational leadership preparation programs for over 50 years (Chance, 1991; Foster & Ward, 1998). Initially borrowed from the field of medicine, internships were intended as a means for practitioners to gain experience near the completion of their formal preparation (Milstein, Bobroff, & Restine, 1991). The focus on practical experience has been described in a variety of ways; however, in their description of internships in educational leadership preparation, Fry, Bottoms, and O'Neill (2005) explained,

> A well-designed internship expands the knowledge and skills of candidates while also gauging their ability to apply new learning in authentic settings as they contend with problems that have real-world consequences. Built right, the internship becomes a sturdy vessel upon which new practitioners can navigate the swift, unpredictable currents that separate classroom theory and on-the-job reality. (p. 3)

In reviewing internships in the field of educational leadership preparation, the purpose of this chapter is to examine the literature describing how internships have been implemented and the effects these clinical experiences have had on aspiring school leaders. To achieve this purpose, we begin by describing the methodology used to review, code, and summarize empirical and nonempirical research dealing with internships. We then provide contextual background about internships, summarizing their historical development in leadership preparation; the purpose and value of these clinical experiences; and criticisms lodged by practitioners, professional associations, and university professors. Next, we examine the types of clinical experiences educational leadership programs currently are implementing and then describe empirical findings about the effects of these experiences on aspiring school leaders. Finally, we conclude by critiquing the existing research literature, exposing weaknesses, and proposing future research to address these shortcomings.

Methodology

In developing this chapter, we conducted an extensive review of literature on internships from various sources, including respected journals in the field of educational administration (e.g., *Journal of Educational Administration, Journal of School Leadership, Educational Administration Quarterly, Planning and Changing*), conference papers from major gatherings in the field (American

Educational Research Association, National Council of Professors of Educational Administration [NCPEA], University Council for Educational Administration [UCEA]), as well as relevant books and chapters. In addition, we reviewed technical reports from organizations focused on policy and practice within educational administration (e.g., Southern Regional Education Board, National Policy Board for Educational Administration [NPBEA], National College for School Leadership), doctoral dissertations, ERIC documents, and various publications from professional organizations in the field (e.g., *AASA Professor, UCEA Review, Teaching in Educational Administration Newsletter*).

We employed a coding scheme to organize documents and guide the analysis. In coding empirical studies, we adapted the Murphy and Vriesenga (2004) category system of recording information on each study's research design, sample, timeframe, and means of data collection (observation, questionnaire, interview, focus group, test, document analysis). We located 29 empirical studies specifically dealing with administrative internships, 12 of which were dissertations (see Table 9.1

Table 9.1 Empirical Studies of Internships in Educational Leadership Preparation

Work by author	Design	Sample	Timeframe	Data collection
1. Bales, 1997	Quantitative	Schools and Staffing Survey national database	One time	Survey: secondary analysis
2. Bradshaw & Buckner, 2000	Mixed method	39 interns in one program	One time	Survey: time spent on internship activities, opportunities to do tasks, recommendations for internships
3. Bratlien, 1993	Quantitative	190 interns in one program	Longitudinal: eight cohorts over 8 years	Survey: rank ordering of entry-level competence and importance for career development
4. Browne-Ferrigno, 2003	Qualitative case study	18 interns in one program	1 year	Interviews, meeting observations, participant narrative questionnaire
5. Cordeiro & Sloan-Smith, 1996	Naturalistic	18 interns and 18 mentors in one program	2 years	Interviews, audiotapes of mentor-intern sessions, artifacts (logs, journals)
6. Daresh, 1986a	Qualitative	36 UCEA institutions	One time	Document analysis: descriptions of field-based activities
7. Daresh, 1986b	Qualitative	12 first- and second-year principals	1 year	Interviews: conditions for supportive professional development
8. Daresh & Playko, 1992	Qualitative	One cohort of principal mentors	One time	Interviews with mentors
9. Finn-Pike, 1999	Qualitative: participant observation	One student intern	One time	Field notes: intern's tasks
10. Fishbein, 2000	Qualitative	9 preservice principal candidates	1 year	Questionnaires and journal documents, semistructured interviews, and audiotaped internship seminar sessions
11. Fry, Bottoms, & O'Neill, 2005	Quantitative	61 preparation programs	One time	Survey: types of activities interns engage in and features of preparation programs
12. Geismar, Morris, & Lieberman, 2000	Quantitative	91 principals	One time	Survey of mentoring competencies needed when working with interns

Table 9.1 Continued

Work by author	Design	Sample	Timeframe	Data collection
13. Gregory, 1993	Quantitative	12 matched pairs of students in two programs	1 year	Survey measuring interns' reflectivity and personal vision
14. Gutterman, 1994	Case study: qualitative	Faculty and students in one program	One time	Observations, interviews, document analysis of interns' experiences
15. Harris, Crocker, & Hopson, 2002	Quantitative	57 interns in one program	One time	Survey: rating of issues mentors discuss with interns
16. Hung, 2001	Mixed method	One program cohort ($N = 25$)	One time	Surveys and interviews of internship elements
17. Keller, 1994	Mixed method	Six intern-mentor dyads	One time	Questionnaires, semantic index instrument, interviews
18. Layton, 1989	Quantitative	30 preparation program graduates with/without internships	One time	Randomized survey
19. Leithwood, Jantzi, Coffin, & Wilson, 1996	Quantitative	11 preparation programs	One time	Survey: value of preparation program elements and colleagues' views of graduates' leadership qualities
20. MacDonald, 2003	Mixed methods	128 educational leadership students	One time	Reasoning About Current Issues test, Experience & Background Inventory, focus group
21. McKerrow, 1998	Qualitative	45 interns in two preparation programs	One time	Document analysis: logs of internship experience
22. Mercado, 2002	Critical ethnography	36 interns in one preparation program	1 year	Interviews focused on internship benefits
23. Notar, 1989	Mixed method	46 mentors in one preparation program	One time	Survey: rating of interns' performance on activities; open-ended responses of interns' strengths and areas for improvement
24. Ovando, 2000	Qualitative	4 interns in one preparation program	One time	Interviews: personal and professional transformation to leadership role
25. Playko & Daresh, 1990	Qualitative case studies	4 prospective principals (while teachers)	1 year (approx.)	Reflective interviews
26. Schmuck, 1993	Action research	Graduates of experimental 2-year program	4 years	Action research (including interviews, focus groups, reflective journals, informal surveys)
27. Spear, 2005	Quantitative: ANOVA	90 Washington state principal program graduates from 1 year	One time	Survey
28. Wells, 1980	Quantitative: ANOVA	131 former ed admin interns from Texas	One time	Survey
29. White & Crow, 1993	Qualitative	54 Bank Street College ed admin interns	1 year	Participants journals, focus groups, reflective papers, field notes

for a summary of these 29 empirical studies). In coding nonempirical studies or other materials, we slightly modified the Murphy and Vriesenga categorization system by noting whether the piece primarily was a program description (5 references), literature review (21 references), or an essay or opinion (18 references).

The Context of Internships in Educational Leadership Preparation

Internships have been used in the preparation of school leaders since the 1940s. Despite this long history, debates continue regarding the best way to structure internships and the relative merits of these clinical experiences. To set the context for our discussion of internships, we begin by summarizing the history of their use in preparation programs, their purported goals and values, and criticisms of internship implementation.

History of Internships

Originally, internships were seen as essential because similar experiences were being required for student teachers (Campbell, Fleming, Newell, & Bennion, 1987). The intent was to allow students to apply information under the supervision of university faculty members and practitioners (Morgan, Gibbs, Hertzog, & Wylie, 1997). Based on this rationale, internships have a long history in the preparation of educational leaders and were first introduced in the 1940s at the University of Chicago and the University of Nebraska (Davies, 1962; McKerrow, 1998; Wheaton, 1950). During their annual meeting in 1947, the NCPEA encouraged the use of internships; by 1950, 17 universities were using internships (Milstein et al., 1991; Short & Price, 1992). The decades of the 1950s and 1960s saw increased calls for clinical experiences in universities. For instance, the preparation program at the University of Maryland advocated for full-time internships (Calabrese & Straut, 1999), and the Kellogg Foundation established the Cooperative Program in Educational Administration by supporting eight universities to use internships, including prestigious institutions such as Harvard, Teachers College at Columbia, and Ohio State University (Milstein et al., 1991). As a result, in the late 1950s and early 1960s, there was a fourfold increase in programs offering internships; however, participation in these clinical experiences was not required, resulting in low enrollments (Murphy, 1992; Ovando, 2000).

This increased attention on internships and program expansion continued for the next two decades. For instance, in the 1960s, 117 institutions of higher education required internships (Hencley, 1963), and from 1940–1970, Educational Specialist, Master of Arts, and EdD programs tripled and PhD programs doubled (Miklos, 1983). This surge of interest was captured by Greenfield (1975):

> Training [of educational administrators] should move away from attempts to teach a broad social science of organizations-in-general towards a familiarity with specific organizations and their problems. That the training should continue to have critical and reflective dimensions should not conflict with this redirection of training programmes. It appears essential also for training programmes to develop a much stronger clinical base than is now common in most of them. In such training, both the theoretician and the practitioner must be intimately involved. (p. 98)

By the 1980s, 25 states required an internship experience for certification (Cordeiro & Sloan-Smith, 1996). These numbers swelled, so that 220 of 252 (87%) universities were using internships by 1990, and 65% required internship for state certification (Milstein et al., 1991; Skalski et al., 1987).

Although internships became part of the formal curriculum, the amount of time devoted to field experiences varied widely. For example, during the 1990s, the average required time in the field was 165 hours (Milstein et al., 1991), UCEA institutions averaged 280 hours (Pautler, 1990), and programs affiliated with the Danforth Program for the Preparation of School Principals averaged 632 hours (Cordeiro, Krueger, Parks, Restine, & Wilson, 1992; Cordeiro & Sloan-Smith, 1996). Despite efforts to increase the number of internship hours in educational leadership preparation programs, they still fall far short of expectations in graduate programs in other disciplines. For example, during the residency component of their graduate education, medical students must complete 80 hours of supervised work per week for 1 year (McLean, 2005; Sectish, Zalneraitis, Carraccio, & Behrman, 2004). Many architecture graduate programs require students to enroll in full-time internships for up to 28 weeks, and the American Institute of Architects (n.d.) requires at least 2 years of internship experience in an architectural firm prior to being eligible to obtain a license.

Within the last decade, calls for reemphasizing internships have surfaced (e.g., Cordeiro & Sloan-Smith, 1996; Glasman & Glasman, 1997; NPBEA, 1995), especially in preparing leaders capable of leading school improvement for improved student learning (McCarthy, 1999). Other trends in the literature on internships encourage full-time internships, student cohorts, school–university partnerships, and quality mentorship experiences (Gregory, 1993).

Goals and Value of Internships

The medical profession provided the genesis of internships in the field of education. For instance, internship experiences in osteopathic medicine are intended to facilitate independent decision making, self-assurance, knowledge development, and integration (Smith, 2004). Similarly, biomedical engineering degree programs expect internships to affect their students' critical thinking, career goals and orientation, professional development, and relationships with the industry (Purdue University Weldon School of Biomedical Engineering, 2006). Therefore, administrative internships, similar to the student teaching experience, have been viewed as an essential capstone experience for preparing effective school leaders (Capasso & Daresh, 2001). Although most internship experiences allow aspirants to engage in leadership tasks conducted by principals and assistant principals, many graduates of preparation programs take on other leadership roles in schools (e.g., department or grade-level chairs) or district offices (e.g., curriculum coordinators, professional development directors). Nevertheless, as highlighted by Greenfield's (1975) earlier quotation, internships provide opportunities to merge theory, research, and practice, an expectation reiterated by recent writers and commissions (Bratlien, 1993; Chance, 1991; National Commission on Excellence in Educational Administration, 1987). Through the process of reflection, aspirants are encouraged to compare and contrast theories of leadership with actual practices in schools (Daresh, 1988; McKerrow, 1998; Milstein, 1990).

The goals or purposes of internships have been identified at two levels: general, or global, outcomes and specific outcomes. At a global level, practicum experiences have been espoused as a means for aspirants to become independent learners (Duley, 1978), practice responsible citizenship (Duley, 1978), and increase self-confidence in their leadership abilities (Creighton & Johnson, 2002; Geismar, Morris, & Lieberman, 2000; Milstein et al., 1991). When describing specific outcomes associated with the internship experience, the literature revealed numerous illustrations. Perhaps the most-often mentioned goal is for potential school leaders to increase their knowledge and skills in communicating, organizing, collaborating, and managing resources (Chance, 1991; Daresh, 1988; Fry et al., 2005; Milstein, 1990; Milstein & Krueger, 1993; NPBEA, 2002). Milstein (1990) made this point explicitly:

> The purpose of clinical experiences is to enable students to be exposed to reality-based programs that permit a balance between *learning about* and *learning how* and that are rooted in a

solid foundation of *learning why*. In the process, students should have multiple opportunities to demonstrate mastery of those skills and knowledge traditionally required of administrative positions as well as those that have not yet been clearly identified but that may be required in the future. (p. 122, emphasis in original)

Besides skill attainment, at least four other espoused outcomes have been identified in the literature:

1. Identify problems and solutions aimed at school improvement and student achievement (Bradshaw, Perreault, McDowelle, & Bell, 1997; Edmonson, 2003; Fry et al., 2005; Jackson & Kelley, 2002).
2. Promote social justice and change in multiple settings, including social service agencies (Pounder, Reitzug, & Young, 2002).
3. Gain insights and awareness about the duties of administrators, such as budget, district operations, and program and personnel evaluation (Chance, 1991; Daresh, 1988; Milstein et al., 1991).
4. Increase commitment to and understanding of a career in school administration (Daresh, 1988; Duley, 1978; McKerrow, 1998).

Although the literature mainly has focused on how aspiring school leaders benefit from engaging in internships, school districts also may derive value from having interns in their schools. For instance, Milstein et al. (1991) claimed that districts benefit in four ways, by (a) identifying high-quality teachers to become administrators, (b) involving them in meaningful leadership experiences, (c) increasing the number of staff who have a comprehensive view of school administration, and (d) evaluating interns' performance prior to appointment.

Criticisms of Internships

Although internships continue to be hailed as an important aspect of leadership preparation, there have been substantial criticisms leveled at their use. In the current era of accountability, one concern is that "too much emphasis has been placed on efficiency and expediency in internships, without a convincing demonstration of effectiveness" (Geismar et al., 2000, p. 234). Recent attacks on educational leadership preparation programs reinforced the notion that little empirical evidence exists regarding the value added to educators who complete graduate programs (e.g., Brent, 1998; Brent & Haller, 1998; Levine, 2005). (Later in this chapter we return to this issue regarding the lack of empirical evidence about how internships have influenced aspirants' actions and attitudes.) Other critics have voiced concerns about (a) inadequate field support and connection with practice, (b) lack of meaningful tasks, and (c) inadequate university support. These issues are explored below.

Field Support and Connection With Practice

A host of problems have been identified as interns are placed in schools. Even with the call for implementing school–university partnerships, there is growing concern there are not enough quality field sites and mentors (i.e., practicing or retired administrators) with whom interns can work (Anderson, 1989; McKerrow, 1998; Milstein, 1990). Similarly, once they have been placed in school settings, questions have been raised about the lack of ongoing support and monitoring for interns (Fry et al., 2005; Milstein, 1990; Pautler, 1990). Because most educational leadership students complete their internships in the same schools where they are teachers, they may not be working alongside highly qualified mentor principals. Finally, the selection and preparation of mentors have been called into question (Barnett, 1991; Crocker & Harris, 2002; Jackson & Kelley, 2002). Muse, Thomas, and Wasden (1992) noted the inherent, and often unaddressed, problems with mentorships: (a) personal agendas of mentors, (b) protective and controlling nature of some mentors, (c) inability of mentors to acknowledge interns' limitations, (d) tendency for interns to become too dependent on mentors, and (e) lack of female mentors. Tillman (2005) has acknowledged another shortcoming, the paucity of educators from underrepresented ethnic groups who are asked to serve as mentors.

Tasks in the Field

One of the espoused purposes of internships is to assist future administrators in identifying problems and assessing the viability of various solutions. Unfortunately, many programs have been criticized because the tasks interns engage in are not linked to meaningful problems of practice, particularly aimed at improved student learning (Creighton, 2002; Dubin, 1987; Fulmer, Muth, & Reiter, 2004; Milstein, 1990; Murphy, 1992). Engaging in menial activities—such as observation, committee work, attendance, lunch and bus duty—tends to predominate (Creighton, 2002; Edmonson, 2003; Fry et al., 2005; Murphy, 1992). Although much of the literature includes speculation about the types of tasks interns are asked to complete, the Southern Regional Education Board's extensive questionnaire study of 61 educational leadership preparation programs in their service region revealed many programs overlook these seven important tasks in their internships (Fry et al., 2005):

1. Of the 61 programs, 66% do not require interns to engage in activities related to student achievement and school improvement.
2. Three quarters do not require interns to assess and develop effective instructional practices.
3. Further, 85% do not require interns to serve on literacy and numeracy task forces.
4. Of the programs, 66% do not require interns to assess student learning.
5. Half do not require interns to analyze school-level data.
6. Half do not require interns to plan, develop, and implement professional development.
7. Finally, 75% of the programs do not require interns to acquire resources aimed at school improvement.

University Guidance

Although most, if not all, universities require an internship, critics contend that often these experiences are delivered haphazardly. The most-often cited criticism is the disconnection between program content and field experiences. In many instances, seminars and analytical activities are sporadic or nonexistent (Dubin, 1987; Milstein, 1990), and little or no direct connection exists between clinical experiences and coursework (Cambron-McCabe, 1999). University supervisors (i.e., full- or part-time department faculty) are expected to visit schools and mentors, facilitate reflective seminars, assist interns in documenting tasks, and intervene if problems arise between mentors and interns; however, serious questions have been raised about the amount and quality of oversight they actually provide (Milstein et al., 1991). Another shortcoming is the lack of attention devoted to mentors' involvement in the program. In many cases, mentors are not thoroughly screened or prepared for their role (Barnett, 1991; Calabrese & Straut, 1999; Crocker & Harris, 2002; McKerrow, 1998). Finally, interns themselves have expressed concerns with the timing of the internship and the short duration of the experience (Gutterman, 1994).

Current Designs and Uses of Internships

In 2006, Murphy indicated that two trends were responsible for the "revitalization of the internship" (p. 53) in educational leadership preparation programs. First, there was increased emphasis on field-based activities directly affecting student learning (e.g., shadowing and interviewing administrators, working on projects affecting students and teachers). Second, more partnerships between university preparation programs and school districts were being forged. As a consequence of these partnerships, Murphy (2006) asserted that the role of practitioners in advising program content and field experiences was legitimized by university faculty. Whether this legitimization of practitioners has translated into greater value being placed on the internship is still debatable.

To determine current internship requirements operating in educational leadership preparation programs across the country, we contacted 48 programs (43 were UCEA institutions). Based on the returns from 40 of these institutions, we found increasing variability in the quality and quantity of specific internship requirements and activities. For example, some internship programs have undertaken substantive transformation from earlier models, which emphasized administrative and managerial skill sets and activities, to designs that reflect instructional leadership, data-driven analysis, and student learning. However, a number of internship programs remain mired in the past, reflecting a disconnect between what principals actually do and what university preparation programs provide aspiring principals (Fry et al., 2005). In addition, in a few states administrative internships have been dropped due to a condition of employment (e.g., Hawaii) or have been made an elective rather than a requirement (e.g., New Jersey). Despite the variability of internship experiences, Murphy's (2006) characterization of administrative internships being revitalized in the field appears to be accurate and also is consistent with what Evers and Gallagher (1994) proposed for internships and field experiences in the 1990s. Only time will tell whether this revitalization of the internship is sustained and widely implemented or just an aberration of innovative programs on the leading edge.

Types of Internship Designs

Carr, Chenoweth, and Ruhl (2003) identified four types of internship experiences: (a) independent, (b) interdependent, (c) embedded, and (d) apprenticeship. From our investigation of internship programs, we have slightly altered their typology, noting that three internship designs tend to dominate the 40 leadership preparation programs we reviewed: (a) full-time, job-embedded internships; (b) detached internships; and (c) course-embedded field experiences in lieu of an internship. These designs deal with the substance and duration of the internship experience. This section describes each of these internship designs by illustrating various required activities and examining the underlying rationale for their inclusion within preparation programs. The section concludes by pointing out several trends affecting current designs and uses of internships and field experiences for aspiring principals.

Full-Time, Job-Embedded Internships

The full-time, job-embedded internship is considered the ideal model for aspiring principals (Carr et al., 2003). This design allows aspiring principals to be immersed in on-the-job learning during their internship experience. While this design represents a small number of internship programs across the country, its appeal is growing, especially if preparation programs are able to establish strong linkages with school districts or capitalize on legislative mandates. For instance, Brigham Young University (BYU) has established a long-standing partnership with Provo (Utah) area school districts, and North Carolina legislation supports full-time paid internship in partnership with local school districts. North Carolina State University (NCSU) and the University of North

Carolina at Chapel Hill (UNC) participate in this program, where interns are paid a $35,000 annual salary for 10 months.

Besides the full-time, job-embedded nature of the BYU internship, other innovative and unique characteristics support the program (BYU, 2007). Interns are required to engage in three field experiences of 12–13 weeks in two schools within their contracted district and in one school outside their contracted district. By providing interns with multisite and multidistrict experiences, interns learn about differing organizational cultures and their operating norms as well as about the degree of vertical and horizontal alignment within the district. The BYU internship is framed around four tenets of leadership: (a) strategic leadership, (b) instructional leadership, (c) operational leadership, and (d) personal leadership. Each of these tenets of leadership is aligned with activities meant to improve student learning. For example, instructional leadership encompasses a variety of areas, including human resources (e.g., staffing, supervision, training, and evaluation) and pedagogy and curriculum (e.g., applied technology, vocational and special programs, and accountability). Emphasizing the human resource element in conjunction with pedagogy and curriculum allows interns to engage in instructional activities geared towards changing the role of the principal from manager to instructional leader. This strong emphasis in instructional leadership fosters the knowledge and skills required to develop professional learning communities as touted by DuFour and Eaker (1998).

Additionally, NCSU and UNC provide two examples of full-time, job-embedded internships. At both NCSU and UNC, the internship program is framed around the Interstate School Leaders Licensure Consortium (ISLLC) and Educational Leadership Constituent Council standards. The full-time, year-long, job-embedded internship is a product of a North Carolina legislative mandate, which provides funding ($35,000 per intern) to support highly selective interns to participate in this internship. In addition to the job-embedded internship, both institutions offer detached internships for students in their regular program.

At NCSU, the internship experience is conceptually framed around the dual themes of learn, educate, apply, and demonstrate (LEAD) and scholarly, ethical, reflective, value diversity, and experienced (SERVE). LEAD represents four forms of knowledge: (a) general pedagogy, (b) content-specific pedagogical strategies, (c) content or discipline knowledge, and (d) knowledge of school settings and their historical perspectives. SERVE focuses on the dispositional qualities of the intern (e.g., being ethical, practicing reflection, and valuing diversity). It is noteworthy that the LEAD portion of the framework is focused on leading through instruction, whereas the SERVE portion of the framework focuses on the interns' emotional and social intelligences (Goleman, 1996, 2006).

Unlike NCSU, the UNC program stresses the themes of social justice and leadership for equity in their internship program. As noted in UNC (2005) mission statement,

> Leadership for equity, social justice, and academic excellence is the conceptual framework for the educational leadership program at the University of North Carolina at Chapel Hill. While we believe that school principals must be proficient in a wide variety of technical skills and tasks to be successful educational administrators, we are first and foremost concerned with the agenda of constructing democratic learning communities which are positioned in the larger society to support an agenda of social action which removes all forms of injustice. (p. 4)

What is unique about UNC's social justice stance is not its appearance of advocacy. Although a growing number of educational leadership preparation programs espouse the value of diversity, UNC's infusion of social justice in students' field experiences addresses an aspect of preparation that Pounder, Reitzug, and Young (2002) maintained has been overlooked in many leadership preparation programs.

One last common, albeit unique, aspect of NCSU and UNC's internship programs is the importance placed on the selection and preparation of mentors for interns. Unlike many internship programs, mentors are not taken for granted. Specific mentoring responsibilities and duties are identified, and mentors are prepared to support their assigned interns.

Detached Internships

A second type of internship design is the detached internship, which continues to be the most prevalent type of internship design used in preparation programs today. In 1992, when Murphy noted that 90% of preparation programs required an internship, a majority of those programs featured detached models of internship. While the detached model continues to dominate the internship landscape, there is wide variability among the depth and breadth of the internship requirements. In some cases there are minimal hourly requirements for interns to document, whereas in other cases the internship is a multisemester, multisite experience requiring hundreds or thousands of hours. Of the 40 internship programs we reviewed, the average requirement is approximately 300 hours, an increase from what Pautler (1990) and Milstein et al. (1991) found in earlier studies. However, this requirement is less than 50% of what was expected at Danforth-funded programs operating in the 1980s and 1990s (Cordeiro et al., 1992; Cordeiro & Sloan-Smith, 1996).

For most detached internships, interns are required to document through a portfolio a list of required activities and write a reflective journal. In contrast to what Fry et al. (2005) reported, our review of 40 internship programs suggests changes may be occurring in the types of activities in which interns engage. Instead of conducting routine tasks (e.g., disciplining students, running faculty meetings, supervising students during lunch), interns are participating in instructionally related activities (e.g., analyzing data, designing professional development programs). Two of the best defined, detached internship programs we reviewed are being delivered at San Diego State University (SDSU) and the University of San Diego (USD). Both programs are tightly linked to the California Standards for Administrative Credentials and the California Professional Standards for School Leaders (SDSU, 2006; USD, 2007). These standards mirror the ISLLC standards.

The unique aspects of the SDSU's internship program are the multicultural, multisite and multilevel experiences and the use of technology for accomplishing tasks and activities. The multicultural experience requires interns to engage in authentic leadership tasks in a school of diverse students. Given San Diego's demographics as a border city, requiring interns to participate in multicultural educational settings provides experiences some aspiring principals would not seek on their own. The multisite and multilevel experience is similar to BYU's requirement to provide interns with differing perspectives of leadership across school systems. SDSU's multifaceted internship provides interns an opportunity not only to examine the vertical alignment of differing school levels within a single district, but also to contrast policies and practices across districts. Another unique component of SDSU's internship program is the emphasis on technology, specifically, the use of TaskStream to document completion of field experience activities. TaskStream is a comprehensive Web-based program with tools for instructional design, program implementation, and e-portfolios. Using TaskStream's capabilities to create e-portfolios is an initial foray into using technology as part of the internship experience.

At USD, the internship experience is a hybrid between the full-time, job-embedded and the detached internship. What separates the USD internship from the SDSU internship is the required 20 days per year of field experiences and the underlying rationale. These field experiences may be accomplished during the summer or intersessions (for year-round schools). In addition to required days of field experience, interns are placed at schools where mentor principals have been selected. In some cases, interns do not conduct their internship at the school where they teach. In contrast to SDSU's strict adherence to the California standards as the driving force in the internship experience, USD's internship program revolves around the concept of problem-based learning. Interns are expected to select projects in consultation with their mentors and design action plans to address specific problems occurring at the school. The action plan represents an authentic leadership experience where interns use their knowledge and skills to deal with the problem.

Course-Embedded Field Experiences

The third type of internship found in practice is the course-embedded field experience. Unlike other internship models, the course-embedded field experience disaggregates the activities contained in a detached internship and places the requisite field experiences in appropriate courses. In other words, there is no stand-alone internship requirement or course section. To exemplify the course-embedded notion, student discipline hearings might be a field experience used in a school law course, while developing a professional development plan might be integrated into a supervision course. Although this model is not widely used due to state certification and licensure mandates requiring an internship, it may become accepted as a secondary means for providing meaningful connections between course content and actual practice in the field.

Several UCEA institutions, such as Florida State University and Ohio State University, have implemented various versions of course-embedded field experiences in lieu of a stand-alone internship. The Florida State University master's degree and principal certification program recently became an online-delivered program, necessitating a rethinking of their internship requirements and how interns would be supervised. At Ohio State University, field experiences are designed as a series of appropriately embedded activities meant to connect course topics to field practice (e.g., students in special education law attend manifestation determination hearings). These course-embedded field experiences are viewed as supplementary activities that add value to students' coursework and provide a path towards students' capstone experience at Ohio State University. As a result, rather than replacing the full-time, job-embedded internship or the detached internship, the course-embedded field experience may represent an ancillary way for preparation programs to provide meaningful authentic practice for aspiring principals (Hoffman, 2007).

Trends in Internships

Based on our examination of the current state of internships in the field, three major trends surfaced: (a) state and national standards emphasize instructional leadership and administrative leadership, (b) tighter linkages between preparation programs and school districts, and (c) technology-driven delivery of preparation programs. Each trend is examined below.

Our review of current internship experiences and requirements suggests that an evolution of activities is occurring. This evolution reflects more authentic leadership activities and projects being engaged by aspiring principals. In contrast to the routine duties implied by the four Bs—budgets, books, butts, and busses—aspiring principals are engaging in more student learning projects and school data related activities. In addition, aspiring principals in many programs are being required to assess the professional development needs of their school and to cultivate the organizational culture to facilitate student achievement and increase faculty effectiveness.

Although similar expectations for certain long-standing activities exist (e.g., shadowing and interviewing administrators, attending placement hearings for special education students), a noticeable emphasis on instructional leadership is emerging. Examples include assessing and providing resources pertaining to student learning, analyzing student-level data, developing professional development for teachers, and working on projects directly related to state or national standards (e.g., California Standards for Administrative Credentials, Texas Examination of Educator Standards, ISLLC, and Educational Leadership Constituent Council). The influence of state and national standards is readily apparent as a major force underlying internship requirements. As state and national standards have codified the importance of instructional leadership, the byproduct is the type of internship activities in which aspiring principals are expected to engage.

The second major trend affecting internships is the creation of tighter linkages between school districts and preparation programs. In the past, most preparation programs tended to operate autonomously from school districts, creating a divide between scholars and practitioners that continues to this date. With increasing pressure from alternative preparation programs and school district based programs, university preparation programs are lowering the gates of the ivory tower to include and value the contributions school districts can provide in a true partnership. By creating stronger linkages to school districts, university preparation programs gain a powerful ally in creating internship experiences that are more authentic and meaningful for aspiring principals. In the end, both school districts and universities win by producing higher quality principals to lead schools where students are expected to learn to their maximum potential.

The final trend affecting internships is the introduction of technology-driven activities. In its simplest form, the internship is about providing real-time experiences that prepare aspiring principals to assume the duties of the job. With the advent of technology-based programs, it remains to be seen what effect this will have on internship and field experiences, particularly the direct contact with mentors, university supervisors, and interns. As Goleman (2006) noted in his latest book, *Social Intelligence*, human beings are social creatures with an innate need to connect with others. Will technology facilitate this connection or create greater levels of isolation among educators? Depending on the outcome, this will shape the substance and form of internships in the future.

Research Evidence of Internship Experience Effects

As noted earlier, the research on internships in educational administration is overwhelmingly descriptive and calls for empirical work focused on effects or outcomes. Scholarship to date has emphasized program models and descriptions as well as prescriptive material to guide program planning. Ironically, there appears to be near-universal agreement that internships are important but limited attention to testing these assumptions with research. Studies tend to place emphasis on describing or evaluating single programs (a common focus in EdD dissertation studies) or chronicling collections of grant-supported programs, such as those funded by the Danforth Foundation in the late 1980s. Consistent with Daresh's (1987a, 1990) characterization of the existing literature, the empirical work on effects or outcomes is quite thin.

Given the limited nature of existing empirical literature, what can be gleaned regarding known outcomes or effects of the internship from the limited sources? Relatively few glimpses of promising work can be located. Findings appear to cluster in five key areas: (a) role conceptions of the principalship; (b) socialization to the principalship and interns' confidence upon entry into the principalship; (c) development of technical expertise, skills, and professional behaviors deemed to be important for leadership; (d) general dissatisfaction with the internship; and (e) role of mentoring in leadership development. A brief discussion follows of each of these emerging, albeit limited, areas of scholarship.

Role Conception and Clarification

For many prospective school administrators, the internship experience provides an early opportunity to "try on" elements of the principal's role. Whereas at least one content analysis of interns' daily logs indicated that internships do not fully expose students to the actual work of administration (McKerrow, 1998), other research suggested that the experience does enable the intern to gain insights about the work of the principalship, particularly related to clarifying conceptions of the role. Findings suggest, for example, that internship experiences tend to change interns' role conceptions about the principalship, grounding perceptions in a new reality of experience (Milstein & Krueger, 1997; White & Crow, 1993). Importantly, a synthesis of research focused on preparation programs engaged in reform suggested that coupling the internship experience with an ongoing, reflective seminar provided interns with a forum for sharing and sense making that deepened the experience (Milstein & Krueger, 1997). This general finding is further supported by the results of a 2-year qualitative study focused on matched pairs of interns and their mentor principals, who demonstrated that the process of reflection is integral to acculturation in the role of principal (Cordeiro & Sloan-Smith, 1995).

Other findings suggest field-based learning develops role clarification and may provide critical opportunities for career decision making (Daresh, 1987b; Daresh & Playko, 1992). Playko and Daresh (1990) conducted a qualitative study in a reform-oriented preparation program, interviewing and observing a small sample of participants over time. They discovered that although role clarification was an important outcome of the internship experience, some participants expressed less inclination to seek formal administrative positions based on their newfound understanding of the principal's role.

Socialization to the Principalship

The initial entry into the principalship can stir up feelings of inadequacy and self-doubt, even for the most seasoned educator. Daresh's (1986a, 1986b) survey study of 1st- and 2nd-year principals suggested that participants' expressions of inadequacy centered, in part, on poor socialization into the profession. Studies focused on principals' socialization revealed the internship can enable particular aspects of socialization and build greater confidence in graduates entering into the principalship. For example, Browne-Ferrigno's (2003) synthesis of research suggested that field-based learning in the internship was highly instrumental in the prospective leader's initial socialization into a new community of practice. Schmuck's (1993) action research study indicated that by participating in field-based internships with seasoned principals, aspiring principals were better prepared and more confident to assume leadership positions.

Findings from another study revealed that the processes of socialization occurring via the administrative internship tended to perpetuate the status quo in power relationships between teachers and administrators. Fishbein (2000) conducted an observation and interview study that explored the informal socialization messages that 9 female administrative interns received during the three-semester internship phase of an administrative preparation program, from which she developed a grounded theory about the power hierarchy. The study pointed out how aspects of the socialization process perpetuated unequal teacher–administrator relationships through unwritten rules that established strict relationship guidelines precluding collegial, collaborative behavior.

Development of Technical Expertise, Skills, and Professional Behaviors

In addition to clarifying role conceptions, other limited findings revealed the internship experience can be beneficial for developing skills and professional behaviors important for the principalship. For example, in their Connecticut study, Cordeiro and Sloan-Smith (1996) employed qualitative methods over a 2-year period and found internships to be useful for acquiring certain types of knowledge: day-to-day understanding of building operations, problem-solving strategies, interpersonal skills, time-management techniques, and reflective thinking. Findings from other studies indicated effects on interns' reflective judgment (MacDonald, 2003) and school governance effectiveness, based on the functionality of a school-site council (Bales, 1997).

Skill development may be related to the nature of the actual work that interns do. For example,

Layton's (1989) survey of interns found relationships between the amount of responsibility given the intern and perceived influence on skills as well as between the areas and levels of involvement of the intern and perceived influence on skills. However, a content analysis of interns' daily logs in another study revealed that two thirds of their time was spent attending meetings, doing office work, or supervising students (McKerrow, 1998). Because interns spent little or no time in an administrative role, the internship experience did not expose students to the actual work of school leaders. Finally, a longitudinal study of interns' preferences found that preservice principals were concerned with instructional leadership and less concerned about certain technical and procedural administrative functions (Bratlien, 1993); however, no empirical evidence could be found to suggest that the internship enables interns to develop their instructional leadership skills.

Dissatisfaction With the Internship

A handful of studies from the 1980s focused on interns' perceptions, finding that, in general, they believed the internship to be an important aspect of preparation but felt it provided inadequate grounding in the work of being a school leader. This small group of studies, all employing survey methods, reported interns' general dissatisfaction with the internship (Daresh, 1986a, 1986b; Notar, 1989; Wells, 1980). Daresh (1986a), for example, found a perceived lack of technical expertise and feelings of inadequate socialization to the profession among early-career principals based on their preparatory experiences. It should be noted that this trend of dissatisfaction with the internship is found in literature that largely predates the most recent reform efforts in principal preparation and may be a function of general dissatisfaction that permeated the field during the 1980s.

Mentoring

Alongside the socialization studies, and related empirical findings, is an emerging emphasis on the role of mentoring in the internship. Mertz (2004) distinguished mentoring from other types of professional relationships, setting apart the notion of mentor as somewhat distinct from that of the intern supervisor. The mentor–mentee relationship can be understood as one aspect of the internship experience; in the best of cases, embedded within an internship is a mentoring relationship. The mentor–mentee relationship has been the basis of empirical examination in the United States (Daresh, 1995; Daresh & Playko, 1992; Muse et al., 1992; Spear, 2005), Great Britain (Bush & Coleman, 1995), and Singapore (Walker & Stott, 1992). The mentoring relationship influenced internship success, entry, practice, and program development and refinement, including reduced feelings of isolation, increased confidence, and therapeutic benefits for mentees (Hobson, 2003). Studies of the personal and contextual variables affecting relationships (Keller, 1994) pointed out the importance of mentor selection and mentor scaffolding of opportunities for interns as keys to in-depth learning (Cordeiro & Sloan-Smith, 1995).

More limited are studies of the specific dimensions of the mentor–mentee relationship. Some research indicated that mentors are perceived to be important to protégés' career development in educational settings (Keller, 1994), but little evidence has been provided about the emotional dimensions of leadership as part of the mentoring process (Spear, 2005). Other findings support the idea that the relationship between mentor and mentee has reciprocal benefits; mentors learn and benefit just as mentees do. For example, Daresh and Playko (1992) conducted a descriptive study of adminstrators' perceptions of their involvement as mentors in what was judged to be an innovative, preservice preparation program. Mentoring was perceived to have parallel benefits for both mentors and protégés, supporting the idea that mentoring for administrators benefits all involved parties. Finally, there is limited evidence about selecting mentors. Geismar et al. (2000)

developed an instrument for helping to select mentors for principal interns that included items designed to measure both "basic" principal competencies as well as a set of mentoring traits. Based on a sample of 91 Broward County, Florida, principals, this method revealed important insights into identifying those judged to be appropriate mentors for prospective principals.

Future Research on Internships

Our review of the scholarship on administrative internships reveals that an overwhelming amount of the overall literature relies on personal essays, opinions, and descriptions of individual preparation programs. In this final section, we begin by critiquing the current methods and findings associated with research on internships before outlining a comprehensive research agenda to discover how internships are delivered and their effects on aspiring school leaders.

Methodological Critique

Based on our efforts to uncover empirical studies of internships, we strongly agree with Murphy and Vriesenga's (2004) conclusion:

> There simply are too few empirical studies to say much about the internship with any degree of confidence. Given the centrality of the internship to the education process (e.g., NCATE), this is troublesome.... In particular, the empirical literature on clinical work provides no insights on how field-based work is woven into and across learning experiences throughout training programs.... The study of field-based work needs considerably more attention than it has received over the last quarter century. (p. 20)

Clearly, the bulk of the literature on educational leadership internships is descriptive. For 20 years, calls for more studies have been raised (e.g., Daresh, 1987a, 1987b, 1988), but little has changed regarding our empirical understanding of how the internship experience affects interns' skills and dispositions. Literature reviews synthesizing the knowledge base on internships exist (e.g., Miklos, 1983; Milstein, 1990; Murphy, 1992; Wheaton, 1950); however, once again, these reviews provide descriptions of internship structures and expectations. A flurry of descriptions of internship programs surface from time to time. A recent example is the Danforth Programs for the Preparation of School Principals (see Cordeiro et al., 1992; Leithwood, Jantzi, Coffin, & Wilson, 1996; Milstein, 1993). Internships are the focus of some doctoral students' research; however, many of these investigations focus on a single program (e.g., Finn-Pike, 1999; Fishbein, 2000; Gregory, 1993; Gutterman, 1994; Hung, 2001; Mercado, 2002).

In summary, our review reveals the following broad research questions have not been addressed adequately:

1. What effects do internships have on interns' attitudes and skills?
2. What are the long-term effects of the internship experience on school administrators' actions once they are on the job?
3. How do internship tasks, program activities, and program designs vary across educational leadership preparation programs?
4. How are mentors selected and prepared, and what influence do they have on interns' development?

Each of these four questions is addressed below. We include promising empirical research designs to improve what is known about internships and their effects.

Future Research Agenda

Attitude and Skill Development

As noted earlier, the field of educational leadership has been criticized roundly for not demonstrating whether program graduates are affected by their preparation experiences. One of the most damning indictments of the influence of educational leadership preparation programs was voiced by Brent (1998):

> Graduate training in educational administration has no significant positive influence on school effectiveness.... If graduate training in school administration improves competence, then the principals of effective schools should, on average, be more highly trained than principals of less effective schools. This is not what we found. (p. 6)

Furthermore, calls for more comprehensive studies of internships abound. Cambron-McCabe (1999) suggested that research is needed to determine whether clinical experiences promote more effective leadership or maintain the status quo. Similarly, Daresh (1988) and Milstein et al. (1991) lamented that few studies or analyses of existing research focus on the effects of internships.

To counter these long-standing criticisms, we recommend conducting studies to determine the degree to which the espoused learning outcomes of internships are occurring. For example, three general outcomes of the internship experience have been advocated: (a) independent learners (Duley, 1978), (b) responsible citizens (Duley, 1978), and (c) self-confident leaders (Creighton & Johnson, 2002; Geismar et al., 2000; Milstein et al., 1991). Comprehensive quantitative and qualitative studies should be conducted to ascertain whether these intended outcomes are being achieved. In addition, studies should focus on the five specific outcomes of internships noted earlier: (a) knowledge and skill attainment (e.g., communicating, organizing, collaborating, and managing resources); (b) problem identification and solution, particularly aimed at school improvement and student achievement; (c) social justice orientation; (d) duties of administrators (e.g., budget, district operations, and program and personnel evaluation); and (e) commitment to a career in school administration.

Most research on internship effects has relied heavily on interns' perceptions at the end of their program of studies. To determine the ongoing effects of the internship, data should be collected from interns and others in the school (a) prior to the internship, (b) during the internship, and (c) at the conclusion of the internship to determine changes in skills and attitudes over time. Several existing lines of research and development can guide this type of data collection. For example, information from teachers and other staff members who work with interns during and following their internships can be obtained. (See Leithwood et al., 1996, for an excellent example of teachers' perceptions of students involved in Danforth principal preparation programs.) In addition, data from mentors who are working directly with interns should be collected. (See Capasso & Daresh, 2001, for various assessment instruments mentors might use to determine interns' readiness to serve as effective leaders.) Finally, information should be collected about how the school's existing policies and practices influence the internship experience and how interns are affecting school improvement efforts and student learning. Although interns cannot be expected to affect these types of outcomes immediately, longitudinal studies (see next section) would be an appropriate research design strategy for obtaining this information.

An added benefit of these types of studies is that they provide a better understanding of how preparation affects interns beyond their surface-level perceptions. Guskey (2000), in his description of the effects of professional development programs, proposed five levels:

1. Participants' reactions (Level 1) are personal reactions to the professional development experience.

2. Participants' learning (Level 2) involves perceptions of what was learned as a result of the experience.
3. Organization support and change (Level 3) shows how the school's current policies and practices support or inhibit the proposed goals of the experience.
4. Participants' use of new knowledge and skills (Level 4) shows how the ideas generated from the experience are being applied.
5. Student learning outcomes (Level 5) determine how student learning has been affected by the experience.

The aforementioned studies would move beyond the typical Level 1 and 2 data and delve into Levels 3, 4, and 5. Such studies would address directly the growing concern about the lack of knowledge regarding program effects.

Long-Term Effects

In general, most studies rely on data collected at the conclusion of the internship and ignore how these experiences may affect school leaders' subsequent actions. A more extensive, longitudinal research design could be implemented by determining if interns who had specific internship experiences (e.g., focusing on school improvement initiatives) are more likely to engage in these activities once they become school administrators. In this sense, a type of quasi-experimental design (Creswell, 2005) would be appropriate. A control group of interns would engage in an internship experience that focuses on typical tasks, such as observing administrators, serving on committees, overseeing attendance, and conducting bus duty. The experimental group of interns would be immersed in additional tasks, particularly those aimed at school improvement as suggested by Fry et al. (2005; e.g., assessing and developing effective instructional practices, serving on literacy and numeracy task forces, and acquiring resources aimed at school improvement). For an excellent example of such a quasi-experimental design, see Leithwood, Riedlinger, Bauer, and Jantzi's (2003) study of how principals' involvement in a professional development program affected school improvement and student learning. Clearly, coordinating this research design would require the cooperation of local districts; however, many programs using partnerships have established intensive internship experiences that extend far beyond the expectations in their traditional program.

Large-Scale Program Trends

A few excellent examples of studies comparing leadership preparation programs across the country do exist, including investigations by Barnett, Basom, Yerkes, and Norris (2000) of 223 programs; Skalski et al. (1987) of 252 programs; Fry et al. (2005) of 61 programs; and Murphy (1999) of 44 programs. However, these studies are the exception, because most investigations of internships either describe one preparation program or report the perceptions of one class or cohort of interns, which usually consists of 40–60 students (e.g., Bradshaw & Buckner, 2000; Cordeiro & Sloan-Smith, 1996; Harris, Crocker, & Hopson, 2002; Ovando, 2000).

We offer two suggestions to learn more about the ongoing trends in internship implementation. First, the sample of educational leadership programs should be expanded beyond single departments or UCEA institutions. For instance, data collected by regional educational organizations (e.g., Southern Regional Education Board) and summaries of NCATE reports would enlarge the pool to include smaller, regional institutions preparing educational leaders. Second, these large-scale investigations should strive to collect information on a common set of independent variables dealing with (a) internship tasks, (b) program activities, and (c) program designs. Based on our earlier review of internship programs, promising independent variables to focus on for each area are listed below.

1. Are important tasks being conducted in the internship? Variables to focus on are (a) school improvement initiatives focusing on student achievement, (b) effective classroom instructional practices, (c) literacy and numeracy task-force participation, (d) authentic assessment of student learning, (e) analysis of school data, and (f) professional development (Fry et al., 2005).

2. Are recommended program activities being implemented? Variables include (a) seminars and analytical activities, (b) mentor preparation, (c) sustained experiences over time, (d) based on standards or defined knowledge, (e) cooperatively implemented with districts, (f) placement within and outsides interns' school districts, and (g) diverse settings used and guided by a prepared mentor.

3. How are internships incorporated in the overall program design? Variables include (a) independent, where internship experiences are not linked to courses; (b) interdependent, where internship experiences are conducted after coursework is completed; (c) embedded, where internship experiences inform courses throughout the program; and (d) apprenticeship, where internship experiences shape the overall structure of the program with readings and theories added as necessary (Carr et al., 2003).

Mentor Involvement and Influence

Because most preparation programs utilize field-based administrators to serve as mentors during the internship, future research should examine their role in interns' development (Crow & Matthews, 1998; Grogan & Crow, 2004). Important information can be gathered about the following: (a) strategies for selecting mentors and matching them with interns, (b) ways mentors are prepared for their role, and (c) influence mentors have on interns' development. Regarding mentor selection and matching, the data collection process can be shaped by the recommendations of Capasso and Daresh (2001) and Daresh (2001, 2006), who strongly have advocated program faculty becoming more diligent about the selection and preparation of field-based mentors. For instance, studies can focus on the eligibility requirements used to select mentors, procedures for nominating mentors, and the criteria for selecting mentors (Capasso & Daresh, 2001; Daresh, 2001). In addition, using the research-based indicators of effective mentoring qualities (Daresh, 2006), data can be collected to determine if the following seven characteristics are taken into account when selecting mentors: (a) reputation as an effective school leader, (b) leadership effectiveness (e.g., communication, intelligence, vision, interpersonal skills), (c) ability to ask good questions, (d) acceptance of alternative points of view, (e) desire to see others expand their capabilities, (f) ability to model continuous learning and reflection, and (g) awareness of the realities of school systems.

Obtaining a better understanding of how mentors are prepared can be guided by existing research and recommendations in the literature. For example, a recent investigation by Weindling (2004) of 43 principal-induction programs from 14 countries revealed that highly reputable programs prepare mentors for their roles. This research design could be replicated to include educational leadership preparation programs across the United States. In addition, the literature on mentor preparation provides useful guidelines for future data collection efforts. Daresh (2001) outlined four areas worth investigating: (a) how mentors are oriented to their roles, (b) how they are initially prepared to work with interns, (c) whether ongoing preparation is provided for mentors, and (d) what human and material resources are required when preparing mentors.

Furthermore, using the potential benefits of mentoring identified in the literature as a guide, large-scale studies could be designed to ascertain the effects on interns and mentors. Information can be gathered from interns to determine whether (a) their confidence has increased, (b) they are able to translate theory into practice, (c) their communication skills have improved, and (d) they feel a greater sense of belonging to the profession (Daresh, 2001). Mentors can provide several types of internship effects data. For instance, they can use formal instruments to assess growth in interns' analytical and organizational capabilities, communication skills, educational values, and skills. (See Capasso & Daresh, 2001, for an excellent example of a formal instrument mentors can use to evaluate interns.) In addition, mentors can assess how they have been affected by the experience by determining whether (a) they feel more satisfied with their work, (b) they receive more recognition from their peers, (c) their careers have advanced, and (d) their enthusiasm for the profession has increased (Daresh, 2001).

Implications

Two final observations about the research on internships are worth noting. First, the present research agenda clearly has been driven by the individual interests of faculty and graduate students, resulting in piecemeal, fragmented efforts to collect and contrast comparable data. Second, employing longitudinal studies in multiple research sites requires a well-supported, coordinated research initiative. Without centralized direction, funding, and oversight, little will change in our empirical understanding of internships in educational leadership preparation.

If these observations are accurate, what organizations and agencies might fund and oversee such coordinated research efforts to learn about the structures and effects of internships? Organizations at the national, regional, and state levels have the potential to make a significant contribution to this research agenda. Each level of support is briefly described.

National-Level Support

Several professional organizations and foundations have the visibility and prestige to launch the research agenda we are proposing. First, the UCEA supports a variety of research centers. In particular, the Center on the Patterns of Professional Preparation in Administration housed at Arizona State University would be the ideal center to undertake such an endeavor. Second, national professional associations can collaborate to support a national data collection effort. While many organizations exist, perhaps the best positioned organization is the NPBEA, based in Washington, DC. The NPBEA membership is composed of 10 major organizations and accrediting bodies in educational leadership (American Association of School Administrators, American Association of Colleges for Teacher Education, Association for Supervision and Curriculum Development, Council of Chief State School Officers, National Association of Elementary School Principals, National Association of Secondary School Principals, National Council for Accreditation of Teacher Education, NCPEA, National School Boards Association, and UCEA). The NPBEA also supports the development of the International Resource Bank. The International Resource Bank is a clearinghouse that documents information about progressive and innovative programs or program elements in educational leadership, one of which is clinical experiences. Therefore, a national request for proposals for research on administrative internships could be overseen by the NPBEA and findings published in the International Resource Bank.

Additionally, numerous foundations, institutes, and centers have supported research on education, most notably the Spencer Foundation, David and Lucille Packard Foundation, Institute for Educational Leadership, Ford Foundation, and the Center for Creative Leadership. Individually, or collectively, these organizations could orchestrate a national call for research on the clinical internship in educational leadership. Finally, the U.S. Department of Education has a history of funding research and development on leadership preparation. Recently, the department funded grants for the School Leadership Program, which supports leadership development programs in high-need school districts.

Regional-Level Support

The Southern Regional Education Board has established a solid track record of collecting and disseminating empirical data about clinical experiences for school administrators (e.g., Fry et al., 2005), commissioning literature reviews on leadership preparation (e.g., Hoachlander, Alt, & Beltranena, 2001), and conducting studies dealing with leadership preparation (e.g., Bottoms & O'Neill, 2001). This organization should be encouraged to continue these lines of research and development. In addition, the Regional Educational Laboratories system, composed of 10 sites across the United States, is another network of agencies that can promote research and dissemination on the internship. For instance, The Laboratory for Student Success at the Mid-Atlantic Regional Educational Laboratory has commissioned literature reviews on educational leadership (e.g., Leithwood, 2005), which should be expanded to include field-based research studies of internships across the region.

State-Level Support

Finally, a variety of state associations or organizations can coordinate and fund research. For instance, philanthropic organizations have the resources to support proposals for research aimed at understanding the structure and effects of administrative internships. Examples of foundations across the country that have invested in educational leadership are the Sid W. Richardson Foundation in Fort Worth, the Wallace Foundation in New York, the Broad Foundation in Los Angeles, and the Meadows Foundation in Dallas. These and other state-level foundations should be encouraged to develop guidelines for research proposals on the internship. In addition, leadership preparation faculty in colleges and universities are required to collect and disseminate new knowledge as part of their jobs. Therefore, university systems, particularly those with multiple campuses, such as the California State Universities, University of Texas System, and the State University of New York, are networks of institutions that can promote and fund multisite research studies. Furthermore, universities in 15 states have formed state affiliates with the NCPEA (2006), which can serve as a coordinating body for intrastate university research collaboration. The research and development offices of these institutions can support interinstitutional research by soliciting grant funding from the state, regional, and national organizations listed above.

Undoubtedly, our proposed research initiative requires high commitment from and collaboration between universities, professional associations, regional centers and laboratories, state agencies, and school districts. To continue relying on individuals or small collections of university preparation program faculty to develop and implement such a comprehensive research initiative about the viability of internships is unrealistic. For far too long, the field of educational leadership has taken a hands-off approach. As our review indicates, the empirical findings on internships are no better now than when Daresh (1988) made this same claim almost two decades ago. The educational leadership profession must provide the direction and resources necessary for the types of studies we envision. If these criticisms and recommendations are minimized or ignored, we run the risk of having the same uninformed discussion about internships 20 years from now.

References

Note: Asterisk (*) used to denote a reference used in the meta-analysis shown in Table 9.1.
American Institute of Architects. (n.d.). *Accord policy on practical experience/training/ internship*. Retrieved March 23, 2007, from http//www.aia.org/SiteObjects/files/Experience.pdf
Anderson, M. E. (1989). Training and selecting school leaders. In S. C. Smith & P. K. Piele (Eds.), *School leadership* (pp. 53–84). Eugene, OR: ERIC Clearinghouse on Educational Management.
*Bales, J. R. (1997). *Graduate preparation in educational administration among high school principals and its relationship to school effectiveness*. Unpublished doctoral dissertation, Illinois State University, Normal.

Barnett, B. G. (1991). School–university collaboration: A fad or the future of administrative preparation? *Planning and Changing, 21*(3), 146–157.

Barnett, B. G., Basom, M. R., Yerkes, D. M., & Norris, C. J. (2000). Cohorts in educational leadership programs: Benefits, difficulties, and the potential for developing school leaders. *Educational Administration Quarterly, 36*(2), 255–282.

Bottoms, G., & O'Neill, K. (2001). *Preparing a new breed of school principals: It's time for action.* Atlanta, GA: Southern Regional Education Board.

*Bradshaw, L. K., & Buckner, K. G. (2000). A comparison of full- and part-time internships in an administrator preparation program. In P. M. Jenlink & T. J. Kowalski (Eds.), *Marching into the millennium: Challenges to educational leaders. The eighth yearbook of the National Council of Professors of Educational Administration* (pp. 160–171). Lanham, MD: Scarecrow Press.

Bradshaw, L., Perreault, G., McDowelle, J., & Bell, E. (1997, November). *Evaluating the results of innovative practices in educational leadership programs.* Paper presented at the annual meeting of the Southern Regional Council on Educational Administration, Charleston, SC.

*Bratlien, M. J. (1993). Competencies and aspirations: Determining internship needs—An eight-year study. *Journal of School Leadership, 3,* 498–509.

Brent, B. O. (1998). Should graduate training in educational administration be required for principal certification? Existing evidence suggests the answer is no. *Teaching in Educational Administration Newsletter, 5*(2), 1, 3–8.

Brent, B. O., & Haller, E. J. (1998). Who really benefits from graduate training in educational administration? *AASA Professor, 21*(1), 1–7.

Brigham Young University. (2007). *Leadership preparation program.* Unpublished manuscript, Brigham Young University, Provo, UT.

*Browne-Ferrigno, T. (2003). Becoming a principal: Role conceptualization, initial socialization, role identity transformation, purposeful engagement. *Educational Administration Quarterly, 39*(4), 468–503.

Bush, T., & Coleman, M. (1995). Professional development of heads: The role of mentoring. *Journal of Educational Administration, 33,* 60–73.

Calabrese, R. L., & Straut, D. (1999). Reconstructing the internship. *Journal of School Leadership, 9,* 400–421.

Cambron-McCabe, N. (1999). Confronting the fundamental transformation of leadership preparation. In J. Murphy & P. B. Forsyth (Eds.), *Educational administration: A decade of reform* (pp. 217–227). Thousand Oaks, CA: Corwin Press.

Campbell, R. F., Fleming, T., Newell, L. J., & Bennion, J. W. (1987). *A history of thought and practice in educational administration.* New York: Teachers College Press.

Capasso, R. L., & Daresh, J. C. (2001). *The school administrator internship handbook: Leading, mentoring, and participating in the internship program.* Thousand Oaks, CA: Corwin Press.

Carr, C. S., Chenoweth, T., & Ruhl, T. (2003). Best practice in educational leadership preparation programs. In F. C. Lunnenburg & C. S. Carr (Eds.), *Shaping the future: Policy, partnerships, and emerging perspectives. The eleventh yearbook of the National Council of Professors of Educational Administration* (pp. 204–222). Lanham, MD: Scarecrow Press.

Chance, E. W. (1991). The administrative internship: Effective program characteristics. *Journal of School Leadership, 1,* 119–126.

Cordeiro, P., Krueger, J., Parks, D., Restine, N., & Wilson, P. (1992). *Taking stock: A study of the Danforth Programs for the Preparation of School Principals.* St. Louis, MO: The Danforth Foundation.

Cordeiro, P. A., & Sloan-Smith, E. (1995, April). *Apprenticeships for administrative interns: Learning to talk like a principal.* Paper presented at the annual meeting of the American Educational Research Association, San Francisco.

*Cordeiro, P. A., & Sloan-Smith, E. (1996). Administrative interns as legitimate partners in the community of practice. *Journal of School Leadership, 6*(1), 4–29.

Creighton, T. B. (2002). Toward a leadership practice field: An antidote for an ailing internship experience. *AASA Professor, 25*(3), 3–9.

Creighton, T. B., & Johnson, J. A. (2002). The need for a leadership practice field: An antidote for an ailing internship experience. In G. Perreault & F. C. Lunnenburg (Eds.), *The changing world of school administration. The tenth yearbook of the National Council of Professors of Educational Administration* (pp. 157–166). Lanham, MD: Scarecrow Press.

Creswell, J. W. (2005). *Educational research: Planning, conducting, and evaluating quantitative and qualitative research* (2nd ed.). Upper Saddle River, NJ: Merrill Prentice-Hall.

Crocker, C., & Harris, S. (2002). Facilitating growth of administrative practitioners as mentors. *Journal of Research for Educational Leaders, 1*(2), 5–20. Retrieved June 3, 2006, from http://www.uiowa.edu/~jrel/spring01/harris_0107.htm

Crow, G. M., & Matthews, L. J. (1998). *Finding one's way: How mentoring can lead to dynamic leadership.* Thousand Oaks, CA: Corwin Press.

*Daresh, J. C. (1986a). Field-based educational administration training programs. *Planning and Changing, 17*(2), 107–118.

*Daresh, J. C. (1986b). Support for beginning principals: First hurdles are the highest. *Theory Into Practice, 25,* 168–173.

Daresh, J. C. (1987a, October). *Administrative internships and field experiences: A status report.* Paper presented at the annual meeting of the University Council on Educational Administration, Charlottesville, VA.

Daresh, J. C. (1987b, October). *Major assumptions of the practicum to prepare administrators: How valid are they?* Paper presented at the annual meeting of the University Council for Educational Administration, Charlottesville, VA.

Daresh, J. (1988). Learning at Nellie's elbow: Will it truly improve the preparation of educational administrators? *Planning and Changing, 19*(3), 178–187.

Daresh, J. C. (1990). Learning by doing: Research on the education administration practicum. *Journal of Educational Administration, 28*(2), 34–47.

Daresh, J. C. (1995). Research base on mentoring for educational leaders: What do we know? *Journal of Educational Administration, 33*(5), 7–16.

Daresh, J. C. (2001). *Leaders helping leaders: A practical guide to administrative mentoring* (2nd ed.). Thousand Oaks, CA: Corwin Press.

Daresh, J. C. (2006) *Beginning the principalship* (3rd ed.). Thousand Oaks, CA: Corwin Press.

*Daresh J. C., & Playko, M. A. (1992). Perceived benefits of a preservice administrative mentoring program. *Journal of Personnel Evaluation in Education, 6*(1), 15–22.

Davies, D. R. (1962). *The internship in educational administration*. New York: Center for Applied Research.

Dubin, A. E. (1987). Administrative training: Socializing our school leaders. *Planning and Changing, 18*(1), 33–37.

DuFour, R., & Eaker, R. (1998). *Professional learning communities at work: Best practices for enhancing student achievement*. Bloomington, IN: National Education Service.

Duley, J. S. (1978). Learning through field experience. In O. Milton (Ed.), *On college teaching: A guide to contemporary practices* (pp. 314–339). San Francisco: Jossey-Bass.

Edmonson, S. (2003). Improving leadership preparation through administrative internships. In F. C. Lunnenburg & C. S. Carr (Eds.), *Shaping the future: Policy, partnerships, and emerging perspectives. The eleventh yearbook of the National Council of Professors of Educational Administration* (pp. 316–328). Lanham, MD: Scarecrow Press.

Evers, N. A., & Gallagher, K. S. (1994). Field-based preparation of educational administrators. *Advances in Educational Administration, 3*, 77–97.

*Finn-Pike, K. (1999). *The roles and responsibilities of a school principal: One intern's perspective*. Unpublished doctoral dissertation, University of Minnesota, Minneapolis.

*Fishbein, S. J. (2000). *Crossing over: The roles and rules of the teacher-administrator relationship*. Unpublished doctoral dissertation, Hofstra University, Hempstead, NY.

Foster, L., & Ward, K. (1998). The internship experience in the preparation of higher education administrators: A programmatic perspective. *AASA Professor, 22*(2), 14–18.

*Fry, B., Bottoms, G., & O'Neill, K. (2005). *The principal internship: How can we get it right?* Atlanta, GA: Southern Regional Education Board.

Fulmer, C., Muth, R., & Reiter, K. F. (2004). Design elements for meaningful clinical practice experiences: The core of principal preparation programs. In C. S. Carr & C. L. Fulmer (Eds.), *Educational leadership: Knowing the way, showing the way, going the way. The twelfth yearbook of the National Council of Professors of Educational Administration* (pp. 190–199). Lanham, MD: Scarecrow Press.

*Geismar, T. J., Morris, J. D., & Lieberman, M. G. (2000). Selecting mentors for principalship interns. *Journal of School Leadership, 10*, 233–247.

Glasman, N., & Glasman, L. (1997). Connecting the preparation of school leaders to the practice of school leadership. *Peabody Journal of Education, 72*(2), 3–20.

Goleman, D. (1996). *Emotional intelligence: Why it can matter more than IQ?* New York: Bantam Dell.

Goleman, D. (2006). *Social intelligence: The new science of human relationships*. New York: Bantam Dell.

Greenfield, T. B. (1975). Theory about organization: A new perspective and its implications for schools. In M. G. Hughes (Ed.), *Administering education: International challenge* (pp. 71–99). London: Athlone.

*Gregory, R. A. (1993). *Leaders for tomorrow's schools: A study of the differences between graduates of traditional/classroom-based and practicum/internship-based programs*. Unpublished doctoral dissertation, University of Wyoming, Laramie.

Grogan, M., & Crow, G. M. (2004). Mentoring in the context of educational leadership preparation and development—Old wine in new bottles? *Educational Administration Quarterly, 40*(4), 463–467.

Guskey, T. R. (2000). *Evaluating professional development*. Thousand Oaks, CA: Corwin Press.

*Gutterman, Y. P. (1994). *Progress and change in leadership preparation. The preparation of educational administrators: Rationales, policies and practices. An examination of one program's approach*. Unpublished doctoral dissertation, University of California, Los Angeles.

*Harris, S., Crocker, C., & Hopson, M. H. (2002). Issues that mentors share with protégés. In G. Perreault & F. C. Lunenburg (Eds.), *The changing world of school administration. The tenth yearbook of the National Council of Professors of Educational Administration* (pp. 199–208). Lanham, MD: Scarecrow Press.

Hencley, S. P. (Ed.) (1963). *The internship in administrative preparation*. Washington, DC: The Committee for the Advancement of Educational Administration.

Hoachlander, G., Alt, M., & Beltranena, R. (2001). *Leading school improvement: What research says*. Atlanta, GA: Southern Regional Education Board.

Hobson, A. (2003). *Mentoring and coaching for new leaders*. Nottingham, England: National College for School Leadership.

Hoffman, D. (2007). *Educational policy and leadership: 896 administrative portfolio development.* Unpublished manuscript, Ohio State University, Columbus.

*Hung, S. S. Y. (2001). *The nature of administrative internships on principal preparation.* Unpublished doctoral dissertation, Columbia University Teachers College, New York.

Jackson, B. J., & Kelley, C. (2002). Exceptional and innovative programs in educational leadership. *Educational Administration Quarterly, 38*(2), 192–212.

*Keller, F. W. (1994). *The personal and contextual variables affecting the relationships between mentors and protégés in a regional program for the preparation of principals.* Unpublished doctoral dissertation, Virginia Polytechnic Institute and State University, Blacksburg.

*Layton, J. C. (1989). *The influence of internships on skills of education administrators.* Unpublished doctoral dissertation, University of Nebraska, Lincoln.

Leithwood, K. (2005). *Educational leadership: A review of the research.* Philadelphia: Mid-Atlantic Regional Educational Laboratory.

*Leithwood, K., Jantzi, D., Coffin, G., & Wilson, P. (1996). Preparing school leaders: What works. *Journal of School Leadership, 6*(3), 316–342.

Leithwood, K., Riedlinger, B., Bauer, S., & Jantzi, D. (2003). Leadership program effects on student learning: The case of the Greater New Orleans School Leadership Center. *Journal of School Leadership, 13*(6), 707–738.

Levine, A. (2005). *Educating school leaders.* Washington, DC: The Education Schools Project.

*MacDonald, M. R. (2003). *The contribution of education, experience, and personal characteristics on the reflective judgment of students preparing for school administration.* Unpublished doctoral dissertation, Andrews University, Berrien Springs, MI.

McCarthy, M. M. (1999). The evolution of educational leadership preparation programs. In J. Murphy & K. S. Louis (Eds.), *Handbook of research on educational administration* (pp. 119–139). San Francisco: Jossey-Bass.

*McKerrow, K. (1998). Administrative internships: Quality or quantity? *Journal of School Leadership, 8*, 171–187.

McLean, T. R. (2005). The 80-hour work week. Why safer patient care will mean more health care is provided by physician extenders. *Journal of Legal Medicine, 26*, 339–384.

*Mercado, L. P. (2002). *The secondary principalship academy: A critical ethnography of the Houston Independent School District and the University of Houston's innovative principal preparation program (Texas).* Unpublished doctoral dissertation, University of Houston, Houston, TX.

Mertz, N. T. (2004). What's a mentor, anyway? *Educational Administration Quarterly, 40*(4), 541–560.

Miklos, E. (1983). Evolution in administrator preparation programs. *Educational Administration Quarterly, 19*(3), 153–177.

Milstein, M. M. (1990). Rethinking the clinical aspects in administrative preparation: From theory to practice. In S. L. Jacobson & J. Conway (Eds.), *Educational leadership in an age of reform* (pp. 119–130). New York: Longman.

Milstein, M. M. (Ed.). (1993). *Changing the way we prepare educational leaders: The Danforth experience.* Newbury Park, CA: Corwin Press.

Milstein, M., Bobroff, B. M., & Restine, L. N. (1991). *Internship programs in educational administration: A guide to preparing educational leaders.* New York: Teachers College Press.

Milstein, M. M., & Krueger, J. (1993). Innovative approaches to clinical internships: The University of New Mexico experience. In J. Murphy (Ed.), *Preparing tomorrow's school leaders: Alternative designs* (pp. 19–38). University Park, PA: University Council for Educational Administration.

Milstein, M., & Krueger, J. (1997). Improving educational administration preparation programs: What we have learned over the past decade. *Peabody Journal of Education, 72*(2), 100–116.

Morgan, P. L., Gibbs, A. S., Hertzog, C. J., & Wylie, V. (1997). *The educational leader's internship: Meeting new standards.* Lancaster, PA: Technomic.

Murphy, J. (Ed.) (1992). *The landscape of leadership preparation: Reframing the education of school administrators.* Newbury Park, CA: Corwin Press.

Murphy, J. (1999). Changes in preparation programs: Perceptions of department chairs. In J. Murphy & P. B. Forsyth (Eds.), *Educational administration: A decade of reform* (pp. 170–191). Thousand Oaks, CA: Corwin Press.

Murphy, J. (2006). *Preparing school leaders: Defining a research and action agenda.* Lanham, MD: Rowman & Littlefield Education.

Murphy, J., & Vriesenga, M. (2004). *Research on preparation programs in educational administration: An analysis* (UCEA monograph series). Columbia, MO: University Council for Educational Administration.

Muse, I. D., Thomas, G. J., & Wasden, F. D. (1992). Potential problems (and solutions) of mentoring in the preparation of school administrators. *Journal of School Leadership, 2*, 310–319.

National Commission on Excellence in Educational Administration. (1987). *Leaders for America's schools: The report of the National Commission on Excellence in Educational Administration.* Tempe, AZ: University Council for Educational Administration.

National Council of Professors of Educational Administration. (2006). *NCPEA state affiliates.* Retrieved April 24, 2007, from https://www4.nau.edu/cee/orgs/ncpea/affiliates.asp

National Policy Board for Educational Administration. (1995). *NCATE guidelines: Curriculum guidelines for advanced programs in educational leadership for principals, superintendents, curriculum directors, and supervisors*. Alexandria, VA: Educational Leadership Constituent Council.

National Policy Board for Educational Administration. (2002). *Standards for advanced programs in educational leadership for principals, superintendents, curriculum directors, and supervisors*. Washington, DC: Author.

*Notar, E. (1989). What do new principals say about their university training and its relationship to their jobs? *National Forum of Applied Educational Research Journal, 1*(2), 14–18.

*Ovando, M. N. (2000). Assessment of interns' performance: A key to enhance school leader preparation for the new millennium. In P. M. Jenlink & T. J. Kowalski (Eds.), *Marching into the new millennium: Challenges to educational leaders. The eighth yearbook of the National Council of Professors of Educational Administration* (pp. 140–159). Lanham, MD: Scarecrow Press.

Pautler, A. J., Jr. (1990, October). *A review of UCEA member institutions clinical experiences/ internship/field experiences for educational leaders*. Paper presented at the annual meeting of the University Council for Educational Administration, Pittsburgh, PA.

*Playko, M., & Daresh, J. (1990, April). *The journey toward educational leadership: Reflective voyages of four teachers*. Paper presented at the annual meeting of the American Educational Research Association, Boston.

Pounder, D., Reitzug, U., & Young, M. D. (2002). Preparing school leaders for school improvement, social justice, and community. In J. Murphy (Ed.), *The educational leadership challenge: Redefining leadership for the 21st century* (pp. 261–288). Chicago: University of Chicago Press.

Purdue University, Weldon School of Biomedical Engineering. (2006). *Internships*. Retrieved July 1, 2006, from: https:// engr.purdue.edu/BME/Academics/Internships/

San Diego State University. (2006). *Field experience in educational leadership handbook*. Unpublished manuscript, San Diego State University, San Diego, CA.

*Schmuck, R. (1993). Beyond academics in the preparation of educational leaders: Four years of action research. *Oregon School Study Council, 33*(2), 1–11.

Sectish, T. C., Zalneraitis, E. L., Carraccio, C., & Behrman, R. (2004). The state of pediatrics residency training: A period of transformation of graduate medical education. *Pediatrics, 114*(3), 832–841.

Short, P. M., & Price, H. J. (1992). Clinical experience in administrator preparation programs: Are we there yet? *UCEA Review, 23*(3), 4–7.

Skalski, J., Lohman, M., Szcepanik, J., Baratta, A., Bacilious, Z., & Schulte, S. (1987, April). *Administrative internships*. Paper presented at the annual meeting of the American Educational Research Association, Washington, DC.

Smith, A. B. (2004). Evaluating the rationale of the osteopathic internship. *The Journal of the American Osteopathic Association, 104*(6), 230–231.

*Spear, L. (2005). *Mentoring the emotional dimensions of leadership: The perceptions of interns*. Unpublished doctoral dissertation, University of Washington, Seattle.

Tillman, L. C. (2005). Mentoring new teachers: Implications for leadership practice in an urban school. *Educational Administration Quarterly, 41*(4), 609–629.

University of North Carolina. (2005). *Preparing leaders in education for equity and excellence in a democratic society*. Chapel Hill: University of North Carolina Educational Leadership Program.

University of San Diego. (2007). *Aspiring leaders handbook*. Unpublished manuscript, University of San Diego, San Diego, CA.

Walker, A., & Stott, K. (1992). Developing school leaders through mentoring: A Singapore perspective. *School Organization, 12*(3), 49–57.

Weindling, D. (2004). *Innovation in headteacher induction*. Retrieved April 19, 2008, from http://www.ncsl.org.uk/media/ F7B/95/randd-innov-case-studies.pdf

*Wells, J. C. (1980). *The status of educational administrative internship programs in Texas institutions of higher education as perceived by former interns*. Unpublished doctoral dissertation, Texas A&M University, College Station.

Wheaton, G. A. (1950). *A status study of internship programs in school administration: A report of a Type C project*. Unpublished doctoral dissertation, Columbia Teachers College, New York.

White, E., & Crow, G. M. (1993, April). *Rites of passage: The changing role perceptions of interns in their preparation for principalship*. Paper presented at the annual meeting of the American Educational Research Association, Atlanta, GA.

10

The Design and Delivery of Leadership Preparation

MARGARET GROGAN, PAUL V. BREDESON, WHITNEY H. SHERMAN,
STACEY PREIS, AND DANNA M. BEATY

Defining good leadership and good leadership preparation has been a challenge for those who have educated and guided generations of school administrators for over 100 years in the United States and elsewhere. Although the principalship as a profession did not begin to formalize until after the Civil War, some evidence of training school leaders dates back to the early part of the 19th century (Murphy, 1998, 2006). For school superintendents, formal preparation specific to educational leadership did not come until after the 1920s, given the emphasis on a business model of school leadership during the Industrial Era (Callahan, 1996). Most of the extant literature on leadership preparation in education in the United States deals with master's or doctoral degree programs designed to prepare principals and assistant principals. In this chapter we review the literature that focuses on delivery models and discussions of delivery of principal preparation programs, since there has been very little research on delivery of superintendent programs. No distinction is made in the literature between doctoral programs and master's programs, though, in practice, we are aware that different principles may guide such programs.

The United States provides us with the most extensive literature on the design and delivery of educational leadership preparation. We focus on this literature in the first half of the chapter. We then draw upon relevant international literature to round out the discussion. The remainder of the chapter is organized into the following nine sections: (a) Examples of Delivery Structures and Components of Various Delivery Models; (b) Cohort Models of Leadership Preparation; (c) Course Delivery Through Distance Technology; (d) Partnerships Between Schools and School Districts, Universities, and Communities; (e) Educational Leadership Preparation Outside of Higher Education; (f) the Design and Delivery of International Programs in Educational Leadership; (g) Stages of Professional Socialization Framework; (h) Suggestions for Further Research; and (i) Conclusions.

Examples of Delivery Structures and Components of Various Delivery Models

The purpose of this section is to provide an overview of what research tells us about common elements found within the various delivery structures. Although each educational leadership preparation program is unique, many contain similar elements. In the United States, most are university based and organized around courses that prepare students for administrative licensure within a degree program, although some students are able to gain licensure by taking a certain set of courses if they already have a master's degree. Most programs include components of practice in addition to coursework such as internships or field-based learning experiences. Commonly, programs are divided into two distinct components: instructional leadership coursework and internship (Hess & Kelly, 2005; Jackson & Kelley, 2002; Milstein & Krueger, 1997). Within the coursework, many programs emphasize case studies, problem-based learning, and hands-on learning experiences (McCarthy, 1999; Milstein & Krueger, 1997). However, although individual features of certain programs have been highlighted as effective in the research literature, very little has been written about what constitutes good or effective models for delivery.

Innovations that break from conventional weekly delivery structures include course modules that are not restricted by the university standard of 45 clock hours being equal to 3 credit hours (Clark & Clark, 1997; Glasman, 1997; Milstein & Krueger, 1997). Online course offerings and weekend class meetings that also can be Web-assisted are viewed as effective ways to better accommodate working professionals (Goldring & Sims, 2005; Hughes, 2005; Jackson & Kelley, 2002). Other features tailored to the working professional include summer institutes or other intensive, time-condensed workshops (Harle, 2000; Jackson & Kelley, 2002). Anecdotal evidence tells us that many preparation programs use a variety of these delivery structures, including coursework delivered in intense units of 1.0–1.5 weekend days three or four times a semester combined with summer intensives of 3–4 weeks of full-day meetings. As yet, there is little research focused on these delivery methods. However, one overarching concept that has been researched is the cohort.

Cohort Models of Leadership Preparation

Barnett and Muse (1993) defined *cohort* as a "group of students who begin and complete a program of studies together, engaging in a common set of courses, activities, and/or learning experiences" (p. 401). The use of cohorts in leadership preparation programs is growing in popularity because it is believed to be both responsive to consumer needs and to address some of the past criticisms of leadership preparation. Barnett, Basom, Yerkes, and Norris (2000) identified cohort programs from as early as the 1950s; however, the incidence of cohort models has increased since the 1987 National Council of Professors in Educational Administration study, *Leaders for America's Schools* (Griffith, Stout, & Forsyth, 1988), which called for a change to leadership preparation programs. The Danforth Foundation grants are most frequently identified with the growth in the number of cohort-based programs of educational leadership preparation (Barnett & Muth, 2003). Most estimates are that over 50% of leadership preparation programs in the United States use the cohort model (Barnett et al., 2000).

Cohort models are often characterized by their common external features such as a standard size (10–25 students) and a common schedule (Barnett & Muse, 1993). In defining a cohort leadership preparation program, proponents argue that the cohort is more than a structure for delivery of a program. Instead, they think of it in terms of a learning model for adult students (Barnett & Muse, 1993; Norris, Barnett, Basom, & Yerkes, 1996). According to proponents of the cohort model, the success of the model is impacted by the degree to which faculty embrace the program at their university and are effective in working with adult learners (Barnett et al., 2000; Browne-Ferrigno & Muth, 2003). However, since there is scant literature focused on other delivery models, this finding might be equally applicable to all leadership preparation models.

As adult learners are self-directed and have strong internal motivation, it is argued that cohort models engage them in a meaningful way (Diller, 2004; McCabe, Ricciardi, & Jamison, 2000). Adult learners have a larger frame of reference from which to draw upon for learning, and, in turn, want to learn about things that are significant and directly applicable to their professional lives (Diller, 2004; McCabe et al., 2000). Donaldson and Scribner (2003) offered structuration theory as a frame for a cohort model where the delivery structure is shaped by the expectations, experiences, and beliefs of the members of the cohort.

Strengths of the Cohort Model

Several studies have reported the benefits of cohorts as perceived by both students and faculty. Engaging in a common curriculum with a fixed group of students was cited most frequently as a benefit for students (Barnett et al., 2000; Barnett & Muse, 1993; Diller, 2004). Students in cohorts view themselves as more than a collection of individuals. They frequently refer to the support, mutual respect, and lifelong relationships they build within the cohort (Bailey, Ruhl-Smith, & Smith, 1999; Norris et al., 1996). Barnett and Muse as well as Browne-Ferrigno and Muth (2003) wrote that students felt a strong sense of community that they attributed in part to taking the same set of courses together. Although the cohort model may seem to some to be too closed or rigid, most cohort students maintain that the structure creates a safe and trusting environment for adult learners (Browne-Ferrigno & Muth, 2003; Milstein, 1995; Norris et al. 1996).

Although acknowledging that critics might be concerned about sacrificing content to enhance the learning experiences of students who must take all courses together, Browne-Ferrigno and Muth (2003) have encouraged continual group-development activities that maintain a positive and emotionally safe environment. Whereas Twale and Kochan (2000) found that women rated the interpersonal aspects of the cohort as more important than men, many students note the appreciation of peer support and the opportunity to learn from others in similar circumstances (Milstein, 1995; Tucker, Henig, & Salmonowicz, 2005). In Diller's (2004) study of Duquesne University's Interdisciplinary Doctoral Program for Educational Leaders, some respondents reported learning more from discussion among the cohort members than from the actual content. In addition, Browne-Ferrigno (2003) reported the positive impact of peer tutoring within the cohort, particularly between the more and less experienced members of the group. Not only are the peer relationships within cohorts strengthened, but a good cohort model also can increase faculty–student connections and develop stronger working relationships (Barnett & Muse, 1993; Barnett et al., 2000). A significant positive effect of the cohort model is the increasing number of students who persist in the completion of the degree (Barnett et al., 2000; Barnett & Muth, in press; McCabe et al., 2000; Milstein, 1995; Milstein & Krueger, 1997; Twale & Kochan, 2000).

Studies of cohorts indicate that the extended opportunities for group work that are characteristic of the cohort model do not distract from individual accomplishment; in fact, often the opposite is true. The benefit is reciprocal: individual successes contribute to the strength and achievement of the cohort, and the cohort provides a resource and support network for the individual (McCabe et al., 2000; Norris et al., 1996; Twale & Kochan, 2000). Additionally, small group projects create a sense of obligation and commitment to other team members; no one is isolated from the group or left behind (Donaldson & Scribner, 2003). When working both individually and as a group, students have time for reflection and consideration of the applications of what they have learned (Barnett & Muse, 1993). Furthermore, cohort curricula are often dependent on discourse among members, a key skill in effective leadership. The ability of students to communicate what they are learning both solidifies their own understanding and can aid in the learning of others (Browne-Ferrigno & Muth, 2003). Continued networking with members of the cohort also benefits the students even after their program is completed (Bailey et al., 1999; Barnett et al., 2000; Barnett & Muse, 1993; Browne-Ferrigno & Muth, 2003; McCabe et al., 2000; Milstein, 1995).

Concerns About the Cohort Model

Tightly structured cohort models that do not allow students to exit and enter along the way pose problems for some students (Barnett et al., 2000). Furthermore, a typical cohort model may limit academic freedom and individual exploration. Some cohort participants have cited this as a disadvantage (Diller, 2004). Universities tend to let scheduling convenience and enrollment increases be the driving force behind implementing a cohort model, which overshadows the value of cohorts as a curricular model (Horn, 2001; Norris et al., 1996).

The course loads may be heavy in some cohort structures, though class meetings are often infrequent. Tucker et al. (2005) found that students early in their program said they regretted the limited contact they had with faculty. Donaldson and Scribner (2003) noted that practical constraints embedded within a program that keeps every student on the same schedule (e.g., time, other commitments, personal issues) restricted the depth in which students were willing to or could explore the concepts covered in the curriculum. Also, when students were preoccupied with the final product of their group work, creativity or divergent ideas were suppressed by other members of the cohort.

Barnett and Muse (1993) and Browne-Ferrigno and Muth (2003) determined that the bond that forms within cohorts may have a downside in that often students become more demanding, even engaging in power struggles with the faculty. Horn (2001) found that since cohort models are so highly structured, students are put into subordinate positions with regard to the faculty who do not encourage democratic decision-making processes. When cohort participants return to their schools, they are inclined to regress into the same traditional power structure that always existed. Horn noted, "The current modernistic power arrangements that are ubiquitous in our educational communities are ineffective in promoting just and caring communities, and in many cases actually reinforce oppression" (p. 324).

Other interpersonal relationships can be detrimental to the effectiveness of the cohort experience that depends so much on group dynamics. Donaldson and Scribner (2003) and Horn (2001) interviewed some women who felt that the men in the cohort attempted to assume a role of authority over the women in the group. Women in both studies felt that to some degree they had been given lesser roles within the group. Cohorts also risk becoming cliquish and isolating to both fellow cohort members and noncohort members pursuing the same degree. In a few instances, cohort members even have reported feelings of insecurity in comparing themselves to their fellow cohort members, particularly if they were entering the same job market (Barnett et al., 2000; Browne-Ferrigno & Muth, 2003; Horn, 2001; McCabe et al., 2000). Additionally, the potential exists for the "one rotten apple" syndrome to negatively affect cohorts (Barnett et al., 2000; Browne-Ferrigno & Muth, 2003; Horn, 2001; Norris et al., 1996). Horn noted that any negative social interaction is magnified in a group setting such as a cohort. The complaints of one quickly can become the complaints of all (Barnett et al., 2000).

One recurring criticism of cohort-based leadership preparation is that no conclusive scientific research exists to substantiate a positive impact on the leadership abilities of the cohort participants versus noncohort participants (Barnett et al., 2000). Our literature search uncovered more conceptual pieces than empirical research studies on cohort models in general. Twale and Kochan (2000) reported that their study could not demonstrate an impact of the cohort training on leadership practices after the completion of the program. However, directing all of the criticism to the quality or structure of the program may be inappropriate. Browne-Ferrigno (2003) found that students who did not enter cohort programs with clear expectations and individual goals were not as likely to feel a sense of accomplishment at the completion of the program.

Most of the literature on cohort and noncohort programs refers to programs that have been delivered mostly or entirely face-to-face with instructors and students together in the same room. However, with increased student access to the Internet and home computing, many leadership programs, both cohort and noncohort, have begun to incorporate at least elements of electronic course delivery.

Course Delivery Through Distance Technology

Universities have experimented with the use of computer technology within the traditional on-campus classroom environment as the number of Internet users has multiplied. Until recently, *distance education* was a term used to denote paper-based class correspondence as well as traditional courses held at off-campus locations, where the instructor goes to a location more convenient for specific groups of students, but where the instruction is still face-to-face. More recently, however, computer technology has become a vital part of distance education, thus prompting the birth of the new term *distance technology*. To clarify, *distance education* focuses on either the distance between instructor and learner (as in a paper-based class correspondence) or the distance between the classroom setting and both the instructor and students (as in traditional course delivery offered in an off-campus location). In contrast, *distance technology* focuses on both the distance between instructor and learner and the use of technology in a course delivery format alternative to the traditional classroom setting. Therefore, we are careful not to confuse *distance education* with *distance technology*, because the two are not synonymous (Guri-Rosenblit, 2005).

The use of distance technology has the potential to lead the way in developing more competent technology leaders as well as reforming preparation and reaching a more inclusive population of administrator aspirants. Proponents argue that distance technology fosters leadership styles that are less traditional and more transformative and relational. The use of distance technology offers opportunities for improvement in the teaching and learning process, an expansion in geographic reach, and more effective service (Broskoske & Harvey, 2000). It breaks from tradition in terms of social dynamics and, with further research, may prove to be a gender, race, and disability equalizer because there may be less potential for bias (Belcher, 1999; Opsal, Brunner, & Virnig, 2005; Savicki, Kelley, & Lingenfelter, 1996; Sullivan, 2002).

Boone (2001) discussed the development of a standards-based superintendent program in Texas in which technology played a significant role in the preparation of school leaders. Utilizing a constructivist approach to learning, technology became, according to Boone, a "virtual partner with the learner as he or she began to construct knowledge," viewing technology as the "intellectual tool kit that enables the learner to build more meaningful personal interpretations of new knowledge" (p. 17). Technology in this circumstance served as the environment in which to engage learners in cognitive learning strategies and critical-thinking skills (Jonassen, Peck, & Wilson, 1999). Smith-Gratto (2000) found that integrating technology in this manner contributed to the social interactions critical to constructivist approaches to learning.

The increasingly global society in which we operate has in many ways demanded a shift in the way individuals construct career paths, problem-solving teams, and intellectual circles. Consequently, the development of a strong and diverse network of peers is an important part of an educational leader's career. In an effort to connect graduate students from two distinct regions of the United States, Borsa, Klotz, and Uzat (1998) utilized distance technology to create a cohort of scholars. Recognizing the importance of considering a less regional perspective when developing a plan for educational change, they created a model that allowed students from the Midwest and Deep South to connect socially and intellectually in an effort to create a broader cohort of scholars than is usually found in one program. In a related effort, Opsal et al. (2005) focused on attitudes in leadership preparation toward members of marginalized groups through their description of a technology-based pedagogical process in a school leadership course. Their technology renders students anonymous to one another and allows them to communicate through a chat room via the Internet and to collaborate on projects before ever meeting one another in person, allowing for the demonstration of leadership skills before any judgment occurs on the basis of gender, disability, or race.

However, university-based leadership preparation does not yet seem to widely embrace distance technology. Sherman and Beaty (2007) conducted an exploratory study of how University Council of Educational Administration member institutions utilize distance technology in the preparation of educational leaders. They found that in all institutions and at all levels (PhD, EdD, EdS, MEd), traditional, face-to-face program structures were the most prevalent forms of program delivery in use. However, respondents indicated that many programs were beginning to utilize hybrid program structures that combine face-to-face delivery and distance technology. The most widely used forms of distance technology were asynchronous Internet programs; synchronous Internet programs; and two-way, interactive video and audio.

Carr-Chellman and Duchastel (2000) warned that despite many positive outcomes that distance technology might provide, its use also runs serious risks of tempering original instruction so that it becomes ineffective. Furthermore, courses that utilize distance technology should not look like traditional courses in sheep's clothing—they indeed should provide something different. The over-reliance on adjuncts; the lack of faculty member interest, technical training, and expertise (Myers, Bennett, Brown, & Henderson, 2004); the absence of sufficient scaffolding for students working from home in terms of modem connect time and high bandwidth needed for successful online experiences (Foshay & Bergeron, 2000); and inadequate access to technology in general (Glass, Björk, & Brunner, 2000) also serve as factors that inhibit quality online environments. Further, Broskoske and Harvey (2000) warned that consideration must be given to the budget (high start-up costs) and marketing (concern with negative reputation associated with the use of distance technology).

Concerns about the use of technology to deliver or help deliver leadership preparation notwithstanding, the traditional models of delivery are being challenged by new approaches. We need to think about effective uses of distance technology, envision what successful distance technology courses look like, and understand how technology might transform both the preparation and practice of educational leaders.

Other new and alternative approaches include the idea of pooling expertise from higher education and from the prekindergarten through Grade 12 (preK–12) arenas. Partnerships between districts, universities, and other professional or community agencies are being created all over the country, particularly since practitioners and others (see Levine, 2005) have criticized university-centric approaches. Yet, Murphy (2006) warned that *alternative* is not necessarily synonymous with *better*.

Partnerships Between Schools and School Districts, Universities, and Communities

Partnerships between schools and universities have the potential to bridge the gap between theory and practice that often has been a criticism of educational leadership preparation offered by universities (Barnett, 2005; Sherman, 2006). They also offer more options for program delivery. A challenge to forming partnerships is that the organizational structures of universities and schools sometimes may seem incompatible (Goldring & Sims, 2005). However, successful partnerships involve collaboration and cooperation at all levels of each participating organization, even if not every level (e.g., university chancellors) will be involved directly (Grogan & Roberson, 2002; Whitaker & Barnett, 1999). Many successful university–school district partnerships have had advisory, development, or redesign committees where all parties were well represented and had input on the structure and expectations for the partnership (Goldring & Sims, 2005). In addition, to be successful, all partners must share a commitment to the partnership and respect what the other partner has to contribute (Whitaker & Barnett, 1999).

Strong collaboration between schools and universities opens up opportunities for collaborative delivery models. For instance, practicing administrators lead seminars or team teach with university faculty (Aiken, 2001; Clark & Clark, 1997; Milstein & Krueger, 1997). Effective veteran administrators are also incorporated into program design by serving as mentors for those in leadership preparation (Aiken, 2001; Whitaker & Barnett, 1999). In addition, a number of university programs offer courses on site within school districts or teach the entire program on site (Grogan & Roberson, 2002; Goldring & Sims, 2005; Jackson & Kelley, 2002; Whitaker, King, & Vogel, 2004). Such collaboration allows the partner districts and university faculty to have equal say in determining what gets taught, how, and when.

Several partnerships go beyond departments or colleges of education and districts and may involve colleges of business or management, state departments of education, corporate leaders, and community organizations. These have not been researched to date, but we provide the following information on some of the new approaches to help map the terrain where the field may be headed.

The Chicago Leadership Academies for Supporting Success (2006), Georgia's Leadership Institute for School Improvement (2006), and the Arkansas Leadership Academy (n.d.) are a few of the leadership preparation programs with extensive partnerships. Chicago Leadership Academies for Supporting Success operates four different leadership preparation models, depending on the needs of the individual and the stage of career. The program partners with the Chicago Public Education Fund as well as with Northwestern University's School of Education and Social Policy and the Kellogg School of Management. Georgia's Leadership Institute for School Improvement partners with the University of Georgia System, Georgia Partnership for Excellence in Education, and the Georgia Department of Education in addition to several other government agencies and business organizations. Georgia's Leadership Institute for School Improvement program lasts approximately 3 years, and most costs are paid by the institute. The program emphasizes performance-based outcomes, with an electronic portfolio used in the first phase of assessment. The Arkansas Leadership Academy has a total of 44 partners statewide, which include universities, government agencies, corporations, and not-for-profit organizations. This program is divided into three phases, with the last two being optional and requiring additional applications. The Arkansas Department of Education covers all of the participants' expenses except travel (Arkansas Leadership Academy, n.d.).

Partnerships provide multiple perspectives and bring together a number of professional strengths that have strong potential for enhancing the depth and quality of educational leadership preparation. The Kentucky Department of Education (2006) collaborates with Western Kentucky University and the Kentucky Alliance of Black School Educators to offer the Minority Superintendent Internship Program. Participants intern in a school district for 1 year while learning about the responsibilities of a superintendent. The city of Boston, in conjunction with Northeastern University and the Fenway Institute for Urban School Renewal, offers the Principal Residency Network through the Center for Collaborative Education (n.d.). Students in this 12- to 15-month program are immersed in field experiences while participating in seminars and completing writing exercises and produce a portfolio of their work by the end of the program (Center for Collaborative Education, n.d.). To cast more light on recent departures from traditional educational leadership preparation, we turn now to available research on programs being delivered outside of institutions of higher education.

Educational Leadership Preparation Outside of Higher Education

In recent years, for-profit and not-for-profit leadership preparation programs have emerged and begun to secure their place in the market of leadership preparation for educational administrators.

These programs outside of higher education are not limited by the constraints inherent in a university setting. Some researchers have argued that these alternative programs are more willing to break from tradition and take risks with new ideas and approaches (Hess & Kelly, 2005).

For example, New Leaders for New Schools (NLNS) recruits applicants from all professions but only accepts a select 5–7% of all applicants. Instructors in NLNS include leaders in both education and business (Hess & Kelly, 2005). NLNS develops the curriculum with input from educators across the country so that their curriculum does not reflect the perspective of only one institution. However, this also can be a liability for NLNS organizers as they try to adapt their programs by state to accommodate each state's licensure standards (Smith, 2005). NLNS self-evaluates, at least in part, through data collected on student achievement in schools led by their graduates (Hess & Kelly, 2005).

Although some researchers have acknowledged the strengths of various characteristics of programs delivered outside of colleges of education, an interesting dilemma exists for many of the programs' graduates. School districts still control the market on educational administration and have demonstrated apprehension at hiring administrators trained outside of an educational environment (Hess & Kelly, 2005). Even programs identified as successful and innovative, such as the National Institute for School Leadership, are seeking partnerships with universities so that their training can be translated into academic credits in a doctoral degree program (Hughes, 2005).

Indeed, the affiliation with higher education has been developed most fully in educational leadership preparation in the United States. As we discuss in the next section, school leaders in other countries take a different route to the principalship.

The Design and Delivery of International Programs in Educational Leadership

In this section of the chapter, we examine the design and delivery of leadership preparation from a global perspective. By *global* we do not mean an exhaustive review of research on all leadership preparation programs around the world. Rather, we use the literature and research on international leadership preparation programs from selected countries to describe important advances in leadership preparation worldwide. We describe factors that have shaped the various designs and delivery strategies used for leadership preparation. Understanding similarities and appreciating distinctive features of leadership preparation among countries will inform international research on leadership preparation as well as serve as a guide to national policy makers and local school leaders.

Factors Shaping Leadership Preparation Programs

The mix of history, culture, educational traditions, governing authority, and pressing challenges has contributed to the design and delivery of preparation programs for school leaders internationally. With full recognition of the mix of these elements internationally, at least eight common factors have shaped the histories, content, and design of leadership training programs. Based on our understanding of current research of leadership development internationally, we identify the following eight common factors: (a) contemporary challenges to educational institutions and waves of reform; (b) cumulative research evidence on leadership; (c) decentralization of educational authority; (d) changing professional socialization patterns for school leaders; (e) historic lack of preservice preparation for school leaders; (f) school leaders rethinking professional needs; (g) increased demands for accountability; and (h) the social, historic, and culture foundations of education in each country.

Contemporary Challenges to Educational Institutions and Waves of Reform

During the last two decades of the 20th century and first years of the 21st century, we have witnessed an unprecedented change and interest in school leader preparation, ongoing professional development, and their work (Bedard & Aitken, 2004; Carter, 1994; Hallinger, 2003; Witziers, Bosker, & Kruger, 2003). Globalization, new information and communication technologies, and the forces of international economic competitiveness have challenged policy makers in every country. In response they have had to rethink their country's position in the world and to examine their national capacity to adjust and compete successfully in what Friedman (2005) referred to as an increasingly flat world. Not surprisingly, each country's educational system has come under greater scrutiny, especially the link between education and economic competitiveness. As business and government turned their attention to education, Hallinger (2003) noted,

> Policymakers seemed, all of a sudden, to *discover* the need for more effective school leadership. This realization has led governments in Europe, North America, and Austral-Asia to establish programs designed to support school leadership and its development throughout the world. (p. 3)

Cumulative Research Evidence on Leadership

Educational research also has shaped current leadership preparation and design. Though scholars in the field of educational administration and leadership long have understood the importance of leaders in educational organizations, historically the focus of educational researchers and policy makers who investigated policy implementation, successful school change processes, and school improvement has been on teachers. An unanticipated yet persistent finding in various large-scale studies conducted in the United States during the 1960s and 1970s was the important role that school principals played in effective policy implementation, successful change, and school improvement (Hallinger, 2003). Effective schools research in the United States (Edmonds, 1979) and in Great Britain (Rutter, Maugham, Mortimore, Ouston, & Smith, 1979) similarly highlighted the important role that principals played in usually effective schools. By the 1990s, the focus on educational reform, bolstered by research confirming the importance of leadership in schools, resulted in a major thrust toward management development in education (Bush & Jackson, 2002; Memom, 2000; Su, Gamage, & Mininberg, 2003).

Decentralization of Educational Authority

As policy makers, academics, and practitioners have come to better understand the cumulative body of research on school leadership and its link to school improvement and policy implementation, they also have recognized that successful implementation of national education policy needs local leadership, not mere compliance by principals who are agents of the national education authority (Höög, Bredeson, & Johansson, 2006; Memom, 2000; Moller & Skedsmo, 2006; Moos, 2000; Tjeldvoll, Wales, & Welle-Strand, 2005). In contrast to the United States, where public education historically has been decentralized to 50 states and currently to some 14,000 local school districts, in Europe, Africa, and Australasia, national education systems have been the norm. Thus, the idea of decentralization in these countries challenged long-standing governing relationships among national, regional, and municipal educational governing authorities. As well, understandings of the role of school leaders (e.g., principals, heads, rectors, and system CEOs—superintendents) continues to change from that of agents of national educational agencies located at the local level to school leaders who increasingly have become more responsible to local authorities and to local constituencies.

Changing Socialization Patterns for School Leaders

The titles of head master and principal are rooted historically in teaching expertise and knowledge, not in administration or leadership. According to *The Education System in the Federal Republic of Germany 2004* (as cited in Cha, 2005), the general pattern of professional socialization to become a school leader was to be a good teacher. In South Korea, principals assume their administrative assignments during the last 4–5 years of their careers after a long apprenticeship in teaching (Cha, 2005).

In national education systems around the world, the administrative structures and governing authorities were already in place in national education agencies. However, in highly decentralized systems like the United States, according to Hart and Bredeson (1996),

> The transformation of the word principal from an adjective to a noun came with the rapid growth of cities and the ever-expanding school-age population. Prior to the 1850s in the United States, most schools, both public and private, tended to be small with only one or two teachers. (p. 104)

Thus, there was little need for full-time administrators beyond the classroom. In contrast to Canada and the United States, where preservice preparation programs for school principals have existed for decades, in most countries it took various waves of education reform and new demands for accountability to heighten awareness of the differences between excellence in teaching and excellence in leadership and management in education (Hallinger, 2003; Huber, 2003; Memon, 2000). The traditional pattern of apprenticeship in many countries, where the route to the principal's role was from teacher to head teacher to department head and then the principalship, is giving way to the creation, and in some case requirements, of some formal preservice training for school administrators (Daresh & Male, 2000; Su, Adams, & Mininberg, 2000; Su et al., 2003).

Historic Lack of Preservice Preparation for School Leaders

The lack of preservice preparation in management, leadership, or systems administration, especially outside of North America, is reflected in the design and delivery of school leader programs in most countries. Without formal preservice programs, new school leaders traditionally have been hired for their expertise and experience as excellent teachers and department heads. Once hired, they were hungry for training and development opportunities that would help them meet the challenges of their daily work in such areas as fiscal management, personnel administration, political negotiations, curriculum management, and assessment. As Bush and Jackson (2002) reported, "The Commonwealth Secretariat (1996) shows that this is certainly a problem in much of Africa where without the necessary skills many heads are overwhelmed by the task … strategies for training and supporting school heads [are] generally inadequate throughout Africa" (p. 418). Thus, the lack of preservice preparation in most countries around the world resulted in a greater reliance on in-service and ongoing professional development. Accordingly, for many new administrators socialization from initial stages of encounter—survival and control, to accommodation and integration, and then on to stabilization—in educational leadership and professional actualization was more tumultuous and took longer than for those administrators who had been socialized in preservice programs (Hart & Bredeson, 1996).

School Leaders Rethinking Professional Needs

In a comprehensive review of the landscape of school leadership development around the world, Hallinger (2003) argued that increased demands from external forces (e.g., policy makers, system administrators, parents, and business and community leaders) have intensified the work of school leaders. He went on to describe how the external forces for change in school leadership also created an inside-the-professional force by school leaders themselves. In a professional field historically dominated by university-delivered degrees and certificates, the intensification of principals' work created new in-service programs and delivery strategies that served school leaders' learning needs within the constraints of their demanding daily work. Graduate degree programs and courses, the traditional currency of higher education institutions, came to be seen as cumbersome and often unrelated to the realities of daily practice. Over the past 20 years, school principals, administrator professional associations, government agencies, school systems, and more recently independent consultants and entrepreneurial groups have created a vast array of in-service programs, including principals' centers, institutes, workshops, and networks to support and enhance the learning of school leaders. We will return to this theme later in the chapter when we discuss emerging challenges in school leadership preparation and ongoing professional development.

Increased Demands for Accountability

Whether as agents of national education authorities or locally autonomous leaders, principals and other administrators always have been held accountable in their work (Bredeson & Kose, 2006; Moller & Skedsmo, 2006; Tjeldvoll et al., 2005). Over the past 15 years in the United States, Great Britain, and Australia, accountability demands have been changed from mere compliance with policy and administrative rules to quality assurance and inspection demands based more on system outputs (student learning outcomes) than on inputs and processes (Bredeson & Johansson, 2006; Bredeson & Kose, 2006). Where national examinations and systems of testing exist (e.g., state testing in the United States, Great Britain, and Australia), school leaders, especially principals, are expected to understand student outcomes in their systems as well as exercise their leadership to ameliorate deficiencies or inequities in student learning outcomes.

From a cynical point of view, it would be easy to argue that this shift in the devolution of authority coupled with greater accountability of principals is a clever ploy by policy makers to center the responsibility for educational outcomes onto local administrators, thereby being able to blame them when national goals or specified educational outcomes are unrealized. By holding principals and teachers more accountable for educational outcomes, policy makers deftly can avoid such nettlesome issues known to affect educational outcomes as inadequate funding, bureaucratic rules and laws that hamstring local autonomy, lack of time and other resources for professional training and development, poverty, and racism, to name a few.

Social, Historic, and Cultural Foundations of Education in Each Country

Given that schools and educational systems, both public and private, are social institutions created to achieve national goals (i.e., academic, social, and civic) and to pass on national culture, history, and aspirations to future generations, it is not surprising that they reflect unique elements within these national settings. Notwithstanding these distinctive histories, the influence of political, economic, cultural, and religious forces evidenced in waves of imperialism, colonialism, and economic domination greatly have affected educational systems around the world. For example, countries currently or formerly part of the British Commonwealth worldwide, from Hong Kong to Barbados, Australia, India, and Pakistan, have national education systems reflecting the British system. Similarly, in Africa, where French, Portuguese, German, and other European countries were colonial powers, national educational systems from Tunisia to South Africa were modeled after European systems. Along with these systems came an understanding of school governance, authority structures, and the role of educational leaders. It is this legacy of history that so powerfully has shaped school leader preparation programs, or lack thereof, and their ongoing professional development programs that exist today.

The eight factors we described above have played out distinctively in each country and have had a powerful influence on the design and delivery of school leader education. They remain part of the legacy upon which policy makers and educators who train and develop school leaders draw. In the next section, we use selected countries to illustrate the impact of these factors on school leader preparation programs and ongoing professional learning.

Approaches to Leadership Development

Though this chapter focuses on contemporary approaches and thinking in leadership development, the idea of formalizing the work and thus the training and preparation of school leaders is not a new one. For instance, in 1537, Johann Sturm, a classically trained renaissance scholar, was hired by the magistrates of Strasburg, Germany, to organize the curriculum, teaching methods, and supervision practices of a local gymnasium. He formalized his work in 1538 in *The Best Mode of Opening Institutions of Learning* (as cited in Hart & Bredeson, 1996). Over the next four centuries, the degree to which formal study and preparation for school leadership positions varied within various national contexts but generally followed a pattern of informal socialization (i.e., teachers with adequate experience and knowledge) moved from the classroom to administrative tasks. By the 18th century the term *headmaster* was in common use, and the roles and responsibilities for these headmasters were focused primarily on discipline and supervision of student life of boys attending schools away from home (Hart & Bredeson, 1996). In Western Europe and in North America the growth of cities during the industrial revolution accompanied by massive social and economic reforms affected the mission, structure, and size of educational institutions, especially public (private in Great Britain) schools. The increase in school size and complexity resulted in the need for *principal teachers* who could spend more time during the day carrying out administrative responsibilities. In like manner, as nations in South America, Africa, Australia, and Asia experienced the effects of the industrial, postindustrial, and information age revolutions, new demands were placed on schools and school leaders.

Formal patterns of professional socialization and preparation programs did not emerge in most countries until late in the 20th century. Bredeson (1996) wrote,

> In the United States, for example, the first college-level, school administration course was offered at the University of Michigan in 1879 (Murphy, 1992). Departments of education existed in colleges and universities, but little if any specific course work or program emphases in school administration existed (Cooper and Boyd, 1987). (p. 252)

However, beginning in the 1960s there was a rapid growth in formal preparation and training programs, first in North America and following in Europe, Australia, and Asia. Despite unique cultural and institutional traditions in these settings, Hart and Weindling (1996) reported that these programs tended to share five features:

1. Programs tend to place more or less emphasis on pre- or postappointment learning.
2. Such programs emphasize formal and informal learning (using deliberately structured processes).
3. Programs depend differentially on experiential learning versus traditional, formal study at a university or college.
4. They pay more or less attention to the postappointment induction.

5. Programs rely more or less on mentors of the preparation of school leaders.

Reporting on an international study of school leadership development, Huber (2003) identified nine general patterns as nations have moved to more formal approaches to school leader development: (a) providing central quality assurance and decentralization, (b) providing preparatory training and development, (c) developing comprehensiveness of programs, (d) providing multiphase designs and modularization, (e) moving from administration and management to leadership for improvement, (f) developing the leadership capacity of schools, (g) moving from acquisition to creation and development of knowledge, (h) shifting from role-based training to personal professional development, and (i) providing new leadership conceptions and an orientation towards values.

To be sure, these patterns have played out differently within distinct national and cultural contexts. These patterns also reflect dimensions and features of the design and delivery of leadership development.

Perhaps one of the most influential patterns is the timing of school leader training and development. That is, how should educators working to prepare school leaders think about and organize programs that stage the professional learning and socialization of school leaders? In the literature we find a number of references to staging the preparation and development of school leaders. Huber (2003) identified four phases in which formal school leader development occurs: (a) orientation, (b) preparation, (c) induction, and (d) continuous development. At the National College of School Leadership (n.d.), the leadership development framework has a plan of activities around five stages in a school leader's career, in which four milestones for headship and national qualification are achieved: (a) emergent leadership, when teachers begin to take on management and leadership responsibilities; (b) established leaders, comprising assistant and deputy heads who will not pursue the headship qualification; (c) entry to headship, teacher preparation for and induction into the headship position in a school; (d) advanced leadership, where school leaders mature in their roles; and (e) consultant leadership, when an able and experienced leader takes on responsibilities to train, mentor, and inspect aspiring and developing school leaders. In the United States, as reported earlier, still another variation of the staging of school leader development is often sponsored collaboratively by school leader professional associations, state departments of education, and university programs. According to Bredeson (2004), stages usually include aspiring-administrator training sessions; formal, university-based principal certification and licensure programs; new-administrator training and induction programs; mentoring; ongoing professional development supported by electronic portfolio documentation; and career-staged licenses (e.g., for school leaders: initial license, professional license, and master administrator).

In the next section, using a professional socialization framework, we review research on school leader preparation from selected countries including the United States to illustrate the range of program designs and delivery structures. School leadership preparation and development programs include orientation, preservice preparation, induction, and ongoing professional development.

To begin, we recognize the importance of informal learning and its impact on school leader development and growth. Within various educational and organizational contexts, aspiring as well as experienced school leaders continually learn new skills, new knowledge, and new ways to think about persistently nettlesome problems and issues in their professional work. "Most on-the-job learning tends to be informal, varied, and multifaceted. Informal learning (everyday learning) is the most important setting for continuous learning" (Rubenson & Schutze, as cited in Bredeson, 2003, p. 79). Notwithstanding the contributions of informal learning to leadership preparation and professional growth, the focus in this chapter is on formal learning structures designed to prepare and enhance the professional growth and practice of school leaders. Next, we use four stages of professional socialization to describe the dominant program design and delivery features of school leadership preparation programs in selected countries.

Stages of Professional Socialization Framework

Orientation

The first stage of professional socialization is *orientation* to school leadership. The United States, Australia, and England provide the best examples of formally structured programs (workshops and structured sessions) designed to help aspiring leaders consider whether or not continued studies and formal preparation and career movement are appropriate for them. These include such programs as a course titled, Becoming a School Leader: Understanding and Managing Yourself and Others (Australia Principals Centre), Emergent Leadership programs and activities (National College for School Leadership), and the Aspiring Principals Program (New York City Leadership Academy). Though common in these countries, early orientation programs designed to move teachers and other educators into more formal preparation programs are rare in other countries.

Preservice Preparation

Formal preservice preparation programs for school leaders, well established in North America, Europe, and Australia, have as a result of education reform and government policy initiatives become much more common throughout the world. Though often available, in most countries they are not mandatory requirements needed to pursue a career as a school leader. Huber (2003), in a study of international school-leader development programs in 15 selected countries, reported that preservice training was mandatory in only 4 countries in his sample and that preservice remained optional in 4 others. Su et al. (2003) wrote, "In China, formal principal training was nonexistent only a few years ago, the National Ministry of Education now requires all the principals to obtain certificates of pre-service training, at least for a few months before they take leadership positions" (p. 51). In such diverse settings as China, Norway, Pakistan, Hong Kong, France, and Singapore, governments have recognized the importance of leadership to school effectiveness and improvement (Bush & Jackson, 2002; Moller & Skedsmo, 2006; Su et al., 2003). Preservice preparation programs, though not ubiquitous, continue to become more available internationally as policy makers and practitioners understand the importance of school leadership to school improvement and success in achieving national economic, political, social, and cultural goals.

Induction

School leaders pass through predictable phases of this important stage of professional socialization. Parkay and Hall (1993) described a continuum of stages, including survival, control, stability, educational leadership, and professional actualization, that newly appointed school leaders move through as they enter and establish themselves in schools. From a global perspective, training and support at the time of induction is likely to be the most prevalent design for school leader preparation and development, whether offered by national education agencies, local municipalities and school districts, or colleges and universities. From a training and development perspective, helping newly appointed heads, principals, and other school leaders successfully navigate these stages of professional socialization in situ is a major program goal. Mentoring, coaching, and internships are common features of induction-based leadership development programs in the United States; Singapore; England; and Ontario, Canada (Bush & Jackson, 2002; Whitaker, 2003).

Huber (2003) identified 9 of the 15 selected countries in his sample as induction-based training and development programs. In some cases the induction training was mandatory, such as in parts of Germany and in Austria, Switzerland, and Hong Kong, whereas in Denmark and Sweden such training was optional. The general assumption in school leader programs designed around induction is that school leaders have met local school leader selection criteria and have been hired; now they need training. This approach stands in sharp contrast to the North American university-based preservice training programs, where academic criteria, prior education training and experiences, personal desire, and educational references are the major factors considered for entry into training programs.

Principal development in Sweden is an example of the design and delivery of an induction-centered, school-leader development program. The National Headteacher Training Programme at Umeå University (2005) in Sweden is described in program information in this way:

> The training programme for school heads is grounded in the state's responsibility to provide education of equal value in which school heads guarantee equality, legal security and quality in the decentralised school system. The training programme will enable those involved to deepen their awareness of the task assigned to schools, enabling school heads to manage and develop their roles in a goal-oriented way. The training programme is based on experience and focuses on procedures. Having completed the training programme, school heads will be expected to be able to implement a management style based on principles of democracy, learning and communication. The training programme provides school heads with a heightened understanding of their tasks which will better equip them to live up to the responsibilities placed on them by curricula and other policy regulations. School heads should also be able to define for their employers the circumstances under which they operate and to assert their needs.
>
> Admission to the training programme takes place in consultation with the training provider and the board of the school to which the school head belongs. The board undertakes to ensure that each participant in the training programme will be granted sufficient time off for self tuition and receives financial support. The training programme comprises a minimum of 30 training days and takes place over a period of at least two and a maximum of three years. Participants will receive a certificate on successful completion of the training programme. (Nature of the Training Programme section)

We highlight several distinguishing features that make the headteacher training program in Sweden unique. First, school leaders already have a context for applying new knowledge and concepts about organizational improvement, leadership, and teaching and learning. Thus, the issue of transfer of learning is reduced. Local school authorities support newly inducted leaders by providing the time, a minimum of 30 days over a 2- to 3-year period, and the financial support to complete the program. Though some countries provide similar support and resources, in most countries participants in school leadership preparation programs, whether preservice, induction, or postinduction, typically pay for their own training and need to find time to participate in and complete those programs after work, during nonschool times, or through employment leaves.

Ongoing Professional Development

With greater attention being paid to school leader development, there is a corresponding interest in the ongoing professional development of school leaders. Historically, preservice preparation and training remained the primary mission of educational leadership programs, especially university-based programs. Once school leaders completed their program requirements, unless they wanted another advanced degree or certification, they did not return for further training. New research findings on leadership and school improvement, new demands on school leaders, and rising expectations for schools and the administrators who lead them have reinforced the idea that school leadership requires more than an acquired set of formal knowledge and skills. It is a commitment over time to continuous learning, development, and improved practice. Bredeson (2003) identified six design themes for professional development.

1. Professional development is about learning.
2. Professional development is work.
3. Professional development is a journey, not a credential.
4. Opportunities for professional learning and improved practice are unbounded.
5. Student learning, professional development, and organizational mission are intimately related.
6. Professional development is about people, not programs.

These design themes resonate with Hallinger's (2003) assertion, "Life-long learning has become a necessary and fundamental facet of the school leader's role" (p. 295). Most researchers and practitioners agree that ongoing professional learning is critical to successful school leadership and improved schools.

A persistent challenge in the preparation and development of school leaders is how to integrate the various stages of professional socialization—orientation, preservice training, induction, and professional development—into a coherent curriculum for school leader development. This problem is especially acute given the fragmentation of programs across these stages and the wide variety of agencies and institutions responsible for delivery of programs. Carter (1994) observed, "The internal and external forces that interact with and shape the character of educational administration and leadership development programmes inevitably influence the executives themselves as they progress in their careers" (p. 31). Thus, the challenge in school leadership development is to think beyond program designs and delivery mechanisms that simply situate leader development within one particular stage of professional socialization. The design and delivery of school leader development programs requires a more holistic and integrated understanding of school leadership as a continuum of learning and practice. Training and development programs designed with an eye toward developing school leaders over the span of their professional careers likely will reassess the content, structure, and delivery strategies employed to accomplish their mission.

Suggestions for Further Research

Current research on leadership preparation programs has centered on how participants and faculty *perceive* the effectiveness of the program and the way it was delivered. However, as more attention is turned toward program outcomes and a greater demand for accountability at all levels, educational researchers must work to *demonstrate* the effectiveness of leadership preparation programs and to inquire into best delivery practices. We first must determine our criteria for effectiveness and then design research studies that will identify delivery methods that meet those criteria. In addition, given the development of new instructional technologies, research is needed on how best to use technology to enhance delivery. Institutions and faculty are conscious of and attentive to how students experience their program, but do not always follow up to determine how or if their learning affects what they do on the job (Barnett et al., 2000; Muth & Barnett, 2001). Both formative and summative research evaluation designs would be helpful here.

In addition to curricular concerns, which will not be dealt with here, leadership programs have not been unaffected by the trend toward a more market-driven system in higher education. Programs may feel pressure to become more responsive and accommodating to the practical needs of the adult learner as well (Browne-Ferrigno & Muth, 2003; Twale & Kochan, 2000). This responsiveness, in turn, may affect delivery options, which can result in very brief face-to-face interactions and fewer demonstrations of learning. Students risk sacrificing quality in pursuit of the easiest and quickest means to a degree or certification. Providers of programs risk catering too much to the demands of the consumer in order to grow or maintain programs, potentially taking shortcuts that could compromise quality (Glasman, Cibulka, & Ashby, 2002). Research into the most effective methods of delivery should not be overshadowed by market influence.

Furthermore, recent research on the effectiveness of preparation programs is limited because it is primarily qualitative, self-reported impressions of participants. To address the lack of research on program effectiveness beyond this will require carefully constructed and executed longitudinal studies (Browne-Ferrigno & Muth, 2003; Diller, 2004). The data must demonstrate the effectiveness of leadership preparation programs through the academic gains of the schools the leaders serve (Barnett & Muth, 2003).

Sherman and Beaty's (2007) research has indicated that the majority of the research-oriented institutions studied continue to rely heavily on face-to-face course delivery. In fact, out of 49 University Council for Educational Administration universities, each with multiple program offerings in the area of educational leadership, only 4 reported a program that was fully online (all at either the EdS or MEd levels). However, as the Internet and instructional technologies become fully integrated into education, we need to concern ourselves with how distance technology can improve course and overall program quality. We might ask: Why do we prefer more traditional methods of delivery? Is it because that is the way we have always prepared leaders? Or, have we not had enough time or resources to become comfortable with distance technology? Further, is there anything to be said for the superiority of the use of distance technology? Or, are we simply trying to make licensure and degree programs more convenient for students? Ideas for further research include exploring how distance technology may be associated with effective school leaders, comparisons of student success with traditional and distance technology courses, student preferences in delivery format, whether the use of distance technology is indeed an equalizer, and the possibilities and potential of global partnerships enhanced by distance technology.

Much more empirical research is needed on program delivery in general. Moreover, the separation of structure from program design and underlying theoretical foundations of leadership preparation is somewhat artificial. Such separation is useful for the purpose of discovering what research already has been conducted in the area, but it is not especially useful for redesigning preparation programs. Still, to understand more fully what delivery means to designers of preparation, we do recommend more micro research on structure.

For instance, if research indicates that approximately half of all educational leadership preparation programs use some type of cohort model (Barnett et al., 2000), we should investigate further to determine what other structures are in place with the other half of the programs. Also, as the various district, agency, and university preparation partnerships multiply, we must look more closely at the delivery structures of those collaborations. In addition, the growth in the number of programs offered outside of higher education provides as yet untapped opportunities for research examining the differences between these programs and university programs. Further, more in-depth studies of nonuniversity programs would help to assess the impact of market influence on the delivery of educational leadership preparation. We also must learn from studies of program design and delivery in other countries.

The need for change in educational leadership preparation, particularly delivery, is questioned by few. Rather, disputes lie in proposed methods for improving the field (Cambron-McCabe & Cunningham, 2002). We need to highlight exceptional programs, spread the word, and create plans for change that are driven by predefined valued ends (Murphy, 2002). We need to stay focused on what leadership preparation is for—enhanced life chances for all students in all our schools. Together with our partners in the field, we need to be ahead of the curve in planning new models of leadership preparation. If we more purposefully can identify good candidates for the next generation of school and district leaders, and what it is that these leaders must do to challenge the status quo effectively, we can work backwards to shape excellent learning experiences for them.

Conclusions

The quest to understand school leadership development from a global perspective is a particularly challenging one. Trying to design and deliver leadership preparation programs based on the study of leadership preparation and development internationally presents both opportunity and risk. On the positive side of the ledger is the undeniably clear message that leadership is critical to education in general and school improvement in particular. International research studies on school leader preparation also provide opportunities to engage in a broader discourse on what is meant by school leadership and what successful school leadership is. It is also clear that educational leadership is a dynamic concept embedded in layers of historic, cultural, political, and social contexts. Our review of the design and delivery of leadership preparation and development programs also reaffirms our belief in an inextricable link between leadership and learning.

We also learned in our review that there are many common features among leadership preparation programs internationally. These commonalities, however, do not suggest the cloning of preparation programs. Like taking school reform initiatives to scale, a familiar choral phrase heard in the United States, the design and implementation of preparation programs for school leaders are highly sensitive to national and local context.

Lastly, we believe a word of caution is necessary regarding the deliverers of leadership development. As the spirit of entrepreneurialism supported by new communications technologies invades the arena of school leadership development, there is the risk of unethical and unprofessional practices in leadership development. A quick search of the Internet provides ample evidence that many rich opportunities for professional learning are accessible to aspiring and practicing school leaders, regardless of location. The same search also reveals scores of consultants and purveyors dubiously qualified yet ready to deliver the latest in leadership topics, tricks of the trade, and career advancement conveniently, at low cost, and with little or no effort by participants. All educational stakeholders have an interest in maintaining integrity and ethical standards in school leadership preparation and development.

Note

An earlier version of this chapter was published as Preis, S., Grogan, M., Sherman, W. H., & Beaty, D. (2007). What the research says about the delivery of educational leadership preparation programs in the United States. *Journal of Research on Leadership Education, 2*(2). Available from http://www.ucea.org/JRLE/pdf/vol2_issue1__2007/Preisetal.pdf

References

Aiken, J. A. (2001). Supporting and sustaining school principals through a state-wide new principals' institute. *Planning and Changing, 32*(3/4), 144–163.
Arkansas Leadership Academy. (n.d.). Home page. Retrieved June 6, 2008, from http://www.arkansasleadershipacademy.org/
Bailey, M. A., Ruhl-Smith, C., & Smith, J. M. (1999). Breaking the mold: A school-university model for preparing principals utilizing the spirit of collaboration. *Catalyst for Change, 29*(1), 22–26.
Barnett, B. G. (2005). Transferring learning from the classroom to the workplace: Challenges and implications for educational leadership preparation. *Educational Considerations, 32*(2), 6–16.
Barnett, B. G., Basom, M. R., Yerkes, D. M., & Norris, C. J. (2000). Cohorts in educational leadership programs: Benefits, difficulties, and the potential for developing school leaders. *Educational Administration Quarterly, 36*(2), 255–282.

Barnett, B. G., & Muse, I. D. (1993). Cohort groups in educational administration: Promises and challenges. *Journal of School Leadership, 3,* 400–415.

Barnett, B. G., & Muth, R. (2003). Assessment of cohort-based educational leadership preparation programs. *Educational Leadership and Administration: Teaching and Program Development, 15,* 97–112.

Barnett, B. G., & Muth, R. (In press). Ensuring research competence: Using doctoral cohort structures to develop scholar-practitioner leaders. In P. M. Jenlick & R. A. Horn (Eds.), *Scholar-practitioner leadership: A post-formal critique.* New York: Peter Lang.

Bedard, G. J., & Aitken, A. (2004). Designing a standards-based master's program in educational leadership: Trends, contexts, and adaptations. *International Electronic Journal for Leadership in Learning, 8,* Article 9. Retrieved from http://www.ucalgary.ca/~iejll

Belcher, D. (1999). Authentic interaction in a virtual classroom: Leveling the playing field in a graduate seminar. *Computers and Composition, 16*(2), 253–267.

Boone, M. (2001, August). *Preparing superintendents through standards-based instruction.* Paper presented at the annual meeting of the National Council of Professors of Educational Administration, Houston, TX.

Borsa, J., Klotz, J., & Uzat, R. (1998, November). *Utilizing distance learning and the case study method to enhance instruction between two universities.* Paper presented at the annual meeting of the Mid-South Educational Research Association, New Orleans, LA.

Bredeson, P. V. (1996). New direction in the preparation of educational leaders. In K. Leithwood, J. Chapman, D. Corson, P. Hallinger, & A. Hart (Eds.), *International handbook of educational leadership and administration* (pp. 251–277). Boston: Kluwer Academic.

Bredeson, P. V. (2003). *Designs for learning: A new architecture for professional development in schools.* Thousand Oaks, CA: Corwin Press.

Bredeson, P. V. (2004). Creating spaces for the development of democratic school leaders: A case of program redesign in the United States. *Journal of Educational Administration, 42*(6), 708–723.

Bredeson, P. V., & Johansson, O. (2006). *Building capacity in schools: Some ethical considerations through a global lens.* Paper presented at the Commonwealth Council for Educational Administration and Management Conference, Lefkosia, Cyprus.

Bredeson, P. V., & Kose, B. (2006, April). *Responding to the education reform agenda: A study of school superintendents.* Paper presented at the annual meeting of the America Educational Research Association, San Francisco.

Broskoske, S. L., & Harvey, F. A. (2000, October). *Challenges faced by institutions of higher education in migrating to distance learning.* Paper presented at the National Convention of the Association for Educational Communications and Technology, St. Louis, MO.

Browne-Ferrigno, T. (2003). Becoming a principal: Role conception, initial socialization, role-identity transformation, purposeful engagement. *Educational Administration Quarterly, 39*(4), 468–503.

Browne-Ferrigno, T., & Muth, R. (2003). Effects of cohorts on learners. *Journal of School Leadership, 13,* 621–643.

Bush, T., & Jackson, D. (2002). A preparation for school leadership. *Education Management & Administration, 30*(4), 417–429.

Callahan, R. E. (1996). Foreword. *Peabody Journal of Education, 71*(2), 1–14.

Cambron-McCabe, N., & Cunningham, L. (2002). National Commission for the Advancement of Educational Leadership: Opportunity for transformation. *Educational Administration Quarterly, 38*(2), 289–299.

Carr-Chellman, A., & Duchastel, P. (2000). The ideal online course. *British Journal of Educational Technology, 31*(3), 229–241.

Carter, D. (1994). A curriculum model for administrator preparation and continuing professional development. *Journal of Educational Administration, 32*(2), 21–34.

Center for Collaborative Education (n.d.). *Greater Boston Principal Residency Network.* Retrieved March 13, 2006, from http://www.ccebos.org/gbprn/

Cha, S. (2005). *The school administrator's transfer enhancing supervisory practice, and their influence on learning.* Unpublished doctoral dissertation, University of Wisconsin, Madison.

Chicago Leadership Academies for Supporting Success (CLASS). (2006). Home page. Retrieved March 16, 2006, from http://www.classacademics.org/

Clark, D. C., & Clark, S. N. (1997). Addressing dilemmas inherent in educational leadership preparation programs through collaborative restructuring. *Peabody Journal of Education, 72*(2), 21–41.

Daresh, J., & Male, T. (2000). Crossing the border into leadership: experiences of newly appointed British headteachers and American principals, *Educational Management & Administration, 28*(1), 89–101.

Diller, P. F. (2004). *Duquesne University IDPEL cohorts: A laboratory for leadership.* Unpublished doctoral dissertation, Duquesne University, Pittsburgh, PA.

Donaldson, J. F., & Scribner, J. P. (2003). Instructional cohorts and learning: Ironic uses of a social system. *Journal of School Leadership, 13,* 644–665.

Edmonds, R. (1979). Some schools work and more can. *Social Policy, 9,* 32–36.

Foshay, R., & Bergeron, C. (2000). Web-based education: A reality check. *Tech Trends, 44*(5), 16–19.

Friedman, T. (2005). *The world is flat: A brief history of the twenty-first century.* New York: Farrar, Straus, & Giroux.

Georgia's Leadership Institute for School Improvement. (2006). *What is GLISI?* Retrieved March 13, 2006, from http://www.galeaders.org/site/aboutus/aboutUs_glisi_I.htm

Glasman, N. S. (1997). An experimental program in leadership preparation. *Peabody Journal of Education, 72*(2), 42–65.

Glasman, N. S., Cibulka, J., & Ashby, D. (2002). Program self-evaluation for continuous improvement. *Educational Administration Quarterly, 38*(2), 257–288.

Glass, T., Björk, L., & Brunner, C. C. (2000). *The 2000 study of the American school superintendency.* Arlington, VA: American Association of School Administrators.

Goldring, E., & Sims, P. (2005). Modeling creative and courageous school leadership through district-university-community partnerships. *Educational Policy, 19*(1), 223–249.

Griffith, D. E., Stout, R. T., & Forsyth, P. B. (Eds.). (1988). *Leaders for America's schools.* Berkeley, CA: McCutchan.

Grogan, M., & Roberson, S. (2002). Developing a new generation of educational leaders by capitalizing on partnerships. *International Journal of Educational Management, 16*(7), 314–318.

Guri-Rosenblit, S. (2005). "Distance education" and "e-learning": Not the same thing. *Higher Education, 49,* 467–493.

Hallinger, P. (Ed.). (2003). *Reshaping the landscape of school leadership development.* Lisse, The Netherlands: Swets & Zeitlinger.

Harle, A. Z. (2000). Leadership academy: One system's solution to leadership training. *Delta Kappa Gamma Bulletin, 67*(1), 56–59.

Hart, A. W., & Bredeson, P. V. (1996). *The principalship: A theory of professional learning and practice.* New York: McGrawHill.

Hart, A. W., & Weindling, D. (1996). Developing successful school leaders. In K. Leithwood, J. Chapman, D. Corson, P. Hallinger, & A. W. Hart (Eds.), *International handbook of educational leadership and administration* (pp. 309–336). Amsterdam: Kluwer Academic.

Hess, F. M., & Kelly, A. P. (2005). An innovative look, a recalcitrant reality: The politics of principal preparation reform. *Educational Policy, 19*(1), 155–180.

Höög, J., Bredeson, P. V., & Johansson, O. (2006). Conformity to new global imperatives and demands: The case of Swedish school principals. *European Educational Research Journal, 5*(3), 236–275.

Horn, R. A. (2001). Promoting social justice and caring in schools and communities: The unrealized potential of the cohort model. *Journal of School Leadership, 11,* 313–334.

Huber, S. (2003). School leader development: Current trends from a global perspective. In P. Hallinger (Ed.), *Reshaping the landscape of school leadership development* (pp. 273–288). Lisse, The Netherlands: Swets & Zeitlinger.

Hughes, R. C. (2005). Creating a new approach to principal leadership. *Principal, 84*(5), 34–39.

Jackson, B. L., & Kelley, E. (2002). Exceptional and innovative programs in educational leadership. *Educational Administration Quarterly, 38*(2), 192–212.

Jonassen, D. H., Peck, K., & Wilson, B. G. (1999). *Learning with technology: A constructivist approach.* Upper Saddle River, NJ: Merrill.

Kentucky Department of Education. (2006). *Minority superintendent internship program.* Retrieved March 16, 2006, from http://www.education.ky.gov/

Levine, A. (2005). *Educating school leaders.* Washington, DC: The Education Schools Project.

McCabe, D. H., Ricciardi, D., & Jamison, M. G. (2000). Listening to principals as customers: Administrators evaluate practice-based preparation. *Planning and Changing, 31*(3/4), 206–225.

McCarthy, M. M. (1999). How are school leaders prepared? Trends and future directions. *Educational Horizons, 77*(2), 74–81.

Memon, M. (2000, January). *Preparing school leaders for the 21st century.* Symposium presentation at the annual meeting of the International Congress for School Effectiveness and Improvement, Hong Kong.

Milstein, M. M. (1995). Progress and perils: Development of the field-based Ed.D. program in educational administration at the University of New Mexico. *Planning and Changing, 26*(3/4), 130–147.

Milstein, M. M., & Krueger, J. A. (1997). Improving educational administration preparation programs: What we have learned over the past decade. *Peabody Journal of Education, 72*(2), 100–116.

Moller, J., & Skedsmo, G. (2006). *Accountability, contexts, and successful schools.* Paper presented at the Commonwealth Council for Educational Administration and Management Conference in Lefkosia, Cyprus.

Moos, L. (2000, January). *Preparing school leaders for the 21st century.* Symposium presentation at the annual meeting of the International Congress for School Effectiveness and Improvement, Hong Kong.

Murphy, J. (1998). Preparation for the school principalship: The United States' story. *School Leadership & Management, 18*(3), 359–372.

Murphy, J. (2002). Reculturing the profession of educational leadership: New blueprints. *Educational Administration Quarterly, 38*(2), 176–191.

Murphy, J. (2006). *Preparing school leaders: Defining a research and action agenda.* Lanham, MD: Rowman & Littlefield Education.

Muth, R., & Barnett, B. (2001). Making the case for cohorts: Identifying research gaps, improving professional preparation, and gaining political support. *Educational Leadership and Administration: Teaching and Program Development,
13*, 109–120.

Myers, C. B., Bennett, D., Brown, G., & Henderson, T. (2004). Emerging online learning environments and student learning:
An analysis of faculty perceptions. *Educational Technology and Society, 7*(1), 78–86.

National College of School Leadership. (n.d.). Home page. Retrieved June 6, 2008, from http://www.ncsl.org.uk

Norris, C., Barnett, B., Basom, M., & Yerkes, D. (1996). The cohort: A vehicle for building transformational leadership
skills. *Planning and Changing, 27*(3/4), 145–164.

Opsal, C., Brunner, C. C., & Virnig, S. (2005, November). *Unprecedented liberation, unparalleled leadership: The case of
a deaf school administrator's superintendency preparation experience.* Paper presented at the annual meeting of the
University Council for Educational Administration, Nashville, TN.

Parkay, F. W., & Hall, G. E. (Eds.). (1993). *Becoming a principal: The challenges of beginning leadership.* Boston: Allyn and
Bacon.

Rutter, M., Maugham, B., Mortimore, P., Ouston, J., & Smith, A. (1979). *Fifteen thousand hours: Secondary schools and their
effects on children.* Cambridge, MA: Harvard University Press.

Savicki, V., Kelley, M., & Lingenfelter, D. (1996). Gender, group composition, and task type in small task groups using
computer-mediated communication. *Computers in Human Behavior, 12*(4), 549–565.

Sherman, W. H. (2006). Transforming the preparation of educational leaders: A case for ethical district-university partnerships. *International Journal of Educational Reform, 15*(3), 309–330.

Sherman, W. H., & Beaty, D. M. (2007). The use of distance technology in leadership preparation. *Journal of Educational
Administration, 45*(5), 605–620.

Smith, L. (2005, May 25). One family, two sides of the debate over preparing school leaders. *Education Week, 24*(38),
30–31.

Smith-Gratto, K. (2000). Strengthening learning on the Web: Programmed instruction and constructivism. In B. Abbey
(Ed.), *Instructional and cognitive impacts of Web-based instruction* (pp. 227–240). Hershey, PA: Idea Group.

Su, Z., Adams, J. P., & Mininberg, E. (2000). Profiles and preparation of urban school principals: A comparative study in
the United States and China. *Education and Urban Society, 32*(4), 455–480.

Su, Z., Gamage, D., & Mininberg, E. (2003). Professional preparation and development of school leaders in Australia and
the USA. *International Education Journal, 4*(1), 42–59.

Sullivan, P. (2002). "It's easier to be yourself when you are invisible": Female college students discuss their online classroom
experiences. *Innovative Higher Education, 27*(2), 129–144.

Tjeldvoll, A., Wales, C., & Welle-Strand, A. (2005). School leadership training under globalization: Comparisons of the
UK, the US and Norway. *Managing Global Transitions, 3*(1), 23–49.

Tucker, P. D., Henig, C. B., & Salmonowicz, M. J. (2005). Learning outcomes of an educational leadership cohort program.
Educational Considerations, 32(2), 27–35. Retrieved November 1, 2005, from http://www.coe.ksu.edu/EdConsider-
ations

Twale, D. J., & Kochan, F. K. (2000). Assessment of an alternative cohort model for part-time students in an educational
leadership program. *Journal of School Leadership, 10*, 188–208.

Umeå University. (2005). *The National Headteacher Training Programme.* Retrieved June 6, 2008, from http://www.pol.
umu.se/CPD/English/courses/headteacher/

Whitaker, K. (2003). Principal role changes and influence on principal recruitment and selection. *Journal of Educational
Administration, 41*(1), 37–54.

Whitaker, K. S., & Barnett, B. G. (1999). A partnership model linking K–12 school districts and leadership preparation
programs. *Planning and Changing, 30*(3/4), 126–143.

Whitaker, K. S., King, R., & Vogel, L. R. (2004). School district-university partnerships: Graduate student perceptions
of the strengths and weaknesses of a reformed leadership development program. *Planning and Changing, 35*(3/4),
209–222.

Witziers, B., Bosker, R. J., & Kruger, M. L. (2003). Educational leadership and student achievement: The elusive search for
an association. *Education Administration Quarterly, 39*(3), 398–425.

11

Student Assessment in Educational Leadership Preparation Programs

Looking at Our Past, Examining Our Present,
and Framing Our Future

FRANCES K. KOCHAN AND DEMETRISS L. LOCKE

Introduction

Although assessing students in higher education has a long history dating back to 1650, when Harvard University instituted oral examinations and senior declamations to determine student knowledge and understanding (El-Khawas, 1989), there is scant research on assessing students of educational leadership preparation programs. This creates difficulties for the authors writing this chapter as well as for members of the educational leadership preparation arenas navigating the current political environment: Baker (2004) wrote,

> When considering funding requests for higher education, financial backers seek evidence of educational quality, student achievement, and institutional accomplishments to foster confidence in higher education's ability and capacity to produce meaningful educational results in an effective and efficient manner. (p. 1)

Thus, educational institutions must be able to demonstrate that they are offering high-quality programs (Lubinescu, Ratcliff, & Gaffney, 2001). The implementation of student assessment programs and processes helps institutions of higher education address inquiries about their political, economic, and educational value as well as demonstrate their value to a wide variety of audiences (Rossman & El-Khawas, 1987).

Hence, it is troubling that only 8% of the articles in the leading educational leadership journals from 1975–2002 dealt with issues related to educational leadership preparation programs. Moreover, most articles were program descriptions or program analyses, and only 3% of these articles were empirical in nature (J. Murphy, 2006). Furthermore, research regarding student assessment in or of educational leadership programs reported student satisfaction with programs rather than issues concerning graduate student performance on program outcomes (Orr & Barber, 2007). Other inquiries focused on program components (Daresh, 1995; Prestine & LeGrand, 1991) as well as on graduate job placements (McFadden & Buckner, 2005). Existing literature dealing primarily with student satisfaction, perceived program benefits, and career advancement utilized single-case groups rather than comparative program studies (Orr, Doolittle, Kottkamp, Osterman, & Silverberg, 2004).

Investigating the research on skills and knowledge gained in educational leadership principal preparation programs, J. Murphy and Vriesenga (2004) found that there were no research articles in the leading journal in the field that directly assessed the skills and knowledge gained in these programs. In addition, none of the articles measured changes in student performance in schools led by program graduates. McCarthy (2006) confirmed the apparent lack of research assessing the skills and knowledge that students gain in educational leadership preparation programs as well as literature documenting possible changes that occur in schools led by graduates of these programs. Orr et al. (2004) examined this topic for the University Council for Educational Administration (UCEA) Task Force and described a similar lack of literature on the topic.

Despite a dearth of research on assessing students in educational leadership preparation programs, the literature does contain prior studies concerning higher education and assessment in general that may prove fruitful to our discussion. In addition, we explore the literature describing a variety of external forces that impact educational leadership programs and their ability to design and implement appropriate assessment agendas. The purpose of this chapter is to examine what we do know about student assessment and evaluation in educational leadership preparation. To provide context, we describe the historical trajectory of assessment from a macro to micro perspective as well as examine the political and other contextual factors that influenced the design and use of assessment and how those practices have changed over time. The components of assessment include coursework evaluation, appraisal of candidates' practical experiences, and exit evaluations that determine recommendations for graduation and licensure.

The chapter begins with an overview of educational assessment in general. We include a definition of assessment, describe related terms, and present the elements of good assessment design. The next section presents a brief historical review of the development of student and program assessment in higher education at the national and state levels and identifies factors that hinder and facilitate the success of assessment programs. This is followed by a review of assessment in colleges of education and in educational leadership programs. Then, we describe factors that hinder and support effective student assessment practices in educational leadership preparation programs. We detail the typical manner in which student assessment is incorporated into educational leadership programs, the primary types of assessment strategies being used to measure student progress and achievement, and some promising research related to measuring student outcomes. The next section identifies challenges and concerns related to student assessment in educational leadership programs. The final section addresses the gaps in the research and proposes future research that should be conducted to fill these gaps.

Overview

The term *assessment* began to emerge in general usage during the late 1930s, when Henry Murray and his associates applied it to the appraisal of individuals (Hartle, 1985). Today the term has varied definitions. Mazzeo (2001) maintained the narrow definition of the past by suggesting that *assessment* and *testing* are so similar that the terms are interchangeable. Others take a broader view; Huba and Freed (2000) maintained,

> Assessment is the process of gathering and discussing information from multiple and diverse sources in order to develop a deep understanding of what students know, understand, and can do with their knowledge as a result of their educational experiences; the process culminates when assessment results are used to improve subsequent leaning. (p. 8)

Marchese (1997) expanded the definition and provided greater clarification:

> Assessment is a process in which rich, usable, credible *feedback* from an act—of teaching or curriculum—comes to be reflected upon by an academic community, and then is acted on by that community—a department or college—within its commitment to get smarter and better at what it does. (p. 3)

Sims (1992) maintained that assessment has multiple meanings to users. For some, assessment refers to the skills and quality of freshmen entering college. For others, assessment refers to the measurement of college-level learning. "Assessment places an emphasis on the results of education—outputs—as opposed to what goes into the educational system as a whole—inputs" (Brown & Faupel, 1986, p. 5). Huba and Freed (2000) emphasized that student assessment in higher education today is part of a movement to change the focus of evaluation from the teaching process to the learning gained.

We have combined the attributes of these definitions and created our own definition of educational assessment. We define *educational assessment* as a comprehensive process by which members of an academic community gather and analyze data about students' knowledge, dispositions, and performance and use that information to revise teaching and learning processes and experiences to assure student success in achieving program goals. We include students, faculty, and stakeholders as part of the academic community that should be engaged in the educational assessment process.

Formative assessment is gathering data at midpoints to improve student learning. *Summative assessment* is gathering data at the conclusion of a series of activities or experiences, such as an internship, a capstone experience, or comprehensive data gathered at program completion. Follow-up data of graduates also would fall within this category. Summative evaluation examines a final outcome and in general is used to judge student and program success (see Niewig, 2004). The best assessment processes are implemented as part of a system that gathers formative and summative data on a consistent and ongoing basis and uses the data as a part of a continuous improvement process. It is essential to realize that student and program assessments are integrated parts of a whole, and it is difficult to separate them (Peterson & Vaughan, 2002). The results of student assessments inform faculty and administrators about their programs so that they can determine what to keep and what to change in admissions, curricular offerings, and assessment strategies. This relationship and connection will be dealt with as appropriate throughout the chapter.

Good assessment design (a) begins with educational values; (b) is ongoing; (c) is built around agreed-upon standards (American Association of Higher Education, 1992); (d) involves formulating statements of intended learning outcomes (Huba & Freed, 2000); (e) includes developing or selecting assessment tools related to learning outcomes (Palomba & Banta, 1999; Wiggins & McTighe, 1998); (f) requires the creation of developmental learning experiences that will lead to the expected outcomes (American Association of Higher Education, 1992); (g) includes analyzing and discussing results with students, advisory groups, and other stakeholders (Kochan & Twale, 1998); and (h) involves using assessment results to improve learning (El-Khawas, 1989; Huba & Freed, 2000; Wiggins & McTighe, 1998). In educational leadership, the values and standards selected must incorporate "visions of society, education, learning, and leadership for schooling in the twenty-first century as well as the values and evidence that define the paths to those visions" (J. Murphy, 1993, p. 2).

Effective student assessment should have a learning-centered focus. The processes and strategies used in assessment should promote high expectations, respect diverse talents and learning styles, promote coherence in learning, synthesize experiences that foster the ongoing practice of skills and abilities, actively involve students in the process, provide prompt feedback, and be part of a larger set of conditions that promote change (American Association of Higher Education, 1992; Huba & Freed, 2000).

Student Assessment in Higher Education

Assessment of students in higher education has received a surge of interest over the past 10 years (El-Khawas, 1989) and is more prominent today than at any time in history (Mazzeo, 2001). The present emphasis on student assessment in higher education is an outgrowth of a 25-year accountability movement in public education which initially focused upon public education from prekindergarten through Grade 12 (preK–12).

This accountability push was stimulated by a general lack of trust in public institutions, labeled by R. Young (1990) as the "crisis of modernity" and the "crisis of education" (p. 5). Habermas (1975) described public distrust of public institutions as the *legitimation crisis*. This lack of trust has resulted in a belief that leaders and staff of governmental institutions such as schools cannot be trusted to do their jobs and must be monitored to demonstrate their value (Cibulka, 1999; Kochan, 2002).

The accountability movement is also an outgrowth of governmental and societal concerns related to the new economics of the global, postindustrial age and technological society as well as the changing demographics of the United States and the world (Bottoms & O'Neil, 2001; J. Murphy, 2006). Some have tied accountability to national security in a time of a competitive global marketplace (Levine, 2005). Disregarding the apparent genesis, it seems in the best interest of universities, colleges of education, and educational leadership programs to demonstrate their value to the public they serve.

History of Student Assessment in Higher Education

The earliest attempt to measure student outcomes dates back to 1918, continuing to 1952 as a period of significant growth for higher education. This vast expansion was fueled by growth in national population and wealth as well as by notable changes in public opinion about the importance of higher education (Cohen, 1998). During this period, educators complained about the incoherence of the curriculum, the low abilities of the students, and the overcrowding of institutions (D. Resnick & Goulden, 1987). Educators also noted the absence of assessment measures that could register the difference between the ideals of a college education and the actual gains made by students (Tatlock, 1924). Tatlock argued, "There is no opportunity to appraise the student as an entire educated human being" (as cited in D. Resnick & Goulden, 1987, p. 86). In addition, course programs were merely "fantastic patchiness, which was sometimes ludicrous" (D. Resnick & Goulden, 1987, p. 80). Written exams and discussion groups became prevalent during this era, which contributed to the increased focus on students' finding and reporting on various sources of research (Cohen, 1998).

Eventually, *comprehensive examinations* were added to the curriculum. Locally designed and administered by the faculty, these summative assessments were expected to bolster integrity of the field by increasing students' desire to learn and giving them the opportunity to demonstrate their command of a field (Sims, 1992). Ralph Tyler and Benjamin Bloom, at the University of Chicago in the 1930s, developed objective, comprehensive exams to measure students' attainment of the goals of Chicago's general education program. According to Pace (1984), "The tests were sophisticated, ingenious, intellectually demanding measures of student outcomes, appropriate to the academically rigorous Chicago general education program and to the high scholastic level of Chicago's student body" (p. 11).

The University of Minnesota, through its Committee on Educational Research, established the General College in 1932 to provide a suitable education for students with moderate academic talents. The General College was created with four tasks at the forefront: (a) to identify the quantifiable, realistic goals and objectives of the program; (b) to measure the knowledge and skill set of students at program entry and exit; (c) to examine character changes, reflected by attitudes and off-campus activities while enrolled at the General College (Sims, 1992); and (d) to determine the attitudes of students toward the General College as an institution (Eckert, 1943).

In an effort to construct reliable and valid examinations, the Committee on Educational Research experimented with various testing types. These included multiple-choice questions, matching, historical sequencing of events, and applying principles to new situations (Sims, 1992). Technical concerns about item discrimination, test reliability, and intercorrelations among different parts of a test were considered (Pace, 1984). Comprehensive examinations for courses in biology, physics, chemistry, and economics were developed. These examinations looked at three aspects of learning: (a) acquiring the terminology or vocabulary distinctive to the course, (b) acquiring principles and other factual information, and (c) applying the knowledge of facts and principles to interpret new situations or problems (Pace, 1984).

Other assessment efforts were initiated during this period. In 1943, Ruth Eckert "compared students who had, and who had not had, certain courses, and retention of information a year after the course" (as cited in Pace, 1984, p. 11). The test also measured attitudes, values, interests, personal and social adjustment, and basic reading and English usage. Eckert also measured religious beliefs, philosophy of life, realism of vocational plans, liberal or conservative attitudes, and overall satisfaction with college. Eckert created assessment measures for students who had graduated, which measured, according to Pace, "job satisfaction, job characteristics related to satisfaction, economic status, leisure activities and interests, civic participation, health practices and many other topics" (p. 11).

National testing agencies had a significant role in measuring student outcomes during this era. The Graduate Record Office of the Carnegie Foundation, which produced the Tests of General Education, and the Cooperative Test Service, known for the General Culture Tests, were of particular significance in the 1940s (Pace, 1984). Pace wrote, "The General Culture Tests covered current social problems, history, and social studies, literature, science, fine arts, and mathematics" (p. 12). The Educational Testing Service, established in 1948, assumed responsibility for the cooperative testing program (Sims, 1992). The General Education Test, which took 8 eight hours to complete, covered general mathematics, physical and biological sciences, literature arts, vocabulary, and effectiveness of expression (Sims, 1992).

The second period of outcomes assessment was 1952–1975. Researchers in education refer to this period as the Golden Age due to expanding enrollments, growth in institutions, and strong financial health in higher education (Cohen, 1998). Cohen referred to this period as "mass higher education in the era of American hegemony" (p. 175). The earlier era had set the stage for growth, which continued during this period. New campuses opened across the nation, a greater variety of students began attending, and new curricula were introduced (Cohen, 1998).

This was the era of optimism. The United States had emerged from World War II as the most powerful nation in the world. The population grew, as did the economy. Economic expansion led to disposable income and a delay in the time when young people entered the workforce, both of which contributed to the massive increase in college enrollments (Cohen, 1998). The number of students enrolled in college increased from 1.5 million to over 11.0 million, while the number of faculty members rose from 150,000 to 628,000. More than 600 public institutions were added; 500 of them were 2-year colleges. "In the private sector, 650 new institutions were opened, but half as many closed, for a net gain of 325" (Cohen, 1998, p. 187). Minority enrollments increased, which lead to the creation of more historically Black colleges and universities. Those returning home from the war were able to attend college at little or no cost under the Servicemen's Readjustment Act of 1944 (Cohen, 1998).

During this period, curricula and foci varied among institutions. Enrollment at single-sex institutions dropped from 25% to 14%, as many institutions closed or became coeducational

(Cohen, 1998). During this phase, academic disciplines were splintered into numerous subfields, which resulted in a greater variety of courses. Course offerings expanded into the arts and sciences as well as into specialized, "esoteric" courses (Cohen, 1998, p. 223). In addition, colleges and universities providing agricultural and mechanical arts curriculums were formed under the Morrill Land Grant Act.

D. Resnick and Goulden (1987) reported major changes that occurred during this second phase; specifically, the portion of students majoring in history, philosophy, math, social science, literature, foreign languages, and science dropped from 40% to 20%. "The major gainer in student majors was business, which was selected by 23 percent of those receiving baccalaureate degrees at the end of this second period of expansion" (D. Resnick & Goulden, 1987, p. 82).

During the 1960s and 1970s, higher education was affected not only by federal policies, but also by changing social attitudes (Aper, 1993). More people were able to go to college due to legislation primarily designed to eliminate discriminatory practices, to provide financial aid to students and institutions, and to promote the development of greater central planning and data collection by the states (Lawrence & Green, 1980)

Higher education reform of the early 1970s, such as nontraditional education, and the professionalization of teaching spurred the use of assessment techniques on college campuses (Sims, 1992). Some of the earliest assessment techniques focused on the returning adult student and on teacher education.

Some private colleges took a leadership role in student assessment during this period. Alverno College, a small private women's college, developed an outcomes-based curriculum in the early 1970s. In partnership with AT&T, Alverno College developed multiple-measure, assessment center programs (Sims, 1992). The programs were designed to help determine whether students were acquiring abilities such as critical thinking, problem solving, effective communication, and decision making as a result of the existing curriculum (Edgerton, 1986).

The student assessment center at Alverno College was designed to emphasize the intellectual and personal development of its students (Sims, 1992). Alverno's student assessment program is comprehensive. Its goals are to provide feedback to individual students for their own progress and to ensure that the curriculum is effectively meeting established educational goals (Ewell, 1985). These goals are met by conducting standardized tests and tests of psychological and personal development to measure individual growth and development.

Students at Alverno College are required to undergo more than 100 performance assessments throughout 4 years of study (Hartle, 1985). The current abilities across the curricula at Alverno are defined by six developmental levels: (a) communication skills; (b) analysis; (c) problem solving; (d) social interaction; (e) effective citizenship; and (f) the development of a global perspective, valuing decision making and aesthetic engagement (Casey, 2004).

Northeast Missouri State University, in Kirksville, began assessing their students in 1971. Founded as a normal school to educate teachers and now a regional comprehensive university (renamed Truman State University), Northeast Missouri State University developed an assessment program with the intention of testing curricular effectiveness. By comparing results obtained by students' college entrance exam scores (e.g., ACT) with graduate and professional school entrance exams (e.g., the Graduate Record Examination [GRE]), Northeast Missouri State University hoped to determine growth of students while attending the university, as compared to national percentages of both testing phases (Sims, 1992). The program was revamped in 1974 to include a value-added approach to determining student outcomes assessment (Hartle, 1985).

The value-added model consisted of three primary goals, according to McClain and Krueger (1985): "the desire to know everything possible about the student, the wish to demonstrate that the university made a positive difference in the student's life, and the desire to demonstrate that students who graduated from the university were nationally competitive" (p. 37). Value-added models, using pre- and posttests, assess student learning from point of entry and then at midpoint in the curriculum (C. Boyer & Ewell, 1988).

The accountability movement gathered momentum during the mid-1980s and affected all public education endeavors from preschool to graduate school. Rising costs and increasing expectations for all public endeavors fueled growing interest of public officials in the effectiveness and efficiency of higher education (Aper, 1993). Historically, higher education institutions have been able to exercise complete autonomy regarding policy and practice. This freedom is slowly being retracted as the battle over the balance between public and institutional expectations continues to escalate (Aper, 1993). The public demands that institutions account for their resources efficiently and effectively to ensure the production of the best education possible at the most reasonable cost (Knight & Yorke, 2003).

Colleges and universities are being asked to explain how money and other resources are being used, especially if there is a need for increased financial support. According to Aper (1993), "The drive for accountability also grew out of the desire of state governments to know more about what institutions of higher education did, and how they managed their affairs" (p. 366).

Both state and federal governments took certain actions to gain information from higher education institutions regarding student outcomes. The federal government became involved in focusing on student outcomes in higher education when a series of reports from state, national, and regional organizations denounced higher education for not providing evidence of its relevance, coherence, and value (Aper, 1993).

Federal Involvement in Student Assessment in Higher Education

Ewell (2002) suggested that the next phase, federal involvement, had its beginnings in the First National Conference on Assessment in Higher Education in the fall of 1985. The meeting was cosponsored by the National Institute of Education and the American Association for Higher Education. Besides utilizing research tools to learn about instructors' own performance, three major recommendations came from that meeting:

1. Set high expectations for students.
2. Involve students in active learning environments.
3. Provide students with prompt and useful feedback.

In 1986, the Task Force on College Quality, convened by the National Governors' Association, met to discuss how colleges and universities could demonstrate that student learning was occurring. The task force stressed the need for these institutions to demonstrate student learning by using multiple assessment measures. They concluded, "Postsecondary institutions must assess student learning and ability, program effectiveness, and institutional accomplishment of mission" (National Governors' Association, 1986, p. 159)

In 1984 and 1986, the Commission on Institutions of Higher Education (now the Higher Learning Commission) surveyed regional, national, and specialized accrediting agencies to determine the emphasis they placed on outcomes assessment in their evaluation process (Sims, 1992). The commission found that "outcomes measurement or evaluation of institution and program effectiveness is an integral part of accrediting agency evaluations, as expressed in their criteria, documents, self-study institutes, and evaluator training programs" (Thrash, 1988, p. 17). The commission also found accrediting commissions disagreed on whether there is or ought to be a relationship between outcomes measurement and public accountability, and whether outcomes and accountability should be viewed as related to educational quality. Furthermore, accrediting commission officials expressed caution about overly narrow definitions of outcomes and the misuse of instruments to measure competence. They valued outcomes as one important aspect of documenting institutional effectiveness but stressed the interrelatedness of outcomes and other criteria that must be applied in making an accrediting judgment, such as purpose, resources, organization, programs, and promise of continuing effectiveness (Thrash, 1988).

This movement toward greater accountability was fostered by the work of the Joint Task Force on Student Learning (1988), which was appointed by the American Association for Higher Education, American College Personnel Association, and the National Association of Student Personnel Administrators. These groups emphasized the notion that student assessment should be part of a comprehensive system of assessment that includes program improvement and student success. Such a recommendation requires higher education institutions and faculty to rethink their roles and the position of assessment and feedback within them (Huba & Freed, 2000; Joint Task Force on Student Learning, 1988).

The most recent student assessment activity at the federal level is a report issued by Secretary of Education Margaret Spellings, addressing the need for a radical change in higher education. The report (Secretary of Education's Commission on the Future of Higher Education, 2006) presented six recommendations, three of which specifically related to changing curricula and measuring student outcomes. These recommendations include a commitment by colleges and universities to embrace new pedagogies, curricula, and technologies to improve student learning, particularly in the area of science and math. The commission also emphasized the need to match higher education curriculum to the changing needs of a knowledge economy. Finally, the commission demanded an increase in transparency and communication by colleges and universities about cost and student success outcomes.

Over the last few decades, federal grants have fostered projects to facilitate and nurture the development of assessment in higher education. The U.S. Department of Education, through the Fund for the Improvement of Postsecondary Education (FIPSE), began funding projects on student outcomes assessment in 1972 (Cook, 1989). FIPSE helped to fund initial assessment development measures. The early assessment efforts brought forth by FIPSE were focused around competency-based learning, which refers to the ability of students to perform an activity. Funded projects involved the following elements, according to Cook: "(1) the identification and formulation of competency objectives; (2) assessment of mastery of competencies; and (3) the design and implementation of learning processes which facilitate the attainment of specified competencies" (p. 1).

FIPSE guidelines shifted in 1976 as testing companies were targeted to design instruments to measure higher order thinking skills (Cook, 1989). Funding was also provided for projects that aligned competency-based testing with giving academic credit for knowledge acquired on the job and volunteer work. Assessment also became an intricate part of providing access to nontraditional students to postsecondary education by providing credit for prior learning (Cook, 1989).

The FIPSE guidelines were rewritten in 1984 and 1985 with an emphasis on the mechanics of the assessment agenda. Cook (1989) observed, "Questions like the following were posed: Should rewards go to programs that do the most for their students, programs that have improved the most, or programs that most need to be improved?" (p. 2).

State Involvement in Student Assessment in Higher Education

In addition to federal involvement, state governments have become very interested in student outcomes assessment in higher education during the last two decades. Some of the pioneer states in student assessment efforts were New Jersey, Georgia, Florida, and South Dakota. In 1982, students in the state of Florida were required to pass the College Level Academic Skills Test in sections in reading, writing, and mathematics in order to receive an associate degree or continue with their junior year of college (Sims, 1992). Entering freshman had to take an evaluation of basic skills at the start of their schooling in addition to the College Level Academic Skills Test. Students who did not score satisfactorily on the test were enrolled in remedial courses (Morante, 1986). Texas followed suit, making it mandatory for incoming freshman to pass a basic skills test before being allowed to start college coursework (Sims, 1992). Some states used early prevention methods, which aimed to detect those who were deficient in an effort to address their needs early on and eventually produce quality students (Sims, 1992).

Most states have established commissions and created general guidelines requiring universities to submit a report that outlines a plan for implementing assessment processes (Sims, 1992). State initiatives on assessment differ from state to state. Some states specifically mandated a standardized process regarding student outcomes information. For example, South Carolina requires each university to submit a detailed report covering all categories of outcome data (Sims, 1992). These policies include strategies to structure relationships and coordinate behavior for collective purposes of the state and nation (Stone, as cited by Mazzeo, 2001).

Some states, such as Maryland and North Carolina, monitor outcomes relating to "student retention, satisfaction and job placement of college graduates, and economic and community development" (Sims, 1992, p. 55). Iowa and Idaho do not monitor these particular areas; however, state colleges are involved in student assessment. Meanwhile, Virginia, Florida, and Colorado have specific state mandates requiring colleges to participate in assessment (Sims, 1992). The areas of assessment mentioned above have shifted over the years from campus-based assessment toward more student-centered and learning-oriented assessment, which is linked to accreditation.

Accreditation and Assessment in Higher Education

Accreditation is the process by which higher education institutions voluntarily police themselves (Sims, 1992; Trivett, 1976). Most states accept accreditation as evidence of sufficient quality to qualify an institution for state licensure (Trivett, 1976). Moreover, the federal government uses accreditation and licensure as preconditions for eligibility for federal funds.

Program accreditation involves a quality assurance process that seeks to verify the quality of academic programs and institutions to external stakeholders (Lubinescu et al., 2001). The accreditation of program quality has two dimensions. First, the goals should be clear, concise, and have courses aligned to attain them. Second, the process should delineate clearly how responsibilities associated with the goals are being carried out and by whom (Ewell, 1987).

Whether regional or institutional, accreditation traditionally has been considered a voluntary association of schools and colleges to facilitate quality control (Ratcliff, 1996). The voluntary nature of accreditation is becoming questionable as institutional eligibility for receipt of federal funding is now attached to regional accreditation (Lubinescu et al., 2001).

Historically, regional accrediting agencies have served three functions, according to Sims (1992): "(1) institutional protector in an effort to distinguish between a college and a high school; (2) insurer of higher education quality; and (3) determiner of outcomes of higher education" (p. 68). The function of accrediting agencies has shifted and expanded over the years to include an emphasis on guaranteeing quality student and institutional assessments. Quality assurance is the basic premise in both assessment and accreditation. There are two parallel continuums in these quality assurance processes, according to Lubinescu et al. (2001): "one detailing the cycle of accreditation and the other student outcomes assessment" (p. 18). Both continuums have now merged.

Six regional associations throughout the United States are responsible for colleges and universities in specific geographical locations: Middle States Association of Colleges and Schools, New England Association of Schools and Colleges, North Central Association of Colleges and Schools, Northwest Association of Schools and Colleges, Southern Association of Colleges and Schools, and Western Association of Schools and Colleges (Sims, 1992). All major accrediting agencies now have linked student assessment to institutional performance to enhance program quality (El-Khawas, 1998; Sims, 1992).

The formal self-study and review process entails key attributes that should be included in the plan (Lubinescu et al., 2001):

1. First, it should be "clear to all parties concerned (government, parliament, higher education institutions staff and students) what may be expected from such a review process" (Vroei-jenstijn, 1995, p. 39). Clear expectations noting the purposes and desired outcomes to be achieved through the review process must be disseminated to everyone involved.
2. The review process should focus on either summative or formative evaluation (Lubinescu et al., 2001). Efforts to use both simultaneously may not lead to desired and valid results.
3. Colleges and universities should have direct responsibility and active engagement in the review process. Involving faculty and administrators in the process allows them to commit to and take ownership of the self-study and student assessment as a means to accountability and improvement.
4. The review procedure represents ongoing processes that should be adapted to changing conditions within and external to the institutional environment. Cyclical reviews help institutions monitor their progress of the system, while allowing them to focus on the types of improvements made after each evaluation cycle (Lubinescu et al., 2001)

The "Secretary's Procedures and Criteria for Recognition of Accrediting Agencies," published in the *Federal Register* in September 1987 (as cited in Sims, 1992), called for each accrediting agency to compel its educational institutions and programs to clearly outline objectives and implement assessment measures to verify and document the extent to which students have achieved the objectives. Though vague, the expectations attempted to prompt improvement and engage institutions in an active review of what they do and how well it is done as well as to identify and address discrepancies in order to improve (Aper, 1993). The areas of assessment have shifted over the years from campus-based assessment to student-centered and learning-oriented assessment (Sims, 1992). The shift from campus-based assessment of the 1980s to the accountability movement of the 1990s has bridged the gap between accreditation and student outcomes assessment (Lubinescu et al., 2001).

The organization that brings various higher education accreditation bodies together, the Council for Higher Education Accreditation, has taken a lead in stressing the notion that institutions and their accrediting bodies must address public demand for evidence of student learning outcomes (Lubinescu et al., 2001). The council suggested that dialogue between internal and external constituencies regarding assessment and accountability should take a variety of forms, such as "implementation of online learning, greater engagement with the communities the institution serves, program renewal, organizational transformation, and changing the accreditation process itself" (Lubinescu et al., 2001, p. 5).

Implementing Successful Student-Assessment Programs

There is a body of knowledge about the elements that make institutional and student assessments succeed or fail in higher education environments. We are presenting this information because we believe it can help inform educational leadership faculty as they seek to develop student assessment strategies and programs.

Factors That Hinder Success in Student and Program Assessment

One of the most comprehensive studies of barriers to creating successful assessment programs in higher education was conducted by the Higher Learning Commission of the North Central Association of Colleges and Schools, previously known as the North Central Association of Colleges and Schools (1996). This group asked institutions within their region to develop a plan to assess student academic achievement, implement it, and then use the results to improve student learning. After 10 years, the Higher Learning Commission examined the results and found that it was very difficult to get the university as a whole to accept the importance of measuring student learning, and the number of programs that actually engaged in the process in a comprehensive manner was small. The North Central Association of Colleges and Schools identified three primary factors that hindered implementation:

1. There were misunderstandings about the purposes and nature of assessment.
2. There was an emotionally based resistance to assessment on the part of university personnel.
3. University personnel had insufficient information and skills to perform the assessment design and implementation processes.

Witters-Churchill and Erlandson (1990) expanded on the issue of personnel resistance noted by the North Central Association of Colleges and Schools (1996). They discovered that university personnel were reluctant to accept the need for a comprehensive approach to assessing students. Some viewed it as an imposition on their professionalism, whereas others believed that what they were already doing was sufficient. Another serious institutional problem they found was a lack of sufficient financial and personnel resources to support assessment efforts.

Other researchers have identified additional barriers to student assessment in higher education. Among them are: a lack of involvement of faculty and students, resulting in a insufficient support and interest, difficulties in developing program goals and measurable objectives, inability to select or develop direct and indirect measures that are aligned with goals and objectives, insufficient processes for collecting and interpreting the data, inadequate dissemination of data because of weak feedback loops, and deficiencies in linking assessment processes with planning and budgeting processes (Huba & Freed, 2000; Lopez, 2004; Peterson & Einarson, 2001).

Factors That Facilitate Successful Student and Program Assessment Initiatives

Many factors influence the success of student and program assessment initiatives. Peterson and Vaughan (2002) have done an excellent job of summarizing the results of a research project of the National Center for Postsecondary Improvement relative to organizational and administrative contextual elements and external influences that facilitate the development and implementation of assessment efforts in higher education. They discovered that the level of institutional support for student assessment can have a positive or negative effect on the degree to which assessment processes are enacted and used for program improvement. Peterson and Vaughan also found that the context of the institution (e.g., public vs. private, size) was related to the types of approaches used in programs and the level of support given to them to engage in assessing students and improving programs, to when and how students are assessed, to the assessment management policies and practices implemented, and to the uses and impact of student assessment upon the institution and its programs.

Other researchers have identified similar factors to creating successful student and program assessment initiatives. Student assessment seems most successful when (a) student assessment processes are developed within the context of a comprehensive institutional assessment that is well supported and publicized (Peterson & Einarson, 2001), (b) faculty see the value of student assessment in improving and are actively engaged in the process (Lopez, 2004), (c) there are clear goals and measurable objectives connected to a mission statement (Maki, 2002), (d) there is faculty development in assessment processes (Maki, 2002), (e) roles and responsibilities are clearly delineated (Maki, 2002), (f) multiple measures are used to collect data (Maki, 2002), and (g) data are shared widely and used to improve programs (Lopez, 2004).

Accountability and Assessment in Colleges of Education

The accountability movement in higher education has had a strong impact on colleges of education, particularly in the areas of teacher education and educational leadership. Following the release of several national reports focusing on preK–12 education, including *A Nation at Risk* (National Commission on Excellence in Education, 1983), the states turned their attention to the quality of education in the public schools. As a result, during the last two decades, the preK–12 sector has been inundated with accountability legislation at the state and national levels, most of it centered on student assessment and improving student learning (May, 2005). The present No Child Left Behind Act of 2001 (NCLB, 2002) mandate, which has been called "the most sweeping change ever made in public education and oversight from the federal government" (Alabama State Department of Education, 2002, p. 1), has expanded the pressure on public schools and the colleges that prepare the teachers and leaders who work in them to demonstrate their value.

Prior to NCLB (2002), all states but Iowa had instituted an assessment system for the public schools. The NCLB legislation requires extensive testing and mandates to measure student success in all 50 states. It also contains language that requires all schools employ teachers who are highly qualified. Although each state can define what *highly qualified* means, the notion of having teachers who can assure that children learn helped bring attention to the programs that prepare these teachers and the administrators who supervise them.

In addition to challenges from external groups to reform colleges of education, there have been calls from within the profession to improve the work being done in colleges of education in the preparation of teachers and leaders (Ewell, 1997; Grogan & Andrews, 2002; McCarthy, 1999, Peterson & Vaughan, 2002). In addition, the Holmes Group (1986), begun by deans of colleges of education from various major research universities, and the Carnegie Forum on Education and the Economy (1986) issued reports calling for the transformation of teaching into a full profession. The Holmes Group also recommended restructuring teacher education programs and building a stronger connection with the field in preparing teachers. The Carnegie Forum on Education and the Economy called for the creation of a national board to develop standards and procedures for screening those entering the teaching profession. The initial version, developed by Schulman and Sykes of Stanford University, required candidates to take written tests as well as teach videotaped lessons for evaluation (Edgerton, 1986; National Commission on Teaching and America's Future, 1996).

The National Council of Accreditation of Teacher Education (NCATE), founded in 1954, heeded the calls from various sectors to revise and expand its accreditation processes from its previous focus on program quality, which included primarily information about inputs, to collecting information about outputs, particularly in the area of student outcomes. It established a standard that requires a comprehensive assessment system that includes extensive student appraisal. Although many colleges of education in the country are not accredited, most of those that are use NCATE for accreditation. NCATE (2007) currently accredits 632 colleges of education, with nearly 100 more seeking NCATE accreditation.

The Teacher Education Accreditation Council (TEAC), founded in 1997, is a nonprofit organization dedicated to improving academic degree programs for educators. TEAC's entire accreditation process is built around a program proving that it prepares competent, caring, and qualified professional educators. In order to receive approval, colleges of education must prove student learning, the validity of the evaluation system, and efforts by the program to achieve continuous improvement and quality control (TEAC, 2007).

Student Assessment in Educational Leadership Programs

The student assessment and accountability movement in higher education and in colleges of education has had an impact on educational leadership programs. Before addressing the present state of affairs, we present a short review of the history of assessment in educational leadership programs in order to create an understanding of how the present situation evolved and where we must focus our future endeavors.

Educational leadership programs are relative newcomers in higher education. School administrators were around before the 1900s. However, little was written on the topic of school leadership (J. Murphy, 1999) because "formal preparation programs for school administrators had not yet developed" (Gregg, 1960, p. 20). The 20th century brought with it the beginning of formal degree programs in school administration (Campbell, Fleming, Newell, & Bennion, 1987), and by 1950, the United States had 125 universities offering graduate programs in educational administration or leadership programs (Silver, 1982). Although extensive assessment systems were not in place in these programs, J. Murphy (2006) noted calls to examine program effectiveness during the transition from the prescriptive era (1900–1946) to the scientific era (1947–1985).

During the scientific era, "prescriptions drawn from practice came to be overshadowed in preparation programs by theoretical and conceptual material drawn from the various social sciences" (J. Murphy, 2006, p. 7). This era was embraced because of its call for a change in the status quo in the way administrators were being prepared, the way school leaders' performance was evaluated, and use of science "that held forth the promise of dramatically improving the education available to prospective school leaders" (J. Murphy, 2006 p. 7).

During this era, four major events influenced the movement to assess students and educational leadership programs:

1. The first, which occurred in 1947, was the creation of the National Conference of Professors of Educational Administration. This organization linked professors together from all over the country, allowing them to contrive new concepts regarding the profession and preparation programs and the evaluation of them (Campbell et al., 1987; Gregg, 1960).
2. The second affair was the creation of the Cooperative Project in Educational Administration. This project consisted of eight universities whose purpose was to regulate changes in school leader preparation programs. The Cooperative Project in Educational Administration

encouraged a multidisciplinary approach when analyzing and educating school leaders (J. Murphy, 2006).

3. The third influential incident was the establishment of the Committee for the Advancement of School Administration in 1955. This committee focused on professional standards of performance, which are essential to creating a student assessment system (J. Murphy, 2006).

4. The final milestone in this era was the establishment of the UCEA in 1956. During the 1960s and 1970s, UCEA was "the dominant force in shaping the study and teaching of educational administration … [and] a major force in the advancement of preparation programs" (Campbell et al., 1987, pp. 182–183). This organization continually has called for the improvement of educational leadership programs. Within its proposals for change, the organization consistently has recommended there be methods to assess the impact of programs upon students prepared in them. These reports and the major historical events of this period, chronicled by J. Murphy (2006), emphasized the need to reform principal preparation programs and to assess their value.

In the 1960s, the National Association of Secondary School Principals (NASSP) established an association to create collaborative relationships between professors and practitioners. This relationship was formalized through the establishment of the Committee of Professors of Secondary School Administration and Supervision in 1969 and resulted in several conferences. In 1973, the results of a conference were summarized in a publication, *Where Will They Find It?* (NASSP, 1973), which called for a competency-based curriculum that encapsulated the idea of assessing student outcomes in educational leadership programs. This approach was re-emphasized at conferences held in 1973 and 1974 (Witters-Churchill & Erlandson, 1990).

In 1975, NASSP created the Assessment Center project, which assessed leadership skills needed for principals and assistant principals and is used by some preparation programs to admit students into their educational leadership programs. Later, this group formed the Consortium for Performance-Based Preparation of Principals (NASSP, 1995). The consortium developed a framework for principal preparation that contained five parts: (a) goals, (b) admission, (c) diagnosis of learning knowledge and skills, (d) design and delivery, and (e) program completion requirements. This framework very clearly emphasized the need to assess students prior to entry, during matriculation, and upon program completion. The group emphasized the need for university preparation programs to stress skill development and engage students in performance-based activities.

The work of NASSP continued. The NASSP (1995) report, *Performance-Based Preparation of Principals: A Framework for Improvement*, commonly referred to as the *red book*, included strategies for program and student evaluation. The report stressed using the 12 generic skills of the NASSP Assessment Center as the overarching standards for developing curriculum, objectives, and assessment. The approach was criticized by some as too costly and requiring too many personnel resources, making it impractical to implement. Some in the university community also suggested that it was redundant, arguing that they were already doing what was proposed (Witters-Churchill & Erlandson, 1990).

In 2000, NASSP issued a report detailing research case studies of program implementation of red book strategies at four institutions across the country (Gagne, 1990). Results indicated that two of the programs implemented competency programs with skill assessment according to the NASSP's competency-based approach and two had a hybrid model. The study also found that the programs were cost effective (Gagne, 1990).

Numerous reports from within the field have dealt with the need to assess students and programs. Among the most prominent has been the work of the UCEA through the National Commission on Excellence in Educational Administration in 1985, the establishment of the Danforth

Foundation projects of the 1980s and 1990s, the 2002 National Commission for the Advancement of Educational Leadership Preparation, and the Wallace Foundation projects, which include a call for enhancing assessment activities as a part of program reform. These have been chronicled in detail by J. Murphy (2006).

Common threads exist in recent urgings for change in educational leadership preparation programs (J. Murphy, 2006). Among those related to student assessment are the development of competency-based curricula, problem-based instruction, and student and program evaluation. Competence is usually equated with the ability to perform skills, to learn objectives, and to demonstrate expected learning objectives at a high level on the job (Palomba & Banta, 2001). Competence may be viewed as "sitting atop the apex of a hierarchy of experiences that have currency for the learning" (Jones & Voorhees, 2000, p. 8). At the base of the hierarchy are personal traits and characteristics. These provide a base for learning. "They are the innate qualities on which learning experiences help to build *skills, abilities, and knowledge*—the next level of the hierarchy" (Jones & Voorhees, 2000, p. 8). The third level of competence is bundles, which are the result of integrative learning experiences in which skills, abilities, and knowledge interact. Jones and Voorhees suggested that in order to determine whether a student has attained an appropriate level of competence, one must (a) be able to describe the competence, (b) have an appropriate means to measure it, and (c) have a standard by which to judge it.

The calls to assess student competence have included strong suggestions that to be truly valid, assessment should examine not simply knowledge, but also performance in creating learning environments that foster positive student outcomes (McCarthy, 2001). Thus, educational leadership program faculty are being encouraged to collaborate with field-based practitioners and to use authentic assessment techniques when judging student competence to perform essential duties of school administrators. These ideas are not new to the field. For example, a study of the Danforth Project programs initiated in the late 1980s featured field-based experiences and authentic student assessment, which included multiple measures of competency (Leithwood, Jantzi, Coffin, & Wilson, 1996; Milstein, 1992).

It is important to note that "*performance assessment* is the formal and informal judgment of how well people complete observable tasks" (Place, 2006, p. 740). Performance assessments are tied to measurable standards. They are only as good as the criteria that are being used to judge performance and are also dependent upon the neutrality of the observer or the systems in place to assure neutrality. The starting point for performance assessment determines the outcomes and standards and matching them with appropriate teaching techniques and environments (Nieweg, 2004). Moreover, *authentic assessment* means assessing a competency in an environment that is very similar if not the same as the environment in which the skill or ability will need to be performed. Typically one must use higher order thinking skills and demonstrate mastery of content at a high level of accomplishment to be consider as having mastered the competency being tested (Wiggins, 1989).

Factors That Hinder and Facilitate Student Assessment in Educational Leadership Programs

Although the calls for program change, which carry with them the need for student and program assessment, have been continuous, it appears that although some changes have occurred, many programs have not engaged in comprehensive reform that includes comprehensive student-assessment processes (Glasman, Cibulka, & Ashby, 2002). Even among those who have developed comprehensive assessment initiatives, the issue of how to adequately assess students to determine program effectiveness has not yet been solved (Shakeshaft, 1999). Factors have hindered the drive toward adequate assessment and other factors have facilitated their development.

Factors Hindering Student Assessment in Educational Leadership Program

Although there have been and continue to be many initiatives aimed at incorporating student assessment into educational leadership programs, there do not appear to be comprehensive and widely accepted approaches in a majority of the programs, even those that are considered to be of high quality. In addition, educational leadership programs have "rarely been evaluated in a systemic and comparative manner, nor have their long-range impacts been measured" (Orr & Pounder, 2006, p. 2). There are many contextual and historical reasons for this situation. Among the most significant are (a) a lack of consensus about standards, (b) a lack of agreement about what kind of leader we need to prepare, (c) a shortage of adequate testing and measurement tools, and (d) the context of educational leadership programs.

Consensus on Standards

One of the most powerful hindrances to the adoption of student assessment processes has been the inability of the field to achieve a consensus on the standards that should be used to develop and assess student outcomes and to determine program success (Bartell, 1994; Finn, 1986; Rodman, 1987). A competency-based program is built upon measuring student success in achieving established standards and goals. This requires program developers to know and agree upon the knowledge, skills, and dispositions required for principals to perform their jobs well in a variety of settings; to agree upon the social, psychological, and cognitive processes by which leadership capacity develops and how and whether it differs in different career stages; and to share common knowledge about the functions and effectiveness of differing strategies and resources needed to promote school leader development (Smylie, Bennett, Konkol, & Fendt, 2005).

Although the field has struggled to develop a knowledge base upon which to build standards for many years, it has been difficult to obtain agreement about what should be taught and learned in leadership preparation programs; there has not been a unified conceptual base within our field (Donmoyer, 1999; Greenfield, 1975). There also have been consistent criticisms that what is taught in educational leadership programs is often irrelevant to the work of the field (Lakomski, 1998; Sergiovanni, 1989). In addition, there has been evidence that field-based internships have tended to be ineffectual and not connected to the content-based work students are doing, with poor assessment techniques to measure both (Milstein, 1999). Difficulties with the content being taught and the methods used to teach such content have made it particularly tricky to measure outcomes, and for years most programs have not even considered doing so (Erickson, 1979; Clark, as cited in J. Murphy, 2006).

As criticisms of program content increased, attempts were made to create a knowledge base for educational leadership programs, including initiatives by the National Commission on Excellence in Educational Administration, the National Policy Board for Educational Administration (NPBEA), and the National Commission for the Principalship. These efforts are detailed by J. Murphy (2006).

In recent years, the Interstate School Leaders Licensure Consortium (ISLLC), under the auspices of the NPBEA, developed a set of standards for school leaders (J. Murphy, 2006). A test was developed by the Educational Testing Service to determine student competency on these standards. The NPBEA set up a working group that used these standards as a foundation for designing a set of performance-based standards for the NCATE to use when reviewing educational leadership programs. Although these standards are being adopted by many programs, they are not universally accepted among all educational leadership faculty or programs, due to existing criticisms by faculty (Anderson et al., 2002; English, 2000, 2001; Reese & Tannenbaum, 1999).

Another complicating factor related to having a common set of standards upon which to build an assessment system in educational leadership is that some leadership preparation programs are being asked to respond to a multiple set of standards and criteria when developing and implementing student assessment programs. Among the various systems are state accrediting systems and national systems such as NCATE and TEAC. All of these entities have different goals, standards, and student output processes.

Defining Leadership

A second reason for a lack of comprehensive student assessment plans in many leadership preparation programs is disagreement about the kind of leadership we need and how we can assess it. Over 10,000 books have been written on the topic of leadership (Yukl, 1989). Despite apparent agreement on the need for strong leadership, there is also concern about assuring that leaders have strong management skills (Kochan & Spencer, 1999) Although many professionals continue to believe that the school leader must be knowledgeable about curricular and instructional issues (Quinn, 2005), some outside the field do not believe that this is true (Fordham Foundation, 2004). There are those who stress the need for leaders to have wisdom and to be moral and just (Dantley, 1990; Quantz & Cambron-McCabe, 1991), whereas others include caring with ethics (Noddings, 1984; Starrat, 1991) and press for school leaders to abide by the moral principles of equity and equality for all children (Goldring & Greenfield, 2002; Scheurich & Skrla, 2003). Some suggest that leaders demonstrate creativity and academic intelligence (Fullan, 2003), whereas others challenge principals to manage learning effectively (M. D. Young & Kochan, 2004) using data-driven processes (Leithwood, 1999; Thornton & Perreault, 2002). Moreover, school leaders are expected by some to have political savvy, energy, resilience, and dedication (Fordham Foundation, 2004).

Thus, it appears that the principal must be all things to all people in all circumstances. This diversity of thought about leadership has made it extremely difficult to sort out what should be taught and measured.

Measurement Tools and Strategies

A third difficulty in developing new program models and assessing their ability to foster student success in achieving program outcomes is identifying or developing measurement instruments and strategies that appropriately measure leadership (Sergiovanni, 1992). The lack of agreement about what constitutes leadership is one element contributing to this problem, leading the National Commission for the Principalship (1990) to suggest that it will be very difficult to develop an assessment package that everyone will be willing to use.

Another problem in assessing leadership is the nature of what is being examined. For example, it is particularly problematic to measure dispositions such as commitment and fairness to all. It also can be difficult to adequately measure conceptual abilities such as problem solving, creative thinking, risk management, managing change, and the interpersonal skill of reflection (Richardson, 1990).

An issue yet unsolved is how to connect the competencies of educational leadership program components to graduates' abilities to create successful schools in which students achieve (McCarthy, 2001; M. D. Young & Peterson, 2002). Jackson and Kelley (2002) analyzed measurements of program effectiveness by examining the following: surveys of student satisfaction, placement rates of students in administrative positions, assessment by school administrators about the effectiveness of the graduates, and passage rates on the licensure examination. No programs reported data related to student learning or school success. Shakeshaft (1999) noted that as a field we do not have reliable data in this area, and until we do, we will not have adequate information to determine the effectiveness of programs. Smylie et al. (2005) stated,

Knowledge of effective leadership practices is not the same thing as knowledge of the capacities required for enactment. Our understanding of effective school leadership practice has grown tremendously in recent years. However, our understanding of the knowledge, skills, and dispositions required for school leaders to be effective is much less well developed. (p. 141)

Program Context

The selection and implementation of assessment systems are also related to the context in which educational leadership programs function. As previously noted, higher education was historically viewed as a valued and necessary part of our society, and faculty were not pressured to be reflective about the extent to which they were fostering student success. Thus, higher education institutions, and the educational leadership programs within them, do not have a lengthy tradition of evaluating student outcomes or their programs and processes (Glasman et al., 2002). Since most universities lack a strong commitment to developing comprehensive assessment programs, educational leadership programs are left to themselves to find resources to support the development and implementation of these assessment endeavors and thus have not adopted such systems (M. D. Young & Peterson, 2002).

Although colleges of education have put a greater emphasis on assessment in recent years through their primary accrediting body, the NCATE, as well as through TEAC, the major focus has been on teacher education, not educational leadership. Within this context, complacency and resistance to change on the part of some educational leadership professors have stifled the development of comprehensive assessment programs (Norton, 2002).

The situation described above is exacerbated by the growing number of educational leadership programs within universities and private profit-making establishments that may or may not have a commitment to quality (Cambron-McCabe, 2002; Norton, 2002). While some program leaders conscientiously may try to develop high-quality assessment programs, establishing universal adoption of model programs is a difficult if not impossible task. Those who do incorporate extensive assessment systems sometimes find that fewer students enroll in their programs because they can get a degree quicker and easier somewhere else (Shakeshaft, 1999). Often, this decrease in enrollment does not sit well with upper level administrators who are not committed to assessment programs, which serves as another disincentive to continue a more rigorous approach to leadership preparation.

Extensive assessment programs require additional personnel resources because of the time-consuming tasks involved (Shakeshaft, 1999). Since the status of colleges of education on many university campuses is not high, and educational leadership programs within them sometimes suffer from having low status within them (J. Murphy, 1999), scarce resources are available to support student assessment processes. In addition, the professional development opportunities that professors may need to implement the assessment processes are often lacking (M. D. Young, Peterson, & Short, 2002).

Factors Influencing Student Assessment in Educational Leadership Programs

Although progress has been slow, and strong barriers hinder the adoption of comprehensive student assessment practices, a number of factors are coalescing to foster increased adoption of student assessment processes in educational leadership programs in higher education institutions. Some factors facilitating change also have elements within them that have hindered this change in the past and may continue to do so in the future. Primary among the facilitating factors are (a) increasing demands for change from external and internal groups; (b) the changing context of higher education; (c) a growing consensus around standards, leadership competencies, and program design and delivery; (d) an expansion of models, tools, and strategies to implement comprehensive assessment systems; (e) an expanding network of groups that are actively engaged in redesigning their programs; and (f) a small but developing body of research related to student assessment in educational leadership programs.

Increasing Demands for Change From Internal and External Groups

Pressures to develop program and student assessment strategies in educational leadership programs come from a variety of forces and are intensified in their stridency (Donaldson, 2001; J. Murphy, 2006). Cambron-McCabe and Cunningham (2002) have stated that the need for change in leadership preparation "is not contested" (p. 289). An essential element of that change is demonstrating program value through student assessment data.

External Forces for Change

Kowalski (2004) identified two groups leading the charge for radical reform in educational leadership. He labeled one group as the antiprofessionalists, composed of those not affiliated with education. The antiprofessionalists come primarily from the business, foundation, political, and reform sectors and are seeking to deregulate the preparation of school leaders as well as move preparation out of universities. Among the most notable are critics Finn (1986) and the signers of the Broad Foundation and Ford Foundation (2003) manifesto, who suggested that university teacher education and educational leadership programs are out of touch with reality.

Finn (1986) has criticized quality-control mechanisms that exist for those who plan to enter teacher education programs, whereas Hess (2004) contended that colleges of education are not capable of producing effective school leaders. Hess wrote, "In general, programs ought to take points to broaden the spectrum of ideas that students encounter, embracing readings and insights from beyond the education community" (p. 514). Hess has favored the abolition of licensure requirements for educational leaders, while proposing and welcoming nontraditional leaders to the field of education. Hess claimed that there is no evidence that educational leadership programs are successful. These criticisms are echoed in the broader environment that is focusing upon "deinstitutionalization, deregulation, and privatization of educational leadership preparation" (J. Murphy, 2006, p. 4).

Some foundations, such as Annenberg and Wallace, have expressed concerns about the state of educational leadership. Rather than suggesting the deinstitutionalization of educational leadership programs, they, like the Danforth Foundation prior to them, have poured large amounts of money into trying to assist with educational leadership reform and assessment of program effectiveness. The Wallace Foundation and the Gates Foundation also have funded alternative programs to prepare leaders on a fast track to leadership preparation through the New Leaders for New Schools (2005) program.

Increasingly, state accountability systems are placing the burden of school success—and individual achievement—squarely on the principal's shoulders. Orr, Silverberg, and LeTendre stated, "Leadership preparation has become this decade's primary approach to educational reform and improved student achievement" (p. 3). The issue has caught the attention of politicians, and as a result governors and legislators throughout the country seeking to reform educational leadership preparation programs believe it is essential to control and structure university programs and in some situations to deregulate the leadership preparation process. As previously noted, many states have initiatives focusing on enhancing and increasing accrediting and licensing standards as well as expanding student and program assessment in university programs.

Adams and Copland (2005) provided an extensive review of the growing trend of stakeholders questioning who should be licensed to lead schools. They found that states and the public are increasingly concerned about the factors that should be considered when licensing school leaders: public safety, legal compliance, accountability, fair access, expert practice, manageable work scope, and leadership development.

Forty-three states and the District of Columbia require a master's degree or equivalent to become a school principal (LeTendre & Roberts, 2005). Over 80% of the states as well as Washington, DC, require some work experience in schools before becoming a leader (National Association of State Directors of Teacher Education and Certification, 2004). Twenty-four states require a test of administrative skills, and 10 others require skill demonstrations. Twenty-eight states include learning-focused knowledge in their criteria. Six other states (Iowa, Louisiana, Massachusetts, New Mexico, North Dakota, and Wisconsin) base their licensing *primarily* on learning-focused knowledge and skills that are directly connected to improve student learning.

Although Adams and Copland (2005) concluded that the learning-focused criteria that these states use in licensing are minimal, the fact that learning is clearly being tied to licensure may be a precursor to an expanding emphasis on this issue. This is another indication of the pressures upon leadership programs to initiate assessment strategies that collect evidence to demonstrate that their graduates have the requisite knowledge, skills, and abilities to create and lead learning-focused schools.

Internal Pressures for Change

In addition to the external groups that are demanding that educational leadership programs assess the effectiveness of their graduates, major research and professional groups within the field are applying pressure as well. For example, the National Association of Professors of Educational Leadership, the UCEA, and the NPBEA also have engaged in extensive efforts to incorporate student and program assessment and evaluation into program design. In addition, these groups are currently reviewing and developing a research agenda around this topic. As M. D. Young and Peterson (2006) so aptly stated, "We need clearly defined and widely accepted leadership goals for our programs … [and] we need evaluative systems based on outcome-related standards that lend themselves to program enhancement" (p. 135).

In 2001, the UCEA and the American Educational Research Association (AERA) Teaching in Educational Administration Special Interest Group (TEA-SIG) created a task force on the topic of evaluating leadership preparation programs. The group is actively engaged in developing and conducting research projects related to this topic. Their work is highlighted in later sections of this chapter. In addition, UCEA is presently revising the program review process for consortium membership. UCEA is also actively seeking to influence accrediting agencies by increasing involvement with them in the accrediting process to enhance student and program assessment processes (M. D. Young & Crow, 2006).

Levine (2005), who is within the higher education profession, has critiqued educational leadership programs quite harshly. Using a set of nine criteria, he indicated that he could not find a single high-quality program in the United States. His criticisms include that the research in educational administration is highly criticized by the academic community at large, admission standards are low, faculty are weak, theory overshadows practice, and there is no evidence of program value. He proposed nine criteria to create high-quality educational leadership programs, including having program faculty engage in continuous self-assessment and performance improvement.

The Southern Regional Education Board (SREB) has criticized educational leadership programs as well. It has established four conditions for redesigning educational leadership programs. The fourth condition focuses on assessment: "Rigorous evaluation of participants' mastery of essential competencies and program quality and effectiveness" (Fry, O'Neill, & Bottoms, 2006, p. 32).

The challenges coming from those outside and inside educational leadership programs are powerful forces in driving the movement toward a more rigorous focus on student assessment within educational leadership programs. Although perhaps not as powerful as these external and internal critiques, the shifting context within which educational leadership programs are operating is also facilitating change.

Contextual Changes

Climates that are conducive to change and climates that encourage evaluation usually appear simultaneously (Glasman & Glasman, 1990). Three primary contextual changes are leading educational leadership faculty to become more attuned to the need to integrate student and program assessment into their programs: (a) a wider acceptance of assessment programs in higher education institutions, (b) a reduction in levels of trust of public institutions, (c) and the changing face of the professorship.

Forces that exert pressure in higher education tend to have an influence upon programs within the institution, such as educational leadership (McCarthy, 1999). As noted earlier, institutions of higher education are becoming more attuned to the need to assess student performance. In fact, most states have an assessment policy affecting public institutions (Ewell, Finney, & Lenth, 1990), with at least 92% of U.S. colleges and universities engaging in some type of assessment activities (Ewell, 1997). This movement toward accountability at the institutional level should assist in creating a climate in which student and program assessment is valued and supported and can lead to greater support for these efforts within educational leadership programs.

Another contextual change in higher education is in the previously described public's growing lack of trust in public institutions. In the past, weaknesses in school systems were "more perceptual than real" to the general public (Lasley, 2004, p. 5). Now, however, the public is questioning the effectiveness of schools as well as the institutions that prepare people to teach in and lead in those schools. The changing demographics of U.S. society, which include an increase in the number of minorities and children in poverty who have not fared well in schools, have contributed to this attitudinal shift (J. Murphy, 2006). NCLB (2002) legislation has had a major impact on publicizing schools that are considered failures. Parents are being given an option to leave these schools and take their children to other places. This has added to the breakdown of trust in schools and programs that prepare the teachers and leaders who work in them.

Closely tied to the decline in public confidence in public schools is the development of a value-added environment (Lasley, 2004) in which public institutions must prove their worth. Educational leadership programs no longer have a monopoly on preparing educational leaders. There is a growing list of private providers who are preparing school leaders who are challenging the value of a university-earned degree. Some states, such as Texas and Ohio, are also creating alternatives to university preparation (M. D. Young et al., 2002).

This question about the value of an educational leadership degree has become more prominent in recent years. Usdan (2002) referred to this as "the secularization of the nation's education leadership" (p. 303). This secularization refers to the influence and power that noneducational groups are exerting over education and the placement of noneducators in positions as principals and superintendents around the country. Although most individuals who fill principalships in the United States have degrees in educational leadership (Feistritzer, 2003), 18 states provide an alternate method for certifying principals to attract people from outside of education to fill these positions (LeTendre & Roberts, 2005). In addition, a growing number of principal preparation programs are being developed outside the university. Barbour (2006) identified five categories of alternate preparation programs: (a) for profit, (b) state-based alternatives, (c) foundation driven, (d) partnership, and (e) outsourced programs. These changes in who prepares principals and who gets hired to lead schools and school systems have fostered a greater sense of urgency among educational leadership professionals in universities to meet public expectations. This also has made the need for student and program assessment more apparent.

The final contextual element that may foster greater acceptance of the need for student assessment relates to the change in faculty who are entering the professorate in educational leadership. Many programs are adding faculty members who have had experience as practitioners. These faculty members, who have been involved in assessment and accountability in the preK–12 sector for many years, may be more accepting of the need to incorporate student assessment into higher education programs. Thus, complacency about assessment among college faculty may decline as these new faculty members come into the professoriate (J. Murphy, 1999).

Consensus About Standards, Competencies, and Program Design and Delivery

Despite many struggles to find common acceptance of educational leadership standards for several years, there does appear to be a growing desire to establish consensus around similar standards as well as agreement concerning the type of leaders and leadership needed in schools. These changes are positively impacting the field's ability to develop and deliver programs that have a learning focus with similar design attributes that include student assessment processes.

Leadership Standards

Although there may not be universal acceptance of the ISLLC standards, as of 2005, 41 states have adopted these leadership standards or standards that are aligned with them (Sanders & Simpson, 2005). The Educational Leadership Constituent Council (ELCC) used the ISLLC standards as the foundation for NCATE program review. The ELCC standards require assessment of student success on individual standards, the aggregation of student assessments within the program, state comparisons on the licensure examination, and job placement and employer and graduate feedback relative to program effectiveness. Over 76 educational leadership programs have received NCATE approval, with 9 programs attempting to receive accreditation status for the first time. Of the 76 programs, 20 submitted documentation or hosted a focused visit to have conditions or provisions removed.

The NCATE/ELCC review process is currently under review. This appraisal will provide useful guidance in developing standards, content, and assessment instruments that will enable the field to come closer to using similar standards in determining performance and program outcomes. Even if there is not complete consensus around these standards in the field, they provide a framework for discussion and deliberation. As Shields (2007) has suggested, regarding the need for discussion around research standards, the purpose of dialogue is to enrich our understanding and practice. This dialogue thus should enhance our capacity to develop and use standards that help us create meaningful student assessment tools and programs and conduct research on them.

Leadership Competencies

In addition to a continued dialogue on the ISLLC standards as a basis upon which to develop program standards, there appears to be a growing consensus around the type of leadership needed to create successful schools. One of the primary reasons for movement toward agreement on a leadership paradigm is that research has demonstrated the influential role of the principal in creating successful schools in which all children can succeed (E. L. Boyer, 1983; Copland, 2003; Cornett, 1983; Erlandson, 1997; Glasman et al., 2002; J. Murphy, 1988, 1990; National Governor's Association, 1986).

Andrews and Soder (1987) found a relationship between teachers' perceptions of principal effectiveness on four interactions (resource provider, instructional resource, communicator, and visible presence) to be directly related to student achievement in reading and mathematics as measured on standardized tests. They found the relationship to be stronger in schools with high percentages of Black students and students on free or reduced-price lunch programs. However, because of the small sample, Andrews and Soder suggested that the results be viewed with caution.

A survey of the literature from 1980–1995 (Hallinger & Heck, 1996) reinforced the connection between strong leadership and student learning. However, Hallinger and Heck found that only school goals appeared to be a mediating variable across all of the studies. They stated that this finding should be viewed with caution because of the diverse ways in which the variable was measured and that the variables that relate to principal effectiveness remain elusive.

More recently, Leithwood, Seashore Louis, Anderson, and Wahlstron (2004) identified three primary abilities of principals who positively impact student achievement: (a) They express a clear vision and actions to achieve it, (b) they develop others, and (c) they create a learning organization that supports teaching and learning by modifying structures. Leithwood et al. (2004) also indicated,

> [The] total (direct and indirect) effects of leadership on student learning account for about a quarter of total school effects.… Leadership is second only to classroom instruction among all school-related factors that contribute to what students learn at school. (p. 3)

Marks and Printy (2003) discovered, "When transformational and shared instructional leadership coexist in an integrated form of leadership, the influence on school performance, measured by the quality of its pedagogy and the achievement of students, is substantial" (p. 370).

Research conducted by SREB posits similar findings. Fry et al. (2006) described leaders who can positively impact student learning as (a) owning the vision; (b) using data to drive change; (c) organizing to improve student learning; and (d) maximizing leadership effectiveness by involving parents, continually learning, and obtaining support from the central office and community members.

These research findings about school success have resulted in a belief that educational leaders must move from a top-down leadership style to a collaborative, nonbureaucratic model. This model encompasses shared and distributed leadership centered upon instruction and a moral imperative to assure high levels of learning for all students (Copland, 2003; Keedy, 1999; Kochan, 2002; Ogawa & Bossert, 1995; M. D. Young & Kochan, 2004). Furman (2007) described this consensus about leadership as the "new narrative of educational leadership" (p. 84). She suggested that all the strands about what we need in educational leaders of the future come together to frame this narrative. Furman described this leadership as primarily a moral and relational practice aimed at specific moral ends; further, this leadership practice is continually constructed anew through the interactions and relationships of multiple participants in unique and dynamic school contexts. (p. 88)

Program Design and Delivery

There also appears to be a growing consensus that preparing school leaders who can implement a collaborative leadership approach focused upon student learning requires that preparation programs develop and implement a curriculum, a teaching and learning model, and an assessment system that engages students in learning and enables them to engage others in learning as well (Orr et al., 2006.) Fry et al. (2006) wrote,

> State leaders have relied on universities to get the job done—with modest state guidance in the form of certification tests, accreditation and program approval, and more recently, school administrator standards. But, as a growing body of research makes clear, many universities *are not getting the job done* and are in no particular hurry to redesign their programs to ensure that aspiring principals are thoroughly prepared for their role in improving curriculum, instruction and student achievement. (p. 3)

In a similar vein, UCEA Executive Director Michelle Young stated that educational leadership professors need not only adopt content standards, but also align their program with standards that look "beyond what's being taught to who's teaching it and how it's being taught" (as cited in Norton, 2002, p. 17). Researchers tend to agree on recommendations for educational leadership reform. J. Murphy's (1990) review of 32 national reports and studies done between 1983 and 1988 indicated that those who are proposing reform recommend that preparation programs emphasize theory and practice, be largely field based, and incorporate clinical practice that focuses upon student learning in the public schools.

Implementing this recommended curricular approach requires a change in teaching models from lecture and discussion to teaching strategies that focus on performance, including activities such as problem-based learning, clinical study, group process training, and games and simulations. In addition, new programs must have a balance of faculty who are practitioners and academics along with rigorous admission requirements and comprehensive assessment systems (Levine, 2005; NASSP, 1995; Sternberg, 2004; Willower & Forsyth, 1999; Witters-Churchill & Erlandson, 1990; M. D. Young et al., 2002). These researchers and others also have stressed the importance of rigorous student assessment activities in program design and delivery (M. D. Young & Kochan, 2004; M. D. Young et al., 2002). Orr (2006) reported that in the past 15 years, there has been an increasing movement toward program redesign including student and program assessment in many colleges throughout the country.

Expanded Measurement Options

The need to assess students' leadership capacity has resulted in the availability of a growing body of measurement techniques and instruments. Lashway (1999) identified 21 instruments that can be used to measure leadership. There are also a number of 360-degree instruments that engage leaders in examining their leadership from a wide variety of perspectives. Moreover, technology promises to expand our ability to measure practices through virtual and distance modalities.

Assessment exists on a continuum. At one end it is intuitive and informal, whereas at the other end it may appear as systematic data in numerical form. However, all assessments include some level of judgment, because even deciding what is measured and how it is measured is a value statement. The important element in successful assessment is to minimize the impact of a judgment being made by a single individual. New models of effective assessment call for multiple measures and multiple assessors (see Lashway, 1999).

Within calls for program reform, educational leadership programs are being encouraged to use student assessment strategies at admission, during matriculation, at completion, and after graduation (Jones & Voorhees, 2000). There are varied types of assessment processes, including indirect and direct measures. Indirect measures tend to assess knowledge in small pieces with little relationship to the real world (L. Resnick & Resnick, 1992), whereas direct measures tend to integrate learning with theory and practice. Indirect strategies include tools such as self-reports and opinion and attitude surveys that generally communicate perceptions. Commonly used methods of garnering opinions include written surveys, telephone surveys, individual interviews, focus groups, observations of behavior, logs of conversations, and suggestions for improvement (Huba & Freed, 2000). Direct assessment strategies are meant to directly measure students' knowledge and skills as well as their ability to apply that knowledge or skills. Direct assessment strategies include projects, exhibitions, performances, case studies, clinical evaluations, portfolios, and oral exams and involve interface between the person being assessed and those conducting the assessment.

Assessment Strategies in Educational Leadership Programs

Assessment strategies used in educational leadership employ direct and indirect data-gathering techniques. Orr et al. (2004) conducted a unique interactive action research activity at the 2003 UCEA convention to gather information about assessment strategies being used by participants, many of whom were preparing for or had completed their ELCC program review. Although Orr et al.'s (2004) research indicated that most assessment strategies were still at the "exploratory stage" (p. 9) and were "limited to low-cost data collection effort," some innovative practices are emerging. Other research and program descriptions detailed by other writers also indicate that there are a growing number of student assessment strategies being used in educational leadership programs at admission, during matriculation and completing, and after program completion.

Assessment and Admission

There is ample evidence that admission requirements in most educational leadership programs lack rigor. Standards are almost open, with people applying based on encouragement by others (Levine 2005; Orr et al., 2006; U.S. Department of Education, 2005). The lack of rigorous screening techniques has resulted in low esteem for these programs and a questionable pool of graduates. In 2002, Jackson and Kelley examined six promising innovative programs to identify similarities and differences. Although these programs were considered promising, only one used leadership experiences and potential as part of the screening process. Other tools used were interviews, recommendations, tests, or a written application.

Astin (1993) emphasized that characteristics of students upon program entry are a factor in their success. If educational leadership programs are going to measure their value based on what their students know and can do, it is imperative that what they know and can do upon entry are considerations in this measurement process.

New models for admission to leadership programs are being developed that hold promise for the future in terms of more rigorous and meaningful methods for program admission. These models stress using a multifaceted approach to selection criteria (Jackson & Kelley, 2002), including (a) engaging multiple stakeholders in the process (SREB, 2002); (b) exploring prior demonstrated leadership, since research has demonstrated such leadership tends to be indicative of future leadership abilities (Jacobson, 1990); and (c) conducting on-site visits to observe and interview students to determine their leadership potential (Orr et al., 2004).

Orr (2006) investigated the roots of leadership development in individuals identified as outstanding leaders and discovered that many had early leadership experiences that were instrumental in developing capacity in themselves and others. In studies conducted by Lad, Browne-Ferrigno, and Shoho (2005), a majority of programs (54% and 62%) were using some type of measurement of leadership potential as selection criteria. Procedures used to screen applicants include modifications of the NASSP Assessment Center approach (Milstein & Krueger, 1993), interviews using a team interviewing process (Lawton, Gilbert, Estabrook, Richtig, & Eddy, 2005; J. Murphy, 1993), portfolios using rubrics (Lawton et al., 2005), and observations by visiting an applicant's classroom to determine the quality of teaching (Orr, 2006). It is important to ensure that such assessments are thorough; make primary use of direct strategies (Huba & Freed, 2000); and are collaborative, including both practitioners and university faculty members (M. D. Young & Peterson, 2002).

Matriculation and Completion

Like assessment strategies for screening, programs are being challenged to include numerous assessment tools, both direct and indirect, during the matriculation process. The emphasis, however, is upon direct assessment, which gives a better indication of learning than do indirect measures.

Orr et al. (2004) found evidence that some programs assess leadership strengths and weaknesses throughout program matriculation using varied techniques, such as the NASSP Assessment Center. They also reported the use of assessment techniques throughout students' programs of study through a revised curriculum that uses strategies such as case studies, problem-based learning, inquiry methods, and action research. Internship assessment used self-report logs, journals, supervisor evaluation, action research, and other projects and portfolios.

In Jackson and Kelley's (2002) study, strategies utilized by programs during matriculation were more comprehensive and broader than the strategies used for admission. Most included some type of joint assessment with the faculty and practitioners. Among the approaches used were portfolios evaluated by two faculty members and a mentor, group assessment of a research project, and interviews after each semester with a job performance evaluation that is used for professional development. Other assessment strategies used within courses and internships include action research that demonstrates ability to apply knowledge and skills, demonstrations, problem solving utilizing case studies, observations with multiple observers and rubrics, and portfolios (Huba & Freed, 2000).

Angelo and Cross (1993) have designed multiple classroom-assessment techniques that can help students and teachers gauge levels of learning in real time. Data in the form of a 1-minute paper, an e-mail paper, a one-sentence summary, and application cards are collected during class time and shared with students during and after classes. Although there is no indication that educational leadership programs are using them, these strategies are an intermediary step in the learning process, techniques that can help keep the concept of assessing learning uppermost in everyone's minds.

Some leadership programs indicate the use of rubrics in program measurement. Rubrics are an essential tool that helps explain the criteria being used to make a judgment about competence. They tend to take a great deal of planning and are sometimes difficult to score. Having more than one person involved can help with issues of validity and reliability. In order to be relevant and useful to the student, the feedback must be timely, presented in a helpful and supportive manner, and focused upon future learning (see Wiggins, 1997; Wiggins & McTighe, 1998).

The fine arts have used portfolios for years. Except for Alverno College, portfolios only have been utilized in non-fine-arts arenas of higher education since about 1980. However, they are increasingly being used in educational leadership programs because they have the potential to measure what students know and are able to do with what they know. In addition, portfolios may be used at any stage of the principal preparation process, from admission to completion, and for a variety of purposes (Schaible-Brandon & Muth, 2006).

The benefits of using portfolios are numerous and include (a) establishing mutual relationships with individual students; (b) helping students, mentors, and faculty members become more aware of abilities, attitudes, values, strengths, and weaknesses; (c) opening up research opportunities related to teaching and learning; (d) examining student learning over time; (e) assessing the program and providing direction for faculty improvement; and (f) assisting students to develop reflective skills and prepare job interviews and careers (Huba & Freed, 2000; Lendley, 1993). However, portfolios can be cumbersome and time-consuming to develop and grade. Making them useful and meaningful requires collaboration among students and professors. Most experts stress the importance of limiting the collection of examples to focus on what is clearly necessary to determine competence. It is also wise to include examples and materials that can demonstrate multiple learning outcomes. Technological advances are making portfolios more usable, accessible, and effective as a measurement tool; however, issues of student privacy must be addressed when creating policies and practices (see Lendley, 1993).

Research describing how programs assess student outcomes at completion and beyond is slim. However, we do know that participants in the Jackson and Kelley (2002) study used indirect and direct measures to determine student achievement of program standards. Among the strategies used was a comprehensive examination based on the ISLLC standards, a portfolio used by a group to assess each competency, and a leadership platform statement. Moreover, participants in the action research study conducted by Orr et al. (2004) reported that students took state ISLLC-based assessment tests.

Follow-Up

The literature lacks sufficient evidence of strategies being used to follow up on graduates or to connect their practice to student learning. Some programs conduct satisfaction follow-up surveys to determine the effectiveness of their programs (D. Murphy, 2004; Orr et al., 2004), but getting an adequate sample to respond is problematic (Pennington, Zvonkovic, & Wilson, 1989). Some programs give their students advance notice about the survey, conduct personal or online interviews or surveys, offer prizes for participation, or conduct surveys at conferences or other meetings to increase their response rates (Orr et al., 2004). Additional programs also use college job-placement data and satisfaction surveys from employers (Jacobson, 1990; Orr et al., 2004).

Although we lack verification that programs are gathering data about the impact of graduates upon learning or their ability to demonstrate leadership, preliminary research in this area is in progress. Such research is discussed later in the section on gaps and future research.

Expanded Redesign Networks and Models

A fourth element that is expanding student assessment practice in educational leadership programs is the rise of networks and models focused on fostering program change that includes assessing student outcomes. Two examples are the redesign efforts of the SREB and multiple efforts that are being led by UCEA.

The SREB has established a redesign effort with a network of 11 university educational leadership programs in the southeast. Among the group are Appalachian State University, Clemson University, East Tennessee State University, Jackson State University, Jacksonville State University, Oklahoma State University, Old Dominion University, Towson University, University of Louisiana at Lafayette, University of North Texas, and Western Kentucky University. Titled the SREB Leadership Initiative, the effort aims to "redesign educational leadership preparation and development programs so that they are aligned with the new accountability systems and standards instituted by the states" (Norton, 2002, p. 1).

This initiative seeks not just to revise programs, but to redesign them. As Fry stated,

Very few, if any, [educational leadership programs] have embraced the kind of continuous, self-directed improvement that would lead to an assessment model linking program preparation to a principal's ability to raise student achievement in a real school.... University design teams will simply have to bite the bullet and do the hard work it will take to develop this kind of outcomes-based assessment.... Somebody will have to become the model. (as cited in Norton, 2002, p. 2)

One of the requirements for entry into the network is that universities must agree to "support faculty with time to conduct school-based research and to participate in an ongoing evaluation about student learning and produce high-achieving schools" (SREB, n.d., p. 5). The conditions for core redesign include four core indicators related to assessment:

1. A regular, formal monitoring process ensures the program meets rigorous quality standards and is aligned with district needs and goals.
2. Candidates are assessed on demonstrated mastery of essential competencies, and the data are used to provide feedback for improvement and determine their status in the program.
3. Decisions about candidates' successful completion of the program are based on clearly defined exit criteria and reliable measures of performance.
4. The evaluation of program effectiveness includes measures of on-the-job performance and results.

The UCEA is a consortium of 77 institutions with educational leadership programs that have competitive membership standards. Among the criteria for entry into this network are recruitment and admission plans and programmatic evaluation. As previously noted, this group is actively engaged in fostering expansion and enhancement of assessment components of member programs as well as actively engaged in fostering research in this area—as evidenced by the publication of this book and this chapter on this topic. In conjunction with the AERA TEA-SIG, UCEA also has created a Task Force on Program Assessment, which includes student assessment and is discussed later in sections on promising research and challenges and cautions in student assessment. UCEA also has instituted the *Journal of Research on Leadership Education* to provide an outlet for research on evaluation, assessment, and other topics related to educational leadership programs.

In addition to educational leadership program networks, some researchers have developed change models that foster the type of leadership that will be needed in the future, along with strategies to assess student competence. One of the most comprehensive of these models was created by Glasman et al. (2002). Glasman et al. suggested that we must build learning communities within our programs in order to prepare leaders who can do likewise in the field. An element of being part of a learning community is continually to seek to learn about what is working and what is not and to use that information in a continuous improvement process. In this model, the program becomes a public case study, around which continuous improvement efforts operate. Glasman et al. suggested this framework also could be useful to schools. Although it has not been implemented in a program setting, the model provides a foundation for discussing what is and what should be occurring while designing assessment strategies for educational leadership preparation programs.

Promising Research to Guide the Field

There are new teaching, learning, and research paradigms as well as new assessment tools for gathering data about student learning and program outcomes. In addition, there are new networks and models of practice designed to propose and implement student assessment and comprehensive, continuous improvement systems in educational leadership programs. Moreover, a vast array of research methods is being used to study our field that will enable us to examine our work at individual institutions as well as across them. Quantitative as well as qualitative methods have become more sophisticated in recent years, lending themselves to examining our work in more powerful and meaningful ways. In addition, computers now allow us to interpret data in more extensive ways and to interpret school performance data along with programmatic information related to students and their abilities (Pounder, 2006).

Also, some foundational studies have taken place that are providing information upon which further research can be conducted. As mentioned earlier, UCEA, in conjunction with the AERA TEA-SIG, has instituted a taskforce on program evaluation. The purpose of this taskforce is to help the leadership preparation field "learn more about how different leadership preparation programs and approaches contribute to the quality and effectiveness of leadership and the school improvement work of graduates who become educational leaders" (Orr & Pounder, 2006, p. 4). The UCEA has developed a research agenda to examine three areas related to program evaluation: (a) a backward mapping study to determine the preparation and early experience factors that lead to effective leadership; (b) an examination of student experiences in programs to determine their relationship to student completion; and (c) a longitudinal study of the impact of public and private preparation programs upon various aspects of student learning, development, and effectiveness. All of these studies will have direct relevance to the design and delivery of student assessment strategies in educational leadership programs and will help facilitate their development and success.

As a part of the work of the task force, Orr et al. (2006) conducted a review of graduates of five NCATE-approved programs to see if students from varied programs differed on outcomes related to what they learned, their leadership orientation, and their career advancement. The purpose of Orr et al.'s (2006) study was to test the assumptions that "core program features have an independent influence on leadership learning, career aspirations and pursuits" (p. 11) as well as whether or not "programs are distinguishable on their core program features" (pp. 11–12). Students were surveyed using the UCEA/TIG-SIG Survey of Leadership Preparation and Practice.

The graduates in one program rated their leadership learning as consistently higher than graduates in the other programs, and one group rated their learning as consistently lower (Orr et al., 2006). Perceived ideas about the principalship and their desire to fill that role were modest. While 55% of the graduates were serving in administrative positions, few were filling the principal role. However, the percentage of graduates who advanced to principal roles increased after a 5-year period (Orr et al., 2006).

Although ratings showing positive beliefs about the principalship were high across all programs, there were some differences based on program attributes, leading Orr et al. (2006) to conclude that program attributes can impact graduate outcomes. Thereafter, they provided ideas about improving the research process, including gathering data on how programs are perceived as preparing people to lead schools as well as measuring the degree to which they are placed in leadership positions.

Byrd and Beach (2004) studied the impact of coursework, grades, and passing rates on the Texas principal certification test. Although they cautioned that principal performance on the examination may or may not be related to their performance as school leaders, they proposed an interesting model for examining possible relationships.

Previous research has demonstrated principals' leadership effects on student achievement (Andrews & Soder, 1987), and recent research helps clarify that impact. Witziers, Bosker, and Kruger (2003) conducted studies to determine any direct relationship between principal leadership and student achievement. Although they found a relationship between the two, effect sizes were very small. They urged further research be conducted and provided specific steps that might be taken.

Leithwood et al. (1996) conducted follow-up studies of 11 redesigned preparation programs to determine program features that were most predictive of principals' effectiveness as reported by teachers. These program features included instructional strategies, cohort groups, and program content. Orr and Barber (2007) compared two university–district partnership programs and one conventional program and also found some program components that appeared to be related to student outcomes: leadership knowledge and skills, career intentions, and career advancement.

Although these research studies have not shown a direct causal effect between leadership preparation and student learning, they provide promising beginnings for connecting student performance to program attributes—a first step in determining the impact of program design. Previous studies also can guide us to identify gaps in the research related to student assessment and help us establish a research agenda for the future.

Framing a Research Agenda

Following the recommendation of the Division A AERA Task Force on Research and Inquiry (Pounder, 2000), it will be important for us to work toward creating a body of knowledge about student assessment processes in educational leadership that can meet the standards of "sustained, disciplined, and focused empirical inquiry" (p. 466). This requires that we develop a comprehensive research agenda that will enable us not only to build effective assessment models into our educational leadership programs, but also to enhance our capacity to judge the viability and effectiveness of program content, delivery systems, and assessment tools.

The members of the UCEA/TEA-SIG task force have proposed a research agenda to aid in overcoming the gap in research literature relative to program impact on effective leadership. The task force has recommended that the research be (a) conceptually based, connecting research on effective leadership, leadership development, and leadership preparation program effectiveness; (b) conceived in a series of outcomes investigated in testable stages; and (c) conducted among multiple leadership preparation programs so that comparisons of program delivery and outcomes can be made. The group also developed an outline for examining the effectiveness of leader-preparation programs with first-, second-, and third-order outcomes and is gathering data from across the country to assemble this information (Orr & Pounder, 2006).

The recommendations adopted by the UCEA/TEA-SIG Taskforce on Evaluation of Leadership Preparation Programs provide a framework for conducting research on student assessment as well as on the effectiveness of educational leadership programs. A myriad of issues in the area of student assessment should be addressed within this framework. We have identified those that we believe are the most significant.

Since little is known about the data collection, analysis, and application methods being used to track student progress within programs or their effectiveness following graduation, we need to initiate studies that will examine the specific manner in which programs are gathering and using student assessment data in educational leadership programs. We might look at this issue from various providers (e.g., research and nonresearch institutions, UCEA and non-UCEA institutions, and public and private providers). We suggest such studies examine information about data collection, analysis, and use in admissions, matriculation, completion, and postgraduate success. It is also vital to examine how collected data are being used to enhance programs.

Research also should be conducted on how effectiveness of graduates is defined, measured, and used. We need to gain an understanding of how these findings are related to program attributes and to personnel and financial resources.

A primary issue in terms of research is to determine the extent to which direct and indirect measures are being used. It appears that most data being collected are still indirect, looking at perceptions rather than measurable outcomes. Research into how to gather direct outcome data and what is being learned from these data should be a primary research focus. There also should be research about whether effectiveness is related to the situation in which graduates are functioning and whether some program attributes appear to enable graduates to operate successfully in diverse environments.

Another research question that should be addressed is the type of student assessment being conducted, to examine where the strategies being used and the type of data collected fit within the paradigmatic families. If educational leadership programs are going to prepare educational leaders who can develop a culture in which every child is valued and succeeds, it is imperative that they engage in assessment activities that foster critical praxis as well as technical skills, meaning making, and problem-solving abilities.

Since our field is emphasizing shared and collaborative leadership, it seems relevant that research studies examine the degree to which programs involve students in developing and using assessment information and their reaction to this participation. One study might address the degree to which students are equipped and ready to participate in self-assessment activities. Most students probably have had little exposure to such methods. Yet, it is important that they gain self-assessment skills and have the capacity to implement them as they lead schools. Likewise, it would be of value to determine the extent to which practitioners are involved in the process and their opinions about it. Additional research might examine the degree to which all involved found the instruments and process useful and beneficial to the teaching and learning process.

There is a body of research about what is needed to make student assessment successful institutionally and to strengthen it programmatically through institutional support (Peterson & Einarson, 2001; Peterson, Einarson, Trice, & Nichols, 1997). However, although we have historical information about what has hindered and facilitated the development of student assessment programs in educational leadership, we do not have comprehensive information concerning what factors university leaders, students, and practitioners perceive as facilitating or hindering the successful implementation of student assessment programs related to and separate from institutional elements. We should gather information about these factors and how people are fostering the facilitative factors and overcoming those that serve as barriers to success. This information would be helpful to institutions and programs as they seek to develop student assessment programs.

Challenges and Cautions

As our field moves into the arena of student assessment in a more comprehensive manner, it is essential that we do not forget the underlying responsibility we have as a field to develop leaders who will not be afraid to question the status quo and who will have the moral integrity to lead so that all children will profit. Thus, student assessment activities and research about them not only should examine what we have learned about our students and programs, but also must address issues of what determines effectiveness, the strategies and processes used to measure them, and who participates in the process.

Measuring Effectiveness

There is intense pressure to prove that leadership preparation programs produce leaders who can foster successful student learning. We should be cautious about this for two reasons. First, we do not have the ability at this time to make this connection (Guskey, 2000; Hallinger & Heck, 1998; J. Murphy, 1998; Witziers et al., 2003). Although it may seem like something we can do, significant elements may prevent this from being a viable approach. Although we must engage in research to investigate the possibility of making this connection, we should be cautious about trying to prove our value based on this one measure of effectiveness alone. In addition, we must be proactive about what is meant by student learning and effective leadership.

At issue here is how student learning is going to be measured and thus how leadership is going to be construed. Thanks to NCLB (2002) legislation, at present, student learning and success are being regarded primarily as performance on standardized tests. If we develop assessment measures that use student performance on standardized test as the true and only measure of leadership, we will be adding to the false notion that learning can and should be addressed in this simplistic manner. Doing so will tend to move our program standards and approaches to a technical and scientific paradigm that will have uncertain effects on our teaching and assessment practices, program approaches, and students' learning.

Assessing graduates' abilities to foster student achievement and learning should include multiple measures of school-related success factors along with individual student success. This will be difficult, as we may not have the tools we need to assess broad measures of student achievement in K–12 schools. However, it is essential that we raise the issue with our K–12 school partners and within our field and build measures into our assessment systems that look beyond standardized test data to measure student and program accomplishment. If we do not become proactive in this area, we most likely will find ourselves trapped on a pathway that may hinder student success in school or life and doubtfully lead to better educational leadership programs.

Likewise, we need to consider how we will measure principal attributes related to the moral and ethical sides of leadership. McCarthy (2001) cautioned that if our tests do not measure essential leadership characteristics that are traditionally difficult to measure, the "tests will take us in directions we may not want to go" (p. 4).

Anderson (2006) and Kochan (2002) recommended that we examine the work of Jürgen Habermas and his cognitive interests in the development and implementation of educational leadership programs. We suggest including this notion in student assessment activities as well. In his writings, Habermas (1971) suggested that knowledge is constructed based upon one's world view and that learning and understanding are acquired using one of these knowledge lenses. He posited that there are three world views: (a) technical, (b) practical, and (c) emancipatory.

The technical view is related to the empirical and analytical paradigm. In this paradigm, the teacher controls the teaching and learning environment. The teacher delivers the knowledge, and the student receives it. In assessment, the focus is on the acquisition of skills, knowledge, and facts in a decontextualized form.

The practical interest is equated with the hermeneutic paradigm, where the emphases are on relationships and constructing meaning. Meaning making is central, as are the interactions among the teachers, the learners, the subject, and the environment. Assessment strategies involve applying knowledge, problem solving, and the construction of meaning.

The emancipatory concentration is related to critical praxis. According to Schubert (1986), it refers to a "freeing of one's self to enable growth and development from the taken-for-granted ideology of social conventions, beliefs, and modes of operation" (p. 318). Teachers and students are colearners in this environment. Together, these colearners deal with ethical and moral issues. They delve into critical questions related to equity, social justice, and the creation of environments that foster both.

Measuring the effectiveness of our graduates and their capacity to lead must include elements from each of these paradigms. Management capacities may fall into the technical paradigm, whereas building learning communities in a collaborative manner assumes a more practical view. Building learning communities that care about and are effective in assuring fairness for all and continually demonstrating the ability to deal with the moral side of leadership fall in the emancipatory realm.

Pounder (2006) cautioned those engaged in educational leadership program design to be sensitive to assuring that the moral and ethical issues principals must deal with not be minimized. We agree with this caution and propose that a part of this sensitivity must include creating learning environments in preparation programs that model an emancipatory approach. We further propose that assessments be conducted to determine the degree to which students perceive that their learning environments are emancipatory and foster critical praxis.

Our assessment endeavors also should seek to determine the learners' commitment to social justice principles and their ability to create such environments themselves. This however, leads to another problematic issue—that of measuring elements of leadership, such as reflection, compassion, and ability to question critically. This is an area that requires additional research and development if we are to create comprehensive programs that include assessment of our students in a holistic manner.

A final caution: Although there is evidence that leadership does relate to the organizational climate and student achievement, many correlates comprise a school, including family culture and socioeconomic status. While accountability entails assuming responsibility for student success, we must refrain from reinforcing expectations that we cannot meet when measuring that effectiveness.

Assessment Strategies and Participation

Just as there should be multiple methods for judging the effectiveness of graduates, there should be multiple strategies, using a variety of cognitive paradigms, to measure student abilities from program entry to program exit. The development of these strategies should be done collaboratively by engaging faculty and school-based partners. Quantitative and qualitative methods should be used to gather and analyze the data. Data should be collected in school sites as well as in college classrooms and settings.

Graduate students and graduates also should be a part of the development and, in some cases, data collection and analysis activities. For example, graduate students could be engaged in action research projects alone or in teams to determine how well their training programs are preparing them to be leaders. Another strategy would be to follow Anderson's (2006) advice and develop some research endeavors using an action research model that would engage program graduates in field-based studies to examine their ability to lead their schools built around their preparation programs' established outcomes.

Students and graduates also should provide feedback on the various data collection strategies used to determine their usefulness and clarity. As educational leadership programs become more engaged in developing partnerships with school systems to develop, implement, and assess their programs, the whole notion of engaging these partners and their students in the assessment process will become a necessity. Likewise, forming advisory councils to help guide program development and assessment can be an important element in ensuring that our programs and methods for assessing them are relevant and effective (Kochan & Sabo, 1995; Kochan & Twale, 1998).

It is essential to realize that school-based partnerships that can develop and implement meaningful assessment strategies will require a long-term commitment, trust, and honesty among the partners as well as shared values. Developing this type of "authentic interdependence" will be a challenge (Cambron-McCabe & Cunningham, 2002, p. 290). The success of these partnerships in creating meaningful student assessment systems will be largely dependent upon the extent to which both partners commit to developing the potential of future leaders and providing support for them throughout their leadership career.

Developing student and program assessment strategies that capture outcomes over time will require staff and material resources. Building support within institutions is a complex process requiring educational leadership faculty demonstrate the value of the work being done. Sharing costs and responsibilities with school-based and other partners may be one way to overcome this challenge.

Final Reflection

As we advance in developing and implementing student assessment activities to determine program and student success, it is important to engage in meaningful research that will enlighten the field and foster our ability to demonstrate our value in preparing effective educational leaders. It is also vital that program data and research about them not only seek to report what currently exists, but also are used to transform our programs and our assessment initiatives, so that those who graduate from our programs will be well prepared and committed to creating schools in which all children are respected, successful, and happy.

References

Adams, J., & Copland, M. (2005). *When learning counts: Rethinking licenses for school leaders.* New York: The Wallace Foundation. (ERIC Document Reproduction Service No. ED491085)

Alabama State Department of Education. (2002). *First look at Alabama schools academic status released.* Retrieved from http://www.alsde.edu/html/home.asp

American Association of Higher Education. (1992). *Principles of good practice for assessing student learning.* Washington, DC: Author.

Anderson, G. L. (2006). Preparing new leaders for the "new economy." In J. Murphy (Ed.), *Preparing school leaders: Defining a research and action agenda* (pp.76–86). Lanham, MD: Rowman & Littlefield Education.

Anderson, G. L., Creighton, T., Dantley, M., English, F., Furman, G., Gronn, P., et al. (2002). Problematizing the ISLLC standards and exam. *AERA Division A Newsletter.* Retrieved May 15, 2007, from http://www.aera.net

Andrews, R. L., & Soder, R. (1987). Principal leadership and student achievement. *Educational Leadership, 44,* 9–11.

Angelo, T. A., & Cross, K. P. (1993). *Classroom assessment techniques: A handbook for college teachers* (2nd ed.). San Francisco: Jossey-Bass.

Aper, J. P. (1993). Higher education and the state: Accountability and the roots of student outcomes assessment. *Higher Education Management, 5*(3), 365–376.

Astin, A. W. (1993). *What matters in college? Four critical years revisited.* San Francisco: Jossey-Bass.

Baker, R. L. (2004). Keystones of regional accreditation: Intentions, outcomes, and sustainability. In R. H. Hernon & R. E. Dugan (Eds.), *Outcomes assessment in higher education: Views and perspectives* (pp. 1–15). Westport, CT: Libraries Unlimited.

Barbour, J. D. (2006, Spring). Non-university based preparation programs: A taskforce summary of alternatives and a research agenda for further study. *Division A: American Educational Research Association Teaching in Educational Administration Special Interest Group Newsletter, 14*(1), 7–8.

Bartell, C. (1994, April). *Preparing future administrators: Stakeholder perceptions.* Paper presented at the annual meeting of the American Educational Research Association, New Orleans, LA.

Bottoms, G., & O'Neil, K. (2001). *Preparing a new breed of school principals: It's time for action* [SREB research monograph]. Atlanta, GA: Southern Regional Education Board.

Boyer, C., & Ewell, P. (1988). *State-based approaches to assessment in undergraduate education: A glossary and selected references.* Denver, CO: Education Commission of the States.

Boyer, E. L. (1983). *High school: A report on secondary education in America.* New York: Harper.

Broad Foundation & Fordham Foundation. (2003). *Better leaders for America's Schools: A manifesto.* Los Angeles: The Broad Foundation. Retrieved February 6, 2009, from http://www.edexcellence.net/detail/news.cfm?news_id=1

Brown, G. H., & Faupel, E. M. (1986). *Postsecondary assessment. Report of a planning conference.* Washington, DC: National Center for Education Statistics. (ERIC Document Reproduction Services No. ED285516)

Byrd, F., & Beach, D. (2004, August). *Evaluating educational administrator preparation programs: A quantitative approach.* Paper presented at the annual meeting of the University Council for Educational Administration, Kansas City, MO.

Cambron-McCabe, N. (2002). Educational accountability in the USA: Focus on state testing. *Education & the Law, 14*(1/2), 117–126.

Cambron-McCabe, N., & Cunningham, L. (2002). National Commission for the Advancement of Educational Leadership: Opportunity for transformation. *Educational Administration Quarterly, 38*(2), 289–300.

Campbell, R. F., Fleming, T., Newell, L. J., & Bennion, J. W. (1987). *A history of thought and practice in educational administration.* New York: Teachers College Press.

Carnegie Forum on Education and the Economy, Task Force on Teaching as a Profession. (1986). *A nation prepared: Teachers for the 21st century.* New York: Author.

Casey, K. (2004). Greater expectations: Teaching and assessing for academic skills and knowledge in the general education history classroom. *The History Teacher, 37*(2), 171–179.

Cibulka, J. G. (1999). Ideological lenses for interpreting political and economic changes affecting schooling. In J. Murphy &

K. Seashore Louis (Eds.), *Handbook of research on educational administration* (2nd ed., pp. 163–182). San Francisco: Jossey-Bass.

Cohen, A. (1998). *The shaping of American higher education.* San Francisco: Jossey-Bass.

Cook, C. (1989). FIPSE's role in assessment: Past, present, and future. *Assessment Update, 1*(2), 1–3.

Copland, M. A. (2003). Building the capacity to lead: Promoting and sustaining change in an inquiry-based model of school reform. In J. Murphy & A. Datnow (Eds.), *Leadership for school reform: Lessons from comprehensive school reform designs* (pp. 159–183). Thousand Oaks, CA: Corwin Press.

Cornett, L. M. (1983). *The preparation and selection of school principals.* Atlanta, GA: Southern Regional Education Board. (ERIC Document Reproduction Service No. ED231053)

Dantley, M. (1990). The ineffectiveness of effective schools leadership: An analysis of the effective schools movement from a critical perspective. *Journal of Negro Education, 56*(4), 585–598.

Daresh, J. C. (1995). Research base on mentoring for educational leaders: What do we know? *Journal of Educational Administration, 33*(5), 7–16.

Donaldson, G. A., Jr. (2001). *Cultivating leadership in schools: Connecting people, purpose, and practice.* Williston, VT: Teachers College Press.

Donmoyer, R. (1999). The continuing quest for a knowledge base: 1976–1998. In J. Murphy & K. Seashore Louis (Eds.), *Handbook of research on educational administration* (2nd ed., pp. 25–43). San Francisco: Jossey-Bass.

Eckert, R. (1943). *Outcomes of general education: An appraisal of the general college program.* Minneapolis: The University of Minnesota Press.

Edgerton, R. (1986). An assessment of assessment. Assessing the outcomes of higher education. In *Proceedings of the 1986 ETS Invitational Conference.*

El-Khawas, E. (1989). How are assessment results being used? *Assessment Update, 6*(4), 1–2.

El-Khawas, E. (1998). Strong state action but limited results: Perspectives on university resistance. *European Journal of Education, 33*(3), 317–330.

English, F. W. (2000, April). *The ghostbusters search for Frederick Taylor in the ISLLC standards.* Paper presented at the annual meeting of the American Education Research Association, New Orleans, LA.

English, F. W. (2001). You say you saw what? Which veil did you lift? *Educational Leadership Review, 2*(2), 22–27.

Erickson, D. A. (1979). Research on educational administration: The state of the art. *Educational Researcher, 8,* 9–14.

Erlandson, D. A. (1997). *The longitudinal study of the professional needs of principals.* College Station: Texas A&M University, Principals' Center. (ERIC Document Reproductive Service No. ED447563)

Ewell, P. T. (1985). *Levers for change: The role of state government in improving the quality of postsecondary education.* Denver, CO: Education Commission of the States.

Ewell, P. T. (1987). *Assessment, accountability and improvement.* Washington, DC: American Association for Higher Education.

Ewell, P. T. (1997). Strengthening assessment for academic quality improvement. In M. W. Peterson, D. D. Dill, & L. A. Mets (Eds.), *Planning and management for a changing environment: A handbook on redesigning postsecondary institutions* (pp. 360–381). San Francisco: Jossey-Bass.

Ewell, P. T. (2002). A delicate balance: The role of evaluation in management. *Quality in Higher Education, 8*(2), 159–171.

Ewell, P. T., Finney, J., & Lenth, C. (1990). Filling in the mosaic: The emerging pattern of state-based assessment. *AAHE Bulletin, 42*(8), 3–5.

Feistrizer, C.E. (2003), *School principal and superintendent certification study results.* Retrieved April 7, 2007, from the National Center for Educational Administration Web site: http://www.ncei.com/publications.html

Finn, C. (1986). Better principals, not just teachers. *Principal, 65*(5), 50–61.

Fordham Foundation. (2004). *Grading the systems: The guide to state standards, tests, and accountability policies.* Washington, DC: Thomas B. Fordham Foundation and Institute. (ERIC Document Reproduction Service No. ED485528)

Fry, B., O'Neil, K., & Bottoms, G. (2006). *Schools can't wait: Accelerating the redesign of university principal preparation programs.* Atlanta, GA: Southern Regional Education Board.

Fullan M. (2003). *The moral imperative of school leadership.* Thousand Oaks, CA: Corwin.

Furman, G. C. (2007). "Scientific" research and the new narrative for educational leadership. In F. W. English & G. C. Furman (Eds.), *Research and educational research: Navigating the new national research council guidelines* (pp. 79–98). Lanham, MD: Rowan & Littlefield Education.

Gagne, M. (1990). Exemplary university preparation programs: Four case studies. In L. Witters-Churchill & D. A. Erlandson (Eds.), *The principalship in the 1990s and beyond: Current research on performance-based preparation and professional development* (pp. 41–48). University Park, PA: The University Council for Educational Administration.

Glasman, N., Cibulka, J., & Ashby, D. (2002). Program self-evaluation for continuous improvement. *Educational Administration Quarterly, 38*(2), 257–288.

Glasman, N. S., & Glasman, L. D. (1990). Educational reform and evaluation. *Educational Administration Quarterly, 24*(4), 438–45.

Goldring, E., & Greenfield, W. (2002). Understanding the evolving concept of leadership in education: Roles, expectations, and dilemmas. In J. Murphy (Ed.), *The educational leadership challenge: Redefining leadership for the 21st century. One hundred-first yearbook of the National Society for the Study of Education* (pp. 1–19). Chicago: National Society for the Study of Education.

Greenfield, W. D. (1975). *Organizational socialization and the preparation of educational administrators.* Paper presented at the annual meeting of the American Educational Research Association, Washington, DC.

Gregg, R. T. (1960). Administration. In C. W. Harris (Ed.), *Encyclopedia of educational research* (3rd ed., pp. 19–24). New York: MacMillan.

Grogan, M., & Andrews, R. (2002). Defining preparation and professional development for the future. *Educational Administration Quarterly, 38*(2), 233–257.

Guskey, T. (2000). *Evaluating professional development.* Thousand Oaks, CA: Corwin.

Habermas J. (1971). *Knowledge and human interests.* Boston: Beacon Press.

Habermas, J. (1975). *Legitimation crisis* (T. McCarthy, Trans.). Boston: Beacon Press.

Hallinger, P., & Heck, R. H. (1996). Reassessing the principal's role in school effectiveness: A review of empirical research 1980–1995. *Educational Administration Quarterly, 34*(1), 5–44.

Hartle, T. W. (1985). The growing interest in measuring the educational achievement of college students. In C. Adelman (Ed.), *Assessment in American higher education: Issues and contexts* (pp. 1–12). Washington, DC: U.S. Department of Education, Office of Educational Research and Improvement.

Hess, F. M. (2004). A license to lead? In T. J. Lasley (Ed.), *Better leaders for America's schools: Perspectives on the manifesto* (pp. 36–51). Columbia, MO: University Council for Educational Administration.

Holmes Group. (1986). *Tomorrow's teachers: A report of the Holmes Group.* East Lansing, MI: Author.

Huba, M. E., & Freed, J. E. (2000). *Learner-centered assessment on college campuses: Shifting the focus from teaching to learning.* Boston: Allyn and Bacon.

Jackson, B. L., & Kelley, C. (2002). Exceptional and innovative programs in educational leadership. *Educational Administration Quarterly, 38*(2), 191–212.

Jacobson, S. L. (1990). Reflections on the third wave of reform: Rethinking administrator preparation. In S. L. Jacobson & J. A. Conway (Eds.), *Educational leadership in an age of reform* (pp. 30–44). New York: Longman.

Joint Task Force on Student Learning. (1988). *Learning principles and collaborative action.* Washington, DC: American Association for Higher Education.

Jones, E., & Voorhees, R. (2000). *Defining and assessing competencies: Exploring data ramifications of competency-based initiatives: Final report of the Working Group on Competency-Based Initiative.* Washington DC: National Postsecondary Education Cooperative.

Keedy, J. (1999). Examining teacher instructional leadership within small group dynamics of collegial groups. *Teaching and Teacher Education, 15*(7), 785–799.

Knight, P. & Yorke, M. (2003). *Assessment, learning and employability.* Maidenhead, England: The Society for Research Into Higher Education and Open University Press.

Kochan, F. (2002). Hope and possibility: Advancing an argument for a Habermasian perspective in educational administration. *Studies in Philosophy and Education, 21*(2), 137–155.

Kochan, F. K., & Sabo, D. (1995). Collaboration in educational leadership programs. *Planning and Changing, 26*(3/4), 168–178.

Kochan, F. K., & Spencer, W. (1999). Preparing leaders for tomorrow's schools: The practitioners' perspectives. *Research in the Schools, 6*(1), 9–16.

Kochan, F. K., & Twale, D. J. (1998). Advisory councils. *Journal of School Leadership, 29*(4), 237–250.

Kowalski, T. J. (2004). The ongoing war for the soul of school administration. In T. J. Lasley (Ed.), *Better leaders for America's schools: Perspectives on the manifesto* (pp. 92–114). Columbia, MO: University Council for Educational Administration.

Lad, K., Browne-Ferrigno, T., & Shoho, A. (2005, November). *Leadership preparation admission criteria: Examining the spectrum from open enrollment to elite selection.* Paper presented at the annual meeting of the University Council for Educational Administration, Nashville, TN.

Lakomski, G. (1998). Training administrators in the wild: A naturalistic perspective. *UCEA Review, 34*(3), 1, 5, 10–11.

Lashway, L. (1999). *Measuring leadership: A guide to assessment for development of school executives.* Eugene: University of Oregon, ERIC Clearinghouse on Educational Management. (ERIC Document Reproduction Service No. ED431209)

Lasley, T. J. (Ed.). (2004). *Better leaders for America's schools: Perspectives on the manifesto.* Columbia, MO: University Council for Educational Administration.

Lawrence, J., & Green, K. (1980). *A question of quality: The higher education ratings game.* Washington, DC: Higher Education Research Institute.

Lawton, S., Gilbert, M., Estabrook, R., Richtig, R., & Eddy, P, (2005). Assessing outcomes from educational leadership programs. In C. L. Fulmer & F. L. Dembowski (Eds.), *National Summit on School Leadership: Crediting the past, challenging the past, and changing the future* (pp. 207–212). New York: Rowman & Littlefield Education.

Leithwood, K. (1999). Foreword. In L. Lashway, *Measuring leadership: A guide to assessment for development of school executives.* Eugene, OR: ERIC Clearinghouse on Educational Management. (ERIC Document Reproduction Service No. ED431209)

Leithwood, K., Jantzi, D., Coffin, G., & Wilson, O. (1996). Preparing school leaders: What works? *Journal of School Leadership, 6,* 316–342.

Leithwood, K., Seashore Louis, K., Anderson, S., & Wahlstron, K. (2004). *Executive summary: How leadership influences student learning.* Minneapolis: University of Minnesota, Center for Applied Research and Educational Improvement.

Lendley, C. B. (1993). Portfolio assessment. In T. W. Banta & Associates, *Making a difference: Outcomes of a decade of assessment in higher education* (pp. 139–150). San Francisco: Jossey-Bass.

LeTendre, B. G., & Roberts, B. (2005). A national view of certification of school principals: Current and future trends. Paper presented at the annual meeting of the University Council for Educational Administration, Nashville, TN.

Levine, A. (2005). *Educating school leaders.* Washington, DC: The Education Schools Project.

Lopez, C. L. (2004). A decade of assessing student learning: What we have learned, and what is next. In P. Hernon & R. E. Dugan (Eds.), *Outcomes assessment in higher education* (pp. 29–71). Westport, CT: Libraries Unlimited.

Lubinescu, E., Ratcliff, J., & Gaffney, M. (2001). Two continuums collide: Accreditation and assessment. *New Directions for Higher Education, 113,* 5–21.

Maki, P. (2002). Developing an assessment plan to learn about student learning. *Journal of Academic Librarianship, 28*(1/2), 8.

Marchese, T. J. (1997). The new conversations about learning. In B. Cambridge (Ed.), *Assessing impact: Evidence and action* (pp. 79–95). Washington, DC: American Association for Higher Education.

Marks, H. M., & Printy, S. M. (2003). Principal leadership and school performance: An integration of transformational and instructional leadership. *Educational Administration Quarterly, 39*(3), 370–397.

Mazzeo, C. (2001). Frameworks of state: Assessment policy in historical perspective. *Teachers College Record, 103,* 367–398.

McCarthy, M. M. (1999). The evolution of educational leadership preparation programs. In J. Murphy & K. Seashore Louis (Eds.), *Handbook of research on educational administration* (2nd ed., pp. 119–139). San Francisco: Jossey-Bass.

McCarthy, M. M. (2001, Fall). Challenges facing educational leadership programs: Our future is now. *Division A: American Educational Research Association, Teaching in Educational Administration Newsletter: AERA Division A, 8*(1), 4–5.

McCarthy, M. M. (2006). Foreword. In J. Murphy, *Preparing school leaders: Defining a research and action agenda.* Lanham, MD: Rowman & Littlefield Education.

McClain, C., & Krueger, D. (1985). Using outcomes assessment: A case study in institutional change. In P. Ewell (Ed.), *Assessing educational outcomes. New Directions for Institutional Research No. 47* (pp. 33–46). New York: Wiley.

McFadden, C., & Buckner, K. (2005). Finishing the preparation of school leaders: Can preparation programs and school districts partner to produce the leaders schools need? In C. L. Fulmer & F. L. Dembowski (Eds.), *National Summit on School Leadership: Crediting the past, challenging the present, and changing the future* (pp. 293–303). New York: Rowman & Littlefield Education.

Milstein, M. (1992, October). *The Danforth Program for the Preparation of School Principals (DPPSP) six years later: What we have learned.* Paper presented at the annual meeting of the University Council for Educational Administration, Minneapolis, MN.

Milstein, M. (1999). Reflections on "The Evolution of Educational Leadership Programs." *Educational Administration Quarterly, 35*(4), 537–545.

Milstein, M., & Krueger, J. A. (1993). Innovative approaches to clinical internships: The New Mexico experience. In J. Murphy (Ed.), *Preparing tomorrow's school leaders: Alternative designs* (pp. 19–38). University Park, PA: University Council for Educational Administration.

Morante, E. A. (1986). The effectiveness of developmental programs: A two-year follow-up study. *Journal of Developmental Education, 9*(3), 14–15.

Murphy, D. (2004). Educational leadership preparation programs: The effectiveness of university off-campus cohort programs and on-campus programs as determined by student course evaluations. *Dissertation Abstracts,* AAT 3122357.

Murphy, J. (1988). Methodological measurement and conceptual problems in the study of administrator instructional leadership. *Educational Evaluation and Policy Analysis, 10*(2), 117–139.

Murphy, J. (1990). The reform of school administration: Pressures and calls for change. In J. Murphy (Ed.), *The reform of American public education in the 1980s: Perspectives and cases* (pp. 277–303). Berkeley, CA: McCutchan.

Murphy, J. (Ed.). (1993). *Preparing tomorrow's school leaders: Alternative designs.* University Park, PA: University Council for Educational Administration.

Murphy, J. (1998). Methodological measurement and conceptual problems in the study of administrator instructional leadership. *Educational Evaluation and Policy Analysis, 10*(2), 117–139.

Murphy, J. (1999). Changes in preparation programs. Perceptions of department chairs. In J. Murphy & P. B. Forsyth (Eds.), *Educational administration: A decade of reform* (pp. 170–191). Thousand Oaks, CA: Corwin Press.

Murphy, J. (2006). *Preparing school leaders: Defining a research and action agenda.* Lanham, MD: Rowman & Littlefield Education.

Murphy, J., & Vriesenga, M. (2004). *Research on preparation programs in educational administration: An analysis.* [UCEA monograph]. Columbia, MO: University Council for Educational Administration.

National Association of Secondary School Principals. (1973). *Where will they find it?* Reston, VA: Author.

National Association of Secondary School Principals. (1995). *Performance-based preparation of principals: A framework for improvement.* Reston, VA: Author.

National Association of State Directors of Teacher Education and Certification. (2004). *NASDTEC manual on the preparation and certification of educational personnel 2004* (9th ed.). Sacramento, CA: Author.

National Commission for the Principalship. (1990). *Principals for our changing schools: Preparation and certification.* Fairfax, VA: Author.

National Commission on Excellence in Education. (1983). *A nation at risk: The importance of educational reform.* Washington, DC: U.S. Department of Education.

National Commission on Teaching and America's Future. (1996). *What matters most: Teaching for America's future.* New York: Author.

National Council of Accreditation of Teacher Education. (2007). *About NCATE.* Retrieved April 7, 2007, from http://www.ncate.org/public/aboutNCATE.asp

National Governors' Association. (1986). *Time for results: The governors' report on education.* Washington, DC: Author.

New Leaders for New Schools. (2005, February 14). *New Leaders for New Schools announces partnership with Oakland Unified School District* [Press release]. Retrieved April 7, 2007, from http://www.nlns.org/NLWeb/resources/Oakland_Press_Release.doc

Nieweg, M. (2004). Case study: Innovative assessment and curriculum redesign. *Assessment & Evaluation in Higher Education, 29*(2), 203–214.

No Child Left Behind Act of 2001, Pub. L. No. 107-110 (2002).

Noddings, N. (1984). *Caring: A feminine approach to ethics and moral education.* Berkeley: University of California Press.

North Central Association of Colleges and Schools. (1996). *Opportunities for improvement: Advice from consultant-evaluators on programs to assess student learning* (Report No. JC020299). Chicago: Author. (ERIC Document Reproduction Service No. ED463790)

Norton, J. (2002, Fall). *Universities in the lead: Redesigning leadership preparation for student achievement* [SREB monograph]. Atlanta, GA: Southern Regional Education Board.

Ogawa, R., & Bossert, S. T. (1995). Leadership as an organizational quality. *Educational Administration Quarterly, 31*(2), 224–243.

Orr, M. (2006). Mapping innovations in leadership preparation in our nation's school of education. *Phi Delta Kappan, 87*(7), 492–499.

Orr, M. T. & Barber, M. (2007). Collaborative leadership preparation: A comparative study of innovative programs and practices. *Journal of School Leadership, 16*(6), 709–739.

Orr, M. T., Doolittle, G., Kottkamp, R., Osterman, K., & Silverberg, R. (2004). What are we learning from the ELCC/NCATE required program evaluations? Findings from real-time action research at the UCEA convention *UCEA Review, 46*(1), 7–10.

Orr, M., & Pounder, D. (2006). *UCEA/TEA-SIG Taskforce on Evaluating Leadership Preparation Programs. Taskforce report: Six years later and future directions.* Unpublished document.

Orr, M., Silverberg, R., & LeTendre, B. (2006, April). *Comparing leadership development from pipeline to preparation to advancement: A study of multiple institutions' leadership preparation programs.* Paper presented at the annual meeting of the American Educational Research Association, San Francisco.

Pace, C. (1984). Historical perspectives of student outcomes: Assessment with implications for the Future. *NASPA Journal, 22*(2), 10–18.

Palomba, C. A., & Banta, T. W. (1999). *Assessment essentials.* San Francisco: Jossey-Bass.

Palomba, C. A., & Banta, T. W. (Eds.). (2001). *Assessing student competence in accredited disciplines: Pioneering approaches to assessment in higher education.* Sterling, VA: Stylus.

Pennington, D. C., Zvonkovic, A. M., & Wilson, S. L. (1989). Changes in college satisfaction across an academic term. *Journal of College Student Development, 30,* 528–535.

Peterson, M., & Einarson, M. K. (2001). What are colleges doing about student assessment? *Journal of Higher Education, 72*(6), 629–669.

Peterson, M., Einarson, M. K., Trice, A. G., & Nichols, A. R. (1997). *Improving organizational and administrative support for student assessment: A review of the research literature.* Stanford, CA: Stanford University, National Center for Postsecondary Improvement.

Peterson, M., & Vaughan, D. S. (2002). A multidimensional strategy for student assessment. *Planning for Higher Education, 30*(2), 13–27.

Place, W. A. (2006). Performance assessment. In F. W. English (Ed.), *Sage encyclopedia of educational leadership* (Vol. 1, p. 740). Thousand Oaks, CA: Sage.

Pounder, D. G. (2000). A discussion of the task force's collective findings. *Educational Administration Quarterly, 36*(3), 465–473.

Pounder, D. G. (2006). Leader preparation research priorities and reform agendas: A response to charting the changing landscape. In J. Murphy (Ed.), *Preparing school leaders: Defining a research and action agenda* (pp. 87–92). Lanham, MD: Rowan & Littlefield Education.

Prestine, N., & LeGrand, B. (1991). Cognitive learning theory and the preparation of educational administrators: Implications for practice and policy. *Educational Administration Quarterly, 27*(1), 61–89.

Quantz, R., & Camron-McCabe, N. (1991). Continuing the conversation: A response to Apple, Johnston, and Sergiovanni. *The Urban Review, 23*(1), 51–57.

Quinn, T. (2005). Principal preparation programs: Problems, prospects, and promising practices. In C. L. Fulmer & F. L. Dembowski (Eds.), *National summit on school leadership: Crediting the past, challenging the present, and changing the future* (pp. 197–206). New York: Rowman & Littlefield Education.

Ratcliff, J. L. (1996). Assessment, accreditation, and evaluation of higher education in the U.S. *Quality in Higher Education, 2*(1), 5–19.

Reese, C., & Tannenbaum, R. (1999). Gathering content-related validity evidence for the school leaders licensure assessment. *Journal of Personnel Evaluation in Education, 13*(3), 263–282.

Resnick, D., & Goulden, M. (1987). Assessment, curriculum and expansion in American higher education: A historical perspective. In D. F. Halpern (Ed.), *Student outcomes assessment: What institutions stand to gain* (New Directions for Higher Education No. 59, pp. 77–88). San Francisco: Jossey-Bass.

Resnick, L., & Resnick, D. (1992). *Report on new standards tasks and protocols for piloting. Project 2.1: Alternative approaches to assessment in mathematics and science. Alternative approaches to assessment in mathematical problem solving* (Report No. R117G10027). Washington, DC: U.S. Department of Education, Office of Educational Research and Improvement. (ERIC Document Reproduction Service No. ED348380)

Richardson, R. (1990). Evaluation of principal performance. In L. Witter-Churchill & D. A. Erlandson (Eds.), *The principalship in the 1990s and beyond: Current research on performance-based preparation and professional development* (pp. 49–61). University Park, PA: The University Council for Educational Administration.

Rodman, B. (1987, March 11). Training programs for administrators are increasingly a target of criticism. *Education Week,* pp. 1, 16.

Rossman, J. E., & El-Khawas, E. (1987). *Thinking about assessment: Perspectives for presidents and chief academic officers.* Washington, DC: American Council on Education and American Association for Higher Education.

Sanders, N. M., & Simpson, J. (2005). *State policy framework to develop highly qualified administrators.* Washington, DC: Council of Chief State School Officers.

Schaible-Brandon, S., & Muth, R. (2006). Portfolios. In F. W. English (Ed.), *Sage encyclopedia of educational leadership* (pp. 777–780). Thousand Oaks, CA: Sage.

Scheurich, J. J., & Skrla, L. (2003). *Leadership for equity and excellence.* Thousand Oaks, CA: Corwin.

Schubert, W. H. (1986). *Curriculum: Perspective, paradigm, and possibility.* New York: Macmillan.

Secretary of Education's Commission on the Future of Higher Education. (2006). *A test of leadership: Charting the future of U.S. higher education.* Washington, DC: U.S. Department of Education.

Sergiovanni, T. J. (1989). Mystics, neats, and scruffies: Informing professional practice in educational administration. *Journal of Educational Administration, 27*(2), 7–21.

Sergiovanni, T. J. (1992). *Moral leadership: Getting to the heart of schooling.* San Francisco: Jossey-Bass.

Shakeshaft, C. (1999). A decade half full or a decade half empty: Thoughts from a tired reformer. In J. Murphy & P. Forsyth (Eds.), *Educational administration: A decade of reform* (pp. 237–250). Thousand Oaks, CA: Corwin Press.

Shields, C. M. (2007). What's a researcher to do? Insights for "post-anything" researchers. In F. W. English & G. C. Furman (Eds.), *Research and educational leadership: Navigating the new national research council guidelines* (pp. 97–118). Lanham, MD: Rowman & Littlefield.

Silver, P. F. (1982). Administrator preparation. In H. E. Mitzel (Ed.), *Encylopedia of educational research* (5th ed., Vol. 1, pp. 49–59). New York: Free Press.

Sims, S. J. (1992). *Student outcomes assessment: A historical review and guide to program development.* New York: Greenwood Press.

Smylie, M. A., Bennett, A., Konkol, P., & Fendt, C. R. (2005). What do we know about developing school leaders? A look at existing research and next steps for new study. In W. A. Firestone & C. Reihl (Eds.), *A new agenda: Directions for research on educational leadership* (pp. 138–155). New York: Teachers College Press.

Southern Regional Education Board. (n.d.). *SREB Leadership Initiative: Creating effective principals who can improve the region's schools and influence student achievement.* Retrieved October 25, 2006, from http://www.sreb.org/main/Leadership/pubs/02V51_LeadershipInitiative.pdf

Southern Regional Education Board. (2002). *Universities in the lead: Redesigning leadership preparation for student achievement.* Atlanta, GA: Author.

Educational Forum, 68(2), 108–114.

Starrat, R. J. (1991). Building an ethical school: A theory for practice in educational leadership. *Educational Administration Quarterly, 27*(2), 185–202.

Tatlock, J. S. (1924). The general final examination in the major study: Report by Committee G. *Bulletin of the American Association of University Professor, 10*, 609–635.

Teacher Education Accreditation Council. (2007). *TEAC guide to accreditation.* Retrieved April 7, 2007, from http://www.teac.org/literature/index.asp

Thornton, B., & Perreault, G. (2002). Connecting the learning organization, strategic planning and public relations. *Journal of School Public Relations, 23*(3), 230–241.

Thrash, P. A. (1988). Educational outcomes in the accrediting process. *Change, 74*(4), 16–18.

Trivett, D. A. (1976). *Accreditation and institutional eligibility* (ERIC/Higher Education Research Report No. 9). Washington, DC: American Association for Higher Education.

U.S. Department of Education. (2005). *FY 2005 school leadership application for grants.* Washington, DC: Author.

Usdan, M. D. (2002). Reactions to articles commissioned by the National Commission for the Advancement of Educational Leadership Preparation, *Educational Administration Quarterly, 38*(2), 300–307.

Vroeijenstijn, A. I. (1995). *Improvement and accountability, navigating between Scylla and Charybdi. Guide for external quality assessment in higher education.* London: Jessica Kingsley.

Wiggins, G. (1989). A true test: Toward more authentic and equitable assessment. *Phi Delta Kappan, 70*(9), 703–713.

Wiggins, G. (1997). Work standards: Why we need standards for instructional and assessment design. *NASSP Bulletin, 81*(590), 56–64.

Wiggins, G., & McTighe, J. (1998). *Understanding by design.* Alexandria, VA: Association for Supervision and Curriculum Development.

Willower, D. J., & Forsyth, P. B. (1999). A brief history of scholarship in educational administration. In J. Murphy & K. Seashore Louis (Eds.), *Handbook of research on educational administration* (2nd ed., pp. 1–24). San Francisco: Jossey-Bass.

Witters-Churchill, L., & Erlandson, D. A. (Eds.). (1990). *The principalship in the 1990s and beyond: Current research on performance-based preparation and professional development.* University Park, PA: University Council for Educational Administration.

Witziers, B., Bosker, R., & Kruger, M. (2003). Educational leadership and student achievement: The elusive search for an association. *Educational Administration Quarterly, 39*(3), 398–425.

Young, M. D., & Crow, G. M. (2006). UCEA's national reform agenda in action: An afterword. In J. Murphy, *Preparing school leaders: Defining a research and action agenda* (pp. 93–99). Lanham, MD: Rowman & Littlefield Education.

Young, M. D., & Kochan, F. K. (2004). Supporting leadership for America's schools. In T. J. Lasley (Ed.), *Better leaders for America's schools: Perspectives on the manifesto* (pp. 115–129) [UCEA monograph]. Columbia, MO: University Council for Educational Administration.

Young, M. D., & Peterson, G. J. (2002). The National Commission for the Advancement of Educational Leadership Preparation: An introduction. *Educational Administration Quarterly, 38*(2), 130–136.

Young, M., Peterson, G. L., & Short, P. M. (2002). The complexity of substantive reform: A call for interdependence among key stakeholders. *Educational Administration Quarterly, 38,* 137–175.

Young, R. (1990). *A critical theory of education: Habermas and our children's future.* New York: Teachers' College Press.

Yukl, G. A. (1989). *Leadership in organizations.* Englewood Cliffs, NJ: Prentice Hall.

12
Program Evaluation in Leadership Preparation and Related Fields

MARGARET TERRY ORR WITH MARGARET E. BARBER

The quality and continuous improvement of educational leadership preparation programs are highly dependent upon the field's engagement in and use of evaluation and related research. Program evaluation in leadership preparation historically has been limited in scope and depth (Glasman, Cibulka, & Ashby, 2002; McCarthy, 2001b; Murphy & Vriesenga, 2006). In recent years, the press of accountability and assessment in kindergarten through Grade 12 (K–12) and higher education and for licensure and certification in educational leadership positions has increased the demand for and expectations of program evaluation in the field (McCarthy, 2001a). National and state accreditation systems for leadership preparation require evidence of program effectiveness (National Policy Board for Educational Administration [NPBEA], 2002). Finally, recent and persistent calls for program-related research and evaluation stress the need to "determine if they [educational leadership preparation programs] are supporting high-quality preparation of educational leaders" (Young, Petersen, & Short, 2002, p. 153) and to determine which program approaches better prepare leaders who can effectively lead school improvement.

For the purposes of this review, educational leadership preparation programs are defined as university-based, graduate programs that prepare aspiring leaders for certification and licensure in school or district educational leadership positions. These programs may lead to a master's degree or certificate of advanced graduate studies. According to recent national estimates, there were 459 master's degree programs in educational leadership in 2003 (Baker, Orr, & Young, 2007), and several certification-only programs exist as well. Demonstrating their effectiveness and fostering continued improvement depend upon their active engagement in program evaluation.

What is program evaluation? Rossi, Freeman, and Lipsey (1999), leading experts in evaluation research, defined program evaluation as

> the use of social research methods to systematically investigate the effectiveness of social intervention programs. It draws on the techniques and concepts of social science disciplines and is intended to be useful for improving programs and informing social action. (p. 35)

Rossi et al. explained that evaluations are usually conducted for four purposes: "program improvement, accountability, knowledge generation, and political ruses or public relations" (p. 40) and typically involve one or more of five program domain assessments: (a) need for the program, (b) program design, (c) the program implementation and service delivery, (d) the program impact and outcomes, and (e) program efficiency. Weiss (1998) extended this program-evaluation purposes framework by outlining five key elements to any evaluation: (a) systematic assessment, (b) the process of the program, (c) the outcomes of the program, (d) standards for comparison, and (e) the purpose of the evaluation as a contribution to program or policy improvement.

Generally, the focus of a program evaluation is determined by two factors: the intended outcomes and the program theory, defined by Rossi et al. (1999) as "a depiction of the significant assumptions and expectations on which the program depends for its success" (p. 90). The first factor, intended outcomes, reflects the larger question concerning what the program is trying to achieve (Weiss, 1998). The second, program theory, reflects the program's theories of change, both what the program is expected to achieve and how. Weiss referred to this latter factor as "the set of beliefs that underlie action" (p. 55). Weiss further explained that program theory refers to the mechanisms that mediate between delivery of a program and the emergence of intended outcomes. She distinguished this type of theory from implementation theory, which she defined as focused on the delivery of program services: what is required to convert the program's objectives into service delivery and program operations. For Weiss, these two theories—program theory and implementation theory—comprise a program's theories of change and are to be the basis for evaluation. Together, they clarify (a) program inputs in terms of resources and organization, (b) program activities and how they are implemented, (c) interim outcomes in response to the activities, and (d) desired end results.

Kirkpatrick (1998), in his foundational work on training evaluation and assessment, clarified interim outcomes and desired end results further in a four-level outcome model, which he conceptualized as a linear chain of effects. Kirkpatrick's four levels are (a) Level 1, reaction (what was the response to the activity and were participants satisfied with the experience?); (b) Level 2, learning (what did participants learn and what knowledge and skills did they gain?); (c) Level 3, application or transfer (how did participants use what they learned?); and (d) Level 4, organizational or business impact (how did the learning transfer affect organizational goals and outcomes?). Guskey (2000) differentiated the Level 4 organizational outcomes further as the changes that result from participants' learning and the organizational outcomes. Phillips (1996) added a fifth level, which is to measure a program's return on investment (ROI) in monetary costs and benefits to participants and their organizations.

Program evaluation, as evaluation experts (Rossi et al., 1999; Weiss, 1998) have stressed, is not simply a research endeavor. Rather, it is a process that can influence resource allocations, institutional decisions, and policy and program reform. It is also fraught with politics over the intended uses of the evaluation, the role of the evaluator as insider or outsider, and the policy-level and program-level interests in the evaluation outcomes. Such interests influence the opportunity for program evaluation, the feasibility and design of program evaluation research, and how results are used.

Thus, to explore the current state of program evaluation in educational leadership preparation requires assessing the policy context for research on evaluation leadership preparation programs (particularly as framed by accreditation, state requirements, licensure testing, federal and foundation evaluation expectations, and private-sector rankings research) and the institutional practice of evaluation research (in national, regional, and state arenas and initiated by external field critics). This review also includes a description and assessment of the current state of evaluation research on educational leadership preparation, as evident in published research, reports, and dissertations.

There is a small and growing body of evaluation research on leadership preparation program models and features, both nationally and internationally. This evaluation research can be found primarily in peer-reviewed research journals, dissertation abstracts, published reports, and peer-reviewed conference proceedings. To shed further light on the state of program evaluation research, this review draws on evaluation research in leadership development as well as in related fields, including international educational leadership preparation, educational leadership development, business education (master's of business administration, or MBA) and leadership development and executive education, where similar questions exist on the effectiveness and impact of various preparation and training approaches. This descriptive review draws on the evaluation design as framed by Rossi et al. (1999) on the types of evaluation, Weiss's (1998) emphasis on program and implementation theories, and Kirkpatrick's (1998) levels of outcomes. An analysis of this body of research is included in this chapter and establishes the current state of evaluation research, reveals its strengths and gaps (particularly as compared to recommended qualities for evaluation research), and offers conceptual and methodological direction for further program evaluation.

Policy Context

The policy context for program evaluation of leadership preparation programs is framed by field-based expectations and emerging concerns about the capacity of programs to prepare high-quality, effective leaders who can contribute to improved education for all children. Field-based expectations for leadership preparation program evaluation come from national organizations, state agencies, and funders. National and state accreditation processes for leadership preparation programs are mandated in some states and programs are indirectly evaluated through state assessments of candidates for licensure and certification. Public and private funding initiatives also encourage state and university reforms of leadership preparation, although their program evaluation roles are more limited. Finally, privately supported institutional rankings provide yet another form of assessment. Little research exists, however, on how these external evaluation mechanisms influence program quality and effectiveness. The impetus for leadership preparation program accreditation and evaluation requirements often stems from changing expectations for school leaders to be able to improve schools and from increased expectations that preparation improve their readiness and leadership effectiveness (Bottoms & O'Neill, 2001; Sanders & Simpson, 2005). Through national and state accreditation processes, two types of program evaluation purposes are specifically encouraged: assessment of program implementation and service delivery and the assessment program's impact and outcomes. Through the state licensure or certification testing, at least one program outcome—candidates' leadership knowledge and skills—is assessed.

National Accreditation

Currently, there are two primary accrediting agencies nationally for schools of education (and, by inclusion, their leadership preparation programs): the National Council for Accreditation of Teacher Education (NCATE), which was established to review the quality of colleges of education every 7 years, and the Teacher Education Accreditation Council (TEAC). Beginning in the late 1990s, NCATE established a process for leadership preparation program reviews. Under NCATE, individual programs, like educational leadership preparation, within colleges or schools of education are reviewed for recognition status by specialized professional associations using nationally recognized standards. The Educational Leadership Constituent Council (ELCC) is the NCATE specialized professional association for leadership preparation and is governed by the NPBEA (n.d.). The NPBEA consists of 10 national administrator stakeholder organizations: (a) American Association of Colleges of Teacher Education (AACTE), (b) American Association of School Administrators, (c) Association for Supervision and Curriculum Development, (d) Council of Chief State School Officers Organization, (e) National Association of Elementary School Principals, (f) NCATE, (g) National Association of Secondary School Principals (NASSP), (h) National Council

8

of Professors of Educational Administration, (i) National School Boards Association, and (j) the University Council for Educational Administration (UCEA). In recent years, ELCC, through the NPBEA, adopted Interstate School Leaders Licensure Consortium (ISLLC) standards for program accreditation. NPBEA (2008) undertook a standards review process in 2006 and 2007, and, after lengthy public review and comment, adopted revised standards in December 2007.

Leadership preparation programs often seek national accreditation in order to meet state requirements and select an accrediting agency based on state preference or institutional interest, if the option exists. As of July 2005, the ELCC had reviewed 201 departments of educational administration in universities in 25 states, as required for state program approval. Another 4 states (Alabama, District of Columbia, Georgia, and Oregon) conduct their own internal reviews but use adapted or revised ELCC (2005) performance standards. Taken together, these programs represent almost half of all leadership preparation programs nationwide (Baker et al., 2007).

ELCC provides both standards and guidelines to programs for the preparation of educational leaders, including expectations for program evaluation. Together, these standards and guidelines clarify expectations against which individual programs can be compared and the kinds of data and outcomes for program implementation and impact assessments. In recent years, ELCC has strengthened its emphasis on assessment, both in the kinds of standards-based data to be collected by programs and how faculty are to use the data for program improvement purposes. ELCC requires seven types of assessments and recommends specific evidence: (a) state licensure assessment or other content-based assessment; (b) assessment of content knowledge in educational leadership, using comprehensive examinations, essays, and case studies; (c) assessment of ability to develop supervisory plan for classroom-based instruction, such as school improvement plans, needs-assessment projects, and faculty intervention plans; (d) assessment of internship and clinical practice using faculty evaluations of candidates' performances, internship and clinical site supervisors' evaluations of candidates' performances, or candidates' formative and summative logs and reflections; (e) assessment of ability to support student learning and development, such as postgraduate 360-degree surveys, employer satisfaction surveys, and community feedback surveys of candidates or graduates; (f) an assessment of the candidates' application of content knowledge in educational leadership (such as action research projects and portfolio tasks); and (g) an assessment of candidates' abilities in organizational management and community relations (such as school-based strategic plans, school simulations, and school intervention plans). To encourage that evaluation data are used for program improvement and improved graduate preparation, ELCC requires that programs describe how their faculty "are using the data from assessments to improve candidate performance and the program, as it relates to content knowledge; pedagogical and professional knowledge, skills, and dispositions; and student learning" (NCATE, 2008, p. 2).

When reviewed by ELCC, programs are rated on their use and quality of these seven types of assessment. Quality is determined by (a) the extent to which the assessment description and scoring guides are aligned to specific ELCC standard elements, (b) how the scoring guide is used to measure progress, (c) how aggregated data are aligned to specific ELCC standards and the assessment scoring guide, and (d) whether results show both areas of candidate success and provide an improvement plan for areas in which candidates are not successful. By setting these expectations, ELCC strives to positively influence how leadership preparation programs evaluate their performance and use their findings to strengthen how well they prepare aspiring leaders, and their future effectiveness.

The second national program accreditation body is the TEAC. Although it is used by fewer institutions and programs nationwide than NCATE, its use is growing, in large part because of differences in assessment expectations. TEAC's (2006) goal for leadership preparation programs is "to prepare 'competent, caring, and qualified' leaders for the schools" (TEAC, 2006, ¶ 1). To qualify for accreditation, programs are to provide evidence that leadership preparation meets three quality principles: (a) evidence of candidate learning (professional knowledge, strategic decision-making, and caring leadership skills as well as the cross-cutting themes of learning how to learn, multicultural perspectives and understandings, and technology), (b) valid assessments of leader learning, and (c) institutional learning (in which faculty demonstrate a viable system of inquiry, review, and quality control for program improvement). TEAC claims that its standards, while not based on the ISLCC or ELCC standards, easily can accommodate these other national standards within its framework.

State Requirements and Mandates

Almost all states now use standards to define the readiness of educational leaders by adopting state and national standards for certification and licensure, and, for many states, by adopting standards and processes for leadership preparation program registration and accreditation. As reported by state education agencies in 2006 (Toye, Blank, Sanders, & Williams, 2007), "Forty-nine states have policies for certifying or licensing school leaders/administrators, and 48 have adopted administrator certification standards" (p. 29). Forty-six states report that their state standards are aligned with the ISLLC (1996) *Standards for School Leaders*, which have become a national model for state leadership standards and were recently updated (NPBEA, 2008).

In 2005, 20 states reported having processes and criteria for approval of administrator preparation programs, including some that specifically require NCATE accreditation or the selection of a national accreditation agency (Sanders & Simpson, 2005). States typically require national accreditation or state review on a 5-year cycle. In addition, several states have implemented aggressive program reviews (e.g., Mississippi and North Carolina) and a few (e.g., Delaware and New Jersey) have used critical friends reviews (Adams & Copland, 2005). Thus, program evaluation is increasingly becoming part of program operations, at least to meet state and national accreditation requirements.

Licensure-Related Testing

In addition to formal program review, many states use standardized assessments—usually for licensure and certification—of leadership preparation graduates to measure leadership knowledge and skills (as readiness for positions) as well as to assess the effectiveness of leadership preparation programs. Presently, 35 states require a standardized assessment for initial administrator certification, 26 of which use commercially developed tests from national assessment contractors; 9 others developed their own initial certification tests.

With regard to program planning and evaluation, state education agency officials use cut-scores as predictors of candidate readiness and, using percentage of graduates with passing scores, as reflections of program effectiveness. States vary in their benchmarks for passing scores on similar tests, however (Toye et al., 2007). Four states (Arkansas, Hawaii, Illinois, and Ohio) can link administrator test results to measures of school and student outcomes, but those state tests have not been validated. Ten states report using initial certification test scores to guide subsequent professional development or induction programs (Toye et al., 2007).

The two most commonly used national leadership preparation assessments are the School Leaders Licensure Assessment and the Praxis II, with subject assessments in educational leadership, administration, and supervision (Jacobson, O'Neill, Fry, Hill, & Bottoms, 2002). The School Leaders Licensure Assessment is a 6-hour, performance-based assessment to determine "whether entry-level principals and other school leaders have the standards-relevant knowledge believed necessary for competent professional practice" (Educational Testing Service, 2008b, ¶ 1). It uses constructed responses, evaluation of 16 short and long action vignettes, two cases studies for information synthesis and problem solving, and teaching and learning documents for analysis and decision making. It was developed through an extensive job analyses, expert panel reviews, pilot testing and validation (Ellett, 1999; Iwanicki, 1999; Reese & Tannenbaum, 1999). The Praxis II uses multiple-choice questions and candidate-constructed responses on knowledge of school leadership (Educational Testing Service, 2008a). Several states, such as Kentucky, Florida and Oklahoma, have their own principal subject test or leadership exam.

While widely used, such tests have been criticized for deprofessionalizing educational leadership (English, 2006) and decontextualizing administrative discourse (Anderson, 2001). According to Sanders (2007), none of the commercially published tests have demonstrated predictive validity in relation to school or student outcomes. Some commercial assessments were developed through job analyses (based on surveys of current and retired administrators that reflect many outdated conceptions of effective leadership); others were developed by selecting components from item banks to represent or align with state standards. Consequently, they vary in their coverage and content across states. Because most commercial assessments used by states measure general knowledge and basic skills, they fail to measure effective leadership strategies or to be accurate gauges of leadership quality. As Sanders noted, a few states are beginning to develop new systems of assessments, including professional portfolios, to remedy the current reliance on tests that lack technical qualities needed to serve multiple purposes of evaluating and improving leader performance. Meanwhile, graduates' performance on these tests becomes a primary gauge for evaluating programs' effectiveness in preparing their graduates.

Federal and Foundation Evaluation Expectations

Recent foundation and federal investments in innovative leadership preparation—such as through the U.S. Department of Education's School Leadership Program and the Wallace Foundation's Leadership for Educational Achievement in Districts (LEAD) grant program—provide additional opportunity for program evaluation but at present only have limited requirements. The U.S. Department of Education's reporting requirements are primarily limited to documentation of program operations, service delivery (number served), and the labor market impact (number who advance into leadership positions). Thus, although these new funding sources are a strong impetus for program innovation (U.S. Department of Education, 2005), they provide limited evidence of effectiveness. The Wallace Foundation, however, has invested in some standards setting for program evaluation, through grant support to the Southern Regional Educational Board (SREB), to established criteria and means of evaluating leadership preparation program quality. The extent to which these standards are shared (and expected) across funded programs, however, is unclear.

Another mechanism for program evaluation standards setting was created through a partnership of a regional federally funded educational laboratory, the Laboratory for Student Success, and the Institute for Educational Leadership. They established a Web-based resource of educational leadership development programs, e-Lead (n.d.), which provides detailed descriptions and evaluation evidence of standards-based programs, many of which are district–university partnerships. To be included in the database, all programs and their curricula must be based on educational leadership standards (e-Lead, n.d.). At present, no external review has been conducted of any of these funded programs or compilations of program descriptions to validate their findings.

Private-Sector Rankings

A nationally standardized means of program evaluation exists through program assessments and rankings by publications such as *U.S. News and World Report*. Annually, its parent company compiles data and ratings to rank U.S. schools of education and their programs, including leadership preparation ("Education Specialties," 2007). It draws on 12 measures to rank schools and calculates schools' total scores using weighted averages. The data sources include (a) a peer assessment score as completed by deans of schools of education; (b) a superintendent assessment score based on a national sample of districts (with only a 23% response rate); (c) mean GRE verbal scores (for doctoral students only if available or all students if not); (d) mean GRE quantitative scores; (e) PhD and EdD acceptance rates (the proportion offered acceptance); (f) the ratio of full-time, degree-seeking students to full-time, tenured or tenure-tracked faculty; (g) the percentage of faculty with awards and editorships; (g) the number of PhDs and EdDs granted each year; (h) the percentage of all students who are PhD and EdD students; (i) annual funded research (in millions) and annual funded research per faculty member (in thousands); and (j) the percentage of faculty engaged in education and school research each year ("Best Graduate Schools," 2008).

Rankings for doctoral program specialties, such as leadership preparation, are based solely upon nominations. Deans of graduate schools of education (with doctoral programs) select up to 10 top programs in each area from the list of all education doctoral programs. Programs are ranked by the number of votes received ("Best Graduate Schools, 2008). A brief review of Web-site links using the Google search engine suggests that the rankings are used primarily for public relations purposes, rather than program improvement, and are more important for some institutions than for others.

Research on the Influence of the Policy Context

Despite the encouragement of and pressure for evaluation and evidence gathered through program accreditation, registration, and external funding or public rankings, there is no research or other documented evidence of their effects on program quality and graduates' effectiveness as educational leaders. Presently, much of the compiled program evidence exists in national and state accreditation and registration reports for individual programs and final reports to funders. Reflection on the use and benefits of these approaches as levers for program improvement has been prospective in nature, suggesting possible benefits (Ellett, 1999). These potential benefits have yet to be realized.

Program Evaluation Efforts Among Professional Groups

In recent years, groups of educational leadership preparation program faculty have convened to discuss program evaluation issues and to collaborate on joint evaluation efforts. Their work, both nationally and within some states and regions, is contributing to increased program evaluation activity and inquiry into the design and use of program evaluation, particularly in defining appropriate outcomes, measuring program features, and establishing comparisons.

National Efforts

In 2001, an informal group of educational leadership preparation program faculty convened at the annual meeting of the UCEA to explore the evaluation needs and priorities of the leadership preparation field (Orr & Pounder, 2006). This group formalized as a national taskforce cosponsored by the UCEA Executive Committee and the Learning and Teaching in Educational Leadership Special Interest Group (LTEL-SIG, formerly the Teaching in Educational Administration [TEA] SIG) of the American Educational Research Association. The Evaluation Taskforce established three purposes: (a) to conduct comparative evaluation of evaluate leadership preparation programs' impact on their graduates and the preK–12 schools that they lead; (b) to develop research designs, methods, and instruments that can be replicated and refined through study in multiple institutions and settings to facilitate ongoing knowledge development on leadership preparation both nationally and internationally; and (c) to engage the leadership preparation field more broadly in the individual and comparative study of their programs' effectiveness and impact.

Since its beginning, the Evaluation Taskforce has made significant progress on all three goals, generating highly relevant research findings, methodology, and instrumentation and greatly broadening the number of researchers and evaluators in the study of leadership preparation and its effectiveness (Orr & Pounder, 2006). The taskforce remains a voluntary group, representing public and private higher education institutions nationwide. Through semiannual work sessions at UCEA and the American Educational Research Association, Evaluation Taskforce members focus on methodology, collaborative evaluation strategies, and research findings. From 2001 to 2008, the Evaluation Taskforce has yielded research findings and methodology on state policy analysis; the nature of the field (in terms of institutions and degree programs); assessment of program impact on graduates and alumni; investigation of exemplary leadership practices; comparison of programs' student selection and support practices; and the means for collaborative, statewide, program evaluation research (Orr, 2008; Orr & Pounder, 2006). Taken together, the taskforce has investigated ways in which programs can assess their effectiveness using Kirkpatrick's (1998) four-level outcome model (participants' reactions, learning, application or transfer of learning, and organizational impact) and Guskey's (2000) recommended fifth level of change that occurs to the organization, in this case, schools led by graduates. Through principal and teacher survey research, taskforce members have developed measures on initial program impacts on graduate learning and career interests and advancement; leadership practices as school leaders, as application of learning; and school improvement practices and improved school climate, as organizational impacts (Orr, 2007). Through work with state data files, taskforce members have developed means of measuring graduates' advancement into and tenure in leadership positions and are investigating ways of linking principals' career information and schools' achievement performance gains (Fuller & Orr, 2006).

Such research has provided critical findings on the field itself, which can be used to benchmark findings for future evaluation research. Moreover, it has provided the means for developing, validating, and assessing the reliability of various evaluation measures, data collection instruments, and methodologies for program evaluation purposes, which many programs are replicating for their own program improvement purposes. One commonly used product is the UCEA LTEL-SIG Survey of Leadership Preparation and Practice, which assesses graduates' program experiences, learning, career advancement, leadership practices, and school improvement work (Orr & Pounder, 2007).

Regional Efforts

One regional evaluation research initiative, an SREB project, is attempting to improve programs through standards setting and evaluation of program design and implementation. The SREB project's aim is to improve the quality and effectiveness of leadership preparation programs in its southern region and to disseminate results for nationwide use. Since the early 2000s, SREB (2006) has worked with 22 "pacesetter" universities to establish formal university–district partnerships for designing and implementing leadership preparation programs that are based on a shared vision of effective school leaders; integrate standards, research-based practices, and real-world problems into course content and learning experiences; provide high-quality field experiences; and systematically use evaluation strategies that provide reliable evidence on the programs and graduates.

Early investigation of the impact of their program improvement work shows how slow and complex university change can be. In 2003, SREB evaluated participating programs' design and redesign progress over 2 or more years using its program standards criteria. SREB staff found that 18 of the 22 universities had made some to substantial progress in forming district partnerships, strengthening their emphasis on leadership knowledge and skills for improving schools and student achievement, and creating well-planned and coordinated field experiences. They found that only one third made substantial progress in their primary criteria for program quality: "developing courses that concentrate on helping candidates master the explicit knowledge and skills they need to lead change in school curriculum and instructional practices" (Frye, O'Neill, & Bottoms, 2006, p. 9).

Despite its value, program evaluation proved to be the most challenging reform strategy for programs to adopt. Frye et al. (2006) argued that program evaluation is integral to effective redesign efforts; should be shared by both universities and districts; and should include "valid and reliable measures of program effectiveness, graduates' on-the-job performance, and school and student achievement results" (p. 22). Frye et al.'s criteria for a rigorous evaluation of participants' mastery and of program quality and effectiveness are (a) having a regular, formal monitoring process that is standards based and aligned with district needs and goals; (b) assessing candidates on mastery of essential skills and using results for improvement; (c) using clearly defined exit criteria and reliable performance measures to evaluate candidates' success program completion; and (d) using measures of on-the-job performance and results for program effectiveness evaluation. Yet, only one program had made some progress toward rigorous program evaluation (defined as planning how to measure graduates' on-the-job performance as instructional leaders and their impact on instruction and student achievement).

Statewide Efforts

Educational leadership preparation programs within several states are now working collectively to establish means of assessing and providing feedback on standards-based program quality and evaluating their programs' effectiveness together, particularly to look beyond initial outcomes of reaction and learning to the more distant outcomes of career advancement, transfer of learning, and organizational impacts. Below are four examples (Kentucky, Indiana, Missouri, and Utah) representing a range of approaches to institutions' collaboration in statewide, program-driven evaluation research and their accomplishments.

In Kentucky, 11 institutions formed the Commonwealth Collaborative of School Leadership Programs for program improvement work statewide. The collaborative meets monthly and proposes recommendations about how to improve leadership program design and instruction at each of the institutions and discusses options for program evaluation and assessment (Sanders & Simpson, 2005).

Faculty at Indiana University at Indianapolis, with support from the Indiana Department of Education, conducted a statewide program study in Academic Years 2006 and 2007. Black, Bathon, and Poindexter (2007) worked with educational leadership faculty representatives from all 17 state-accredited, building-level-administrator preparation programs in Indiana to study program features and outcomes and report policy recommendations to the Indiana Department of Education. Drawing on program survey results and other state data sources, Black et al.'s report shows how programs differ in rationale, size, student selection, faculty composition, course structure and curriculum, field experiences, teaching methods, and assessments. The report highlights areas in which programs meet nationally recommended standards for programs; provides benchmarks for program design and delivery; and highlights policy and program priorities, particularly where wide variability exists.

In recent years, the Missouri Professors of Educational Administration—representing all 17 institutions in the state with leadership preparation programs—formed an evaluation subcommittee and have engaged in ongoing collaborative evaluation efforts. The group compiled program documentation information on program practices and reviewed state leadership assessments by institution to identify patterns and implications. The group meets regularly to review the findings and to discuss their program and policy implications (Friend, 2007). All programs agreed to field the UCEA LTEL-SIG Survey of Leadership Preparation and Practice with one cohort of graduates, using a common online survey resource, with the intention of using survey findings for within-program improvement as well as for comparison and discussion (anonymously) across programs (Friend, Watson, & Waddle, 2006).

Similarly, the five educational leadership preparation programs in Utah conducted a multiphase study of school leadership preparation programs and their effectiveness. The Utah Consortium for Educational Leadership includes administrator professional associations, the Utah State Office of Education, and five universities (including a new institution). All five programs completed Self-Report Program Narratives describing core program elements, and faculty members conducted student and faculty focus-group interviews in each other's institutions (Pounder & Hafner, 2006b). All programs then surveyed their 2006 program graduates on their program experience, job intentions, and initial career outcomes (Pounder & Hafner, 2006a).

Presently, these state efforts have yielded significant descriptive findings on programs and graduates that enable program comparison and identification of common and outlier practices (such as overuse of adjunct faculty or unusually large enrollments). In some cases, the findings are to be used for state policy purposes to inform accreditation and program registration expectations and are available for within and among program discussions. The effects of such research on program improvement, however, have not yet been investigated.

Critics of the Field

Finally, there have been two recent research indictments on the state of the leadership preparation field, released in non-peer-reviewed reports and disseminated through press conferences and the Internet. The first, *Educating School Leaders,* was undertaken independently by Levine (then president of Teachers College) and Sanoff (a former senior staff member of *U.S. News & World Report*'s annual rankings project) with funding support from various national foundations. Levine (2005) concluded, from his 28 case-study schools of education and surveys of 2,200 education school faculty and over 700 principals, that most educational administration programs were weak or inadequate. Based on his criteria of program quality—which were not based on national or professional standards for leadership preparation or any other documented higher education criteria—only a few programs were "strong" and none were "exemplary." He criticized programs for their recruitment and selection, poor curriculum scope and quality, and weak faculty. Levine offered provocative recommendations to replace the current system but provided little to no descriptive evidence. The report and related Web site (Education Schools Project, 2005) provided little data or conceptual and methodological information. Subsequently, the report was soundly criticized by the leadership preparation field for wasting a critical program evaluation opportunity and its methodological and interpretative shortcomings (Young, Crow, Orr, Ogawa, & Creighton, 2005).

Concurrently, Hess and Kelly (2005) published a report through the Progressive Policy Institute, in which they criticized the curricular content of leadership preparation programs in the field. Although innovative in its attempt to analyze the content of what students read for leadership preparation courses, their study fell short of its aims both methodologically and conceptually. Hess and Kelly used a small sample size (31 programs) and relied on course syllabi and textbooks (but not articles or other course-related readings) as the primary information sources on course content—while attempting to generalize to the field as a whole. Conceptually, the analysis was not grounded in either nationally recognized leadership standards or research-based exemplary leadership practices or preparation.

Despite their methodological limitations, both studies sparked institutional interest in reviewing affiliated leadership preparation programs and encouraged more attention to specific degree programs, particularly rethinking the EdD as advanced degree in educational leadership practice (Orr, Young, & Baker, 2006). Such interest greatly improved the climate for and support of program evaluation within and among institutions.

Program Evaluation Practice in Educational Leadership Preparation

Despite these new and emerging evaluation research initiatives, the educational leadership preparation field long has been sharply criticized for its lack of evaluation practice. As McCarthy (1999) decried in her research review on leadership preparation, "there is insufficient research documenting the merits of program components in relation to administrator performance" (p. 133). Her assessment characterizes the available research as meager and calls for research that "evaluates the elements of redesigned preparation programs in relation to student performance in schools where graduates are employed (p. 134). McCarthy (1999) argued further that more and better evaluation research is needed to justify the expense of such programs, provide a rationale for program practices, and eliminate ineffective practices.

Bredeson (1996), in his research review, drew similar conclusions about the criticisms of leadership preparation programs. He identified three national and regional initiatives that address these weaknesses: (a) the UCEA Knowledge Base Project, (b) the Danforth Programs for the Preparation of School Principals, and (c) the NPBEA. Of these, only the Danforth programs supported formative and summative evaluation research. In the late 1980s, the Danforth Foundation funded 22 university-based programs that were designed or redesigned to be more responsive to current leadership needs, using a constructivist approach and a commitment to success for all children and the empowerment of students and teachers. These 22 programs in turn became the basis for research on leadership preparation program models and claims of effectiveness, providing first-time evidence on the link between preparation and principal practices (Leithwood, Jantzi, Coffin, & Wilson, 1996; Milstein, 1993; Milstein & Kruger, 1997).

A more recent review of the state of research on leadership preparation generally drew similar conclusions about the paucity of research and identified several reasons for its limitations: insufficient faculty engagement in research generally and the limited scope and focus among the most research-active faculty; the lack of cumulative knowledge development; and a reliance on ad hoc research inquiries, including an overreliance on survey research and descriptive studies (Murphy & Vriesenga, 2006). Other scholars have noted a weak tradition for programs' self-evaluation generally (Glasman et al., 2002). Still others have found significant conceptual and methodological limitations to rigorous evaluation research in this field (McCarthy, 1999; Orr, 2003). Focus-group discussions among leadership preparation professors confirmed these findings, revealing that their program evaluations are often limited to measuring program satisfaction and career advancement, without comparison groups (Orr, Doolittle, Kottkamp, Osterman, & Silverberg, 2004).

Despite these limitations, some evaluation research in educational leadership preparation programs is evident in searches of research databases and a review of leadership preparation research by Murphy and Vriesenga (2004). A systematic analysis of these studies clarifies the current state of the field conceptually and methodologically. In 2004, Murphy and Vriesenga catalogued leadership preparation research in four leading journals, spanning 1975–2002. Additional Web-based searches of educational leadership dissertation databases and the ProQuest and ERIC research journal databases supplement the Murphy and Vriesenga (2004) research for purposes of this review. Finally, professional association newsletters, published reports, and conference programs provide a final, informal source of data for evidence on evaluation practice.

What did these searches yield? Murphy and Vriesenga (2004) reviewed all the articles between 1975 and 2002 from four leading journals in school leadership—*Journal of Educational Administration, Educational Administration Quarterly, Planning and Changing*, and *Journal of School Leadership*—to identify those that dealt at least in part with empirical research on preservice education of school administrators and leaders. Taken together, they identified 56 articles, the majority of which were published in the *Journal of School Leadership*. A significant portion of the research (and even essays and descriptive work) on educational leadership preparation found in these four journals could be traced to two UCEA initiatives and the Danforth Foundation work of the early 1990s.

A Web-based search of dissertations on educational leadership or administration preparation and research or program evaluation for the 15-year period 1993–2007 yielded 116 dissertations. A Web-based search of peer-reviewed journal articles in national and international journals (as indexed through ProQuest or ERIC) was also conducted, using search terms such as *leadership preparation, principal preparation, leadership education*, and *administration preparation*, coupled with *evaluation* or *research*. This search, coupled with the Murphy and Vriesenga (2004) search, yielded 64 peer-reviewed journal articles, mostly from the same four journals they reviewed and a few articles from journals such as *Peabody Journal of Education* and the *International Journal of Educational Management*.

Next, the articles and dissertations were coded further based on program evaluation focus (implementation study, outcome study, comparative program evaluation, and effects study), type of sample and sources of data, types of program and outcome measures, and theory used to guide the evaluation research design. They were also thus analyzed using Rossi et al.'s (1999) five assessment designs, Weiss's (1998) program and implementation theories, and types of outcomes using on Kirkpatrick's (1998) four levels.

Much of the program evaluation research for leadership preparation was conducted either by faculty on their own programs or as dissertation research by graduate students. A small number of studies were conducted with foundation support, but much of this research is in published reports rather than peer-reviewed research articles. Almost all the dissertations and most of the published research were focused on the United States (program, region, state, or nation as a whole); very few international studies of program evaluation were found that might reflect the limitations of searches of international research.

The available published and unpublished research on leadership preparation was then culled further for program evaluation studies that included two or more programs, with the purpose of making some form of comparison. Taken together, this yielded 31 published articles, 1 non-peer-reviewed research study, and 37 dissertations (1993–2007). The 69 studies were then grouped based on four overarching purposes for the program evaluation research: (a) 16 journal articles and 16 dissertations that were implementation studies on the extent to which two or more programs adhere to standards or theoretical or field-related priorities, (b) 9 journal articles and 13 dissertations as outcome studies on the extent to which current leaders' skills and practices are related to their prior preparation generally (such as sufficiency, level, or combination of experiences), (c) 3 peer-reviewed journal studies (and 1 published study) and 8 dissertations that compare program features and models on graduate outcomes as school leaders (such as job attainment, competency and performance), and (d) 3 effects studies (plus 1 in press, which we did not include in our count of 69).

These studies were then analyzed in five ways: (a) type of study design, (b) sample, (c) program measures, (d) outcome measures, and (e) theories or conceptual frameworks that guided the research. This analysis illuminates the extent to which patterns exist among these studies and compares their evaluation designs to Weiss (1998) and Rossi et al.'s (1999) frameworks and to Kirkpatrick's (1998) levels of measures. In the review of research, an additional 32 peer-reviewed articles based on single program studies were found; most were implementation studies of program innovations.

Implementation Studies

The most commonly conducted studies (both peer-reviewed journal articles and dissertations) were implementation studies. There were 16 implementation studies in peer-reviewed journals (see Table 12.1). Most were focused on the prevalence and use of a specific instructional or organizational strategy (distance learning, cohorts, internship, portfolios, advisory groups, and student selection). The second most common focus was on the prevalence and use of specific types of instructional content (social justice, special education, understanding poverty, and parental engagement as well as the integration of theory and practice). The remaining implementation studies were focused on the features of multiple programs and on the faculty characteristics. The samples ranged from the comparison of multiple programs within one institution, to the comparison of two programs, to a national study of 450 programs. Most studies were primarily descriptive, using qualitative content

Table 12.1 Peer-Reviewed Studies of the Need for and Implementation of Leadership Preparation Standards, Program Content, or Features, Nationally and in Selected States and Regions

Authors	Sample	Program measures	Outcome measures	Theory
Hackman & Berry, 1999	109 doctoral programs	Institution type	Use of distance learning	Atheoretical
Epstein & Sanders, 2006	161 schools and universities	Structural, organizational, and attitudinal factors (including officials' beliefs about importance of the topics)	Coverage of partnership topics, preparedness of graduates to conduct family and community involvement activities, and prospects for change	
Sirotnik & Kimball, 1994	23 administration programs 10 principals	Students and faculty	Content analysis of preparation, as pertains to special education	Atheoretical
Lyman & Villani, 2002	279 programs	Institution type Degrees offered	How programs emphasis understanding the complexity of poverty and its effects	Causes of poverty
Twale, Reed, & Kochan, 2001	33 leadership preparation programs		Academic, sociocultural, program, and professional development activities to foster collaborative communities	Collaborative learning communitiesand authors' prior research
Creighton, 2002	450 programs	Admissions criteria and extent to which nonbehavioral and behavioral-based measures are used	Whether focus on analytical ability, leadership potential or teaching success	Atheoreteical
Sherman & Beaty, 2007	49 higher education institutions		Utilize distance technology in the leader preparation Overall program structures; types of distance technology; goals, problems and factors that affect the expansion of the use of distance technology	Atheoretical

(continued)

Table 12.1 Continued

Authors	Sample	Program measures	Outcome measures	Theory
Kochan & Twale, 1998	36 UCEA-affiliated programs	Use of advisory group	Membership Types of activities in which groups are involved How advice is used	Atheoretical
McDaniel, Furtwengler, & Furtwengler, 1999	Four programs in Midwest Exemplar university staff informants	Levels of reform proficiency (isolated, emerging, embraced, and institutionalized) Sample type (unreformed, transition, progressive, exemplary)	Reform themes and categories (political, professional and curricular)	Atheoretical
Barnett, Basom, Yerkes, & Norris, 2000	Multiple programs	Benefits and difficulties with cohort use	Preparedness for leadership roles	Group dynamics theory
McCarthy & Kuh, 1998	Multiple programs 449 faculty	Institutional contexts New and experienced faculty With and without administrative experience	Faculty characteristics, activities and attitudes	Atheoretical
Norton, 2004	Multiple programs	Degree level	Use of student portfolios and applications	Atheoretical
Townley & Sweeney, 1993	Multiple programs 78 faculty members	Institutional type (public/private)	Faculty characteristics	Atheoretical
McClellan & Dominguez, 2006	Two doctoral programs (community college and educational leadership) in one New Mexico institution	Institutional power structures	transformation to a social justice content	School reform and social justice Organizational openness
Wilmore & Thomas, 1998	Two programs: University of Texas at Arlington and Texas Christian University	Institutional context	Program features Instructional strategies Theory to practice links	Linking theory and practice in preparation
McKerrow, 1998	Two programs in two Midwestern universities 45 interns	Independent and dependent of mentor	Time spent by type of administrative activity Based on logs and description	Anticipatory socialization of internships Legitimate peripheral participation Reflection on practice

analyses or survey research. Many were atheoretical, focusing on describing patterns and trends, drawing on research about leadership preparation and leadership, but lacking an overarching theory or framework. A few studies drew on theory on learning communities, group dynamics, and organizations.

In all, there were 16 dissertation studies on leadership preparation (studies of doctoral programs were excluded from the dissertation analyses) that looked at the extent to which leadership preparation programs adhered to state and national standards (ISLLC, ELCC, or SREB's standards; 5 studies); focused preparation on instructional leadership, antiracism, special education, law, technology, and philosophy (7 studies); or used one or more active learning strategies to improve preparation, such as standards-aligned field experiences and cohort structure (4 studies). Most of these studies were descriptive in design, compiling information from programs, their faculty, and sometimes students or graduates. Most drew on national or state standards to evaluate the quality of program content or best-practices research on program features. Many were atheoretical, drawing on standards to frame their research. The exceptions were studies that drew on learning, organizational, and critical theory (see Table 12.2).

Table 12.2 Dissertation Studies of the Need for and Implementation of Leadership Preparation Standards, Program Content, or Features in Selected States and Regions

Name	Sample	Program measures	Outcome measure	Theory
Harpin, 2003	Three programs	Preparation program content	Use of standards	Standards
Henwood, 2000	Faculty and students from four programs	Program course content	standards included and are important	Standards
Vick, 2004	Multiple programs	Perceived preparation and outcomes	Use of SREB critical success factors	SREB standards, (Bottoms & O'Neil, 2001) Standards (Murphy)
Wilson, 2006	Three programs	Program features and practices	None; descriptive	ISLLC standards and research on program features (e.g., Jackson & Kelley, 2002)
Dyce Faucett, 2005	349 principals from 7 community types in New York state who had participated in multiple programs	Extent program prepared principals in standards	Extent to which standards are important to the principalship	NPBEA standards
Kibble, 2004	49 faculty from 40 nationally sampled programs (7 were traditional)	Traditional and restructured programs Faculty respondent demographics	Importance and emphasis of instructional leadership in program content	NCATE program standards for instructional leadership Institutional homogenization
Lightfoot, 2003	Three programs	Program features, organization and faculty	How antiracism and cultural awareness are addressed	Critical race theory
Narducci, 1997	Chairs of four programs	Danforth program model features	Program attributes and philosophy Change process Outcomes	Critical theory Cultural perspective on organizations Change process
Palm-Leis, 2005	Program faculty interviews from 12 programs	Types of treatment of ethics in programs Institution	Nature of ethics taught and how offered	Framework on ethics in educational leadership preparation
Reale-Foley, 2003	38 programs in New England	Preparation strategies Institutional characteristics: NCATE accreditation, funding, faculty rewards and development, faculty knowledge of technology	Technology leadership content implementation	Organizational change theory

(continued)

Table 12.2 Continued

Name	Sample	Program measures	Outcome measure	Theory
Witt, 2003	94 program chairs	Content and instruction Institutional characteristics (program size, NCATE accreditation, UCEA affiliation)	Extent to which special education topics are taught	Atheoretical
Schlosser, 2006	362 participants of 21 programs	Legal instruction and textbooks used	school law knowledge	Atheoretical
McRae, 2000	147 programs	Program attributes Institutional attributes (e.g. UCEA membership, Carnegie classification, degrees)	Use of alternative delivery	Atheoretical
Copeland, 2004	Two samples: 61 programs and 24 programs in 16 states	Field experience attributes Level of leadership opportunities	SREB's 13 critical success factors recommended for principal preparation	Vroom's expectations theory on how much programs value and hold as important to motivation SREB's research on principal knowledge and skills and leadership preparation NPBEA standards
Poimbeauf, 2004	201 participants of four programs	Cohort or not Participant school level, gender	Perceptions of essential cohort components (e.g., networking, community for learners)	Structural and learning attributes of cohorts
Lin, 2005	14 elementary school principals in both countries, from multiple programs	American, Chinese	Adequacy of the selection criteria Preparation program effectiveness Helpfulness and satisfaction with development programs	Atheoretical

Outcome Studies

The second most commonly conducted studies were those that investigated program outcomes for groups of educational leaders, either as a whole or by type of program or combination of preparation and development experiences. There were nine studies in peer-reviewed journal articles that used two or more programs to investigate program outcomes, most commonly leadership readiness and perceived availability and adequacy of leadership preparation (see Table 12.3). Other outcomes investigated were related to the demographics of graduates and the extent to which patriarchy is encouraged formally or informally.

There were also 13 dissertation studies on the outcomes of leadership preparation programs (see Tables 12.4 and 12.5). Two were of international samples (England and Columbia), 2 were national samples (using Schools and Staffing Survey [SASS] national principal and teacher data sets), 9 were state or regional samples (Indiana, Florida, Kansas, Missouri, and Texas) or a city or region within a state (Minnesota, northwest Tennessee, and three school divisions in Virginia).

The studies were focused on the leadership outcomes for a group as a whole (1st-year principals, middle-level school assistant principals, elementary principals, high school principals), in comparing alternate types of programs (clinically or theoretically oriented; innovative or not), levels of

Table 12.3 Peer-Reviewed Studies of Leadership Preparation Outcomes for Special Samples

Author	Sample	Program or other independent measures	Outcome measures	Program theory
Furtwengler & Furtwengler, 1998	One university	Tested five performance rubrics, job-related criteria, and multiple evidence for determining leadership expertise	Inquiry-oriented helping behaviors Interrelated problem-solving strategies Belief in others' value	Leadership expertise
Rucinski & Bauch, 2006	106 doctoral program graduates and 113 coworkers	Graduate age, gender, and position (i.e., higher education, preK–12, or other)	Perceptions of use of reflective, ethical and moral dispositions, and leadership practices	Reflection Reflection on action Ethical and moral leadership Ethic of care
Scollay & Logan, 1999	28 programs		Gender demographics of students and faculty	Atheoretical
Rapp, Silent X., & Silent Y., 2001	Four programs	Doctoral program experiences	How patriarchy is encouraged formally and informally	
Hewitson, 1995	Multiple programs 36 principals 6 principal interviews	Preparation program and other forms of preparation	Perceived preparedness for principalship	Leadership forces hierarchy
Nicholson & Leary, 2001	Multiple programs 103 principal mentors		Helpfulness of courses and other experiences	Postmodern perspective Theory to practice
Shen & Hsieh, 1999	Multiple programs 147 professors 457 students		Dimensions of instructional leadership and their importance in preparation programs	Leadership theory
Dunning, 1996	Multiple programs British primary headteachers	Preparation, induction and continuing professional development Demands of the recent education reform	Adequacy and availability of training and professional development	
Restine, 1997	Multiple programs 3 states 104 principals	Nature and quality of experiences Traditional and nontraditional preparation Postpreparation experiences	Building human capacity through involvement, opportunity, participation, and advocacy	Adult development phases and stages

advanced preparation (master's, specialist, or doctorate), and mix of pre- and postdegree leadership preparation and development (leadership preparation program or district program). The data were primarily quantitative surveys or qualitative interviews. Only one study drew on three samples: (a) school leaders, (b) their teachers, and (c) their supervisors. A second study compared the perspectives of 1st-year principals and their district leaders. The rest were single sample studies.

The studies were primarily designed to assess the outcomes of interest, skills, and roles of school principals in one of two ways—levels of perceived effectiveness (three studies) or extent and usefulness of preparation in these areas (nine studies). These were either generically determined skill areas, standards-based definitions of skills, or theoretically developed domains of principal effectiveness (such as transformational leadership or school effectiveness leadership). Only one study (Martin, 2002) investigated school leaders' self-reported task performance and time spent in these areas as their outcome measure.

Table 12.4 Dissertation Studies of Leadership Preparation Outcomes for International or National Samples

Author	Study design	Sample	Program measures	Outcome measure	Theory
International					
Alonso, 1993	Comparison of graduates of four programs on effectiveness of preparation and leadership performance	260 elementary and high school principals who graduated from one of four universities in the city, in Columbia.	Clinically-oriented or theoretically-oriented preparation program	Relevance to principal role performance in five areas	
Hvizdak, 2001	Outcome analysis—effects of preparation on principal practice	Head teachers in England who had multiple programs and experiences	Preservice training, experience, or both	Extent of preparation for 28 leadership roles	Policy and historical context; atheoretical concepts
National					
Bales, 1997	Outcome analysis-relationship between degree earned and internship, and school effectiveness outcomes	National sample of high school principals (SASS)	Level of advanced leadership preparation (masters, specialist, doctorate) and whether had an internship	Four indices of school effectiveness (leadership, school environment, graduation rate; and use of site councils)	School effectiveness research and the recommendations of the Commission on the Restructuring of the American High School (NASSP) NASSP's recommendations for graduate preparation Replication of Haller, Brent, & McNamara study
Perdue, 1997	Outcome analysis—relationship between leadership preparation and school effectiveness	3,999 public school elementary principals (SASS)	Graduate preparation degree, university sponsored program or not; and internship or not.	Teachers' ratings of perceived school effectiveness (based on 25 items	NPBEA and NASSP recommendations for leadership preparation

Most of this research was atheoretical, drawing on the research literature to provide an historical and policy context for the research, but not to frame the research design's assumed relationship between preparation (as measured here) and the leadership outcomes. There was little consensus among the more theoretically derived research on appropriate program and outcome measures. The program measures were drawn from Daresh's model (as cited in Alonso, 1993) and Milstein's research (as cited in J. J. Poole, 1999) on effective preparation. The leadership outcomes were drawn from Sergiovanni's model of five principal roles (as cited in Alonso, 1993), Smith and Piele's five key areas of effective instructional leadership (as cited in Perdue, 1997), Boone and Mizelle (both as cited in Martin, 2002) on assistant principal responsibilities, Kriekard (as cited in Crain, 2004) on assistant principals' basic competencies, King (as cited in Crain, 2004) on CTE leader competencies, Daresh & Playko (as cited in J. J. Poole, 1999) on effective principal skills, or Kouzes and Posner (1995) on transformational leadership. Four studies drew on national standards, including NASSP, NBPEA, ISLLC and SREB, for leader competency measures.

Table 12.5 Dissertation Studies of Leadership Preparation Outcomes for State and Special Samples

Author	Study design	Sample	Program measures	Outcome measure	Theory
States					
Bordeaux, 1994	Survey and interview on principal satisfaction with university preparation by skill domains	101 randomly selected current elementary principals in Missouri state	Satisfaction with content and instructional styles; date of initial certification	Appropriate to role expectations in six generic skill domains	A theoretical
Cox, 1998	Outcome analysis—impact of preparation on principal practice	Case studies of three districts Interviews of 19 first-year principals and 9 district leaders from three Florida school districts	Content of district-based leadership preparation programs and transfer of learning	Perceived preparedness of 1st-year principals for job demands	Research-based conceptual framework on effective leadership preparation (content, process, context) and research on individual components; on the transfer of training
Jolly, 1995	Two-way survey comparison—faculty to administrators on what programs provide; what received and what is needed for secondary school leaders	31 faculty 312 secondary school leaders, who had prepared in one of six Kansas public universities	Rate preparation qualities and content; and skills, knowledge, and experience	Strength of usefulness rating and whether received	Atheoretical on program content, functions, and organizational problems and secondary school leader competencies
J. J. Poole, 1999	Survey research comparison between importance and preparedness of critical skills and differences by program type	86 new principals from traditional (56) or nontraditional preparation (30) programs, in Indiana	Program type (traditional, nontraditional)	Importance and preparedness of critical skill areas	On preparation program innovation; on critical principal skills
Crain, 2004	Relationship between type of school, leadership position, and school location on perception of preparation effectiveness	88 career and technical education superintendents and directors from Ohio	All types of leadership preparation including advanced degree or certification coursework and professional development	Importance and effectiveness of 8 areas of CTE leadership preparation	Study of assistant principals' basic competencies and on CTE leader competencies
Region or district					
Border, 2004	Comparison between presence and value of program characteristics and mastery and importance of principal competencies for graduates and supervisors	163 graduates and 20 supervisors from 10 Texas institutions	Program characteristics presence and value	Principal competencies mastery importance	NCAELP on program characteristics NPBEA on principal competencies

(continued)

Table 12.5 Continued

Author	Study design	Sample	Program measures	Outcome measure	Theory
Martin, 2002	Outcome analysis—relationship of preparation to assistant principal practice	99 assistant middle school principals who attended multiple preparation programs regionally (2/3 attended one of six regional institutions)	Perceptions of sufficient preparation for the tasks	Task performance, time spent, and degree of mission importance	Study on asst. principal preparation and task performance research on assistant principal responsibilities
Neuman, 1999	Self-assessment of preparation program attributes and competencies	172 principals in two urban cities, Minnesota	Helpfulness of program attributes, primarily internship and assessment	31 competencies	NPBEA competencies
Quenneville, 2007	Qualitative inquiry on attributes of leadership preparation from university and district programs	19 educational leaders from three districts, who attended multiple programs	Program type Program attributes	Preparedness learning	NPBEA and ISLLC on standards Adult learning theory

Only one study (Cox, 1998) tried to model the relationship between preparation and leadership practices by drawing on Broad and Newton's transfer of training theory and on Guskey and Sparks to frame the investigation of leadership preparation in terms of content, process, and context. Only two studies replicated prior research—Bales (1997) replicated Haller, Brent, and McNamara's study by looking narrowly at the sample of high school principals, and Martin (2002) replicated Brinegar's dissertation research on assistant principal preparation. None of the studies investigated the relationships among their measures beyond group comparisons. For example, perceptions of preparation were not related to perceptions of task performance and time spent.

Comparative Program Evaluation Studies

Two peer-reviewed journal articles and eight dissertation studies could be classified as comparative program evaluation studies that looked at the relationship between multiple program features and graduate outcomes for a group of programs, a comparison of innovative and conventional programs, or a comparison between preparation and leadership development experiences (see Tables 12.6 and 12.7). One journal article compared a U.S. and a Mexican program, whereas the other compared an innovative and conventional program. Six dissertation studies were based in one of six states (Alabama, Kansas, Mississippi, Oregon, Tennessee, and Texas); the other two were in Los Angeles and New England. Seven of the eight dissertation studies used mixed research designs, surveying one or two samples other than program graduates (e.g., supervisors, coworkers, or faculty), generating comparisons among the samples as well as between program models.

Among the published research studies, only three could be classified as comparative program evaluations. All three used a multiple-program comparison design approach to relate differences in quality program features and graduate learning and career outcomes. A published report also fits this category.

Table 12.6 Comparative Program Evaluation Studies on Preparation and Outcomes, 1993–2007, Journal Articles

Author	Sample	Program measures	Outcome measure	Theory
Slater et al., 2003	Two programs, U.S. and Mexico 47 students	Focus groups of students in two programs	Types of transformational change (e.g., professional skills, confidence) Quality of their experience (e.g., internship, cohort, application)	Cultural differences (Hofstede) Leadership models
Hermond, 1999	Two programs, one new cohort program ($n = 15$) and one comparison ($n = 29$)	Cohort vs. noncohort	Meeting program objectives in developing leadership qualities	Evaluation model Exemplary leadership priorities (Kouzes & Posner, 1995) Cohort and other program features (Griffiths, Stout, & Forsyth, 1988)
Orr & Barber, 2007	Two partnership and one conventional program	Program features	Leadership aspirations Perceived preparedness	Transformational leadership
Darling-Hammond, Meyerson, LaPointe, & Orr, 2007 (published study)	4 innovative programs, their graduates who became principals (2000–2005), and a national comparison group of principals	Innovative program features, work	Learning, leadership practices, and school improvement	Effective leadership practices

In the most recent published study, Orr and Barber (2007) compared graduates of two university–district partnership programs (which had many of innovative program features as defined by Jackson and Kelley, 2002) and a conventional program (which had fewer). They found that graduates' ratings of supportive program structures; comprehensive, a standards-based curriculum; and broader, more intensive internships were significantly but differentially related to graduates' leadership knowledge and skills, career intentions, and career advancement.

One published report, Darling-Hammond, Meyerson, LaPointe, and Orr (2007), with Wallace Foundation funding, investigated how exemplary educational leadership preparation and professional development programs develop strong school leaders and foster school improvement. The study identified the qualities of four innovative preparation programs and compared their principals and a national comparison group of principals on their instructional and organizational leadership practices and school improvement using survey research. Darling-Hammond et al.'s results showed that the two groups of principals differed significantly on their preparation experiences (particularly in terms of program focus, content, pedagogy, and internship quality) and in turn differed significantly on how frequently and extensively they practiced instructional leadership actions and had gains in improved school effectiveness.

Only one dissertation study (B. J. Poole, 1994) developed a theoretical model to investigate the relationship between preparation and program outcomes. B. J. Poole (1994) used Kirkpatrick's (1998) four levels of outcome for determining program effectiveness as the broad rationale for looking at program effects in leaders' practice, and drew on Baldwin and Ford's theory of transfer of training and Fugan and Parks's theories of career advancement for both relationships and outcomes to investigate. The rest of the studies drew on existing research to frame their program (McCarthy, 1999; Barnett et al., 2000, on nontraditional programs) and outcome measures (Kouzes and Posner, 1995, on effective leadership) or national standards (ISLLC and NPBEA for leadership standards

Table 12.7 Comparative Program Evaluation Studies on Preparation and Outcomes, 1993–2007, Dissertation Studies

Author	Sample	Program measures	Outcome measure	Theory
Sharps, 1993	24 students in each of two programs in Oregon	Program type Program features on recruitment and selection, coursework, and internship	Program efficacy	Atheoretical
B. J. Poole, 1994.	1 program and all programs statewide, 281 graduates surveyed 60 supervisors, coworker or subordinates for 10 graduates, Alabama	Program type Program features (internship, sponsorship, subject matter)	Job title Degree attained Certificate attained Self-rated skills and competencies Job performance Time to advancement	Kirkpatrick's (1998) 4 levels for determining program effectiveness Theory of transfer of training Theories of career advancement
Jones, 1999	136 students (in focus groups), 12 graduates, 15 mentors, 17 faculty, for three Texas programs	Program design and delivery	Successes Challenges	Atheoretical National and state standards
Kraus, 1996	Five programs, 25 administrators, 361 teachers, and 8 supervisors, New England	Whether preparation program was innovative (Danforth)	Job preparedness	Educational administration job preparedness survey and innovative preparation
Hale, 1999	34 superintendents with at least 2 years' experience and 128 principals (3–5 per superintendent) in Los Angeles County, with different preparation and development experiences	Attributes of formal preparation based on the leadership training survey (type, impact on leadership development in 13 areas); degree earned; post-preparation training	Transformational leadership behavior based on leadership practices inventory	Kouzes and Posner's theory of Transformational leadership
Dodson, 2006	170 northeast Tennessee principals from 16 districts, with different preparation and mentoring experiences	Whether had formal mentoring Type of degree (masters or higher) One institution vs. others; cohort or not; classroom vs. hands-on; year degree earned	Perceived adequately prepared to be successful in 13 critical success factors (SREB)	SREB's research on leadership factors critical to school success Literature on effective mentoring
Shaw, 2005	41 licensed administrators who completed one of two versions of a Mississippi university's program after 1998 (nontraditional) and 35 who completed before (traditional) and were working in the Delta region	Program type	Leadership Practices Inventory (Kouzes & Posner)	Barrett et al. (2000) on nontraditional programs Kouzes and Posner on effective leadership
Franklin, 2006	5 principals from a Texas innovative program and 5 principals from traditional, matched design 10 faculty interviews Quantitative program and graduate career outcome data as of 1996–97 (50 innovative and 109 traditional program graduates)	Core program features Mission Recruitment and selection Cohort Curriculum Number of credits Faculty quality	Job attainment Graduates' perception of impact Preparedness	McCarthy; Leithwood and Jantzi on effective preparation qualities Leadership standards

and NCAELP for program characteristics). Three studies were fairly atheoretical, reviewing the research literature but not drawing on specific research to frame research design or measures.

The studies ranged in the levels of their outcomes from only feedback on the quality and efficacy of the preparation (two studies), to career advancement and time to advancement (two studies), to perceived leadership performance and effectiveness (five studies). Their program measures included program type (innovative or traditional), program features (recruitment and selection, coursework, and internship, faculty, instructional strategies, and quality). All the studies relied on statistical comparison of groups on the measures and did not investigate the relationships among the program measures and outcome measures.

Models of Large-Scale Effects Studies of Leadership Preparation

Several researchers have stressed the need to evaluate leadership preparation programs' influence on graduates' organizational and student achievement contributions (Gonzalez, Glasman, & Glasman, 2002), representing Kirkpatrick's (1998) Level 4 outcome assessments for program evaluation. A few, large-scale evaluation studies of leadership preparation have attempted to ascertain the effects of leadership preparation on schools and school outcomes. These studies differ in their statistical modeling by using a direct-effects design or an indirect-effects design and by using different measures of program participation and the type of outcome effects measured. According to Muller and Judd (2005), direct effects are the portion of the relationship between an independent and a dependent variable that do not go through a mediator variable, whereas indirect effects are those that do.

The difference between these two models is important when applied to Kirkpatrick's (1998) four-level outcome model. A direct-effects study design assumes that the program participation (the independent measure) would have a direct impact on each of the four levels of outcomes in Kirkpatrick's model and even on Guskey's (2000) fifth-level outcome (how the graduates' impact on their organization affects others). An indirect-effects design assumes that the outcome measures are themselves relational and the influence of program participation on the levels of outcomes would be only direct on the first-level outcomes and indirect on the remaining ones, through the mediating effects of these intermediary outcomes—Kirkpatrick's second- and third-level outcomes of learning and transfer of learning to practice. The two types of designs and their program and outcome effect measures are discussed below.

Direct Effects

In the last 10 years, three published studies have modeled the direct effects of leadership preparation on school outcomes and found no effects. Two measured program participation dichotomously; one used teacher perceptions as outcomes, and the other used student achievement gains. A third study looked at variations in program feature experiences and related these to teachers' perceptions of graduates who had become principals. The first study tested the relationship between principals' graduate degrees earned in educational administration and five indices of school effectiveness as measured by their teachers' perceptions, using national principal and teacher survey data—the 1987–1988 SASS. Having had graduate preparation in educational administration (in contrast to other degree areas) was found to have no positive association with teachers' perceptions of school leadership on school effectiveness (Haller, Brent, & McNamera, 1997). These findings build on and extend other unpublished work using the same data set that found that principals' training in educational administration was unrelated to their teachers' perceptions of their instructional leadership practices (Zheng, 1996).

A second, more recent study (Vanderhaar, Muñoz, & Rodosky, 2006) again found no direct effects on student outcomes of whether principals had district preparation experiences (including a district–university preparation program) and had attended one metropolitan area university. Using one district's principals with 2–6 years of experience, Vanderhaar et al. compiled district data to identify which principals had participated in one of three leader education programs (certification, aspiring principals, and year-long internship) and had attended one metropolitan university (or not), as well as schools' achievement test performance, principal experience, and school factors on student poverty and teacher experience. Vanderhaar et al. acknowledged, however, that a direct-effects model "is not a comprehensive framework for viewing the principal's role in school effectiveness" (p. 30). It is even less sufficient for looking at the effects of preparation.

The third study was Leithwood et al.'s (1996) follow-up study of graduates of leadership preparation programs that recently had been redesigned as part of the Danforth Foundation initiative. Using case study evaluation research and follow-up survey research of graduates and sampled teachers in their schools, the researchers investigated the effects of innovative preparation on graduates who had become principals for 11 programs. They found that some innovative program features—instructional strategies, cohort membership, and program content—were most predictive of teacher perceptions of principals' leadership effectiveness.

The Vanderhaar et al. (2006) study findings are consistent with leadership effectiveness research that similarly has found no direct effects of leadership on student outcomes (Leithwood & Jantzi, 2005). The conflicting results between the Haller et al. (1997) and Leithwood et al. (1996) studies on the influence of leadership preparation on teachers' perceptions of leadership practice and school effectiveness suggest that more robust measurements of preparation can distinguish among preparation experiences and find associated effects on leadership outcomes. Moreover, these results suggest that the effects of preparation on leadership practices may be indirect, mediated by other factors.

Indirect Effects

Recent program evaluation research that accounts for indirect effects of differences in leadership preparation on school outcomes has yielded positive findings (see Table 12.8). Only one study (Orr & Orphanos, in press) examined the relationship between preparation and school effectiveness, by constructing an indirect effects model and a more robust set of measures for leadership preparation experiences than used in other studies. Using the Stanford University study survey data of principals who had graduated from one of four innovative leadership preparation programs and comparison principals, Orr and Orphanos tested the relationship among these experiences and outcomes, using structural equation modeling. Their results showed that principals who had completed an innovative program were significantly more likely to have had quality preparation and internship experiences. These in turn had a strongly positive effect on what principals learned about instructional leadership and school change and on how they focused their leadership practices on teaching and learning. These practices, in turn, had a strongly positive effect on school improvement outcomes and improved school effectiveness, even when other school and district factors (such as student poverty and extent of school problems) are taken into account (Orr & Orphanos, in press).

These results confirm that leadership preparation effects on leadership practices and organizational outcomes are mediated through more intermediate outcomes of the quality of preparation and what graduates learned about leadership. These relationships and their mediating effects are consistent with the Kirkpatrick (1998) levels of outcome framework, suggesting that a more fully defined measurement model—that takes into account measurement of each outcome level—can demonstrate program effects on graduates' leadership practices and their schools.

Table 12.8 Direct- and Indirect-Effects Studies of Educational Leadership Preparation

Author	Sample	Program measures	Outcome measure
Leithwood, Jantzi, Coffin, & Wilson, 1996	11 programs, their graduates and their teachers	Program features	Teachers' perceptions of leader effectiveness
Vanderhaar, Muñoz, & Rodosky, 2006	Three programs 91 principals	Principal preparation in primary program or not Participated in district preparation program or not Principal experience School context	Student achievement
Haller, Brent, & Mc-Namera, 1997	National sample of principals and teachers	Master's degree or not Educational administration major or not	Teacher perceptions of leader effectiveness
Orr & Orphanos, in press	Four innovative preparation programs' graduates and a national sample of principals	Innovative or conventional program Program and internship quality measures	Leadership learning Leadership practices School improvement progress School effectiveness climate

Summary

Taken together, there has been a large body of program evaluation research on educational leadership preparation, although primarily dissertation research. Much of the research is of two types outlined by Rossi et al. (1999): program implementation and service delivery, and program impact and outcomes. When analyzed according to Weiss's (1998) five key elements, several patterns emerge. First, only a few studies have used measures of both program processes and program outcomes. The needs-assessment and implementation studies provide the most detail on program features, particularly as grounded in research on best practices for leadership preparation and national and other standards for quality preparation. The leadership preparation outcome studies have used only simple categorical measures of preparation experiences (such as program type or degree earned) but demonstrate a range of possible program outcomes, primarily related to feedback on the relevance of the preparation for principal roles and responsibilities and perceived effectiveness in these roles. While such research associates preparation and outcomes, it falls short by under-measuring preparation processes. Finally, the comparative program evaluation studies have used more detailed measures of program experiences and more varied program outcomes, including both feedback on preparation relevance and perceived role effectiveness, as well as career-related outcomes such as job attainment and time to advancement.

Much of the research summarized here has drawn on national or other standards as a source of comparison on leadership preparation content and leadership outcomes, particularly the ISLLC and ELCC standards. All the studies were included because they were based on two or more programs, and most studies used these multiple programs for purposes of comparison, primarily between innovative and conventional programs and leadership preparation and development programs. A few studies drew comparisons among sources of evidence, comparing teachers or supervisors' views of principals and the principals' self-assessments.

The range of program and outcome measures used across the various studies suggests that the field is still at an exploratory stage of measurement development. When evaluated using Kirkpatrick's (1998) and Guskey's (2000) levels of outcomes, several patterns are evident among program outcomes. First, the commonly used outcome measures of preparation as job relevant and perceived leadership effectiveness could be classified as Level 1, reactive, and Level 3, application, respectively. Yet, even among these measures, there was little standardization, with similar concepts measured differently among the studies. Second, only the published direct- and indirect-effects research attempted to measure either Level 2, learning, or Level 4, organizational impact outcomes. None attempted to investigate Phillips's (1996) proposed measure of ROI.

In measuring program processes and outcomes and in making comparisons, however, very few authors clarified a program or implementation theory that guided their inquiry. A few studies drew on available research on effective preparation, but such research served as more as standards of effectiveness, rather than a representation of the program's theory of action. The few exceptions are the studies that were grounded in adult learning theory (as the program implementation theory) on the transfer of training. Finally, with a few exceptions, only the direct and indirect studies modeled and tested the relationship among program processes and outcomes, and only three studies (Leithwood et al., 1996, Orr & Barber, 2007; Orr & Orphanos, in press) attempted to relate fairly robust measures of program processes with multiple outcomes. The wealth of dissertation research and emerging published research in the field provides a foundation for further measurement development and evaluation design modeling.

International Program Evaluation on Leadership Preparation

Some limited international research exists on program evaluation practices, and findings are similar to studies of U.S. programs. The primary research comes from Huber's (2004) comparative international study of school leadership development in 15 countries, drawing on case studies of program designs and their policy and country contexts. In his study of program features and practices, Huber noted that program evaluation recently had become a central policy concern, particularly in some countries. He found evidence of program evaluation for only very few countries, which he attributed to programs' newness and competitiveness, and only limited evaluation research designs. In cases where evaluation evidence was provided, Huber found the information to be unsystematic, informal, and primarily concerned with participant satisfaction, with almost no follow-up assessments or external evaluations. Although a few countries or programs had evaluation studies underway, comparative evaluations of the effectiveness of different program models remain nonexistent.

Some published research on leadership preparation internationally explores the national context for leadership preparation and its design implications. Reilly and Brown (1996), for example, identified a range of cultural, political, and educational issues that influenced developing a school leadership preparation program in the Republic of Georgia. These include the culture and educational system structure of the country, the need for school leaders, the country's vision for its educational system and leader approach, the degree of centralization in school governance, and accountability and assessment systems (Reilly & Brown, 1996). Similar research has focused on superintendent training needs in Palestine (Kanan, 2005) and on the training needs of educational leaders in Africa (Bush & Oduro, 2006) and Spain (Immegart & Pascual, 1994).

In a few cases, researchers from around the world have begun evaluating the effectiveness of new leadership preparation programs. This research includes the evaluation of the program experiences and early leadership outcomes of three cohorts completing a Palestine university (Kanan & Baker, 2006) and a training program for aspiring and current principals in Hong Kong (Wong, 2004). Much of this research has paralleled U.S. program evaluation research, drawing on similar standards for leadership and effective program design, but differs by focusing on the economic, political, and educational contexts (Kanan & Baker, 2006).

Evaluating Educational Leadership Development Programs

While there is limited published program evaluation research of educational leadership development programs (as postpreparation experiences) and participants, existing evaluation research designs are instructive, particularly on how they address several measurement issues. Several regional, national, and international initiatives in educational leadership development provide opportunity for program evaluation research and methodological lessons, as all the studies attempted to look at multiple levels of evaluation outcomes or explore comparisons. These include the National College for School Leadership in England (Brundrett, 2006; Bush, 2006; Crow, 2004); the Blue Skies model in Hong Kong (Walker & Dimmock, 2006); the Leadership Development Programme for Serving Headteachers (Watkins, 2000); the New Orleans School Leadership Center (Leithwood, Riedlinger, Bauer, & Jantzi, 2003); Western Australia's principal professional development program (Wildy & Wallace, 1995); and Darling-Hammond et al.'s (2007) comparative study of four innovative, district-based, leadership development programs. Three different program evaluation models are evident in these examples.

The first model is a post-only program evaluation research design, in which all participants received a common leadership development experience that emphasized the leadership competencies that were then assessed. For example, the Leadership Development Programme for Serving Headteachers program in the United Kingdom focused on improving headteachers' leadership styles, effective leadership practices, and the organizational climate of their schools. Two-thousand headteachers participated in a 4-day workshop, Web-site resources, Internet conferencing with their cohort, and a 1-day follow-up. The results were quite positive, showing that high-achieving schools had headteachers who used more leadership styles and scored higher on school climate measures (Watkins, 2000).

The second type of program evaluation model investigated the relationship between participation in a range of professional development opportunities and personal and organizational outcomes. Three cohorts of principals who participated in year-long fellows program and used other related leadership education services and resources of the New Orleans Leadership Center were compared on their leadership practices and student achievement for three cohorts of principals (Leithwood et al., 2003). The researchers used an indirect-effects research model to evaluate program influences on student achievement outcomes and found that participating principals had increases in teachers' perceptions of the quality and effectiveness of their leadership and management, which in turn were positively associated with gains in student achievement and school improvement conditions (Leithwood et al., 2003).

Darling-Hammond et al. (2007) compared the experiences of new and experienced principals who had participated in one of four exemplary, district-sponsored, in-service programs with a national sample of principals on the extent of their professional development, its perceived helpfulness, and their leadership practices and school improvement work. The exemplary-in-service principals reported significantly more mentoring and coaching and visits to other schools than did other principals. They in turn reported significantly more engagement in effective leadership practices (such as guiding curriculum and instruction and fostering teacher professional development) and working more hours weekly than did comparison principals. They also reported more organizational changes in their schools, as indicators of organizational improvement and teacher effectiveness (including job satisfaction and more attention to low-performing students).

Similarly, positive relationships were found between principal professional development on their leadership practices and schools (Wildy & Wallace, 1995). Wildy and Wallace, in evaluating an innovative leadership development program for principals and assistant principals in Australia using reports from colleagues, found a positive relationship between program participation and leadership practices. The greatest impact was found in principals' improved data analysis, in problem-solving and communication skills, and in encouraging staff to develop new strategies for improvement.

A third evaluation approach has been to use leadership assessment as both a learning strategy in the program and as means of pre- and postprogram evaluation. Avolio, Clapp, Vogelgesang, and Wernsing (2005), in their evaluation of the Nebraska Educational Leadership Institute program for educational leaders in the state, used personal assessment as a primary learning strategy, providing feedback for direction and for baseline and follow-up evidence of progress. Through the program, participants develop and revise a vision statement, attend a developmental assessment center, participate in leadership simulations, receive strengths feedback, and engage in developmental planning. Participant feedback was very positive. Avolio et al. reported strong self-reports on leadership development gains throughout the program and demonstrated quality of participants' individualized leadership development plans to impact their schools.

Supplementing these research studies are several dissertation studies of district and state leadership academies, which range in focus from being prospective (McGinn, 2004; McNamara, 2001), to evaluating program design and implementation (Robinson, 2001), to ascertaining participants' reactions to and perceived benefits of their participation (Bell, 2005; Garcia, 2003; Morman, 2001; Talnack, 2000). Only one dissertation attempted to ascertain the impact of leadership development participation for school or district staff on their schools and student outcomes (Anthony, 1999). Anthony examined the effect of school district staff involvement in the Arkansas Leadership Academy on their schools' student outcomes, comparing measures 2 years before involvement through 2 years after involvement. Anthony found statistically significant differences over time by level of involvement in the Arkansas Leadership Academy in reducing dropout rates and increasing student attendance rates. The impact on achievement tests was less clear because of testing changes during the years of the study, according to Anthony.

In addition to these program evaluation studies, other researchers have explored critical issues for program evaluation of leadership development programs. These include the context, governance, and costs and funding for leadership preparation programs (Thody, 1998) as well as methodological issues in measuring the impact of educational leadership development (Earley & Evans, 2004). Earley and Evans used two very large sample surveys (as baseline and follow-up studies) of school heads and deputies in England on the adequacy of leadership preparation and the role of the National College for Educational Leadership (as a leadership development program). Earley and Evans explored potential impact measures. The results showed slight improvement in the degree to which heads felt prepared prior to and after taking their leadership post over the 2 years prior (2001, 2003). The comparison results showed that once in position, heads felt less prepared for the position than prior, although slightly less so in 2003 than 2001. They attributed participants' sense of preparedness to on-the-job experience, however, rather than to formal training. Earley and Evans questioned whether cross-sectional surveys of the field over time, such as these, could be used to evaluate the effectiveness of the National College and suggested instead that both forward mapping and backward mapping methodologies be used, particularly by selecting highly effective leaders and exploring how they have used their leadership development experiences.

This evaluation research, while still in an exploratory stage of research development, adds measurement and evaluation design insight to the foundation of research on leadership preparation. Unlike the bulk of the research on leadership preparation, which focuses primarily on leadership practices outcomes (primarily perceived effectiveness), this research offers more examples of measurement on teacher and organizational changes (Kirkpatrick's Level 4 outcomes). The studies also illustrate how to investigate the effects of programs that are variable rather than standardized "treatments." As well, they address the challenges of investigating changes in leadership practices and organizational practices that may be attributable to leadership education, by highlighting the career- and context-related factors that may be confounding. In particular, Anthony's (1999) study shows the value of longitudinal research both prior to and following leadership education to ascertain more reliably the effects on leaders and their schools.

Evaluating the MBA

Program evaluation research on the MBA can shed further light on evaluation design and measurement considerations for leadership preparation program evaluation. There are strong parallels between the fields on the current state of evaluation research, challenges to program quality and effectiveness both in institutions and the field as a whole, and potential benefits for using evaluation research. Among the parallels are the steps being taken to establish national (and even international) standards, the role of published rankings, and criticisms of program effectiveness, particularly from leaders in the business education field. The available research is suggestive of future research options in the leadership preparation field. Below is a review of current research and recommendations on evaluation research on MBA program quality and effectiveness on implications currently being drawn for the use of standards and program reform.

Evaluations of Program Quality

Like the debates over program quality and its measurement for university-based educational leadership preparation programs, the MBA field has had many debates over standards for program evaluation and had several recent critical reviews of the state of the programs, from both inside and outside the field.

The Association to Advance Collegiate Schools of Business (AACSB) International is the oldest and largest accrediting body for business schools worldwide (551 accredited business schools in 30 countries). While AACSB accredited business schools represent less than 10% of all business schools worldwide, its accredited schools represent significant diversity, a range of missions and contexts (Saunders, 2007). In 2002, AACSB established a commission to evaluate the nature and challenges of management education. Within a year, the commission returned with findings outlining the changing context for the field and need for program innovation (Management Education Taskforce, 2002). The taskforce found that while the demand for business education is growing worldwide, there are more nontraditional competitors, students want more flexible options, and educational markets increasingly have become international. At the same time, there is an increasing doctoral faculty shortage, caused by narrow, discipline-based training and a traditional system of tenure. With a global, dynamic marketplace, business schools must have both a relevant curriculum and effective instructional practices to enhance learning. The taskforce strongly recommended more clinical content and experiences, innovative program models, and networking, while teaching core management skills. Nondegree programs, particularly corporate based, the taskforce argued, compete for students and faculty and are blurring the distinctiveness of traditional programs.

Like educational leadership preparation programs, business schools are ranked by *U.S. News & World Report* and other news publications, with each publication using somewhat different measures, methods, and sources of data. There has been significant field-related concern over the impact of these rankings on programs (Taskforce of AACSB International's Committee on Issues in Management Education, 2005). An AACSB International taskforce investigated the consequences of the rankings on business schools and found that the rankings do not measure quality but add expenses to schools to provide the data, lead to reallocated resources to enhance rankings (making programs more expensive), and frequently yield inconsistent definitions and verification processes.

The taskforce challenged the field to make better use of its own accreditation systems (as designed by AACSB) as more valid, reliable, and quality-based indicators of performance.

Evaluations of Program Effectiveness

Several leading field experts recently reviewed available research on MBA program effectiveness, looking at graduates' career-related outcomes and proposed field-related reforms. Pfeffer and Fong (2002) synthesized the available research literature on the effectiveness of business schools. According to their review, available research is very limited on graduates and the profession of management, and available results suggest that business schools are not very effective. They found that grades earned in an MBA program or having an MBA did not correlate with career success (when compared to others who did not have an MBA)—as measured by number of job offers, job performance, earnings, retention, promotion, job satisfaction, or fit—or with management practice. The exception was the most selective business schools, suggesting that their selectivity matters most.

In addition, Pfeffer and Fong (2002) argued that grades and degree completion may not provide evidence of learning, as almost no one fails. Business schools in fact have been criticized for adopting academic (rather than practice-based) paradigms; giving insufficient attention to problem-finding, leadership, and interpersonal skill development; and overemphasizing analysis in skill development. Consequently, the authors argued, the content of MBA programs may be a poor fit to what is important in business success. They also argued that programs may have incorrect assumptions about learning, by offering very little experiential learning. Pfeffer and Fong found that programs that are trying to become more relevant are focused more on experienced students who more easily can transfer learning; are multidisciplinary; are focused on learning concepts, techniques, and changing how people think about business issues; and have an experiential component. They recommended that business schools learn more from other professional schools and incorporate more educational evaluation in their improvement work

Similarly, Bennis and O'Toole (2005), in what has been termed a "scorching indictment," sharply criticized MBA programs for how they evaluate quality and effectiveness:

> During the past several decades, many leading B schools have quietly adopted an inappropriate—and ultimately self-defeating—model of academic excellence. Instead of measuring themselves in terms of the competence of their graduates, or by how well their faculties understand important drivers of business performance, they measure themselves almost solely by the rigor of their scientific research. (p. 1)

Bennis and O'Toole argued that this "scientific model" does not fit a field that trains practitioners, and they advocated for a professional model, as used by institutions that prepare doctors and lawyers. They criticized business schools for being organized around the scientific model—particularly in their faculty hiring and tenuring processes, and curriculum and instructional practices—and being too divorced from the practice of business. They advocated that business schools create their own standards of excellence and use their personnel policies in recruitment, promotion, tenure, and rewards to forge a professional model of education.

Similarly, Gosling and Mintzberg (2004, 2006) sharply criticized the content and pedagogy of MBA programs, stressing their inattention to the practice of managing. They advocated for redesigning programs around the art and craft of managing, rather than around business skills, and developed their own innovative program model. Their program design principles focus on selecting experienced practitioners, integrating education and practice throughout the program, leveraging work and life experiences, reflection, organizational development, and interactive learning among faculty and participants.

Much of the focus on evaluation in management education, based on a content analysis of journal articles in the *Journal of Management Education*, is either on the nature and use of evaluation data—primarily student course evaluation—or descriptions of innovative programs. Only a few studies have investigated the quality and effectiveness of instructional innovations. For example, one group of field experts investigated how to improve faculty research on managerial practice, using action learning as a means of improving teaching and program content (Tushman, O'Reilly, Fenollosa, Kleinbaum, & McGrath, 2007). Among these, only a very few are comparative evaluations of MBA programs. One study compared general and specialized MBA programs in one urban university (Baruch, Bell, & Gray, 2005). Using a survey of alumni, Baruch et al. found most were now working managers, valued their degree and the competencies and skills they had gained, and reported career success benefits based on internal and external measures.

Finally, there has been some effort to assess the ROI of MBA programs as a means of program evaluation. Van Auken, Wells, and Chrysler (2005) assessed the relative value of one private university's standards-based MBA program's purpose, content, and teaching methods, using alumni's perceptions, knowledge, and skill development. Van Auken et al. also assessed the relative value of their ROI, using the AACSB ROI metric. The authors found that knowledge-based understandings and case and computer simulations were significantly associated with ROI.

Taken together, MBA program evaluation research strongly parallels the educational leadership preparation program evaluation research as a field improvement endeavor. Change forces within the field and outside are similarly pushing for program standards, more field-relevant programs and evaluation research that demonstrates program effectiveness. The two fields, however, differ in the types of graduate outcomes used, including the types of organizational impact measures considered. Much of the MBA program evaluation research has focused on measures of individual job performance, some of which has utility for educational leadership preparation program evaluation, particularly on job retention and promotion. In contrast, the educational leadership preparation program evaluation research is moving toward Kirkpatrick's (1998) Level 4 impacts of organizational outcomes, using student achievement gains. The MBA program evaluation research provides insight into additional program effects measurement considerations—particularly ROI—which has not been used in the educational leadership preparation field.

Evaluating Leadership Development and Executive Education

Finally, the larger field of management development and executive education also offers insights into models and methods for program evaluation. Like the field of educational leadership development, this too is an evolving field, with related implications for definitions, purposes, and related evaluation and research. Similarly, much of the leadership development evaluation research is dominated by case studies (Giber, Carter, & Goldsmith, 2000). Several meta-analyses of evaluation research in the field provide useful insights and direction.

One recent meta-review of the management development literature offers a framework of perspectives and research (Cullen & Turnbull, 2005). Cullen and Turnbull identified nine literature reviews from 1986 (Wexley & Baldwin, 1986) to 1997 (Easterby-Smith & Thorpe, 1997). In their analysis of these reviews, Cullen and Turnbull concluded that available research ranged on several dimensions, including the individual participant or organizational context, the provision of services (e.g., costs, time, and number of individuals trained), and the impact of learning processes on individuals and organizational cultures as recipients of training. They identified a shift in the field over time from management development to management learning. With this came a shift in research focus from training methods and organizational impact to theoretical approaches that address the process of learning and how it can be develop within the organization. From Thomson and others, Cullen and Turnbull drew out four theoretical contributions to understanding management development: (a management learning (individual), (b) organizational processes (organization), (c) organizational contingency (sector), and (d) human capital and labor market (macro sector or state).

Burke and Day (1986), in their meta-analysis of 70 managerial training studies, looked for patterns among program content, training methods, and subjective and objective learning and results. They found positive effects of training on subjective learning and, to a lesser extent, objective learning, but negative results for problem-solving and decision-making training (in part due to the small number of studies). Programs that focused on increasing motivation or improving values as measured by objective learning criteria were quite effective. Self-awareness training yielded the highest mean effect but used only self-reported measures of behavior change. In terms of the training methods, behavioral modeling strategies (e.g., role playing and modeling) led to positive behavior change in new situations, and the lecture method in training generalized across situations to some degree. Burke and Day concluded that different methods of training are on average moderately effective in improving learning and job performance.

In a later review, Collins (2002) analyzed evaluation methods used in management development program studies from 1986–2000. She noted that while attention to evaluation has grown, limited evaluation research focused on the organizational benefits of these programs. She analyzed 18 studies with performance outcomes, using the high-performance leadership competency model to categorize training content areas, and labeled the types of interventions (both formal programs and other learning opportunities). The studies varied widely in their time period (1–15+ years). Most programs focused on developing strategic leadership capacities. Most used survey research or mixed methods. She found only two studies that tested the relationship between performance measures at different levels of analysis: how process and individual outcomes related to organizational outcomes. More typically, evaluations assessed just the individual learner outcomes or organizational (performance-level) outcomes. In her discussion, Collins argued that the human resource development field should "take the lead in combining evaluation theory with performance-based management development theory to create the appropriate system for measurement of organizational-level performance improvement" (p. 106).

A few examples of innovative programs and evaluation research exist and are instructive. First, the Center for Creative Leadership has developed several approaches, many in recent years, to evaluate leadership development programs for a variety of public and private sectors (Hannum, Martineau, & Reinelt, 2007). According to Hannum et al., leadership development programs and interventions can have an impact on several different domains, broadening Kirkpatrick's (1998) definitions of impacts to including the individual participants' groups or teams that may be the target of the intervention; the organization (such as on strategy and performance indicators); and, more broadly, communities, fields, networks and systems. They recommended that program evaluation research consider the following factors: how the program or intervention is implemented, program duration, embeddedness of the program, continuum of learning or mastery, domain of outcomes, levels of training, levels of outcomes and measures, and timing of outcomes and impact.

Second, the W. K. Kellogg Foundation, which has invested significantly in leadership development programs over the past few years, commissioned a study on evaluation of change-oriented leadership education programs (Russon & Reinelt, 2004). The results, based on a scan of 55 programs that give priority to leadership for social change, showed that most programs commonly focused on individual outcomes (e.g., knowledge, skills, and attitudes), changes in behavior and beliefs, leadership paths, and relationships. Some outcomes also addressed organizational and community changes. Most programs lacked an explicit program theory to connect program activities and the hoped-for outcomes and limited their evaluation designs to short-term outputs to meet funder information needs. Commonly used sources of data were surveys, interviews, observations, and focus groups, collected from participants, mentors, supervisors, and others, with data most often collected from participants. A model for conceptualizing and designing leadership development program evaluation research—EvaluLead—was then created for the foundation and field tested with 22 programs (Grove, Kibel, & Haas, 2005). This model provides a lens for both conceptualizing core program features and measuring outcomes at the individual, organizational, and societal levels.

Similar large-scale leadership development evaluation research has been conducted internationally. Boaden (2006) evaluated the outcomes of the UK National Health Service leadership development programs. Three cohorts of human resource managers and directors participated in a series of residential course (half-week blocks every 2–4 months), service improvement projects, learning sets, and Web-site support. Evaluation results showed positive program effects on personal development, professional knowledge, and organizational contribution. Boaden noted how organizational instability made it challenging for some participants to put what they learned into practice, and some changed jobs to find better fits.

Some research has begun to focus on selected management education strategies. Kayes (2002) identified four agendas in management learning: (a) action, (b) cognition, (c) reflection, and (d) experience. Action-based learning approaches learning as a process of improving managerial behaviors in problem solving; cognitive approaches to management learning focus on managers' thinking processes. Reflective approaches focus on the processes of self-discovery and questioning to gain a more comprehensive view of practice. According to Kayes, experiential approaches use new experiences to foster development and motivation, through which managers gain more holistic views of themselves, with knowledge development individualized.

Despite the encouragement of Kirkpatrick's (1998) Level 3 (transfer of learning to practice) and Level 4 (organizational development) outcome investigations, such evaluations of leadership development programs are difficult, in part due to challenges in accounting for disparate, intervening influences and isolating the effects of development program experiences on outcomes (Stevenson & Warn, 2003). Stevenson and Warn explored this challenge in measuring the extent to which participants' mental models of leadership changed through leadership education, training, and experience and tested a card-sorting measurement technique. They found the technique effectively to differentiate more and less effective leaders and leaders at different levels (from trainee to senior management) in whether they cluster concepts by strategy or task, and along transformational lines.

Very few studies are longitudinal. One exception is a multiyear study of one open-enrollment, executive education program (Yorks, Beechler, & Ciporen, 2007). Yorks et al. had found little evidence of impact studies of management development programs over time and none of open-enrollment senior executive programs; they acknowledged the challenges of achieving "a degree of robustness in terms of conventional validity criteria" (p. 311). They pointed to the complex learning, the diverse and nonstandardized workplace contexts of participants, the inability to establish a control group, and the proprietary nature of unit performance data. The 4-week, in-resident, general management course they evaluated was designed around the assumption that the value added by executive leaders is impacted by the quality of how they think and learn. Thus, the program focused on developing both a learning mind-set and a learning community and was evaluated using an action-learning-research process over 3 years. Yorks et al. used a pre- and post-test, 360-degree leadership assessment survey (drawing data from managers, peers, direct reports and participants themselves), pre- and postimplementation qualitative interviews using a critical incident methodology, and a self-appraisal of the program's impact on their work. Self, manager, and peer ratings improved on almost all 14 leadership competencies assessed, but direct reports did not. Interviews showed the greatest impact on self-awareness, sensitivity to diversity, broader and more global thinking, and reflection but mixed organizational support for learning transfer. Yorks et al. concluded that such program evaluations need to be situated in the theories on learning transfer (Holton & Baldwin, 2003) and program evaluation (Kirkpatrick, 1998) that connect program design, participant learning, application and performance, and organizational impact.

One novel study integrated the two fields by comparing the effects of formal and informal mentoring relationships in both corporate and K–12 school contexts (Sosik, Lee, & Bouquillon, 2005). Sosik et al. measured mentoring functions in terms of career development, role modeling and psychosocial support, and outcomes in terms of organizational commitment and career satisfaction; they found a significant interaction effect between context, formal and informal mentoring, and outcomes. Teachers in K–12 schools benefited more from informal mentoring, whereas protégés in high-tech firms benefited more from formal mentoring, which the authors attributed to sector differences and how organizational structures and processes influence mentoring functions and relationships.

In contrast to the educational leadership preparation program evaluation field, the leadership development and executive education field has yielded much more extensive research using a fuller range of outcome measures, reflecting Kirkpatrick's (1998) four outcome levels and the work of Guskey (2000) on more differentiation among these outcomes and Phillips (1996) on ROI. There is also greater use of adult learning theory to establish the principles for the programs' theories of change—both program theory and implementation theory—as Weiss (1998) recommended. Finally, there is greater use of participants' leadership assessment as part of program delivery as well as evaluating program effects over time. Like the available program evaluation research on educational leadership development, evaluation research in this field accounts for considerable challenges in measuring both the level and quality of the educational experiences as well as the effects on participants, given varied organizational contexts and conditions.

Conclusions and Implications

Program evaluation research in educational leadership preparation is in an emerging state, both conceptually and methodologically. A comparison of the current state of this field with other related fields in education and leadership development helps to situate this work in this stage of research development and offers promising directions for advancing the quality and sophistication of further research.

This review of peer-reviewed journals and dissertation research in the educational leadership preparation field shows that there is a solid foundation of research on implementation studies of individual programs or the field as a whole to mark trends and patterns on program approaches and features. This work has shaped current definitions of best practices and exemplary program features (Jackson & Kelley, 2002; Orr, 2006), which serve as a foundation for program comparison (Darling-Hammond et al., 2007). There is also a solid foundation of work assessing leadership readiness and the responsiveness of existing and new programs to the practices and challenges of school and district leaders. While little of this work has been synthesized, its compilation here shows the breadth of this work and the influence of leadership standards in framing these initial program outcomes. The most limited research has been comparative program evaluations and effects studies of multiple programs. Such research holds promise for teasing out the effects of different types of preparation on leaders and their work in schools and, as illustrated here, shows the importance of measuring differences in program features as well as stages of outcomes, as defined by Kirkpatrick's (1998) four levels of outcomes.

The growth of dissertation research in particular in recent years, especially for leadership outcomes studies, appears to have been triggered by the standards movement in educational leadership and the evaluation expectations of national accreditation systems like NCATE and ELCC. Thus, as the ELCC strengthens its program evaluation expectations for program accreditation and as states implement leadership assessments for certification and licensure, there will be even greater program and institutional support for program evaluation and outcome assessments. As of yet, although most outcome studies assess similar concepts (of leadership readiness and preparedness), there are few commonly used measures or methods. Thus, there is a need for field-based agreement on outcome measures and methodology that would facilitate cumulative knowledge development and comparison across studies.

Comparing the current state of program evaluation research in the educational leadership preparation field with other related fields shows the differences in the fields' objectives—and thus the focus of their program evaluations—and offers insights for conceptual and methodology considerations. Only the leadership preparation field looks beyond the benefits to its program graduates to consider the impact of the graduates on the organizations (and their clients, the students) that they eventually lead. Other fields focus more specifically on the career benefits of the programs (such as MBA programs) on graduates. The exception is executive leadership development programs, which are often offered as an organizational change strategy and thus are intended to lead to organizational change through leadership development. Evaluations of these latter types of programs offer examples of more theory-guided program evaluation, as recommended by Weiss (1998), and consideration of stages of outcomes, as recommended by Kirkpatrick (1998) and Guskey (2000). Such program evaluation models may be applicable to the educational leadership preparation field and at the very least underscore areas for further conceptual and methodological development.

The review above shows that the field is ready to move beyond documenting outcomes to looking at the relationship between program features and approaches and various leadership and organization outcomes. Such research has begun to explore the validity and effects of different types of outcomes to add to an understanding of the effects of preparation on leadership practice. Such research, however, must be based on multiple programs, both to offer comparisons and to gain sufficient sample size for robust analyses. The emerging trend of leadership preparation programs working collaborative at the state and national level (particularly through the UCEA LTEL-SIG Taskforce on Evaluating Leadership Preparation Programs) is extremely promising. This work enables shared knowledge development on program effects and outcomes while addressing individual program and institutional evaluation needs for accreditation and program improvement. Creating shared research communities of practice will enable the field to develop agreed-upon measures and standards for program evaluation and makes use of more advanced evaluation research designs.

What future directions in program evaluation does this review suggest? There is now a foundation of research on the presence or absence of key program features (such as rigorous selection and cohort structures) and essential content (such as attention to special education and technology). Research allows us to look more deeply at our program theories—as learning theories of individual change and as instrumental for the field of education generally. It is also evident that program evaluation research in our field continues to be driven primarily by individual faculty interest and initiative. External forces—such as accreditation and licensure requirements—are widening the field of interest in program effectiveness, and thus evaluation research, and are engaging institutional support for conducting program evaluations. However, these forces are insufficient to advance program evaluation research. Much of the research has been made possible by the voluntary efforts of individual faculty or their service to the field through their state and national professional associations. Faculty interest and commitment to learning more about best practices and the effects of preparation on leadership practices remain the primary drivers for advancing program evaluation research in our field.

References

Note: Asterisks indicate references that were part of the meta-analysis.

Adams, J., & Copland, M. A. (2005). *When learning counts: Rethinking licenses for school leaders.* Seattle: University of Washington, Center for the Study of Teaching and Policy.

*Alonso, C. (1993). *Usefulness of educational administration programs in the performance of school principalship roles in Bogota, Republic of Colombia.* Unpublished doctoral dissertation, State University of New York, Buffalo.

Anderson, G. (2001). Disciplining leaders: A critical discourse analysis of the ISLLC national examination and performance standards in educational administration. *International Journal of Leadership in Education: Theory and Practice, 4*(3), 199–216.

Anthony, B. L. (1999). *The effect of Arkansas Leadership Academy involvement on student outcomes in Arkansas school districts.* Unpublished doctoral dissertation, University of Arkansas.

Avolio, B. J., Clapp, R. O., Vogelgesang, R. R., & Wernsing, T. (2005). *Nebraska Educational Leadership Institute (NELI) Project.* Lincoln, NE: The Gallup Leadership Institute.

Baker, B., Orr, M. T., & Young, M. D. (2007). Academic drift, institutional production and professional distribution of graduate degrees in educational leadership. *Educational Administration Quarterly, 43*(3), 279–318.

*Bales, J. R. (1997). *Graduate preparation in educational administration among high school principals and its relationship to school effectiveness.* Unpublished doctoral dissertation, Illinois State University, Normal.

*Barnett, B. G., Basom, M. R., Yerkes, D. M., & Norris, C. J. (2000). Cohorts in educational leadership programs: Benefits, difficulties, and the potential for developing school leaders. *Educational Administration Quarterly, 36*(2), 255–282.

Baruch, Y., Bell, M. P., & Gray, D. (2005). Generalist and specialist graduate business degrees: Tangible and intangible value. *Journal of Vocational Behavior, 67*(1), 51–68.

Bell, M. S. (2005). *The relationships among selected demographic variables, school settings, attendance in leadership academies, and the self-perceptions of secondary school principals.* Unpublished doctoral dissertation, Louisiana Tech University, Ruston.

Bennis, W. G., & O'Toole, J. (2005). How business schools lost their way. *Harvard Business Review, 83*(5), 1–10.

Best graduate schools: Education methodology. (2008, March 26). *U. S. News & World Report.* Retrieved from http://www.usnews.com/articles/education/best-graduate-schools/2008/03/26/education-methodology.html

Black, W. R., Bathon, J., & Poindexter, B. (2007). *Looking in the mirror to improve practice: A study of administrative licensure and master's degree programs in the state of Indiana.* Indianapolis: Indiana University, Center for Urban and Multicultural Education.

Boaden, R. J. (2006). Leadership development: Does it make a difference? *Leadership & Organizational Development Journal, 27*(1/2), 5–28.

*Bordeaux, J. A. (1994). *The efficacy of university preparation to meet the expectations of the role of elementary principal in Missouri: An analysis of the perception of current principals.* Unpublished doctoral dissertation, Saint Louis University, Saint Louis, MO.

*Border, K. (2004). *University-based principal preparation programs in Texas: Perceptions of program completers and supervisors in the Texas Lighthouse Project.* Unpublished doctoral dissertation, Baylor University, Waco, TX.

Bottoms, G., & O'Neill, K. (2001). *Preparing a new breed of school principals: It's time for action.* Atlanta, GA: Southern Regional Education Board.

Bredeson, P. V. (1996). New directions in the preparation of educational leaders. In K. Leithwood, J. Chapman, D. Corson, P. Hallinger, & A. Hart (Eds.), *International handbook of educational leadership and administration* (pp. 251–274). Dordrecht, The Netherlands: Kluwer Academic.

Brundrett, M. (2006). Evaluating the individual and combined impact of national leadership programmes in England: Perceptions and practices. *School Leadership & Management, 26*(5), 473–488.

Burke, M. J., & Day, R. R. (1986). A cumulative study of the effectiveness of managerial training. *Journal of Applied Psychology, 71*(2), 232–245.

Bush, T. (2006). The National College for School Leadership: A successful English innovation? *Phi Delta Kappan, 87*(7), 508–511.

Bush, T., & Oduro, G. K. T. (2006). New principals in Africa: Preparation, induction and practice. *Journal of Educational Administration, 44*(4), 359–375.

Cockrell, K., Caplow, J., & Donaldson, J. (2000). A context for learning: Collaborative groups in the problem-based learning environment. *Review of Higher Education, 23*, 347–364.

Collins, D. B. (2002). Performance-level evaluation methods used in management development studies from 1986 to 2000. *Human Resource Development Quarterly, 1*(1), 91–110.

*Copeland, S. (2004). *A study of field experiences and leadership opportunities in principal preparation programs in the 16 SREB member states.* Unpublished doctoral dissertation, University of Memphis, Memphis, TN.

*Cox, H. S. (1998). *Effectiveness of principal preparation in Florida as perceived by selected superintendents, first-year principals and other key informants.* Unpublished doctoral dissertation, Florida State University, Tallahassee.

*Crain, J. (2004). *Perceptions of career and technical education superintendents and secondary directors in Ohio on leadership preparation experiences.* Unpublished doctoral dissertation, Bowling Green State University, Bowling Green, OH.

*Creighton, T. (2002). Standards for educational administration preparation programs: Okay, but don't we have the cart before the horse? *Journal of School Leadership, 12*(5), 526–551.

Crow, G. M. (2004). The National College for School Leadership: A North American perspective on opportunities and challenges. *Educational Management Administration & Leadership, 32*(3), 289–3607.

Cullen, J., & Turnbull, S. (2005). A meta-review of the management development literature. *Human Resource Development Review, 4*(3), 335–355.

*Darling-Hammond, L., Meyerson, D., LaPointe, M., & Orr, M. T. (2007). *Preparing leaders for a changing world*. Palo Alto, CA: Stanford University.

*Dodson, R. B. (2006). *The effectiveness of principal training and formal principal mentoring programs*. Unpublished doctoral dissertation, East Tennessee State University, Johnson City.

Dunning, G. (1996). Preparing for primary school management: Training providers, task preparation and support— Perceptions of new headteachers. *The International Journal of Educational Management, 10*(4), 33–43.

*Dyce Faucett, K. J. (2005). *Perceptions of the efficacy of the National Policy Board for Educational Administration Standards in guiding principal preparation: A survey of New York State principals*. Unpublished doctoral dissertation, University of Rochester, Rochester, NY.

Earley, P., & Evans, J. (2004). Making a difference? *Educational Management Administration & Leadership, 32*(3), 325–338.

Easterby-Smith, M., & Thorpe, R. (1997). Research tradition in management learning. In J. Burgoyne & M. Reynolds (Eds.), *Management learning: Integrating perspectives in theory and practice* (pp. 38–53). London: Sage.

Education Schools Project. (2005). *Report No. 1: Educating school Leaders*. Retrieved September 1, 2008, from http://www.edschools.org/reports_leaders.htm

Education specialties: Administration/supervision. New! Ranked in 2007: U.S. News & World Report. (2007). *U. S. News & World Report*. Retrieved September 1, 2008, from http://grad-schools.usnews.rankingsandreviews.com/usnews/edu/grad/rankings/edu/brief/edusp01_brief.php

Educational Leadership Constituent Council. (2005, August). *A listing of nationally recognized educational leadership preparation programs at NCATE accredited colleges and universities*. Retrieved September 1, 2008, from the National Policy Board for Educational Administration Web site: http://www.npbea.org/ELCC/ELCC-approved_and_denied_list_0805.pdf

Educational Testing Service. (2008a). *For test takers: Praxis II overview*. Retrieved September 1, 2008, from http://www.ets.org

Educational Testing Service. (2008b). *Test content: The School Leaders Licensure Assessment*. Retrieved September 1, 2008, from http://www.ets.org

e-Lead. (2007). *Professional development programs*. Retrieved September 1, 2008, from http://www.e-lead.org/programs/index.asp.

Ellett, C. D. (1999). Developments in the preparation and licensing of school leaders: The work of the Interstate School Leaders Licensure Consortium. *Journal of Personnel Evaluation in Education, 13*(3), 201–204.

English, F. W. (2006). The unintended consequences of a standardized knowledge base in advancing educational leadership preparation. *Educational Administration Quarterly, 42*(3), 461–472.

*Epstein, J. L., & Sanders, M. G. (2006). Prospects for change: Preparing educators for school, family, and community partnerships. *Peabody Journal of Education, 81*(2), 81–120.

*Franklin, S. H. (2006). *Exploratory comparative case studies of two principal preparation programs*. Unpublished doctoral dissertation, The University of Texas, Austin.

Friend, J. (2007, April). *State-Wide Program Improvement Initiative: UCEA/TEA-SIG Alumni Survey*. Paper presented at the meeting of the Missouri Professors of Educational Administration, Columbia, MO.

Friend, J., Watson, R., & Waddle, J. (2006). *Looking in the mirror to improve practice: Discussing statewide leadership preparation studies*. Paper presented at the annual meeting of the University Council for Educational Administration, San Antonio, TX.

Frye, B., O'Neill, K., & Bottoms, G. (2006). *Schools can't wait: Accelerating the redesign of university principal preparation programs*. Atlanta, GA: Southern Regional Educational Board.

Fuller, E., & Orr, M. T. (2006, April). *Texas leadership preparation programs and their graduates' school leadership advancement: A trend comparison of institutional outcomes, 1995–2005*. Paper presented at the annual meeting of the University Council for Educational Administration, San Antonio, TX.

*Furtwengler, W., & Furtwengler, C. (1998). Performance assessment in the preparation of educational administrators. *Journal of School Leadership, 8*(1), 65–85.

Garcia, V. C. (2003). *Ethical relational leadership: A case study of a holistic model for the professional development of school administrators*. Unpublished doctoral dissertation, University of New Mexico, Albuquerque.

Giber, D., Carter, L., & Goldsmith, M. (2000). *Linkage Inc.'s best practices in leadership development handbook*. San Francisco: Pfeiffer.

Glasman, N. S., Cibulka, J., & Ashby, D. (2002). Program self-evaluation for continuous improvement. *Educational Administration Quarterly, 38*(2), 257–288.

Gonzalez, M., Glasman, N. S., & Glasman, L. D. (2002). Daring to link principal preparation programs to student achievement in schools. *Leadership and Policy in Schools, 1*(3), 265–283.

Gosling, J., & Mintzberg, H. (2004). The education of practicing managers. *MIT Sloan Management Review, 45*(4), 19–22.

Gosling, J., & Mintzberg, H. (2006). Management education as if both matter. *Management Learning, 37*(4), 419.

Griffiths, D. (1995). Theoretical pluralism in educational administration. In R. Donmoyer, M. Imber, & J. Scheurich (Eds.), *The knowledge base in educational administration: Multiple perspectives* (pp. 302–311). Albany: State University of New York Press.

Griffiths, D. E., Stout, R. T., & Forsyth, P. B. (Eds.). (1988). *Leaders for America's schools: The report and papers of the National Commission on Excellence in Educational Administration.* Berkeley, CA: McCutchan.

Grove, J. T., Kibel, B. M., & Haas, T. (2005). *EvaluLead: A guide for shaping and evaluating leadership development programs.* Oakland, CA: The Public Health Institute.

Guskey, T. R. (2000). *Evaluating professional development.* Thousand Oaks, CA: Corwin Press.

*Hackman, D., & Berry. (1999). Distance learning in educational administration doctoral programs: The wave of the future? *Journal of School Leadership, 9*(4), 349–367.

*Hale, C. L. (1999). *Effect of formal training on the transformational leadership behaviors of superintendents.* Unpublished doctoral dissertation, University of La Verne, La Verne, CA.

*Haller, E. J., Brent, B. O., & McNamera, J. H. (1997). Does graduate training in educational administration improve America's schools? *Phi Delta Kappan, 79,* 222–227.

Hannum, K., Martineau, J., & Reinelt, C. (2007). *The handbook of leadership development evaluation.* San Francisco: Center for Creative Leadership.

*Harpin, L. T. (2003). *Integration of ISLLC leadership standards into Rhode Island principal preparation programs.* Unpublished doctoral dissertation, Johnson & Wales University, Providence, RI.

*Henwood, J. (2000). *The influence of Colorado licensure standards on principal preparation programs.* Unpublished doctoral dissertation, University of Denver, Denver, CO.

Hermond, D. (1999). Evaluating a leadership preparation program: Participants' perspectives. *Planning and changing, 30*(3/4), 198–217.

Hess, F. M., & Kelly, A. M. (2005). *Learning to lead? What gets taught in principal preparation programs.* Washington, DC: American Enterprise Institute for Public Policy Research.

*Hewitson, M. T. (1995). The preparation of beginning principals in Queensland: An overview of findings. *Journal of Educational Administration, 33*(2), 20–30.

Holton, E. F., & Baldwin, T. T. (2003). Making transfer happen: An action perspective on learning transfer systems. In E. F. Holton & T. T. Baldwin (Eds.), *Improving learning transfer in organizations* (pp. 3–5). San Francisco: Jossey-Bass.

Huber, S. G. (2004). *Preparing school leaders for the 21st century: An international comparison of development programs in 15 countries.* London: RoutledgeFalmer.

*Hvizdak, M. (2001). *Preservice training and experience and English headteachers' preparation for the headship.* Unpublished doctoral dissertation, the University of Texas, El Paso.

Immegart, G. L., & Pascual, R. (1994). International co-operation in the preparation of school directors in Spain. *Journal of Educational Administration, 32*(3), 5–17.

Interstate School Leaders Licensure Consortium. (1996). *Standards for school leaders.* Washington, DC: Council of Chief State School Officers.

Iwanicki, E. F. (1999). ISLLC standards and assessment in the context of school leadership reform. *Journal of Personnel Evaluation in Education, 13*(3), 283–294.

Jackson, B. L., & Kelley, C. (2002). Exceptional and innovative programs in educational leadership. *Educational Administration Quarterly, 38*(2), 192–212.

Jacobson, A., O'Neill, K., Fry, B., Hill, D., & Bottoms, G. (2002). *Are SREB states making progress? Tapping, preparing and licensing school leaders who can influence student achievement.* Atlanta, GA: Southern Regional Educational Board.

*Jolly, R. A. F. (1995). The effectiveness of secondary educational administration preparation programs at Kansas Regents universities. *Dissertation Abstracts International, 56*(11), 4224. (UMI No. AAI96099508)

*Jones, J. L. H. (1999). A qualitative analysis of collaborative, field-based principal preparation programs in Texas. *Dissertation Abstracts International, 60,* 11A. (UMI No. AAI9949291)

Kanan, H. M. (2005). Assessing the roles and training needs of educational superintendents in Palestine. *Journal of Educational Administration, 43*(2), 154–169.

Kanan, H. M., & Baker, A. M. (2006). Student satisfaction with an educational administration preparation program. *Journal of Educational Administration, 44*(2), 159–169.

Kayes, D. C. (2002). Experiential learning and its critics: Preserving the role of experience in management learning and education. *Academy of Management Learning & Education, 1*(2), 137–149.

*Kibble, L. (2004). How instructional leadership is addressed in educational administration/leadership programs. *Dissertation Abstracts International, 55*(02). (UMI No. 3122214)

Kirkpatrick, D. L. (1998). *Evaluating training programs: The four levels* (2nd ed.). San Francisco: Berrett-Koehler.

*Kochan, F., & Twale. (1998). Advisory groups in educational leadership: Seeking a bridge between town and gown. *Planning and Changing, 29*(4), 237–250.

Kouzes, J., & Posner, B. (1995). *The leadership challenge: How to keep getting extraordinary things done in organizations.* San Francisco: Jossey-Bass.

*Kraus, C. M. (1996). Administrator preparation programs: Impact on job preparedness and learning. *Dissertation Abstracts International-A, 57*(04), 1419. (AAT 9625562)

Leithwood, K., & Jantzi, D. (2005, April). *A review of transformational school leadership research.* Paper presented at the annual meeting of the American Educational Research Association, Montreal, Quebec, Canada.

*Leithwood, K., Jantzi, D., Coffin, G., & Wilson, P. (1996). Preparing school leaders: What works? *Journal of School Leadership, 6*(3), 316–342.

Leithwood, K., Riedlinger, B., Bauer, S., & Jantzi, D. (2003). Leadership program effects on student learning: The case of the greater New Orleans School Leadership Center. *Journal of School Leadership, 13*, 707–738.

Levine, A. (2005). *Educating school leaders.* Washington: The Education Schools Project.

*Lightfoot, J. D. (2003). Toward a praxis of anti-racist school leadership preparation. Unpublished doctoral dissertation, University of Illinois, Chicago.

*Lin, J. (2005). *Perception of principals in the southern, urban United States and eastern, urban China regarding the selection, preparation, and professional development of elementary principals.* Unpublished doctoral dissertation, Texas A&M University, College Station.

*Lyman, L., & Villani, C. (2002). The complexion of poverty: A missing component of educational leadership programs. *Journal of School Leadership, 12*(3), 246–280.

Management Education Taskforce. (2002). *Management education at risk.* Tampa, FL: AACSB International.

*Martin, T. P. (2002). *The perception of middle-level school assistant principals regarding their administrative preparation and the tasks they perform.* Unpublished doctoral dissertation, Dowling College, Oakdale, NY.

McCarthy, M. M. (1999). The evolution of educational leadership preparation programs. In J. Murphy & K. Seashore Louis (Eds.), *Handbook of research on educational administration: A project of the American Educational Research Association* (pp. 119–139). San Francisco: Jossey-Bass.

McCarthy, M. M. (2001a). Challenges facing educational leadership programs: Our future is now. *Newsletter of the Teaching in Educational Administration Special Interest Group, 8*(1), 1, 4.

McCarthy, M. M. (2001b). Educational leadership preparation programs: A glance at the past and an eye toward the future. *Leadership and Policy in Schools, 1*(3), 201–221.

*McCarthy, M. M., & Kuh, G. (1998). A new breed of educational leadership faculty members. *Journal of School Leadership, 8*(4), 360–372.

*McClellan, R., & Dominguez, R. (2006). The uneven march toward social justice. *Journal of Educational Administration, 44*(3), 225–238.

*McDaniel, R., Furtwengler, W. J., & Furtwengler, C. B. (1999). Doctoral preparation programs in educational administration: The status of reform in four midwestern universities. *Journal of School Leadership, 9*(1), 26–50.

McGinn, A. (2004). *A study of social and political acumen in dynamic educational leadership and the implications for leadership development programs.* Unpublished doctoral dissertation, University of Calgary, Calgary, Alberta, Canada.

*McKerrow, K. (1998). Administrative internships: Quality or quantity? *Journal of School Leadership, 8*(2), 171–186.

*McRae, T. (2000). *Alternative delivery of educational administration academic and licensure programs in the United States and Canada.* Unpublished doctoral dissertation, the University of Texas, San Antonio.

McNamara, P. A. (2001). *Professional development for principals: Road to a leadership academy in rural west Texas.* Unpublished doctoral dissertation, Texas A&M University, College Station.

Milstein, M. M. (1993). *Changing the way we prepare educational leaders: The Danforth experience.* Newbury Park, CA: Corwin Press.

Milstein, M. M., & Kruger, J. (1997). Improving educational administration preparation programs: What we have learned over the past decade. *Peabody Journal of Education, 72*(2), 100–116.

Morman, O. C. (2001). *Is there a statistical difference in perceptions of professional preparations of elementary and middle school administrators who attend a leadership academy?* Unpublished doctoral dissertation, the Union Institute, Cincinnati, OH.

Muller, D., & Judd, C. M. (2005). Direct and indirect effects. In *Encyclopedia of statistics in behavioral science.* Hoboken, NJ: Wiley. Retrieved from http://mrw.interscience.wiley.com/emrw/9780470013199/esbs/article/bsa173/current/abstract (DOI no. 10.1002/0470013192.bsa173)

Murphy, J., & Vriesenga, M. (2004). *Research on preparation programs in educational administration: An analysis.* Memphis, TN: Vanderbilt University.

Murphy, J., & Vriesenga, M. (2006). Research on school leadership preparation in the United States: An analysis. *School Leadership & Management, 26*(2), 183–195.

*Narducci, D. M. (1997). *The preparation of educational administrators for the 21st century: A changing paradigm.* Unpublished doctoral dissertation, Fordham University, New York.

National Council for Accreditation of Teacher Education. (2008). *Program report for the preparation of educational leaders (school building leadership level)*. Retrieved September 1, 2008, from http://www.ncate.org/ProgramStandards/ELCC/ELCCWebReport(SchoolBldgLevel)July1.doc

National Policy Board for Educational Administration. (n.d.). Home page. Retrieved September 1, 2008, from http://www.npbea.org

National Policy Board for Educational Administration. (2002). *Instructions to implement standards for advanced programs in educational leadership for principals, superintendents, curriculum directors and supervisors*. Arlington, VA: Author.

National Policy Board for Educational Administration. (2008). *Educational leadership policy standards: ISLLC 2008*. Austin: University of Texas. Retrieved September 1, 2008, from http://www.npbea.org/projects.php

*Neuman, J. M. (1999). *Preparation of the urban principal*. Unpublished doctoral dissertation, University of Minnesota.

*Nicholson, B., & Leary, P. A. (2001). Appalachian principals assess the efficacy and appropriateness of their training. *Planning and Changing, 32*(3/4), 199–213.

*Norton, M. S. (2004). Student learning portfolios: How they are being implemented in educational administration preparation programs. *Planning and Changing, 35*(3/4), 223–235.

Orr, M. T. (2003, April). *Evaluating educational leadership development: Measuring leadership, its development and its impact*. Paper presented at the annual meeting of the American Educational Research Association, Chicago.

Orr, M. T. (2006). Mapping innovation in leadership preparation in our nation's schools of education. *Phi Delta Kappan, 87*(7), 492–499.

Orr, M. T. (2007, November). *Evaluating leadership preparation programs: Current findings and future directions*. Paper presented at the annual meeting of the University Council for Educational Administration, Alexandria, VA.

Orr, M. T. (2008, April). *UCEA/LTEL-SIG Taskforce on Evaluation Leadership Preparation Programs (ELPP) updates*. Paper presented at the American Educational Research Association, New York.

*Orr, M. T., & Barber, M. E. (2007). Collaborative leadership preparation: A comparative study of partnership and conventional programs and practices. *Journal of school leadership, 16*(6), 709–739.

Orr, M. T., Doolittle, G., Kottkamp, R., Osterman, K., & Silverberg, R. (2004). What are we learning from the ELCC/NCATE required program evaluations? Findings from real-time action research at the UCEA convention. *UCEA Review, 46*(1), 7–10.

*Orr, M. T., & Orphanos, S. (in press). How preparation impacts school leaders and their school improvement: Comparing exemplary and conventionally prepared principals. *Educational Administration Quarterly*.

Orr, M. T., & Pounder, D. G. (2006). *UCEA/TEA-SIG Taskforce on Evaluating Leadership Preparation Programs. Taskforce report: Six years later and future directions*. Austin, TX: University Council for Educational Administration. Retrieved from http://www.ucea.org/evaluation/pdf/reportfinal.pdf

Orr, M. T., & Pounder, D. G. (2007, November). *Comparing leadership education from pipeline to preparation to advancement: A study of multiple institutions' leadership preparation programs*. Paper presented at the annual meeting of the University Council for Educational Administration, Alexandria, VA.

Orr, M. T., Young, M. D., & Baker, B. (2006). *Promoting researcher integrity—From case study to field action*. Unpublished manuscript, Bank Street College of Education, New York.

*Palm-Leis, M. (2005). *Status of a philosophy of educational administration in programs that prepare educational leaders in the state of Wisconsin*. Unpublished doctoral dissertation, Edgewood College, Madison, WI.

*Perdue, J. S. (1997). Graduate preparation in educational administration among elementary principals and its relationship to school effectiveness. *Dissertation Abstracts International, 58*(07-A), 2483.

Pfeffer, J., & Fong, C. T. (2002). The end of business schools? Less success than meets the eye. *Academy of Management Learning & Education 1*(1), 78–95.

Phillips, J. J. (1996). ROI: The search for best practices. *Training & Development, 50*(2), 42–48

*Poimbeauf, R. P. (2004). *Administration students' perceptions of their experience in a leadership cohort*. Unpublished doctoral dissertation, University of Houston, Houston, TX.

*Poole, B. J. (1994). *The quality of job performance and career advancement of individuals completing the University of Alabama's Innovative Principalship Program during the years 1988 through 1991 compared to individuals completing traditional certification programs*. Unpublished doctoral dissertation, University of Alabama.

*Poole, J. J. (1999). *Perceptions of preparedness of critical skills based on type of principal preparation program; traditional or non-traditional*. Unpublished doctoral dissertation, Indiana State University, Terre Haute.

Pounder, D. G., & Hafner, M. (2006a, April). *Utah leadership preparation: Initial findings of a longitudinal study*. Paper presented at the annual meeting of the University Council for Educational Administration, San Antonio, TX.

Pounder, D. G., & Hafner, M. (2006b, April). *Utah leader preparation study: Preliminary report of Stage 1 research*. Paper presented at the annual meeting of the American Educational Research Association, San Francisco.

*Quenneville, J. M. (2007). *Preparing school leaders: School administrators' perceptions of traditional and district level training programs*. Unpublished doctoral dissertation, University of Virginia, Charlottesville.

*Rapp, D., Silent X., & Silent Y. (2001). The implications of raising one's voice in educational leadership doctoral programs: Women's stories of fear, retaliation, and silence. *Journal of School Leadership, 11*(4), 279–295.

*Reale-Foley, L. B. (2003). *How New England graduate programs in school administration are preparing aspiring school administrators to become technology leaders*. Unpublished doctoral dissertation, University of Hartford, Hartford, CT.

Reese, C. M., & Tannenbaum, R. J. (1999). Gathering content-related validity evidence for the school leaders licensure assessment. *Journal of Personnel Evaluation in Education, 13*(3), 163–282.

Reilly, D. H., & Brown, J. (1996). Issues in developing a school leadership preparation programme in a post-communist republic of the former Soviet Union. *Journal of Educational Administration, 34*(4), 5–23.

*Restine, L. N. (1997). Experience, meaning and principal development. *Journal of Educational Administration, 35*(3), 253–267.

Robinson, W. L. (2001). *The Sarasota County, Florida, school district leadership training program: A descriptive case study.* Unpublished doctoral dissertation, Virginia Polytechnic Institute and State University, Blacksburg.

Rossi, P. H., Freeman, H. E., & Lipsey, M. W. (1999). *Evaluation: A systematic approach* (6th ed.). Thousand Oaks, CA: Sage.

*Rucinski, D. A., & Bauch, P. A. (2006). Reflective, ethical, and moral constructs in educational leadership preparation: effects on graduates' practices. *Journal of Educational Administration, 44*(5), 487–508.

Russon, C., & Reinelt, C. (2004). The results of an evaluation scan of 55 leadership development programs. *Journal of Leadership & Organizational Studies, 10*(3), 104–108.

Sanders, N. M. (2007). *2006 key state policy indicators for improving administrator quality* [Draft]. Washington, DC: Council of Chief State School Officers.

Sanders, N. M., & Simpson, J. (2005). *State policy framework to develop highly qualified administrators.* Washington, DC: Council of Chief State School Officers.

Saunders, D. (2007, October 4). *RE: Interim report from the AACSB Strategic Directions Committee and request for feedback* [Memo]. Tampa, FL: Association to Advance Collegiate Schools of Business. Retrieved from http://www.aacsb.edu/sdc/SDCrpt-02oct07.pdf

*Schlosser, R. A. (2006). An analysis of principal interns' legal knowledge and legal instruction in principal preparation programs. *Dissertation Abstracts International, 67*(09). (UMI No. 3233261)

*Scollay, S., & Logan, J. P. (1999). The gender equity role of educational administration: Where are we? Where do we want to go? *Journal of School Leadership, 9*(2), 97–124.

*Sharps, C. J. (1993). Innovative and traditional principal preparation in Oregon: A study of matched pairs. *Dissertation Abstracts International, 54*(08A).

*Shaw, G. (2005). *Examination of leadership practices of graduates from traditional and nontraditional educational leadership programs at a regional university.* Unpublished doctoral dissertation, Delta State University, Cleveland, MS.

*Shen, & Hsieh. (1999). The instructional goals of the school leadership program: Future school leaders and educational leadership professors' perspectives. *Journal of school leadership, 9*(1), 79–91.

*Sherman, W. H., & Beaty, D. M. (2007). The use of distance technology in educational leadership preparation programs. *Journal of Educational Administration, 45*(5), 605–620.

*Sirotnik, K., & Kimball, K. (1994). The unspecial place of special education in programs that prepare school administrators. *Journal of School Leadership, 4*(6), 598–630.

*Slater, C. L., McGhee, M. W., Capt, R. L., Alvarez, I., Topete, C., & Iturbe, E. (2003). A comparison of the views of educational administration students in the USA and Mexico. *International Journal of Leadership in Education, 6*(1), 35–55.

Sosik, J. J., Lee, D., & Bouquillon, E. A. (2005). Context and mentoring: Examining formal and informal relationships in high tech firms and K–12 schools. *Journal of Leadership & Organizational Studies, 12*(2), 94–108.

Southern Regional Education Board. (2006). *Schools can't wait: Accelerating the redesign of university principal preparation programs.* Atlanta, GA: Author.

Stevenson, E., & Warn, J. (2003). Quantifying changing understanding: Level 3 evaluation of leadership development interventions. *Evaluation Journal of Australasia, 3*(1), 56–60.

Talnack, A. S. (2000). *A case study: The impact of the Santa Cruz County Educational Leadership Consortium Academy on the skill development and practices of school principals.* Unpublished doctoral dissertation, University of La Verne, La Verne, CA.

Taskforce of AACSB International's Committee on Issues in Management Education. (2005). *The business school ranking dilemma.* Tampa, FL: AACSB International.

Teacher Education Accreditation Council. (2006). *TEAC accreditation process: TEAC's accreditation goal, principles, and standards for educational leadership.* Retrieved September 1, 2008, from http://www.teac.org/educaleadership/index.asp

Thody, A. (1998). Training school principals, educating school governors. *International Journal of Educational Management, 12*(5), 232–239.

*Townley, A. J., & Sweeney, D. P. (1993). Who is teaching California school administrators? A profile of California professors of educational administration. *Journal of School Leadership, 3*(3), 329–343.

Toye, C., Blank, R., Sanders, N. M., & Williams, A. (2007). *Key state education policies on P–12 education: 2006. Results of a 50 state survey.* Washington, DC: Council of Chief State School Officers.

Tushman, M. L., O'Reilly, C. A., Fenollosa, A., Kleinbaum, A. M., & McGrath, D. (2007). Relevance and rigor: Executive education as a lever in shaping practice and research. *Academy of Management Learning & Education, 6*(3), 345–362.

*Twale, D. J., Reed, C. A., & Kochan, F. R. (2001). Creating collaborative communities for part-time students in educational leadership programs. *Planning and changing, 32*(3/4), 214–225.

U.S. Department of Education. (2005). *Innovations in education: Innovative pathways to school leadership.* Washington, DC: Author.

Van Auken, S., Wells, L. G., & Chrysler, E. (2005). The relative value of skills, knowledge, and teaching methods in explaining Master of Business Administration (MBA) program return on investment. *Journal of Education for Business, 81*(1), 41–45.

*Vanderhaar, J. E., Muñoz, M. A., & Rodosky, R. J. (2006). Leadership as accountability for learning: The effects of school poverty, teacher experience, previous achievement, and principal preparation programs on student achievement. *Journal of Personnel Evaluation in Education, 19*(1–2), 17–33.

*Vick, R. C. (2004). *Use of the SREB leadership development framework in preservice principal preparation programs: A qualitative investigation.* Unpublished doctoral dissertation, East Tennessee State University, Johnson City.

Walker, A., & Dimmock, C. (2006). Preparing leaders, preparing learners: The Hong Kong experience. *School Leadership & Management, 26*(2), 125–147.

Watkins, C. (2000). The leadership programme for serving headteachers: Probably the world's largest leadership development initiative. *Leadership & Organizational Development Journal, 21*(1/2), 13–20.

Weiss, C. H. (1998). *Evaluation: Methods for studying programs and policies* (2nd ed.). Upper Saddle River, NJ: Prentice Hall.

Wexley, K. N., & Baldwin, T. T. (1986). Management development. *Journal of Management, 12,* 277–294.

Wildy, H., & Wallace, J. (1995). School leadership development in Western Australia: An impact study. *Journal of school leadership, 5,* 248–271.

*Wilmore, E. L., & Thomas, C. (1998). Linking theory to practice: Authentic administrative preparation. *International Journal of Educational Reform 7*(2), 172–177.

*Wilson, T. M. (2006). *The features and practices of three mid-south principal preparation programs.* Unpublished doctoral dissertation, University of Memphis, Memphis, TN.

*Witt, D. E. (2003). *An examination of how educational administration programs prepare principals in special education issues.* Unpublished doctoral dissertation, University of Cincinnati, Cincinnati, OH.

Wong, P. (2004). The professional development of school principals: Insights from evaluating a programme in Hong Kong. *School Leadership & Management, 24*(2), 139–162.

Yorks, L., Beechler, S., & Ciporen, R. (2007). Enhancing the impact of an open-enrollment executive program through assessment. *Academy of Management Learning & Education, 6*(3), 310–320.

Young, M. D., Crow, G., Orr, M. T., Ogawa, R., & Creighton, T. (2005). An educative look at "Educating School Leaders." *UCEA Review, 46*(2) 1–5.

Young, M. D., Petersen, G. J., & Short, P. M. (2002). The complexity of substantive reform: A call for interdependence among key stakeholders. *Educational Administration Quarterly, 38*(2), 137–175.

Zheng, H. (1996, April). *School contexts, principal characteristics, and instructional leadership effectiveness: A statistical analysis.* Paper presented at the annual meeting of the American Educational Research Association, New York.

13

Comprehensive Leadership Development

A Portrait of Programs

CAROLYN KELLEY AND JAMES J. SHAW

School leaders play a critical and measurable role in shaping school effectiveness (Hallinger & Heck, 1998; Leithwood & Riehl, 2003; Leithwood & Seashore Louis, 2004; Mortimore, 1993; Scheurich, 1998; Waters, Marzano, & McNulty, 2003). In fact, principal leadership behaviors have been found to be second only to teacher effects in their impact on student learning. Although modeling school effects on student learning leaves a significant share of student learning unexplained, about one quarter of the total school effects can be attributed to principal leadership (Hallinger & Heck, 1998; Leithwood & Seashore Louis, 2004).

Yet, despite the critical role that principals play in shaping school effectiveness, insufficient attention has been paid to providing ongoing, meaningful professional growth opportunities for principals to advance student learning. Principal professional development is often fragmented and poorly targeted to the needs of principals at different career stages (Jackson & Kelley, 2002; Peterson & Kelley, 2002). Despite a growing awareness and the emergence of new models to address principal development across the career stages, models of expert practice and comprehensive leadership development that move practicing principals from "good to great" (Collins, 2001) or from mid-career, journeyman-level practice to advanced or expert-level practice are underdeveloped. The failure to address the developmental needs of principals at various career stages is exemplified by the literature on principal professional development, which is itself often difficult to extract from the broader literature on principal preparation and training (Lammert, 2004; Nicholson, Harris-John, & Schimmel, 2005).

In this chapter we examine two critical questions relevant to advancing principal professional development programs. First, what do we know about the design of professional development programs for school leaders that advance individual, organizational, and student learning outcomes? Second, what do we need to know to advance professional development designs that more effectively support principals in leading and managing schools to advance student learning? We draw from three bodies of knowledge to examine what we know: (a) research, (b) theory, and (c) practice. From the research literature, we review existing research on professional development programs for school leaders; from theory, we examine some of the theoretical foundations of professional development design; and from practice, we try to capture some of what we know but have not well documented from the significant experiential base of program providers. In the concluding section, we consider some of the questions that still need to be answered to advance a more complete knowledge base related to the quality and effectiveness of school leadership development programs.

What Do We Know?

A significant body of research has identified critical elements of school leadership that advance organizational effectiveness and student learning. In a review of research linking school leadership to student learning, Leithwood and Seashore Louis (2004) suggested that critical leadership practice is transformational and involves setting direction, developing people, and redesigning the organization. Others have identified such important dimensions of leadership as establishing trust (Bryk & Schneider, 2002), shaping school culture (Deal & Peterson, 2003), providing instructional leadership (Fullan, Hill, & Crevola, 2006; Hallinger, 2000), supporting systems of distributed leadership (Gronn, 2002; Spillane, 2006), and actively engaging the community to help address critical context variables that shape student outcomes (Rothstein, 2004; Warren, 2005).

This work is carried out in the context of a job characterized by brevity, variety, and fragmentation (Mintzberg, 1973; Peterson, 1982, 1989). More than 80% of the principal's day is spent in verbal interactions, many lasting less than a minute, with little time for reflection and with unexpected and nonroutine problems occurring with regularity (Peterson, 1982, 1989).

Thus, effective principal leadership advances student learning using the vehicle of fragmented daily work. To do so, principals need to have a significant understanding of critical issues of context; the ability to communicate with, motivate, and develop people (both internal and external stakeholders); and the ability to utilize a broad and deep knowledge and skill base to solve problems and advance school goals. Leaders advance school goals by creating a shared vision and communicating it effectively to others; involving staff in leadership processes; improving curriculum, learning, and teaching quality; raising achievement and improving students' attitudes and behaviors; engaging the community; and obtaining external support to advance student learning (Keys, Sharp, Greene, & Grayson, 2003).

The current accountability environment adds another dimension of complexity to the skill set required of school leaders, as they not only must orchestrate leadership to maintain quality, but also must move the organization continuously forward, raising levels of productivity by increasing student learning gains consistently over time in order to be viewed as effective. Clearly, research and policy suggest that the role of the principal is complex and challenging, requiring a significant and broad skill set that in turn requires training and experience to develop.

The development of this skill set depends on many factors, from recruitment and selection into the profession to the quality of leadership preparation, induction, and mentoring, and to ongoing work to develop and refine principal's leadership practice. Other chapters in this volume focus on leadership development through the initial stages of the principal's career. Yet, even assuming excellence in selection, preparation, mentoring, induction, and day-to-day experience on the job, the demands of the principalship suggest a need for professional growth opportunities beyond these basic levels. The growing interest in the creation of professional development that can advance principal leadership at journeyman or advanced levels of administrative practice has led to some growth in professional development opportunities specifically targeted at experienced, practicing principals. The next section examines the features of these programs as identified in the research literature.

Professional Development for Principals

The literature on professional development for principals highlights the critical role of principals and the importance of training to ensure that principals are effective (Nicholson et al., 2005). However, at the same time research points to the limited evidence that existing professional development for principals has the quality and focus needed to produce measurable results in student learning (Achilles & Tienken, 2005; Scherer, 2002; Schmoker, 2004).

The descriptive literature that exists documents the landscape of professional development for practicing principals, which includes a variety of programs that vary in focus and purpose, including the development of organization-specific knowledge; updating principals on rapidly changing information, knowledge, and skills; and providing an opportunity for personal renewal, reflection and redirection. Programs also vary in curricular coherence, instructional strategies, length and time structure, connection to state educational initiatives and policies, and links to district values and specific educational initiatives (Peterson & Kelley, 2002).

Pierce and Fenwick (2005) identified three different approaches to the design of education and professional development for principals: (a) the *traditional management approach*, used by many universities in principal preparation programs, in which principals learn research, management principles, and general rules of administrative behavior, typically in a classroom setting; (b) the *craft model*, in which principals are trained by experienced administrators through job shadowing, internships, and field experiences; and (c) the *reflective inquiry model*, in which learning is context embedded, values are made explicit, and principals are active participants in their own learning through self-reflection and engagement in real school settings. Other research supports the reflective inquiry model as an effective approach to principal leadership development. The Educational Research Service (as cited in Sparks & Hirsh, 2000, Professional Development for School Leaders section) suggested that effective staff development for administrators is "long-term, planned, and job-embedded; focuses on student achievement; supports reflective practice; and provides opportunities to work, discuss, and solve problems with peers."

However, the traditional management model still appears to describe a large portion of professional development available to principals (Pierce & Fenwick, 2005). A project designed to document professional development for principals in the state of Virginia identified 131 different professional development programs and activities (see e-Lead, n.d.-a), which varied in focus to include orientation workshops, information updates, state-sponsored sessions to encourage implementation and compliance with state regulations and initiatives, programs that focus on development of specific skills, and programs designed for a broad audience that includes principals. They ranged in length from 2 hours to multiple sessions over the course of a year. Most programs were evaluated through participant reactions to a postworkshop survey but did not assess or follow up on actual implementation or development of knowledge and skills at the school level. Many reflected the traditional management model of professional development.

In contrast, a comprehensive review of the research on evaluation of professional development programs identified four recurring themes that appear in schools and districts in which professional development practices and strategies have led to improved results in terms of student learning: (a) a clear focus on learning, (b) an emphasis on individual and organizational change, (c) small changes guided by a grand vision, and (d) ongoing professional development that is procedurally embedded (Bredeson, 2002; Guskey, 2000). To these criteria, e-Lead (n.d.-b) added that professional development should be embedded in the broader district context, including a shared, research-based vision of leadership that is aligned with district goals and objectives for long-term improvement, and evaluated based on efforts that seek to measure meaningful results.

Research on evaluation of professional development in education and other fields has described evaluation data as a continuum of assessment, with four stages: (a) participant reactions or satisfaction with the experience; (b) participant learning; (c) transfer, including the application of knowledge by the leader and the resulting organizational effects; and (d) results, often defined as improvements in student learning or other desired outcomes (Guskey, 2000; Kirkpatrick, 1994). Outcome-based evidence is critical to assess program effectiveness, but Kirkpatrick argued that assessment should capture all four elements to provide a full understanding of the quality and impact of professional training programs.

As recently as 2005, researchers have argued that the lack of evidence that links principal professional development to student learning or other educational outcomes is alarming (Achilles & Tienken, 2005). However, emerging research is beginning to provide a foundation for research-based understandings of the design and effectiveness of school-leadership development programs. Darling-Hammond, LaPointe, Meyerson, and Orr (2007) examined four in-service principal development programs as part of a larger study of preservice and in-service programs. The programs were identified as exemplary due to participant reports of the relationship between participation in the program and stakeholder reports of leadership effectiveness and student learning outcomes. The exemplary in-service programs shared the following design features, according to Darling-Hammond et al.: a "learning continuum" that recognized and addressed distinct learning needs from preservice to mature leaders, programs "organized around a model of leadership and grounded in practice," and "collegial learning networks ... that offer communities of practice and support for problem-solving" (pp. 8–9). They also identified leadership, institutional partnerships, and financial support as critical factors shaping program success and institutionalization.

The research by Darling-Hammond et al. (2007) provides an important foundation for further study of principal professional development program design and effectiveness. In addition, the National Institute for School Leadership (NISL) recently has commissioned a large-scale evaluation of their leadership development programs, which includes the development of research instruments to better measure leadership behaviors and link those to participation in professional development and resulting student learning (Camburn, Spillane, & Sebastian, 2006; Goldring, Spillane, Huff, Barnes, & Suppovitz, 2006; Huff, 2006; Spillane, Camburn, Lewis, & Pareja, 2006). When complete, this research promises to broaden and deepen our knowledge base about the ability of professional development programs for principals to advance student learning and organizational effectiveness. The evaluation also will provide research instruments that can be used by other programs to assess the impact of professional development on principal leadership behaviors and outcomes.

Theoretical Foundations of Professional Development Programs

While the literature described above has identified a number of features of effective programs, few connections have been made to the theoretical foundation for the design of professional development programs. An exception is a chapter by Goldring and Vye (2004) that described learning theory (Bransford, Brown & Cocking, 1999) as the foundation for the design of the Institute for School Leadership at Vanderbilt University. The program uses a multimedia, case-based approach to professional development for practicing school leaders. Further work is needed to continue to advance our understanding of learning theory and its relationship to school leadership and leadership development. Here, we identify and briefly discuss some areas of the theoretical literature that have important implications for the design of school leadership development programs.

First, we know that learning is based on experience. According to Bransford et al. (1999, p. 10), "In the most general sense, the contemporary view of learning is that people construct new knowledge and understanding based on what they already know and believe" (e.g., Piaget, 1952, 1973a, 1973b, 1977, 1978; Vygotsky, 1962, 1978). Learning is also based on understanding, organized around important concepts, and active in nature. Application of knowledge occurs after individuals develop a sufficient threshold of initial learning to support transfer. Learning with understanding is more likely to support transfer than memorization, and knowledge taught in a variety of contexts is more likely to support flexible transfer than knowledge taught in a single context (Bransford et al., 1999).

Second, learning is a social process. Social development and social learning theories (Bandura, 1977; Vygotsky, 1978) suggest that learning occurs first on a social level and later on an individual level. In short, people learn from observing others. Bandura noted, "Most human behavior is learned observationally through modeling: from observing others one forms an idea of how new behaviors are performed, and on later occasions this coded information serves as a guide for action" (p. 22).

These basic principles of learning theory, social development theory, and social learning theory have clear implications for professional development design. Further elaboration and exploration of the theoretical relationships underlying leadership development will provide a stronger theoretical foundation for program development, design, experimentation, and evaluation to identify a more fully elaborated theoretical foundation for school leadership professional development programs. By better understanding and articulating the theoretical foundation for the features of effective programs, we can enrich our understanding of why these features are important and provide better guidance for strengthening the field.

But in order to advance student learning, school leaders need to do more than learn and apply knowledge. To produce learning gains for students, the educational leader is like the conductor of a symphony orchestra, eliminating systemic barriers to success, leading, motivating, nurturing, and directing others. The leader develops leadership around him or her, utilizes the expertise of others, and develops supports and addresses barriers to enable individuals and groups to work together to advance their understanding and effectively contribute to the whole. Thus, theories of implementation, organizational change, and organizational learning (Argyris & Schön, 1996; Fullan, 2007; Honig, 2006; Wenger, McDermott, & Snyder, 2002) have clear implications for the design of professional development programs for school leaders.

A clearer understanding of the problems to be addressed and the nature of the system (its boundaries, supports, and obstacles to change) also can help us to create professional development experiences that support leaders in effectively engaging in organizational and systemic change (Honig, 2006). This level of theoretical articulation of the leadership challenge and its implications for professional development program design have yet to be explored. By better articulating systemic connections and system learning needs and opportunities, professional development might better target cohort groups of participants to advance collaborative learning among key stakeholders in reform of critical systems. This targeted approach could advance the development of systemic leadership rather than focusing on the development of the school leader as an individual and leaving it up to that leader to mobilize and develop leadership in others to advance system change. Clearly, further development of the theoretical foundations of professional development for school leaders significantly could advance purposeful program design for individual, organizational, and system learning to advance specific, targeted goals.

Experiential Knowledge: Case Examples of School-Leadership Professional Development Programs

In this section, we summarize the features of five school-leadership development programs to consider what we might learn from a direct look at what we know from experience with professional development programs. The programs were identified through a reputational sample, using recommendations by experts and programs identified in the research literature as potentially useful models for replication. The programs are all relatively new and reflect a growth in the field in the development of programs targeted to address the needs of experienced principals to advance leadership and student learning. We recognize that many other programs could have been identified for inclusion in this study; these programs were chosen to represent a variety of institutional arrangements and to be comprehensive in their effort to advance leadership for student learning.

ng progress toward goals. Once participants have completed the program, they lead professional development for others in the district using the NISL model.

including opportunities for networking among headteachers, access to research on evidence-based interventions to improve student learning, and processes to document and assess learning gains.

The professional development offered by the NCSL (n.d.-a) at different career stages is based on 10 school leadership propositions that assert that all leadership must (a) be purposeful, inclusive, and values driven; (b) embrace the context of the school; (c) promote active learning; (d) be instructionally focused; (e) be distributed throughout the school community; (f) build capacity by developing a learning community; (g) be futures oriented and strategically driven; (h) use experiential and innovative methodologies; (i) be supported by a coherent policy context; and (j) be supported by NCSL. In addition to the 10 propositions, the NCSL promotes leadership development that is driven by the needs and learning styles of the learners, is context specific but part of a national strategy to improve education, is a blend of individual private study and interaction between colleagues, and builds toward a Leadership Development Portfolio.

The view of leadership as distributed in a community of practice is reflected in the unique leadership structure of NCSL that is an amalgam of bureaucratic, university, and private-sector organizational features. The NCSL has a governing council composed of business leaders, headteachers, teacher leaders, and leaders of government agencies. The governing council works with NCSL's chief executive and a leadership team composed of individuals with varied backgrounds in higher education, kindergarten through Grade 12 education, and business. The college is staffed by faculty with backgrounds as school heads and university researchers to integrate practice and theory in the context of local schools. According to research reported by the NCSL, 86% of headteachers are aware of the purpose of the college and 80% have participated in a college activity, reflecting the broad impact of the NCSL on school leaders throughout the United Kingdom.

The recently adopted corporate goals of the NCSL reflect its strong focus on measurable results. The college is developing capacity to document measurable results and is committed to publishing in its annual report on participating schools' progress toward achieving national targets, judgments on the quality of leadership and management in schools, their ability to recruit participants for the National Professional Qualification for Headteachers, stakeholder and customer views about the quality and impact of the college's activities and its overall effectiveness, organizational efficiency, and staff turnover and satisfaction (NCSL, 2005).

The Arkansas Leadership Academy

The Arkansas Leadership Academy is a state-funded partnership of 13 universities; 9 professional associations; 15 educational cooperatives; the Arkansas Department of General Education, Department of Higher Education, and Department of Workforce Education; the Arkansas Educational Television Network; Tyson Foods; and the Walton Family Foundation, which is designed to support school leadership development in the state of Arkansas. The Arkansas Leadership Academy Principals' Institute was developed based on a review of the research literature and model programs and professional associations, including the Harvard Principals' Center, the National Association of Elementary School Principals, the American Association of School Administrators, the National Association of Secondary School Principals, the National Staff Development Council, and others including leadership training programs for business as well as education.

The Master Principal Institute includes three one-year phases with three to four residential sessions each. The residential work is directly connected to continuous job-embedded learning experiences, research, reflective practice, inquiry, and study. There is ongoing electronic communication with other principals, coaches, and Arkansas Leadership Academy staff through electronic mailing lists, phone conferences, Web conferences, and distance-learning opportunities.

The curriculum for the program is continuously assessed for alignment to benchmark standards, practice, and research results in the field of leadership development. The program is focused on developing and documenting leadership that advances systemic reform to support student learning. Participants are expected to both utilize and affect broad policy, social, and economic systems in the support and advancement of student and organizational learning.

The institute focuses on five purposive leadership processes: (a) vision, (b) leading and managing change, (c) building and maintaining accountability systems, (d) deep knowledge about teaching and learning, and (e) building and maintaining relationships. While all three phases of the Master Principal Institute focus on individual, group, and organizational change in the five performance areas, the first phase of the Master Principal Institute (open to practicing principals with 3 years of experience and their superintendent's recommendation) focuses on individual change: principal knowledge, skills, and experiences for each of the five performance areas. The second phase focuses on the principal extending the knowledge, skills, and experiences of all adults within the school in the five performance areas. The third phase focuses on the principal being successful at effecting system-level change. Participants in the Master Principal Institute develop a portfolio of work that documents their progress in advancing student and organizational learning. The portfolios are assessed using rubrics developed by the institute that assess performance in the five leadership dimensions.

The application for Phase II involves the submission of a portfolio that includes narrative descriptions of success in the five performance areas and contextual data. Phase III applicants follow a portfolio process that is more rigorous than that for Phase II in that the application of the knowledge and skills of the five performance areas is applied at the level of system change, which may be beyond the principal's school and district.

Applicants respond to portfolio prompts that ask for evidence that addresses the five performance areas through narratives that describe the story of their school using Coburn's (2003) lenses of depth, breadth, sustainability, and shift in reform responsibility. Evidence of performance in these areas must indicate a higher level of performance above that of the previous portfolio application for Phase II. Phase III applicants also must provide a list of references who are interviewed about the applicant's performance in the five areas of the program. Additional interviews other than those names supplied by the candidate are also conducted. Phase III applicants are expected to be involved in various leadership roles at least at the district and regional levels. Evidence of improvement in student achievement must be apparent. A principal designated as a Master Principal by the Arkansas Leadership Academy is eligible to receive $5,000 annual bonuses for 5 years and an additional $25,000 annually for 5 years for serving in a high-need school (Elliott & Morledge, 2005).

The Wisconsin Urban Schools Leadership Project

The Wisconsin Urban Schools Leadership Project is a partnership of the Department of Public Instruction, the Governor's Office, two public and one private university, five urban school districts, the Milwaukee Partnership Academy, and the Association of Wisconsin School Administrators. The program recruits 30 exceptionally strong principals in cohorts based on a record of improved student learning and recommendations from their school district to participate in a 2-year leadership development program. Groups of 10 principals work with a university partner around a curriculum designed to advance mastery as defined by the research literature, the master principals, the state standards, and the state's master administrator licensure assessment process. The partnership is unique in that in addition to seeking the master license, these principals are providing feedback to the state in the development and refinement of the master licensure assessment process.

Principals create and utilize learning communities within their schools, districts, and cohort groups. Leadership is defined as strategic (data driven), instructional, and ethical (with a focus on equity in student learning). Principals evaluate data and document school-based leadership initiatives that produce measurable improvement in student or organizational outcomes. Site visits, which take the form of a school audit, are used to assess leadership in context. Critical areas of leadership assessed by the portfolio process include advancing equity in student learning, building professional learning communities, leading and managing the organization, and building and engaging community. The Wisconsin Urban Schools Leadership Project builds on prior work on administrative mastery at the University of Wisconsin-Madison and was supported by the Wallace Foundation and the partnering organizations.

The CASL

The CASL is a district-level program delivered in cooperation with the Chicago Principals and Administrators Association, designed to support Chicago Public Schools site-based management reforms and to help principals become stronger instructional leaders. Three cohort programs are offered by the Chicago Leadership Academies for Supporting Success for (a) aspiring principals (Leadership Academy and Urban Network for Chicago), (b) 1st-year principals (Leadership Initiative for Transformation), and (c) practicing principals (CASL). The CASL 1-year program is constructivist in nature and involves a mixture of case study, simulations, collaborative learning, and role playing. It does not subscribe to a particular definition of leadership but aspires to develop facilitative leaders who are strong and open to change. The program is embedded in the school context and places a heavy emphasis on professional development and creating professional learning communities, both within the cohort of principals going through the program as well as within the Chicago Public Schools campuses.

The curriculum is linked to the Interstate School Leaders Licensure Consortium (1996) standards and the Chicago Public Schools leadership standards. The program provides 12 days of curricular focus in the areas of leadership, data-driven instruction, and principals as change agents. Seminar participants develop and present a portfolio to the CASL and to their own school stakeholders that illustrates the impact that the program has had on their leadership.

Analysis

The research literature provides a consistent picture across studies of the features of professional development programs that are thought (and in a few cases, shown) to be related to organizational change and improved achievement outcomes for students. Many of these features are consistent with the broader literature on professional development for teachers (see e.g., Desimone, Porter, Birman, Garet, & Yoon, 2002; Desimone, Porter, Garet, Yoon, & Birman, 2002; Garet, Porter, Desimone, Birman, & Yoon, 2001). These five features suggest that comprehensive school-leadership development programs should do the following:

1. Recognize that principal skills fall on a continuum from novice to mastery. They target professional learning with an understanding of how school leaders learn and how they develop skills and dispositions at various stages of their careers (Darling-Hammond et al., 2007; Smylie & Bennett, 2005).
2. Provide coherence around a model of leadership that is context-embedded. In other words, the model of leadership is understood and shared by school and district stakeholders and is consistent with district culture and policies related to leadership. The model should recognize important contextual issues that shape leadership behaviors (Darling-Hammond et al., 2007; Desimone, Porter, Birman et al., 2002; Smylie & Bennett, 2005).

3. Carry out a change process based on collegial problem solving (Darling-Hammond et al., 2007; Sparks & Hirsh, 2000) in which leaders engage with teachers and other stakeholders to identify and address challenges (Sparks & Hirsh, 2000).

4. School leadership programs should be long term and job embedded (Guskey, 2000; Pierce & Fenwick, 2005; Sparks & Hirsh, 2000).

5. Programs should be evidence based, meaning that the programs themselves are evaluated and modified based on a range of feedback factors, including participant satisfaction, participant learning, the application of knowledge, and organizational and student learning outcomes (Guskey, 2005; Kirkpatrick, 1994).

Table 13.1 applies these criteria to the sample of programs, describing the ways in which the programs address these five critical features of professional development programs designed for comprehensive school leadership development. As Table 13.1 shows, each of the five programs recognizes a continuum of leadership experience, but the definitions vary greatly across programs. These are variously defined by roles, years of experience, recommendations, review of a portfolio of work, and interviews with others who have worked with the individual. The NISL accepts principals from novice to experienced but requires that principal participants be willing to serve as trainers to other principals in the district, which may influence which principals are selected for participation.

Each program also defines the model of leadership underlying the program and provides various approaches to ensure coherence with organizational context, policy and culture. Leadership in the programs is variously defined as strategic, instructional, distributed, ethical, and transformational, with data-based decision making, accountability, and equity as important areas of focus. Programs provide various approaches to creating coherence, including focusing the professional development on cohorts of leaders from the district (NISL); representation of key stakeholders on coordinating or governing teams for the programs (Wisconsin and Arkansas); creating structural connections to policy makers (NCSL, Arkansas, Chicago Public Schools); or connecting content to national, state, or district standards (NCSL, Arkansas, Wisconsin, Chicago Public Schools).

The programs develop collegial problem solving through cohort design that involves key district decision makers (NISL); curriculum content and application (all programs); and the development of a portfolio that describes and documents work (Arkansas and Wisconsin), in one case with a site-visit audit of the school (Wisconsin). The Arkansas Leadership Academy defined multiple communities of focus for collegial problem solving by focusing on the development of the individual leader, then the school, and then on broader system change (which could include system changes at the state, district, community, or professional levels).

One issue that was not fully addressed in our case analysis is the extent to which the partnerships created through these collegial problem-solving processes reflected the diversity of the target schools and communities. Our sense is that more needs to be done to advance representation of diverse ideas and opinions to ensure that leaders are sensitive to and adept at addressing problems in increasingly diverse and challenging school and community contexts.

The programs ranged in length from 12 to 35 days over a 1- to 3-year period. All were job embedded in that the focus of the work was on accessing data from the leader's school or district, analyzing the data, and working through a collaborative change process to address identified needs.

The evidence base for the programs includes all four levels of evaluation data: (a) participant satisfaction, (b) learning, (c) application, and (d) outcomes. All of the programs collect satisfaction surveys of participants and do some work to assess participant learning. Two of the programs (NISL and NCSL) are gearing up for major evaluations of participant learning and program effectiveness. In the Arkansas, Wisconsin, and Chicago programs, participants develop a portfolio of their

Table 13.1 Features of Sample Programs

National Institute for School Leadership (NISL)	National College for School Leadership (NCSL)	Arkansas Leadership Academy	Wisconsin Urban Schools Leadership Project	Chicago Academy of School Leadership (CASL)
Continuum				
Principals must have 1–5 years of experience & be willing to train others; novice to expert principals are accepted.	Targets five levels of leadership: emergent, established, entry to headship, advanced, & consultant leadership	Master Principal Institute open to principals with 3+ years of experience. Principals must master prior phase to continue to next phase.	Principals must have 3 years of experience & be identified by their district & by student learning outcomes as strong school leaders with a record of school improvement.	Targeted programs for aspiring, novice, & experienced principals
Coherence				
Strategic, instructional, & ethical leadership with strong emphasis on data & equity. Contextual coherence is created by involving district team as the focal learning community.	Ten propositions define leadership as strategic, instructional, distributed, & ethical. Professional development is context specific but part of a national strategy to improve schools.	Five purposive leadership processes: vision, leading & managing change, building & maintaining accountability systems, knowledge about teaching & learning, & building & maintaining relationships. Context specific to Arkansas	Consistent with state standards; designed by participants to reflect state, urban, district, school, & community contexts. Leadership defined as instructional, strategic, and ethical leadership.	Leadership is strategic and transformational. Consistent with Chicago Public Schools & state standards; focused on supporting implementation of district school improvement initiatives
Collegial problem solving				
Cohort includes superintendent, principal, central office staff, university rep, & often business community members from a single district.	Strong emphasis on distributed leadership; programmatic focus on school leadership development for teachers & headteachers	Strong emphasis on distributed leadership, organizational & system change that requires collaboration with school & other stakeholders; participants carry out program-related school improvement activities with others at their schools	Cohorts of 30 principals from five districts work with three university partners to identify leadership challenges & opportunities and to document mastery through a portfolio process. Principals work with their school communities to advance & document school effectiveness.	Cohorts of principals from across the district work together through simulations & case studies; principals work with stakeholders in their own schools to apply learning
Long term and job embedded				
Fourteen units lasting 35 days completed over 13–24 months. Standard curriculum applied to specific district context & problems.	Job-embedded, long-term professional development opportunities for networking among headteachers	Master-level program is three 3-year units with three to four residential sessions each. The work is long term & job embedded.	Sixteen days of content over a 2-year period; university faculty & cohort principals conduct site visits to identify challenges, establish leadership goals, & assess program outcomes.	Twelve days of content spread over the course of a year; principals use knowledge base to address challenges in their own schools

(continued)

Table 13.1 Continued

National Institute for School Leadership (NISL)	National College for School Leadership (NCSL)	Arkansas Leadership Academy	Wisconsin Urban Schools Leadership Project	Chicago Academy of School Leadership (CASL)
Evidence based				
NISL has commissioned a large-scale evaluation to assess impact on leadership & learning outcomes.	NCSL recently adopted corporate goals to build capacity to assess & annually publish measurable results, including operational efficiency, participant & stakeholder satisfaction, leadership, management, & learning outcomes.	ALC is research based & continuously benchmarked to effective practices in other programs. Principal portfolios document improvements in student learning & broader system outcomes (including district & state policies & programs)	Research based & uses feedback from principals, university faculty, & districts as well as portfolios to assess program effectiveness & provide feedback to the state on the development & refinement of its master administrator licensure assessment process.	Program uses satisfaction surveys; portfolios provide data to program & school stakeholders on principal learning, organizational & student outcomes.
Program genesis				
Program grew out of a research study commissioned by National Center on Education and the Economy to reflect a broad research base drawing from professional standards & leadership development across a variety of fields.	Nationally funded effort to advance leadership quality in England; strong research base	Program is governed by leaders from public and private sectors; state funded; state incentives attached to mastery; strong research base	Foundation-, state-, & university-funded collaborative venture of governor, Department of Public Instruction, two public & one private universities, five urban school districts & professional association; linked to state master-level principal license	Program originated from union-management collaborative venture to improve the quality of school leadership in Chicago Public Schools; standards-based

work, which provides evidence of participant learning, application, and outcomes. The programs all clearly have a commitment to linking participation to student learning outcomes and assess these impacts in various ways.

The range of approaches that these programs take to the five features of professional development programs described above provides some interesting natural variation. Such varying approaches could be examined to identify features of programs that are consistent with the theoretical foundations of professional development design and that produce the most significant and cost-effective outcomes. The opportunities for research and exploration are significant and could greatly inform the development and direction for future programming.

Conclusions: What Do We Need to Know?

This review of the research, theory, and practice of school-leadership professional development programs provides a foundational knowledge base from which to build and raises questions that need to be addressed through future research. Although not a complete list, below we identify three questions that provide opportunities for further research. To these questions, we would add the importance of further elaboration and articulation of the theoretical foundations of school-leader professional development design.

1. The body of knowledge related to school leadership in both the research literature and the sample programs is immense. Despite the relatively long-term investment of the sample programs in professional development (12–35 days), the bodies of knowledge identified by these programs, and by the research literature, as critical knowledge for school leaders are inconsistent in focus and overwhelming in scope. For example, among a list of five purposive processes, the Arkansas Leadership Academy suggests that principals need to possess "deep knowledge about teaching and learning." Deep knowledge of teaching and learning could include expertise in evaluation, teaching, curriculum design, differentiated instruction, content-based pedagogy, learning needs of English language learners, and so on. Any one of these areas could be the focus of a 12-day program, let alone the many other goals for the development of knowledge, skills, and dispositions identified by the program.

   We derive one of two conclusions from this. One possibility is that the body of required knowledge for master-level school leaders is not as large as it would appear from these ambitious descriptions, and greater clarity is needed to narrow the body of knowledge to the specific aspects of teaching, learning, and leadership that school leaders really need to know. Perhaps the knowledge base is context specific, and leadership professional development programs need to be able to better target their focus to critical skill subsets (as some do). Alternatively, if leaders need to deeply master knowledge in a variety of complex domains, it may be necessary to identify ways to supplement targeted professional development programs with ongoing, embedded structures and expectations to support career development of the large and complex knowledge and skill sets required of school leaders. This could be done through human resource management and incentive structures, such as knowledge and skills-based pay that supports the development of such skills, or through the advancement of professional norms that support knowledge and skill development throughout the leadership career.

2. The unit of analysis for professional development needs to be more carefully considered. For most professional development programs, the unit of analysis is the participant. However, for school leaders working to enhance student learning outcomes, the unit of analysis may be the communities of practice in the school, a leadership team across the district, or groups of community activists working with the school to advance community support for student health care and safety. In the NISL example, the cohort group included members of a district-level leadership team of district administrators, principals, university, and sometimes community members. The other programs all created cohorts of principals who learned together and from each other and then were asked to apply that knowledge to their own school settings. The district-level teams provide opportunities to create coherence within the district setting. The principal cohort model provides opportunities for the principals to build on the broader experience base of the cohort group and for the development of a supportive community of practice among principals. Yet, both of these approaches leave it to the principals to apply knowledge from this experience to their own school settings. Further research is needed to better understand the trade-offs and effectiveness of the use of different professional development targets, to understand what the implications are of considering the unit of analysis or focus for professional development to be groups of principals, school leadership teams, district leadership teams, community partnerships, or other target groups.

3. Further research is also needed to inform assessment of school-leadership professional development. Critical context factors, underlying values that shape goals for school improvement, and factors within and outside the span of control of the participants (leadership mobility, boundary changes, policy goals, etc.) play important roles in shaping the leadership challenge. These factors are central to the nature of the leadership challenge and reflect the focus

of the work of the school leader and leadership teams. Further research is needed to design assessment systems that can capture the interrelated web of influence that leadership and context have in shaping who is at the table in leadership decisions (with implications for who should be involved with what role in the professional development design), the baseline conditions of the school, the nature and focus of educational goals, what factors emerge as organizational supports and constraints, the strength of communities within and around the school, and their willingness to support change efforts.

In short, a deeper knowledge base is needed to better understand the relationships among district, school, and community context; program design; and student outcomes. Ultimately, we need to know this: How does school-leader professional development impact teaching and learning?

References

Achilles, C. M., & Tienken, C. (2005). Professional development and educational improvement. In L. W. Hughes (Ed.), *Current issues in school leadership* (pp. 303–320). Mahwah, NJ: Erlbaum.

Argyris, C., & Schön, D. (1996). *Organizational learning II: Theory, method and practice.* Reading, MA: Addison Wesley.

Bandura, A. (1977). *Social learning theory.* Englewood Cliffs, NJ: Prentice Hall.

Bransford, J. D., Brown, A. L., & Cocking, R. R. (Eds.). (1999). *How people learn: Brain, mind, experience, and school.* Washington, DC: National Academy Press.

Bredeson, P. (2002). *Designs for learning: A new architecture for professional development in schools.* Thousand Oaks, CA: Corwin Press.

Bryk, A. S., & Schneider, B. (2002). *Trust in schools: A core resource for improvement.* New York: Russell Sage Foundation.

Camburn, E., Spillane, J., & Sebastian, J. (2006, April). *Measuring principal practice: Results from two promising measurement strategies.* Paper presented at the annual meeting of the American Educational Research Association Conference, San Francisco.

Coburn, C. (2003). Rethinking scale: Moving beyond numbers to deep and lasting change. *Educational Researcher, 32*(6), 3–12.

Collins, J. (2001). *Good to great: Why some companies make the leap … and others don't.* New York: HarperCollins.

Darling-Hammond, L., LaPointe, M., Meyerson, D., & Orr, M. (2007). *Preparing school leaders for a changing world: Executive summary.* Stanford, CA: Stanford University, Stanford Educational Leadership Institute.

Deal, T. E., & Peterson, K. D. (2003). *Shaping school culture: The heart of leadership.* San Francisco: Jossey-Bass.

Desimone, L., Porter, A. C., Birman, B. F., Garet, M. S., & Yoon, K. S. (2002). How do district management and implementation strategies relate to the quality of the professional development that districts provide to teachers? *Teachers College Record, 104*(7), 1265–1312.

Desimone, L. M., Porter, A. C., Garet, M. S., Yoon, K. S., & Birman, B. F. (2002). Effects of professional development on teachers' instruction: Results from a three-year longitudinal study. *Educational Evaluation and Policy Analysis, 24*(2), 81–112.

e-Lead. (n.d.a). *Principles of professional development.* Retrieved June 1, 2008, from http://www.e-lead.org/principles/

e-Lead. (n.d.b). *Va-Lead: Complete list of programs.* Available from http://e-lead.org/states/va/programs.htm

Elliott, B. C., & Morledge, K. L. (2005, April). *Arkansas Leadership Academy Master Principal Program.* Paper presented at the annual meeting of the American Educational Research Association, Montreal, Quebec, Canada.

Fullan, M. (2007). *The new meaning of educational change* (4th ed.). New York: Teachers College Press.

Fullan, M., Hill, P., & Crevola, C. (2006). *Breakthrough.* Thousand Oaks, CA: Corwin Press.

Garet, M. S., Porter, A. C., Desimone, L., Birman, B. F., & Yoon, K. S. (2001). What makes professional development effective? Results from a national sample of teachers. *American Educational Research Journal, 38*(4), 915–945.

Goldring, E., Spillane, J., Huff, J., Barnes, C., & Suppovitz, J. (2006, April). *Measuring the instructional leadership competence of school principals.* Paper presented at the annual meeting of the American Educational Research Association, San Francisco.

Goldring, E. B., & Vye, N. (2004). We must model how we teach: Learning to lead with compelling models of professional development. In W. Hoy & C. Miskel (Eds.), *Educational administration, policy and reform* (pp. 189–218). Greenwich, CT: IAP.

Gronn, P. (2002). Distributed leadership. In K. Leithwood & P. Hallinger (Eds.), *Second international handbook of educational leadership and administration* (pp. 653–696). Dordrecht, The Netherlands: Kluwer.

Guskey, T. (2000). *Evaluating professional development.* Thousand Oaks, CA: Corwin Press.

Hallinger, P. (2000, April). *A review of two decades of research on the principalship using the "Principal Instructional Management Rating Scale."* Paper presented at the annual meeting of the American Educational Research Association, Seattle, WA.

Hallinger, P., & Heck, R. (1998). Exploring the principal's contribution to school effectiveness: 1980–1995. *School effectiveness and school improvement, 9*(2), 157–191.

Honig, M. (2006). *New directions in education policy implementation: Confronting complexity.* Albany, NY: SUNY Press.

Huff, J. (2006, April). *Measuring a leader's practice: Past efforts and present opportunities to capture what educational leaders do.* Paper presented at the annual meeting of the American Educational Research Association, San Francisco.

Interstate School Leaders Licensure Consortium. (1996). *Standards for school leaders.* Washington, DC: Council of Chief State School Officers. Retrieved March 31, 2005, from http://www.ccsso.org/content/pdfs/isllcstd.pdf

Jackson, B. L., & Kelley, C. (2002). Exceptional and innovative programs in educational leadership. *Educational Administration Quarterly, 38*(2), 192–212.

Keys, W., Sharp, C., Greene, K., & Grayson, H. (2003). *Successful leadership of schools in urban and challenging contexts: A review of the literature.* Nottingham, England: National College for School Leadership.

Kirkpatrick, D. (1994). *Evaluating training programs: The four levels.* San Francisco: Berrett-Koehler.

Lammert, J. (2004). *Review of the research: Key components of effective principal training.* Charleston, WV: Appalachia Educational Laboratory.

Leithwood, K. A., & Riehl, C. (2003). *What we know about successful school leadership.* New Brunswick, NJ: Center for Educational Policy Analysis. Retrieved January 25, 2007, from http://www.cepa.gse.rutgers.edu/whatweknow.pdf

Leithwood, K., & Seashore Louis, K. (2004). *How leadership influences student learning.* New York: Wallace Foundation.

Levine, A. (2005). *Educating school leaders.* Washington, DC: The Education Schools Project. Retrieved March 31, 2005, from http://www.edschools.org/pdf/Embargoed_Report_050315.pdf

Mintzberg, H. (1973). *The nature of managerial work.* New York: Harper & Row.

Mortimore, P. (1993). School effectiveness and the management of effective learning and teaching. *School Effectiveness and School Improvement, 4*(4), 290–310.

National College of School Leadership. (n.d.a). Home page. Retrieved June 1, 2008, from http://www.ncsl.org.uk

National College of School Leadership. (n.d.b). *LDF implications.* Retrieved June 1, 2008, from http://www.ncsl.org.uk/publications/ldf/publications-ldf-implications.cfm

National College of School Leadership. (2005). *Corporate plan, 2005–08.* Retrieved February 4, 2007, from http://www.ncsl.org.uk/media/9E1/E2/543-CorpPlan-AW1.pdf

Nicholson, B., Harris-John, M., & Schimmel, C.J. (2005). *Professional development for principals in the accountability era.* Charleston, WV: Appalachia Educational Laboratory.

Peterson, K. D. (1982). Making sense of principals' work. *Australian Administrator, 3*(3), 1–4.

Peterson, K. D. (1989). *Secondary principals and instructional leadership: Complexities in a diverse role.* Madison: University of Wisconsin, National Center on Effective Secondary Schools.

Peterson, K. D., & Kelley, C. (2002). Principal in-service programs: A portrait of diversity and promise. In M. S. Tucker & J. B. Codding (Eds.), *The principal challenge: Leading and managing schools in an era of accountability* (pp. 313–346). San Francisco: Jossey-Bass.

Piaget, J. (1952). *The origins of intelligence in children.* New York: International Universities Press.

Piaget, J. (1973a). *The child and reality: Problems of genetic psychology.* New York: Grossman.

Piaget, J. (1973b). *The language and thought of the child.* London: Routledge and Kegan Paul.

Piaget, J. (1977). *The grasp of consciousness.* London: Routledge and Kegan Paul.

Piaget, J. (1978). *Success and understanding.* Cambridge, MA: Harvard University Press.

Pierce, M. C., & Fenwick, L. (2005, Winter). Professional development of principals. *Professional Development From the Inside Out: District and School-Level Strategies. The Newsletter of the Comprehensive Center–Region VI, 8*(1), 32–33.

Rothstein, R. (2004). *Class and schools: Using social, economic, and educational reform to close the Black-White achievement gap.* Washington, DC: Economic Policy Institute.

Scherer, M. (2002). Perspectives: Job One. *Educational Leadership, 59*(6), 5.

Scheurich, J. J. (1998). Highly successful and loving, public elementary schools populated mainly by low-SES children of color: Core beliefs and cultural characteristics. *Urban Education, 33*(4), 451–491.

Schmoker, M. (2004). Tipping point: From feckless reform to substantive instructional improvement. *Phi Delta Kappan, 85*(6), 424–432.

Smylie, M. A., & Bennett, A., with Konkol, P., & Fendt, C. R. (2005). What do we know about developing school leaders? A look at existing research and next steps for new study. In W. A. Firestone & C. Riehl (Eds.), *A new agenda for research in educational leadership* (pp. 138–155). New York: Teachers College Press.

Sparks, D., & Hirsh, S. (2000). *Learning to lead, leading to learn: Improving school quality through principal professional development.* Oxford, OH: National Staff Development Council. Retrieved June 1, 2008, from http://www.nsdc.org/library/leaders/leader_report.cfm

Spillane, J. (2006). *Distributed leadership.* San Francisco: Jossey-Bass.

Spillane, J., Camburn, E., Lewis, G., & Pareja, A. (2006, April). *Taking a distributed perspective in studying school leadership and management: Epistemological and methodological trade-offs.* Paper presented at the annual meeting of the American Educational Research Association, San Francisco.

Tucker, M. S., & Codding, J. B. (2002). *The principal challenge: Leading and managing schools in an era of accountability.* San Francisco: Jossey-Bass.

Vygotsky, L. S. (1962). *Thought and language.* Cambridge, MA: MIT Press.

Vygotsky, L. S. (1978). *Mind in society: The development of the higher psychological processes.* Cambridge, MA: The Harvard University Press.

Warren, M. R. (2005). Communities and schools: A new view of urban education reform. *Harvard Education Review, 75*(2), 133–173.

Waters, J. T., Marzano, R. J., & McNulty, B. A. (2003). *Balanced leadership: What 30 years of research tells us about the effect of leadership on student achievement.* Aurora, CO: Mid-continent Research for Education and Learning.

Wenger, E., McDermott, W. M., & Snyder, W. M. (2002). *Cultivating communities of practice.* Boston: Harvard University Press.

14

Establishing Meaningful Leadership Mentoring in School Settings

Transcending Simplistic Rhetoric, Self-Congratulation, and Claims of Panacea

STEVEN JAY GROSS

Overview

In light of the complexity and growing demands that define school leadership in this era, it is natural for scholars and practitioners to worry about those aspiring to the principalship, especially during their early years in office. One response to this concern is a rise in the number and kind of leadership mentoring programs available for in-service school administrators. While the concept of matching a novice school leader with a wise veteran guide seems logical enough, the field of leadership mentoring for educators is complex, dynamic, and typified by contradictions. Some programs are of relatively short duration, lasting only a few months, whereas others continue for 3 years. Some designs are modeled on corporate mentoring plans, whereas others reject business values in favor of ideals found in school settings. Some planners desire future educational leaders to respond mainly to state accountability regimes, whereas others seek what they call democratic ethical leadership. Even the meaning of mentoring itself is open to debate. The paucity of studies focused on program effectiveness only adds to our uncertainty and underscores the need for greater consideration of the concept of leadership mentoring for educators.

Since we are working on a multifaceted problem, several interrelated questions arise. This chapter was written to establish a foundation for future program planning by looking into the following four issues, or research questions:

1. What difficulties do today's principals face that make mentoring a relevant idea?
2. What models exist for leadership mentoring programs?
3. What qualities should mentoring programs embody?
4. What future research priorities should be taken in the field?

Question 1: What Difficulties Do Today's Principals Face That Make Mentoring a Relevant Idea?

Being a principal has never been easy. However, there are reasons to believe that additional help will be needed to secure the next generation of principals.

Losing a Generation of School Leaders Without Sufficient Replacements

One thing that becomes clear to those studying the issue of the principalship is that we are in the midst of a generational turnover in building leadership. Looking at educational administrators as a group, the U.S. Department of Labor's Bureau of Labor (2005) statistics show that in 2002 there were 427,000 jobs held in the field. While this included all educational administrators, in public and private practice and at all levels, a large proportion worked in the public K–12 school system, according to the U.S. Department of Labor. Currently, it is estimated that there are 93,200 school principals in the United States (Blackman & Fenwick, as cited in Crocker & Harris, 2002). This large group of school leaders is in the midst of a changing of the guard. Since 1993, we have known that 55% of school principals planned to retire within a decade (National Association of Elementary School Principals [NAESP], National Association of Secondary School Principals, & Educational Research Service, 1998). Simply looking at the average age of sitting principals tells a good deal of the story. In 1993 the average age of principals was 47.7, and 37% of principals were already over age 50 (NAESP et al., 1998). The aging of principals is a clear national pattern. In New York City, for example, approximately 1,100 schools face the retirements of 260 principals, and as of 2002, half of the schools were run by people with fewer than 3 years of experience as principals (Archer, 2002).

No level of the K–12 system is free from the threat of principal shortage, according to the studies. Only 9% of elementary schools across the United States had a surplus of qualified principal candidates, for instance, while 47% had a shortage (NAESP et al., 1998). In the case of middle schools and high schools, the situation is worse. In both of these, only 6% responded that they had a surplus of candidates, and 55% found themselves facing a shortage (NAESP et al., 1998). Thomas F. Koerner, the National Association of Secondary School Principals executive director in 1998, stated, "Schools are going without principals, retired principals are being called back to full time work and districts have to go to great lengths to recruit qualified candidates" (as cited in Hopkins, 1998).

While principal preparation programs produce certified graduates, many of these people chose not to seek administrative positions (NAESP et al., 1998). This leads us to the question: Why are people electing not to become principals just when we need a new generation of building leaders?

Pressures Faced by Today's Principals

The job of principal has never been an easy one (Aiken, 2002). However, recent research has cast new light on traditional job pressures while revealing new conflicts in the role.

Lashway (2003) described five specific causes of stress in new leaders that bear watching:

1. Complexity: The job of principal is complex. Simply put, the principal is asked to work rapidly on issues ranging from bus schedules to safety to performance on academics. The obvious problem of juggling multiple issues that vary in priority requires a blend of wisdom and maturity. New people are unlikely to possess these qualities at the start of their careers in administration.

2. Isolation: When a new teacher comes into the profession, she or he enters into a building filled with experienced colleagues. The confusion of the first several years is normal, and schools do lose too many promising new educators during that period. However, imagine the situation facing new principals where they have no colleagues in the building with similar responsibilities. Even in the district context, there may not be a collegial relationship among the principals. This means that the principal's isolation is hard-wired into the job description in most districts.

3. Lonely job: Coming from the ranks of teachers, it might be natural to suppose that one will maintain a warm collegial relationship with faculty once becoming a principal. This is often not the case. Becoming an administrator often means an immediate switch from being one of "us" to becoming one of "them." This, logically enough, means a lonely life to many school principals. The very same personality traits that made a person attractive during the hiring process, such as superb human relation skills, can make a people person susceptible to feeling lonely. As one writer put it, "Voices stop when you walk into the teachers' lounge" (Curtis, as cited in Lashway, 2003).

4. Assimilation: There are no generic schools. Each school has its own context. The community each school serves has a history, traditions, and an evolving set of accomplishments and challenges. Each school system has its own evolution of norms and forces propelling it. For the new principal, the question is this: How are things done and how are they done here (Crow & Matthews, 1998)? Without clear guidance, how is a new leader to know? With the press of this complex job, when is there time for a person to become familiar with the rich history and mores of the school unaided?

5. Role conflict: The job of the principal also has a series of potentially conflicting demands. Are school goals aligned with district goals? If not, how does a building principal support the school without getting into trouble with the district? Does the principal find that the school's reform agenda is reasonable and in keeping with his or her philosophy? Looking at the national picture, can the principal be effective in dealing with such issues as Adequate Yearly Progress on the one hand and support hands-on instruction or multidisciplinary investigation on the other? Is the principal merely an agent from the district or state or a professional with deeply held beliefs based upon ethical reasoning (Gross & Shapiro, 2004)?

Of course, there is much more to the job of principal than these five areas of stress. Still, these issues alone clarify that, for many, being the person on the other side of the principal's desk is not an easy career move. In short, this is not an attractive job to people who are otherwise qualified. Added to this, other writers have pointed out that there is too much reliance on on-the-job training for new principals (Brown, Anfara, Hartman, Mahar, & Mills, 2001).

New Leadership Demographics

Another important trend is the rise in the number of women and heretofore underrepresented minority group members in the principalship. In 1988, only 2% of principals were women. By 2000, however, 35% of all principals were women (Blackman & Fenwick, as cited in Malone, 2001). At that time, 13% of principals were members of minority groups. Younger women and minority group members, who were underrepresented in building and district leadership roles so recently, cannot depend upon mentors who share their backgrounds and who know from life experiences their struggles. Yet, the good news that leadership positions are more available to women and minority group members helps to point out a striking need for quality and sensitive mentoring that incorporates diversity as a crucial value.

Question 2: What Models Exist for Leadership Mentoring Programs?

Clearly, districts face a serious problem of securing the services of qualified leaders now and in the near future. With a generational turnover increasing the need to find principals on the one hand and a job that comes across as increasingly unattractive on the other hand, it is doubly important to make sure that school systems do everything possible to keep promising new leaders. One strategy that makes sense for planners is mentoring for new school principals. Mentoring is an ancient concept whose name dates back to Homer's *Odyssey*. Boon (1998) reminded us that Mentor was entrusted with watching over King Odysseus's son Telemachus while Odysseus was at war. Currently a variety of organizations around the world use mentoring as a way of helping junior-level employees advance. In educational administration, the practice of mentoring is well known among aspiring principals. Daresh and Playko (1993) described satisfaction that mentors experience in their new roles as teachers of a new generation as well as the need to study how these relationships are formed and maintained.

While mentoring may be an idea with a long history found in and outside of educational settings, it is important to learn from concrete examples. The purpose of the following section is not to attempt an exhaustive review of existing mentoring programs but to provide some examples that may be helpful to planners who want to learn about options. Below, we examine specific mentoring programs to consider part of the range of possible approaches to this process.

A District-Based Program

Districts are a major site for mentoring programs and may be either independently organized or designed in cooperation with other institutions such as state agencies or universities. Criticism of the former (Browne-Ferrigno & Muth, 2004) stems from the potential for state programs to fail to attend to the needs of new leaders. Browne-Ferrigno and Muth advocated a strong university–district partnership to assure a reasonable connection between theory and practice, although other studies (Kiltz, Danzig, & Szecsy, 2004) described the challenges in proving the utility of theory to busy district practitioners and the meaning of practice to theory-based university scholars. Still, Browne-Ferrigno and Muth found it possible to establish the benefits of this combination to both groups. Studies of mentoring programs in the United States (Williams, Matthews, & Baugh, 2004) and the United Kingdom (Bush & Glover, 2005) also supported the integration of experiential learning with theoretical perspectives.

Beginning Principals' Mentoring Program

One program comes from Prince George's County, Maryland, which is the19th largest U.S. school district, including 193 schools and 135,000 students (Bundy & McKay, 2004). The Beginning Principals' Mentoring Program was organized in 1998 with the cooperation of the University of Maryland in response to a state and county superintendent request for help. The program included 113 new principals in five cohorts. The size of cohort ranged from 15–27 as of 2004 and lasted 18 months. The program included five content areas for mentors and protégés: (a) instructional leadership (knowledge of research on teaching methodology, curriculum, instructional strategies and assessment), (b) supervision and evaluation of teachers, (c) data analysis, (d) shared decision making (with teachers and parents, planning by the whole group), and (e) school reform and continuous improvement.

A Regional Mentoring Plan

Some mentoring programs grow out of individual contacts and needs. In New York State, such a support network developed between three administrators, according to Riede (2003). While they were superintendents, their collegial support could work just as easily for building principals, in the same district or between districts. In this case, the journaling triad, as they called themselves, agreed to write four times each week. In this way, a flow of communication was developed as well as an increasing level of understanding. As the e-mail dialogue deepened, it became clear that this small network of support was helpful in the daily tasks of leadership. As one member said, "It's a safe environment to get some really critical feedback" (as cited in Riede, 2003).

International Examples of Mentoring

The challenge of helping new principals succeed is shared by schools everywhere, and some of the most interesting examples of mentoring programs come from the international community. Southworth (1995) studied the use of mentors to help new school leaders in Britain. He found that mentoring helped new leaders overcome isolation and allowed the pair (mentor and protégé) to "consider and reconsider" events. Problems regarding mentoring included finding a compatible pair and making sure that mentoring leads to better preparation for schools in the future rather than socializing a new generation to the practices of the past. Boon (1998) studied 27 pairs of mentors and protégés in Singapore and found that mentors felt they improved their professional knowledge by taking on their new roles and that protégés became part of a wider network of colleagues while developing greater self-confidence.

More recent studies in Singapore (Lim & Low, 2004) indicated the development of new habits such as admitting mistakes and building effective relationships as a result of participating in a mentor–protégé relationship. Coleman, Low, Bush, and Chew (1996) also studied mentoring practices for new and aspiring school leaders in the UK and Singapore and reported that in the British schools, new leaders appreciated working with a nonjudgmental colleague. Coleman et al. also found important differences between the two systems, such as duration of the mentoring process.

Erasmus and Westhuizen (1994) wrote guidelines for mentoring new principals in South Africa and advised that mentors tasks should include consulting, guiding and role modeling. Recent international studies also have reminded scholars and practitioners to contextualize mentoring programs by placing them in the larger arena of professional development for all leaders, novices and veterans (Walker & Dimmock, 2006). Walker and Dimmock's description of the Hong Kong Blue Skies mentoring design reflected a sensitivity to the emerging school leader's needs and argued against rigid conformity in program structures. They referred to Huber's finding that "effective programmes focused on long-term skill development, not just on-the-job training, and actively involved participants through stressing the central role of collaboration" (as cited in Walker & Dimmock, 2006, p. 137).

The First Time Principals Programme in New Zealand (University of Auckland School Leadership Centre, n.d.) includes 200 hundred new principals who work with 22 highly experienced mentors. A strong emphasis is placed on interpersonal skills, and the program is part of national educational network. The University of Auckland conducts training for the principals, often in the form of residential courses. For 3 half-days per year, the protégés and mentors work together, using e-mail and telephone conversations between meetings. By design, the First Time Principals Programme concentrates on issues selected by the new principal. The project director of the First Time Principals Programme stated, "If a mentoring relationship is working well, then the mentor can see if the principal is under stress, talk with them about it and advise them where to seek additional help" (as cited in Nelson, 2003).

Question 3. What Qualities Should Leadership Mentoring Programs Embody?

The literature supports consideration of five program principles for leadership mentoring programs:

1. First, we need to remember the big picture as we plan. Where does mentoring fit into the larger work of bringing new leaders into our district? Where might we need to watch out for potential downsides to mentoring?
2. Next, we need to understand that good mentors share specific qualities. Many assert that not everyone is destined to be a teacher. The same is true for mentoring. It is imperative for us to know the dispositions of effective mentors regardless of program structure. Likewise, qualities typifying effective protégés deserve consideration.
3. Once we identify potential mentors, we must know how to prepare them for their work. What are effective professional development strategies for this group?
4. Matching mentors with protégés is not a simple task, and the literature helps us to understand this process better.
5. Finally, we need some practical advice on such specifics as program length and cost.

Seeing the Big Picture

While the task at hand is the creation of a successful leadership mentoring program, we need to step back and recognize this as one piece in the larger picture of leadership development, recruitment, and induction. Mentoring programs will mean little without these efforts, as a clear understanding of larger issues like leadership succession (see Gross, 2004) are highly relevant. Replacing a leader who has done an effective job is a difficult task; finding the best person to succeed a less than re- markable leader is even more challenging. Board and district leaders are well advised to consider the state of each school as they approach the job of identifying the traits needed for school leaders, as this is their most important job as representatives of the community. Finding new leaders is a serious expense in time, money, and organizational energy.

Once a recruitment process is underway, districts need to have an attitude that will promote mutual benefit. The best candidates likely will have many choices and, at their best, schools may be in the same situation. Candidates rightly assume that they will have to compete for a position in schools. School leaders need to understand that they, too, compete for these candidates. In this way, recruitment needs to focus on fit between a candidate's skills and the needs of the school at the time of the search. There will not be a generic or universally appropriate candidate for a given school, of course, just as there is no universally perfect school for a specific aspiring administrator.

After the conclusion of the hiring process, which includes successfully working through salary and benefit negotiations, the induction process begins. *Induction* refers to the integration of the new school leader into a new setting (Lashway, 2003). Boards and district administrators must beware of the overuse of this term, however. As Morgan (1997) noted, each metaphor illuminates and obscures. Induction as a metaphor illuminates the process by making us aware that we need to bring an outsider into a system as an intentional act, that is, to recognize that the transition into a school system will not occur by accident or through osmosis. Taking responsibility for organizing the transition of a new principal into the district is at the heart of any rationale for developing a mentoring system in the first place.[1]

Here is another irony: Mentoring is a powerful idea that holds many potential benefits for school systems, yet we need to be aware of the dangers of the concept of mentoring as well. The literature has suggested five downsides:

1. First, mentors can have selfish or ulterior motives (Crow & Matthews, 1998; Muse, Wasden, & Thomas, 1988). Why someone wishes to become a mentor is a personal and powerful question that deserves consideration.
2. Mentors can be too protective (Crow & Matthews, 1998; Daresh & Playko, 1993), which

means that program designers need to be aware of the subtle difference between a generative behavior on the part of the mentor and one that smothers the protégé.

3. Mentors may have too much attachment to a single style of leadership (Crow & Matthews, 1998). "Mentoring may encourage cloning" (Hay, as cited in Crow & Matthews, 1998, p. 8) or "constrict innovation" (Hart, as cited in Crow & Matthews, 1998, p. 8). Southworth (1995) raised the possibility of mentors' socializing protégés simply to replicate the past rather than to prepare new leaders for the challenges of the future. Long-range studies of the socialization process also have been advocated (Enomoto & Gardiner 2006).

4. Another area of caution is the possibility of mentors' being too controlling (Lashway, 2003).

5. Finally, mentoring merely may be bent on molding a new person to the needs of a given district. In that way, mentoring is merely an artifact of the machine metaphor (Morgan, 1997), rather than the evolving and continually learning brain metaphor.

Looking at leadership mentoring as a panacea is another danger. Enthusiasm for mentoring is moderated by our understanding that it is but one element in the professional development process and not a stand-alone cure-all. The fact that mentoring has become a kind of catch phrase today means that too many people may be expecting too much, thereby placing this very promising idea among the fads that have haunted other innovations in education.

Uneven availability of mentoring is an additional challenge for principals and assistant principals. Dunavin's (2004) study of a "large, essentially urban and culturally diverse public school district" in the Southwest (student enrollment of 85,000) found that of the 118 principals and assistant principals returning surveys, 27% participated in formal induction programs for new administrators (p. 3). Additionally, 60% received mentoring as part of their induction, 75% of principals received mentoring as part of their induction in Year 1, and 33% of new assistant principals had the same kind of support.

Qualities of Successful Mentors and Protégés

Several personal qualities that make someone a poor mentor have just been enumerated. Yet, a skilled mentor is not just an educator who is not burdened with these drawbacks; the literature has shown important qualities that merit the attention of practitioners and scholars of the field. Planners are wise to identify people who are trusted guides (as in the original use in Homer's *Odyssey*), teachers (Levinson, Darrow, Klein, Levinson, & McKee, 1978), sponsors (Schein, 1978), challengers (Daloz, 1983), and confidents (Gehrke & Kay, 1984). Others have emphasized qualities such as acceptance of multiple alternative solutions to complex problems, decisiveness, the habit of asking the right question (Wunsch, 1994), and mutual trust (Daresh & Playko, 1993; Enz, 1992).

It is imperative to describe clearly what is meant by mentor in the first place (Healy & Welchert, 1990). Carefully defined mentoring can be distinguished from related but distinct forms of what Mertz (2004) called "supportive relationships" (p. 543). Drawing on a broad selection of mentoring literature, Mertz developed a conceptual model that significantly clarified what mentoring means in terms of intent and involvement. According to this model, two concepts relate to mentoring, namely the intent of the mentor and the degree of involvement. At the base of the triangular model, the intent is one of modeling and the degree of involvement is one of the role model, peer pal, or supporter (involvement Level 1) or teacher or coach (involvement Level 2). Higher up is the intent of advising and matched with the involvement of the counselor, advisor, or guide (involvement Level 3). At the top of the intent hierarchy is the role of the broker and the intent of the sponsor or benefactor (involvement Level 4), with the patron or protector (involvement Level 5) finally placing the involvement of the mentor at the very top. Clearly, Mertz has made mentoring a most serious enterprise filled with the deepest commitments.

It is important to consider the very definition of mentoring in light of these variables. On one hand, if any helping relation is considered mentoring, then schools may be simply building a superficial plan that will disappoint everyone. On the other hand, if mentoring is defined as too demanding, they may find it difficult to recruit mentors willing to dedicate the emotional effort to live up to such weighty responsibilities. Lincoln (1999) described four levels of mentoring; many mentoring plans in the literature appear to be working on the fourth level, collegial and collaboration.

The selection of mentors is a crucial element of any program. Geismar, Morris, and Lieberman (2000) described a Mentor Identification Instrument used to screen for those with the likely qualities of a good mentor. This instrument was also mentioned by Malone (2001) in connection with the Haberman Urban Principal Selection Interview. The goal seems to be to identify great potential principals for urban schools and to pair them with likely good mentors.

Part of the challenge for those wishing to design an effective program is to remember that the qualities of good mentors described above are those that many people may think they possess, since they reflect values of a caring, committed person. Planners must seek ways to find evidence of these qualities in the *performance* of mentor candidates as they have lived their professional lives. This implies making the role of mentor so prestigious that highly talented and motivated leaders will aspire to it. Potential mentors also should be made aware of the research-based findings of benefits, which include an appreciation of professional development and increased sense of performance as leaders (Hobson & Sharp, 2005). The development of theory and practice into the nature of equity in mentoring programs is also evident. University–school partnerships also have been used to invent new, more egalitarian relationships between mentors and protégés, referred to as comentoring partnerships (Mullen, 2000).

While it is natural to spend a good deal of time thinking through what personality traits make for an effective mentor, concern also needs to focus upon the qualities of a good protégé. Looked at one way, this may seem unnecessary, since any new principal may be required to participate in the leadership-mentoring program. However, merely going through the motions of a mentoring program likely will be a superficial experience. The hiring decision itself is a reasonable time to pose the question: Does this candidate approach his or her professional life in a way that values opportunities such as a research-based mentoring program? This question is not easily answered with a simple affirmation. Search committees need to probe candidates to find out when they have had similar experiences, where they worked closely with a senior colleague. It is also logical to look for individuals whose confidence is so authentic that they are comfortable making mistakes and anxious to learn from them. The qualities of a successful protégé seem specifically related to the qualities that will make this individual successful as an administrative leader in a district. Recent studies have indicated that protégés can look forward to a combination of emotional support and practical advice as major benefits from participating in a mentoring relationship (Hobson & Sharp, 2005).

Preparing Mentors to Help New Principals

Finding potential mentors may be a daunting task, but it is only the first step. The leadership mentoring plan next needs to consider preparation of mentors to work effectively with protégés. Peel, Wallace, Buckner, Wrenn, and Evans (1998) highlighted the need for the careful training of mentors. Mentors need to be advised that they face serious challenges (Crocker & Harris, 2002) in simply assuming their role. They will be responsible for supporting, assisting, and guiding the process of the relationship as well as facilitating self-reliance in the protégé (Crocker & Harris, 2002). Next, mentors must understand the richness of the task itself. Mentors will take on multiple roles, including that of a trusted colleague and encouraging developer (Head, Reiman, & Thies-Sprinthall, 1992). While mentors are clearly role models, Restine (1993) pointed out that this is not a question of asking people merely to imitate an experienced veteran.

Next, mentors must be prepared to understand the relationship. One aspect of the connection between mentor and protégé is its complexity and the need for mutual trust and mutual valuing (Playko, 1991). Establishing clear expectations and an expectation of confidentiality are key elements of this relationship (Dukess, 2001). Mentors need to be sensitive to the depth of that relationship while not forgetting that it is also a professional association. Mentor and protégé are also engaged in an evolving partnership by the very nature of the work. Of course, one expects that the protégé will grow as a result of the support of the mentor's guidance; that is the primary purpose. This growth means that the kind of help needed by the protégé will change with time if the program is working as planned. The mentor also must understand that the protégé will grow in independence and honor this development.

Considering the maturation of the protégé is only one side of the equation. There is the growth of the mentor to consider as well, because this relationship is an important professional development for mentors as well (Cordeiro & Smith-Sloan, 1995). Being committed to mentoring, giving help to a new generation of leaders, and sharing expertise consistently likely will lead to changes in self-image and will raise the need to gain a broader perspective. A leadership mentoring program of high quality should include plans for the development of mentors into increasing levels of responsibility as they evolve.

Learning to Become an Effective Mentor

Selecting potentially gifted mentors and preparing them to have the right approach with protégés is a critical step, leading logically to the question of content and process in the mentoring relationship. Simply put, what will the learning agenda be for protégés? If we look at this issue in the way we look at other learning experiences, three questions emerge:

1. First, what will the learning agenda be? Normally, we refer to this as the curriculum.
2. How will the content be shared with learners? This is another way to describe instruction.
3. Finally, how will learners demonstrate what they have learned? Of course, this is an issue of assessment.

These three elements have been used to describe the work of innovating schools in the United States and Canada (Gross, 1998), where a change in one of these elements has been shown to lead to a change in the other two. For instance, by expanding the curriculum to include local history, changes in instruction and assessment would follow quickly from the older approach of lecturing and testing. While this initially may look a little awkward, because it is more typically found in discussions about learning experiences designed for students, this three-element model it is useful for mentoring purposes because it helps organize the leadership mentoring program in a way that covers three issues: (a) What content matters, (b) how will we share that content, and (c) how will we know that the protégé has learned the content?

The literature on mentoring programs has shown that the work between mentor and protégé normally occurs through dialogues. These are not simple talking sessions but are well organized and thoughtfully conducted (Barnett, 1991). In these discussions, the mentor typically helps the protégé strike a balance between the natural need of the new principal to gain control of vital technical information and the requirement of school leaders to build a rich understanding of the larger picture of their school and education in general (Lashway, 2003). New principals will fail if they have a poor understanding of how their district's budgeting system works, for instance. Yet, they also will fail to live up to their role as true educational leaders if they have no conception of national educational policy and its transformation over recent history or the need to make well-reasoned ethical decisions. One way for mentors to understand the problem of balancing the dialogues with protégés is to ask them to recall models of development such as Maslow's (1970) hierarchy of needs.

It could be said that the need for new principals to get a handle on the concrete parts of their job is closely related to the lower end of the hierarchy where people focus on survival. Will the principal get through the day successfully? Only after understanding the needs of the protégé as they evolve can the successful mentor guide the protégé to more abstract, yet equally vital topics. This does not necessarily mean that a linear model of learning needs to be followed, whereby new principals only focus on the technical side of their work to the exclusion of larger issues.

Moving from this overview, program planners can turn to the kinds of content that the literature suggests for leadership mentoring programs. One promising plan describes four areas of technical learning for the protégé that seem appropriate for the early stages of the program: (a) daily operations, (b) information collection and problem-solving strategies for these tasks, (c) ways to work with a variety of adults, and (d) time management in the face of multiple tasks (Cordeiro & Smith-Sloan, 1995).

Bolman and Deal (1993) used the case study of a new principal's 1st year and his reflections with a mentor to highlight five major lessons important to new principals: (a) mapping the school's politics, (b) empowering people, (c) aligning the structure with the job at hand, (d) celebrating the school's culture, and (e) reframing using a variety of perspectives to understand a problem. If these four areas are reasonable parts of the early learning agenda or curriculum, others have depicted ways of sharing the agenda. Again, a four-step strategy is used to share the agenda: (a) Teach them how, (b) let them do, (c) help them learn from having done, and (d) accept them unconditionally.

Kay (as cited in Crocker & Harris, 2002) discussed training to deliver a four-step strategy. This four-step strategy is a way of thinking through instruction between mentor and protégé with the last step, accepting the protégé unconditionally, implying elements of assessment. Acceptance follows results of the protégé working through the process of doing their work and learning new tasks. Acceptance of the protégé does not imply ignoring problems, as clear feedback is essential to the task of mentoring. It means valuing the person regardless of results.

A third model (Cordeiro & Smith-Sloan, 1995) describing the development of protégé learning goes further than the ideas above by taking mentoring from the early days, when new principals typically have a limited grasp of the job, to a much later stage, when they have high "self and cultural awareness" (p. 27). Cordeiro and Smith-Sloan described five stages:

1. Initial contact creates a formal relationship. The protégé or intern is still a stranger.
2. The liminal stage is when the stress of the job begins, as the protégé dives into the work.
3. The settling-in stage involves "reflecting with mentors, scaffolding of tasks, and knowing there is a safety net" (Cordeiro & Smith-Sloan, 1995, p. 30).
4. The efficacy stage allows more autonomy for the intern as well as creativity. Cordeiro and Smith-Sloan (1995) noted, "Interns consider themselves to be full members of their community" (p. 30).
5. At the interdependence stage, great mutual benefits are seen. Thoughts of leaving are stressful.

Gross and Shapiro (2004) demonstrated the relevance of multiple ethical paradigms (including the ethics of justice, care, critique, and the profession) combined with turbulence theory (including the four levels of light, moderate, severe, and extreme) in a multiyear mentoring program. Findings in their case study demonstrated that mentoring dialogues enabled a protégé to respond to complex ethical dilemmas while reducing the level of organizational and personal turbulence that threatened to damage the chances of sustained educational innovation. Through these allied approaches the mentor and protégé were able to address and respond to challenging ethical dilemmas.

Matching of Mentors and Protégés

It is possible to identify seasoned educators with the potential to be superb mentors. Such educators can learn effective approaches and specific content to share with protégés. The next step is the more tangible work of bringing mentors and protégés together. Whereas some districts opt for an assigned mentoring program, such a process may be inadequate to the task of forging meaningful relationships. Holding to the standards set in the literature for a leadership mentoring program requires a high degree of sensitivity to that relationship as a long-range, career-changing process for both the mentor and the protégé.

Equally important, potential difficulties with mentoring have been described by scholars in this field. Geography may be a problem. Lashway (2003) noted the special problem of rural school districts, where a lack of money and personnel may make the matching process more difficult. Yet, geography is not a barrier limited to rural districts. Large cities have their own limiting factors of distance and financial limits, as do many large suburban districts. Yet, creative planners can find ways to transcend these constraints.

A more daunting challenge in matching mentors to protégés is the question of gender and racial balance. Currently, 60% of school principals are White males, and 35% are females. Only 13% of school principals are men and women from racial minorities (Malone, 2001). Finding sufficient female role models has been a long-standing problem. Pavan (1986) examined mentoring relationships in Pennsylvania schools and school districts. Among her findings were the importance of mentoring aspiring female leaders, the lack of female mentors, and the fact that psychosocial functions (such as support and encouragement) were seen as most helpful. Matters (1994) described a mentoring program in Australia designed to encourage more women to become school leaders. Difficulty in finding female mentors and the brevity of the program (2 weeks of mentoring) were listed as problems to overcome. The Principal's Institute (Bank Street College, 1992) focused on increasing the number of women and minorities in leadership positions in public schools. Mentoring in this program lasted one semester and was considered to be the project's most useful aspect. Feedback from participants indicated that this preservice model would have been more useful if the mentoring relationship had been sustained longer. Cohn and Sweeny (1992) connected the role of school districts in establishing effective mentoring programs with helping underrepresented groups such as women and minorities in becoming principals.

Completing the picture, high percentages of White males continues to run the school system at the central office and on school boards. If programs are committed to matching protégés with mentors of the same gender or same racial group, and if program developers insist on choosing mentors from among their employees, they may not be able to sustain a viable system. Again, the standard of quality of the relationship is vital. How similar do mentor and protégé need to be? This is a complex and highly sensitive question. Although it is likely some of the pairs will not come from the same backgrounds, vast differences in the perspectives of the mentor and the protégé are not inevitable—if and only if planners are dedicated to the concept of true empathy and deep understanding on the part of the mentor. Obviously, this means a great deal of attention paid to the selection and education of mentors.

Time Requirements

Clearly, the creation of a promising leadership mentoring system requires attention to a range of issues that include abstract, ethical problem solving as well as concrete technical issues. In this way the plan mirrors the learning curve of the protégé, who also must blend learning specifics with gaining perspective of the larger, current issues in education. Some design qualities may appear to be deceptively simple technical issues that actually require complex handling. One such issue is time and the related concern of cost. How long should a mentoring program last? How much should it cost the district? Schools have finite resources of time and money as well as competing demands for both.

The literature has suggested a great variety of models. Malone (2001) found varied lengths of the mentoring relationship, from 165 hours to 632 hours. Dunavin (2004) reported that a multiyear program would be beneficial:

> Evidence encouraged maintaining a structured mentor/coach relationship for the first three years of the new administrators' tenure. Further, as the mentoring progressed, a long-term model which incorporated evaluation promoted professional relationships in which learning goals were either achieved or re-negotiated (Daresh, 2001; Walker & Stott, 1994; Wilmore, 1995; Zachary 2000). (p. 11)

Gross (2002) also described a multiyear program that resulted in a successful transition for a new high school principal. Through consistent, structured mentoring, supported at the district level, the mentor in Gross's study was able to help her protégé keep this high school on its track of deep reform during a period of high challenge.

Duration is only the most obvious aspect of the time issue. How often mentors and protégés are able to meet is just as important for planners to contemplate. Frequency has been a challenge for past programs. Barnett (1995) emphasized the need for frequency as a key constant in program design. Crocker and Harris (2002) advocated for extra time to spend with protégés. Yet, scheduled time needs to be focused; Crocker and Harris recommended, "Specific guidelines should be available to the mentor outlining roles for the mentee that include meaningful activities and delineate ways to involve mentees in these experiences" (p. 19).

Time constraints are equally important for this kind of mentor–protégé relationship for assistant principals in a given district who wish to advance to the principalship. Calabrese and Tucker-Ladd (1991) looked at the kinds of issues that a mentoring principal should discuss with an assistant principal. They suggested taking time each day to debrief and ask questions such as the following: Why did you respond this way? What were the alternatives? Calabrese and Tucker-Ladd also raised the question of separation: When and how should the mentoring relationship end? Crow and Matthews (1998) described peer mentoring for midcareer leaders and discussed a year-long plan. Patience, understanding, and tolerance are among the required qualities for mentors, in their opinion.

Question 4. What Future Research Priorities Should Be Taken in the Field?

Looking Beyond the Current State of Research Into Mentoring Programs in Educational Settings

Although a considerable body of literature exists that describes leadership mentoring programs in school settings, there is an unmet need for further studies that consider unexplored and underexamined aspects of this practice, especially for studies that pose and produce findings on specific benefits and challenges in the field. At this point, it is reasonable to state that the topic of leadership mentoring, as an area of scholarly research, is at an early stage of its evolution, justifying new research projects. Specifically, four major areas of potential investigation are apparent:

1. First, there is a need for more evidence-based program evaluations that describe the effectiveness of leadership mentoring.
2. By analyzing mentoring programs outside of education and raising similar questions in the field, we may be able to expand the depth of our knowledge of mentoring dynamics more deeply.
3. We would benefit from examining current, multiple field studies that cut across boundaries of profession, country, culture, and sponsoring agency. This would enable us to design future research to extend those studies.
4. Last, we need to recall the larger question of motivation for mentoring. This raises the question of the values and ethical paradigms that undergird our programs and help us define them. A consideration of each of these research fronts is explored briefly below.

More Evidence-Based Program Evaluations

The literature has shown a clear need for evidence of program effectiveness. Currently the field is criticized for programs evaluated on participant testimonials (Ehrich, Hansford, & Tennent, 2004; Hobson & Sharp, 2005). Agreeing with Huber (2003), Walker and Dimmock (2006) reminded students of mentoring, "Few studies have adequately explored whether the programmes really make a difference to improving leadership and student learning" (p. 137). Not only is there a need to enlarge the quality of leadership mentoring program evaluation, the scope also needs to expand dramatically to include the impact of programs on the school organization as well as the mentor–protégé dyad (Ehrich et al., 2004). Given the multiyear duration of many programs and their potential for long-term career impact, longitudinal studies of the range of leadership mentoring programs' effectiveness represent a reasonable priority for the field.

Thoughtful Analysis of Mentoring Programs Outside of Education

Important research questions for mentoring programs have been raised in fields outside of education that could inspire the pursuit of new avenues for those focused on school-based programs. Typical of this group are a pair of studies conducted in business settings (Godshalk & Sosik, 2000; Sosik & Godshalk, 2005). Godshalk and Sosik's study in 2000 raised the question of perceived versus actual influence of mentors on protégés. Mentors in 199 mentor–protégé dyads were studied and grouped according to the influence they suspected they had on their protégés. Findings indicated that those mentors who understated their impact had the greatest influence on protégés. In their 2005 study, Sosik and Godshalk raised the question of gender and supervisory status in mentor-protégé relationships. Did it matter if a protégé's mentor was also that person's supervisor? Did it also matter if the mentor and protégé were of the same gender? Findings in that study pointed to greater support from cross-gendered dyads. Supervisory mentors seemed to have a greater benefit to protégés in career advancement. In both cases, parallels to education are clear. Mentors in school settings very likely have a range of self-concepts about their influence. Studies like these can help us better understand the possible relationship between mentor self-concept and actual performance. They also can help us to design education-specific studies that question the relevance of this finding in our field.

Likewise, as mentor–protégé matching is a crucial element in nearly every program studied, questions of same-sex matches and supervisor or nonsupervisor mentors are highly relevant for our field. As in the first case, future studies located in school settings that investigate these questions will help us to see where useful comparisons may be drawn from industry examples and where these break down. For instance, reflection was a major outcome for educational mentoring programs reviewed by Ehrich et al. (2004) but not an important outcome for programs they considered in medicine or industry. This is a clear example of the difference in professions and may reflect differences in underlying values and cultures that planners of educational mentoring programs need to take into account.[2] Even fundamental questions of mentoring program effectiveness need to be considered as this analysis moves forward. Scandura and Schriesheim (1994) pointed out that mentoring for career outcome variables in corporate culture typically includes rate of advancement, salary growth, and supervisory rating of performance. While these categories have some reasonable analogues in education, a wholesale transfer seems ill advised.[3] In each instance, the exercise of this type of future research will deepen our understanding and help us to transcend our current state of knowledge.

Development of Multiple Field Studies That Cut Across Boundaries of Profession, Country, Culture, and Sponsoring Agency

Just as a systematic reflection of mentoring dynamics in noneducational settings suggests new avenues of research on school-based programs, we would also be wise to launch research projects that include diverse, professional, national, and cultural locations. Ehrich et al.'s (2004) meta-analysis of previous studies described patterns among mentoring programs in education, business, and medical professionals. Their finding that mentoring is a highly complex relationship leads to inevitable questions about the profession-specific mentoring complexity versus transcendent issues that cut across all fields, all of which deserve further illumination. Diversity in leadership norms in the UK, Canada, and Australia was the focus of Kakabadse et al.'s (2003) study. Their work clarified that context, in this case national setting, is a critical variable to understand. This means elevating our sensitivity as program designers and as researchers to national norms and expectations while simultaneously expanding our grasp of leadership mentoring program qualities that seem universal. Again, this raises the need for further study in multiple countries. Although many comparative international studies include advance economies, attention needs to be paid to a wider spectrum of countries than has been the case.

No matter what nations are included in such research, sensitivity to cultural diversity within those countries is also a high priority. Méndez-Morse (2004) described Latina school leaders who sought out their own mentors from a variety of nontraditional backgrounds. Questioning the need for mentors to be matched from above in the educational organization, she offered the possibility of horizontal development of helping relationships. Is the possibility of constructing such relationships culturally grounded or more universal? Again, further study is warranted and would help those interested in mentoring better related to all of the potential mentors and protégés in leadership positions.

Finally, there is the boundary of program sponsorship to consider. In this case, researchers have vast and fertile fields to investigate in the form of mentoring programs funded by philanthropic organizations. In the past few years, leadership mentoring programs such as NYC Emeritus Corps, New Visions for Public Schools, and New Leaders for New Schools have been created. Adding to the list are leadership-training initiatives from the Wallace Foundation and the Broad Foundation as well as umbrella projects such as the Educational Alliance at Brown University. Although several of these have reported success in attaining programmatic goals, further evaluation questions arise. What values do these programs instill in participants? What assumptions about educational leadership and its relevance to other professions are made and why? How do these programs compare to each other and to those established by districts alone? To what degree do these programs model the qualities that are supported by research findings?

Improving our understanding of program evaluation also includes a serious reflection on the deeper meaning of continuously learning leadership. For instance, Lim and Low (2004) pointed out the need for aspiring leaders to develop relationship skills. What this brings to mind is the promulgation of a disposition for educators to identify mentors or potential mentors in their environment throughout the career cycle as well as the disposition to be a mentor. Méndez-Morse (2004) alluded to this practice as well in her description of emerging Latina educational leaders. Realizing that any given organization likely will have one or more individuals willing and capable of guiding a new leader is in itself an important awareness. As in Méndez-Morse's case, these people may not hold a title that makes their mentoring potential obvious. Learning how to identify these people and build mutually rewarding relationships is both a disposition and a skill that transcends any specific mentoring program. Allied with this disposition is the possibility of altering the balance between mentor and protégé. Rather than assuming a guiding and giving role as the inevitable and sole property of the mentor (and the corollary of a strictly following and receiving duty of the protégé), writers such as Mullen (2000) have described newer concepts such as comentoring partnerships, where learning and relationship status can be more equally shared.

Raising the Question of the Values and Ethical Paradigms That Undergird Leadership Mentoring Programs in the First Place

A final direction for future research requires us to explore the values and ethical perspectives upon which we build leadership mentoring programs in the first place. This speaks to the purpose of the principal's role and certainly the form and intention of any mentoring program. In this case, a dichotomy appears to be emerging in the field of educational leadership that amplifies the need for such reflection. On one hand, programs that lean toward hierarchical management, borrowing design components from business and aimed at creating a cadre of leaders who can follow state and national standard-driven mandates, clearly have found room in the expanding universe of mentoring programs. Harris, Ballenger, and Leonard (2004) advised selecting mentors who model priorities in state mandates, as protégés will be influenced by their mentor and the mentor's values. Despite an inherent logic in this perspective, in the extreme, it describes the principal mainly as a bureaucratic functionary implementing but not exercising judgments about policies.

Countering this perspective are calls from the field for an emphasis on values of democracy and ethical decision making in leadership mentoring programs (Gross, 2006; Gross & Shapiro, 2004). These are supported by earlier calls for a profession-changing, social-justice orientation in mentoring programs for teachers (Hargreaves & Fullan 2000). It is useful to note that this debate is part of a larger contest in the field. Framing a broader vision for the field, many scholars and practitioners from the United States, Canada, UK, Australia, and Taiwan have begun to organize in a movement they call the New DEEL (Democratic Ethical Educational Leadership). According to proponents, educational leaders come from many quarters, including administration, faculty, students, families, and the community (Dantley, 2005; Davis, 2001; Mitra, 2004; Young, Petersen, & Short, 2002). Such proponents believe it is the job of educational leaders to pursue and sustain a democratic society (Begley, 1999; Begley & Zaretsky, 2004; Boyd, 2000; Burford, 2004; Crow, 2006; Gutmann, 1999; Normore, 2004; O'Hair, McLaughlin, & Reitzug, 2000; Sernak, 1998; Shapiro & Purpel, 2004). While acknowledging the need for educational leaders to understand and observe current policy mandates, these writers have criticized the principal-as-state-functionary model as a case of the ethic of justice standing alone (Shapiro & Stefkovich, 2005; Starratt, 1994). Several of these scholars have pointed to the need for other ethical perspectives to be used in nurturing new leaders. These include the ethics of care (Gilligan, 1982), critique (Giroux, 1994), the profession (Shapiro & Stefkovich, 2005), and the community (Furman, 2003). Gross (1998, 2004, 2006) included the need for emerging leaders to understand the concept of turbulence in the context of these ethical lenses. Clearly, this vision requires a very different set of leadership skills than needed for those who advocate accountability management as the central duty of the principal.

Conclusion

Establishing meaningful leadership mentoring in school settings is an evolving process. Although the practice of mentoring is ancient, its systematic application in educational leadership is recent and varied. This chapter highlighted four aspects of leadership mentoring with the intention of contextualizing the issue, offering examples of current practice, suggesting important elements of program design and implementation, and forecasting future directions for scholars and practitioners to consider.

There are clear problems facing principals in any era. However, today such issues as the national accountability movement and a generational change make the job of finding, nurturing, and keeping high-performing principals is an especially challenging priority for almost every district. Mentoring has a long and well-documented history from which we can learn. Clearly, the relationship between an older, generative guide and a younger, maturing professional is found throughout history and has special relevance to our profession. Care, however, must be taken to ensure that these relationships are authentic and carry more than simply the name of mentoring. Models of mentoring in North America and around the world also teach us that this is a pervasive phenomenon. Of equal importance, while program designs vary, certain patterns emerge, in program duration and learning content especially.

Good programs clearly place mentoring into the larger program of leadership induction. Care must be taken, however, to expand the traditional meaning of the word *induction* into a more flexible, bidirectional process. Of equal significance, the literature tells us a great deal about the type of person who will make a good mentor as well as the type of person who will value the role of protégé. Mentorship education and the task of matching mentors to protégés are discussed in the literature. Sensitivity in matching women and underrepresented minorities with appropriate mentors is imperative. Finally, the literature teaches us that longer programs, often extending to 3 years, deserve serious consideration.

Moving leadership mentoring beyond its current state of development is crucial if this promising practice is to reach its potential to nurture the next generation of school leaders. The most obvious need is attention to more studies on program effectiveness. What evidence is there that leadership mentoring makes a difference in the first place? Although the field is not at baseline zero, much work, including longitudinal research, needs to be undertaken. New dimensions in the practice of mentoring need to be uncovered and explored. These may be identified through reflections on mentoring research in other professions, though care must be exercised in identifying differences in organizational culture and values. Expanding research on educational leadership mentoring by including school-based programs with mentoring programs in other fields also will aid in finding commonalities as well as profession-specific areas of difference. Finally, articulating the undergirding values of any mentoring program is essential. Planners who aspire to design and construct effective leadership mentoring programs must hold a clear vision of the type of educational leader they wish to nurture. Everything else flows from this step. In any era this would be a priority. In our times, so characterized by turbulence and challenges to democratic life, it is an ethical imperative.

Notes

1. Ironically, induction, taken out of context, brings to mind entering the military or similar organization. In that case, the organization demands change from the individual, with little apparent room for reciprocal change expected, because a new person has joined the group. This may be appropriate for some organizations but is not what schools, as learning organizations, are trying to emulate. First, schools should not be run as authoritarian organizations but as institutions whose central mission is the promotion of a democratic way of life. Schools must continue to cultivate life skills for students, chief among these being the ability to find and keep meaningful employment. However, it is the more difficult challenge of engaging responsibly in a democratic society that remains their primary goal. As such, district leaders must honor relationships that are mutual in character. Certainly, districts have much to share with any new person joining their ranks, from the new student and their family to the new school principal. But the spirit of democratic life compels leaders to remember that each new person has much to offer the school system's organization. Their perspective, their experiences, and their needs and aspirations are all part of what should define the district's future, if, as a society, we really believe in the equality of people. Induction, looked at in this way, is inadequate for the task of mutual development. Our field needs to have a process that welcomes and educates the new person to a school system and also honors the new person by listening, responding, and *changing* to reflect that person's energy and goals. Perhaps we need to infuse the concept of induction with the concept of development.
2. Literature on mentoring in corporate settings correctly points out the differences in culture to illustrate the need to recognize relevant values of a given context. Godshalk and Sosik (2000), for instance, explained crucial dissimilarities separating business culture from the military: "Relative to military contexts, mentoring relationships in corporate business contexts may afford safe havens for one to let his or her guard down and be modest, humble, and more realistic regarding self-assessments of leadership qualities" (p. 10). Such behaviors in a military context could be destructive to the career of a junior officer, according to the authors. Given this sensitivity to context, it is ironic to witness the mushrooming of corporately cloned mentoring programs sprouting upon the landscape of educational leadership practice.
3. In an analogue to the divide separating the culture of schools and that of corporate life, Kakabadse, Korac-Kakabadse, and Kouzmin (2003) described the difference between public sector values and private sector responsibilities:

    For example, leaders need to show how to serve "clients" or "customers" in particular contexts and to balance that with the interests and rights of "citizens." Because the sum and balance of these interests define public interest, or the common good, equity, citizenship, democracy, the public interest and the needs of clients are all public service values that produce tensions—they carry with them different sets of assumptions in different contexts. (p. 493)

    Kakabadse et al. demonstrated the pursuit of nonhierarchical, noncorporate values to inform public sector service is not limited to education. Referring to the Canadian Public Service Values and Ethics Taskforce, they illustrated four groups of values:
    - "democratic" values include loyalty to the public interest (a fundamental value enshrined in law and Constitution, from which other values such as integrity; equity; fairness; impartiality and anonymity are linked); accountability, and responsibility.
    - "professional" values consist of old values (excellence; professional competence; continuous improvement; merit; effectiveness; economy; frankness; objectivity; and impartiality in advice; "speaking truth to power"; balancing complexity and fidelity to the public trust) and new, emerging values (innovation; initiative; creativity; and teamwork).
    - "ethical" values include integrity; honesty; impartiality; taking responsibility; and building accountability; probity; prudence; honesty; equity; objectivity; disinterestedness; selflessness; trustworthiness; discretion; respect for law and due process; and the careful stewardship of public resources; and
    - "people" values consist of four sub-groups; existential values (courage; moderation; decency; reasonableness; balance; responsibility; humanity); values shown to others (respect; concern; civility; tolerance; patience; benevolence; reciprocity; courtesy; receptivity; openness; fairness; caring); leadership/management values (participation; involvement; collegiality; consultation; and communication); and Canadian values (diversity and respect for other collective or individual rights). (pp. 487–488)

References

Aiken, J. (2002). The socialization of new principals: Another perspective on principal retention. *Education Leadership Review. 3*(1), 32–40.

Archer, J. (2002, May 29). Novice principals put huge strain on NYC schools. *Education Week, 21*(38), 1, 15.

Bank Street College. (1992). *The Principals' Institute 1990–1992.* New York: New York City Board of Education.

Barnett, B. G. (1991). School-university collaboration: A fad or the future of administration preparation? *Planning and Changing, 21,* 146–157.

Barnett, B. G. (1995). Developing reflection and expertise: Can mentors make the difference? *Journal of Educational Administration, 33,* 45–59.

Begley, P. T. (Ed.). (1999). *Values and educational leadership.* Albany: State University of New York Press.

Begley, P. T., & Zaretsky, L. (2004). Democratic school leadership in Canada's public school systems: Professional value and social ethic. *The Journal of Educational Administration, 42*(6), 640–655.

Bolman, L., & Deal, T. (1993) *The path to school leadership: A portable mentor.* Newbury Park, CA: Corwin Press.

Boon, S. L. Z. (1998). Principalship mentoring in Singapore: Who and what benefits?" *Journal of School Administration, 36,* 29–43.

Boyd, W. L. (2000) The r's of school reform and the politics of reforming or replacing public schools. *Journal of Educational Change, 1*(3), 225–252.

Brown, K., Anfara, V., Hartman, K., Mahar, R., & Mills, R. (2001, April). *Professional development of middle-level principals.* Paper presented at the annual meeting of the American Educational Research Association, Seattle, WA.

Browne-Ferrigno, T., & Muth, R. (2004). Leadership mentoring in clinical practice: Role socialization, professional development, and capacity building. *Educational Administration Quarterly, 40*(4), 468–494.

Bundy, B., & McKay, B. (2004). *Beginning principals' mentoring program Prince George's County, Maryland.* London: National College for School Leadership.

Burford, C. (2004, October). *Ethical dilemmas and the lives of leaders: An Australian perspective on the search for the moral.* Paper presented at the annual meeting of the Values and Leadership Conference, Christ Church, Barbados.

Bush, T., & Glover, D. (2005). Leadership development for early headship: The new visions experience. *School Leadership and Management, 25*(3), 217–239.

Calabrese, R. L., & Tucker-Ladd, P. R. (1991) The principal and assistant principal: A mentoring relationship. *NASSP Bulletin, 75,* 67–74.

Cohn, K. C., & Sweeny, R. C. (1992, April). *Principal mentoring programs: Are school districts providing the leadership?* Paper presented at the annual meeting of the American Educational Research Association, San Francisco. (ERIC Document Reproduction Service No. ED345376)

Coleman, M., Low, G. T., Bush, T., & Chew, O. A. J. (1996, April). *Re-thinking training for principals: The role of mentoring.* Paper presented at the annual meeting of the American Educational Research Association, New York. (ERIC Document Reproduction Service No. ED397479)

Cordeiro, P., & Smith-Sloan, L. (1995, April). *Apprenticeships for administrative interns: Learning to talk like a principal.* Paper presented at the annual meeting of the American Educational Research Association, San Francisco.

Crocker, C., & Harris, S. (2002). Facilitating growth of administrative practitioners as mentors. *Journal of Research for Educational Leaders, 1*(2), 5–20.

Crow, G. (2006). Democracy and educational work in an age of complexity. *UCEA Review, 48*(1), 1–5.

Crow, G. M., & Matthews, L. J. (1998). *Finding one's way: How mentoring can lead to dynamic partnership.* Thousand Oaks, CA: Corwin.

Daloz, L.A. (1983). Mentors: Teachers who make a difference. *Change, 5,* 24–27.

Dantley, M. E. (2005). Moral leadership: Shifting the management paradigm. In F. W. English (Ed.), *The Sage handbook of educational leadership: Advances in theory, research, and practice* (pp. 34–46). Thousand Oaks, CA: Sage.

Daresh, J., & Playko, M. (1993, February). *Benefits of a mentoring program for aspiring administrators.* Paper presented at the annual meeting of the American Association of School Administrators, Orlando, FL. (ERIC Document Reproduction Service No. ED354603)

Davis, J. E. (2001). Transgressing the masculine: African American boys and the failure of schools. In W. Martino & B. Meyenn (Eds.), *What about the boys?* (pp. 140–153). Philadelphia: Open University Press.

Dukess, L. (2001). *Meeting the leadership challenge: Designing effective principal mentoring programs.* New York: New Visions for Public Schools.

Dunavin, R. (2004, April). *School leaders are not developed equally: Principals' and assistant principals' differing induction and professional development experiences.* Paper presented at the annual meeting of the American Educational Research Association, San Diego, CA.

Ehrich, L. C., Hansford, B., & Tennent, L. (2004). Formal mentoring programs in education and other professions: A review of the literature. *Educational Administration Quarterly. 40*(4), 518–540.

Enomoto, E. K., & Gardiner, M. E. (2006). Mentoring within internships: Socializing new school leaders. *Journal of School Leadership, 16*(1), 34–60.

Enz, B. J. (1992). Guidelines for selecting mentors and creating an environment for mentoring. In T. Bey & C. Holmes (Eds.). *Mentoring contemporary principles and issues* (pp. 65–77). Reston, VA: Association of Teacher Educators.

Erasmus, M., & Westhuizen, P. C. van der. (1994, May). *Guidelines for the professional development of school principals by means of a mentoring system in a developing country.* Paper presented at the International Intervisitation Programme, Buffalo, New York. (ERIC Document Reproduction Service No. ED371440)

Furman, G. (2003). Moral leadership and the ethic of the community. *Values and Ethics in Educational Administration, 2*(1), 1–8

Gehrke, N. J., & Kay, R. S. (1984). The socialization of beginning teachers through mentor-protégé relationships. *Journal of Teacher Education, 35,* 21–24.

Geismar, T. J., Morris, J. D., & Lieberman, M. G. (2000). Selecting mentors for principalship interns. *Journal of School Leadership, 10,* 233–247.

Gilligan, C. (1982). *In a different voice: Psychological theory and women's development.* Cambridge, MA: Harvard University Press.

Giroux, H.A. (1994). Educational leadership and school administrators: Rethinking the meaning of democratic public culture. In T. Mulkeen, N. H. Cambron-McCabe, & B. Anderson (Eds.), *Democratic leadership: The changing context of administrative preparation* (pp. 31–47). Norwood, NJ: Ablex.

Godshalk, V. M., & Sosik, J. J. (2000). Does mentor-protégé agreement on mentor leadership behavior influence the quality of a mentoring relationship? *Group and Organizational Management, 25*(3), 291–317.

Gross, S. J. (1998). *Staying centered: Curriculum leadership in a turbulent era.* Alexandria, VA: The Association for Supervision and Curriculum Leadership.

Gross, S. J. (2002). Passing a torch: Sustaining change through leadership mentoring at one reforming high school. *Journal of In-Service Education, 28,* 35–56.

Gross, S. J. (2004). *Promises kept: Sustaining school and district leadership in a turbulent era.* Alexandria, VA: The Association for Supervision and Curriculum Leadership.

Gross, S. J. (2006). *Leadership mentoring: Maintaining school improvement in turbulent times.* Lanham, MD: Rowman & Littlefield, the American Association of School Administrators.

Gross, S. J., & Shapiro, J. P. (2004). Using multiple ethical paradigms and turbulence theory in response to administrative dilemmas. *International Studies in Educational Administration, 32,* 47–62.

Gutmann, A. (1999). *Democratic education.* Princeton, NJ: Princeton University Press.

Hargreaves, A., & Fullan, M. (2000). Mentoring in the new millennium. *Theory Into Practice, 39,* 50–56.

Harris, S., Ballenger, J., & Leonard, J. (2004). Aspiring principal perceptions: How often do mentor principals model Texas instructional leadership standards? *Journal of Mentoring and Tutoring, 12*(2), 155–172.

Head, F. A., Reiman, A. J., & Thies-Sprinthall, L. (1992). The reality of mentoring: Complexity in process and function. In T. Bey & C. Holmes (Eds.). *Mentoring contemporary principles and issues* (pp. 5–24). Reston, VA: Association of Teacher Educators.

Healy, C. C., & Welchert, A. J. (1990). Mentoring relations: A definition to advance research and practice. *Educational Researcher, 19*(9), 17–21.

Hobson, A. J., & Sharp, C. (2005). Head to head: A systematic review of the research evidence on mentoring new head teachers. *School Leadership and Management, 25*(1), 25–42.

Hopkins, G. (1998). Help wanted: Qualified principal. *Education World.* Retrieved November 10, 2004, from http://www.educationworld.com/a_admin/admin067.shtml

Huber, S. G. (2003). *Preparing school leaders for the 21st century.* London: Routledge.

Kakabadse, A., Korac-Kakabadse, N., & Kouzmin, A. (2003). Ethics, values, and behaviours: Comparison of three case studies examining the paucity of leadership in government. *Public Administration, 81*(3), 477–508.

Kiltz, G., Danzig, A., & Szecsy, E. (2004). Learner-centered leadership: A mentoring model for the professional development of school administrators. *Mentoring and Tutoring, 12*(2), 135–153.

Lashway, L. (2003). *Inducting school leaders.* Eugene, OR: CEPM Clearinghouse on Educational Management. Retrieved January 22, 2009. from http://eric.uoregon.edu/publications/digests/digest170.html

Levinson, D. J., Darrow, C. N., Klein, E. B., Levinson, M. H., & McKee, B. (1978). *The seasons of a man's life.* New York: Ballantine.

Lim, L. H., & Low, G. T. (2004). Relevance and significance of relationships: The Singapore experience in mentoring. *International Studies in Educational Administration, 32*(3), 34–43.

Lincoln, Y. S. (1999, February). *Mentoring in the moment.* Paper presented at the annual meeting of the Southwest Educational Research Association, San Antonio, TX.

Malone, R. J. (2001). *Principal mentoring.* Eugene, OR: CEPM Clearinghouse on Educational Management. Retrieved May 11, 2008, from http://eric.uoregon.edu/publications/digests/digest 149.html

Maslow, A. (1970). *Motivation and personality* (2nd ed.). New York: Harper & Row.

Matters, P. (1994, January). *Mentoring partnerships: Key to leadership success for principals and managers.* Paper presented at the annual meeting of the International Congress for School Effectiveness and Improvement, Melbourne, Victoria, Australia. (ERIC Document Reproduction Service No. ED366113)

Méndez-Morse, S. (2004). Constructing mentors: Latina educational leaders' role models and mentors. *Educational Administration Quarterly, 40*(4), 561–590.

Mertz, N. T. (2004). What's a mentor, anyway? *Educational Administration Quarterly, 40,* 541–560.

Mitra, D. L. (2004). The significance of students: Can increasing "student voice" in schools lead to gains in youth development? *Teachers College Record, 106*(4), 651–688.

Morgan, G. (1997). *Images of organization.* Thousand Oaks, CA: Sage.

Mullen, C. A. (2000). Constructing co-mentoring partnerships: Walkways we must travel. *Theory Into Practice, 39*(1), 4–11.

Muse, I. D., Wasden, F. D., & Thomas, G. J. (1988). *The mentor principal: Handbook.* Provo, UT: Brigham Young University Press.

National Association of Elementary School Principals, National Association of Secondary School Principals, & Educational Research Service. (1998). *Is there a shortage of qualified candidates for openings in the principalship?* Washington, DC: Educational Research Service.

Nelson, B. (2003). Help for first-time principals. *Education Gazette*. Retrieved May 11, 2008, from http://www.edgazette. govt.nz/articles/show_articles.cgi?

Normore, A. H. (2004). Ethics and values in leadership preparation programs: Finding the North Star in the dust storm. *Values and Ethics in Educational Administration, 2*(2), 1–8.

O'Hair, M. J., McLaughlin, H. J., & Reitzug, U. C. (2000). *Foundations of democratic education*. Cambridge, MA: Thomson Wadsworth.

Pavan, B. (1986, April). *Mentors and mentoring functions perceived as helpful to certified aspiring and incumbent female and male public school administrators*. Paper presented at the annual meeting of the American Educational Research Association, San Francisco. (ERIC Document Reproduction Service No. ED269884)

Peel, H. A., Wallace, C., Buckner, K. G., Wrenn, S. L., & Evans, R. (1998) Improving leadership preparation programs through a school, university and professional organization partnership. *NASSP Bulletin, 82*(602), 26–34.

Playko, M. A. (1991). Mentors for administrators: Support for the instructional leader. *Theory Into Practice, 30,* 124–127.

Restine, L. N. (1993). Mentoring: Assisting and developing the new generation of leaders. *People and Education, 1*(1), 42–51.

Riede, P. (2003). Electronic mentoring: Three school leaders across upstate New York advise each other through e-mail. *School Administrator*. Retrieved May 11, 2008, from http://www.aasa.org/publications/saarticledetail.cfm?ItemNumber= 1581&snItemNumber=950&tnItemNumber=1995)

Scandura, T. A., & Schriesheim, C. A. (1994). Leader-member exchange and supervisor career mentoring as complementary constructs in leadership research. *Academy of Management Journal, 37*(6), 1588–1602.

Schein, E. H. (1978). *Career dynamics: Matching individual and organizational needs*. Reading, MA: Addison-Wesley.

Sernak, K. (1998). *School leadership—Balancing power with caring*. New York: Teachers College Press.

Shapiro, H. S., & Purpel, D. E. (Eds.). (2004). *Critical social issues in American education: Democracy and meaning in a globalizing world* (3rd ed.). Mahwah, NJ: Erlbaum.

Shapiro, J. P., & Stefkovich, J. A. (2005). *Ethical leadership and decision making in education: Applying theoretical perspectives to complex dilemmas* (2nd ed.). Mahwah, NJ: Erlbaum.

Sosik, J. & Godshalk, V. M. (2005). Examining gender similarity and mentors' supervisory status in mentoring relationships. *Mentoring and Tutoring, 13*(1), 39–52.

Southworth, G. (1995) Reflections on mentoring for new school leaders. *Journal of Educational Administration, 33,* 17–28.

Starratt, R. J. (1994). *Building an ethical school*. London: Falmer Press.

U.S. Department of Labor. (2005). *Occupational outlook handbook, 2004–2005 edition* (Bulletin 2750). Washington, DC: U.S. Government Printing Office.

University of Auckland School Leadership Centre. (n.d.). *First time principals programme*. Retrieved May 11, 2008, from http://www.firstprincipals.ac.nz/

Walker, A., & Dimmock, C. (2006). Preparing leaders, preparing learners: The Hong Kong experience. *School Leadership and Management, 26*(2), 125–147.

Williams, E. J., Matthews, J., & Baugh, S. (2004). Developing a mentoring internship model of school leadership: Using legitimate peripheral participation. *Mentoring and Tutoring 12*(1), 53–70.

Wunsch, M. (1994). *Mentoring: Making an impact on individuals and institutions*. San Francisco: Jossey-Bass.

Young, M. D., Petersen, G. J., & Short P. M. (2002). The complexity of substantive reform: A call for interdependence among key stakeholders. *Educational Administration Quarterly, 38*(2), 136–175.

Conclusion

Moving Forward on Research for Enriching
the Education of School Leaders

GARY M. CROW, MICHELLE D. YOUNG, JOSEPH MURPHY,
AND RODNEY T. OGAWA

Charles Handy (1989) tells the story of a meeting of the General Synod of the Church of England in the 1980s debating the ordination of women to the priesthood: "A speaker from the floor of the Chamber spoke with passion, 'In this matter,' he cried, 'as in so much else in our great country, why cannot the status quo be the way forward'" (p. 3). In similar fashion, the status quo still characterizes the content and methods of much of the research on school leader preparation. Leadership development research, as this handbook demonstrates, struggles like many issues of our field with the tension between status quo and moving forward.

In this concluding chapter, we try to create, as the introduction suggested, "the broad contours as well as the integrative architecture for leadership preparation in school administration." This chapter provides a general depiction of these broad contours by examining what the chapter authors have identified of what we know about research on the education of school leaders and what we need to know. Following these highlights, we propose a plan for moving us forward in this research.

Before presenting these broad contours, we remind the reader of the purposes of the handbook. This handbook provides an in-depth portrait of what constitutes research on leadership development and a game plan for strengthening the research-based education of school leaders. Ultimately, the handbook should contribute to the improvement of leadership development in order to impact leadership's influence on student engagement and learning. Explicit in the purpose and implementation of the reviews in this handbook is the value placed on research-based practice in leadership development. We believe that rigorous, substantive, and relevant research has the potential to contribute to the improvement of leadership development. This handbook both extols what quality research has been able to contribute and critiques the gaps that future research needs to address.

What We Know About Research on the Education of School Leaders

The handbook authors have provided excellent depictions of the contours of what we know about research on leadership development. In this section, we identify several of the highlights of their content and methodological conclusions. Clearly, the chapters have identified a great deal of information from research regarding leadership development. The findings identified in this concluding chapter are by no means exhaustive of what the previous chapters have so skillfully presented. Rather, these are highlights that are chosen because they seem to provide some indications of the contours of leadership development.

General Patterns

Before identifying some of the highlights of what we know about specific components of leadership development, we begin with some general patterns found across many of the chapters. First, the analyses in this handbook expose the glaring scarcity of empirical research on the education of school leaders. Although much has been written, little has been systematically and rigorously investigated. As Kottkamp and Rusch described it in chapter 1, "There are multiple bricks missing in the leadership preparation research wall. In fact, our data suggest there is not much of a wall at all." This dearth of empirical research is disappointing, given the critical need for research on leadership development to inform the development of high-quality preparation and professional development programs for leaders. It does, however, provide an opportunity for serious research agendas that can contribute to research, policy, and practice.

Second, another clear conclusion is that the bulk of research on leadership development focuses on the perceptions of those involved in this process. A significant amount of research provides ample evidence regarding what students, faculty, and graduates of leadership preparation programs perceive to be the strengths and weaknesses. Understanding the perspectives of these stakeholders may not be the complete story on leadership development, but it is an important piece of the narrative. These perspectives tell us how students and faculty make sense of their work and study.

Third, the chapter authors also conclude that we have a significant storehouse of descriptions of programs and models. In some components of leadership development, for example internships, research has identified an array of diverse programs and program components that can be used to inform the development of alternative approaches to leadership preparation. Although in chapter 9 Barnett and his colleagues acknowledge a lack of evidence of the effectiveness of some of these internship programs, research that describes program components is aiding preparation programs in developing a range of innovations.

Fourth, several chapters, especially those by McCarthy and Forsyth, LaMagdeleine et al., and Lumby et al. (chapters 2–4), provide excellent discussions of the contextual factors that influence leadership development programs. Understanding the external and internal influences (e.g., the rise of new public management, globalization, accreditation, and accountability) that create the environment in which leadership development occurs is particularly helpful in designing empirical investigations and critiquing overly narrow and partial perspectives in leadership development.

Fifth, some chapters, particularly those by Browne-Ferrigno and Muth and by Hackmann et al. (chapters 5 and 6), note evidence of increasing research on leadership preparation candidates and faculty and a strong interest in developing national databases to follow candidates into their leadership careers. For example, in the case of candidates, preparation programs and accreditation agencies are beginning to amass a significant amount of data on individuals that would permit analysis of not only who is involved in leadership development programs, but also where and to what positions these individuals are appointed and their effectiveness for enhancing school improvement and student learning. As McCarthy (1999) has urged, we need national databases to inform research, policy, and practice concerning the candidates of leadership development. The handbook chapters indicate that there is at least a growing interest and some data to build this foundation.

Finally, several chapters, especially those by Kochan and Locke (chapter 11) and Orr and Barber (chapter 12), demonstrate the growing attention to research on leadership development program outcomes. Again, the research is only beginning in this area, but there is cause for optimism as researchers increasingly acknowledge the importance of investigating the effectiveness of program components for school improvement, student achievement, and other outcomes.

Specific Program Components

We already have noted that the Browne-Ferrigno and Muth and the Hackmann et al. chapters presented a growing body of research on two important stakeholders in leadership development—the candidates and faculty. There is increasing attention in a few states regarding who candidates are and some information on admissions and recruitment patterns. However, as we will discuss later, this tends to be more at the program level rather than large-scale studies at state or national levels. In terms of faculty, the studies conducted by McCarthy and colleagues over the years have provided useful trend data (e.g., the move from a homogeneous to a more diverse professorate). These classic studies provide not only important details regarding the personal and professional characteristics of faculty, but also a model of the type of rigorous, longitudinal studies that could benefit our understanding of other components of leadership development.

In terms of curriculum, Osterman and Hafner (see chapter 7) conclude that programs differ and curriculum matters. Although there are commonalities in U.S. educational leadership programs, there are also important differences. This conclusion in some respects differs from some of the highly visible critiques of leadership programs that have castigated the irrelevant curricula in many programs. Recognizing that curricular differences exist provides an important argument for conducting studies on how these differences relate to leadership outcomes.

Another highlight is from Taylor, Cordiero, and Chrispeel's finding in chapter 8 that, despite a lack of substantive research on pedagogy generally, there is research that informs us of leadership candidates' perspectives on one area: Candidates perceive that they benefit more from authentic, field-based pedagogies than the typical lecture-and-discussion formats of coursework. This finding suggests why promising trends in various pedagogies, such as cases and problem-based learning, are engaging candidates in enriched learning experiences.

Not surprisingly, the literature on design and delivery, reviewed by Grogan and colleagues (chapter 10), has included extensive research on the use of cohort models. These authors found useful research that identifies the strengths and weaknesses of cohort programs, such as student persistence, student engagement, and the problems of limiting academic freedom and individual exploration. The authors also note that we have information on how participants and faculty perceive the effectiveness of cohort programs and their delivery.

Student assessment is one of the most glaring areas lacking research. This is reflected in annual meeting and dissertation topics, as Kottkamp and Rusch's analyses demonstrate in chapter 1, and in other types of published research, as Kochan and Locke found (chapter 11). However, Kochan and Locke conclude that we do know how satisfied students are, what they perceive the benefits of programs are, and how they believe programs affect their career advancement. Most would agree that this research on student assessment is limited at best, but the level of satisfaction of students in leadership development programs is an important issue that informs our practice.

One of the most needed and evolving areas of research on leadership development is program evaluation. A growing body of evaluation research, which by no means is extensive or exhaustive yet, is informing practice in leadership development programs. One promising area is the significant amount of program evaluation being conducted by accreditation organizations, state government agencies, licensing exams, foundations, and other organizations (see Orr and Barber's chapter 12). This has the potential of providing national databanks to support large-scale studies of leadership development programs. Orr and Barber also note the growing number of indirect-effect studies, which are demonstrating positive effects of certain types of preparation programs on leadership practices. This research on indirect effects also has identified supportive program structures; comprehensive, standards-based curricula; and broader, more intensive internships as related to graduates' subsequent leadership knowledge and skills.

Kelley and Shaw extend the examination of the leadership development continuum by reviewing the research on professional development in chapter 13. The largely descriptive research available emphasizes the variety in focus, purpose, instructional strategies, length and time, connection to state educational initiatives, and curricular coherence. They conclude that there is limited evidence that existing principal professional development has the quality and focus needed to measurably affect student learning. However, research has identified four features of professional development that lead to student learning results: (a) clear focus on learning, (b) emphasis on instructional organizational change, (c) small change guided by grand vision, and (d) ongoing professional development that is procedurally embedded. Kelley and Shaw also found that literature emphasizes three effective design features: (a) professional development seen as part of a learning continuum, (b) programs organized around a model of leadership and grounded in practice, and (c) collegial learning networks.

Mentoring has become one of the most popular strategies for leadership development in preparation, induction, and midcareer stages. Gross, in his review in chapter 14 of the research on mentoring, highlights the varied and complex nature of the field. However, he identifies five principles of leadership mentoring programs found in the literature: (a) Mentoring needs to be considered in context as leaders plan new programs, (b) mentors share specific qualities, (c) mentors need to be prepared for their work, (d) matching mentors with protégés is not a simple task, and (e) program length and cost become important aspects of the programs in order to integrate mentoring with other leadership development initiatives.

Methodological Considerations

What we know about research in the education of school leaders is based on a limited set of methodological approaches: descriptive, survey, and cross-sectional. Admittedly, there is value to the ample number of descriptive studies of leadership preparation programs for identifying potential components and models. This information is useful for developing program innovations and for understanding the commonalities and differences among programs. This understanding of the variety in program elements could be useful in designing and conducting studies of program outcomes, for example, how different types of delivery modes impact leadership knowledge and skills.

The studies identified by the chapter authors tended to use surveys of participants or faculty as primary data sources. This, too, has relevance and value for providing overviews of program features and participant perspectives. Surveys provide evidence of participant satisfaction, employer assessment of leaders, and areas of program strength and weakness from the participants' perspectives. These types of surveys have become a major feature of National Council for Accreditation of Teacher Education (NCATE) reviews.

The majority of research reviewed in this handbook also tended to be cross-sectional rather than longitudinal. This type of approach provides some depth in our understanding of particular leadership development programs, allowing researchers to explore the various elements in programs and to make comparisons between and among programs.

What We Need to Know About the Education of School Leaders

As in the previous section, this review of the highlights from the chapters of what we need to know about leadership development is organized in terms of general patterns, gaps in research in specific program areas or components, and methodological considerations that need to be addressed. Not surprisingly, what we need to know far outweighs what we know.

General Patterns

Overall, five general patterns regarding gaps in the research on leadership development have been identified by several authors, especially Kottkamp and Rusch, McCarthy and Forsyth, Pounder et al., and Lumby et al. First, the authors point to the lack of recent studies in several areas; they mention the dependence on 15- to 20-year-old studies. Ample evidence is available that the roles of school leadership and school leaders have changed in relation to a variety of contextual factors, including the knowledge society, technology, globalization, and accountability. Thus, many of the studies that we depend on for information about leadership development are seriously outdated or at least might be questioned in regard to their relevancy.

Second, authors of several chapters, including the historical, international, faculty, and pedagogy chapters, point to the atheoretical character of much of the research. These authors argue for research that is informed by theoretical concepts, such as the nature of leadership, adult learning theory, context, diversity, and culture. The international chapter by Lumby and colleagues, for example, notes the importance of understanding leadership in order to understand leadership development and the important ways culture influences these understandings. Taylor et al., in their review of the research on pedagogy, stress the importance of a theoretical framework for studying leadership development that considers the nature of leadership, adult learning theory, context, and so forth.

The third general pattern in authors' reviews is the importance of understanding the education of school leaders as a continuum. Kelley and Shaw mention this in relation to their review of the research on professional development. Yet, the idea of leadership development as a continuum also informs how early stages of leadership development connect with later stages. There is a tendency across several areas to examine a slice of the leadership development landscape, which may assume that preparation, induction, or later professional development are unrelated to each other.

Fourth, most of the research tends to be descriptive investigations of single programs rather than large-scale studies involving multiple programs. Although these single-program descriptions can be helpful, the field of research in leadership development clearly has reached a stage in which larger scale research projects are needed to be able to draw conclusions about national and international trends and outcomes.

Finally, while we have acknowledged for some time that context matters when it comes to leadership, we have not always recognized the influence of context on leadership development. LaMagdeleine and colleagues identify the contextual factors that influence the education of school leaders. Several other authors provide examples of how some cultural and societal factors can influence leadership development and thus should be considered in the design of research on leadership development. Lumby and associates emphasize, as later chapters demonstrate, the importance of culture. These authors provide a very useful analysis of the effects of culture and also recommend an international perspective to help understand the contextual and cultural relevance of preparation programs and to avoid privileged, Western views of leadership and leadership development. McCarthy and Forsyth point to the need to examine various contextual features that influence leadership and in turn leadership development, such as how leadership preparation is being altered to respond to demographic changes in schools and among candidates. These authors and

Lumby et al. also point to the need to examine whether external factors such as standards-based accountability have narrowed the focus of leadership development programs and what has been ignored in the process (Gronn, 1999). Research that acknowledges the influence of context and avoids the privileging of certain contexts for understanding leadership and leadership development is sorely missing, as evidenced by the reviews in this handbook.

Specific Program Components

The authors in this handbook have identified an excellent list of areas for further research on the various components of leadership development. Here we highlight some of the most significant research needs.

Significant gaps in the research on leadership preparation program candidates have been identified by Browne-Ferrigno and Muth. They maintain that demographic information on program participants is routinely overlooked. These authors along with others also reveal that information on what happens to these candidates after they complete programs is missing. Furthermore, although some admission and recruitment research is available, there is little evidence about how admission and recruitment practices influence leadership preparation program quality and subsequent leadership effectiveness.

In regard to research on faculty, Hackmann and colleagues point to several gaps. One of these is the lack of information on the characteristics of non-tenure-track faculty. There is an overall increase in part-time university faculty; 47.5% of faculty overall in 2005 were part-time, according to the National Center for Education Statistics (2006). This, together with the encouragement by various organizations to include practicing administrators as faculty in preparation programs, has given rise to questions about the characteristics of these non-tenure-track faculty and how the composition of tenure-track versus non-tenure-track faculty influences the quality of leadership preparation. The chapter authors also call attention to the need to understand better how educational leadership faculty are prepared and what types of ongoing professional development exist. The recent increase in expectations for faculty to increase their involvement in service to schools and districts also raises important questions for research. How does this field-service expectation influence the attractiveness of the professorate (Pounder, Crow, & Bergerson, 2004) and the balancing of research, teaching, and service obligations? In addition, while the professorate is becoming somewhat more diverse, Hackmann et al. identify the need to examine the effectiveness of strategies for increasing diversity of faculty in leadership development programs.

Major conclusions from the Osterman and Hafner chapter on curriculum emphasize the scarcity of research on the actual enacted curriculum in educational leadership development programs and on the learning process itself. These authors quite appropriately urge us to broaden our understanding of curriculum, as Glatthorn (2006) recommended, to include the taught, assessed, learned, and enacted curriculum. Doing so will provide a more complete and extensive understanding of what is actually taught and learned in leadership development programs—information that would permit a more in-depth and credible response to many of the recent critiques of leadership preparation. Interestingly, Kottkamp and Rusch found the topic of curriculum to be the most recommended area for research by authors of dissertations. Osterman and Hafner also wisely recommend investigations that examine the relationship between different types of curricula. For example, they suggest the importance of investigating whether social justice topics, recommended in the literature, are actually being taught in leadership development courses.

Like curriculum, research on the pedagogy of leadership development is missing. As Taylor et al. suggest, research in this area would enable us to make wise decisions regarding how best to prepare future administrators. A theoretical framework for these types of studies of pedagogy, according to these authors, should include the application of themes on how adults learn leadership development pedagogy.

A specific area of pedagogy relates to practice experience, which has gained attention in the last several years. Barnett et al. acknowledge that despite near universal agreement on the importance of internships, there is limited attention to testing the effectiveness of internships. They recommend examining the long-term effects of practice experiences, such as internships. Do different types of internships influence leadership practices well into the job?

Grogan and colleagues, in their review of the literature on program design and delivery, acknowledge that there is limited research on program delivery in general and very little on what constitutes good or effective models. They offer the example of research on cohort models of delivery. Although there are ample descriptive studies of cohort programs, there is no scientific evidence that substantiates the effect of cohort versus noncohort programs on leadership skills and effectiveness. These authors suggest some other useful areas for research that relate to recent work in leadership development. Additional research is needed, according to Grogan et al., on the effectiveness of district–university partnerships for quality leadership development. In addition, they suggest the need for studies that compare traditional and nontraditional modes of delivery (e.g., distance learning) in regard to their outcomes for leader effectiveness. They wisely caution against allowing market considerations to take precedence over actual research studies in determining the selection of program design and delivery.

Other chapter authors, including Lumby et al. and McCarthy and Forsyth, point to another area of research related to instructional delivery systems. They urge researchers to examine whether leadership-development effectiveness criteria should stress the optimization or diversity in delivery models. Or, as Lumby et al. suggest, we need to consider the homogenizing versus diversifying effects of various modes of program delivery.

As we mentioned before, some of the most exciting work in leadership development is in the area of program effectiveness. Although the research is still limited, there is growing awareness of the importance of this area and an evolving development of research designs and tools to investigate this topic. Orr and Barber examine some recent useful studies of the indirect effects of programs on learner and school outcomes. Certainly more needs to be done in this area. They also recommend examining the effects of accreditation on program quality, noting a near absence of research in this area.

Kelley and Shaw maintain that insufficient attention has been paid to research on the professional growth of principals. They argue that studies in this area typically lack a connection to theoretical foundations and that we need more work applying adult learning theory to professional development practices (Merriam, Caffarella, & Baumpartner, 2007). They further identify the need to design systems for assessing professional development that recognize the interacting influences of leadership and context.

In the final chapter, Gross examines the lack of rigorous empirical research on mentoring effectiveness and outcomes. Like internships and cohorts, mentoring has become a panacea for remedying leadership development deficiencies. Yet, little evidence is available to explore assumptions regarding the value of mentoring for improving leadership practice or for examining whether mentoring makes a difference in improving schools and increasing student learning. Gross also encourages us to look not only at the impact of mentoring on the individual leader or aspiring leader, but also at the effect on the school. He also recommends that researchers examine investigations of mentoring in other fields and conduct multiple field studies that cut across boundaries of profession, country, culture, and sponsoring agency. Gross astutely urges researchers to examine the varied purposes of mentoring and, particularly, whether current mentoring programs primarily focus on creating leaders who respond to governmental standards and mandates or who respond to the need for democratic and ethical decision making.

Methodological Considerations

In addition to gaps in the content on various aspects of leadership development, the chapter authors identify several methodological considerations that need to be attended to in developing agendas for research in leadership development. First, Taylor et al. criticize the lack of sustained research agendas on aspects of leadership development. In a recent examination of research on educational leadership in general, Firestone and Riehl (2005) found a similar lack of sustained, focused research agenda. This situation limits the depth of research that enables policy recommendations, program innovations, and more relevant and rigorous research directions.

Second, a strong pattern of critique from many of the chapter authors is that research on leadership development needs to be more rigorous. These comments about rigor take many forms, including some of the other methodological considerations we identify in the following discussion. Yet, the critique of research in this area is about not only the need for different types of methodological designs, but also the importance of timely, well-designed, and carefully executed research studies that permit us to answer the important questions identified in this handbook and to gain information that is both relevant to and credible for advancing policy and practice in leadership development.

Third, several authors criticize the narrow range of methodologies used in the research on leadership development. Typically, surveys, self-report, descriptive studies, and cross-sectional methodologies and designs are used, not only in published research, but also, as Kottkamp and Rusch found, in annual meeting presentations and dissertations. Hackmann and his colleagues emphasize the valuable yet limited use of surveys for research on faculty in leadership development and urge researchers to conduct qualitative studies to understand faculty perspectives in more in-depth ways. They also urge the use of comprehensive case studies, quasi-experimental and experimental designs that would permit us to ask more relevant questions about faculty effectiveness. Osterman and Hafner also recommend qualitative studies about how the curriculum of leadership development relates to outcomes—the nature of the transformation and what deeper understanding students gain from leadership preparation programs and courses. The use of more experimental designs to investigate program components and effectiveness also would seem to be timely and useful for responding to critiques and developing innovative program designs.

Fourth, these handbook authors stress the need for large-scale studies. Typically, research on various components of leadership development relies on descriptive studies of individual programs. As we mentioned, this has been useful for developing and changing programs. However, descriptive studies neither provide an understanding of trends and patterns nor allow for more sophisticated analyses of program or program component effectiveness. Osterman and Hafner found that many of the studies on curriculum in leadership development were conducted in UCEA institutions. This, however, does not demonstrate what goes on in the other institutions, where the majority of school administrators are prepared. Barnett et al. recommend the development of national databases (e.g., accreditation reports) that would permit large-scale studies of internships and their effectiveness for later practice.

Fifth, several authors urge researchers to design longitudinal studies that would permit us to know how leadership preparation programs influence ongoing leadership practices. Taylor et al. emphasize the need for longitudinal studies of the effects of various pedagogical tools, such as case studies and problem-based learning. Barnett et al. also encourage the use of longitudinal studies of the effects of internship experiences on long-term leadership practice and effectiveness. Orr and Barber recommend the value of longer term studies of the effects of preparation on induction and later leadership practices as well as student learning and school improvement.

Finally, Kelley and Shaw make a very useful recommendation that research on professional development should attend to alternative units of analysis. Typically, studies—not only on professional development, but also on other leadership development components—focus on how leadership development affects the individual student or future administrator. However, as Kelley and Shaw recommend, decisions about the unit of analysis for research should consider communities of practice in the school, leadership teams, and so forth.

An Immodest Proposal for Supporting and Disseminating Research on the Education of School Leaders

A major aim of this handbook is to encourage future initiatives that expand and enrich the research on leadership development. The chapter authors have presented insightful recommendations for research on various aspects of leadership development. In this final section, we make several more global recommendations that we hope will encourage the support and dissemination of rigorous, varied, and relevant research to enrich leadership development.

One of the opportunities and challenges of research in a profession such as educational leadership is the dynamic nature of the field. Educational leadership, like most knowledge work, is affected by the rapid and evolving demands of a knowledge society, the persistent demographic changes of schools, and the increasing complexity of the job of school leader (Crow, 2006). Thus, leadership development must respond to this new world with curricula, pedagogy, and so forth that are dynamic and relevant. In like manner, research on leadership development may be a moving target. This suggests that research needs to focus on content and to use methodologies and designs that permit the investigation of dynamic and responsive leadership development. Yet, it also means that the way research on leadership development is disseminated may need to change, or at least expand, to permit more accessible means for acquiring and using research in the field.

We propose that to address the need for dynamic and accessible research on leadership development, a variety of organizations need to support the type of large-scale, varied designs and longitudinal research that the chapter authors recommend. First, the National Center for Education Statistics should develop a national database of candidates in leadership development—including the types of leadership development programs they experienced. In addition, we propose that the National Center for Education Statistics revise the School and Staffing Survey to include an expanded set of variables and more attention to school leaders. These two initiatives would permit national data on candidates in leadership development to be linked to the School and Staffing Survey so that researchers can follow candidates through their careers. This would permit the type of longitudinal, large-scale research that several chapter authors recommend, thus enabling us to investigate the relationship between leadership development programs and leadership outcomes.

In addition, as Taylor et al. recommend, states could join forces in developing databases on preparation programs. This database would allow research on national trends in pedagogy and curriculum. The Education Commission of the States could promote the development of these databases with common variables that would permit comparative studies of different leadership development approaches.

A more grandiose, perhaps, but valuable source of data could be created by the Organization for Economic Co-operation and Development (OECD) by developing an international database of information regarding leadership development practices worldwide. Developing an international database, similar to the Programme for International Student Assessment (PISA), would permit international and comparative research that would expand the ideas for innovative leadership development, test assumptions, and encourage dialogue. These data would help to avoid the narcissism that Lumby and associates critique in regard to leadership preparation programs and would encourage a rich exchange of ideas for leadership development research.

In addition to government and international organizations, the accreditation associations

NCATE and Teacher Education Accreditation Council (TEAC) could provide support for research in leadership development by making available their extensive reports on program assessments. This would allow not only descriptions of curriculum, pedagogy, and program designs, but also assessments of programs and program components.

Other agencies such as foundations, universities, and professional organizations such as UCEA, AERA, National Council of Professors of Educational Administration (NCPEA), National Association of Elementary School Principals (NAESP), National Association of Secondary School Principals (NASSP), and Association for Supervision of Curriculum and Development (ASCD) could support valuable research initiatives by encouraging and underwriting various large-scale, longitudinal studies to answer relevant questions about leadership development. The National Policy Board on Educational Administration could be the vehicle for creating research collaboration among these organizations. Collaborating on research on important questions that need answering but are difficult for an individual university or faculty member to support would be valuable for both preparation programs and professional development organizations, thus enriching the research on the leadership development continuum. This also would allow cross-institutional research that moves beyond single program designs.

In addition to the support for research, it is important to develop more dynamic and accessible ways to disseminate research. Several vehicles are appropriate to improve dissemination. First, the UCEA *Journal of Research on Leadership Education* is a powerful tool for disseminating this research. Due to its design as a Web-based journal, research can be published more quickly and is more accessible to a larger number of recipients—policy makers, practitioners, and researchers. LaMagdeleine et al., in their chapter on context, recommend other accessible formats that move beyond the few top-tier journals in the field, such as the *CONNEXIONS* project at Rice University sponsored by NCPEA. The rapidly changing nature of technology presents new opportunities everyday to disseminate research in highly accessible ways. While not diminishing the importance of traditional prestigious journal formats for disseminating research, it is important to find ways to get abbreviated but relevant and rigorous research results in the hands of policy makers, practitioners, professors, and other researchers quickly and easily. Organizations such as OECD, the U.S. Department of Education, the Educator Certification System, Southern Regional Education Board, state agencies, and professional associations already have valuable vehicles that could be used to make this research more accessible.

A contrasting suggestion, proffered by Kottkamp and Rusch, involves the format of presentations at professional conferences. These authors argue that more sophisticated, large-scale, and longitudinal studies could be more fully discussed and debated at professional conferences if larger blocks of time were allotted for these types of research. More time would allow more substantive and critical conversations to develop, which could spawn subsequent and sustained research agendas.

Finally, as LaMagdeleine and colleagues recommend, it is important to hold a national conversation on leadership development based on this handbook. UCEA's National Commission for the Advancement of Educational Leadership Preparation forums have been useful and should be continued in order to encourage greater collaboration among government, university, nontraditional preparation programs, foundations, and so forth to support and disseminate research ideas and initiatives. As Young, Petersen, and Short (2002) argued, such conversations and the collaborative initiatives that result are key to substantive reform.

The success of this handbook in part will be evidenced by the quality of research that it encourages. This research must respond to the dynamic quality of education for leaders of today and tomorrow's schools that enables us and them to move forward rather than maintain the status quo.

References

Crow, G. M. (2006). Complexity and the beginning principal in the United States: Perspectives on socialization. *Journal of Educational Administration, 44*(4), 310–325.

Firestone, W., & Riehl, C. (2005). *A new agenda for research in educational leadership.* New York: Teachers College Press.

Glatthorn, A. A. (2006). *The principal as curriculum leader: Shaping what is taught and tested* (2nd ed.). Thousand Oaks, CA: Corwin Press.

Gronn, P. (1999). *The making of educational leaders.* London: Cassell.

Handy, C. (1989). *The age of unreason.* Boston: Harvard Business School Press.

Merriam, S. B., Caffarella, R. S., & Baumpartner, L. M. (2007). *Learning in adulthood: A comprehensive guide.* San Francisco: Wiley.

McCarthy, M. M. (1999). The evolution of educational leadership preparation programs. In J. Murphy & K. Seashore Louis (Eds.), *Handbook of research on educational administration* (2nd ed., pp. 119–139). San Francisco: Jossey-Bass.

National Center for Education Statistics. (2006). *Employees in postsecondary institutions, Fall 2005, and salaries of full-time instructional faculty, 2005–06.* Washington, DC: Author.

Pounder, D. G., Crow, G. M., & Bergerson, A. (2004). Job desirability of the university professorate in the field of educational leadership. *Journal of School Leadership, 14*(2), 497–529.

Young, M. D., Petersen, G. J., & Short, P. M. (2002). The complexity of substantive reform: A call for interdependence among key stakeholders. *Educational Administration Quarterly, 38*(2), 137–175.

Contributors

Margaret E. Barber, EdD, is an Assistant Professor in the Educational Leadership program in the College of Education at Lehigh University. Her primary research interests are in the design and evaluation of leadership preparation and development of school leaders. Her work has been published in the *Journal of School Leadership*.

Bruce G. Barnett is a Professor in the Educational Leadership and Policy Studies Department at the University of Texas at San Antonio. His research interests include the use of cohorts in leadership preparation, mentoring and coaching programs for school leaders, leadership for school improvement, and the realities of beginning principals. Bruce's work in these areas appears in a variety of books, book chapters, and journals, including the *Educational Administration Quarterly, Journal of School Leadership, Journal of Educational Administration, Educational Leadership and Administration,* and *Leading and Managing*.

Scott C. Bauer (PhD, Cornell University) is an Associate Professor in the Education Leadership program at George Mason University. His most recent publications deal with the design of distributed leadership processes in schools, the development of teacher leaders, and the redesign of school leadership preparation programs. He serves on the editorial boards of the *Journal of School Leadership* and *Journal of Research for Educational Leaders* and as an officer for the Learning and Teaching in Educational Leadership and the Leadership for School Improvement special interest groups in AERA.

Danna M. Beaty is an Assistant Professor at Tarleton State University. Her research interests include: leadership preparation and mentoring; gender and equity issues in leadership; early career superintendents. She has published in journals including the *Journal of Educational Administration, Journal of Research on Leadership Education,* and *Journal of Women in Educational Leadership*.

Lars G. Björk, PhD., is a Professor and Chair of the Department of Educational Leadership Studies, University of Kentucky, and was named as a Fulbright Scholar to Finland during Spring 2009. Dr. Björk has authored and coedited several books, including *Higher Education Research and Public Policy* (1988), *Minorities in Higher Education* (1994), *The New Superintendency* (2001), *The Study of the American Superintendency: A Look at the Superintendent of Education in the New Millennium* (2000), *The Superintendent as CEO* (2005), and *The Contemporary Superintendent* (2005).

Paul V. Bredeson is Professor and Chair of the Department of Educational Leadership and Policy Analysis at the University of Wisconsin-Madison. Dr. Bredeson is also an International Faculty Associate at Umea University in Umea, Sweden. Two major books, *The Principalship: A Theory of Professional Learning and Practice* (1996), coauthored with Ann W. Hart, and *Designs for Learning: A New Architecture for Professional Development in Schools* (2003), are used in graduate educational leadership and policy programs across the United States, Canada, Australia, Russia, Sweden, and Hong Kong.

Tricia Browne-Ferrigno is an Associate Professor in the Department of Educational Leadership Studies at the University of Kentucky. She evaluated the Principals Excellence Program, funded through the U.S. Department of Education School Leadership Development Program and a multipartner project to develop broad-based leadership teams in rural high schools supported by the U.S. Department of Education Teacher Quality State Grant Program. Dr. Browne-Ferrigno is chair of the LTEL SIG of AERA and a founding member of the UCEA/LTEL-SIG Taskforce on Evaluating Educational Leadership Preparation.

Miles Bryant is a Professor of Educational Administration at the University of Nebraska-Lincoln. He has taught in the United States, China, and Israel and has worked with doctoral students from many different countries. His research work has examined how culture shapes leadership behaviors. He teaches a popular graduate course on the topic of cross-cultural leadership.

Tony Bush is Professor of Educational Leadership at the University of Warwick, England. He is a prolific author on many aspects of educational leadership. His many funded research projects include several for the English National College for School Leadership. He is the editor of the leading international journal, *Educational Management, Administration and Leadership*.

Nelda H. Cambron-McCabe is Professor of Educational Leadership at Miami University. She is coauthor of *Public School Law: Teachers' and Students' Rights* (Allyn and Bacon, 6th ed., 2009), *The Superintendent's Fieldbook: A Guide for Leaders of Learning* (Corwin, 2005), and *Schools That Learn* (Doubleday, 2000). She has served as president of both the Education Law Association and the American Education Finance Association and as editor of *the Journal of Education Finance*.

Janet H. Chrispeels is Professor in Education Studies and director of the Joint Doctoral Program in Educational Leadership at the University of California, San Diego. Her research and publications focus on shared and team leadership, school and system restructuring, teacher and administrative professional development, and parent education programs that promote the social and intellectual capital of diverse families. She has served as president of the International Congress for School Effectiveness and Improvement and is on the editorial boards of the *Journal for Effective Schools, School Effectiveness and School Improvement* and *Leadership and Policy in Schools*.

Michael A. Copland is Associate Professor of Educational Leadership and Policy Studies in the College of Education at the University of Washington. His research interests include issues related to the preparation and professional development of school and district leaders, school and district reform, central office and comprehensive high school transformation, and distributed leadership. Dr. Copland's recent publications include the book *Connecting Leadership With Learning*, from ASCD, as well as pieces in *Phi Delta Kappan, Journal of School Leadership, Educational Evaluation and Policy Analysis*, and *Educational Administration Quarterly*.

Paula A. Cordeiro has been Dean of the School of Leadership and Education Sciences at the University of San Diego since 1998. Dr. Cordeiro has published three books and recently completed the fourth edition of her coauthored text, *An Introduction to Educational Leadership: A Bridge From Theory to Practice* (2008). Paula's research is in the areas of school leadership, cross-cultural leadership, and international education. In 2006, Dr. Cordeiro was appointed by Governor Schwarzenegger to the California Commission on Teacher Credentialing, and in 2007 she was appointed to the board of the James Irvine Foundation in San Francisco.

Gary M. Crow is Professor in the Department of Educational Leadership and Policy Studies at Indiana University. His research interests include work socialization of school site leaders, school leadership, and school reform. His most recent book is *Being and Becoming a Principal* (coauthored with Matthews, Allyn and Bacon). Articles authored by Crow have appeared in the *Educational Administration Quarterly, Educational Management, Administration and Leadership, Journal of Educational Administration*, and *American Educational Research Journal*.

Patrick B. Forsyth, Department of Educational Leadership and Policy Studies, The University of Oklahoma. He conducts research on school trust, academic performance, and affective and structural dimensions of schools. His books include *Educational Administration: A Decade of Reform*, with Joe Murphy; *City Schools: Leading the Way*, with Marilyn Tallerico; and *Effective Supervision: Theory Into Practice*, with Wayne K. Hoy. In addition to five books, he has written numerous book chapters, refereed articles and papers.

Margaret Grogan is Professor and Dean, School of Educational Studies at Claremont Graduate University, Claremont, California. A past president of the University Council for Educational Administration (UCEA), she has researched educational leadership preparation and development, women in leadership, the superintendency, the moral and ethical dimensions of leadership, and leadership for social justice. Together with Cryss Brunner, she has just published *Women Leading School Systems: Uncommon Roads to Fulfillment* (2007, Rowman & Littlefield Education).

Steven Jay Gross is Professor of Educational Leadership at Temple University. His interests include initiating and sustaining deep, democratic reform in schools; leadership mentoring; and turbulence theory. His books include *Ethical Educational Leadership in Turbulent Times* (with Joan Shapiro, 2007), *Leadership Mentoring: Maintaining School Improvement in Turbulent Times* (2006), and *Promises Kept: Sustaining School and District Leadership in a Turbulent Era* (2004).

Donald Gene Hackmann is an Associate Professor and Interim Head of the Department of Educational Organization and Leadership at the University of Illinois at Urbana-Champaign. His research interests include leadership preparation programming, the principalship, and middle level education. He has published recently in the *Journal of School Leadership* and the *Journal of Research on Leadership Education*.

Madeline M. Hafner is the Executive Director of the Minority Student Achievement Network at the Wisconsin Center for Education Research, University of Wisconsin-Madison. She works with school districts and universities across the country to collaboratively conduct research, engage in interventions, and convene practitioners and students in order to understand and eliminate racial achievement gaps that exist in our schools.

Carolyn Kelley is a Professor of Educational Leadership and Policy Analysis at the University of Wisconsin-Madison. Her research focuses on human resource management in schools, principal preparation, licensure, and expert practice. Recent publications include "Developing School Leaders: Issues in Professional Development" (with Kent Peterson, in Simmons, *Breaking Through: How to Transform the Results of Urban School Districts*, 2005), and "Teacher Compensation and Teacher Workforce Development" (with Kara Finnigan, in Smylie & Miretzky, *Developing the Teacher Workforce*, 2004).

Frances K. Kochan is Dean of the College of Education and Professor in Educational Leadership in the College of Education at Auburn University. She has written articles on collaboration and leadership and has published books and articles on mentoring and organizational change. Dr. Kochan's research interests embrace the relationship between beliefs and practice and collaboration at the individual, organizational, and cross-system levels; the principalship; and mentoring.

Robert B. Kottkamp is Professor Emeritus of Foundations, Leadership and Policy Studies, Hosfstra University. His career long interest in study of leadership preparation has been manifested through numerous presentations at AERA and UCEA, journal articles, and *Reflective Practice for Educators* (with Karen F. Osterman). He is a founding member and former chair of the AERA Learning and Teaching in Educational Leadership special interest group.

Donald LaMagdeleine is a sociologist whose research interests have included the sociology of religion, educational policy, and qualitative research methods. His publications in educational research mostly have concerned federal and state desegregation policy. His current research focuses on U.S. literacy programs' consequences on urban districts. Don currently serves as Chair of the Department of Leadership, Policy, and Administration in the School of Education at the University of St. Thomas.

Demetriss L. Locke is a doctoral student in Higher Education Administration within the Department of Educational Foundations, Leadership, and Technology at Auburn University. He is currently a graduate research assistant for the Office of Diversity, Recruitment, and Retention and the Dean's Office within the College of Education. His dissertation topic relates to support staff members' perception of campus climate for diversity within higher education.

Jacky Lumby is Professor of Education at the University of Southampton, England. She has taught in a range of educational settings, including high schools, community and technical education. She has researched leadership in the United Kingdom, South Africa, Hong Kong, and the Republic of China and is particularly interested in diversity issues in leadership and in comparative and international perspectives. She has published widely on leadership and management in schools and colleges in the U.K. and internationally.

Brendan D. Maxcy is an Assistant Professor in the Department of Educational Leadership and Policy Analysis at the University of Missouri-Columbia. Maxcy was awarded Outstanding Dissertation in the Politics of Education, 2004–2006 by the Politics of Education Association. His research draws on critical and postcolonial theories to examine the interplay of leadership, management, and public-sector reform policies and discourses in schools. His work has been published in the *Educational Administration Quarterly, Educational Policy* and *The Journal of Educational Administration* (South Korea).

Martha M. McCarthy, Chancellor's Professor, chairs the Educational Leadership and Policy Studies Department at Indiana University. She has served as President of the Education Law Association and the University Council for Educational Administration (UCEA) and Vice-President (Division A) of the American Educational Research Association. She has authored or coauthored 11 books and more than 250 articles on various aspects of education law and leadership preparation. Among recent honors, she received the Living Legend Award from the National Council of Professors of Educational Administration and the Campbell Lifetime Achievement Award from UCEA.

Joseph Murphy is Associate Dean and Professor of Education at Peabody College of Education of Vanderbilt University. His work is in the area of school improvement, with special emphasis on leadership and policy.

Rodney Muth, a professor of educational leadership at the University of Colorado Denver, focuses on many aspects of professional preparation programs, including doctoral programming, portfolios, and research. His latest publications include *Principal Accomplishments: How School Leaders Succeed* (Teachers College Press, 2007, with Bellamy, Fulmer, & Murphy).

Rodney T. Ogawa is Professor of Education at the University of California, Santa Cruz. His research has examined educational leadership, school organization and educational reform. His current research focuses on two topics: (a) how the structure of educational organizations shape contexts for learning and teaching and (b) school factors that affect the retention and development of teachers of color.

Margaret Terry Orr, PhD, is faculty member of Bank Street College and director of the Future School Leaders Academy. Her research centers on evaluation of leadership preparation programs and leadership practices for school improvement. She has published extensively in the *Educational Administration Quarterly, Phi Delta Kappan, the Journal of School Leadership*, and other journals and received the Distinguished Researcher Award (2008) from the Learning and Teaching in Educational Leadership special interest group of the American Educational Research Association.

Karen F. Osterman is Professor and Chairperson in the Department of Foundations, Leadership, and Policy Studies at Hofstra University. Her teaching and research focus broadly on motivation in a social context, with particular emphasis on organizational structures and processes that affect the workplace behavior of adults and students. Particular areas of interest include the use of reflective practice for professional development, interpersonal and organizational communication, and systemic violence.

Diana G. Pounder is Professor and Chair of the Department of Educational Leadership and Policy at the University of Utah-Salt Lake City and current Editor of *Educational Administration Quarterly (EAQ)*. Dr. Pounder's work appears in *Educational Administration Quarterly, Journal of School Leadership, the Australian Journal of Education, Educational Leadership, the School Administrator*, and other prominent publication outlets. Her research awards include the 1996 Davis Award for Outstanding *EAQ* article (coauthored with Rod Ogawa and Ann Adams) and the University of Utah College of Education research award.

Stacey Preis is a doctoral student in Educational Policy Studies in the Department of Educational Leadership and Policy Analysis at Virginia Commonwealth University. She is coauthor of two published articles on educational leadership, one evaluating the first-year cohort of the St. Louis New Leaders Program and the other a review of the literature and research on leadership preparation programs. In addition, she and a graduate school colleague presented a paper at the 2006 UCEA Convention on a case study they conducted to examine the relationship between a superintendent and school board in a high-achieving district.

David M. Quinn is an Assistant Professor of Educational Administration and Policy at the University of Florida. Dr. Quinn's teaching, research, and service interests focus on technology leadership issues, data-driven decision making, and organizational change and culture. He recently has published in the *Educational Administration Quarterly* and *Journal of Educational Administration*.

Cynthia J. Reed is Director of the Truman Pierce Institute, a research and outreach unit in the College of Education at Auburn University, and an Associate Professor of Educational Leadership. She is cochair of the District 5 Education Committee for the Alabama Rural Action Commission and is a commissioner on the Education Committee of the Governor's Black Belt Action Commission. Her research and publications focus on applied transformational leadership, educational policy, leadership development and preparation, and collaborative educational reform efforts. She is an active member of UCEA and AERA.

Edith A. Rusch is an Associate Professor of Educational Leadership at the University of Nevada-Las Vegas. Dr. Rusch researches educational settings engaged in profound cultural change and the developmental traits of educational leaders who practice their craft in democratic ways. She also examines the intractability of gender and race as an issue in educational settings. Her recent work has appeared in the *Review of Higher Education, Educational Administration Quarterly*, and the *International Journal of Leadership in Education*. She currently serves as the editor of UCEA's *Journal of Research on Leadership Education*.

James J. Shaw is a Clinical Professor and Director of the Wisconsin Idea Executive Ph.D. program in the Department of Educational Leadership and Policy Analysis at the University of Wisconsin-Madison. His research interest is social learning and social development theory and its relationship to school leadership and leadership development. Before coming to the university, Jim was a highly acclaimed educator and administrator in K–12 public education in Wisconsin. He is a former Wisconsin Superintendent of the Year and has been recognized by both public and private sector organizations for his leadership and contributions to public education.

Whitney H. Sherman is an Assistant Professor at Virginia Commonwealth University. Her research interests include leadership preparation and mentoring, women in leadership, and social justice and ethics in leadership. She has published in journals including the *Educational Administration Quarterly, Educational Policy, Journal of Educational Administration, Journal of Research on Leadership Education*, and *International Journal for Qualitative Studies in Education*.

Alan R. Shoho is a Professor of Educational Leadership and Policy Studies at The University of Texas at San Antonio. His research focuses on high school leadership and reform along with school organizational cultures and how they affect the sense of alienation, trust, and ethical behavior of their stakeholders. He received his BS in electrical engineering at California State University at Fullerton, MEd at the University of Hawaii, and his EdD at Arizona State University.

Dianne L. Taylor is an Associate Professor in the Department of Educational Theory, Policy, and Practice at Louisiana State University. She is on the editorial board of the *Educational Administration Quarterly* and is a past editorial board member of the *Journal of School Leadership*. She is active in UCEA, for which she is a past cochair for the annual convention; in AERA, particularly Division A and the Leadership for Social Justice Special Interest Group; and in the Southwest Educational Research Association, of which she is a past president.

Allan Walker is Chair Professor and Chair of the Department of Educational Administration and Policy at The Chinese University of Hong Kong. He is also Associate Director of the Hong Kong Centre for the Development of Educational Leadership. Allan's research interests include principalship preparation and development, cultural influence on school leadership, school improvement, strategic planning, professional learning communities, and leadership needs analysis. His most recent work includes his published book *Educational Leadership, Culture and Diversity*, coauthored with C. Dimmock, and findings from a study of cultural influences on school leadership across three societies.

Michelle D. Young is Associate Professor of Leadership and Policy at the University of Texas and serves as the Executive Director of the University Council for Educational Administration. Dr. Young is nationally recognized for her work on the preparation, practice, and evaluation of educational leaders and education policies that facilitate equitable and quality experiences for all students and adults who learn and work in schools.

Index

Page numbers in italic refer to Figures or Tables.

external influences, 142–150
faculty recruitment, 138–140
faculty retention, 138–140
faculty reward and incentive systems, 135–138
faculty roles and responsibilities, 132–135
history, 130–132
implications for leader preparation, 148–150
internal influences, 132–142
internal tension, 129–130
Interstate School Leaders Licensure Consortium
    standards, 145–146, 149–150
market-oriented approach, 142
New Public Management, 144–147
operating in and responding to current conditions,
    146–148
public education critiques 1980s, 143–144
recentering of profession, 131
shift in institutional mission, 132–133
as skilled craft, 130
standards, 130–131
systemic overhaul, 131
theories, 130
University Council for Education Administration,
    148
University Council for Education Administration, 1,
    10–12, 430
annual convention, 25
case methods, 340
Joint Research Taskforce on Educational Leadership
    Preparation, 11–12
knowledge development, 110–111
National Commission on the Advancement of
    Educational Leadership Preparation, 10–11,
    112
1975 nationwide study, 323
professional development, 113–114
program evaluation, 12, 463–464, 466
simulations, 346
student assessment, 436
    expanded redesign networks and models,
    443–444
Taskforce on Evaluating Leadership Preparation
    Programs, 79–80
early history, 79
structure, 79
supporting processes, structures, and
    organizations, 79–80
University–field connections, 15
University–school district partnerships, 400–401
school leadership preparation, 210
students, 210
U.S. Department of Education, Integrated
    Postsecondary Education Data System, 292
Utah, principals, 203

V
Valuation, 86
conceptualized, 86
practice knowledge, 87
technical-rational knowledge, 87

Values, 14, 242, 243–244
attitudes, 242–243
faculty, research recommendations, 261
mentoring, 529–530
school leadership preparation, 4
written curriculum, 293–294
Video technology, pedagogy, 339
Voucher programs, 103

W
Wallace Foundation, 10, 113
knowledge gaps, 114
principals, statewide studies, 200–204
program evaluation, 462
school leadership preparation, 210–211
students, 210–211
Web-based courses, 351
Wisconsin Urban Schools Leadership Project, 506–
    507, 508–510, *509–510*
Witters-Churchill study, 332
Women, 6, 322
African Americans, as principals, 320
history, 319
mentoring, 517
new leadership demographics, 517–518
superintendents, 321
tenure-track faculty, 231–232
    characteristics, 231–232
Workplace realities, 5
Written curriculum, 270, 283–294
alternative delivery formats, 283–284
change, 286
classroom instruction management, 294
cognition, 284–285
course content, 291–294
course requirements, 283–290
courses, 290–291
decision making, 291
enacted curriculum, alignment, 305–307
external leadership, 294
functionalism, 292
general managerial competencies, 289–290
general systems theory, 292
instructional leadership, 288
Interstate School Leaders Licensure Consortium
    standards, 289
leadership competencies, 288–290
leadership theory, 294
managing for results, 293
norms, 293–294
personnel management, 293
program descriptions, 283–290
program reform, 284–285
program themes, 283–290
recommended curriculum, alignment, 305–307
school change, 286
school culture, 294
school improvement, 286
self-awareness, 284–285
social justice, 286–288